ABOUT THE AUTHOR

Photo: Vando Rogers

Noted author, scholar, educator, and librarian Jessie Carney Smith is Dean of the Library and William and Camille Cosby Professor in the Humanities at Fisk University, Nashville, Tennessee. She is a graduate of North Carolina A&T State University, Michigan State University, and Vanderbilt University, and she holds a Ph.D. from the University of Illinois.

In addition to the first and second editions of *Black Firsts,* her Visible Ink publications are *Black Heroes* and, with Linda T. Wynn, *Freedom Facts and Firsts: 400 Years of the African American Civil Rights Experience.* Other important works that she has written or edited include *Encyclopedia of African American Popular Culture* (3 volumes), *Notable Black American Women* (Books I, II, and III), *Notable Black American Men* (Books I and II), *Encyclopedia of African American Business* (2 volumes), *African American Almanac* (8th edition), *Ethnic Genealogy,* and *Black Academic Libraries and Research Collections.*

Dr. Smith had been honored widely with recognitions such as the National Women's Book Association Award; the Candace Award for excellence in education; the Anna J. Cooper Award for research on African American women from *Sage* magazine; the Academic/Research Librarian of the Year Award from the Association of College and Research Libraries; the Distinguished Alumni Award from the University of Illinois, Graduate School of Library and Information Science; and the Research Career Award from Fisk University.

ALSO FROM
VISIBLE INK PRESS

African American Almanac: 400 Years of Triumph, Courage and Excellence
by Lean'tin Bracks, Ph.D.
ISBN: 978-1-57859-323-1

Black Heroes
by Jessie Carney Smith
ISBN: 978-1-57859-142-8

Freedom Facts and Firsts: 400 Years of the African American Civil Rights
   Experience
by Jessie Carney Smith and Linda T. Wynn
ISBN: 978-1-57859-192-3

The Handy History Answer Book, Third Edition
by David L Hudson, Jr.
ISBN: 978-1-57859-372-9

Please visit us at www.visibleinkpress.com.

BLACK FIRSTS

4,000 GROUND-BREAKING AND PIONEERING HISTORICAL EVENTS

Third Edition

JESSIE CARNEY SMITH

Detroit

BLACK FIRSTS

Copyright © 2013 by Visible Ink Press®

This publication is a creative work fully protected by all applicable copyright laws, as well as by misappropriation, trade secret, unfair competition, and other applicable laws.

No part of this book may be reproduced in any form without permission in writing from the publisher, except by a reviewer who wishes to quote brief passages in connection with a review written for inclusion in a magazine, newspaper, or website.

All rights to this publication will be vigorously defended.

Visible Ink Press®
43311 Joy Rd., #414
Canton, MI 48187-2075
Visible Ink Press is a registered trademark of Visible Ink Press LLC.

Most Visible Ink Press books are available at special quantity discounts when purchased in bulk by corporations, organizations, or groups. Customized printings, special imprints, messages, and excerpts can be produced to meet your needs. For more information, contact Special Markets Director, Visible Ink Press, www.visibleinkpress.com, or 734-667-3211.

Managing Editor: Kevin S. Hile
Art Director: Mary Claire Krzewinski
Typesetting: Marco Di Vita
Proofreaders: Chrystal Rosza and Sarah Trenz
Indexing: Shoshana Hurwitz

ISBN 978-1-57859-369-9
Cover images: Shutterstock.

Library of Congress Cataloging-in-Publication Data

Black firsts : 4,000 ground-breaking and pioneering events / [edited by] Jessie Carney Smith. — 3rd ed.
    p. cm.
Includes bibliographical references and index.
ISBN 978-1-57859-369-9 (pbk. : alk. paper)
  1. African Americans—History—Miscellanea. 2. Blacks—History—Miscellanea. 3. World records—United States—Miscellanea. I. Smith, Jessie Carney, 1930-
E185.B574 2013
920.009296′073—dc23
[B]
2012034407

Printed in the United States of America
All rights reserved
10 9 8 7 6 5 4 3 2 1

CONTENTS

v

PHOTO CREDITS

ACKNOWLEDGMENTS

Research projects such as *Black Firsts* often engage numerous contributors—from those who are involved in the intricate research project, to those who submit names that they know, to those who take a critical look at what has been said, or simply those who offer words of praise and encouragement throughout the project. I must not overlook those who appreciate the first two editions, often expressing their love for them and defining the project's helpfulness in their teaching or quest for knowledge. Simply saying thank you is never enough, but it is at least a way of publicly acknowledging that their efforts and words were sustenance to me.

I could not have predicted that a whole family would join the project as if it were their own. My library colleague at Fisk, Cheryl Jones Hamberg, and the Hamberg family—her husband, Dr. Marcelle, and son Marc—devoted an unbelievable amount of time to this work. They remained alert to the various new firsts that emerged and discovered others who had achieved previously and were already selected for the current edition. "Do you have this person?" they asked, and marveled when I did or felt a sense of helpfulness when I didn't. They read and corrected entries that I felt inadequate to handle, and even built a chart. As this project became a family affair, we began to refer to the book as "our book." Thank you, my friends, the Hamberg family.

Others on my staff at Fisk helped to make the book possible as well. Thank you, Kathy Harrell, for searching references and for your extensive photocopying of materials needed for the book—and for enjoying the entire process. This facilitated my work more than you will never know. And Jason Harrison, you were always ready to retrieve materials from our Special Collections, copy articles, and return items to the shelves—something that I never liked to do. Thank you, Jason, for your work and the pleasant attitude that you demonstrated during the process. I am grateful to other staff members, as well, who handled a myriad of activities, from retrieving faxes to re-shelving books and more. I appreciate your assistance Susie Harris, Mattie McHollin, Ester McShepard, Mike Powell, and researcher Vanessa Smith of libraries at Fisk and Meharry Medical College. It is painful to remember the help of Beth Howse, our Special Collections Librarian, who recently outran us to the great beyond. Let this be a posthumous thanks to Beth for always lending much-needed support. For all of my friends (especially former Fisk dean Carrell Horton) and Fisk colleagues, thank you for your suggestions and understanding when I put you on hold as I worked on the research project. I appreciate and thank all of my readers who made suggestions, corrected errors, and made the work a better product. I thank all of you for joining me in anticipating this new edition. And to my son, Rick Smith, thank you for keeping my old computer alive, rebuilding it, and finally replacing it as a beautiful birthday gift.

Thank you Roger Jänecke of Visible Ink Press for continuing to believe in me, for offering me contracts over and over again, and for continuing to assign Kevin Hile as my editor. We work together so well. Thanks, Kevin, for your continuous support and guidance through this third edition of *Black Firsts*. There are other Visible Ink staffers, including typesetter Marco Di Vita, page and cover designer Mary Claire Krzewinski, indexer Shoshana Hurwitz, and freelance proofreaders Crystal Rosza and Sarah Trenz, whose work on the book I may never know, but in the end I always see a good project.

INTRODUCTION

The experience of conducting research and writing about African Americans who are first achievers continues to be an exciting moment in my rigorous pursuit of facts or of untold or uncelebrated moments in our history. A person's fame was never a consideration here; instead, the focus remains on first accomplishments. Rayford W. Logan and Michael R. Winston had at least a passing concern for "the first" blacks in particular professions once "closed to them by law or custom." In their work *Dictionary of American Negro Biography* (1982) these editors decided to avoid giving "heavy weight to 'firsts,'" for they found "dozens or more 'firsts,' all of whom may have believed they enjoyed this 'distinction' simply because they were ignorant of the others and the frequent absence of any clear record." While this never hampered their research, Logan and Winston found that such firsts "multiplied rather spectacularly" and, like many other researchers, they were hopelessly confused by claims of one being the "first Negro physician" as well as who was really the "first Negro college graduate."

Cited in Dreck Spurlock Wilson's *African American Architects: A Biographical Dictionary 1865–1945* (2004), Valencia Hollins Coar stated in *A Century of Black Photographers: 1840–1960* her intention to "correct or reform the exclusionist traditions in our histories." Wilson followed Coar in this direction and found a dearth of information on his subject which made his task difficult. Three of his contributors reported that the architects they found each claimed to be the first black architect in Virginia, either because their research was incomplete or because they believed that no such architects practiced as early as the 1890s and 1900.

Both in the case of Logan and Winston and Dreck Wilson, and others who have become bewildered by the confusion of "firsts," it is often important to qualify the claim by a simple statement, such as "first woman to finish the gentleman's course," the "first black architect in modern times," the "first black architect with a college degree," or the "first in fifty years." Consistently, in my reporting I found it necessary to add a qualifier and then to list several people with similar claims—all firsts and all noteworthy.

Becoming a black first can be a daunting experience. For some, it may be a dream come true; with others, the goal was not necessarily to be the first but to reach a particular milestone. Whatever the aim, becoming a black first can be challenging. Sometimes the world has to become comfortable with a black person in a highly visible position. Consider the circumstances surrounding Henry Ossian Flipper (1856–1940), who became a cadet at the U.S. Military Academy at West Point: he suffered four years of exclusion and ostracism by white cadets but went on to become the first black to graduate from the academy. Try to understand the story of Jesse Owen (1913–1980), the son of an Alabama sharecropper, who won gold for the long jump in the Berlin Olympics held in 1936 and tied the Olympic record for the 100-meter run. The world was stunned when Adolph Hitler publicly and adamantly refused to acknowledge him and the medals that he won. Think of baseball legend Jackie Robinson (1919–1972), who in 1947 joined the Brooklyn Dodgers as a third baseman and became the first black in the major leagues of the modern era. When the season opened, Robinson soon began to receive verbal abuse, death threats, and misgivings among his white teammates and opponents, and he was denied lodging in certain hotels when the team traveled. Still, in later years, the circumstances surrounding Ruby Bridges [Hall], the first black student enrolled at William Frantz Elementary School in New Orleans, are disturbing, particularly considering the young child that she was. Her effort required federal marshals to escort her to school in 1960, as she faced the jeers and taunts of angry white students and their parents, who did not want the public schools integrated. Or think about Tiger Woods (1975–), who in 1997 won the crown jewel of golf matches—the Masters, held at Augusta, Georgia—and became the youngest ever to win the prestigious event and the first black to win a major professional tournament. But on his journey he endured the taunts and jeers of white spectators, as well.

The pinnacle of successful firsts, however, is unquestionably the 2008 election of Barack Hussein Obama (1961–) as the first black president of the United States. He won world-wide recognition and approval for his accomplishment in both the United States and abroad, and his race was duly cited.

I refocus the African proverb "It takes a village to raise a child" and say that it takes a nation to revise and expand *Black Firsts*. Clearly this has been the case with the second edition, and now the third, for in each case I asked readers to provide firsts that I may have overlooked, lacked an opportunity to uncover, or erroneously described. The responses were numerous and served the dual purpose of providing previously unknown entries as well as satisfying my need to produce a comprehensive work.

As in previous editions of this work, and in addition to citing a specific accomplishment that made a person a "first," in most cases the entries provide background information on the person or event. This edition updates much of the historical information given in the earlier editions with full knowledge that many careers are still developing or in progress and, like works of a biographical nature, revisions are constantly needed.

This third edition differs from the first two in several ways: it contains a number of new subheadings; new lists or new tables are included; existing tables have been expanded; sometimes, when there is information on a particular person with multiple firsts, the entry is combined so the person appears only once rather than in several listings; some topics are rearranged; and some entries have been deleted entirely because the only documentation was an Internet source that is no longer available and documentation with one or more references remains an essential part of this work. As was noted in the first edition, I ended the collection of data as close as possible to the publication date of *Black Firsts*. Some 3,000 entries were included in that edition. The same pattern followed in the second edition, yet it was expanded and revised with over 4,000 firsts included. The work grew from fifteen chapters to sixteen. For the present edition of *Black First*, I continued the previous and deliberate focus on women who have been overlooked in our history far too often and too consciously by those who deemed their work inconsequential.

As with other reference works, readers are advised to explore the detailed index for single as well as multiple references to people, places, and events. And some high achievers, like Venus and Serena Williams, Usain Bolt, and Condoleezza Rice, kept on reaching new heights.

Although this work is comprehensive, I am convinced that there is still much more to know than I have cited in well over 4,000 new and expanded firsts. Print and electronic media do much to impart information, yet we never know how many facts, whether historical or current, remain obscure. When I received an email from reader Monet Winkler, who reported that her grandmother Ida Mae Legett, Olympic gold medalist Wilma Rudolph's cousin, was the first African American woman admitted to the bar in Idaho in 1992 and the first African American appointed to the bench in Idaho, I was convinced that my suspicion was substantiated. This information arrived too late to be added to the text, but it is noted here out of appreciation for Winkler's concern for my book's inclusiveness.

Due to space limitations, many newly found firsts are deliberately omitted, particularly when they were similar to others reported, such as first black dean of a college or first black woman president of an organization. Yet for Legett, we know that few black firsts are reported for Idaho, and her inclusion is needed. What is rewarding, however, is the extent to which the first and second editions of *Black Firsts* have been so well received and the third edition so eagerly anticipated. On the other hand, my editor and I worked up to the last minute after the 2012 Olympics in London to cite newsworthy Gabby Douglas (1995), member of the U.S. Women's Gymnastics team, who was the first African American to win gold in the women's all-around final competition. Notwithstanding the space limitations and fear that important details remain lacking, I still want to tell it all!)

ARTS &
ENTERTAINMENT

Architecture

1892 • The first black to earn a bachelor of science degree in architecture was Robert Robinson Taylor (1868–1942). He was the first black admitted to the School of Architecture at Massachusetts Institute of Technology in 1888 and the only black in the first-year class. After graduating, educator Booker T. Washington hired him as a teacher in the Mechanical Industries Department and as campus architect, planner, and construction supervisor for the Tuskegee Institute in Alabama. Taylor designed twenty-eight buildings for Tuskegee, including Booker T. Washington's residence, known as "The Oaks," and a laundry that later became the George Washington Carver Museum. In 1912 he prepared the first plans for the rural schools that Julius Rosenwald funded under Washington's request. And in 1914 he designed an industrial building and a teachers' home for the schools. Taylor also chaired the Tuskegee, Alabama, chapter of the American Red Cross—the only black chapter in the nation.

Sources: Hoffschwelle, *The Rosenwald Schools of the American*, pp. 52–53; Wilson, *African American Architects*, pp. 393–96.

1897 • John A. Lankford (1874–1946) opened one of the first black architectural offices in Washington, D.C. A year later he designed and supervised construction of a cotton mill in Concord, North Carolina. He served as an instructor of architecture at several black colleges and superintendent of the Department of Mechanical Industries at Shaw University in Raleigh, North Carolina. As national supervising architect for the African Methodist Episcopal Church, he designed "Big Bethel," the landmark located in Atlanta's historic Auburn Avenue district. His other designs included churches in South and West Africa. He was commissioned to design the national office for the Grand Fountain United Order of the True Reformers, which organized one of the first black-owned banks. In the 1930s Lankford helped to establish the School of Architecture at Howard University.

Sources: Salzman, *Encyclopedia of African-American Culture and History*, vol. 1, p. 172; Wilson, *African American Architects*, pp. 253–57.

1902 • George Washington Foster Jr. (1866–1923) was the first black architect to practice in New Jersey. He studied at Cooper Union in New York and was a draftsman in Henry J. Hardenberg's architectural firm. He is claimed to have worked on the Flatiron Building in New York City in 1903, when he was a member of Daniel Burnham's firm. Foster was commissioned to build Mother African Methodist Episcopal Zion Church on 137th Street in Harlem.

Sources: Salzman, *Encyclopedia of African-American Culture and History,* vol. 1, p. 172; Wilson, *African American Architects,* pp. 156–58.

1904 • Julian Francis Abele (1888–1950) became the first black architect at the firm Horace Trumbauer and Associates in Philadelphia. That same year, Abele became the first black to graduate from the Pennsylvania School of Fine Arts and Architecture. Trumbauer sent Abele to study at L'Ecole des Beaux Arts in Paris, from which Abele received a diploma in 1906. He became chief designer for the firm in 1908. During his career with the firm he designed a number of major buildings, including Philadelphia's Free Library and Museum of Art; the Widener Library at Harvard University; and the chapel, the Allen administration building, and much of the campus at Trinity College in Durham, North Carolina (now Duke University). Abele's work on the Duke campus gained him membership to the American Institute of Architects. He is credited as being "the first black American architect to have an impact on the design of large buildings" and was known for modernizing classical forms when designing structures.

Sources: Salzman, *Encyclopedia of African-American Culture and History,* vol. 1, p. 5.

1906 • William Sidney Pittman (1875–1958) became the first black to receive a federal contract. Pittman won a competition in the fall of this year for the design of the Negro Building at the Jamestown Tercenennial Exposition held in Virginia. Partial support for the exposition came from the U.S. Congress and the secretary of the treasury supervised the work. Pittman's contract required him to supervise construction of the Negro Building, which opened in 1907; it also helped to launch the architect's career. Also in 1907, Pittman married Portia Marshall Washington, the daughter of Tuskegee Institute founder Booker T. Washington. A native of Montgomery, Alabama, Pittman graduated in 1897 with a degree in mechanical and architectural drawing. He earned a diploma in architectural drawing from Drexel Institute in 1900 and returned to Tuskegee as an assistant in the Division of Architectural and Mechanical Drawing. He provided blueprints for several campus buildings. Pittman relocated to Washington, D.C. in May 1905 and became a draftsman in the office of prominent architect John Anderson Lankford. Lankford also entered the contest for the Tercentennial project but his design was second to Pittman's. Pittman went on to design churches, institutional buildings, YMCA buildings, buildings for fraternal organizations, and homes. The Jamestown Tercentennial was an example of expositions, or giant fairs held throughout the South from the last quarter of nineteenth-century America until well into the twentieth century. As cities and states sponsored the exhibitions, they gradually provided for a Negro building to allow blacks to display and promote their works. Pittman moved to Dallas in the late 1920s; he later became eccentric and died destitute.

Sources: "A Successful Architect," *Colored American Magazine* 11 (1906): 424–25; Smith, *Encyclopedia of African American Popular Culture,* vol. 2, p. 478–81; Wilson, *African American Architects,* pp. 319–21.

1908 • Birmingham, Alabama, became the home of the first black-owned architectural firm in the state when Wallace Augustus Rayfield (1874–1941) opened his office in that city. He collaborated with black contractor Thomas C. Windham and together they changed the architectural face of black Birmingham. His business became known as W. A. Rayfield & Co., Architects. Rayfield was born near Macon, Georgia, and in 1896 graduated from Howard University. He received a certificate from Pratt Polytechnic Institute and then earned a bachelor of architecture degree from Columbia University in 1899. He became the second black architect formally trained (Robert Robinson Taylor, 1868–1942, was first). While at Columbia, Booker T. Washington, founder of the Tuskegee Institute in Alabama, recruited him to join the Tuskegee faculty. There he taught mechanical and architectural drawing and worked with architect Robert Robinson Taylor. Rayfield left Tuskegee in 1907 and moved to Birmingham. He was already an established architect, having built a mail order business to market his plans nationally. He designed over four hun-

Selected Black Exhibition Buildings, 1895–1936

Year	Building	Location
1895	Cotton States and International Exhibition Negro Building	Atlanta, GA
1897	Tennessee Centennial and International Exposition Negro Building	Nashville, TN
1901	South Carolina Interstate and West Indian Exhibition Negro Building	Charleston, SC
1906	Alabama State Fair Negro Building	Montgomery, AL
1907	Jamestown Tercentennial Exposition Negro Building	Jamestown, VA
1910	Appalachian Exposition Negro Building	Knoxville, TN
1933	Century of Progress Exhibition, DeSaible Cabin	Chicago, IL
1936	Texas Centennial Exhibition Hall of Negro Life	Dallas, TX

Sources: Wilson, *African American Architects: A Biographical Directory 1865–1945.*

dred buildings in at least twenty states and in Liberia; these included theaters, schools, and homes (especially for prominent black professionals). Perhaps the most famous of these is the Sixteenth Avenue Baptist Church in Birmingham, completed in 1911, where four little black girls were killed when the church was bombed on September 15, 1963, during the Civil Rights Movement. The church had been the site of numerous planning activities and events for the movement. Rayfield also became the chief architect for the A.M.E. Zion Churches of America and designed churches and parsonages throughout the nation; he was also superintending architect for the Freedmen's Aid Society. He died destitute during the beginning of World War II and remained largely forgotten until 1993, when 411 of his plates showing drawings of churches, schools, and advertisements for his company were discovered and brought forth to restore his legacy.

Sources: Brown, *W.A. Rayfield: Pioneer Black Architect of Birmingham, Alabama*; Ward, "Rediscovering Mr. Rayfield." *Preservation*: 63 (January/February 2011): 16–23; Wilson, *African American Architects,* pp. 338–40.

1908 • Vertner W. Tandy, Sr. (1885–1949) was the first black architect registered in New York State. Tandy is also known as a founder of Alpha Phi Alpha fraternity at Cornell University. In 1909 he established a partnership with architect George Washington Foster that lasted until 1915. Through the partnership the men received several significant commissions, including St. Philips Episcopal Church and its Queen Anne-style parish house (1910–11) and the Harlem townhouse of black-hair care magnate Madame C. J. Walker. Later, after the partnership ended, in 1917 he designed the country mansion Villa Lewaro, in Irvington-on-Hudson, for Madame Walker. His other works include Small's Paradise, the Harlem Elks Lodge, and in the 1940s the Abraham Lincoln Houses in the Bronx.

Sources: *Who's Who in Colored America, 1929*, p. 352; Salzman, *Encyclopedia of African-American Culture and History,* vol. 1, pp. 173–75; Wilson, *African American Architects,* pp. 389–92.

1930s • David Augustus Williston (1868–1962) was the first black landscape artist to establish his own practice. Although the date is uncertain, by 1934 he was living and practicing in Washington, D.C. Williston was born in Fayetteville, North Carolina, the second of thirteen children. Each child was responsible for a garden plot of his or her own. Young Williston used his to grow flowers, which he did in abundance. He studied at Howard University's Normal School from 1893 to 1895 and went on to Cornell University. In 1898 he became the first black to graduate from Cornell with a bachelor's degree in agriculture. Williston taught agriculture and horticulture at several black colleges, including Tuskegee Institute and Fisk University. By 1910 he was in charge of landscape planning and construction at Tuskegee. He did planting designs for The Oaks, the home of Booker T. Washington, as well as the George Washington Carver Museum and other facilities at Tuskegee. While there he established a lifetime friendship with George Washington Carver. From 1900 to 1932 Williston worked almost exclusively with the leading black land-grant col-

New York's First Black Woman Architect

In 1954 Norma Merrick Sklarek (1928–) became the first black woman registered architect in New York State. In 1962 she became the first black woman licensed in California. She was also the first black woman fellow of the American Institute of Architects in 1980. Sklarek was born in New York City and received a bachelor of architecture degree from Barnard College of Columbia University. In 1955 she joined the architectural firm of Skidmore, Owens, Merrill and in 1960 moved to Gruen and Associates in Los Angeles where she remained for twenty years. Sklarek, in 1966, became the first woman director of architecture with twenty architects on staff. That same year she was the first woman honored with a fellowship in the American Institute of Architects. In 1985 she founded her own architectural firm, Siegel, Sklarek, Diamond.

Sources: Hine, *Black Women in America*, pp. 1042–43; Lanker, *I Dream a World*, p. 41; Smith, *Notable Black American Women*, p. 1027; *The Black New Yorkers*, p. 280.

leges as landscape designer and consultant and was virtually the only black teaching horticulture and site planning. While in Washington he was landscape artist for five buildings at Howard University. He and architect Hilyard R. Robinson did the site planning and landscape design for the Langston Terrace Housing Project, the nation's first federal housing project. Among his other projects were the plan for Fisk University campus, Roberts Airfield, the president's residence at Atlanta University, and Catholic University of America. He died on July 28, 1962.

Sources: *Landscape Architecture* 72 (January 1982): 82–85; Wilson, *African American Architects*, pp. 453–55.

1935 • John Lewis Wilson (1898–1989) was the only black appointed to a team of seven architects to design the Harlem River Houses in New York. Wilson came from a prominent Mississippi family. He was the first black student to attend Columbia University's School of Architecture in 1923.

Sources: Salzman, *Encyclopedia of African-American Culture and History*, vol. 1, p. 175; Wilson, *African American Architects*, pp. 456–58.

1937 • Langston Terrace, the first public housing program built in Washington, D.C., opened this year. A part of the New Deal's Public Works Administration, it was to accommodate black low-income, working-class families. Hilyard Robinson was the architect; this was deemed his most outstanding project. Located at the corner of Benning Road and 21st Street in northeast Washington, the $1.8 million complex overlooks the Anacostia River. Consisting initially of 274 units, 34 additional units were built north of the original site in 1965. In 1987 the National Park Service listed Langston Terrace on its National Register of Historic Places. Robinson, a native of Washington, incorporated in his design his commitment to his race and his concern for the families who would be housed there. Robinson was trained in architecture at the University of Pennsylvania, the Columbia University School of Architecture, and the University of Berlin. For thirteen years he was professor of architecture and head of the department at Howard University. In 1993 Robinson organized Washington's housing survey. In 1934 he became consulting architect to the National Capitol Advisory Committee and senior architect for the United States Suburban Resettlement Administration.

Sources: *The Negro Almanac*, 5th ed., p. 1090; "Langston Terrace Dwellings/Hilyard Robinson, African American Heritage Trail." http://www.culturaltourismdc.org/things-do-see/langston-terrace-dwellingshilyard-robinson-african-american-heritage-trail.

Howard University's School of Architecture

In 1949 Howard University's School of Architecture became the first predominantly black architecture school to receive accreditation. In 1968 the school was still the only accredited program at a black college. By 1990, however, accredited programs in either architectural engineering and/or professional architecture also existed at Hampton University, Southern University in Baton Rouge, Tuskegee University, Florida A & M University, Morgan State University, Prairie View A & M University, and the University of the District of Columbia.

Sources: Salzman, *Encyclopedia of African-American Culture and History,* vol. 1, p. 177.

1952 • John Saunders Chase (1925–2012) opened the first black architectural firm in Texas and became the first black licensed to practice architecture in the state. After the 1950 landmark United States Supreme Court decision *Sweatt v. Painter* integrated graduate programs, Chase—a decorated World War II soldier—became the first black student in the University of Texas at Austin Graduate School of Architecture. While at the school he met intense racial prejudice and isolation, and no white architectural firm in Houston would hire him after graduating with a master's degree in architecture. He accepted a position as assistant professor at historically black Texas Southern University (TSU). Chase also opened his own business. He became the first black member of the Houston chapter of the American Institute of Architecture. Later, he opened branches of his firm in Washington, D.C., Houston, and Dallas. In 1971, Chase and twelve other black architects from across the country formed the National Organization of Minority Architects (NOMA); there are now chapters in eighteen states. In 1980 President Jimmy Carter appointed Chase to the U.S. Commission on the Fine Arts, the first black to hold that appointment. (The commission later picked the design for the famous Vietnam Veterans Memorial.) His work at TSU includes the Thurgood Marshall School of Law, several residence halls, the Martin Luther King School of Education, and the student center. He was also associate architect for the Federal Reserve Bank of Dallas.

Sources: BusinessMakers, "John Chase Biography," http://www.thehistorymakers.com/biography/biography.asp; "Building a Legacy: Following historic enrollment, African American Architect John Saunders Chase lays a foundation of firsts." University of Texas at Austin, http://www.utexas.edu/features/2008/chase/; Salzman, *Encyclopedia of African-American Culture and History,* vol. 1, p. 180.

1953 • Paul Revere Williams (1894–1980) was the first black architect to become a fellow of the American Institute of Architects. Certified in California in 1915, he designed homes and buildings for Hollywood luminaries. His clients included Frank Sinatra, Lucille Ball and Desi Arnaz, Zsa Zsa Gabor, and William "Bojangles" Robinson. In addition to designing more than three-thousand homes, ranging in value from $10,000 to $600,000, Williams served as associate architect for the $50 million Los Angeles International Airport. Born in Los Angeles, Williams attended the Los Angeles School of Art and also took classes at the Los Angeles component of the Beaux Arts Institute of Design. He worked as a draftsman and later with Wilbur D. Cook, a planner and landscape architect. He enrolled in the University of Southern California's engineering school but left in 1919 without graduating. While there he designed fraternity and sorority houses on campus. In 1921 Williams opened the architectural firm Paul R. Williams and Associates and at first saw many potential customers who turned away when they realized he was black. He won a contract from automobile magnate E. L. Cord to build his thirty-two-room mansion and eighteen-car garage, and as his business flourished, he received more contracts from wealthy white clients. He also built nonresidential projects in the black community, including schools, churches, and other facilities. His career spanned six decades, ending in retirement in 1973. Williams served on numerous boards of directors and commissions.

Paul Revere Williams

President Calvin Coolidge appointed him to the National Monuments Committee in 1929, and President Dwight D. Eisenhower named him to the Advisory Committee on Government Housing Policies and Programs in 1953. Twice he was delegate to the National Republican Convention.

Sources: Robinson, *Historical Negro Biographies,* pp. 262–63; Wilson, *African American Architects,* pp. 447–52; Smith, *Notable Black American Men,* pp. 1238–41.

Cartoons

George Herriman

1910 • George Herriman (1880–1944) was the first black to achieve fame as a syndicated cartoonist. On July 26, 1910, the prototype of Ignatz Mouse hit the prototype of Krazy Kat with a brick. The strip "Krazy Kat" was extremely popular, especially among intellectuals, in the 1920s, and continued with somewhat diminished success until July 25, 1944. Herriman was born in New Orleans in a family classified as black, and the family moved to Los Angeles to escape racial labeling. Some of his friends called him "The Greek," but he never openly divulged his background.

Sources: McDonnell, O'Connell, de Havenon, *Krazy Kat,* pp. 30–31, 55.

1933 • E[lmer] Simms Campbell (1906–1971) was the first black cartoonist to work for national publications. Born in Saint Louis, he lived in Chicago while completing his high school education. He studied at the Art Institute of Chicago for three years. After returning to St. Louis, he was discouraged from becoming a commercial artist because the field was not a viable one for blacks. After working with a local commercial art studio for one year, he moved to New York City where he hoped to become a freelance cartoonist. There he worked for a local advertising studio and sold some of his work to other artists. He enrolled in the Academy of Design and also studied at the Art Students League under printmaker George Grosz. After publishing his well-known "A Night-Club Map of Harlem" that included such sites as the Lafayette Theater, Small's Paradise, and the Cotton Club, Campbell began to receive a number of commissions. He contributed cartoons and other art work to *Esquire* (he was in nearly every issue from 1933 to 1958), *Cosmopolitan, Redbook, New Yorker, Opportunity,* and syndicated features in 145 newspapers. Campbell created the character "Esky," the pop-eyed mascot who appeared on the cover of *Esquire.* He worked tirelessly and became one of the highest paid commercial artists, often creating three-hundred full-page drawings a year. In 1957 Campbell and his family moved to Switzerland. Fourteen years later, after his wife died, he returned to the United States and died a year later.

Sources: *Dictionary of Black Culture,* p. 81; *Encyclopedia of Black America,* p. 214; *Who's Who in Colored America, 1950,* p. 592; Smith, *Notable Black American Men,* pp. 169–71.

1933 • Artist and cartoonist Oliver Harrington (1912–1995), one of America's most popular social satirists, created the first cartoon to focus on black American life. His early characters portrayed life during the Harlem Renaissance. His first comic strip, "Boop" was featured in the *Pittsburgh Courier* on March 11, 1933. (It was renamed "Scoop" on March 18.) On May 25, 1935, Harrington published a panel in New York's *Amsterdam News* entitled "Dark Laughter." On December 28 that same year he introduced the Bootsie character to the panel, who continued in the newspaper for several years and was published later in the *Courier.* For forty years Bootsie appeared in black newspapers. Harrington was born in the Valhalla community of West Chester County near New York City. He arrived in Harlem toward the end of the Harlem Renaissance and supported himself by working as a freelance artist. In 1940 he graduated from Yale University and started work on a master of fine art degree. Harrington was well known for his work as cartoonist for the black press and for his illustrations in children's books. He illustrated Ellen F. Tarry's *The Runaway Elephant,* published in 1950. The American Institute of Graphic Arts selected both the book's cover and illustrations as one of the Fifty Best American Books that year—the first time the institute had so recognized a black artist. His book *Bootsie and Others,* an anthology of cartoons, was published in 1958.

Sources: *Jet* 85 (14 February 1994): 36; 89 (27 November, 1995): 17; Smith, *Notable Black American Men,* pp. 511–12; Inge, *Dark Laughter: The Satiric Art of Oliver W. Harrington.*

1937 • Zelda Jackson "Jackie" Ormes (1917–1986) became the first nationally syndicated black woman cartoonist. In this year she began her cartoon "Torchy Brown in Dixie to Harlem," that ran in the *Pittsburgh Courier.* She also created the strips "Patty Jo n' Ginger," and "Candy." Born in Pittsburgh, Ormes studied in art schools before joining the *Pittsburgh Courier* around 1936, where she was a feature writer and contributor of artwork. She married and moved to Chicago in the early 1940s. There she was a general assignment reporter for the *Chicago Defender* and at the same time enrolled in the Art Institute of Chicago. Ormes published her second cartoon, "Patty Jo n' Ginger," but by the late 1960s she suffered from rheumatoid arthritis, which forced her to give up cartooning. She then devoted her time to the Chicago community and served as a board member of the DuSable Museum of African American History and Art. Her work was syndicated in black newspapers nationwide, and until the 1990s she was the only nationally syndicated black woman cartoonist. She died on January 2, 1986.

Sources: Hine, *Black Women in America,* vol. 2, p. 903.

1964 • Morrie (Morris) Turner (1923–), cartoonist and educator, created "Wee Pals," the first integrated comic strip. Influenced by Charles Schulz's "Peanuts" and inspired by Dick Gregory, "Wee Pals" was first published in the black newspaper, the *Chicago Defender.* When, in 1964, the strip became nationally syndicated and appeared in all of the large daily and Sunday papers, Turner became the first black to receive national distribution by a major syndicate. Nippie, the main character in "Wee Pals," was named for the comedian Nipsey Russell. While serving during World War II, Turner drew comic strips for service publications. He continued to draw part-time, while working for eleven years as a civilian clerk in the Oakland police department. In recognition for his work, the National Conference of Christians and Jews presented him the Brotherhood Award and the B'nai Brith Anti-Defamation League gave him its Intergroup Relations Award. Turner was born in California and began drawing during childhood.

Sources: *Contemporary Authors,* vol. 29–32, p. 646; *Ebony Success Library,* vol. 1, p. 311; *Essence* 5 (July 1974): 58–59, 64, 67; "'Wee Pals' Integrate the Comics," *Sepia* 18 (April 1969): 49–51; Salzman, *Encyclopedia of African-American Culture and History,* vol. 2, pp. 624–25.

1991 • Barbara Brandon (1958–) became the first black woman cartoonist nationally syndicated in the white press. Her comic strip "Where I'm Coming From" appeared first in the *Detroit Free Press,* and was acquired by Universal Press Syndicate in 1991. Her cartoons were the first to center on black women. Brandon was born in Brooklyn, New York, and attended Syracuse University. Her father, Brumsic Brandon Jr., was the creator of the "Luther" comic strip that first appeared in the late 1960s. In the 1980s she served as a fashion and beauty writer for *Essence* magazine. In 1982 she created "Where I'm Coming From" and took it to the editors of the black woman's magazine *Elan.* Although the magazine accepted her strip, it ceased publication before her strip appeared. When *Essence* magazine had no space for the cartoon, her father informed her of the *Detroit Free Press* and its interest in featuring more black cartoonists. The paper first published her strip in 1989 and two years later it went national. Brandon was only the eighth black cartoonist to have work syndicated.

Sources: Hine, *Black Women in America,* pp. 161–62; *Contemporary Black Biography,* vol. 3, pp. 16–17.

1992 • Alonzo Lavert Washington (1967–) created the first black comic book to deal with social issues and established the largest black comic book publishing firm. Born in Kansas City, Kansas, he studied at Kansas City Community College, Pioneer Community College, and Kansas City Media Project Communications. He developed an interest in comic books while growing up in the inner city; however, he was unable to relate to the characters. Whenever black characters appeared in books, they were either criminals or athletes, or they played a subordinate role to whites. He first created his own black superheroes by painting the white action figures black and giving them Afro hairstyles. He later began to produce comics of his own—all dealing with social issues—and sold them to his classmates. In 1992 Washington promoted his first comic, "Original Man," by targeting churches, bookstores, and organizations in the community and collected $1,000 in advance orders. That printing quickly sold out, prompting him to print ten thousand more. He made $30,000 in sales from his first issue. By 1998 his firm, Omega 7, had become the largest black-owned comic book company in the nation. He created a cast of action figure characters that included, among others, Omega Man, Lady Ace, and Original Woman, all with black features. His company was the first to offer black action figures on the market. He secured a deal with Toys R' Us® to distribute his toy characters, but generally marketed them in minority areas.

Sources: *Contemporary Black Biography,* vol. 29, pp. 178–79; *Who's Who among African Americans,* 26th ed., p. 1288.

Circus

1966 • The first black showgirl with Ringling Brothers Circus was Toni Williams (1943–) of Reading, Pennsylvania. Since then she has formed a trapeze act of her own.

Sources: Alford, *Famous First Blacks,* p. 71; *Essence,* 8 (March 1978): 56, 58, 60.

1968 • Promoter Irving Field signed up the King Charles Troupe, the first all-black circus act in America. The troupe of basketball-playing unicycle riders, discovered auditioning on the sidewalk outside Madison Square Garden, also performed on television, appearing on such shows as *The Tonight Show.* Field introduced the troupe to the circus, billing them as "the first all-black circus act in America." Jerry King, architect of the act, first saw a unicycle act used in a small circus in Florida in 1916. Forty-two years later he taught his son, Charles King, and others in their Bronx, New York, neighborhood to ride the unicycle. To this the young riders added their basketball skills, created a special act, and became something like the Harlem Globetrotters on wheels. Charles King became the group's leader.

Sources: Culhane, *The American Circus,* pp. 326–27.

1977 • Bernice Collins (1957–) was the first black woman clown with Ringling Brothers. The Kansas City native decided to become a clown when she was fourteen years old.

Sources: *Essence* 8 (March 1978): 58.

1994 • The first black man to train and perform with tigers in the Ringling Brothers/Barnum and Bailey Circus was Tyrone Taylor. For seventeen years before becoming a performer, he had assisted with circus animals, such as tigers and elephants.

Sources: *Jet* 85 (2 May 1994): 36–37.

1998 • Johnathan Lee Iverson (1976–) signed on with Ringling Brothers/Barnum and Bailey's "The Greatest Show on Earth" as ringmaster of the Red Unit, one of the troupe's two traveling shows. He was the first black and the youngest ringmaster in the history of the Ringling Brothers Circus. The son of a postal worker and a firefighter, Iverson was born in New York City. At age eleven he joined the Boys' Choir of Harlem and won several awards. He also sang on the soap opera *As the World Turns.* He graduated from Hartt School of Music in Connecticut and won a role in "The Fireside Christmas Show" held in Fort Atkinson, Wisconsin. It was there that Iverson's vocal talent captured the attention of the director of the show, who had also directed the circus. Iverson was encouraged to audition for the ringmaster's role, winning it after the first rehearsal.

Sources: *Jet* 95 (18 January 1999): 39; *New York Times* (24 June 2000); "Ringling Bros." First Black Ringmaster," *Ebony* 54 (May 1999): 152–56; *Who's Who among African Americans,* 26th ed., p. 631.

Comedy Shows

2007 • Star comedian Dave Chappelle (1973–) set an endurance record of six hours and twelve minutes with his stand-up comedy show, telling jokes at a Los Angeles club. He broke his own record of six hours and seven minutes set in mid-April this year. Comedian Richard Pryor set a record in 1980, telling jokes in a stand-up show for two hours and forty-one minutes (his record was shattered in early April 2007, when Dane Cook performed for three hours and fifty minutes).

Sources: *Jet* 112 (24–31 December 2007): 44.

2008 • Comedian Chris Rock (1965–) became the first comedian to perform during a stand-up comedy act before 15,900 fans at O2 Arena in London, England, and set a new record in British history for largest comedy audience with 15,900 fans in attendance. He broke the existing record of 10,108 fans that British comedian Lee Evans set in 2005. The number of ticket stubs collected at the box office was used to measure the crowd's size.

Dave Chappelle

Sources: *Jet* 113 (16 June 2008): 38.

Dance

1845 • Master Juba (William Henry Lane, 1825?–1852) was the first black dance star. He took his stage name from the African dance, the juba. In 1845, Lane won the title "King of All Dancers" after three challenge contests. He toured with three white minstrels, receiving top billing, and garnered acclaim for his 1848 performance in London. Lane died in 1852, without ever returning to the United States.

Sources: Emery, *Black Dance*, pp. 185–90; Thorpe, *Black Dance*, pp. 42–44.

1876 • The Hyers Sisters Comic Opera Company was organized. This was the first permanent black musical-comedy troupe. Sam B. Hyers, the Hyers sisters' father, led his daughters to success from the post-Civil War period until the 1890s. The sisters, Anna Madah Hyers (1856?–1930s) and Emma Louise Hyers (1858?–1899?), were born in Sacramento, California, and at an early age revealed their talents. They received their early musical training from their parents, and later they studied voice and piano with a German professor and a former Italian opera singer. On April 22, 1867, the sisters made their professional debut at the local Metropolitan Theater and received rave reviews in the press. They left the stage to continue study and to prepare for a national tour. Their first major recital came on August 12, 1871, in Salt Lake City, Utah, and had successful concerts in principal cities all over the country. By the mid-1870s, when the sisters were at the height of their popularity, their father changed the concert company into a musical comedy company, the Comic Opera Company. They toured the country under the Redpath Lyceum Bureau. The first and only black repertory company, for more than a decade, they were the nation's most celebrated troupe.

Sources: Smith, *Notable Black American Women*, pp. 550–52; Hine, *Black Women in America*, vol. 2, p. 1162; Southern, *Music of Black Americans*, pp. 240, 250–51.

1923 • In October, 1923, *Running Wild* was the first black show to introduce the Charleston to non-black audiences. After its appropriation by a white show in 1926, the dance achieved a worldwide popularity second only to the black-inspired Tango, which came to Europe and America from Argentina. A third black dance to achieve wide success in the 1920's was the Black Bottom, which reached New York in *Dinah* at Harlem's Lafayette Theater in 1924. Both the Charleston and the Black Bottom were theatrical adaptations of dances known to blacks in the South for a decade or more.

Sources: Emery, *Black Dance*, pp. 226–28; Johnson, *Black Manhattan*, pp. 189–90.

1932 • Buddy [Clarence] Bradley (1905-1972) was the first black to choreograph a show of white dancers. He was hired to prepare the London production of *Evergreen* for which he was in charge of sixty-four dancers. Bradley received full credit in the program. His career from this time on was mainly in Europe, where he was an important figure in popular dance.

Sources: Thorpe, *Black Dance,* pp. 106–07.

1932 • Hemsley Winfield (1906–1934) was the first black dancer to be involved in ballet. He choreographed and performed with his own company in the Metropolitan Opera's production of Louis Gruenberg's *The Emperor Jones.* This was a one-time exception to the rules—management did not list the dancers in the program. The next black dancer did not appear with the company until 1951. Winfield's mother was a playwright, and he made his debut in one of her plays, *Wade in the Water* (1926). He became a dancer and a pioneer in black concert dance, organizing the Negro Art Theater Dance Group. This group gave its first concert on April 29, 1931, and appeared in Hall Johnson's *Run Little Chillun* in 1933.

Sources: Emery, *Black Dance,* pp. 242–43, 320; Thorpe, *Black Dance,* pp. 112–14.

1940s • The Four Step Brothers, who were billed as "eight feet of rhythm," appeared annually for ten years at Radio City Music Hall and were the hall's first black act. The group was formed around 1925, when Maceo Anderson (1910–2001) and two other dancers persuaded agents at the Cotton Club to allow them to perform there with Duke Ellington. They remained with the club for four years and in the 1930s added the fourth dancer. By then the dancers were Rufus "Flash" McDonald (1919–?), Prince Spencer (1917–?), Al Williams, and Anderson. The group also performed at the Roxy and with Frank Sinatra at the Paramount. They later toured on the Keith-Orpheum circuit, as well as on black circuits, and many times were the first blacks to perform in theaters. Their act included singing, acrobatics, comedy and vernacular dance as well as traditional tap. Each dancer tried to top another's dance steps. Their trademark was an escalation of speed and complexity. Until they disbanded in the 1960s, the group played at top nightclubs and theaters around the world and danced for the queen of England and for Japanese leader Hirohito. They also starred in numerous films, including *Here Comes the Girls* and *Johnny Comes Marching Home,* and on television shows such as *The Ed Sullivan Show* and in Bob Hope specials. On July 14, 1988, the dance quartet was honored with a star on the Hollywood Walk of Fame, under a new category called live theater. They had become one of the most celebrated and enduring tap acts in the nation, and their act was one of the most imitated in show business. They had also helped break the color barrier in entertainment. The last surviving member of the group, tap-dancer and exuberant clown Maceo Anderson, died on July 4, 2001.

Sources: *Ebony* (8 April 1953): 74; *New York Times* (14 July 2001); Frank, *Tap,* pp. 211–30.

Pearl Primus

1943 • Pearl Primus (1919–1994) was the first dancer to present the African American experience within a framework of social protest, in such dances as *Strange Fruit, Hard Times Blues,* and *The Negro Speaks of Rivers.* She began to create and perform the dances around 1943, and she gave her first professional dance concert at the New York Men's Hebrew Association. Born in Trinidad, Primus moved to the United States in 1921. She received a bachelor of arts degree from Hunter College in 1940 and a doctorate from New York University in 1978. She formed her own dance company in the 1940s and later became a nightclub performer. She and her troupe appeared on Broadway at the Belasco and Roxy theaters. Primus danced in a revival of *Show Boat* in 1946; later she toured with her company, concentrating their appearances in the South. Sometime later she opened a dance school in New York. With a Rosenwald Foundation fellowship, she studied dance in Africa. In 1949 she became the first director of the African Performing Arts Center in Monrovia, Liberia. Primus brought African dance to the United States in the 1960s and 1970s, to schoolchildren and to dance companies. Three of her social protest dances were revived in 1988 and presented at Duke University for the American Dance Festival. The Alvin Ailey American Dance Theater, under the direction of Judith Jamison, presented her piece *Impinyuza* at New York's City Center in 1990.

Sources: *Contemporary Black Biography,* vol. 6, pp. 214–17; Smith, *Notable Black American Women,* pp. 878–81.

1951 • Janet Collins (1917–2003) was the first black prima ballerina at the Metropolitan Opera Company, a position she held for three years. She made her debut in *Aida* on November 13 and had the lead in *Carmen, La Gioconda,* and *Sampson and Delilah.* Collins was born in New Orleans on March 2, 1923, and her family settled in Los Angeles shortly after her birth. At a young age she was determined to study ballet but racial discrimination prevented her from being accepted in dance classes; instead, she was trained under a private instructor. Collins studied under Katherine Dunham, who was known for her landmark modern dance company, the Dunham Dance Company. Collins graduated from Los Angeles City College and Arts Center School. She moved to New York in search of a career in dance and made her debut in 1949. In 1950 she appeared in Cole Porter's *Out of the World,* in which she danced the role of "Night." She taught at the School of American Ballet, performed in concerts and on television, but became known chiefly for her choreography and her dance instruction. In the mid-1950s Collins left the stage and taught dance in the Bronx, at St. Joseph School for the Deaf. She died on May 28, 2003.

Janet Collins

Sources: Emery, *Black Dance,* pp. 320–22; *Encyclopedia of Black America,* p. 279; *Negro Almanac,* p. 1429; Smith, *Notable Black American Women,* pp. 210–11; "Profiles Northwest: The Blazing Steps of Janet Collins," *Seattle Times,* Lifestyles (23 January 2000); *Jet* 112 (19 November 2007): 20.

1955 • The first black dancer in the country to become a member of the New York City Ballet was Arthur Mitchell (1934–). He made his debut with the company in November, when he appeared in *Western Symphony.* He remained the company's principal dancer from 1955 to 1969. Born in New York City, Mitchell studied at the city's High School of Performing Art and at the School of American Ballet. Renowned choreographer George Balanchine, who directed the latter school, became his teacher. He continued to study while performing as a modern dancer with such groups as the Donald McKayle Company, the New Dance Group, and with Sophie Maslow's and Anna Sokolow's companies. Mitchell's first appearance on Broadway was in 1954, when he appeared in *House of Flowers.* Other dancers in that production included Geoffrey Holder, Carmen De Lavallade, Juanita Hall, and Alvin Ailey. He joined the John Butler Company in 1955 and performed with that group until he joined the New York City Ballet. In February 1969 he founded the Dance Theatre of Harlem as a school of dance—especially classical ballet—for children, regardless of race. The first black classical ballet company in the United States, they made their debut at the Guggenheim Museum of Art in New York City. In 1988 the company was the first black cultural group to tour the Soviet Union under the renewed cultural exchange program. Mitchell was a dance educator as well. He taught at the Katherine Dunham School of Dance, the Karel Shook Studio, and the Melissa Hayden School of Ballet in Washington, D.C. In 1993 Mitchell received the National Medal of Arts and the next year the National Endowment for the Arts named him ambassador-at-large. He was awarded a MacArthur Fellowship in 1994 and in 1995 he received the School of Ballet Lifetime Achievement Award.

Arthur Mitchell

Sources: Emery, *Black Dance,* pp. 279–84; *Encyclopedia of Black America,* p. 564; *Jet* 74 (23 May 1988): 56; Garrett, *Famous First Facts about Negroes,* p. 44; Smith, *Notable Black American Men,* pp, 819–21.

1963 • Katherine Dunham (1909–2006) was the first black choreographer to work at the Metropolitan Opera House. A dancer, choreographer, school founder, and anthropologist, she was born in Glen Ellyn, Illinois, and graduated from the University of Chicago and Northwestern University. As early as the 1930s Dunham incorporated her training in anthropology and her study of African and West Indian dances into her own techniques and dance instruction. In the early 1940s her professional troupe, the Dunham Dancers, was a first for black Americans, setting the stage for the Alvin Ailey American Dance Theater and Arthur Mitchell's Dance Theater of Harlem. On November 17, 1989, she was awarded the National Medal of Arts. Other recognitions include the Kennedy Center Honor for Lifetime Achievement and the NASACM Image Award.

Katherine Dunham

Sources: Emery, *Black Dance,* pp. 251–60; Smith, *Notable Black American Women,* pp. 296–301; Thorpe, *Black Dance,* pp. 124–30; *Jet* 94 (23 November 1998): 20.

Los Angeles' First Blacks Dance Studio

In 1916 Lauretta Green Butler (1881–1952) opened the first black professional dance studio in Los Angeles. Born in Los Angeles, Butler began her musical career while serving as a church pianist. She later performed with some of the country's best black orchestras. When she returned to Los Angeles, she gave up her musical career and opened a professional dance studio for children— the first such venture in the country. The studio, which taught children age two to teenagers, taught dance, singing, and mime. Butler presented her first Kiddie Minstrel Review in 1917, establishing herself as the foremost producer of children's acts. The studio was renamed the Kiddie Review around 1923, eliminating blackface makeup. The "Butler Kids," as her students became known, were in constant demand. They performed for social events, on military bases, in the movie industry, and elsewhere. Black as well as white children were trained in the studio, including some members of *The Little Rascals* and *Our Gang*. Among the legendary stage and screen stars trained there was Dorothy Dandridge. Butler Studio closed in the late 1940s.

Sources: Hine, *Black Women in America*, vol. 1, pp. 207–08.

1984 • The Alvin Ailey Dance Theater was the first black modern dance troupe to perform in New York's Metropolitan Opera House. Founded in 1958 by Alvin Ailey (1931–1989), the troupe has performed before more than an estimated fifteen million people throughout the world. In 1962 the company was the first black dance group to travel abroad under the International Exchange Program. The company was also America's first modern dance group to perform in the Soviet Union since the 1920s and in 1985 they were the first U.S.-sponsored company to tour the People's Republic of China since Sino-American relations were improved. Ailey's best-known work, "Revelations," based on his childhood experiences in black Baptist churches, was created in 1961. Among the notable companies for which Ailey created ballets were the American Ballet Theatre, the London Festival Ballet, Paris Opera Ballet, and La Scala Opera Ballet. A pioneer in modern dance as well as a choreographer, Ailey was born in Rogersville, Texas. In 1942 Ailey moved to Los Angeles where his mother had relocated. He enrolled in the University of California, Los Angeles and studied dance at night at the Lester Horton Theater. He moved to San Francisco and later enrolled in San Francisco State College. Ailey took Lester Horton's advice and left school to become a dancer. He returned to the Horton Company in 1953 and became choreographer after Horton died. Ailey joined the cast of the Broadway musical *House of Flowers* and never returned to California. After he founded the Alvin Ailey Dance Theatre, where he showcased his own talent as well as that of other black dancers, he had a flourishing career in dance.

Sources: Emery, *Black Dance*, pp. 272–79; Hornsby, *Chronology of Twentieth Century African-American History*, pp. 432–33; Thorpe, *Black Dance*, pp. 131–35; Smith, *Notable Black American Men*, pp. 8–11.

Drama, Dramatists, and Theater

1821 • The African Company was the first black theatrical company. They performed at the African Grove, which was located at the corner of Beeker and Mercer Streets in New York City. Henry Brown formed the group, which lasted until at least 1823, when a playbill announced a benefit performance for Brown. The company's building was destroyed in 1823.

Sources: Bergman, *The Chronological History of the Negro in America*, pp. 117–18; Emery, *Black Dance*, p. 180; Johnson, *Black Manhattan*, pp. 78–80; Southern, *Biographical Dictionary of Afro-American and African Musicians*, p. 178.

New York City Ballet's First Black Performer

In 1950 the first black to become a member of the New York City Ballet was Arthur Bell (1927?–). Although two black dancers, Talley Beatty and Betty Nichols, danced with George Balanchine's Ballet Society in the late 1940s, it was not until later that Balanchine transformed the society into the New York City Ballet. While still a child, Bell's family moved around in the South before settling in Tampa, Florida. Following high school, he moved to New York and worked in the garment district. He studied with Katherine Dunham and in 1945 performed the role of "The Boy Possessed" in the Broadway show *Carib Song,* with Dunham as choreographer. Bell later landed a role in "Illuminations," with British choreographer Frederick Ashton. He moved to Paris in the 1950s and played in "Night Is a Witch" at the Palais Garnier. He remained out of public view and separated from his family for forty years, until he was found homeless and nearly frozen on a Brooklyn street.

Sources: *Jet* 93 (4 May 1998): 24–25; *New York Times* (25 March 1998).

1823 • In June 1823, *The Drama of King Shotaway* was the first play by a black to be produced in the United States. Written by Henry Brown and produced by the African Company, it dealt with the insurrection of the Caravs on Saint Vincent and featured actor and singer James Hewlett. The text is not extant, but the play may have been founded on personal experiences of the author, who came to New York from the West Indies.

Sources: Southern, *The Music of Black Americans,* p. 120.

1826 • The first black actor to attain international renown was Ira Frederick Aldridge (1805–1867), one of the leading Shakespearean actors of the century. Born in New York City, he attended the local African Free School No. 2 until age sixteen and then left home. From 1821 to 1824 Aldridge worked with the African Theater Company in New York City, and later moved to Europe, where he studied briefly at the University of Glasgow in Scotland. His first professional engagement in London was in October 1825 with the Coburg Theater. For three decades his fame on the continent exceeded his high standing in England. Aldridge won acclaim for his portrayal of tragic, melodramatic, and comic roles, but was best known for his portrayal of Othello.

Sources: Logan and Winston, *Dictionary of American Negro Biography,* pp. 8–9; *Encyclopedia of Black America,* pp. 96–97; Johnson, *Black Manhattan,* pp. 80–87; Smith, *Notable Black American Men,* pp. 12–15.

Ira Frederick Aldridge

1858 • William Wells Brown (1814?–1844), abolitionist, author, and reformer, wrote *The Escape, or A Leap to Freedom,* the first play written by a black American. (Henry Brown, the author of *The Drama of King Shotaway,* was from the West Indies.) The play was published in Boston, but probably not produced, although Brown gave lyceum readings from it.

Sources: Abramson, *Negro Playwrights,* pp. 8–14; Logan and Winston, *Dictionary of American Negro Biography,* pp. 71–72; *Encyclopedia of Black America,* p. 532; Smith, *Notable Black American Men,* pp. 138–41.

1891 • *The Creole Show,* an all-black production in New York City with a white promoter, John Isham, was the first minstrel show to introduce black women into the cast. In the finale Dora Dean and Charles Johnson introduced the first theatrical cake-walk, derived from the old plantation chalk-line walk. It also is one of the first shows in which black performers did not wear black face.

Sources: Emery, *Black Dance,* pp. 207–09; Johnson, *Black Manhattan,* pp. 95–96; Thorpe, *Black Dance,* pp. 28–29, 53.

The First Black Minstrel Company

In 1865 Charles "Barney" Hicks, a black showman, organized the first permanent black minstrel company, the Georgia Minstrels. Black entertainers had appeared in troupes as early as the 1840s, and one all-black company, Lew Johnson's Plantation Minstrel Company, was formed in the early 1860s. Organized in Indianapolis, Indiana, the celebrated Georgia Minstrels' tours included performances in Germany and Great Britain. Hicks faced great difficulties in dealing with white theater managers, and sold his rights in 1872 to Charles Callender. The troupe was then known as Callender's Georgia Minstrels.

Sources: Johnson, *Black Manhattan*, pp. 89–93; Southern, *The Music of Black Americans*, p. 229; Thorpe, *Black Dance*, p. 48.

1897 • *Oriental America* was the first show to play on Broadway and the first to break away from playing in burlesque theaters. The production followed the minstrel pattern, but the after-piece was a medley of operatic selections. It had only a short run.

Sources: Emery, *Black Dance*, pp. 208–09; Johnson, *Black Manhattan*, pp. 96–97; Thorpe, *Black Dance*, p. 55.

1898 • *A Trip to Coontown* was the first full-length black musical comedy. It was also the first black show to draw a large white audience, and it played for the first time on Broadway this year. In a break with the minstrel tradition, it had a cast of characters involved in a story from beginning to end. The show was written and produced by Robert "Bob" Cole (1863?–1911), a composer, dancer, singer, musician, and actor. The first black show to be organized, produced, and managed by blacks, it ran for three seasons after its April 1898 debut in New York.

Sources: Logan and Winston, *Dictionary of American Negro Biography*, pp. 121–22; *Encyclopedia of Black America*, p. 530; Johnson, *Black Manhattan*, p. 102; Southern, *The Music of Black Americans*, p. 297.

1898 • The operetta *Clorindy—The Origin of the Cake-Walk,* based on Paul Laurence Dunbar's book with the same title, was the first show to introduce syncopated ragtime music to New York City theatergoers. It opened after *A Trip to Coontown* and ran the summer season at the Casino Roof Garden. The composer, Will Marion Cook (1869–1944), was composer-in-chief and musical director for the George Walker–Bert Williams company.

Sources: Emery, *Black Dance*, pp. 209–10; *Encyclopedia of Black America*, p. 530; Johnson, *Black Manhattan*, pp. 102–03; *Negro Almanac*, p. 1118; Southern, *The Music of Black Americans*, pp. 268–69.

1901 • Bert Williams (1873–1922) and his partner George Walker (1873–1911) became the first black recording artists; they were also among the first black best-selling artists. Williams starred in the first black musical comedy to open on Broadway, *In Dahomey*. During the 1908–09 season Williams and Walker toured with the production of *Bandanna Land*. Their show was the first black show to play at the formerly whites-only Belasco Theater in Washington, D.C. Williams went on to become the first major black star featured in a motion picture, *Darktown Jubilee*.

Sources: Badger, *A Life in Ragtime*, p. 41. *Bert Williams: A Biography of the Pioneer Black Comedian*, p. xi.

1905 • The Pekin Theater in Chicago was the first black-owned theater in the United States. Founded by Robert Mott (?–1911), the theater was important not only for stage productions, but also for its concert series. The Pekin Stock Company was the first black repertory company in this century. The theater ceased operation in 1916.

Sources: Logan and Winston, *Dictionary of American Negro Biography,* p. 261; Southern, *The Music of Black Americans,* p. 291.

1913 • Black showman Sherman H. Dudley (1872–1940) organized the first black theater circuit; this led the founding of the Theatre Owners Booking Association, or TOBA.

Sources: Southern, *The Music of Black Americans,* 2nd ed., p. 218.

1915 • Anita Bush (1883–1974), dancer and actress, organized the Anita Bush Players and became the first black woman to run a professional black stock dramatic company in the United States. Her company was also the first stock company in New York since the African Players of 1821. The players opened at the New York City's Lincoln Theater on November 15, 1915, with *The Girl at the Fort.* They had a short but successful run, and by December 27, 1915, had transferred to the larger Lafayette Theatre, where they became the Lafayette Players. Bush grew up in Brooklyn and began to appear on stage when she and her sister had extra roles in *Anthony and Cleopatra.* She joined Williams and Walker Company when she was sixteen and toured England with them in the smash hit *In Dahomey.* She formed her own dance group about 1909 and toured with the four or five other women members until she was injured in a serious accident in 1913. After the Anita Bush Players ended their short life, Bush continued to perform.

Sources: Hine, *Black Women in America,* pp. 205–06; Kellner, *The Harlem Renaissance,* p. 63; Smith, *Notable Black American Women,* pp. 142–43.

1916 • *Rachel,* a play by Angelina Grimké (1880–1958), was the first known play written by a black American and presented on stage by black actors in the twentieth century. It portrayed a respectable black family destroyed by prejudice. The play was first produced by the Drama Committee of the NAACP at Myrtilla Miner Normal School, in Washington, D.C. Grimké, a poet, was born in Boston and taught school in Washington.

Sources: *Encyclopedia of Black America,* p. 532; Hine, *Black Women in America,* vol. 1, pp. 504–05; Smith, *Notable Black American Women,* pp. 416–21.

1917 • Black actors in serious drama first won the attention of mainstream audiences and critics on April 5, 1917, when three one-act plays written for blacks were presented at the Garden City Theater. Playwright Ridley Torrence was white, but this production marked the first serious use of black life on a commercial stage. The trilogy features a folk comedy, a tragedy, and a religious play that broke stereotypes which had imprisoned black actors.

Sources: Bergman, *The Chronological History of the Negro in America,* p. 384; *Encyclopedia of Black America,* p. 532; Johnson, *Black Manhattan,* pp. 175–78.

1919 • Mary P. Burrill (1884?–1946) published her play, *They That Sit in Darkness.* This was possibly the first black feminist drama ever published. One of her two known published plays, it appeared in *Birth Control Review* in September 1919, in a special issue on "The Negroes' Need for Birth Control, as Seen by Themselves." The play advocated access to birth control for every woman. Later she revised the work and called it "Unto the Third and Fourth Generation." Burrill was born in Washington, D.C., and graduated from the M Street School, later renamed Dunbar High School. In 1929 she received a bachelor of literary interpretation degree from Emerson College of Oratory, later to become Emerson University. She spent most of her career at Dunbar High School where she taught English, speech, and dramatics. Playwrights Willis Richardson and May Miller were among her students. Burrill directed the Washington, D.C., Conservatory of Music and School of Expression from 1907 to 1911 and while there she taught elocution, public speaking, and dramatics.

Sources: Hine, *Black Women in America,* vol. 1, p. 198.

1920 • Charles Sidney Gilpin (1878–1930) was the first black to star in a major American play, Eugene O'Neill's *The Emperor Jones.* He has been called "the first modern American Negro to establish himself as a serious actor of first quality." Born in Richmond, Virginia, he received little education. In 1896 Gilpin began traveling with vaudeville troupes, a practice which he followed for two years. In 1907 he joined the Pekin Stock

Charles Gilpin

Company of Chicago as a dramatic actor, and in 1916 joined the Lafayette Theater Company in Harlem. Gilpin played the lead in *The Emperor Jones* from 1920 to 1924, winning the Spingarn Award in 1921 for his theatrical accomplishment.

Sources: Bergman, *The Chronological History of the Negro in America*, pp. 284, 400; Logan and Winston, *Dictionary of American Negro Biography*, pp. 261–62; Johnson, *Black Manhattan*, pp. 182–85; Kellner, *The Harlem Renaissance*, pp. 137–38; *Negro Almanac*, p. 1140; Smith, *Notable Black American Men*, pp. 460–62.

1922 • Singer and dancer Maude Rutherford (1897?–2001) is said to have been the one who introduced the Charleston on Broadway. She appeared on Broadway in the all-black revue *Liza*, with lyrics and music by Maceo Pinkard, and led the chorus girls in the dance called the Charleston. Some critics claim, however, that the Charleston was brought to Broadway in 1923, in the show *Runnin' Wild*. Rutherford also worked with Josephine Baker, Fats Waller, and Pearl Bailey, and was billed as the Slim Princess. She was also a favorite at Harlem's Cotton Club. Rutherford was born in Texas to a black mother and white father; laws against interracial unions prevented the parents from living together. Her theater credits included *Dixie to Broadway* (1924), *Chocolate Scandals* (1927), and *Keep Shufflin'* (1928). Sometime in the fifties she left show business and in 1953 married for the fifth time. Rutherford later became a switchboard operator in an Atlantic City hotel. She died on March 8, 2001, at her home in Atlantic City.

Sources: *New York Times* (29 March 2001).

1923 • The first nonmusical play by a serious black writer to reach Broadway was *Chip Woman's Fortune*, a one-act play presented by the Ethiopian Art Players on May 7, 1923, along with Oscar Wilde's *Salome* and an interpretation of Shakespeare's *The Comedy of Errors*. Written by Willis Richardson (1889–1977), it was presented at the Frazee Theater and was the only play on the bill to be fully approved by the critics. The North Carolina native wrote and published several other plays, but he had little commercial success.

Sources: Brawley, *Negro Genius*, pp. 282–84; Johnson, *Black Manhattan*, pp. 190–91; Kellner, *The Harlem Renaissance*, p. 302; Rush, *Black American Writers*, vol. 2, pp. 629–30; *Who's Who in Colored America, 1927*, pp. 167–68.

1925 • The first black woman to headline at a Broadway venue was Florence Mills (1896–1927). She became the preeminent woman jazz dancer during the Harlem Renaissance. Born in Washington, D.C., she demonstrated her talent as a singer and dancer early and was called a child prodigy. By age eight, she was a stage phenomenon, having been guided by the accomplished performer Aida Overton Walker. Mills sang "Miss Hannah from Savannah" in the musical comedy *Sons of Ham* that led to her work with a vaudeville company beginning 1905. In 1921 Mills joined Noble Sissle and Eubie Blake's production of *Shuffle Along*. Her success in the musical led Lew Leslie to hire her to perform at the Plantation Club on Broadway. When the musical comedy *From Dixie to Broadway* opened in New York in October 1924, Mills sang "I'm a Little Blackbird Looking for a Bluebird" and was a showstopper. The revue, along with the work of Mills and other black performers, helped eradicate the racial stereotypes that up to this time characterized blacks. Mills' heavy workload contributed to her declining health and eventual death on November 1, 1927. During her grand funeral in Harlem, it has been said that a flock of blackbirds flew over her funeral procession as it made its way up Seventh Avenue to Woodland Cemetery in the Bronx.

Sources: *Contemporary Black Biography*, vol. 22, pp. 149–51; Smith, *Notable Black American Women*, pp. 752–56.

1933 • The first folk opera by a black to reach Broadway was *Run, Little Children*, by [Francis] Hall Johnson (1888–1970). It ran 126 performances. Johnson was one of the most successful choral directors of his time and had been choral director of *Green Pastures* in 1930.

Sources: Robinson, *Historical Negro Biographies*, pp. 211–12; Southern, *Biographical Dictionary of Afro-American and African Musicians*, pp. 207–8; Southern, *The Music of Black Americans*, pp. 411–13.

1935 • *Mulatto,* by Langston Hughes (1902–1967), was the first play by a black author to be a long-run Broadway hit. It opened at the Vanderbilt Theatre on October 24, 1935, and played continuously until December 9, 1937. The poet and author was born James Mercer Langston Hughes in Joplin, Missouri, and graduated from Lincoln University, Pennsylvania. His first volume of poetry, *Weary Blues,* was published in 1926, the year he returned to college to complete his degree. The following year he published *Fine Clothes to the Jew.* By this time he had become a celebrated young talent of the Harlem Renaissance era. He wrote prolifically and published ten volumes of poetry; more than sixty short stories; a number of dramas, operas, and anthologies; as well as two autobiographies, *The Big Sea* (1940) and *I Wonder as I Wander* (1956). Hughes created the black folk character Jess B. Simple, and wrote about him in *Simple Speaks His Mind* (1950), and *Simple Stakes a Claim* (1957). For twenty-two years, Hughes wrote a weekly newspaper column for the *Chicago Defender* and then for the *New York Post.* Twenty years after his death, his cremated remains were interred under a floor map in the Schomburg Center for Research in Black Culture. In February 2002 the U.S. Postal Service issued a Black Heritage postage stamp in honor of Hughes, the 25th in that stamp series. The stamp marked Hughes's one hundredth birthday.

Sources: Bontemps, *Harlem Renaissance Remembered,* pp. 90–102; Logan and Winston, *Dictionary of American Negro Biography,* pp. 331–34; *Encyclopedia of Black America,* p. 456; Smith, *Notable Black American Men,* pp. 580–84.

1939 • Ethel Waters (1896–1977), as Hagar in *Mamba's Daughters,* became the first black woman to perform the leading role in a dramatic play on Broadway. She made her first public appearance at the age of five as a singer in a church program. Waters appeared in nightclubs and vaudeville, and in 1927 made her Broadway debut in *Africana.* When she toured in *As Thousands Cheer* (1934), she became the first black person to co-star with white players below the Mason-Dixon line. Her greatest role came in 1940, when she appeared on stage in *Cabin in the Sky;* she appeared in the movie version in 1943. From 1957 to 1976 she toured with evangelist Billy Graham and achieved wide recognition for the gospel hymn "His Eye Is on the Sparrow." In 1950 Waters was the first black to star in a scheduled comedy program on television. She appeared in *Beulah* on ABC on October 3, taking over the role played by Hattie McDaniel (1895–1952) on the radio. Waters' health allowed her to film only a few episodes.

Sources: *Encyclopedia of Black America,* p. 724; *Negro Almanac,* p. 1162; Smith, *Notable Black American Women,* p. 1225; Southern, *Biographical Dictionary of Afro-American and African Musicians,* p. 393.

Ethel Waters

1943 • Paul Robeson (1898–1976) was the first black to play Othello on an American stage with a white cast. The son of a former slave, he was born in Princeton, New Jersey, and graduated from Rutgers University and Columbia University School of Law. At Rutgers, he was an All-American athlete and elected to Phi Beta Kappa. Robeson developed an international career on stage and in film, as well as in concert, and became a recording star. His work with the Progressive Party, the Council on African Affairs, the National Negro Congress, the left-wing unions of the CIO, and his early call for a militant black movement made him a hero in Communist and Third World countries, and led the U.S. State Department to revoke his passport. Robeson held fast to his convictions and in 1958 published his autobiography, *Here I Stand.* Well after his death Robeson remains highly celebrated; his life has been depicted in exhibits, films, festivals, and lectures. On the centennial of his birth, the United States and many foreign countries held celebrations to recognize his work and his legacy.

Sources: Duberman, *Paul Robeson;* Hornsby, *Milestones of Twentieth-Century African-American History,* pp. 263–66; *Encyclopedia of Black America,* p. 732; Lee, *Interesting People,* p. 57; Smith, *Notable Black American Men,* pp. 1013–16.

Paul Robeson

1950 • Zelma Watson George (1903–1994), singer, social worker, actress, and educator, was the first black woman to play a leading role in an American opera on Broadway. She was cast in a revival of composer Gian-Carlo Menotti's opera, *The Medium.* George was born in Hearne, Texas and graduated from the University of Chicago, where she endured racial discrimination. She received both her master's and doctoral degrees from New York University. In 1960 George was approved as alternate to the United States Delegation to the Fifteenth General Assembly of the United Nations and was in great demand as a speaker and lecturer.

Sources: Smith, *Notable Black American Women*, pp. 393–97; *Tennessean* (6 July 1994).

1959 • Harry [Harold George] Belafonte Jr., (1927–) singer, actor, and civil rights crusader, was the first black to have an hour-long special on television. Born in New York City, he lived in Jamaica from 1935 to 1940. He received a Tony Award in 1954 for a supporting role in *John Murray Anderson's Almanac*. In 1966 Belafonte was the first black to produce a major show for television. During President John F. Kennedy's administration, he became the first cultural advisor to the Peace Corps. In 1990 he was the first person to receive the Nelson Mandela Courage Award of TransAfrica Forum.

Sources: *Current Biography, 1956*, pp. 45–47; *Ebony Success Library*, vol. 2, pp. 6–9; *Encyclopedia of Black America*, p. 170; *Jet* 78 (23 April 1990): 6; 81 (18 November 1991): 6, 8; Smith, *Notable Black American Men*, pp. 68–71.

1959 • Playwright and activist Lorraine Hansberry (1930–1965) was the first black woman to premiere a play on Broadway; it opened at the Barrymore Theatre on March 11. The play tells the story of a black family's struggle to have a better life in South Side Chicago. Hansberry took the title of her play, *A Raisin in the Sun*, from Langston Hughes' poem "Harlem"; it was the first serious black drama to impact the dominant culture. New York's most influential critics gave the play positive reviews, and both black and white audiences were overwhelmingly favorable towards the play. Her 1964 play, *The Sign in Sidney Brustein's Window* never became the commercial success that *Raisin* had been primarily because her audiences failed to understand its intellectual content. *Les Blancs*, her unfinished play, was produced in 1970 but received mixed reviews and had a short run. Robert Nemiroff selected scenes from Hansberry's writings that NBC commissioned and produced as a book, *To Be Young, Gifted and Black*. He adapted the work into a play that was produced in 1969 and aired on television in 1972. In 1973 the musical *Raisin*, a revival of her play, won the Tony Award for best musical. Born in Chicago on May 19, 1930, Hansberry studied at the University of Wisconsin and the Art Institute of Chicago. In addition to plays, Hansberry's works include poems, articles, and books. Hansberry died of cancer in New York City when she was only thirty-five years old.

Sources: Abramson, *Negro Playwrights in the American Theatre*, pp. 239–54; Hine, *Black Women in America*, pp. 524–29; *Encyclopedia of Black America*, p. 425; Smith, *Notable Black American Women*, pp. 452–57.

1959 • Lloyd Richards (1919–), who directed Lorraine Hansberry's *Raisin in the Sun*, was the first black director of a play on Broadway. Richards was born in Toronto, Ontario, Canada, to Jamaican immigrants. The family moved to Detroit where Richards graduated from Wayne State University. After serving in World War II and later working as a social case investigator in Detroit, he studied in New York with Paul Mann. He was head of actor training at New York University School of the Arts from 1966 to 1972; appointed head of the Eugene O'Neill Theater Center in Waterford, Connecticut, in 1969; and from 1979 to 1991 Richards was dean of the Yale School of Drama. Richards in 1986 received a Tony Award as director of *Fences*. On retirement from Yale in 1991, the school established an endowed chair in his honor, the first of its kind named for a black American.

Sources: Bergman, *The Chronological History of the Negro in America*, p. 562; Hornsby, *Milestones in Twentieth-Century African-American History*, p. 62; *Jet* 81 (18 November 1991): 12; Salzman, *Encyclopedia of African American History and Culture*, vol. 4, p. 2332.

1962 • Diahann Carroll (1935–) starred in *No Strings* and became the first black to star in the romantic lead of a white Broadway play. Her work earned her a Tony Award.

Sources: *Jet* 89 (15 April 1996): 19.

1964 • Frederick Douglass O'Neal (1905–1992), stage, movie, and radio actor, was the first black president of the Actor's Equity Association, and later the first black international president of the Associated Actors and Artists of America. The actor and director was born in Brookville, Missisippi, and studied at the New Theatre School and the American Theatre Wing in New York City.

Sources: *Current Biography, 1946,* pp. 438–40; *Encyclopedia of Black America,* pp. 655–56; *State of Black America, 1993,* p. 295; Smith, *Notable Black American Men,* pp. 885–88.

Ruby Dee

1965 • Ruby Dee (1924–) was the first black actress to play major parts at the American Shakespeare Festival in Stratford, Connecticut, where she played Kate in *The Taming of the Shrew* and Cordelia in *King Lear.* Born Ruby Ann Wallace in Cleveland, Ohio, she is a graduate of Hunter College. Dee is known for her appearances in Broadway performances, including *A Raisin in the Sun* (1959) and *Purlie Victorious* (1961). She and her late husband, Ossie Davis, shared careers in television, stage, screen, and other public appearances, and were active in civil rights.

Sources: Hine, *Black Women in America,* pp. 313–15; *Current Biography, 1970,* pp. 107–10; *Encyclopedia of Black America,* p. 30; Smith, *Notable Black American Women,* pp. 260–62.

1970 • Maya Angelou [Marguerite Johnson] (1928–), actress, dancer, and writer, was the first black woman to have an original screenplay produced, *Georgia, Georgia,* which she directed. Angelou was also the first black woman to have a work on the nonfiction bestseller list. Her autobiographical *I Know Why the Caged Bird Sings* (1969) evoked images of a black girl's childhood in the South, and was nominated for a 1974 National Book Award and aired as a television movie in 1979. An artist of wide-ranging talents, she was nominated for a Tony Award for acting and a Pulitzer Prize for poetry.

Sources: *Current Biography, 1974,* pp. 12–15; *Jet* (8 February 1993): 4–10; Lanker, *I Dream a World,* p. 162; Smith, *Notable Black American Women,* pp. 23–27.

1970 • Margaret Rosezarian Harris (1943–2000), musician, prominent conductor, and educator, worked on Broadway, notably as music director of *Hair.* She took over that position this year on a regular basis, a pioneering engagement for a black woman. Harris was also the first black woman to conduct the symphony orchestras of Chicago, Detroit, Los Angeles, St. Louis, Minnesota, and eleven other cities in America. She gained the most prominence as a conductor; however, she also composed two ballets, an opera (*King David*) and two piano concertos. In 1995 the United States Information Service of the United States Embassy in Tashkent, Uzbekistan, invited her to serve as American cultural specialist for a local production of *Porgy and Bess.* Harris was born in Chicago on September 15, 1943, and was recognized as a gifted musician early in life. Before she was four years old, she gave a public piano recital, playing eighteen short pieces and three encores, all from memory. At age ten she performed with the Chicago Symphony Orchestra. She graduated from Julliard School with both the bachelor's and master's degrees. Harris died before assuming the position associate dean of the Pennsylvania Academy of Music.

Sources: *New York Times* (22 March 2000).

1973 • Shirley Prendergast (1932–) became the first black woman lighting designer on Broadway. She worked with the Negro Ensemble Company's *The River Niger.* After passing the lighting examination in 1969, she became one of the first black women to gain admission into the lighting division of United Scenic Artists Association. She has designed for a number of theaters, including the Alvin Ailey American Dance Theatre, New York Shakespeare Festival, and the New Federal Theatre. Prendergast was born in Boston and graduated from Brooklyn College.

Sources: Hine, *Black Women in America,* pp. 939–40.

1976 • Vinnette Justine Carroll (1922–2002) became the first black woman to direct a Broadway musical, *Your Arms Too Short to Box with God.* In the summer of 1975 the play was commissioned for the Spoleto Festival in Italy, and the next year opened to rave reviews in New York. She won an Obie Award in 1961 for *Moon on a Rainbow Shawl* and an

Emmy Award in 1964 for *Beyond the Blues*. She received three Tony Award nominations, including one for *Don't Bother Me, I Can't Cope*. Carroll was born in New York City and grew up in Jamaica, West Indies. She received degrees from Long Island University and New York University. She did doctoral study in psychology at Columbia University, and later did post-graduate study in a dramatic workshop. After completing post-graduate studies in theater, Carroll became the first black woman to play the role of Ftatateeta in George Bernard Shaw's *Caesar and Cleopatra*.

Sources: Smith, *Notable Black American Women*, pp. 81–82; *The Black New Yorkers*, p. 360; McClinton, *The Work of Vinnette Carroll, an African American Theatre Artist*; Salzman, *Encyclopedia of African-American Culture and History*, vol. 1, p. 503.

1983 • Lonette McKee (1954–) became the first black woman to star as Julie on Broadway, in the Houston Grand Opera's version of *Show Boat*. The character of Julie, the product of a mixed-race relationship, required her to pass for white as she headlines on a show sailing down the Mississippi River in the late 1880s. Detroit native McKee made a number of theater appearances on Broadway (*Showboat*, 1983), and off-Broadway (*Lady Day at Emerson's Bar and Grill*, 1986–87). Her film appearances include *The Cotton Club* (1984), *Jungle Fever* (1991), and *Malcolm X* (1992). Among her television appearances are *The Women of Brewster Place* (1989) and *Queen* (1993).

Sources: *Jet* 86 (31 October 1994): 36–39; *Contemporary Black Biography*, vol. 12, pp. 134–37.

1985 • August Wilson (1945–2005) was the first black American to have two concurrent plays on Broadway. His play, *Fences*, written in 1983, opened at the Forty-sixth Street Theatre on Broadway in April 1985. It depicts the personal and economic problems of black families. The play grossed $11 million in one year and broke the record of earnings for nonmusical plays. In 1987 Wilson won a Pulitzer Prize and a Tony Award for the play. While *Fences* was still running on Broadway, Wilson's *Joe Turner's Come and Gone*, written in 1984, opened at the Ethel Barrymore Theater. The play explores the after-effects of slavery in 1911 in Pittsburgh and the Southern black migration to the urban North. Originally named Frederick August Kittel, Wilson was born in Pittsburgh on April 27, 1945, the son of Fritz Kittel who considered himself German but was an Austro-Hungarian citizen. His parents divorced and Wilson assumed his mother's maiden name. His mother remarried, and in the 1950s the family moved from a poor Hill district to the white Hazelwood neighborhood in the suburbs. After a high school teacher gave him a non-passing grade on his research paper on Napoleon, he dropped out of school without his mother's knowledge. He spent the rest of the year reading in the local library. Over the next four years he read an estimated 300 books on a variety of topics and learned well the works of black writers. Meanwhile, his mother concluded that he had squandered his potential and that "he was no good" and "would amount to nothing." In the midst of their now stormy relationship, Wilson left home in 1963 and joined the army. He took the Officer Candidate School test and scored second in his battalion. However, he could not become an officer because he was two years too young. He left the army in 1964. On April 1, 1964, Wilson purchased a typewriter with the money he had earned by writing a term paper for his sister Freda, and, from his basement apartment in the Hill district where he now lived, he tried his hand at writing poetry. For the next dozen years or so, he worked odd jobs with low pay and began to publish his poems in small magazines, but failed to gain recognition for his work. He became a founder of two black organizations: the Center Avenue Poets Theater Workshop (1965) and Black Horizons Theatre, a black activist company (1968). For Horizons Wilson wrote his earliest one-act plays—*Recycle* (1973), *The Homecoming* (1976), and *The Coldest Day of the Year* (1977). Wilson moved to St. Paul, Minnesota, in 1977, married, and became a liberated playwright, writing such works as *Jitney!* and *Fullerton Street* (both in 1982). His play *Ma Rainey's Black Bottom* (1983), first produced by the Eugene O'Neill National Playwrights Conference, was Wilson's big breakthrough. It opened at the Cort Theater on Broadway in 1984 and ran for 175 performances, bringing him national success. His next works included *Fences* (1983, for which he won a Tony Award in 1986–87), *Joe Turner's Come and Gone* (1984), and *The Piano Lesson* (1987). The latter play was made into a television movie in 1995, with Wilson as producer. In 1990 Wilson won a second Pulitzer Prize for *Fences* and became the seventh playwright to win the prize at least twice. He also wrote *Two Trains Running* (1990), which opened on Broadway in 1992 and won the New York Drama Critics Circle Award for Best Play. His play *King Hedley II* was first produced in Pittsburgh on January 12, 2000, and opened in New York in May 2001.

Sources: *Contemporary Black Biography,* vol. 7, pp. 297–300; *The Dramatic Vision of August Wilson,* 1994; Smith, *Notable Black American Men,* pp. 1241–44; *New Yorker* (April 16, 2001): 50–65; Salzman, *Encyclopedia of African-American Culture and History,* vol. 5, pp. 2858–59.

1990 • The first black and the youngest person to become artistic director of Atlanta's Alliance Theatre was Kenny Leon (1957?–). He was raised by his grandmother in Tallahassee, Florida. In the mid–1980s he graduated from Clark Atlanta University and went on to become an actor and director at the Academy Theatre in Atlanta. He served with several theater companies, including Center Stage Theatre in Baltimore, Goodman Theatre in Chicago, and Huntington Theatre Company and Boston University Theatre in Boston.

Sources: *Contemporary Black Biography,* vol. 10, pp. 151–53.

1995 • Hope Clark (1943?–) was the first black person to direct and choreograph a major staging of the opera-musical *Porgy and Bess.* A Washington, D.C. native, she was principal dancer with the Katherine Dunham Company and the Alvin Ailey American Dance Theater during the 1960s. She also appeared in a number of television shows, including *Hill Street Blues, The Jeffersons,* and *As the World Turns.* Clark's Broadway appearances include *Don't Bother Me I Can't Cope* and *Purlie.* Her choreography for *Jelly's Last Jam* (1992) earned her a Tony Award nomination. In 1995 she won the award for directing *Porgy and Bess.*

Sources: *Contemporary Black Biography,* vol. 14, pp. 48–50.

1997 • The Ford Foundation, located in New York City, named Anna Deavere Smith (1950–) its first artist-in-residence. Her seven-month assignment was to help plan a "new initiative on the civic role of the arts." She was also asked to assist the foundation in integrating artistic and cultural perspectives across its program areas. In 1996 Smith also received a Genius Award for theater work from the John D. and Catherine T. MacArthur Foundation. The Baltimore-born playwright, performance artist, and actress is known for her unique performance. Her plays give a cross-section of Americans from the 1980s to the 1990s. She has also taught in a number of top dramatic arts programs.

Sources: *Jet* 91 (3 February 1997): 19; Salzman, *Encyclopedia of African-American Culture and History,* Supplement, p. 250; *Who's Who among African Americans,* 26th ed., pp. 1138–39.

2001 • Gordon J. Davis (1941?–) was the first black president of Lincoln Center for the Performing Arts in New York City. He had a stormy nine-month tenure with the center, then resigned abruptly. Lincoln Center is comprised of thirteen constituent arts organizations, including the New York Philharmonic, the Metropolitan Opera, the New York City Opera, and the Julliard School. An estate lawyer, Davis was the city's first black parks commissioner and for more than twenty years he was a member of the Lincoln Center board. In 1990 he was the founding chairman of what became known as Jazz at Lincoln Center. Davis grew up in Chicago near a university campus that had rich offerings in the arts.

Sources: *New York Times* (28 October 2000); (28 September 2001); (29 September 2001).

Festivals

1949 • [Daniel] Louis "Satchmo" Armstrong (1900–1971), jazz trumpeter, was the first black to preside over the New Orleans Mardi Gras. His lifelong dream came true when he was selected Mardi Gras King of the Zulu Social Aid and Pleasure Club; that led to his appearance on the cover of *Time* magazine for February 21, 1949. Born in New Orleans, he

Louis Armstrong

claimed to have been born on the Fourth of July, rather than on August 4. He learned to play the coronet and read music while in the Negro Waifs Home for Boys and later became leader of its band. Between 1917 and 1922, he played with various Dixieland jazz bands in New Orleans, including that of Kid Ory. Armstrong moved to Chicago in 1922 where he became second cornetist with King Oliver's Creole Jazz band. He was also Oliver's protégé. He married Lil Harding in 1924 (whom he later divorced); she became a strong influence in his life. Harding persuaded him to become independent of Oliver. He left Oliver's band and later moved to New York where he provided a spark in Fletcher Henderson's band and made the jazz band a viable entity. In 1927 Armstrong formed a band called Louis Armstrong and His Stompers. During the early years of Great Depression he was unemployed for a while, but from 1932 to 1935 he toured Europe, playing before King George V of England. He appeared in several noteworthy films, including *Pennies from Heaven* and *Cabin in the Sky*. At the height of his popularity in the 1950s and 1960s, Armstrong had become well known as an entertainer. His recording of "Hello Dolly," which he made in the 1960s, brought him to the top of the charts. His hits "Mack the Knife" and "Blueberry Hill" added to his popularity. Although he took a stance against racial segregation by refusing to play in New Orleans for many years, blacks often misunderstood Armstrong and accused him of pandering to whites. They also criticized his wide grin and use of a large white handkerchief—his trademark—to wipe perspiration from his face. In time, however, he became recognized as one of the most influential jazz artists. A superb showman, he was known for his gravelly, growling vocal style. In 1932 an editor of *The Melody Maker* gave him the nickname "Satchmo."

Sources: Southern, *Biographical Dictionary of Afro-American and African Musicians,* pp. 17–18; Southern, *The Music of Black Americans,* pp. 373–77; Smith, *Notable Black American Men,* pp. 29–34.

1987 • The first National Black Arts Festival in the United States was held in Atlanta. Patron of the arts and educator Michael L. Lomax (1947–) founded the world-class celebration. Its mission is "to engage, cultivate and educate diverse audiences about the arts and culture of the African Diaspora and provide opportunities for artistic and creative expression."

Sources: *Jet* 74 (25 April 1988): 51; Smith, *Encyclopedia of African American Popular Culture,* vol. 3, pp. 992–93.

Film

1902 • The first appearance of blacks in film came in *Off to Bloomingdale Asylum.* The slapstick comedy was made in France and produced by George Méliès. The black characters were probably played by white actors.

Sources: Bergman, *The Chronological History of the Negro in America,* p. 338; *Negro Almanac,* p. 1234.

1905 • *The Wooing and Wedding of a Coon* is the earliest known American-made film with an all-black cast. A derogatory one-reel film, it presented undisguised mockery of black life and featured the first movie version of a "coon." One of the most insulting black caricatures, the coon (a short version of raccoon) depicted the person as lazy, inarticulate, easily frightened, and a buffoon. The caricature was born during the slavery period and reflected the masters' and overseers' view of their slaves as "slow," "lazy," and "trifling." Hollywood films as well as minstrel shows did much to extend the coon image and to lay the groundwork for movies of the 1930s and 1940s that used the image.

Sources: Bergman, *The Chronological History of the American Negro in America,* p. 347; Klotman, *Frame by Frame,* p. 585; *Negro Almanac,* p. 1234; "The Coon Caricature," http://www.ferris.edu/news/jimcrow/coon/.

1914 • Sam Lucas [Samuel Milady] (1840–1916) was the first black to play the title role in *Uncle Tom's Cabin* on film. This may have made him also the first black man to have a leading role in film. Lucas had been the first black man to play Uncle Tom on stage in

1878. Born in Washington, Ohio, Lucas performed with major minstrel troupes, wrote one of the most popular minstrel songs of the 1870s ("Carve dat 'Possum"), appeared in vaudeville, and starred in musical comedies, including *A Trip to Coontown* (1898). He is also known as the first black composer of popular ballads.

Sources: Emery, *Black Dance,* pp. 205, 209; Johnson, *Black Manhattan,* pp. 90–92, 102, 113; Southern, *The Music of Black Americans,* p. 237; Richards, *African American Films through 1959,* p. 177.

1915 • Madame Sul-Te-Wan [Nellie Conley] (1873–1959) was the first black American to be hired by a major movie producer on a continuing basis. D. W. Griffith hired her after she worked on *Birth of a Nation*. Born in Louisville, Kentucky, she later moved to Cincinnati and continued theatrical work begun earlier. There she organized her first company, The Black Four Hundred, and the next year she formed The Rair Black Minstrels; both contributed to her success. She married and moved to California around 1912 but had little success on stage. Then she turned to D. W. Griffith for employment. Sul-Te-Wan appeared in about eleven films between 1915, when *Birth of a Nation* opened, and 1940, when the Twentieth Century-Fox film *Maryland* opened. She also had fleeting appearances as an extra in other films.

Sources: Beasley, *The Negro Trail Blazers of California,* p. 237; Hine, *Black Women in America,* pp. 1129–32; *Our World* 9 (February 1954): 80–82; Smith, *Notable Black American Women,* pp. 1093–94.

1916 • The Lincoln Motion Picture Company, founded on May 24, was the first movie company organized by black filmmakers. On January 20, 1917, the state of California formally incorporated the company and on April 30, 1917, Lincoln issued 25,000 shares of common stock. Actor Noble Johnson was the company's founding president. Other officers included actor Clarence A. Brooks; James T. Smith, a druggist; and Dudley A. Brooks, treasurer and assistant secretary. The film company's first production was *The Realization of a Negro's Ambition,* released in mid 1916. Other films were *Trooper of Troop K* (*Trooper of Company K,* 1916), *The Law of Nature* (1917), *Lincoln Pictorial* (1918), *A Man's Duty* (1919), *By Right of Birth* (1921), and *A Day with the Tenth Calvary at Fort Huachua* (1922). White cameraman Harry Gant handled the cinematography and directed most of the company's productions; blacks, however, still managed Lincoln. Publicity materials noted that the company expected to reach millions of people, and it booked its films in theaters and arranged for showings in churches, halls, schools, and small towns without theaters. Nevertheless, it closed in 1921.

Sources: Birchard, *Lincoln Motion Picture Company* (1916–1921), pp. 1–3; Richards, *African American Films Through 1959*.

1921 • Anita Bush, Lawrence Chenault, Bill Pickett, Steve Reynolds, and thirty black cowboys appeared in the first all-black Western movie, *The Crimson Skull* (also known as *The Scarlet Claw*) . The 30mm, silent, black-and-white movie was filmed on location in the all-black town of Boley, Oklahoma.

Sources: Richards, *African American Films through 1959,* p. 42; Hine, *Black Women in America,* pp. 1320.

1926 • Stepin Fetchit [Lincoln Theodore Monroe Andrew Perry] (1902–1985) and Carolynne Snowden played in the first onscreen black romance in the movie, *In Old Kentucky*. Fetchit, an actor and comedian, was the first black actor to receive feature billing in movies and the first black to appear in films with stars like Will Rogers and Shirley Temple. He appeared in films in the 1920s and 1930s. The Key West, Florida, native took his stage name from a race horse on which he had bet in Oklahoma, before he left for Hollywood in the 1920s.

Sources: *Encyclopedia of Black America,* p. 38; Hornsby, *Milestones in Twentieth-Century African-American History,* pp. 345–46; Dates and Barlow, *Split Image,* p. 138.

1928 • The first black sound film was *Melancholy Dame,* a comedy two-reeler, starring Evelyn Preer, Roberta Hyson, Edward Thompson, and Spencer Williamson.

Sources: Klotman, *Frame by Frame,* p. 347.

1929 • The first two full-length films with all-black casts were *Hearts in Dixie,* starring Daniel Haynes, Nina Mae McKinney, and Victoria Spivey; and *Hallelujah,* starring Clarence Muse, Stepin Fetchit, and Mildred Washington. *Hearts in Dixie* was also the first black-oriented all-talking, all-singing film from a major company.

Sources: Bergman, *The Chronological History of the Negro in America,* p. 447; Kane, *Famous First Facts,* p. 401; Klotman, *Frame by Frame,* pp. 217–18, 227; Southern, *The Music of Black Americans,* pp. 436–437.

1929 • Nina Mae McKinney (1912–1967) was cast in the starring role as Chick in King Vidor's film *Hallelujah*—the first all-black musical—and in March became the first "black temptress" in talking pictures. In that role she also became the first recognized black woman actor in a Hollywood film. McKinney was born on June 12, 1912, in Lancaster, South Carolina. She lived there with her grandmother until the age of twelve, when she moved to New York City to live with her parents and attend school. When she was sixteen, the self-taught dancer was spotted in the chorus line of Lew Leslie's *Blackbirds* (1929) and was hired for the role in *Hallelujah.* With her dance of seduction, the Swanee Shuffle, she became the first leading lady to create a tradition of style that Lena Horne and Dorothy Dandridge would express. Although she signed a five-year contract with MGM when she was only seventeen, Hollywood had no place for beautiful, sexy, mulatto women; the movie industry cast her in minor roles in obscure films while the American film public ignored her. McKinney moved to Europe in December 1929 where she was billed as the black Garbo. She sang in cellars and cafes and later starred with Paul Robeson in *Congo Road* (1930) and *Sanders of the River* (1935). She returned to the United States in 1940 and sang and toured the country with her own band. Eleven years after her death, McKinney was inducted into the Black Filmmakers Hall of Fame.

Sources: *The Black New Yorkers,* p. 205; Smith, *Notable Black American Women,* pp. 707–08.

1934 • When Etta Moten Barnett (1091–2004) sang at a White House dinner in January before President Franklin D. Roosevelt and his guests, she became the first black movie actress to entertain there. In the 1930s she was one of the first black actresses to be cast in a romantic role in film. Born in Weimar, Texas, she moved about with her family, living in California and later in Kansas City, where Barnett sang with the Jackson Jubilee Singers. She graduated from the University of Kansas. Her senior concert recital led to an invitation to join the Eva Jessye Choir. After moving to New York, Barnett began to appear in Broadway musicals, yet sometimes only her voice was used. Her singing voice was used in several films, but it was not until *The Gold Diggers of 1933* that she actually appeared on screen. In 1934 she sang "Carioca" in *Flying Down to Rio,* starring Ginger Rogers and Fred Astaire, and for the first time actually received screen credit. Barnett made her concert debut in New York's Town Hall and from 1942 to 1945 she toured with the show *Porgy and Bess,* singing opposite Todd Duncan as Porgy. Her singing career tapered off in the early 1960s. After that, Barnett became active with the Alpha Kappa Alpha Sorority, the Links Incorporated, and served on numerous boards. She was twice married, the second time to Claude Barnett, who headed the Associated Negro Press. In the fall of 2001 entertainers and more than 400 other friends joined her in Chicago in celebration of her 100th birthday.

Sources: Smith, *Notable Black American Women,* pp. 51–55; Potter and Claytor, *African-American Firsts,* p. 61; *Contemporary Black Biography,* vol. 18, pp. 128–30.

1937 • Fredi Washington (1903–1994), actress, dancer, and civil rights activist, founded the Negro Actors Guild of America and became its first executive secretary. Born Fredericka Carolyn Washington in Savannah, Georgia, she moved to New York and completed studies at Egri School of Dramatic Writing and the Christophe School of Languages. She landed a spot in the chorus line in the 1921 production of the musical *Shuffle Along.* Her role in the 1926 Broadway play *Black Boy* typecast her as the tragic mulatto and led her to leave stage and screen. In the late 1920s Washington toured Europe and returned to the United States to star in a series of films. By the 1930s she had become one of the country's great black dramatic actresses, appearing in strong roles in such movies as *The Emperor Jones* (1933), *the Old Man of the Mountain* (1933), and *Imitation of Life* (1934). She returned to the Broadway stage in the late 1930s, where she played opposite Ethel Waters in *Mamba's Daughters*. Despite some success, Washington sensed that the stereotyped roles she played stalled her career and turned to politically oriented activities. She founded the Negro Actors Guild of America in 1937 to create jobs for black actors and to eliminate stereotyped roles. She was theater editor and columnist for *The People's Voice* and used her column to criticize injustices to blacks in the arts.

Sources: *Contemporary Black Biography,* vol. 10, pp. 247–49; Smith, *Notable Black American Women,* pp. 1212–14.

Fredi Washington

1940 • *Son of Ingagi* was the first black-cast horror film. Originally titled *House of Horror,* the seventy-minute film was in black and white with sound. The black cast included Laura Bowman, Spencer Williams (who wrote the story), Daisy Bufford, Alfred Grant, Earl J. Morris, Arthur Ray, Jesse Graves, and The Four Toppers.

Sources: Hine, *Black Women in America,* pp. 154, 1323; Richards, *African American Films Through 1959,* pp. 157–58.

1944 • The first United States Army training film favorably depicting blacks was made. It was designed to introduce black and white soldiers to the contributions of blacks in military history. Producer Frank Capra, black writer Carlton Moss (1900–1997), and a large group of black soldiers were among those who created *The Negro Soldier.*

Sources: Dates and Barlow, *Split Image,* p. 150; Smith, *Notable Black American Men,* pp. 841–43; *Contemporary Black Biography,* vol. 17, pp. 131–33.

1948 • *No Time for Romance* was the first all-black cast film in Cinecolor. Vivian Cosby wrote the original story that recounts the struggle of a young musician of superior talent who is successful in his efforts to reach the top. The film's cast included forty-six black actors and actresses.

Sources: Richards, *African American Films through 1959,* p. 126.

1959 • *Odds Against Tomorrow* was the first modern film produced by a black American, Harry Belafonte (1927–).

Sources: *The Black New Yorkers,* p. 290.

1963 • Wendell Franklin (1920?–) was assistant director for the film *The Greatest Story Ever Told,* breaking Hollywood's color bar against blacks as production personnel, and was the first black to have an important creative post on a major movie. Previously he had staged a number of musical events and had been state manager at NBC-TV in Hollywood. Franklin studied under Laura Bowman and the Lafayette Players. During World War II, he created and staged army productions, and for two years he worked with the *Carmen Jones* company.

Sources: "Hollywood Hires a Negro Director," *Sepia* 12 (April 1963): 35–38.

1971 • Richard Roundtree (1942–) became the first black private detective and super-hero in a motion picture role in the trendsetting movie, *Shaft.* Born in New Rochelle, New York, he attended Southern Illinois University on a football scholarship, but became interested in acting in campus theater. In 1967 he was a model for the Ebony Fashion Fair and later advertised hair care products for black men in *Ebony* magazine. After Bill Cosby advised him to study dramatic arts in New York, Roundtree joined the Negro Ensemble Company and appeared in three of their productions.

Sources: *Ebony Success Library,* vol. 2, pp. 224–27.

Richard Roundtree

Hollywood's First Black Producer

In 1968 Gordon A. Parks Sr. (1912–2006) produced *The Learning Tree,* and he helped to break down racial barriers in Hollywood when he became the first black to produce, direct, and score a film for a major studio, Warner Bros. The film, *Seven Arts,* was based on his autobiographical novel published in 1963. On September 19, 1989, the film became one of the first registered in the Library of Congress's national film registry. Other highly commercial films directed by Parks included *Shaft* (1971), *Shaft's Big Score* (1972), and *The Super Cops* (1974) all for MGM. After it had been struggling for some time, the "Shaft" films enabled MGM to become financially sound again.

Sources: *Contemporary Black Biography,* vol. 1, pp. 184–88; Smith, *Notable Black American Men,* pp. 907–11; Salzman, *Encyclopedia of African-American Culture and History,* vol. 4, pp. 2101–02; *Jet* 96 (20 September 1999): 19.

1982 • The first black American woman to direct a feature-length film, *Losing Ground,* was Kathleen Collins. She also wrote the screenplay.

Sources: Hine, *Black Women in America,* p. 1331.

1989 • Euzham Palcy was the first black woman director of a full-length film for a major American studio. *A Dry White Season,* starring Donald Sutherland and Susan Sarandon, deals with apartheid in South Africa. Palcy was born in Martinique and educated at the Sorbonne in Paris, with a bachelor's degree in French literature. She also received a degree in filmmaking from Vaugiard in Paris.

Sources: *Jet* 81 (18 November 1991): 62; *Movies on TV and Videocassette,* 1993–94, p. 295; *Who's Who among African Americans,* 13th ed., p. 1022.

1989 • Lenny Henry (1958–), British comedian, actor, writer, and director, was the first British comedian to make a live stand-up comedy film, *Lenny Henry Live and Unleashed.* Born in Dudley, Great Britain, he distinguished himself early on as a comic. He left school at age fifteen to work on his comedy. He imitated Elvis Presley at the Queen Mary Ballroom in Dudley, his first stage appearance. In 1975 Henry received his first big break, winning a television talent show *New Faces.* He moved on to the variety club circuit, performing in discos and clubs. He was hired on the children's cult television program *Tiswas* in 1978, and three years later appeared in the adult version of the program, called *O.T.T.* (*Over the Top*). Other shows followed, including *Three of a Kind* and *The Lenny Henry Show.* His character Delbert Wilkins, seen in the latter show, was popular with viewers who liked the loud-dressing, fast-talking hustler; however, the British government urged the British Broadcasting Corporation to kill off the shady character. In 1989 Henry published a spin-off of the show called *Lenny Henry's Well-Hard Paperback.* It was in that year that he made a live stand-up comedy film, *Lenny Henry Live and Unleashed,* a first for a British comedian. In 1988 he launched the independent production company, Crucial Films, a company that encourages the work of minority artists.

Sources: *Contemporary Black Biography,* vol. 9, pp. 114–17.

1992 • Julie Dash (1952–) became the first black woman writer and director to have a feature-length film in national distribution. The film, *Daughters of the Dust,* is the story of one day in the lives of a black family living on Ibo Island, South Carolina. Dash was born in New York City and graduated from City College of New York with a degree in film production. She moved to Los Angeles in search of a career in filmmaking. Dash became sound assistant for the film *Passing Through* in 1973 and continued her studies at the Center for Advanced Film Studies at the American Film Institute. With a Guggenheim Grant in 1981, Dash began work on a series of films about black women. Her drama *Illusions* was highly acclaimed and received the 1989 Jury Prize for the Black Filmmakers Foundation's

Best Film of the Decade. Although she began work on *Daughters of the Dust* in 1975, Dash continued to work on the project throughout the 1980s. She relocated to Atlanta in 1986, founded Geechee Girls Productions, Inc., in 1988, and released *Daughters of the Dust,* which catapulted her to national attention.

Sources: Hine, *Black Women in America,* pp. 301–2; *Essence* 22 (February 1992): 38; Smith, *Notable Black American Women,* Book II, pp. 159–61.

1994 • When Whoopi Goldberg (1950–) hosted the sixty-sixth annual Academy Awards telecast on March 21, she became the first black and the first solo woman ever to host the event. More than one billion people watched the Oscars that year. She followed a long line of comedians, including Billy Crystal, Johnny Carson, Bob Hope, and others, who had previously hosted the show and she went on to serve as host three additional times. Born Caryn Johnson in New York City, Goldberg lived with her mother in a housing project in the Chelsea section of Manhattan. She started acting at age eight, having been influenced by established actresses including Gracie Allen, Carole Lombard, and Claudette Colbert. She dropped out of school at age seventeen. During the 1960s Goldberg was a hippie and participated in civil rights marches and student protests at Columbia University. Goldberg moved to the West Coast in 1974 to begin a new life with her daughter and to pursue an acting career. She made her film debut in *The Color Purple* (1985). For her lead role as Celie, Goldberg won a Golden Globe Award, the NAACP Image Award, and an Academy Award nomination. She won an Academy Award as best supporting actress in the film *Ghost* in 1991, the second black actress to win the award (Hattie McDaniel was the first in 1939). Her other films include *Jumpin' Jack Flash* (1986), *Fatal Beauty* (1987), *Homer and Eddie* (1989), *The Long Walk Home* (1990), *The Player* (1992), *Sister Act* (1992), *The Lion King* (1994), *How Stella Got Her Groove Back* (1998), and *Rat Race* (2001). In 1992 she hosted the talk show *The Whoopi Goldberg Show* and has co-hosted a number of television shows. She has also participated in a number of benefits, including Comic Relief. Her various television appearances include *Star Trek: The Next Generation* (1987–94) and *Baghdad Café* (1990). Whoopi Goldberg became the only black performer to win an Oscar (1991), Tony (2002), Emmy (2002), and Grammy (1985), as well as the Mark Twain Prize for American Humor (2001), for which she was the first woman honoree.

Whoopi Goldberg

Sources: *Contemporary Black Biography,* vol. 4, pp. 102–6; *Jet* 85 (21 February 1994): 55, 113 (14 April 2008): 60; 85 (11 April 1994): 54–55; Smith, *Notable Black American Women,* pp. 409–10.

1995 • Laurence Fishburne (1961–) became the first black American to play Othello in film. Fishburne was born in Augusta, Georgia, but the family relocated to New York when he was a young child. Fishburne began his acting career at age eleven when he began a three-year appearance in the soap opera *One Life to Live.* Filmmaker Spike Lee cast him in the film *School Daze,* but Fishburne refused to play in Lee's 1988 hit *Do the Right Thing.* He was involved in a number of television projects, including episodes of *Hill Street Blues* and *CSI.* Other film appearances include *the Color Purple* (1985), *Boyz N the Hood* (1991), *Just Cause* (1995), and the *"Matrix"* movies (1999-2003). He appeared in various stage productions, such as *Two Trains Running* (1992), *Tuskegee Airmen* (1995) and *Miss Evers Boys* (1997). He is an advocate for positive roles of blacks on stage and screen.

Sources: Salzman, *Encyclopedia of African-American Culture and History,* Supplement, pp. 93–94; *Contemporary Black Biography,* vol. 22, pp. 72–77.

Laurence Fishburne

1997 • Michael Jai White became the movies' first black superhero with his role in *Spawn.* In this movie with dazzling special effects, White played Al Simmons, a government agent. Following the film's introduction, the comic book it was based upon became a national bestseller.

Sources: *Jet* 92 (22 September 1997): 35.

1997 • New Millennium Studios became the first full-service Hollywood film production studio in Virginia. Founders of the new company were Tim Reid, co-star of the television sitcom *Sister, Sister;* his wife Daphne Maxwell Reid, a star on *The Fresh Prince of Bel-Air;*

and their partners Dan Hoffler and Mark Warner. Reid formed New Millennium Studios Picture Corporation to concentrate on films and Tim Reid Productions to concentrate on television. *Jet* 92 (4 August 1997): 38.

2001 • When Whoopi Goldberg (1950–) won the Mark Twain Prize for American Humor, she was the first woman and only the fourth person to earn the honor. The award ceremony was held at the John F. Kennedy Center for the Performing Arts and was televised on November 21 on PBS.

Sources: *Jet* 100 (5 November 2001): 12.

Tyler Perry

2008 • Tyler Perry (1969–) actor, playwright, screenwriter, television and film producer, and director—opened Tyler Perry Studios on October 4, and became the first black American owner of a major television and film studio. Located on over thirty acres in Atlanta, his studio is housed in a 200,000-square-foot production complex featuring five soundstages, a post-production facility, a 400-seat theater, private screening rooms, and areas for entertaining and other events. In his work Perry concentrates on themes such as drama, humor, religion, racism, love, and other subjects. After his career in playwriting began in the late 1990s, he reached an untapped audience and rocketed to success and acclaim. His works also revitalized urban theater and redefined gospel theater. Perry is known for his beloved character "Madea," a term of endearment often used by blacks to refer to their grandmothers; it is also used to refer to a composite of women in the black community that Perry has known. Perry has produced eleven films, eleven plays, a best-selling novel, and two popular television programs. He got his start with his first play, *I Know I've Been Changed* (1998), and Perry followed with a succession of plays, including *I Can Do Bad All by Myself* (1999), *Diary of a Mad Black Woman* (2001), *Madea's Family Reunion* (2002), *Madea's Class Reunion* (2003), *Why Did I Get Married?* (2004), *Madea Goes to Jail* (2005), and others. His film career began in 2005, and he adapted many of his plays into film. In *Diary of a Mad Black Woman* (2005) he cast himself as three characters: Madea, Joe Baker, and Brian Baker. *The Family That Preys* was released in 2009 and was written and directed by Perry. In 2010, he directed and produced Ntozake Shange's play, *for colored girls,* into a film; it met mixed reviews. In 2012 he released *Good Deeds* and *Madea's Witness-Protection,* both of which he wrote, directed, and starred in. Perry also produced *Tyler Perry's House of Payne* and *Meet the Browns,* both popular television shows. By 2012, Perry was still writing plays and directing and producing films and television shows. Madea remains at the center of much of Perry's work. Tyler Perry (Emmitt R. Perry Jr.) was born in New Orleans on September 14, 1969. He moved to Atlanta in 1992 and, after struggling for a time, fulfilled his dream of having his writing catapult him to success.

Sources: *Contemporary Black Biography* 54, 2006; *Jet* 116 (19–26 October 2009): 20; Christian, "Becoming Tyler," *Ebony* 63 (October 2008): 83.

2009 • The full-length movie, *The Princess and the Frog,* opened on December 11 with the first black female lead in a Disney animated feature. Rising black star and Tony Award–winning actress Anika Noni Rose provides the voice for the princess. The story is like an old fable in which a frog asks a princess to kiss him on the promise that he will turn into a prince. Instead, when she does kiss the frog she becomes a frog as well. The film is set in New Orleans (The Big Easy) and its boggy surroundings in the 1910s and '20s. The heroine, Tiana, is a hard-working culinary prodigy who aims to open a restaurant in the French Quarter. Once Tiana becomes a frog, she and Prince Naveen of Maldonia (already transformed into a frog by a witch doctor) go into the bayou filled with swamp creatures. The movie highlighted the spirit of black Cajun soul that defines the culture of New Orleans.

Sources: "Disney Charms Again with 'Princess'," *Tennessean* (11 December 2009); "Holiday Movie Preview 2009," *Time* 174 (7 December 2009): 105; "The Top 10 Everything of 2009," *Time* 174 (21 December 2009): 82; Robertson, "The Princess Diaries," *Essence* 40 (January 2010): 90–93.

Museums

2005 • The founding director of the National Museum of African American History and Culture is Dr. Lonnie G. Bunch III (1952–). The first national museum founded to showcase the work of African Americans, the NMAAHC was established on December 19, 2003; it is the nineteenth museum to open as a part of the Smithsonian Institution. Architect David Adjaye designed the building, which features a crown motif from Yoruban sculpture. It will be erected on the National Mall in Washington, D.C.; construction began in February 2012 and is scheduled to be completed in July 2015. In addition to overseeing the building's design, Bunch sets the museum's mission, engages in fundraising and membership campaigns, develops collections, and establishes cultural partnerships. The NMAAHC opened "Let Your Motto Be Resistance: African American Photographs," its inaugural exhibition, in May 2007 at the International Center of Photography in New York City. Another exhibit, "Slavery at Jefferson's Monticello: Paradox of Liberty," was at the National Museum of History in 2012 and received nationwide attention. Bunch has served as president of the Chicago Historical Society, associate director for curatorial affairs at the Smithsonian, education specialist at the Smithsonian's National Air and Space Museum, and curator of history for the California Afro-American Museum in Los Angeles (1983–89). President George W. Bush appointed Bunch to the Commission for the Preservation of the White House in 2002. In 2005, the American Association of Museums named Bunch one of the 100 most influential museum professionals of the twentieth century. The Newark, New Jersey, native received his bachelor's, master's, and doctoral degrees from the American University.

Sources: "Lonnie Bunch Biography." http://clas.asu.edu/bunch-bio; Newsdesk—Pressroom of the Smithsonian Institution. "Staff Biographies, Lonnie G. Bunch." http://newsdesk.si .edu/about/bios/Lonnie-g-bunch; *Who's Who among African Americans,* 26th ed., p. 178.

Music

1551 • Vincente Lusitano (d. 1561?), of Portugal, published a book of twenty-three motets, or sacred music, "Liber primus epigramatum," and became the first black composer known to have music published. His family name is unknown ("Lusitano" simply means "Portuguese"). He became a priest and taught in Padua and Viterbo. Nothing is known of him after 1561.

Sources: *New York Times* (13 September 1999); Sadie, *New Grove Dictionary of Music and Musicians,* vol. 15, pp. 326–27.

1764 • Newport Gardner [Occramer Marycoo] (1746–1826) was the first black American to compose in the European tradition. An African, he was sold into slavery in Newport, Rhode Island, at age fourteen. In 1764 he began to write music, and it is likely that Gardner became one of the first black music teachers in the new nation in 1783. In 1791 he purchased freedom for himself and his family, and established a singing school in Newport. "Crooked Shanks," which he may have composed, was probably the first musical composition by an American black to be published in 1803. The text of *Promise Anthem,* one of his choral pieces performed in Newport and Boston, still exists.

Sources: *Detroit Free Press* (9 February 1992); Hornsby, *Chronology of African-American History,* p. 10; Southern, *Music of Black Americans,* pp. 69–70; Southern, *Readings in Black American Music,* pp. 36–40.

1782 • The first known printing of a "Negro Jig" appeared in *A Selection of Scotch, English, Irish and Foreign Airs,* a dance collection published by James Aird in Scotland. This tune may represent the earliest evidence of slave music influence on white colonists. The "Negro Jig" in this published work may or may not have been of slave origin, but it may have been composed to imitate a slave dance tune. It was clear, however, that the colonists had become aware of the distinctive qualities of Negro music and used it for dancing.

Sources: Southern, *The Music of Black Americans,* 2nd ed., pp. 46, 61.

Elizabeth Taylor Greenfield

1818 • Frank [Francis] Johnson (1792–1844), composer and bandleader, was the first black American musician to publish sheet music. This is perhaps the earliest of a long series of firsts: He was also the first black to win wide acclaim as a musician in the United States and in England, the first to give formal band concerts, and the first to tour widely in the United States. In the 1843–44 season Johnson produced the first racially integrated concerts in United States history. He was the first American musician of any race to take a musical group abroad to perform in Europe, and he introduced the promenade concert to the United States. Said to have been born in Martinique, Johnson migrated to the United States in 1809 and settled in Philadelphia.

Sources: *Black Perspective in Music,* 5 (Spring 1977): 3–29; Southern, *Biographical Dictionary of Afro-American and African Musicians,* pp. 205–07; Southern, *The Music of Black Americans,* pp. 107–10, 112–16.

1853 • Elizabeth Taylor Greenfield (1819?–1876), the nation's first black concert singer, became the first black singer to give a command performance before royalty when she appeared before Queen Victoria on May 10, 1853. Born in Natchez, Mississippi, she was called "The Black Swan" because of her sweet tones and wide vocal compass. Greenfield toured the United States and Canada extensively during her career and became the best-known black concert artist of her time. In the 1860s, she organized and directed the Black Swan Opera Troupe.

Sources: Logan and Winston, *Dictionary of American Negro Biography,* pp. 268–70; Smith, *Notable Black American Women,* pp. 412–16; Southern, *The Music of Black Americans,* pp. 103–04.

1858 • The first black pianist to win national fame was Thomas Greene Bethune [Blind Tom] (1849–1909). He was also the first black artist known to have performed at the White House. Then about ten years old, he played the piano for President James Buchanan. Born a blind slave near Columbus, Georgia, Bethune's talent as a composer and a pianist was soon recognized by Colonel Bethune, who had purchased him in 1850. The child prodigy made his debut in Savannah, Georgia, and for more than forty years amazed his audiences "with his artistry and his gift for total recall" of the more than seven hundred pieces that he played. Bethune had sporadic formal training and is said to have composed more than a hundred works. The most celebrated of the early black pianists, he began a tour of Europe in 1866 that netted $100,000.

Sources: Logan and Winston, *Dictionary of American Negro Biography,* pp. 43–44; *Encyclopedia of Black America,* p. 174; Southern, *The Music of Black Americans,* pp. 246–47; Garrett, *Famous First Facts about Negroes,* pp. 122–23; *American Visions* (February-March 1995): 22–25.

Thomas Greene Bethune

1867 • The first collection of plantation, or slave, songs appeared in print, in *Slave Songs of the United States,* edited by William Allen, Charles Ware, and Lucy McKim Garrison. While several attempts had been made to write down the refrains as early as 1800 and to notate the music in the 1830s, it was not until 1867 that they were actually published.

Sources: Southern, *The Music of Black Americans,* 2nd ed., p. 151.

1868 • The first black composer to write an opera was John Thomas Douglass (1847–1886). In this year his three-act *Virginia's Ball* was registered with the United States Copyright Office but was later lost. The opera was performed in 1868 at the Stuyvesant Institute on Broadway in New York City. Reputedly, a wealthy patron sent Douglass abroad for study. He settled in New York by the late 1860s and for the next decade presented enough concerts to become known as "the master violinist" and "one of the greatest musicians of his race."

Sources: Southern, *The Music of Black Americans,* 2nd ed., p. 248.

1873 • The first black opera troupe organized to present complete operas in the United States was the Colored American Opera Company of Washington, D.C. They received critical acclaim for their production of Julius Eichberg's *The Doctor of Alcantara,* but the company was short-lived. The first lasting black opera company was the Theodore Drury

The First Black Classical Composer

During the 1770s the Chevalier de Saint-Georges [Joseph Boulogne] (1739?–1799) was the first black classical composer of note. Between 1772 and 1779 he published most of his instrumental music, and made his debut as an operatic composer in 1777. Although little is known about his musical training, it is said that he took violin lessons from his father's plantation manager (and possibly with Leclair), and studied composition with Gossec in France. One of the finest swordsmen in Europe, Saint-Georges also excelled in dancing, swimming, skating, and riding. He was born of racially mixed parents near Basse Terre, Guadeloupe.

Sources: *Black Perspective in Music,* 7 (Fall 1979): 143; *Detroit Free Press* (9 February 1992); *New Grove Dictionary of Music and Musicians,* pp. 391–92; Phillips, *Piano Music by Black Composers,* p. 218.

Colored Opera Company, which began in Brooklyn, New York, in 1889. Drury (1860s–1940s), singer and music teacher, achieved a series of nine consecutive annual performances from 1900 to 1908. His last production was *Carmen,* in Philadelphia, in 1938.

Sources: Garrett, *Famous First Facts about Negroes,* p. 125; Moses, *Alexander Crummell,* p. 202; Southern, *The Music of Black Americans,* pp. 256, 288.

1878 • James Bland (1854–1911), composer and minstrel entertainer, was the first black to compose a song that became an official state song. "Carry Me Back to Old Virginny," was adopted by the state in April 1940, although few knew that it was by a black composer. Bland wrote approximately seven hundred songs in his career, including "Oh, Dem Golden Slippers" and "In the Evening by the Moonlight." Born in Flushing, New York, he attended Howard University Law School but gave up his law studies to join the entertainment world.

Sources: Logan and Winston, *Dictionary of American Negro Biography,* pp. 46–47; *Encyclopedia of Black America,* p. 184; Southern, *The Music of Black Americans,* pp. 234–37.

1886 • Gussie Lord Davis (1863–1899), songwriter, wrote "'Neath the Maple on the Hill" and persuaded Helling & Company to publish the song for a twenty-dollar fee. He also wrote the successful song "The Lighthouse By the Sea" which resulted in a contract in 1885 with publisher Groen & Company. Later George Propheter took Davis to New York where, within a few years, the leading publishers in New York's commercial music district, or Tin Pan Alley, were publishing his songs. In 1886 Davis was perhaps the first black American to sign a contract and to have his songs published by white publishing houses. He was born in Whitestone, New York, and obtained his musical education through private tutoring at the Nelson Musical College in Cincinnati. He was denied admission to the school because of his race. However, the school's administration hired him as a janitor and paid him fifteen dollars a month, which he used for his private lessons. He became a prolific songwriter and wrote in a variety of forms, including sacred, sentimental, comic, black, and Irish. By the end of the nineteenth century Davis was one of the top two or three songwriters in the nation. His best-known work was "In the Baggage Coach Ahead" that sold more than a million copies.

Sources: Southern, *Biographical Dictionary of Afro-American and African Musicians,* p. 95; Sadie, *New Grove Dictionary of Music and Musicians,* 2nd ed., vol. 7, p.77.

1886 • Walter Craig (1854–1920) became the first black musician to be admitted to the Musician's Mutual Protective Union. He was called "the Prince of Negro Violinists" as well as a "perfect master of his instrument." Craig made his debut in 1870 at Cooper Hall in New York and was known for his society dance orchestra.

Sources: Southern, *The Music of Black Americans,* 2nd ed., p. 248.

James Bland

The Fisk Jubilee Singers

In February 1882, the Fisk Jubilee Singers, who introduced the spiritual to the world as an American art form, became the first black choir to perform at the White House. Their rendition of "Safe in the Arms of Jesus" moved President Chester Arthur to tears. The night before their performance, the singers were denied lodging in every hotel in the district. On October 6, 1871, the nine men and women singers —all former slaves or freedmen—set out on their first tour to raise money to save fledgling Fisk University located in Nashville, Tennessee. Under the direction of George Leonard White, their first tour took them to Ohio. While there, they assumed the name Jubilee Singers, after the Year of the Jubilee in the Old Testament. Although they were hungry and cold, they donated their first purse of less than fifty dollars to the Chicago Relief Fund to aid victims of the great Chicago fire. After that, they traveled widely, singing in the Boston Coliseum, in churches, and electrified audiences wherever they performed. They sang the songs of their ancestors—slave songs, and spirituals. Following a successful performance in New England, President Ulysses Grant invited them to sing at the White House. The singers made their first tour of England in 1873–74, where they sang before royalty and in cathedrals and palaces. Queen Victoria was so impressed with them that she commissioned her court painter, George Edmund Havel, to paint a portrait of the group that now totaled eleven members. His life-size rendition now hangs in Fisk's Jubilee Hall, the residence hall that the school erected in 1875 from funds that the singers earned while on tour. The singers toured Europe in 1875 and continued to sing throughout the United States, electrifying audiences with their moving rendition of slave songs and spirituals. In November 2000 the current singers were inducted into the Gospel Music Hall of Fame in Nashville, Tennessee. President George W. Bush awarded the singers the National Medal of the Arts, in 2008.

Sources: *American Visions* (February-March 1995): 23; Ward, *Dark Midnight When I Rise*; Fox, "The Jubilees Forever."

1889 • Composer Will Marion Cook (1869–1944) formed an orchestra for the black community of Washington, D.C., with Frederick Douglass as its president. Saxophonist and orchestra leader Elise Hoffman gave what was probably the first solo by a black American on a saxophone at the orchestra's concert in Grand Army Hall on September 26.The orchestra disbanded after a couple of tours of the eastern seaboard and then Cook left for New York.

Sources: Badger, *A Life in Ragtime,* p. 24.

1897 • In December 1897, the first piano rag by a black, "Harlem Rag," was published. Its composer, Thomas Million Turpin (1873–1922), was a bar owner in Saint Louis's Tenderloin district and eventually became the owner of the Booker T. Washington Theater in that city.

Sources: Southern, *The Music of Black America,* pp. 291, 316, 323.

1901 • Bert [Egbert Austin] Williams (1873–1922) was the first black to record with Victor Talking Machine Company. Between 1901 and 1903 he recorded fifteen titles, primarily show tunes or comedy routines that he had done on stage. In 1910 he was the first black to receive feature billing in the Ziegfeld Follies and remained with them until 1919. Williams was born in Antigua, British West Indies, and moved with his family to New York and California. He studied civil engineering for a period, before entering show business. He and George Nash Walker formed a successful vaudeville team that reached New York City in 1896. Their show, *In Dahomey,* opened in a Times Square theater in 1902 and had a command performance during a tour abroad in 1903. The team became known for their characterizations—Walker as a citified dandy, and Williams as a blackface comic, wearing an outlandish costume and using black dialect. In 1914 Williams became the first black to star in a movie, *Darktown Jubilee*. The film is said to have caused a race riot when it was shown in Brooklyn. *Darktown Jubilee* was his only movie. Williams's trademark was the song "Nobody," which he wrote and sang. He is regarded by many as the greatest black vaudeville performer in American history.

Sources: Logan and Winston, *Dictionary of American Negro Biography,* pp. 653–54; Emery, *Black Dance,* pp. 211–13; *Encyclopedia of Black America,* p. 857; Johnson, *Black Manhattan,* pp. 104–08.

Ma Rainey

1902 • Ma Rainey [Gertrude Pridgett] (1886–1939), of the Rabbit Foot Minstrels, was the first black to sing the blues in a professional show. She learned a blues song from a local woman in Missouri, and audience response was such that she began to specialize in blues and became known as the "Mother of the Blues." Born in Columbus, Georgia, she began public appearances at age fourteen, performing in a local talent revue. She went on to perform in tent shows and sing the blues until around 1902. After marrying Will Rainey, the husband-and-wife team traveled with the Rabbit Foot Minstrels and performed as "Ma" and "Pa" Rainey. They toured the South with several companies. Ma Rainey became especially popular, receiving separate billing. She sang in a raw and gritty style and became a flashy dresser who loved jewelry and glitter. Rainey met Bessie Smith sometime between 1912 and 1916 and greatly influenced Smith's musical career. Rainey extended her audience through the recordings that she made with Paramount Record Company beginning December 1923, and through performances on the Theatre Owners Booking Association (TOBA) circuit. After the TOBA collapsed around 1931, at the time of the depression, Rainey's career suffered as well. In 1935 she returned to her native home in Columbus and operated two theaters that she owned.

Sources: Bergman, *The Chronological History of the Negro in America,* p. 336; Smith, *Notable Black American Women,* pp. 913–16; Southern, *The Music of Black Americans,* p. 330.

1902 • Chicago's Local 208, a black musicians union, became the first such union incorporated into the American Federation of Musicians.

Sources: Southern, *The Music of Black Americans,* 2nd ed., p. 218.

1903 • Wilbur Sweatman (1882–1961) and his band were the first black dance band to record. They played Scott Joplin's "Maple Leaf Rag" in a music store in Minneapolis, Minnesota. Sweatman was noted for playing three clarinets at the same time.

Sources: Southern, *The Music of Black Americans,* pp. 305–06.

1904 • *In Dahomey,* by George Walker and Bert Williams, premiered at the Shaftesbury Theatre in London and became the first black musical show to be performed abroad.

Sources: Southern, *The Music of Black Americans,* 2nd ed., p. 218.

1905 • The Memphis Students, a vaudeville act organized by Ernest Hogan (1865–1909), a multitalented black entertainer, presented the world's first syncopated music show. The group's members were not students or from Memphis, but did include twenty talented, experienced performers such as singer Abbie Mitchell (1884–1960) and dancer Ida Forsyne (1883–?). New Yorkers were the first exposed to syncopated music played by a group of instrumentalists, including saxophonists. New Yorkers also witnessed the first singing band, the first dancing conductor, and the first drummer (Buddy Gilmore) to perform stunts while drumming. The Memphis Students' initial two-week engagement lasted five months. Will Marion Cook (1869–1944) later led the group on a European tour lasting several months.

Sources: Bergman, *The Chronological History of the Negro in America,* p. 346; Johnson, *Black Manhattan,* pp. 120–22; Southern, *The Music of Black Americans,* pp. 297, 343–44.

1908 • The first black bandmasters were appointed to the U.S. Army Ninth and Tenth Cavalry regiments and the Twenty-fourth and Twenty-fifth Infantry regiments. President Theodore Roosevelt signed a special order in November ordering black bandmasters as-

The First Black Jazz Band

In 1891 Charles "Buddy" Bolden (1877–1931) was the first black to form what may have been a real jazz band, in New Orleans. His band incorporated blues and ragtime. He has been called the patriarch of jazz, and because of his fierce, driving tone, he was known as "King Bolden." A plasterer by trade, Bolden developed a cornet style that influenced musicians such as King Oliver and Dizzy Gillespie. Bolden was born in New Orleans and took his first formal music lesson from a neighbor around 1895. Soon he adapted his own style of playing from the music that he heard around town, in barbershops, and parades. He also played in small string bands, often for parties and dances. A friendly and gregarious person, Bolden was a ladies' man. As a performer, he was more comfortable in uptown New Orleans than downtown and never played at the Creole society halls. His greatest rival was John Robichaux, a Creole whose band played for wealthy plantation owners, brokers, and other white professionals. Bolden's popularity peaked in 1905. In an effort to remain ahead of his competitors, he took on more and more jobs but soon realized that his style was no longer new. Frustrated, he began to drink heavily, had spells of depression, and sometimes was jailed for his behavior. He was diagnosed as paranoid in 1907, and on June 5 that year he was committed to East Louisiana State Hospital in Jackson, Louisiana, where he spent the last twenty-four years of his life. While there, however, he played a horn on some occasions, but was not a member of the patients' band. He died in Parker Hospital on the grounds of the institution where he had been institutionalized, on November 4, at age fifty-four.

Sources: *Encyclopedia of Black America*, p. 603; *Negro Almanac*, p. 1204; Southern, *The Music of Black Americans*, pp. 340–41, 375; Williams, *Jazz Masters of New Orleans*, pp. 2–25; Marquis, *In Search of Buddy Bolden*.

signed to the four regular military regiments; white bandmasters were to be transferred out of these units as soon as possible. Four bandmasters were then promoted to the rank of chief musicians: Wade Hammond, Alfred Jack Thomas, William Polk, and Egbert Thompson.

Sources: Southern, *The Music of Black America*, 2nd ed., p, 301.

1909 • "Memphis Blues," by W[illiam] C[hristopher] Handy (1873–1958), composer, cornetist, band leader, and publisher, was the first written blues composition. It was also the first popular song to use a jazz break. Written in 1909 as a campaign song for legendary "Boss" Edward H. Crump, when he ran for mayor of Memphis, it was published in 1912. The song was the third blues song published; black songwriter Artie Matthews published the first, "Baby Seals Blues" in August 1912, a white composer published the second in September 1912, and Handy's song came three weeks later. Handy led the way in the adaptation of Southern black folk blues into popular music. His "St. Louis Blues," published two years later, carried the blues all over the world. Handy was born in a log cabin in Florence, Alabama, and began playing in a minstrel band at a young age. He was bandmaster and director of a dance orchestra in the Mississippi Delta, and then returned to Memphis where he continued band activities. In 1918, he established himself in New York City, where he made his first recordings and co-founded a music company. Handy lost his sight after World War I, partially regained it, but became totally blind in 1943. Over the years he continued to write music, arrange spirituals and blues, and compose marches and hymns. One of the most celebrated musicians of his time, Handy is known as the "Father of the Blues."

Sources: Bergman, *The Chronological History of the Negro In America*, pp. 273–74; Cantor, *Historic Landmarks of Black America*, pp. 127–28; Logan and Winston, *Dictionary of American Negro Biography*, pp. 282–83; *Encyclopedia of Black America*, p. 415; Southern, *Biographical Dictionary of Afro-American and African Musicians*, pp. 165–66; Southern, *The Music of Black Americans*, pp. 336–38.

1911 • Scott Joplin's opera *Treemonisha*, the first black folk opera written by a black composer, was first performed in private. A talented musical composer, Joplin (1868?–1917) was born in northeastern Texas. Around 1875 the family relocated to Texarkana. By the late 1880s Joplin had settled in St. Louis and later in Sedalia, Missouri. He studied at George R. Smith College in Sedalia. Joplin established himself as a composer of instrumental rags. His first major success was "Maple Leaf Rag" which earned him the title "King of Ragtime." He worked with several publishers but changed frequently in search of better terms. In 1913 he established his own publishing company. After his first major success, Joplin continued to compose. His works included the full-length ragtime opera, *A Guest of Honor* (1903), *Treemonisha* (written in 1910 and published a year later), and *Magnetic Rag* (1914). He moved from St. Louis, where he had settled again, to New York City in July 1907, and earned his living as a composer and teacher. After he died, he was remembered for little more than "Maple Leaf Rag" until the 1960s, when he was rediscovered and this work became the score for the movie *The Sting*. On January 28, 1972, *Treemonisha* premiered in Atlanta and was well received. For his contribution to American music, in 1976 Joplin received a special Bicentennial Pulitzer Prize.

Scott Joplin

Sources: Southern, *The Music of Black Americans*, 2nd ed., p. 218; Smith, *Notable Black American Men*, pp. 661–64; Logan and Winston, *Dictionary of American Negro Biography*, pp. 369–71.

1912 • James Reese Europe (1880–1919) and his Clef Club Orchestra—the leading black orchestra in the country—held a concert on May 2 for a largely white audience at Carnegie Hall in New York City for a historic first "Concert of Black Music" by black singers and instrumentalists. The program was more comprehensive than others that Europe had directed and reflected a full range of African American musical expression, including secular, religious, traditional, modern, vocal, and instrumental. Reese was born in Mobile, Alabama, and moved to Washington, D.C. He took violin lessons from Joseph Douglass, who was Frederick Douglass's grandson, and later switched to the mandolin and piano. To hone his skills in music, Europe was active in musical and dramatic activities at his church. He became active in the musical theater and directed the orchestra for such productions as *A Trip to Africa* (1904) and *Shoo-Fly Regiment* (1905). Europe became a successful bandleader and officer in the U.S. Army. On December 29, 1913, Europe, with his Society Orchestra, began a historic series of recordings of dance music for Victor Records. Europe received one of the first contracts that a major record company had given to a black musician and the musical group received the first ever given to a black orchestra. On January 12 the next year, Europe led the first black orchestra to perform at a leading white vaudeville theater, at the Palace Theater in New York City. During this performance the group complied with the union's band on black musicians by appearing on stage and not in the orchestra pit. While touring in 1914, Europe, who often experimented with new musical ideas, was the first bandleader to play W. C. Handy's "Memphis Blues."

Sources: Smith, *Notable Black American Men*, pp. 382–86; Badger, *A Life in Ragtime*, pp. 89, 115.

1915 • "Jelly Roll Blues," by Jelly Roll Morton [Ferdinand Joseph La Menthe] (1885–1941), was the first published jazz arrangement. Morton was the first true jazz composer and the first to notate his jazz arrangements. Born in Gulfport, Mississippi, he soon became immersed in the music world of New Orleans.

Sources: Logan and Winston, *Dictionary of American Negro Biography*, pp. 445–56; Southern, *The Music of Black Americans*, pp, 376–77.

1916 • Harry T. Burleigh's solo arrangements of spirituals, *Jubilee Songs of the United States of America*, was issued and became the first publication of a collection of spirituals arranged for solo voice. Before this, spirituals were performed on a concert stage but only in ensemble or choral arrangements. Burleigh's work made spirituals set in the manner of art songs available to concert singers for the first time. Later, many concert singers closed their recitals with a group of Negro spirituals. Burleigh was born on December 2, 1866 and died on September 12, 1949.

Sources: Southern, *The Music of Black Americans*, 2nd ed., pp. 219, 268.

Roland Hayes

1917 • Roland Hayes (1887–1976) became the first black to sing in Symphony Hall in Boston. Born in Curryville, Georgia, the son of former slaves, Hayes studied at Fisk University where he was a member of the Fisk Jubilee Singers. He left Fisk to study voice in Boston, then traveled and studied in Europe. The 1917 concert did not attract much public attention but another in the same venue on December 2, 1923, was a triumph. It was the beginning of a major career for Hayes. In 1923 he sang with the Boston Symphony, and may have been the first black to sing with a major orchestra. Hayes became the first black to give a recital at Carnegie Hall in 1924. He was known in the United States for his interpretation of classical lieder and Negro spirituals, and was the leading black singer of his time.

Sources: *Encyclopedia of Black America*, p. 424; *Negro Almanac*, p. 1184; Southern, *Biographical Dictionary of Afro-American and African Musicians*, p. 173; Southern, *The Music of Black Americans*, pp. 400–402.

1919 • Lucie [Lucy] Campbell [Williams] (1885–1963) published "Something Within" and became the first black woman composer to have a gospel song published. In her lifetime she wrote more than eighty songs—a number of them became classics in the field of gospel. These included "Jesus Gave Me Water," "There Is a Fountain," and "In the Upper Room with Jesus"; her songs for liturgical use included "This Is the Day the Lord Has Made." Campbell, along with Charles A. Tindley (1851–1933) and Thomas Andrew Dorsey (1899–1993), is considered a gospel music pioneer. Campbell, who had a great influence on Tindley, selected songs for his hymnal, *Gospel Pearls*. Born in Duck Hill, Mississippi, Campbell graduated from Rust College in Holly Springs, Mississippi, in 1927 and received a master of science degree from Tennessee State University in 1951. A self-taught musician, she played the piano and organ at the Metropolitan Baptist Church in Memphis. In 1909 she began to organize young people's choirs and by 1916 she was musical director of the Sunday School and Baptist Young People's Union. Her songs are still heard at Baptist Conventions and at the Grand Ole Opry in Nashville. In addition to her musical talent, Campbell was a dynamic speaker.

Sources: Smith, *Notable Black American Women*, pp. 154–55; Broughton, *Black Gospel: An Illustrated History of the Gospel Sound*, p. 39; Hine, *Black Women in America*, pp. 217–18.

1921 • Lillian "Lil" Harding Armstrong (1898–1971) joined "King" Oliver's Creole Jazz Band as pianist and is believed to have been the first woman to enter the jazz field. She was the first woman to play piano with jazz bands and led many of the finest black bands from the 1920s on, including the Dreamland Syncopators (also known as Lil's Hot Shots). "Miss Lil," as she was called, married Louis Armstrong in 1924 and was a positive influence on his career. Except for a few years in New York City, she spent her professional life in Chicago and performed in the finest clubs and theaters in the United States, Canada, and Europe. Born in Memphis, she studied at Fisk University but moved to Chicago with her family and never returned to graduate. Armstrong earned a teacher's certificate from Chicago College of Music and a post-graduate diploma from New York College of Music.

Sources: Smith, *Notable Black American Women*, pp. 27–28; Handy, *Black Women in American Bands & Orchestras*, pp. 168–69; Potter and Claytor, *African-American Firsts*, p. 194.

1921 • The Bethel Church choir in Chicago performed the first opera to be sung by blacks in that city. The opera was presented on successive nights in December. Accompanied by members of the Chicago Symphony, the Bethel choir presented Von Flotow's *Martha*. The orchestral accompaniment marked another first for blacks in Chicago. Old-line churches in black Chicago were prominent cultural forces in Chicago around the turn of the century. They also established choral study clubs. To obtain funds, personnel, and a place to perform classical music, the choral and study clubs associated themselves with the churches. The Bethel choir was the result of such union.

Sources: Harris, *The Rise of Gospel Blues*, p. 107.

The First Black Record Company

In 1921 the Pace Phonograph Company, which used the Black Swan label, was the first record company owned and operated by a black. It was established in January 1921 by Henry Pace (1897–1943), who had been owner of a music publishing company with W. C. Handy. Two former workers for the Pace-Handy Company joined him: Fletcher Henderson (1897–1952) as a recording manager and William Grant Still (1895–1978) as an arranger. In spring 1921 Ethel Waters (1896–1977) recorded the company's first hit, "Down Home Blues/Oh, Daddy." During its first six months the company reportedly sold more than half a million records. It went broke in 1923, and was sold to Paramount Records the following year.

Sources: Southern, *The Music of Black Americans,* pp. 366–67.

1922 • Kid [Edward] Ory (1886–1973), jazz trombonist, and his Sunshine Orchestra made the first instrumental jazz recording for the Nordskog label in Los Angeles in June 1922. King [Joseph] Oliver (1885–1938) and his band, often cited as the first to record, did not actually make their first record until April 6, 1923. George Morrison (1891–1974), who headed big bands operating out of Denver, Colorado, made recordings in March and April 1920, but they were never released.

Sources: Garrett, *Famous First Facts about Negroes,* p. 129; Southern, *Biographical Dictionary of Afro-American and African Musicians,* pp. 295–96; Southern, *The Music of Black Americans,* pp. 373, 379.

1923 • "Downhearted Blues/Gulf Coast Blues" was the first record by a black to sell more than a million copies. Singer Bessie Smith (1894–1937) became one of the most important women in the history of American music, both as a stage performer and recording star. Between 1923 and 1933, she gave us such works as "Backwater Blues" and "Do Your Duty," which became twentieth-century landmarks. Born in Chattanooga, Tennessee, Smith first performed on the city streets. She eventually performed with Ma [Gertrude] Rainey (1866–1939), the first professional to sing blues, in the Rabbit Foot Minstrels. Smith's only movie appearance was in the first film short featuring black musicians, *Saint Louis Blues,* later retitled *Best of the Blues,* in 1929.

Sources: Logan and Winston, *Dictionary of American Negro Biography,* pp. 561–62; *Encyclopedia of Black America,* p. 797; Smith, *Notable Black American Women,* pp. 1041–45; Southern, *Biographical Dictionary of Afro-American and African Musicians,* p. 343; Southern, *The Music of Black Americans,* pp. 368–69, 437.

Bessie Smith

1923 • In October the first male to record the blues guitar, either as solo or accompaniment, was Sylvester Weaver (1897–1960). However, the first to achieve success was "Papa" Charlie Jackson (?–1938), who recorded "Lawdy, Lawdy Blues" and "Airy Man Blues" in August 1924. These men represented the down-home blues as opposed to the classic city blues of the great women blues singers.

Sources: Southern, *The Music of Black Americans,* p. 369; Salzman, *Encyclopedia of African-American Culture and History,* vol. 4, p. 2286.

1924 • Sidney Bechet (1897?–1959), an outstanding representative of the New Orleans tradition, became the first black to achieve recognition on the soprano saxophone. He was also one of the first blacks recognized in classical music circles. Born in New Orleans, he was playing the clarinet by age six. In his early teens he played professionally, working with famous bands and orchestras, including King Oliver's and Jack Carey's, and made his first recording in 1924. A statue of Bechet was erected in Antibes in honor of his work in France.

Sources: Logan and Winston, *Dictionary of American Negro Biography*, p. 36; Garrett, *Famous First Facts about Negroes*, p. 129; *Negro Almanac*, p. 1203.

DeFord Bailey Sr.

1924 • DeFord Bailey Sr., (1899–1982), a harmonica player, became the first black musician to perform on the Grand Ole Opry in Nashville, Tennessee, on December 26, 1924. Originally called "The Barn Dance," the show's name was changed to "The Grand Ole Opry" in the autumn of 1927. Bailey was perhaps the first black heard on nationwide radio. The next year, he was the first black to have a recording session in Nashville, Tennessee. Bailey recorded eight sides for RCA. Known for his train sounds, he was one of the most influential harmonica players in blues and country music, and one of the most popular performers in the first fifteen years of the Opry, the longest-running radio show in the country. Bailey was fired in 1941 as a result of the dispute between ASCAP and the newly formed BMI over payment for music played on the radio. In 1991, a memorial marker was erected near his birth site in Wilson County, Tennessee.

Sources: Dates and Barlow, *Split Image*, p. 176; *Essence* 7 (September 1977): 154–55; Morton, *DeFord Bailey*; Smith, *Notable Black American Men*, pp. 43–46; *Tennessean* (18 December 1991).

Eva Jessye

1926 • Eva Jessye (1895–1992), composer, musician, choral director, educator, writer, and actress, became the first black woman to achieve acclaim as director of a professional choral group. The Eva Jessye Choir performed regularly at New York City's Capital Theater from 1926 until 1929. Jessye directed the choir in Hollywood's first black musical, *Hallelujah*, in 1929. She was born in Coffeyville, Kansas, graduated from Western University (Quindaro, Kansas), and later attended Langston University in Oklahoma. In 1935 Jessye became choral director for the premiere of George Gershwin's *Porgy and Bess*.

Sources: Hine, *Black Women in America*, pp. 635–36; Smith, *Notable Black American Women*, pp. 573–75; Southern, *Music of Black Americans*, pp. 429–35.

1927 • Lillian Evanti (1890–1967), a singer and composer, was the first black American to sing opera with an organized European opera company, performing *Lakmé* in Nice, France. She could sing in five languages and was fluent in them as well. She was born Annie Lillian Evans in Washington, D.C. and attended Howard University. Novelist Jessie Fauset suggested the name Evanti, a contraction of her maiden name and her married name. She was a founder of the Negro Opera Company in Washington. Presidents Dwight D. Eisenhower and Harry S. Truman invited her to sing at the White House during and after World War II. She also began her own publishing company, the Columbia Music Bureau.

Sources: Logan and Winston, *Dictionary of American Negro Biography*, pp. 215–16; Smith. *Notable Black American Women*, pp. 329–31; Southern, *The Music of Black Americans*, p. 406.

1928 • The first black-music survey was held at Carnegie Hall. The concert included spirituals, jazz, and symphonic music. W. C. Handy's Orchestra and Jubilee Singers performed.

Sources: Southern, *The Music of Black Americans*, 2nd ed., p. 357.

1930 • The first woman to lead an all-male band was Blanche Calloway (1902–1973), one of the most successful bandleaders of the 1930s. Born in Baltimore, Maryland, she studied at Morgan State College, and later moved to Miami, Florida, where she became the first woman disc jockey on American radio. For a while, she and her brother, Cab, had their own act. Calloway toured from 1931 to 1944 with The 12 Clouds of Joy as singer, dancer, and conductor.

Sources: Hine, *Black Women in America*, p. 216; *Encyclopedia of Black America*, p. 212; Smith, *Notable Black American Women*, pp. 152–53.

1930 • The National Baptist Convention, U.S.A., was the first major religious group to publicly endorse gospel music. From this endorsement followed the first choruses, the first publishing houses, the first professional organizations, and the first paid gospel concerts. Thomas Dorsey (1899–1993), the "Father of Gospel," founded the first gospel choir in the world with Theodore Frye at Chicago's Ebenezer Baptist Church in 1931. He established the first music publishing firm, Dorsey Music, dedicated only to gospel music in 1932. The action of the Baptist convention, which had been carried away by Dorsey's "If You See My Savior," called public attention to a major change that had been taking place in the music of black churches, and is often considered the starting point for the history of gospel music. Dorsey wrote more than two thousand blues and gospel songs during his lifetime. "Precious Lord, Take My Hand" has been declared one of the most profound expressions of Christian faith ever published. Dorsey was born in Villa Rica, Georgia, to an itinerant preacher who moved about until he settled in Atlanta. Dorsey left school after grade four, when he was around the age of thirteen. By age fourteen was playing for dances at rent parties and in brothels. By 1919 he had settled in Chicago where he enrolled in the Chicago School of Composition to develop his skills. He became music director at New Hope Baptist Church and began to write songs; his first religious piece was "If I Don't Get There." He was soon earning his living by arranging music. He wrote the famous "Precious Lord, Take My Hand" after mourning the loss of his newborn son.

Thomas Dorsey

Sources: Sadie, *The New Grove Dictionary of Music and Musicians,* 2nd ed., vol. 7, pp. 510–11; Southern, *The Music of Black Americans,* pp. 451–53, 472; Smith, *Notable Black American Men,* pp. 319–22; *Jet* 96 (5 July 1999): 19.

1931 • William Grant Still (1895–1978) was the first black to have a symphony performed by a major orchestra, when on October 29, the Rochester Philharmonic Orchestra presented his first work—the *Afro-American Symphony.* Born in Woodville, Mississippi, he studied at Wilberforce University, Oberlin Conservatory of Music, and the New England Conservatory of Music. Still worked in a great variety of musical settings, from playing in dance and theater orchestras, to supplying arrangements of popular music for black show people, and was a prolific composer in the art music tradition. In 1936 he was the first black to conduct a major symphony orchestra, the Los Angeles Philharmonic, and became the first black American to have an opera performed by a major opera company in 1949, when New York City Opera put on *Troubled Island.*

Sources: Abdul, *Blacks in Classical Music,* pp. 29–32; Bergman, *The Chronological History of the Negro in America,* p. 316; *Encyclopedia of Black America,* p. 809; Southern, *Biographical Dictionary of Afro-American and African Musicians,* pp. 359–61; Southern, *The Music of Black Americans,* pp. 406, 423–27.

William Grant Still

1932 • Don [Donald Matthew] Redman (1900–1964), jazz saxophonist, bandleader, and arranger, was the first orchestra leader to have a sponsored radio series. He was a pioneer jazz arranger-composer and contributed significantly to the development of the big band sound of the 1920s and 1930s. A child prodigy, Redman was born in Piedmont, West Virginia, and studied at music conservatories in Boston and Detroit.

Sources: Chilton, *Who's Who of Jazz,* pp. 313–14; *Encyclopedia of Black America,* p. 729; Southern, *Biographical Dictionary of Afro-American and African Musicians,* p. 318.

1933 • When Caterina Jarboro (1898?–1986) sang *Aida* at New York City's Hippodrome Theater, she became the first black to sing with an all-white company. She was also the first black to sing with the Chicago Opera Company. Born Catherine Yarboro in Wilmington, North Carolina, she began her career in Broadway musicals, including *Shuffle Along* (1921) and *Running Wild* (1923). Differing accounts of Jarboro's life exist. According to some sources, she was born Katherine Yarborough in Wilmington, North Carolina, and changed her name to Catarina Jarboro. After her early education, she moved to Brooklyn to continue her education. In 1926 she went to Paris to continue her education and to become a classical singer. She studied with Nino Campinno in Italy and in 1930 made her debut at the Puccini Opera House in Milan. She returned to the United States in 1932 and received a number of singing engagements.

Sources: *Encyclopedia of Black America,* p. 469; Southern, *Biographical Dictionary of Afro-American and African Musicians,* pp. 200–01; Southern, *The Music of Black Americans,* p. 407; Smith, *Notable Black American Women,* Book II, pp. 326–28.

Catarina Jarbaro

1933 • Florence Beatrice Smith Price (1888–1953) was the first black woman to have a symphony performed by a major orchestra. The Chicago Symphony, under Frederick Stock, first played her *Symphony in E-minor* at the Chicago World's Fair. Price was born in Camden, New Jersey. The first black woman to achieve distinction as a composer, Price was a graduate of the New England Conservatory of Music in 1906 and furthered her music education at Chicago Musical College, the American Conservatory, the University of Chicago, Chicago Teachers College, and elsewhere. She taught music at Shorter College in Arkansas from 1906 until 1910 and gave private lessons in violin, piano, and organ from 1910 until 1912. One of her mentors, Margaret Allison Bonds, later became known in the music world. Price won her first Harmon prize for composition in 1925. She wrote a number of works, many of which were published. She also made recordings, but no extensive list of these works is known to exist.

Sources: Hine, *Black Women in America,* pp. 940–41; Smith, *Notable Black American Women,* pp. 872–74; Southern, *The Music of Black Americans,* pp. 416–19.

1933 • The first production on Broadway of a black folk opera written by a black composer, Hall Johnson's *Run Little Chillun,* was presented.

Sources: Southern, *The Music of Black Americans,* 2nd ed, p. 358.

Margaret Allison Bonds

1933 • Margaret Allison Bonds (1913–1972) became the first black American guest soloist with the Chicago Symphony Orchestra, performing Price's *Piano Concerto in Fminor* at the 1933 World's Fair. Although Bonds was a skilled composer, her output is largely in the area of vocal music. Her arrangements of spirituals for solo voice and chorus are well known. Her arrangement of "He's Got the Whole World in His Hands," commissioned and recorded in the 1960s by Leontyne Price, is among Bonds's best-known pieces. Bonds was born in Chicago into a music family. In high school she studied piano and composition with Florence Price and later William Dawson. She received her bachelor of music degree in 1933 and her master of music degree in 1934 from Northwestern University. She remained active as a concert musician.

Sources: Smith, *Notable Black American Women,* pp. 95–96; Southern, *Biographical Dictionary of Afro-American and African Musicians,* pp. 313–14; Sadie, *New Grove Dictionary of American Music,* 2nd ed, vol. 20, p. 314.

1934 • Opening on February 22, 1934, *Four Saints in Three Acts,* by Virgil Thompson, was the first black-performed opera on Broadway. The first opera that had nothing to do with black folk life, it is a non-logical presentation of European saints.

Sources: Southern, *The Music of Black Americans,* pp. 439–41.

1934 • On November 14, 1934, William Levi Dawson's (1899–1990) first symphony, the *Negro Folk Symphony,* was the first work by a black composer to use black folk themes and to be performed by a major orchestra. He substantially revised the work in 1952, after a visit to West Africa. Born in Anniston, Alabama, Dawson began to compose at age sixteen. He is also known for his leadership of the internationally renowned Tuskegee Choir.

Sources: *Encyclopedia of Black America,* p. 305; Kane, *Famous First Facts,* pp. 72, 630; Southern, *Biographical Dictionary of Afro-American and African Musicians,* pp. 98–99; Southern, *The Music of Black Americans,* pp. 418–19.

1936 • Thomas Andrew Dorsey (1899–1993) was one of the first to promote a "battle of song," between Roberta and Sallie Martin, at DuSable High School in Chicago. He charged an admission fee of fifteen cents; the first time an entrance fee was charged for a concert of sacred music. Traditionally, church music concerts were free of charge, with voluntary offerings acceptable. Dorsey's program was so successful that from then on gospel music concerts with paid admission continued.

Sources: Southern, *The Music of Black Americans,* 2nd ed., p. 455.

1937 • La Julia Rhea (1908–1992) was the first black to sing with the Chicago Civic Opera Company during the regular season. She opened December 26, 1937, in the title role of Verdi's *Aida*.

Sources: Lee, *Interesting People,* p. 69; Southern, *Biographical Dictionary of Afro-American and African Musicians,* pp. 319–20; Southern, *The Music of Black Americans,* pp. 407–08.

1937 • When jazz great Billie "Lady Day" Holiday (1915–1959) teamed up with the Artie Shaw Band and toured the country, this was the first time a black woman and a white band shared the same stage. She was born Elenora Fagan in Baltimore, Maryland. She later moved to New York and, at age fifteen, sought work in various nightspots. Although she had no formal training as a singer or dancer, customers liked her and she was hired. She became a regular in Harlem clubs and was in demand as a singer. In 1937 she toured with Count Basie's orchestra and became soloist with Artie Shaw's white band. Jazz saxophonist Lester Young nicknamed her "Lady Day" when she was with Count Basie's band. She assumed the name "Billie" from movie star Billie Dove. Holiday was known for wearing gardenias in her hair and she performed with her eyes nearly closed. Her protest song "Strange Fruit" was a ballad about lynching; the fruit represented black men hanging from trees. At the peak of her career in the late 1930s and early 40s, she began to struggle with drug and alcohol addiction. After being jailed on a drug charge, she tried to recapture her life, but her addiction led to poor health and death.

Billie Holiday

Sources: *Jet* 88 (17 July 1995): 22; Smith, *Notable Black American Women,* pp. 497–502; *African-American Biography,* vol. 2, pp. 351–54.

1938 • "Sister" Rosetta Tharpe [Rosetta Nubin] (1921–1973) was the first black to take gospel music into a secular setting, when she sang on a Cab Calloway show from the Cotton Club. When she signed with Decca, she became the first gospel singer to record for a major company. Born in Cotton Plant, Arkansas, and raised in the Church of God in Christ, a Pentecostal denomination, Tharpe began touring as a professional when she was six. She took the lead in bringing gospel music to the mainstream. Tharpe was the first major gospel singer to tour extensively in Europe, and in 1943 she was the first to sing gospel at the Apollo Theater in New York City.

Sources: Smith, *Notable Black American Women,* pp. 1120–21; Southern, *The Music of Black Americans,* pp. 456, 472; Salzman, *Encyclopedia of African-American Culture and History,* vol. 5, pp. 2636–37.

1939 • Singer Marian Anderson (1897–1993) became the first black to sing before a reigning British monarch at the White House. She sang earlier in an informal setting in the Monroe Room on February 19, 1936, but this time she sang for King George VI and Queen Elizabeth of England on their visit to the White House. This was the first visit of a reigning British monarch to the United States, and President Franklin Roosevelt and Eleanor Roosevelt had planned an "Evening of American Music" in which Anderson sang Schubert's "Ave Maria."

Marian Anderson

Sources: *American Visions* (February-March 1995): 24; Keiler, *Marian Anderson,* p. 201.

1940 • "Surely God Is Able," written by W. Herbert Brewster Sr. (1897–1987), a Memphis Baptist minister, and recorded by the Ward Singers, is said to be the first gospel recording by a black singing group to sell more than one million copies. Principal singers in the group were organizer Gertrude Ward (1901–1983) and Clara Mae Ward (1924–1973). In 1957 the group was the first to perform at the Newport Jazz Festival. They were also the first to appear in nightclubs in 1961, and the first to sing at Radio City Music Hall in New York City in 1963.

Sources: *Ebony* (6 December 1950): 95; *Encyclopedia of Black America,* p. 832; Heilbut, *Gospel Sound,* pp. 137–43; Smith, *Notable Black American Women,* pp. 1202–05; Southern, *The Music of Black Americans,* pp. 468–69.

1941 • The first black electric guitarist to use single-string solos was Charlie Christian (1919–1942). He was also a pioneer in the development of the jazz revolution later named

Bop. Christian was one of a group of musicians meeting after hours at Minton's Playhouse, a Harlem nightclub. The group usually included Thelonious Monk, Kenny Clarke, and Dizzy Gillespie. From 1939 until 1941, he played in Benny Goodman's band.

Sources: Chilton, *Who's Who of Jazz,* p. 72; *Encyclopedia of Black America,* p. 226; Southern, *The Music of Black Americans,* pp. 474–75.

1941 • Dean Charles Dixon (1915–1976) was the first black to conduct the New York Philharmonic and was possibly the first black American recognized as a symphonic conductor of international stature. He was the first to hold permanent positions for long periods with symphony orchestras and toured worldwide as a guest conductor. Born in New York City, Dixon was educated at Julliard School of Music and Columbia University Teachers College. In 1949 he settled in Europe, where he remained until 1970.

Sources: *Ebony Success Library,* vol. 1, p. 96; *Encyclopedia of Black America,* 318; Garrett, *Famous First Facts about Negroes,* pp. 131–32; Southern, *Biographical Dictionary of Afro-American and African Musicians,* pp. 107–08; Southern, *The Music of Black Americans,* p. 510.

1941 • Mary Lucinda Cardwell Dawson founded the first permanent black opera company, the National Negro Opera Company, in Pittsburgh. The company functioned through 1962.

Sources: Hine, *Black Women in America,* vol. 1, pp. 311–12.

Dorothy Donegan

1943 • Jazz pianist Dorothy Donegan (1922–1998) became the first black musician to play in Chicago's prestigious Orchestral Hall. She was born in Chicago and began piano lessons when she was eight years old. She later became a church organist and played in small clubs on Chicago's South Side. Donegan made her professional debut in 1943 at Orchestral Hall. During the 1940s and 1950s she played at top clubs in New York, Chicago, and Los Angeles, but with the advent of rock music in the 1960s, she had difficulty finding work. By the 1970s, however, she was playing at festivals in the United States and abroad. Until health problems forced her to end her career in 1997, Donegan continued to perform and to receive favorable press.

Sources: *Jet* 94 (8 June 1998): 38–39; Smith, *Notable Black American Women,* pp. 283–85; "Wonder Woman," *New Yorker* 60 (18 February 1991): 37–38, 40–41.

1943 • Muddy Waters [McKinley Morganfield] (1915–1983) was the first person to combine blues and amplified guitar to create urban blues. A guitarist and singer, he was born in Rolling Fork, Mississippi, and grew up in Clarksdale, Mississippi. It is said that he was nicknamed Muddy because, as a child he liked to play in the mud; the name Waters was added later. He left the Mississippi Delta and toured with the Silas Green tent show. In 1943 he settled in Chicago, where he adopted the electric guitar. Waters was discovered by folklorist Alan Lomax. In 1948 Waters signed a recording contract and became known as the "King of the Delta (or Country) Blues."

Sources: *Encyclopedia of Black America,* p. 847; Lee, *Interesting People,* p. 95; Southern, *The Music of Black Americans,* pp. 493–94; Smith, *Notable Black American Men,* pp. 850–53.

1944 • The first black American to receive the Walter Naumberg Award was Carol Brice (1918–1985). Born Carol Lovette Hawkins Brice in Sedalia, North Carolina, she was a child prodigy who traveled with her school's glee club. She also toured as soloist with the Palmer Institute Singers when she was fourteen. Brice graduated from Talladega College in 1939 and enrolled at Juilliard School of Music that fall. While a soloist at St. George's Episcopal Church in New York City, she worked with the noted black baritone Harry T. Burleigh. She made her Town Hall debut in 1945. She had stage roles in such musical works as *Show Boat, Gentlemen, Be Seated,* and *Porgy and Bess.* Brice toured extensively and made a number of recordings as well. She has been described as having one of the most outstanding voices of the twentieth century.

Sources: Smith, *Notable Black American Women,* pp. 104–05; Southern, *Biographical Dictionary of Afro-American and African Musicians,* pp. 47; Turner, *Afro-American Singers,* p 14.

1945 • When Robert Todd Duncan (1903–1998) appeared as Tonio in *I Pagliacci* with the New York City Opera Company in September, he became the first black to sing with a major American operatic company. He was the original Porgy in Gershwin's *Porgy and Bess,* playing the role more than 1,800 times. Duncan also starred on stage in Vernon Duke's *Cabin in the Sky* (1940) and in Kurt Weill's *Lost in the Stars* (1944). The baritone was born in Danville, Kentucky, and graduated from Butler University and Columbia University. As a concert singer, he gave more than 2,000 performances in fifty-six countries. He also taught music at Howard University and was a private voice instructor and coach in his home in Washington, D.C.

Sources: *Ebony Success Library,* vol. 1, p. 100; *Encyclopedia of Black America,* p. 329; Southern, *The Music of Black Americans,* pp. 406–07; Salzman, *Encyclopedia of African-American Culture and History,* vol. 2, p, 813; *Jet* 93 (16 March 1998): 17.

1945 • As soloist for the New Orleans Symphony in 1945, Orrin Clayton Suthern (1912–), a college professor and organist, was the first black to perform with a white Southern orchestra. He was also the first black organist to perform on the CBS network. Born in Renovo, Pennsylvania, Suthern studied at Case Western Reserve, Cleveland Institute of Music, Northwestern University, and Columbia University.

Sources: *Encyclopedia of Black America,* p. 812; *Negro Yearbook,* 1952, p. 63; Southern, *Biographical Dictionary of Afro-American and African Musicians,* pp. 363–64.

1945 • Camilla Ella Williams (1919–2012) was the first black woman to sing with the New York City Opera when she performed the title role in Puccini's *Madama Butterfly.* The next year she became the first black to sign a full contract with a major opera company in the United States. In 1954 she was the first black singer to appear on the stage of the Vienna State Opera. Born in Danville, Virginia, Williams graduated from Virginia State College, studied voice in Philadelphia, and became known as an interpreter of lieder.

Camilla Ella Williams

Sources: *Current Biography, 1952,* pp. 632–34; *Encyclopedia of Black America,* p. 857; Southern, *Biographical Dictionary of Afro-American and African Musicians,* p. 403; Story, *And So I Sing,* pp. 72–75; *Jet* 90 (20 May 1996): 20.

1945 • Nora Douglas Holt (1885?–1974) became the first black American member of the Music Critics Circle of New York. Born Lena Douglas in Kansas City, Kansas, she began piano lessons at age four. She earned a bachelor of arts degree at Western University in Quindaro, Kansas and moved to Chicago around 1916. The next year she received a bachelor's degree in music from the Chicago Musical College. In 1918 Holt completed study at the Chicago Music School and she may have been the first black American to receive a master's degree in music. She became music critic for the *Chicago Defender.* From 1919 until 1921 she published the magazine *Music and Poetry.* Holt helped to establish the National Association of Negro Musicians. By 1943 she was music critic for the *Amsterdam News* and beginning in 1956 she held the same position at the *New York Courier.*

Sources: Smith, *Notable Black American Women,* pp. 509–11; Southern, *Biographical Dictionary of Afro-American and African Musicians,* p. 187; Dannett, *Profiles of Negro Womanhood,* vol. 2, p. 145–49.

1948 • William Clarence "Billie" Eckstine (1914–1993) was the first black ballad singer to become successful as a soloist independent of a dance band. When he recorded such pop songs as "I Apologize" and "My Foolish Heart," his deep-voice vibrato caused teenagers to swoon. Eckstine was perhaps the first black male pop idol. Eckstine began his singing career with jazz orchestras. He recorded "Skylark" in 1942 with Earl Hines's band. He left two years later and emerged as an independent soloist before organizing his own big band. It was not until 1948 that he signed a contract with MGM and toured and recorded with a studio band.

"Billie" Eckstine

Sources: Southern, *The Music of Black Americans,* 2nd ed., p. 497; Salzman, *Encyclopedia of African-American Culture and History,* vol. 2, p. 826; Smith, *Notable Black American Men,* pp. 357–59.

Lionel Hampton

1949 • Lionel Hampton (1908–2002) was the first black musician to perform for a presidential inauguration, for Harry S. Truman. On April 17, 2002, Hampton's ninety-fourth birthday, the U.S. Congress honored him by passing a resolution describing him as one of the all-time great jazz musicians. Hampton was born in Louisville, Kentucky, and around 1919 he and his mother relocated to Chicago. The Chicago environment enabled Hampton to develop his musical talents; he played the drums in school and also joined the newsboy's band of the *Chicago Defender.* He also accompanied his uncle Richard Morgan to parties where he was exposed to the great jazz musicians Jelly Roll Morton, Louis Armstrong, King Oliver, and others. He moved to Hollywood in the early 1920s and became known as one of the top drummers on the West Coast. He learned to play the vibraphone and joined Benny Goodman's Quartet in 1936, where he still played that instrument. Hampton formed his own band in summer 1940, with his wife Gladys as his manager, and became internationally known. Among the well-known performers who got their start with Hampton's band were Quincy Jones, Dinah Washington, and Joe Williams. Hampton died on August 31, 2002.

Sources: Smith, *Notable Black American Men,* pp., 506–08; *Jet* 101 (13 May 2002): 10.

1950 • Joe Bostic, the "Dean of Gospel Disc Jockeys," produced the Negro Gospel and Religious Music Festival at Carnegie Hall in New York, the first all-gospel concert. The show featured Mahalia Jackson (1911–1972), whose recording of "Move On Up a Little Higher" (1946) was the second gospel recording to sell more than a million copies in a year. Through her recording she became the first to bring gospel singing to the general public. Acclaimed as America's greatest gospel singer, Jackson was the first gospel singer to appear on the *Ed Sullivan Show* and became the first gospel artist to sing at the Newport Jazz Festival in 1958. She was known as the "Queen of the Gospel Song." Born in New Orleans, she moved to Chicago at age sixteen, and met Thomas A. Dorsey, her musical advisor and accompanist.

Sources: *Encyclopedia of Black America,* p. 467; Smith, *Notable Black American Women,* pp. 557–59; Southern, *The Music of Black Americans,* pp. 467–68, 472–73.

1953 • Mattiwilda Dobbs (1925–), who sang at all of the major opera houses in Europe, was the first black woman to sing a principal role at La Scala, in Milan, Italy, where she played Elvira in Rossini's *L'Italiana in Algieri.* On November 9, 1956, she became the third black to sing at the New York City's Metropolitan Opera, and as Gilda in *Rigoletto,* she was the first black to sing a romantic lead there. Born in Atlanta, Dobbs graduated from Spelman College and studied at Columbia University.

Sources: *Ebony Success Library,* vol. 1, p. 96; *Encyclopedia of Black America,* p. 318; *Negro Almanac,* p. 1181; Smith, *Notable Black American Women,* pp. 280–83.

1953 • Dorothy Maynor (1910–1996), opera singer, choral director, and school founder, became the first black to sing at a presidential inauguration when she sang "The Star Spangled Banner" at Dwight D. Eisenhower's swearing-in. Born Dorothy Leigh Mainor, in Norfolk, Virginia, on September 3, 1910, she graduated from Hampton Institute (now Hampton University). In 1965 she founded the Harlem School of the Arts.

Sources: *Encyclopedia of Black America,* p. 548; Smith, *Notable Black American Women,* pp. 739–40; Southern, *The Music of Black Americans,* p. 405.

1954 • "Sh-Boom" was the first rock 'n' roll record. Recorded by a black male rhythm blues group, it went to the top of that chart and then went to the top of the pop chart. At first, most of the records of this kind were covers of black recordings by white groups and soloists. It was some time before white consumers began to seek out records cut by blacks.

Sources: Southern, *The Music of Black Americans,* pp. 504–05.

1954 • Alex Bradford (1926–1978) organized Bradford Specials, the first all-male gospel choir in history. He attended Snow Hill Institute in Snow Hill, Alabama. When he was thirteen he joined a children's gospel group in Bessemer, Alabama, called the Protective Harmoneers. He also had his own local radio show. Bradford settled in Chicago following

The Metropolitan Opera's First Black Principal

In 1955 Marian Anderson (1897–1993), one of the twentieth century's most celebrated singers, was the first black to sing a principal role with the Metropolitan Opera. She made her debut as Ulrica in Verdi's *Un Ballo in Maschera* on January 7 and remained with the opera for seven performances. In October 1930 Anderson received critical acclaim for her concert at the Bach Saal in Berlin and from there embarked on an extensive tour of Europe. She made national news in 1939 when the Daughters of the American Revolution refused to allow her to appear at their Constitution Hall. Anderson continued to tour until her farewell trip in the 1964–65 season.

Sources: Hine, *Black Women in America*, pp. 29–33; *Current Biography Yearbook, 1940*, pp. 17–19; 1950, pp. 8–10; Smith, *Notable Black American Women*, pp. 14–20; Story, *And So I Sing*, pp. 37–58.

World War II and was in frequent contact with such gospel leaders as Thomas A. Dorsey, Roberta Martin, Sallie Martin, and Mahalia Jackson. He also sang with various gospel groups and in 1954 he organized an all-male group called Bradford Specials. By the 1960s he was involved with gospel theater. In 1961 Langston Hughes wrote *Black Nativity* especially for Bradford, Marion Williams, and Princess Stewart. In 1972 he appeared in the Broadway show *Don't Bother Me, I Can't Cope,* winning an Obie Award. In addition to writing music, he directed musicals, such as *Your Arms Too Short to Box with God* (1976). During his lifetime, he composed more than three hundred gospel songs, including "He'll Wash You Whiter Than Snow" and "Too Close to Heaven." Bradford was a minister as well, but he moved gospel out of the church. In the 1970s he founded the Creative Movement Repertory Company.

Sources: Boyer, *How Sweet the Sound*; Heilbut, *The Gospel Sound*; Southern, *The Music of Black Americans,* 2nd ed., p. 469.

1955 • Robert McFerrin (1921–2006) made his debut as the first black man to join the Metropolitan Opera and the first black singer to have a permanent position with the opera on January 27. Born in Marianna, Arkansas, he was a graduate of Chicago Music College and sang with the National Negro Opera from 1949 until 1952.

Sources: *New Grove Dictionary of American Music*, p. 147; *New York* (24 February 1992); Southern, *Biographical Dictionary of Afro-American and African Musicians*, p. 258; Southern, *Music of Black Americans*, pp. 513–24.

1955 • Conductor and musician Everett Lee directed the New York Opera's performance of *La Traviata* and became the first black to conduct a professional grand opera or Broadway show in the nation.

Sources: *Jet* 89 (22 April 1996): 20.

1956 • Dizzy [John Birks] Gillespie (1917–1993) was the first black to make an overseas tour sponsored by the United States Department of State. The jazz trumpeter and bandleader was born in Cheraw, South Carolina, and studied harmony and theory at Laurinburg Institute in North Carolina. He played in Cab Calloway's band from 1939 until 1941 and, along with Oscar Pettiford and Charlie "Bird" Parker, pioneered the formation of the jazz style called Bop. He earned a Grammy Award in 1974 and again in 1980.

Sources: Bergman, *The Chronological History of the Negro in America*, pp. 383, 493, 515; *Encyclopedia of Black America*, p. 405; Southern, *The Music of Black Americans*, pp. 475–78.

1956 • Vocalist Frankie Lymon (1942–1968) became the first black American teen heartthrob. He also inspired a number of younger musicians, including Michael Jackson. Born in Harlem, he became a singer of doo-wop, performing with his friends for donations on

Dizzy Gillespie

the streets of New York. They later created the quartet that would be known as the Teenagers. In January 1956 they released "Why Do Fools Fall in Love?" and it reached the number one position on the Rhythm and Blues charts and number six on the pop charts. Lymon left the Teenagers and recorded the moderately successful "Goody, Goody." After experimenting with drugs, his career began to falter. His life was the subject of a movie titled after his famous song, "Why Do Fools Fall in Love?"

Sources: *Contemporary Black Biography*, vol. 22, pp. 137–39.

1957 • The Famous Ward Singers—Clara, Gertrude, and Willa—were the first gospel group to sing at the Newport Jazz Festival. In 1961 they were the first gospel group to move into nightclubs and in 1963 the first to sing at New York City's Radio City Music Hall. They were among the first gospel groups to appear in films and gospel musicals. In 1963, Clara Ward played a leading role in Langston Hughes's *Tambourines to Glory*.

Sources: Southern, *The Music of Black Americans,* 2nd ed., p. 469.

1958 • Errol Louis Gardner (1921–1977) was the first black pianist to give a jazz concert in Carnegie Hall. Born in Pittsburgh, Pennsylvania, he had no formal music training but became one of the most important jazz pianists.

Sources: *Encyclopedia of Black America,* p. 402; Southern, *Biographical Dictionary of Afro-American and African Musicians,* p. 143; Thorpe, *Black Dance,* pp. 162–65.

Ella Fitzgerald

1959 • Ella Fitzgerald (1918–1996) was the first black woman to win a Grammy. Fitzgerald was born April 25, 1918, in Newport News, Virginia, and moved to Yonkers, New York. She began her career at age fifteen, at the Harlem's Apollo Theater where she won an amateur contest. In 1935 she was hired by Chick Webb's band to sing at a dance at Yale University. Fitzgerald recorded the well-known "A Tisket-A-Tasket" in 1938 and it became the band's first hit. Following Webb's death in 1939, Fitzgerald kept the band together for several years. She developed her famous skat singing style while on a tour with Dizzy Gillespie. Known as the "First Lady of Jazz," Fitzgerald became one of the most celebrated singers of the century. During her career she recorded more than 250 albums and won thirteen Grammys. She also won the Kennedy Center Honor, the National Medal of the Arts, and the American Black Achievement Award.

Sources: Smith, *Notable Black American Women,* pp. 346–49; *Jet* 81 (18 November 1991): 12; 90 (1 July 1996): 58–63; Southern, *Biographical Dictionary of Afro-American and African Musicians,* pp. 133–34.

1959 • Bessie Griffin was the first gospel singer to move to cabaret. She sang a leading role in *Portraits in Bronze* at New Orleans's Cabaret Concert Theatre. The show was called the first gospel musical in history. After that, other gospel singers began to appear in coffeehouses and nightclubs.

Sources: Southern, *The Music of Black Americans,* 2nd ed., p. 473.

1960 • Rock singer Chubby Checker [Ernest Evans] (1941–) became well known for his recording of "The Twist." The song remains the first and only record to have reached number one on the pop charts two times, in 1960 and 1962. He introduced a dance by the same title and set off the greatest dance craze since the Charleston of the 1920s.

Sources: *Split Image,* p. 85; Southern, *Biographical Dictionary of Afro-American and African Musicians,* p. 129; *Ebony* 16 (January 1961): 40–44.

1961 • The first black to perform at the Wagner Bayreuth Festival was Grace Ann Bumbry (1937–) as Venus in *Tannhäuser* on July 23, 1961. Her selection by Wieland Wagner, the composer's grandson, caused an international stir. Greatly influenced by Marian Anderson, Bumbry won critical acclaim for her lieder and other art songs. She was born in Saint Louis and studied at Northwestern University, where she became a protégée of Lotte Lehmann.

Sources: *Current Biography, 1964,* pp. 60–62; Smith, *Notable Black American Women,* pp. 126–28; Southern, *Biographical Dictionary of Afro-American and African Musicians,* p. 55.

The First Black Man to Win a Grammy Award

In 1959 Count [William] Basie (1904–1984) was the first black man to win a Grammy. He was also the first black from the United States to have a band give a command performance before Queen Elizabeth. Born in Red Bank, New Jersey, he began playing the piano as a teenager and studied with Fats Waller. Basie's own band, formed in 1935 in Kansas City, Missouri, took the flowering of that city's style to Chicago and New York City. He is said to have helped to invent big-band swing. The band established itself as one of the leaders in jazz.

Sources: *Encyclopedia of Black America*, p. 168; *Jet* 81 (18 November 1991): 12; Southern, *Biographical Dictionary of Afro-American and African Musicians*, pp. 29–30; Southern, *The Music of Black Americans*, pp. 384–85.

Count Basie

1961 • Quincy [Delight] Jones Jr. (1934–), composer, was the first black vice president of a white record company, Mercury. By 1991 he had become the first black to win six Grammy awards in one year, for *Back on the Block,* and won a total of twenty-five awards (second only to Georg Solti, the orchestra and opera conductor, who won twenty-eight). Born in Chicago, he grew up in Seattle and attended Berklee College of Music. Jones also composes in large forms, such as his *Black Requiem,* performed by the Houston Symphony and an eighty-voice choir, with Ray Charles as a soloist. In 2001 Jones published *Q: The Autobiography of Quincy Jones.*

Sources: *Negro Almanac*, pp. 1147–48; Southern, *Biographical Dictionary of Afro-American and African Musicians*, p. 219; Southern, *The Music of Black Americans*, pp. 543, 544; Smith, *Notable Black American Men*, pp. 656–60.

1961 • The Marvelettes released "Please Mr. Postman" on September 4 this year. It hit the top spot on the Rhythm and Blues charts on November 13. By December 3 it was the number-one Rhythm and Blues single and Motown's first record to hit number one on the pop charts. By December 11 it was the number-one pop single.

Sources: *Jet* 91 (9 December, 1996): 20.

1962 • Robert Starling Pritchard (1927–) became the first black American to perform at the Lincoln Center for the Performing Arts in New York City. Born in Winston-Salem, North Carolina, Pritchard was educated at Syracuse University, where he received a bachelor of arts degree in 1948 and later a master's and doctorate. He launched his international music career in 1957, when he performed in the State Department's cultural exchange program. He was the first black solo concert pianist to tour North America, Europe, and the Middle East. He helped establish music education programs in Africa and the Caribbean universities, and in 1959 he founded the music department at the University of Liberia. His proposal for the first Festival Mondial des Arts Negres (First World Festival of Negro Arts) was implemented in 1966, sponsored by the government of Senegal and UNESCO.

Sources: *Contemporary Black Biography,* vol. 21, pp. 139–42.

1964 • Jimmy [James Oscar] Smith (1925?–2005) was the first black to win the *Downbeat* magazine award for jazz when a category for organ was first included. He won *Playboy* magazine's Jazz Poll in 1969, the year in which it too added a category for organ. Smith continued to win recognition from both jazz polls for a number of years. Born in Norris-

"Duke" Ellington

town, Pennsylvania, he studied piano at the Ornstein School of Music and formed his own jazz trio by 1954.

Sources: *Ebony Success Library,* vol. 1, p. 284; Salzman, *Encyclopedia of African-American Culture and History,* vol. 5, p. 2496.

1965 • Edward Kennedy "Duke" Ellington (1899–1974) held a sacred music concert at Grace Cathedral Church in San Francisco, the first jazz concert ever held in a major church.

Sources: Southern, *The Music of Black Americans,* 2nd ed., 359.

1966 • On September 16, 1966, Leontyne [Mary Violet Leontine] Price (1927–) was the first black to open a Metropolitan Opera season and to sing the title role at the opening of a new Metropolitan Opera house. Samuel Barber wrote the role in his new opera *Anthony and Cleopatra* for her; unfortunately, the opera did not enjoy great success. She played Flora Tosca in Puccini's *Tosca,* which was televised on NBC's *Opera Workshop* in 1955 and became the first black to appear in opera on television. Emerging in the 1950s as a major artist, Price was the first black lyric soprano to achieve international diva status. Born in Laurel, Mississippi, she graduated from Julliard School of Music.

Sources: *Encyclopedia of Black America,* p. 707; Lee, *Interesting People,* p. 142; Smith, *Notable Black American Women,* pp. 874–78; Story, *And So I Sing,* pp. 100–14.

Charlie Pride

1967 • Charley Pride (1939–), singer and guitarist, became the first black singer with the Grand Ole Opry. His interest at first was in baseball, and at age sixteen he left his home state of Mississippi to seek employment with the now-defunct Negro American Baseball League. He was pitcher-outfielder with the Memphis Red Sox, later played with the Birmingham Black Barons, and in 1961 played in the majors with the Los Angeles Angels. Opry star Red Foley heard Pride sing country music in 1963 and encouraged him to go to Nashville, where he charmed RCA Records and entered the country music field. The white audience at his first major concert in 1967 did not know his race until he appeared on stage. His recording "Just Between Me and You" launched him into super-stardom and made him a number-one country music attraction. In 1971 Pride was the first black named Entertainer of the Year and Male Vocalist of the Year in the field of country music.

Sources: *Current Biography, 1975,* pp. 329–32; *Ebony Success Library,* vol. 2, pp. 212–15; Southern, *Biographical Dictionary of Afro-American and African Musicians,* p. 314; Smith, *Notable Black American Men,* pp. 966–68.

1968 • When Henry Jay Lewis (1932–1996) conducted the New Jersey Symphony Orchestra, he became the first black permanent conductor of a leading American symphony. Lewis was born on October 16, 1932, in Los Angeles. When he was sixteen, he became the youngest and the first black instrumentalist with a major orchestra, the Los Angeles Philharmonic.

Sources: *Encyclopedia of Black America,* p. 505; Southern, *Biographical Dictionary of Afro-American and African Musicians,* pp. 244–45; *Tennessean* (29 January 1996).

1970 • James Anderson DePriest (1936–) was the first black to conduct an entire program in the regular series of the National Symphony in Washington. (Howard University's Warner Lawson had conducted portions of a program when his choir performed with the symphony.) Born in Philadelphia, DePriest received his bachelor's and master's degrees from the University of Pennsylvania. He held positions with a number of symphony orchestras, including the New York Philharmonic, where he was assistant conductor to Leonard Bernstein; and the National Symphony Orchestra, where he was associate conductor and later principal guest conductor. DePriest wrote music for concert and ballet and also two volumes of poetry.

Sources: *Jet* 39 (17 December 1970): 61; Southern, *Biographical Dictionary of Afro-American and African Music,* p. 100; *Encyclopedia of African-American Culture and History,* vol, 2, p. 750; *Who's Who among African Americans,* 26th ed., p. 335.

1971 • The first black American composer to be honored with an Academy Award was Isaac Hayes (1942–2008). The honor was for the best song from a motion picture, for the song title "Shaft." Hayes was born in poverty in Covington, Tennessee. In the early 1960s he performed in various bands in Memphis. He and his friend, David Porter, had two big hits as a song-writing team—"Soul Man" and "Hold On, I'm Coming." Hayes' record "Hot Buttered Soul" launched his career. His recording of "Shaft," the song for which he is best known, reached number one on the pop charts and earned him an Academy Award and a Grammy Award.

Sources: *Contemporary Black Biography,* vol. 20, pp. 82–84.

1972 • Henry Jay Lewis was engaged by the Metropolitan Opera to conduct *La Bohème* and became the first black to conduct in that house. He had many subsequent engagements with the Met, including its 1975 tour of Japan.

Sources: Smith, *Notable Black American Men,* pp. 716–18; *The Black New Yorkers,* p. 354.

1975 • The first black women to perform on the Grand Ole Opry, in Nashville, Tennessee, were the Pointer Sisters. The sisters, called the "musical darlings" of the 1970s and 1980s, returned on June 8, 2002, to perform at Nashville's most prestigious social event, the Swan Ball. The sisters, Ruth (1946–), Anita (1948–), Bonnie (1951–), and June (1954–2006), were born in Oakland, California. They sang in the choir of West Oakland Church of God where their parents were ministers. Two of the sisters, Bonnie and June, formed a group known as Pointers and performed in the Bay area. Anita later joined the group and, in 1972, Ruth was the last to join.

Sources: Ciulla, "The Pointer Sisters—Biography," *Tennessean* (25 January 2002).

1977 • Chuck Berry's song "Johnny B. Goode," and Blind Willie Johnson's 1927 recording, "Dark Was the Night, Cold Was the Ground," were the first songs by blacks to be sent out of the solar system. When *Voyager I* was sent into outer space, it carried a copper phonograph record containing the songs, as well as other musical selections and greetings in a hundred languages, on the chance that aliens might find it. Chuck [Charles Edward Anderson] Berry (1926–) was the first black to receive four Special Commendation awards from Broadcast Music, Inc. (BMI) in 1981. His first song, "Mabelline," received wide attention, and "Roll Over Beethoven" became one of his best-known songs. Blind Willie Johnson (1902?–1950?), gospel singer and guitarist, was born in Marlin, Texas, and blinded at age seven. He sang at Baptist Association meetings and rural churches near Hearne, Texas, accompanying himself on the guitar. He made several recordings of exceptionally high quality between 1927 and 1930 and strongly influenced other gospel singers. After the depression, Johnson returned to street singing.

Chuck Berry

Sources: Cohn, et al, *Nothing But the Blues,* pp. 119–26; *Current Biography, 1977,* pp. 57–60; *Essence* 24 (May 1993): 40; *Jet* 60 (21 May 1981): 62; Southern, *Biographical Dictionary of Afro-American and African Musicians,* p. 33.

1977 • Alberta Hunter (1895–1985) was the first black to record a best-selling album at age eighty-three. Born in Memphis, Tennessee, she moved to Chicago, where her singing career began. During her early career she performed at various clubs and cabarets for blacks. In 1915 she moved to one of the top spots for whites, the Panama Cafe. Elite black performers, such as Florence Mills and Ada "Bricktop" Smith appeared downstairs, while Hunter sang upstairs with the barrelhouse singers. She became so popular that composers paid her to showcase their songs—"Sweet Georgia Brown" and "Saint Louis Blues" were examples. In 1921 she cut her first record for the Black Swan label, but, feeling neglected in favor of Ethel Waters, she switched to Paramount, where she recorded her own "Down Hearted Blues." She moved to New York where she performed in *How Come?* at the Apollo Theater, then went on the road with the show. She also worked in vaudeville on the Keith Circuit. Hunter worked in Paris and on the French Riviera in 1927, and a year later she opened in the London production of *Show Boat.* She returned to New York in 1929, occasionally touring Europe where she had successful performances. When she later undertook a USO tour of Europe and Korea, she became the first black woman performer to visit the war zone in Korea. Hunter left show business to work as a practical nurse for twenty years; forced to retire from nursing, she returned to music. During her career she appeared on the vaudeville circuit, on stage, recorded extensively, appeared on radio and television, sang on film tracks, and performed in numerous nightclubs.

Sources: Lee, *Interesting People,* p. 47; Smith, *Notable Black American Women,* pp. 524–29; Southern, *Biographical Dictionary of Afro-American and African Musicians,* pp. 190–91.

1977 • The first black vice president of Black Music Marketing for CBS Records was H. LeBaron Taylor (1935–2000). He joined the company in 1974 as vice president for special markets. In his new position he had responsibility for Jazz/Progressive Marketing and was successful in bringing the label's efforts in black music to a leadership position. Black Music Marketing then became the model for the record industry as a whole. Taylor was born in Chicago and graduated from Wayne State University. His numerous awards for professional achievement included two Congressional Black Caucus Chair Awards, the NAACP Image Corporate Award, and the Highest Public Service Honor from the National Urban League. The Black Employees Organization of CBS recognized him for mentoring and promoting the growth and development of minority employees with the company.

Sources: *Jet 98* (7 August 2000): 37.

1978 • Simon Lamont Estes (1938–), bass-baritone and opera singer, was the first black man to sing at the Bayreuth Festival when he appeared in the title role of *Der Fliegende Hollander.* In 1966 he also won the first International Tchaikovsky Vocal Competition in Moscow. Born in Centerville, Iowa, Estes attended the University of Iowa and Julliard School of Music.

Sources: Abdul, *Blacks in Classical Music,* pp. 118–19; *Ebony Success Library,* vol. 1, p. 107; Southern, *The Music of Black Americans,* pp. 516–17; Smith, *Notable Black American Men,* pp. 381–82.

1978 • President Jimmy Carter on October 8 inaugurated a series of nationally televised concerts from the White House. Opera singer Leontyne Price (1927–) was the first black American to present works at the concerts. She presented works by Handel, Richard Strauss, and Puccini and closed with a group of American songs and spirituals.

Sources: *American Visions* (February-March 1995): 22.

Ray Charles

1979 • Ray Charles [Ray Charles Robinson] (1930–2004) was the first person of any race to perform before the Georgia Assembly. Born in Albany, Georgia, he moved to Florida as a young child and was blinded by glaucoma at about six. Charles formed a trio in 1950, but the next year he formed a larger and more successful rhythm and blues group. He made a number of records, including "Georgia on My Mind," which set new sales records in 1959. It is said that Charles developed the concept of soul, merging gospel, rhythm and blues, and popular music into a musical entity.

Sources: *Current Biography, 1965,* pp. 59–62; Southern, *Biographical Dictionary of Afro-American and African Musicians,* p. 68; Smith, *Notable Black American Men,* pp. 186–89.

1979 • The first two rap records were "King Tim III (Personality Jock)," recorded by the Fatback Band, a Brooklyn group, and "Rapper's Delight," by the Sugar Hill Gang, with a New Jersey-based label. Bronx-style rapping can be traced back to 1976, but was not recorded until 1979.

Sources: *Split Image,* p. 112.

1981 • James Cleveland (1931–1991), minister, gospel singer, pianist, composer, arranger, choir director, and recording artist, was the first black gospel artist to receive a star on Hollywood's Walk of Fame. He was accompanist for the Caravans and the Roberta Martin Singers and later formed the James Cleveland Singers and the Southern California Community Choir. In 1968 Cleveland founded and was national president of Gospel Music

Workshop of America. He was born in Chicago, and attended Roosevelt University. Known as the "Crown Prince of Gospel," he received four Grammy awards.

Sources: *Ebony Success Library,* vol. 1, p. 71; Heilbut, *Gospel Sound,* pp. 233–47; *Who's Who among Black Americans, 1992–93,* p. 1595.

1982 • Max [Maxwell Lemuel] Roach (1924–2007), was the first black percussionist inducted into the Percussive Art Society. Roach was a moving force in the development of modern jazz. A founding member of Bebop and a member of Dizzy Gillespie's 1945 quintet, which gave the name to the music, he pioneered in exploiting the drums as melodic as well as rhythmic instruments. From 1946 to 1948 he was Charlie Parker's drummer. He assembled the Clifford Brown-Max Roach Quintet in 1954, one of the most innovative quintets in the history of jazz. His concern for racial oppression in the United States and South Africa led him in the 1960s to mix politics and music. In 1960 Roach, Oscar Brown Jr., and Abbey Lincoln, then his wife, collaborated in creating the album *We Insist: The Freedom Now Suite.* The album was one of the first jazz works to concentrate on civil rights. He joined the faculty at the University of Massachusetts, Amherst in the 1960s. In addition to receiving several honorary doctorates, in 1988 he became the first jazz musician to receive a MacArthur Foundation Genius Award. Roach was born in Elizabeth City, North Carolina, and raised in Brooklyn. He received music lessons from his mother while he was a child and in the early 1950s studied composition and tympani at the Manhattan School of Music. He inspired a number of jazz drummers and was a leading figure in the development of black culture.

Sources: *Jet* 63 (20 December 1982): 21; 93 (12 January 1998): 20; Feather, *Encyclopedia of Jazz,* p. 398; Southern, *Biographical Dictionary of Afro-American and African Musicians,* p. 322; Southern, *The Music of Black Americans,* pp. 476–77; Salzman, *Encyclopedia of African-American Culture and History,* vol. 4, pp. 2343–44.

1983 • Michael Jackson's album *Thriller* was the first to produce five top singles—"The Girl is Mine," "Billie Jean," "Beat It," "Wanna Be Startin' Somethin'," and "Human Nature." In 1981 the *Guinness Book of Records* certified *Thriller,* for which Jackson (1958–2009) won eight Grammy Awards, as the best-selling album to date. *Guinness* also cited Jackson for winning the most awards (seven) at the American Music Awards in 1984. Jackson was born in Gary, Indiana, into a musical family. The Jackson brothers—Jackie, Tito, Jermaine, Marlon, and Michael—became known as The Jackson Five and received their first big break at Harlem's Apollo Theater in 1968. They caught the attention of Motown and its president Barry Gordy and in 1969 made their debut album, *Diana Ross Presents the Jackson Five.* Michael Jackson began his solo career by acting in the 1977 movie *The Wiz.* His enormous record sales and success in concerts earned him the title "King of Pop." Since his death in 2009, sales of his works have soared.

Michael Jackson

Sources: *Jet* 81 (18 November 1991): 60; Obituary, *Who's Who among African Americans,* 24th ed., p. 1377; Smith, *Notable Black American Men,* pp. 605–7.

1984 • Wynton Marsalis (1961–), trumpeter and bandleader, was the first black instrumentalist to simultaneously receive Grammy awards as best classical and jazz soloist. Born in New Orleans into a musical family, Marsalis was trained in both jazz and classical traditions. He released his first album in 1981.

Sources: Hornsby, *Milestones in Twentieth Century African-American History,* p. 343; *Negro Almanac,* p. 1217; *Contemporary Black Biography,* vol. 16, pp. 150–55.

1987 • The first black to occupy a chief position with the Royal Ballet was Isaiah Jackson (1945–). Born in Richmond, Virginia, Jackson graduated from Harvard University in 1966 and studied music at Stanford University, receiving his master's degree in 1967. He also studied at Julliard School of Music, receiving a master's degree in 1969 and doctor of musical arts in 1973. He was founder and conductor of the Julliard String Ensemble. Jackson held positions with a number of orchestras, including the Baltimore Symphony, the Rochester Philharmonic, the Detroit Symphony, the Boston Pops, and the Berlin Symphony.

Sources: *Encore* (December 1974): 37; *Jet* 70 (16 June 1986): 54; Southern, *Biographical Dictionary of Afro-American and African Musicians*, p. 196; *Contemporary Black Biography*, vol. 3, pp. 95–96.

1988 • Cab [Cabell] Calloway III (1907–1994), bandleader, singer and entertainer, was the first black winner of the ASCAP Duke Award. Born in Rochester, New York, Calloway and his family later moved to Chicago, where he studied at Crane College. He was an important big band leader of the 1930s and 1940s, and used as his theme song "St. James Infirmary." He played at the Cotton Club, then calling his band the Cab Calloway Cotton Club Orchestra and later the Cab Calloway Band. He also appeared in several movies, including the role of Sportin' Life in *Porgy and Bess* (1953), *Stormy Weather* (1943), *Hello Dolly* (1967), and *The Blues Brothers* (1980). He was a flamboyant dresser who often performed in a zoot suit—his most famous was yellow, with a matching hat—and pleased his audiences with his famous scat singing style— "Hi-de-ho-de-ho-de-hee."

Cab Calloway

Sources: Bogle, *Toms, Coons, Mulattoes, Mammies, and Bucks*, pp. 131–32; *Jet* 74 (30 May 1988): 36; Southern, *Biographical Dictionary of Afro-American and African Musicians*, pp. 61–62; Smith, *Notable Black American Men*, pp. 162–66.

1988 • Queen Latifah [Dana Owens] (1970–) was one of the first women to make a breakthrough in the male-dominated field of rap music. She was born in Newark, New Jersey and, as a child, sang in the Bloomfield's Shiloh Baptist Church Choir. She attended the Borough of Manhattan Community College but left college once her career as an entertainer blossomed. In 1989 Queen Latifah had several successes—she made her first European tour, first appeared at the Apollo in Harlem, made her first video, "Dance for Me," and the album *All Hail the Queen*. In 1990 she was recognized with an award for best new artist. She later appeared in such films as *Juice, Jungle Fever, House Party 2, Chicago, Ice Age 2 and 3,* and *Joyful Noise*. Her television appearances include *Fresh Prince of Bel-Air, Living Single* and *Joyful Noise*.

Sources: Smith, *Notable Black American Women*, Book II, pp. 393–94; *Jet* 94 (20 July 1998): 34–38; *Contemporary Black Biography*, vol. 16, pp. 172–74.

1988 • The duo DJ Jazzy Jeff and the Fresh Prince became the first rap group to win a Grammy Award, for the hit "Parents Just Don't Understand." Music partners Jeff Townes and Will Smith teamed up in 1987 to form the group. Smith went on to have a successful career in television and movies.

Sources: *Jet* 92 (21 July 1997): 36.

1988 • The first black Rockette at Radio City Music Hall was Jennifer Jones (1968?–). A fill-in, she was scheduled to be called whenever there was a vacancy.

Sources: *Jet* 73 (18 January 1988): 8.

1989 • The first black woman vice president of a major record company, Atlantic Records, was Sylvia Rhone (1952–). Rhone began her career in banking and finance. Born in Philadelphia, Pennsylvania, and raised in New York City, Rhone graduated from the Wharton School of Finance and Commerce at the University of Pennsylvania. Before moving into higher management, she directed promotional work for various record labels and gained a reputation as one who discovered and shaped black talent. In 1991 she was named co-president and chief executive officer of Atlantic's East-West Records, and became chair and chief executive officer of Atlantic's newly formed Atco-East/West label.

Sources: *Contemporary Black Biography*, vol. 2, pp. 194–94; Smith, *Notable Black American Women*, pp. 550–52; *Who's Who among African Americans*, 26th ed., p. 1048.

1992 • Boyz II Men, of Philadelphia, was the first black group to have a record at the top of *Billboard's* Hot One Hundred chart. For twelve consecutive weeks, "End of the Road" held first place and became the longest-running pop single—even breaking the record set by Elvis Presley. Their debut album, *Cooleyhighharmony*, went quadruple platinum.

Sources: *Time* 140 (2 November 1992): 77.

The Rock and Roll Hall of Fame Inducts Aretha Franklin

In 1986 Aretha Franklin (1942–), the "Queen of Soul," was the first black woman selected for induction into the Rock and Roll Hall of Fame and Museum. At the age of twelve, Franklin sang her first solo in New Bethel Baptist Church in Detroit, where her father was pastor. She later joined the quartet directed by James Cleveland. She turned to blues in the 1960s, and in 1967 two of her albums sold more than a million copies each. Franklin won more than fifteen Grammy awards and in 1994 received the Grammy Legend Award. Aretha Franklin was born on March 25, 1942, in Memphis, Tennessee; when she was two years old the family moved to Detroit.

Sources: *Encyclopedia of Black America*, p. 393; *Jet* 71 (13 October 1986): 54; Smith, *Notable Black American Women*, pp. 364–68.

Aretha Franklin

1992 • RuPaul [Andre Charles] (1960–) became the first drag queen recording star. His "Supermodel (You Better Work!)" made its debut in November at designer Todd Oldham's spring showing and became one of the most asked-for videos on MTV. Born in New Orleans, Charles is a seven-foot-tall black man known for his signature long and flowing white-blond hair. In 1995 RuPaul became spokesmodel for M.A.C. (Makeup Art Cosmetics), the choice of makeup companies for models and stylists; he was the first drag queen to secure such a contract. Since 1981 he has been a multimedia entertainer, actor, singer, dancer, as well as a talk-show host.

Sources: *New Yorker* (22 March 1993): 49; *New York* 28 (March 13, 1995): 16; *Contemporary Black Biography*, vol. 17, pp. 161–65.

RuPaul

1992 • The first black pianist to win the Naumburg Competition for young musicians was Awadagin Pratt (1966–). Pratt was born in Pittsburgh and in 1975 his family moved to Normal, Illinois. While a student at Peabody Conservatory of Music in Baltimore, Pratt received a five-thousand-dollar prize, two major residencies with national arts organizations, and forty concerto and recital appearances. He has appeared in concert at the White House at the invitation of President Bill Clinton and Hilliary Rodham Clinton, performed at the Aspen Festival, and has had engagements with numerous symphony orchestras in the United States and abroad.

Sources: *Jet* 82 (1 June 1992): 22; Smith, *Notable Black American Men*, pp. 961–63.

1996 • Composer George Theophilus Walker (1922–) was awarded the Pulitzer Prize in music for his composition *Lilacs* (for voice and orchestra), making him the first black to win the award in the area of music. Walker was born in Washington, D.C. His father was a physician, and his mother a pianist. He began playing piano at age five under the supervision of his mother. With a four-year scholarship, he began study at Oberlin Conservatory of Music at age fifteen. After graduating with a bachelor of music degree at age eighteen, he earned an artist diploma from the Curtis Institute where he studied piano with Rudolph Serkin and composition with Rosario Salro and Gian Carlo Menotti. He later studied piano with Robert Cadeuseus at the American Academy in Fontainbleau, obtaining a second diploma in music. In 1957 he received a doctor of musical arts degree from the Eastman School of Music. With a Fulbright Scholarship, he returned to Paris to study composition with Nadia Boulanger and Gregor Piatigorsky. He has served on a number of faculties, receiving appointments from such schools as Dillard University, Smith College, the University of Colorado, Peabody Conservatory of Music, and the University of Delaware. While at Delaware he was Distinguished University Professor. After twenty years, he retired from Rutgers University, where he had been department chair and Distinguished Professor. Walker has received a number of commissions—from the New York Philharmonic, the Cleveland Orchestra, Eastman School of Music, Kennedy Center for the Performing Arts, National Endowment for the Humanities, and elsewhere. *Lilacs* was commissioned by the Boston Symphony Orchestra as a tribute to tenor Roland Hayes. More than eighty of his compositions have been published.

Sources: Salzman, *Encyclopedia of African-American Culture and History,* vol. 5, p. 2763; *Jet* 89 (29 April 1996): 24; "George Walker," http://georgetwalker.com/bio.html.

1997 • The first jazz artist to win a Pulitzer Prize was Wynton Marsalis (1961–), who won the award in April for his jazz opera *Blood on the Fields.* Although music was added in 1943 as category for recognition, until 1997 no jazz artist had been so honored.

Sources: *The Black New Yorkers,* p. 419; Smith, *Notable Black American Men,* pp. 758–62.

1999 • Norma Solomon White became the first woman to direct the Florida A & M "Marching 100." White directed the band during the pre-game activities for the sixty-second Orange Blossom Classic in Jacksonville, when Florida A & M played Howard University. When White was a student at the university (1951–55), she was the first female member of the band. She was also the twenty-fifth national president of her sorority, Alpha Kappa Alpha.

Sources: *Jet* 95 (18 January 1999): 10.

2000 • Charley Pride (1939–) became the first black American voted into the Country Music Hall of Fame located in Nashville, Tennessee. He and singer Faron Young were the seventy-third and seventy-fourth members to be inducted into the Hall of Fame at the thirty-fourth annual Country Music Association Awards. Their selection was the result of the votes of about 350 CMA members. During Pride's extraordinary career, he had twenty-nine country hits, representing the first major success by a black American in commercial country music. During the awards program Pride performed "Kiss An Angel Good Mornin'," "Crystal Chandeliers," "Is Anybody Goin' to San Antone," and "Kaw-Liga." Pride was honored again, on May 14, 2001, when the Country Music Hall of Fame held its first official event at its new facility in Nashville, receiving a medallion commemorating his induction into the hall in the previous year.

Sources: Charley Pride, http://www.answers.com/topics/charley-pride; *Tennessean* (14 May 2001).

2000 • The first black president of Notre Dame's men's glee club was Austin Stephen Smith (1979?–). A marketing major in his senior year, Smith and four other members of the glee club performed at the Capitol in Washington, when the university's president emeritus, Reverend Theodore Hesburgh, received the Congressional Gold Medal. Smith is from Country Club Hills, Illinois.

Sources: *Jet* 98 (27 November 2000): 38.

2001 • Gordon J. Davis (1941–) became the first black president of New York City's Lincoln Center for the Performing Arts. Davis served in the top position for only nine months, resigning in November 2001. Davis had served on the Lincoln Center board for over twenty years. The Lincoln Center includes such heralded arts organizations as the Juilliard School, the Metropolitan Opera, the New York City Ballet, and the New York Philharmonic. But Davis was best known for being the chairman of Jazz at Lincoln Center, the largest not-for-profit institute for jazz in the world. During his brief tenure as president, Davis, a successful real estate attorney, helped raise and manage $1.5 billion to renovate the Center's eighteen acres. He also secured a ten-year, $240 million grant from the City of New York, the largest grant made by the city to an arts organization. Davis previously served in the New York City government as planning commissioner in the John Lindsay administration and as parks commissioner in the Ed Koch administration. As parks commissioner, he created the popular free concerts series that highlighted the likes of Diana Ross and Simon and Garfunkel. Davis also played a pivotal role in helping to establish

New York's Central Park Conservancy. He continued his involvement with Jazz at Lincoln Center, whose artistic director is famed jazz musician Wynton Marsalis, until his resignation in 2001.

Sources: *Jet* 99 (26 February 2001): 25; "Gordon J. Davis," topics.nytimes.com/topics/reference/timestopics/people/d/Gordon_j_davis/index.html

2008 • Former frontman with the rock band Hootie & the Blowfish, Darius Rucker (1966–), a successful pop singer-songwriter, made his debut in country music in 2008, producing his debut disc, *Learn to Live,* with three hit singles. The disc went No. 1 on the country charts. With that success, Rucker became the first black singer to win the Best New Artist Award at the Country Music Association Awards in November 2008. Rucker calls himself a country singer. "I've always liked country music but never really told anybody," he said. Some sources say that Rucker is "sitting on top of the country music world." His single "Come Back Song" was in *Billboard's* Top 10 country singles. *Charleston, SC 1966,* his 2010 CD, was No. 1 on *Billboard's* top country CDs and, after two months was still in the Top 20. Rucker is the first black to crack country music's top twenty singles since 1988 and the first black to reach No. 1 since 1983, when Charley Pride achieved that honor. He is also the first black with a No. 1 country CD or album since 1985, when Ray Charles achieved that success. A singer and songwriter, Rucker was born on May 13, 1966, in Charleston, South Carolina. He graduated from the University of South Carolina and in 1986 cofounded the band Hootie & the Blowfish, named after two of their college classmates. They played the college circuit for several years and toured full time, breaking into mainstream in 1994. Rucker continues his relationship with the band. His new album is due out in fall of 2012.

Darius Rucker

Sources: *Contemporary Black People Biography,* vol. 72, pp. 133–35; vol. 74, pp. 140–43; *Jet* 118 (13 December 2010): 42–43; *People* (30 November 2009): 17; *Tennessean* (12 November 2009).

2010 • The first basketball player of any race to conduct the Boston Pops was Shaquille O'Neal (1972–), a center with the Boston Celtics. The event took place at a holiday concert on Monday, December 20, at Boston's Symphony Hall, when O'Neal led the chorus and orchestra through "Sleigh Ride," "Can You Feel It" by the Jackson Five, and "We Are the Champions," by Queen. "I have a whole new respect for conductors," O'Neal said. "I went through a rehearsal today, and my arms are shot right now."

Sources: "Jet" 119 (17 January 2010): 27; NBC News (21 December 2010); *Who's Who among African Americans,* 26th ed., p. 950.

Organizations

1998 • Jeanie Weems became the first black assistant vice president for the American Society of Composers, Artists, and Publishers (ASCAP), the world's largest performing rights society. Since 1998 Weems had worked with ASCAP's film and television division.

Sources: *Jet* 94 (27 July 1998): 20.

1998 • When Susan Davenport's peers elected her as chair of the Board of Directors of Broadcast Music Inc. (BMI), she became the first woman and the first black woman to serve in that capacity. She moved up from the post as vice chair. She previously worked at Goldman, Sachs, & Co. Davenport is a graduate of Harvard University and Stanford University Graduate School of Business.

Sources: *Los Angeles Sentinel* (15 March 2012).

Painting

1600s • The painting of Giulia de' Medici, by Pontormo, is the first known European portrait of a young woman of African descent. A seventeenth-century inventory of Portormo's portrait described the child. She is captured in a portrait with her aunt, Maria Salviati. While portraits of young African men, particularly as slaves and shown in exotic costume, predate this painting, young African women were missing from portraits before now. Giulia de' Medici was the daughter of Alessandro de' Medici, the first duke of Florence. Alessandro's mother was a black slave from Northern Africa identified as Simunetta. His father was Giulio de' Medici, later a cardinal and then Pope Clement VII. After the murder of her father by an insane cousin, she became a very rich girl when she was about six years old. For nearly a century the painting had been in the United States; however, it was not until 1994 that Giulia's identity became known. In 1902 Henry Walters purchased the painting from an Italian collection. It was later displayed at the Walters Art Museum in Baltimore. Originally only a portion of the images in the painting were visible, until a routine x-ray and cleaning, thirty-five years later, revealed another figure in front of the larger image. In fall 2001 the National Gallery of Art in Washington, presented the painting as "The First Portrait of a Girl of African Descent in European Art."

Sources: *Washington Post* (25 November 2001).

1798 • Joshua Johnston (1765–1830) was the first black portrait painter to win recognition in America. Born a slave, he lived and worked in the Baltimore, Maryland area. A highly accomplished craftsman, Johnston was probably the first black professional artist in America. An advertisement in the *Baltimore Intelligencer* on December 19, 1798, described Johnston as a "self-taught genius." He painted many prominent citizens and his works are in many museum collections.

Sources: Logan and Winston, *Dictionary of American Negro Biography,* p. 362; *Encyclopedia of Black America,* p. 118; Garrett, *Famous First Facts about Negroes,* p. 17.

1842 • Robert Scott Duncanson (1817–1872) was the first black American painter to win acclaim at home and abroad as a serious landscape artist and muralist. Born in New York, he received his early education in Canada before moving to Ohio in 1841–42. He traveled in the northern United States and made three trips to Europe.

Sources: Cederholm, *Afro-American Artists,* pp. 83–85; Logan and Winston, *Dictionary of American Negro Biography,* p. 203; Dwight, *Negro History Bulletin* 18 (December 1954): 53; Smith, *Notable Black American Men,* pp. 347–48.

1876 • Edward Mitchell Bannister (1828–1901) was the first black to achieve full recognition in America as a painter. The most renowned black artist of the nineteenth century, he specialized in landscapes. Bannister received the gold medal in the Philadelphia Centennial Exhibition of 1876 for his huge landscape *Under the Oaks.* He was one of the founders of the Providence Art Club, which developed into the Rhode Island School of Design.

Sources: Cederholm, *Afro-American Artists,* pp. 15–16; Logan and Winston, *Dictionary of American Negro Biography,* pp. 25–26; Garrett, *Famous First Facts about Negroes,* p. 18.

1928 • Archibald J. Motley Jr. (1891–1981) was the first artist of any race to have one of his works published on the first page of the *New York Times.* Although he spent time in New York during the Harlem Renaissance, he lived most of his life in Chicago. Born in New Orleans, Motley moved to Chicago with his family during the northern migration of that period. He was also the first black artist to depict urban social life in his art.

Sources: Smith, *Notable Black American Men,* pp. 843–45.

1941 • Jacob Lawrence Jr. (1917–2000) became the first black artist represented by a New York gallery, helping to set a standard for future generations of black artists. His work is characterized by small-scale genre paintings of black Americans and their political and social struggles. He presented much of his work in series—between 1940 and 1941 he developed sixty panels of paintings into what he called *The Migration of the Negro,* illustrating the black exodus from South to North. Although Lawrence had other successful works, the migration series continues to enjoy success and has been called his greatest single achievement.

Sources: *Contemporary Black Biography,* vol. 4, pp. 151–55; Smith, *Notable Black American Men,* pp. 702–05; Wheat, *Jacob Lawrence: American Painter.*

1950 • The first black instructor at the Art Students League in Manhattan was Charles Henry Alston (1907–1977). Alston was born in Charlotte, North Carolina, and received both his bachelor's and master's degrees from Columbia University. In 1935–36 he directed the work of thirty-five artists who, along with Alston, painted murals for Harlem Hospital for the Federal Arts project. He collaborated with Hale Woodruff in 1948 in painting murals for the Golden State Insurance Company in Los Angeles. In addition to his work at the Art Students League, he taught at the Museum of Modern Art and City College of New York.

Charles Henry Alston

Sources: *The Black New Yorkers,* p. 274; Salzman, *Encyclopedia of African-American Culture and History,* vol. 1, pp. 103–04.

1972 • Alma Woodsey Thomas (1891–1978) became the first black woman to have a solo exhibit at the New York's Whitney Museum of American Art. Thomas was born in Columbus, Georgia. She received her bachelor's degree from Howard University and her master of fine arts degree from Columbia University. From 1924 to 1960 she taught at Shaw Junior High School in Washington. Her works show a variety of themes, including science, economics, religion, and society. Thomas was deeply inspired by the space program and did a number of "Space Paintings." Her most popular painting, *The Eclipse,* features a dark circle surrounded by mosaic squares in many colors. She was eighty-one at the time of the Whitney exhibit.

Sources: Bontemps, *Forever Free: Art by African-American Women, 1862–1980,* pp. 132–33; Smith, *Notable Black American Women,* pp. 1121–26.

1973 • The first black artist to have a solo exhibit at the Boston Museum of Fine Arts was Lois Mailou Jones (1905–1998). A Boston native, Jones studied drawing at the Boston Museum and served an apprenticeship with a Rhode Island School of Design teacher. She graduated from the Boston Museum School of Fine Arts and later studied at the Designers' Art School of Boston. In 1945 she received a bachelor's degree from Howard University. Jones was responsible for organizing the art department at Palmer Memorial Institute in Sedalia, North Carolina. She left two years later for a teaching position at Howard University, where she remained for nearly fifty years. She was highly successful as teacher and artist, and influenced the lives of many fledgling black artists. She had more than fifty one-person shows in her lifetime.

Sources: Bontemps, *Forever Free: Art by African-American Women 1862–1980,* pp. 94–95; Smith, *Notable Black American Women,* pp. 597–600.

1991 • Esther Mahlangu (1932?–), South African master painter and muralist, became the twelfth artist and the first and only woman artist to paint a BMW Art Car for the National Museum of Women in the Arts exhibition in Washington, held from September 15 through November 13. The show was titled "Esther Mahlangu, South African Muralist: The BMW Art Car and Related Works." Mahlangu used tribal traditions and high technology as inspiration for her design. Other artists who have contributed to the Art Car collection include Andy Warhol, Robert Rauschenberg, Roy Lichtenstein, and Alexander Calder. In addition to her work on the Art Car collection, she also painted a mural on a building next to the National Museum of Women in the Arts. In 1992 she was commissioned to paint a five-story mural on the Johannesburg Civic Theater. Mahlangu, from the rural KwaNdebele region of South Africa, learned the tribal art form of painting murals on clay huts. Her works brought her acclaim from exhibitions in Paris, Lisbon, Tokyo, and Kassel, Germany.

Sources: "The Living Art of Esther Mahlangu," *Washington Post* (4 September 1994).

Esther Mahlangu

1992 • Corinne Howard Mitchell (1914–1993) became the first black American to have a solo exhibit, *A Glimpse of Joy,* at the National Museum of Women in the Arts, located in Washington. Born in Mecklenburg, Virginia, Mitchell graduated from St. Paul's College, Virginia State College, and George Washington University. She responded to the race problems in America by painting; for example, she reflected on the 1963 March on Washington by painting *The March* (1965). After lung cancer forced her to stop painting in 1991, she reduced her activities and explored sculpture and African masks until she died two years later.

Sources: *Contemporary Black Biography*, vol. 8, pp. 171–73.

1996 • Hillary Rodham Clinton, who had searched for two years to acquire a work by a famous black artist for the White House's permanent art collection, selected Henry O. Tanner's *Sand Dunes at Sunset, Atlantic City*. The painting became the first by a black artist to be included in the White House collection. Measuring fifty-eight by thirty inches, the painting captures a shadowy beach and sand dunes made pink by the late afternoon sun. The White House Endowment Fund underwrote the $100,000 price tag.

Sources: *Jet* 91 (18 November 1996): 24–25; 94 (22 June 1998): 19.

2002 • The first black to paint a commissioned portrait of Britain's Queen Elizabeth II was Chinwe Chukwuogo-Roy. The painting was unveiled on Commonwealth Day, March 12 this year, at Marlborough House in London and marked the Queen's Golden Jubilee. Nigerian-born Chukwuogo-Roy received a bachelor's degree with honors in graphic design in England and moved immediately to complete her commissioned piece.

Sources: *Jet* 102 (1 April 2002): 29.

2002 • Artist Simmie Knox (1935–) was the first black artist to paint the official portrait of a U.S. president—that of Bill Clinton. Knox won the commission just before Clinton left office in January 2001. He also painted a portrait of former first lady and U.S. senator, and now U.S. Secretary of State Hilliary Rodham Clinton. The oil on linen portraits of both Clintons took two years each to complete; they were unveiled during a ceremony in the East Wing of the White House on June 18, 2004. President Clinton's portrait hangs alongside those of other former presidents. In 1989 Knox was the first black artist commissioned to paint an official portrait of a Supreme Court Justice, Thurgood Marshall. When he painted a portrait of educator and school founder Mary McLeod Bethune, his was the first by a black artist to hang in the South Carolina State Capitol. Knox's portrait of Maryland state senator Verda F. Welcome was the first by a black artist to be included in the official Maryland State Collection of Art. Knox's other portraits include such luminaries as black senator Blanche K. Bruce of Mississippi, Supreme Court justice Ruth Bader Ginsburg, philanthropist Camille Cosby (of whom he has done multiple portraits), abolitionist Frederick Douglass, civil rights leader Martin Luther King Jr., activist Fannie Lou Hamer with civil rights worker Ella Baker, baseball legend Hank Aaron, boxer Muhammed Ali, television mogul Oprah Winfrey, actor Paul Robeson, former New York City mayor David Dinkins, former Howard University president H. Patrick Swygert, and historian John Hope Franklin and his wife Aurelia. Knox was born an only child in Aliceville, Alabama. His parents divorced while he was a child, and he grew up on a farm in Leroy, Alabama, with an aunt. He went to school only when the farming season was slow and he was not needed as a worker. After he moved to Mobile, Alabama, to live with his father and attended the Heart of Mary school; the sisters at the school recognized his artistic talent. Knox received his first commission to paint when he was in the fifth grade, painting the church's religious statues as well as the Stations of the Cross. After a stint in the army, he joined his father and stepmother in Delaware and attended Delaware State College where he majored in biology. So detailed were his biology drawings that his professor encouraged Knox to study art. Knox transferred to the University of Delaware and prepared to become an art teacher. He earned a master of fine arts degree from Temple University's Tyler School of Art. For eighteen years he also taught in public schools, colleges, and universities in Delaware, Maryland, Pennsylvania, and Washington. D.C.

Sources: *Crisis* 109 (May/June 2002): 45–48; *Jet* 111 (18 June 2007): 20; Smith, *Notable Black American Men*, Book II, pp. 407–10.

Photography

1884 • James Conway Farley (1854–1910) of Richmond, Virginia, was the first black American to gain recognition as a photographer. He won first prize at the Colored Industrial Fair in Richmond in 1884 and a premium at the New Orleans World Exposition in 1885, where he exhibited with white photographers. In 1873 Farley was employed as a photo technician with C. R. Rees and Company, a downtown Richmond photography firm. By 1875 he was setting scenes and making pictures for another downtown firm, the G. W. Davis Photo Gallery. While with the Davis firm, some white employees wanted him fired, but the gallery owner fired them instead. In 1895, Farley opened his own studio, the Jefferson Fine Arts Gallery, where he specialized in transferring the pictures he made of individuals and groups into greeting cards. The Valentine Museum in Richmond had one of his photographs on display as late as 1982. Of his many photographs, only one remains that can be attributed to him.

Sources: Logan and Winston, *Dictionary of American Negro Biography,* p. 219; Salzman, *Encyclopedia of African-American Culture and History, Supplement,* p. 91; Richings, *Evidence of Progress among Colored People,* p. 495; Simmons, *Men of Mark,* pp. 801–04.

1967 • Ken Hamblin (1940–) became the first black photographer hired by the *Detroit Free Press.* The son of West Indian parents, he was born in Brooklyn. He was active in the civil rights struggle of the 1960s, and from 1969 until 1976 he worked as a documentary film producer and host-producer for the Detroit PBS affiliate. Hamblin operated a cable television station in Dillon, Colorado, from 1976 until 1983, while he continued to produce documentary films. After working in a number of jobs, he landed his own show on Denver's Entertainment Radio Network called *The Ken Hamblin Show.* He contributes to columns in the *Denver Post* and the New York Times Syndicate.

Sources: *Contemporary Black Biography,* vol. 10, pp. 83–85; *Tennessean* (13 March 1944).

Radio

1903 • Victor Talking Machine Records issued the first recording of any kind of black music. The records featured Dinwiddie Colored Quartet's Jubilee and Camp Meeting Shouts. Joseph Douglass, a gifted violinist and the grandson of abolitionist and statesman Frederick Douglass, was the first black violinist to make recordings for Victor. Joseph Douglass also performed at the White House for President William McKinley and later for President William Howard Taft.

Sources: *American Visions:* 22–25.

1920s • Banjoist Jack McVea was the first black radio host in Los Angeles. His show, *The Optimistic Doughnut,* was broadcast throughout the early 1920s on station KNX.

Sources: *New York Times* (15 January 2001).

1922 • *Shuffle Along,* a black musical by Eubie Blake (1883–1983) and Noble Sissle (1889–1975), aired in Boston in early November to become the first known live radio performance of a Broadway musical with original cast. The stage show played before black and white audiences in New York for more than a year, receiving rave reviews, before it went on the road. Blake and Sissle led the show, while female vocalist Lottie Gee was featured. The show had such a large following when it played in Boston that white entrepreneur John Shepard III, owner of radio station WNAC, decided to put the cast on the air. The concert was held during the Boston Exposition. This may have been the first appearance of Blake and Sissle on radio.

Sources: Halper, Donna, "African Americans and Early Radio," http://www.coax.net/people/lwf/AAER.HTM.

1922 • Jack L. Cooper (1889–1970), black radio pioneer and ventriloquist, emulated vaudevillian Bert Williams's comedy routine, which enabled him to claim to be "the first four Negroes on radio." He was first black disc jockey with a commercially sustained radio show. There is some dispute over the exact date that he became an announcer; however, his broadcasting career started sometime between 1922 and 1924 on station WCAP in Washington, D.C. He was also the first black sports announcer. He moved to Chicago in

Eubie Blake

1926, and in 1927 originated a community news broadcast on WSBC called *The All-Negro Hour.* This was a pioneering achievement that set precedents in black radio history. Cooper, the only broadcaster to play popular black music on race labels, built up a loyal black audience. He gathered news from black publications to develop the first daily black newscast. He avoided black dialect in favor of middle-American speech patterns, and the information he gave appealed to the black community. Cooper financed his shows with money from national advertisers. He created a missing persons bureau to help itinerant black migrants locate relatives who had moved to Chicago. His radio career in Chicago spanned more than thirty years. By 1949 Cooper owned his own broadcast studio and advertising agency, and had become a millionaire.

Sources: *Ebony* 3 (December 1947): 47; 7 (July 1952): 14; 12 (July 1957): 5; Garrett, *Famous First Facts about Negroes,* p. 166; *Negro Digest* 3 (February 1945): 11–12; Dates and Barlow, *Split Image,* pp. 182, 185–86.

1929 • The Harlem Broadcasting Corporation was established and became the first black radio venture of its kind. It operated its own radio studios at Lenox Avenue and 125th Street in Harlem, leased time on local radio outlet WRNY, and operated an artist bureau for black radio talent.

Sources: Dates and Barlow, *Split Image,* p. 185.

1929 • The Mills Brothers were the first black group to have commercial sponsorship on a national network, CBS. They first broadcast over WLW in Chicago in 1929. The longest-lived group of modern times, the Mills Brothers performed from about 1922 until 1982. During this period, there were only two changes in personnel—bassist John Jr., died in 1936, and was replaced by his father, who retired in 1954. The quartet then became a trio.

Sources: Southern, *The Music of Black Americans,* pp. 437, 498.

1933 • The first black hero to be heard on network radio was Juano Hernandez's depiction of "John Henry: Black River Giant," which he performed in a series broadcast on CBS.

Sources: Dates and Barlow, *Split Image,* p. 187.

1943 • *King Biscuit Time* was the first live black country blues program. The program was heard on KFFA in Helena, Arkansas, until 1981, although the music was not always live. Harmonica-player Rice [Willie] Miller (1899–1965), also known as "Sonny Boy Williamson, No. 2," and guitarist Junior [Robert] Lockwood (1915-2006) began the program in November. For the first time, black Americans in the South developed their own radio programs.

Sources: Dates and Barlow, *Split Image,* p. 208; Southern, *The Music of Black Americans,* pp. 492–93.

1945 • Station WSM, in Nashville, Tennessee, provided the first clear-channel broadcasting oriented at blacks in the South. The success of this format was a stimulus for the growth of radio programming aimed at black audiences in the South.

Sources: *Tennessean* (20 February 1992).

1947 • Earl Wright (1915?–1999), pioneering radio personality, was hired at Clarksdale's WROX Radio and became the first black disc jockey in Mississippi. He was known for his nightly *Soul Man* broadcast that ran for fifty years. Wright, who retired in 1998, hosted one of this nation's longest continuously running radio shows. He interviewed a number of celebrities for the show, including Elvis Presley, Muddy Waters, B.B. King, Ike and Tina Turner, and country singer Charley Pride. He also attracted the national media to his hometown's blues and gospel heritage.

Sources: *New York Times* (14 December 1999).

1948 • Nat King Cole [Nathaniel Coles] (1919–1965) led the first black jazz group to have its own sponsored program on radio. Cole soon began to concentrate his attention on his singing, and by 1952 he was one of the most successful singers of popular music.

Nat King Cole

In 1956 and 1957 he was the second black to host a nationwide network television show. Born in Montgomery, Alabama, his family moved to Chicago, and by 1936 he was piano player for the touring black revue, *Shuffle Along.* He formed the King Cole Trio, which toured the country and made recordings. "Straighten Up and Fly Right," his first record, sold more than five hundred thousand copies. "Nature Boy" (1948), "Mona Lisa" (1949), and "Too Young" (1951) are among his most successful hits.

Sources: Logan and Winston, *Dictionary of American Negro Biography,* pp. 120–21; *Encyclopedia of Black America,* p. 277; Southern, *Biographical Dictionary of Afro-American and African Musicians,* p. 76; Southern, *The Music of Black Americans,* pp. 497–98; Smith, *Notable Black American Men,* pp. 215–17.

1948 • Hal Jackson (1915–2012) was the first black announcer and disc jockey on WOOK, in Washington, D.C., when the station changed to a black format. Known as the dean of broadcasting, he was also the first black master of ceremonies for a network jazz show, the first black to host an interracial network jazz show, the first black host of an international network television presentation, and the first minority person inducted into the National Association of Broadcasters' Hall of Fame. Jackson founded the Miss Black Teenage America Pageant (now the Miss United States Talented Teen Pageant).

Sources: Dates and Barlow, *Split Image,* p. 212–13; Tenth Anniversary, Candace Awards, Program, 22 June 1992.

1949 • WDIA in Memphis, Tennessee, a white-owned radio station, became the first to feature all black-oriented programming. The station hired Nat D. Williams (called Nat D) (1907–1983), who became the first black disc jockey in the South, and the first black announcer in the South to play popular rhythm and blues records on the air. On October 21, 1948, the station launched *Tan Town Jamboree,* its first black show; it was the first all-black format radio station. Memphis became a center for blues broadcasting. The station aired such musicians as B. B. [Riley] King (1925–) and his band.

Sources: *Jet* 65 (5 December 1983): 18; Southern, *The Music of Black Americans,* p. 493; Dates and Barlow, *Split Image,* pp. 209–10; *Tennessean* (29 February 1992).

1949 • The first black-owned radio station, in Atlanta, Georgia, was WERD, purchased on October 4, 1949, by J. B. Blayton. Broadcasting began on October 7. Jack "The Rapper" Gibson (1920–2000) was the first black program director in Georgia. In 1955 Gibson organized the National Association of Radio Announcers (NARA) to give the original thirteen black disc jockeys a voice in the broadcasting industry. WERD station signed off the air, was sold, and relocated in 1957.

Sources: Alford, *Famous First Blacks,* p. 76; Bergman, *The Chronological History of the Negro in America,* p. 521; Mason, *Going Against the Wind,* pp. 123, 161; Dates and Barlow, *Split Image,* p. 213.

1954 • W. Leonard Evans Jr., (1914–2007) publisher of the black radio trade magazine *Tuesday,* a Sunday magazine supplement appearing in twenty papers, founded the National Negro Network. The first black radio network, it began programming on January 20, 1954, and was carried on forty stations. Juanita Hall starred in the first program, *The Story of Ruby Valentine,* a soap opera.

Sources: Dates and Barlow *Split Image,* p. 226; *Encyclopedia of Black America,* p. 378; *Negro Almanac,* p. 1429.

1955 • The National Association of Radio Announcers (NARA) was the first black disc jockey trade organization. It was organized and run by a group that became known as the "Original Thirteen." By 1967 NARA faced an internal crisis that destroyed it as a viable organization—a militant new breed of disc jockeys made a number of angry demands and tried to change its name to NARTA, to include television announcers. The organization was unable to overcome this conflict.

Sources: *Split Image,* pp. 216, 226.

1960s • William Roscoe Mercer (1927–2000) was a disc jockey who broke several barriers. He was the first black news announcer on station WINS in New York in the early 1960s, known by his fans simply as "Rosko," and was the first black disc jockey in KBLA in Los Angeles. Mercer was a pioneer of free-form FM radio in New York City. Born on May 25, 1927 in New York City, Mercer was a charity student at a Catholic boarding school in Pennsylvania. He began his radio career as a jazz disc jockey at Chester, Pennsylvania's station WHAT. He moved to WDAS in Philadelphia and later to WBLS in New York. In the late 1950s he played rhythm and blues on WNJR in Secaucus, New Jersey. Mercer was blacklisted for six months for refusing to cross a picket line during a demonstration to establish a union for disc jockeys. After becoming an announcer for station WINS, KDIA in Oakland hired him as disc jockey. When radio station KGFJ in Los Angeles tried to hire him, their efforts resulted in a precedent-setting lawsuit that established a new procedure for preparing disc jockey's contracts. During the early 1960s Mercer broadcasted live and on tape on Oakland's KGFJ six nights a week, spending the seventh night live on Oakland's KDIA. Radio station KBLA, at first an all-white station, hired him to play rock and rhythm and blues. In 1966 he returned to New York, working at several stations until 1970, before moving to France for five years, where he broadcast for the Voice of America. When he returned to New York, he returned to radio and was known especially for his announcements on *CBS Sports*.

Sources: *New York Times* (6 August 2000).

1967 • Chicago radio executive Bernadine Washington (1920s–1993) became the first black woman vice president of a radio station—WVON radio, in Chicago. Originally a women's clothes buyer, she joined WVON in 1963 and was named vice president four years later. Still later, she was named general manager. She hosted the popular show *On Scene with Bernadine* that presented the latest trends in the black community, including fashion and politics. Washington was born in New Orleans and attended Fisk University.

Sources: *Jet* 84 (18 October 1993): 17.

1972 • The first black-controlled station of the National Federation of Community Broadcasters was KPOO-FM in San Francisco. Called "Poor People's Radio," it was founded by Lorenzo Milam to serve the black community and inner-city poor.

Sources: Dates and Barlow, *Split Image,* p. 233.

1972 • John H. Johnson (1918–2005), publisher and editor, purchased Chicago radio station WGRT and became the first black in the city to own a broadcasting outlet.

Sources: *Ebony Success Library,* vol. 2, pp. 132–37; Smith, *Notable Black American Men,* pp. 630–34.

1975 • Catherine "Cathy" Liggins Hughes (1947–), who has been called "Ms. Radio," became the first female radio general station manager in Washington, D.C. She began in radio as an administrative assistant to Tony Brown at Howard University in 1971. Her diligent work led to her transfer to Howard's radio station in 1973, and by 1975 she was vice president and general manager of the station. Today she is owner and CEO of Radio One, Inc.

Sources: *Contemporary Black Biography,* vol. 27, 2001, pp. 87–89; *Ebony* 55 (May 2000): 100–05

Mamie Smith

Recording

1920 • On February 14, 1920, Mamie Smith (1883–1946) was the first black woman to make a record. She recorded "You Can't Keep a Good Man Down" and "This Thing Called Love." These songs were written by her black manager, Perry Bradford, who also wrote the next two songs she recorded, "It's Right Here for You" and "Crazy Blues." The first blues song ever recorded, "Crazy Blues" sold 790,000 copies in the first year. Its success led O-

Keh Records to establish "Original Race Records" series under black musical director Clarence Williams (1893–1965).

Sources: *Encyclopedia of Black America,* p. 599; Smith, *Notable Black American Women,* pp. 1048–49, *Biographical Dictionary of Afro-American and African Musicians,* p. 347; Southern, *The Music of Black Americans,* p. 365.

1926 • The Reverend J. M. Gates recorded the first successful "sermons with singing" on record. He was discovered when Columbia, a major record company, sent a field agent to Atlanta to make recordings of black singing groups. They recorded four of his "sermons with singing." In his sermon "Death's Black Train Is Coming," two women from his congregation featured singing. During the sermon, Gates declares, "I want to sing a song tonight, and while I sing I want every sinner in the house to come to the angel's feet and bow and accept prayer—you need prayer." Columbia's engineers were even able to add a train's whistle to the background while the singers warned of the railroad to hell. Two sides of the recording were issued in October 1926, bringing a massive 34,025 orders for copies. Gates never entered a contract with Columbia but for six years worked on six different labels, recording forty-two sides in three weeks. He used dramatic titles for his sermons such as "Tiger Flower's Last Fight," "God's Wrath in the St. Louis Cyclone," "Hitler and Hell, or Will Hell Be Your Santa Clause." Gates influenced other singing preachers, many of them signing on with record companies.

Sources: Broughton, *Black Gospel: An Illustrated History of the Gospel Sound,* p. 41.

1960 • Moms [Jackie] Mabley (1894–1975) was the first black comedienne to have a best-selling record. For many years she was the only black woman comedienne in the country and was the first to become widely recognized. Mabley portrayed a cantankerous, raucous old woman who dressed shabbily and had a toothless smile. She had a gravelly voice, often told off-color jokes, and levied insults on men. In real life, however, she was a compassionate woman. Born Loretta Mary Aiken in Brevard, South Carolina, she was one of twelve children. She moved to Cleveland at age fourteen. Mabley traveled on the vaudeville circuit and often appeared with "Pigmeat" Marcum, Bill "Bojangles" Robinson, and Cootie Williams. The team Butterbeans and Susie discovered Mabley in the mid–1920s and brought her to New York where she made her debut at Connie's Inn. She was a regular at the Apollo in Harlem in 1939, made several recordings, and appeared in Broadway shows, on television, and had bit parts in films. She died on May 23, 1975, after more than sixty years in entertainment.

Sources: *Current Biography, 1975,* pp. 216–64; Lee, *Interesting People,* p. 56; Smith, *Notable Black American Women,* pp. 688–90.

Sculpture

1870 • [Mary] Edmonia "Wildfire" Lewis (1845–1890?) was the first black American sculptor to study abroad, and in 1871 was the first black artist to exhibit in Rome. Lewis was born of black and Native American heritage. Her birthplace—either Greenhigh, Ohio; Greenbush, New York; or somewhere near Albany, New York—cannot be verified. After studying at Oberlin College, Ohio, she opened a studio in Boston and earned enough money to move to Europe. Lewis received commissions for her neoclassical sculpture from all over the United States. She received national recognition at Philadelphia's Centennial Exhibition in 1876.

Sources: Cederholm, *Afro-American Artists,* pp. 176–78; Logan and Winston, *Dictionary of American Negro Biography,* pp. 393–95; Smith, *Notable Black American Women,* pp. 663–66.

1934 • Augusta Christine [Fells] Savage (1892–1962), a sculptor and educator, was the first black member of the National Association of Women Painters and Sculptors. One of her major commissions was the creation of sculpture for New York World's Fair 1939–40, *Lift Every Voice and Sing,* a sculptural group symbolizing blacks' contribution to music, which became Savage's best known and most widely recognized work. Another of her most

Edmonia Lewis

The Museum of Modern Art Exhibits William Edmondson

In 1937 William Edmondson (1874–1951) was the first black artist to be featured in a solo exhibit at New York's Museum of Modern Art from October 20 to December 12, 1937. Edmondson, an untrained sculptor, grew up on the Compton plantation near Nashville, Tennessee, and later moved to that city. To help sustain himself and his family during the Depression, he began to fashion cheap tombstones, religious folk items and other works to sell to black customers. In 1935 white artists from nearby Peabody College discovered Edmondson and helped to promote him and his work. In recent years his works have been promoted in exhibitions at the Tennessee State Museum and at the Cheekwood Museum in Nashville. A small park on Charlotte Avenue in Nashville and a plaque on his home site now commemorate Edmondson.

Sources: Smith, *Notable Black American Men*, pp. 359–61; Fuller, *Visions in Stone: The Sculpture of William Edmondson*; Jones, *Ever Day in Tennessee History*, p. 28; Lovett, *The African-American History of Nashville, Tennessee, 1780–1930*, pp. 103–04.

successful works was *The Negro Urchin*. Born in Green Cove Springs in northern Florida, Savage moved to New York City in 1920 and studied sculpture at Cooper Union. In 1937 she became the first director of the Harlem Community Art Center and organized programs in education, art, and recreation. Savage was also an organizer of the Harlem Artists Guild. She presented the first annual Exhibition Salon of Contemporary Negro Art at her studio in New York City on June 20, 1937. She was devoted to the efforts of black artists and continued to recognize and promote their work.

Sources: *Encyclopedia of Black Culture*, p. 741; Hine, *Black Women in America*, pp. 1010–13; *Jet* 90 (24 June 1996): 20; Smith, *Notable Black American Women*, pp. 979–83.

1943 • Selma [Hortense] Burke (1900–1995), sculptor, educator, and school founder, was the first black sculptor to design a United States coin. She won a competition to design the portrait of President Franklin D. Roosevelt that appeared on the dime. Born in Mooresville, North Carolina, Burke moved to New York and studied at Cooper Union. She received her master of fine art degree from Columbia College in 1941. She founded the Selma Burke School of Sculpture in New York. In 1983 the Selma Burke Gallery opened at Winston-Salem State University, where many items from her private collection are gathered. This marks the first time a gallery has been named for a black American woman artist. Amid some controversy, in 1990 the gallery was moved to Johnson C. Smith University in Charlotte.

Sources: Hine, *Black Women in America*, pp. 190–95; Cederholm, *Afro-American Artists*, p. 41; Smith, *Notable Black American Women*, pp. 128–30; *Who's Who in Colored America, 1950*, p. 77.

1945 • Richmond Barthé (1901–1989) was the first black sculptor elected to the National Academy of Arts and Letters. He is noted for his sensitive small bronzes and monumental statues, and in 1946 he was commissioned to sculpt the bust of Booker T. Washington to be placed in the American Hall of Fame at New York University. Born in Bay St. Louis, Mississippi, Barthé studied at the Art Institute of Chicago where he began modeling in clay. He moved to New York City in 1929 and continued his education at the Art Students League. He held a number of solo exhibits and in 1929, 1931, and 1933 exhibited in group shows for the Harmon Foundation and other museums. In the 1930s he created sculptures of black male nudes, one of the first black American artists to do so. He was a remarkable sculptor whose spiritual pieces, genre scenes, portraits, and other works demonstrate compelling themes.

Sources: Cederholm, *Afro-American Artists*, pp. 17–18; *Encyclopedia Americana*, 1988, vol. 3, p. 278; Garrett, *Famous First Facts about Negroes*, p. 175; Smith, *Notable Black American Men*, pp. 60–64.

Richmond Barthé

2000 • The White House displayed the bust of civil rights leader Martin Luther King Jr., in commemoration of Black History Month. This marked the first time that an image of a black person was displayed in public spaces of the White House. The bronze bust by artist Charles Austin stands 12⅝ inches high and was on extended loan from the Smithsonian Institution's National Portrait Gallery. Austin sculpted the bust in 1970.

Sources: *Jet* 97 (13 March 2000): 22.

Television

1939 • Ethel Waters (1896–1977) became the first black singer to appear on television and the first black American to star to appear in her own television show, *The Ethel Waters Show.* This was an experimental, one-night event for the new medium of television. She returned to television eleven years later as the star of *Beulah.*

Sources: Bogle, *Primetime Blues,* p. 1; *Contemporary Black Biography,* vol. 7, pp. 285–88; Smith, *Notable Black American Women,* pp. 1225–29.

1948 • Timmie Rogers (1914–2006), entertainer, comedian, dancer, singer, composer, and musician, launched the first all-black variety show, *Sugar Hill Times,* on CBS television. Known for his trademark "Oh, Yeah!," he was sometimes called the "dean of black comedians" and inspired such black entertainers as Redd Foxx, Dick Gregory, Nipsey Russell, and Slappy White. He also wrote hit songs for Nat King Cole and Sarah Vaughan.

Sources: *Ebony Success Library,* vol. 1, p. 268.

Timmie Rogers

1949 • *Happy Pappy* was the first television variety talent show with an all-black cast. First televised on April 1, 1949, on WENR-TV in Chicago, the jazz-oriented show featured the Four Vagabonds and the Modern Modes. Ray Grant was master of ceremonies.

Sources: Kane, *Famous First Facts,* p. 657.

1950 • When DuMont Network launched *The Hazel Scott Show* on July 3, Hazel Scott (1920–1981) became the first black television show host presented in musical format. The show was first broadcast as a local program but became a network show in 1950. At first the show ran for fifteen minutes on Friday evenings, but it later moved to three days a week. Most television hosts at that time were men; Scott, however, broke new ground. While the show looked promising, especially for the image of the black American women, Scott was accused of being either a Communist or Communist sympathizer and her contract was not renewed. Her program went off the airways on September 29. Scott, a musician, singer, actress, social activist, and child prodigy was born in Port-of-Spain, Trinidad, and moved to the United States. She studied at Juilliard School of Music.

Sources: Feather, *Encyclopedia of Jazz,* p. 412; Bogle, *Primetime Blues,* pp. 15–19; Smith, *Notable Black American Women,* pp. 997–98.

1951 • William Warfield (1920–2002) and Muriel Rahn (1911?–1961) appeared on the *Ed Sullivan Show,* marking the first appearance of black concert artists on a television show. (Marian Anderson followed the next year.) William Caesar Warfield was born in West Helena, Arkansas, but later moved to Rochester, New York. He graduated from Eastman School of Music in 1942. Warfield's debut recital on March 19, 1950 at New York's Town Hall was well received and led to numerous invitations for appearances. He married soprano Leontyne Price and the two performed together— they had joint leads in the folk opera *Porgy and Bess*—but divorced later. His career soared and in 1961 he appeared in a revival of that opera as well as in *Showboat.* He taught at the University of Illinois from 1974 to 1990, then held adjunct and visiting professorships. He died in 2002. Muriel Rahn joined the casts of at least two Broadway musicals, *Black Birds of 1929* and *Hot Chocolates* (1929–30). She also became a star in the original production of *Carmen Jones* and co-starred in *The Barrier.* She was also in the opera *Salome,* where she performed in "The Dance of Seven Veils." In her career Rahn combined concert and theater and made extensive concert tours. The gifted singer, opera star, and stage personality was born in Boston and relocated with her mother to New York. Rahn graduated from the Music Conservatory of the University of Nebraska, took special course work at Teachers' College, Columbia University, and later taught school in Winston-Salem, North Carolina. She returned to New York and studied voice at the Juilliard School of Music.

Sources: Southern, *The Music of Black Americans,* 2nd ed., p. 359; Smith, *Notable Black American Men,* pp. 1179–81 (Warfield); *Ebony* 10 (January 1955): 66–68; *Jet* 20 (24 August 1961): 48; Smith, *Notable Black American Women,* pp. 911–13.

1955? • Maude Eudora McClennan Boxley (1882–1970) was the first black woman to host a Southern television cooking show, demonstrating cooking techniques. Aired on WLAC, Channel 5, in Nashville, Tennessee, the show was known as the *Eudora Boxley Cook Show.* It aired during the Jim Crow era when blacks were rarely seen on television, especially with their own show. Boxley and her daughters also had a successful catering business in Nashville; it was regarded as the number one business of its kind in Nashville. The business catered to wealthy families in the area and had a staff of approximately fifty. When Boxley became ill, daughter Lucille took her place on television and continued until the end of her mother's contract. Thus, Lucille Boxley Frierson was the second black woman to have a cooking show on local television. When popular entertainers, such as Little Richard, Fats Domino, Jackie Wilson, and Joe Tex came to town, they often took meals at Boxley's home on Jefferson Street, in the black community. Maude Boxley, known locally as MomMu, was born in Arkansas and raised in Tennessee. She graduated from Fisk University.

Sources: Frierson, "The First African American Woman to Host a Southern TV Cooking Show: Maude Eudora McClellan Boxley." Undated document, Special Collections, Franklin Library, Fisk University.

1955 • Leontyne Price (1927–) became the first black American to appear in a televised production of an opera, performing in *Tosca.*

Sources: *Generations in Black and White,* p. 150.

1956 • Entertainer Nat King Cole (1919–1965) became the first major black performer to host his own television show, *The Nat King Cole Show.* The show was first aired on October 3 and ran for sixty-four weeks. The show received low ratings from the start. When no commercial sponsor could be secured, the show was cancelled and went off the air in December 1957.

Sources: Bogle, *Primetime Blues,* pp. 75–77; *Contemporary Black Biography,* vol. 17, pp. 37–41; Smith, *Notable Black American Men,* pp. 215–17.

1957 • The first black producer of network television programs at NBC was George E. Norford (1918–?). He had also been the only black correspondent on the staff of the army weekly magazine *Yank* during World War II. Born in New York City, Norford studied journalism and playwriting at Columbia University and attended the New School for Social Research.

Sources: *Ebony Success Library,* vol. 1, p. 237.

1958 • Acclaimed jazz pianist and composer Bill Taylor (1921–2010) was the first black to lead a television studio orchestra, on NBC's *The Subject is Jazz.* In the 1940s he moved to New York to establish a career as a jazz pianist. Later, he led the Billy Taylor Trio, composed dozens of pieces for ensembles, including over three hundred songs. In 1949 he was hired as house pianist at Birdland, where he played with such legendary musicians as Charlie Parker, Miles Davis, John Coltrane, Stan Getz, and Art Blakey. Taylor joined the staff of radio station WNEW and became the first black to host a daily show on a New York station. He cofounded Jazzmobile in 1964, which brought top jazz artists to poor urban areas where they performed for free. From 1977 to 1982, Taylor hosted a popular and weekly jazz show, *Jazz Alive,* that aired on National Public Radio. He won an Emmy Award for his 1983 segment on Quincy Jones, and won Downbeat's Lifetime Achievement Award in 1984. Even more significant was the profile of musicians that he did for *Sunday Morning,* a CBS program. In 1989 he formed his record label, Taylor Made, and released four albums under his label. The popular song, "I Wish I Knew How It Would Feel to be Free," composed in 1954 and popularized during the Civil Rights Movement, was one of his most famous works. Taylor became artistic advisor on jazz at the Kennedy Center. Born in Greenville, North Carolina, Taylor grew up in Washington, D.C., and graduated from Virginia State College (now University). He earned a master's and doctorate from the University of Massachusetts-Amherst. He was a Duke Ellington Fellow and held the Wilber D. Barrett Chair of Music at the university as well. His numerous awards include the National Medal of Arts, which he received in 1992.

Sources: *Contemporary Black Biography*, vol. 23, pp. 186–89; *Jet* 119 (7 February 2011): 20.

1963 • Actress Cicely Tyson (1942–) won a regular feature role in *East Side, West Side* and became the first black to appear in a key part on a television series. Born in East Harlem, New York, and raised in poverty, she studied acting at the Actors Playhouse and made her Broadway debut with a hit role in *The Dark of the Moon*. Tyson had successful roles in a number of films and was universally hailed by critics for her portrayal of a sharecropper's wife in *Sounder*. She is regarded as one of the most gifted actresses in Hollywood.

Sources: *Current Biography, 1975*, pp. 422–25; *Ebony Success Library*, vol. 2, pp. 264–67; Smith, *Notable Black American Women*, pp. 1160–64.

Cicely Tyson

1965 • Bill Cosby (1937–), a comedian and actor, broke the color barrier in television and became the first black in a non-traditional role when he co-starred in the network television series, *I Spy*. Cosby was also the first black star in a television series that excluded racial themes. After appearing on *The Tonight Show* this year, his career blossomed. In 1966 and 1967 he became the first black actor to win Emmy awards for best actor in a running series. In 1968 he narrated the seven-part series, "Of Black America" that aired on *CBS News Hour*. Cosby made a number of television appearances and later had his own show. *The Bill Cosby Show* was aired on NBC from 1969 to 1971 and he appeared on the *Electric Company* on PBS from 1971 to 1976. *The New Bill Cosby Show* ran on CBS from 1972 to 1973, *The Cosby Show* aired on NBC from 1984 to 1992, and *Cosby* aired on CBS from 1996 to 2000. In the 1970s he preserved in cartoons some of his elementary school friends and he recreated them in characters such as Fat Albert and Weird Harold. *Fat Albert and the Cosby Kids* (later renamed *The New Fat Albert Show*) aired on CBS from 1972 to 1984. Other shows include *You Bet Your Life* and *Kids Say the Darndest Things*. Cosby appeared in a number of films, including *Uptown Saturday Night* (1974), *A Piece of the Action* (1977), and *Jack* (1996). He has written a number of books, including *Fatherhood* (1986) and a series of books for children. Born in Germantown, Pennsylvania, he began comedy routines when he was in the fifth grade. Cosby entered Temple University on a track and football scholarship, dropped out in his sophomore year to perform in Philadelphia coffee houses, and later completed his doctorate degree there. The outspoken critic of black images in television made a bid to purchase the National Broadcasting Company on October 28, 1992. Cosby and his wife Camille are strong supporters of education; they have given generously to several black colleges, including Fisk University and Spelman College.

Sources: *Ebony Success Library*, vol. 1, p. 80; *Encyclopedia of Black America*, pp. 289, 724; Lee, *Interesting People*, p. 154; *Tennessean Showcase*, 26 April 1992; Smith, *Notable Black American Men*, pp. 230–34; *Primetime Blues: African Americans on Network Television*, 115–26.

Bill Cosby

1968 • *The Xernona Clayton Show* was first broadcast this year. Host Xernona Clayton (1930–) became the first black person in the South to have her own show and the first black woman in the South to host a regularly scheduled primetime television talk show. Xernona Brewster Clayton and her identical twin sister were born in Muskogee, Oklahoma. She graduated from Tennessee State University and later taught in the Chicago public schools. After moving to Atlanta, Clayton and her husband Edward worked with the Southern Christian Leadership Conference and were involved in speechwriting and engagements for Martin Luther King Jr. and Coretta Scott King. Early in 1966 Xernona Clayton became involved in efforts to desegregate Atlanta's hospitals. Her friendship with journalist Ralph McGill led to her career in television.

Sources: *Jet* 93 (24 November 1997): 36–37; Smith, *Notable Black American Women*, Book II, pp. 96–99; *Contemporary Black Biography*, vol. 3, pp. 34–36.

Diahann Carroll

1968 • Diahann Carroll (1935–), actress and singer, was the first black woman to star in a non-stereotypical role on television, in the weekly NBC series *Julia*. (She won the 1968 Golden Globe Award for Best Female TV Star for her role.) Born Carol Diahann Johnson in the Bronx, New York City, she graduated from the High School of Music and Art. She began singing at age six at Harlem's Abyssinian Baptist Church. In the 1980s she appeared in other nighttime soaps, such as *Dynasty* and *The Colbys* and in 2006–07 in the popular *Grey's Anatomy*. Her autobiography *Diahann!* was published in 1987 and her latest memoir, *The Legs Are the Last to Go,* was published in 2008. In 2011 she was inducted into the Television Academy Hall of Fame.

Sources: *Contemporary Black Biography,* vol. 9, pp. 39–42; *Current Biography,* 1962, pp. 74–76; *Ebony Success Library,* vol. 1, p. 59; Jet 116 (21–28 September 2009): 16; Smith, *Notable Black American Women,* pp. 160–63.

1968 • Charles Hobson, broadcast journalist and educator, wrote what may have been the nation's first black-produced community program on television, *Inside Bedford-Stuyvesant,* while he was with WNEW-TV in New York City. He has also served as writer-producer for the National Educational Television series *Black Journal*.

Sources: *Ebony Success Library,* vol. 1, p. 153.

1968 • Otis Young (1932?–2001) was the first black actor to star on a television Western series, playing a former slave turned bounty hunter in *The Outcasts*. Young's best-known film role was as a career sailor in *The Last Detail* (1973). In the 1980s he made occasional television appearances, including an appearance in the miniseries *Palmerstown USA*. He was also a minister and a college instructor.

Sources: *Jet* 100 (10 December 2002: 18; *New York Times* (20 October 2001); (23 October 2001).

Della Reese

1969 • Della Reese (1932–) was the first black woman to host a television variety show, *The Della Reese Show.* The show was aired five days a week for the 1969–70 season. She later became the first woman of any race to host *The Tonight Show.* Reese also appeared in the television shows *Chico and the Man* (1976–78) and *The Royal Family* (1991–92). Reese's career was revitalized beginning in 1994 when she began playing Tess on *Touched by an Angel.* She was recognized in 1994 with a star on the Hollywood Walk of Fame. Born Deloreese Patricia Early in Detroit, she attended Wayne State University. Reese sang with Mahalia Jackson's chorus and also appeared with Erskine Hawkins' band.

Sources: Hine, *Black Women in America,* p. 967; *Current Biography, 1971,* pp. 338–40; *Encyclopedia of Black America,* p. 729; Southern, *Biographical Dictionary of Afro-American and African Musicians,* p. 319; Smith, *Notable Black American Women,* Book II, pp. 546–48; Bogle, *Primetime Blues,* pp. 426–29.

1970 • Comedian Flip [Clerow] Wilson (1933–1998) was the first black man to have a weekly primetime comedy television show in his own name. He was most known for his impersonation of a black woman, "Geraldine," and became a regular at the Apollo Theater in Harlem. He left the show in 1974 and went into semi-retirement, appearing in television specials, a television game show, a situation comedy, and several movies. Born in Jersey City, New Jersey, Wilson was one of twenty-four children. He was shifted from one foster home to another and then spent some of his early years in a reformatory. He later served in the United States Air Force.

Sources: Bogle, *Primetime Blues,* pp. 176–78; *Current Biography, 1969,* pp. 454–56; *Ebony* 25 (December 1970): 176–82; 27 (December 1971): 67; *Encyclopedia of Black America,* p. 860; Salzman, *Encyclopedia of African-American Culture and History,* Supplement, p. 283.

1971 • *The Audrey Thomas Show* became the first black half-hour news and talk show on WSNS-TV in Chicago. Host Audrey Thomas (1933–1996) had been a fashion model during the 1960s, appearing in such magazines as *Ebony* and *Vogue*.

Sources: *Jet* 91 (18 November 1996): 18.

1971 • WABC-TV news reporter Melba Tolliver (1939–) caused a stir when she changed her hair from straightened to natural, becoming the first black woman news reporter to do so. She was assigned to cover the White House wedding of Tricia Nixon that summer. Studio executives described her appearance as less attractive and warned her that she could not appear on-air until she changed her hairstyle. She refused and, after public pressure because of the mandate, the station relented. Tolliver was born in Rome, Georgia, and moved to New York after completing high school. She graduated in 1959 from New York University-Bellevue School of Nursing and became an operating nurse. She left nursing in 1967 and became a secretary and assistant at ABC network television. She completed a training program in broadcast journalism, including study at New York University School of Journalism; she then became a television news reporter.

Sources: Smith, *Notable Black American Women,* Book II, pp. 651–53; *The Black New Yorkers,* pp. 350–51.

1972 • The first black television show sponsored by a black business was *Soul Train.* Johnson Products, Inc., supported the show, which began locally in Chicago then spread nationwide. The show became a television staple and, in the 1980s, was the primary video exposure for black talent.

Sources: Alford, *Famous First Blacks,* p. 76; Salzman, *Encyclopedia of African American Culture and History,* vol. 4, p. 2290.

1975 • *The Jeffersons,* which ran eleven seasons, made its debut. Starring Isabel Sanford (1917–2004), Sherman Hemsley (1938–2012), and Marla Gibbs (1931–), the show became the longest-running black series. The show was also the first to feature a married interracial couple, the Willises.

Sources: *Jet* 81 (18 November 1991): 45; Bogle, *Primetime Blues,* pp. 210–19.

Marla Gibbs

1975 • Williams Venoid Banks (1903–1985) became the first black American owner of a television station. Banks was born in Geneva, Kentucky, the son of a tenant farmer. He received his bachelor's degree from Detroit City College and his law degree from Detroit College of Law. He also received a doctor of divinity degree from Detroit Baptist College. He was a prominent business leader, an active Republican, and an active member of the International Free and Accepted Masons. His relationship with the Republican Party led to an invitation to the White House from President Richard M. Nixon, who helped him politically in his bid to purchase a television station. In 1964 Banks and the Masons purchased an FM radio station in Detroit. He secured a license from the Federal Communications Commission and in September 1975, with the help of the Masons, Banks launched WGPR-TV. After his death in August 1985, the Masons sold the station to CBS. Black business leaders protested, pointing out the station's historical significance to the black community.

Sources: *Contemporary Black Biography,* vol. 11, pp. 12–14.

1977 • The television series *Roots* became the most-watched dramatic show in television history. It aired on ABC as an eight-episode miniseries and some 130 million viewers watched the series. Alex [Alexander Murray Palmer] Haley (1921–1992) became the first black to win a Pulitzer Prize for his book *Roots* on which the television movie was based. When he was six weeks old, Haley and his mother moved to Henning, Tennessee, where they lived at her family home. In 1939 after two years of college, he volunteered in the United States Coast Guard. Haley devoted much of his free time to reading, writing letters, and writing adventure stories. The coast guard created the position of chief journalist for him in 1949, and he retired ten years later to become a full-time writer. In 1962 *Playboy* magazine retained Haley to write a series of interviews including one with Malcolm X, which led him to write *The Autobiography of Malcolm X* (1964), a bestseller that outsold *Roots.* Haley launched upon a twelve-year venture to track the ancestry of his mother's family. His search eventually took him to Gambia in West Africa, where his fourth great-grandfather, Kunte Kinte, had been born. A blend of fiction with fact, *Roots: The Saga of an American Family* (1976), brought Haley prompt renown. By February 1977, it had become the No. 1 best-selling book in the nation. Haley received a Pulitzer Prize, a National Book Award, and numerous other honors. The book was translated into thirty languages.

Sources: *Current Biography,* 1977, pp. 184–87; *Ebony Success Library,* vol. 1, p. 136; Funeral Program, February 1992; *Encyclopedia of Black America,* pp. 411–12; Hornsby, *Milestones in 20th-Century African-American History,* pp. 283, 488; *Jet* 110 (29 January 2007): 20; Smith, *Notable Black American Men,* pp. 496–99.

1980 • Robert L. Johnson (1946–) was the first black to found and own a black-oriented cable television network, Black Entertainment Television (BET). BET premiered on January 25, 1980, and marked the first time that viewers had access to quality programming that reflected the needs, interests, and lifestyles of black Americans.

Sources: Hornsby, *Milestones in Twentieth-Century African-American History,* p. 494; *Jet* 77 (16 October 1989): 40; Smith, *Notable Black American Men,* pp. 640–41.

1982 • The first black co-host of *The Today Show* was Bryant Charles Gumbel (1948–). He replaced Tom Brokaw as co-host of the show after sitting in for him for a several months. Prior to his work on *Today,* most of Gumbel's broadcast experience had been in sports, which he acknowledges as his true love. He had been co-host of NBC's Rose Bowl Parade since 1975, worked as chief anchor of NBC's televised football games, and in 1977 was co-host for Super Bowl XI. In 1988 he was NBC's host for the Olympic games in Seoul, South Korea. Gumbel was born in New Orleans, Louisiana, but the family moved to Chicago when Bryant and his older brother Greg were infants. He is a graduate of Bates College, where he played both baseball and football. He was a semi-dilettante for a brief time after graduation in 1970 and focused on becoming a sports director. He wrote an article about Harvard's first black athletic director for *Black Sports,* which led to a contract with the magazine and to his becoming its editor nine months later. He became a weekly sportscaster for Los Angeles' KNBC-TV in 1972, moved to sportscaster on the evening news, and to sports director in a span of just eight months. For a time he worked for both KNBC and as co-host of the NFL pre-game show, commuting between Los Angeles to New York. He began to do more shows for NBC, and in 1980 was assigned to do three sports features a week for *Today.* When he took over the plum job of co-host of the show, the show was in second place in the ratings. By spring 1985, the show had moved to first place. His stay on "Today" was not without controversy. Gumbel is regarded as a hard taskmaster and was given to expressing his opinions about aspects of the show and its cast members, sometimes in unflattering terms. Creative differences between Gumbel and the producers led in part to his decision to leave the show in January 1997. He soon accepted a CBS offer to host *Public Eye,* a weekly primetime magazine interview show. This show lacked *Today*'s longevity, and later Gumbel returned to the morning show beat as co-host of the CBS *The Early Show,* which competed with *Today* in many markets. In May 2002 he left *The Early Show.* He has always maintained multiple projects and continued his HBO sports show, *Real Sports.* Over the years he has earned three Emmys and numerous other awards and honors, including two Image Awards from the NAACP and Journalist of the Year from the Association of Black Journalists in 1993. He has also become known for his philanthropies, particularly his work on behalf of the UNCF.

Sources: Dates and Barlow, *Split Image,* p. 389; *Contemporary Black Biography,* vol.14, pp. 109–12; Smith, *Notable Black American Men,* pp. 492–95; *Who's Who among African Americans,* 26th ed., p. 507.

1985 • Danitra Vance (1959–1994) was the first black woman to join the regular *Saturday Night Live* cast, joining in the 1985–86 season. A native of Chicago and Roosevelt University graduate, she also performed with Chicago's Second City comedy troupe.

Sources: *Jet* 86 (12 September 1994): 59.

1986? • Oprah Winfrey (1954–) became the first black woman to host a nationally syndicated weekday talk show, *The Oprah Winfrey Show,* on February 8. She started her career at WTVF, a CBS local affiliate in Nashville, Tennessee, (where in 1971 she was the first woman co-anchor) and later moved to Chicago. In 1984 Winfrey took over *A.M.*

Chicago, which aired opposite Phil Donahue, and later expanded to a one-hour television show. She formed Harpo Productions, which enabled her to develop her own projects, and in 1989 bought her own television and movie production studio. She is the first black woman in television and film to own her own production company. After twenty-five seasons, she ended the show with the 2011 "farewell season" with the final show on May 25. On January 1, 2011, Winfrey launched the series premier of her network called OWN (Oprah Winfrey's Network) a joint venture with Discovery Communications. Winfrey was born in Kosciusko, Mississippi. For a while she lived with her mother in Milwaukee, then with her father in Nashville. She enrolled at Tennessee State University with an academic scholarship from the local Elks and also worked as a news announcer for WVOL, a local black-owned-and-operated station. WLAC, a major radio station in Nashville, hired her and later she moved to WLAC-TV (now WTVF). She left Nashville shortly before graduation, and it was not until 1988 when she delivered the commencement address at TSU that she was awarded a bachelor's degree. Oprah's Book Club, an on-air reading club that ran from 1996 to 2002, aided in promoting reading nationwide. In 1997 Winfrey launched Oprah's Angel Network that encouraged people to help others who are in need. In addition to her television show, she has appeared in a number of films, including *The Color Purple,* and *Beloved.* Her television movies include *The Women of Brewster Place.* With Hearst Magazines, in April 2000 Winfrey introduced *The Oprah Magazine,* a monthly publication that became the most successful journal launched in recent history. Oprah Winfrey is the richest woman in television history. For several years she has appeared on *Forbes* Celebrity 100 list of the world's most powerful celebrities in the world, claiming the No. 1 spot for several years. In December 2010 Winfrey was an honoree at the 33rd annual Kennedy Center Honors.

Oprah Winfrey

Sources: *Contemporary Black Biography,* vol. 2, pp. 262–66; vol. 15, pp. 230–34; vol. 61, pp. 177–82; Hine, *Black Women in America,* vol. 2, pp. 1274–76; "Oprah Winfrey Biography," Oprah.com; Smith, *Notable Black American Women,* pp. 1273–76; *Who's Who among African Americans,* 26th ed. p. 1371.

1986 • WLBT-TV, in Jackson, Mississippi, was the first black-owned network affiliate; the owner was the Civic Communications Corporation.

Sources: *Jet* 71 (13 October 1986): 17.

1986 • Don Cornelius (1936–2012) held the first *Soul Train Music Awards,* the first musical awards show dedicated exclusively to black musicians. The *Soul Train* music show, conceived by Cornelius in the late 1960s, first aired on August 17, 1970, and went national on October 2, 1971. Similar to Dick Clark's *American Bandstand, Soul Train* followed a black music format attracting black audiences. Cornelius often added to the show's attraction by dressing in flashy clothing. By 1992 *Soul Train* had become the longest-running syndicated music program. Cornelius was born in Chicago and studied art at DuSable High School, where he drew cartoons for the school's newspaper. He joined the U.S. Marines in 1954, returning to Chicago after eighteen months of service. He worked as a part-time announcer with radio station WVON, but later moved to WCIU-TV when his superior and mentor left the radio station for television. It was there that he established *Soul Train.*

Sources: *Contemporary Black Biography,* vol. 4, pp. 29–52; *African American Biography,* vol. 1, pp. 168–70.

1986 • The first black general manager of a network-owned television station was Johnathan Arlin Rodgers (1946–). Born in San Antonio, Texas, Rogers received his bachelor's degree from the University of California at Berkeley in 1967 and his master's from Stanford University in 1972. His various positions included reporter and later associate for *Sports Illustrated*; writer-producer for WNBV-TV in New York City; executive producer, news director, and station manager for KNXT-TV (now KCBS-TV in Los Angeles); and executive producer for *CBS Morning News* and other programs in New York City. From 1986 to 1990 he served as vice-president and the first black general manager of WBBM-TV in Chicago. He was appointed president of CBS Television Stations Division in 1990.

Sources: *Contemporary Black Biography,* vol. 6, pp. 229–32.

1989 • Comedian Arsenio Hall (1960–) was the first black to host a talk show on national television. Hall was born in Cleveland, Ohio, and began his career as a standup comic. He starred with Eddie Murphy in the film *Coming to America.*

Sources: *Negro Almanac,* p. 1142; *Who's Who among African Americans,* 26th ed., p. 514.

1989 • Jennifer Karen Lawson (1946–) became executive vice president of programming for the Public Broadcasting Service in Washington. As the highest-ranking black woman to serve in public television, she managed the creation, promotion, and scheduling of national programming for 330 stations. For the first time, her appointment centralized national program decision-making in one executive. *The Civil War,* which was aired under her administration, drew more than fifty million viewers and became the most-watched show in PBS history. Lawson was born in Fairfield, Alabama, and graduated from Columbia University.

Sources: *Contemporary Black Biography,* vol. 1, pp. 137–38; *Essence* 21 (August 1966): 37; Smith, *Notable Black American Women,* Book II, pp. 395–98.

Robin Roberts

1990 • Television sportscaster Robin Roberts (1960–) became the first on-air black anchorwoman for ESPN. In 1996 she was named new host of *ABC's Wide World of Sports,* the first black woman to hold that position. She was also the first black woman to host a network-televised NFL pre-game show. It was no accident that Roberts became a sportscaster. She was a talented college athlete as an honor roll student, but she turned down better-paying jobs to pursue a career as a sportscaster. Roberts was born in Pass Christian, Mississippi, into a family where "firsts" were not a novelty. Her father was one of the Tuskegee Airmen, and her mother had served on the Mississippi Board of Education. Both parents set high standards for their daughter. Her first sport of note was bowling; Roberts was a Mississippi state champion when she was ten years old, and she became a state basketball champion in high school. It was her older sister, who was a television anchorman, who drew Roberts' attention to broadcasting. She majored in communications at Southeastern Louisiana University, and graduated cum laude in 1983, after having starred as a scorer and rebounder on the basketball team. She took positions in Mississippi and in Atlanta before she agreed to take the ESPN post. In 1994 she had a series of her own on ESPN, *In the Sports Light,* and she anchored ABC's coverage of the U.S. Figure Skating Championships in 1996. Roberts has won two Emmy awards and the DAR Television Award for Merit. She was inducted into the Women's Institute on Sports and Education Foundation Hall of Fame in 1994 and the Women's Basketball Hall of Fame in 2012. In 2005 Roberts became co-anchor of *Good Morning America.* She took a hiatus from the show in 2012 to undergo a bone marrow transplant to treat MDS, myelodysplastic syndrome.

Sources: *Contemporary Black Biography,* vol. 16, pp. 183–85; *Jet* 88 (21 August 1995): 22; *Who's Who among African Americans,* 26th ed., p. 1059.

1991 • Kathleen Bradley became the first black model on the daytime television game show *The Price Is Right,* starring Bob Barker. More than seventeen million viewers tune in to the show daily.

Sources: *Jet* 90 (3 June 1996): 60–61.

1994 • Diann Burns became the first black woman anchor at a network station in Chicago. She joined Capital Cities/ABC's WLS in Chicago as a general assignment reporter and was promoted in 1994.

Sources: *Jet* 86 (23 May 1994): 20.

1995 • Halle Maria Berry (1968–) became the first black to play the role of Sheba on television. The television movie, *Solomon and Sheba,* is based on the Old Testament of the Bible and premiered on February 26. It tells of the legendary love of Solomon, King of Israel, and Nikiaule, the Queen of Sheba. Born in Cleveland, Ohio, Berry dropped out of Cuyahoga Community College where she studied broadcast journalism and turned to modeling. Her first film, *Jungle Fever* (1991), set her on the road to stardom. In 2002 Berry was voted best female actor for the film *Monster's Ball* (2001) at the 74th Annual Academy Awards, becoming the first black woman to win the award. Her other films appearances include *Boomerang* (1992), and *Honor Among Thieves* (1993), *Who Do Fools Fall in Love?* (1998), *Gothica* (2003), *X-Men: The Last Stand* (2006), and *Cloud Atlas* (2012). Among her television appearances have included a recurring role in *Knots Landing,* the miniseries *Queen* (1993), and *Introducing Dorothy Dandridge* (1999).

Sources: *Jet* 87 (27 February 1995): 57; Smith, *Notable Black American Women,* Book II, pp. 30–33; "Halle Berry," http://us.imdb.com/Name?Berry,+Halle; *Tennessean* (11 March 2002).

1996 • The first movie cable channel to concentrate on black film artists was launched, a joint venture between BET Holdings, Inc. and Encore Media Corporation.

Sources: *Jet* 90 (14 October 1996): 33.

1996 • Lori Stokes became the first anchor on Microsoft and NBC's cable news network, MSNBC, on July 15. The daughter of U.S. Representative Louis Stokes of Cleveland, she was promoted from anchor on *Good Morning Washington,* a weekend program.

Sources: *Jet* 90 (1 July 1996): 20.

1999 • The first black woman executive at Twentieth Century-Fox Film Corporation in Los Angeles was MaryAnn Johnson. The fourteen-year veteran with the corporation was named director of television music administration. Her responsibilities were to track music in the corporation's television shows, which included *Ally McBeal, The XFiles,* and *The Simpsons.*

Sources: *Jet* 96 (4 October 1999): 20.

1999 • The first black woman weekend anchor for the nationally syndicated entertainment magazine *Access Hollywood* was Shaun Robinson. Prior to this appointment, Robinson was the morning and noon anchor at WSVN-TV in Miami, a Fox affiliate. She was also named correspondent for the program's daily edition.

Sources: *Jet* 96 (16 August 1999): 20; *Black Manhattan,* pp. 175–8.

1999 • A pioneer in his field, Ken Rudulph became the first television host on the horse racing network TVG, in July. The wagering network TVG is one of the world's most widely distributed horse racing networks. By 2008 he remained the only black on-air host for such a network in North America. Rudulph called his start "baptism by fire. I had never been to the racetrack in my life. I had no idea where this would take me." The former TV anchor and sports reporter is also a guitarist and singer. He calls his work "the ultimate test of intellect and your integrity." He weaves music into every show, earning him the moniker "music man."

Sources: *Jet* 114 (10 November 2008): 26.

Shaun Robinson

2002 • Vecepia "Vee" Towery (1966?–) became the first black to win $1 million on CBS's show, *Survivor,* in May. The Portland, Oregon, native was a member of the network's fourth installment of *Survivor* called *Survivor: Marquesas*; for the first time as well, two women remained in the final competition. In November 2001, sixteen contestants equipped with minimal supplies joined a television production crew on the island of Nuku Huiva in the South Pacific. They were divided into two tribes of eight players each. Every three days one player was voted off the island. The show was taped over a thirty-nine-day stay on the island.

Sources: *Jet* 101 (3 June 2002): 16.

2005 • The first African American woman to create and produce a top-ten series on network television was Shondra Lynn Rhimes (1970–). The award-winning film and television writer, director, and executive producer is best known for the popular medical drama *Grey's Anatomy,* first produced on ABC this year. By the time this series was aired, she had already become one of Hollywood's hottest writers. *Grey's Anatomy* features a racially-diverse cast of African Americans, Asians, and Latinos who work together in a hospital setting. The show ranked among the top ten most-watched television programs during its first four seasons. It received an NAACP Image Award, a Producers Guild Award, and a Writers Guild of America Award for best new series. Rhimes launched a spin-off of the show in 2007, with *Private Practice.* Most recently, she was executive producer of *Off the Map,* also on ABC. The Chicago native graduated from Dartmouth College and received an MFA from the University of Southern California, School of Cinema-Television.

Sources: *Contemporary Black Biography,* vol. 67, pp. 129–31; *Ebony* 60 (October 2005): 204–06; *Jet* 119 (21–28 March 2011): 20–21.

2007 • Black Entertainment Television's *Celebration of Gospel 07* was the most watched inspirational and religious program in television history, on January 28. This was a show-stopping, "hand-clapping, foot-stomping two-hour revival filled with rousing performances." Those contributing to the spiritually-uplifting performance were Shirley Caesar, Bobby Jones, Quincy Jones, Fantasia, Yolanda Adams, Kirk Franklin, and The Caravans. Filmmaker Tyler Perry, who was honored during the presentation, said that "gospel music is our heritage," and "to have BET honor me within a gospel celebration was an amazing thing."

Sources: *Jet* 111 (5 March 2007): 44.

BUSINESS

Advertising

1893 • Nancy Green (1834–1923), a former slave from Montgomery County, Kentucky, was the first Aunt Jemima and the world's first living trademark. She made her debut at age fifty-nine at the Columbian Exposition in Chicago, where she dressed in costume and served pancakes in a booth. The Aunt Jemima Mills Company distributed a souvenir lapel button that bore her image and the caption, "I'se in town honey." The caption later became the slogan on the company's promotional campaign. Green was the official trademark for three decades, touring the country and promoting Aunt Jemima products. The Aunt Jemima character, a variant of the mammy image, has perpetuated racial and gender stereotyping. Characteristically, the mammy icon in American culture is that of a plump black woman household servant who is soft-witted, comical, and headstrong and who nurtures the children of her white master. Aunt Jemima, on the other hand, is a polite, indulgent cook who is closely associated with pancakes and kitchen products. Her image has been used on products that bore the Aunt Jemima label while the mammy and Jemima images have been seen in housewares, dolls and other toys, household decorations, in literature, films, radio, and elsewhere. Both images are now generally considered derogatory.

Sources: *Black Ethnic Collectibles,* p. 18; *They Had a Dream,* vol. 3, p. 29; Hine, *Black Women in America,* pp. 53–54; vol. 2, pp. 781–82.

1956 • Vince Cullers Advertising, Inc., located in Chicago, was the first black advertising agency in the United States. Founder Vincent T. Cullers attended the Art Institute of Chicago; he graduated from the American Academy of Art and the University of Chicago.

Sources: *Black Enterprise* 1 (February 1971): 15–22; *Ebony Success Library,* vol. 1, p. 82; *Who's Who among African Americans,* 14th ed., p. 296.

1971 • Barbara Gardner Proctor (1933–) opened her own agency this year and became the first black woman in Chicago to found an advertising agency. Born in Black Mountain, North Carolina, Proctor earned bachelor's degrees in English education and in psychology and social science from Talladega College in Alabama. She wrote descriptive comments for jazz album covers and also worked in several advertising companies, before deciding to form her own company.

Sources: Salem, *African American Women,* pp. 407–08; Smith, *Notable Black American Women,* pp. 887–90.

1977 • Richard A. Guilmenot III (1948–) was the first black vice president of a major advertising agency, Batten, Barton, Durstine and Osborne (BBDO) in New York.

Sources: *Jet* 52 (21 April 1977): 19; *Who's Who among Black Americans* 26th ed., p. 506.

1977 • Caroline Robinson Jones (1942–2001) was the first black female vice president of a major advertising agency, Batten, Barton, Durstine and Osborne (BBDO). Her career began in 1963 when she was hired by the J. Walter Thompson firm as a secretary and copywriter trainee. She progressed to the position of creative director. In 1968 she was one of the co-founders of Zebra Associates, a full-service agency. During the 1970s and 1980s she worked for several agencies before helping to found Mingo Jones in 1977. In 1986, she established her own agency, called initially Creative Resources Management, which was later operated as Caroline Jones Advertising and Caroline Jones, Inc. She remained president of Caroline Jones, Inc., until her death. The Jones firm served both domestic and international clients, specializing in public relations and special events, as well as advertising. One of the firm's most recognized slogans was "We do chicken right," developed for Kentucky Fried Chicken. She became an advertising pioneer who broke race and sex barriers in the industry. She was active in professional organizations and civic affairs and the recipient of many awards and honors. She was also involved in the establishment of the Caroline Robinson Jones Permanent Collection at the Smithsonian in 1997. Jones was born in Benton Harbor, Michigan. She received her bachelor's degree from the University of Michigan in English and science. Rather than become a doctor as she had envisioned, Jones became highly successful in the field of advertising.

Sources: *Contemporary Black Biography*, vol. 29, pp. 86–88; *Jet* 100 (23 July 2001): 30; *Who's Who among African Americans*, 13th ed., pp. 728–29.

1998 • When actress Lark Voorhies (1974–) was named national advertising campaign spokesmodel for Head & Shoulders, she became the first black woman celebrity in the country to fill that role. Voorhies has appeared on television in such shows as *Saved By the Bell*, *In the House*, *Days of Our Lives*, and *The Bold and the Beautiful*. She also starred in the Def Jam movie *How to Be a Player*.

Sources: *Jet* 94 (28 September 1998): 54; *Who's Who among African Americans*, 26th ed., p. 1266.

Automobile Industry

1915 • Frederick Douglas Patterson (?–1932) was the first black to manufacture cars. Between 1915 and 1919 Patterson built some thirty Greenfield-Patterson cars in Greenfield, Ohio. He was the youngest of four children born to former slave Charles "Rich" and Josephine Patterson. The family was already successful when Frederick was born; the father had bought out his white partner and owned C. R. Patterson and Sons Carriage Company in Greenfield and made the most popular carriages of the day. Frederick Patterson was the first black American to graduate from the local high school and then entered Ohio State University where he was the first black to play on the football team. He left three years later and taught school in Kentucky for two years, before returning to Greenfield to work in the family's carriage business. Frederick's father died shortly after his return home, leaving him and other relatives to operate the business. While traveling with his sales manager, he made note of some "funny-looking horseless" carriages. When he returned, he persuaded his company's board to build these horseless carriages, or cars, and his bold plan resulted in the automobile known as the Patterson-Greenfield. Patterson's first car—a two-door coupe—rolled off the line on September 23, 1915. The car reportedly had a forty horsepower Continental four-cylinder engine and reached a top speed of fifty miles per hour. The company's two models—a roadster and a big four-door touring car—both sold for $850. Insufficient capital and slow car sales led to the car company's demise. Patterson went on to produce school bus bodies that were in great demand. The bus business closed in 1939.

The First Black Car Dealership

In 1939 Edward Davis (1911?–1999) opened his first automobile business, a used-car lot, in downtown Detroit. Two years later the used car business was turned into a Studebaker dealership, and Davis became the first black American to own a new-car dealership. He retained the franchise until 1956, when the manufacturer went out of business. When Davis was awarded a Chrysler-Plymouth dealership in November 1963, he became the first black American to run a Big Three franchise. Before operating his own business, Davis worked at a Dodge plant and later sold cars for a Chrysler-Plymouth dealership. Forbidden to sell on the showroom floor with white salespersons, he was successful in promoting himself in Detroit's black community. After retiring from his Chrysler dealership in 1971, he became manager for the city bus system and worked as a consultant to minority automobile dealers. In 1993 the National Association of Minority Automobile Dealers honored Davis by establishing the annual Edward Davis Pioneer Award. The Edward Davis Scholarship Fund, in his honor, was established to support black students interested in the automotive field. In January 1999 Davis was inducted into the Automobile Hall of Fame Museum, the first black man to be so honored. Davis is the author of the book *One Man's Way*.

Sources: "Edward Davis, First Black Auto Dealer, Honored in Detroit," *Jet* 95 (1 February 1999): 46–48; *New York Times Obituaries* (5 May 1999); *Contemporary Black Biography*, vol. 24, pp. 48–51.

Sources: "Forgotten Faces: Black Automaker among Early Trailblazers," *African Americans on Wheels* 2 (Winter 1996): 10–11; Reasons, *They Had a Dream*, vol. 3, p. 48.

1967 • Albert William Johnson Sr. (1926–2010) was the first black to be awarded an Oldsmobile dealership. A native of St. Louis, Missouri, Jackson gained the franchise in a predominantly black area of Chicago. In less than four years his success led to a Cadillac dealership.

Sources: *Ebony Success Library*, vol. 1, p. 175; *Black Enterprise* 8 (June 1978): 98–102; Obituaries, *Who's Who among Black Americans*, 26th ed., p. 1411.

1970 • Nathan G. Conyers (1932–) opened an automobile dealership in Detroit; as of 2002, it is the oldest black-owned dealership in the United States and the only one in Detroit. Conyers was born in Detroit and received his law degree from Wayne State University. He worked as an attorney for the Small Business Administration, in private law practice, and as special assistant to the attorney general for the state of Michigan, before becoming partner in the law firm Keith, Conyers, Anderson, Brown & Wahls, P.C. Conyers serves as the company's president.

Sources: *Contemporary Black Biography*, vol. 24, pp. 38–40.

1972 • The first major black-owned automobile dealership in New York City opened in the Bronx, when Richard D. "Dick" Gidron (1939–2007) opened Dick Gidron Cadillac, Inc. Prior to opening the dealership, Gidron worked as general manager of Cadillac Motors in Chicago (1959–72). He later opened a second automobile dealership, Dick Gidron Ford, Inc., also in the Bronx and served as its president. Born in Chicago, Gidron was educated at Bryant and Straton College.

Sources: *The Black New Yorkers*, p. 354; *Who's Who among African Americans*, 14th ed., p. 471.

1987 • Barbara Jean Wilson (1940–) was the first black woman automobile dealer. She received special recognition from the Carats, Inc., Detroit Chapter, in 1979 and the Candace Award for Businesswoman of the Year in 1987. Wilson was president of Porterfield-Wilson Pontiac, GMC Truck, Mazda, Honda (1979–84), Ferndale Honda, Ferndale,

Michigan, (1984–) and Porterfield's Marina Village, Detroit (1989–). Born in Dallas, Texas, she graduated from Prairie View Agricultural and Mechanical College in 1960.

Sources: *Jet* 72 (6 July 1987): 51; *Who's Who among African American,* 26th ed., p. 1361.

1987 • The first black American to become a vice president at Ford Motor Company was Elliott Sawyer Hall (1938–). Hall was born in Detroit and earned a bachelor's degree from Wayne State University. His career includes attorney (1965), corporation counsel for the city of Detroit (1974–75), chief assistant prosecutor for Wayne County (1983–85), and full partner in the firm Dykema, Gossett, Spencer, Goodnow and Trigg. Hall also served as president of the United Black Coalition and the Detroit chapter of the NAACP. He retired from Ford in 2002 and returned to the law firm.

Sources: *Contemporary Black Biography,* vol. 24, pp. 70–72; *Who's Who among African Americans,* 26th ed., p. 515.

1990 • Sheleme S. Sendaba was the first black vice president of Nissan Motor Corporation in the United States. Born in Ethiopia, Sendaba holds a master's degree in business administration from the Walter Heller Graduate School of Business (1977). Sendaba worked at General Motors before going to Nissan.

Sources: *Jet* 79 (22 October 1990): 29; *Who's Who among Black Americans, 1992–93,* p. 1259.

1994 • When Ford Motor Company named Deborah Stewart Kent (1953–) manager of the Ohio Assembly Plant in Avon Lake, she became the first black woman to manage an assembly plant in the firm's worldwide manufacturing system. In 1992 she became the first black woman in the history of the company to serve as assistant plant manager in an assembly plant. By 1993 Stewart worked through her Chicago office to oversee the work of 2,700 employees. After her appointment in Chicago, the Taurus/Sable became the best-selling car in the nation. Kent first worked with General Motors for ten years where she received several promotions in plants in St. Louis; Bowling Green, Kentucky; and Detroit. As production superintendent at the Pontiac Assembly Plant in Detroit in 1985, she helped to bring about a twenty-five percent per year cost reduction for the plant. She joined Ford in 1987 as chassis area manager at its Wixom, Michigan, assembly plant. During her employment, the 1988 Town Car and the 1989 Lincoln Continental were rated best in their class for chassis. While manager in Dearborn, the assembly plant won several awards, including the Q–1 and Preventive Maintenance Awards, and the Ford Mustang received top customer satisfaction numbers. Kent was born and raised in St. Louis' inner city, third in a family of nine children. She graduated from Southern Illinois University at Carbondale and received her master's degree from Washington University in St. Louis.

Sources: Mowris, "Head of the Line," *Washington University Magazine and Alumni News* 63 (Winter 1993): 25–27; *Jet* 86 (10 October 1994): 32; *Who's Who among African Americans,* 26th ed., p. 719.

1994 • When Ronald Eugene Goldsberry (1942–) was appointed vice president and general manager for customer service for Ford Motor Company, he became the first black to head an operations division and only the second black vice president in the company's history. He was born in Wilmington, Delaware. He received a bachelor's degree from Central State University, a master's degree in business administration from Stanford University, and a doctorate from Michigan State University. With a background in chemistry, he served as assistant professor of chemistry at the University of California at San Jose and as research chemist. He also served as vice president for business development with Occidental Chemical Corporation.

Sources: *Contemporary Black Biography,* vol. 18, pp. 56–58; *Who's Who among African Americans,* 26th ed., p. 472.

1999 • David Stephens beat out nearly one hundred applicants to become the first black American Jaguar dealer in the United States. With a $1 million loan from Ford Motor Company, the owner of Jaguar, he renovated a former Jaguar dealership and established

Stephens Automotive Group's Millennium Motor Cars in Plano, Texas. Stephens repaid the loan in five months. In his first year of operation the company sold over one thousand cars, with sales of $48 million. The eldest of nine children, Stephens grew up on a farm in Washington, Louisiana. He graduated from Southern University in Baton Rouge, Louisiana, with a degree in marketing. In 1977 he joined Ford Motor Company in Atlanta where he worked in field operations. He held a number of management positions, including franchising and merchandising manager, before becoming a dealer. He entered a two-year dealer-training program but left training in 1992 to become general manager of a Lincoln-Mercury dealership in Texas. The next year he opened Falls Lincoln-Mercury in Wichita Falls, Texas. After receiving the Jaguar dealership, he sold his Wichita Falls business to concentrate on the luxury car business.

Sources: *Black Enterprise* 31 (June 2001): 166–72.

1999 • Ellenae L. Henry-Fairhurst (1943–) became the first black to own a Nissan-Infinity car dealership in North America. The dealership, which is a part of Nissan North America's initiative to assist minority entrepreneurs, opened this year in Huntsville, Alabama. Until then only thirteen of the approximately 1,070 Nissan dealerships in North American were black-owned, and none of the black-owned dealerships carried the luxury Infinity line. Born in Dayton, Ohio, she received her bachelor's degree from Miami University and her master's degree from the University of Detroit. For more than ten years Henry-Fairhurst had been involved in dealerships with Ford, Chrysler-Plymouth, and other automakers in Detroit and Huntsville.

Sources: *Black Enterprise* 30 (December 1999): 26; *Jet* 97 (1 November 1999): 40; *Who's Who among African Americans,* 26th ed., p. 571.

2007 • A former vice president for Volvo Parts North America, Stephanie Dawkins was promoted to senior vice president at AB Volvo, making her the company's first black senior vice president. Her responsibilities included overseeing labor and employment relations, health, safety, performance management, organizational effectiveness, and policy harmonization. Volvo is recognized worldwide as one of the leading manufacturers of trucks, busses, and construction equipment; aerospace components and services; and other works. She now is president and CEO of Stephanie R. Dawkins International, Inc.

Sources: *Jet* 111 (30 April 2007): 22.

2007 • Alicia Boler-Davis joined General Motors in 1994 as a manufacturing engineer and steadily climbed the ranks. In 2007 she became the first black woman plant manager at a General Motors Corporation vehicle-assembly plant. She began her new post in October, at the GM plant in Arlington, Texas. Previously, Boler-Davis was assistant plant manager at the Pontiac Assembly. "You can be successful in manufacturing, a male-dominated field," she said. "I look at that significance more so than being the first African American female," she continued. Her goal is to become an officer at GM. Her plant assembled the Chevrolet Tahoe, GMC Yukon, and the Cadillac Escalade. Boler-Davis, a Michigan native, graduated from Northwestern University with a bachelor's degree in chemical engineering, and received her master's degree in engineering from Rensselaer Polytechnic Institute in New York.

Sources: *Jet* 112 (8 October 2007): 46–47.

2008 • Crystal Windham, who was appointed director of General Motors North American Passenger Car Design, became the first black woman director in the carmaker's history. The appointment meant that she oversees interior design for GM's Global Midsize Car, Global Compact Car, and Global Small Car. After being with the company fifteen years, Windham was a lead designer on the 2008 Chevy Malibu. Automotive journalists with the North American Car and Truck of the Year awards named the Malibu "Car of the Year" for 2008. Windham was also a major player in designing the 2007 award-winning Saturn Aura. The Detroit native received her bachelor's degree in industrial design from the Center of Creative Studies in her hometown and a master's degree in business administration from the University of Detroit-Mercy.

Sources: *Jet* 114 (19–26 January 2009): 28.

Banking

1888 • The True Reformers' Bank of Richmond, Virginia, and the Capital Savings Bank of Washington, D.C., were the first black-created and black-run banks. The True Reformers' Bank, or the Savings Bank of the Grand Fountain of the United Order of True Reformers, was chartered on March 2 and opened for business on April 3. The Capital Savings Bank was organized on October 17, and it was the first black bank to have no fraternal connections.

Sources: Kane, *Famous First Facts,* p. 93; *Negro Year Book, 1913,* p. 230; *Twenty-five Years History of the Grand Fountain of the United Order of True Reformers, 1881–1905,* p. 95.

1889 • The Mutual Bank and Trust Company of Chattanooga, Tennessee, was the first black bank in the state. It failed during the panic of 1893.

Sources: *Negro Year Book, 1913,* p. 230.

1890 • The Alabama Penny Savings Bank was the first black-owned bank in Alabama. It opened in Birmingham on October 15 and was in business until 1915.

Sources: *Negro Year Book, 1913,* p. 230.

Jesse Binga

1908 • Jesse Binga (1865–1950) was the founder of the first black-owned bank in Chicago, Binga State Bank. It was also the first bank owned, managed, and controlled by blacks in the North. Beginning as a private bank, the institution received a state charter in 1920. When it closed during the Great Depression of 1932, Binga lost his fortune and thousands of black Chicagoans lost their savings as well. Binga was born in Detroit and left a promising business career to travel about Missouri, Minnesota, and Washington. He opened several barbershops and later made a handsome profit from land investments in Pocatello before settling in Chicago in the mid-1890s. By 1910 Binga, also a real estate agent and philanthropist, was Chicago's leading businessman.

Sources: *Encyclopedia of Black America,* p. 180; Gosnell, *Negro Politicians,* p. 107; Hornsby, *Chronology of African-American History,* p. 53; Smith, *Notable Black American Men,* pp. 75–76.

1913 • The Atlanta State Savings Bank was the first chartered black banking institution in Georgia. Atlanta Mutual, North Carolina Mutual, Pilgrim Health and Life, and Standard Life insurance companies were among its depositors.

Sources: Mason, *Going Against the Wind,* p. 53.

1942 • Channing Heggie Tobias (1882–1961) was elected to membership on the board of directors of the Modern Industrial Bank in New York City and became the first black elected to the board of a major bank. Tobias was born in Augusta, Georgia and received his early education at the historic Haines Institute. He received his bachelor's degree in 1902 from Paine Institute (now Paine College) and later taught there. He received his bachelor of divinity degree from Drew Theological Seminary in 1905 and was ordained in the Colored Methodist Episcopal Church. He later studied at the University of Pennsylvania. By 1911 he had become interested in the YMCA and two years later left teaching to become student secretary of the international Committee of the YMCAs. From 1923 until 1946 Tobias served as senior secretary of the Colored Men's Department of the National Council. He moved to the Phelps Stokes Fund, later serving as its first black director from 1946 to 1953. There he supported the fund's mission as he worked to improve educational opportunities for blacks. He fought against segregation in the armed services during World War II and discrimination against black nurses during the war, and sought compliance with the government order that barred racial discrimination in industries that held war contracts. Former secretary of the U.S. Treasury Henry Morgenthau Jr. nominated Tobias to the Modern Industrial Bank board of directors.

Sources: Smith, *Notable Black American Men,* pp. 1122–25; *Current Biography,* 1945, pp. 609–12; "Mystery Man of Race Relations," *Ebony* 6 (February 1951): 15–21.

The First Black Woman Bank President

Maggie Lena Walker

In 1903 Maggie Lena Walker (1865–1934) became the first black woman bank president on July 28, when she founded the Saint Luke Penny Savings Bank in Richmond, Virginia. The bank began as an insurance society in which Walker became active at the time of her marriage in 1886. When she retired due to ill health in 1933, the bank was strong enough to survive the Great Depression, and it is still in existence. The bank had a marked effect on black life in Richmond. Walker urged blacks to save their nickels and dimes, turning them into dollars, and to finance their own homes since white-owned banks would not do so. Walker also became a visible force in other areas. An ardent feminist, she urged women to improve themselves educationally and economically. She fought for women's suffrage and also worked in voter registration campaigns. She was also an instrument in the formation of the Virginia Lily-Black Republican Party. In March 1902, Walker founded *The St. Luke Herald,* a newspaper that illuminated black concerns and strengthened communication between the community and the Order of St. Luke, a black organization that dealt with the concerns of the race. The daughter of a former slave washerwoman, she became one of the wealthiest and most influential black women of the early twentieth century. Her spacious home in Richmond has been declared a National Historic Landmark.

Sources: *Encyclopedia of Black America,* pp. 152, 830; *Negro Almanac,* pp. 231, 1394; Smith, *Notable Black American Women,* pp. 1188–93.

1953 • James Del Rio (1924–) was the first black licensed mortgage banker in the United States and established one of the first black mortgage companies in the country. Del Rio was a successful real estate broker in Detroit. He later served for eight years in the Michigan legislature, until 1973 when he became a Detroit Recorder's Court judge.

Sources: *Ebony* 18 (February 1963): 55–60; 29 (June 1974): 90–92; *Ebony Success Library,* vol. 1, p. 93.

1953 • The Sivart Mortgage Company of Chicago, Illinois, was the first black mortgage banking firm. The firm was established by Chicago businessman Dempsey J. Travis (1920–2009). In 1961 the company was the first black-owned firm approved by the Federal Housing Administration and the Veterans Administration.

Sources: Alford, *Famous First Blacks,* p. 16; *Ebony Success Library,* vol. 2, pp. 256–59; *Who's Who among Black Americans,* 26th ed., pp. 1243–44.

1965 • The Freedom National Bank was Harlem's first black-chartered and black-operated bank. It was in business until November 5, 1990, when it was closed by federal regulators amid considerable controversy.

Sources: Hornsby, *Milestones in Twentieth-Century African-American History,* p. 459; *Negro Almanac,* p. 218.

1970 • Thomas A. Wood (1926–) was the first black to serve on the board of Chase Manhattan Bank. Wood received his bachelor's degree in electrical engineering from the University of Michigan. In 1968 he founded TAW International Leasing, a New York-based firm operating principally in Africa.

Sources: *Ebony* 27 (March 1972): 88–96; *Ebony Success Library,* vol. 2, pp. 302–5; *Encyclopedia of Black America,* p. 867.

1977 • The first woman to become vice president of Continental Bank of Philadelphia was Emma Carolyn [Bayton] Chappell (1941–). Chappell was born in Philadelphia and was influenced greatly by her pastor, Reverend Leon H. Sullivan (1922-2001) of the Zion Baptist Church, an advocate of black economic development. Chappell graduated from Temple University and did graduate work in banking at Rutgers University. She was a teller and loan review specialist at Continental, before moving up to become the bank's first black and first woman vice president. She was a founder of the Rainbow Coalition and served as treasurer of Jesse Jackson's campaign for President of the United States.

Sources: *Contemporary Black Biography,* vol. 18, pp. 25–27; Smith, *Notable Black American Women,* Book II, pp. 90–92; *Who's Who among African Americans,* 26th ed., p. 229.

1982 • Mildred Glenn became president of the New World National Bank in Pennsylvania and was the first black woman bank president in the state. New World National Bank is the only minority bank in the state.

Sources: *Jet* 62 (14 June 1982): 47.

1986 • Nathan A. Chapman Jr. (1957–) became founder and chief executive officer of the Chapman Company, the first black-owned investment banking firm in America.

Sources: *Contemporary Black Biography,* vol. 37, pp. 37–39.

1988 • Richard Dean Parsons (1948–) became the first black American to manage a major lending company, when he became Dime Savings Bank of New York's chief operating officer. When he engineered a merger between Anchor Savings Bank and the financially troubled Dime Savings to create Dime Bancorp in 1995, he helped to create the nation's fourth largest savings bank.

Sources: *Contemporary Black Biography,* vol. 11, pp. 185–88; Salzman, *Encyclopedia of African-American Culture and History,* Supplement, pp. 214–15; *Jet* 87 (14 November 1994): 24; *New Yorker* (October 29, 2001): 58–61.

1990 • Emma Carolyn Chappell (1941–) became the first chair and chief executive officer of the newly founded United Bank of Philadelphia, which opened for service on March 23, 1992. Leading blacks from Philadelphia's business community saw a need for a black-controlled bank in the area as early as 1987 and approached Chappell about heading the bank. She helped raise funds by soliciting in churches and searching for small investors. The board of directors contributed funds themselves and asked large banks to provide start-up money. The bank grew, withstood setbacks, and by 1995 was named *Black Enterprise* magazine's Financial Company of the Year. Through her efforts, Chappell contributed significantly to economic development of Philadelphia's black community.

Sources: *Contemporary Black Biography,* vol. 18, pp. 25–27; Smith, *Notable Black American Women,* Book II, pp. 90–92; *Who's Who among African Americans,* 26th ed., p. 229.

1994 • Catherine Davis-Cartey became the first black vice president of Michigan National Bank's private banking division in Farmington Hills, Michigan. Prior to her appointment, she was a relationship manager for high network clients at the bank.

Sources: *Jet* 85 (14 March 1994): 20.

1994 • Sworn in by treasury secretary Lloyd Bentsen, Alice M. Dear was the first black woman and the second black American to serve as U.S. executive director of the African Development Bank headquartered in Abidjan, Ivory Coast. Her responsibilities included oversight of the bank's portfolio and management of its financial, operational, and administrative operations. Dear, a Gary, Indiana, native, graduated from Howard University. She was a flight attendant for Pan American World Airways and later vice president and marketing officer for New York's Irving Trust Company where she handled banking services in Africa and the Middle East. In 1981 Dear, a pioneering entrepreneur, opened her own consulting firm and directed a wide range of global businesses.

Sources: *Jet* 86 (16 May 1994): 20.

1995 • Nashville's Citizens Savings Bank & Trust Company, the oldest continuously operating minority-owned bank in the country, named Deborah Scott-Ensley its chief executive officer and seventh president. With the appointment, she became the first woman to hold the post at the bank. She headed the bank when it closed its downtown office and relocated to the black community near Fisk and Tennessee State universities and Meharry Medical College. There the bank aimed to strengthen its focus as a community-oriented institution. A Nashville native, Scott-Ensley had served the institution for sixteen years.

Sources: *Metropolitan Times* (1 August 1995): 20; *Jet* 88 (31 July 1995): 19.

1998 • Norman B. Rice (1943–) became the first black head of the Federal Home Loan Bank board in Seattle. In 1999 Rice, former mayor of Seattle, became president and chief executive officer of the bank.

Sources: *Jet* 93 (30 March 1998): 10.

1998 • The first black to head the top bank in Detroit, one of the largest banks in the country, was Walter C. Watkins Jr. (1946?–). Born in Nashville, Tennessee, Watkins graduated from Fisk University in 1968 with a bachelor's degree in business administration. In 1977 he received his master's degree in business administration from Wayne State University. His interest in banking led to his appointment as branch manager of National Bank of Detroit in 1972, and in 1980 he was promoted to vice president of the Midwest banking division. Watkins continued to move up the corporate ladder. In 1985 he was named first vice president and in 1988 head of the Eastern group. Watkins served as executive vice president of First Chicago NBD and head of regional banking in Michigan from 1987 until 1998. Since 1998 he has served as bank president. He serves as board member of several corporate and community groups and as a member of the Board of Trustees of his alma mater, Fisk University.

Sources: *Contemporary Black Biography,* vol. 24, pp. 178–79.

2008? • Kimberly Young Lee is the first black woman president and chief executive officer of New Orleans-based Dryades Savings Bank. Federally chartered in 1994, the bank is a leading black-owned financial institution that serves Orleans and Jefferson Parishes. Lee is former vice president of Entergy Corporation in New Orleans.

Sources: *Jet* 113 (4 February 2008): 19.

Insurance

1810 • The African Insurance Company of Philadelphia is the first known black insurance company. It was not incorporated, but had capital stock in the amount of five thousand dollars. Its president was Joseph Randolph; treasurer, Carey Porter; and secretary, William Coleman.

Sources: Kane, *Famous First Facts*, p. 322; *Negro Year Book, 1913*, p. 300; *Negro Year Book, 1916–17*, p. 318.

1893 • The North Carolina Mutual Life Insurance Company, founded in this year in Durham, North Carolina, was the first black insurance company to attain $100 million in assets. The success of the company was largely due to the work of Charles Clinton Spaulding (1874–1952), who became general manager of the company in 1900 and was president from 1923 until his death.

Sources: Alford, *Famous First Blacks,* p. 16; Logan and Winston, *Dictionary of American Negro Biography,* pp. 567–68; *Encyclopedia of Black America,* p. 207, 806.

The First Black Actuary

I n 1932 Asa T. Spaulding (1902–1990) became the first black actuary in the United States. After earning a bachelor's degree (magna cum laude) in accounting from New York University in 1930, and a master's degree from the University of Michigan in 1932, Spaulding went to work for the North Carolina Mutual Life Insurance Company in Durham, North Carolina. He became president of the company in 1959 and retired in 1968. He was also the first black to serve on the board of directors of a major non-black corporation, W. T. Grant (1964), and the first black elected to the Durham County Board of Commissioners. He is a member of the state Business Hall of Fame.

Sources: *Ebony Success Library*, vol. 1, p. 289; *Encyclopedia of Black America*, p. 806; *Jet* 78 (24 September 1990): 15; *Who's Who among Black Americans, 1992–93*, p. 1610.

1931 • Alexander and Company General Insurance Agency of Atlanta, Georgia, established by Theodore Martin Alexander Sr. (1909–2001) was the first black-owned and black-controlled general insurance brokerage and risk management agency in the South. It eventually grew to be the largest.

Sources: *Jet* 61 (24 September 1981): 16; 77 (19 March 1990): 15–16; *Who's Who among Black Americans*, 13th ed., p. 16.

1957 • Cirilo A. McSween (1926–2008) was the first black to represent a major white-owned insurance company, New York Life Insurance Company, and the first black to sell a million dollars worth of life insurance for any company in one year. McSween went on to surpass this feat in later years: He was the first black to sell a million dollars of insurance in one month and became a qualifying member of the industry's Million Dollar Round Table, whose membership is comprised of a top insurance professionals who are recognized for superior work. McSween was also one of the first owners of McDonald's restaurants in Chicago; he operated five franchises including those at O'Hare airport. Born in Panama City, Panama, he was a varsity letterman at the University of Illinois, where he received his bachelor's degree in 1954. In 1984 the Chicago business leader became the first black elected to Chicago's State Street Council. He was also a civil rights leader with a close relationship with Martin Luther King Jr., and was a pallbearer at King's funeral in 1968.

Sources: *Ebony* 20 (May 1965): 207–8; *Ebony Success Library*, vol. 1, p. 213; *Jet* 114 (24 November–1 December 2008): 43; *Who's Who among Black Americans*, 18th ed., p. 857.

1977 • The E. G. Bowman Company was the first major American black-owned commercial insurance brokerage firm on Wall Street. Ernesta G. Procope (1931–) founded the company in 1953 and named it for her husband, who had died the previous year, and led it as it grew. Her present husband is editor and publisher of the *Amsterdam News*.

Sources: Smith, *Notable Black American Women*, pp. 885–86; *Who's Who among African American*, 14th ed., p. 1059.

Labor Unions

1850 • In July of 1850 in New York, Samuel Ringgold Ward (1817–1864) was the first president of the American League of Colored Workers; Frederick Douglass was a vice president. Ward is primarily known as a lecturer and the author of *The Autobiography of a Fugitive Negro* (1855). The league was primarily interested in industrial education rather than trade unionism. Ward, an abolitionist, journalist, and religious worker, was born a slave on Maryland's Eastern Shore. His parents resettled near Greenwich, New Jersey and later in New York City. Ward attended the Free African School; among his classmates were abolitionists Henry Highland Garnet, Alexander Crummell, and Charles Lewis Reason. In

The First Black Labor Union

In July 1858 the Association of Black Caulkers in Baltimore, Maryland, became the first black labor organization on record. While earlier organizations were more mutual aid societies and fraternal organizations than labor unions, the Association of Black Caulkers was formed to resist the efforts of white workers to drive blacks from a line of work blacks had traditionally controlled.

Sources: *Encyclopedia of Black America*, p. 491; Foner, *Organized Labor and the Black Worker*, p. 11.

November 1839 he became a traveling agent for the American Anti-Slavery Society and later held the same post with the New York Anti-Slavery Society. The Anti-Slavery Society of Canada hired him as lecturer in late 1851. Ward was an imposing figure and a leading black orator for the abolitionist movement.

Sources: Foner, *Organized Labor and the Black Worker*, p. 11; Logan and Winston, *Dictionary of American Negro Biography*, pp. 631–32; *Negro Almanac*, pp. 13, 1017; Smith, *Notable Black American Men*, pp. 1177–79.

1862 • The American Seamen's Protective Association was the first seaman's organization in the United States. (In 1850 nearly half of the 25,000 seamen on American ships were black.) Its founder was William M. Powell, born in New York City of slave parents. In 1870 he reported that 3,500 black seamen were headquartered in the city.

Sources: Foner, *Organized Labor and the Black Worker*, pp. 14–15.

1869 • The Colored National Labor Union was the first attempt to build a black labor organization that would paralleled the National Labor Union. Established in 1866, the National Labor Union (a forerunner of the Knights of Labor) and its affiliate unions excluded blacks, and the continued hostility of white workers undermined attempts to develop black labor organizations. The Colored National Labor Union held its organizational meeting on December 6 in Washington, D.C. Isaac Myers (1835–1891) was elected president. Among the delegates were the Caulker's Trade Union Society and the Colored Engineers Association.

Sources: Logan and Winston, *Dictionary of American Negro Biography*, pp. 468–69; *Encyclopedia of Black America*, p. 491; Foner, *Organized Labor and the Black Worker*, pp. 30–46.

1925 • A. Philip Randolph (1889–1979) founded the Brotherhood of Sleeping Car Porters on August 25, the first major nationwide black union. It would take ten years of struggle and new federal labor legislation before the union established a collective bargaining agreement with the Pullman Palace Car Company. Thus the union became the first official bargaining agent for black Pullman workers on October 1, 1935. Randolph became active in civil rights as well. He used his power and reputation gained from his work with the Brotherhood of Sleeping Car Porters to call for a March on Washington in 1942. This planned protest against the government's indifference to the war efforts and black rights led to advances in civil and economic rights for blacks. In 1957 Randolph became a vice president of the American Federation of Labor and Congress of Industrial Organizations (AFL-CIO) representing the Pullman porters; he served until 1968. Randolph was born in Crescent City, Florida. He graduated from Cookman Institute (now Bethune Cookman University) in Jacksonville in 1907 and held several short-lived jobs. In 1912 he enrolled in City College in New York where he associated with student radicals and adopted a belief in socialism. From 1918 until 1927 Randolph served as editor of the *Messenger*, a magazine geared to radical groups. He is regarded as one of the most important labor leaders of his time.

A. Philip Randolph

Sources: Bennett, *Before the Mayflower*, pp. 366, 525, 532; *Encyclopedia of Black America*, pp. 727–28; Foner, *Organized Labor and the Black Worker*, pp. 177–87; Jet 81 (13 April 1992): 32; *Negro Almanac*, p. 560l; Smith, *Notable Black American Men*, pp. 983–86.

1934 • A group of young black cooks and waiters, including George Ellington Brown Jr. (1906–1951), organized the Dining Car employees Local 370 in New York City and in 1935 elected Brown president. As head of the union, Brown, then thirty-five years old, became the first black to head a labor union for dining car employees nationwide. Among other issues, the waiters and cooks protested the requirement that they sleep on small cots in the dining car when on overnight runs. They also protested the low wages that they were paid. After unsuccessful attempts to address the workers' demands, Brown took the matter to Pennsylvania's state representatives. In 1937 the Pure Food Law was amended and railroads in that state were forced to abolish that practice. Large railroads elsewhere followed. Top leaders of the Hotel, Restaurant and Bartenders International Union, with which Local 370 was affiliated, recognized Brown's potential as a leader. In August 1938, Brown became the first black and youngest person elected as vice president of the American Federation of Labor (AFL), representing the Dining Car Workers and Hotel and Restaurant Employees. At the same time he became president-at-large of the railroad division and held that office until he died. Brown was born in Hoboken, New Jersey, the son of a steamship porter and former horse trainer. His mother was of Senegalese and German origin. He became a dining car cook for the Pennsylvania Railroad in 1925 and later served as a waiter.

Sources: "Associate Foretold Death of Railroad Labor Leader," *Washington Afro-American*, (22 December 1951); email, Awo Ojelola Ifasakin (Eric Franklin Brown) to Jessie Carney Smith, 27 April 2010; Hogans, "Among Railroad and Pullman Workers," *Washington Afro-American* (27 August 1938).

1936 • The opening of the National Negro Congress, the first attempt at a united front organization to try to better the conditions of black workers, was on February 14, 1936. A. Philip Randolph was its first president. It supported the unionization efforts of the CIO. The organization ran into trouble as a Communist front in 1940 and by 1950 it ceased to exist.

Sources: Bennett, *Before the Mayflower*, pp. 361, 531; Foner, *Organized Labor and the Black Worker*, pp. 213–14.

1938 • Ferdinand C. Smith (1894–1961) was a founder of the National Maritime Union and in 1938 served as the first black vice president. When that office was abolished in 1939, he became the first black national secretary. In 1943 he became the first black member of the CIO executive board. He was influential in recruiting the mixed crew for Hugh Mulzac (1886-1971), who set sail as the first black captain of a merchant ship on October 20, 1942. A native of Jamaica and an alleged subversive because of his Communist ties, in 1948 Smith was arrested and deported as an undesirable alien.

Sources: Logan and Winston, *Dictionary of American Negro Biography*, pp. 562–64; Foner, *Organized Labor and the Black Worker*, pp. 227, 231, 285.

Cleveland Robinson

1950 • Cleveland Robinson (1914–1995) became the first black officer of the American Federation of Labor and Congress of Industrial Organizations (AFL-CIO) and led some 30,000 members who worked in small shops and department stores in New York City. Between 1950 and his retirement in 1992, he led the District 65 United Auto Workers of the AFL-CIO. He was a close ally of Martin Luther King Jr. and a member of the Southern Christian Leadership Conference's board. Robinson figured prominently in the 1963 March on Washington, serving as chairman for the historic event. He was born Cleveland Lowellyn in Swabys Hope, a parish in Jamaica. He immigrated to the United States in 1944.

Sources: *Jet* 88 (18 September 1995): 56–57.

1954 • The first woman president of a packinghouse local was Addie L. Wyatt (1924–2012). Wyatt was born in Brookhaven, Mississippi, but moved to Chicago. When she failed to get a clerical job at a meat packinghouse, she took a union position, joined the United Packinghouse Workers, and later became the union local's president. In 1968 the union merged with the Amalgamated Meat Cutters Union.

Sources: Salem, *African American Women*, pp. 566–67; Smith, *Notable Black American Women*, Book II, pp. 723–25; *Who's Who among African Americans*, 26th ed., p. 1389.

1962 • Nelson Jack Edwards (1917–1974) was the first black member of the United Auto Workers (UAW) international executive board and in 1970 became the first black vice president of that union. Born in Lowndes County, Alabama, Edwards moved to Detroit in 1937 and found work in a Chrysler foundry. He left that position and joined Ford Motor Company's Lincoln plant. About 1937 he joined UAW and rose steadily to the head of the organization's independent parts department. Edwards worked in the interest of pension reform and the reinsurance of the union's pension plans. The U.S. Congress later approved the program. He also served as a bridge between UAW and the black community.

Sources: *Ebony Success Library*, vol. 2, pp. 68–71; *Encyclopedia of Black America*, p. 352; *Negro Almanac*, pp. 1405–6; Bailey, *They Too Call Alabama Home*, p. 125.

1966 • The South's first regional director of the United Automobile Workers Union was George L. Holloway Jr.

Sources: Jones, *Everyday in Tennessee History*, p. 165.

1969 • Lonnie L. Johnson (1932–1989) was the first black national president of the Mail Handler's Union, AFL-CIO. Born in Hickory, Mississippi, Johnson attended Chicago's Roosevelt University. His involvement in labor activities began in 1963. Moving up the ladder, from shop steward to local vice president, Johnson became local president of his union. In 1965 he became national education director for the Mail Handlers and in 1970 he became the organization's first black national director. He also established the firm Johnson Consultant Company, a labor-consulting firm.

Sources: *Who's Who among African Americans*, 18th ed., p. 1440.

1974 • William E. Pollard (1915–2003) was the first black to head the American Federation of Labor and Congress of Industrial Organizations (AFL-CIO) civil rights department in Washington, D.C. Pollard began his union career as secretary-treasurer of Dining Car Employees, Local 582 in 1941. In 1945 he became general chairman of the Dining Car Employees locals 456 and 482. From 1959 until 1964 he served as vice president of the Los Angeles County Federation of Labor. He held the AFL-CIO civil rights post until 1986, when he joined the NAACP as deputy executive director. Pollard was born in Pensacola, Florida, and was educated at the University of California, Los Angeles and Los Angeles City College.

Sources: *Ebony* 29 (October 1974): 32; *Jet* 62 (12 April 1982): 16; 70 (21 April 1986): 4; Obituary, *Who's Who among African Americans*, 18th ed., p. 1455.

1976 • As vice president, Leon Lynch (1935–2012) was the first black national officer of the American Federation of Labor and Congress of Industrial Organizations (AFL-CIO) Steel Workers Union. Lynch began to work for the Youngstown Sheet and Tube Company as a loader in 1956. He was born in Edwards, Mississippi. He earned a bachelor of science degree at Roosevelt University in Chicago, Illinois, in 1967. He began to work as a union staff representative for United Steelworkers of America in 1968. In 1973 Lynch became international representative for the union and in 1976 he became international president of human affairs.

Sources: *Jet* 56 (26 July 1979): 10; *Who's Who among African Americans*, 26th ed., p. 796.

1976 • As a member of the national executive board of the Amalgamated Meat Cutters and Butcher Workmen, Addie L. Wyatt (1924–2012) was the first black woman labor executive. Wyatt became an international vice president of the union this year and was the first black woman to hold this leadership role in an international union.

Sources: *Ebony* 32 (August 1977): 70; 39 (March 1984): 104; Lee, *Interesting People*, p. 196; *Notable Black American Women*, Book II, pp. 723–25; *Who's Who among African Americans*, 26th ed., p. 1389.

1981 • Barbara B. Hutchinson was the first black woman member of the American Federation of Labor and Congress of Industrial Organizations (AFL-CIO) executive council.

Hutchinson was director of women's affairs for the American Federation of Government Employees. Her choice as director was the occasion of some controversy.

Sources: *Jet* 61 (10 December 1981): 8; 64 (21 March 1983): 9.

1984 • Michelle V. Agins (1956–) was the first black woman still photographer admitted to the International Photographers of the Motion Picture and Television Industries union. She was personal photographer to then-Chicago mayor Harold Washington.

Sources: *Jet* 66 (9 April 1984): 8; *Negro Almanac*, p. 1067.

1984 • Jacqueline Barbara Vaughn (1935–1994) was the first black woman president of the Chicago Teachers Union. Vaughn graduated from Chicago Teachers College and began teaching in the Chicago schools in 1956. In 1968 she became a secretary for the Illinois Federation of Teachers, and in 1972 she was elected union vice president. For nearly ten years she led the nation's strongest local union and, as result of the strikes that she led in 1985 and 1987, teachers saw a number of salary increases and perks. Her showdowns with the school board brought national attention. Union concessions in fall 1993 were made to advert a strike that might have shut down the school system. Vaughn was born in St. Louis and moved to Chicago with her mother when she was two years old; her father had just died and her mother died two years later. A local teacher, Mae Alice Bibbs, became her guardian and encouraged her to become a teacher as well.

Sources: *Jet* 66 (30 July 1984): 21; 67 (19 November 1984): 40; 85 (7 February 1994): 54; 85 (7 February 1994): 54; *Who's Who among Black Americans, 1992–93*, p. 1432.

1984 • Althea Williams was the first black woman president of the Michigan State Employees Union. Williams was a 1981 graduate of Wayne State University, Detroit, where she earned her degree in psychology.

Sources: *Jet* 66 (27 August 1984): 12.

1988 • Edgar O. Romney (1943–) was the first black vice president of the International Ladies' Garment Workers Union. Romney has held a number of positions with the union since 1966, including director of organization, assistant manager, and manager/secretary. In 1989 he was named executive vice president. Since 1995 he has been executive vice president of UNITE! He serves on the New York State Department of labor Garment Advisory Council and has served on numerous labor boards. Romney was born in New York City and educated at Hunter College and Empire State Labor College.

Sources: *Jet* 76 (17 July 1989): 38; *Who's Who among African Americans*, 26th ed., p. 1075.

1988 • John Nathan Sturdivant (1938–1997) was the first black president of the American Federation of Government Employees, American Federation of Labor and Congress of Industrial Organizations (AFL-CIO). A native of Philadelphia and a 1980 graduate of Antioch College, Ohio, Sturdivant has worked for the union since 1962, serving as president for nine years until his death.

Sources: *Jet* 75 (3 October 1988): 10; *Who's Who among Black Americans, 1992–93*, p. 1351.

1990 • Lee Jackson was the first black to head the Kentucky Association of State Employees/FSE. Jackson was program supervisor at the Department for Employment Services, Lexington, Kentucky.

Sources: *Jet* 78 (22 October 1990): 20.

1995 • The first black board director of New York City Police Department's Patrolmen's Benevolent Association was Warren Binford (1958?–). Binford, who had served as delegate to the association for eight years, would now become financial secretary to the board of directors, representing precincts in borough of Queens. He told the New York press that his work and dedication to the union led to his appointment.

Sources: *Jet* 87 (27 February 1995): 36.

2001 • William Burrus was installed as president of the American Postal Workers Union, becoming the first black elected president of a major national union. He was also appointed to the AFL-CIO executive council. Burrus had served as executive vice president of the union since November 1980. By mail ballot, he was elected president, receiving 53 percent of the vote in a three-way contest. Burrus is a native of Wheeling, West Virginia. He attended West Virginia State College and served in the 101th Airborne Division.

Sources: *Jet* 100 (10 December 2001): 5.

Manufacturing

1798 • James Forten Sr. (1766–1842) established the first major black-owned sail making shop in Philadelphia. His financial worth soon reached $100,000. Forten was a leader in the radical abolitionist movement. An organizer of the American Anti-slavery Society (1833), he also supported women's suffrage and temperance. He inspired his daughters Margaretta, Sarah, and Harriet, and his granddaughter Charlotte Forten Grimké, in their efforts on behalf of blacks. He was born in Philadelphia to free blacks and attended a school that Quaker Anthony Benezet operated for blacks. After his father died Forten ended his education and went to work to help support his family. He worked in various positions, including that as a powder boy on the *Royal Louis* beginning in 1781. He later became a sailor on a ship bound for Liverpool and arrived there around March 1785. There he was in contact with abolitionists Granville Sharp and Thomas Clarkson. He returned to America by fall 1786 and became apprentice to sail maker Robert Bridges. In 1793 he met Paul Cuffe (1759-1818), the black captain of a small ship. In summer 1798 Forten bought out Bridges, became master of the sail loft, and soon became successful.

Sources: Logan and Winston, *Dictionary of American Negro Biography,* pp. 234–35; *Encyclopedia of Black America,* p. 391–92; *Negro Almanac,* pp. 234, 808; Smith, *Notable Black American Men,* pp, 408–11.

1818 • Thomas Day (1800?–1861), a free black, was the first widely recognized black furniture and cabinet maker in the deep South. He operated one of North Carolina's largest furniture enterprises, making sofas, chairs, chests, tables, and bedsteads from walnut, mahogany, and oak. He also built coffins and did fine interior work, such as stairways and trims. His ornately carved work was represented in homes of distinguished families throughout the state. Day was recognized as one of the finest artisans of the day. He worked in Milton, North Carolina, and his workshop, the Yellow Tavern, is a National Historical Landmark. He was born in Halifax County, Virginia, and moved to Milton in 1823, where he opened his shop.

Sources: Cantor, *Historic Landmarks of Black America,* p. 231; Logan and Winston, *Dictionary of American Negro Biography,* pp. 162–63; *Negro Almanac,* pp. 221–22; Smith, *Notable Black American Men,* pp. 275–76.

1885 • D. Watson Onley built the first steam saw and planning mill owned and operated entirely by blacks in Jacksonville, Florida. After the mill was destroyed by fire set by an incendiary, Onley worked for Florida State Normal and Industrial College (later Florida A&M University), attended Howard University School of Dentistry, and established practice in Washington, D.C.

Sources: Culp, *Twentieth Century Negro Literature,* opposite p. 347.

1910 • Madame C. J. Walker (1867–1919) is believed by some to be the first black woman to become a millionaire. However, supporters of Annie Turnbo Malone (1869–1957) dispute this. Both women produced hair-care products for black women during the period; it is asserted that Walker worked as a salesperson for Malone products. Both became very wealthy by around 1910, but by 1927 Malone's business began to run into difficulties due to poor management. Sarah Breedlove McWilliams Walker, known as Madame C. J. Walker, was born in Louisiana to indigent former slaves. She became interested in the hair problems of black women and, after moving to Denver, she began to manufacture hair products, including her Wonderful Hair Grower, and eventually produced five hair-care products. Her company began with door-to-door selling techniques; she eventually established a chain of beauty parlors across the country, the Caribbean, and South America. In 1910 Walker selected Indianapolis as her headquarters. She employed five thousand black commissioned agents, who demonstrated her techniques and sold her products. She became wealthy and built a palatial mansion, Villa Lewaro, on the Hudson River in Irvington, New York. Enrico Caruso gave the home its name. It became a gathering place for black leaders and entertainers. Walker lived there barely a year before she died. In 1993 investment banker Harold Doley bought the house and in 1958 turned it into a temporary decorators' museum to attract black designers and raise money for charity. The mansion has since changed ownership. Annie Minerva Turnbo Pope Malone was born in Metropolis, Illinois, and was orphaned at an early age. By 1900 she had developed successful straighteners, hair growers, special oils, and other products. Malone also manufactured and sold Wonderful Hair Grower and, with her assistants, sold products door-to-door. She opened Poro College in St. Louis in 1902, where she trained women as agents for the Poro system. Students were also taught how to properly walk, speak, and eat. By 1905 Madame C. J. Walker was one of Malone's first students. Poro claimed to employ 75,000 agents throughout the United States, the Caribbean, and other parts of the world. In 1930, Malone relocated the college and the business to Chicago. Her business was poorly managed and also fell victim to several lawsuits. By 1950 most of the Poro property was sold.

Sources: Logan and Winston, *Dictionary of American Negro Biography,* p. 621 (Walker); *Encyclopedia of Black America,* p. 545 (Malone); p. 830 (Walker); *Negro Almanac,* pp. 1393–94 (Walker); Smith, *Notable Black American Women,* pp. 724–27 (Malone); 1184–93 (Walker).

1962 • Harvey Clarence Russell Jr. (1918–1998) was the first black vice president of a leading national corporation, Pepsico. Born in Louisville, Russell served in the U.S. Coast Guard during World War II and, though advised that he would not receive the position, became one of the coast guard's first black deck officers. He joined a Manhattan advertising firm, where he was placed in charge of marketing. At Pepsico Russell was put in charge of "Negro sales" and by 1958 managed its ethnic marketing department. In 1962 he was appointed vice president in charge of special markets for the company, in 1965 he was appointed vice president in charge of planning, and vice president for community affairs in 1969. He retired in 1983.

Sources: *Black Enterprise* 2 (September 1971): 15–18; *Ebony* 17 (June 1962): 25–32; *Encyclopedia of Black America,* p. 737; *Jet* 93 (16 March 1998): 18; *Who's Who among Black Americans, 1992–93,* p. 1232.

1963 • James Phillip McQuay (1924–) was the first and only black in wholesale-retail fur manufacturing. McQuay, who operated his fur business in New York City, won fur designer awards in 1970, 1975, and 1976. He was born in White Plains, New York.

Sources: *Ebony* 24 (July 1969): 38; *Encyclopedia of Black America,* p. 552; *Negro Almanac,* pp. 1412–13; *Who's Who among African American,* 26th ed., p. 862.

1969 • Stanley W. Tate (1924?–1995), advocate for minority entrepreneurs, was the first black to have a Hamm's beer distributorship. He was also successful in the banking industry, serving from 1973 until 1980 as vice president/director of marketing for Chicago's Independence Bank and as senior vice president of Highland Community Bank. Tate headed the Chicago office of the State of Illinois Office of Minority Business Enterprise and was co-chair of the Minority Banking Task Force of Chicago United. He served as regional director for the U.S. Department of Commerce's Minority Business Development Agency, retiring in 1988. In 1980 President Jimmy Carter recognized Tate for outstanding leadership.

Sources: *Jet* 87 (6 February 1995): 58.

1970 • Clarence C. Finley (1922–) was the first black president of a major white firm, Charm-Tred-Monticello, a division of Burlington Industries. Finley began work for Charm-Tred Company as a file clerk in 1942.

Sources: Alford, *Famous First Blacks,* pp. 16–17; *Ebony* 26 (February 1971): 58–65; *Jet* 93 (12 January 1998): 20; *Ebony Success Library,* vol. 2, pp. 72–75.

1971 • When Melvin R. Wade (1936–) purchased the Eastern Rubber Reclaiming Company of Chester, Pennsylvania, he became the first black to own a rubber recycling plant. Prior to purchasing the plant, Wade worked as a technician for General Electric.

Sources: *Ebony Success Library,* vol. 1, p. 314.

1986 • William R. Harvey (1941–) was the first black to be the sole owner of a major soft-drink bottling franchise, a Pepsi plant in Houghton, Michigan. A native of Alabama, Harvey holds his doctorate in education from Harvard University (1971), and became president of Hampton University in 1978.

Sources: *Jet* 70 (7 April 1986): 8; Smith, *Notable Black American Men,* pp. 516–19; *Who's Who among African Americans,* 26th ed., p. 551.

1990 • Bertram M. Lee (1939–2003) was the first black to serve of the board of directors of Reebok International. Born in Lynchburg, Virginia, Lee has a bachelor's degree from North Central College and did graduate study at Roosevelt University from 1963 to 1965. In 1969 he was appointed president of BML Associates Inc. and in 1986 president of Kellee Communications Group. In 1989 he, along with Peter Bynoe, became part owners of the Denver Nuggets Corporation, where Lee served as president until 1992. He has also been active in many other businesses.

Sources: *Jet* 78 (1 October 1990): 35; *Who's Who among African Americans,* 14th ed., p. 783.

1994 • Corporate executive Ann M. Fudge (1951–) became the first African American woman to head a major company, when she was appointed president of the Maxwell House Coffee division of Kraft General Foods in 1994. Her success in corporate America began in 1977, when Fudge joined Minneapolis-based General Mills Company and in 1978 was named assistant product manager. Four years later she was made product manager with responsibility for four brands. Honey Nut Cheerios was developed under her leadership and became one of the division's top performers. Fudge left the company in 1986 and joined Kraft General Foods where she revived old brands such as Shake `N Bake and Stove Top Stuffing, both high profit-makers for Kraft. She held a number of management positions, before being named executive vice president in 1993 and a year later president. Fudge's success brought the attention of a number of boards that invited her to join; these included Allied Signal, Liz Claiborne, Inc., Simmons College, and Harvard Business School Alumni Association. Born in Washington, D.C., she graduated from Simmons College in 1973 and in 1977 received her master's in business administration from Harvard Business School. In 1991 *Black Enterprise* recognized her accomplishments by naming her one of the country's "21 Women of Power and Influence."

Sources: *Contemporary Black Biography,* vol. 11, pp. 97–99; Salzman, *Encyclopedia of African-American Culture and History,* Supplement, p. 103; *Essence* 26 (May 1995): 112–150.

1999 • On April 14, John W. Thompson (1949–) became the first black president and chief executive officer of Symantec Corporation, a major computer software company. Based in Culpertino, California, the firm became known for its anti-virus products. His focus on corporate security solutions led to a profit for the company and an increase in the value of its shares. Thompson was born on a military base in Fort Dix, New Jersey. Later the family settled in West Palm Beach. He received his bachelor's degree from Florida Agricultural and Mechanical University and his master's degree from Massachusetts Institute of Technology. In 1971 he joined IBM and moved through the management ranks, and was later named general manager of its Personal Software Products division. He left in 1996 and headed IBM Americas, an organization that supported technology products.

Sources: *Black Enterprise* (June 1997): 80; *Contemporary Black Biography,* vol. 26, pp. 167–69; *New York Times* (19 November 2000); Salzman, *Encyclopedia of African-American Culture and History,* Supplement, p. 260.

Miscellaneous Industries

William Leidesdorff

1846 • William Leidesdorff (1810–1848) opened the first hotel in San Francisco. He is also credited with organizing the first horse race and operating the first steamboat (1847). In April 1848, he was the chair of the board of education that opened California's first public school. Leidesdorff was born in the Virgin Islands, the son of a Danish man and an African woman. In 1841 he settled in the Mexican province of California and became a Mexican citizen in 1846 in order to acquire extensive land holdings. He is recognized as an important figure in California history. He was a civic leader in California and deeply involved in the activities that led to the United States' annexation of California. When he became a United States vice consul in 1845, he was probably the first black in United States history to hold a diplomatic post. Leidesdorff followed a somewhat circuitous route to California. He first worked in his father's cotton business in New Orleans from about 1834 until his father's death in 1840. He then moved to New York, where he worked as a seafarer, serving as a ship's master on several voyages, participating in shipping and commercial trading until 1845. His move to California coincided with the period of controversy over whether California should remain in alliance with Mexico, become independent, or be annexed by the United States. His close friendship with the American Consul resulted in a diplomatic appointment and his personal involvement in the controversy. He was active in real estate and successful as a merchant, trader, and shipper. After an initial underevaluation, Leidesdorff's estate was valued at $1.5 million; this high value was in large part due to the presence of gold on his land.

Sources: Ingham and Feldman, *African-American Business Leaders,* pp. 424–29; Logan and Winston, *Dictionary of American Negro Biography,* pp. 392–93; Katz, *The Black West,* pp. 117–19; Smith, *Notable Black American Men,* pp. 711–13.

Robert Church Sr.

1899 • Robert Reed Church Sr. (1839–1912) founded Church Park in Memphis, Tennessee, and became the first to provide recreational facilities for black residents who had been denied access to such public facilities. Church served as the park's owner and manager. He was born a Mississippi slave, the son of a white riverboat captain and his legal property, a slave seamstress. Although he was emancipated in 1863, Church never considered himself a slave. After his mother died in 1851, he lived with his father and learned the riverboat trade. Church settled in Memphis where he began a career of personal and professional services to others. In Memphis he acquired a number of prime properties, including a hotel downtown. By the 1870 he had built a small fortune and continued to make money primarily from real estate. Church became known as the South's first black millionaire. Church Park and Auditorium, purchased in 1899, became the cultural center for black Memphis and a site for conventions, concerts, and large public ceremonies. Church also helped to establish the Solvent Savings Bank and Trust company in 1906. Although he had little interest in politics, he served as a delegate to the Republican National Convention in 1900, where he supported William McKinley. He had several marriages, the second of which produced the prominent civil rights leader and educator Mary Church Terrell (1863–1954). The most prominent child of his third marriage was Robert Jr., who was known as the "Dictator of the Lincoln Belt," a political organization in West Tennessee.

Sources: Smith, *Notable Black American Men,* pp. 200–203.

1951 • The Ben Moore Hotel was founded in Montgomery, Alabama, and opened for business on September 23; it was the first black hotel in the city. Its owner, Matthew F. Moore (?–1956), named the business in honor of his father, a former slave born in Alabama. At first a truck farmer, Moore closed his farming business after opening the hotel. Along with sleeping rooms, the hotel contained the Majestic Café, a grocery store, a drug store, and a rooftop garden.

Sources: Bailey, *They Too Call Alabama Home,* pp. 36–37.

1959 • Ruth Jean Bowen (1924–2009) was the first black woman to establish a successful booking and talent agency in New York City. She had done personal relations work for Dinah Washington, and her firm, Queen Booking Corporation, has represented such artists as Ray Charles, Sammy Davis Jr., Lola Falana, Aretha Franklin, Marvin Gaye, Gladys Knight, Patti LaBelle, Smokey Robinson, and the Staples Singers. Bowen began in 1959 with an initial five-hundred-dollar investment and within ten years owned the largest black-owned agency in the world. Ruth Jean Baskerville Bowen was born in Danville, Virginia, and relocated to New York City with her family. She attended New York University for two years. She married Wallace "Billy" Bowen, a member of the original Ink Spots, a renowned singing group. At one time she was publicist for singer Dinah Washington, who encouraged Bowen to pursue a career as publicist. Bowen retained David Dinkins, later mayor of New York City, as her attorney and then obtained a booking license from the State of New York. As she devoted more time to Washington and became her personal manager, she hired other personnel to help with her publicity business, then known as Queen Artists.

Sources: *Encyclopedia of Black America,* p. 188; Lerner, *Black Women in White America,* p. 151; *Negro Almanac,* pp. 1375–76; Smith, *Notable Black American Women,* Book II, pp. 48–51; *Who's Who among Black Americans, 1992–93,* p. 135.

1964 • Joseph Jacob "Jake" Simmons Jr. (1901–1981) broke the color barrier in the oil industry and became the first black in the world to represent a major oil company abroad. In 1964 Phillips Petroleum hired Simmons as corporate ambassador for its permanent office in Lagos, Nigeria. They knew him as an articulate and persuasive salesman who helped to bridge the distrust between new African states like Nigeria and Ghana and American multinationals like Phillips Petroleum, Texaco, and Signal. He has been called the most successful black American in the history of the oil business. Simmons was born in Muskogee, Oklahoma, the great-grandson of Cow Tom, one of the only black chiefs to lead an American Indian tribe. He graduated from Tuskegee Institute (now Tuskegee University) in Alabama, where he learned the art of public speaking. He worked for a short time as a machinist in a Detroit automobile factory but returned to Oklahoma. Simmons began to broker oil leases for black farmers in Oklahoma and Texas, helping to prevent big oil companies from exploiting them. When he arrived in Africa in the mid–1960s, he found the new African states eager to become independent from Britain's petroleum giants and that nation's political domination. They welcomed Simmons, respected his fierce racial pride, and vested their trust in him. By 1968 he had spent two years helping the Ghanaian Ministry of Lands and Mineral Resources develop its first comprehensive petroleum investment code. He also negotiated deals between some of the world's largest oil companies and the Ghanaian government. Over the next decade, Simmons' work resulted more than $150 million worth of oil company investment in Ghana.

Sources: Greenberg, *Staking a Claim.*

1967 • Israel Tribble Jr. (1940–2003), who accepted a position with Pacific Telephone's Management Achievement Program in Sunnyvale, California, became the first black telephone company commercial manager in California. Tribble was born in Philadelphia and educated at Montclair State College (B.A., 1962), California State University at Hayward (M.S., 1972) and Stanford University (M.A., 1975, Ed.D., 1976). He held a number of teaching positions in California, before moving into administrative positions. He was provost at Bethune-Cookman College (1977–78), vice president and dean of academic affairs at Edward Waters College (1978–80), and became special assistant to the secretary, U.S. Department of Education (1980–81). He held posts with the American Association of State Colleges and Universities, the U.S. Department of Defense, and the Board of Regents of the State University System of Florida. Since 1985 Tribble had been president and chief executive officer for the Florida Education Fund (previously known as the Florida Endowment Fund for Higher Education). He published his ideas about American education in two books, *Making Their Mark* (1992) and *If You Can Talk You Can Sing, If You Can Walk You Can Dance: A Successful African-American Doctoral Program* (1994).

Sources: *Contemporary Black Biography,* vol. 8, pp. 248–51; *Who's Who among African Americans,* 14th ed., p. 1301.

1972 • On May 16, 1972, the Johnson Publishing Company headquarters was dedicated. The eleven-story edifice was the first building built by blacks in downtown Chicago since the time of Jean Baptiste Point Du Sable. Black architect John Warren Moutoussamy (1922–1995), managing partner in the architectural and engineering firm Dubin, Dubin and Moutoussamy, designed the building.

Sources: *Ebony Success Library,* vol. 2, p. 1355; *Jet* 88 (22 May 1995): 15; *Who's Who among Black Americans 1994/95,* 8th ed, p. 1076.

1975 • Willie E. Gary (1947–) founded the first black law firm in Martin County, Florida, and became its only attorney. He rose from poverty to become a highly successful and visible personal injury and malpractice lawyer. Born in Eastman, Georgia, he came from a family of eleven children. The family relocated to Silver City, Florida, where they lived in a tiny wooden shack and worked as migrant workers. Later the family relocated to Indiantown, Florida, where he and his father opened a business, selling produce from a truck that Gary had bought his father from money he earned in his own lawn-mowing business. In search of a football scholarship, he went first to Bethune-Cookman College (later University) in Daytona Beach and then to Shaw University in Raleigh, North Carolina, where, at first, he was denied a spot on the team. To sustain himself while at Shaw, Gary slept in dormitory lounges, ate food that was smuggled to him, cleaned the locker room, and aided the football team. He was later assigned to the team and awarded a scholarship. While still a student, Gary launched a successful lawn-care business, receiving large contracts and hiring others to do the work. He graduated from Shaw in 1971 with a bachelor's degree in business administration. He enrolled in North Carolina Central University's law school and graduated in 1974. His road to success was swift. After opening a law firm, he was successful in two high profile cases that established him as an able lawyer. By the 1980s he was grossing over $100 million a year. His successful suit against the Florida Power & Light Company for the electrocution death of a Jupiter, Florida, family put him in the national spotlight. Among his numerous financial contributions is his 1992 gift of $10 million to his alma mater, Shaw University—then the largest cash donation to a black college. Since 1975 he has been senior partner at the law firm of Gary, Williams, Parenti, Finney, Lewis & McManus in Stuart, Florida. He is also president of Gary Enterprises.

Sources: *Contemporary Black Biography,* vol. 12, pp. 53–55; *Who's Who among African Americans,* 26th ed., pp. 451–52.

1977 • Harambee House, Washington, D.C., was the first large hotel designed and built by blacks. The hotel was designed by Sulton-Campbell and Associates, and was owned by the Peoples Involvement Corporation, a local citizens group. The hotel is now owned by Howard University and operates as the Howard Inn.

Sources: *Jet* 52 (24 March 1977): 13.

1977 • Kenwood Commercial Furniture was the first black-owned company to sign a $1 million contract with Consolidated Edison. The firm, established by Kenneth N. Sherwood (1930–1989), was to furnish and install carpet in all the utility company's offices in New York City and Westchester County.

Sources: *Ebony* 28 (August 1973): 168–73; *Ebony Success Library,* vol. 2, pp. 236–39.

1984 • The first black to enter the high-stakes world of billion-dollar business takeovers was Reginald F. Lewis (1942–1993). Lewis created TLC Pattern (the Lewis Company) on July 29, 1983, with the intention of taking over McCall Pattern Company. His holding company was known as TLC Group. On January 29, 1984, he acquired McCall, doubled the company's profits, engaged in other maneuvers and then sold the company in 1987 for a ninety-to-one gain. In 1987 as well, he acquired Beatrice International for $985 million and now headed the largest black-owned business in the country and the only black-owned company with over $1 million in revenues. Beatrice International was comprised of sixty-four companies in thirty-one countries; its parent company was Beatrice Foods, then the thirty-fifth largest industrial corporation in the United States. Lewis became one of the four hundred wealthiest entrepreneurs in the United States. Born in Baltimore, Maryland, Lewis graduated from Virginia State College (now Virginia State University) in Petersburg and received his law degree from Harvard Law School. After graduating in 1968, he joined one of New York City's bluechip law firms, Paul, Weiss, Rifkind, Wharton & Garrison. Two years later he became a partner with Murphy, Thorp and Lewis, one of Wall Street's first black law firms. Later he bought out two of his partners and renamed the firm Lewis and Clarkson. Within a few years the firm had among its major clients General Foods, the Ford Foundation, Aetna Life, and Equitable Life.

Sources: *Contemporary Black Biography,* vol. 6, pp. 175–78; Smith, *Notable Black American Men,* pp. 720–23; Ingham and Feldman, *African-American Business Leaders,* pp. 434–40.

1990 • Errol B. Davis Jr. (1943–) was the first black to head a major utility company, Wisconsin Power and Light. Davis graduated from Carnegie-Mellon University with a bachelor of science degree in electrical engineering in 1965 and from the University of Chicago with a master's of business administration in 1967. He served as a member of the Corporate Finance Staff for Ford Motor Company from 1969 to 1973 and at Xerox Corporation in Rochester, New York from 1973 to 1978. At Wisconsin Power and Light he served as vice president for finance from 1978 to 1982, and vice president for finance and public affairs from 1982 to 1984. Davis continued as executive vice president, president, and then chief executive officer. From 1990 to 1998 he was president and CEO of WPL Holdings. He also served as chairman of the board for Alliant Energy.

Sources: *Jet* 78 (30 July 1990): 16; *Who's Who among African Americans,* 26th ed., p. 314.

1992 • Roberta Palm Bradley (1947–) was the first woman to head a major public utility, Seattle City Light. She has served on a number of boards, including United Way, Vallejo Chambers of Commerce, and the Vallejo Salvation Army. A native of Frederick, Maryland, she took a degree in English at Morgan State University in 1969 and completed the program for management development at Harvard University School of Business in 1991. B'nai Brith awarded her the Woman of the Year Certificate in 1990.

Sources: *Ebony* 47 (September 1992): 10; *Who's Who among African Americans,* 14th ed., p. 130.

1993 • Pearline Motley was the first black honored as American Business Woman of the Year. She received the award from the American Business Women's Association in 1993. Motley was the manager of the Federal Women's Program of the Agricultural Stabilization and Conservation Service in Kansas City, Missouri.

Sources: *Jet* 83 (28 December 1992): 20.

1995 • Henry Wadsworth McGee III (1953–) became the first black president of HBO Home Video in New York City. Prior to this promotion, he was the company's senior vice president of programming. McGee was born in Chicago and received his bachelor of arts degree (*magna cum laude*) from Harvard University in 1947; he received his master's degree in business administration from Harvard Business School in 1979. From 1974 to 1977 he was a reporter for *Newsweek* magazine, in New York and in Washington, D.C. McGee served as manager of film acquisition for HBO in New York (1979–80), director of program acquisitions for Time-Life Television (1980–81), and director of budgeting and planning for Cinemax (1981–82). He held various positions with HBO Enterprises, when he became president of HBO Home Video. McGee is president of the Film Society of Lincoln Center, director of the Black Filmmaker Foundation, and president of the Alvin Ailey Dance Theater Foundation.

Sources: *Jet* 87 (3 April 1994): 21; *Who's Who among African Americans,* 26th ed., p. 846.

1995 • Mark E. Dean (1957–) became the first black IBM fellow. By 1997 Dean had become vice president of performance for IBM's RS/6000 division located in Dallas. He became known for his pioneering work with high-performance computer software and in 1997 he held more than twenty patents. In recognition of his work, in 1997 Dean was elected to the National Inventors Hall of Fame. Dean received his bachelor's degree from the University of Tennessee, a master's from Florida Atlantic University, and a doctorate from Stanford University.

Sources: *Jet* 92 (4 August 1997): 10; *Who's Who among African Americans,* 26th ed., p. 327.

1995 • One of the first two individuals approved to operate a riverboat casino in Gary, Indiana, was Detroit entrepreneur Don H. Barden (1943–2011). Nineteen companies applied for a license from the Gaming Commission. Barden, chair and chief executive officer of the Barden Companies, Inc., would operate the first riverboat casino with minorities as the main investors. Barden owned 42.5 percent and local black investors held 15 percent. His company's interests included cable television franchises. Born in Detroit, Michigan, Barden attended Central State University.

Sources: *Jet* 119 (6 June 2011): 20; *Who's Who among African Americans*, 26th ed., p. 67.

1995 • Miller Brewing Company, headquartered in Milwaukee, named I. Patricia Henry (1947–) manager at its North Carolina brewery in Eden. With the appointment, Henry became the first woman to hold a top management post at an American brewery. She directed a staff of 878 and oversaw of all of the plant's operations, including the production of eight million barrels of beer annually. Prior to her promotion, the seventeen-year veteran served as brew master. The Reidsville, North Carolina, native received her degree in chemistry (*summa cum laude*) from Bennett College for Women and studied at Harvard University and Siebel's Institute of Brewing Technology.

Sources: *Ebony* 50 (September 1995): 9; *Jet* 88 (5 June 1995): 25; *Who's Who among African Americans*, 26th ed., p. 570.

1995 • Quentin Redman became the first black manager of advanced systems economic analysis for Hughes Missile Systems Company in Tucson, Arizona. Before his promotion, Redman was the company's senior engineering specialist.

Sources: *Jet* 88 (18 September 1995): 24.

1996 • Nathaniel Berger was the first black partner in JMGR's ninety-six-year-history. JMGR is the oldest architecture and engineering firm in Memphis. Berger's responsibilities were to manage the firm's projects as it expanded into new markets and to recruit and develop new minority employees. He received a bachelor's degree in architecture from Carnegie-Mellon University.

Sources: *Jet* 91 (16 December 1996): 22; *Who's Who among African Americans*, 26th ed., p. 95.

1996 • Judith Alane Colbert became the first black woman in Oklahoma to be named a shareholder and partner in a major law firm, when she became a partner with Hall, Estill, Hardwick, Gable, Golden & Nelson, P.C., located in Tulsa.

Sources: *Jet* 89 (22 April 1996): 19.

1996 • The president and chief executive officer of Soft Sheen Products, Inc. in Chicago, Terri Gardner was the first woman to hold the office. With fifteen years of experience as an international marketer for Soft Sheen, Gardner positioned the firm to continue its record-breaking success as the top black hair-care products company. Prior to her promotion, she had held several posts with the company, including executive vice president of advertising and president of Brainstorm Communications, the company's advertising agency. She is the daughter of the firm's founders, Edward and Bettiann Gardner.

Sources: *Jet* 90 (28 October 1996): 19.

1996 • Pamela Thomas-Graham was named partner in the largest management consulting firm in the world, McKinsey & Company—the first black woman to hold this post at the firm. Prior to her promotion, she was the company's senior engagement manager.

Sources: *Jet* 89 (18 March 1996): 20.

1996 • Named general manager of the original Harrah's Tunica Casino in Tunica, Mississippi, Karen Sock became the first black woman to hold such a position. She gave oversight to Harrah's daily operations and was placed in charge of five hundred employees and a $50 million operation. She left in 1997 and became senior vice president of administra-

The First Black Fortune 500 Executive

In 1992 A. Barry Rand (1944–) became the first black chief executive officer of a Fortune 500 company, Xerox Corporation. Rand was born in Washington, D.C. He received his bachelor's degree from American University in 1968 and master's degrees in 1972 and 1973 from Stanford University. At Xerox he served as vice president of field operations, eastern operations, corporate vice president, senior vice president and president of U.S. Marketing Group, and since 1992 executive vice president of operations. He serves on numerous boards, including Honeywell Inc., Abbott Laboratories, the College Retirement Equities Fund (CREF), and the U.S. Chamber of Commerce.

Sources: *Contemporary Black Biography,* vol. 6, pp. 218–20; *Who's Who among African Americans,* 26th ed., p. 1024.

tion and assistant general manager of Grand Casino Tunica. Before her Tunica appointments, Sock was director of workforce diversity at Harrah's Memphis.

Sources: *Jet* 90 (20 May 1996): 8; 29 (1 September 1997): 19.

1997 • Mary K. Bush (1948–), president of the international consulting firm Bush and Company, Washington, D.C., was the first black woman elected to the board of directors of Texaco, Inc. Bush graduated from Fisk University in 1969 and received a master's degree in business administration from the University of Chicago in 1971. Experienced in economics and international business, she held positions at Chase Manhattan Bank N.A., Citibank N.A., and was vice president for the world corporate department at Bankers Trust Company. She also held posts with the U.S. Treasury Department and the International Monetary Fund.

Sources: *Jet* 92 (4 August 1997): 19; *Who's Who among African Americans,* 26th ed., p. 188.

1997 • Robert L. Clayton became the first black managing partner with a major law firm in Louisiana. He left his partnership with Chaffe, McCall, Phillips, Toler & Sarpy, L.L.P. to join the newly opened office of Vial, Hamilton, Koch, & Knox, L.L.P., in New Orleans.

Sources: *Jet* 92 (15 September 1997): 19.

1997 • When Robert L. Johnson (1946–), CEO and chairman of BET Holdings, Inc., was approved as director in the Hilton Hotels Corporation to hold a gaming license in Nevada, he became the first black to be approved by the state as director of a major public corporation.

Sources: *Jet* 91 (19 May 1997): 36; *Who's Who among African Americans,* 14th ed., p. 701.

1997 • Inez Y. Kaiser was named the 1997 National Minority Advocate of the year. She was the only black included in the National Hall of Fame of Women in Public Relations.

Sources: *Jet* 93 (29 December 1997–5 January 1998): 10.

1997 • Edith Stubblefield Washington, a certified construction specialist and president of the Stubblefield Group in Toledo, Ohio, was elevated to fellow at the Constructions Specifications Institute. She became the first black so honored for service to the institute and for contributing to continuing education for those in the building industry.

Sources: *Jet* 92 (25 August 1997): 20; *Who's Who among African Americans,* 26th ed., p. 1289.

1998 • Roberts Wireless Communications (RWC) became the first black-owned affiliate with Sprint PCS. RWC agreed to build cell sites and to market wireless service in Missouri, serving one million residents in areas outside of St. Louis and Kansas City. The company is owned by brothers Steven and Michael V. Roberts, who in 1974 founded

Roberts-Roberts & Associates, a conglomerate of entities that managed minority-and women-owned businesses. They expanded their business to include other enterprises, including television broadcasting, and wireless communications. Steven Roberts (1952–) received his bachelor's degree from Clark University and his law degree from Washington University. Michael Roberts (1948–) graduated from Lindenwood College, received his law degree from St. Louis University Law School and certificates from the Hague Academy of International Law in Holland and the International Institute of Human Rights in Strasbourg, France.

Sources: *Black Enterprise* 30 (June 2000): 172–74; *Who's Who among African Americans,* 14th ed., p. 1104.

1998 • Denise Grant became the first black partner with the international corporate law firm Shearman & Sterling located in New York City. She graduated from Georgetown University Law Center in 1989 and then joined the firm's project development and finance group.

Sources: *Jet* 93 (2 March 1998): 20; *Who's Who among African Americans,* 14th ed., p. 494.

1998 • When Clarence Vanzant McKee Jr. (1942–) was elected into the Tampa Business Hall of Fame, he became its first black member. As president, CEO, and owner of McKee Communications, McKee Holdings, and McKee Acquisitions Corporation, McKee's responsibilities included advising and helping public, community, and media businesses. He also assisted individual buyers of radio and television stations. Born in Buffalo, New York, he received his bachelor's degree from Howard University and then graduated from the Howard University School of Law. McKee has held a number of federal positions. He was also co-owner, CEO, chairman, and president of WTVT, Channel 13 in Miami, from 1987 to 1992.

Sources: *Jet* 93 (13 April 1998): 22; *Who's Who among African Americans,* 26th ed., p. 851.

1998 • Ricky A. Raven, at first an associate at Woodard, Hall & Primm, P.C., in Houston, Texas, became the first black partner with the thirty-eight-year-old firm. He specialized in toxic tort, environmental law, commercial litigation, and personal injury. Raven is affiliated with the Ronald McDonald House and the Houston Symphony.

Sources: *Jet* 93 (2 March 1998): 20; *Who's Who among African Americans,* 26th ed., p. 1028.

1998 • Preston Davis became the first minority president of the ABC-TV. The Norfolk, Virginia, native was named president of Broadcast Operations and Engineering in New York City.

Sources: *Jet* 94 (13 July 1998): 10; *Who's Who among African Americans,* 14th ed., p. 325.

1999 • Deval Patrick (1956–) was named general counsel and vice president of Texaco, Inc., and became the company's first black vice president. The company, headquartered in White Plains, New York, received national attention on November 4, 1994, when the *New York Times* made public an audiotape containing racially disparaging remarks by company officials, including a reference to black employees as "black jelly beans." The black employees of the company filed a racial discrimination suit against the company—the largest ever. On November 15, 1996, the company agreed to a $176.1 million settlement and to establish an external task force to monitor its diversity program. Patrick, then the U.S. Justice Department's civil rights enforcer and chair of a task force overseeing the company's progress in race relations, was named a company official. He was born in Chicago and graduated from Harvard College and then Harvard Law School. He was law clerk to Judge Stephen Reinhardt of the U.S. Court of Appeals, Ninth Circuit; assistant counsel for the NAACP Legal Defense and Education Fund; and then partner at Hill and Barlow law firm. President Bill Clinton on February 1, 1994, nominated Patrick to the post of assistant attorney general for civil rights; he was confirmed on March 17, 1994. While in this role, his department settled a racial discrimination lawsuit against Denny's restaurant.

Sources: *African American Almanac,* 8th ed, 2000, pp. 78–79; *Jet* 95 (18 January 1999): 10; *Contemporary Black Biography,* vol. 12, 1996, pp. 161–65.

1999 • MaryAnn Johnson (1948–) was promoted to director of TV Music Administration for Twentieth Century Fox Film Corporation in Los Angeles, becoming the first black woman executive in the department. Born in Memphis, she completed her education at Griggs Business College in 1967. Her positions with Twentieth Century Fox Film Corporation included manager and later associate director of TV music administration.

Sources: *Jet* 96 (4 October 1999): 20; *Who's Who among African Americans,* 14th ed., p. 698.

1999 • When named vice president of human resources at MGM Grand Detroit Casino, Lisa J. Lindsay Wicker became the first black woman to hold the position at the casino. Her responsibilities included recruitment, benefits, career development, and community affairs.

Sources: *Jet* 96 (14 June 1999): 24; *Who's Who among African Americans,* 14th ed., p. 1385.

1999 • Joset Wright became the first black president of Ameritech Illinois. Based in Chicago, she was placed in charge of government, regulatory, and external relations in the state. Wright joined the company in 1987 and moved up to become vice president of procurement and property services in 1987. Her other positions with Ameritech included vice president and general counsel of its enhanced business services and vice president and general counsel of Ameritech Indiana. She also held a number of other legal positions. A resident of Evanston, Wright graduated from Denison University and received her law degree from Georgetown University Law Center.

Sources: *Jet* 96 (8 November 1999): 22.

2000 • Business executive and lawyer Kenneth I. Chenault (1952–) became president and chief operating officer of American Express, the first black to hold either position. In April 1999 his predecessor, Harvey Golub, declared Chenault as his CEO-designee, having tapped him two years early as president of the company. The appointment makes him one of the most visible and highest-ranking blacks in corporate America. Since 1981 when he joined the company, Chenault has held a number of high positions with American Express. These include vice president of merchandise services and then senior vice president and general manager of the division, and top positions in the Platinum/Gold Card Division, the Personal Care Division, the Consumer Card and Financial Services Group, and American Express Travel Related Services. Born in Hempstead, New York, Chenault graduated from Bowdin College and then Harvard Law School. From 1977 to 1979 he was associated with the corporate law firm Rogers & Wells in New York City, and later joined the business consulting firm Bain & Company in Boston before leaving the firm in 1981 for American Express.

Sources: *Contemporary Black America,* vol. 4, pp. 38–41; *Jet* 91 (17 March 1997): 8–9; Smith, *Notable Black American Men,* pp. 191–93; Hoekstra, "Power Under Pressure," *Northwest Airlines World Traveler* (March 2001): 36–40.

2000 • The Greater Columbus Chamber of Commerce elected its first black chairman, Alex Shumate. Shumate, managing partner with Squire, Sanders & Dempsey, an international law firm in Columbus, was responsible for working with local businesses to strengthen economic development in central Ohio.

Sources: *Jet* 97 (5 June 2000): 33.

2000 • Myrtle Stephens Potter (1958–) became the first black woman to head a department in a major pharmaceutical business when she was named president of the Bristol-Myers Squibb U.S. Cardiovascular/Metabolics business. Born in Las Cruces, New Mexico, she graduated from the University of Chicago in 1980. After serving as a marketing intern with IBM, she held a variety of positions with such firms as Procter & Gamble, Merck Sharp & Dohme, and Astra/Merck.

Sources: *Ebony* 55 (May 2000): 10; *Who's Who among African Americans,* 26th ed., p. 1006.

2001 • Lawyer, political advisor, and corporate executive Richard Dean Parsons (1948–) was named chief executive officer of AOL-Time Warner and became the first black to head the world's largest media conglomerate. He took office on May 16, 2001. He was chief executive officer and chair of the Time Warner Inc. board for four years and then on October 1, 1995, was named president of the leading media and entertainment conglomerate in the world at that time. He was its first black president. With the appointment he became one of the highest-ranking blacks in corporate America. He guided the company into greater prosperity in 2000 when it merged with America Online. Parsons grew up in Queens, New York, and graduated from the University of Hawaii and Union University's Albany Law School. In 1971 he joined New York governor Nelson Rockefeller as assistant counsel. During Rockefeller's term as vice president, Parsons served as general counsel and associate director of the White House Domestic Council. In 1977 he joined the law firm Patterson, Belknap, Webb & Tyler and two years later was named a managing partner. He was one of New York mayor Rudolph W. Giuliani's first-term campaign team members and in 2001 became a member of Mayor-elect Michael R. Bloomberg's transition team. Earlier in 2001 President George W. Bush appointed Parsons to co-chair, with former U.S. Senator Daniel Patrick Moynihan, a commission to recommend changes in the country's Social Security program.

Sources: *Contemporary Black Biography,* vol. 11, pp. 185–88; *Jet* 87 (14 November 1994): 24; *New York Times* (6 December 2001); *New Yorker* (29 October 2001): 58–61; Salzman, *Encyclopedia of African-American Culture and History,* Supplement, pp. 214–15.

2001 • The first woman and the first black senior vice president of Aerospace's Engineering and Technology Group was Wanda M. Austin. Born in New York City, she received her bachelor's degree from Franklin & Marshall College in 1975 and her master's degree from the University of Pittsburgh in 1977. In 1987 Austin received a doctorate from the University of Southern California. Since 1979 she has been employed with the Aerospace Corporation. Before her promotion to senior vice president, she was general manager of the firm.

Sources: *Jet* 100 (24 September 2001): 21; *Who's Who among African Americans,* 26th ed., p. 49.

2002 • Developer R. Donahue Peebles became the first black to develop and own a major convention/resort hotel. The 422-room Royal Palm Crowne Plaza, reportedly built at the cost of $84 million, opened on May 15, after a two-year delay. Donahue, a former Washington resident, relocated to Miami Beach in 1996. He bought a dilapidated Art Deco hotel and was awarded a municipal bid to erect another hotel adjacent to an oceanfront lot. His new venture came as activists, city officials, and lodging executives reached a settlement over their disagreement, at the end of a three-year black tourism boycott of South Florida. The new hotel committed itself to hiring minorities to comprise about half of its staff and at least a quarter of senior management. Peebles is president and chief executive officer of Peebles Atlantic Development Corporation, based in Miami.

Sources: *Jet* 101 (3 June 2002): 22; *Tennessean* (15 May 2000).

2002 • The first black to wholly own a national casino company, the Majestic Star Casino in Gary Indiana, was businessman Don H. Barden (1943–2011). His company also acquired three Fitzgerald casinos located in Tunica, Mississippi; Black Hawk, Colorado; and Las Vegas, Nevada.

Sources: *Jet* 101 (7 January 2002): 33–34.

2002 • Frank M. Clark was promoted to president of the Chicago-based ComED, becoming the first black to hold that post at the electric utility company. He joined ComEd in 1966 as mailroom clerk. He serves also as senior vice president of Exelon Corporation, ComEd's parent company. Exelon oversees the delivery of electricity in northern Illinois, serving over 3.4 million customers.

Sources: *Jet* 101 (7 January 2002): 20.

2007? • James Moss became the first black American to head U.S. Global Marketing Group, the world's largest marketing alliance. He provides marketing strategies in business and is a member of a network of marketing professionals and service providers nationwide.

He also represents alliance members in Atlanta, New York, California, Nevada, and Hawaii in their efforts to establish new initiatives.

Sources: *Jet* 111 (16 April 2007): 31.

2008 • Named managing partner of the Washington, D.C., office of the International law firm Reed Smith, A. Scott Bolden is the first black to hold that post and to be named managing partner. Reed Smith is one of the fifteen largest firms in the world. Bolden continues his active practice and focuses on civil and criminal defense litigation.

Sources: *Jet* 113 (30 June 2008): 26.

2009 • Ursula Burns (1958–), president of Xerox Corporation, became the company's chief executive officer on July 1 and the first black woman to head the company. Xerox, the printer- and copier-maker, is the largest company in the United States to be headed by a black woman. She is also the first black female CEO of a Fortune 500 company and the first of her race and gender to run an S&P 100 company, with sales of $17.6 billion in 2008. Burns is the middle of three children of a single mother who worked to support her family by taking in ironing and babysitting in a Manhattan housing project. A graduate of Polytechnic Institute of New York University, Burns interned at Xerox while completing her master's degree in mechanical engineering at Columbia University. At Xerox she quickly distinguished herself by multitasking successfully and flagging problems that she observed. She helped lead the push for color copying and focused on improving customer service and the company's financial health. Her rise to the top reflected Xerox's commitment to gender and racial diversity. "I'm in this job because I believe I earned it through hard work and high performance…" she said. "I went to work for a company that was openly seeking to diversify its workforce. So I imagine race and gender got the hiring guy's attention. And then the rest was really up to me." In 2010, Burns and TV mogul Oprah Winfrey were listed on Forbes magazine's 50 Most Powerful Women in Business, an honor they have held for several years.

Ursula Burns

Sources: *Business Week* (8 June 2009): 5–6, 18–21; *Jet* 112 (22 October 2007): 26; 115 (15 January 2009): 11.

2011 • Kenneth C. Frazier (1954–) became the first black chief executive officer and president of Merck & Co., the nation's second largest pharmaceutical company. He joined Merck in 1992 in its public affairs division and moved up the corporate ladder. Now he sits on the company's board. The Philadelphia native holds degrees from Pennsylvania State University and Harvard Law School. He volunteers for organizations that serve the underprivileged.

Sources: Beighley, email to the author, 11 May 2011; "Kenneth C. Frazier," http://blackhis tory.psu.edu/timeline/kenneth_c._frazier_ba_lib_1975_becomes_the_ceo_and_president_ of_merck_co.

Publishing

1938 • John H. Johnson (1918–2005), the founder of *Ebony* (1945) and *Jet* (1951), was the first black named as one of the country's "Ten Outstanding Young Men" by the United States Junior Chamber of Commerce. This was the first of many awards for Johnson. In 1972 he became the first black to receive the Henry Johnson Fisher Award from the Magazine Publishers Association, the most prestigious honor in that field. He was also the first black inducted into the Arkansas Business Hall of Fame in 2001. Johnson was born poor in Arkansas City, Arkansas, and moved to Chicago during the Great Depression. He attended the University of Chicago part-time while he worked at Supreme Life Insurance Company. Between 1943 and 1957, however, he had little contact with Supreme Life. The new black consciousness of the World War II era stimulated Johnson to begin a publication to show the public the achievements of blacks; he founded the Negro Digest Publishing Company and began issuing *Negro Digest* in November 1942. The magazine grew and established new records as a black journal. Johnson saw a market for another magazine—

one modeled after *Life* magazine. On November 1, 1945, he founded *Ebony;* the magazine's first run of 25,000 copies quickly sold out. In 1949 Negro Digest Publishing Company became Johnson Publishing Company. Johnson's company published a number of other magazines, including *Jet,* which was launched on November 1, 1951, and also had a book-publishing arm. The company later diversified and established Fashion Fair Cosmetics subsidiary and entered the television market, sponsoring such programs as "Ebony Music Awards," "American Black Achievement Award," and "Ebony/Jet Showcase." Johnson rose from poverty to become a wealthy entrepreneur with an international reputation.

Sources: *Ebony Success Library,* vol. 2, p. 132–37; *The Negro Almanac,* pp. 1261–62; Smith, *Notable Black American Men,* pp. 630–34; *Who's Who among African Americans,* 14th ed., p. 693.

1960 • Charles F. Harris (1935–), an editor at Doubleday, established Zenith Books, the first series to present minority histories for the general and educational markets. Harris was born in Portsmouth, Virginia. A graduate of Virginia State College in 1955, Harris worked for the publishing firms Doubleday, John Wiley, and Random House before joining the Howard University Press in 1971.

Sources: *Ebony* 20 (March 1965): 6; *Ebony Success Library,* vol. 1, p. 143; *Who's Who among African Americans,* 26th ed., p. 536.

1970 • Earl G. Graves (1935–) founded a new publishing venture, Earl Graves Ltd., located in New York City, and in November became editor and publisher of the first African American business journal, *Black Enterprise.* The magazine turned a profit by its tenth issue. Graves established BCI Marketing, a development and market research firm to examine the buying patterns of potential readers and then enticed general and black businesses to subscribe to and advertise in his journal. *Black Enterprise* publishes articles on a variety of issues including economics, science, technology, health, and politics. Graves had worked in a variety of occupations, including administrative assistant on the staff of Senator Robert F. Kennedy. In 1968 he founded Earl G. Graves Associates, a management consulting firm specializing in urban affairs and economic development. The experiences of his company propelled him to study black-owned businesses in Caribbean countries and to develop a business plan and editorial prospectus for the business periodical that he envisioned. In 1970, with a $150,000 loan from the Manhattan Capital Corporation of Chase Manhattan Bank, he began his publishing venture. Graves was born in Brooklyn and graduated from Morgan State University.

Sources: *The Black New Yorkers,* p. 348; *Contemporary Black Biography,* vol. 1, pp. 95–96; Smith, *Notable Black American Men,* pp. 475–78.

1979 • Dolores Duncan Wharton (1927–) was the first black and the first woman on the board of Gannett Company. She is also the first black and first woman director for the Kellogg Foundation and Phillips Petroleum. Wharton was the founder and president of the Fund for Corporate Initiatives based in Cooperstown, New York. The New York City native graduated from Chicago State University. She founded the Fund for Corporate Initiatives Inc. and became its chair and corporate director. She is married to educator and organization executive Clifton R. Wharton Jr.

Sources: *Blackbook,* 1984, p. 79; *Jet* 56 (12 April 1979): 21; *Who's Who among African Americans,* 14th ed., p. 1371.

Real Estate

1866 • Biddy Mason (1818–1891) was the first known black woman property owner in Los Angeles, California. Born into slavery in Georgia or Mississippi and named Bridget, she and her master, Robert Smith, took the strenuous journey first to the Utah Territory and then to California, where Mason legally gained her freedom on January 21, 1856. All members of her family were freed as well. Mason worked as nurse and midwife— as she had done en route to the West—and saved her money. Her earnings and careful investment became the foundation that enabled her grandson Robert to be called the richest black in Los Angeles around 1900. A very religious and charitable woman, Mason opened her house for the establishment of the first African Methodist Episcopal church in the city in 1872. She is also said to have opened the first day care nursery for homeless community children.

Sources: Katz, *The Black West*, pp. 129–30; Smith, *Notable Black American Women*, pp. 732–34; *Sepia* (April 1960): 71.

1905 • Phillip A. Payton Jr. (1876–1917) was the first black to open Harlem to black residents. Payton was born in Westfield, Massachusetts, and graduated from Livingstone College in Salisbury, North Carolina. He settled in New York City. He held several odd jobs, including that as janitor in a real estate firm around the turn of the century. This gave him his first exposure to the real estate business. With a partner, he opened Brown and Payton Realty Company in October 1900, but the business was short-lived. He continued to market himself as a real estate agent and in 1901 and began to manage properties particularly for black tenants. He founded the Afro-American Realty Company in 1904 and centered its activities in Harlem. He persuaded persons who had overbuilt apartments to rent to blacks. The company operated in the midst of turmoil and became riddled with internal dissension involving Payton and stockholders. In 1907 Payton was arrested on fraud charges concerning financial statements, but was soon cleared. By 1908 Payton controlled more than a half-million-dollars worth of property in New York City. Unfortunately, he spent money as quickly as he made it, and, after his company closed in 1908, he went broke.

Sources: *Black Enterprise* 6 (June 1976): 126–27; *Encyclopedia of Black America*, p. 417; Lewis, *When Harlem Was in Vogue*, pp. 25–26; Ingham and Feldman, *African-American Business Leaders*, pp. 517–25.

Retail

1834 • David Ruggles (1810–1849) was the first known black bookseller and the first black to have an imprint in a book, when he published *The "Extinguisher" Extinguished* in 1834. From 1829 to 1833 Ruggles was a grocer and butter merchant in New York. He opened his bookstore the next year, selling anti-slavery works and stationery and engaging in a variety of publishing tasks, including the composition of letters for those who were unable to write. His New York City shop was unfortunately burned out by a white mob in September 1835, fueled no doubt by his activities as an active abolitionist and worker on the Underground Railroad. The destruction did not stop Ruggles. He continued to live at the same address and to maintain his status as an anti-slavery advocate and agent for abolitionist papers. He was a secretary of the New York Vigilance Committee and was noteworthy for his aggressive and daring activities on behalf of former slaves. When his health began to fail, Ruggles spent his last years as a hydrotherapist and is believed to have been the first black hydrotherapist. He was arrested twice, once for assault and later in connection with a case in which a former slave was accused of theft. In the latter case, which occurred during 1839, he stood accused of a major crime for seventeen months before he was discharged without a trial.

Sources: Logan and Winston, *Dictionary of American Negro Autobiography*, pp. 536–38; Smith, *Notable Black American Men*, pp. 1034–35.

1950s • Alvenia Fulton (1907?–1999), trailblazing nutritionist, became the first black to establish a health food store and vegetarian restaurant in Chicago. After opening her businesses in the late 1950s, she continued to work in Fultonia Health and Fasting Institute until illness in 1999 forced her to retire. Fulton encouraged what she called therapeutic healing and recommended that her clients cleanse the body, allowing the body to cleanse itself. Born in middle Tennessee, her parents, Richard and Mahala Moody, taught her the importance of natural foods, herbs, and the various cures of nature. She graduated from Lincoln College of Naturopathy and Natural Medicines in Indianapolis, with an N.D. and a Ph.D. degree. She became the first woman to enroll and graduate from Payne Theological Seminary in Birmingham, Alabama; then she pastored St. John's AME Church in

The First Black Millionaire

In 1890 Thomy Lafon (1810–1893) was thought to be the first black millionaire. He was a New Orleans real estate speculator and moneylender. He was recognized as a community activist and philanthropist before the Civil War, when he was still a young man. He was listed as a merchant in the New Orleans City Directory in 1842; in 1868 the directory listed him as a broker, and he was considered the city's second leading black broker until 1870. As his wealth grew, he gave freely to those less fortunate, including religious and anti-slavery causes, and supported the Lafon Orphan Boys' Asylum and the Home for Aged Colored Men and Women, both of which he founded. The Thomy Lafon School, dedicated in 1898, made him the first black man and the second black person in New Orleans to have a school named for him. The Wall of Fame at the 1939–40 New York World's Fair listed his name along with those of other blacks, Native Americans, and foreign-born Americans who were notable contributors to American progress and culture. He lived frugally, and despite his philanthropic gifts, his estate was valued at nearly half a million dollars. Lafon's will provided for his relatives and friends, but he left the bulk of his estate to charity.

Sources: Logan and Winston, *Dictionary of American Biography*, pp. 379–80; *Dictionary of Black Culture*, p. 261; *Efforts for Social Betterment Among Negro Americans*, pp. 40–41; Smith, *Notable Black American Men*, pp. 692–93.

Louisville, St. Stephens AME church in Birmingham, and later St. Johns AME church in Manhattan, Kansas. Fulton was the author of *The Fasting Power* and *The Nutrition Bible*.

Sources: *Jet* 95 (15 March 1999): 22.

1968 • Leon Howard Sullivan (1922–2001) developed the first major black-sponsored shopping center, Progress Plaza, in Philadelphia, Pennsylvania. This center grew out of an investment group he founded (Zion Investment Associates) that built inner city housing and shopping centers and also established the first black-owned aerospace supply agency, Progress Aerospace Enterprises. He was a Baptist minister in Philadelphia for more than thirty-eight years, during which time he was active in civil rights and urban affairs, as well as the development of black business. A childhood experience with segregation is said to have had a profound effect on him. This experience and the influence of the grandmother who raised him are likely to have contributed to his strong civil rights views. General Motors recognized his business acumen when, on January 4, 1971, he became the first black chosen to sit on the GM board. Sullivan spent two years in New York under the tutelage of Adam Clayton Powell before moving to Philadelphia. While there, he was hired by Bell Telephone Company as their first black coin-box operator. He also met and was influenced by A. Philip Randolph, president of the first major black American union, the Brotherhood of Sleeping Car Porters. Born in Charleston, West Virginia, Sullivan graduated from West Virginia State College (B.A., 1943), Union Theological Seminary (1954), Columbia University (M.A., 1947), and Virginia Union University (D.D.).

Sources: *Current Biography, 1969*, pp. 419–21; *Ebony Success Library*, vol. 2, pp. 248–51; *Encyclopedia of Black America*, p. 811; Hornsby, *Chrononolgy of African-American History*, pp. 158, 250–51; *Negro Almanac*, pp. 61, 618, 1417; Obituary, *Who's Who among African Americans*, 14th ed., p. 1477; Smith, *Notable Black American Men*, pp. 1089–92.

1968 • Frederick D. Wilson Jr. (1921–) was the first black vice president of Macy's. Wilson had joined the retail chain in 1948, after distinguished service in the wartime army, followed by a master's degree in business administration from Harvard University.

Sources: *Ebony Success Library*, vol. 2, pp. 288–91.

1968 • The nation's first black-owned McDonalds opened in Chicago, with pioneering businessman Herman Petty as owner. The historic building was rebuilt and reopened on its original site, at 65th Street and Stony Island Avenue, and had a grand reopening in 2008. Yolanda Travis, owner and operator of the rebuilt structure, said "Breathing new life into this historic landmark franchise demonstrates McDonald's commitment to education and employment in our community."

Sources: *Jet* 113 (11 February 2003): 51.

1975 • Wally "Famous" Amos (1937–) was the first black to open a cookie-only retail store; his was the first black-owned gourmet cookie company to build a national following. Amos was born in Tallahassee, Florida, but by age twelve he relocated to New York City where he lived with his Aunt Della. She loved to cook, often preparing her special chocolate chip cookie for him. He dropped out of high school and joined the U.S. Air Force, receiving his general education diploma while in service. After returning to civilian life, Amos held a variety of jobs, including mail clerk for the William Morris Company in New York. The company made him its first black agent and executive vice president with responsibility for booking such acts as the Temptations, the Supremes, and Marvin Gaye. He left the company in 1967 and moved to Los Angeles where he worked on his own as a talent agent. To supplement his income, he used his Aunt Della's recipe and began baking chocolate chip cookies that he distributed to his clients and friends. He borrowed $25,000 from a number of people, including Marvin Gaye, and opened a small shop on Sunset Boulevard in Hollywood. His shop became the first of its kind dedicated to chocolate chip gourmet cookies. Two years after he founded Famous Amos Chocolate Chip Cookies, the company was grossing two million dollars a year. His profits grew and his cookies were nationally distributed. Although he made millions in his business, by 1985 the company began to report a loss in revenue. Rather than lose the company, Amos sold the controlling share to the Bass Brothers of Fort Worth, Texas. He remained on the company's board as vice chairman, but later was no more than a company spokesman. He left the company in 1989. In 1992 he started another company, The Uncle Noname Cookie Company and offered five varieties of gourmet Cookies. He was prevented from using the Famous Amos name.

Sources: *Jet* 72 (30 March 1987): 6; *Sepia* 27 (June 1978): 22–28; *Time* 109 (13 June 1977): 72, 76; *Contemporary Black Biography*, vol. 9, pp. 5–7; *Who's Who among African Americans*, 14th ed., p. 26.

1977 • Jesse Hill Jr. (1927–) was the first black person appointed to the board of directors of Rich's department store in Atlanta.

Sources: Smith, *Notable Black American Men*, pp. 549–52; *Contemporary Black Biography*, vol. 13, pp. 103–05; *Who's Who among African Americans*, 26th ed., p. 583.

1982 • Sybil Collins Mobley (1925–) was the first black woman member of the board of Sears, Roebuck and Company. The Shreveport, Louisiana, native graduated from Bishop College in Marshall, Texas, and Wharton School of Finance and Commerce at the University of Pennsylvania, where she received a master's degree in business administration. In 1964 she received a doctorate from the University of Illinois. Mobley taught in the business school of Florida Agricultural and Mechanical College (later Florida A & M University), where she became a dean in 1974. She has led the business school to national prominence. At first only a few companies recruited from the school's business department, but she was able to convince a number of Fortune 500 companies to recruit her students. She groomed her students for success and taught them what it takes to succeed in corporate America. Mobley has become highly respected in the business community and is sought out for her expertise. Her board memberships include Anheuser-Busch Company, Hershey Foods Corporation, Southwestern Bell Corporation, and Champion International Corporation. She holds a number of honorary degrees, including those from Wharton School of Finance and Hamilton College.

Sources: *Jet* 62 (30 August 1982): 38; *Who's Who Among Black Americans*, 26th ed., p. 889; Smith, *Notable Black American Women*, Book II, pp. 480–82.

1983 • Ben F. Branch (1924–1987) was the president of the nation's first black-owned soft drink company, Dr. Branch Products, in Chicago, Illinois. Branch was also a civil rights activist and a musician. He combined these interests by organizing the SCLC Operation Breadbox Orchestra, the world's only gospel orchestra.

Sources: *Jet* 72 (14 September 1987): 55.

1986 • Eldo Perry was the first black vice president/region manager in St. Louis, Missouri, for Church's Fried Chicken.

Sources: *Jet* 69 (24 February 1986): 20.

1996 • Coleman Hollis Peterson (1948–), executive vice president of the People Division of Wal-Mart Stores, Inc., became a member of the fifth class of Fellows of the National Academy of Human Resources in New York, and was the first black accepted in the prestigious institution in human resources. Peterson's responsibilities at Wal-Mart include directing human resources and setting company personnel direction and strategies for over 500,000 associates internationally. In 1976 he initiated one of the company's first minority networks to help develop and retain minority executives. He was a key sponsor of the Wal-Mart Women in Leadership Group. Born in Birmingham, Alabama, Peterson graduated from Loyola University with a bachelor's degree in 1972 and a master's degree in 1977. In 1998 the Black Retail Action Group named him Executive of the Year.

Sources: *Jet* 91 (9 December 1996): 33; *Who's Who among African Americans,* 26th ed., p. 987.

1997 • The first black member of the board of directors for Profitt's Inc. was Julius W. "Dr. J." Erving (1950–). Based in Knoxville, Tennessee, the company had some 176 stores in twenty-four states. A former professional basketball star, Erving played with the Virginia Squires, the New York Nets, and the Philadelphia 76ers. Near the end of his basketball career, Erving purchased shares in the New York Coca-Cola Bottling Company and three years later purchased the larger Philadelphia Coca-Cola Bottling Company, the world's fifteenth largest bottling facility. He and partner Bruce Llewellyn shared one of the world's largest black-owned businesses. He was elected to the Basketball Hall of Fame and in 1996 was voted one of the top fifty players in NBA history. In 1997 Erving became executive vice president of the Orlando Magic professional basketball franchise.

Sources: *Contemporary Black Biography,* vol. 18, pp. 35–38; *Jet* 92 (20 October 1997): 39; Smith, *Notable Black American Men,* pp. 375–78.

1998 • When Katherine Johnson opened her own Harley-Davidson motorcycle dealership in Horn Lake, Mississippi, on December 12, she became the first black woman licensed for the dealership in the company's ten-year history. Her business, Harley-Davidson of Desoto County, Inc., serves a variety of customers, including doctors, lawyers, and executives. As she searched for a new business venture, a black recruiter at Harley's Milwaukee headquarters encouraged the fifty-year-old mother and grandmother of seven to consider the motorcycle business. Her store includes a full-service repair shop and sells clothing and accessories that bear the Harley logo.

Sources: *Jet* 97 (3 April 2000): 23–24.

1999 • Maytag Corporation, one of the nation's largest appliance makers, appointed Lloyd David Ward (1949–) chairman and chief executive officer, making him the first black American to hold the post and the second to head a major United States corporation. He took over the reins in August but resigned fifteen months later, citing differences with the company's directors. Like other big appliance makers, Maytag's profits began to erode from its peak in July. Ward became chairman and chief executive of iMotors, an Internet start-up company that sells used cars online. He left that position in May 2001 to head the U.S. Olympic Committee. He has held positions with Procter & Gamble, Pepsico, and Frito-Lay. Ward was born in Romulus, Michigan, and graduated from Michigan State University (B.S., 1970) and Xavier University (M.B.A, 1984). He is a black belt in karate.

Sources: *New York Times,* (10 November 2000, 7 February 2001); *Who's Who among African Americans,* 26th ed., p. 1283; *Jet* 100 (3 December 2001): 48.

1999 • When Paula A. Sneed (1947–) was named chief marketing officer for Kraft Foods in Northfield, Illinois, she became the first black to hold this position at the company. She was made responsible for media services, advertising services, ethnic marketing, and other operations. Sneed was born in Everett, Massachusetts. She graduated from Simmons College in 1960 with a bachelor's degree. In 1977 she received a master's degree in business administration from Harvard University. She has held a number of positions, including education supervisor and female coordinator for Outreach Program for Problem Drinkers (1971–82) and program coordinator, Boston Sickle Cell Center (1972–75). Sneed joined General Foods Corporation in 1977 and held several posts before being promoted to executive vice president and general manger of the Desserts Division (1991–95). Since joining Kraft Foods North America, she was senior vice president of marketing services (1995–99) and then she was named chief marketing officer in 1999. Sneed was also president of Kraft's E-Commerce Division. In 2005, she became executive vice president for the firm Global Market Resources and Initiatives. Highly recognized for her achievements, Sneed was named in 1991 and 1997 by *Black Enterprise* magazine one of the 21 Most Influential African American Women in Corporate America. In 1994 *Executive Female* named her one of 1992 America's 50 Most Powerful Women Managers. Other honors followed.

Sources: *Jet* 96 (7 June 1999): 32; *Who's Who among African Americans,* 26th ed., p. 1158; *Contemporary Black Biography,* vol. 18, pp. 172–74.

1999 • Brentwood Baptist Church in Houston became the first church in the nation to receive a McDonald's hamburger franchise. McDonald's approved the church's request in May, when the Joe Ratliffe Lifelong Learning Center, named for its senior pastor, was under construction. The new restaurant and drive-through windows were allotted 3,000 square feet for operations. Senior pastor Joe Ratliffe (1950–) conceived of the idea after observing that McDonald's was establishing restaurants in gasoline stations, schools, and hospitals. Church deacon Ernest Redmond, who owns four McDonald's restaurants in the Houston area, assisted in developing a business plan to present to the company. Redmond and the church established a limited partnership that calls for him to oversee the business through his franchise license. The church receives 100 percent of the profits. The restaurant has become popular with the church's more than 10,000 active members who attend the three services, Bible study, Boy Scout meetings, and other church functions. A high school and elementary school in the vicinity also support the restaurant.

Sources: *Black Enterprise* 32 (September 2001): 24.

2000 • Don Thompson became the first black American president of McDonald's Midwest division located in Oak Brook, Illinois. His responsibilities include working with the company's U.S. leadership team to forge new growth. Thompson, a Chicago native, graduated from Purdue University with a bachelor's degree in electrical engineering.

Sources: "Speaking of People," *Ebony* 56 (February 2001): 10; *Jet* 98 (4 December 2000): 22.

2012 • Wal-Mart Stores Inc., the world's biggest retailer, named Rosalind Brewer (1963–) as CEO and president of Sam's Club, making her the first woman and the first black CEO of one of its business units. Previously, Brewer held a number of executive positions at Kimberly-Clark Corporation.

Sources: Brewer, "Named First Woman, African-American, CEO of Sam's Club," http://www.huffingtonpost.com/2012/01/20/rosalind-brewer-sams-club_n_1219076.html, accessed September 13, 2012.

Stock Brokerage

1967 • Pioneering entrepreneur and educator William H. Ross III (1925?–2000) became Maryland's first black stockbroker and was one of fifty black registered representatives in the United States. Earlier he was also the first black sales representative for Gunther Brewing Company in Baltimore. A pioneer educator as well, Ross became the first black teacher in Baltimore City College's history department.

Sources: *Jet* 97 (13 March 2000): 54.

1970 • On February 13, 1970, Joseph L. Searles III (1940–) became the first black member of the New York Stock Exchange. The former director of local business development for New York City, Searles began training as a floor partner for the Newburger firm, Loeb & Company. He graduated from Kansas State University and later was vice president of Manufacturers Hanover Trust Company's public finance department. Searles served in several federal, state, and municipal agencies with an interest in urban affairs and economic development.

Sources: *Black Enterprise* 1 (October 1970): 19; *Jet* 37 (19 February 1970): 20; 69 (17 February 1986): 22; *Negro Almanac,* p. 1430; *Statistical Record of Black America,* p. 474.

1971 • On June 24, 1971, the brokerage of Daniels and Bell was the first black company to become a member of the New York Stock Exchange. The firm was founded by Willie L. Daniels (1937–), and Travers Bell Jr. (1942-1988).

Sources: *Ebony Success Library,* vol. 1, p. 86; *Negro Almanac, 1976,* p. 1024; *Sepia* 21 (June 1972): 67–70.

1972 • Jerome Heartwell "Brud" Holland (1916–1985) was the first black to serve on the board of the New York Stock Exchange, taking his seat in 1972. Holland had been an All-American football player at Cornell University, New York, where he took his B.S. (1939) and M.S. (1941) degrees, excelling in academics and athletics. He was the first black player on the Cornell football team. He was also to become Cornell's first black member of the Board of Trustees. These achievements at Cornell are particularly noteworthy since Holland was initially denied admission to the institution on the grounds that his academic credentials were not satisfactory and was faced with racial discrimination once he was admitted. After Cornell, Holland did some college teaching at Lincoln University in Pennsylvania, served as a director of personnel for a Pennsylvania firm, and taught and coached football at Tennessee Agricultural and Industrial State University in Nashville (now Tennessee State University). While working in Nashville, he was also pursuing study toward a doctoral degree at the University of Pennsylvania. He received his degree in 1950, and in 1953 became president of Delaware State College (now University), serving from 1953 to 1960. He left Delaware State to become president of Hampton Institute, (now University) where he served from 1960 to 1970, when he became ambassador to Sweden. He remained in this post until 1972. Upon his return to the United States, Holland served on many corporate boards and participated actively in community organizations. The high school football stadium in his Auburn, New York, hometown was named after him and is only one of the many honors that recognized his service and leadership to education, corporate America, and the country.

Sources: *Ebony Success Library,* vol. 2, pp. 104–7; *Encyclopedia of Black America,* p. 443; *Jet* 68 (6 May 1985): 54; Smith, *Notable Black American Men,* pp. 558–60.

1984 • Christine Bell was the first black woman financial futures specialist for Prudential-Bache Securities in Chicago.

Sources: *Jet* 66 (26 March 1984): 38–39.

1995 • Ariel Mutual Funds in Chicago named Bert Norman Mitchell (1938–) chair of the board of trustees, making him the first black American ever to chair a public mutual fund. Mitchell was chair and chief executive officer of Mitchell, Tutus & Company, an accounting firm in Chicago. Mitchell graduated from City College of New York in 1963 and in 1968 received a master's degree in business administration from the school. He also attended the Harvard Graduate School of Business in 1985. He has held positions with the Ford Foundation, J. K. Lasser & Company, Interam Insurance Company, and Lucas Tucker & Company. In 1973 Mitchell founded and became chairman of Mitchell & Titus, LLP, in New York City. He has served on the board of directors for the Harvard Business School, the Association of Black Accountants, and the Consolidated Corporate Fund for Lincoln

The First Black Company on the Stock Exchange

In 1971 Johnson Products became the first black firm to be listed on a major stock exchange when it was listed on the American Stock Exchange. The firm was founded by George Ellis Johnson Sr. (1927–) in 1954. Johnson was the first black elected a director of the board of Commonwealth Edison, in 1971. Johnson was born in Richton, Mississippi, to sharecroppers. He relocated to Chicago with his mother, and attended Wendell Phillips High School until he was forced to drop out to help support his family. He joined Fuller Products and later became a production chemist, developing hair relaxer for men. In 1954 Johnson borrowed $250 from a finance company to establish Johnson products. Later he and his wife turned the company into a multimillion-dollar enterprise known for innovations in the beauty care products industry. In the mid–1980s he lost the company in a divorce settlement.

Sources: *Ebony Success Library,* vol. 2, pp. 126–31; *Encyclopedia of Black America,* p. 473; *Jet* 69 (18 November 1985): 16; *Who's Who among African Americans,* 26th ed., p. 669.

Center. His honors include the Alumni Achievement Award from Harvard Business School. He has published over fifty articles in professional journals.

Sources: *Jet* 87 (1 May 1995): 20; *Who's Who among African Americans,* 26th ed., p. 883.

1996 • Ashanti Goldfields Company, Limited, based in Accra, Ghana, became the first African company in operation to be listed on the New York Stock Exchange. The company's shares were already on the Official List of the London Stock Exchange as well as the First List of the Ghana Stock Exchange.

Sources: *Jet* 89 (18 March 1996): 46.

1998 • Chapman Holdings, Inc., located in Baltimore, was the first black-owned securities brokerage firm to be publicly traded. Under the symbol CMAN, in February company president and chief executive officer Nathan A. Chapman Jr. (1957–) offered one million shares for public trading on the NASDAQ market, giving the firm an edge over any other black brokerage firm. The company pioneered in the Domestic Emergency Markets (DEM) investments strategy works in the interests of minorities and invested funds into U.S companies owned by blacks, Asian Americans, Latin and Hispanic Americans, and by women. Born in Baltimore, Chapman graduated from the University of Maryland at Baltimore County in 1979. He was a certified public accountant for Peat, Marwick & Mitchell accounting firm and later was a securities representative with Alex, Brown & Son, Inc., an investment banking firm. In 1986 he established The Chapman Company and its affiliates, Chapman Capital Management, Inc. His first account was Park's Sausage Company. The next year he began a U.S. Treasury money-market fund, the first mutual fund initiated and sold by a black-owned company. Chapman serves as chairman of the Board of Regents for the University System of Maryland.

Sources: *Contemporary Black Biography,* vol. 21, pp. 37–39; *Jet* 94 (27 July 1998): 23; *Who's Who among African Americans,* 26th ed., p. 228.

1999 • Radio One, founded by Catherine "Cathy" Liggins Hughes (1947–), became the first company headed by a black woman to be traded on the stock exchange. The company, which went public in May 1999, was the largest black-owned and operated broadcast company in America, owning twenty-six stations. According to a recent NAMME report, the network now has sixty-two stations and a current value of more than $2 billion. All of this growth has taken place since founder Hughes bought her first station in Washington, D.C., in 1980. The network has stations in Los Angeles, Detroit, Philadelphia, Atlanta, and over a dozen more major cities, but at last report had yet to tap Chicago and New York. Radio One concentrates on an urban-oriented format, offering a blend of music and talk. Hughes' son, Alfred C. Liggins, III, took over as CEO in 1999 after having managed the day-to-day operations since 1994; Hughes herself became chairperson of the board. The company targets its broadcasts to a primarily African American audience and has more than a thousand African American employees. Its urban-oriented format, however, gives it some crossover appeal. Radio One is recognized for its strong community involvement. Further growth is anticipated.

Sources: *Contemporary Black Biography*, vol. 27, pp. 87–89; *Ebony* 55 (May 2000): 102–5; *New York Times* Premium Archive, (25 December 2000).

2000 • Merrill Lynch chose Ernest Stanley O'Neal (1951–) to run its U.S. Private Client Group, and he became the first black person to run the nation's largest brokerage business. He is also the first person to hold that position that had not been a stockbroker. O'Neal, the oldest of four children, was born poor in eastern Alabama; his grandfather had been a slave. He studied in a one-room schoolhouse and also worked in the cotton fields alongside his family. When he was thirteen, the O'Neal family moved to a federal housing project in Atlanta and later on he worked in an automobile plant in Doraville, Georgia. He graduated from General Motors Institute, a cooperative college, working two years as foreman at Doraville, and then enrolled in the Harvard Business School, graduating with a master's degree in business administration. O'Neal joined General Motors' treasury office in New York and in the 1980s worked on some of the company's biggest financial deals. He left in 1987 for Wall Street, where he joined Merrill Lynch.

Sources: *New York Times* (29 October 2000); (25 July 2001).

2000 • Darien Dash (1972?–) founded Digital Mafia Entertainment, known as DME Interactive Holdings, the first new technology firm owned by a black from to be traded on Wall Street. With funds from a deal with Roc-A-Blok that he made with Columbia Records, as well as financial support from family and friends, he founded the company in 1994, running it from his bedroom. In June 1999 DME acquired the automobile leasing company Pride Automotive Group, and later in the year the company acquired the multimedia consulting firm Kathoderay. The U.S. Department of Commerce in 1999 recognized the company's success and named it the minority technology firm of the year. That same year the company partnered with Places of Color and provided low-cost Internet service to subscribers. In 2000 DME and Hewlett-Packard entered a project to sell personal computers for less than $250, to include free Internet access in New York and New Jersey. Dash was born in New York City and graduated from the University of Southern California. Before founding his own company, he was vice president of sales for Digital Music Xpress.

Sources: *Contemporary Black Biography*, vol. 29, pp. 47–49.

2005 • The first black president and CEO of Sears Holdings Inc. was Aylwin B. Lewis (1954-?). Sears Holdings, based at the Hoffman Estates in Illinois, operated about 3,800 Sears and Kmart stores in the United States and Canada. Lewis was a major player in Sears' merger with Kmart this year and, according to the company's chairman in 2008, he was committed to "Sears during a critical time in the company's history." He stepped down from the company's helm in 2008, as sales and profit continued to slump. Lewis is an MBA graduate of the University of Houston. His previous posts included that as director, CEO, and president of Kmart, and president and chief multibranding and operating officer of YUM! Brands Inc.

Sources: *Jet* 113 (18 February 2008): 16.

Transportation

1784 • Paul Cuffe (1759–1817) was the first black to sail as master of his own ship. His father was an Ashanti slave who was brought from Africa. His father's second owner was a Quaker, who freed the senior Cuffe three years after purchasing him. The freedman married a Native American woman, and Paul Cuffe was thus born free. He went to sea at age fourteen, working as a sailor. By 1777 he was involved with maritime trade as a blockade-runner. During the Revolutionary War, he was plagued by issues of taxation and was once imprisoned by the British for three months after they seized an American vessel. When the war ended, Cuffe broadened his seafaring activities and bought property from which he operated his business. By 1800 his investment in ships, a waterfront farm, and a windmill resulted in assets of nearly $10,000, which may have made him the wealthiest African American in the U.S. at the time. Cuffe launched his ship *Alpha* in 1806 and served as its captain. An American-imposed embargo on international trade with Europe led to his interest in Africa and abolition of slave trade. His Quaker heritage facilitated this interest as he worked with white Quaker abolitionist James Pemberton. Cuffe later developed trade with Sierra Leone, where he encouraged missionary work and colonization. His plans included carrying emigrants to Sierra Leone, and he launched the first black-led return to Africa in 1815. Although the voyage was successful, financial problems doomed his hope of making a yearly voyage. He tried to work with the newly formed white American Colonization Society. The organization seemed to attract persons who supported colonization for racist reasons and was condemned by black leaders in 1817, a few months before Cuffe's death. His name is sometimes given as Cuffee.

Sources: Logan and Winston, *Dictionary of American Negro Biography,* pp. 147–48; *Encyclopedia of Black America,* pp. 280–296; *Negro Almanac,* pp. 9, 209, 234; Smith, *Notable Black American Men,* pp. 241–43.

1831 • John Mashow was the first black to establish a prominent shipbuilding firm. He was active in South Dartmouth, Massachusetts, until shortly before the Civil War.

Sources: James, *The Real McCoy,* p. 33.

1866 • On February 12, the Chesapeake Marine Railway and Drydock Company of Baltimore, Maryland, was the first major black ship-fitting company. Organized by Isaac Myers, it was in business until 1884. The company was formed by and for black workers driven from longshoremen and caulkers' jobs by white strikers.

Sources: Logan and Winston, *Dictionary of American Negro Biography,* pp. 468–69; *Encyclopedia of Black America,* p. 201; Foner, *Organized Labor and the Black Worker,* pp. 22–23.

1979 • The Kent-Barry-Eaton Connection Railway Company was the first minority-owned company to operate a railroad. The line ran forty-two miles between Grand Rapids and Vermontville, Michigan.

Sources: *Jet* 56 (23 August 1979): 24.

1985 • Robert Joe Brown (1935–) was the first black member of the board of directors of the Norfolk Southern Railroad Company.

Sources: *Jet* 69 (2 December 1985): 18; *Who's Who among Black Americans,* 26th ed., p. 165.

1987 • Vander Brown Jr. was the first black to head a division of Greyhound Lines, Western Greyhound, one of the four regional divisions. Brown was born in Bakersfield, California, and had worked for the company for eighteen years.

Sources: *Jet* 72 (29 June 1987): 38–39.

CIVIL RIGHTS & PROTEST

Abolition

1644 • The first blacks emancipated in North America consisted of eleven men freed during the Dutch and Indian War. Their emancipation took place on February 25 at Fort Amsterdam, in the vicinity of Bowling Green, Kentucky.

Sources: "The Freedom Trail," www.nytimes.com/library/photos/021300freedom-trail.7 .html.

1688 • The Mennonite Quakers at Germantown, Pennsylvania, adopted and signed the first formal abolitionist document in United States history. After the Society of Friends declared that slavery violated the rights of man and was in opposition to Christianity, the Mennonite Anti-Slavery Resolution was approved by the group on February 18.

Sources: Garrett, *Famous First Facts about Negroes,* p. 1; Hornsby, *Chronology of African-American History,* p. 4; Kane, *Famous First Facts,* p. 598; *Negro Almanac,* p. 3.

1775 • Organized on April 14, 1775, the Pennsylvania Society for the Abolition of Slavery was the first abolition society. Its first president was John Baldwin. After reorganizing and adopting a new constitution, it was incorporated on December 8, 1775, as the Pennsylvania Society for Promoting the Abolition of Slavery, for the Relief of Free Negroes Unlawfully Held in Bondage, and for Improving the Condition of the African Race.

Sources: *Encyclopedia of Black America,* p. 789; Hornsby, *Chronology of African-American History,* p. 7; Kane, *Famous First Facts,* p. 1; *Negro Almanac,* pp. 5, 812.

1777 • Vermont became the first colony to abolish slavery on July 2, 1777. Although the results were gradual, by 1804 all states north of Delaware had taken action to abolish slavery.

Sources: Bennett, *Before the Mayflower,* p. 446; Hornsby, *Chronology of African-American History,* p. 8.

1793 • The first Fugitive Slave Act was passed by Congress on February 12, 1793. The law made it a crime to harbor a fugitive slave or to interfere with the slave's arrest. Penalties were levied against those who aided or abetted a slave's attempt to escape bondage.

Sources: Hornsby, *Chronology of African-American History,* p. 11; *Negro Almanac,* 5th ed., pp. 118–19.

113

Dates of Emancipation in the Northern States

Year	State
1777	Vermont
1780	Pennsylvania
1783	Massachusetts
1783	New Hampshire
1784	Rhode Island 1799 New York[1]
1804	New Jersey[2]

[1]Gradually instituted. [2]Gradually instituted; abolition completed by statute in 1846.
Sources: Hornsby, *Chronology of African-American History,* p. 8.

1797 • On January 30, 1797, the first recorded anti-slavery petition was presented to Congress. The petition, which was rejected by Congress, was brought by North Carolina blacks seeking "redress against a North Carolina law which requires that slaves, although freed by their Quaker masters, be returned to the state and to their former condition."

Sources: Hornsby, *Chronology of African-American History,* p. 12; *Negro Almanac,* p. 8.

1832 • A group of "females of color" in Salem, Massachusetts, formed the Salem Female Anti-Slavery Society on February 22, 1832. The abolitionist press documents the existence of a variety of women's anti-slavery societies during this period, and free black women actively participated in the racially mixed societies.

Sources: Hine, *Black Women in America,* vol. 1, p. 8; Sterling, *We Are Your Sisters,* p.113; Yee, *Black Women Abolitionists,* pp. 6, 87.

1832 • Maria W. Stewart (1803–1879), women's rights activist, journalist, and educator, was the first American-born woman to speak publicly on political themes to a mixed audience of men and women. On September 21, 1833, she was perhaps the first black woman to lecture in defense of women's rights. Her public speeches, delivered in Boston during a two-year period, also made Stewart the first black woman to lecture on anti-slavery issues. The importance of education and the need for blacks to be unified in the struggle for liberation were also themes in her speeches and writings. Abolitionist and newspaper publisher William Lloyd Garrison, who recruited her to write for *The Liberator* in 1831, published three of her speeches individually and the text of all four speeches collectively in 1835. Stewart was an acknowledged militant who was willing to accept armed conflict if necessary. Her militancy was intricately entwined with her religious commitment. Although she was deeply religious during her early years, the deaths of her husband and black anti-slavery activist David Walker in 1830 led to a "born again" experience from which she emerged with a view of herself as an advocate for oppressed Africa, freedom, and God's cause. In her final speech delivered in 1833, titled a farewell address, Stewart noted the disfavor with which the black community viewed her. After this speech she moved to New York; in 1853 she moved to Baltimore; she settled finally in Washington, D.C. in the early 1860s, remaining there until her death. In all three locations, Stewart taught school. In Washington, she also worked at Freedmen's Hospital, opened a Sunday School for neighborhood children, and succeeded in obtaining a government pension as the wife of a Navy veteran. She used this money to print an expanded version of a book she had written earlier. Stewart was both an example of and an advocate for the right of women to be heard on the important issues of the day.

Sources: Hine, *Black Women in America,* vol.2, pp. 1113–14; Smith, *Notable Black American Women,* pp. 1083–87; Yee, *Black Women Abolitionists,* p. 26.

1838 • The first known black regular lecturer in the anti-slavery cause and the first major black abolitionist was Charles Lenox Remond (1810–1873). His fame soared, following a triumphant tour of England. He was one of the seventeen members of the New England Anti-Slavery Society, the first anti-slavery society in America. Remond was born in Salem,

Massachusetts and educated in the local public schools. He became active in the abolitionist and reform movements early, and may have become involved in the black Massachusetts Anti-Slavery Society, the state's first anti-slavery organization, founded in 1832. His oratorical skills led to the position as first black lecturer for the American Anti-Slavery Society. He toured Maine, Massachusetts, and Rhode Island on behalf of the society, and he lectured throughout the North, although most of his work was centered in New England. While Remond was a significant orator and leader in the abolition movement, the work and oratorical skills of Frederick Douglass upstaged him and led to a quarrel between the men. His sister, Sarah Remond, began speaking publicly on abolition as early as 1842, and often joined him on the anti-slavery lecture circuit.

Sources: Bennett, *Before the Mayflower,* 161–62; Logan and Winston, *Dictionary of American Negro Biography,* pp. 520–22; Robinson, *Historical Negro Biographies,* pp. 115–16; Smith, *Notable Black American Men,* pp. 1003–1005.

Charles Lenox Remond

1846 • The first known black organization in Saint Louis dedicated to the overthrow of slavery, the Knights of Liberty, was formed by Moses Dickson and eleven other free blacks. After a decade, the organization turned its primary attention to helping slaves escape to freedom. Dickson established the Knights and Daughters of Tabor Society in 1871 as a memorial of this group.

Sources: *Negro Year Book, 1921–22,* p. 158.

Government Action

1776 • Laws offering freedom to slaves who served in the American army were enacted.

Sources: Southern, *Music of Black Americans,* 2nd ed., p. 51.

1854 • The first successful suit to end segregation in street cars was won this year. Until that time blacks in New York were restricted to certain cars marked "Colored People Allowed in This Car." A black public school teacher and protester, who had been dragged out of her seat, took her case to court. Future U.S. president Chester A. Arthur was one of her lawyers.

Sources: Johnson, *Black Manhattan,* p. 46.

1857 • Dred Scott (1795–1858), a Virginia slave, sued for his freedom after living on free soil in Missouri. The decision in *Dred Scott* v. *Sandford* rendered on March 6 this year was the first decision by the Supreme Court denying blacks citizenship. The ruling stated that blacks could not be citizens of the United States, even though they might be citizens of their states. Prior to this decision, Scott had many times attempted to purchase his freedom with no success. He had also been denied freedom after suing in the lower courts. A county court first denied his suit for freedom and damages but set a new trial date for December 1847. Scott then filed suit in the state circuit court in St. Louis. He actually won this suit, based on the fact that he had lived for five years with one of his owners in two areas that did not support slavery—the territory of Wisconsin and the state of Illinois. The Missouri Supreme Court overturned this decision, and the U.S. Supreme Court agreed in the 1857 ruling. The doctrine of dual citizenship remained important and resurfaced in the post–Civil War attack on black rights. In 1873 the Supreme Court again affirmed the doctrine of dual citizenship, federal and state, and suggested that most civil rights fell under state citizenship, and so were not protected under the Fourteenth Amendment.

Dred Scott

Sources: Bennett, *Before the Mayflower,* pp. 178, 262, 463; Logan and Winston, *Dictionary of American Negro Biography,* pp.548–49; Smith, *Notable Black American Men,* pp. 1049–50.

1862 • Slavery was abolished in the District of Columbia when "an act for the release of certain persons held to service or labor in the District of Columbia," was passed on April 16, 1862. The law stated that persons held "by reason of African descent are hereby discharged and freed from all claim to such service or labor" and "neither slavery nor involuntary servitude ... shall hereafter exist in said district." Slave owners were compensated, and $100,000 was appropriated to support emigration of former slaves from the United

An Act to Prohibit the Importation of Slaves

An Act to Prohibit the Importation of Slaves became effective on January 1, 1808. It was passed in March 1807 and was first law prohibiting the importation of slaves into the United States. First the Treasury Department, then the Secretary of the Navy, and at times the Secretary of State were responsible for enforcing the law. Although it was poorly enforced, the law helped to end slavery in the United States by prohibiting the transportation of slaves from Africa to the United States and its territories. It prompted some Southern states to pass similar laws, while other states refused to act.

Sources: *Negro Almanac,* 5th ed, pp. 121–22; Hornsby, *Chronology of African-American History,* p. 13.

States. However, a law passed on April 2, 1862, offering compensated emancipation to the border slave states found no takers.

Sources: Hornsby, *Chronology of African-American History,* p. 34; Kane, *Famous First Facts,* p. 598; *Negro Year Book* 1921–22, p. 134.

1866 • Citizenship was first conferred upon blacks by the Civil Rights Bill of 1866, an "Act to Protect all Persons in the United States in their Civil Rights and Furnish the Means of Their Vindication." The bill also gave blacks "the same right, in every State and territory … as is enjoyed by white citizens." Enacted during the first session of the thirty-ninth Congress on April 9, 1866, the bill passed over the president's veto.

Sources: Bennett, *Before the Mayflower,* p. 476; Hornsby, *Chronology of African-American History,* p. 41; Kane, *Famous First Facts,* p. 170.

1867 • Black males were first granted the right to vote by an act of January 8, 1867, which was "to regulate the elective franchise in the District of Columbia." The right was given to every male person twenty-one years of age, except those who were paupers, under guardianship, convicted of infamous crimes, or who had voluntarily aided rebels. President Andrew Johnson vetoed the bill on January 5, 1867, but both the Senate and the House of Representatives voted to override the veto, and the bill became law.

Sources: Clayton, *The Negro Politician,* pp. 23–24; Kane, *Famous First Facts,* p. 234; Hornsby, *Chronology of African-American History,* p. 40; *Negro Almanac,* p. 17.

1868 • Black Americans were granted citizenship and equal protection under the law for the first time with the passage of the Fourteenth Amendment on July 28, 1868.

Sources: Bennett, *Before the Mayflower,* pp. 260–61, 483; Hornsby, *Chronology of African-American History,* p. 42; *Negro Almanac,* p. 17.

1870 • Thomas Mundy Petersen [Petersen-Munday], a school custodian from Perth Amboy, New Jersey, became the first black person to vote as a result of the adoption of the Fifteenth Amendment on March 31, 1870, one day after the ratification of the amendment. A special election was called to ratify or reject a city charter, and Petersen was appointed to the committee to revise the charter—which was adopted in the election. He later became a delegate to the Republican national convention.

Sources: Cantor, *Historic Landmarks of Black America,* p. 87; *Jet* 58 (3 April 1980): 20; 72 (6 April 1987): 18; Kane, *Famous First Facts,* p. 233.

1875 • The U.S. Congress passed the Civil Rights Bill of 1875, prohibiting for the first time discrimination in places of public accommodation. The accommodations included theaters, public conveyances, and places of public recreation. The bill declared that every

Thirteenth Amendment to the Constitution

After it was ratified by twenty-seven states, U.S. secretary of state William Seward declared the Thirteenth Amendment to the Constitution in effect on December 18, 1865. The amendment stated that "neither slavery nor involuntary servitude, except as a punishment for crime, whereof the party shall have been duly convicted, shall exist within the United States." That amendment abolished slavery.

person in the United States was entitled to enjoy public accommodations whether or not they were ever in servitude. In 1883 the U.S. Supreme Court overturned the law.

Sources: Hornsby, *Chronology of African-American History*, p. 45.

Anti-slavery Laws

Date	Law
August 6, 1861	The congressional confiscation bill freed slaves who were forced to fight against the United States government or to work in support of the rebellion.
July 22, 1862	The District of Columbia passes a law abolishing slavery.
January 1, 1863	Emancipation Proclamation.
June 19, 1863	West Virginia admitted as a state with a constitution forbidding slavery.
January 11, 1864	Missouri amends constitution, forbidding slavery.
March 14, 1864	Arkansas amends constitution, forbidding slavery.
May 11, 1864	Louisiana amends constitution, forbidding slavery.
June 28, 1864	Fugitive Slave Acts of 1793 and 1850 repealed.
July 6, 1864	Maryland amends constitution, forbidding slavery.
June 19, 1865	Texas slaves are informed by proclamation that they are free.
July 13, 1865	The provisional governor of Georgia abolishes slavery by proclamation.
July 20, 1865	The provisional governor of Arkansas abolishes slavery by proclamation.
July 21, 1865	Mississippi amends constitution, forbidding slavery.
August 3, 1865	The provisional governor of Florida abolishes slavery by proclamation.
September 28, 1865	South Carolina amends constitution, forbidding slavery.
October 2, 1865	North Carolina amends constitution, forbidding slavery.
December 18, 1865	The Thirteenth Amendment, which abolished slavery in the United States, was adopted.

Sources: Bennett, *Before the Mayflower*, p. 463; Hornsby, *Chronology of African-American History*, p. 39; *Negro Almanac*, p. 16; *Negro Year Book, 1921–22*, pp. 134–35.

1881 • Tennessee was the first state to require the separation of the races in railway cars. This is usually taken as the beginning of the oppressive "Jim Crow" legislation that changed a largely *de facto* system of segregation into a legally defined system throughout the South. The test of a similar 1890 law in Louisiana led to the Supreme Court's decision in *Plessy v. Ferguson* on May 18, 1896. The court's doctrine of "separate but equal" became the legal underpinning of segregation for the next sixty years.

Sources: Bennett, *Before the Mayflower*, p. 267; Hornsby, *Chronology of African-American History*, pp. 50, 55; *Negro Almanac*, pp. 150–52; *Negro Year Book, 1921–22*, p. 171.

1941 • The U.S. Supreme Court declared on April 28 that black passengers are entitled to accommodations on Pullman cars in the railroad and to other first-class services. This was the first such ruling concerning railroad sleeping cars. The ruling settled a case that

Representative Arthur Mitchell, a Democrat from Illinois, filed after he was removed from a Pullman car and sent to a segregated car in April 1937.

Sources: *Jet* 95 (3 May 1999): 19.

1944 • Irene Morgan (Kirkaldy) (1917–2001), civil rights pioneer, refused to give up her seat on an interstate bus to a white person in Gloucester, Virginia. She was jailed and fined $100 for resisting arrest. This occurred nearly a decade before Rosa Parks gained recognition for a similar action on a local bus in Alabama. In July 1944 Morgan, who lived in Baltimore, boarded a bus in Hayes Store, took a seat in the rear, and refused to give her seat to a white couple. Morgan resisted and was fined for kicking the Middlesex County sheriff who tried to remove her and for scratching the deputy who took her to jail. NAACP lawyer Thurgood Marshall was successful in his appeal to the U.S. Supreme Court on Morgan's behalf. The court then struck down segregation in interstate transportation. Kirkaldy ran a child-care center in Queens on Long Island, where she lived after leaving Baltimore. She graduated from St. John's University when she was sixty-eight years old, and later earned a master's degree in urban studies from Queens College. Gloucester County honored her on its 350th anniversary in 2000, and in 2001 President Bill Clinton awarded her the Presidential Citizens Medal for "taking the first step on a journey that would change America forever."

Sources: *New York Times* (5 August 2000); (13 August 2007); Smith and Wynn, *Freedom Facts and Firsts,* p. 176.

1950 • Elmer Henderson (1913?–2001) was the civil rights activist whose case before the U.S. Supreme Court ended segregation in railway dining cars. In 1942 he experienced the segregation firsthand, when he traveled from Washington to Birmingham as a field representative for the President's committee on Fair Employment Practices. The railroad used a curtain to separate the races and allotted ten tables for whites and only one for blacks. In 1949 the federal government joined Henderson's fight and asked the court to end such segregation. For eight years Henderson challenged the Southern Railway for segregating blacks in its dining cars; the Supreme Court later ruled that segregation in the dining cars violated the Interstate Commerce Act. Henderson then targeted segregation in railroad and bus company waiting rooms. A native of Baltimore, Henderson graduated from Morgan State College (later Morgan State University). He received his master's degree from the University of Chicago and his law degree from Georgetown University. During his early years, he concentrated on the Civil Rights Movement, later teaching at Howard University. Henderson served as Midwest regional director for the Fair Employment Committee in the 1940s, after President Franklin D. Roosevelt issued an order banning discrimination in employment in government and defense industries. From 1948 until 1955 he directed the American Council on Human Rights. He was also advisor to Democratic presidential candidate Adlai Stevenson in the mid–1950s. In 1955 Henderson was appointed legal counsel and later general counsel to the Government Operations Committee, the primary investigating arm of the U.S. House of Representatives.

Sources: Smith and Wynn, *Freedom Facts and Firsts*, p. 176; *Washington* Post *(18 July 2001).*

1953 • The Government Contract Commission was established to insure racial parity in government contracts with employers for the first time. President Dwight D. Eisenhower established the fifteen-member committee on August 15.

Sources: *Jet* 96 (16 August 1999): 19.

1957 • The Montgomery Bus Boycott of 1955 and subsequent arrest of Rosa Parks on December 1 catapulted Martin Luther King Jr. (1929–1968) to leadership of the modern movement for civil rights; he became the first person in the nation to lead a massive and successful nonviolent protest movement for this cause. He combined Christian theology, moral suasion, and nonviolent protest in his fight against racial segregation and discrimination. In 1957, King organized the Southern Christian Leadership Conference (SCLC) to help in the cause. He led boycotts and marches for the next eleven years primarily in the South. King's protest activities resulted in his numerous arrests. He was arrested and jailed in Birmingham, Alabama, for demonstrating without a permit but this, too, brought him and the movement more national visibility. While incarcerated, he wrote his famous "Letter from Birmingham Jail," which is often cited in civil rights literature for its advocacy of nonviolent direct action. Perhaps the milestone of his career came on August 28, 1963, with the highly recognized March on Washington, representing the efforts of several groups. It was the nation's largest civil rights demonstration ever held. King delivered before the crowd his "I Have a Dream" speech, which also became an historical document. The march and its advocacy for civil rights provided the impetus for the impending Civil Rights Act and paved the way for ratification of the Twenty-fourth Amendment to the U.S. Constitution, affecting the voting rights of citizens. King's dream continued and was seen in such activities as the passage of the Voting Rights Act and Poor People's Campaign to address unemployment and poverty. These activities underway, in March 1968 he traveled to Memphis to support the cause of sanitation workers and led a march which turned violent. On April 4, an assassin fatally shot King as he stood on the balcony of the Lorraine Hotel. Following the tragedy, violence erupted in 130 American cities and thousands were arrested. In time, the nation looked favorably on King's work as an ambassador of peace and named schools, streets, educational programs, and a national holiday in his honor.

King was born in Atlanta and educated at Morehouse College. Later he enrolled in Crozer Theological Seminary and was ordained a Baptist minister. In 1955 he received his Ph.D. in Theology from Boston University. He married Coretta Scott and moved to Montgomery to become pastor of Dexter Avenue Baptist Church, where he began his civil rights activities.

Sources: Branch, *Parting the Waters,* 1968; Garrow, *Bearing the Cross,* 1986; Smith, *Notable Black American Men,* pp. 686–91.

1957 • The first city to legislate against race or religious discrimination in housing was New York City. On December 5 the city adopted a Fair Housing Practices Law.

Sources: *The Black New Yorkers,* p. 283.

1964 • The Civil Rights Act of 1964 became law on July 2. President Lyndon B. Johnson signed what was regarded as the strongest and most far-reaching civil rights legislation since Reconstruction. Among its various provisions, the new act guaranteed blacks the right to vote, provided blacks access to public accommodations, authorized the federal government to sue to desegregate public schools and facilities, extended the life of the Civil Rights Commission, and authorized the Department of Justice to enter into pending civil rights cases.

Sources: Adams and Burke, *Civil Rights,* p. 147; *Jet* 100 (9 July 2001): 19.

1967 • A Mississippi jury found seven Ku Klux Klansmen guilty of violating the civil rights of three activists—James Cheney, Andrew Goodman, and Michael Schwerner—on October 20, marking the first time a Mississippi jury convicted Klansmen in the death of a black person or civil rights workers. The three civil rights activists, who were members of the Congress of Racial Equality (CORE), were killed in Philadelphia, on June 21, 1964, when they participated in a voter-registration campaign during Freedom Summer. They had been arrested on traffic charges, released, and then pulled over by police accompanied by Klansmen.

Sources: *Jet* 113 (23 June 2008): 18.

1968 • The Civil Rights Act of 1968 (also known as the Fair Housing Act) is signed by President Lyndon B. Johnson on April 11. The act made discrimination in the sale or rental of housing illegal.

Sources: *African American Almanac,* 6th ed., p. 205.

Group Action

1830 • The first National Negro Convention met at Mother Bethel Church in Philadelphia September 20–24, 1830, "to devise ways and means for bettering of our condition," to fight oppression, to promote universal education, and inspire other pursuits. Richard Allen presided. After the Civil War, the conventions focused on voting, fair employment, education, citizenship rights, and the repeal of discriminatory laws.

Selected Protests in the Modern Civil Rights Movement

Date	Event
December 1, 1955	Arrest of Rosa Parks in Montgomery sparks Civil Rights Movement
December 1955	Massive bus boycott held in Montgomery, AL, marked beginning of the modern black Civil Rights Movement
February 1, 1960	First Sit-In Movement to receive major results began in Greensboro, NC
May 4, 1961	Freedom Rides, Washington, D.C. to New Orleans
August 28 1963	March on Washington to support pending civil rights legislation
March 25, 1965	Selma to Montgomery march, concluding with "Bloody Sunday"

Sources: Baer and Singer, *African-American Religion in the Twentieth Century,* p. 26; *Encyclopedia of Black America,* p. 834; Hornsby, *Chronology of African-American History,* p. 18.

Marcus Garvey

1914 • Marcus [Mozian Manaseth] Garvey (1887–1940), black nationalist, orator, and organizer, formed the first black mass movement organization, the United Negro Improvement Association (UNIA). The organization aimed to unite blacks under the motto "One God! One Aim! One Destiny!" Its divisions and subsidiaries later included the African Legion and the Black Cross Nurses. Garvey was born in St. Ann's Bay, Jamaica, traveled to England in 1912, and returned to Jamaica in 1914. He came to America on March 23, 1916, and one year later established a branch of UNIA in Harlem. This branch immediately became the headquarters of Garvey's international movement. He founded a weekly newspaper, *Negro World,* in 1918, which spread his word. By mid–1919 he had launched the Black Star Shipping Line to help create economic opportunities for blacks, who bought stock in the line. Garvey and his stockholders later expanded the business to form a cross-continent steamship trade. In 1923, he was convicted and jailed for mail fraud. He was pardoned and deported in 1927, when he moved to London. He wrote extensively about his movement and race philosophy, and with more than a million followers, he had built the largest and most powerful black mass movement in American history.

Sources: Franklin and Meier, *Black Leaders of the Twentieth Century,* pp. 104–38; *Contemporary Black Biography,* vol. 1, pp. 75–78; Logan and Winston, *Dictionary of American Negro Biography,* pp. 254–56; Katz, *Eyewitness: The Negro in American History,* pp. 399–400; Smith, *Notable Black American Men,* pp. 441–45.

Charles Houston

1935 • Lawyer and educator Charles Hamilton Houston (1895–1950) became the first full-time paid special counsel for the NAACP. He devised a strategy at the NAACP that led to school desegregation. The campaign against discrimination in education ended two decades later, after Houston's death, when the *Brown v. Board of Education* decision of 1954 declared segregation in public schools unconstitutional. During his career, Houston helped prepare civil rights cases in lower federal and state courts, and argued such cases before the United States Supreme Court. Houston was born in Washington, D.C., and graduated from Amherst College and Harvard Law School, where he studied under Supreme Court Justice Felix Frankfurter. He was the first black to serve as editor of the *Harvard Law Review.* Early in his career he joined his father's Washington, D.C., law firm, Houston and Houston. His work with the firm included many cases addressing discrimination in employment and specific aspects of discrimination in Washington. He remained a member of the firm until his death. In 1929 he became vice-dean of Howard University Law School, Washington, D.C. and led the school into full accreditation by the American Bar Association. Civil rights and civil libertarian groups acknowledged Houston for his work at Howard and his philosophy of social engineering. He combined teaching, litigating, and serving as a mentor for over two decades. While serving as special counsel for the NAACP, he handled numerous cases involving due process and jury discrimination in addition to education cases. According to *Notable Black American Men,* some gave him the title of "Mr. Civil Rights." In 1938 Houston won the NAACP'S first case in the U.S.

Supreme Court, *Missouri ex rel. Gaines v. Canada*. This case concerned the obligation of providing separate but equal public education. For his pioneering work in developing the NAACP legal campaign, he was awarded the Spingarn Medal posthumously on September 27, 1950.

Sources: Bennett, *Before the Mayflower*, pp. 363, 546; Franklin and Meier, *Black Leaders of the Twentieth Century*, pp. 220–40; Logan and Winston, *Dictionary of American Biography*, pp. 328–30; Smith, *Notable Black American Men*, pp. 575–78.

1941 • Publishers of the Atlanta telephone directory announced on December 22 that black women who were married would be identified by the title "Mrs." in front of their names—the same format traditionally used for white women. The action came after a strong protest from the Atlanta Urban League.

Sources: *Jet* 93 (22 December 1997): 19.

1947 • The first known freedom ride occurred April 9, 1947, when the Congress of Racial Equality (CORE) and the Fellowship of Reconciliation tested the South's compliance with the court's decision of June 3, 1946, which banned segregation on interstate buses. CORE sent twenty-three black and white riders through the South. While the freedom rides of May 1961 were more widely publicized, this was the first challenge to segregation on interstate buses. The freedom rides led to a firm policy on desegregation of interstate travel. In May 2001 Congressman John Lewis led a delegation of former riders and civil rights supporters on a tour, retracing the historic journey.

Sources: Bennett, *Before the Mayflower*, p. 542; Hornsby, *Milestones in 20th-Century African-American History*, p. 44; *Negro Almanac*, p. 27; *Jet* 99 (14 May 2001): 10.

1957 • The first organization to coordinate the work of nonviolent groups devoted to racial integration and improved life for black Americans was the Southern Christian Leadership Conference (SCLC). Known in the Southern Civil Rights Movement for its nonviolent and direct action, SCLC grew out of the 1955–56 Montgomery Bus Boycott. It was founded by Martin Luther King Jr., Bayard Rustin, and Stanley Levinson.

Sources: Alford, *Famous First Blacks*, p. 26; *Contemporary Black Biography*, vol. 1, pp. 132–33; *Encyclopedia of Black America*, pp. 804–5; *Negro Almanac*, p. 30.

1958 • The first sit-ins to win concessions in a Southern state in modern times occurred in restaurants in Oklahoma City, on August 19, 1958. The NAACP Youth Council members sat at lunch counters and were served without incident or publicity.

Sources: Alford, *Famous First Blacks*, p. 25; Bennett, *Before the Mayflower*, p. 556.

1960? • The first sit-in movement to achieve major results began February 1, 1960, when four students from North Carolina Agricultural and Technical College (now known as A&T State University) sought service at a Greensboro F. W. Woolworth store's lunch counter reserved for whites. The students were Ezell Blair, Franklin McCain, David Richmond, and Joseph McNeil. The movement, patterned after the passive resistance techniques of Mahatma Gandhi, gained momentum and by February 10, 1960, had spread to fifteen southern cities in five states. On March 16, 1960, San Antonio, Texas, became the first city to integrate its lunch counters as result of the movement. On the fortieth anniversary of the Greensboro sit-ins, in 1994 the Smithsonian Institution recreated an eight-foot section of the counter, four stools, a soda fountain, and other items from F. W. Woolworth's Greensboro store. A&T erected on its campus a life-size monument of the four student leaders, called February 1. The Woolworth's site became the International Civil Rights Center and Museum and opened on February 1, 2010. The fiftieth anniversary of the sit-in movement was celebrated in many sites across the nation. The Atlanta movement and the 1960s protest against racial segregation, for example, was celebrated with the renaming of Fair Street, SW to the Atlanta Student Movement Boulevard.

Sources: Alford, *Famous First Blacks*, p. 25; Bennett, *Before the Mayflower*, pp. 383–84, 557; Cantor, *Historic Landmarks of Black America*, pp. 229–31; Hornsby, *Milestones in 20th-Cen-*

tury African-American History, pp. 63, 66; *Jet* 99 (6 February 2001): 20; 118 (13 December 2010): 41; Salzman, *Encyclopedia of African-American History and Culture,* Supplement, pp. 2242–43.

1960 • Marion Shepilov Barry (1936–) was the first national chairman of the Student Nonviolent Coordinating Committee (SNCC). A native of Itta Bena, Mississippi, Barry and his family moved to Memphis, Tennessee, after his father died. He graduated from LeMoyne College in Memphis in 1958. While in college, Barry became president of the college chapter of the NAACP. He earned a master's degree in chemistry from Fisk University, where he also helped form a chapter of the NAACP. At Fisk he participated in workshops in nonviolence and helped to organize the lunch counter sit-ins in Nashville in 1960. He joined Martin Luther King Jr. and others at Shaw University in Raleigh and together they founded the SNCC, a vital force in the Civil Rights Movement. After teaching at various universities and pursuing doctoral work, Barry devoted full-time service to SNCC. In the 1960s he devoted his efforts to Youth Pride, a month-long project for black youths to clean the streets of Washington, D.C; he later expanded the program to become Pride Economic Enterprises. In 1970 Barry won a seat on the school board and later became its president, and in 1975 he was elected to the city council. Barry was elected mayor of Washington, D.C., in 1979 and was re-elected to the position for two terms. He resigned before the end of his third term and served a jail sentence for a misdemeanor charge of drug usage. He later reentered politics as a member of the city council.

Sources: *Ebony* 23 (December 1976): 82–89; *Ebony Success Library,* vol. 1, p. 21; *Who's Who among African Americans,* 26th ed., p. 72.

Martin Luther King Jr.

1963 • The first March on Washington was held on August 28; it was a peaceful demonstration to focus national attention on equality for blacks as well as to advance the civil rights bill that was before Congress. A quarter of a million people participated, making it the largest single protest march in the country up to that time. This was one of the most historical events in the Civil Rights Movement; it was at this march that Martin Luther King Jr. stood before the Lincoln Memorial and gave his famous "I Have a Dream" speech. He first gave the speech seven years earlier at Bethel AME Church in Atlanta. After the march, civil rights leaders met with President John F. Kennedy at the White House; Kennedy promised to push for anti-discrimination legislation. It was Lyndon B. Johnson, however, who became president on November 22, 1963, after the assassination of Kennedy, who gave the bill top priority. He signed the omnibus Civil Rights Act on July 2, 1964.

Sources: *Jet* 96 (30 August 1999): 19; Hornsby, *Chronology of African-American History,* pp. 115–16; Jordan, *Vernon Can Read,* p. 82; Salzman, *Encyclopedia of African-American Culture and History,* vol. 2, p. 567.

1964 • The first wave of riots to hit black urban neighborhoods during the 1960s occurred in the Harlem section of New York July 18–22. The riots then spread to the Bedford-Stuyvesant section of Brooklyn, Rochester, New York City, and Jersey City and Paterson, New Jersey.

Sources: Bennett, *Before the Mayflower,* p. 571; Hornsby, *Milestones in 20th-Century African-American History,* p. 78; *Negro Almanac,* p. 32.

1964 • Civil rights activist Stokely Carmichael (1941–1998) was the first person to popularize the phrase "Black Power" as a slogan during James Meredith's voter registration drive in Mississippi. As Carmichael conceptualized the term, it was intended to develop black consciousness in Mississippi and Alabama by stressing separatism along with black power. In 1966 he became head of the Student Nonviolent Coordinating Committee (SNCC) and altered its orientation from nonviolent protest to black liberation. Carmichael was born in Trinidad; he came to the United States at age eleven. He later graduated from Howard University in Washington, D.C. During the turbulent atmosphere of the 1960s Carmichael was considered a radical. He was a member of the second group of Mississippi Freedom Riders, which originated in Washington, D.C. He left SNCC in 1967 to join

The Montgomery Bus Boycott

Rosa Parks

The boycott of public buses in Montgomery, Alabama, marked the beginning of the modern black Civil Rights Movement. On December 1, 1955, Rosa Parks (1913–2005) was jailed for refusing to give up her seat on a city bus to a white passenger, thus prompting the historic 381-day Montgomery Bus Boycott. The local black community then formed the Montgomery Improvement Association (MIA) to join the fight to desegregate the busses and elected Martin Luther King Jr. as president. The MIA filed a suit in the U.S. District Court on February 1, 1956, designed to declare Alabama's segregation laws unconstitutional. On June 2 a lower court declared such segregation unconstitutional and the Supreme Court upheld the ruling, ordering integration on December 20, 1956.

Sources: Southern, *The Music of Black Americans,* p. 359; *Contemporary Black Biography,* vol. 1, pp. 130–35 (King); vol. 1, pp.189–92 (Parks); Smith, *Notable Black American Women,* pp. 820–23 (Parks); Smith. *Notable Black American Men,* pp.686–91 (King).

the more militant Black Panthers. By 1968 he was prime minister of the Panthers' most militant group, but in 1969 he left to join the Pan-African Movement, which emphasized cultural nationalism. Carmichael's activities often placed him at odds with other well-known African Americans. He moved to Guinea to flee from police harassment. In Guinea, he became involved with the Marxist party and continued to espouse his revolutionary ideas. In 1978 he changed his name to Kwame Ture to honor African leaders Kwame Nkrumah and Ahmed Sekou Toure.

Sources: Alford, *Famous First Blacks,* p. 24; *Encyclopedia of Black America,* p. 215; *Negro Almanac,* pp. 240–42; Smith, *Notable Black American Men,* pp. 173–76.

1967 • The first Black Power Conference met in Newark, New Jersey, on July 20. The four-day conference followed the violent Newark race riot that left twenty-three dead. Delegates at the conference represented forty-two cities and thirty-six states, and constituted the largest and most diverse group of civil rights activists assembled up to that time.

Sources: *Jet* 94 (20 July 1998): 19.

1984 • The first Black Family Summit was held at Fisk University, in Nashville, Tennessee, in May 1984. The summit was in response to Benjamin Hooks' and the NAACP's call to bring together organizations and other resources to map plans for family survival.

Sources: *Negro Almanac,* pp. 258–59.

1989 • Barbara Arnwine (1951?–) became the first black woman to head the male-dominated Lawyers Committee for Civil Rights Under Law. Arnwine grew up in a housing project in the Watts section of Los Angeles. She received scholarships to Scripps College in Claremont, California, and to Duke Law School in Durham, North Carolina. After graduating from Duke in 1976, she became a Reginald Huber Smith fellow and worked for the Durham Legal Assistance Program. She later moved to Raleigh to work at the head office. There she handled affirmative action policies and helped open new legal aid programs throughout North Carolina. In the early 1980s Arnwine served as executive director of the Boston Lawyer's Committee for Civil Rights. Arnwine left that position in 1989 to become executive director of the national branch of the Lawyers Committee for Civil Rights, a group that John F. Kennedy founded. Her concern for women's rights and the need to clarify the real roles that black women play in this country led her to organize the National Conference on African-American Women and the

Law. Arnwine and four hundred charter members launched the National Network for African-American Women and the Law. She has received numerous awards, including a 2011 Gruber Prizes for Justice.

Sources: *Contemporary Black Biography,* vol. 28, pp. 5–7.

1994 • The first black to become executive director of the International Human Rights Law Group was Gay Johnson McDougall (1947–). Born in Atlanta, she graduated from Bennington College in Vermont in 1969 and obtained her law degree from Yale Law School in 1972. Following graduation, McDougall was hired by a New York corporate law firm. She later became an unpaid employee of the National Conference on Black Lawyers in Washington, an organization that worked to help minorities and the poor with legal problems, race matters, and voter's rights and to address international law issues. In 1978 she received a master of laws degree from London School of Economics and Political Science, with a concentration in public international law. After a year as associate counsel in the New York City deputy mayor's office, McDougall became director of the Southern Africa Project of the Lawyer's Committee for Civil Rights under Law. This led to her selection as a key overseer of the elections in South Africa in 1994. In 1994 McDougall was named to the Independent Electoral Commission in South Africa, whose charge was to run South Africa's first all-race elections. In her position as executive director of the International Human Rights Law Group, she is an advocate for human rights around the world.

Sources: *Contemporary Black Biography,* vol. 11, pp. 156–59; *Jet* 86 (17 October 1994): 12; Smith, *Notable Black American Women,* Book II, pp. 442–45.

1995 • The first Million Man March and Day of Absence, masterminded by Louis Farrakhan (1933–), was held on October 16, 1995, twenty-one blocks from the Capitol Building in Washington, D.C. It was to be a national day of atonement, with thousands gathering for spiritual, economic, or political reasons. The men were to unite and pledge to take responsibility for themselves. Parallel activities, along with church services, rallies, and other gatherings, occurred in cities and towns across the country. Joining in the protest were black leaders from all walks of life; they included Rep. Charles Rangel, Rev. Jesse Jackson, Isaac Hayes, and Stevie Wonder. Women were excluded as marchers but were asked to lend support by staying at home to pray, fast, or to speak out in support of the march. Some women, such as activist Angela Davis, criticized the exclusionary nature of the march. The march was deemed a success due to the large number of participants and the cross-section of the black community represented.

Sources: *The African American Almanac,* 8th ed., p. 611; 11th ed., p. 818; *Jet* 112 (22 October 2007): 32; Smith and Wynn, *Freedom Facts and Firsts,* pp. 49–50.

1997 • The first Million Woman March was held in Philadelphia on October 26. More than 300,000 American women attended. Speakers included Congressman Maxine Waters, Winnie Mandela, and Sister Souljah. Organizers of this march aimed to strengthen the cohesiveness of black women from all walks of life. The women addressed such issues as women in prison, the beginning of independent black schools, employment, and women in politics and business.

Sources: *The African American Almanac,* 8th ed., p. 611; Smith and Wynn, *Freedom Facts and Firsts,* pp. 50–51.

2008 • The first Recommitment March to reconnect with the spirit of Martin Luther King Jr. and to celebrate and honor his civil rights work was held in Memphis on April 4, forty years after King's assassination. The Reverend Al Sharpton and Martin Luther King III cochaired the event. Participants from all over the nation, represented by different racial and economic groups, marched side-by-side from City Hall to the Lorraine Motel, where King was assassinated. Participants included retired sanitation workers, Harry Belafonte, Rev. Jesse Jackson, Rev. Bernice King, Tavis Smiley, and Cornel West. Politicians seeking national office included Sen. John McCain and Barack Obama. Speaking of King, Tavis

Smiley said, "This 40th anniversary of his assassination reminds us of our role and responsibility of his legacy of love."

Sources: *Jet* 113 (21 April 2008): 6, 8, 10, 62–63.

Miscellaneous

1936 • Sue Bailey Thurman (1903–1997) was the first black woman to have an audience with human rights leader Mahatma Gandhi. She met with Gandhi to discuss nonviolent resistance in the struggle for political freedom and social change. She is also credited with helping to establish the first integrated church in the United States and with being the first black student to be awarded the bachelor's degree in music by Oberlin Conservatory (1926). After graduation from Oberlin, she obtained a position teaching music at what was then Hampton Institute, but did not find teaching music fulfilling and left in 1930 to become traveling secretary of the YWCA national staff. In 1932 she married Howard Thurman, who was then a professor of theology and dean of the chapel at Howard University. With this marriage, the Thurmans became true partners, not just in marriage but also in their goals and interests. A month-long visit to Burma (now Myanmar), Ceylon (now Sri Lanka), and India as guests of the Student Christian Fellowship resulted in their commitment to the idea of nonviolent resistance and to the establishment, with Presbyterian minister Dr. Alfred Fisk, of the Church for the Fellowship of All Peoples in San Francisco. During their ten years there (1944–54), Sue Thurman served as chairperson of the Intercultural Workshop. Community involvement characterized Thurman throughout her life, whether in Washington, San Francisco, or at Boston University with her husband from 1953 to 1964. Her activities celebrated black people and black life. After her husband's death in 1981, she took over administration of the Howard Thurman Educational Trust, which offers grants to black college students and presents seminars and workshops pertinent to educational achievement.

Sources: *Jet* 91 (20 January 1997): 17; Smith, *Notable Black American Women*, pp. 1139–42.

2000 • John Robert Lewis (1940–) received the Wallenberg Medal from the University of Michigan—the first American-born recipient of the award. (Raoul Wallenberg, an alumnus and international humanitarian, engineered the rescue of thousands of Hungarians from the Nazis in World War II.) During a ceremony at the university, Lewis was honored for his civil rights contributions and delivered a public lecture on "Civil Rights—Past, Present, and Future." Lewis was born in Pike County, near Troy, Alabama, to parents who were sharecroppers until they established a peanut business. He received a bachelor's degree from American Baptist Theological Seminary (now American Baptist College) in Nashville, Tennessee, in 1961, and a bachelor's degree in religion and philosophy from Fisk University in 1967. While in Nashville he became interested in civil rights activities. He attended local workshops on nonviolent techniques and became a student of Septima Clark of the Highland Folk School in Monteagle, Tennessee. Lewis was one of the local students who launched a test sit-in in Nashville in November and December 1969, predating the Greensboro, North Carolina, sit-ins by two months. He was arrested several times for his sit-in activities. By June 1960 the student movement had helped to desegregate lunch counters in seven Tennessee cities. Lewis also became a founder of the Student Nonviolent Coordinating Committee (SNCC) and participated in the Freedom Rides that the Congress of Racial Equality (CORE) organized in 1961. He and his fellow riders were attacked on their trip from Washington, D.C., to New Orleans, on May 4. Nevertheless, the protest was successful and in September the Interstate Commerce Commission outlawed racial segregation in bus stations. He dropped out of college to serve as chair of SNCC from 1963 until 1965, and he worked on the August 23, 1963 March on Washington. Lewis was active in the Mississippi Freedom Summer in 1964 and in the Montgomery-to-Selma march held on March 7, 1965. His work with SNCC led to his being arrested over forty times, numerous physical attacks, and injuries, yet his commitment to nonviolent social change endured. After graduating from Fisk, he directed the Voter Education Project for the Southern Regional Council. In 1977 Lewis was unsuccessful in his bid for a seat in Georgia's Fifth Congressional District. He won a seat on the Atlanta City Council in 1981, and in November that year he defeated state senator Julian Bond to become U.S. representative for the Fifth Congressional District. He continues his tenure in Congress, sits on influential committees, and supports civil rights issues.

Sources: *Jet* 97 (31 January 2000): 20; Smith, *Notable Black American Men,* pp. 718–20; *Contemporary Black Biography,* vol. 2, pp. 137–39.

Slave Revolts

1526 • The first recorded slave revolt in North America occurred this year, after Spanish explorers brought Africans to land known later as South Carolina. The escaped Africans settled with American Indians.

Sources: *Negro Almanac,* p.2.

1663 • The first major conspiracy between black slaves and indentured servants occurred in Gloucester County, Virginia, on September 13, 1663. The conspiracy was betrayed by an indentured servant.

Sources: Alford, *Famous First Blacks,* p. 27; Hornsby, *Chronology of African-American History,* p. 3; *Negro Almanac,* p. 3.

1712 • The first major slave revolt occurred in New York City on April 7, 1712. As a result, twenty-one blacks were executed, and six others committed suicide. The men had met about midnight on April 6 to take revenge for their masters' abuse. Some were armed with firearms, swords, knives, and hatchets. Paul Cuffe set fire to his master's house, which attracted a crowd of townspeople. The revolt grew as the insurgents opened fire on the crowd, killing nine whites and wounding five or six more.

Sources: Hornsby, *Chronology of African-American History,* p. 4; Johnson, *Black Manhattan,* pp. 7–8; *Negro Almanac,* p. 4; *Negro Year Book, 1921–22,* p. 149.

1720 • The first insurrection of slaves in South Carolina occurred in 1720, when whites were attacked on the streets and in their houses in Charleston. Twenty-three slaves were arrested, six convicted, and three executed.

Sources: *Negro Yearbook, 1921–22,* p. 149.

1739 • The first serious slave revolt in South Carolina took place when a slave named Cato led an uprising at Stono, about twenty miles west of Charleston. After killing two warehouse guards and securing arms and ammunition, the slaves headed south, hoping to reach Florida. As they marched to drum beats, they killed twenty to thirty whites who had attempted to interfere. Armed whites captured all but a dozen slaves, and more than thirty blacks, who were alleged participants, were killed.

Sources: Hornsby, *Chronology of African-American History,* p. 4.

1791 • Toussaint L'Ouverture [Francois Dominique Toussaint Breda] (1743–1803) led the first slave revolt against the French in Haiti to liberate the colony. A self-educated slave, this insurgent, soldier, statesman, and martyr was imprisoned by Napoleon. He is ultimately responsible for making Haiti the first independent, black-ruled country in the Western Hemisphere.

Sources: Bennett, *Before the Mayflower,* pp. 117, 118, 120–23; *Negro Almanac,* p. 7; *Negro History Bulletin* 15 (November 1951): 38, 40–41.

Toussaint L'Ouverture

1822 • The first revolt leader of note was Denmark [Telemaque] Vesey (1767–1822), who in May 1822 organized a slave revolt in Charleston, South Carolina. Vesey and nearly fifty others were executed after the revolt, one of the most elaborate on record. Vesey, a sailor and a prosperous merchant carpenter, had been free since 1800. While still in his teens, he opened his own master carpenter shop in Charleston. He found himself, however, in a strange position as a free man in a slave society in which many free blacks owned slaves

The First Slave Revolt

In Southampton County, Virginia, on August 21 and 22, 1831, Nat Turner (1800–31), minister and slave, led what has been recognized as the first slave revolt of magnitude. The revolt was crushed but only after Turner and his band had killed some sixty whites and threw the South into panic. After hiding out, Turner was captured on October 30, 1831, and hanged in Jerusalem, Virginia, on November 11. Thirty other blacks were also implicated and executed. It was not until John Brown's 1859 raid on Harpers Ferry, Virginia, that another slave revolt or conspiracy became known. Turner was born to African-born slaves of Benjamin Tucker, in the Tidewater region of southeast Virginia, near North Carolina. After several attempts to escape slavery, his father finally succeeded and immigrated to Liberia. Although slaves were forbidden to read or write, Turner did so with ease and became a wonder to the slave community. Turner styled himself as a Baptist preacher and in 1825 held his first "praise meetings." He became an itinerant preacher, using his travel to learn the terrain of Southampton. He also identified slave and free blacks who would attend his sessions and prepare for what he called the great "mission" that God envisioned for them. Turner also claimed to have received signs that it was time for him to lead his rebellion. Finally, on the night of August 21, when whites had left their churches and settled in for the night, Turner and his insurrectionists moved swiftly in a surprise attack on plantations in the Southampton countryside. After he lost his tactical advantage, Turner grew concerned for his own survival and hid underground for six weeks. He was captured on October 30; he offered no testimony in court, nor did he allow defense on his behalf. His famous deposition became known as the *Confessions of Nat Turner*. The document was published and copies sold out quickly.

Nat Turner

Sources: Bennett, *Before the Mayflower*, pp.131–39; Hornsby, *Chronology of African-American History*, p. 18; *Negro Almanac*, p. 11; Smith, *Notable Black American Men*, pp. 1137–42.

and participated in slave trading. He viewed this as moral corruption in the free black community, and he became determined to uproot slavery. State laws that prevented children from being free if their mother was a slave, difficulties arising when Charleston blacks left the white-dominated Methodist Church for the new African Methodist Episcopal Church (AME), and fines and taxes aimed at restricting the mobility of free blacks also contributed to his determination. Vesey had a revolutionary perspective and actively recruited followers for his cause, planning the uprising over several years. Five thousand blacks were prepared to participate in the revolt that was originally set for July of that year but moved up to June when Vesey learned that authorities had learned of his plans from traitorous insiders. Subsequently he tried to postpone the revolt once more, but it was too late for word to reach everyone and the uprising proceeded. Vesey was arrested and tried the day after his arrest. Throughout the days following his arrest, however, Vesey and his co-leaders who had remained faithful refused to disclose any information; they are considered martyrs. Vesey was hanged two weeks after his arrest. On one July morning, twenty-two men were killed in a mass execution. After the insurrection occurred, South Carolina and other states passed laws to control free blacks, to tighten the reins on slaves, and to keep watch on possible revolts. Morris Brown (1770–1849), a prominent leader in the AME Church, became a suspect and fled to the North, where he succeeded Richard Allen as AME bishop. Another well-known slave revolt leader was Gabriel Prosser (1775?–1800), who planned a revolt for August 30, 1800, which subsequently failed. Vesey, however, is considered to be the first to use pan-Africanism as an organizing principle for his liberation movement.

Sources: Bennett, *Before the Mayflower*, pp. 127–31; Hornsby, *Chronology of African-American History*, pp. 15–16; *The Negro Almanac*, p. 10; Smith, *Notable Black American Men*, pp. 1158–63.

1839 • A group of Africans launched the first revolt at sea that resulted in the legal freedom of the rebels. They seized the slave ship *Amistad* and brought it into Montauk, Long Island, New York. The ship came into American custody on August 26, 1839. Cinqué, the young African leader, and his followers were tried in court, defended by former President John Quincy Adams. The Supreme Court decision to free them was handed down on March 9, 1840. The thirty-five surviving Africans were returned to Africa on November 25, 1841.

Sources: Bennett, *Before the Mayflower*, p. 457; Hornsby, *Chronology of African-American History*, p. 1838; *Negro Almanac*, p. 12.

Slavery

1619 • Twenty unnamed persons of African extraction were the first blacks in Virginia. They arrived in Jamestown in August, transported by a Dutchman who sold them to the planter colonists as indentured servants.

Sources: Bennett, *Before the Mayflower*, p. 441; Kane, *Famous First Facts*, p. 598; *Negro Almanac*, p. 2.

1622 • Anthony and Mary Johnson and family were the first known free blacks. They lived in Old Accomack, later Northampton County, in the Virginia colony. In 1651, Anthony Johnson, John Johnson, and John Johnson Sr., were the first black landowners in Virginia, receiving grants totaling 850 acres, and in the same year, Richard Johnson appears to have been the first black to enter Virginia as a free man. Anthony Johnson and his wife were among the twenty-three black servants in the 1624–25 census of the colony. In 1653, Anthony Johnson became the first black on record as a slave owner. However, by 1662 slavery had been made hereditary in the colony by a decree assigning freedom or slavery according to the condition of the mother. Still, free blacks in Virginia did not lose the right to vote until 1723.

Sources: Bennett, *Before the Mayflower*, pp. 35–38; *Encyclopedia of Black America*, p. 37; *Negro Year Book, 1921–22*, pp. 126–27.

1640 • The first known black "servant for life," or more plainly, slave, was John Punch, who had run away with two fellow white servants. All three were whipped. The indentures of the whites were extended five years, while Punch was bound for life.

Sources: *Negro Year Book, 1921–22*, p. 126.

1641 • The first colony to legalize slavery and to forbid use of "unjust violence" in the capture of slaves was Massachusetts.

Sources: Hornsby, *Chronology of African-American History*, p. 3; *Negro Year Book, 1921–22*, p. 126.

1642 • The colony of Virginia was the first to pass a fugitive slave law. The law stated that following a second escape attempt slaves would be branded. The law probably also applied to servants. Seven years later there were only four hundred blacks in the colony. The first formal recognition of slavery is 1661.

Sources: *Negro Almanac*, p. 2; *Negro Year Book, 1921–22*, p. 127.

1643 • The first inter-colony agreement over fugitive slaves was made in the New England Confederation. Certification by a magistrate could convict an escaped slave.

Sources: *Negro Almanac,* p. 2.

1664 • The lower house of the Maryland legislature asked the upper house to draft an act declaring that baptism of slaves did not lead to their freedom. At least six of the colonies had laws making this specific declaration by 1710. This is the first known attempt to resolve the question by statute.

Sources: Rabotecau, *Slave Religion,* p. 99.

1786 • The first evidence of the existence of an "underground railroad," in the sense of people organized to help fugitive slaves escape, refers to a group of Quakers in Philadelphia. Between 1812 and the Civil War, the necessarily clandestine organizations became more widespread and more effective. From 1830 to 1860, it is estimated that some nine thousand fugitives passed through Philadelphia, and some forty thousand through Ohio. One of the most famous conductors was Harriet Tubman (1820?–1913), who in a ten-year period made at least ten trips from the North into Southern states and led over two hundred slaves into free states of the North.

Sources: *Negro Year Book, 1921–22,* pp. 153–54; Smith, *Notable Black American Women,* pp. 1151–55.

1842 • Frederick Douglass (1818–1895) made his first appearance in print as he agitated for the freedom of George W. Latimer, an escaped slave. Latimer had been captured, leading to the first of several famous fugitive slave cases. Boston abolitionists later purchased Latimer's freedom. On September 6, 1866, Douglass gave a stirring address before the Republican Convention in Rochester, New York, that promoted suffrage and laid the groundwork for the Fifteenth Amendment. George Latimer was the father of Lewis Howard Latimer (1848–1928), the inventor who revolutionized the lighting industry.

Sources: Logan and Winston, *Dictionary of American Negro Biography,* p. 385; *Negro Almanac,* p. 12; Smith, *Notable Black American Men,* pp. 698–700.

EDUCATION

Awards and Honors

1907 • Alain Locke (1885–1954), educator, interpreter, and promoter of black culture, was the first black Rhodes scholar. Established in 1902, the Rhodes Trust awarded the prestigious scholarship. It was not until 1960 that the second black Rhodes scholar, Joseph Stanley Sanders, was selected. Locke studied at Oxford University in England from 1907 to 1910, at the University of Berlin in Germany from 1910 to 1911, and at the Collège de France in Paris the following year. Locke was a logical first choice. He came from a family with a rich educational tradition. His grandfather had studied at Cambridge University in England, and his parents were descendants of educated free blacks in the North. Locke was born in Philadelphia, where his family was part of the black elite. He graduated second in his high school class and first in his class at the School of Pedagogy. At Harvard he continued this record, graduating *magna cum laude* and being elected to Phi Beta Kappa. In England Locke experienced racial discrimination, including being denied admission to several Oxford colleges before being accepted at Hertford College. When he returned to the United States, few job opportunities were commensurate with his educational preparation, and he spent six months searching in the South before he was appointed assistant professor of English and instructor of philosophy and education at Howard University. In 1916 he returned to Harvard, where he completed requirements for his doctorate, and in 1918 he was the first black person to receive a doctorate in philosophy from that institution. He resumed his position at Howard, where he remained until 1924. Locke's views, which tended to make him popular with students, made him less so with administration. He was nonetheless re-hired by Howard in 1928, where he continued to write critical essays and to promote black culture as expressed in art and literature. Locke's belief that black cultural expressions should be an essential component of education are said to have led to the revision of Howard's liberal arts curriculum during the late 1930s; his efforts were recognized by the American Association for Adult Education when he was elected its president in 1945. Although Locke taught for brief intervals at other institutions, Howard University was always his home base. When he retired in 1953, Howard awarded him an honorary Doctor of Humane Letters. Following his retirement, Locke moved to New York; his health declined and he died almost one year after leaving Howard.

Alain Locke

Sources: Alford, *Famous First Blacks,* p. 35; Bennett, *Before the Mayflower,* p. 642; Logan and Winston, *Dictionary of American Negro Biography,* pp. 398–404; Hornsby, *Milestones in Twentieth-Century African-American History,* pp. 8–9; Smith, *Notable Black American Men,* pp. 728–32.

1993 • Nima Warfield, of Plainfield, New Jersey, an English major at Morehouse College, became the first student from an historically black college to win a Rhodes Scholarship. Warfield had a perfect 4.0 grade point average and was one of thirty-two Rhodes Scholars chosen from 1,200 applicants. With the scholarship, he studied at the School of Modern History and English at Oxford in fall 1994. He planned to teach in the public school system in Plainfield.

Sources: *Journal of Blacks in Higher Education* (Spring 1994): 9.

1995 • Oseola McCarty (1908–1999) contributed her life savings, $150,000, to the University of Southern Mississippi, establishing a scholarship fund for black students. This was the first time that a black person had funded such a program at the school. McCarty was born in Wayne County, Mississippi, and moved to Hattiesburg when she was very young. With only a sixth-grade education, she dropped out of school to care for her sick aunt and grandmother. By 1967 all of her close relatives, including her mother, had died, leaving McCarty small amounts of money that she saved. For seventy-eight years McCarty worked as a washerwoman. Without the modern conveniences of a washer and dryer, she used a large pot and scrub board. As she continued to save money and to invest it wisely, she accumulated an estate, the bulk of which she gave to the University of Southern Mississippi, where a scholarship fund was established in her name. The community matched the $150,000 that she gave, bringing the total to $300,000. Interest from the funds was made available to other deserving students. She received wide recognition, including an honorary degree from Harvard University in 1996, a Trumpet Award from Turner Broadcasting in 1997, and the Fannie Lou Hamer Award from the National Council of Negro Women in 1997. Carletta Barnes, who graduated with honors with a bachelor's degree in chemistry, was the first recipient of the Oseola McCarty Endowed Scholarship in 1998.

Sources: *Jet* 94 (8 June 1998): 24; *Contemporary Black Biography*, vol. 16, pp. 159–62.

2000 • The first endowed professorship in African American studies funded by a corporation, Time Warner, Inc., was established at Harvard University. It was named for legendary producer, arranger and composer Quincy Jones (1933–).

Sources: *Black Issues in Higher Education*, vol. 17 (21 December 2000): 34, 35.

College Administrators

Daniel A. Payne

1863 • Historian, educator, and African Methodist Episcopal minister Daniel A. Payne (1811–1893) was the first black president of a black college, Wilberforce University. He spent most of his life working in education and promoting expansion of the black church. On Payne's advice, the AME Church purchased Wilberforce University, which had been founded in 1856 by the Methodist Episcopal Church. The university, which had been closed since 1862, was officially transferred on March 30, 1863. Payne became president in July of that year. He served as president for sixteen years. Payne was born in Charleston, South Carolina, to parents of mixed racial heritages. Both of his parents had died before he reached age ten; Payne was raised by his great-aunt. As a child, he worked for a carpenter and a tailor and had little formal schooling. It was his religious conversion at age eighteen, following his study in a Methodist class, which is said to have shaped the rest of his life. He opened his first school in 1829, when he was still a teenager, and continued his own education. When the state of South Carolina took steps to prevent the education of blacks, Payne, in 1835, moved to New York, where letters of introduction enabled him to be chosen for training at a seminary in Gettysburg. Thus began his pathway to the ministry, and by 1852 he had progressed to the position of bishop in the AME Church. He retained this position while serving as Wilberforce's president. He turned to writing in his later years and produced several works. His most important works were *The History of the African Methodist Episcopal Church* (1891) and *Recollections of Seventy Years* (1888).

Sources: Logan and Winston, *Dictionary of American Negro Biography*, pp. 484–85; Bennett, *Before the Mayflower*, pp. 173, 463; *Negro Almanac*, p. 1010; Simmons, *Men of Mark*, 1078–85; Smith, *Notable Black American Men*, pp. 917–20.

1906 • Scholar and minister John Wesley Edward Bowen, Sr. (1855–1933) was the first black president of Gammon Theological Seminary in Atlanta, Georgia. He served as president from 1906 to 1910 and was also the first black to teach at the school. In 1904 he founded and edited *The Voice of the Negro*, a publication appealing to the black middle class in the South. Born in New Orleans, Bowen was a member of the first graduating class at New Orleans University. In 1885 he received a bachelor of sacred theology and in 1887 a doctorate, both from Boston University. While at Boston he also taught at Morgan College (later Morgan State University) and at Howard University, and served as minister to congregations in Washington and in Baltimore. Bowen served as field secretary for the Methodist Missionary Board and later a faculty member at Gammon Theological Seminary.

Sources: Logan and Winston, *Dictionary of American Negro Biography*, pp. 52–53; *Encyclopedia of Black America*, pp. 187–88; Shockley, *Heritage and Hope*, p. 92; Salzman, *Encyclopedia of African-American Culture and History*, vol. 1, pp, 411–12.

First Black Presidents
of Selected Black Colleges, 1863–1955

Year Selected	Name	College	Year Founded
1863	Daniel A. Payne	Wilberforce College (Wilberforce, OH)	1854
1871	Hiram Rhodes Revels	Alcorn College (Lorman, MS)	1871
1881	Booker T. Washington	Tuskegee Institute (Tuskegee, AL)	1881
1882	John Mercer Langston	Virginia State College (Petersburg, VA)	1882
1904*	Mary McLeod Bethune	Bethune Cookman College (Daytona Beach, FL)	
1904	Artemisia Bowden	St. Phillips Junior College and Industrial School (San Antonio, TX)	1917
1926	Mordecai Wyatt	Howard University (Washington, DC)	1867
1930	Mary E. Branch	Tillotson College (San Antonio, TX)	
1937	Dwight Oliver Holmes	Wendell Morgan State College (Baltimore, MD)	1867
1945	Horace Mann Bond	Lincoln University (Lincoln University, PA)	1854
1946	Charles Spurgeon Johnson	Fisk University (Nashville, TN)	1866
1946	Harold L. Trigg	Saint Augustine's College (Raleigh, NC)	1867
1949	Alonzo G. Morón	Hampton University (Hampton, VA)	1868
1952	Arthur D. Gray	Talladega College (Talladega, AL)	1867
1953	Albert Edward Manley	Spelman College (Atlanta, GA)	1881

*Although the institution dates back to 1904, Bethune founded Bethune Institute this year and became founding president; the institution merged with Cookman Institute in 1929 to become Bethune-Cookman College and offered its first baccalaureate degree.

1906 • The first president of Morehouse College was John Hope (1868–1936). Hope was born in Augusta, Georgia. He graduated from Worcester Academy in Massachusetts in 1886 and entered Brown University on a scholarship. In June 1890 he graduated from Brown with honors and gave one of the class orations. From 1894 to 1898 he taught at Roger Williams University in Nashville. In 1898 he joined the faculty at Atlanta Baptist College and served as bookkeeper. In 1906 Hope was named president. When the college was renamed Morehouse College in 1913, Hope continued as president.

Sources: Smith, *Notable Black American Men*, pp. 568–71; *Contemporary Black Biography*, vol. 8, pp. 122–26.

1926 • Mordecai Wyatt Johnson (1890–1976), clergyman, educator, administrator, and public speaker, was the first black president of Howard University. He remained in this position until his retirement in 1960. Under his administration, the faculty and student body tripled in size, twenty new buildings were erected, three professional schools (law, medical, and dental) were strengthened, and graduate programs were accredited. The NAACP recognized his achievements after only three years in office at Howard and awarded him the Spingarn Medal in 1929. He also had a direct influence on the movement of nonviolent resistance. Martin Luther King Jr. heard Johnson lecture about his trip to India, in which Johnson spoke of Mahatma Gandhi's life and teachings. After hearing Johnson's lecture, King purchased books on Gandhi's life and works, and became committed to nonviolent resistance. Born in Paris, Tennessee, Johnson overcame humble circumstances to obtain three bachelor's degrees, a master's degree in theology, and two doctor of divinity degrees. However, he had no terminal academic degree when he was named Howard's president, and this exposed him to criticism and opposition. He was also criticized for his administrative style, which was considered too autocratic. Johnson, however, had the backing of university trustees, and in time his accomplishments overshadowed the criticism. He was recognized as an outstanding orator, and he traveled extensively, lecturing primarily on racial issues. He was a strong leader who never wavered in his goals for Howard or in his penchant to speak against racial injustice.

Sources: Bennett, *Before the Mayflower,* p. 526; *Encyclopedia of Black America,* p. 475; *Jet* 91 (13 January 1997): 22; 92 (23 June 1997): 19; Katz, *Eyewitness,* pp. 507–8; Smith, *Notable Black American Men,* pp. 635–38.

1937 • Dwight Oliver Wendell Holmes (1877–1963), educator and writer, became the first black president of Morgan State College (now Morgan State University), where he guided the transition of the school from Methodist control to state control. He served until 1948, when he retired. Holmes is known also for his book *Evolution of the Negro College,* published in 1934. Through his career and his writings, he significantly influenced black higher education.

Sources: Logan and Winston, *Dictionary of American Negro Biography,* pp. 320–21; *Encyclopedia of Black America,* p. 443; *Who's Who in America, 1946–1947,* p. 1106.

Charles Spurgeon Johnson

1946 • Charles Spurgeon Johnson (1893–1956), sociologist, editor, writer, and educational statesman, became the first black president of Fisk University on September 1, 1946. He was born in Bristol, Virginia, the grandson of a slave, but with a father whose education had been fostered by the slave master. Because of the racial discrimination in Bristol and Richmond at the time, Johnson attended the high school associated with Virginia Union. He graduated from Virginia Union University and in 1916 went to the University of Chicago to do doctoral study. He never completed his doctoral work but became a close associate of Chicago sociologist Robert E. Park. He later directed research and records at the Chicago Urban League, while Park was its president. Johnson interrupted his stay in Chicago to enlist in the army in 1918. A race riot that took place in Chicago in 1919 led to his appointment as associate director of the committee studying the riot and to the 1922 report, *The Negro in Chicago,* which was primarily Johnson's work. In 1923 Johnson was named editor of the Urban League's *Opportunity* magazine; throughout the 1920s the magazine served as an outlet for works by the Harlem Renaissance literary and artistic figures. His work became the model for sociological research based on facts that provoked and warranted social commentary. After a time he broadened his perspective and directed attention to the people and events that together made up the Harlem Renaissance. He left the Urban League in 1929 to accept a teaching position at Fisk, where he hoped to conduct a monumental study of racial conditions in the South and to use the results in the fight against racism. Johnson drew criticism because of his willingness to work with members of all races; some members of his own race, including W. E. B. Du Bois and E. Franklin Frazier, who with Johnson are considered founding fathers of black sociology, perceived him as too conservative. The establishment of the Race Relations Institute, which brought scholars and researchers to the Fisk campus was an essential component of the total social science program. Under Johnson's leadership, Fisk became known as a center for social science research. His own role in this process was acknowledged when the Southern Sociological Society elected him president in 1946. When he assumed the Fisk presidency, Johnson had become acknowledged as an accomplished researcher, educator, and writer. One of his works, *Shadow of a Plantation,* was reprinted in 1996, sixty-two years after the date of its first publication. As Fisk's president, his personal writing declined, but his fight for racial justice continued. He died in Louisville while on his way to a Fisk Board of Trustees meeting in New York.

Sources: Logan and Winston, *Dictionary of American Negro Biography,* pp. 347–49; Hornsby, *Milestones in Twentieth-Century African-American History,* pp. 45–46; Smith, *Notable Black American Men,* pp. 616–19.

First Black Women Presidents of Selected Black Colleges and Universities

Year	Name	College
1904	Mary McLeod	Bethune Institue (Bethune-Cookman College)*
1917	Artemisia Bowden Sr.	Phillips Junior College and Industrial School
1930	Mary E. Branch	Tillotson College
1955	Willa B. Player	Bennett College
1974	Mabel Parker McLean	Barber-Scotia College
1981	Yvonne Kennedy	Bishop State Community College
1984	Yvonne Walker-Taylor	Wilberforce University
1987	Johnnetta Betsch Cole	Spelman College
1987	Niara Sudarkasa	Lincoln University (PA)
1988	Dolores M. Spikes	Southern University and A & M College
1990	Sebetha Jenkins	Jarvis Christian College
1991	Mary Levi Smith	Kentucky State University
1991	Dolores M. Spikes	Southern University and A & M College System
1993	Joann Horton	Texas Southern University
1994	Shirley A. R. Lewis	Paine College
1994	Dorothy Cowser Yancy	Johnson C. Smith University
1995	Lois Stovall Williams	Knoxville College
1996	Portia Holmes Shields	Albany State University
1996	Dolores M. Spikes	University of Maryland, Eastern Shore
1997	Marie V. McDemmond	Norfolk State University
1998	Marguerite Archie-Hudson	Talladega College
1999	Dolores E. Cross	Morris Brown College
1999	Trudie Kibbe Reed	Philander Smith College
1999	Diane Boardley Suber	Saint Augustine's College
2001	Algeania Freeman	Livingstone College (NC)
2001	Carolynn Reid-Wallace	Fisk University
2005	JoAnn Haysbert	Langston University
2010	Carolyn W. Meyers	Jackson State University
2011	Portia Holmes Shields	Tennessee State University

Some are also first woman of any race to head the college, or first woman president of a state-supported college.

*Although the institution dates back to 1904, Bethune founded Bethune Institute in 1904 and became founding president; the institution merged with Cookman Institute in 1929 to become Bethune-Cookman College and offered its first baccalaureate degree.

Sources: *Crisis* 108 (March/April 2001): 26–28; Smith, *Notable Black American Women*; Smith, *Notable Black American Women, Book II;* Spradling, *In Black and White,* 3rd ed., vol. 1, p. 634.

1946 • The first black president of Saint Augustine's College in Raleigh, North Carolina, was Harold L. Trigg. The college was founded in 1867 by the Freedman's Commission of the Protestant Episcopal Church, a group that included clergy and laymen of North Carolina's Episcopal diocese.

Sources: *Encyclopedia of Black America,* p. 739.

1949 • The first black president of Hampton Institute (now Hampton University) was Alonzo Graseano Morón (1909–1971), who moved up from his position as acting president. He was elected in April and installed as president in October. Born in Saint Thomas, he graduated from Hampton's trade school in 1927 and enrolled at Brown University in 1928. He was elected to Phi Beta Kappa in his senior year and graduated in 1932. He received a master's degree from the University of Pittsburgh in 1933. With a Rosenwald Fellowship, Morón enrolled in Harvard Law School in 1944 and received his law degree in 1947. His career experiences were varied. In 1933 he became the first black to be employed by the Emergency Relief Commission in Baltimore. That same year the governor of the Virgin Islands appointed Morón as commissioner of public welfare for the islands. Three years later he moved to Atlanta to become assistant administrator to the acting president of Atlanta University. For four years he managed a 675-unit housing project for blacks in Atlanta; later he also managed Atlanta's John Hope Homes and lectured at Atlanta University on housing and housing problems. He also published a number of articles on housing and the black community. In 1946, while still in law school, he worked as business management consultant at Hampton, and the next year he was named business manager at the school. After Hampton's president resigned, Morón chaired the interim administrative committee and became acting president in October 1948.

Sources: *Current Biography, 1949,* pp. 435–36; Hornsby, *Milestones in Twentieth-Century African-American History,* p. 157.

1952 • The first black president of Talladega College was Arthur Douglass Gray (1907–1979). He was inaugurated on September 1. Gray was born in Sheffield, Alabama, and graduated from Talladega College in 1929. He received a second bachelor's and a master's degree from Chicago Theological Seminary. In 1949 he received an honorary doctor of divinity degree from the seminary. He served as pastor of Plymouth Congregational Church in Washington (1934–44) and then pastor of the Church of Good Shepherd in Chicago (1944–52), one of the nation's largest Christian churches. In 1962, during the civil rights demonstrations, he supported the students' protests and won their respect. During his tenure at Talladega enrollment increased, the curriculum was revised, the physical plant upgraded, and the Southern Association of Colleges and Schools accredited the school. Gray resigned in August 1963 to become pastor of the Congregational Church of Park Manor in Chicago.

Sources: Bailey, *They Too Call Alabama Home,* pp. 148–49.

1953 • Albert Edward Manley (1908–1997) became the first black president of Spelman College. He served until 1976, when he became president emeritus. Born in San Pedro Sula, Spanish Honduras, he graduated from Johnson C. Smith University in North Carolina, Columbia Teachers College, and Stanford University. He was a faculty member and administrator at North Carolina College in Durham from 1946 to 1953. He was also a guest lecturer at Harvard University in summers 1970 through 1975.

Sources: *Ebony Success Library,* vol. 1, p. 215; *Who's Who among African Americans,* 10th ed., p. 963

1960 • James Madison Nabrit Jr. (1908–1997) and Samuel Milton Nabrit (1905–2003) became the first black brothers to simultaneously hold the presidencies of two of the largest black universities. James Nabrit, a lawyer, educator, and civil rights advocate, served as president of Howard University from 1960 to 1969, while educator Samuel Nabrit was president of Texas Southern University from 1947 to 1966. Born in Macon, Georgia, Samuel attended Morehouse College (B.A., 1925) and Brown University (M.S. in 1928 and Ph.D. in 1932). He was the first black to receive a doctorate in biology from Brown. He returned to Atlanta after his Brown graduation, and worked in the biology department at Atlanta University from 1932 to 1947. He was promoted to dean in 1947, but left to assume the presidency of Texas Southern. Samuel Nabrit held a number of important posts, including serving on the National Science Board, being appointed to the Atomic Energy Commission by President Lyndon Johnson, and serving as director of the Southern Fellowships Fund from 1967 until he retired in 1981. Both Morehouse and Texas Southern have named science buildings in honor of Samuel Nabrit.

Sources: *Encyclopedia of Black America*, pp. 611–12; *Who's Who among Black Americans*, 1992–93, p. 1045; *Wormley, Many Shades of Black*, pp. 61, 159; Salzman, *Encyclopedia of African-American Culture and History*, Supplement, p. 201.

1966 • James Colston (1909–1982) became the first black to head a college in New York State when he was appointed president of Bronx Community College. He graduated from Morehouse College in Atlanta and obtained his doctorate from New York University. He served as president of Knoxville College in Tennessee from 1951 until his new appointment in 1966 at Bronx Community College, where he served until 1976.

Sources: *Jet* 61 (11 February 1982): 54; *Negro Almanac, 1976*, p. 1023; *Who's Who among Black Americans, 1980–81*, p. 165.

1969 • William M. Boyd, III (1942–) was the first black on the board of trustees of Williams College in Massachusetts. He served as president from 1969 to 1972. The Tuskegee native graduated from Williams College and the University of California, Berkeley, and was a Peace Corps volunteer in Cameroon from 1963 to 1965.

Sources: *Ebony Success Library*, vol. 1, p. 38.

1969 • A[loyisus] Leon Higginbotham Jr., (1928–1998) lawyer, judge, and graduate of the Yale Law School, was the first black elected to the university's board of trustees, the Yale University Corporation. He defeated five other candidates in the April and May nationwide balloting. Higginbotham, who became one of the most prominent black judges, was born in Trenton, New Jersey. His parents were blue-collar workers, and the Bible and a dictionary were the only books in their home. Higginbotham, nevertheless, was a serious and high-achieving student. When he graduated from the previously all-white high school he helped to integrate, he enrolled at Purdue University, with the intent of becoming an engineer. A racial incident involving housing for black students led to his withdrawal from Purdue and transfer to Antioch College in Ohio. After his graduation from Antioch, Yale accepted him in 1949, and he earned a bachelor's degree in sociology. He was admitted to the Pennsylvania bar in 1953 and soon joined a firm in which he became a partner in 1954. He remained with the firm until 1962, while also serving as a hearings officer for the U.S. Department of Justice. When he left the law firm in 1962, he became the youngest person and the first black to serve on the Federal Trade Commission. His appointment to the U.S. District Court of the Eastern District of Philadelphia came two years later. He remained a judge for thirteen years and was host to several law clerks who later became national political figures. He was appointed judge of the U.S. Court of Appeals for the Third District (Philadelphia) in 1977, and in 1989 he became chief judge for the U.S. Court of Appeals. He retired from the bench in 1993, having earned distinction as a jurist and an author. His 1978 book, *In the Matter of Color: Race and the American Legal Process*, garnered awards from the American Bar Association, the National Bar Association, the National Association of Black Journalists, and the National Conference of Black Lawyers; the work also received a 1981 nomination for the American Book Award. As a jurist, Thurgood Marshall was Higginbotham's mentor, and Higginbotham was an active advocate for racial justice. While on the bench, Higginbotham also taught and held administrative posts at several colleges. Upon retirement, he became a professor of law at Harvard University. He was given the nation's highest civilian honor, the Presidential Medal of Freedom, by President Bill Clinton in 1995, and the NAACP's Spingarn Medal in 1996. His second study of race and the law, *Shades of Freedom*, was published in 1996.

Sources: *Encyclopedia of Black America*, pp. 436–37; Garrett, *Famous First Facts about Negroes*, pp. 162–63; Salzman, *Encyclopedia of African-American Culture and History*, Supplement, pp. 128–29; Smith, *Notable Black American Men*, pp. 548–49; *Who's Who in America, 1982–83*, vol. 1, p. 1332.

1970 • The first black president of a major American university in the twentieth century was Clifton Reginald Wharton Jr. (1926–), who on January 2, 1970, became president of

Michigan State University. Wharton was born in Boston and graduated from Harvard University in 1947 and Johns Hopkins University in 1948. He was the first black to earn a doctorate in economics from the University of Chicago in 1958. After leaving Michigan State, he became chairman and chief executive officer of the Teachers Insurance and Annuity Association and the College Retirement Equities Fund (TIAA-CREF). He became the first black chancellor of the State University of New York in 1978. In 1993 he was named Deputy U.S. Secretary of State. He is now a New York Stock Exchange director and continues as a TIAA overseer.

Sources: *Encyclopedia of Black America,* pp. 851–52; Garrett, *Famous First Facts about Negroes,* pp. 61–62; *Who's Who among African Americans,* 26th ed., pp. 1313; *Jet* 98 (23 October 2000): 19.

**Marian Wright
Edelman**

1972 • The first black woman elected to the Yale University Corporation was Marian Wright Edelman (1939–), a lawyer, children's rights activist, and head of the agency that she founded in 1973, the Children's Defense Fund. In 1980 she became the first black (and the second woman) to head the Spelman College Board of Trustees. Edelman, born in Bennettsville, South Carolina, was raised by her family with the expectation that she would help her community. She entered Spelman in 1956. While there, she earned scholarships for study abroad and studied at the Sorbonne University in Paris and the University of Geneva in Switzerland; she also spent two months in the Soviet Union. When she returned to Atlanta in 1959, she became a very active participant in the student protests in the South and was arrested after a large sit-in at Atlanta's City Hall. Her decision to go to law school was crystallized at this time, and she entered Yale University, as a John Hay Whitney Fellow, after her 1960 graduation from Spelman. She earned her law degree from Yale in 1963, and took her first job as one of the first two interns with the NAACP's Legal Defense and Education Fund in Jackson, Mississippi. She later opened her own law office. In 1968 she moved to Washington with a grant to study how to obtain legal justice for the poor. She directed the Harvard's Center for Law and Education from 1971 to 1973, but also continued work on her Washington project while establishing the Children's Defense Fund. She and her husband returned to Washington in 1979. The organization she founded has dealt effectively with a broad range of family and children's issues, particularly those that impacted the poor. Edelman serves on a number of boards and has received awards from a wide variety of sources. She has been profiled by the *New Yorker* magazine, named by *Time* magazine one of America's 200 young leaders in 1971, and named by the *Ladies' Home Journal* one of the 100 most influential women in America in 1985. Her services have been utilized by the government through a number of committee appointments; she has received a multitude of distinguished service awards; and holds more than thirty honorary degrees. Edelman has written extensively, with most of her works pertaining to children's issues. Her name is synonymous with dedicated service on behalf of children.

Sources: Hine, *Black Women in America,* vol. 1, pp. 377–78; *Encyclopedia of Black America,* p. 331; Smith, *Notable Black American Women,* pp. 309–12. *Who's Who among African Americans,* 26th ed., pp. 373.

1972 • James J. Gardner (1931?–1998) was the first black chairman of Florida's Board of Regents. A graduate of Florida A & M University in Tallahassee, he worked to keep the historically black school a separate entity within the state's university system. He had served as principal of several elementary and high schools in Florida and as assistant to the superintendent of Broward County schools. He served two terms and was later appointed assistant to the president of Nova Southeastern University in the Fort Lauderdale area.

Sources: *New York Times* (27 August 1998).

1974 • Charles Shelby Rooks (1924–2001) was named the first black president of Chicago Theological Seminary on April 8, 1974, and remained in the position until January 1984. He left to become executive vice president of the United Church Board for Homeland Ministries in New York City. He was born in Beaufort, North Carolina, did his undergraduate work at Virginia State College (later University), and received the master of divinity degree from Union Theological Seminary. He holds the Doctor of Divinity degree from the College of Wooster (1968), Interdenominational Theological Center (1979), and Virginia Union University (1980). He held pastorates in churches in Orangeburg, South Carolina, and Washington, D.C., and served as executive director of the Fund for Theological Education in Princeton, New Jersey before assuming the Homeland Ministries presidency. He retired from this position in 1992.

Sources: Hornsby, *Chronology of African-American History,* pp. 218–19; *Jet* 66 (18 June 1984): 26; *Who's Who among African Americans,* 14th ed., p. 1121.

1977 • Wenda Weekes Moore (1941–), a Minneapolis civic leader, was the first black chairperson of the University of Minnesota Board of Regents, from 1975 to 1983. She was appointed to the board in 1973, elected to the board in 1975, elected vice chair of the board in 1975, and then moved up to become chair. In 1979 she was leader of the First Educational Exchange Delegation, University of Minnesota, to the People's Republic of China. Moore was born in Boston and graduated from Howard University in Washington. She also completed two years of graduate work at the University of Southern California.

Sources: *Jet* 53 (29 September 1977): 24; *Who's Who among African Americans,* 26th ed., p. 900.

1977 • Jesse Hill Jr. (1927–) became the first black member of the Georgia Board of Regents. Born in St. Louis, Missouri, Hill demonstrated his aptitude for business at an early age. He worked with his grandfather and uncles who operated the Dennis Moving and Furniture Company. Hill started his own newspaper business in St. Louis and carried all of the black newspapers published around the country. He received a bachelor's degree in mathematics and physics from Lincoln University (Missouri) in 1947. Two years later he received a master's degree in business administration from the University of Michigan. In 1973, living in Atlanta and serving as vice president and chief actuary of Atlanta Life Insurance Company, he was made president and chief executive officer when Norris B. Herndon stepped down from office. Under Hill's watch, Atlanta Life reached its highest level of growth in assets and shareholder value. During the 1950s he was active in voter-registration and other civil rights activities, which propelled him to local prominence. He worked with the Atlanta Cooperative Action, a group of entrepreneurs and educators that challenged Georgia's segregated system of higher education. He also worked with local black college students who sought to desegregate lunch counters in public places. To fill the void in reporting news from the black community, in 1960 he founded the *Atlanta Inquirer.* A participant in political activities, in the late 1970s Hill was fundraiser and campaigner for President Jimmy Carter. His alma mater, the University of Michigan, recognized him in 1987 by awarding him the Business Leadership Award and again in 1996 by awarding him an honorary doctorate. Hill retired from his post at Atlanta Life in 1993 but remained chairman of the board until 1995.

Sources: *Contemporary Black Biography,* vol. 13, pp. 103–05; Smith, *Notable Black American Men,* pp. 549–52; *Who's Who among African Americans,* 26th ed., p. 583.

1980 • Benjamin Lelon McGee (1943–) became the first black chairperson of the Arkansas State University Board of Trustees—the first in the South to attain that position at a predominantly white institution. McGee was born in Booneville, Mississippi, and graduated from Arkansas Agricultural, Mechanical, and Normal College in Pine Bluff (as it was known then). He did further study at Memphis State University (now the University of Memphis). Among his career accomplishments, he was a compliance supervisor with the U.S. Department of Agriculture from 1967 to 1975. Since 1977 he has been owner of Liquor Center in Memphis.

Sources: *Jet* 59 (18 September 1980): 30; *Who's Who among African Americans,* 26th ed., p. 845.

1981 • Jewel Plummer Cobb (1924–) became president of California State University at Fullerton. She was the first black woman appointed in the system and is believed to be the first to head a major public university on the West Coast. She was born in Chicago, into a family that emphasized the accomplishments and concerns of black people. Her father practiced medicine and her mother once taught interpretive dance. Although Cobb grew up in comfortable circumstances, she was also aware of the obstacles that black people encountered. Her family changed residences several times while she was growing up, always moving to a better location, into a section of town that had experienced white flight. Cobb began her college study at the University of Michigan, but transferred to historically black Talladega College after three semesters. Talladega did not accept transfer credits, but Cobb graduated after three and one-half years by taking examinations and summer classes. She was awarded a fellowship to do graduate work at New York University (NYU) and earned both a master's degree in 1947 and doctoral degree in biology in 1950. As a cell biologist, Cobb has concentrated on cell research and specifically melanin, a brown or black pigment that colors the skin. She is also credited with pioneering research on the study of drugs used in the treatment of cancer. She served on the faculty at NYU from 1955 to 1960. She continued to do research while also serving as an academic administrator at both Sarah Lawrence College in New York and Connecticut College. She discontinued her research only when she moved to Douglass College of Rutgers University in New Jersey in 1976 to serve as dean. Cobb held this position until she was named president of California State University at Fullerton. While there, she expanded both the curriculum and the physical facilities and changed the institution from a commuter college to one with student housing. She has written extensively, often about the role of women in science. Her appointment as Trustee Professor at California State College, Los Angeles, has allowed her to continue her efforts to motivate minorities to study science and engineering. Her work as a biologist is praised in scientific circles; buildings bear her name at Douglass College and at California State, Fullerton; and her portrait, as a distinguished black scientist, hangs in the National Academy of Science.

Sources: Hine, *Black Women in America,* vol. 1, pp. 257–68; Smith, *Notable Black American Women,* pp. 195–98; *Who's Who among African Americans,* 26th ed., p. 250; Warren, *Black Women Scientists in the United States,* pp. 40–49.

1981 • Walter J. Kamba was installed as the first black president of the University of Zimbabwe. A Yale Law School graduate, he taught at several European universities before locating in Zimbabwe.

Sources: *Jet* 61 (22 October 1981): 22.

1981 • Yvonne Kennedy (1945–) became the first black woman junior college president in Alabama in 1981, when she took the position at Bishop State Community College in Mobile. She also became the first black woman to head a state college in Alabama. Born in Mobile, she is the eleventh of twelve children; her family represents several generations of Mobile natives. She graduated from Bishop State Junior College with an associate in arts degree and entered Alabama State College (now Alabama State University), where in 1965 she was elected Miss Alabama State University. While there she joined civil rights protesters in the Selma to Montgomery march and was deeply touched by the experience. She graduated in 1966 with a degree in English and social sciences. In 1968 she received a master of arts degree in English from Morgan State College (now Morgan State University). She received her doctorate degree from the University of Alabama, Tuscaloosa. She also served as a member of the Alabama House of Representatives, where she chaired the Black Caucus.

Sources: *Jet* 61 (19 November 1981): 24; *Who's Who among African Americans,* 26th ed., p. 719.

1981 • The first black rector of James Madison University in Virginia was James H. Taylor Jr. The Tuskegee University graduate received his doctorate from Duke University and served as the assistant superintendent of city schools in Lynchburg, Virginia.

Sources: *Jet* 62 (6 September 1982): 22.

1984 • The first woman of any race to become president of Wilberforce University was Yvonne Walker-Taylor (1916–2006). She was named the sixteenth president of Wilberforce, the same institution at which her father, D. Ormonde Walker, had served as the tenth president. Walker-Taylor was born in New Bedford, Massachusetts. Her father was an African Methodist Episcopal minister, who later became a bishop. Her tie with Wilberforce, a school founded by the AME Church in 1856, began early; she graduated from Wilberforce the year her father was named its president. She went on to earn a master's degree from Boston University in 1938 and an educational specialist degree from the University of Kansas in 1964. She joined the faculty at Wilberforce in 1955, after teaching at the Wilberforce Academy and a Boston high school. Walker-Taylor served Wilberforce in a variety of positions and was responsible for significant program additions before becoming president. She organized the institution's first reading clinic and initiated a Cooperative Education Program, making Wilberforce the first black college to require cooperative education. She held the administrative positions of dean and vice president—both "firsts" for a woman at Wilberforce. She maintained strong ties with the AME Church and represented Wilberforce at all church conferences. She retired from the presidency in 1987, having improved fund-raising efforts, expanded curricular offerings and the physical plant, and enhanced the quality of student life. After retiring, she was named president emeritus. Walker-Taylor was highly visible nationally, appearing on television, testifying before Congressional committees, and participating in a variety of professional and community associations. A dynamic woman, who once wanted to be a jazz singer, Walker-Taylor has been recognized as both an educator and a humanitarian. From 1990 to 1996, she continued her active involvement with higher education as distinguished presidential professor at Central State University, also in Wilberforce, Ohio.

Sources: *Jet* 66 (12 March 1984): 23; Smith, *Notable Black American Women,* Book II, pp. 670–72; *Who's Who among African Americans,* 14th ed., pp. 1334.

First Black Women Presidents
of Selected Mainstream Colleges and Universities in the U.S.

Year	Name	College
1981	Jewel Plummer Cobb	California State University, Fullerton
1986	L. Eudoria Pettigrew	College of Old Westbury
1988	Blenda Jacqueline Wilson	University of Michigan, Dearborn
1990	Marguerite Ross Barnett	University of Houston
1990	Dolores E. Cross	Chicago State University
1994	Carol Surles	Texas Women's University
1992	Blenda Jacqueline Wilson	California State, Northridge
1995	Jacqueline M. Belcher	DeKalb (GA) College
1995	Ruth J. Simmons	Smith College
1998	Joyce Brown	State University of New York, Fashion Institute of Technology
1998	Glenda D. Price	Marygrove College
1999	Shirley Ann Jackson	Rensselaer Polytechnic Institute
2001	Ruth J. Simmons	Brown University

Sources: *Crisis* 108 (March/April 2001): 26–28; Smith, *Notable Black American Women*; Smith, *Notable Black American Women,* Book II.

1985 • Elridge W. McMillan (1934–), prominent Atlanta educator and executive director of the Southern Education Foundation (SEF), became the first black vice-chairperson of the Board of Regents of the University System of Georgia. He went on to serve as the board's chairperson from 1986 until 1987. He was born in Barnesville, Georgia, but the family moved often as his Methodist minister father was assigned new pastorates. McMillan entered Clark College in Atlanta at age sixteen and graduated in 1954 with an A.B. degree in English. He taught in Atlanta public schools during the summers, while he did graduate work at Columbia University's Teachers College. After receiving his master's in guidance and school student personnel administration in 1959, he worked as a resource counselor for a division of the Atlanta schools. McMillan stayed with the school system until 1965, when he became the first black hired by the new Office of Economic Opportunity. In 1968 he began his work with the SEF as a program associate; a year later he was promoted to associate director, and then to executive director in 1978. His title was changed to president in 1983, when the structure of the organization was changed. McMillan is given credit for changing SEF from a private foundation to a public charity that collaborates with and obtains funds from other organizations concerned with equality of education for blacks in the South. He first became a member of the Georgia Board of Regents in 1975. He holds several honorary doctorate degrees and has received a number of awards, including the NAACP's W. E. B. Du Bois Award in Education in 1982, 1987, and 1992.

Sources: *Jet* 68 (12 August 1985): 22; 74 (11 July 1988): 15; Smith, *Notable Black American Men,* pp. 797–98; *Who's Who among African Americans,* 14th ed., p. 889.

1985 • The first black chancellor of California's 106 community colleges was Joshua L. Smith (1934–), former president of Manhattan Borough Community College. Smith was born in Boston and graduated from Boston University. He received his master's and doctorate from Harvard Graduate School of Education. Smith's other positions include program officer for the Ford Foundation, dean of the school of education at City College of the City University of New York, president of Brookdale Community College, and interim chair of the Department of Education at Baruch College.

Sources: *Jet* 69 (13 January 1986): 11; *Who's Who among African Americans,* 26th ed., p. 1149.

1985 • David Hall (1950–) was named associate dean and professor at Northeastern University School of Law, the first black to head a Boston-area law school. He was named provost and senior vice president in 1998—the school's first black to hold the senior slot. He is an expert on civil rights and legal education. Hall was born in Savannah, Georgia, and graduated from Kansas State University (B.A.), the University of Oklahoma (M.A. and J.D.), and Harvard Law School (LL.M., SJD). He was staff attorney for the Federal Trade Commission and also held teaching positions in law schools at the University of Mississippi and the University of Oklahoma.

Sources: *Jet* 94 (13 July 1998): 20; *Who's Who among African Americans,* 26th ed., p. 514.

1986 • Niara Sudarkasa (1938–), educator and anthropologist, became the first woman president of Lincoln University in Pennsylvania. She was the unanimous choice of the board of trustees, chosen from a field of 103 candidates. Born Gloria A. Marshall in Fort Lauderdale, Florida, she entered Fisk University as an early entrant in 1952, at age fourteen. After spending her junior year as an exchange student at Oberlin College, she transferred to Oberlin and graduated in 1957. She entered Columbia the next year and was awarded the master's degree in anthropology in 1959. She received her doctorate from Columbia University in New York in 1964. Between 1959 and 1964 she held three different fellowships that supported her study, including periods of study in London and in Nigeria. After graduation, she taught briefly at Columbia and at New York University before moving to the University of Michigan in 1967, where she remained for nearly twenty years. She was, in 1976, the first black woman promoted to full professor in the arts and sciences division and the first tenured black woman professor. She was appointed associate vice president for academic affairs at Michigan in 1984. Sudarkasa gives Oberlin the credit for sparking her interest in Africa, which has been the subject of much of her research. Her research on African women and the application of this research to the African American family structure has contributed to her international reputation as a researcher. She is also well known for her political activism, which came to the fore during the 1970s with the increase of black students at major universities and their pleas for black studies programs. Her activism has been extended to stress the need for equal access to higher education. Gloria Marshall changed her name to emphasize her ties to Africa. Niara Sudarkasa further emphasized these ties when she was inaugurated as Lincoln's president. Both her inaugural robe and her inaugural ball gown used kente cloth from Ghana. Her honors include recognition by the Michigan Senate and the Michigan House of Representatives. She was also named Distinguished Visiting Scholar in the College of Liberal Arts at Florida Atlantic University. She remained president of Lincoln University until 1998.

Sources: Hine, *Black Women in America,* vol. 2, pp. 1123–24; *Jet* 71 (27 October 1986): 22; Smith, *Notable Black American Women,* pp. 1089–93; *Who's Who among African Americans,* 26th ed., p. 1191.

1987 • Educator and anthropologist Johnnetta Betsch Cole [Robinson] (1936–) became the first black woman president of Spelman College. She was affectionately called "Sister President," a title that she gave herself in 1987. At Spelman, Cole increased the endowment from $40 million to more than $143 million. She led a campaign that raised $114 million, the largest amount ever raised by a black school. During her stay at Spelman, the school was listed in the top ten of the one hundred top colleges as rated by *Money* magazine. She resigned from the Spelman post in June 1997, and after a year's leave she became a member of the faculty at Emory University. Then she became president of Bennett College for Women. She retired from Bennett in 2007 and, since 2009, has served as director of the Smithsonian Institution's National Museum of African Art. Born in Jacksonville, Florida, Cole was influenced considerably by Mary McLeod Bethune and other black women associated with nearby Bethune-Cookman University; these women along with her own mother, who was a teacher and registrar at Edward Waters College in Jacksonville, became her role models. She enrolled in Fisk University, but after a year joined her older sister at Oberlin College and graduated in 1957. She earned her master's and doctorate degrees in anthropology from Northwestern University, completing the doctorate in 1967. Cole taught at Washington State University for two years, at the University of Massachusetts-Amherst (where she was promoted from professor to provost of undergraduate education), and at Hunter College of the City College of New York before going to Spelman. She has a record of distinguished achievement wherever she has been. Her landmark book, *All American Women,* published in 1986, broke new ground in women's studies with its emphasis on ethnicity, race, and class. She has more than forty honorary degrees and prestigious awards. In 1998 she was profiled on the PBS show *Bridgebuilders,* and in 1999 she was given the McGovern Behavioral Science Award. Born into the family that owned the Afro-American Life Insurance Co., founded by her maternal grandfather, Cole broke with family tradition when she opted not to join the family business. When she married a white fellow graduate student at Northwestern in 1959, there were threats from the Jacksonville white community, which speaks to the attitude existent toward interracial marriage at the time. Cole retired in 1997 and the next year she became Presidential Distinguished Professor of Anthropology, Women's Studies, and African American Studies at Emory University. In 2002, she came out of retirement to become president of Bennett College for Women. She is the only person to have served as president of two historically black colleges for women.

Sources: Hine, *Black Women in America,* vol. 1, pp. 260–61; *Jet* 90 (23 September 1996): 8; 97 (20 December 1999): 10; *Negro Almanac,* pp. 97, 1081; Smith, *Notable Black American Women,* pp. 198–201; *Who's Who among African Americans,* 26th ed., p. 253.

1987 • Marilyn Virginia Yarbrough (1945–) became the first black law school dean in the South and the only black woman law school dean in the country, when she was hired at the University of Tennessee at Knoxville. Yarbrough came to the school from the University of Kansas, where she was law professor and associate vice chancellor. She left Tennessee in 1991 and became professor of law at the University of North Carolina, Chapel Hill. Born in Bowling Green, Kentucky, she is a graduate of Virginia State University in Petersburg and received her law degree from the University of California, Los Angeles.

Sources: *Black Issues in Higher Education* 7 (28 February 1991): 25; *Jet* 73 (5 October 1987): 39; *Who's Who among African Americans,* 14th ed., p. 1446.

1987 • The first black to become dean of a New York state law school was W. Haywood Burns (1940–1996). He was named dean of the law school of the City University of New York and served from 1987 to 1994. He served as professor and administrator in the City University of New York for seventeen years, working as vice provost and as dean of Urban and Legal Problems. Born in Peekskill, New York, Burns was a graduate of Harvard University and Yale Law School. In 1966–67 he was law clerk to Judge Constance Baker Motley. Burns became known in the late 1960s and early 1970s as attorney for activist Angela Davis, who faced kidnapping charges. After the rebellion in Attica prison in 1971, he worked on behalf of the inmates. He also worked with Martin Luther King Jr.

Sources: *Jet* 89 (29 April 1996): 22–23; *Who's Who among African Americans*, 9th ed., p. 214.

1988 • Clark University and Atlanta University merged in July 1988 to become Clark Atlanta University. Thomas Winston Cole Jr. (1941–) became the first president. A native of Vernon, Texas, he graduated from Wiley College in Marshall, Texas, and received his doctorate degree from the University of Chicago. He taught at the University of Illinois and Massachusetts Institute of Technology. He was president of West Virginia State College from 1982 to 1986 and chancellor of the West Virginia Board of Regents from 1986 to 1988.

Sources: *Jet* 77 (16 October 1989): 16; *Who's Who among African Americans*, 26th ed., p. 253.

1988 • Blenda Jacqueline Wilson (1941–) became the first black woman to head a public university in Michigan when she was appointed chancellor of the University of Michigan, Dearborn. Wilson was born in Perth Amboy, New Jersey, where her mother, who had been a teacher in Georgia, encouraged her daughter's dreams of teaching and reducing the inequities in education. Wilson grew up in the mostly white community of Woodbridge, New Jersey, where she was one of only two black children in her kindergarten class. She made trips on Sunday to attend an African American Baptist Church in Perth Amboy, her primary exposure to black culture. When she graduated from high school, she chose to enter Cedar Crest College in Allentown, Pennsylvania, one of the few colleges that offered merit scholarships to women, without regard to race. She graduated from Cedar Crest in 1962, and began her teaching career in Woodbridge that same year. Wilson earned a master's degree from Seton Hall University in 1965, and she moved to New Brunswick, New Jersey, in 1966, taking one of the first jobs offered through the Lyndon Johnson administration's War on Poverty. While there, she wrote a grant for the state's first Head Start program. In 1968 she became executive director of the Middlesex County (New Jersey) Economic Opportunities Corporation, but left in 1969 to become executive assistant to the provost at Rutgers University. This was to mark the beginning of her career in educational administration. While at Rutgers, Wilson enhanced her administrative skills by attending the Institute for Educational Management at Harvard Business School. In 1972 she became associate dean for administration at Harvard and was named senior associate dean in 1975. This position allowed her to attend graduate school at Boston University, and she received her doctorate in higher education administration in 1979. From 1982 to 1984 she served as vice president for sector management at Independent Sector, an organization designed to improve management in nonprofit organizations. In 1984 she became executive director of the Colorado State Department of Higher Education and a state cabinet officer. She left Denver in 1988 to accept the Michigan position, where she remained until 1992. From 1992 to 1999, she was president of California State University at Northridge, the only woman in the United States to head a branch of the nation's largest public university system at the time. Beginning in 1999, Wilson became president and chief executive officer of the Nellie Mae Education Foundation, which is based in Quincy, Massachusetts.

Sources: *Detroit Free Press* (21 May 1992); Smith, *Notable Black American Women*, Book II, pp. 719–22; *Who's Who among African Americans*, 26th ed., p. 1361.

1989 • The first black chancellor of Los Angeles Community Colleges was Donald Gayton Phelps (1929–2003). He was inaugurated in May 1989 to head the nine-campus system, the largest community college system in the world. Born in Seattle, he graduated from Seattle University and received his doctorate from the University of Washington. His administrative experiences include director of the National Institute on Alcohol Abuse and Alcoholism, president of Seattle Central Community College, and chancellor, Seattle Community College District VI.

Sources: *Jet* 76 (17 April 1989): 37; *Who's Who among African Americans*, 14th ed., p. 1029.

1990 • Marguerite Ross Barnett (1942–1992) took office as the first woman and first black president of the University of Houston on September 1, 1990. In 1986 she had been named the first black woman chancellor of the University of Missouri, Saint Louis. She was noted for her strong fund-raising activities at both institutions. The Charlottesville, Virginia, native did her undergraduate work at Antioch College in Ohio and received her master's and doctorate in political science from the University of Chicago. She received her master's degree in 1968, and was hired by the University of Chicago as a lecturer in 1969. Her other early positions included teaching posts at Princeton University, Howard University, Columbia University, and City University of New York (CUNY). She also served as vice chancellor of CUNY from 1983 until 1986, when she left for the University of Saint Louis. When appointed at the University of Houston, she became one of only three women who lead institutions with more than 30,000 students and the only black to head a major research institution at the time. She wrote extensively, publishing articles and books, and is the recipient of many awards.

Sources: Hine, *Black Women in America*, vol. 1, pp. 89–90; *Jet* 78 (21 May 1990): 36; Smith, *Notable Black American Women*, pp. 55–56.

1990 • Dolores E. Cross (1938–) was the first black woman president of Chicago State University. She was appointed in May and took office on September. She was also the first woman to head a four-year college in the Illinois system of public higher education. Her accomplishments at Chicago State included expansion of the physical plant, increase in the number of bachelor's degrees awarded annually, and an increase in the retention rate. In 1997 she stepped down from the post to take a position with the General Electric Company, where she headed the GE fund to support education. After serving for two years as the GE Fund Distinguished Professor in Leadership and Diversity at the City University Graduate School and University Center in New York, she became in 1999 the first woman president of Morris Brown College in Atlanta. Born in Newark, New Jersey, Cross graduated from Seton Hall and Hofstra universities before receiving her doctorate degree from the University of Michigan in 1971. Cross's positions prior to assuming her first college presidency reflect her commitment to higher education. She began her career with a teaching post at Northwestern University in Illinois; she was later the first black American woman to hold a teaching post at the Claremont Graduate School in California. She also held an academic administrative post at City University of New York, and she was the first black senior administrator at the University of Minnesota. An advocate of achieving a healthy balance physically, emotionally, and spiritually in personal and professionally life, Cross became an accomplished marathon runner. She finished first in her category in the Houston Marathon. She recounts her experiences in achieving a healthy balance in the book *Breaking through the Wall: A Marathoner's Story* (1999).

Sources: *Jet* 78 (18 June 1990): 22; 79 (15 April 1991): 22; 92 (23 June 1997): 32; 97 (24 April 2000): 20; *Who's Who among African Americans*, 26th ed., p. 288.

1990 • Otis L. Floyd (1928–1993) became chancellor of the Board of Regents in Tennessee on June 29, 1990. He was the first black person ever to head a university system in Tennessee. He served as vice president for administration at Middle Tennessee State University and acting commissioner of education for the Tennessee Department of Education. Floyd served as president of Tennessee State University in Nashville from 1987 until his new appointment. Born in Selmer, McNairy County, Tennessee, he began his career as a teacher in a one-room school in Purdy. He graduated from Lane College in Jackson (Tennessee), Tennessee State University, and received his doctorate in education from Memphis State University (now the University of Memphis).

Sources: Jones, *Every Day in Tennessee History*, p. 33; *Nashville Banner* (19 May 1993); *Tennessean* (20 May 1993).

1991 • The first black president of Andover Newton Theological School in Newton Centre, Massachusetts, the oldest theological school in the nation, was David Thomas Shannon Sr. (1933–2008). Shannon, an Old Testament scholar, was born in Richmond, Virginia. He graduated from Virginia Union University, Virginia Union School of Religion, and Oberlin Graduate School of Theology. He also received a doctorate from Vanderbilt University in Nashville and the University of Pittsburgh. He pastored several churches and served on

Stanford's First Black Academic Officer

In 1993 Condoleezza "Condi" Rice (1954–) became the youngest and first black chief academic officer at Stanford University on September 1, 1993. Rice served as senior director of Soviet and East European Affairs on the National Security Council from 1991 to 1993, for President George Bush. For Bush's son, President George W. Bush, she was confirmed as head of the National Security Council in 2001. Born in segregated Birmingham, Alabama, Rice has risen to prominence and esteem as an academician and an expert in international relations. Her father was a university administrator, and her childhood circumstances were comfortable despite her experiences with segregation. Political science was not her first choice for a college major. Initially a music major at the University of Denver, Rice changed her major and graduated in 1974 at age nineteen. A master's degree from the University of Notre Dame followed in 1975, and she was awarded the doctorate in international studies from the University of Denver in 1981. One of the internships she held while pursuing her doctorate was with the U.S. Department of State. After receiving the degree, she taught at Stanford from 1981 to 1989; her teaching was recognized with an award in 1984. A fellowship in 1987 allowed Rice to serve as special assistant to the director of the Joint Chiefs of Staff, whose assignment was Strategic Nuclear Policy. Rice has an enviable list of scholarly publications and has been called by some one of the "new breed of young black conservatives."

Sources: *Contemporary Black Biography,* vol. 3, pp. 206–8; *Jet* 84 (7 June 1993): 22; Smith, *Notable Black American Women,* Book II, pp. 552–54; *Who's Who among African Americans,* 26th ed., pp. 1043–44.

the faculty at Virginia Union, Howard University, Bucknell University, Pittsburgh Presbyterian Theological Seminary, and elsewhere. He served as president of Virginia Union from 1979 to 1985. He left Andover Newton in 1994 to become president of Allen University.

Sources: *Jet* 80 (14 October 1991): 36; *Who's Who among African Americans,* 14th ed., p. 1161.

1991 • James E. Walker (1941–2006) became the first black president of Middle Tennessee State University in Murfreesboro and the first black head of a majority-white state institution in Tennessee. A native of Phoenix City, Alabama, he did his undergraduate work at Alabama State University and went on to earn a doctorate in education from Pennsylvania State University. His first postgraduate job was teaching special education courses at Southern Illinois University. From there, he went to a series of academic administration posts. He served as provost and vice president for academic affairs at the University of Northern Colorado when he was tapped for the MTSU presidency. Under Walker's leadership, MTSU's enrollment grew by thousands, academic standards were raised, and the physical plant was greatly improved.

Sources: *Jet* 80 (27 May 1991): 38; (14 August 2000): 38; *Tennessean* (13 August 2000).

1991 • Delores Margaret Richard Spikes (1936–) became president of the Southern University and A & M College system, the first woman in the United States to head a university system. She was also the first woman to head a public college or university in Louisiana. Her route to the presidency started in 1981, with a position as part-time assistant to Southern's chancellor while also serving as a full-time faculty member. She served as system president until 1996 and was named president emeritus. On January 13, 1997, Spikes took office as president of the University of Maryland, Eastern Shore (Princess Anne). A native of Baton Rouge, Louisiana, she attended both public and private schools before enrolling in Southern University. She holds a bachelor's degree from Southern, a master's degree from the University of Illinois at Urbana, and a doctorate from Louisiana

State University, all in mathematics. Spikes was both the first black graduate and the first Southern University graduate to earn a doctorate in mathematics from LSU, in 1971. Southern University named her "Alumnus of the Century" at its centennial celebration.

Sources: Hine, *Black Women in America*, vol. 2, pp. 1097–98; *Crisis* 108 (March/April 2001): 28; *Ebony* 55 (October 1999): 198; *Who's Who among African Americans*, 14th ed., p. 1218; *Contemporary Black Biography*, vol. 18, pp. 175–77.

1992 • Belle Smith Wheelan (1951–) became president of Central Virginia Community College on January 1. She was the first black woman to serve as president of a two-or-four-year public institution of higher education in the Commonwealth of Virginia. On July 1, 1989, she began her tenure as president of Northern Virginia Community College, the nation's largest community college college.

Sources: *Who's Who among African Americans*, 26th ed., p. 1165.

1993 • Barbara Williams White (1943–) became the first black dean at the University of Texas at Austin, where she headed the School of Social Work. A native of Macon, Georgia, she holds a bachelor's degree from Florida A & M University and a master's and doctorate from Florida State University.

Sources: *Ebony* 50 (August 1995): 10; *Who's Who among African Americans*, 26th ed., p. 1316.

1993 • Joann Horton became the first woman president of Texas Southern University, one of the nation's largest historically black colleges. Born in Lenoir, North Carolina, she received her bachelor's and master's degrees from Appalachian State University and her doctorate from The Ohio State University. Among the positions held before moving to Texas Southern, she headed the fifteen institutions and twenty-eight campuses of the Iowa community college system. She left the post in 1995, and in 1998 became president of Kennedy-King College in Chicago.

Sources: *Jet* 84 (23 August 1993): 16; *Who's Who among African Americans*, 26th ed., p. 606; *Ebony* 50 (May 1995): 7.

1994 • Carol Surles (1947?–) was named president of Texas Woman's University, the first black to hold the post. She was the unanimous choice from among the three finalists for the position and took office in the summer of this year. The university has campuses in Denton, Dallas, and Houston. Surles was serving as vice president for administration and business affairs at California State University at Hayward when she was tapped for the Texas post. She had also held administrative posts in Florida, Mississippi, and Michigan earlier in her career. Surles holds a bachelor's degree in psychology from Fisk University, a master's degree in counseling from Chapman College, and a doctorate in education from the University of Michigan. Since her Texas appointment, in 1999 she has been named president of Eastern Illinois University in Charleston, the first black woman to hold this position.

Sources: *Crisis* 108 (March/April 2001): 28; *Jet* 86 (6 June 1994): 24; Smith, *Notable Black American Women*, Book III, pp. 571–74 .

1994 • The first black president of Wright State University in Ohio, Harvey Flack, took office on February 1. He was also the first black president of any mainstream institution in the state. Flack left his position as executive vice-president and provost of Rowan College in Glassboro, New Jersey, where he had served since 1989 to move to Ohio. His previous positions include academic vice president for the State University of New York at Old Westbury, and dean of the College of Allied Health Sciences at Howard University. He is a graduate of The Ohio State University and Kent State University; he holds a doctorate from the State University of New York at Buffalo.

Sources: *Jet* 85 (10 January 1994): 32.

1994 • Johnson C. Smith University in Charlotte, North Carolina, named Dorothy Cowser Yancy (1944–) its twelfth president and the first woman to head the school in its 127-year history. She was born in Cherokee City, Alabama, and graduated from Johnson C. Smith

(A.B. in history, 1964); the University of Massachusetts, Amherst (M.A. in history, 1965); and Atlanta University (Ph.D. in political science, 1978). Yancy is also recognized as a labor arbitrator and holds a certificate in management from Harvard University and certificates in labor arbitration and mediation. She began her career as a teacher in 1965 at Albany State College (Georgia), and taught at Hampton Institute (now Hampton University) from 1967 to 1969, in the Evanstown township from 1969 to 1971, and Barat College (Lake Forest, Illinois) from 1971 to 1972, before moving to the Georgia Institute of Technology in 1972. She was named Outstanding Teacher of the Year there in 1985. She had been on the institute's faculty twenty-two years, moving through the ranks as assistant professor, associate professor, and then professor. She left that position in 1994 to become president of Johnson C. Smith.

Sources: *Crisis* 108 (March/April 2001): 28; *Jet* 87 (21 November 1944): 22; *Who's Who among African Americans,* 26th ed., p. 1392.

1994 • The Board of Regents of Texas A & M University appointed Woodrow Jones dean of the College of Liberal Arts in College Station, making him the first black to hold the post.

Sources: *Jet* 86 (4 July 1994): 20.

1994 • Retia Scott Walker was appointed dean of the University of Kentucky's College of Human Environmental Sciences, making her the first black woman to hold the post. Walker was previously faculty administrator at the University of Maryland, Eastern Shore.

Sources: *Jet* 87 (28 November 1994): 20.

1994 • C[ecelia] Ellen Connally (1945–) became the first black to head the Board of Trustees of Bowling Green State University. She was born in Cleveland and graduated from Bowling Green State University and Cleveland State University. She also received her law degree from Cleveland State. Since 1980 she has served as a municipal court judge in Cleveland.

Sources: *Who's Who among African Americans,* 26th ed., pp. 265–66; *Jet* 86 (13 June 1994): 20.

1994 • The University of Mississippi named Louis Westerfield (1949–1996) to head its law school, making him the first black dean of the law school. He applied for the position earlier but was turned down. He insisted that racism was not a factor. His previous positions included dean of Loyola University School of Law, law professor at the University of Mississippi, dean of the law school at North Carolina Central, and assistant district attorney in New Orleans. Westerfield was born in DeKalb, Mississippi; his family moved from rural Mississippi to New Orleans and lived in Fischer public housing development. He became determined to move ahead, however, and placed a high value on reading and on education. He graduated from Southern University in New Orleans (B.A.), Loyola University School of Law (J.D.), and Columbia University School of Law (LL.M). He died in 1996.

Sources: *Black Issues in Higher Education,* 11: 8–9; *Who's Who among African Americans,* 13th ed., p. 1604; *Jet* 90 (16 September 1996): 52; *Ebony* 50 (August 1995): 128–32.

1994 • Shirley A. R. Lewis (1937–) was named president of Paine College in Augusta, Georgia, and became the first woman president in the school's 112-year history. Lewis had a wealth of academic and administrative experience before being named president of Paine. She had worked at both Vanderbilt University and Meharry Medical College; she was the first associate dean of academic affairs at Meharry. She was executive director of the Black College Fund for the United Methodist Church for five years, after which she was promoted to assistant general secretary for the General Board of Higher Education and Ministry of the United Methodist Church in Nashville, Tennessee; she was in this position when she accepted the post at Paine. A native of Winding Gulf, West Virginia, Lewis spent her early years living alternately with her mother and her father, who had divorced when she was young. After a succession of different residences, she and her mother settled in Berkeley, California. Both her parents were supportive and encouraged her early interest in reading. She also showed an early interest in politics, exhibited by her running for class offices in school. Lewis was elected vice president of the student body at her Berkeley junior high school, where she was the only black student, and was a class officer throughout high school. Lewis earned a bachelor's degree in Spanish and speech from the University of California at Berkeley in 1960 and did further study at the school's San Francisco and Hayward branches to become eligible for teacher certification. Early in her career she taught in California, Ohio, and New York. She and her husband have made several trips to Africa; both hold certificates of African studies as a result of courses taken at the University of London and the University of Ghana. In 1968 Lewis returned to Berkeley and received her master's degree in social work in 1970. Some years later, in 1979, she earned a doctorate from Stanford University. The Lewis family later moved to Nashville, Tennessee, where she served as an adjunct faculty member at George Peabody College of Vanderbilt University. When she became president of Paine, she was one of only four women presidents in the forty-one colleges that comprised the United Negro College Fund. Her career has been characterized by high expenditure of personal energy and a history of success in her endeavors. She retired from the school in 2007 and is now a consultant for various schools.

Sources: *Contemporary Black Biography,* vol. 14, pp. 151–54; *Crisis* 108 (March/April 2001): 27; *Ebony* 55 (October 1999): 96; Smith, *Notable Black American Women,* Book II, pp. 408–11.

1995 • Jacquelyn M. Belcher was named president of DeKalb College in Georgia and became the first black woman to head the third largest institution in the University System of Georgia. She was also the first black woman head of any institution in the system and the first black person to head a Georgia institution that is not historically black. A former president of Minneapolis Community College, Belcher was inaugurated in 1996 as only the fifth president in DeKalb's thirty-two-year history. She has since become head of Georgia Perimeter College. Her honors include Outstanding Alumnus by Marymount College in 1990 and Woman of the Year by the Girl Scouts of America in 1989.

Sources: *Jet* 88 (21 August 1995): 22; 90 (17 June 1996): 20; *Who's Who among African Americans,* 26th ed., p. 84.

1995 • Ruth Simmons (1945–) became the first black president to lead one of the "Seven Sisters" schools, Smith College in Northampton, Massachusetts. She was also the first black to head an upper-tier college. Smith was founded in 1871 and became a part of the "Seven Sisters," a group of elite, private women's colleges whose other members include Barnard, Mount Holyoke, Bryn Mawr, Radcliffe, Wellesley, and Vassar. Simmons came to Smith from Princeton, where she served as vice provost. She was born in Grapevine, Texas—one of twelve children whose parents were sharecroppers— and grew up in Houston. She graduated *summa cum laude* from Dillard University. Following graduation, she used a Fulbright grant to study in France for a year. She earned a master's degree in 1970 and a doctorate in romance languages in 1973 from Radcliffe College (now a part of Harvard University). Simmons held positions at several colleges between 1970 and 1990, including teaching positions at Radcliffe and the University of New Orleans. She was a program coordinator for the National Endowment for the Humanities at the University of California at Northridge, and associate dean at the University of Southern California at Los Angeles and at Princeton University. During her first tour of duty at Princeton, as director of the black studies program, Simmons brought such notable persons as novelist Toni Morrison to the faculty. In 1989 she moved to historically black Spelman College as provost, where she stayed until she returned to Princeton in 1992. When Smith College tapped her for the presidency, she was the unanimous choice from among the 350 candidates. Much of her scholarly research has focused on Caribbean and African literature; she has also published a book on education in Haiti. Under Simmons' leadership, Smith's endowment was doubled; the first engineering program at a women's college was established; and curriculum changes, including a paid internship for every undergraduate and a focus on public speaking, were introduced. She also took steps to increase minority enrollment at Smith, creating a partnership with a New York City high school, through which Harlem high school students could visit the college. She left Smith in 2001 to assume the presidency at Brown University. She is credited as being one of the most admired college presidents and has been honored with television appearances and network awards. She was among the women *Vanity Fair* profiled in its 1998 photo portfolio, *Women of America: A Portrait of Influence and Achievement,* and she is a Fellow of the American Academy of Arts and Sciences.

Sources: *Crisis* 108 (March/April 2001): 22–25; Salzman, *Encyclopedia of African-American Culture and History,* Supplement, pp. 247–48; *Tennessean* (16 December 1994); *Who's Who among African Americans,* 14th ed., p. 1176.

1995 • Psychologist Harvette Grey became founding director of the Women's Center at DePaul University.

Sources: *Jet* 88 (16 October 1995): 22.

1995 • Lois Stovall Williams became the first woman president of Knoxville College and the twenty-second president in the college's 120-year history. Her previous experience includes a tenured faculty position at Norfolk State University, director of the Center for Teaching Excellence at Hampton University, and dean of instruction at Passaic County Community College in New Jersey. The Mocksville, North Carolina, native graduated from Morgan State University and Loyola College; she received her doctorate from the University of Connecticut. She also received certification from Harvard University's Institute for Educational Management.

Sources: *Ebony* 50 (June 1995): 6–7; *Who's Who among African Americans,* 26th ed., p. 1347.

1996 • Pennsylvania State University elected Hugh Jesse Arnelle (1933–) as president of its board of trustees, the first black elected to this position. He has been a senior partner in Arnelle, Hastie, McGee, Willis and Greene, a corporate law firm, since 1985. He was born in New Rochelle, New York, and graduated from Pennsylvania State and Dickinson School of Law, where he received his law degree. He was admitted to practice in California and in Pennsylvania, and before the United States Supreme Court. During his college days, Arnelle achieved All-American status in basketball and an honorable mention for football. He has received a number of honors, including a 1977 election to the New York Hall of Fame.

Sources: *Jet* 89 (18 March 1996): 20; *Who's Who among African Americans,* 26th ed., p. 41.

1996 • Corporate executive Benjamin S. Ruffin (1941–) was elected vice chairman of the University of North Carolina Board of Governors, the first black to hold the post. His duties include membership on the executive committee and the search committee for the new university president. Ruffin became vice president of corporate affairs for R. J. Reynolds Tobacco Company. He graduated from North Carolina Central University and served as senior vice president and special assistant to the president of North Carolina Mutual Life Insurance Company.

Sources: *Jet* 90 (26 August 1996): 20; *Who's Who among African Americans,* vol. 14, p. 1128.

1996 • Elson S. Floyd (1956–) became the first black vice chancellor at the University of North Carolina. Born in Henderson, North Carolina, he received his bachelor's, master's, and doctoral degrees from the University of North Carolina. Floyd, whose doctoral degree is in higher and adult education, held administrative posts at Eastern Washington University and with the Washington State Higher Education Coordinating Board before taking his first position at the University of North Carolina as assistant dean for student life in 1978. In 1998 he became president of Western Michigan University and from 2003 to 2007 he was president of the University of Missouri.

Sources: *Jet* 89 (15 January 1996): 10; *Who's Who among African Americans,* 26th ed., p. 417.

1996 • Mamphela Ramphele (1947–), civil activist, physician, and educator, was promoted to vice chancellor of the University of Capetown in South Africa. She was the first black African and the first woman to hold the post, which is equivalent to the presidency of an American university. The daughter of schoolteachers, she was born in a rural part of the South Africa's Northern Province. She received a bachelor's degree and diplomas in tropical health and hygiene, and public health, as well as a bachelor's of commerce in administration from the University of Witwatersrand. In 1991 she received a doctorate in anthropology from the University of Capetown, and in 1992 she received a medical degree from Natal Medical School. In 1992 she founded the Zanempilo Community Health Center, the first black-owned and black-operated center in King Williamstown. In 1999 she was the highest ranking African member of the World Bank, serving as managing director for human resources. Ramphele's writings include *Across Boundaries: The Journal of a South African Woman* (1997).

Sources: *Contemporary Black Biography*, vol. 29, pp. 130 –33.

1997 • New Mexico governor Gary E. Johnson named Richard Toliver (1939-) to the Board of Regents of the University of New Mexico, making him the first black on the board. The state senate confirmed him for a six-year term beginning March 1. Toliver is a retired colonel from the U.S. Air Force. He is the author of the memoir *Uncaged Eagle* (2010).

Sources: *Jet* 92 (7 July 1997): 20.

1997 • The first black to lead a Lutheran seminary in North America was James Echols (1952?–). He became president of the Lutheran School of Theology in Chicago, after serving as its academic dean since 1991. The school is one of eight seminaries of the Evangelical Lutheran Church in this country. Echols graduated from Temple University and Lutheran Theological Seminary. He received other degrees including a doctorate in history of Christianity from Yale University.

Sources: *Jet* 92 (18 August 1997): 37.

1997 • Georgia State University's College of Business Administration named Sidney E. Harris (1949–) the university's first black dean. He left his position as professor of management at the Peter F. Drucker Center at the Claremont Graduate School in California to accept the new position. Of the 667 business schools in the nation, blacks headed only three percent. Harris was born in Atlanta and graduated from Morehouse College. He holds a master's and doctorate from Cornell University.

Sources: *Jet* 92 (26 May 1997): 20; *Who's Who among African Americans,* 26th ed., p. 543.

1997 • Marie V. McDemmond (1946–), the first woman and the third president of Norfolk State University, took office in July. She came to the university from Florida Atlantic University, where she was vice president for finance and chief fiscal officer (the first woman to hold that post in the Florida State University System). While at Florida Atlantic, she was elected president of the Southern Association of College and University Business Officers (the first black woman to hold this office). She also held other positions, including finance officer at Atlanta University, the University of Massachusetts at Amherst, and Emory University (Georgia). McDemmond is a native of Louisiana and earned her first two postsecondary degrees at Xavier University and the University of New Orleans; she holds a doctorate from the University of Massachusetts at Amherst. During a gala event at Norfolk State a month before McDemmond assumed the presidency, two prominent black Virginians congratulated her—Robert C. Scott, Virginia's first elected black congressman since Reconstruction, and former Virginia governor L. Douglas Wilder, who was the first black governor since Reconstruction.

Sources: *Crisis* 108 (March/April 2001): 27; *Jet* 88 (October 16, 1995): 22; 92 (2 June 1997): 33; 92 (4 August 1997): 23; *Who's Who among African Americans,* 26th ed., p. 841.

1997 • Wayne State University in Detroit named its first black president, Irvin D. Reid (1941?–). Reid had served as president of Montclair State University in New Jersey since 1989. He was born on Pawley's Island, South Carolina, into a family of ministers and educators. He holds bachelor's and master's degrees from Howard University, and a master's and doctorate from Wharton School of Business. He has held teaching posts at Howard University and at the University of Tennessee at Chattanooga. He was later named head of the Department of Marketing and Business Law at Tennessee, leading the school to its first certificate of national accreditation. In 1989 Reid was named president and chief executive officer of Montclair College and reorganized the school to become Montclair State University. He was installed as the ninth president of Wayne State in late 1997.

Sources: *Contemporary Black Biography,* vol. 20, pp. 184–87; *Jet* 92 (22 September 1997): 22; 93 (26 January 1998): 22; *Who's Who among African Americans,* 26th ed., p. 1037.

1998 • Philander Smith College in Little Rock named Trudie Kibbe Reed (1947–) as president. She was the school's eleventh president and first woman president. Reed left her post as dean of the Leadership Institute and director of the graduate program at Columbia College in South Carolina to accept the position. She founded and was editor of *A Leadership Journal: Women in Leadership—Sharing the Vision.* Reed also held a senior management position within the United Methodist Church with which Columbia and Philander Smith are affiliated. She holds a master's degree from the University of Texas and a doctorate from Columbia University. Reid left her post in 2004 to become president of Bethune Cookman University until retiring in 2012.

Sources: *Crisis* 108 (March/April 2001): 27; *Jet* 93 (2 March 1998): 22.

1998 • The appointment of Joyce F. Brown (1946–) as president of the Fashion Institute of Technology in New York made her the first black and first woman head of the school. She took office on June 8 and served as both president and chief executive officer of the school's advisory group, the Educational Foundation for the Fashion Industries. Brown was professor of clinical psychology at the Graduate School and University Center of the City University of New York. In 1990 she was acting president of Baruch College. Born in New York City, Brown received her bachelor's degree from Marymount College and a master's and doctorate from New York University.

Sources: *Jet* 93 (18 May 1998): 34; *Who's Who among African Americans,* 26th ed., p. 160.

1998 • Adam W. Herbert Jr. (1943–) became the first black chancellor of the State University System of Florida. The system includes ten public universities in the state. He had previously served as president of the University of North Florida in Jacksonville.

Sources: *Jet* 93 (26 January 1998): 23; (2 February 1998): 8–9; *Who's Who among African Americans,* 26th ed., p. 572.

1998 • Marguerite Archie-Hudson (1937–) became the first woman president of Talladega College in Alabama. She was only the seventh president in the school's 132-year history. (Former slaves and the American Missionary Association founded the liberal arts college in 1867.) Archie-Hudson was born in Yonges Island, South Carolina. She received a scholarship to Talladega and graduated in 1958. She received a master's degree from Harvard University in 1962 and a doctorate from the University of California, Los Angeles. She served Talladega as interim president from July 1998 until she was named president later that year. Her career has included public service as a California state legislator, a Los Angeles city commissioner, and an Emmy award as host of a public affairs program. Before going to Talladega, Archie-Hudson served as an associate dean at California State University. She left Talladega in 2001.

Sources: *Jet* 40 (2 November 1998): 40; *Crisis* 108 (March/April 2001): 26; *Contemporary Black Biography,* vol. 21, pp. 4–8.

1998 • Benjamin S. Ruffin (1941–) was elected chairman of the board of the University of North Carolina, Chapel Hill, the first black to hold the post. As chairman, he headed the thirty-two-member board for the state's sixteen public campuses. Ruffin, a Durham native, graduated from North Carolina Central University and the University of North Carolina. At the time of his appointment he was vice president of R. J. Reynolds Tobacco Company based in Winston-Salem. He has served as vice president for the North Carolina Mutual Life Insurance Company and as special assistant to North Carolina Governor Jim Hunt.

Sources: *Jet* 94 (10 August 1998): 27; *Who's Who among African Americans,* 14th ed., p. 1128.

1998 • The first black female layperson to be named president of Marygrove College in Detroit was Glenda Delores Price (1939–). A former provost of Spelman College, Price took office on July 1, becoming the seventh president of the Catholic, liberal arts college. Price was born in York, Pennsylvania, and received her bachelor's, master's, and doctoral degrees from Temple University. She obtained her master's degree in 1969, and worked as a clinical laboratory professor at Temple from 1969 until 1979, when she received her doctoral degree. She then spent seven more years at Temple as assistant dean in the College of Allied Health. In 1986 she moved to the University of Connecticut as assistant dean in its School of Allied Health and remained in this post until she went to Spelman in 1992. Price is a past president of the American Society for Medical Technology. She has a number of publications, including a textbook of clinical laboratory science, published in 1988.

Sources: *Contemporary Black Biography,* vol. 22, pp. 162–63; *Crisis* 108 (March/April 2001): 28; *Jet* 94 (1 June 1998): 20; *Who's Who among African Americans,* 26th ed., p. 1013.

1999 • Shirley Ann Jackson (1946–) became the first black president of Rensselaer Polytechnic Institute in Troy, New York, the oldest university in the nation dedicated to science and engineering. Shortly after she took office, the school received the largest financial donation in its history when an anonymous donor contributed $360 million in unrestricted funds. Jackson, who was born in Washington, D.C., was renowned as a distinguished theoretical physicist well before she was chosen for the Rensselaer presidency. Her parents believed strongly in education, and accelerated mathematics work plus good teachers at her high school prepared her well for college work. She was valedictorian of her high school class and entered Massachusetts Institute of Technology in 1964. She was one of the students who organized MIT's Black Students Union. Jackson received the bachelor's degree in physics in 1968 and became the first black woman to earn a doctorate from MIT in 1971. She spent two years as a research associate at the Fermi National Accelerator Laboratory in Illinois and a year as a visiting scientist at the European Center for Nuclear Research in Geneva, Switzerland. When she returned to the United States in 1976, she took a position at AT & T Bell Laboratories in Murray Hill, New Jersey, continuing her research in several areas of theoretical physics. In July 1995 she took office as chairman of the United States Nuclear Regulatory Commission, making her the first woman and the first black to hold that office. She has published more than one hundred scientific articles and abstracts. The scientific community has recognized the excellence of her work by giving her numerous honors and awards, including election as a fellow of the American Physical Society. She has served on a number of state and federal government committees, as a faculty member at Rutgers, and as a trustee of MIT. She is a member of the National Women's Hall of Fame and the Women in Technology International Foundation Hall of Fame.

Sources: *Crisis* 108 (March/April 2001): 27; *Jet* 99 (16 April 2001): 10; 100 (2 July 2001): 19; *New York Times* (21 August 1999); Smith, *Notable Black American Women,* pp. 565–66; Warren, *Black Women Scientists in the United States,* pp. 127–34; *Who's Who among African Americans,* 26th ed., p. 644.

1999 • The first black chairman of the University System of Maryland Board of Regents was Nathan A. Chapman Jr. (1957–). Thirteen colleges and universities make up the system. Chapman is president and chief executive officer of The Chapman Company. He is a graduate of the University of Maryland, Baltimore County, where he earned his bachelor's in two-and-one-half years.

Sources: *Jet* 96 (2 August 1999): 23; *Who's Who among African Americans,* 26th ed., p. 228.

1999 • Gail F. Baker became the first black to hold the title of vice president at the University of Florida. She was promoted from her position as director of university communications to vice president for public relations. She was also the chair of the Department of Public Relations in the College of Journalism and Communications.

Sources: *Jet* 96 (15 November 1999): 24.

1999 • St. Augustine's College (now University) in Raleigh, North Carolina, named Dianne Boardley Suber (1949?–) president, making her the first woman president of the school. She took office January 1, 2000, as the school's tenth president. Suber graduated from Hampton and received her doctorate in education from Virginia Technological University. She served Hampton University in various positions since 1986, including vice president for administrative services.

Sources: *Jet* 96 (18 October 1999): 24–25; 99 (28 May 2001): 24.

1999 • Theoretical physicist George Campbell (1945–) was named president of the Cooper Union for the Advancement of Science and Art in New York. He is the first black to head the school in its 141-year history and the school's eleventh president. The institution, founded in 1859 by an industrialist, was one of the first schools to prohibit racial discrimination in enrollment. It is one of a few private colleges in the country that provides full scholarships and that offers an exclusively engineering, art, and architecture curriculum. Campbell was appointed at a time when colleges and universities were struggling to increase minority enrollment in engineering. Campbell graduated from Drexel University, where he was a Simon Guggenheim Scholar (1963–67) and received his doctorate from Syracuse University, specializing in theoretical high-energy physics. He later completed the Executive Management Program at Yale University and spent twelve years with AT & T Bell Laboratories. Since 1989 Campbell has been an emeritus member of the Secretary of Energy Advisory Board. In his position as president of the National Action Council for Minorities in Engineering, he has provided scholarships in engineering and other science-based disciplines for minority students who are economically disadvantaged. He is also a member of the Congressional Commission on the Advancement of Women and Minorities in Science, Engineering and Technology and the socioeconomic and workforce panel of the President's Information Technology Advisory Committee.

Sources: *Jet* 97 (10 January 2000): 37; *New York Times* (18 November 1999); *Who's Who among African Americans,* 26th ed., pp. 202–3.

1999 • Johnnie L. Early became the first black dean of the University of Toledo College of Pharmacy. He was previously the head of the pharmacy school at the University of South Carolina.

Sources: *Jet* 97 (15 May 2000): 10.

1999 • Warrick L. Carter (1942–) became the first black president of Columbia College in Chicago. He took office on July 1 as head of the independent graduate liberal arts college. He had been director of entertainment arts for Walt Disney Entertainment and held a number of positions in academic institutions, including provost and vice president of academic affairs, Berkelee College of Music (1995–96); guest lecturer, School of Music, University of Sao Paulo Brazil (1976); and dean of the faculty, Berkelee College of Music (1984–95). Carter was born in Charlottesville, Virginia, and received a bachelor's degree from Tennessee State University. He studied advanced percussion at Blair Academy of Music in Nashville from 1954 to 1955, and received a master's of music and a doctorate from Michigan State University. In 1983 *School Musician* named him one of the ten Outstanding Music Educators.

Sources: *Jet* 97 (17 April 2000): 8; *Who's Who among African Americans,* 26th ed., pp. 220–21.

1999 • On October 1, James E. Walker (1941–2006) left the presidency at Middle Tennessee State University (MTSU) to become president of Southern Illinois University, and to oversee both the Carbondale and Edwardsville campuses. He is the first black to hold that office. Middle Tennessee State University is recognized for its remarkable record of achievement and growth under Walker's leadership. In returning to Southern Illinois, Walker returned to the institution at which he held his first academic position, as an assistant professor. The challenges he faced as president were said to be similar to those he faced when he took over at MTSU.

Sources: *Jet* 80 (14 August 2000): 38; *Tennessean* (13 August 2000).

2001 • Phillip L. Clay (1946?–) was named chancellor at Massachusetts Institute of Technology, making him the highest-ranking black administrator in the institution's 136-year history. He became the second in command at the school. He was assistant director of the MIT-Harvard Joint Center for Urban Studies and headed the Urban Studies and Planning Department. He is known for his work in housing policies. Clay, a native of Wilmington, North Carolina, graduated from the University of North Carolina at Chapel Hill and in 1975 received his doctorate from MIT. He wrote one of the first studies on urban gentrification, and the Housing Act of 1990 incorporated some of the policies that he helped to formulate.

Sources: *Jet* 100 (9 July 2001): 25.

2001 • Livingstone College in Salisbury, North Carolina, named Algenia W. Freeman (1949–) its eleventh president, making her the first woman to head the 122-year-old institution. Freeman received her master's degree from Southern Illinois University and her doctorate from Ohio State University. She has served as administrator or member of the faculty at a number of institutions, including Morgan State University, East Tennessee State University, and Orange Coast College. Before moving to Livingston, she was professor at Norfolk State University.

Sources: *Jet* 99 (29 January 2001): 54; *Who's Who among African Americans,* 26th ed., p. 436.

2001 • The first black and first woman president of an Ivy League school took office on July 1, when Ruth Simmons (1945–) became president of Brown University in Providence, Rhode Island. A former president of Smith College, she is also the first woman to head two of the nation's premier institutions. Simmons, who can trace her maternal ancestry back to slaves, became the president of a university named for a wealthy slave trader, John Nicholas Brown. Founded in 1764, Brown University is the seventh oldest school in the country, and Simmons is its eighteenth president. Neither of Simmons' parents went beyond the eighth grade, but they provided the stable and nurturing environment that allowed her to go from humble beginnings to unparalleled success as an educator who happens to be black. She serves on the boards of Pfizer, Metropolitan Life, Texas Instruments, and the Goldman Sachs Group. She and Brown made a good match; the institution is considered one of the most liberal in the nation. Simmons retired in 2012.

Ruth Simmons

Sources: *"Speaking of People," Ebony* 51 (January 2001): 10; *Jet* 98 (27 November 2000): 37; *Who's Who among African Americans,* 14th ed., p. 1176; *Crisis* 108 (March/April 2001): 22–25; Salzman, *Encyclopedia of African-American Culture and History,* Supplement, pp. 247–48; *"Speaking of People," Ebony* 51 (January 2001): 10; *Who's Who among African Americans,* 14th ed., p. 1176.

2001 • Carolynn Reid-Wallace (1947–) became the first woman president of Fisk University. Her career prior to her Fisk appointment include a variety of administrative posts in higher education, the Corporation for Public Broadcasting, and the National Endowment for the Humanities. President George Bush appointed her assistant secretary for post-secondary education at the Department of Education in 1991. When Reid-Wallace moved to the Corporation for Public Broadcasting in 1992, Washington became her home base, where she was widely known as an education consultant and lecturer. Her experiences at Fisk include six years of service on the institution's Board of Trustees. She is the second Fisk graduate and the first woman to ascend to the presidency, having graduated in 1964, and the university's thirteenth leader.

Sources: *Fisk University Reports* 8 (Summer 2001): 1–2; *Jet* 99 (19 May 2001): 18; *Tennessean* (6 May 2001); (8 May 2001).

2002 • Darlyne Bailey became dean and vice president for academic affairs at Teachers College, Columbia University. She also became a full professor in the university's School of Social Work. Bailey has served as dean of the Mandel School of Applied Social Sciences at Case Western Reserve University in Cleveland.

Sources: *Jet* 100 (30 July 2001): 19.

2008 • Claudette Williams is installed as the 28th president of the historically black Edward Waters College in St. Augustine, Florida, becoming the first women to head the 143-year-old institution.

Sources: *Jet* 113 (7 April 2008): 24.

2008 • Harvard College, the undergraduate division of Harvard University, named Evelynn M. Hammonds (1953–) dean of that division, making her the first black and the first woman to hold that post. She took office on June 1. In 2005, she became the first black senior vice provost for diversity at Harvard. Before coming to Harvard, in 2001–02 Hammonds was the founding director of the Massachusetts Institute of Technology Center for the Study of Diversity in Science, Technology, and Medicine. Hammonds was born in Atlanta and received a dual degree in physics from Spelman College and a B.E.E. degree in electrical engineering from Georgia Institute of Technology. She holds a master's degree in physics from Massachusetts Institute of Technology and a Ph.D. degree in history of science from Harvard.

Sources: *Contemporary Black Biography*, vol. 69, pp. 66–68; *Jet* 113 (24 March 2008): 30.

2009 • Autumn Adkins became the sixteenth president and the first black woman to head Girard College; she took office on July 1. The boarding school, located in Philadelphia, was founded by a nineteenth-century merchant banker who wrote in his will that he wanted to educate many "poor, White, male, orphans." The school educates students from the first through the twelfth grade. Martin Luther King Jr. and other civil rights protesters spent seven months working to integrate the school. The first black students—four boys—were finally admitted in 1965. It was not until 1984 that girls were admitted to the school. By 2009, the enrollment was 80 percent black. Before joining Girard, Adkins was assistant principal at Friends Seminary, a Quaker school in New York City. She is also former dean of the Upper School at Sidwell Friends School in Washington, D.C. Adkins was educated at the University of Virginia and Columbia University.

Sources: *Crisis* 116 (Spring 2009): 10; *Jet* 115 (4 May 2009): 13.

2009 • The first black and the first woman to be named dean of Columbia College was Michele Moody-Adams. She moved up from her position as Hutchinson Professor and director of the program on ethics and public life. Previously, Moody-Adams was vice provost for undergraduate education at Cornell University and associate dean for undergraduate education at Indiana University. She received a bachelor's degree from Wellesley College and a second bachelor's from the University of Oxford. Her master's and doctoral degrees are from Harvard University.

Sources: *Jet* 115 (23–30 March 2009): 20.

2011 • Portia Holmes Shields took the top seat on January 2 as the interim president of Tennessee State University, becoming the first woman to head the school. From 2007 to 2009, she was chief executive officer and chief academic officer of Concordia College in Selma, Alabama, and the first woman to hold that post. Shields was the seventh president of Albany State University in Albany, Georgia, from 1996 to 2005, and the first woman to lead that institution as well. When she stepped down, the state senate recognized her for outstanding service to the university. She has also held administrative posts at Howard University in Washington, D.C. A native of Washington, D.C., Shields graduated from the District of Columbia Teachers College, George Washington University, and holds a Ph.D. from the University of Maryland.

Sources: "New TSU President Promises Change," *Tennessean* (17 January 2011).

College Buildings

1881 • Allen Hall, located on the Huston-Tillotson College campus in Austin, Texas, is believed to be the first building in Texas (and the first west of the Mississippi) built to educate blacks. The college was founded in 1876, when Sam Huston College and Tillotson College merged.

Sources: *Encyclopedia of Black America,* p. 457–58.

1887 • The first gymnasium erected on a black college campus was at Fisk University in Nashville, Tennessee. The building is now known as the Van Vechten Gallery of Art.

Sources: Fisk University, *Mission and Management,* part 6, p. 60.

1990 • The first building named in honor of a black at Louisiana State University in Baton Rouge, was Alexander Pierre Tureaud Sr. Hall. Tureaud was recognized for his dedication to civil rights: his legal work had opened the doors of the university to black students forty years earlier. He was the only black practicing attorney in the state from 1938 to 1947. He initiated students' suits to enter LSU's law school, medical school, and graduate school, and filed suits at other public colleges and universities in the state. He initiated more than thirty public school district desegregation cases and filed suits to desegregate buses, parks, playgrounds, and public facilities before the passing of the 1964 Civil Rights Act.

Sources: *Jet* 78 (28 May 1990): 24.

1993 • After receiving a record gift of $3 million from Reginald F. Lewis (1942–1993), the largest donation from an individual in the history of the law school, Harvard University responded on April 23 by naming a building in his honor, the first building at the university named in honor of a black American. Lewis graduated from Harvard Law School in 1968 and became a supporter of the school. After becoming a financier and philanthropist, he gave the record gift to fulfill a long-term commitment to the school. Lewis went on to become one of the four hundred wealthiest entrepreneurs in the United States.

Sources: *New York Times,* n.d. (in the author's possession); Smith, *Notable Black American Men,* pp. 720–23.

1995 • North Carolina Central University School of Law, located in Durham, established the first endowed chair in constitutional law and named it in honor of civil rights lawyer Charles Hamilton Houston (1895–1950). Businessman Franklin Anderson and his wife, lawyer Susan R. Powell, contributed $667,000 and the state legislature added $333,000 to endow the chair. During a public occasion to accept the donation, the school also dedicated a bronze relief of Houston created by artist Gail Fulton.

Sources: *Jet* 87 (10 April 1995): 12.

1995 • The University of North Carolina, Chapel Hill, completed a $9.7 million School of Social Work building and named it in honor of John B. Turner (1922–2009), dean emeritus. Others who shared in the honor were the CBS News correspondent Charles Kuralt and John A. "Jack" Tate, a philanthropist. Called the Turner-Kuralt-Tate Building, it was the first academic building on campus named in honor of a black achiever. Turner established the first development office at UNC and strengthened the school's social work program; it ranked twelfth among the top 120 social work programs in the country. Turner, who was born in Fort Valley, Georgia, received a bachelor's degree from Morehouse College and both a master's degree and doctorate in social work from Case Western Reserve in Cleveland. His experiences in academia include Kenan professor at the School of Social Work at the University of North Carolina, Chapel Hill, dean of the school (1981–93), and also professor emeritus. In 1977 he edited the *Encyclopedia of Social Work.* He was also a pilot in the U.S. Air Force (1943–45).

Sources: *Who's Who among African Americans,* 14th ed., p. 1308; *Jet* 88 (6 December 1994–2 January 1995): 32.

2001 • University of Georgia in Athens renamed and dedicated a building in honor of its first black students—Charlayne Hunter-Gault (1942–) and Hamilton Earl Holmes (1941–1995)—on the fortieth anniversary of the school's integration. The structure that became the Holmes-Hunter Academic Building is the same structure at which the two tried to register forty years earlier. Hunter-Gault is now the South Africa bureau chief for CNN.

Holmes became the first black graduate of Emory University's medical school and was a distinguished orthopedic surgeon in Atlanta.

Sources: *Jet* 89 (22 January 1996): 99; (29 January 2001): 26–27.

College Degrees

1734 • Anthony William Amo (1700?–1759?), an African born in Guinea, was the first known black to obtain a European medical doctorate. He attended the University of Wittenberg and eventually returned to Africa after a thirty-year stay in Europe.

Sources: Simmons, *Men of Mark,* pp. 617–19.

George Vashon

1844 • George Boyer Vashon (1824–1878), lawyer, educator, and writer, was the first black to receive a bachelor's degree from Oberlin College in Ohio. He was born in Carlisle, Pennsylvania, but moved with his family to Pittsburgh in 1829, where his father was actively involved in the education of blacks. When he was only fourteen years old, Vashon became secretary of the Juvenile Anti-Slavery Society. While enrolled at Oberlin, he also taught school in Chillicothe, Ohio. Following graduation he read law with Walter Forward, a lawyer in Pittsburgh. He was admitted to the New York bar in 1847. He taught at a college in Haiti for two years, before returning to Syracuse, New York, where he practiced law for four years. Vashon held a number of positions during the course of his life, most of them as a teacher in higher education institutions. In 1867 he became the first black to receive a teaching appointment in the evening school of Howard University's Normal Department. His last known position was on the faculty of Alcorn Agricultural and Mechanical College (now Alcorn University) in Mississippi from 1874 to 1878. Vashon was also a poet, with his first known work, "Vincent Oge," appearing in an 1833 anthology and his last known work, "Ode on the Proclamation of the Fifteenth Amendment," being read at a Washington church.

Sources: Logan and Winston, *Dictionary of American Negro Biography,* p. 617; Bennett, *Before the Mayflower,* pp. 172, 460; *Encyclopedia of Black America,* p. 826; Smith, *Notable Black American Men,* pp. 1157–58.

1850 • The first black woman to graduate from college was Lucy Ann Stanton [Mrs. Levi N. Sessions] (d. 1910). She completed the two-year "ladies'" course and received the bachelor's degree from Oberlin College on December 8, 1850. She taught school in the South during Reconstruction. Two other women also have been called the first black woman college graduate. Grace A. Mapps was the first black woman to obtain a degree from a four-year college— Central College, McGrawville in New York. She apparently finished in 1852 and joined Charles Lewis Reason (1818–1893), then recently named head, at the Institute for Colored Youth in Pennsylvania. Mary Jane Patterson (1840–1894) was the first black woman to earn a bachelor's degree from the four-year "gentleman's" course at Oberlin College in 1862.

Sources: Baskin, *Dictionary of Black Culture,* p. 399; Jackson-Coppin, *Reminiscences of School Life, and Hints on Teaching,* p. 149; Kane, *Famous First Facts,* p. 118; Lane, *William Dorsey's Philadelphia and Ours,* pp. 137, 139.

1865 • Patrick Francis Healy (1834–1910), a Jesuit theologian, passed his final examination on July 26, 1865, and received a doctorate from Louvain University in Belgium, to become the first black American to receive an earned doctorate. Healy was born on a Jones County, Georgia, plantation to an Irish father and a mulatto slave mother. He received his bachelor's degree from Holy Cross College and taught at St. Joseph's College in Philadelphia and at Holy Cross. He became America's first black president of a predominantly white university when he was inaugurated on July 31, 1871, as president of Georgetown University, the oldest Catholic university in America. However, it was not until after World War II that the institution admitted its first black students. Healy had moved up from professor to become dean of the college, then vice rector, and finally president. He resigned the position in 1884 due to ill health. Georgetown had been a small liberal arts college that

The First Black College Graduate

In 1823 Alexander Lucius Twilight (1795–1857) was the first known black to graduate from an American college, when he received a bachelor's degree from Middlebury College in Vermont. Twilight, who was born in Bradford, Vermont, went on to become an educator, preacher, and legislator. He taught in Peru, New York, studied theology, and was licensed to preach by the Champlain Presbytery in New York. He was school principal in Brownington, Vermont, and at the same time minister of the local church. He became one of the first blacks elected to a state legislature, serving Montpelier, Vermont, from 1836 to 1837. Other black college graduates from this early period include: Edward A. Jones, who received his degree from Amherst College in Massachusetts; and John Brown Russwurm, first black graduate from Bowdoin College in Maine. Both graduated in 1826, with Jones graduating a few days ahead of Russworm. By 1860 only about twenty-eight blacks had received baccalaureate degrees from American colleges.

Sources: Bennett, *Before the Mayflower*, p. 172; Bowles and DeCosta, *Between Two Worlds*, pp. 12–13; Logan and Winston, *Dictionary of American Negro Biography*, p. 613.

Healy modernized by changing its curriculum and expanding the number of departments. He built a seven-story building that was named for him after his death; his work at Georgetown led him to be called the school's second founder.

Sources: Bennett, *Before the Mayflower*, pp. 474, 641; Logan and Winston, *Dictionary of American Negro Biography*, pp. 304–05; *Encyclopedia of Black America*, p. 433; Salzman, *Encyclopedia of African-American Culture and History*, vol. 3, p. 1260.

1867 • Robert Tanner Jackson became the first black to receive a degree in dentistry, on February 6.

Sources: *Crisis* 106 (January-February 1999): 41; *Jet* 91 (10 February 1997): 19.

1869 • George Lewis Ruffin (1834–1886) was the first black to graduate from Harvard University Law School, and perhaps the first black obtain a law degree from a university law school. The same year that he graduated from Harvard, he became one of the first blacks to practice law in Boston. He went on to become judge of the District Court of Charlestown, Massachusetts, on November 19, 1883, and he was a member of the Common Council of Boston in 1875 and 1876. He has the distinction of being the first black elected to the Massachusetts legislature. His wife, Josephine St. Pierre Ruffin (1842–1924), was a leader in the black women's club movement. When Ruffin graduated from Harvard, the Emancipation Proclamation was only four years old. His way at Harvard was not easy; he faced the challenge of his studies as well as his classmates' racism. It is to his credit that he survived and went on to prosper in the legal profession.

Sources: Logan and Winston, *Dictionary of American Biography*, pp. 535; Simmons, *Men of Mark*, pp. 740–43; *Crisis* 108 (March/April 2001): 45.

1870 • Richard Theodore Greener (1844–1922), educator, lawyer, consular officer, and reformer, was the first black to graduate from Harvard University. In October 1873 he became professor of metaphysics at the University of South Carolina. In addition to his primary teaching duties, he assisted in the departments of Latin, Greek, mathematics, and constitutional history. He was acting librarian, arranging the university's book collection of 27,000 volumes, and beginning preparation of a catalog. During this same time, Greener studied law. In 1876 he graduated from the university's law school. He was admitted to the Supreme Court of South Carolina in 1877, and the next year practiced at the District of Columbia bar. He remained at South Carolina until March 1877, when the Wade Hampton legislature abruptly closed the door of the university to black students. He headed the

George Lewis Ruffin

Richard Theodore Greener

law school at Howard University and developed a considerable reputation as a speaker and writer. Greener became active in the foreign service, serving in Bombay and Vladivostok. He retired in 1905.

Sources: Bennett, *Before the Mayflower,* p. 642; Sollors, *Blacks at Harvard,* pp. 36–41; Logan and Winston, *Dictionary of American Negro Biography,* pp. 267–68; Robinson, *Historical Negro Biographies,* pp. 83–84; Simmons, *Men of Mark,* pp. 326–35; Smith, *Notable Black American Men,* pp. 483–84.

1874 • Edward Alexander Bouchet (1852–1918), the first black to attend Yale, graduated this year. He was also the first to receive a doctorate from an American university when he was awarded the doctorate from Yale in 1876. The Institute for Colored Youth of Philadelphia, with which he was subsequently associated for twenty-six years as a teacher of chemistry and physics, supported his graduate work in physics. Bouchet was born in New Haven, Connecticut, and attended the oldest of four primary schools for blacks in that city. He was later able to attend the private Hopkins Grammar School, from which he graduated as valedictorian. He continued to be an outstanding student when he entered Yale College in 1870, which no doubt served to call him to the attention of the Institute for Colored Youth. While teaching there he became actively involved with the affairs of Philadelphia's black community. He also maintained a connection with Yale through his membership in the Yale Alumni Association. Bouchet, along with other faculty members at the Insititute, was fired in 1902, on the grounds that the facility's academic department was being closed. The school did move and reopened at what became Cheyney Training School of Teachers. In its new location, the curriculum followed the model of Hampton and Tuskegee, with an industrial arts focus that Bouchet found unpalatable. Between 1902 and 1905, he held various positions in St. Louis, including teacher at a public high school, business manager of Provident Hospital, and U.S. Inspector of Customs at the Louisiana Purchase Exposition. He spent the next three years as director of the academic department and teaching courses in several subjects at St. Paul's Normal and Industrial School in Lawrenceville, Virginia. He also served as principal at a high school in Gallipolis, Ohio, and faculty member at Bishop College in Marshall, Texas before retiring for health reasons in 1916. Bouchet returned to New Haven and died less than two years later. In 1998 Yale unveiled a granite memorial at his previously unmarked gravesite in New Haven's Evergreen Cemetery.

Sources: Logan and Winston, *Dictionary of American Negro Biography,* pp. 50–51; *Encyclopedia of Black America,* p. 187; Lane, *William Dorsey's Philadelphia and Ours,* p. 144; Smith, *Notable Black American Men,* pp. 97–99.

Edward Alexander Bouchet

1875 • Virginia E. Walker [Broughton] (1856?–1934) studied at Fisk University for ten years before receiving her bachelor's degree in May of this year and is said to be the first black woman in the South to graduate from college. She went on to teach in the public schools of Memphis and became active with Christian missionary activities. In both areas of endeavor, Broughton was often the victim of gender bias. As a teacher, a male teacher was given the promotion she should have received. As a woman missionary, male preachers often resented her efforts because she was more literate than they. Even her own husband initially questioned her dedication to missionary work. She is recognized as a religious feminist who was one of several Baptist women who used the Bible to defend women's rights during the latter decades of the nineteenth century and early in the twentieth century. She taught, lectured, and wrote throughout her life. Fisk University awarded her an honorary degree in 1878. She was a widow living in Memphis at the time of her death.

Sources: Smith, *Notable Black American Women,* Book II, pp. 57–60; Higginbotham, *Righteous Discontent: The Women's Movement in the Black Baptist Church, 1880–1920,* pp. 70–73, 124–25; Broughton, *Twenty Years' Experience of a Missionary,* reprinted in *Spiritual Narratives.*

Virginia E. Walker

1877 • Inman Edward Page (1853–1936) and George Washington Milford became the first blacks to graduate from Brown University. As a result of Page's later achievements, he alone is often recognized as the university's first black graduate. He was born to slave par-

The African-American Pioneers of Higher Education at the Nation's Highest-Rated Universities

Year	Institution	First Black Graduate
1828	Dartmouth College	Edward Mitchell
1870	Harvard University	Richard T. Greener
1870	University of Michigan	Gabriel F. Hargo
1874	Yale University	Edward A. Bouchet
1877	Brown University	Inman Page, George Washington Milford*
1883	University of Pennsylvania	William Adger
1889	Washington University	Walter Moran Farmer
1892	Mass. Inst. of Technology	Robert R. Taylor
1895	Stanford University	Ernest H. Johnson*
1896	University of Chicago	Corabelle Jackson
1897	Cornell University	Sarah W. Brown
1903	Northwestern University	Lawyer Taylor
1905	Univ. of Calif., Berkeley	Charles E. Carpenter*
1922	Carnegie Mellon University	Esther B. Summers
1926	Univ. of Calif., Los Angeles	James C. Williamson*, Hilda I. Johnson*, Jefferson Brown*
1932	Calif. Inst. of Technology	Grant D. Venable Jr.
1946	Johns Hopkins University	Reginald G. James
1947	Princeton University	John Howard*
1947	University of Notre Dame	Frazier L. Thompson
1952	Georgetown University	Samuel Halsley Jr.
1959	University of Virginia	Robert Bland
1967	Duke University	Nathaniel White Jr., Mary Mitchell Harris, Wilhelmina R. Cooke
1967	Vanderbilt University	Maxie T. Collier
1967	Emory University	Charles L. Dudley
1970	Rice University	Linda Faye Williams

As rated by *U.S. News & World Report*. Universities originally listed in rank order. *Information obtained from sources other than official university graduation records. Note: The first blacks to earn college degrees in the United States appear to be at Middlebury College (1823), Amherst College (1826), and Bowdoin College (1826).

Sources: Adapted from JBHE research department, *Journal of Blacks in Higher Education,* no. 4 (Summer 1994): 48.

ents in Warrenton, Virginia. Later the family moved to Washington, D.C., where Page worked as an errand boy and attended Howard University soon after it opened. In 1873 he left Howard to study at Brown. He was elected class orator for his graduation in 1877. He taught at Natchez Seminary in Mississippi, the only black teacher at the school, and was later named president of Lincoln Institute (now Lincoln University) in Missouri. George Milford, who graduated from Brown with Page, became a lawyer.

Sources: Savage, *The History of Lincoln University,* pp. 40–43.

1880 • The first black person to graduate from Maryville College in Maryville, Tennessee, was William H. Franklin (1852–1935). Born to free parents in Knoxville, he attended school in Knoxville. In 1870 he left to teach in Hudsonville, Mississippi, and with the money he earned, he entered Maryville College two years later. During his first year at Maryville he was vice president of the Athenian Society. Following his graduation from Maryville in 1880, he entered Lane Theological Seminary. He graduated from Lane in 1883 and moved to Rogersville, Tennessee. He established Swift Memorial College only a few months after the Union Presbytery, Synod of Tennessee, ordained him. Among those who graduated from the school under his administration was William A. Scott, who founded of Scott Newspaper Syndicate. Franklin was also a journalist who wrote for several newspapers, including *The Tennessee Star, The Herald Presbyter,* and *The Critic.* He was a special correspondent for the *New York Age* and the *Negro World.*

Sources: Penn, *The Afro-American Press and Its Editors,* pp. 1347–52.

1883 • William Adger (1857–1885) was the first black to receive a bachelor's degree from the University of Pennsylvania. In 1879 he had been the first black to enter the college department. A native of Philadelphia and a graduate of the Institute for Colored Youth, he died during his senior year at the Episcopal seminary.

Sources: Coppin, *Reminiscences of School Life,* pp. 150–51.

1885 • Blanche Ketene Bruce (1859-1952) was the first black to graduate from the University of Kansas. For the next fifty years he served as principal of Sumner School in Levenworth. He was the nephew of Blanche Kelso Bruce (1841–1898), the first black elected to a full term in the U.S. Senate, 1875–81.

Sources: Kansapedia, Kansas Historical Society, http://www.kshs.org/kansapedia/blanche-ketene-bruce/11996, accessed September 15, 2012.

1888 • Aaron Albert Mossell Jr. (1863–1951) was the first black to graduate from the University of Pennsylvania Law School. Mossell did his undergraduate work at Lincoln University (Pennsylvania) and began practicing law in Philadelphia after he was admitted to the bar in 1895. He later served as attorney for the Frederick Douglass Memorial Hospital in Philadelphia, where his brother, Nathan Francis Mossell, was superintendent. He was born in Ontario, Canada, but his family moved to Lockport, New York, after the Civil War. He and his siblings were the first blacks to attend an integrated school there, which may have been facilitated by the fact that his father donated the brick for the Lockport Public School building. Aaron Albert Mossell Jr. was the father of Sadie Tanner Mossell, one of the first three black women to earn a doctorate. Not satisfied with his progress in Philadelphia, Mossell moved to Cardiff, Wales, in 1899, leaving his wife and children behind.

Sources: Lane, *William Dorsey's Philadelphia and Ours,* pp. 172–73, 181–82; Smith, *Notable Black American Women,* p. 5.

1888 • Tucker E. Wilson became the first black to graduate from DePauw University. The university honored him in 1997.

Sources: *Jet* 92 (7 July 1997): 10.

1889 • Alfred Oscar Coffin (1861–?), zoologist and biologist, was the first black American to obtain a doctorate in biological science, from Illinois Wesleyan University. Later he was professor of romance languages at Langston University. Coffin received his bachelor of arts degree from Fisk University in 1885.

Sources: "Faces of Science: African Americans in the Sciences," https://webfiles.uci.edu/mcbrown/display/faces.html.

1889 • Harriet [Hattie] Aletha Gibbs Marshall (1869–1941), concert artist, pianist, and educator, was the first black to complete the entire course at Oberlin Conservatory of Music in Ohio. Her degree was awarded in 1906 because the school did not actually give degrees in music when she completed her course. To help preserve the rich heritage of black music, in 1890 Marshall founded a music conservatory at Eckstein-Norton University in Cane Springs, Kentucky. This was the first and for a time the only such school for blacks. She was appointed director of music for Washington, D.C.'s "colored public schools" in 1900. In 1903 she established the Washington Conservatory of Music in Washington, D.C., which she directed until 1923. Marshall moved to Haiti with her husband that year, where she founded an industrial school and collected folk music. She returned to the United States in 1936, and established a National Negro Music Center in association with the Washington conservatory. Born in Vancouver, British Columbia, the daughter of Mifflin Gibbs, Marshall was a pioneer in her efforts to bring black concert artists from all over the nation to Washington, D.C.

Sources: *Encyclopedia of Black America*, p. 546; Logan and Winston, *Dictionary of American Negro Biography*, p. 426; *Notable Black America*, p. 546; Southern, *Biographical Dictionary of Afro-American and African Musicians*, pp. 264–65; Smith, *Notable Black American Women*, Book II, pp. 431–33.

First Black Holders of Doctorates in Education

Year	Recipient	Granting Institution
1925	Charles H. Thompson	University of Chicago, Chicago, IL
1928	Althea Washington	Ohio State University, Columbus, OH
1928	Jennie Porter	University of Cincinnati, Cincinnati, OH
1931	Ambrose Caliver	Columbia University, New York City, NY

Sources: Greene, *Holders of Doctorates among American Negroes*, pp. 82–83.

1895 • The first black to receive a doctorate from Harvard University was W[illiam] E[dward] B[urghardt] Du Bois (1868–1963), educator, writer, and Pan-Africanist. He was also the first black to obtain a Ph.D. in history. While Du Bois is universally recognized as an important and influential leader, controversy surrounded his leadership and his progressive ideas on black-white relations often brought him into conflict with black leaders who espoused less radical approaches. He was born in Great Barrington, Massachusetts, to a black single mother (nee Burghardt) and a mulatto father of French Huguenot ancestry, Alfred Du Bois. He had little contact with his father, who moved to Connecticut after his birth and died soon after. W. E. B. Du Bois was the first of the Burghardts to graduate from high school in 1884. His near-perfect high school record also foreshadowed his later achievements; he was the valedictorian of his graduating class and the only black student in the class. Even so, he could not meet Harvard's admission standards when he graduated and enrolled instead at Fisk University in 1885, classified as a sophomore. It was there that he first learned more about the achievements of black people and about the conditions of black life in the South. He saw Fisk students as part of the "elite" who would work toward

W. E. B. Dubois

and effect advancement of black people. Du Bois enriched his educational training while further developing his literary skills, teaching school in rural Tennessee during the summers. His graduation from Fisk led to acceptance at Harvard in 1888, but as an undergraduate. He earned three degrees from Harvard in the space of seven years: bachelor's degree in 1890, master's degree 1891, and doctorate in 1895. In between the latter two degrees, he studied at the University of Berlin and traveled extensively in Europe. Du Bois was turned down for faculty posts by several institutions before taking a job at Wilberforce University. He stayed at Wilberforce only a year, leaving to join the faculty at the University of Pennsylvania in 1896. He left Pennsylvania in 1898 for a position at Atlanta University, where he remained for eleven years. His work, *The Philadelphia Negro,* published in 1899, is widely credited as providing the model for urban sociology studies. In 1903 he published what would be his best-known work, *The Souls of Black Folk.* Du Bois' views were often challenged by Booker T. Washington, whose approach to the race problem was more moderate; the sharp contrast between the two is believed to have led to establishment of The Niagara Movement in 1905. The Niagara Movement, which started in Canada, was designed to provide an organizational vehicle for Du Bois' principles. The group that was to become the National Association for the Advancement of Colored People evolved from Niagara, and Du Bois became its director of publications and research, including serving as founding editor of its signature publication, *The Crisis.* He proved to be more radical than the NAACP Board and in 1934, after years of dissension, Du Bois retired from the board and returned to Atlanta University as chairperson of the sociology department. When the university's president, John Hope, who brought him back to Atlanta, died in 1936, Du Bois lost much of his influence and retired in 1943, only to return to the NAACP. Du Bois had been an active supporter of Pan-Africanism since the end of World War I, and continued his vocal and active support until his death. He also seemed to become progressively more radical, and was perceived as leaning toward socialism. He was on the Justice Department's list of people it considered subversives, and he was once indicted by the department and jailed briefly in New York. Du Bois was a man of strong opinions, who expressed them vigorously in his prolific writings and his career activities. He joined the Communist Party in 1961 and moved to Ghana, where he became a citizen at age ninety-five. He was given a state funeral in Ghana when he died in 1963, on the eve of the March on Washington.

Sources: Smith, *Notable Black American Men,* pp. 336–41; Logan and Winston, *Dictionary of American Negro Biography,* pp. 193–200; Garrity and Carnes, *American National Biography,* vol. 6, pp. 942–43.

First Black Holders of Doctorates in Biological Sciences

Year	Recipient	Granting Institution
1889	Alfred O. Coffin	Illinois Wesleyan University, Bloomington, IL (Biology)
1916	Ernest E. Just	University of Chicago, Chicago, IL (Physiology and Zoology)
1940	Roger Arliner Young	University of Pennsylvania, Philadelphia, PA (Zoology)

Sources: Greene, *Holders of Doctorates among American Negroes,* pp. 182–83.

1897 • Anita Hemmings was the first black to graduate from Vassar College in Poughkeepsie, New York. Since she was very light-skinned, not many realized that she was black and her declaration of racial identity upon graduation created a sensation in the press and caused "dismay" for the college administration.

Sources: Lane, *William Dorsey's Philadelphia and Ours,* p. 273.

1897 • The first black woman to graduate from a law school in the South was Lutie A. Lytle (1875?–1950?), who received her law degree from Central Tennessee College. (Some sources erroneously cite her as the first black woman lawyer in the United States. Charlotte E. Ray [1850–1911], who graduated from Howard University Law School in 1872, holds this distinction.) The daughter of a barber, Lytle was born in Topeka, Kansas. After graduating from high school, she was a compositor on a local black newspaper. She married and also used the names Lytle-McNeil and Cowan. Her exposure to politics inspired her to become a lawyer. At age twenty-two she moved to Chattanooga, Tennessee, taught school for two years, and saved money to support her law school education. Central Tennessee College, located in Nashville, was founded in 1865 and, according to the *Nebraska Lawyer,* by 1897 claimed to be "the first and leading school established for the education of colored attorneys in the whole South." Lytle graduated on June 1 this year and on September 8 was admitted to the Criminal Court in Memphis. At age twenty-six, she was the first black woman licensed to practice law in Tennessee and perhaps in the South. Later in September this year she returned to Topeka, where she became the first black woman admitted to the Kansas bar. Lytle received favorable attention in the press and in the black community. Rather than practice in Topeka, in 1898 she returned to Central Tennessee College and joined the law faculty, becoming the first woman law professor at a chartered law school in the country and perhaps in the world. Around the turn of the century, she moved to New Paltz, New York. In the 1920s she began to support Marcus Garvey and his Universal Negro Improvement Association.

Sources: Connolly, "Attorney Lutie A. Lytle: Options and Obstacles of a Legal Pioneer," *Nebraska Lawyer* (January 1999): 6–12; Smith, *Emancipation,* pp. 344, 353–54, 365, 501–02.

1900 • The first black woman to graduate from Smith College in Northampton, Massachusetts was Otelia Cromwell (1873–1972), educator and author. Cromwell was born in Washington, D.C., where her father, John Wesley Cromwell, had established himself as an editor, scholar, educator, and lawyer. Her mother died when she was twelve years old. She graduated from Miner Normal School and taught in Washington public schools for six years, before she entered Smith. After graduating from Smith, she returned to Washington, where she taught in elementary schools until 1922. She obtained a master's degree from Columbia

First Black Holders of Doctorates in Languages and Literature

Year	Recipient	Granting Institution
1893	William L. Bulkley	Syracuse University, Syracuse, NY (Latin)
1896	Lewis B. Moore	University of Pennsylvania, Philadelphia, PA (Greek and Latin)
1920	Harry S. Blackiston	University of Pennsylvania, Philadelphia, PA (German)
1921	Georgianna Rose Simpson	University of Chicago, Chicago, IL (German) (first woman in German)
1921	Eva Beatrice Dykes	Radcliffe College, Cambridge, MA (English)
1925	Anna Haywood	Cooper University of Paris, France (French)
1931	Valaurez B. Spratlin	Middlebury College, Middlebury, VT (Spanish)

Sources: Greene, *Holders of Doctorates among American Negroes,* pp. 163–64.

University and studied abroad in Germany and at the University of Pennsylvania. In 1923 Cromwell became head of the English and history department in Washington's junior and senior high schools. She received her doctorate in English literature from Yale in 1926, and the university published her dissertation two years later. In 1930, Cromwell returned to Miner Normal School, which had moved from junior college to a four-year college as an assistant professor; she stayed at Miner until she retired in 1944. She was an acknowledged scholar and teacher, and one of only three women on the board of directors of the *Encyclopedia of the Negro* in 1932. Smith awarded her an honorary law degree in 1950. *The Life of Lucretia Mott,* published by the Harvard University Press in 1958, is considered to be a major scholarly work. Cromwell lived all of her life with three of her younger siblings in the same Washington house that had been their parent's home; she was the last of the siblings to die.

Sources: *Encyclopedia of Black America,* pp. 295–96; Smith, *Notable Black American Women,* pp. 241–43.

1909 • Gilbert H. Jones received a doctorate in German from the University of Jena and reportedly became the first black American to receive this degree from a German University.

Sources: *Negro Year Book, 1921–22,* p. 27.

1910 • Samuel Eddy Cary [Carey] (1886–1961), a Providence, Kentucky native, was the first African American graduate of Washburn University School of Law in Topeka, Kansas. In 1914 he was elected county attorney of Russell Springs. He relocated to Denver in 1919 and on October 6 that year he was admitted to the Colorado Bar, becoming the first black attorney licensed to practice law in the state and one of the earliest African American pioneers in law in the American West. He established a criminal law practice and served clients rejected by mainstream lawyers: blacks, Asians, Native Americans, and poor whites. Cary was disbarred on September 30, 1926 due to complaints that he neglected his clients. Many considered the punishment overly harsh, unjust, and possibly due to racial prejudice. To support his family, he worked as a waiter for the Denver Rio Grande Railroad until he was reinstated to the bar on October 1, 1935 and permitted to practice law again. Cary retired in 1945 due to illness. The Sam Cary Bar Association in Colorado was created in his memory in September 1971. In 2011, Washburn's law school honored him posthumously with the Lifetime Achievement Award.

Sources: Harmon, email, (12 June 2011); "Lifetime Achievement Award for 2011: Samuel E. Cary, 1910," http://washburnlaw.edu/alumni/association/lifetime/2011/cary-samuel.php, accessed September 16, 2012. Sam Cary Bar Association website, http://samcarybar.net/Our History.html, accessed September 16, 2012.

1920 • The first black graduate of Chicago's John Marshall Law School was Lincoln T. Beauchamp Sr. (1904?–1996). He practiced in the black community of Chicago's South Side for thirty years.

Sources: *Jet* 91 (9 December 1996): 18.

First Black Holders of Doctorates in Social Sciences

Year	Recipient	Granting Institution
1895	W. E. B. Du Bois	Harvard University, Cambridge, MA (Social Science)
1906	R. L. Diggs	Illinois Wesleyan, Bloomington, IL (Sociology)
1911	Richard Robert Wright Jr.	University of Pennsylvania, Philadelphia, PA (Sociology; first from organized graduate school)
1921	Sadie T. Mossell Alexander	University of Pennsylvania, Philadelphia, PA (Economics)
1925	Charles H. Wesley	Harvard University, Cambridge, MA (concentration in History)
1931	Laurence Foster	University of Pennsylvania, Philadelphia, PA (Anthropology)
1934	Ralph J. Bunche	Harvard University, Cambridge, MA (Political Science)
1937	Anna Johnson Julian	University of Pennsylvania, Philadelphia, PA (Sociology)
1941	Merle Johnson	State University of Iowa, Ames, IA (History)
1941	Merze Tate	Radcliffe College, Cambridge, MA (Political Science and International Relations)

Sources: Greene, *Holders of Doctorates among American Negroes*, pp. 46–47.

1921 • Eva Beatrice Dykes (1893–1986), Sadie Tanner Mossell Alexander (1898–1989), and Georgianna R. Simpson (1866–1944) were the first three black American women to earn doctorates. All three received their degrees in 1921. Dykes was the first to complete requirements for a Ph.D. She was born in Washington, D.C., where her family had close ties to that city's Howard University. Four of her relatives, including her father, were Howard graduates. One of her sisters taught at Howard after graduating from the institution. Dykes herself graduated from Howard *summa cum laude* in 1914. She taught at the now closed Walden University (Nashville, Tennessee) for a year, and then enrolled at Radcliffe College, where she was accepted as an unclassified student. She went on to earn three degrees from Radcliffe: A.B. in English, *magna cum laude*, honors in English, and election to Phi Beta Kappa (1917); A.M. (1918); Ph.D. (1921). Before joining Howard's faculty in 1929, Dykes taught at what became Paul Laurence Dunbar High School in Washington; she retained her Howard position until 1944. She published several works while there. When she left Howard, she became the first woman to join the faculty at Oakwood College, a Seventh Day Adventist junior college in Huntsville, Alabama. Dykes, who was known for her musical ability and her commitment to the Seventh Day Adventist Church in addition to her commitment to education, remained the only faculty woman for ten years. The rest of her career was spent at Oakwood. She first retired in 1968, came back in 1970 to teach a full load for three years, and taught a reduced load from 1973 until she retired permanently in 1975. During her stay at Oakwood, Dykes chaired the committee whose work led to Oakwood's accreditation in 1958 and directed several Oakwood music groups. She was also instrumental in helping to establish a separate black conference of the Adventist Church. Of the three black women who obtained doctorates in 1921, Dykes completed her requirements first. However, the commencement exercises of Sadie Alexander and Georgianna Simpson were both held before hers. Alexander received her degree in economics (the first black American to earn a degree in the field) from the University of Pennsylvania and Simpson earned her degree in German at the University of Chicago. Simpson attended commencement exercises on June 14, making her the first black American woman to earn a doctorate.

Sources: Bennett, *Before the Mayflower,* p. 523; Hine, *Black Women in America,* vol. 2, pp. 1038–39; *Jet* 90 (17 June 1996): 19; 94 (15 June 1998): 19; Smith, *Notable Black American Women,* pp. 5–8, 304–06.

1923 • Virginia Proctor Powell Florence (1903–1991) became the first African American woman to receive professional training in librarianship in the United States. She received her training at Carnegie Library School. Florence graduated from Oberlin College in 1919, and was admitted to the library school in 1922. Although she completed her course in one year, the school withheld her diploma for seven years due to uncertainty about placing their first black graduate in a position. Florence served in the New York Public Library from 1923 until 1927. In 1927 she was the first African American to sit for and pass the New York high school librarian's examination; she was then appointed librarian at Brooklyn's Seward High School where she remained until 1931. She later served as a librarian at Cardozo High School in Washington, D.C., and at Maggie Walker Senior High School in Richmond, Virginia.

Sources: Hine, *Black Women in America,* vol. 1, pp. 439–40; *American Libraries* 20 (February 1989): 154–57.

First Black Holders of Doctorates in Psychology and Philosophy

Year	Recipient	Granting Institution
1903	T. Nelson Baker Sr.	Yale University, (New Haven, CT) (Philosophy)
1920	Francis Cecil Sumner	Clark College (Atlanta, GA) (Psychology)
1934	Ruth Howard Beckham	University of Minnesota (Child Welfare and Psychology)

Sources: Greene, *Holders of Doctorates among American Negroes,* pp. 199–200.

1927 • Sadie Tanner Mossell Alexander (1898–1989) was the first black woman to receive a law degree from the University of Pennsylvania School of Law. Later in 1927, she became the first black woman to enter the bar and practice law in Pennsylvania. Alexander, who was born in Philadelphia, grew up in a family that could count two generations of distinguished members. Her maternal grandfather, Benjamin Tucker Tanner (1835–1923), was an editor and a bishop in the African Methodist Episcopal Church. Tanner and his wife Sadie's children included painter Henry Ossawa Tanner (1859–1937) and Alexander's father, Aaron Mossell, who was the first black graduate from the law school from which his daughter earned her law degree. Alexander, who obtained bachelor's, master's, and doctoral degrees in economics from the University of Pennsylvania before entering law school, was ostracized by the other women students and encountered much prejudice. She was one of the first three black women who earned a doctoral degree in the United States. Despite the honors and awards that accompanied her degrees, Alexander experienced difficulty finding a position after receiving her doctorate. She worked for two years with the black-owned North Carolina Mutual Life Insurance Company in Durham, where she again faced prejudice. This time it came from people of her own race who were wary of her northern roots. Alexander returned to Washington in 1923 and soon thereafter married Raymond Pace Alexander (1897–1974). She entered law school in 1924, and when she graduated she joined her husband in his Philadelphia law practice. Their law firm grew and prospered. When her husband became a judge in 1959, she established her own law firm. Although the majority of her legal work related to domestic cases, she and her husband were both active in civil rights, fighting segregation and discrimination in Philadelphia. Alexander was the first black woman to serve as assistant city solicitor in Philadelphia and as secretary of the National Bar Association. In 1978, at the age of eighty-one, President Jimmy Carter appointed her chairperson of the White House Conference on Aging, where she remained until 1981. She was an active member of more than thirty local and national organizations, but became a victim of Alzheimer's disease in 1982. She was forced her to retire from her law practice and from public life. Her papers are held in the University of Pennsylvania Archives.

Sadie Alexander

Sources: Hine, *Black Women in America,* vol. 1, pp. 17–19; *Encyclopedia of Black America,* p. 98; *Jet* 90 (17 June 1996): 19; Lee, *Interesting People,* p. 59; Smith, *Notable Black American Women,* pp. 5–8.

1927 • Edith Sampson (1901–1979) was the first woman of any ethnic background to receive a master of laws degree from Loyola University in Chicago. She was admitted to the

Illinois bar the same year she graduated and she was among the first black women to practice before the Supreme Court (1934). Sampson was also the first black person to be appointed a delegate to the United Nations (1950), and the first black woman elected judge in the United States (1962). Sampson, who was born in Pittsburgh, Pennsylvania, was one of seven children. The family was poor, and Edith first began working when she was in grade school; at fourteen, she worked in a fish market. After graduating from high school, she took a job with Associated Charities. She enrolled in New York University School of Social Work. After completing her degree in social work, Sampson later enrolled in law school. She completed the course of study at Chicago's John Marshall School of Law, while working during the day and taking courses at night. She managed to maintain careers in social work and law for much of her life. She worked for the Juvenile Court of Cook County, Illinois, for eighteen years, while also practicing law. She gained international experience when she went on a seventy-two-day trip around the world in the late 1940s. The trip was a part of the *Town Meeting of the Air* radio program, and its travelers represented various groups. Sampson was the representative of the National Council of Negro Women; she was also chairwoman of that group's executive committee. The World Town Hall Seminar grew out of this trip; Sampson was elected president of the group. During her years as a delegate to the United Nations, speeches Sampson made about the status of blacks in the United States opened her to criticism from some of her black colleagues, who felt that she painted too glowing a picture; she continued to speak against communism and to point out the achievements of blacks under America's capitalist system. Sampson's first judgeship was in the Municipal Court of Chicago, and she became judge of a branch of the Circuit Court of Cook County late in the decade of the 1960s. She had no children, but two of her nephews followed in her footsteps and became lawyers; both also were named judges.

Sources: *Jet* 88 (28 August 1995): 19; Smith, *Notable Black American Women,* pp. 969–73; Hine, *Black Women in America,* vol. 2, pp. 1002–03.

1929 • Jane Ellen McAllister (1899–1996) became the first black woman in the United States to receive a doctorate in education. She received the degree from Teachers College of Columbia University in New York. McAllister was born in Vicksburg, Mississippi. Her parents had attended the seminary that became Jackson State. Through her mother's friendship with the school's president, she was exposed to experiences that were uncommon for blacks at the time, which included spending summers at Martha's Vineyard in Massachusetts. She did her undergraduate work at Talladega College and graduated in 1919 and in 1921 graduated with the first class to receive a master's from the University of Michigan. McAllister's first teaching appointment was at Southern University in Louisiana. In 1925 she was involved in opening the first extension classes for black teachers in Louisiana. She was also an early user of technology, being the first person to import tele-lectures, broadcast by telephone or satellite, to Jackson State University in Mississippi and several other regional historically black colleges from other parts of the world. From 1951 to 1957 she taught at Jackson State and implemented some of the school's first significant outreach programs in education. McAllister was an innovator, and her ideas always served to benefit the institutions, students, and communities she served. From 1933 to 1968 she served on the board of trustees at Talladega. In 1971 the Jackson State School of Education and the Student National Education Association established the Jane McAllister Lecture Series on Jackson State's campus. The institution honored her again in 1989, when it named a women's residence hall in her honor, McAllister-Whiteside Hall. (Mary Whiteside was one of McAllister's colleagues.)

Sources: *Jet* 89 (11 March 1996): 22–23; Smith, *Notable Black American Women,* pp. 690–92.

1929 • Louis L. Redding (1901–1998) broke the color barrier of the Bar Association in Delaware to become the first black lawyer in the state. At the age of twenty-eight, he graduated from Harvard University's law school, went into practice in Wilmington, Delaware, and became involved in several landmark civil rights decisions that resulted in the desegregation of public schools throughout the nation. Until Redding openly challenged public school segregation in the courts, no real progress toward school desegregation was made in Delaware.

First Black Holders of the Doctor of Education (Ed.D.) Degree

Year	Recipient	Granting Institution
1933	Howard H. Long	Harvard University, Cambridge, MA
1933	Edgerton Hall	Rutgers University, New Brunswick, NJ
1939	Rose Butler Browne	Harvard University (first black woman to receive a doctorate from Harvard)

Sources: Greene, *Holders of Doctorates among American Negroes,* p. 83.

Sources: *New York Times* (30 September 1998); Salzman, *Encyclopedia of African-American Culture and History,* vol. 2, p. 741; Smith, *Notable Black American Men,* Book II, pp. 566–68.

1931 • The first black woman to graduate from the Yale University Law School was Jane Matilda Bolin (1908–2007). At age thirty-one, she became the first black woman judge in the United States when she was appointed a judge in the Domestic Relations court (later known as Family Court) of New York City. She is a native of Poughkeepsie, New York. Her mother was born in England; her father, Gaius C. Bolin, was in 1889 the first black American graduate of Williams College and practiced law in Poughkeepsie for more than fifty years. She received her undergraduate degree from Wellesley College in 1928. After her Yale graduation, she clerked in her father's office for six months in order to fulfill a New York State requirement for being admitted to the bar. Once she was admitted to the bar, Bolin moved to New York City after practicing briefly in Poughkeepsie. In New York City, she practiced at first with her husband, but moved rapidly through the professional legal hierarchy. She was appointed New York City's assistant corporation counsel in 1937, a position she held until appointed judge for a ten-year term by Mayor Fiorello LaGuardia. Three successive mayors each appointed her to ten-year terms, and she retired in 1979, when retirement became mandatory. Throughout her career, Bolin fought racial discrimination in child placement facilities, the assignment of probation officers, in a treatment facility for delinquent boys, and in other arenas. Bolin was an active member of the New York community, serving on a number of boards and becoming a member of such organizations as the Urban League and the Committee Against Discrimination in Housing. Once retired, Bolin continued to be active. She was for a time a volunteer reading teacher in the New York City public schools, after which she was appointed to the Regents Committee of the New York State Board of Regents. Among her many recognitions is one that focused on characteristics other than legal prowess: John Powers, who headed of one of the nation's best-known modeling agencies, included her on his list of the most beautiful black women in America.

Jane Bolin

Sources: *Contemporary Black Biography,* vol. 59, pp. 17–19; Hine, *Black Women in America,* vol. 1, pp. 145–47; Smith, *Notable Black American Women,* pp. 94–95.

1931 • Ambrose Caliver (1894–1962) became the first black to receive the doctorate in education from Columbia University. Born in Saltsville, Virginia, Caliver graduated from Knoxville College in Tennessee in 1915 and received a diploma in industrial arts from Tuskegee Institute in Alabama a year later. In 1919 he received a diploma in personnel management from Harvard University. He received his master's degree from the University of Wisconsin in 1920. In summer 1927 he became dean of Fisk University, the first black to hold that post. Caliver went on leave in 1930 to work on his doctorate at Columbia but never returned to Fisk. He instead joined the U.S. Office of Education as senior specialist in Negro education. He received several promotions, becoming an assistant to the U.S. commissioner of education and later chief of the Adult Education section of the U.S. Office of Education, while still assistant to the commissioner. He conducted and published a number of studies and published the results, including *Bibliography on Education of the Negro* (1931), *Rural Elementary Education among Negroes under Jeanes Supervising Teach-*

ers (1933), and *Sources on Instructional Materials for Negroes* (1946). Caliver spent a life-time in education and was perhaps the best authority in his field.

Sources: Smith, *Notable Black American Men*, pp. 160–62; Lykes, *Higher Education and the United States Office of Education (1867–1953)*, pp. 185–86.

1932 • Virginia Lacy Jones (1912–1984) became the first black woman to earn an advanced degree in library science, when she graduated from Columbia University with a master's in library science. Jones was born in Cincinnati, Ohio, but her parents moved to Clarksburg, West Virginia, when she was a child. While still in high school she began to show her affinity for books, when she headed the development of a library at her St. Louis school. After graduation from high school, Jones returned home to West Virginia and worked to earn enough money to enter what was then Hampton Institute. She earned her first library degree from Hampton in 1933 and followed this with a degree in education in 1936. Between the two degrees, she took her first job as a professional librarian at the Negro branch of the University of Louisville. She also worked with the librarian at Kentucky State College (later University) to organize the librarians' section of the Kentucky Negro Education Association, was involved with in-service programs for black librarians at the Negro branch of the Louisville Public Library, and guided the move of the Louisville Municipal Library into its new building. These activities were but a prelude of what she was to achieve. Just as she received her second Hampton degree, a plan was developed to train badly-needed black librarians at four regional centers in the South. Jones was named director of the center in Prairie View, Texas. To further enhance her own training, she entered the University of Illinois in 1937. In 1936, there were protests at the meeting of the American Library Association's meeting in Richmond, Virginia, and racism was rampant throughout her stay at the University of Illinois. Jones prevailed, however, and graduated with a master's degree. In 1941 she joined the faculty at Atlanta University, teaching cataloguing and classification in Atlanta's new library school. She was not yet through with her own scholarly training. Jones entered the University of Chicago in 1943 to work toward a doctorate; she completed her dissertation and received the degree in 1945. She returned to Atlanta and became the second dean of Atlanta University's School of Library Service, where she served until 1981. During this period she did much to strengthen the library and the library education program at Atlanta, while playing an increasingly important role among professional librarians. She was given honorary membership in the American Library Association in 1976 and is the recipient of numerous other awards. When the Atlanta University Center consortium of four historically black Atlanta institutions was formed in 1981, Jones was named director of the Center's Robert R. Woodruff Library. She resigned in 1983 due to ill health. The trustees gave her the title of dean emeritus and named the campus exhibition gallery in her honor. She was too ill to attend the dedication ceremony and died soon thereafter.

Sources: Hine, *Black Women in America*, vol. 1, pp. 657–58; Smith, *Notable Black American Women*, pp. 606–09.

1933 • N. Naylor Fitzhugh became the first black to receive a master's in business administration from the Harvard Business School. He had a long career at Harvard and was known there as the "dean of black business."

Sources: Salzman, *Encyclopedia of African-American Culture and History*, vol. 4, p. 2237.

1933 • The first black woman to earn a doctorate in bacteriology was Ruth Ella Moore (1903–1994).

Sources: Brown, "The Faces of Science: African Americans in the Sciences," https://web-files.uci .edu/mcbrown/display/faces.html.

1935 • Roger Arliner Young (1899–1964) received a doctorate in zoology, becoming the first black woman to do so. Young was born in Clifton Forge, Virginia, and grew up in Burgettstown, Pennsylvania. She received her bachelor's degree from Howard University in 1923, then taught at Howard to earn money for graduate study. She conducted research with biologist Ernest Everett Just and in 1924 published her first article in *Science*, making her the first black woman in her field to conduct research and publish the findings professionally. In 1926 Young received her master's degree from the University of Chicago. She did research at the Marine Biological Laboratory at Woods Hole, Massachusetts in summer 1927 and 1928. After receiving her doctorate from the University of Pennsylvania, she taught at North Carolina College for Negroes (as it was known then) in Durham and later became head of the biology department at Shaw University in Raleigh. She held a number of other posts primarily at black colleges. Young was plagued by personal and financial problems and died poor and alone in New Orleans.

Sources: *Contemporary Black Biography,* vol. 29, pp. 195–97.

1937 • The first black to receive a doctorate in sociology was Anna J. Johnson Julian (1904–1994), who graduated from the University of Pennsylvania. She also earned her bachelor's and master's degrees there and was the first black person there to be awarded Phi Beta Kappa honors. Julian was a visible victim of racism when the home she shared with husband Dr. Percy Julian in a previously all-white Chicago suburb was firebombed. Bodyguards were hired to protect the home. She was respected as a professional sociologist and recognized as a social activist, but was also known as an officer of Julian Chemical Company and of Julian Research Institute. Her involvement with civic affairs led to several appointments to state and federal committees and to awards and honors from local and national groups. In 1986, in the same community in which her house had been firebombed, she was given the first Shalom Award from the Oak Park Community of Churches. Following her husband's death, Julian established Percy L. Julian scholarships at DePauw University and MacMurray College, and funded an award to the highest-ranking student at Percy L. Julian High School in Phoenix. She continued to live in Oak Park until her death.

Sources: *Jet* 86 (15 August 1994): 18; Smith, *Notable Black American Women,* pp. 614–15.

1937 • Clara B. Williams (1886?–1994) became the first black to receive a bachelor's degree from New Mexico College of Agriculture and Mechanic Arts (now New Mexico State). When she graduated some students boycotted ceremonies. However, when the school awarded her an honorary degree in 1980, she received a standing ovation. She was born in Plum, Texas, the daughter of sharecroppers. Williams worked as a teacher and also owned drug stores in Texas and New Mexico. She was valedictorian of her 1905 class at Prairie View State Normal and Industrial College. In 1910 she attended the University of Chicago summer session. She worked with her sons to establish the Williams Medical Clinic in Chicago. She died in a Chicago hospital when she was 108 years old.

Sources: *Jet* 86 (25 July 1994): 52.

1937 • The first black woman to earn a doctorate from Harvard University's Graduate School of Education was Rose Butler Browne (1897–1986). Born in Boston, Browne was one of seven children; her mother was a laundry worker and her father a bricklayer. They had high regard for education and cultural activities. The family moved to Newport when Browne was ten years old. With several scholarships, she entered Rhode Island Normal School and graduated with a bachelor's degree. Unable to find a teaching position in the area, she obtained a master's degree in engineering from the University of Rhode Island. She taught at Virginia State College (now Virginia State University) in Petersburg, and protested the imbalance in salaries for blacks and whites. Browne was a faculty member at North Carolina College (now North Carolina Central University) for twenty years, first as teacher and later as head of the Department of Educational Psychology. In 1969 her alma mater, now known as Rhode Island College, dedicated a women's residence hall and medical facility in her honor.

Sources: "Psychology's Feminist Voices: Rose Butler Browne." www.feministvoices.com/rose-butler-browne, accessed September 16, 2012.

1939 • The first black woman certified public accountant was Mary T. Washington. She graduated from Northwestern University.

Sources: Hine, *Black Women in America,* p. 1322.

1940 • Elizabeth Catlett (1915–2012) was the first person to receive a master of fine arts degree in sculpture from the University of Iowa. She went on to become an internationally celebrated artist who was known for her figurative sculpture and prints, and as a cultural nationalist and civil rights activist. Catlett was born in Washington, D.C., and in 1936 graduated from Howard University where she studied under art under Lois Mailou Jones, James Lesene Wells, and James A. Porter. Mexican muralists Diego Rivera and Miguel Covarrubias greatly influenced her later art work. She taught high school in Durham, North Carolina, became active in the North Carolina Teachers Association, and fought to equalize salaries for black teachers with those of whites in the state. When she studied at Iowa, she was denied living quarters in the residence halls because of her race. American Realist painter Grant Wood, who was on Iowa's faculty, influenced her to depict her race in her work; as result, she did a limestone sculpture of a black American mother and child for her thesis. For this work she won first prize in sculpture from the American Negro exposition in Chicago in summer 1940. That same summer Catlett taught at Prairie View Agricultural and Mechanical College (now University) in Texas and also won first prize in sculpture in the Golden Jubilee National Exposition held in Chicago. She headed the art department at Dillard University in New Orleans and in summer 1941 studied ceramics at the Art Institute of Chicago. While there she married artist Charles White and after their divorce, she married artist Francisco Mora. Among her works are portrayals of nineteenth-century abolitionists, a lifesize bronze bust of Louis Armstrong for the City Park of New Orleans, and images of women that focus on the themes nobility, action, and motherhood. Her works have been exhibited widely and she has held many one-woman shows.

Sources: Bontemps, *Forever Free,* pp. 68–69, 174–76; Hine, *Black Women in America,* vol. 1, pp. 229–32; Smith, *Notable Black American Women,* pp. 172–77.

1942 • Geologist and geographer Marguerite Thomas Williams (1895–1991?) became the first black person to earn a doctorate in geology in the United States. She was born in Washington, D.C. and graduated from Howard University in 1923. In 1930 she received a master's degree from Columbia University. She received her doctorate from Catholic University of America. Williams taught at Minor Teachers College from 1923 to 1929. She chaired the division of geology, taught as an assistant professor, and later full professor in the Department of Social Sciences at Minor from 1943 to 1955. She also taught in evening school at Howard in 1944.

Sources: "The Faces of Science: African Americans in the Sciences," https://webfiles.uci .edu/mcbrown/display/marguerite_williams.html.

1947 • The first black students to graduate from Princeton University were John Howard, who received his degree on February 5; "Pete" Wilson, whose degree was conferred on June 9; and James War, who received his degree on October 1. They were in a special wartime training program. It was not until the 1960s that Princeton began admitting black students to its regular program.

Sources: *New York Times* (3 September 2001).

1947 • The first black to be admitted to and to graduate from the University of Notre Dame was Frazier L. Thompson. In 1997 the university remembered him by naming an award in his honor. The first recipient was Percy Pierre, a graduate of the institution, a member of its board of trustees, and vice president of research and graduate studies at Michigan State University.

Sources: *Jet* 92 (21 July 1997): 27.

1949 • The first two black women to receive doctorates in mathematics were Marjorie Lee Browne (1914–1979), from the University of Michigan, and Evelyn Boyd Granville (1924–), from Yale University. Granville was born in Washington, D.C. and graduated with honors from Smith College in 1945. After receiving her doctorate, she taught at Fisk University then returned to Washington where she was a mathematician at the National Bureau of Standards. Later she held positions with IBM in New York City and then in Washington with IBM's contract for the U.S. space program, first for NASA's Project Vanguard and then for Project Mercury. She also taught at California State University in Los Angeles and at Texas College, a black institution in Tyler. Marjorie Lee Brown was born in Memphis. She graduated from Howard University in 1935 and received her master's degree from the University of Michigan in 1939. She was a teaching fellow at Michigan in 1947–48. She moved to North Carolina College in Durham (now North Carolina Central University), where she was professor and chair of the Department of Mathematics from 1949 to 1970.

Sources: Sammons, *Blacks in Science and Medicine,* p. 41 (Browne); "Evelyn Boyd Granville," www.answers.com/ topic/evelyn-boyd-granville, accessed September 16, 2012.

1950 • Juanita E. Jackson Mitchell (1913–1992) was the first black woman to graduate from the University of Maryland law school and the first black woman to practice law in Maryland. Mitchell was born in Hot Springs, Arkansas, but by the time she graduated from high school, her family was living in Baltimore. While still in her teens, she witnessed her parents' active protests of racial injustice in Baltimore and in Princess Anne, Maryland. Originally denied admission to the University of Maryland in 1927, she attended Morgan State College and transferred to the University of Pennsylvania after two years. She received a bachelor's degree in education in 1931 and a master's degree in sociology in 1935. In 1942 Mitchell organized a citizens' march on the state capitol in Annapolis, which resulted in appointment of the Governor's Interracial Commission, black police officers, and investigation of charges of police brutality. This was the backdrop against which her battle to be admitted to the University of Maryland was renewed. With legal support from the Baltimore branch of the NAACP, which her mother headed, Mitchell was admitted when the university dropped its racial barriers. She received her law degree from the University of Maryland twenty-three years after it had denied her admission. She believed strongly in fighting battles with the ballot, public opinion, and the courts, and she won major battles in desegregation suits. She and her husband, Clarence M. Mitchell Jr., lawyer and civil rights activist (1911–1984) never moved from the home they bought in the black community. When, as a widow, she was struggling to pay legal expenses for one of her sons, she borrowed on her house and was unable to repay the loan; the bank foreclosed. As a measure of the esteem in which she was held, Baltimore leaders raised more than $93,000 in two weeks, and she was able to keep her home. Mitchell was appointed to White House commissions by three different presidents—Franklin D. Roosevelt, John F. Kennedy, and Lyndon B. Johnson.

Sources: Hine, *Black Women in America,* pp. 804–5; *Ebony* 12 (October 1957): 17–24; Smith, *Notable Black American Women,* pp. 757–59.

1950 • The first black to graduate from the Columbia University Business School was George A. Owens (1919–). Owens was born in Hinds County, Mississippi, and graduated from Jackson State College and Tougaloo College (both now Universities) before entering Columbia. He held several administrative posts at Tougaloo before becoming acting president in 1964 and president from 1965 to 1984. Owens was named interim president of LeMoyne College in Memphis in 1986–87. He also served as a trustee of the Pension Board. The school saluted him on February 10, 1995, by giving him an outstanding leadership award and a reception.

Sources: *Who's Who among African Americans,* 14th ed., p. 992; *Pension Pointers* (February 1995): 4.

1952 • Floyd Bixler McKissick (1922–1991) was the first black to graduate from the University of North Carolina Law School. Born in Asheville, North Carolina, to parents who were both college graduates, he worked after high school graduation to obtain enough money to pay his tuition at Morehouse College. McKissick left school when World War II began. When he returned, he served as youth counsel for the NAACP and also worked with the Congress of Racial Equality (CORE). He made his first application to the University of North Carolina Law School during this time. When he was denied admittance, he took a number of temporizing steps: he worked for a year as a waiter, returned to Morehouse for a second undergraduate year, and then enrolled in the law school for blacks at North Carolina College (now North Carolina Central), after filing suit to gain admission

Floyd McKissick

to the University of North Carolina. He started his own firm in 1955, after working with another Durham law firm for three years. He specialized in civil rights cases. He served as legal counsel for CORE, was its national chairman from 1963 to 1966, and in 1966 succeeded James Farmer as its national director. McKissick was actively involved in the sit-in movement and the 1963 March on Washington. He encountered racism early in his childhood, and this may have influenced his later activism. Disenchantment with the provisions of the Civil Rights Bill caused him to shift his political allegiance from Democrat to Republican during the 1970s. In 1972 he formed Floyd B. McKissick Enterprises, which in 1974 organized Soul City, a new town in North Carolina that he hoped would become a model integrated community. He was appointed judge for the North Carolina Judicial District in 1990. When he died, he was buried in Soul City after a funeral in Durham.

Sources: *Current Biography, 1968,* pp. 238–41; Hornsby, *Milestones in Twentieth-Century African-American History,* pp. 82, 471; Robinson, *Historical Negro Biographies,* p. 225; Smith, *Notable Black American Men,* pp. 795–97.

1952 • Yvonne Clark (1929–) became the first woman to complete the requirements for a bachelor's degree in mechanical engineering from Howard University; the degree was conferred at the annual Commencement in 1952. She became head of the Department of Mechanical Engineering at Tennessee State University. When Clark graduated from Howard, she was hired, after almost three months of job seeking, as an engineer at the Frankford Arsenal Gage Laboratory in Philadelphia. She encountered some gender prejudice, both in receiving this job and in obtaining a promotion. She left Frankford Arsenal for a job in industry with RCA, where she stayed until she moved to Nashville after her marriage in 1955. This time, both racial and gender prejudice led her to seek employment at Tennessee State Agricultural and Industrial State College, where she has been employed ever since. Clark combines her academic career with summer work in industry. She was the first woman ever hired by the Nashville Ford Motor Company at their glass plant. Despite applying during the 1950s, she was not hired until 1971.

Sources: *Graduating Engineer* (Women's Issue, February 1984):51; Warren, *Black Women Scientists in the United States,* pp. 37–40.

1953 • Nathaniel Ridley (1910–1996) graduated from the University of Virginia's Curry School of Education and was believed to be the first black to receive a degree of any type from a traditional Southern white college or university. He was born in Newport News, Virginia. After completing his studies, he was dean of St. Paul's College in Lawrenceville, Virginia. Ridley became the fifth president of Elizabeth City State College (now University) in North Carolina in 1958. Later in his career and until retirement, he was a distinguished scholar at West Chester University in Pennsylvania. He was named president emeritus at Elizabeth City and West Chester. In 1987 the University of Virginia honored him by creating a privately funded scholarship for black students in his name.

Sources: *Jet* 90 (21 October 1996): 59.

1954 • The first black woman to receive a doctorate in political science was Jewel Limar Prestage (1931–). She became dean and professor of political science in the Benjamin Banneker Honor College at Prairie View Agricultural and Mechanical College in Texas. A native of Louisiana, she did her undergraduate work at Southern University and Agricultural and Mechanical College and earned master's and doctoral degrees from the University of Iowa. Prestage began teaching at Prairie View in 1954, and moved to Southern in 1956, where she progressed to the position of dean of the School of Public Policy and Urban Affairs by 1983. She served in this position until she accepted the interim dean position at Prairie View in 1989. Prestage was named dean in 1990. The University of Iowa gave her a Distinguished Alumni Achievement Award in 1986. She became a member of the Judicial Council of the national Democratic Party in 1977.

Sources: Hine, *Black Women in America,* vol. 2, p. 940; *Jet* 61 (31 December 1981): 23; *Who's Who among African Americans,* 26th ed., p. 1012.

1956 • Lila Fenwick became the first black woman to graduate from the Harvard Law School. The school was one of the first university law schools to admit blacks, but one of the last to admit women.

Sources: *Crisis* 108 (March/April 2001): 45.

1960 • Charles Edward Anderson (1919–1994) received his doctorate in meteorology from Massachusetts Institute of Technology, becoming the first black to hold that degree. Born on a farm in University City, Missouri, Anderson received his bachelor's degree from Lincoln University in Missouri in 1941. In 1943 he received his master's degree from the University of Chicago, which certified him in meteorology. Anderson earned a second master's degree from the Polytechnic Institute of Brooklyn in 1948. He worked at the Air Force Cambridge Research Center in Massachusetts from 1948 to 1961. During World War II he was a captain in the U.S. Air Force and also weather officer for the Tuskegee Airmen in Tuskegee, Alabama. Anderson held a number of other positions, serving with the U. S. Department of Commerce and with the University of Wisconsin in Madison, where he was a professor of meteorology. In 1970 he was appointed professor of Afro-American studies and chair of the meteorology department, and in 1978 he became associate dean of the university. He moved to North Carolina State University in Raleigh as professor in the Department of Marine, Earth and Atmospheric Sciences, where he remained from 1987 until he retired in 1990.

Sources: "Charles Edward Anderson—Meteorologist." *BlackFacts.com.* http://www.black facts.com/fact/1cec6dd9-68f3-46b4-a865-4d53eccc0b8c. Accessed October 9, 2012.

1964 • Jessie Carney Smith (1930-) became the first black to receive a Ph.D. degree in library science from the University of Illinois. In 1976–77, she became the first black national president of Beta Phi Mu, the honor society for persons with graduate degrees in library science. Smith was honored again in 1985, this time as the first black to be named Association of College and Research Librarian of the Year. She is dean of the library and William and Camille Cosby Professor in the Humanities at Fisk University.

Jessie Carney Smith

Sources: Hine, *Black Women in America,* 2nd ed., vol. 3, p. 158; *Who's Who among African Americans,* vol. 26, pp. 1147–48; *Who's Who in America,* 65th ed., Biography, http://www.ans wers/com/topic/jessie-carney-smith-1.

1967 • Percy A. Pierre (1939–), electrical engineer and mathematician, became the first black to receive a doctorate in electrical engineering. Pierre was born in St. James Parish, Louisiana. He received his bachelor's degree in engineering in 1961 and a master's in electrical engineering in 1963, both from Notre Dame University. In 1976 he graduated from the Johns Hopkins University with a doctorate, and then served a postdoctoral appointment at the University of Michigan. After a year with the Rand Corporation in 1968–69, he served as White House Fellow for the Executive Office of the President in 1969–70, and then returned to Rand. Howard University appointed him dean of the School of Engineering in 1971. Pierre left in 1981 to become assistant secretary for research, development, and regulation for the U.S. Department of the Army. He was president of Prairie View Agricultural and Mechanical University from 1983 to 1989. From 1990 to 1995 he was vice president for research and graduate studies at Michigan State University.

Sources: *Contemporary Black Biography,* vol. 46, pp. 131–33; *People Weekly* (25 September 2000).

1969 • Lillian Lincoln Lambert, a one-time maid, was the first black woman to earn an MBA degree from Harvard Business School. She enrolled in Howard University on a scholarship and received a B.A. degree in 1966. While there her mentor was H. Naylor Fitzhugh, who was the first black to receive a Harvard MBA in 1933. In 1967 she entered Harvard Business School. While at Harvard, she and other black students began a recruitment program to attract more black students and also established an African American student union. Prior to completing her Harvard degree, in 1976 she founded a janitorial services company, Centennial One Inc., on an investment of several thousand dollars. She was chief executive officer and president before selling her company in 2001, then worth $20 million in sales. She also taught at Bowie State University in the mid–1970s. Lambert was born in 1940 and grew up on a farm in a Powhatan County, Virginia, where she worked in the fields, read widely, and maintained a thirst for knowledge. Harvard recognized her contributions and in 2003 gave her the business school's Alumni Achievement Award— its highest honor for alumni. She has received numerous awards and honors as well. Now a successful writer and speaker, Lambert likes to promote her memoir, *The Road to Some-place Better: From the Segregated South to Harvard Business School and Beyond.* It is a powerful reflection of her diligence, creativity, and vision.

Sources: "Lillian Lincoln Lambert," http://www.lillianlincolnlambert.com, accessed September 15, 2012. "Virginia Women in History," http://www.lva.virginia.gov/public/vawomen/2011/lambert.htm, accessed September 15, 2012.

1969 • The first black American to receive a doctorate in computer science was Skip [Clarence A.] Ellis. Born in Chicago in 1943, Ellis grew up in a poor neighborhood. De-termined to succeed, he took a double major in physics and mathematics at Beloit College in Wisconsin. While studying for his doctorate at the University of Illinois, Ellis worked on hardware, software, and various applications of the Illiac 4 Supercomputer at the school. After graduation, he worked on supercomputers for Bell Telephone Laboratories. Ellis has taught at Stanford University, the University of Texas, Massachusetts Institute of Technol-ogy, Stevens Institute of Technology, and held an overseas teaching fellowship in Taiwan. He has published widely in his field and has additional experiences in research, spending some time at Xerox Palo Alto Research Center. Currently Ellis is professor of computer sci-ence and director of the Collaboration Technology Research Group at the University of Colorado at Boulder.

Sources: *Contemporary Black Biography,* vol. 38, pp. 54–56.

1970 • Elaine R. Jones (1944–) graduated from the School of Law at the University of Vir-ginia and became the first black woman to be admitted and to graduate from the school. As a student there, she was once mistaken for a cleaning woman and was asked to clean out a refrigerator. Jones was born in Norfolk, Virginia into a family that she has described as one of words and ideas. Her undergraduate work was done at Howard University in Washington, D.C. When she received her law degree, she was offered a job with a Wall Street law firm, but chose instead to become managing attorney in the New York office of the NAACP's Legal Defense and Education Fund (LDF). She briefly left LDF for a position as special assistant to the U.S. Secretary of Transportation from 1975 to 1977. When she returned to her post, she became LDF's first official legislative advocate on Capitol Hill. A promotion in 1988 led to her being named deputy director-counsel; she became president of the Fund in 1993. Jones is recognized as a tireless and effective civil rights worker, and under her leadership equal education and voting rights legislation have received contin-uing attention. She is a member of several bar associations and has served on the arbitra-tion panel of the American Stock Exchange.

Sources: *Jet* 94 (19 October, 1998): 19; Smith, *Notable Black American Women,* Book II, pp. 348–50; *Who's Who among African Americans,* 26th ed., p. 691.

1972 • Kellis E. Parker (1942–2000) became the first black law professor at Columbia University. He also became the first black professor to receive tenure there in 1975. Parker, along with four other black students, is credited with integrating the University of North Carolina. He graduated in 1960, and entered Howard University, graduating with a law de-gree in 1968. In 1968–69 Parker was a law clerk for Judge Spottswood W. Robinson III, who in 1966–92 served on the U.S. Court of Appeals in Washington, D.C. Parker also taught law at the University of California in 1969–72.

Sources: *Jet* 98 (4 December 2000): 18; *Who's Who among African Americans,* 13th ed., p. 1027.

1972 • Willie Hobbs Moore (1934–1994) became the first black woman to receive a doc-torate in physics. Born in Atlantic City, she received three degrees from the University of Michigan. In 1958 she was awarded the bachelor of science in electrical engineering, in

1961 the master of science in electrical engineering, and in 1972 she received her doctorate. Much of her research has been published in scientific journals. She held engineering positions at Bendix Aerospace Systems Division, Barnes Engineering Company, and Sensor Dynamics Inc. She later became an executive with Ford Motor Company, working with the warranty department of automobile assembly. She died at home in Ann Arbor, Michigan.

Sources: Mickens, "Willie Hobbs Moore: The First African American Woman Doctorate in Physics," *National Society of Black Physicists Newsletter,* Conference 2000 ed., p. 23.

1973 • Shirley Ann Jackson (1946–) received a doctorate in theoretical elementary particle physics. She was the first black woman in the United States to receive a doctorate in physics from Massachusetts Institute of Technology. In 1976 she joined AT & T Bell Laboratories, where she conducted research on topics relating to theoretical material sciences.

Sources: *Negro Almanac,* pp. 106, 1084; Smith, *Notable Black American Women,* pp. 565–66; *Contemporary Black Biography,* vol. 12, pp. 92–95.

1980 • Lewis V. Baldwin (1949–), a minister, educator, and author, became the first black to receive a doctorate in history from Northwestern University. Born in Camden, Alabama, Baldwin graduated from Talladega College (B.A., 1971) and Crozer Seminary (M.A, 1973 and M.Div., 1975). On December 31, 1973 he was ordained and licensed to preach; the event took place at his father's church, the Pine Level Baptist Church No. 2 in Greenville, Alabama. He taught at Wooster College from 1981 to 1982, Colgate University and Colgate Divinity School from 1982 to 1984, and then moved to Vanderbilt University where he continues to teach religious studies. Baldwin is a prolific writer whose works include *Freedom Is Never Free: A Biographical Profile of E. D. Nixon, Sr.* (1992) and *There Is a Balm in Gilead: The Cultural Roots of M. L. King Jr.* (1991).

Shirley Ann Jackson

Sources: Bailey, *They Too Call Alabama Home,* pp. 28–29; *Who's Who among African Americans,* 26th ed., p. 59.

1981 • The first black woman to earn the doctor of science degree in chemical engineering was Jennie R. Patrick [Yeboah] (1949–) of Gadsden, Alabama. She received her degree from the Massachusetts Institute of Technology. Though neither of her parents had gone beyond the sixth grade in school, and both had humble jobs—her mother worked as a maid, and her father worked as a janitor—Patrick-Yeboah credits them both with inspiring her to strive for and attain excellence. She found a different academic setting when she entered Gadsden's newly-integrated high school in 1964, where violence and harassment were frequent. Nevertheless, she graduated with honors. Pursuing her early interest in engineering, she entered Tuskegee Institute (now Tuskegee University) in Alabama, and remained there for three years, leaving when the chemical engineering program was discontinued. She obtained her bachelor's degree in chemical engineering from the University of California in Berkeley in 1973. While completing her bachelor's degree, Patrick-Yeboah worked as an assistant engineer for Dow Chemical Company and Stouffer Chemical Company. While at MIT, she was a research assistant and worked for Chevron and Arthur Little Company as a chemical engineer. Patrick-Yeboah has worked for several companies since earning her doctoral degree and is credited with developing significant research programs at each. She returned to Tuskegee in 1993, as 3-M Eminent Scholar and Professor of Chemical Engineering. Years of work with chemicals have resulted in an illness referred to as "multiple chemical sensitivity," but this has not caused her to cease her work. She became senior consultant for Raytheon Engineers and Constructors in 1997. Patrick-Yeboah also devotes much of her time to young blacks, hoping to facilitate their progress in the nation. She includes among her honors the National Organization of Black Chemists and Chemical Engineers Outstanding Women in Science and Engineering Award in 1980.

Sources: *Jet* 57 (6 December 1979): 21; Smith, *Notable Black American Women,* Book II, pp. 516–18; *Who's Who among African Americans,* 26th ed., p. 968.

First Black Holders of Doctorates in Physical Sciences

Year	Recipient	Granting Institution
1916	Saint Elmo Brady	University of Illinois, Urbana, IL (Chemistry)
1925	Elbert Cox	Cornell University, Ithaca, NY (Mathematics)
1942	Marguerite Thomas Williams	Catholic University of America, Washington, DC (Geology; first woman in the field)

Sources: Greene, *Holders of Doctorates among American Negroes,* p. 140.

1994 • Gail Marie Hawkins received a doctorate in genetics from Stanford Medical School, becoming the first black ever to receive the degree. She was also the first black woman to graduate from the University of California at Davis with a bachelor's degree in genetics.

Sources: *Jet* 86 (9 May 1994): 17.

1995 • Cassandra Swain became the first black woman to earn a doctorate in electrical engineering from Vanderbilt University. She worked as an engineering researcher for AT & T Bell Laboratories in Holmdel, New Jersey.

Sources: *Jet* 88 (3 July 1995): 21.

1996 • Illinois Circuit Court Judge Mary Maxwell Thomas (1943–) became the first black woman judge to receive a master of judicial studies degree from the University of Nevada, Reno. The program was available to sitting judges who graduated from law schools accredited by the American Bar Association. Thomas was born in Waukegan, Illinois; she attended Michigan State University and graduated from New Mexico State University and the University of Chicago Law School. She has held several positions in Chicago, including that of assistant U.S. attorney and a partner with the firm Sulzer and Shapiro, Ltd.

Sources: *Who's Who among Africans,* 14th ed., p. 1277; *Jet* 90 (8 July 1996): 19.

1996 • Cylenthia Latoye Miller (1962–) was the first black woman to serve as president of her law school class at the Detroit College of Law. This is the oldest, independent, continuously operating law school in the country. Miller was born in Pine Bluff and received her bachelor's degree from Wayne State University and juris doctor degree (cum laude) from the Detroit College of Law. She is a member of several law associations, including the Women Lawyers Association of Michigan.

Sources: *Who's Who among African Americans,* 26th ed., p. 122; *Jet* 90 (29 July 1996): 19.

1998 • The first black woman to graduate from the University of Arizona in Tucson with a degree in mining engineering was Erica Baird. She was an honor graduate of the five-year program, graduating one semester early. She became a marketing management trainee with Caterpillar Inc. in Peoria, Illinois.

Sources: *Jet* 93 (12 January 1998): 19.

1998 • The first all-woman class of doctoral graduates from the United Theological Seminary of Dayton, Ohio, graduated this year. They were also the first class of all black women in the school's 150-year history. The women were Michele DeLeaver Balamani, Shirlimarie McAroy-Gray, Barbara A. Reynolds, and Cynthia Wimbert-James. Six more black women were expected to graduate later in the year.

Sources: *Jet* 93 (26 January 1998): 23.

2000 • Colleen Samuels (1960?–) received a law degree as well as a master's degree in social work from Yeshiva University in New York, becoming the first person to simultaneously earn the two degrees there. A native Jamaican and mother of ten, Samuels spent four years commuting each day by bus, riding six hours round trip from Stroudsburg, Pennsylvania, to New York City to attend Benjamin N. Cardozo School of Law and Wurzweiler School of Social Work at Yeshiva. After graduation she passed the New York State bar examination on her first attempt and became an associate with the firm Sciretta & Venterina. In 1996 Samuels graduated (cum laude) from the State University of New York at Stony Brook, completing four years in less than two years. From there she entered law school and then began her social work degree.

Sources: *Jet* 99 (15 January 2001): 55.

2001 • The first black woman to receive a doctorate from NASA's Goddard Space Flight Center was Aprille Ericsson-Jackson. She was also the first black woman to receive a doctorate in Mechanical Engineering from Howard University as well as the first American to receive a doctorate with the aerospace option. She was born in Brooklyn and grew up in the Bedford Styvesant neighborhood. At age fifteen she moved to Cambridge to live with her grandparents and attend the Cambridge School of Weston. She received her bachelor's degree from the Massachusetts Institute of Technology in aeronautical/astronautical engineering. As an engineer with NASA's Goddard Space Flight Center, she has also taught at Bowie State University in Maryland and at her alma mater, Howard University.

Sources: *Contemporary Black Biography,* vol. 28, pp. 64–66; *Jet* 99 (4 January 2001): 8.

2007 • Ashley, Brittany, and Courtney Henry received bachelors degrees from Dartmouth College, becoming the first set of triplets to graduate from the Ivy League school. The triplets, then twenty-one years old, have remained together through life. They were born on the same day, attended the same schools, and always lived together. They attended a Christian Seventh Day Adventist school and graduated in 2003 with the shared distinction as "valedictorian" of their sixty-student class.

Sources: *Jet* 111 (2 July 2007): 26.

2007 • Girl genius Brittney Exline, then fifteen years old, became the youngest black female ever accepted to an Ivy League school; the University of Pennsylvania. The Colorado Springs, Colorado native received a full scholarship that covers the $50,000 tuition at the university. "I think it's cool and I'm proud of myself for holding that record," she said. Exline was sitting up at 4 ½ months, making designs in blacks when she was 6 months old, walking at 8 months old, and by 15 months, completing jigsaw puzzles with 24 to 100 pieces. In high school Exline studied Spanish, French, Japanese, Russian, Arabic, and German. A gifted dancer as well, she has studied jazz, tap, and ballet. Her recognitions include the title Miss Colorado Pre-Teen (2004) and Miss Colorado Jr. National Teenager (2006). She is the daughter of Christopher and Chyrese Exline and has one brother.

Sources: *Jet* 111 (11 June 2007): 26.

2009 • The first black woman to earn a Ph.D. degree in mathematics from Florida Atlantic University was Mary Hopkins; she graduated in May. Her dissertation evolves around communicative ring theory, a part of abstract algebra.

Sources: *Jet* 114 (12 January 2009): 24.

2009? • Andrew Williams was the first black American to earn a Ph.D. degree in engineering from the University of Kansas. He later became a computer science professor at historically black and all-female Spelman College. Born to an African American father and a Korean-born mother, he comes from Junction City, Kansas, where he grew up with five brothers and sisters. At Spelman, in 2004 Williams formed the SpelBots (short for Spelman College robotics team), then the only all-black and all-female robotics team. The six-student-team was required to know electronics, mechanics, and software in order to master the design, manufacture, and application of robots.

Sources: *Jet* 115 (18 May 2009): 16.

College Faculty

1849 • The first black faculty member on a white college campus was hired at Central College in McGrawville, New York. Charles Lewis Reason (1818–1893), reformer and

Charles Reason

writer, was named professor of mathematics, belles lettres, and French in October 1849. A native of New York, Reason received his early schooling at the African Free School. He began teaching at age fourteen, under the supervision of another teacher. After earning a degree at Central College, he was hired to teach there. In 1852 he became principal of the Institute for Colored Youth in Philadelphia. He stayed in Philadelphia for three years, before returning to New York, where he worked as a teacher and principal in the city's black schools until 1890. Reason is given credit for rescuing and strengthening the Institute for Colored Youth, which was struggling to maintain itself when he arrived. He was also active in the abolitionist movement in Philadelphia, and continued his efforts on behalf of equal rights in New York, where he became a community leader. His activism began early in life. As a teenager, he helped to form the Young Men's Convention in 1837, which was founded to challenge New York State's restrictive suffrage provision. He was co-secretary of the black convention of 1840, which continued the drive for equal suffrage rights. Reason once wanted to be an Episcopal priest, but was denied because of his race. He became instead a person considered a master teacher and an advocate for his race. Other black faculty members of the time included William G. Allen and George Vashon (1824–1878). Allen, professor of Greek and German languages, rhetoric, and belles letters, married one of his white students and later was forced to flee with her to England. George Vashon joined the McGrawville faculty in 1854.

Sources: Jackson, *A History of Afro-American Literature,* vol. 1, p. 126; Lane, *William Dorsey's Philadelphia and Ours,* p. 137; Logan and Winston, *Dictionary of American Biography,* pp. 516–17; Smith, *Notable Black American Men,* pp. 998–1000; Woodson, *The Education of the Negro Prior to 1861,* p. 280.

1859 • Sarah Jane Woodson Early (1825–1907) became the first regular black teacher at Wilberforce, where she served as principal for several years. While not officially given the title of professor, she taught courses in literature. Early had as good an education as was possible for the times; she studied first at Albany Manual Labor Academy in Ohio and graduated from Oberlin in 1856. For more than thirty years, she taught as she and her minister husband moved to his various appointments. She was an active worker in behalf of anti-slavery and temperance causes. Her efforts resulted in recognition from the state committee of Tennessee's Prohibition Party, who hired her to lecture throughout the state in 1887. She was also the only woman delegate from the Southern states at the Congress of Representative Women in 1893 at the Columbian exposition in Chicago. It has been suggested that Early's father, Thomas Woodson, was the child of Sally Hemings and Thomas Jefferson. At the time of her death, Early was residing in Nashville, Tennessee.

Sources: Buck, *The Progression of the Race in the United States and Canada,* pp. 51–52; Smith, *Notable Black American Women,* Book II, pp. 198–200.

1870 • The first black teacher to be engaged by the Freedmen's Aid Society to teach at Claflin College, in South Carolina, was William Henry Crogman (1841–1931), a scholar and writer. He was president of Clark College, in Atlanta, Georgia, from 1903 to 1910. He is known for his early histories of blacks, *Progress of a Race* and *Citizenship, Intelligence, Affluence, Honor and Trust.* The last work was revised and published as *The Colored American.*

Sources: Logan and Winston, *Dictionary of American Negro Biography,* pp. 140–41; Shockley, *Heritage and Hope,* pp. 91–92.

1870 • The first black to teach white college students in Kentucky was Julia Britton Hooks (1852–1942), who was instructor of instrumental music at Berea College in Kentucky. She was one of the first black women in this country to attend Berea. Hooks, who was born in Lexington, lived during three major wars: the Civil War, World War I, and World War II. Her mother, who was also a talented musician, recognized her musical talents early. It is said that her mother's white father paid for piano lessons for Hooks. In 1869, the Hooks family moved to Berea. She married in 1872 and moved to Greenville, Mississippi, where her minister husband had opened a free school for blacks. She taught in the school until she moved to Memphis in 1876. Her husband had died in 1873, and she married Charles Hooks in 1880. Hooks taught music in Memphis, both in the public schools and privately.

W. C. Handy, one of the early trailblazing black musicians, was one of her students. She was an active advocate for the Memphis black community, and used proceeds from her concerts to found the Negro Old Folks and Orphans Home in 1891. She was also involved in establishing the Negro Juvenile Court Detention Home, where her second husband, who was a truant officer there, was killed by one of its residents. She later opened her own music school, which welcomed both black and white students. She was the grandmother of Benjamin Hooks Jr. (1925–2010), who was to become executive director of the NAACP.

Sources: Hine, *Black Women in America*, pp. 572–73; Smith, *Notable Black American Women*, pp. 511–13.

1878 • George Franklin Grant (1846–1910) was the first black member of the Harvard University faculty. He was the second black graduate of the dental school in 1870. He taught as "demonstrator" and instructor from 1878 to 1889. One of his personal patients was Charles William Eliot, president of Harvard. Grant also invented the golf tee.

Sources: Sollors, *Blacks at Harvard*, p. 6.

1932 • James Weldon Johnson (1871–1938), educator, lyricist, consul, author, editor, poet, and civil rights activist, was appointed in January 1932 to teach creative writing at Fisk University, where he held the Adam K. Spence Chair of Creative Literature and Writing. He was the first poet to teach writing at a black college. Born in Jacksonville, Florida, Johnson's accomplishments were so varied and so notable that they almost defy brief summary. His mother, who is said to have been the first black woman public school teacher in Florida, was one of his teachers when he attended Stanton elementary school for black children in Jacksonville. With no local high school available, Johnson was sent to Atlanta University's preparatory school in 1887; he graduated in 1894 and returned to Jacksonville to become principal of Stanton. One of his early achievements was extension of the curriculum through the high school years. He founded a newspaper in 1895, and may be best known for his 1900 collaboration with his brother, J. Rosamond, to write "Lift Every Voice and Sing," which became known as the Negro National Anthem. Johnson moved to New York in 1902 to devote more time to writing song lyrics for Broadway productions, again collaborating with his brother and producer Bob Cole. When the three went on tour in 1905, the tenor of the times was such that they could not get acceptable lodging in Salt Lake City. Somewhat concurrently, he was plunged into diplomatic work, serving as U.S. Consul in Venezuela from 1904 to 1909 and in Nicaragua until 1912. He became more visible as a civil rights activist when he returned to the United States after resigning the Nicaragua post. He allied himself with the NAACP, serving as a minor officer twice before he became its first nonwhite executive secretary in 1920. He also had many publications during the flowering of the Harlem Renaissance in the 1920s. He turned to writing nonfiction in the next decade, including publications made while he was a Fisk professor, the position he held until his death.

James Weldon Johnson

Sources: Kane, *Famous First Facts*, p. 476; Logan and Winston, *Dictionary of American Negro Biography*, pp. 353–57; Smith, *Notable Black American Men*, pp. 626–30.

1946 • Allison Davis (1902–1983), psychologist and educator, was the first black professor at the University of Chicago. The next year he became the first black professor to receive tenure at a major predominantly white northern university. In 1970 he became the first John Dewey Distinguished Service Professor of Education. He was the first in education from any race to become a fellow in the American Academy of Arts and Sciences, and one of the first to challenge the accuracy of the IQ test for "measuring accurately the educational potential of children from low-income families." Born in Washington, D.C., to a relatively prosperous family, Davis graduated from Williams College in Massachusetts, where he was forbidden from living on the rigidly segregated campus. He graduated valedictorian of his class in 1924. Davis earned two master's degrees from Harvard University and a doctorate from the University of Chicago. Later he studied at the London School of Economics. Davis spent more than forty years on the Chicago faculty. He was hired only after philanthropist Julius Rosenwald offered to cover his salary. He also taught at a number of institutions, including Dillard, Hampton, Harvard, and Yale and was visiting scholar at Columbia, Smith, the University of Michigan, and elsewhere. Davis published ten books, including a study of twentieth-century cotton plantation systems called *Deep South*. On February 1, 1994, the U.S. Postal Service issued a twenty-nine-cent stamp in his honor, a part of the Postal Service's Black Heritage Series.

Sources: *Encyclopedia of Black America,* p. 302; Garrett, *Famous First Facts about Negroes,* pp. 62, 185; *Jet* 65 (12 December 1983): 15; *Who's Who in America, 1982–1983,* p. 766; Smith, *Notable Black American Men,* pp. 252–53; *Journal of Blacks in Higher Education,* p. 23.

1946 • After she received her master's degree in 1946, Estelle Massey Riddle Osborne (1901–1981) became the first black woman instructor in New York University's department of nursing education. She received a bachelor's degree in nursing education from Columbia University in 1931. She did her undergraduate work at Prairie View State College (later University) in Texas. While studying at Columbia, she taught at Lincoln Hospital School for Nurses in the Bronx. After graduation, she became the first educational director of nursing at Freedmen's Hospital School of Nursing, later to become the college of Nursing at Howard University in Washington, D.C. She became the first black director of nursing at City Hospital No. 2, known later as the Homer G. Phillips Hospital Training School. In 1943 she became consultant to the National Nursing Council for War Service and was the first black consultant on the staff of any national nursing organization. She remained an advocate for black nurses and was active in the National Association of Colored Graduate Nurses and later the American Nurses Association. Osborne was born in Palestine, Texas, the eighth of eleven children.

Sources: Hine, *Black Women in America,* pp. 903–5; *Negro Almanac,* pp. 1389, 1426; *Who's Who among Black Americans, 1980–81,* p. 607; Salzman, *Encyclopedia of African-American Culture and History,* vol. 4, p. 2070.

1948 • The first black faculty member at Oberlin College in Ohio was Wade Ellis Sr.

Sources: "Mathematicians of the African Diaspora," http://www.math.buffalo.edu/mad/PEEPS/ellis_wade.html, accessed September 16, 2012.

1949 • J. Saunders Redding (1906–1988) is believed to be the first black faculty member to teach at an Ivy League university. While on leave from a teaching position at Hampton Institute, as it was known then, Redding was visiting full professor at Brown University, his alma mater. Redding was born in Wilmington, Delaware, the third of seven children. He earned a bachelor of philosophy degree in 1928 and a master of arts degree in 1932, both from Brown University. Although he met the requirements for membership in Phi Beta Kappa while he was at Brown, racism in the 1920s prevented his acceptance into the scholarly society and it was not until 1943 that he was awarded the honor. He continued graduate study at Columbia University in 1933–34. His negative feelings about black college administrators never deterred him from teaching at a number of them, including Morehouse College, Southern University, Elizabeth City State Teacher's College, and Hampton Institute (now Hampton University). After a stint with the Division of Research and Publications for the National Endowment for the Humanities, in 1970 he joined the English Department at Cornell University, becoming the first black appointed to the rank of professor in the College of Arts and Sciences as well as the first to hold an endowed chair. In 1975 he was named the Ernest I. White professor of American Studies and Humane Letters Emeritus. Redding wrote a number of fiction and nonfiction works; among them were *To Make a Poet Black* (1939), *No Day of Triumph* (1942), *They Came in Chains* (1950), *Stranger and Alone* (1950), and *The Lonesome Road* (1958). He was twice a Guggenheim fellow (1944–45 and 1959–60) and a Ford Foundation Fellow at Duke University (1964–65). William Augustus Hinton (1883–1959), the second black faculty member at Harvard and a pioneering syphilogist, held annual appointments as instructor in the Medical School beginning in 1918. Harvard University promoted Hinton to professor of bacteriology and immunology; he became the first black on the Harvard Medical School faculty to attain that rank.

Sources: *Contemporary Black Biography,* vol. 26, pp. 122–25; Smith, *Notable Black American Men,* pp. 1000–1002; Sollors, *Blacks at Harvard,* p. 6; Logan and Winston, *Dictionary of American Negro Biography,* pp. 315–6; *Jet* 90 (1 July 1996): 22.

1950 • Ralph J. Bunche (1903–1971) was the first black person named to the faculty of Arts and Sciences at Harvard, when he became professor of government. He resigned in 1952 because of pressing obligations at the United Nations, where he was Undersecretary General. From 1959 to 1969 he served as the first black member of Harvard's board of overseers. Bunche, who was born in Detroit and traced his mother's family ancestry back to slavery, knew much less about his father's roots. Bunche's childhood was punctuated by his mother's death in 1917, and after that he never saw his father again; he moved to Los Angeles with his grandmother in 1918, and it was she who encouraged him to attend college. He graduated *summa cum laude* from the University of California at Los Angeles in 1922. A fellowship from Harvard led to his earning a master's degree in 1928, after which he declined Harvard's offer of support for doctoral study and accepted an offer to organize the political science department at Howard University. Bunche took leave the next year, however, and returned to Harvard for doctoral study. In 1934 he won the prize for the best dissertation. His first book, *World View of Race,* followed two years later. Bunche had a rich catalog of scholarly research experience, doing fieldwork in the South as he worked with Swedish social scientist Gunnar Myrdal on the project that was published in 1944 as *An American Dilemma: The Negro Problem and American Democracy*. Rejected for the World War II draft for physical reasons, he worked for the National Defense Program Office of Information and then for the State Department. He participated in conferences relating to formation of the United Nations, and became the first black to serve on the U.S. delegation to the United Nations General Assembly. When he was appointed undersecretary, he became the highest-ranking U.S. official at the United Nations. One of his crowning achievements was receipt of the Nobel Peace Prize in 1950; he was the first black person to receive the honor. He remained at the United Nations until 1971, when his poor health resulted in his being relieved of his duties. Despite the recognition and general acclaim that Bunche received for his work at the United Nations, he was considered too conservative and too racially conciliatory by some of the black leaders of his day. His papers are housed at UCLA and at the U.N. archives in New York.

Ralph Bunche

Sources: Sollors, *Blacks at Harvard,* p. 6; Smith, *Notable Black American Men,* pp. 152–56.

1956 • Joseph Applegate (1925-2003), who was assistant professor of modern languages at the Massachusetts Institute of Technology, was the school's first black faculty member.

Sources: *New York Times* (6 March 2001).

1966 • Vivienne Malone-Mayes (1932?–1995) became the first black professor at Baylor University in Waco, Texas. She had been denied admission to the university just five years earlier. Before moving to Baylor, Malone-Mayes served as chair of the mathematics department at Paul Quinn College and at Bishop College, both in Texas.

Sources: *Jet* 88 (26 June 1995): 17.

1966 • The U.S. Naval Academy in Annapolis, Maryland, appointed its first black faculty member, Samuel P. Massie (1919–2005). He taught chemistry and was co-founder of the Black Studies Program. Massie was born in North Little Rock, Arkansas, and graduated from Arkansas Agricultural and Mechanical, and Normal College (now the University of Arkansas at Pine Bluff). He received a master's degree in chemistry from Fisk University and a doctorate in organic chemistry from Iowa State University. He returned to teach at Fisk after serving in World War II, and worked to strengthen the master's degree in his field. In 1960 he held a post with the National Science Foundation and was part-time chair of the department of pharmaceutical chemistry at Howard University, both in Washington, D.C. In 1963 he became president of North Carolina College (now North Carolina Central University) in Durham. From there Massie moved to the Naval Academy. He was honored in 1997 when the National Academy of Science Gallery included his picture in its collection. In 1998 he was the only black scientist honored on the *Chemical and Engineering News'* list of the seventy-five greatest contributors to the field of chemistry. In 1997 he became vice president for education of Bingwa Multicultural Software.

Sources: *Jet* 93 (1 December 1997): 10; 94 (13 July 1998): 32; Smith, *Notable Black American Men,* pp. 775–76.

1968 • Jacquelyne Johnson Jackson (1932–), sociologist and civil rights activist, became the first full-time black faculty member at Duke University Medical School. In 1971 she received tenure and became the medical school's first black tenured faculty member. She was also the first woman chair of the Association of Black Sociologists. The Winston-Salem native received her doctorate in 1960, becoming the first black woman to earn the doctorate in sociology from The Ohio State University. As a child, her family was part of the black academic elite. Both of her parents had earned master's degrees; her father earned his from New York University and was head of the Tuskegee Institute School of Business. Growing up in Tuskegee, Jackson was surrounded by such luminaries as George Washington Carver and by black people who fought for racial equality. She did her undergraduate and master's work at the University of Wisconsin in Madison, and was the first black postdoctoral fellow at Duke's Center for the Study of Aging and Human Development. Jackson taught at several historically black institutions in the South before going to Duke, first at Southern University in Louisiana, then at Jackson State College in Mississippi, and later at St. Augustine's College in Virginia. She also served on the faculty at Howard University in Washington. She was actively involved in the Civil Rights Movement and participated in the 1963 March on Washington and was in Jackson, Mississippi, during the riot when three young black men were shot. Jackson served as a professor at Duke until 1988 and was awarded emeritus status when she retired. She is the author of a number of works on aging, with special emphasis on minority aging, and was the first black to edit a journal of the American Sociological Association.

Sources: *Ebony Success Library,* vol. 1, p. 167; Smith, *Notable Black American Women,* pp. 554–56; *Who's Who among African Americans,* 14th ed., p. 657.

1969 • Constitutional law scholar Derrick Albert Bell Jr. (1930–2011) became the first black law professor at Harvard Law School. In 1971 he became the first black tenured law professor. He was a civil rights scholar who joined others in establishing the field of critical race theory. Bell was born in Pittsburgh, Pennsylvania, to parents who influenced his development as an activist. He was a first-generation college student when he entered Duquesne University, from which he received his bachelor's degree in 1952. After two years of military service, Bell entered law school at the University of Pittsburgh, with the career goal of becoming a civil rights lawyer, and graduated in 1957. His first job after graduation was with the Civil Rights Division of the U.S. Justice Department. He resigned in 1959, when the Department considered his NAACP membership a conflict of interest. He worked with the NAACP and its Legal Defense and Educational Fund until 1967. After serving as director of the University of California's Western Center on Law and Poverty for two years, Bell was appointed as a lecturer in law at Harvard. Only two years later he was promoted to professor and given tenure. He continued his activism while at Harvard, and in 1990, after twenty-three years, he began an unpaid leave of absence to protest Harvard's hiring policies. Earlier, he had taken a five-year leave of absence, from 1980 to 1986, to serve at the University of Oregon Law School. He was dismissed from Harvard in 1992, when it was claimed that he exceeded his two-year maximum leave. Bell held various visiting professor or other special appointments at New York University Law School starting in 1991. He wrote numerous publications relating to racial justice and injustice.

Sources: *Contemporary Black Biography,* vol. 6, pp. 33–36; Smith, *Notable Black American Men,* pp. 71–73; *Who's Who among African Americans,* 26th ed., p. 84 .

1969 • The first chairperson of Harvard University's Department of Afro-American Studies was Ewart Guinier (1911–1990). His daughter, (Carol) Lani Guinier, gained national recognition in 1993, when President Bill Clinton chose her to head the U.S. Department of Justice's civil rights division. Clinton later withdrew the nomination.

Sources: *Jet* 84 (21 June 1993): 4–7; *Who's Who among Black Americans, 1988,* p. 282.

1969 • Kelly Miller Smith Sr., (1920–1984), clergyman and writer, became the first black faculty member in the Vanderbilt University Divinity School in Tennessee. He later became assistant dean. The Mound Bayou, Mississippi, native was Martin Luther King's associate in Nashville, Tennessee, during the civil rights struggle of the 1960s.

Sources: *Ebony Success Library,* vol. 1, p. 285.

1976 • Eileen Jackson Southern (1920–2002) was the first African American woman to received a tenured professorship in any discipline at Harvard. A specialist in Renaissance European and African American music, she was professor of music and Afro-American studies at the university from 1974 to 1987. Previously, Southern chaired the university's Afro-American Studies Department (1975–79). In 2007, Southern's portrait was unveiled at Harvard as a part of the Harvard Foundation's Portraiture Project that S. Allen Counter, a Harvard professor, initiated in 2002 "to increase the number of portraits at Harvard of minorities who have served the university for many years with distinction."

Sources: *Contemporary Black Biography*, vol. 56, pp. 138–40; *Encyclopedia of African American Culture and History*, 2d ed., vol. 6, p. 1560; Gates and Higginbotham, *African American National Biography*, vol. 7, pp. 335–36; *Jet* 111 (5 March 2007): 26.

1976 • The first black woman to head a major research university in this country was Mary Frances Berry (1938–). She was named chancellor of the University of Colorado at Boulder this year. Berry has had an enviable career in a variety of spheres. A Nashville, Tennessee native, she was born into a family of extremely poor circumstances, which resulted in her being placed in an orphanage for a period of time. She credits mentorship from one of her black high school teachers with motivating her and helping her to overcome the trauma of her early years. Berry worked her way through school to earn a bachelor's degree from Howard University in 1961, a master's degree one year later form Howard, and a doctorate and law degree from the University of Michigan in 1966 and 1970, respectively. She began her career as an academician, working at colleges in Michigan and Maryland before taking a faculty position at the University of Colorado in 1970. She was Colorado's first director of the Afro-American Studies in 1972 and was named provost for the Division of Behavioral and Social Sciences in 1974. After a year as chancellor, Berry remained on the faculty at Colorado until 1980. She was assistant secretary of education in the U.S. Department of Health, Education, and Welfare from 1977 to 1980. She was the first black woman to be named chief educational officer of the United States, serving from 1977 to 1979. In 1980 she joined the faculty at Howard University and was appointed to the U.S. Commission on Civil Rights that same year. In 1987 she became the Geraldine R. Segal Professor of American Social Thought at the University of Pennsylvania. An accomplished and highly published author, Berry has earned praise for her expertise in legal and African American history. She has been a consultant for numerous boards and organizations, holds more than eighteen honorary degrees, and has received many national awards for her scholarship and public service.

Sources: Potter and Claytor, *African-American Firsts,* pp. 35–36; Salzman, *Encyclopedia of African-American Culture and History,* Supplement, pp. 16–17; Smith, *Notable Black American Women,* pp. 80–86; *Who's Who among African Americans,* 26th ed., p. 98.

1978 • Barbara T. Christian (1944?–2000) was the first black tenured professor at the University of California, Berkeley. In 1986 she was the first black promoted to full professor and in 1991 the first black to receive the Distinguished Teaching Award from the university. Christian, an acclaimed professor in African American Studies, was considered one of the first scholars to focus national attention on such black women writers as Toni Morrison and Alice Walker. She joined the faculty at Berkeley in 1972 and remained there until her death. She played a central role in founding the African-American studies department. In 2000 she received Berkeley's highest honor, the Berkeley Citation.

Sources: *New York Times* (29 June 2000).

1979 • The first black woman to become tenured at Yale University was Sylvia A. Boone. Born in Mt. Vernon, New York, she graduated from Brooklyn College and Columbia University. Later she earned her master's and doctoral degrees from Yale. She did further study at the University of Ghana. She was visiting lecturer in Afro-American studies at Yale and taught a course on black women. She also began a black film festival.

Sources: Potter and Claytor, *African-American Firsts*, p. 36.

1980 • The first black dean at the University of Oregon Law School was Derrick Albert Bell Jr. (1930–2011). He was also the first black ever to head a non-black law school. On leave from his position at the Harvard School of Law, Bell was scheduled to be at Oregon from 1980 to 1986, but left the post in 1985 when he protested a faculty directive to deny an Asian American woman a post on the faculty and re-open the search. He spent the last year of his leave as a professor at Stanford University, where he encountered another situation that evoked a similar protest.

Sources: Smith, *Notable Black American Men*, pp. 71–73; *Contemporary Black Biography*, vol. 6, p. 35; *Who's Who among African Americans*, 26th ed., p. 84.

1982 • Glenn Cartman Loury (1948–), an economist, became the first tenured professor in the economics department at Harvard University. Born on Chicago's South Side, he received both his bachelor's and master's degrees from Northwestern University. In 1976 he received his doctorate from Massachusetts Institute of Technology. After teaching posts at the Northwestern and the University of Michigan, he taught at the John F. Kennedy School of Government at Harvard from 1982 to 1991. He was named professor of economics at Boston University in 1991, university professor in 1994, and since 1997 he has been director of the Institute on Race and Social Division. Loury has published widely, writing on such topics as negative stereotypes, self-censorship, and race.

Sources: *New York Times* (20 January 2002); *Who's Who among African Americans*, 26th ed., p. 789.

1985 • The first black tenured professor at Harvard Business School was James Ireland Cash Jr. (1947–). He is a specialist in the management of information systems technology in large corporations. Cash is a native of Fort Worth, Texas, who received his undergraduate degree from Texas Christian University in 1969, and master's and doctoral degrees from Purdue in 1974 and 1976, respectively. He held computer-related positions in academia and in industry before becoming an assistant professor in the Harvard Graduate School of Business Administration in 1976. He was elected to the Texas Christian University Hall of Fame in 1982 and is the author of three books and numerous papers in his field.

Sources: *Jet* 68 (22 July 1985): 21; *Who's Who among African Americans*, 26th ed., p. 222.

1997 • The first black faculty member of the National Defense University in Washington, D.C., was Nedra Huggins-Williams. A graduate of Fisk University, she received her doctorate from the University of Utah.

Sources: *Jet* 91 (14 April 1997): 10; *Who's Who among African Americans*, 26th ed., p. 616.

1998 • The first tenured minority woman on the Harvard Law School faculty was [Carol] Lani Guinier (1950–). She made headlines in 1993 when President Bill Clinton nominated her to head the Civil Rights Division of the U.S. Department of Justice. She later withdrew her name, citing concern over allegedly controversial ideas relating to race and voting rights in some of her writings. Guinier, who was born in New York City, came naturally to the legal profession. Her grandfather and her father were both lawyers. She also came naturally to Harvard. Her father was the first chair of Harvard's Department of African-American Studies. Her parents, a black father and a Jewish mother, exposed Guinier to both black and Jewish cultures. She did her undergraduate work at Radcliffe College, graduating in 1971, and earned her law degree from Yale University in 1975, attending classes with Bill and Hillary Clinton. She held several positions before accepting her first teaching appointment at the University of Pennsylvania Law School. She worked in the Civil Rights Division of the Justice Department during the Jimmy Carter administration; and, notably, she was the chief litigator on voting rights for the NAACP Legal Defense and Education Fund from 1981 until she moved to Pennsylvania in 1988. Many of her writings appeared after her work with the NAACP, where her experiences in the courts may have helped to shape her views.

Lani Guinier

Guinier has defended her writings, which were criticized widely by conservatives. She is highly regarded as an advocate for racial equality and was given the Torch of Courage award by the NAACP's magazine, *Crisis*, in 1993. Members of the Congressional Black Caucus refused to meet with President Clinton after he withdrew Guinier's nomination. Her 1998 book, *Lift Every Voice*, describes her experience with nomination and withdrawal.

Sources: *Contemporary Black Biography*, vol. 7, pp. 107–12; *Jet* 93 (16 February 1998); 93 (20 April 1998): 20; Smith, *Notable Black American Women*, Book II, pp. 261–63; *Who's Who among African Americans*, 26th ed., pp. 506.

1998 • Marilyn K. Easter (1957–) became the first black associate professor and chair at the College of Notre Dame in Belmont, California. She was named chair of a new program, Health Services. Born in Oklahoma City, she has degrees from the University of Colorado (B.A.), Denver University (M.A., M.S.W.), and the University of San Francisco (Ed.D.). She was a marketing consultant from 1979 to 1982, heading the firm Marketing by Marilyn. She has teaching experiences at several institutions, including California State University and St. Mary's College.

Sources: *Who's Who among African Americans*, 26th ed., p. 371; *Jet* 93 (15 December 1997): 20.

1998 • Fannie G. Gaston-Johansson became the first black woman tenured professor at Johns Hopkins University. In 2007, she became the first chair of the School of Nursing in the Department of Acute and Chronic Care at the university. Internationally renowned nursing educator, researcher, and clinical practitioner, Gaston-Johansson also directs the Center on Health Disparities Research and leads the international and interdisciplinary Minority Global Health Disparities Research Training Program. Her recognitions include the National Black Nursing Association's Trailblazer Award and citations from the U.S. Congress and the government of Sweden for notable international and domestic research initiatives.

Sources: Johns Hopkins University, Elsie M. Lawler Chair http://webapps.jhu.edu/named professorships/professorshipdetail.cfm?professorshipID=12. Accessed September 16, 2012.

1999 • Bill Duke (1943–), actor, producer, and director, was appointed the first Time Warner Professor at Howard University. He was also named chairman of the Department of Radio, TV, and Film in the School of Communications. Time Warner, Inc., endowed the chair through a $2 million gift, the largest corporate gift ever for the School of Communications. As a producer, Duke has a number of films to his credit, including *Hoodlum*, *Deep Cover*, *Sister Act 2*, *Back in the Habit*, and *Rage in Harlem*. He was born in Poughkeepsie, New York, and holds a bachelor's degree from Boston University and master's degrees from New York University and the American Film Institute. He has directed for Disney, New Line Cinema, Miramax, Harpo Productions, American Playhouse, and PBS. He has won several awards, including an NAACP Image Award for Special Achievements in Directing in 1991.

Sources: *Jet* 95 (12 April 1999): 24–25; *Contemporary Black Biography*, vol. 3, pp. 58–61; *Who's Who among African Americans*, 26th ed., p. 360.

1999 • Larry Earl Davis (1946–) was named the first E. Desmond Lee Professor of Racial and Ethnic Diversity at Washington University in St. Louis. Born in Saginaw, Michigan, he completed undergraduate studies at Michigan State University and holds a master of social work, a master of arts, and a doctorate from the University of Michigan. He has published and co-published a number of articles and books on race and gender, including *Working with African-American Males: A Guide to Practice* (1999).

Sources: *Jet* 95 (17 May 1999): 20; *Who's Who among African Americans*, 26th ed., p.317.

1999 • The first Ida B. Wells Barnett University Professor at DePaul University in Chicago was Michael Eric Dyson (1958–), who was also tenured in the school's department of religious studies. The nationally known author, scholar, and Baptist minister was distinguished visiting professor of African American studies at Columbia University when he received the DePaul position. He is now University Professor of Sociology at Georgetown

Michael Eric Dyson

University. Dyson, who was born in Detroit, graduated *magna cum laude* from Carson New-man and went on to earn his master's and doctorate from Princeton University, receiving the latter degree in 1993. Among his published works are *Making Malcolm: The Myth and Meaning of Malcolm X* (1995); *Race Rules: Navigating the Color Line* (1997); *Holler If You Hear Me* (2001); *Is Bill Cosby Right* (2005); and *Can You Hear Me Now?* (2009).

Sources: *Contemporary Black Biography*, vol. 11, pp. 69–72; *Jet* 95 (17 May 1999): 20; *Who's Who among African Americans*, 26th ed., p. 368.

First Black Holders of Doctorates in Professional and Vocational Fields

Year	Recipient	Granting Institution
1887	John Wesley E. Bowen Sr.	Boston University, Boston, MA (Religion)
1915	Julian H. Lewis	University of Chicago, Chicago, IL (Medicine)
1923	Charles Hamilton Houston	Harvard University, Cambridge, MA (Law)
1932	Frederick Douglas Patterson	Cornell University, Ithaca, NY (Agricultural Science)
1934	George M. Jones	University of Michigan, Ann Arbor, MI (Engineering)
1936	Flemmie P. Kittrell	Cornell University, Ithaca, NY (Home Economics)
1939	Maurice W. Lee	University of Chicago, Chicago, IL (Business)
1940	Eliza Atkins Gleason	University of Chicago, Chicago, IL (Library Science)
1941	Alfred B. Turner	Pennsylvania State University, University Park, PA (Industrial Education)
1942	Oscar A. Fuller	University of Iowa (Music)
1960	Charles Edward Anderson	Massachusetts Institute of Technology (Meteorology)
1967	Percy A. Pietta	Princeton University (Electrical Engineering)
1969	Skip Clarence A. Ellis	University of Illinois (Computer Science)

Sources: Greene, *Holders of Doctorates among American Negroes*, p. 115; "Computer Scientists of the African Diaspora," http://www.math.buffalo.edu/mad/computer-science/ellis_clarencea.html.

2001 • The University of Iowa College of Law named Adrienne Katherine Wing (1956–) as the Bessie Dutton Murray Distinguished Professor of Law. The author of more than sixty publications, Wing is the first black woman to be awarded an endowed chair at the 154-year-old institution. She has been professor of law since 1987. Born in Oceanside, California, Wing holds degrees from Princeton University (A.B. 1978), the University of California at Los Angeles (M.A. 1979), and Stanford Law School (J.D. 1982). Her professional experiences include an internship with the United Nations in 1981, a member of the law firms Curtis, Mallet, et. al. from 1982 to 1986, and Rabinowitz, Boudin, et. al., since 1987. She holds membership in numerous organizations and serves on a number of advisory boards.

Sources: *Who's Who among African Americans*, 26th ed., pp. 1371–72 ; *Jet* 100 (10 December 2001): 20.

College Foundings

1833 • The first college in the United States founded with a mission to educate blacks was Oberlin College in Ohio. One of the elements creating the institution was Lane Seminary in Cincinnati. When many of the students converted to abolitionism, it became expedient to move to northern Ohio and join the nucleus of students and instruction already established there. By the time of the Civil War, one-third of the student body was black.

Sources: *Negro Almanac*, p. 11; Woodson, *The Education of the Negro Prior to 1861*, pp. 275–76, 300.

1854 • Lincoln University (Pennsylvania) and Wilberforce University (Ohio) are the oldest historically black colleges established in America. Unlike Cheyney State, which had its

The Country's Oldest Black College

Cheyney State College, sometimes referred to as the oldest black college in the United States, had its beginning in 1832. Richard Humphreys, a Philadelphia Quaker, willed $10,000 to a board of trustees to establish a school for blacks. A school for black boys was eventually established in 1839 and incorporated in 1842. The school became known as the Institute for Colored Youth in 1852. It reorganized in 1902 and moved to Cheyney, Pennsylvania, where it was renamed. It became a teacher training school in 1914 and a normal school in 1921, when it was purchased by the state. Since 1932 Cheyney State College (now Cheyney University of Pennsylvania) has been a degree-granting institution.

Sources: *American Colleges and Universities, 1983*, p. 1565; Bowles and DeCosta, *Between Two Worlds*, pp. 23–24; Lane, *William Dorsey's Philadelphia and Ours*, pp. 338; Woodson, *The Education of the Negro Prior to 1861*, pp. 268–70.

origin in 1832, these institutions are still in their original locations and were the first to indicate their aim to award baccalaureate degrees and develop fully into degree-granting institutions. Lincoln University, the outgrowth of Ashmun Institute, was incorporated January 1, 1854, and opened its doors to young black men on August 30, 1856. Wilberforce University was incorporated in 1856 and awarded its first baccalaureate degree in 1857. In 1862, Wilberforce came under black control, making it the oldest college controlled by blacks.

Sources: Bennett, *Before the Mayflower*, pp. 457, 462–63, 641; Bowles and De Costa, *Between Two Worlds*, p. 20; Woodson, *The Education of the Negro Prior to 1861*, pp. 268–72.

1858 • Berea College in Kentucky was the first college south of the Ohio river established specifically to educate blacks and whites together. Activities of the college were temporarily suspended during the Civil War in 1865. The integrated school received numerous threats of violence, but also experienced periods without friction. The Kentucky legislature passed a law forbidding the racial mix, which ended the biracial experiment abruptly in 1904.

Sources: Holmes, *Evolution of the Negro College*, pp. 81–82.

1866 • Edward Waters College in Jacksonville, Florida, became the first institution of higher learning for blacks in Florida. The African Methodist Episcopal Church founded the school in Live Oak, Florida. It was later renamed Brown University and moved to Jacksonville. In 1892 it was incorporated under its present name of Edward Waters College.

Sources: *Encyclopedia of Black America*, pp. 352–53.

1866 • The first institution of higher learning for blacks in Mississippi was Rust College, in Holly Springs. Founded by the Methodist Episcopal Church as Shaw University; the name was changed in 1890, presumably to avoid confusion with the school in Raleigh, North Carolina. The school was then named for Richard Rust, a white anti-slavery advocate who supported the Freedmen's Aid Society of the church.

Sources: Cantor, *Historical Landmarks of Black America*, p. 172; *Encyclopedia of Black America*, p. 737.

1867 • The first black college founded in Tennessee, and still in existence, is Fisk University. Although work on the founding of the school was begun in October 1865, it was incorporated under the laws of the State of Tennessee in August 22, 1867, under the auspices of the American Missionary Association. The institution opened on January 9, 1866. It was named in honor of General Clinton B. Fisk of the Freedmen's Bureau.

Sources: *Fisk University Bulletin, 1986–89*, p. 4; Richardson, *A History of Fisk University 1865–1946*.

1867 • On January 8, 1867 Howard Theological Seminary changed its name to Howard University. On that date the university, located in Washington, D.C., became the first black school to establish undergraduate, graduate, and professional schools. The school was established under the auspices of the Freedmen's Bureau and named in honor of General Oliver O. Howard, who headed the Bureau.

Sources: *Encyclopedia of Black America*, p. 455; Hornsby, *Chronology of African-American History*, p. 40; *Jet* 81 (13 January 1992): 38.

1867 • The first college open to blacks in Alabama was Talladega College. Founded by the American Missionary Association as a primary school, the first college program was published in the 1890 catalogue. The first class graduated in 1895.

Sources: *Encyclopedia of Black America*, p. 813.

1871 • The first land grant college for blacks was Alcorn Agricultural and Mechanical College in Lorman, Mississippi. This was made possible under the Morrill Act of 1862. Ironically, the college was named in honor of James L. Alcorn, a Reconstruction governor of the state who led the white branch of the Republican Party, and who opposed black legislators during his term of office. Hiram Rhoades (Rhodes) Revels (1822–1901) and a former U.S. Senator, was the first president. The college maintained, for a considerable period, a liberal arts curriculum, in spite of the disapproval of the legislature.

Sources: Cantor, *Historic Landmarks of Black America*, pp. 168–69; *Encyclopedia of Black America*, p. 96; *The Negro Almanac, 1976*, p. 532.

1872 • The Disciples of Christ founded the Southern Christian Institute (SCI) in Jackson, Mississippi, the first denominational school for blacks in Mississippi. The school closed in 1932. After the black Disciples of Christ were organized, blacks became concerned with education, evangelism, and other issues. White groups assisted in their efforts, especially where education was concerned. A white husband and wife team, Randall and Letitia Faurot, worked among black Disciples in Mississippi; Randall preached while Letitia ran a school and encouraged blacks to attend. They formed a corporation to aid them in establishing a school designed specifically to train blacks, the SCI. In 1863 Randall Faurot also helped to establish a school in Hillsboro, Tennessee, that was the foundation for the Southern Christian Institute in Mississippi. Other schools that the Disciples established whose mission was to train blacks were Louisville Bible College (1893–1916) in Lexington, Kentucky; Piedmont Christian Institute (1904–1916) in Martinsville, Virginia; and Jarvis Christian College (1912–) in Hawkins, Texas.

Sources: Jordan, *Two Races in One Fellowship*, p. 51.

1872 • Paul Quinn College was the first black college founded in Texas. It was founded by a group of African Methodist Episcopal circuit riders who saw a need for a trade school to train newly freed slaves. The college is still in existence.

Sources: Paul Quinn College website, http://www.pqc.edu. Accessed September 16, 2012.

1875 • Emerson Institute, in Mobile, Alabama, became that state's first black college. The American Missionary Association founded the school before the end of the Civil War. Its students included many blacks of wealth, who went on to enjoy lucrative careers.

Sources: Bailey, *They Too Call Alabama Home*, p. 16.

1883 • Hartshorn Memorial College, the first black women's college in the country, opened on November 7. It began in Richmond, Virginia, in the basement of Ebenezer Baptist Church, with fifty-eight students. It was chartered on March 13 by the Virginia legislature as "an institution of learning of collegiate grades for the education of young women." The college awarded its first degrees in 1892, when three young women graduated: Mary Moore Booze, Harriet Amanda Miller, and Dixie Erma Williams. The college was never well funded and struggled to fulfill its mission as a college for black women. In 1918 Hartshorn students began enrolling in courses at Virginia Union University; by 1922 Hartshorn had entered into an agreement for educating its students at Virginia Union.

Tuskegee Institute

In 1881 Booker T. Washington (1956–1915), with the assistance of his wife Fanny Norton Smith Washington, founded Tuskegee Institute in Alabama on July 4. He was born a slave in Virginia, where he remained until he moved with his mother and siblings to join his stepfather in West Virginia after the end of the Civil War. He received his first formal schooling in Malden, West Virginia, but was unable to attend regularly. Despite this, at age sixteen he entered Hampton Institute, which taught normal school classes and trades. It is said that the school's founder, who is alleged not to have believed in social equality for black people, became Washington's father figure. Washington did well at Hampton, and when he graduated he taught public school in Malden from 1855 to 1877. After studying briefly at Wayland Seminary in Washington, D.C., he returned to West Virginia. In 1879 he took a teaching job at Hampton, where he remained until he was asked in 1881 to open a new school in Alabama. He accepted, and in July of that year Tuskegee Normal and Industrial Institute was born. He was at first the only teacher, and Washington had to work to establish support of the white community. He followed the Hampton model, preparing students for crafts and encouraging them to be public school teachers. As the school prospered, so too did Washington's reputation as a leader. He became known increasingly for his conservative stance on racial issues, which were attributed to his belief that agitation by black people would not yield positive results. In time, other black figures, including W.E.B. Du Bois, emerged to question Washington's philosophy. A number of works list Washington as the author, although some are known to have been ghostwritten. Both the Library of Congress and the Tuskegee Institute Library have collections of his papers.

Sources: Logan and Winston, *Dictionary of American Negro Biography,* pp. 633–38; *Contemporary Black Biography,* vol. 4, pp. 252–56; Smith, *Notable Black American Men,* pp. 1181–86; Smith, *Notable Black American Women,* Book II, pp. 683–85; Harlan, *Booker T. Washington: The Making of a Black Leader, 1856–1901.*

Rather than merge with Virginia Union, in June 1928 Hartshorn officials closed the college department and focused on its high school. In 1932 the college trustees conveyed the school's property to Virginia Union, merged with the school, and became Hartshorn Memorial College in the Virginia Union University.

Sources: Hine, *Black Women in America,* pp. 543–47.

1874 • Alabama State University was founded at Salem, as the State Normal School and University for Colored Students and Teachers. It was the first state-supported institution in the United States to train black teachers. In 1887 the institution moved to its present site in Montgomery.

Sources: Bowles and DeCosta, *Between Two Worlds,* p. 292; *Encyclopedia of Black America,* p. 95.

1876 • Knoxville Freedmen's College, the first institution of higher learning in East Tennessee for blacks, was dedicated. The institution's forerunner was founded in 1863. The institution educated preachers as well as male and female teachers. It continues as Knoxville College and is listed on the National Register of Historic Places.

Sources: Jones, *Every Day in Tennessee History,* p. 173.

1877 • The first normal school for blacks in North Carolina was Fayetteville State. Until 1960, the only major the school offered was education. The first four-year class graduated in 1939. The school graduated its first white student in 1969. It is now known as Fayetteville State University.

Sources: Cantor, *Historical Landmarks of Black America*, p. 350; *Encyclopedia of Black America*, p. 384.

1881 • Spelman College in Atlanta was the first institution of higher education established in Georgia to educate black women. Sponsored by philanthropist John D. Rockefeller, the school opened on April 11, 1881, as the Atlanta Baptist Female Seminary. In 1884 the name Spelman was adopted in honor of Mrs. John D. Rockefeller's parents.

Sources: Hine, *Black Women in America*, pp. 1091–95; *Encyclopedia of Black America*, p. 807; Hornsby, *Chronicle of African-American History*, p. 50; Read, *The Story of Spelman College*.

Mary McLeod Bethune

1904 • Mary McLeod Bethune (1875–1955) became founder and president of Daytona Normal and Industrial Institute in Daytona Beach, Florida. In 1923 the school merged with Methodist-supported Cookman Institute in Jacksonville, which promoted Bethune's desire to maintain a college. In 1929 the institution changed its name to become Bethune-Cookman College (now University) and retained Bethune as its president. Born in Sumter County, near Mayesville, South Carolina, she was the fifteenth of seventeen children. She attended a rural Presbyterian mission school in the area and came under the influence of Emma Jane Wilson, a pioneer black teacher. She later attended Scotia Seminary (now Barber-Scotia College), a Presbyterian school in North Carolina. After graduation she enrolled in the Bible Institute for Home and Foreign Missions (now Moody Bible Institute) in Chicago where she prepared to enter foreign missions and become an African missionary. The Presbyterian church, however, did not place black missionaries in Africa. Bethune went on to teach at the Presbyterian-supported Haines Institute in Augusta. There she came under the influence of Lucy Craft Laney, the school's founder and principal. In 1900 Bethune founded a Presbyterian school in Palatka, Florida, then established an independent school. On October 3, 1904, in a sparsely furnished rented house, she founded Daytona Educational and Industrial Institute. Financial support from the Methodist church helped Bethune with some of the school's financial problems. In 1926 she accepted a full-time federal position in Washington, D.C., and the school suffered as she continued to divide her attention between the two positions. After a life-threatening illness, she resigned the presidency in 1942 but worked her way back into that office until 1947. Bethune was well known for her work in the black women's club movement. In 1920 she founded and became president of the Southeastern Association of Colored Women. From 1924 to 1928 she served as president of the National Association of Colored Women, an organization of some 10,000 women. On December 5, 1935, she founded the National Council of Negro Women and later pushed the organization into extensive lobbying in Washington. D.C. Under her leadership the organization sponsored the *SS Harriet Tubman* in 1944, the first liberty ship to honor a black woman and fought for the acceptance of black women in the armed forces. Bethune wrote for several journals as well as a column for the *Pittsburgh Courier* and the *Chicago Defender.* One of her best-known works is her "Last Will and Testament," that serves as an inspiration for black people; it was subsequently published in a number of sources. Bethune was highly honored for her activities as an educator, clubwoman, and orator.

Sources: Smith, *Notable Black American Women*, pp. 86–92; *Contemporary Black Biography*, vol. 4, pp. 17–21; Hine, *Black Women in America*, pp. 113–27.

1925 • The first black state-supported liberal arts college was North Carolina Central University in Durham. Founded in 1910 by James E. Shepard, the school was first chartered as the National Religious Training School and Chautauqua. It later became a state normal school. In 1925, as North Carolina College for Negroes, it became a liberal arts college.

Sources: *Encyclopedia of Black America*, p. 651.

1929 • The first and only black college consortium, the Atlanta University System, was founded in 1929. John Hope (1868–1936) became the first president of the system when Atlanta University (a co-educational institution), Spelman College (an undergraduate college for women), and Morehouse College (an undergraduate college for men), entered a consortia arrangement. Later Clark and Morris Brown colleges and the Interdenomina-

The First Black Catholic College

In 1915 Xavier University in New Orleans was founded by Katherine Drexel and the Sisters of the Blessed Sacrament. It opened on September 27, 1915, as a high school. The college department was added in 1925. Xavier was the first (and remains the only) black Catholic college.

Sources: Alford, *Famous First Blacks in the United States*, p. 32; Davis, *The History of Black Catholics*, p. 254; *Encyclopedia of Black America*, p. 871.

tional Theological Seminary (all co-educational) joined to form the largest educational center in the world for blacks. Atlanta and Clark merged in 1988, to become Clark Atlanta University, which remains a part of the center.

Sources: *Encyclopedia of Black America*, p. 144; Hornsby, *Chronology of African-American History*, p. 82; Hornsby, *Milestones in Twentieth-Century African-American History*, p. 30; *Jet* 52 (2 June 1977): 15.

1948 • The first institution for higher learning for blacks during the period of segregation established by the Churches of Christ was Southwestern Christian College. Located in Terrell, Texas, it opened in the fall of this year with forty-five students. The college began in Fort Worth under the name Southern Bible Institute. It moved into buildings that once housed Texas Military College and changed its name to Southwestern Christian College. Though founded to educate blacks, it has maintained an open door policy to students regardless of race. The institution became a four-year college in the 1970s. The campus contains the first dwelling erected in Terrell—an octagonal-shaped house built by a man named Terrell. It exists as one of the twenty surviving Round Houses in the country.

Sources: Southwestern Christian College History, http://www.swcc.edu/about.htm. Accessed September 16, 2012.

College Fund-Raising

1981 • Lou Rawls' "Parade of Stars," a national fundraiser to benefit the United Negro College Fund (now The College Fund, UNCF) begun five years earlier, in 1981 became the first nationally televised benefit for education. Co-hosted by Rawls and Marilyn McCoo, the show received pledges from across the country to support the forty-two historically black member institutions. UNCF was founded on April 24, 1944, to coordinate fundraising efforts of private black colleges.

Sources: Hornsby, *Milestones in Twentieth-Century African-American History*, pp. 41, 340; *Jet* 67 (21 January 1985): 22.

1992 • Spelman College in Atlanta became the first black college to receive a single gift of $37 million, the largest gift ever made to a historically black college. The gift from the DeWitt Wallace/Spelman College fund was established in the New York Community Trust by the Reader's Digest Association. The funds were earmarked for scholarships and to build a curriculum development program within the honors program.

Sources: *Jet* 82 (25 May 1992): 22.

2007 • The first Historically Black College and University (HBCU) to divest from Sudan was Howard University. The Board of Trustees passed a resolution to cut ties with Sudan and any company transacting business with Sudan, whose government has been involved in ethnic cleansing since 2003. The conflict there resulted in the killing of 450,000 or more people, displacing 2.5 million and looting and destruction of 90 percent of villages in Darfur. Patrick Swygert, president of Harvard at the time, said that the university's actions represented its "commitment to social justice in its governance policies," and that "Clearly, it is the right thing to do."

Sources: *Jet* 111 (16 April 2007): 46.

College Integration

1868 • The University of South Carolina was first opened to all races on March 3, 1868. B. A. Boseman and Francis L. Cardozo were elected to the board of trustees. There was a long series of disturbances occurred between July 8 and October 26, 1876, and federal troops were sent in. During this period, Democratic as well as Republican state governments were established in South Carolina. The deal that elected Rutherford B. Hayes president of the United States was struck on February 26, 1877. Democrats took over South Carolina on April 10, 1877, when federal troops were withdrawn.

Sources: Bennett, *Before the Mayflower,* p. 485.

1935 • Alice Jackson Stewart (1913–2001) attempted to integrate the University of Virginia. She became the first known person to seek admission to a white graduate or professional school in the state. After her admission was denied, the state set up a tuition supplement for black students to study in graduate schools outside Virginia. She accepted the supplement and enrolled at Columbia University. After graduation, she taught at a number of high schools and universities, including Howard University. In 1950 the supplement program was declared unconstitutional and the state's public university graduate programs were gradually integrated. Stewart was born June 2, 1913, in Richmond and completed her undergraduate degree at Virginia Union University. She joined the NAACP's lawsuit challenging segregation in public colleges and universities.

Sources: *New York Times* (14 June 2001).

1949 • Nancy Randolph Davis became the first black student to enroll at Oklahoma State University. Much later the university dedicated a new residence hall in her honor and named a series of scholarships after her. The scholarships benefit incoming freshmen as well as continuing and graduate students.

Sources: *Jet* 101 (25 February 2002): 12.

1949 • Ada Lois Sipuel Fisher (1924–1995) became the first black admitted to the University of Oklahoma Law School. She graduated from historically black Langston University (Oklahoma) in 1945 and for two years was denied admission to Oklahoma's law school. The letter denying her admission stated quite clearly that her race was the reason she was denied; the institution's president had earlier acknowledged that Fisher was academically qualified for admission. She filed a suit in state courts in 1947, which upheld the position of the University of Oklahoma. The United States Supreme Court heard the appeal in January 1948, reversed the state court's decision, and ordered the state court to provide a legal education for Fisher without delay. Before the second semester started, however, the State Board of Regents voted to establish a segregated law school at all-black Langston University, intending for Fisher to enroll there. She was not deterred. She filed a petition in state courts, again asking to be admitted to the University of Oklahoma, contending that the new law school would provide separate but not equal education. This petition was denied in August 1946. It was not appealed, because the NAACP, who provided the legal assistance for Fisher, was concentrating on the case of George McLaurin, a Langston professor who was seeking admission to Oklahoma's doctoral program in education. In 1949 a law was passed by the state legislature allowing admission of blacks to Oklahoma graduate courses on a segregated basis. When Fisher finally entered Oklahoma, it was more than three years after her initial application. Thurgood Marshall, then an attorney for the NAACP, handled her case. In 1950 the United States Supreme Court overturned all laws requiring segregation at the graduate level. Fisher received her law degree in 1951. She began to practice law immediately after graduation but returned to Langston to teach in 1957. She began working part-time on a master's degree in history at the University of Oklahoma at the same time and received the degree in 1968. She remained at Langston until her retirement. Born in Chickasha, Oklahoma, Fisher's perseverance and resolve changed the education landscape. The Fisher and McLaurin cases did away with the legal basis for segregation in graduate education. The University of Oklahoma recognized her in 1978 by having a day in her honor and in 1991 by awarding her an honorary doctorate. An anonymous donor established a $100,000 scholarship in her name in 1991, and she was named to the Board of Regents of the University of Oklahoma Law School in 1992.

Sources: Salzman, *Encyclopedia of African American Culture and History,* Supplement, p. 94; Smith, *Notable Black American Women,* pp. 344–46.

1950 • Louis L. Redding (1901–1998), Delaware's first black lawyer, represented nine black students from Delaware State College who sought admission to the University of Delaware. He was successful, making the University of Delaware the first state-supported undergraduate school to be desegregated by court order. In 1950 as well, Sarah Bulah, a black woman, complained that school buses carrying white children refused to bring her daughter to a black school. Louis Redding took the case on condition that Bulah agreed to petition to have her daughter attend the white school. In 1952 he won the case in state court; the appeal was incorporated into the U.S. Supreme Court decision of *Brown v. Board of Education.* This decision set in force the desegregation of the nation's public schools.

Sources: *New York Times* (30 September 1998); Smith, *Notable Black American Men,* Book II, pp. 566–68.

1953 • Joseph A. Johnson Jr. (1914–1979) became the first black student at Vanderbilt University in Nashville on May 2, 1953. By vote of the board of trustees, who said that "Christianity is not the exclusive possession of any one nation or race," he was admitted to the Vanderbilt's divinity school. He was also the first black to graduate and receive a doctorate from Vanderbilt in 1958. He then served on the school's board of trustees. The Shreveport native later became a presiding bishop in the Christian Methodist Church.

Sources: *Ebony Success Library,* vol. 1, p. 178; *Jet* 60 (7 May 1981): 18; 84 (3 May 1983): 32; *Who's Who among Black Americans, 1980–81,* p. 431.

1956 • After three and a half years of legal efforts on the part of the NAACP, Autherine Juanita Lucy [Foster] (1929–) became the first black student admitted to the University of Alabama on February 3, 1956. A riot followed, and she was suspended that evening. She was expelled February 29 for making "false" and "outrageous" statements about the school. Lucy had completed her undergraduate degree at Miles College in Alabama. In 1989 she entered the Alabama's graduate program in elementary education. She and her daughter, Grazia, graduated in the spring of 1992. Lucy received a master's degree in education; her daughter earned a degree in corporate finance.

Sources: Bennett, *Before the Mayflower,* p. 552; Hine, *Black Women in America,* pp. 448–49; *Ebony* 11 (June 1956): 93; 12 (March 1957): 51–54; Salzman, *Encyclopedia of African-American Culture and History,* vol. 3, p. 1666; Hornsby, *Milestones in Twentieth-Century African-American History,* p. 59; *Jet* 81 (18 November 1991): 10; 95 (8 February 1999): 20.

1961 • Charlayne Hunter-Gault (1942–) and Hamilton Earl Holmes (1941–1995) were the first black students to enroll at the University of Georgia, on January 10. Students rioted in protest of their admission, and they were temporarily suspended in the interest of their safety. Nevertheless, both students graduated from the institution in 1963. Holmes, who the university initially rejected as academically unqualified, graduated Phi Beta Kappa. He became the first black medical student at Emory University in 1967 and went on to a career as an orthopedic surgeon. Holmes later became the first black trustee of the University of Georgia Foundation. Hunter-Gault, whose Georgia degree was in journalism, worked at the *New Yorker* magazine until a 1967 Russell Sage Fellowship led her to study social science at Washington University in St. Louis. A trip to Washington, D.C., to cover the Poor People's Campaign, led to her employment as an investigative reporter and evening news anchorwoman at WRC-TV. In 1968 she began a ten-year stay on the staff of the *New York Times,* primarily covering stories in Harlem. She joined PBS in 1978 and advanced to a position of prominence as national correspondent for *The News Hour* with Jim Lehrer. In 1994 she leveled criticism at PBS for using primarily white males for anchors of prime-time shows; rejection of her own show, *Rights and Wrongs,* for national distribution; and for failing to feature her enough on what was then the McNeil-Lehrer show. She joined a news firm in South Africa in 1997.

Sources: *Ebony Success Library,* vol. 1, p. 122; Hine, *Black Women in America,* vol. 1, pp. 595–96; *Jet* 89 (15 January 1996): 19; 89 (22 January 1996): 60; Smith, *Notable Black American Women,* pp. 535–36; Smith, *Notable Black American Women,* Book II, p. 780; *Who's Who among Black Americans,* 26th ed., p. 674 (Holmes): 704 (Hunter-Gault).

1962 • The first black admitted to the University of Mississippi was Air Force veteran James Howard Meredith (1933–). Meredith was admitted after being denied admission three times. Although the U.S. Supreme Court ordered Meredith's admission, Governor Ross R. Barnett defied the decision. United States marshals were called to escort Meredith to classes on October 1, and federal troops were called out to quell disturbances. They remained on campus to protect Meredith until he graduated on August 18, 1963, with a bachelor's degree in political science. He went on to earn a law degree from Columbia University Law School in 1968. An account of his experiences at Ole Miss was presented in his first book, *Three Years in Mississippi,* published in 1966. In that same year, he organized the "Walk Against Fear," a march from Memphis, Tennessee, to Jackson, Mississippi, to call attention to black voting rights and to try to overcome black concerns about violence. He was shot during the walk, triggering a wave of protests from prominent civil rights activists. A native of Kosciusko, Mississippi, Meredith had to walk more than four miles a day each way to attend the Attala County Training School, which served black youth for elementary and high school; there was no bus available, and there were no teachers who had a college degree. After his junior year in high school, Meredith's parents sent him to live with relatives in St. Petersburg, Florida, where he graduated from Gibbs High School in 1951 and promptly joined the air force. He took college courses while stationed in Kansas, and when he left the air force in 1960, he entered Jackson State University as an advanced junior. He completed all graduation requirements by the end of 1961. He first applied to the University of Mississippi during his second quarter at Jackson State. In 1968 Meredith received an LL.B. degree from Columbia University. He returned to Mississippi in 1971. He has run for public office several times without success. He has often flirted with controversy—once in 1989 when he briefly held a position he was offered by Senator Jesse Helms, a conservative North Carolina Republican; and again in 1991 when he endorsed David Duke, a former Ku Klux Klan leader, as a candidate for governor of Louisiana. He established a publishing company in 1991, and published a treatise on Mississippi titled *Mississippi: A Volume of Eleven Books.* He also organized a solo march in 1996 to promote reading and writing in standard English. Illness prevented him from completing the last fifty miles on foot. In 1997 he created the Meredith Institute at Ole Miss.

Sources: *Crisis* 70 (January 1963): 5–11; *Encyclopedia of Black America,* p. 553; Hornsby, *Milestones in Twentieth-Century African-American History,* p. 71; *Jet* 71 (1 December 1986): 8; Katz, *Eyewitness,* pp. 483, 496–97; Smith, *Notable Black American Men,* pp. 801–3; *Who's Who among African Americans,* 13th ed., p. 922.

1963 • Harvey Bernard Gantt (1943–1995) was the first black student admitted to Clemson University in South Carolina, where he studied architecture. He graduated in 1965. A native of Charleston, South Carolina, Gantt enrolled at Iowa State University before transferring to Clemson. He earned his master's degree from the Massachusetts Institute of Technology in 1970. His career has had several facets. He worked with several architectural firms in Charlotte, North Carolina, before he obtained his graduate degree; and was a planner for activist Floyd McKissick's planned integrated community in North Carolina, Soul City, in 1970–71. He worked as a lecturer at the University of North Carolina and as visiting critic at Clemson. He then turned his interest to government, serving on the Charlotte City Council for four years, from 1974 to 1979. After serving as mayor *pro tempore,* Gantt was elected mayor of Charlotte in 1983 and served in that capacity until 1987. He was a Democratic candidate for the U.S. Senate in 1990. He is a partner in the Charlotte architectural firm of Gantt Huberman Architects. In 1995, President Bill Clinton named him chair of the National Capital Planning Commission, the government's central planning agency. Clemson has awarded him an honorary degree.

Sources: *Contemporary Black Biography,* vol. 1, pp. 72–74; *Jet* 88 (22 May 1995): 38; *Who's Who among African Americans,* 26th ed., p. 447.

1965 • The first black student to graduate from the University of Alabama, on May 30, 1965, was Vivian Malone [Jones] (1942–1995). In 1956 Autherine Lucy [Foster] (1929–) was the first black student enrolled in the university. Malone along with another black student, James Hood, had to be escorted by the National Guard to registration. The Alabama experience strengthened her motivation to be active in civil rights, and after graduation she looked for jobs that would allow her to be a positive force in the struggle for civil rights. She spent most of her career employed by the federal government, working for the Justice Department, the Veteran's Administration Hospital in Atlanta, and retiring in 1996 from her position as director of the Federal Office of Environmental Justice in the Environmental Protection Agency. She also served as the executive director of the Voter Education Project. Malone has been honored for her civil rights efforts. In 1995 the University of Alabama celebrated the 30th anniversary of her graduation by establishing the Vivian Malone Jones Scholarship Fund. The next year, former Governor Wallace and Malone met prior to her being awarded the first Lurleen B. Wallace Award of Courage in a ceremony held at the state capitol. The award was named in memory of George Wallace's deceased wife and is given to women whose activities result in major improvements in Alabama. James Hood, who had dropped out the summer after his enrollment, later transferred to Wayne State University in Detroit, Michigan, where he earned a bachelor's degree. This was followed by a master's degree from Michigan State University. He returned to the University of Alabama in fall 1995 as a doctoral student.

Sources: *Jet* 88 (6 November 1995): 25; 90 (28 October 1996): 6; 99 (4 June 2001): 19; *Negro Almanac, 1976,* p. 39; Smith, *Notable Black American Women,* pp. 727–28.

Extension Programs

1906 • Thomas Monroe Campbell (1883–1956) was the first black farm field agent in the United States. He held the position until 1953, working with Tuskegee Institute president Booker T. Washington and Seaman A. Knapp to revolutionize farming in the South by taking education directly to the farmers. He received little education while growing up outside the city limits of Bowman, Georgia, where he was born. At age fifteen, Campbell had a cumulative total of twelve months of education. Pursuing his desire to go to Tuskegee, he walked there despite being discouraged by people along the way and arrived almost penniless. He did not get admitted to a class until his second year there, but he graduated with honors in 1906 after eight years. At the same time, Knapp, who was considered the father of farm demonstration work, arrived at Tuskegee determined to improve Southern farming techniques. Knapp hired Campbell as his farm demonstrator. They, along with Booker T. Washington, are credited for revolutionizing farming in the South. Campbell worked as a farm agent until his retirement in 1953, traveling throughout the South and in Africa and India. Upon his retirement, the staff of the United States Department of Agriculture honored him for his long and valued service.

Sources: Bailey, *They Too Call Alabama Home,* pp. 62–64.

Honorary Degrees

1804 • Lemuel Haynes (1753–1833) was the first black to receive an honorary degree in the United States. Middlebury College in Vermont awarded Haynes a master's degree at its second commencement. Haynes has been regarded as a trailblazer in practically every aspect of black life. Born in West Hartford, Connecticut, to a white mother and an African father, he was abandoned by both his parents. While still an infant, he was taken to Middle Granville, Massachusetts, and classified as an indentured servant. He was raised on a farm, and credits this upbringing with establishing his religious orientation. His indentured status ended when he was twenty-one, and he enlisted in the army as a Minute Man. He later served with Ethan Allen's Green Mountain Boys and was one of the three blacks who participated in the capture of Fort Ticonderoga. He was an early anti-slavery advocate, writing and speaking on the topic years before Frederick Douglass. Haynes had little formal schooling. He had a chance to enter Dartmouth College after his army service ended, but he studied instead with pastors in Granville and taught school. He was pronounced eligible to preach in 1780 and was soon named pastor of a new Congregational church in Granville. This was the start of a fifty-three-year ministry, during which he served at least five white congregations. Of these, his longest pastorate was in West Rutland, Vermont, where he served for thirty years. His last pastorate was in Granville, New York, where he served from 1822 until his death. During his ministerial career, some of his sermons were published, and he was often consulted on questions of theology by the Yale University and Amherst College presidents. Haynes did not confine himself to theological and anti-slavery treatises; he also wrote a short story, "Mystery Developed," about a real-life murder case, which is said to be one of the early short stories written by a black writer.

Sources: Logan and Winston, *Dictionary of American Biography*, pp. 300–301; Smith, *Notable Black American Men*, pp. 532–33.

1896 • Educator, school founder, and race leader Booker T. Washington (1856–1915) was the first black recipient of an honorary degree from Harvard University—the master of arts. He is also recognized by some as the first national black leader after slavery, whose trademark beliefs were self-help and hard work.

Sources: Alford, *Famous First Blacks*, p. 35; Logan and Winston, *Dictionary of American Negro Biography*, pp. 633–38; Hornsby, *Chronology of African-American History*, p. 55.

1946 • On February 21, 1946, Mary McLeod Bethune (1875–1955), educator and civic leader, became the first black to receive an honorary degree from a white college in the South; she received the degree from Rollins College, Winter Park, Florida.

Sources: Garrett, *Famous First Facts about Negroes*, pp. 59, 122–23, 161; *Jet* 82 (6 July 1992): 32; Kane, *Famous First Facts*, p. 216.

1973 • B. B. [Riley B.] King (1925–) received a honorary doctorate from Tougaloo College in Mississippi, becoming the first black musician to receive an honorary degree for work in the blues. He also holds an honorary degree, conferred in 1977, from Yale University, and is the recipient of multiple Grammys and other awards. King, who never finished high school, was born in Indianola, Mississippi. He began his musical career singing with a gospel group in 1940, but soon learned he could earn more money by playing and singing the blues on the street. In 1946 he moved to Memphis, Tennessee, where he had his own radio show, and in 1950 he was a disc jockey. By the 1960s he was a successful performer. In 1979 he was the first black blues artist to perform in what was the Soviet Union. The recordings of such musicians as Blind Lemon Jefferson (1897–1929) influenced his early style. King participated in the Vatican's 1997 Christmas concert, after which he and a group of international artists held a special audience with Pope John Paul II. At the end of the concert, King donated "Lucille," his famous fifty-year-old guitar, to the pontiff. His love for music and women, and his struggles to succeed in the music business are among the details of his life included in his middle 1990s autobiography, *Blues All around Me: The Autobiography of B. B. King*. He is noted for his philanthropy, including a huge gift of vintage, collector's-item records to the University of Mississippi, and organization of benefit concerts.

Sources: *Current Biography, 1970*, pp. 226–27; *Encyclopedia of Black America*, p. 489; Smith, *Notable Black American Men*, pp. 683–86; *Jet* 90 (4 November 1996): 32–37; 93 (12 January 1998): 25; Southern, *Biographical Dictionary of Afro-American and African Musicians*, p. 232; *Who's Who among African Americans*, 26th ed., p. 724.

Law Schools

1868 • In October 1868 John Mercer Langston (1829–1897) founded and organized the Law School at Howard University, the first in a black school. He headed the department when classes formally began on January 6, 1869, and was its dean for seven years. From 1873 to 1875 he was also vice president and acting president of the university. Langston was born in Louisa County, Virginia, son of a black former slave mother and her white former owner. By the time he was four, both his parents were dead and friends of his father became his guardians, moving him to Chillicothe, Ohio. He moved several times after that, but went on to graduate from Oberlin College and read law with an abolitionist lawyer in Oberlin. He returned to the study of law in 1853, after earning a degree in theology at Oberlin. He studied with a leading attorney and newspaper publisher, with whom he had become acquainted while working with the Free Democratic Party. Because Ohio laws prohibited blacks from suing whites, the district court could not qualify him to practice law. They found a way to qualify him, on the grounds that he was closer to white than black, based on his complexion. Langston changed his political philosophy several times. He worked with the black convention movement in Ohio and was at first in favor of black emigration to form separate black communities; by 1854 he had become an opponent of emigration. He developed a successful law practice and was elected to several local government positions between 1854 and 1860. He moved to Washington, D.C., in 1867 to serve as inspector-general of the Freedmen's Bureau, and was recruited subsequently for the Howard position. His last few years at Howard found Langston in somewhat of a state of flux. He resigned as vice president in January 1875, but consented to serve briefly as acting president and did not resign as dean of the law school. He resigned from both positions in June 1875. He later went on to hold both appointive and elective positions in Washington, D.C., and the state of Virginia. He also served as the president of Virginia Normal and Collegiate Institute from 1885 to 1887.

John Mercer Langston

Sources: Logan and Winston, *Dictionary of American Negro Biography,* pp. 382–83; Logan, *Howard University,* pp. 55–62; Smith, *Notable Black American Men,* pp. 693–97.

1990 • The first black student to become editor of the *Harvard Law Review* was U.S. President Barack Obama (1961–). A second-year law student and a native of Hawaii, Obama was employed in social work on Chicago's South Side before entering law school.

Sources: *Jet* 77 (26 February 1990): 10.

2009 • The first African American to serve as dean of the University of Maryland's School of Law is Phoebe Haddon. She joined the 185-year-old law school's administration on July 1 as its ninth dean, after serving as a distinguished member of Temple University's Beasley School of Law. Of her appointment at Maryland, Haddon said, "it has a social justice mission" and that she would "like to make sure that other students have the ability to come to law school and be successful and go into productive professions." Haddon graduated from Yale Law School and the Duquesne University School of Law. In 1976, the fourth-generation lawyer became the first black American to edit the *Duquesne Law Review.*

Sources: *Crisis* 116 (Spring 2009): 10; *Jet* 115 (4 May 2009): 13.

Libraries, Archives, Collections

1905 • The first public library to provide service exclusively for the black community, with all-black staff, was the Louisville Branch Library. Thomas F. Blue (1866–1935) was the first librarian of this segregated branch. Blue graduated from Hampton Institute (now Hampton University) in 1888 and in 1898 from Richmond Theological Seminary (now Virginia Union University). It was under his administration that the library flourished and became a model program. He provided training workshops for his staff and guided those from other cities where black branches existed or were planned. When a new branch was added in 1915, Blue was named director of Colored Branches.

Sources: "A Separate Flame", http://www.lfpl.org/western/htms/sepflame.htm; Josey, *The Black Librarian in America,* p. 177.

1924 • J. P. Morgan Jr., incorporated his library of rare books and manuscripts into an educational institution dedicated to the memory of his father. He named Belle Da Costa Greene (1883–1950) as the first library director, a position she held until she retired on November 30, 1948. At first a clerk in Princeton University Library, she guided the collecting and organizing of the treasures in the Morgan library since 1905, when J. Pierpont Morgan owned it; she made it into one of the world's greatest libraries. She was known and respected in libraries, museums, galleries, and aristocratic houses throughout Europe and she stood as one of the great figures in the art and bibliophile world. When she represented the Morgans abroad, Greene wore couturier clothes and patronized luxury hotels. At work in the library in her early years, she wore Renaissance gowns and appropriate jewelry. Greene was named to the Committee for the Restoration of the University of Louvain Library, the Librarian's Advisory Council of the Library of Congress, and held other important boards and memberships. She was one of the first women fellows of the Mediaeval Academy of America and a fellow in perpetuity of the Metropolitan Museum of New York. Greene was the daughter of Richard Theodore Greener, the first black to graduate from Harvard University, a professor at the University of South Carolina in 1873, acting librarian and curator of rare books at the school, and later a lawyer and head of the Howard University Law School. (Belle Greene dropped the second "r" from the spelling of her last name.)

Sources: Garrity, *Dictionary of American Biography,* Supplement Four, pp, 344–46 (Greene), pp. 346–447 (Greener); Logan and Winston, *Dictionary of American Negro Biography,* pp. 267–68; Strouse, *Morgan, American Financier,* pp. 509–21.

1924 • The first black appointed as a branch librarian for the Chicago Public Library was Vivian Gordon Harsh (1890–1960), who was appointed on February 26. In 1941 the branch library was named in her honor. Born in Chicago, Harsh was educated at Simmons College, Columbia University, and the Graduate Library School of the University of Chicago. When the George Cleveland Hall Branch Library opened on January 16, 1932, Harsh was at its helm. She received a grant in 1934 from the Julius Rosenwald Fund to travel to leading bookselling centers in the country to buy books about blacks for the library. When the books arrived, she placed them in one wing of the library and named the collection the Special Negro Collection. Harsh also began a series of public forums and invited as speakers such noted blacks as Zora Neale Hurston, Carter G. Woodson, and Charles S. Johnson. She also developed lifetime friendships with leading black writers, including Richard Wright and Langston Hughes. After she died, the Chicago Public Library renamed the collection the Vivian G. Harsh Collection of African American History and Literature. That name was retained when the collection was moved to new quarters in the Carter G. Woodson Regional Library Center.

Sources: Smith, *Notable Black American Women,* pp. 474–75; Schultz and Hast, *Women Building Chicago 1790–1990,* pp. 359–61; *Contemporary Black Biography,* vol. 14, pp. 113–16.

Fannie Barrier Williams

1924 • Fannie Barrier Williams (1855–1944), lecturer, civic leader, clubwoman, and journalist, was the first black—and the first woman—to serve on the Library Board of Chicago. She held the position for two years. In 1895 she had been the first black member of the Chicago Women's Club, a membership she held for thirty years. In 1891 she also assisted Daniel Hale Williams in the founding of Provident Hospital and Training School for Nurses, one of the first black-controlled medical centers in the country. Williams was born in Brockport, New York, and in 1870 graduated from the academic and classical course of the State Normal School in Brockport. She taught school in the South and in Washington, D.C. After she married S. Laing Williams, she moved to Chicago where she led a high-profile life for more than thirty years. She saw that blacks held a prominent place in the World's Columbian Exposition of 1893. She was a founder of the National League of Colored Women in 1893 and was one of its primary leaders. She joined Mary Church Terrell in founding the successor organization, the National Association of Colored Women. In addition to her prominent work in the black women's club movement, Williams, once a voice of militant protest, joined Booker T. Washington and his conciliatory approach to matters affecting race and became one of Washington's ardent supporters. She worked with W. E. B. Du Bois and the newly founded NAACP and also became active in the women's suffrage movement.

Sources: Logan and Winston, *Dictionary of American Negro Biography,* pp. 656–57; Smith, *Notable Black American Women,* pp. 1251–54; Hine, *Black Women in America,* pp. 1259–61.

1926 • The New York Public Library appointed Catherine Ann Latimer (1895?–1948) as reference librarian in charge of the Division of Negro Literature and History located in the 135th Street Branch, making her the first black professional librarian in the system. Born in Nashville, Tennessee, she was educated at Howard University and did graduate work at Tuskegee Institute (now Tuskegee University). After one year at Tuskegee as assistant librarian, she moved to the New York Public Library. Latimer had a reading knowledge of German and was fluent in French, having spent some of her early life in France and Germany. She headed the Division of Negro Literature Branch, established in 1925, until bibliophile Arthur A. Schomburg took over. After Schomburg died in 1938, she headed the collection until historian Lawrence D. Reddick assumed leadership in 1939. The collection later became known as the Schomburg Center for Research in Black Culture and is recognized as the world's leading library on African American materials. Latimer lectured widely at such institutions as Wellesley, Vassar, and Smith colleges. She retired in 1946 and died two years later.

Sources: Smith, *Notable Black American Women,* pp. 474–75; Schultz and Hast, *Women Building Chicago 1790–1990,* pp. 657–58; Kellner, *The Harlem Renaissance,* p. 215.

1935 • The first public library for blacks in Raleigh, North Carolina, opened in a storefront on East Hargett Street with 890 books. Mollie Huston Lee (1907–1982) was its founder. Lee received private contributions, gift books, equipment and supplies, and moved the library into a house; it was a memorial to black stage actor Richard B. Harrison. Later the Richard B. Harrison Library, as it was named, received national recognition for its service to the aged, disadvantaged, blind, and illiterate. The collection, basically one of black books and materials, grew in quality and later the library received annual appropriations from the North Carolina State Library. Through interlibrary loan services, materials were available to public libraries throughout the state. In 1972 the collection was officially named the Mollie Huston Lee Collection of Black Literature. Lee also trained personnel to serve black libraries, using the Harrison library as a practical laboratory for students from library education programs at North Carolina Central in Durham, the University of North Carolina at Chapel Hill, and Atlanta University. She was supervisor of Negro School Libraries in North Carolina from 1946 to 1953, and was instrumental in the founding in 1934 of the North Carolina Negro Library Association. Mollie Huston Lee was born in Columbus, Ohio, and received her first undergraduate degree from Howard University in 1929. She was librarian at Shaw University in Raleigh from 1930 to 1935. She continued her education and received a second bachelor's degree, in library science, from Columbia University in 1935. While at Shaw she identified a need for black American literary collections in library settings in the black community, thus founding the public library for blacks in Raleigh.

Sources: Smith, *Notable Black American Women,* Book II, pp. 406–8.

1946 • Doris Evans Saunders (1921–) was the first black reference librarian in the Chicago library system. A Chicago native, Saunders became librarian for the Johnson Publishing Company in 1949, and head of the company's book division in 1961, a position she held until 1966. She influenced Johnson Publishing to fill the gap in information about black people and publish more books on black themes. A native Chicagoan, Saunders completed the Chicago Public Library Training Class, studied at Northwestern University, and received a master's degree in journalism as well as a master's degree in Afro-American Studies from Boston University. In 1983 she began work toward her Ph.D. in history at Vanderbilt University. Saunders grew up under the influence of librarian and children's writer Charlemae Hill Rollins, who encouraged her to read widely and to become a librarian. After her experiences as a librarian, she held several other posts, including head of her own public relations firm. A writer as well, her works included *The Day They March*

(1963), *The Kennedy Years and the Negro* (1964), *Negro Handbook* (1966), and *Black Society* (with Geraldyn "Gerri" Major, 1976).

Sources: *Ebony Success Library,* vol. 1, p. 274; Smith, *Notable Black American Women,* pp. 977–78; *Who's Who among African Americans,* 26th ed., p. 1096.

1998 • Gloria Twine Chisum (1930–), psychologist and library administrator, was the first black and first woman chair of the board of trustees of the Free Library of Philadelphia. She was born in Muskogee, Oklahoma, and graduated from Howard University (B.S.,1951; M.S., 1953) and the University of Pennsylvania (Ph.D., 1960). Before her retirement in 1990, she was a research psychologist, lecturer in psychology, head of a vision laboratory (1965–80), and head of a research team in environmental physiology (1980–90).

Sources: *Jet* 77 (5 February 1990): 20; *Who's Who among African Americans,* 26th ed., p. 235–36.

1998 • Hampton University in Virginia established the nation's first African American Poetry Archive, in the summer of this year. The archive is housed in the museum. In 1996 the museum took on management and operation of the *International Review of African American Art.* It is the only publication primarily geared to black American art.

Sources: "Hampton's Museum," http://oaa.hamptonu.edu/museum.cfm. Aaccessed September 17, 2012.

Schools

1750 • Anthony Benezet led the Philadelphia Quakers in opening the first free school for blacks. It was an evening school taught by Moses Patterson. Benezet left money at his death to continue the school.

Sources: Garrett, *Famous First Facts about Negroes,* p. 48; *Negro Almanac, 1976,* pp. 528–29.

1787 • The African Free School was the first free secular school in New York City. Organized by the Manumission Society, the African Free School was opened on November 1, 1787, before there was a free school for whites. It began as a one-room school, and the first permanent building was erected in 1796. After this building burned, African School No. 2 was opened in 1815, with room for five hundred pupils. There were seven African Free Schools by 1834, and they were eventually incorporated into the public school system.

Sources: Hornsby, *Chronology of African-American History,* pp. 8–9; Horton, *Free People of Color,* pp. 59, 153; Johnson, *Black Manhattan,* pp. 20–23; *Negro Almanac, 1976,* p. 429.

1829 • Saint Francis Academy of Rome in Baltimore, Maryland, was the first boarding school for black girls. The school was established by the Oblate Sisters of Providence, a group of black nuns who were French-educated. The school opened with twenty-four girls. The only secondary school for black women, Saint Francis became well known and attracted young women from all across the country as well as from Canada. The school had become coeducational by 1865 and was known then as the Saint Francis Academy.

Sources: Hine, *Black Women in America,* p. 382; Garrett, *Famous First Facts about Negroes,* p. 49; Smith, *Notable Black American Women,* pp. 813–14.

1833 • The first known school for free blacks in Nashville, Tennessee, opened on the first Monday in March. It was located on Church Street, between College and Summer streets. Alphonso M. Sumner, a teacher and barber, opened the school with the understanding that "none but free children should attend." The school had an enrollment of twenty students and lasted for six weeks. Due to illness among the students, the school closed temporarily for two weeks. During this time, however, Sumner was accused of writing and sending two important letters to two fugitives who lived in Detroit. After whites intercepted the letters, Sumner was nearly beaten to death and forced to leave the state permanently. Fearing the harsh sentiment toward black schools, free blacks, then totaling about two hundred, decided to wait "until the storm blew over" before continuing their school. No other school was known to exist until January 1838, when free blacks petitioned to have another school, this time with a white teacher.

Sources: *History of the Colored Schools of Nashville, Tennessee,* pp. 4–5.

1835 • The Abiel Smith School, the first combined primary and secondary public schools for blacks opened in Boston this year. It operated for twenty years and closed in 1855. Although slavery was illegal in Massachusetts, schools were still segregated by race. Primary schools for blacks were established as early as the 1820s, but public secondary schooling was unavailable to blacks until white businessman Abiel Smith provided the city $2,000 in endowment to educate black youth. As many as five hundred students enrolled. Blacks, however, protested the city's continuing segregation policy and boycotted the new school. After the state legislature outlawed segregated schools in 1855, Abiel Smith School closed. In 2000, it reopened as a part of the Museum of Afro-American History, serving as monument to the city's turbulent history of race in the school system.

Sources: *New York Times* (22 February 2000).

1849 • Benjamin Roberts filed the first petition to abolish segregated schools. Roberts filed the school integration suit on behalf of his five-year-old daughter, Sarah C. Roberts, against the city of Boston, which had a local ordinance requiring separate schools. Charles Sumner argued the case *Roberts v. Boston* before the Massachusetts Supreme Court on December 4, 1849. In his opening argument he asked, "Can any discrimination, on account of color or race, be made, under the Constitution and Laws of Massachusetts, among the children entitled to the benefit of the public schools?" Further, he noted that, under the state's laws and constitution, the School Committee was entrusted with the power to exclude black children from public schools and compelled them to set up separate schools. The court rejected the suit. Separate schools were not abolished by state law until 1855, which resulted in Boston being the first major city to eliminate segregated schools.

Sources: Cantor, *Historic Landmarks of Black America,* p. 70; Garrett, *Famous First Facts about Negroes,* p. 49; *Negro Almanac, 1976,* p. 531; *Argument of Charles Sumner, Est., against the Constitutionality of Separate Colored Schools, in the case of Sarah C. Roberts vs. the City of Boston.*

1862 • Perhaps the first black school in Tennessee that merged with another institution and continues to exist was established. Lucinda Humphrey, a hospital nurse at Camp Shiloh, in West Tennessee, began to teach by candlelight small groups of "contraband Negroes." The school moved to Memphis in 1863 and grew to become known in 1866 as Lincoln School and later as Lincoln Chapel. Race riots that followed resulted in the destruction of Lincoln Chapel. It was rebuilt quickly and reopened in 1867 with 150 students and six teachers. Faced with financial problems, the school managed to survive, but only through the efforts of Francis Julian LeMoyne, a prominent physician of Washington, Pennsylvania, and a life member of the American Missionary Association. He gave the school $20,000. The school was renamed in 1871 in honor of its benefactor and became known as LeMoyne Normal and Commercial School. It had a long history of educating blacks and, in 1901, expanded to include regular high school. The school grew to become a junior college in 1924, and in 1934 the State of Tennessee chartered LeMoyne College as a four-year, degree-granting institution. LeMoyne College merged with Owen College in fall 1968 and became LeMoyne-Owen.

Sources: Price, "An Historical Perspective of the American Missionary Association and Its Establishment of LeMoyne College," pp. 31–44; Salzman, *Encyclopedia of African-American History and Culture,* Supplement, p. 165.

1863 • Sarah J. [Smith] Thompson Garnet (1831–1911) was the first black woman to be appointed principal in the New York public school system. She had been a teacher at the African Free School in Williamsburgh, Brooklyn, since 1854. Her second marriage, in about 1879, was to the prominent abolitionist and Presbyterian minister Henry Highland Garnet (1815–1882). In 1892 Sarah Garnet and a number of prominent black women raised funds to replace the destroyed presses of Ida B. Wells' Memphis newspaper. Garnet

The First Black Teacher

In 1861 Mary Smith Kelsick Peake (1823–1862), a free woman of color, was the first teacher for freed slaves. Supported by the American Missionary Association, she was appointed to teach children at Fort Monroe, Virginia, and on September 17, 1861, she opened a school in Hampton, Virginia, marking the beginning of the general education of blacks in the South. The school started as a day school, providing elementary education for children. A night school for adults was soon added. Hampton Institute (now Hampton University) had its roots in this school. Peake was born in Norfolk, Virginia, daughter of a prominent Englishman and a free mulatto woman. At age six, she was sent to live with relatives in Alexandria, Virginia, to attend a private school for free blacks. When Virginia passed laws closing all schools for blacks, she returned to Norfolk, where she became established as a seamstress. She moved to Hampton, Virginia, when her mother married in 1847. Concern for her people led her to begin teaching children in her home. The Hampton home she shared with her husband was burned shortly after the Civil War began, which led the Peakes and other blacks to seek harbor at Fortress Monroe. Unfortunately, Peake's health failed shortly after establishment of the school, and she died of tuberculosis on February 22, 1862.

Sources: Cantor, *Historic Landmarks of Black America*, pp. 253–54; Logan and Winston, *Dictionary of American Negro Biography*, p. 486; *Negro Yearbook, 1921–22*, pp. 230–31; Smith, *Notable Black American Women*, pp. 834–35.

was a founder of one of Brooklyn's first equal rights organizations, the Equal Suffrage League, and superintendent of the Suffrage Department of the National Association of Colored Women. One of her sisters was the pioneer woman physician Susan Maria Smith McKinney Steward (1847–1918). Garnet was born in Queens County, New York, to parents with a mixed racial heritage. Little is known about her education or the founding of the African Free School at which she taught. It is known that for all of her career in New York's public schools, Garnet supervised an entirely black staff, although white students were present after 1883. Garnet retired from her principalship in 1900. She was also a seamstress, and she maintained the shop she opened in 1883 until her death. She worked to achieve suffrage for women for most of her life. Barely two months before her death, she was in London for the first Universal Races Congress. Garnet died on September 17, eight days after the Equal Suffrage League gave her a welcome home reception at her home.

Sources: Hine, *Black Women in America*, vol. 1, p. 479; Logan and Winston, *Dictionary of American Negro Biography*, pp. 253–54; Smith, *Notable Black American Women*, pp. 388–91; *The Black New Yorkers*, p. 86.

Francis L. Cardozo

1865 • Francis Louis Cardozo (1837–1903) was the first black principal of what was to become Avery Normal Institute, in Charleston, South Carolina. Avery was an agent of the American Missionary Association (AMA) who performed pioneer work in the education of the newly freed slaves. Cardozo, who was born in Charleston to a Jewish father and a mother of mixed ancestry, was educated abroad and was very active in reconstruction politics. He served in several high governmental positions, including South Carolina Secretary of State; he later was principal of both the Colored Preparatory High School and its successors, the M Street High School and the Paul Laurence Dunbar High School in Washington, D.C. As a youth, he served an apprenticeship with a carpenter and worked as both an apprentice and a journeyman. He attended the free schools for black children, but went to Great Britain to study in 1848, with letters of recommendation from the pastor of Charleston's Second Presbyterian Church. He spent seven years there, studying at the University of Glasgow and at Presbyterian seminaries in London and Edinburgh. Upon his return to the United States, Cardozo assumed the pastorate of a Congregational church in New Haven, Connecticut, although his career goal was education, not ministry. His brother

Thomas had been named to head the Charleston AMA school in April 1865, but troubles involving relationships with a student at his teaching position in Flushing, New York, led the AMA to appoint Francis instead; he took over in August of this year. It was Francis Cardozo who was able to obtain funding from the Avery estate and the Freedmen's Bureau that resulted in Avery Institute in 1867. He had to relinquish his position with Avery when he was elected Secretary of State in 1868; he was the only black person on the state-wide Republican ticket. He continued an active involvement with government and South Carolina Republican politics until he moved to Washington, D.C., in 1877, where he accepted a Treasury post. He was charged with fraud by South Carolina Democrats, but was later pardoned. Cardozo returned to education when he left the Treasury Department, and between 1884 and 1896 developed the Washington high school into what was considered the nation's best black preparatory school. He is nevertheless regarded as an effective educational leader and a dedicated public servant.

Sources: Logan and Winston, *Dictionary of American Negro Biography*, pp. 89–90; *Dictionary of Black Culture*, p. 81; *Encyclopedia of Black America*, p. 102; Smith, *Notable Black American Men*, pp. 171–73.

1867 • The City of Nashville, Tennessee, bought Belleview House, a seven-room home located at 305 North Summer Street, installed seats for 351 children, hired George W. Hubbard as principal and hired four teachers. At the same the city opened another facility, Lincoln Hall School located at Lincoln Allen and Cherry Street and hired six teachers. These two institutions were the first public schools established in the city specifically to educate black children.

Sources: *The African-American History of Nashville, 1730–1930*, p. 135.

1869 • Fanny Jackson Coppin (1837–1913) became the first black woman to head a major educational institution for blacks, the Institute for Colored Youth of Philadelphia. The Society of Friends founded the school in 1837, and when Coppin graduated from Oberlin College in 1865, she became principal of the Institute's female department. The Institute was a prestigious school with a faculty consisting of some of the most highly educated blacks of the period. She retired in 1902. Coppin was born a slave in Washington, D.C. After an aunt purchased her freedom, she moved to New Bedford, Massachusetts, where educational opportunities were better, to live with the wife of her uncle. The next year, the family moved to Newport, Rhode Island, again to improve Coppin's educational opportunities. She worked as a servant in the home of Mary Stuart Calvert, a descendant of Mary, Queen of Scots; and it was here that she developed her appreciation of the literary arts. She began her college work at Rhode Island Normal School. Her life at Oberlin was both rich intellectually and challenging, since few women had graduated from Oberlin's college department at the time. Coppin began her teaching career while still an Oberlin student, teaching voluntarily in an evening school that she established for newly freed blacks. When she moved to Philadelphia, her activities resulted in establishment of a home and nurse training courses for poor black women in 1888, opening of the industrial department of the Institute in 1889, and another school, the Women's Exchange and Girls' Home, in 1894. She was also active politically, although women did not yet have the right to vote. Coppin was forty-two when she married Levi Coppin, a man who was fifteen years younger than she. He was a minister, and despite the fact that poor health had caused her to retire, she went with her husband to Capetown, South Africa, where her health continued to decline. When she died, people from all over the country attended her funeral in Philadelphia, and separate memorial services were conducted in Washington, Baltimore, and Philadelphia.

Fanny Jackson Coppin

Sources: Hine, *Black Women in America*, vol. 1, pp. 281–83; Lane, *William Dorsey's Philadelphia and Ours*, pp. 135, 142–47; Smith, *Notable Black American Women*, pp. 224–28.

1870 • Snowden School, Virginia, was the first state school for blacks. The school was short-lived.

Sources: Kane, *Famous First Facts*, p. 563.

1870 • The Preparatory High School for Colored Youth, the first public high school for blacks in the country, opened in the basement of the Fifteenth Street Presbyterian Church in Washington, D.C. It moved to its first permanent location in 1891, when it occupied a building on M Street, N.W. It then became known as the M Street High School, and twenty-five years later, was renamed to honor Paul Laurence Dunbar. The M Street/Dunbar High School was acknowledged as the best public high school for blacks in the country.

Sources: Badger, *A Lifetime in Rag,* p. 18; Hutchinson, *Anna J. Cooper,* pp. 66–83.

Josephine Silone Yates

1879 • Josephine Silone Yates (1859–1912), teacher, journalist, and clubwoman, was the first black American certified to teach in the public schools of Rhode Island. In 1877 she had been the first black to graduate from Rogers High School in Newport, Rhode Island. She later became an outstanding teacher at Lincoln Institute in Jefferson, Missouri, and president of the National Association of Colored Women. Yates was born in Mattituck, Suffolk County, on Long Island. When she was eleven, she was sent to live with her maternal uncle in Philadelphia and studied at the Institute for Colored Youth for a year. She progressed rapidly and was later sent to live with her maternal aunt in Newport to finish grade school and enroll in high school. She completed the four-year high school course in three years, excelling in all of her courses. She was the only black in her class and her class valedictorian. After graduation, she chose to prepare for a teaching career by taking the teaching course at Rhode Island State Normal School, where she again graduated with honors. She went to Lincoln in 1879, and when she resigned to get married in 1889, she was a full professor and head of the department of natural science. While there, Booker T. Washington offered Yates the position of lady principal at Tuskegee; she refused the offer. Her marriage led to a move to Kansas City, Missouri, where her husband W. W. Yates was principal of an elementary school that was later renamed for him. Yates continued her teaching career in Kansas City and also became active as a clubwoman. She organized the Kansas City Women's League in 1893 and shortly thereafter became president of the federated clubs. She was the second president of the National Association of Colored Women. She is known to have written for newspapers, writing poetry and prose. Yates continued to teach in Lincoln High School in Kansas City until she died suddenly after a two-day illness.

Sources: Hine, *Black Women in America,* vol. 2, pp. 1297–98; Smith, *Notable Black American Women,* pp. 1286–87.

1879 • Austin High School was founded in Knoxville, Tennessee, becoming the first public high school in the city to educate black students. John W. Manning, the first black principal, arrived in fall 1881 and retired in 1912. A native of Edenton, North Carolina, Manning graduated from Yale University earlier in 1881. Before retiring in 1912, Manning developed the school's curriculum and saw the first tenth-grade class graduate in 1888. Austin High was located in a high-crime area, drawing the protest of black leaders. Around the turn of the century, the school was relocated and renamed Knoxville Colored High School in 1916. A new Austin High was built in 1928 and by 1952 yet another Austin High was erected. After schools were integrated in Knoxville in 1968, the school was combined with all-white East High; the merged institution was named Austin East High School.

Sources: Lovett and Wynn, *Profiles of African Americans in Tennessee,* pp. 4–5.

1882 • The first black member of the Brooklyn, New York, Board of Education was Philip S. White. In 1898 the public schools came under the control of the New York City Board of Education.

Sources: *The Black New Yorkers,* p. 107.

1895 • Mary Church Terrell (1863–1954) was the first black woman to serve on the Washington, D.C., Board of Education. She served from 1895 to 1901, and again from 1906 to 1911. In 1896 she was the co-founder and first president of the National Council of Colored Women. Terrell was born in Memphis, Tennessee, to parents who were former slaves. Her father was the son of his owner and opened a successful saloon after Emancipation. Her mother ran an equally successful hair salon. She was sent to Ohio for her early schooling, attending first the Antioch College Model School, then a public school in Yellow

Mary Church Terrell

Springs, and finally the public high school in Oberlin. During this time, her mother moved to New York while Terrell was away in school. She graduated from Oberlin College in 1884 and returned to Memphis, where her father, Robert Reed Church Sr. (1839–1912), had become wealthy. In 1885 she began her professional career at Wilberforce College, but left after a year to teach in the Latin department of the Colored High School in Washington, D.C. She completed work for her master's from Oberlin in 1888, while working in Washington. After spending two years traveling and studying abroad, she returned to Washington and married Robert H. Terrell (1857–1925) in 1891. Robert Terrell was a Harvard graduate who later became a judge in the District of Columbia. At the time, married women were barred from working, and she contented herself with a quiet life until a Memphis friend was lynched in 1892. That same year, she became the leader of the Colored Women's League. This group later merged with Boston's Federation of American Women and two other groups to become the National Council of Negro Women. The new group concerned itself with all aspects of equal rights and justice, with its main focus on the fight for equal rights for all women, but black women in particular. Terrell traveled and lectured extensively. She was the only representative of any of the nonwhite races when she spoke at the 1904 Berlin International Congress of Women. Her address was given with presentations in three languages: English, French, and German. She later made two more presentations abroad to an international audience. She became known for her work as a political activist and civil rights pioneer. She once led successful desegregation protests against discrimination in restaurants, in Washington. During the last decade of the nineteenth century, Terrell became a professional lecturer for the Slayton Lyceum Bureau. Her career as a public lecturer lasted thirty years. She was also active in church and community work. She and her husband are counted among the founders of the Lincoln Temple Congregational Church in Washington, and she was the first black woman elected president of the Bethel Literary and Historical Association, also in Washington. She worked actively with the Republican Party and with the NAACP. Through her club work, public speaking, and political activism, her name is associated with some of the major causes of her day. One source quotes her as saying that she labored under the dual handicap of race and gender, but a review of her life indicates that these handicaps apparently did not lessen her effectiveness. A school in Washington and several women's clubs are named after Terrell. She was living in Annapolis, Maryland, when she died.

Sources: Hine, *Black Women in America*, vol. 2, pp. 1157–59; Hornsby, *Milestones in Twentieth-Century African-American History*, pp. 49, 55; *Jet* 94 (15 June 1998): 19; Smith, *Notable Black American Women*, pp. 1115–19.

1904 • Mother Academy, a private school and high school, was established and became the first such Catholic school for blacks in Tennessee. Katherine Mary Drexel, who died on March 3, 1955 at age ninety-six and was canonized a saint on October 1, 2000, by Pope John Paul II, purchased the land off Seventh Avenue South to build the school. The nuns of Katherine Drexel's order staffed the school. In 1919 the primary division was renamed Holy Family, and in 1954 the Mother Academy closed. Mother Drexel went on to found St. Vincent de Paul School in 1932—a predominantly black school on Heiman Street in North Nashville, near Fisk University and Meharry Medical College. The school closed in 2000.

Sources: *Jet* 98 (23 October 2000): 24; *Nashville Tennessean* (18 March 2000); *Jet* 98 (23 October 2000): 24.

1907 • Charlotte Hawkins Brown (1883–1961) became the founding president of Palmer Memorial Institute in Sedalia, North Carolina. Brown, who was named "Lottie" at birth, was the granddaughter of slaves and born on a plantation in Henderson, North Carolina. Her grandmother had been a favored slave, and Brown grew up understanding the importance of education. At age five, she and eighteen other members of her family moved to Cambridge, Massachusetts, in search of better educational opportunities. Her exceptional abilities were exhibited early, including a talent for oratory and leadership as well as artistic ability. She came to the attention of Alice Freeman Palmer, the second president of Wellesley College, just as she was about to graduate from high school. This encounter changed the course of her life. In 1900 the newly renamed Charlotte Eugenia Hawkins

Charlotte Hawkins Brown

graduated from Cambridge High School. She changed her name because she thought "Lottie" was too undignified for a diploma, and she entered State Normal with a "dignified" name and the assurance that Palmer, who became her benefactor, would pay her school expenses. A job offer from the American Missionary Association (AMA) led to Brown's departure from State Normal at the beginning of her second and what would have been her last year there. She began her career as an educator in 1901 in a rural school near McLeansville, North Carolina. When the AMA closed its small schools because of funding problems in 1902, she had other job offers, but decided to stay in the area and open her own school. With help from Palmer and other Northerners, and the donation of land and an old blacksmith shop by members of the Sedalia community, the Alice Freeman Palmer Institute was born. The school offered black youth industrial and vocational education as well as academic subjects. Its name was changed to Palmer Memorial Institute in 1907, some time after Palmer's death. In the interim, Brown had raised funds for a new campus building and continued her own studies. She completed work at State Normal, receiving a diploma, and did further study during the summers at three Massachusetts institutions— Harvard University, Radcliffe College, and Simmons College. Despite fires that damaged the Palmer campus in 1907 and 1922, Palmer Memorial flourished. The class of 1922 was its first graduating class as an accredited institution. Soon thereafter the curriculum emphasis was placed more on secondary and postsecondary components and less on industrial and vocational education. In time, the school began to attract increasing numbers of black youth from upper-middle class black families and families from outside the South. It became known as a "finishing school," as well as a first-rate academic institution. Both Brown and Palmer students were active participants in the Sedalia community, seeking to improve life conditions and to foster racial harmony through the national leaders Brown brought to the campus. As she pursued her activities, she became even more widely known and her influence increased accordingly. She was appointed to membership in the YWCA by its national board in 1921, a first for a black person; and she was inducted into the Hall of Fame of the North Carolina Board of Education in 1926. Many more honors were to come her way. In 1928 she became first black member of the 20th Century Club of Boston. Membership in the club included distinguished artists, scientists, and theologians. When Brown retired from the presidency of Palmer in 1952 after a half-century of service, she had been through a third campus fire and withdrawal of state subsidies for the school. After resigning the presidency, Brown stayed involved with the school, serving as vice chairman of the board of trustees and director of finances until 1955. Her contributions to education in North Carolina went beyond the establishment of Palmer Memorial and served to improve the quality of education for blacks throughout the state. She published her first book when she was eighteen, and while the school was still demanding much of her time and attention, she managed to raise seven of her nieces and nephews on the Palmer campus. In 1971 still another fire damaged the Palmer campus. The school became a part of historically black Bennett College in Greensboro, North Carolina, but its site was not used. The Charlotte Hawkins Brown Historical Foundation was incorporated in 1983; its exhibits and a state visitors' center are housed in the former Carrie M. Stone Teachers Cottage. The entire campus was designated a state historic site in 1987.

Sources: *Encyclopedia of Black America*, p. 194; Smith, *Notable Black American Women*, pp. 109–14; Robinson, *Historical Negro Biographies*, pp. 25–26; Wadelington and Knapp, *Charlotte Hawkins Brown & Palmer Memorial Institute*, p. 158.

1908 • Virginia Estelle Randolph (1870–1958) was the first black Jeanes teacher. Anna T. Jeanes, a Philadelphia teacher, provided one million dollars to initiate a fund for teachers who worked with other teachers to encourage improvements in small black rural schools. Randolph was one of the most effective educators of her day. The Jeanes teacher program was fashioned after her notable practices in Henrico, Virginia. Through the Jeanes movement that covered the period from 1908 to 1968, Randolph was instrumental in bringing about improvements in the lives of thousands of teachers, children, and community residents. Born in Richmond, Virginia, to parents who were slaves, her early years were difficult. Her father died when she was young, and she took her first job when she was eight years old. After attending schools in Richmond, she obtained a job teaching in a county school at age sixteen, and moved to the Henrico school three years later. Her many achievements there extended beyond the regular school week; she organized a Sunday school, and taught in it herself for five years. Randolph left the Henrico school when she became a Jeanes teacher, working over time in Virginia, North Carolina, and Georgia. Her success led to expansion of the Jeanes movement, with Jeanes teachers supervising industrial education and building community support for black schools all over the South. The program was later broadened to include supervision of instruction in regular academic curricula. The Virginia Randolph Fund, established as a tribute to her in 1936, was merged with the Anna T. Jeanes Foundation, which had been renamed the Negro Rural School Fund. These funds were later merged with others that became the Southern Education Fund. It has been said that confusion over the role of the Jeanes teachers, whose successes were unquestioned, when desegregation was begun contributed to the death of the program. Many tributes to Randolph exist, including a Virginia museum named for her, which was designated a national historic landmark in 1976. She was living in Richmond at the time of her death.

Sources: Hine, *Black Women in America,* vol. 2, pp. 962–63; Smith, *Notable Black American Women,* pp. 918–21; *Who's Who in Colored America, 1937,* p. 429.

1909 • Charlotte Andrews Stephens (1854–1951) became the first black to have a school named in her honor, in Little Rock, Arkansas. A larger school was later erected on the same site and named in her honor a well. It was dedicated on October 8, 1950. Stephens was born in Little Rock and worked with her parents, who had been slaves most of their lives, to establish a school to educate blacks in Little Rock as early as 1864. The first such school was established in her father's small Methodist church. She was taken from her parents when she was seven years old and enslaved as plantation housemaid some ten miles away. After slavery ended two years later, Stephens was reunited with her family. By then she had gained bits and pieces of knowledge from the plantation. With that, and her father's lessons, she trained to become a teacher. For seventy years until she retired in 1939, Stephens taught at every level in Little Rock's schools as well as in schools in other areas. She was Little Rock's first black teacher. Her dedication to teaching led officials to name a school in her honor.

Sources: *Contemporary Black Biography,* vol. 14, pp. 202–4; Smith, *Notable Black American Women,* Book II, pp. 616–17.

1911 • The first black permanent teacher in Albany, New York, was Harriet Lewis Van Vranken (1892?–1996). She also became the first black social worker in that city in 1939. Two years later, she became the first black senior social worker in upstate New York, a post that she retained until she retired in 1958. Born in Albany, she attended the local public schools and graduated from Albany Teachers College, now the State University of Albany. She did graduate work at Wesleyan University and the New York School of Social Work. Van Vranken died in 1996, at age 104.

Sources: *Jet* 89 (15 April 1996): 51.

1922 • Bessye Jeanne Banks Bearden (1888–1943), political and civic worker, was the first black woman member of the New York City Board of Education. Bearden was very dynamic in Democratic Party politics; she founded and was the first president of the Colored Women's Democratic League. She also worked closely with the National Council of Negro Women. She had a major role in political, civic, and social activities both in her Harlem community and nationwide. Bearden was born in Goldsboro, North Carolina, but raised in Atlantic City, New Jersey, where she is considered a native. She graduated from Virginia Normal and Industrial Institute and did later work at the University of Western Pennsylvania and at Columbia University in New York. During the early years of her marriage, Bearden and her husband moved often, living first in New York, then in Charlotte, North Carolina, back to New York, then Canada, and finally back to New York City. She was a cashier in a theater and the manager of a real estate office before her 1922 appointment to the Board of Education. She was the first black woman in the country to sign public school diplomas, after having become chair of the board. Bearden achieved another first when she became deputy collector in internal revenue for New York's Third Collection District in

1935. Romare Bearden (1911–1988), renowned African-American artist, was her son. She served on several committees and boards, including the planning committee of the Negro March on Washington, and chair of the New York State Committee to Abolish the Poll Tax. After a long illness, she died in Harlem Hospital.

Sources: Hine, *Black Women in America,* vol. 1, pp. 97–98; *Encyclopedia of Black America,* p. 169; Smith, *Notable Black American Women,* pp. 70–72.

1930 • Sadie Delany (1889–1999) became the first black domestic science teacher at the high school level in New York City public schools. She was born in Raleigh, North Carolina, on the campus of St. Augustine College, where her parents taught. When she graduated from St. Augustine, she took a job supervising the domestic science curriculum in the black schools of Wake County, North Carolina. She moved to Harlem when she was in her early twenties, seeking to add to her formal education, and enrolled at Pratt Institute in New York, which was a two-year college at that time. When Delany completed Pratt's domestic science course, she entered Columbia University's Teachers college and received a bachelor's degree in 1920 and a master's degree in education in 1925. After teaching first at a mostly all-black elementary school, she obtained her position as New York's first black high school domestic science teacher with a measure of subterfuge—to keep from being identified as a black person, she did not report for the job until the first day of class, having skipped the face-to-face interview. She continued to teach in New York high schools until her retirement in 1960. Delany's life became inextricably entwined with that of her sister, Bessie, who was two years younger than she, when they moved to Harlem together. The sisters were the second and third of the ten Delany children. Bessie graduated from Columbia's dental school in 1919 and received her D.D.S. degree in 1923. Both Delany sisters were thus on the path to success and service. Both had experienced some racial prejudice in North Carolina, and Bessie had serious encounters with racism as a black dentist and in an encounter with the Ku Klux Klan in New York. By 1926, all ten Delany siblings were living in the same Harlem apartment building, and their mother moved to New York in 1928 after the death of her husband. In 1993, Sadie and Bessie's autobiography, *Having Our Say: The Delany Sisters' First 100 Years,* was published, and celebrity came to the sisters. Their captivating anecdotes about their lives, set in the context of black history, and their longevity combined to result in a best seller, complete with television appearances. A second book, *The Delany Sisters' Book of Everyday Wisdom,* was published in 1994. At the time, they were the world's oldest living coauthors. Neither sister ever married; Bessie offered this fact as one of the factors contributing to their longevity.

Sources: Delany, *Having Our Say,* 1993; *Jet* 84 (18 October 1993): 34–37; Smith, *Notable Black American Women,* Book II, pp. 170–73.

1933 • Ethel Thompson Overby (1892–?) became the first black woman principal in the Richmond, Virginia, school system. She headed Elba School and later the Albert V. Norrell School. Overcrowded conditions at Elma spurred Overby to push for a twelve-month school program. She was successful and included parent education in the curriculum. During her tenure salaries for white were significantly higher than those for blacks. She protested and became a leading advocate for equalization of teachers' salaries. She began her college education in summer 1929 at Columbia University and graduated later on with a degree in supervision and administration of elementary schools. During this time she taught seventh grade at Booker T. Washington School where, with donations and some state funds, she started a library.

Sources: *Ethel Thompson Overby.*

1935 • Alvin Demar Loving Sr., (1907–?) educator, was the first black high school teacher in the Detroit public schools. He later was a professor and associate dean at the University of Michigan. He set up universities in Nigeria and India and, as result, he became an important figure in international education. The Indian government hired Loving as a consultant to advise them on the reorganization of their secondary school system.

Sources: *Who's Who among Black Americans, 1978,* p. 566; Salzman, *Encyclopedia of African-American Culture and History,* vol. 3, p. 1662.

1936 • Gertrude Elise McDougald Ayer (1884–1971), activist, educator, and writer, was the first black woman to have a full-time principalship in a New York City public school after desegregation of the school system. (Sarah Garnet was the first black woman principal in 1863, in a black school.) Ayer was strongly committed to the education and training of African Americans. She wrote a number of articles relating to gender and racial inequality, and a chapter on women in Alain Locke's *The New Negro,* the seminal work on the Harlem Renaissance. A native of New York City, her father was a physician there. She attended New York Training School for Teachers from 1903 to 1905 and also studied at Hunter College, Columbia University, College of the City of New York, and New York University. Her first job was as a teacher in a Manhattan public school, but she worked with the Urban League, served as head of the Woman's Department in the Harlem bureau of the U.S. Labor Department Employment Bureau and headed the initiation of the counseling department into New York public schools in 1918 before becoming an assistant principal in 1924. Ayer remained in this position for three years. After her 1936 appointment as a full-time principal, she retained that position until her retirement in 1954, being transferred from the first appointment to a second public school in 1945. Ayer never earned a college degree. Her teaching philosophy, which combined academic learning with practical knowledge, served her well.

Sources: Smith, *Notable Black American Women,* pp. 29–31; *Who's Who in Colored America, 1950,* p. 585.

1939 • Midian Othello Bousfield (1885–1948), a physician, insurance executive, and army officer, was the first black to serve as a member of the Chicago Board of Education. Among his service to the local schools, he was school health officer and school tuberculosis physician. Bousfield was the first black colonel in the Army Medical Corps. During World War II, Bousfield, along with thirty-five other black officers, organized Station Hospital Number One, a 1,000-bed hospital at Fort Huachuca, in the Arizona desert, for the all-black Ninety-third Division. Bousfield also became commanding officer for the hospital. He also helped to incorporate Liberty Life Insurance Company and continued his service after the company's 1929 merger that created Supreme Life Insurance Company. Born in Tipton, Missouri, Bousfield graduated from the University of Kansas. He received his medical degree from Northwestern School of Medicine and completed an internship at Freedmen's Hospital in Washington, D.C. He set up practice in Chicago.

Midian Othello Bousfield

Sources: Logan and Winston, *Dictionary of American Negro Biography,* pp. 51–52; *Dictionary of Black Culture,* p. 61; *Journal of the National Medical Association* 49 (May 1948): 20.

1939 • Walter S. Mills (1909–1994) stood alone in the nation's first suit to equalize teacher's pay and was successful in bringing equity in teacher's salaries in Maryland. The school principal from Annapolis, Maryland, argued the case as he stood beside NAACP counsel Thurgood Marshall. This occurred fifteen years before the 1954 school desegregation ruling and became one of only two such cases discussed in law books. In 1984 the National Education Association honored Mills by giving him the Whitney Young Memorial Award for educators. Mills grew up on a farm in Maryland and graduated from Hampton Institute (now Hampton University). He taught for forty-six years.

Sources: *Jet* 86 (8 August 1994): 15.

1944 • Ruth Wright Hayre (1910–1998) was the first black to become a regular high school teacher in Philadelphia, at William Penn High School. She was the daughter of African Methodist Episcopal Bishop Robert Richard Wright Jr. and the granddaughter of the pioneer black banker and entrepreneur Robert Richard Wright Sr. She co-edited, with her father, an edition of the poetry of Phillis Wheatley. In 1985 she was elected to the Philadelphia Board of Education, and in 1990 she was the first black (and the first woman) elected president of the board. Hayre was born in Philadelphia and grew up in a family with strong ties to the AME Church, which was founded there in 1794, and a commitment to education. Her early education came from white public schools. She entered the University of Pennsylvania when she was fifteen years old, having won scholarships from both her city and her state. She graduated in four years and stayed on to earn a master's degree in 1931. After that she taught for several years in Arkansas, Ohio, and Washington, D.C., before moving back to Philadelphia in 1939. In 1949, she received a doctorate in English literature and languages from the University of Pennsylvania, which gave Hayre and her father the distinction of being the first father-daughter pair to earn doctorates from that institution. She was made a district superintendent in Philadelphia in 1963. She retired from the Philadelphia school system in 1978, but her contributions to education did not stop then. In 1988 Hayre told the 119 sixth-grade students at two public schools in north Philadelphia that her "Tell Them We Are Rising" fund would pay for their college educations at any accredited school. One of the schools, Richard R. Wright Elementary, was named for her grandfather. The other school, Kenderton Elementary, was chosen because of the reading achievement of its students and its good academic reputation.

Sources: *Marketing* (14 April 1992): 7; Smith, *Notable Black American Women*, Book II, pp. 279–82; *Who's Who among Black Americans, 1992–93*, p. 630.

1953 • Rufus Early Clement (1900–1967) was the first black elected to a school board in the deep South since Reconstruction. Clement was elected to the Atlanta Public School board by both black and white citizens. In 1925 he was the youngest academic dean in America, at Livingstone College in Salisbury, North Carolina. He later became dean of Louisville Municipal College in Kentucky. In 1936 he became president of Atlanta University and was instrumental in fostering their newly formed graduate school (1929), as well as enlarging the influence of the Atlanta University Center. In 1966 *Time* magazine chose Clement as one of the fourteen most influential university presidents in America. He was always identified with organizations in the South directed toward the healing of race relations, and the eradication of all forms of discrimination.

Sources: Bacote, *The Story of Atlanta University*, pp. 316–30, 344–82; Logan and Winston, *Dictionary of American Negro Biography*, p. 117; *Encyclopedia of Black America*, p. 275; Hornsby, *Chronology of African-American History*, p. 99; *Time* 87 (11 February 1966): 64; Smith, *Notable Black American Men*, pp. 208–11.

1954 • The U.S. Supreme Court ruled racial segregation in public schools unconstitutional. The historic decision, which was handed down on May 17, came in the form of a landmark ruling, *Brown v. Board of Education of Topeka*. The decision declared unconstitutional the *Plessy v. Ferguson* case of 1896, which allowed school segregation in the South, and the "separate but equal" doctrine that denied black children their basic rights.

Sources: Smith and Wynn, *Freedom Facts and Firsts*, pp. 164–65.

1956 • John Henrik Clarke (1915–1998), editor, writer, teacher, and historian, was the first black licensed to teach African and African American history in New York State public schools. He was best known as a critic, anthologist, and editor; he has also written short stories and poetry. He was the co-founder of the *Harlem Quarterly*, book review editor of the *Negro History Bulletin*, and associate editor of *Freedomways: A Quarterly Review of the Negro Freedom Movement*. He also co-founded the Black Academy of Arts and Letters. He became a lecturer at Hunter College of the City University of New York in 1969, where he helped to establish a black studies program. In that year he also helped to found the black studies program at Cornell University. The next year he was associate professor in the Department of Black and Puerto Rican Studies at Hunter and remained there until he retired in 1985. His writings as well as his numerous lectures reflect considerable political and racial controversy. Clarke was born in Union Springs, Arkansas, to a sharecropper father and a laundrywoman. He was the first in a family of nine children to learn to read. He dropped out of school in the eighth grade and worked to help support his family. Clarke hopped a freight train to New York when he was seventeen, held a number of low-paying jobs, and spent considerable time researching in libraries and writing poems and short stories. Although he went on to become a well-known educator and Afrocentric scholar, he followed an unorthodox academic career path. He studied at New York University, Columbia University but never graduated. He received a teaching license from People's College, Malverne, Long Island. At age seventy-eight he received a doctorate from Pacific Western University, an unaccredited institution in Los Angeles. He had become blind late in his life; he died on July 16, 1998, at age eighty-three.

Sources: *African American Almanac,* 8th ed., p. 385; *Contemporary Black Biography,* vol. 20, pp. 38–41; *Encyclopedia of Black America,* p. 273; *Who's Who among African Americans,* 10th ed., p. 280.

1956 • On August 26, twelve black teenagers enrolled in Clinton High School, desegregating Tennessee's—and the South's—first public, all-white high school. Located in the eastern region of the state, in Anderson County, civil rights activities began in Clinton, Tennessee, shortly after World War II, when black parents sought equitable facilities for their children. In 1950, blacks filed suit against the county because four black students were refused admission to Clinton High School. The case *McSwain et al. v. County Board of Education of Anderson County, Tennessee,* became the state's first school desegregation case and involved, among other black lawyers, Thurgood Marshall, then of the NAACP. The case was denied but the ruling was overturned in January 1956. On May 17, 1957, Robert "Bobby" McCain Jr., the only senior among the twelve blacks who enrolled, graduated from Clinton High School.

Sources: Smith and Wynn, *Freedom Facts and Firsts,* pp. 114–15.

1957 • Daisy Bates (1920–1999), then president of the Arkansas state branch of the NAACP, led nine black students to integrate Central High School in Little Rock, Arkansas, on September 25 of this year. For their efforts, Bates and the "Little Rock Nine," as they came to be known, received the NAACP's Spingarn Medal on July 11, 1958. The medal was given "in grateful acknowledgement of their courageous self-restraint in the face of extreme provocation and peril." In 1998 the U.S. Senate voted to award Congressional gold medals to the nine at a White House ceremony and made the awards in 1999. Bates was recognized again when the state of Arkansas declared the third Monday in February in her honor. Bates was born in Huttig, Arkansas, and was raised by adoptive parents. She grew up in a positive relationship with her surrogate parents and attended the poorly equipped segregated schools in her hometown. When she married in 1941, she moved with her husband to Little Rock, where she and her husband leased the *Arkansas State Press.* The paper's report of the beating death of a black army sergeant by a local white policeman led to loss of its advertising from white businessmen, but it survived and gained stature as an independent voice of the people, which worked to improve conditions for blacks throughout the state. When Arkansas moved slowly to follow the U.S. Supreme Court's 1954 desegregation order, the NAACP, under Bates' leadership, protested and developed several strategies to force quicker action. Daisy Bates and other NAACP officials surrendered to police on October 25, 1957, following an arrest order issued by the Little Rock City Council that charged the organization with violation of a new law requiring organizational information. Bates was convicted and fined, but the decision was later reversed. The *Arkansas State Press* ceased publication in 1959, but Bates continued to be active in voter registration drives and in work with the Democratic National Committee; the paper resumed publication in 1985. When Bates died, she had received more than two hundred citations and awards. Her body was held in state for a day to allow public viewing, authorized by the city of Little Rock. Her papers are on file at the State Historical Society of Wisconsin, Archives Division, in Madison.

Fifty years after Central High School's integration, the nation reflected on the legacy of the town and the Little Rock nine in a week-long celebration in Little Rock that included speeches by the Nine (all of whom attended), the opening of the school as a National Historic Site (with a museum), a commemorative coin, and a speech by former President Bill Clinton. Thousands, including local citizens, civil rights leaders, and students attended the activities.

Sources: *Jet* 96 (22 November 1999): 58–59; 98 (September 25, 2000): 19; 100 (16 July 2001): 19; Smith, *Notable Black American Women,* pp. 64–69.

1958 • Ernest Gideon Green (1941–), investment banker and government worker, was the first black graduate from the Little Rock, Arkansas, Central High School. Green was one of the "Little Rock Nine," the black students who integrated the Little Rock public schools under the watch of the federal troops called out by President Dwight D. Eisenhower in 1957. Along with the other students and advisor Daisy Bates, Green was the recipient of the NAACP'S Spingarn Medal in 1958. Born in Little Rock, he received his bachelor's and master's degrees from Michigan State University, and went on to become an investment banker in Washington, D.C. He served as the Assistant Secretary for the U. S. Department of Labor from 1977 to 1981, and was part owner of his own firm before taking a position with the D.C. firm. Michigan State awarded him an honorary doctorate degree in 1994.

Sources: Cantor, *Historic Landmarks of Black America,* pp. 147–48; Hornsby, *Chronology of African-American History,* p. 106; *Who's Who among African Americans,* 26th ed., p. 492.

1958 • Helen Walker Williams became the first black woman hired as a permanent teacher in the Rhode Island school system. She was hired as an English and social studies teacher at Esek Hopkins Junior High School in Providence. Williams was born in Henderson, North Carolina, and graduated from Spelman College and the University of Michigan. She received a doctorate from Boston College. Her sorority, Delta Sigma Theta, honored her before her death by naming her "Teacher of the Year." Williams was sister of Eunice W. Johnson of Johnson Publishing Company and director of Ebony Fashion Fair.

Sources: *Jet* 90 (2 September 1996): 17.

1960 • Ruby Bridges [Hall] (1954–) became the first black student enrolled at William Frantz Elementary School in New Orleans. On that day she was escorted to school by federal marshals, who joined her at the school for celebration of Black History Month in 2001. The significance of Hall's enrollment was recognized in Norman Rockwell's painting, *The Problem We All Live With,* which shows Hall entering school. Hall never attended college, but the trauma of her brother's murder in New Orleans triggered reflection and action, leading to her volunteer work as a parental liaison at William Frantz. In 1995 *The Story of Ruby Bridges,* her picture book for children, on which Harvard psychologist Robert Cole collaborated, was published. The book's success led to establishment of the Ruby Bridges Foundation, which focuses on helping schools establish diversity programs. *Through My Eyes,* published by Bridges in 2000, describes her first year at William Frantz and has been made part of an elementary school reading program in New Orleans. William Frantz, however, still has little diversity. Its students now are predominantly black, as are students in most New Orleans public schools.

Sources: *Jet* 91 (10 March 1997): 21.

1964 • Harlem School of the Arts was the first school in the state of New York founded to offer preprofessional training to mostly black and Latino children. The noted opera singer and school founder Dorothy Maynor (1910–1996) was the first executive director of the school. The school provided performing arts instruction for underprivileged community children. Maynor served as its director until 1979, culminating a forty-year career that began with her historic Town Hall voice recital in 1939. She was internationally acclaimed as a leading soprano and an interpreter of German lieder.

Sources: Hine, *Black Women in America,* pp. 761–62; Smith, *Notable Black American Women,* pp. 739–40; *Contemporary Black Biography,* vol. 19, pp. 155–58.

1967 • Benjamin Elijah Mays (1895–1984), college president, clergyman, and educational administrator, was elected the first black president of the Atlanta Public School Board of Education. He had retired as president of Morehouse College in this same year. He was born to tenant farmers in South Carolina. As a child, he had to face both racial problems and family problems. His father was prone to alcohol binges and was sometimes abusive to Mays' mother. Despite these problems, and with his mother's backing, he demonstrated early on a desire for education. Dissatisfied after attending county schools and a church-run school in McCormick, South Carolina, he entered the high school de-

partment of South Carolina State College in Orangeburg in 1911, and graduated as valedictorian in 1916. He had paid much of his own way by working as a Pullman porter, because his father stopped financial support when Mays refused to return to the farm during
the summers. He entered Bates College in New England in 1917, graduated with honors
in 1920, and began further study at the University of Chicago. These studies were interrupted by his first involvement with Morehouse, as a teacher of mathematics. He would
pursue doctoral study on and off, while doing other things, until he received his degree in
1935. Before becoming president of Morehouse in 1940, Mays taught at Howard University and held a number of Baptist church pastorates. He was Morehouse's president for
twenty-seven years, and is credited by some as its most effective president. He was also a
brilliant civil rights advocate. Martin Luther King Jr. was a student at Morehouse during
Mays' tenure as president, and Mays delivered the eulogy at King's funeral. In January
1984 Mays was inducted into the South Carolina Hall of Fame and cited for his long career in education and civil rights. His name has been given to schools and streets in both
Greenwood County, South Carolina, and Atlanta. His life is chronicled in his autobiography, *Born to Rebel,* published in 1971.

Benjamin Mays

Sources: *Black Enterprise* 7 (May 1977): 26–29; *Ebony* 33 (December 1977): 72–80;
Hornsby, *Chronology of African-American History,* pp. 131, 142, 327, 329; Smith, *Notable
Black American Men,* pp. 780–84.

1970 • Elbert E. Allen (1921–1999), a dentistry graduate of Meharry Medical College
(1947), was the first black since Reconstruction to hold office in Shreveport, Louisiana,
when he was elected to the Caddo Parish School Board. In the same year of his election to
the school board, Allen also became head of the American Woodmen, a fraternal organization with some forty thousand members.

Sources: *Ebony Success Library,* vol. 1, p. 9; *Who's Who among Black Americans, 1992–93,*
p. 22.

1970 • Wilson Camanza Riles (1917–1999) was the first black elected to a statewide office in California and served as the state's leading schools advocate. He was opposed to
mandatory busing of students and advocated higher testing standards. He began work
with the California State Department of Education in 1958, holding first the position of
head of the Bureau of Intergroup Relations and becoming associate superintendent of the
department in 1965. In 1970 he was elected state superintendent of public instruction
and director of education. He served as state superintendent from 1971 to 1983, directing
the country's largest education system. His achievements in reshaping California's educational system were recognized by the NAACP in 1973, when he was awarded the Spingarn
Medal. Following his tenure in the department of education, he established Wilson Riles
and Associates, an educational consulting firm. Riles was born in rural Louisiana and had
lost both his parents before he was twelve years old. He was raised by a married couple who
had been friends of his deceased parents. He attended high school in New Orleans and
moved with his surrogate family to Arizona after high school graduation. Riles worked
his way through Arizona State College, where he was the only black student at the school
at the time. After graduation his first job was as a teacher at an Indian reservation. He
worked in Arizona public schools for fourteen years, taking time along the way to earn a
master's degree in school administration from Northern Arizona University in 1947. He
held nine honorary doctorate degrees and many other awards. He was a resident of Sacramento when he died.

Sources: *Current Biography, 1971,* pp. 348–50; *Ebony Success Library,* vol. 2, pp. 216–19;
Who's Who among African Americans, 10th ed., p. 1267; Smith, *Notable Black American
Men,* pp. 1011–13.

1971 • Roland Nathaniel Patterson (1928–1982) was the first black appointed superintendent of schools in Baltimore, Maryland. Patterson came from the Seattle, Washington,
school system.

Sources: *Who's Who among Black Americans, 1977–78,* p. 697.

The First Black School Superintendent since Reconstruction

▌n 1969 John W. Porter (1931–2012), educator, became the first black state superintendent of public instruction since Reconstruction. Porter was appointed to the position by Michigan governor William G. Milliken. He was president of Eastern Michigan University from 1979 to 1989.

Sources: *Ebony* 14 (February 1959): 6; Garrett, *Famous First Facts about Negroes*, p. 61; *Who's Who among Black Americans, 1978*, p. 723.

1973 • On July 1, 1973, Alonzo A. Crim (1928–2000) became the first black superintendent of schools in Atlanta, Georgia. A native of Chicago, Illinois, Crim held the position until 1988, when he became a professor at Georgia State University. He obtained his early postsecondary degrees from schools in Chicago, earning a bachelor's degree from Roosevelt College in 1950 and a master's degree from the University of Chicago in 1958. In 1969 Harvard University awarded him the doctorate in education. From 1954 to 1963 he was a teacher in the Chicago public school system. He served as superintendent there for one year, in 1968–69. Thereafter he worked in California public schools until he moved to Atlanta in 1973. His last post was as a professor at Spelman College. Crim was the recipient of numerous awards and honorary degrees, the latter being given by both black and white institutions of higher education.

Sources: Hornsby, *Chronology of African-American History*, pp. 207–28; *Negro Almanac*, p. 69; *Who's Who among African Americans*, 13th ed., p. 1509.

1973 • Marianna White Davis (1929–) was the first black woman member of the South Carolina Board of Education, on which she served from 1973 to 1976. She later served as acting president of Denmark Technical College in South Carolina in 1985–86. Born in Philadelphia, she earned degrees from South Carolina State College (B.A., 1949) and New York University (M.A., 1953), before receiving her doctorate in education from Boston University in 1966. Davis began her career as a teacher in the South Carolina public schools and went on to teach at several historically black institutions in South Carolina between 1956 and 1982. She also spent a year as a visiting professor at Boston College. In 1996 she became special assistant to the president of Benedict College in South Carolina. She was among the persons named as an Outstanding Educator of America in 1970–71, and received a Distinguished Alumni award from Boston College in 1981. She has also received numerous awards and recognitions for her work. In 1989 she was executive producer of the PBS black history teleconference, "The Struggle Continues." She is a prolific writer, with more than a dozen books and many articles published.

Sources: Hornsby, *Chronology of African-American History*, pp. 207–28; *Negro Almanac*, p. 69; *Sepia* 28 (November 1979): 72–76; *Who's Who among African Americans*, 26th ed., pp. 317–18.

1977 • John D. O'Bryant (1931–1992) was the first black member of the Boston School Committee. The Boston-born educator began his career in the Boston schools in 1956 after earning a master's in education from Boston University.

Sources: *Jet* 82 (27 July 1992): 22; *Who's Who among Black Americans, 1992–1993*, p. 1069.

1979 • Willie W. Herenton (1940–) became the first black superintendent of the Memphis City school system in 1979 and held that position until 1992. Herenton had begun his teaching career in the elementary schools of Memphis in 1963. He was elected the first black mayor of that city in 1992. A Memphis native, he received two of his three postsecondary degrees from Memphis institutions—a bachelor's degree from LeMoyne-Owen and a master's degree from Memphis State University—and earned a doctorate from Southern Illinois University.

Sources: *Ebony* 47 (March 1992): 106–8; *Jet* 93 (20 April 1998): 20; *State of Black America, 1992,* pp. 383–84; *Who's Who among African Americans,* 26th ed., p. 572.

1981 • Ruth Burnett Love [Holloway] (1935–) was the first black and the first woman to serve as superintendent of the Chicago school system. She served from 1981 to 1984 and was faced with an extremely difficult situation for a newcomer to the state and the system: The system had budget problems, the desegregation plan was under discussion with the courts and the Justice Department, and additional political issues arose under the leadership of newly elected mayor Jane Byrne. Although Love could not overcome fully the problems she faced in Chicago, she did institute some programs, including discipline codes and "Adopt-a-School," that had positive results. She held the Chicago position for three years, after which she returned to California and formed Ruth Love Enterprises, an educational consulting firm based in San Francisco. She also became co-publisher of *The Sun Reporter,* which issues seven weekly newspapers in the Bay Area; Love publishes the *California Voice.* Born in Lawton, Oklahoma, Love grew up in Bakersfield, California, and obtained all of her postsecondary degrees in California schools. Her bachelor's degree in elementary education was obtained from San Jose State University, followed by a master's degree in guidance and counseling from San Francisco State University, and a doctorate in human behavior from United States International University in San Diego. During the early years of her career, Love taught in California and in England, and did counseling in Africa. She began her work as a school administrator in California, where she was first hired as a teacher in 1954. Her career in school administration began in 1965, when she became director of the "Right to Read" program in the U.S. Department of Education, where illiteracy was the major concern. She remained with this program for six years. In 1975 she became superintendent of the Oakland Unified School District, where student achievement increased markedly during her term of office. She left Oakland to accept the position in Chicago. Love has received a Certificate of Recognition from the Department of Health, Education, and Welfare.

Sources: Smith, *Notable Black American Women,* pp. 685–87; *Who's Who among African Americans,* 14th ed., p. 818.

1982 • Bettye J. Davis (1938–), state representative, was the first black woman elected to the Anchorage, Alaska, Board of Education. Born in Louisiana, Davis first completed training as a practical nurse, then graduated from Grambling State University in 1971, and later attended the University of Alaska. Her first job after she obtained her college degree was with the YWCA in San Bernardino, California, where she was assistant director. She held several positions in Alaska, beginning in 1975 as a child care specialist with the Youth Services Department. While most of her positions have utilized her talents as a social worker, she served as director of the Alaska Black Leadership Educational Program from 1979 to 1982. She was elected to the Alaska legislature in 1991. Her numerous awards include a Woman of Achievement award from the YWCA in 1991, and a 1992 Outstanding Leadership award from the California Assembly.

Sources: *Who's Who among African Americans,* 26th ed., p. 310.

1982 • Charles Albert Highsmith (1921–) was the first black superintendent of the Philadelphia, Pennsylvania, public schools.

Sources: *Who's Who among Black Americans, 1992–93,* p. 652.

1985 • Laval S. Wilson (1935–) was the first black superintendent of schools in the Boston public school system. A native of Jackson, Tennessee, he received all of his three postsecondary degrees from institutions in the Chicago area, earning a bachelor's degree from Chicago State Teachers College, a master's from the University of Chicago, and a doctorate from Northwestern University in 1967. Wilson worked as a teacher and educational administrator in a number of places before taking the Boston post. In the last two posts prior to Boston, he served as superintendent of the Berkeley, California, schools from 1974 to 1980 and as superintendent of the Rochester, New York, schools from 1980 to 1985. He left the Boston system in 1990.

Sources: *Who's Who among African Americans,* 26th ed., p. 1365.

1986 • Ethel Harris Hall (1928–2011) and Willie Paul were the first blacks elected to the Alabama Board of Education. Born in Decatur, Alabama, Hall became an associate professor at the University of Alabama in 1978. Hall received the Doctor of Social Work from the University of Alabama in 1979, after earning degrees previously at Alabama Agricultural and Mechanical University (B.S. 1948), and the University of Chicago (M.A. 1953). She began as a public school teacher, went on to serve as director of the neighborhood Youth Corps for five years, and was on the faculty of the University of Montevallo for seven years, just before taking the position at the University of Alabama. Paul headed the Montgomery Head Start Program.

Sources: *Jet* 70 (14 July 1986): 16; *Who's Who among African Americans,* 26th ed., p. 515.

1988 • Marvin E. Edwards (1943–) was the first black to be named general superintendent of the Dallas, Texas, Independent School District. He held this position for five years. Born in Memphis, he received a bachelor's degree from Eastern Illinois University in 1967, a master's degree from Chicago State University in 1969, and a doctorate in education from Northern Illinois University in 1973. He had extensive teaching and administrative experience in public school systems prior to being named to the Dallas post. He had been a teacher, principal, assistant superintendent, or superintendent in various cities in Illinois, and in Richmond, Virginia, and Topeka, Kansas. In 1993 he became superintendent of the Elgin (Illinois) Area School District. He is the recipient of several awards, including Distinguished Alumni awards from Northern Illinois and Eastern Illinois, and the Outstanding Texas Award from the Texas Legislative Black Caucus.

Sources: *Who's Who among African Americans,* 26th ed., p. 377–78.

1988 • Richard R. Green was named the first black chancellor of the New York City school system, the largest in the country.

Sources: *Jet* 73 (18 January 1988): 8; 74 (8 August 1988): 12.

1990 • Gwendolyn Calvert Baker (1931–) was the first black woman president of the New York City Board of Education. She has been National Executive Director of the YWCA of America and president of the United States Committee for UNICEF Children's Fund. Baker, who was born in Ann Arbor, Michigan, earned all of her postsecondary degrees from the University of Michigan, culminating with a doctorate in education in 1972. Her path to this achievement was not, however, uninterrupted. She married after her freshman year and withdrew from college to raise a family. Ten years later, in 1964 she earned her bachelor's degree in elementary education. Baker then began teaching in Ann Arbor's elementary schools, where she worked from 1964 to 1969. Along the way, two significant events occurred: In 1968 she earned a master's degree in elementary education, and in that same year she received the University of Michigan's Ann Arbor Teacher of the Year Award, in recognition of her skills in supervising student teachers. The award carried with it a year's assignment on the Michigan faculty. This led to a full-time position, and Baker taught at the University of Michigan from 1970 to 1976. She remained there for two more years as director of affirmative action programs. During the administration of President Jimmy Carter, in 1978, she moved to the nation's capitol to become chief of Minorities and Women's Programs for the National Institute of Education. She later served (1981 to 1984) as vice-president and dean of Graduate and Children's Programs at the prestigious Bank Street College of Education. When she moved to the YWCA in 1984, she continued to use her experience as an educator, and her reorganization of that agency is said to have resulted in better services and a balanced budget. She remained in the post until 1993, when she moved to UNICEF. Baker is noted for her abiding interest in multicultural education, which has served as the focus for many of her projects. She is also recognized as an outstanding administrator, which is credited with giving her another "first:" She was named to the board of the Greater New York Saving Bank in 1992, the first black and the first woman ever chosen. Many other honors have come her way, including a $5,000 scholarship established in her name by the New York Alliance of Black School Educators. She became president of Calvert Baker and Associates in 1997, and also accepted a post as director of social justice at the American Educational Research Association.

Sources: *Chicago Defender* (13 July 1993); *Jet* 79 (1 April 1991): 31; Smith, *Notable Black American Women,* Book II, pp. 20–24; *Who's Who among African Americans,* 26th ed., pp. 57–58.

1992 • The first black and the first woman to be named superintendent of the South Bend Community School Corporation in Indiana was Virginia Brown Calvin (1945–). In 1996 she was named Superintendent of the Year, the first black to hold that honor.

Sources: *Jet* 89 (12 February 1996), p. 20; *Who's Who among African Americans,* 14th ed., p. 198.

1994 • Frances Edwards became the first black woman elected chair of the school board for DeKalb County, Georgia. Previously she was vice chairperson of the board.

Sources: *Jet* 85 (21 February 1994): 20.

1994 • Charles E. Coleman was named superintendent of Marion Community Schools in Indiana. Previously he was area administrator for Fort Wayne Community Schools.

Sources: *Jet* 87 (3 April 1994): 21.

1995 • John Stanford (1938–1999) was selected the Seattle, Washington, superintendent of schools, for a system serving more than 47,000 students. He was the first black to hold that post. Born in Darby, Pennsylvania, he received his bachelor's degree in 1961 from Pennsylvania State University and his master's degree from Central Michigan University. While in college, he was a member of the ROTC and upon graduation he was commissioned a second lieutenant in the U.S. Army. Stanford held several assignments in the army, becoming military assistant to the Undersecretary of the Army from 1977 to 1979, executive assistant to the Secretary of Defense from 1981 to 1984, and then was promoted to major general on May 1, 1988. After serving as director of plans, programs, and policy of the U.S. Transportation command at Scott Air Force Base in Illinois, he retired on August 1, 1991. From 1991 to 1995 he served as county manager for Fulton County, Georgia, and left to become superintendent of schools in Seattle. Stanford kept a sense of urgency about his mission to establish innovative programs in the schools; however, his health failed before he could realize his mission. He died of leukemia in 1999.

Sources: *Contemporary Black Biography,* vol. 20, pp. 194–98; *Jet* 88 (28 August 1995): 23; 95 (14 December 1999): 18.

1995 • Lillie Ransom became the first black president of Maryland School for the Deaf, located in Frederick, Maryland. She is an expert in deaf education and was vice president of the Board of Trustees for the school.

Sources: *Jet* 88 (21 August 1995): 22; *Who's Who among African Americans,* 14th ed., p. 1070.

1996 • Charles Larke became the first black superintendent of the Augusta, Georgia, school system. He had served the Richmond County Board of Education for twenty-six years, and had been assistant superintendent for vocational services as well as interim superintendent.

Sources: *Jet* 90 (26 August 1996): 20.

1996 • Virginia Brown Calvin (1945–) became the first black to be named Indiana State Superintendent of the Year. She was also the first black and first woman superintendent in the history of the district that the South Bend Community School Corporation embraces. Calvin was born in Lake Providence, Louisiana, and received her bachelor's degree from Alcorn State University, master's from New Mexico Highlands University, and doctorate in education from Texas Women's University. She has also studied at North Texas State University and the University of South Bend. Since 1992 she has been superintendent of schools for the South Bend Community School Corporation.

Sources: *Jet* 89 (12 February 1996): 20.

1997 • Rosa A. Smith was named superintendent of the Columbus, Ohio, public schools, becoming the first woman to head the 63,000 student district. In 1997 the former superintendent of the Beloit, Wisconsin, school district was named Superintendent of the Year in Wisconsin.

Sources: *Jet* 92 (22 September 1997): 19.

1999 • James N. Allen was appointed to the Independent School Board in Amarillo, Texas, becoming the first black member. Allen was vice president of Installment Lending for the Amarillo National Bank and had served the bank for ten years. He graduated from Morehouse College in Atlanta, West Texas Agricultural and Mechanical College, and the American Institute of Banking.

Sources: *Jet* 96 (22 November 1999): 20.

2006 • Urban Prep Academy, a charter school, opened in the Englewood community on Chicago's South Side, as the first black all-boys public charter high school in the country. In 2010, all of the school's 107 graduates were accepted into different colleges and universities, including the University of Illinois, Northwestern, and historically black Fisk University, Morehouse College, and Howard University. Tim King, the academy's founder, said of the school, "We are doing everything that we should to prepare the students for the academic rigors of college." The school "promotes a spirit of brotherhood from the students' earliest days in high school." It also promotes a spirit of brotherhood, family, and community. Eighty-five percent of the students are from low-income households and unable to pay college expenses. So that the students may have access to the administrators and teachers at all times, Urban Prep's staff are given cell phones; all have access to email. Black males comprise 60 percent of the staff.

Sources: *Jet* 117 (19–26 April 2010): 16–19.

2009 • Mark Reed (1965?–) broke uncharted waters when he became the first black to head prestigious Charlotte Country Day School in Charlotte, North Carolina, in July. He was appointed the eleventh head of the school, then in its nearly seventy-year history. He would work in an area where 89 percent of the 1,600 pre-K students and 90 percent of the nearly 300 faculty and staff were white. The board of trustees' chair said that "race was not a factor in the search" and that Reed had "the right experience and perspectives, the proven professional commitment and leadership, and the personal qualities to serve" and lead the school "exceptionally well." Reed had experienced diversity in education when he became the first black male faculty member at St. John's School in Houston. There for nineteen years, he was teacher, coach, and administrator. When approached about the Charlotte school, he was in his fifth year as assistant headmaster at St. John's. Reed was born and raised in Great Falls, Montana, where his parents moved so that his father could play baseball in the minor leagues. His father had played with the old Negro Leagues when the family lived in Alabama.

Sources: *Crisis* 116 (Fall 2009): 6.

GOVERNMENT: COUNTY & STATE

Alabama

1948 • Mahala Ashley Dickerson (1912–2007) was the first black woman attorney in Montgomery and until 1952 the only black woman lawyer in Alabama. On August 6, 1995, she was one of five women who received the Margaret Brent Award from the American Bar Association's Commission on Women in the Profession. The award, named for the country's first woman attorney, honored the recipients as outstanding women attorneys in the United States; Hillary Rodham Clinton and Ruth Bader Ginsburg are among previous recipients. Dickerson was born in Montgomery and graduated *cum laude* from Fisk University and Howard University Law School. While practicing in Montgomery, she argued a number of cases involving land titles and civil rights. She moved to Indianapolis for a while, where she became the first black woman attorney in the city and the second in the state. Dickerson returned to Alabama to argue a case before the Federal District Tax Court in Birmingham.

Sources: *Tennessean* (20 July 1995); *They Too Call Alabama Home,* pp, 115–16.

1967 • On January 16, 1967, Lucius D. Amerson (1934–1994) became the first black sheriff in the South since Reconstruction. Amerson held the office of Macon County sheriff until 1987, and paved the way for many blacks. Born on a small farm in Clinton, Greene County, he was educated at Tuskegee Institute (now Tuskegee University). He served as a paratrooper in the Korean War and served tours of duty in Japan and Germany. He later worked for the postal service in Montgomery and in Denver, Colorado. His employment with the Veterans Administration took him back to Tuskegee. By then he had a growing ambition to become a law enforcement officer. He enrolled in class at night to study police methods, despite opposition from some blacks who were concerned that no blacks were on the state trooper force. Using the theme "Now Is the Time," Amerson ran for sheriff of Macon County and won. Suffering from poor health and the effects of a stroke, he died at home at age sixty.

Sources: Bailey, *They Too Call Alabama Home,* pp. 17–18; Bennett, *Before the Mayflower,* p. 578; Hornsby, *Chronology of African-American History,* pp. 131, 164, 172; *Negro Almanac,* p. 44.

1970 • Fred Davis Gray (1930–) and Thomas J. Reed (1927–1997) were the first blacks elected to the Alabama legislature in modern times. An attorney and a minister, Gray was Rosa Parks' lawyer during the Montgomery Bus Boycott and Martin Luther King Jr.'s first lawyer. Gray was born in Montgomery and graduated from Alabama State University in 1951. He received his law degree from Case Western Reserve University in 1954. He worked to advance the rights of black Americans particularly in the 1960s. He worked with Vivian Malone in her suit to enroll at the University of Alabama, with Harolyn Franklyn to desegregate Auburn University, and he filed a suit to desegregate the state's public schools. Gray served in the legislature for four years (1970–74). Reed served in the legislature from 1980 to 1988, and again from 1994 to 1998. Reed received his degree in economics from Tuskegee Institute. Also a civil rights activist, he was instrumental in getting the legislature to hire the first black page.

Sources: *Ebony Success Library*, vol. 1, pp. 131 (Gray), 260 (Reed); *Jet* 38 (18 June 1970): 10; 43 (16 November, 1972): 5; 46 (17 July 1974): 14–16; *Who's Who among Black Americans, 1992–93*, p. 550 (Gray), 1175 (Reed); Bailey, *They Too Call Alabama Home*, pp. 149–51 (Gray), 321 (Reed).

1970 • The first black coroner in Bullock County was Raymond "Ray" W. Allen Jr. (1935–1996), who served until 1978. Allen attended Tuskegee Institute (now Tuskegee University) and later became owner of Allen Funeral Home in Union Springs and Dothan.

Sources: Bailey, *They Too Call Alabama Home*, p. 16.

1974 • Jesse J. Lewis (1925–) was the first black cabinet officer in Alabama in modern times. Lewis was named to head the Office of Highway Traffic Safety by Governor George Wallace. He held this position until 1978. He became president of Lawson State Community College in Birmingham, Alabama. Lewis was born in Tuscaloosa, Alabama, and earned his bachelor's degree from Miles College in 1951 and master's degree from Troy State University in 1977. In 1954 he opened the first black-owned advertising agency in Alabama.

Sources: Hornsby, *Chronology of Black America*, p. 248; *Who's Who among African Americans*, 26th ed., p. 770.

1977 • A businesswoman who became interested in politics while visiting a coffee shop, Louphenia Thomas (1918–2001) became the first black woman elected to the Alabama legislature. A Democrat from Birmingham, she represented the thirty-ninth district in the state house from 1977 to 1978. Although the turnout was light, she won a special election in July to fill the seat of John Porter, defeating William Fred Horn. When the regular election was held the next year, however, she lost to Horn. After leaving the legislature, she remained active in politics, serving on the Democratic National Committee. Thomas graduated from Miles College in Birmingham and did graduate study at Alabama Agricultural and Mechanical University in Huntsville. In 1961 Thomas was unsuccessful in her bid for a seat on the city council. She served in the Women's Division of the Jefferson County Progressive Democratic Council and the Alabama Democratic Conference.

Sources: Bailey, *They Too Call Alabama Home*, p. 368; *New York Times* Obituaries (12 February 2001).

1977 • John T. Porter was the first black member of the Pardon and Parole Board. Porter was a first-term legislator at the time of his appointment and served the Sixth Avenue Baptist Church in Birmingham for fourteen years.

Sources: *Jet* 52 (28 April 1977): 9.

1977 • Howard A. Gunn was the first black member of the Tenn-Tom Waterway Board of Directors. Gunn was also president of the Ministerial Institute and College, West Point, Mississippi.

Sources: *Jet* 53 (10 November 1977): 28.

1979 • Cain James Kennedy (1937–) was the first black appointed circuit judge in Alabama in this century. Kennedy was born in Thomaston, Alabama, and took his law degree at George Washington University in 1971.

Sources: *Jet* 57 (20 December 1979): 55; *Who's Who among Black Americans, 1992–93*, p. 813–14.

1980 • Oscar William Adams Jr. (1925–1997) was appointed to fill the remaining term of Justice James Bloodsworth, becoming the first black in the state's history to serve on the state supreme court. Two years later he was elected to the court, becoming the first black in Alabama's history elected to statewide office. In 1969 he founded Adams, Baker & Clemon, the first black law firm in Birmingham. After thirteen years on the bench, he retired on October 31, 1993. He was also the first black member of the Birmingham Bar Association. Adams grew up in Birmingham and graduated from Talladega College. He received his law degree from Howard University.

Sources: Bailey, *They Too Call Alabama Home,* pp. 6–9; *New York Times* (18 February 1997).

1983 • On May 24, 1983, Jesse L. Jackson (1941–) was the first black to address a joint session of the legislature in the twentieth century.

Sources: *Negro Almanac,* p. 86.

1984 • Jackie Walker was the first black woman tax collector in Dallas County.

Sources: *Jet* 67 (29 October 1984): 18.

1992 • Earl Frederick Hilliard (1942–) was the first black elected to the U.S. House of Representatives since Reconstruction. In 1974 he chaired the first Black Legislative Caucus in the state. The Birmingham native graduated from Morehouse College in 1964, Howard University School of Law in 1967, and Atlanta University School of Business in 1970. After serving as assistant to the president at Alabama State University in 1968–70, he became a partner in the law firm Pearson & Hilliard in 1972–73. He served as a state representative in Alabama from 1970 to 1972 and state senator from 1980 to 1992. He was elected to the U.S. House of Representatives in 1992 and re-elected in 1994, 1996, and 1998.

Earl Hilliard

Sources: *Contemporary Black Biography,* vol. 24, pp. 82–84; *Encyclopedia of African-American Culture and History,* Supplement, pp. 130–31; *Who's Who among African Americans,* 26th ed., p. 585.

1993 • Birmingham judge Ralph D. Cook, the first black circuit court judge in the Tenth Judicial Circuit (Bessemer), was appointed a justice on the state supreme court. Cook replaced Oscar William Adams Jr., who retired from the bench on October 31 this year. The state legislature created the tenth circuit along with another new district judgeship when it reapportioned Jefferson County. Cook previously served as a district court and family court judge. He graduated from Tennessee State University and the Howard University School of Law.

Sources: *Jet* 85 (6 December 1993): 26; Bailey, *They Too Call Alabama Home,* p. 90.

1994 • Willie Abner Alexander, commander of the 122nd Support Group in Selma, was promoted to brigadier general in the Alabama National Guard and became the first black to hold that position. Alexander's military career began in 1959; he served military police force units in Fort Bragg, North Carolina, and in Germany and Korea. A graduate of Alabama State, he joined the Alabama National Guard in 1972, and serve the guard continuously since then. He also worked as a senior auditor with AT&T in Atlanta, Georgia.

Sources: *Jet* 86 (3 October 1994): 36.

1999 • For the first time, the nine member state supreme court had two black justices serving concurrently. In this year Governor Don Siegelman appointed John Henry England Jr. to the court. England, a judge for the Sixth Judicial Circuit in Tuscaloosa County and the first black circuit judge in Tuscaloosa in the twentieth century, graduated from the University of Alabama School of Law. He was in private practice for twenty years and served on the Tuscaloosa City Council. The other black state justice, Ralph Cook, replaced black justice Oscar William Adams Jr., in 1993, when he retired.

Sources: *Jet* 96 (20 September 1999): 6; 85 (6 December 1993): 26.

2000 • David E. Gay Jr. was named director of Bryce Hospital in Tuscaloosa, becoming the first black director in the institution's 140-year history. The hospital, which also operates two nursing homes, was the largest state-run mental health facility. Gay previously served as director of Tuscaloosa's Taylor Harding Secure Medical Facility.

Sources: *Jet* 98 (13 November, 2000): 36.

Alaska

1959 • Mahala Ashley Dickerson (1912–2007) was admitted to the state bar and became the first black attorney in Alaska.

Sources: Bailey, *They Too Call Alabama Home,* pp. 115–16.

1960 • Blanche Preston McSmith was the first black state legislator.

Sources: *Ebony* 16 (March 1961): 148; 25 (November 1969): 132; Garrett, *Famous First Facts about Negroes,* p. 186.

1982 • Walt Furnace was the first black Republican elected to public office in the state. He was elected to the state legislature.

Sources: *Jet* 64 (23 May 1983): 21.

1993 • Larry D. Card (1948?–) was appointed a Superior Court judge, making him the first black judge in the state. The Kansas native served in the U.S. Air Force and in 1976 was assigned as U.S. Air Force attorney in Alaska. Before becoming judge, he did criminal defense work and had a mixed civil practice.

Sources: *Jet* 85 (29 November 1993): 39.

1995 • Nicholas Douglas was promoted from chief of the Division of Minerals in the Bureau of Land Management, Bakersfield, California, to district manager of the bureau in the Anchorage District. He was the first black to hold the position.

Sources: *Jet* 88 (3 July 1995): 21.

Arizona

1967 • Cloves C. Campbell (1931–) was the first black elected to the state senate.

Sources: *Encyclopedia of Black America,* p. 234.

1980 • Cecil Booker Patterson Jr. (1941–) was the first black to sit on the Maricopa County Superior Court. He held the post until 1991. He later served as chief counsel in the Human Services Division of the attorney general's office. From 1995 to 2003 he held a seat on the Arizona Court of Appeals. Patterson was born in Newport News, Virginia, and graduated from Hampton University. He took his law degree at Arizona State University in 1971.

Sources: *Jet* 59 (4 December 1980): 4; *Who's Who among African Americans,* 26th ed., p. 968.

Arkansas

1919? • Scipio Africanus Jones (1863?–1943) was the first black lawyer to handle a major case for the NAACP in a Southern state—the appeal process of twelve blacks sentenced to death for the Elaine, Arkansas, riot of October 1919. In 1923 the U.S. Supreme Court, hearing the case *Moore v. Dempsey,* overturned the lower court's verdicts. In 2007, Jones was honored for his pioneering and activist work when the U.S. Post Office in Little Rock was renamed the Scipio A. Jones Post Office Building.

Sources: *Encyclopedia of Black America,* pp. 500, 618; *Jet* 112 (15 October 2007): 25; Logan and Winston, *Dictionary of American Negro Biography,* pp. 368–69; *Negro Almanac,* pp. 314–15; *Negro Year Book,* 1921–22, pp. 78–79; Smith, *Notable Black American Men,* pp. 660–61.

1987 • George Hammons was the first black appointed to the state racing commission. Hammons is a professor at Philander Smith College, Little Rock. The state position is unsalaried and has a five-year term.

Sources: *Jet* 71 (16 February 1987): 17.

1988 • Kathleen Bell, Jesse L. Kearney (1950–), and Joyce Williams Warren (1949–) were the first blacks appointed to circuit chancery judgeships to oversee the juvenile division. These were newly established positions. Warren was the first black woman judge in Pulaski County, and Bell was the first black in the First Judicial District.

Sources: *Jet* 77 (9 October 1989): 22; *Who's Who among African Americans,* 26th ed., p. 713 (Kearney), p. 1286 (Warren).

1988 • Tommy Sproles was the first black chair of the state Game and Fish Commission. The Little Rock businessman became the first black on the commission when he was appointed to a seven-year term in 1983.

Sources: *Jet* 76 (11 September 1989): 47.

1988 • Joyce Williams Warren (1949–) was the first black to chair the state board of law examiners. Warren became a county judge in 1983, and a state judge in 1989. She received her law degree at the University of Arkansas at Little Rock in 1976. She was an administrative assistant to Governor Bill Clinton in from 1979 to 81.

Sources: *Jet* 77 (15 January 1990): 38; *Who's Who among African Americans,* 26th ed., p. 1286.

1990 • Lottie H. Shackelford (1941–) was the first black chair of the state Democratic Party. A native of Little Rock, Shackelford was executive director of the Urban League of Greater Little Rock from 1973 to 1978. At the time of her selection, she was serving on the Arkansas Regional Minority Council. She was also the first woman elected mayor of Little Rock in 1987. She graduated from Philander Smith College in 1979 and was a fellow in the John F. Kennedy School of Government at Harvard University in 1983.

Sources: *Jet* 71 (9 February 1987): 57; 78 (30 April 1990): 33; *Who's Who among African Americans,* 26th ed., p. 1111.

1991 • Daniel Terry Blue Jr. (1949–) was the first black speaker of the state house of representatives, and thus the first black speaker in any Southern state since Reconstruction. Born in Dillon, South Carolina, Blue graduated from North Carolina Central University and received his law degree from Duke University. He was organizer of the first successful effort to desegregate Woolworth's, the bus depot, and other facilities in Orangeburg in 1959–60.

Sources: *Jet* 79 (21 January 1991): 27; *State of Black America, 1992,* p. 364; *Who's Who among African Americans,* 26th ed., p. 113.

1993 • Jerry Donal Jewell (1930–) was the first black to serve as governor of Arkansas. A dentist and the president pro tempore of the state senate, Jewell held the post for three days, as Governor Jim Guy Tucker attended the presidential inauguration of former governor Bill Clinton.

Sources: *Jet* 83 (8 February 1993): 22–23.

California

1919 • Frederick Madison Roberts (1880–1952) was the first black to serve in the California legislature. Reputedly a great-grandson of Thomas Jefferson and Sally Hemings, Roberts was born in Ohio and moved to California while young. He became a mortician and the publisher of the *New Age.* He held his seat until he was defeated in 1934, by a black Democrat, Augustus F. Hawkins.

Sources: Logan and Winston, *Dictionary of American Negro Biography,* pp. 526–27; *Encyclopedia of Black America,* p. 83.

Frederick Madison Roberts

1944 • Doris E. Spears was the first black woman deputy sheriff in the United States.

Sources: Lee, *Interesting People,* p. 19.

1946 • In January 1946 Pauli Murray became the first black deputy attorney general of California. Due to illness, she held the position only briefly.

Sources: Hine, *Black Women in America,* pp. 825–26; *Encyclopedia of Black America,* p, 584; Lee, *Interesting People,* p. 83; Smith, *Notable Black American Women,* pp. 783–88.

1966 • Carlton Goodlett (1914–1997) became the first black American since Reconstruction to mount a serious candidacy for the governorship of California. He was a physician and newspaper publisher who used his power to campaign for civil rights. Born in Chipley, Florida, Goodlett graduated from Howard University and became one of the first blacks to receive a doctorate in psychology from the University of California at Berkeley. He taught for a few years and then studied medicine at Meharry Medical College in Nashville, Tennessee, graduating in 1944. The next year he established a general private practice in San Francisco and used his earning to buy a tiny weekly handout called *The Reporter.* He merged the paper with its rival, *The Sun* to form the weekly *Sun-Reporter.* He built the paper into the Reporter Publishing Company and issued nine weeklies. He became an influential voice in the Democratic Party; in 1966 Goodlett announced his intent to run for governor of California. He faced Democratic incumbent Edmund G. "Pat" Brown" who was challenged by the Republican Ronald Reagan.

Sources: *New York Times* Obituaries (2 February 1997).

1967 • Yvonne Watson Braithwaite Burke (1932–) was the first black woman elected to the state assembly. In 1993 she became the first black on the powerful Los Angeles County Board of Supervisors. She was later named chair of that five-member team.

Sources: *Encyclopedia of Black America,* pp. 199–200; *Jet* 70 (14 July 1986): 14; Smith, *Notable Black American Women,* pp. 130–32; Smith, *Notable Black American Women,* pp. 130–32; *Who's Who among African Americans,* 26th ed., p. 181.

1974 • Mervyn M. Dymally (1926–) was the first black to be elected lieutenant governor of California on November 5, 1972. Dymally was an educator who had served in the assembly and senate since 1963. In 1980 he was elected to the U.S. House of Representatives.

Sources: *Ebony* 29 (January 1974): 37; 30 (March 1975): 128; *Ebony Success Library,* vol. 1, p. 102; *Who's Who among African Americans,* 26th ed., p. 368.

1977 • Wiley E. Manuel (1928–) was the first black state supreme court judge.

Sources: *Ebony* 33 (March 1978): 25; *Jet* 51 (10 March 1977): 45.

1978 • Florence Stroud was the first black, the first woman, and the first non-physician to head the California Board of Medical Quality.

Sources: *Jet* 53 (9 February 1978): 18.

1978 • Diane Edith Watson (1933–) was the first black woman elected to the state senate. She held the post from 1978 to 1998. Born in Los Angeles, Watson received a doctorate in educational administration from Claremont College in 1976 and worked in the Los Angeles United School District from 1956 to 1975, when she became a member of the Board of Education. She later became ambassador to Micronesia. Watson was successful in her bid for public office again in 2001 and was sworn in as the fifteenth black woman member of the U.S. House of Representatives. She replaced Julian Dixon who died on December 8, 2000, and who represented the Thirty-second Congressional District. Then the House had the largest number of black women ever elected to the body.

Sources: *Jet* 59 (19 February 1981): 21; 100 (25 June 2001): 30; *Who's Who among African Americans,* 26th ed., p. 1298.

Diane Watson

California's First Black Highway Patrol Officer

In 1942 Homer Garrott (1915?–1998) became California's first black highway patrol officer. For thirteen years he remained the only black on the force. He spent a number of years on motorcycle duty. From 1964 to 1967 Garrott was a deputy public defender and from 1967 to 1968 a Juvenile Court referee. He was a Los Angeles Municipal Court commissioner from 1968 to 1973, until Governor Ronald Reagan named him to the Compton Municipal Court. He retired in 1984.

Sources: *New York Times* Obituaries (20 March 1998).

1980 • Willie Lewis Brown Jr. (1934–) became the first black speaker of the California State Assembly. Brown was born in Texas and took his law degree in 1958. He was first elected to the assembly in 1964. He has been active in both state and national politics.

Sources: *Contemporary Black Biography,* vol. 7, pp. 27–31; *Ebony Success Library,* vol. 1, p. 47; *Jet* 59 (18 December 1980): 5; *Who's Who among African Americans,* 26th ed. p. 168.

1982 • Democrat Thomas Bradley (1917–1998) was the first black nominated by a major party as a candidate for governor. He was narrowly defeated in the election, losing to state attorney general George Deukmejian.

Sources: *Contemporary Black Biography,* vol. 20, pp. 25–28; *Negro Almanac,* p. 428; Smith, *Notable Black American Men,* pp. 104–8; *Who's Who among Black Americans, 1992–93,* p. 144

1983 • Raymond L. Johnson (1936–) was the first black chief of the southern district of the California Highway Patrol. Before joining the highway patrol, he worked in the Bakersfield police department. He later served as chief of the Inglewood police department and as executive director of the Office of Criminal Justice and Planning. Johnson was born in Arkansas and educated at California State University in Sacramento.

Sources: *Jet* 64 (27 June 1983): 21; *Who's Who among African Americans,* 26th ed., p. 678.

1983 • Charles E. Bell (1947?–) became the first black chief sergeant–at–arms of a state legislature. He held the position until 1996. A native of Dayton, Ohio, he was a scholar and athlete at Sacramento State College, where he graduated with a bachelor's and a master's degree.

Sources: *Jet* 89 (1 April 1996): 5.

1992 • Willie L. Williams (1943–) became the first black police chief in Los Angeles, on July 1, 1992. This was the nation's third-largest police force. Born in Philadelphia, he received a bachelor's degree from the Philadelphia College of Textiles and Science and later a master's degree from St. Joseph's University. He has a certificate of police administration from Northwestern University, a certificate from Harvard University's Police Executive Research Forum, and certificates from other training programs he has attended. His career includes a variety of law enforcement positions in Philadelphia as he rose through the ranks to become police detective, police captain and commander, and, immediately before leaving for Los Angeles, police commissioner. He moved to Los Angeles after the nationally publicized beating of Rodney King in March 1991 eroded public confidence in law enforcement in that city. Williams moved swiftly to counter wide claims of police brutality and to improve relations between the police force and citizens. After serving a five-year term, a storm of controversy arose in 1997 when the Los Angeles Police Commission denied him a second term.

Sources: *Jet* 91 (31 March 1997): 39; *Contemporary Black Biography,* vol. 4, pp. 278–81; *Who's Who among African Americans,* 26th ed., p. 1356.

1996 • Janice Rogers Brown (1950?–), a political conservative and California Court of Appeals judge since 1994, was appointed to the California Supreme Court, making her the first black woman to serve on the highest court in the state. Brown received her bachelor's degree from California State University in Sacramento in 1974 and a law degree from the University of California, Los Angeles in 1977. In 1987 she was appointed deputy secretary general counsel for the California Business, Transportation and Housing Agency. From 1979 to 1987 Brown was deputy attorney general for California's Department of Justice. From 1991 to 1994 she was legal affairs secretary to Governor Pete Wilson, who appointed her to her post on the high court.

Sources: *Jet* 89 (29 April 1996): 36–37; *Who's Who among African Americans,* 26th ed., p. 158.

1996 • Willard H. Murray, state assemblyman from the Fifty-second Assembly District and serving his third consecutive term, swore in his son Kevin Murray to represent the Forty-seventh Assembly District. The two were the first father and son members to serve in the same assembly in the history of the state.

Sources: *Jet* 88 (6 December 1994–2 January 1995): 38.

2008 • Los Angeles lawmaker Karen Bass became the first black woman, the first Democratic woman, and the sixty-seventh person elected speaker of the California State Assembly. Her post is recognized as the second most powerful position in the state's government. In 2004, Bass was elected to the eighty-member chamber. She is recognized for writing legislation to support child welfare and social justice.

Sources: *Jet* 113 (25 March 2008): 16; 113 (2 June 2008): 20.

Karen Bass

2010 • Kamala Devi Harris (1964–) became Attorney General-elect for California, becoming the first woman as well as the first black and Indian American elected to that post. Harris was deputy district attorney in Alameda County (1990–98) and in August 2000 became managing attorney of the Career Criminal Unit, Office of the San Francisco District Attorney. Born in Oakland to a Jamaican father and Indian mother, Harris was raised in Berkeley. Both parents were active in the Civil Rights Movement and instilled in their daughter a strong commitment to justice and public service. She received her bachelor's degree from Howard University in 1986. In 1989, she received her Juris Doctor from the University of California's Hastings College of Law. In 2006, Howard gave her its Outstanding Alumni Award "for extraordinary work in fields of law and public service." Harris is included in *Newsweek's* America's 20 Most Powerful Women. *Ebony* magazine and the *New York Times* named her one of seventeen most likely to become the nation's first female president.

Sources: *Howard University News* (17 December 2010).

Colorado

1956 • George L. Brown (1926–2006) was the first black elected to the state senate. In 1969 Brown became the first executive director of the Metro-Denver Urban Coalition. In 1974 he became the first black elected lieutenant governor of the state. George L. Brown and Mervyn Dymally of California were both elected lieutenant governor of their states on the same day in 1974. After 1979 his career was primarily as a business executive for the Grumman Corporation.

Sources: *Ebony* 30 (March 1975): 129; 33 (October 1978): 91; *Ebony Success Library,* vol. 1, p. 44; *Encyclopedia of Black America,* p. 194; *Who's Who among African Americans,* 13th ed., p. 156.

1985 • The first black to serve as presiding judge of Denver County Court was Robert L. Patterson (1945–). Patterson was born in Detroit and received his bachelor's degree from Colorado State University and law degree from the University of Colorado. He directed the black education program at the University of Colorado and later served at Colorado State University as assistant director of Project Go. He became a staff attorney for the Legal Aid

Society then an attorney for the Colorado Public Defender's office. Patterson was assistant federal defender for the Federal Public Defender and the assistant attorney general for Colorado until he became presiding judge.

Sources: *Jet* 93 (16 February 1998): 40; *Who's Who among African Americans,* 26th ed., p. 970.

1991 • Gregory K. Scott was the first black named to the Colorado Supreme Court, a post he assumed in January 1992. A native of California and holder of a law degree from Indiana University, Scott was a law professor at the University of Denver.

Sources: *Jet* 82 (5 October 1992): 28.

1994 • Victoria "Vikki" Buckley (1947–1999) rose from the welfare rolls to become the first black woman in Colorado to hold a statewide office and the first black woman to become Colorado's secretary of state. She was also the highest-ranking Republican woman in a statewide office. Born in Denver, Buckley received an associate's degree from Sieble School of Drafting and Engineering in 1968 and attended the University of Colorado and Metropolitan State College, both in Denver. She was a draftsperson for Humble Oil (1969–70), director of Opportunities Industrialization (1971–73), and office manager with Public Service Careers (1973–74). From 1974 to 1994 Buckley was an administrative officer in the Colorado Secretary of State's office, and then became secretary of state. She was elected to a second term and sworn in office in January 1999. She died of a heart attack on July 13, 1999, at age fifty-one.

Sources: *Contemporary Black Biography,* vol. 24, pp. 25–27; *Jet* 94 (23 November 1998): 13; *New York Times* (15 July 1999).

1995 • Claudia J. Jordan was sworn in as a member of the Denver County Court Bench making her the first black woman judge in the city. Jordan was a noted local attorney in private practice. A member of the Colorado Bar Association and the Sam Carey Bar Association, she is in Colorado's Black Hall of Fame.

Sources: *Jet* 88 (5 June 1995): 22; *Who's Who among African Americans,* 26th ed., p. 705.

1997 • A captain with the Denver Sheriff's Department, Carlos Jackson was promoted to major and became the highest ranking black in the department as well as the first black to hold the post. He was placed in charge of the Internal Affairs Bureau at the department.

Sources: *Jet* 91 (13 January 1997): 20; *Who's Who among African Americans,* 26th ed., p. 634.

1998 • Joe Rogers, a lawyer, was elected lieutenant governor and became the first black to hold that post in the state. He was elected on the Republican ticket with white gubernatorial candidate Bill Owens.

Sources: *Jet* 94 (23 November 1998): 12.

Connecticut

1980 • Carrie Saxon Perry (1931–) was the first black woman elected to the state legislature.

Sources: *Negro Almanac,* pp. 430–31; *Notable Black American Women,* pp. 837–40; *Who's Who among African Americans,* 12th ed., p. 1037.

1987 • Robert Davis Glass (1922–2001) became the first black member of the state supreme court. He achieved several other firsts as well. In 1962 he set up practice in Waterbury, becoming the state's first black lawyer. He was the state's first black, full-time prosecutor. He was the first black assistant U.S. attorney in the district of Connecticut from 1966 to 1967. In 1967 he was named a Juvenile Court judge, the first black to hold that post in the state. He was a Superior Court judge for the Waterbury Judicial District from 1984 to 1987. Glass was associate justice for the Connecticut Supreme Court in 1987 until he retired in 1992. The son of a farmhand and a domestic worker, Glass was born in Wetumpka, Alabama. He received his bachelor's degree in 1949 and his law degree in 1951, both from North Carolina Central University in Durham.

Sources: *Who's Who among African Americans*, 13th ed., p. 479.

1991 • Joseph Perry Jr. became the first black commander of the Connecticut State Police.

Sources: *State of Black America, 1993*, p. 275.

Delaware

1901 • The first black to win public office in Delaware was Thomas Postles. He was elected to the Wilmington City Council this year.

Sources: Salzman, *Encyclopedia of African-American Culture and History*, vol. 2, p. 741.

1947 • William J. Winchester became the first black elected to the Delaware General Assembly.

Sources: Salzman, *Encyclopedia of African-American Culture and History*, vol. 2, p. 741.

1964 • Herman M. Holloway, Sr. (1922–1994) was the first black to serve in the Delaware Senate. A native of Wilmington, Holloway was a building inspector and had long been active in politics. In 1963 he served in the house, filling an unexpired term. He is a graduate of Hampton Institute (now Hampton University).

Sources: *Ebony Success Library*, vol. 1, p. 154; *Who's Who among African Americans*, 14th ed., p. 610.

1970 • Henrietta Johnson (1914?–1997) became the first black woman elected to the general assembly in Delaware. She died in Wilmington at age eighty-three.

Sources: *Jet* 91 (17 November 1997): 18.

1994 • Margaret R. Henry became the first black woman state senator in Delaware. In a special election, she won the seat left open when the state's first black senator, Herman M. Holloway, died.

Sources: *Jet* 86 (23 May 1994): 18.

1995 • Janet K. Smith became the first black woman captain in the Police Department of New Castle County, Delaware. She had been with the department since 1973 and was promoted from lieutenant to the higher rank.

Sources: *Jet* 88 (3 July 1995): 21; *Who's Who among African Americans*, 26th ed., p. 1147.

Florida

1897 • James Weldon Johnson (1871–1938) passed the Florida bar; this may be the first time in Duval County or in Florida that a black sought admission to the Florida bar through open examination in a state court. Johnson and a friend from childhood, Judson Douglass Wetmore, practiced law in Florida from 1898 to 1901.

Sources: Johnson, *Along This Way*, pp. 142–43; Smith, *Notable Black American Men*, pp. 626–30.

1968 • In November 1968, Joe Lang Kershaw became the first black elected to the Florida legislature in the twentieth century.

Sources: Hornsby, *Chronology of African-American History*, p. 134.

1970 • Gwendolyn Sawyer Cherry (1923–1979) was the first black woman in the state legislature. Cherry taught in the Dade County schools for eighteen years. When the Uni-

Florida's First Black Justice

On September 2, 1975, Joseph Woodrow Hatchett (1932-) was sworn in as the first black state supreme court justice in the South since Reconstruction. Hatchett graduated from Florida Agricultural and Mechanical College (now Florida A & M University) and served two years in the army. He graduated from Howard University School of Law and later was named assistant U.S. attorney in Jacksonville. He served as a U.S. magistrate for the Middle District of Florida and was later appointed to the state supreme court. When he was re-elected to that court, he became the first black elected to a statewide office since Reconstruction. In 1979 President Jimmy Carter named him to the Fifth U.S. Court of Appeals.

Sources: *Jet* 88 (4 September 1995): 19.

versity of Miami's law school opened to blacks, she attended and became a lawyer. She also worked for the Coast Guard. Cherry was killed in an automobile accident during her fourth term.

Sources: *Ebony Success Library,* vol. 1, p. 65; *Essence* 4 (March 1974): 20; *Jet* 55 (1 March 1979): 18; Lee, *Interesting People,* p. 130.

1979 • Wallace E. Orr was the first black secretary of labor in the state. He had served as president of the Florida Education Association.

Sources: *Jet* 56 (26 April 1979): 11.

1982 • Carrie Meek (1926–) was the first black state senator since Reconstruction. A graduate of Florida Agricultural and Mechanical University, Meek served in the state house for three years.

Sources: *Jet* 62 (23 August 1982): 27; *Notable Black American Women,* Book II, pp. 467–70; *Contemporary Black Biography,* vol. 6, pp. 192–95.

1982 • Cynthia Reese, a resident of Riviera Beach, was the first black woman state trooper.

Sources: *Jet* 61 (15 February 1982): 39.

1982 • By gaining the position of county judge in Miami, Leah Simms became the first black woman state judge. Simms holds a law degree from Willamette University Law School and has served as assistant state's attorney and assistant U.S. attorney for Southern Florida.

Sources: *Jet* 61 (4 February 1982): 22.

1990 • Leander J. Shaw Jr., (1930–) was the first black state supreme court chief justice and the first black to head any branch of government in Florida. Shaw was first appointed to the court in 1983. Shaw was born in Salem, Virginia, and graduated from West Virginia State College in 1952. He took his law degree at Howard University in 1957. He had wide experience in government service and private practice at the time of his selection.

Sources: *Jet* 77 (2 April 1990): 8; 78 (23 July 1990): 33; *Who's Who among African Americans,* 26th ed., p. 1115.

1995 • Nat Glover (1943–) won a landslide victory over two white opponents to become the first black sheriff in Florida. He won in Jacksonville where blacks comprise only twenty-five percent of a population of 700,000. Glover had served on the police force for twenty-nine years, having taken charge of the consolidated force for Duval County and Jacksonville.

Sources: *Jet* 88 (17 July 1995): 24; *Who's Who among African Americans,* 26th ed., p. 470.

1997 • Thirty-three-year-old Julia L. Johnson (1963–) became the youngest elected chairman of the Florida Public Service Commission (PSC) and the first black woman to serve on the commission. The commission regulates the state's $15 billion utility district. Born in Clermont, Florida, Johnson graduated from the University of Florida with a bachelor's degree and three years later with a law degree. She was an associate with the law firm Maguire, Voorhis and Wells, and assistant general counsel for the Department of Community Affairs. Then she became director of legislative affairs. She became a PSC commissioner in 1993.

Sources: *Jet* 91 (24 February 1997): 19; *Who's Who among African Americans,* 26th ed., pp. 672–73.

2002 • The first black fire chief to head the Miami-Dade Fire Rescue Department was Charles U. Phillips, a twenty-eight-year veteran of the department. He was previously deputy director for operations and interim fire chief, overseeing a staff of nearly 1,900.

Sources: *Jet* 101 (22 April 2002): 19.

2008 • Justice Peggy A. Quince (1948–) became the first black woman to be Chief Justice of the Florida Supreme Court or any branch of the state's government. On December 8, she was jointly appointed by the outgoing and incoming governors, Lawson Chiles and Jeb Bush, respectively. A Norfolk, Virginia native, Quince attended Virginia's racially-segregated schools. She is a graduate of Howard University and earned her Juris Doctorate from Columbus School of Law at the Catholic University of America. She left office in 2010 and has received numerous awards. Her appointment to the 2nd Court of Appeals in 1993 made her the first black woman to serve in any appellate court in Florida.

Peggy A. Quince

Sources: *Contemporary Black Biography,* vol. 69, pp. 123–25; *Jet* 113 (14 April 2008): 14; *Who's Who among African Americans,* 26th ed., p. 2021.

2011 • The fall 2010 midterm elections put many Republicans in political power, among them unprecedented numbers of African Americans, including Lt. Governor-elect Jennifer Carroll (1959–), the first black woman and the first woman elected to that post. She took office on January 4, 2011. A member of the Clay County Republican Committee, Carroll was unsuccessful in two previous bids for the U.S. House of Representatives. In 2003 she won a special election, becoming the first black woman Republican elected to the state's legislature. Born in Port of Spain, Trinidad, Carroll moved to the United States when she was eight years old. After high school, Carroll enlisted in the U.S. Navy and in 1985 became an Aviation Maintenance Officer. She spent twenty years in the U.S. Navy before retiring as Lieutenant Commander. Then she received an A.A. degree from Leeward Community College, a B.A. degree from the University of New Mexico, and an M.B.A. degree from St. Leo University. Married and the mother of three, her son, Nolan, is a member of the Miami Dolphins professional football team.

Jennifer Carroll

Sources: *Jet* 118 (27 December 2010–3 January 2011): 12–14.

Georgia

1964 • On February 4, 1964, Austin T. Walden (1885–1965) became the first black judge in the state since Reconstruction. He was a municipal judge in Atlanta. Walden obtained a law degree from the University of Michigan in 1911, and was admitted to the Georgia bar the following year. He began his law practice in Atlanta in 1919.

Sources: *Chronology of African-American History,* p. 117; *Negro Digest* 8 (August 1950): 65–69. *Who's Who in America, 1966–1967,* p. 2214.

1967 • Grace Towns Hamilton (1907–1992) was the first black woman in the state legislature and became known as "The Lady from Fulton." She lost her bid for reelection in 1984. A native of Atlanta, Georgia, she graduated from Atlanta University in 1927 and received her master's degree from The Ohio State University in 1929. Hamilton was active in social work and from 1943 to 1960 was executive director of the Atlanta Urban League.

She worked through the Urban League to establish a hospital for nonindigent blacks and a training program for doctors and nurses, resulting in the development of West Side Health Center that opened in September 1944. She also worked through the league to find housing for veterans by surveying and locating land. Her work resulted in the construction of the High Point Apartments in 1950, the Carver Public Housing Development in 1953, the Perry Homes in 1955, and new single–family housing in 1955.

Sources: *Encyclopedia of Black America,* p. 413; *Notable Black American Women,* pp. 444–48; *Who's Who among Black Americans, 1992–93,* p. 587.

1967 • James Edward Dearing (1935?–1995) became the first black special agent for the Georgia Bureau of Investigation. In this year he also became one of the first black officers in the Savannah Police Department, where he remained until 1972. Then he became chief of police and director of safety at Georgia State University in Atlanta. He strengthened the force at Georgia State, moving it from a security force to a full-fledged police force. For many years Dearing was a member of the Georgia Police Officers Standards and Training Council.

Sources: *Jet* 88 (23 October 1995): 18.

1969 • Edith Jacqueline Ingram-Grant (1942–) was the first black woman judge in the state, when she became a judge of the Hancock County Court of Ordinary. In 1973 she became judge in that county's probate court. Ingram-Grant was born in Hancock County, Georgia, near Sparta, and graduated from Fort Valley State College (now Fort Valley State University) in 1963. She taught in public schools in Griffin and in Sparta, Georgia.

Sources: *Encyclopedia of Black America,* p. 463; *Notable Black American Women,* p. 553; *Who's Who among African Americans,* 14th ed., p. 644.

1977 • Horace T. Ward (1927–) was the first black to serve on the Fulton County Superior Court. Ward was born in La Grange, Georgia, and received his bachelor's degree from Morehouse College in Atlanta, a master's degree from Atlanta University, and his law degree from Northwestern University in 1959. He was elected to the Georgia State Senate in 1964. Ward was a civil court judge from 1974 to 1977, before joining the Superior Court. In 1979 he became a U.S. District Court judge.

Sources: *Ebony* 20 (September 1965): 50; *Jet* 46 (30 May 1974): 5; Hornsby, *Chronology of Black-American History,* pp. 296–97; *Who's Who among African Americans,* 26th ed., p. 1282.

1982 • Charles S. Johnson was the first black member of the Georgia Board of Bar Examiners. In 1987 Johnson became the first black chair of the organization.

Sources: *Jet* 63 (20 December 1982): 46; 72 (13 July 1987): 20.

1984 • Robert Benham (1946–) was the first black named to the state court of appeals. In 1989 Benham became the first black state supreme court justice. A native of Cartersville, Georgia, he graduated from Tuskegee Institute (now Tuskegee University) in 1967 and took his law degree at the University of Georgia in 1970. In 1990 he received his master of laws degree from the University of Virginia. He has served as president of the Cartersville Bar Association.

Sources: *Jet* 66 (23 April 1984): 12; 77 (25 December 1989): 6; *Who's Who among African Americans,* 26th ed., p. 91.

1985 • Gloria Butler was the first black and first woman to chair the state Campaign and Financial Disclosure Commission. Butler was executive director of Augusta Opportunities Industrialization Center. Before her election, she served as vice-chair of the state commission.

Sources: *Jet* 69 (30 September 1985): 37.

1985 • Clarence Cooper (1942–) was the first black to serve on the state supreme court in the twentieth century when he temporarily filled in for a sitting judge. Cooper became associate judge of the Atlanta Municipal Court in 1979 and later a superior court judge in

Georgia's First Black Legislator

In 1962 Leroy Reginald Johnson (1928–) was the first black elected to a southern legislature since Reconstruction. He represented Fulton County's Thirty-eighth District and served for twelve years. Johnson received his master's degree in 1951 and a law degree in 1957. He taught in the Atlanta Public School System from 1950 to 1954, and was a criminal investigator for the solicitor general's staff, Fifth Judicial District in Atlanta, from 1957 to 1962.

Sources: *Encyclopedia of Black America*, p. 475; Hornsby, *Chronology of African-American History*, pp. 113, 249; *Ebony* 18 (March 1963): 25–28; 30 (January 1975): 35; *Who's Who among African Americans*, 14th ed., p. 695.

Fulton County. He was later named U.S. District Court judge for the Northern District of Georgia.

Sources: *Jet* 68 (29 April 1985): 4; *Who's Who among African Americans*, 26th ed., p. 270.

1985 • Thelma Wyatt-Cummings Moore (1945–) was the first black woman appointed judge in the State Court of Fulton County, a position that she held until 1990. In 1998 she became the first black woman judge on Fulton County's Superior Court. Moore was born in Amarillo, Texas, and graduated from the University of California in 1965. She received her law degree from the Emory Institution School of Law in 1971 and had become a judge on the Municipal Court of Atlanta in 1977, a position she held until 1980. She serves on the board of directors for the National Center for State Courts.

Sources: *Jet* 68 (8 July 1985): 37; 94 (27 July 1998): 53; *Who's Who among African Americans*, 26th ed., pp. 899–900.

1988 • Thomas Edison Brown Jr. (1952–) was the first black director of public safety in DeKalb County. Brown began his career with the Atlanta Fire Bureau in 1972 and became fire chief of DeKalb County in 1985. Brown was born in Atlanta and was trained in emergency medical service and in fire science at DeKalb Community College in Clarkston, Georgia. He then attended the Brenau Professional College in Gainesville.

Sources: *Who's Who among Black Americans*, 26th ed., p. 166.

1990 • Glenda Hatchett (1951–) was appointed judge of Fulton County Juvenile Court, becoming Georgia's first black chief presiding judge of a state court. She stepped down in 1999 and later starred on the syndicated television series *Judge Hatchett*.

Sources: *Jet* 100 (22 October 2001): 18; *Who's Who among African Americans*, 26th ed., p. 553.

1991 • Paul Lawrence Howard Jr. (1951–) was the first black to be elected Fulton County solicitor. He has held a number of positions in Fulton County, including deputy solicitor for the City of Atlanta's municipal court and assistant district attorney. Howard was born in Waynesboro, Georgia, and is a graduate of Morehouse College. He holds a law degree from Emory University.

Sources: *Jet* 83 (27 December 1992): 28; *Who's Who among African Americans*, 26th ed., p. 610.

1992 • Jacquelyn "Jackie" H. Barrett (1950–) was the first black woman to be elected sheriff, winning the Fulton County post on November 3. Barrett had sixteen years' experience in law enforcement; as sheriff she supervised more than seven hundred employees. Barrett was born in Charlotte, North Carolina, and received a degree in criminal justice from Beaver College in Pennsylvania. She later received a master's degree in sociology from Clark Atlanta University. Barrett was a member of the Georgia Officers Standards and Training Council from 1976 to 1985. She was chief administrative officer in the sheriff's office from 1985 to 1987. She directed the county's Public Safety Training Center from 1987 to 1992. Her election in 1992 signaled a major change in the image of a typical law enforcement officer in the South. Under her administration the sheriff's office provided security for a Democratic National Convention and the 1996 Summer Olympics.

Sources: *Jet* 83 (23 November 1992): 58–59; (11 January 1993): 18; *Contemporary Black Biography*, vol. 28, pp. 11–13; *Who's Who among African Americans*, 26th ed., p. 71.

1992 • M. Yvette Miller became the first woman director and judge of the appellate division of the State Board of Worker's Compensation.

Sources: *Jet* 97 (10 January 2000): 37.

1992 • The first woman and the second black to serve on the Georgia Supreme Court was Leah J. Sears-Collins (1955–). She was first appointed to the seat, but in the same year she won a permanent seat in a statewide election. She was born in Heidelberg, Germany, while her father was stationed there in the U.S. Army. She graduated from Cornell University and received her law degree from Emory University. Sears-Collins served as a trial lawyer, judge on the Atlanta Traffic Court and in 1988 on the Fulton County Superior Court, the youngest person in Georgia to sit on that court.

Sources: *Contemporary Black Biography*, vol. 5, pp. 246–48; *Encyclopedia of African-American Culture and History*, vol. 2, p. 741; *Jet* 84 (25 October 1993): 10; *Who's Who among African Americans*, 14th ed., p. 1155.

1993 • Charles W. Walker Sr. became the first black senator elected chairman of the state Senate Democratic Caucus, the highest ranking black member of the caucus. On November 13, 1996, he was elected Senate Majority Leader, becoming the first black to hold that post. Walker is founder and president of the Walker Group in Atlanta.

Sources: *Jet* 20 (20 December 1993): 20; *Who's Who among African Americans*, 26th ed., p. 1270.

1994 • Karen Elaine Webster (1960–) became the first woman chief of staff for the Fulton County commissioner. Born in Atlanta, Webster graduated from the University of Virginia and Georgia State University. She has served Fulton County as law clerk and as executive assistant to the county manager.

Sources: *Jet* 86 (20 June 1994): 20; *Who's Who among African Americans*, 26th ed., p. 1306.

1994 • The first black politician in Georgia elected from a rural, white majority district since Reconstruction was Floyd Lee Griffin Jr. (1944–). Griffin was elected to the state senate representing the Twenty-fifth District (encompassing Baldwin County in east-central Georgia) about ninety miles south of Atlanta. He defeated Wilbur Baugh. He is a Milledgeville, Georgia, native and was educated at Tuskegee Institute (now University) and Florida Institute of Technology.

Sources: *Jet* 86 (19 September 1994): 6; *Who's Who among African Americans*, 26th ed., p. 501.

1995 • Sybil Carter Hadley became the first woman chairperson and chief registrar of the Fulton County Board of Elections and Registration in Atlanta. The Dallas native also served as senior associate attorney with the firm Swift, Currie, McGhee and Hiers.

Sources: *Jet* 88 (18 September 1995): 24; *Who's Who among African Americans*, 26th ed., p. 510.

1995 • The state supreme court unanimously elected Robert Benham (1946–) as chief justice, the first black to head the state's judiciary. He succeeded Chief Justice Willis B. Hunt Jr. who became a U.S. District Court judge. Benham was sworn in on July 29.

Sources: *Jet* 88 (26 June 1995): 4; *Who's Who among African Americans*, 26th ed., p. 91.

1995 • Garfield Hammonds Jr. became chairman of the Georgia State Board of Pardons and Paroles, the first black man to hold the post. He was appointed in 1995 and in the same year the board elected him chairman. He previously served in Drug Enforcement Administration and in the Department of Juvenile Services.

Sources: *Jet* 90 (22 July 1996): 32; *Who's Who among African Americans,* 26th ed., p. 522–23.

1996 • Charles W. Walker Sr. became the state's first black senate majority leader on November 13. With the election, he became the fourth highest elected official in Georgia. His responsibilities included sponsoring and working to help pass proposals recommended by the Democratic Caucus. He served on the Democratic Caucus Policy Committee as well as the Senate Administrative Affairs Committee, overseeing senate operations. Walker was also chief executive officer of The Walker Group, a consortium of service enterprises whose membership includes the *Augusta Focus* newspaper, Georgia Personnel Services, and other businesses.

Sources: *Jet* 91 (16 December 1996): 34; (17 March 1997): 19; *Who's Who among African Americans,* 26th ed., p. 1270.

1997 • Paul Lawrence Howard Jr. (1951–) became Georgia's first black elected district attorney. He had served as deputy solicitor in Atlanta's municipal court, as assistant district attorney for Fulton County, and now serves as district attorney for the state court.

Sources: *Jet* 91 (20 January 1997): 12; *Who's Who among African Americans,* 26th ed., p. 610.

1997 • Moses Ector became chief of staff of the Georgia Bureau of Investigation in Decatur, making him the highest-ranking black in the bureau and the first black to become chief. Formerly a bureau supervisor, he developed the Adopt–A–School program.

Sources: *Jet* 92 (6 October 1997): 20.

1997 • Governor Zell Miller appointed Thurbert E. Baker (1952–) to the post of attorney general, filling an unexpired term. The appointment made him the first black to hold that position in Georgia. Baker captured a full-term victory in the 1998 election. Baker was born in Rocky Mount, North Carolina, and received his bachelor's degree from the University of North Carolina at Chapel Hill and his law degree from Emory University. In 1998, Michael Thurmond also won the labor commissioner's race and became Georgia's first black labor commissioner. Thurmond and Thurbert E. Baker then became the first two blacks elected to office in a non–judicial statewide race in Georgia since Reconstruction.

Sources: *Jet* 94 (23 November 1993): 10; 92 (2 June 1997): 8; *Who's Who among African Americans,* 26th ed., p. 58 (Baker).

1998 • The first black to be named chaplain of the Georgia Bureau of Investigation in Decatur was Raleigh Rucker. He had been active in law enforcement and community projects in the Atlanta area and was chaplain of the Georgia State Patrol and the Georgia chapter of the national Organization of Black Law Enforcement Executives.

Sources: *Jet* 93 (16 February 1998): 38; *Who's Who among African Americans,* 26th ed., p. 1081.

1999 • Gwendolyn R. Keyes became the first black, the first woman, and, at thirty years old, the youngest person elected to the post as Solicitor General of DeKalb County. Her responsibilities included supervising and training twenty staff attorneys and thirty support personnel.

Sources: *Jet* 95 (15 February 1999): 19.

1999 • Penny Brown Reynolds was named chief executive counsel in the office of Georgia Governor Roy Barnes. She was the first black to hold the position. The former chief of staff in the lieutenant governor's office advises the governor on policy and legislative matters. She also works with state agencies on behalf of the governor.

Sources: *Jet* 95 (15 February 1999): 19.

2000 • State representative and telecommunications consultant Vernon Jones was elected the first black chief executive officer of DeKalb County, the second largest county in the state. The post is the county's top office. One of only three black county executives in the United States, Jones was successful in a runoff election against the incumbent, who had served eight years in the Georgia House.

Sources: *Jet* 98 (13 November 2000): 36.

2000 • The first black woman to serve on the state's Court of Appeals was M. Yvette Miller. Georgia governor Roy Barnes appointed her to the post. She began her legal career in the Fulton County State Court where she was a law clerk.

Sources: *Jet* 97 (10 January 2000): 37.

Illinois

1871 • John Jones (1816–1879) was the first black elected to public office in Cook County. A native of North Carolina and the son of a free black mother and a white father, Jones had been apprenticed to a tailor in Tennessee and came to Chicago in 1845. He was elected to a one-year term on the county board in 1871, to a three-year term in 1872, and defeated in 1875. No other black was elected to the board until Theodore W. Jones won in 1894.

Sources: Logan and Winston, *Dictionary of American Negro Biography,* pp. 366–67; Gosnell, *Negro Politicians,* pp. 81–82; *Chronology of African-American History,* pp. 37–38; Katz, *The Black West,* pp. 67–70.

1917 • James G. Cotter was the first black assistant attorney general in Illinois. Cotter, a graduate of Fisk University and the Illinois College of Law, entered private practice in 1919.

Sources: Gosnell, *Negro Politicians,* p. 213.

1920 • Violette Neatley Anderson (1882–1937) was the first black woman admitted to the Illinois bar. Born in London, England, Anderson received her law degree from the University of Chicago in 1920 and became the first woman assistant prosecutor in Chicago in 1922. She was the first black woman lawyer admitted to practice before the U.S. Supreme Court on January 29, 1926. She urged congressmen from Illinois to pass the Bankhead-Jones Bill in 1936. The bill aided black tenant farmers and sharecroppers in receiving low-interest loans to buy small farms. The bill passed in 1937.

Sources: Garrett, *Famous First Facts about Negroes,* p. 94; *Opportunity* 4 (March 1926): 107; Smith, *Notable Black American Women,* Book II, pp. 12–15; *Who's Who in Colored America,* pp. 13–14.

1924 • Adelbert H. Roberts was the first black elected to the Illinois Senate. Roberts was a native of Michigan who moved to Chicago early in the 1890s. After taking a law degree, he became a clerk for the municipal court. He took office on January 10, 1925, and held his senate position until 1934.

Sources: Clayton,*The Negro Politician,* p. 46; Gosnell, *Negro Politicians,* pp. 69–71; Hornsby, *Chronology of African-American History,* p. 75.

1947 • Edith Spurlock Sampson (1901–1979) became the first black woman named an assistant attorney for Cook County.

Sources: Schultz and Hast, *Women Building Chicago, 1790–1990,* pp. 775–78; Smith, *Notable Black American Women,* pp. 969–73.

1958 • Floy Clements was the first black woman elected to the Illinois legislature.

Sources: Clayton, *The Negro Politician,* p. 147.

1969 • Ralph Metcalf (1910–1978) became the first black elected to the post of president *pro tempore* of the Chicago City Council. He was a protégé of U.S. Representative William

Illinois's First Black State Appointment

In 1889 E. H. Wright was the first black to be appointed to a major state post when he became a bookkeeper and railroad incorporation clerk in the office of the secretary of state. In 1920 he became the first black ward committeeman in Chicago.

Sources: *Clayton, The Negro Politician,* pp. 46–48; *Gosnell, Negro Politicians,* pp. 153, 213.

Dawson and won Dawson's seat in 1970, when Dawson retired from Congress. Metcalf also was re-elected to Congress three times.

Sources: Smith, *Notable Black American Men,* pp. 803–6.

1970 • Ronald Townsel (1934–) was the first black superintendent of adult parole in Illinois. Townsel was a twelve-year veteran of the parole system, where he served first as a youth parole agent and later as state superintendent of adult parole. He had also served as a youth gang worker and a teacher in Chicago. He subsequently retired. Townsel was born in Chicago and received his bachelor's degree from at George Williams College and master's degree from Governors State University.

Sources: *Ebony Success Library,* vol. 1, p. 308; *Who's Who among African Americans,* 26th ed., p. 1242.

1971 • Dora B. Somerville (1920–1994) was the first black woman to hold the position of correctional programs administrator for the Illinois Department of Corrections. Somerville had a distinguished career in juvenile work and corrections, and was coauthor of *The Delinquent Girl* (1970). She received her bachelor's degree from Ursuline College in 1939, master's degree from Catholic University of America in 1942, and master's in social work from Loyola University in 1948. Before assuming the position with the Department of Corrections, she was the first woman member of the Illinois Parole and Pardon Board. Somerville was born in Greensboro, Alabama.

Sources: *Ebony Success Library,* vol. 1, p. 228; Obituary, *Who's Who among African Americans,* 9th ed., p. 1731.

Roland Wallace Burris

1978 • Roland Wallace Burris (1937–) was the first black elected to statewide office as comptroller of the state. In 1987 Burris became the first comptroller elected to three consecutive terms. He held the office until 1991, when he became state attorney general, the second black to hold such a position, and the first black Democrat. In 1963 he had also been the first black hired by the U.S. Treasury Department as a bank examiner. In 1977 he announced his bid for the Illinois Governor's seat. He made other important contributions to the state, notably the creation in 1992 of the Women's Advocacy Division in the Attorney General's Department. He also established a Children's Advocacy Division in 1993, a first for child abuse victims in the state. A civil rights advocate, Burris led a drive to create the Civil Rights Division in 1993. Burris was born in Centralia, Illinois, and earned a bachelor's degree in 1959 from Southern Illinois University. He did postgraduate studies as an exchange student at the University of Hamburg in West Germany. He earned his law degree from Howard University Law School in 1963.

Sources: *State of Black America, 1992,* pp. 360–61; *Who's Who among African Americans,* 26th ed., p. 185; *Notable Black American Men,* pp. 158–59; *Contemporary Black Biography,* vol. 25, pp. 37–39.

1979 • Agaliece Miller (1911?–1996) became the first woman and the first black administrator of the Illinois Department of Labor's Bureau of Employment Security. She held the post until 1982.

Sources: *Jet* 91 (2 December 1996): 16.

1980 • Joyce Tucker was the first black woman to serve in the state cabinet, as director of the Department of Human Rights. A graduate of the University of Illinois, a Chicago lawyer, and a judge on the U.S. Court of Appeals, Washington, D.C., Tucker was nominated in 1990 to the U.S. Equal Employment Opportunity Commission by President George Bush.

Sources: *Jet* 58 (10 July 1980): 30; 78 (30 July 1990): 14.

1990 • Charles Eldridge Freeman (1933–) became the first black elected to the Illinois Supreme Court. He had served as assistant attorney general (1964), assistant state's attorney (1964), assistant attorney for the Board of Election Commissioners (1964–65), arbitrator for the Illinois Industrial Commission (1965–73), and commissioner for the Illinois Commerce Commission (1973–76). In 1976 he was elected to the Circuit Court of Cook County, and from 1986 to 1990 he served on the First District of Illinois, Appellate Court. Freeman was born in Richmond, Virginia, and received his bachelor's degree from Virginia Union University in 1954. After serving in the U.S. Army as a courts and boards reporter, he returned to civilian life and moved to Chicago. He earned a law degree from John Marshall Law School in 1962.

Sources: *Jet* 91 (19 May 1997): 15; *Who's Who among African Americans,* 14th ed., p. 443; *Contemporary Black Biography,* vol. 19, pp. 79–82.

1994• Cook County Commissioner John Herman Stroger Jr. (1929–2008), a Democrat, became the first black president of the county board. He won the election across racial lines in all of Chicago's fifty wards and received 46 percent of the suburban vote. He worked his way up the political ladder, serving as personnel director of the Cook County Jail from 1955 to 1959 and had served the Cook County Board of Commissioners since 1968. During his tenure the county built a new Cook County Hospital and named the facility after him. It was one of Chicago's most expensive public works projects. When he resigned from office in July 2006 due to health reasons, the Stroger family and allies supported Stroger's son Todd for that post. He was elected in November 2006. Stroger was born in Helena, Arkansas, and received a bachelor's degree from Xavier University in New Orleans (where he chaired the Board of Trustees) and a law degree from DePaul University School of Law.

Sources: *Jet* 87 (28 November 1994): 9; 88 (26 December 1994–2 January, 1995): 38; 113 (4 February 2008): 39; *Who's Who among African Americans,* 14th ed., p. 1241.

1997 • Howard A. Peters III became the first black secretary of the Illinois Department of Human Services. He previously served as deputy chief of staff to Illinois Governor Jim Edgar.

Sources: *Jet* 91 (7 April 1997): 19.

1997 • Howard A. Peters III became the first black secretary of the Illinois Department of Human Services. He previously served as deputy chief of staff to Illinois Governor Jim Edgar.

Sources: *Jet* 91 (7 April 1997): 19.

1997 • Charles Eldridge Freeman (1933–) became the first black chief justice of the Illinois Supreme Court. Although his name was not widely known, the quiet and unassuming Freeman had been involved in a number of local black political activities.

Sources: *Jet* 91 (19 May 1997): 15; *Contemporary Black Biography,* vol. 19, pp. 79–82.

1998 • The first black to become secretary of state in Illinois was Jesse C. White Jr. (1934–). A former teacher, he was a state representative in the Illinois General Assembly (1975–77) and served as Cook County Recorder of Deeds. White was born in Alton, Illinois, and graduated from Alabama State College (now Alabama State University) in 1957. He also did graduate work at North Texas State University. From 1957 to 1959 White served in the U.S. Army's 101st Airborne. White founded the well-known Jesse White Tumbling Team for youths.

Sources: *Jet* 95 (1 February 1999): 36; *Who's Who among African Americans,* 26th ed., p. 1318; *Contemporary Black Biography,* vol. 22, pp. 192–95.

The Illinois Senate's First Black President

In 1971 Cecil A. Partee (1921–1994) was the first black to head a state legislative chamber since Reconstruction, when he became president *pro tempore* of the Illinois senate. Born in Blytheville, Arkansas, he graduated from Tennessee State University. He was denied admission to the University of Arkansas Law School, because the school was still racially segregated. The State of Arkansas instead paid his tuition at Northwestern University's law school, where he earned a degree in law. Partee, a Chicago lawyer, was elected to the Illinois House of Representatives in 1956. He was elected to the state senate in 1967 and served two terms as president (1971–73 and 1975–77). In 1971 he became the first black to serve as governor in the nation since Reconstruction, and the first ever in Illinois, when he briefly held the position from 9:15 A.M. to 11:00 P.M. He was the first black in the state to be nominated for attorney general in 1976. Partee left the general assembly and became Human Services commissioner. He was treasurer of Chicago for three terms. In 1989 Partee was appointed Cook County state's attorney.

Sources: *Ebony* 27 (April 1972): 195; *Encyclopedia of Black America,* p. 665; Obituary, *Who's Who among African Americans,* 9th ed., p. 1729; *Jet* 86 (5 September 1994): 16.

Indiana

1881 • James Sidney Hinton (1834–?) was the first black elected to the Indiana House of Representatives.

Sources: *Encyclopedia of Black America,* p. 439.

1990 • Robert D. Rucker Jr. (1952?–) was the first black appointed to the Indiana Court of Appeals. He was deputy prosecutor in Lake County, Indiana, and deputy city attorney for the City of Gary. From 1985 to 1990 he was in private practice. Rucker was born in Canton, Georgia, and graduated from Indiana University. He took his law degree at the Valparaiso University School of Law.

Sources: *Jet* 78 (8 October 1990): 31; *Who's Who among African Americans,* 26th ed., p. 1081.

1991 • Pamela Lynn Carter (1949–) was the first black woman in the United States to be elected state attorney general and the first woman to be elected to the position in the state. Carter was the second black elected to a statewide office. (Dwayne Brown, elected state clerk of the courts in 1990, was the first.) Carter was born in South Haven, Michigan, and earned a bachelor's degree from the University of Detroit in 1971, a master's in social work from the University of Michigan in 1973, and a law degree from Indiana University in 1984.

Sources: *Jet* 83 (23 November 1992): 58; *Who's Who among African Americans,* 26th ed., p. 219.

1998 • Indiana's first black American sheriff was Oates Archery (1937–), who was also the first black to head any of the state's ninety-two counties. He was also the first Democrat to hold that office in twenty years. In 1959 he sought a teaching position in Marion, Indiana, but was refused; instead, he was hired as a janitor. He later became a teacher, a professor at Ball State University, an FBI special agent, and head of security for the 1996 World Cup Soccer Games in Pasadena, California. Archery was born in Marion and was educated in the local schools and graduated from Grambling State University in Louisiana. Although he did not play football at Grambling, legendary football coach Eddie Robinson was his mentor.

Sources: *Muncie Times* (21 January 1999).

Iowa

1918 • Gertrude E. Durden Rush (1880–1962) was the first black woman admitted to the Iowa bar. From the beginning of her practice until the 1950s, she was the only black woman to practice law in Iowa. She was also a co-founder of the National Bar Association. Rush was born in Navasota, Texas, and graduated from Des Moines College in 1914. In that year as well, she completed her law training by correspondence at LaSalle Extension University. In 1919 Rush graduated from Quincy Business College. She was active with women's groups, particularly the Iowa Federation of Colored Women's Clubs and the National Baptist Women's Convention. She founded the Charity League in 1912, whose primary concern was with the welfare of blacks in Des Moines. In 1924 she served as attorney for the Women's Auxiliary of the National Baptist Convention.

Sources: *Jet* 52 (4 August 1977): 18; 60 (6 August 1981): 23; Smith, *Notable Black American Women,* Book II, pp. 575–77.

1977 • Shirley Creenard Steele was the first black woman assistant attorney general of the state.

Sources: Hornsby, *Chronology of African-American History,* pp. 280–81; *Jet* 52 (12 May 1977): 26.

1983 • Thomas J. Mann Jr. (1949–) was the first black state senator. The Brownsville, Tennessee, native graduated from Tennessee State University in 1971. He took his law degree at the University of Iowa Law School in 1974, and served as an assistant state attorney general from 1974 to 1976, and from 1980 to 1982. From 1978 to 1979, he was executive director of the Iowa Civil Rights Commission.

Sources: *Jet* 63 (10 January 1983): 6; *Who's Who among African Americans,* 26th ed., p. 808.

2001? • Ramonda D. Belcher became the first African American woman to be Polk County District Associate Judge in Iowa. For the previous fifteen years she was assistant Polk Count attorney and has prosecuted juvenile, civil, and criminal cases. The North Carolina native graduated from Howard University in 1990 and in 1995 from Drake University's law school in Des Moines. In 2008 she graduated from the Scott Hawkins Leadership Institute, Cohort II.

Sources: *Linked I* (Winter/Spring 2001): 66.

Kansas

1882 • Edward (Edwin) P. McCabe (1850–1920) was the first black elected to state office outside the deep South when he became state auditor. McCabe moved to Oklahoma in 1889 and was one of the founders of Langston City, Oklahoma.

Sources: *Encyclopedia of Black America,* p. 83; Katz, *The Black West,* pp. 254–61; Logan and Winston, *Dictionary of American Negro Biography,* pp. 410–13.

Kentucky

1936 • Charles W. Anderson Jr. (1907–1960) was the first black elected to the Kentucky state legislature, in which he served six consecutive terms. He was also the first black legislator in the South since Reconstruction. In May 1946 he became the first assistant Commonwealth's attorney for Jefferson County. A long-time Republican, in 1949 he was narrowly defeated in his bid to become the Republican nominee for judge in Louisville's Third District Municipal Court. Anderson helped dismantle legal segregation in the state when his bill allowing black and white nurses to go to the same school was passed in 1948. The bill further allowed black physicians to take residencies at white hospitals. He fought to integrate the state's public universities and helped to defeat a bill to segregate people on public transportation, in libraries, and in other public places. Anderson was born in Louisville and received a bachelor's degree from Kentucky State College (now Kentucky State University) and a second bachelor's from Wilberforce University. He earned his law degree from Howard University and in 1933 he was admitted to the Kentucky bar. He set up a law practice in Louisville, became a successful trial attorney, and as an NAACP representative, in 1934 he helped prosecute seven whites for lynching a black man in Hazard, Kentucky.

Sources: *Jet* 51 (6 January 1977): 25; Clayton,*The Negro Politician,* pp. 118–19; *Encyclopedia of Black America,* p. 265; Smith, *Notable Black American Men,* pp. 24–26.

1969 • Georgia M. Davis Powers (1923–) was the first black, and the first woman, elected to the Kentucky State Senate. Prior to the election, she was a Louisville businesswoman and civil rights worker. She entered politics in 1962, when she trained volunteers for Wilson Wyatt's campaign for the U.S. Senate. The experience was challenging and prompted her to work as chairperson for candidates running for the national office. Powers was elected to the Jefferson County Democratic Executive Committee in 1964. In 1968 she spoke at the Democratic National Convention on behalf of Hubert H. Humphrey. Active in civil rights as well, in 1964 Powers was an organizer of the Allied Organizations for Civil Rights. The next year she helped organize the Kentucky Christian Leadership Conference and she participated in the Selma-to-Montgomery March. She marched for open housing in Louisville and joined Martin Luther King Jr. in the march in Memphis to support the sanitation workers. She was a local organizer for the Poor People's Campaign held in Washington, D.C. Powers was born in Springfield, Kentucky, and educated at Louisville Municipal College. She is author of *I Shared the Dream* (1995) and *The Adventures of the Book of Revelations* (1998).

Sources: *Ebony Success Library,* vol. 1, p. 88; Smith, *Notable Black American Women,* pp. 867–69; *Who's Who among African Americans,* 26th ed., p. 1010.

1980 • As secretary of the Department of Justice, William Eugene McAnulty was the first black to serve in the state cabinet.

Sources: *Jet* 57 (28 February 1980): 53.

1988 • Gary D. Payne (1948–) was the first black judge in Fayette County, the location of Lexington. A native of Paducah, Kentucky, Payne graduated from Pepperdine University in Malibu, California, in 1976 and took his law degree from the University of Kentucky in 1978. Before becoming a judge, he was staff attorney for the Kentucky Corrections Cabinet in Frankfort. He also held a number of positions, including estate attorney with the Internal Revenue Service, partner with the law firm of Crenshaw and Payne, and assistant county attorney.

Sources: *Jet* 76 (10 April 1989): 22; *Who's Who among African Americans,* 13th ed., p. 1037.

1991 • Janice R. Martin (1956?–) was the first elected black woman judge in the state. The thirty-six-year-old graduate of the University of Louisville and its law school was a Jefferson District judge in Louisville, Kentucky. She has been in private law practice and head of the Juvenile Division of the Jefferson County Attorney's Office.

Sources: *Jet* 83 (1 February 1993): 18; *Who's Who among African Americans,* 26th ed., p. 818.

2000 • Governor Paul Patton appointed Ishmon F. Burks commissioner of the Kentucky State Police, making him the first black to head Kentucky's top law enforcement agency. A native of Kentucky, Burks was a retired military officer and had served as executive vice-president and chief operating officer of Spaulding University in Louisville.

Sources: *Jet* 98 (23 October 2000): 20.

Louisiana

1868 • Oscar James Dunn (1820?–1871) was nominated and elected lieutenant governor of the state; he took office on June 13, becoming the first black to hold that post. Born in New Orleans, he was the son of a free woman of color who operated a boarding house.

From her customers, Dunn learned to read, write, and play the violin. After working as a music teacher and a barber before the Civil War, he enlisted in the Union Army, joining the first unit of black soldiers formed in 1862. He became a captain but resigned in 1863 in protest of a white officer's promotion to a rank which Dunn thought he deserved instead. He became active in civil rights and worked with a group at the New Orleans *Tribune* which, toward the end of the war, demanded black suffrage. He continued to play a prominent role in suffrage, particularly at the black suffrage convention held in January 1865. He attended the founding convention of the state Republican Party in September 1865 and in that same year became active in the New Orleans Freedmen's Aid Association. In 1871 he chaired the state Republican committee and by now headed a powerful faction of the state Republican Party. There are unsubstantiated claims that his sudden death in 1871, sometimes attributed to poisoning, was the work of his political foes who opposed the idea that he might become the Republican nominee for governor. The first black state treasurer, Antoine Dubuclet, a planter who was freeborn was also named in the 1868 election.

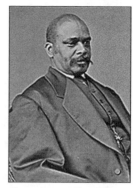

Oscar James Dunn

Sources: Bennett, *Before the Mayflower*, p. 481; Foner, *Freedom's Lawmakers: A Directory of Black Officeholders during Reconstruction*, pp. 67–68; Hornsby, *Chronology of African-American History*, pp. 41–42; Logan and Winston, *Dictionary of American Negro Biography*, pp. 204–05.

1951 • Kermit Parker was the first black to qualify as a Democratic party primary candidate for the nomination for governor.

Sources: *Jet* 65 (17 October 1983): 22.

1967 • Ernest Nathan "Dutch" Morial (1929–1989) was the first black elected to the state legislature since Reconstruction. Prior to his election to the House of Representatives, Morial was the first black graduate of the Louisiana State University Law School, Louisiana's first black assistant U.S. attorney, and the first black juvenile court judge.

Sources: *Encyclopedia of Black America*, p. 568; Smith, *Notable Black American Men*, pp. 831–32; *Who's Who among Black Americans, 1992–93*, p. 1605.

1971 • Dorothy Mae Taylor was the first black woman elected to the Louisiana legislature. In 1986 she was elected the first councilwoman-at-large of New Orleans, and was also the first woman to serve as acting mayor of the city.

Sources: *Jet* 70 (28 July 1986): 20.

1974 • Sidney John Barthelemy (1942–) was the first black elected to the state senate in this century. In 1986 he became mayor of New Orleans and held the post until 1993. From 1974 until the year of his election as mayor, Barthelemy was associate professor of sociology at Xavier University. Other positions he held include director of the city's Welfare Department, councilman-at-large, interim director of the Adult Basic Education Program, and director of social services. He has also served as adjunct professor at the Kennedy School of Government, Tulane University School of Public Health, and the University of New Orleans School of Education. Barthelemy was born in New Orleans and graduated from St. Joseph Seminary in 1967 and Tulane University in 1971.

Sources: *Negro Almanac*, p. 427; *Who's Who among African Americans*, 26th ed., p. 72.

1976 • James Davis Wilson (1937–) was the first black appointed to the state Board of Pharmacy. Wilson was educated at Morehouse College in Atlanta and was a 1963 graduate of the Xavier University College of Pharmacy. He also graduated from Texas Southern University in Houston. From 1963 to 1969 Williams worked as a pharmacist and manager for a Walgreens Drug Store. He has received an award for being the first black owner of a surgical supplies company. Wilson was born in Kingstree, South Carolina.

Sources: *Jet* 51 (16 December 1977): 24; *Who's Who among Black Americans*, 14th ed., p. 1426.

1984 • Joan Bernard Armstrong became the first black woman state judge when she was appointed to the state court of appeal. Born in New Orleans, Armstrong graduated from

The First Black Governor

In 1872 Pinckney Benton Stewart Pinchback (1837–1921) became the first black governor of any state. He served from December 9, 1872, to January 13, 1873, while Louisiana governor Henry Clay Warmoth faced impeachment proceedings. Born of a white father and a freed slave mother in Mississippi, Pinchback had been sent to Ohio for an education. He became active in Louisiana politics; his election to the U.S. House of Representatives in 1872 was disputed, as was his election to the U.S. Senate in 1873. He became surveyor of customs in New Orleans about 1883. In the 1890s he moved permanently to Washington, D.C.

Sources: Logan and Winston, *Dictionary of American Negro Biography*, pp. 493–94; *Encyclopedia of Black America*, p. 677; Hornsby, *Chronology of African-American History*, p. 45; Kane, *Famous First Facts*, p. 290; Smith, *Notable Black American Men*, pp. 938–41.

Pinckney Pinchback

Xavier University in 1963 and took her law degree at Loyola University School of Law in 1967. In 1974 she received a college certificate from the National College of Juvenile Justice. She served as New Orleans Parish Juvenile Court judge from 1974 to 1984.

Sources: *Jet* 67 (24 September 1984): 32; *Who's Who among Black Americans*, 26th ed., p. 40.

1992 • Revius Ortique Jr. (1924?–2008) became the first black justice on the Louisiana Supreme Court. He served until 1994, when he retired. He was also a civil rights attorney.

Sources: *Jet* 113 (7 July 2008): 9.

1993 • Alonzo Harris (1961–), a District Court judge in St. Landry Parish, became the first black judged elected in the parish and, at age thirty-one, the youngest to hold such a position in the state. Born in Opelousas, Louisiana, Harris graduated from Southern University in 1983 and received his law degree from the Southern University Law Center in 1986. He was an attorney with Harris and Harris Law Firm from 1983 to 1987.

Sources: *Jet* 85 (29 November 1993): 39; *Who's Who among African Americans*, 26th ed., p. 534.

1994 • Bernette Joshua Johnson (1943–) became the first black woman to sit on the Louisiana Supreme Court. Previously, Johnson was chief justice for the Civil District Court. She was a community organizer with the NAACP Legal Defense Fund from 1964 to 1966 and held a summer internship with the U.S. Department of Justice in 1967. From 1969 to 1973 Johnson was an attorney with the New Orleans Legal Assistance Corporation and then became a self-employed lawyer. From 1977 to 1981 she was director of the AFNA National Education Foundation and then became deputy city attorney for the City of New Orleans. Johnson was born in Donaldsonville, Louisiana. She graduated from Spelman College in 1964 and received her law degree from the Louisiana State University Law Centers in 1969.

Sources: *Jet* 87 (19 December 1994): 22; *Who's Who among African Americans*, 26th ed., p. 664.

Cleo Fields

1995 • Cleo Fields (1962–), a U.S. congressman, became the first black since Reconstruction to run for governor in Louisiana. The Democratic congressman ran against state senator Mike Foster, who switched to the Republican Party in September. Analysts predicted that Fields had little chance to win the election primarily because of his liberal Democratic voting record, his stance on affirmative action, opposition to the death penalty, support of gun control, and advocacy for government set-aside contracts for minorities. Foster won the election by a large margin. In 1996 Fields was volunteer senior advisor to the Clinton-Gore presidential campaign. He was born in Port Allen, Louisiana, to a dock-worker and a maid. He received two degrees from Southern University in Baton Rouge—a bachelor's in 1984 and a law degree in 1987.

Sources: *Contemporary Black Biography,* vol. 13, pp. 50–53; *Jet* 89 (13 November 1995): 5; *Tennessean* (18 November 1995); (19 November 1995).

Maine

1971 • Gerald Edgerton Talbot (1931–) was the first black member of the Maine legislature. There he introduced legislation for a Martin Luther King Jr. holiday. At the time of his election this Maine native was a newspaper compositor. Among his numerous other achievements, he served as chair of the Maine Board of Education in 1983–84. Talbot was born in Bangor, Maine, and in 1970 took diploma lessons in printing. In 1972 he received a certificate of apprenticeship for printing, approved by the State Apprenticeship Council.

Sources: *Crisis* 80 (February 1973): 69; *Ebony Success Library,* vol. 1, p. 298; *Who's Who among African Americans,* 26th ed., p. 1199.

Maryland

1958 • Irma Dixon (1917–2011) and Verda Freeman Welcome (1907–1990) were the first black women elected to the Maryland House of Delegates. The two represented bitterly opposed factions in the Democratic Party. In 1962 Welcome became the first black woman elected to the state senate.

Sources: Hine, *Black Women in America,* pp. 1241–42 (Welcome); Clayton, *The Negro Politician,* pp. 145–47; *Ebony* 19 (June 1964): 139 (Dixon); 20 (April 1965): 195 (Dixon); *Ebony Success Library,* vol. 1, p. 324 (Welcome); *Sepia* 13 (October 1964): 8–12 (Welcome); *Who's Who among Black Americans, 1992–93,* p. 1613 (Welcome); Smith, *Notable Black American Women,* Book II, pp. 698–700 (Welcome).

1967 • Victorine Quille Adams became the first black woman elected to the City Council in Baltimore. She was elected in the 4th District. In 1946 she began a drive to elect blacks to political positions in the city. Adams was born in Baltimore and educated at Morgan State University and Coppin State Teachers College. For twelve years she was executive director of the Health and Welfare Council of Central Maryland.

Sources: *Jet* 91 (18 November 1996): 12; *Who's Who among African Americans,* 14th ed., p. 8.

1977 • Claudia H. Payne was the first black to head 4-H home economics activities in the state. She was a state 4-H program leader for the U.S. Department of Agriculture.

Sources: *Jet* 53 (29 December 1977): 20.

1978 • Aris Allen (1910–1991) was the first black to run for statewide office in Maryland. A Republican, Allen ran for the office of lieutenant governor. A physician and graduate of Howard University Medical College (1944), he entered the Maryland legislature in 1966. In 1977 he served as the first black chair of the state Republican Party.

Sources: *Encyclopedia of Black America,* p. 99; *State of Black America 1992,* p. 367; *Who's Who among Black Americans, 1988,* p. 1591.

1982 • Delawrence Beard was the first black superior court judge in Montgomery County. Beard received law degrees from the University of Maryland and Georgetown Law School, and spent three years as head of the Public Defender's Office before his appointment.

Sources: *Jet* 62 (10 May 1982): 40.

1984 • Julia Davidson-Randall was the first black woman state registrar of vital records in the United States.

Sources: *Jet* 66 (21 May 1984): 14.

1991 • Vera Hall, a member of the Baltimore City Council, was the first black woman chair of the Democratic Party of Maryland.

Sources: *Jet* 82 (17 August 1992): 7; *State of Black America, 1993*, p. 291.

1994 • Wayne K. Curry became the first black county executive in Prince Georges County, in Maryland. The heavily Democratic county, a suburb of Washington, D.C., had become the largest political subdivision in the nation. During the election, for the first time four blacks captured Democratic nominations for the county council. A well-known attorney, Curry had served as president of the Prince George's County Chamber of Commerce.

Sources: *Jet* 86 (3 October 1994): 8–9, 87 (20 February 1995): 19; "Blacks Rise in Power," *New York Times* (1 July 2001).

1995 • Donna Hill Staton (1957–) became the first black circuit court judge in Howard County. Since 1997 she had been Maryland's first black deputy attorney general. Born in Chester, Pennsylvania, Staton graduated from Princeton University in 1979 and George Washington University School of Law in 1982. She was judicial law clerk from 1982 to 1983 and an associate with Piper and Marbury from 1983 to 1993.

Sources: *Jet* 91 (17 March 1997): 19; *Who's Who among African Americans*, 26th ed., pp. 1173.

1995 • Dianna D. Roseborough, press secretary to Governor Parris Glendening, was named press secretary to the governor. A radio and television traffic reporter for Baltimore, she was the first black to hold that post.

Sources: *Jet* 87 (13 February 1995): 38.

1996 • Richard Nathaniel Dixon (1938–), a conservative from suburban Carroll, Maryland, became the first black state treasurer for the state of Maryland. Since 1983 Dixon has been a member of the Maryland House of Delegates. In this year Dixon made it possible for minority-owned financial institutions to receive a share of the hundreds of millions of dollars that the state treasurer invests. Born in Westminster, Maryland, Dixon received a bachelor of arts degree and master of arts in business administration degree from Morgan State College (now University). He has served as hospital administrator for Provident Hospital and was associate professor in the School of Business at Morgan State. Dixon was delegate/stock broker and assistant vice president for Merrill Lynch.

Sources: *Jet* 89 (19 February 1996): 6; *Who's Who among African Americans*, 26th ed., p. 344.

1996 • Robert Mack Bell (1943–) became the first black chief of the Court of Appeals in Maryland. From 1969 to 1974 he was an associate with Piper and Marbury. One of the state's most experienced judges, he was a judge of Maryland District Court, First District, in Baltimore, from 1975 to 1980. When he took office, he was the youngest judge in the state. From 1980 to 1984 Bell was associate judge in Baltimore's City Circuit Court, Eighth Judicial Circuit. From 1984 to 1991 he was judge on the Court of Special Appeals, Sixth Appellate Circuit in Annapolis. He became associate judge on Maryland's Court of Appeals in Baltimore in 1991 and held that post until 1996, when he became chief judge on that court. Bell was born in Rocky Mount, North Carolina. He attended Morgan State College and received his law degree from Harvard Law School.

Sources: *Jet* 91 (25 November 1996): 46; *Who's Who among African Americans*, 26th ed., p. 87; *Contemporary Black Biography*, vol. 22, pp. 29–31.

1998 • Economic development consultant Joseph J. James became the first black director of Prince George's County Economic Development Corporation. The New Jersey native held membership on numerous economic development boards.

Sources: *Jet* 93 (18 May 1998): 18; *Who's Who among African Americans*, 26th ed., p. 87.

1998 • The first black judge on the Baltimore County Circuit Court was Alexander Wright Jr. Wright graduated from Morgan State College (later University) and the University of Maryland Law School.

Sources: *Jet* 94 (13 July 1998): 38.

1998 • Alonzo D. Black became the first black elected sheriff in Prince George's County.

Sources: *Jet* 94 (23 November 1998): 13.

Massachusetts

1845 • Macon B. Allen (1816–1894) of Worcester was the first black formally admitted to the bar in any state on May 3, 1845. He had been allowed to practice in Maine two years earlier. Born in Indiana, Allen had been a businessman in Portland, Maine. He moved to Massachusetts to practice law. By 1870 he had moved to South Carolina, where he entered politics, and in 1873 became one of the first black judges, as a judge of the Inferior Court. (Miflin W. Gibbs was the first black judge that year in the municipal court of Little Rock.) Little is known of Allen's life after the 1870s; in 1894, he died in Washington, D.C.

Macon B. Allen

Sources: Garrett, *Famous First Facts about Negroes,* p. 93; Logan and Winston, *Dictionary of American Negro Biography,* pp. 11–12; *Negro Almanac,* p. 13.

1866 • Charles Lewis Mitchell (1829–1912) and Edward Garrison Walker (1831?–1910) were the first blacks elected to a state legislature. Walker would jokingly claim to be the first on the grounds that the polls in his ward closed a few hours earlier than those in Mitchell's. Mitchell, who had lost his foot during war service, served as the first black inspector of customs in Boston. He retired in 1909. Walker became a prominent Boston lawyer and a Democrat, a surprising switch at this time. (Walker was the son of David Walker, who issued the inflammatory tract *David Walker's Appeal.*)

Sources: Bennett, *Before the Mayflower,* p. 477; Logan and Winston, *Dictionary of American Negro Biography,* pp. 443–44 (Mitchell), 623 (Walker); *Negro Almanac,* pp. 16, 1425.

1960 • Edward William Brooke (1919–) was the first black to be nominated to run for statewide office in Massachusetts. He lost this election, but in 1962, he was the first black to be elected Massachusetts attorney general.

Sources: *Current Biography Yearbook, 1967,* pp. 40–43; *Ebony Success Library,* vol. 2, pp. 16–21; *Who's Who among African Americans,* 26th ed., p. 146; Smith, *Notable Black American Men,* pp. 121–24.

1987 • Deborah Boutin Prothrow-Stith (1954–) became the first woman and the youngest commissioner of public health for the Commonwealth of Massachusetts. She was born in Marshall, Texas, and received her bachelor's degree from Spelman College in 1975 and medical degree from Harvard University Medical School in 1979. Between 1984 and 1987 she was co-principal investigator on numerous adolescent violence projects. She had held a number of positions with Boston City Hospital, the Commonwealth of Massachusetts, and Harvard University. She was recognized nationally for her work on violence and the prevention of violence among adolescents.

Edward Brooke

Sources: *Contemporary Black Biography,* vol. 10, pp. 213–17; Smith, *Notable Black American Women,* Book II, pp. 530–32; *Who's Who among African Americans,* 26th ed., p. 1017.

1988 • Henry Tomes Jr., (1932–) was the first black commissioner of the Department of Mental Health. A native of San Antonio, Texas, Tomes took his bachelor's degree from Fisk University and his doctorate from the Pennsylvania State College in 1963. He had a distinguished career in teaching, and as an administrator in the field of mental health.

Sources: *Jet* 76 (7 August 1989): 20; *Who's Who among Black Americans,* 8th ed., p. 1465.

1993 • The first black appointed to the Probate and Family Court of Massachusetts is Judith Nelson Dilday (1943–), who received a lifetime position. She is one of four black women judges in the state judiciary. In 1989 Dilday became a founding partner of Burnham, Hines & Dilday, the only law firm in Boston owned by black women. Born in Pittsburgh, Pennsylvania, she graduated from the University of Pittsburgh with a B.A. degree, and then earned graduate credits in French at Millersville State College. She earned her law degree from Boston University School of Law. Her experiences include teaching French in the Pittsburgh schools, assistant district attorney with the Suffolk County District Attorney, attorney with the firm Stern and Shapiro, and attorney advisor in the Office of the Solicitor, U.S. Department of the Interior. She was the first black president of the Women's Bar Association in 1990–91.

Sources: *Jet* 85 (29 November 1993): 36; *Who's Who among African Americans*, 26th ed., p. 340.

1994 • Ralph C. Martin II became the first black district attorney in Suffolk County. Governor Weld appointed him to the vacant post.

Sources: *Jet* 87 (28 November 1994): 9; *Who's Who among African Americans*, 26th ed., p. 819.

1997 • Roderick Louis Ireland (1944–) was confirmed as a justice on the state's supreme court, becoming the first black to hold the post. Until his appointment, Ireland was associate justice of the Massachusetts Appeals Court, beginning in 1990. From 1977 to 1990 he served as a judge on the Boston Juvenile Court. From 1975 to 1977 he was counsel to the secretary of Administration and Finance and director of the Roxbury Defenders Committee from 1971 to 1974. A native of Springfield, Massachusetts, Ireland received his bachelor's degree from Lincoln University, law degree from Columbia University Law School, master of law degree from Harvard Law School, and the doctorate degree from Northeastern University. He joined the faculty of both Northeastern University School of Law and Northeastern University's College of Criminal Justice. Ireland is an expert in juvenile law and wrote a volume of the Massachusetts Practice Series called *Massachusetts Juvenile Law*.

Sources: *Jet* 92 (1 September 1997): 8; *Who's Who among African Americans*, 26 ed., p. 628.

2007 • Deval Patrick (1956–) was installed as Massachusetts' first black governor; he was only the second black in U.S. history to become an elected governor. This was his first try for a political office. In 1989, L. Douglas Wilder of Virginia became the nation's first black elected governor. Patrick was re-elected to office in 2010.

Sources: *Contemporary Black Biography*, vol. 12, pp. 161–65; vol. 61, pp. 128–32; Finkelman, *Encyclopedia of African American History*, vol. 4, pp. 64–65; Gates and Higginbotham, *African American National Biography*, vol. 6, pp. 262–63; *Jet* 110 (22 January 2007), p. 8.

Michigan

1893 • William Webb Ferguson, a Republican from Detroit, became the first black elected to the state House of Representatives. He served two terms, from 1893 to 1896.

Sources: *African American Legislators in Michigan 1893–2002*, pp. 4, 31.

1950 • Charline White (1920–1959) was the first black woman elected to the Michigan legislature.

Sources: Clayton, *The Negro Politician*, pp. 138–39; *Ebony* 11 (August 1956): 82; 21 (August 1966): 97.

1952 • Cora M. Brown (1914–1972) was the first black woman in the United States to be elected to a state senate. Since the only previous woman senator in Michigan had been appointed, she was the first woman of any race elected to the Michigan Senate. After supporting Eisenhower in the 1956 election, she was appointed special associate general counsel of the U.S. Post Office Department on August 15, 1957, becoming the first black woman member of the department's legal staff.

Sources: Alford, *Famous First Blacks*, p. 45; Clayton, *The Negro Politician*, pp. 139–43; *Ebony* 22 (September 1967): 27–28.

1960 • On November 8, 1960, Otis M. Smith (1922–1994) became the first black to win a statewide election since Reconstruction when he was elected auditor general of Michigan. He also was a Michigan State Supreme Court justice from 1961 to 1966. He was the first black to serve in this capacity in any state since Reconstruction. Smith was born in the slums of Memphis, Tennessee, the son of a black domestic worker and her prominent white employer. During World War II he was a journalist with the all-black Tuskegee Airmen.

Sources: *Ebony* 16 (March 1961): 75–80; 33 (December 1977): 33–42; 37 (March 1982): 130; *Ebony Success Library,* vol. 1, p. 286; *Encyclopedia of Black America,* p. 798; *Who's Who among Black Americans, 1992–93,* p. 1309; *Looking Beyond Race: The Life of Otis Milton Smith.*

1970 • Richard H. Austin (1913–2001) became the first black secretary of state in modern times when he assumed that position in Michigan. He held the post from 1970 to 1994, winning reelection five times and becoming Michigan's longest-serving secretary of state. He was also the nation's longest-serving black state official. The position as secretary of state made Austin second in succession to the office of the governor. During Reconstruction, nine other black Americans served in that capacity in other states. He is credited with creating the country's first "motor voter" law by working to make Michigan the first state to register voters in the same office in which drivers were registered. He also was successful in lobbying for one of the first mandatory seat belt laws in the nation, with establishing a motorcycle helmet law, and for streamlining the method of renewing driver licenses and vehicle registration. Austin became the first black licensed certified public accountant in the state in 1941. He worked in the private arena before his election. Austin was born in Stouts Mountain, Alabama, and lived in Sipsey and Pratt City before moving to Pennsylvania. After his father, an itinerant coal miner died, the family moved to Detroit in 1925. Austin attended Wayne State University, graduating later from the Detroit Institute of Technology. In 1971 the Detroit College of Business awarded him the honorary L.L.D. degree. He became an accountant with the firm Austin, Washington and Davenport, and then had a meteoric rise in politics. He was precinct delegate and later district chair. He became Wayne County auditor and soon was elected secretary of state. After reelection in 1982 and 1986, he was known as Michigan's most popular elected official.

Sources: Alford, *Famous First Blacks,* p. 48; *Ebony* 26 (January 1971): 94; *Ebony Success Library,* vol. 1., p. 15; *Who's Who among Black Americans,* 13th ed., p. 48; Bailey, *They Too Call Alabama Home,* pp. 23–25.

1979 • Loren Eugene Monroe was the first black state treasurer.

Sources: *Negro Almanac,* p. 1432.

1997 • The first black elected chief justice of the Michigan Supreme Court was Conrad L. Mallett Jr. (1953–). In 1990 Governor James Blanchard appointed him to the Court; in 1992 Mallett was elected to serve a two-year term and in 1994 to a full eight–year term. While he was executive assistant to Detroit mayor Coleman Young, *Ebony* magazine in March 1985 named him one of the thirty Leaders of the Future. Mallett was born in Detroit and educated at the University of California, Los Angeles (B.A., 1975) and the University of Southern California (M.P.A. and J.D., 1979).

Sources: *Jet* 91 (3 February 1997): 34; *Who's Who among African Americans,* 26th ed., p. 805.

Minnesota

1991 • Alan Cedric Page (1945–) was the first black elected to the state supreme court. Page had played professional football as a member of the Minnesota Vikings. He was inducted into the National Football League Hall of Fame in 1988. He graduated from Notre Dame University in 1967 and took his law degree at the University of Minnesota Law School in 1978.

Sources: *Jet* 83 (23 November 1992): 58–59; (1 February 1993): 22; *Who's Who among African Americans,* 26th ed., p. 957.

1994 • Ed Toussaint became the first black member of the Minnesota Court of Appeals. He was previously Hennepin County District Court judge.

Sources: *Jet* 87 (3 April 1994): 21.

Mississippi

1868 • Charles Caldwell (?–1875) was the first black in the state to be accused of the murder of a white man and found "not guilty" by an all-white jury. While he was attending the state constitutional convention, Caldwell killed the son of a white judge in self-defense. In 1870 Caldwell was elected to the state senate, and on December 25, 1875, he was assassinated in Clinton, Mississippi.

Sources: Bennett, *Before the Mayflower,* pp. 245, 497; *Encyclopedia of Black America,* p. 221.

1964 • Aaron "Doc" Henry (1922–1997) became the first black chairman of the state's Democratic party. He was also the first chair of the splinter group, the Mississippi Freedom Democratic party. Henry was born in Dublin, Mississippi, and received a bachelor's degree from Xavier University in New Orleans. He was a practicing pharmacist and co-owner of two pharmacies.

Sources: Branch, *Pillar of Fire; Contemporary Black Biography,* vol. 19, pp. 103–6; Salzman, *Encyclopedia of African-American History and Culture,* Supplement, pp. 127–28.

1968 • Robert G. Clark (1929–) was the first black elected to the state legislature since Reconstruction. He later lost in two bids to become a U.S. Congressman. A native of Ebenezer, Mississippi, Clark was a graduate of Jackson State College (1953), Michigan State University (1959), and Florida Agricultural and Mechanical University (1960). In addition to his legislative duties, he ran the House of Clark Furniture Store.

Sources: *Ebony* 23 (February 1968): 26; *Ebony Success Library,* vol. 1, p. 68; *Jet* 62 (9 August 1982): 12; *Who's Who among African Americans,* 26th ed., p. 240.

1971 • [James] Charles Evers (1922–), who had become the first black mayor of Fayette, Mississippi, on May 13, 1969, was the first black candidate for governor in modern times. He was mayor from 1979 to 1989; in 1968 he ran for a seat in the Mississippi State Senate but was unsuccessful. A 1951 graduate of Alcorn State University, this civil rights activist is the brother of the slain Medgar Evers.

Sources: Alford, *Famous First Blacks,* p. 39; *Current Biography, 1969,* pp. 134–36; Fax, *Contemporary Black Leaders,* pp. 131–48; *Negro Almanac,* p. 51; *Who's Who among African Americans,* 26th ed., p. 393.

1981 • Reuben Vincent Anderson (1942–?) was the first black circuit court judge in the state. Born in Jackson, Mississippi, he graduated from Tougaloo College in 1964 and took his law degree at the University of Mississippi Law School in 1967. He became a municipal judge in 1975, and a county judge in 1977. From 1982 to 1985 he was circuit judge on the Seventh Circuit Court. From 1985 to 1990 Anderson served on the Mississippi Supreme Court, the first black to hold that post. Governor Bill Allain selected him to replace Justice Francis S. Bowling, who retired on January 1. He has served as a trustee for Tougaloo College and since 1980 he has been a trustee of Piney Woods School, both in Mississippi. From 1997 to 1998, he was president of the Mississippi Bar Association. He is a senior law partner with the Jackson firm Phelps Dunbar LLP.

Sources: *Jet* 61 (19 November 1981): 22; 99 (15 January 2001): 19; Hornsby, *Chronology of African-American History,* p. 336; *Who's Who among African Americans,* 10th ed., pp. 36–37.

1985 • Alyce Griffin Clarke (1939–) was the first black woman member of the state house of representatives. She was appointed to fill the term of Fred Banks, who had been appointed a circuit judge. Born in Yazoo, Clarke was educated in Mississippi schools, taking four master's degrees, each at a different school—Alcorn State University, Tuskegee University, Mississippi College, and Jackson State University. She worked as a public school teacher and as a nutritionist.

Sources: *Jet* 68 (22 April 1985): 5; *Who's Who among African Americans,* 26th ed., pp. 241–42.

1987 • Beverly Wade Hogan (1951–) was the first black and the first woman commissioner of the state's Workers' Compensation Commission. A native of Louisiana, Hogan took a bachelor's degree at Dillard University, and a master's degree at Fisk University. At the time of her appointment she was executive director of federal-state programs in the governor's office.

Sources: *Jet* 72 (24 August 1987): 20; *Who's Who among African Americans,* 26th ed., pp. 590–91.

1987 • Rosie S. Simmons was the first black elected in a countywide election since Reconstruction, when she was elected to the position of Bolivar County circuit clerk. A 1967 graduate of Tuskegee, Simmons had been deputy circuit clerk for seven years at the time of her election.

Sources: *Jet* 72 (14 September 1987): 6.

1992 • David Lee Jordan (1933–) became the only political candidate in the country to hold two elective posts concurrently. He was elected to the City Council in Greenwood, the first black to sit on the council. In 1985 the council became predominantly black in membership and he was elected president, again the first black to hold that post. He was successful in his bid for the state Senate this year and now held two elective jobs. He successfully sued the state of Mississippi to redraw the Second Congressional District; he later became the first black elected to Congress.

Sources: *Jet* 87 (3 April 1995): 39; *Who's Who among African Americans,* vol. 26, p. 705.

1994 • Robert G. Clark (1929–), Mississippi's first black state representative, became the first black House speaker in modern times. He was also the first black person to have a Mississippi state building named in his honor.

Sources: *Jet* 85 (28 March 1994): 19; *Who's Who among African Americans,* 26th ed., p. 240.

1995 • Jannie Lewis (1958?–), sworn in as a circuit judge, became the first black judge in two of the counties in her district. She spent ten years with the Legal Services Corporation and in private practice and became a highly regarded attorney in Tchula, Mississippi.

Sources: *Jet* 87 (17 April 1995): 40; *Who's Who among African Americans,* 26th ed, p. 770.

1996 • Fred Johnson became the first black sheriff in Pike County. Previously, he served as a police officer for the county.

Sources: *Jet* 89 (12 February 1996): 20.

Missouri

1920 • Walthall M. Moore was the first black elected to the Missouri legislature in modern times.

Sources: Garrett, *Famous First Facts about Negroes,* p. 186.

1962 • Deverne Lee Calloway (1916–1993) was the first black woman to be elected to state office in Missouri, when she became a member of the state house of representatives. Calloway held the legislative position for nine consecutive terms. She was born in Memphis and was educated at LeMoyne-Owen College in that city. She taught school in Vicksburg, Mississippi, and in Cordele, Georgia. During World War II, she worked for the United States Service Organization (USO) in Philadelphia and at Fort Huachuca, Arizona, and later joined the American Red Cross. After the war, she moved to Chicago and was a contributor to *Our World.* She was also a cofounder of the Congress on Racial Equality

(CORE). After she moved to St. Louis in 1950, she ran for the state house of representatives, won the race, and held the post until 1982.

Sources: *Ebony* 20 (April 1965): 196; *Ebony Success Library*, vol. 1., p. 57; *Encyclopedia of Black America*, p. 231; *Who's Who among Black Americans, 1992–93*, p. 221; Smith, *Notable Black American Women*, Book II, pp. 78–80.

1977 • Gwen B. Giles (1933?–1986) was the first black woman elected to the state senate. She served as city assessor in Saint Louis from 1981 until her death.

Sources: *Jet* 70 (14 April 1986): 18.

1983 • Evelyn Marie Baker was the first black woman circuit court judge in the state. She was the third woman, and the second black, to be a judge in Saint Louis.

Sources: *Jet* 64 (2 May 1983): 30.

1983 • Cheryl Holland was the first black in the state to hold the position of clerk of the superior court, in Gates Country.

Sources: *Jet* 63 (24 January 1983): 21.

1991 • Appointed to her post as associate circuit judge of the 21st Judicial Circuit in St. Louis in March, Sandra Farragut-Hemphill became the first black to serve on the Circuit Court bench in St. Louis County, Missouri. From 1979 to 1986, she was a partner in the firm Cahill, White & Hemphill. Her legal career included assistant county counselor for St. Louis County and staff attorney at Legal Services of Eastern Missouri. She remained committed to teaching law and taught law at St. Louis University School of Law and Washington University School of Law. She was an active member of the Missouri judiciary and served on various state and local court committees. In 1998, she was elected the first black president of the Missouri Association of Probate and Associate Circuit Judges. Judge Hemphill graduated from Spelman College and the University of Florida School of Law.

Sources: Email from Mound City Bar Association, St. Louis, to Sandra Farragut-Hemphill, March 3, 2010; "Hon. Sandra Farragut-Hemphill, Biographical Information," email from Judge Hemphill to Jessie Carney Smith, March 3, 2010.

1995 • Ronnie L. White (1953–) was named to the Missouri Supreme Court, becoming the first black to hold that post. He was previously a judge in the Missouri Court of Appeals, an assistant public defender, a member of the state legislature, and served on the St. Louis City Council. The St. Louis native received his bachelor's degree from St. Louis University and his law degree from the Missouri-Kansas City School of Law.

Sources: *Jet* 12 (21 July 1997): 4; *Who's Who among African Americans*, 13th ed., p. 1419.

1996 • The first woman elected comptroller in St. Louis was Darlene Green. She was also the first woman elected to the city's Board of Estimate and Apportionment, responsible for the city's budget.

Sources: *Jet* 90 (9 September 1996): 25; *Who's Who among African Americans*, 26th ed., p. 492.

1999 • Amber Boykins and her mother, Billie Boykins, became the only mother-daughter combination to serve in the Missouri House of Representatives. The youngest black woman legislator in the history of the Missouri House of Representatives, Amber Boykins represents the Sixtieth District. She was elected to her first term in 1998. From 1978 to 1982 Billie Boykins served in the house and, at the time, was the youngest black woman legislator.

Sources: *Jet* 96 (22 November 1999): 37.

Montana

1974 • Geraldine Travis was the first black elected to the Montana legislature. She was the wife of an Air Force sergeant.

Sources: *Negro Almanac*, p. 331.

Nebraska

1892 • Matthew O. Ricketts, a former slave, was the first black elected to the state legislature from Omaha. A physician who graduated from the University of Nebraska College of Medicine in 1884, the Omaha resident served two terms.

Sources: Katz, *The Black West,* p. 177; *Jet* 58 (3 April 1980): 20.

1971 • Elizabeth Davis Pittman (1922?–1998) became the first woman judge and the first black judge in the state. She left her position as deputy Douglas County attorney when Governor J. J. Exon appointed her to the Omaha Municipal Court bench this year. When the municipal courts in Omaha and Lincoln merged into the county system in 1985, Pittman became a county judge. She retired from the Douglas County Court in 1986.

Sources: *New York Times* Obituaries (10 April 1998).

Nevada

1995 • Yvonne Atkinson Gates was elected chair of the Clark County Commission in Las Vegas, becoming the first black woman to hold that position. She served two years.

Sources: *Jet* 88 (22 May 1995): 24; *Who's Who among African Americans,* 26th ed., p. 454.

New Hampshire

1974 • Henry B. Richardson (?–1981) was the first black state representative. Richardson was a retired U.S. Army major.

Sources: *Jet* 60 (2 April 1981): 14.

New Jersey

1920 • Walter Gilbert Alexander (1880–1953) was the first black elected to the New Jersey legislature. Alexander was a physician who first practiced medicine for a year in his native West Virginia, and then established himself in Orange, New Jersey, in 1904.

Sources: Garrett, *Famous First Facts about Negroes,* p. 186; *Encyclopedia of Black America,* p. 98.

1957 • Madaline A. Williams (1895–1968) was the first black woman to serve in the state assembly. Williams became a member of the state Migrant Labor Board in 1952. She served two terms in the legislature and then became Essex County registrar, a position she held at the time of her death.

Sources: *Crisis* 65 (June/July 1958): 364–67; *Ebony* 21 (August 1966): 97; *Jet* 61 (17 December 1981): 28.

1960 • Roger M. Yancey (1904–1972) was the first black county court judge in the state.

Sources: *Encyclopedia of Black America,* p. 871.

1970 • James Rankin Cowan (1916–1995) was the first black in the United States appointed to a governor's cabinet as commissioner of health. He held the cabinet position from 1970 to 1974. A distinguished physician, Cowan earned his bachelor's degree in 1939 from Howard University, master's degree in 1940 from Fisk University, and his medical degree from Meharry Medical College in 1944. Cowan was senior vice president of Blue Cross & Blue Shield of Greater New York in 1976. He was assistant secretary of defense for Health and Environment from 1974 to 1975, and has held other positions. He was also in private practice from 1953 to 1970. In 1990 he was indicted on charges of accepting bribes and in 1992 pled guilty to a count of corporate misconduct and received probation, community service, and paid $100,000 to the hospital.

Sources: *Ebony* 27 (April 1972): 96; *Ebony Success Library,* vol. 2, p. 81; *Who's Who among African Americans,* 14th ed., p. 282.

1971 • Leonard [Bud] Simmons (1920–2007) was the first black to serve on the New Jersey Civil Service Commission. He was also the first black police officer in Roselle, New Jersey. A native of Goldsboro, North Carolina, Simmons had been active in politics in the Roselle borough, serving as city councilman and member of the board of education, as well as being commissioner of police. Earlier he had been the first black policeman in Roselle, and later he would become the first (and only) black to serve on the original New Jersey Lottery Commission.

Sources: *Ebony Success Library,* vol. 1, p. 282; *Who's Who among African Americans,* 14th ed., p. 1176.

1971 • Winona Lipman (1929?–1999) became the first black woman elected to the state senate. She said later that, at the time of her election, the senate had no restroom facilities for women. She was also the longest-serving member of the upper house. Lipman championed the causes of women, minorities, children, and small businesses. She proposed a number of bills that became law, such as stronger penalties for adults who patronized child prostitutes and expansion of laws to protect domestic violence victims and to increase services for children.

Sources: *New York Times* Obituaries (11 May 1999); *Jet* 95 (31 May 1999): 54.

1986 • Herbert Holmes Tate Jr. (1953–) was the first black prosecutor for Essex County, which is the location of the city of Newark. Tate was born in Karachi, Pakistan, and received his bachelor's degree from Wesleyan University. He took his law degree at Rutgers University School of Law in 1978, and had extensive experience in both government and private practice.

Sources: *Jet* 70 (1 September 1986): 12; *Who's Who among Black Americans,* 26th ed., p. 1202.

1995 • New Jersey Supreme Court justice James H. Coleman (1933?–) was sworn in and became the first black to hold that post in the state. His confirmation the previous year was by unanimous vote in the senate.

Sources: *Jet* 87 (21 November 1994): 37; 88 (9 January 1995): 6.

1998 • Patricia Hurt was sworn in as Essex County prosecutor, becoming the first black and the first woman to hold the post. Governor Christine Todd Whitman appointed her to a five-year term. When she took office, she was the only black prosecutor in the state. Hurt was previously deputy administrator for Essex County.

Sources: *Jet* 93 (16 March 1998): 19.

2000 • The first black woman to become director of the New Jersey Division on Civil Right in Trenton was O. Lisa Dabreu. She oversees the division's operation as it fulfills the mandate under the New Jersey Law Against Discrimination as well as the New Jersey Family Leave Act.

Sources: *Jet* 98 (4 December 2000): 22.

New York

1855 • Frederick Douglass (1817–1895) was the first black candidate for state office. The Liberty Party nominated him for secretary of state.

Sources: *Negro Almanac,* p. 14.

1916 • Edward A. Johnson (1860–1944) was the first black elected to the New York Assembly. He won in Manhattan's Nineteenth Assembly District. Registered black voters in both the nineteenth and the twenty-first districts were sufficiently large to prompt the Democratic and Republican parties to run blacks for office. Before becoming interested in politics, Johnson was an educator who, in 1890, published *A School History of the Negro Race in America from 1619 to 1890*. In 1891 Johnson became a lawyer. A native of Raleigh, North Carolina, a city where he was elected alderman in 1897, Johnson moved to New York City in 1907.

Sources: *The Black New Yorkers*, p. 143; Clayton, *The Negro Politician*, p. 62; Hamilton, *Adam Clayton Powell Jr.*, p. 112; Logan and Winston, *Dictionary of American Negro Biography*, pp. 349–50.

1920 • The first black nominated for a high-level statewide post was A. Philip Randolph (1889–1979), who ran for state comptroller as the Socialist Party candidate. Although he lost the election, he received 202,361 votes.

Sources: *The Black New Yorkers*, pp. 169–70.

1922 • Henry W. Shields was elected to the state legislature as a Democrat. He was the first black Democrat elected to any political office.

Sources: Work, *The Negro Yearbook, 1925–26*, p. 63.

1945 • On March 12, 1945, New York was the first state to establish a Fair Employment Practices Commission.

Sources: Hornsby, *Chronology of African-American History*, p. 92.

1952 • Julius A. Archibald was the first black elected to the state senate. Born in Trinidad, Archibald was a schoolteacher.

Sources: *Jet* 57 (8 November 1979): 18.

1953 • The first black assemblyman for the predominantly black and Puerto Rican Seventh District was Walter Gladwin. The assistant district attorney in the Bronx, Gladwin was elected to the New York State Assembly on November 3.

Sources: *The Black New Yorkers*, p. 277.

1954 • Bessie Allison Buchanan (1902–1980) was the first black woman elected to the state legislature. The New York City native was active in social welfare and civil rights issues. From 1963 to 1967, she served on the New York State Human Rights Commission, the first black woman to serve on the seven-member commission. Before her marriage in 1929 to Charles P. Buchanan, the owner of the Savoy Ballroom, she had been a singer and dancer at the Cotton Club. Buchanan served with distinction for eight years.

Sources: Clayton,*The Black Politician*, pp. 143–45; *Ebony* 11 (August 1956), cover and p. 80; Smith, *Notable Black American Women*, Book II, pp. 73–75.

1955 • Robert Clifton Weaver (1907–1997) became New York State rent commissioner, the first black to hold cabinet rank in the state. The following year, Weaver became the first black to hold federal government cabinet rank as secretary of housing and urban development.

Sources: Baskin and Runes, *Dictionary of Black Culture*, p. 464; *Encyclopedia of Black America*, p. 849; *Who's Who among Black Americans, 1992–93*, p. 1478; Smith, *Notable Black American Men*, pp. 1195–98.

1964 • Constance Baker Motley (1921–2005) was the first black woman to win a seat in the state senate on December 10. (She had been appointed to fill an unexpired term the previous year.) Before becoming the first black woman federal judge, Motley was also the first woman New York City borough head in 1965.

Sources: *The Black New Yorkers*, p. 300; *Encyclopedia of Black America*, p. 582; *Negro Almanac*, pp. 344–55; Smith, *Notable Black American Women*, pp. 779–82; *Who's Who among African Americans*, 14th ed., p. 951.

1967 • Ersa Hines Poston (1921–2009) was the first black president of the New York State Civil Service Commission. A native of Kentucky, Poston took a master's degree in social work from Atlanta University in 1946, and went to work for the Tuberculosis and

Health Association in Connecticut. When she moved to New York City, her rise in government service was rapid. In 1977 she became vice-chair of the United States Merit Systems Protection Board.

Sources: *Ebony Success Library*, vol. 2, pp. 198–201; *Encyclopedia of Black America*, p. 697; *Negro Almanac*, pp. 1389, 1413; Smith, *Notable Black American Women*, pp. 864–65; *Who's Who among Black Americans, 1992–93*, p. 1139.

1971 • Carmel Carrington Marr (1921–) became the first woman to serve on the New York State Public Service Commission when she was named its commissioner in 1971. From 1953 to 1971, Marr, a graduate of the Columbia University Law School in 1948, served as a lawyer on the staff of the United Nations, and in New York state government. She served on the Public Service Commission until her retirement in 1986.

Sources: Christmas, *Negroes in Public Affairs and Government*, p. 33; *Crisis* 78 (March 1971): 48–52; *Encyclopedia of Black America*, p. 546; *Who's Who among African Americans*, 26th ed., p. 811.

1974 • The first black person appointed to the New York State Board for Public Accountancy was William Aiken (1934–). He was born in New York City and received his bachelor's degree in business administration from City College in 1963 and master's degree in business administration from Baruch College in 1970. He was a state insurance examiner from 1963 to 1967, Certified Public Accountant with the firm Aiken & Wilson from 1972 to 1978, and assistant deputy commissioner for the New York City Human Resources Administration from 1978 to 1980. He was a partner with Main Hurdman from 1980 to 1987 and with Peat Marwick Main and Company in 1987.

Sources: *The Black New Yorkers*, p. 357; *Who's Who among African Americans*, 26th ed., p. 12.

1981 • Lillian Roberts (1928–) was the first black woman to head the New York State Department of Labor. She held the appointed position until 1986. Roberts is a native of Chicago. She studied at the University of Illinois in 1944–45 and at Roosevelt University Labor School from 1958 to 1960. She is experienced in labor activities, serving as labor organizer for mental health employees in Chicago and as associate director of District Council 37, AFSCME, AFL-CIO in New York City. She was senior vice president for Total Health Systems from 1987 to 1990 and in 1991 she became a consultant with Signa.

Sources: *Black Enterprise* 13 (August 1983): 92; *Negro Almanac*, p. 1390; *Who's Who among African Americans*, 26th ed., p. 1058.

1984 • John W. Heritage III was the first black captain in the New York State Police. He had entered the State Police Academy in 1967. In 1986 he became the first black major in the force.

Sources: *Jet* 67 (22 October 1984): 4; 70 (1 September 1986): 22.

1985 • Fritz W. Alexander II (1926–) was the first black to serve full-time on the state court of appeals. Alexander had become a municipal district judge in 1970, and an associate justice of the appellate division in 1977. A native of Florida, he was educated at Dartmouth and received his law degree from the New York University School of Law in 1952.

Sources: *Jet* 67 (28 January 1985): 23; *Who's Who among Black Americans, 1992–93*, p. 15.

1990 • The first black woman elected to a judgeship in Queens County was Patricia Polson Satterfield (1942–). She was elected to the Civil Court in the November elections. Satterfield was born in Christchurch, Virginia. She received her bachelor's degree from Howard University in 1964, master's degree from Indiana University in 1967, and law degree from St. Johns University School of Law in 1977. She has served as assistant deputy counsel and senior counsel with the USC Counsels Office of Court Administration (1979–80), judge in the Unified Court System of the State of New York (1991–94), and acting supreme court justice (1994–98). Since 1998 she has been supreme court justice for the state of New York.

Sources: *The Black New Yorkers,* p. 396; *Who's Who among African Americans,* 26th ed., p. 1095.

1994 • H. Carl McCall (1935–) was elected state comptroller and became the first black in New York to garner a statewide victory. He was chosen by the legislature in 1993 to fill an unexpired term and the next year won the seat in his own right. A longtime Democrat, he won a second term in the 1998 elections with 2.9 million votes, topping the number of votes of any candidates in the statewide elections that year. In 2001 McCall, an ordained minister, announced his candidacy for governor in the 2002 election and became the first black man to win the state Democratic party's nomination for governor. McCall graduated from Dartmouth College and received his master of divinity degree from Andover-Newton Theological Seminary. From 1974 to 1979 he served as state senator and in 1982 was nominated for lieutenant governor. He served as vice president of Citicorp from 1985 to 1993. From 1991 to 1993 he served as president of the New York City Board of Education.

Sources: *Contemporary Black Biography,* vol. 27, pp. 132–34; *Jet* 87 (28 November 1994): 7; 99 (19 February 2001): 24; 101 (10 June 2002): 7; *New York* Times (25 January 2002); *Who's Who among African Americans,* 26th ed., p. 833.

2007 • Floyd Madison, pioneering firefighter, became the first black to oversee the state's Office of Fire Prevention and Control. New York Governor Eliot Spitzer appointed Madison to the post. Madison was also the first black fire chief for the city of Rochester, from 1995 to 2007.

Sources: *Jet* 112 (19 November 2007): 26.

2007 • Melodie Mayberry-Stewart (1948–) became the first black female chief information officer of state, in May. "As the governor's top information technology adviser, she developed and oversaw IT investments for the $134 billion state enterprise and over 190,000 employees." She left the post in 2011. Stewart enjoyed a number of firsts. She was the first CTO and CIO for Cleveland, Ohio, in 2002. When she graduated from the Peter F. Drucker Graduate School of Executive Management (Claremont Graduate University in California), she was the first black woman to earn a doctorate from the school. Mayberry-Stewart also holds an M.A. degree from the University of Nebraska, an MBA from Pepperdine University, and an M.A. from Claremont.

Sources: "Melodie Mayberry-Stewart Blazes a Trail as New York State CIO," Public CIO, http://www.govtech.com/pcio/articles/Melodie-Mayberry-Stewart-Blazes-a-Trail-as.html, accessed September 19, 2012;

2008 • David Alexander Paterson (1954–) was sworn in office as the 55th governor, becoming the first black governor of the state. He is also the state's first legally blind governor. In 2006 he ran on a ticket with Eliot Spitzer and became the state's first black lieutenant governor. Paterson succeeded Spitzer, who resigned amid a sex scandal. Paterson completed Spitzer's term which ended on December 31, 2010 and chose not to seek reelection amid accusations of witness tampering and a fiscal crisis in the state. In 1985 Paterson was elected to the New York state senate as a representative from Harlem, becoming the youngest state senator in Albany. He was elected minority leader of the senate in 2003, the first non-white to hold that post. In 2004 he addressed the Democratic National Convention and was the first visually-impaired person to do so. The Brooklyn native lost most of his eyesight in childhood when he had an infection that left no sight in his left eye and only partial sight in the right. Rather than use Braille, he presents all of his speeches from memory. Paterson is the son of Basil A. Paterson, New York's first secretary of state and the first black vice chair of the National Democratic Party. David Paterson graduated from Columbia University and received his law degree from Hofstra Law School. He has taught at Columbia's School of International and Public Affairs.

David Paterson

Sources: *Contemporary Black Biography,* vol. 59, pp. 140–42; Finkelman, *Encyclopedia of African American History,* vol. 4, pp. 140–42; *Jet* 113 (31 March 2008): 8.

North Carolina

1969 • Henry E. Frye (1932–) was the first black member of the state legislature in modern times. In 1983 Frye became the first black on the state supreme court. Frye was born in Richmond County, North Carolina, and received his undergraduate degree from North Carolina Agricultural and Technical State University in 1953. He earned his law degree in 1959 from the University of Carolina Law School.

Sources: *Ebony Success Library,* vol. 1, p. 119; Hornsby, *Chronology of African-American History,* p. 134; *Jet* 71 (27 October 1986): 20; *Who's Who among African Americans,* 26th ed., p. 439–40.

1971 • As superior court judge, Sammie Chess Jr. (1934–) was the first black judge in North Carolina. He served from 1971 to 1975. A native of Allendale, South Carolina, Chess took a law degree at North Carolina Central University. His appointment also made him the first black superior court judge in the South in modern times.

Sources: *Ebony Success Library,* vol. 1, p. 65; *Encyclopedia of Black America,* p. 225; *Who's Who among African Americans,* 26th ed., p. 251.

1971 • In November, 1971, Elizabeth Bias Cofield (1920–2009) was the first black, and the first woman, elected to the Wake County, North Carolina, Board of Commissioners. She was director of student life at Shaw University at the time of her election, and had previously been elected to a four-year term on the Raleigh school board in 1969. The Raleigh native was educated at Hampton Institute (now Hampton University) in Virginia and received her master's degree from Columbia University.

Sources: *Ebony Success Library,* vol. 1, p. 74; *Who's Who among African Americans,* 14th ed., p. 252.

1983 • Harvey Bernard Gantt (1943–) won 52 percent of the overall vote and 36 percent of the white vote to become the first black mayor of Charlotte. He held the office for two terms, from 1983 to 1987. Although he made a strong showing in his bid to become the state's first black senator since Reconstruction—and in the process won national attention and respect—he lost the election to conservative Jesse Helms. Gantt was born in Charleston, South Carolina. While in his teens, he took part in sit-ins in Charleston that first aimed to desegregate lunch counters. He received a bachelor of architecture degree in 1965 from Clemson University. He was the school's first black student. After graduating, he worked as an architect while studying for his master's degree. He received his master's degree in 1970 from Massachusetts Institute of Technology. After that he worked with Floyd B. McKissick, the civil rights activist, in planning for North Carolina's Soul City. In 1971 he returned to Charlotte and established a business in architecture. When Gantt was appointed to the Charlotte City Council in 1974, his political career was launched. He was elected to the council in 1975, lost the election in 1979, and regained his seat in 1981.

Sources: *Contemporary Black Biography,* vol. 1, pp. 72–74; *Who's Who among African Americans,* 26th ed., p. 447.

1988 • Everett Blair Ward (1958–) was the first black executive director of the state Democratic party. A native of North Carolina, and a graduate of Saint Augustine's College (1982), Ward had served since 1983 as political director of the party at the time of his selection.

Sources: *Jet* 77 (20 November 1989): 20; *Who's Who among African Americans,* 26th ed., p. 1282.

1991 • Ralph Campbell Jr. was the first black elected to a statewide position, when he won the race for state auditor. Campbell had served on the Raleigh City Council for six years.

Sources: *Jet* 83 (23 November 1992): 58.

1998 • Lieutenant Colonel Richard Holden became the first black commander of the North Carolina Highway Patrol.

Sources: *Jet* 95 (5 April 1998): 8.

2008 • State representative Thomas Wright (1956?–), Democrat representing New Hanover, was removed from office after a vote by the General Assembly. The 109–5 vote led to his expulsion, making him the first legislator in the General Assembly to be removed from office since 1880. Wright was accused of campaign finance fraud in Raleigh. He consistently denied that he hid or mishandled $340,000 in loans and campaign and charitable contributions.

Sources: *Jet* 113 (7 April 2008).

Ohio

1855 • John M. Langston (1829–1897), who had been admitted to the Ohio bar in the previous year, became the first black elected to office in the United States. He was elected clerk of Brownhelm Township in Lorain County. Among his other achievements were election to Congress from Virginia in 1888.

Sources: Bennett, *Before the Mayflower,* p. 462; Cantor, *Historic Landmarks of Black America,* p. 40; Logan and Winston, *Dictionary of American Negro Biography,* pp. 382–84; Hornsby, *Chronology of African-American History,* pp. 27–28; Smith, *Notable Black American Men,* pp. 693–98.

1879 • George Washington Williams (1849–1891) was elected to the state legislature, becoming the first black to win such office in the state. He is principally remembered for his major, two-volume historical work, *History of the Negro Race from 1619 to 1880,* the first documented history of black America. A multitalented man, Williams was also the first black to write a column for a white newspaper. He was a lawyer, a soldier in the Civil War, and a minister who pastured leading Baptist churches. Williams was born of mixed parentage in Bedford, Pennsylvania. He attended the Baptist-supported Wayland Seminary in Washington, D.C., and in 1870 was admitted to Newton Theological Institution near Boston. He graduated from Newton on June 10, 1874, and was ordained the next day. While pastoring Twelfth Baptist Church in Boston, he wrote his first historical work, *History of Twelfth Baptist Church.* He established a short-lived newspaper, the *Commoner.* In February 1876 Williams became pastor of Union Baptist Church in Cincinnati. While there, he became politically active and also wrote for the *Cincinnati Commercial Appeal,* using the name Aristides; he was then the first black columnist to write for a white newspaper. In January 1880, he became the first black legislator in Ohio. In December 1882 he published the first volume of his seminal work, *History of the Negro Race from 1619 to 1880.* He published another extensive work in 1887, *History of the Negro Troops in the War of the Rebellion.* John Hope Franklin's biography of Williams illuminated his life, making him known for much more than the black history that he wrote.

George Washington Williams

Sources: Smith, *Notable Black American Men,* pp. 1233–36; Franklin, *George Washington Williams.*

1885 • Benjamin William Arnett (1838–1906) was the first black to represent a majority white constituency in a state house of representatives. A bishop of the AME church, he represented Green County from 1885 to 1887. In 1864 Arnett was the first and, for a period, the only black teacher in Fayette County, Pennsylvania. As a legislator, Arnett helped abolish discriminatory laws in Ohio. In addition to his purely religious work, he remained influential in many fraternal organizations and in politics, especially through his friendship with William McKinley Jr., who became president in 1897. He was born in Brownsville, Pennsylvania, and attended Wilberforce University and Cincinnati's Lane Theological Seminary.

Sources: Logan and Winston, *Dictionary of American Negro Biography,* pp. 17–18; Kane, *Famous First Facts,* p. 347; *Negro Almanac,* p. 1425; Smith, *Notable Black American Men,* pp. 34–36.

1937 • H. Elsie Austin was appointed assistant state attorney general, becoming the first black woman in the nation to hold that post.

Sources: Salzman, *Encyclopedia of African-American Culture and History,* vol. 3, p. 1588.

1960 • Merle M. McCurdy (1912–1968) was the first black public defender in Cuyahoga County, the county where Cleveland is located.

Sources: Christian, *Negroes in Public Affairs and Government,* p. 150; *Jet* 36 (17 July 1969): 11; *Encyclopedia of Black America,* p. 550.

1963 • As director of industrial relations, William O. Walker (1896–1981) was the first black cabinet member in the state. A 1916 graduate of Wilberforce University, Walker became a journalist. In 1932 he founded the *Call and Post* newspaper in Cleveland, Ohio. He was elected to the Cleveland City Council in 1939.

Sources: *Ebony* 5 (September 1950): 49; *Ebony Success Library,* vol. 1, p. 317; Hill, *Who's Who in the Negro Press,* pp. 31–33; Lee, *Interesting People,* p. 51.

1994 • J. Kenneth Blackwell (1948–) became the first black to hold a non-judicial statewide office in Ohio. Governor George Voinovich appointed the Cincinnati Republican state treasurer to fill out a vacant term. Blackwell's political career began in 1977 when he was elected to the Cincinnati City Council. He won election to the council six times; he served also as Cincinnati's mayor and vice mayor. Blackwell is a Cincinnati native and graduated from Xavier University with a bachelor's and a master's degree. In 1981 he studied in Harvard University's Program for Senior Executives in State and Local Government. He has teaching experience in Cincinnati's public schools and at the University of Cincinnati. Among other experiences, Blackwell was vice mayor of Cincinnati in 1977–78, mayor in 1979–80, and again vice mayor from 1985 to 1987. He served as U.S. Department of Housing and Urban Development under secretary from 1989 to 1991 and confirmed at the rank of ambassador, and in 1991 U.S. representative to the United Nations Human Rights Commission. He holds membership in numerous organizations and has received wide recognition from academic institutions and other organizations.

Sources: *Jet* 85 (7 March 1994): 35; *Who's Who among African Americans,* 26th ed., p. 107–8.

1995 • Ohio state senator Ben E. Espy became the first black assistant minority leader of the Democratic Caucus for Ohio's 121st General Assembly. With this he reached the highest level for any minority in the state legislature.

Sources: *Jet* 87 (13 March 1995): 22; *Who's Who among African Americans,* 26th ed., p. 389.

1997 • Veroman D. Witcher Jr., became the first black to win the State Trooper of the Year award. The Ohio State officer joined the patrol in 1985 and graduated in the 115th Academy class. Then he was assigned to a post in Xenia. A background investigator and field training office, he also addresses safety issues through education and enforcement.

Sources: *Jet* 93 (16 March 1998): 19; *Who's Who among African Americans,* 26th ed., p. 1374.

1999 • Michael Bennett Coleman (1954–) received 60 percent of the vote and became the first black mayor of Columbus. He was also the first Democrat to win the post in thirty-two years. Coleman was educated at the University of Cincinnati, where he received a bachelor's and master's degree, and at the University of Dayton School of Law, where, in 1981, he received a law degree. After serving on the city council since 1992, he was elected mayor this year and took office in 2000. While on the council, he held an Urban Recovery Fair to repair and rebuild the inner city. He sponsored a Boys to Men Volunteer Fair, a mentoring program, and sat on the Bikeways Advisory Committee, which constructed bikeways and bikepaths.

Sources: *Jet* 96 (22 November 1999): 4; *Who's Who among African Americans,* 26th ed., p. 256; *Contemporary Black Biography,* vol. 28, pp. 53–54.

Oklahoma

1964 • Edward Melvin Porter (1930–) was the first black elected to the Oklahoma senate. Porter was born in Okmulgee, Oklahoma, and graduated from Tennessee State University in Nashville in 1956. He took his law degree from the Vanderbilt School of Law in 1959. He was co-owner and publisher of *Black Voices* magazine.

Sources: *Ebony Success Library,* vol. 1, p. 252; *Who's Who among African Americans,* 26th ed., p. 1004.

1968 • Hannah Diggs Atkins (1923–2010) was the first black woman elected to the state house of representatives. She was born in Winston-Salem, North Carolina, and grew up during the Great Depression. She received a bachelor's degree in library science from the University of Chicago Graduate Library School in 1949. Until her election to the legislature, Atkins worked primarily as a librarian at Fisk University in Nashville, in the school system in Winston-Salem, in Oklahoma City's public library, at Oklahoma State Library, and at Oklahoma City University. From 1983 to 1987 she served as assistant director of the state Department of Human Services and from 1988 to 1991 as secretary of state/cabinet secretary of human resources. The appointment was the first time a black had occupied a cabinet position in Oklahoma.

Sources: *Ebony Success Library,* vol. 1, p. 14; *Homecoming,* 9 (No. 1: Spring 1992): 6; Smith, *Notable Black American Women,* Book II, pp. 17–18; *Who's Who among African Americans,* 24th ed., p. 45.

1986 • Vickie Miles LaGrange was the first black woman elected to the state senate. She was the third black elected: the first was E. Melvin Porter, whom she defeated in a run-off election. LaGrange is a native of Oklahoma City and an attorney.

Sources: *Jet* 71 (10 November 1986): 5.

Oregon

1993 • James "Jim" Hill (1947?–), a Democrat, was the first black man to hold statewide office in Oregon. For ten years he was a state legislator representing Salem. In 1992 he was elected state treasurer and served two four-year terms. He announced his candidacy for governor in August 1999 and in July 2001 continued to call for a "rainy day" fund for schools, the use of technology to stimulate the economy, and downsizing the cost of government by reducing the state's workforce as people retire.

Sources: *The Medford (Oregon) Mail Tribune* (21 July 2001).

Pennsylvania

1938 • Crystal Dedra Bird Fauset (1893–1965) was the first black woman elected to a state legislature in the United States. Born in Princess Anne, Maryland, Fauset was one of nine children. After her parents died, she moved to Boston to live with her aunt. There she attended Boston Normal School, graduating in 1914. In 1918 she began work with the YMCA in New York as the first secretary for younger black girls. She later worked with the American Friends Service Committee, and the Works Progress Administration (WPA) before going into politics. Fauset was known for her superior ability as a public speaker and charmed large audiences. She used her public lectures to encourage all citizens, particularly black women, to become politically active. She resigned from the legislature after a year to return to Pennsylvania's WPA. Her relationship with Eleanor Roosevelt and her involvement in Franklin D. Roosevelt's election campaigns led to her position in 1941 as special consultant to the director of the Office of Civilian Defense. She continued a career of government service and active involvement in politics. In 1931 she received a bachelor's degree from Columbia University's Teachers College.

Crystal Fauset

Sources: Hine, *Black Women in America,* pp. 410–11; *Negro Almanac,* pp. 25, 1426; Smith, *Notable Black American Women,* pp. 333–36.

1955 • Andrew M. Bradley (1906–1983) was the first black to hold cabinet rank in the state. An accountant, Bradley became secretary of property and supplies.

Sources: *Ebony* 13 (May 1958): 79–84; *Encyclopedia of Black America,* p. 189.

1959 • Juanita Kidd Stout (1919–1998) was the first woman judge in the state. Stout was appointed to the Philadelphia Municipal Court in September, and won election to a ten-year term in November of 1959. Born in Wewoka, Oklahoma, she studied at Lincoln University in Jefferson City, Missouri, and transferred to the University of Iowa in Iowa City, where Stout received a bachelor's degree in music in 1939. Since childhood her ambition was to become a lawyer. She completed her law degree at Indiana University, specializing in legislation. She taught grade school at various locations in Oklahoma until the outbreak of World War II, when she went to Washington. In 1954 she passed the Pennsylvania bar examination. After ten years on the municipal court, she spent twenty years on the court of common pleas. On March 3, 1998, she became the first black woman to serve on any state supreme court. She reached the state's mandatory age limit and retired two years later; she then returned to the Common Pleas Court where she was a senior judge until she died.

Sources: *Contemporary Black Biography,* vol. 24, pp. 160–62; *Encyclopedia of Black America,* p. 811; *Negro Almanac,* p. 1392; Smith, *Notable Black American Women,* pp. 1087–89.

1967 • Herbert Arlene (1917–1989) was the first black state senator. Arlene had long been active in Philadelphia Democratic politics and had served in the state house from 1959 to 1967.

Sources: *Ebony Success Library,* vol. 1, p. 13; *Who's Who among Black Americans, 1992–93,* p. 41.

1969 • K. Leroy Irvis (1919–2006) was the first black majority leader in the Pennsylvania house of representatives. A native of New York State, he took his law degree at the University of Pittsburgh Law School, and was first elected to the Pennsylvania house in 1958. In 1977 he was elected the first black speaker of the house, a first for the state and for the nation. He held the position until his retirement in 1988. He was recognized as a versatile man and a leader who was instrumental in getting legislation passed to support community colleges, the arts, civil rights, and human services. In 1993 the Alpha Kappa Alpha Sorority, Inc., unveiled a bust of Irvis at the State Museum in Harrisburg. In 1999 the state honored Irvis by naming the east wing the state capitol for him.

Sources: *Ebony* (April 1972): 95; Hornsby, *Chronology of African-American History,* p. 197; *Jet* 84 (11 October 1993): 39; 96 (22 November 1999): 14; *Negro Almanac* (1976), pp. 360–61; *Who's Who among African Americans,* 14th ed., p. 647.

1971 • [Cynthia] Delores Nottage Tucker (1927–2005) became the first black woman cabinet member in Pennsylvania when she was appointed secretary of state in 1971. She held the position until 1977. Tucker was very active in politics on the state and national level. She was the first black and the first woman member of the Philadelphia Zoning Board. In 1989 she became a newspaper executive on the *Philadelphia Tribune.* Tucker was a founding member of the National Women's Political Caucus and cofounder of the Black Women's Political Caucus. She became an outspoken critic of "gangsta" rap. As chair of the National Political Caucus, she criticized Tupac Shakur's music, alleging that the music caused her emotional distress. She filed a $10 million law suit against Shakur's estate, after he was killed on September 30, 1996. A Philadelphia native, Tucker attended Temple University, Pennsylvania State University, and the University of Pennsylvania.

Sources: *Ebony Success Library,* vol. 2, pp. 260–63; *Jet* 92 (1 September 1997): 62; Smith, *Notable Black American Women,* pp. 1155–57; *Who's Who among African Americans,* 14th ed., p. 1303.

1977 • Ethel S. Barnett (1929–) was the first black woman member of the state Civil Service Commission. Born in Macon, Georgia, Barnett was from 1961 to 1971 a police officer in the City of Philadelphia Police Department.

Sources: *Jet* 51 (3 March 1977): 26; *Who's Who among African Americans,* 26th ed., p. 70.

1984 • On January 6, 1984, Robert N. C. Nix Jr. (1928–2003) became the first black state supreme court justice. Nix, who began his career as a criminal lawyer, had become a judge in the common pleas court of Philadelphia County in 1968. In 1984 he became the chief justice of the state supreme court. He was also a prominent lawyer during the Civil Rights Movement and a partner in the law firm Nix, Rhodes & Nix. After serving the court system for over a quarter of a century, he retired in 1996. Born in Philadelphia, Nix was a 1955 graduate of the University of Pennsylvania School of Law. He is the namesake son of Philadelphia's first black congressman.

Sources: *Contemporary Black* Biography, vol. 51, pp. 105–06; Hornsby, *Chronology of African-American History*, p. 327; *Jet* 65 (30 January 1984): 4; 78 (23 July 1990): 33; *Who's Who among African Americans*, 14th ed., p. 975.

1986 • Therese L. Mitchell was the first black chair of the state Civil Service Commission. Mitchell had served as deputy press secretary to Governor Dick Thornburgh.

Sources: *Jet* 71 (29 September 1986): 64.

1987 • Ronald M. Sharpe (1940–) was the first black commissioner of the state police. Sharpe started his career with this law enforcement agency in 1962. He had served as acting commissioner for several months.

Sources: *Jet* 73 (2 November 1987): 47; *Who's Who among Black Americans, 1992–93*, p. 1264.

1990 • Cynthia A. Baldwin (1945–) was the first black woman elected to the Allegheny County bench, for a ten-year term. The county is the location of Pittsburgh. In her career she has served as assistant dean of student affairs at Pennsylvania State University, McKeesport; deputy attorney general and later attorney-in-charge for the Office of the Attorney General in Pennsylvania; faculty member, Duquesne University law school; and part-time family division judge civil division, Court of Common Pleas for Allegheny County. A native of McKeesport, Pennsylvania, she took her law degree at the Duquesne University School of Law in 1980. Baldwin was also the first black woman installed as president of the Penn State Alumni Association.

Sources: *Jet* 78 (30 April 1990): 5; *Who's Who among African* Americans, 26th ed., p. 59.

1995 • The Pennsylvania State Police promoted Virginia L. Smith (1947?–) to the rank of major, making her the first woman in the department's eighty-nine-year history to hold that rank. During her twenty-year tenure with the department, in 1993 she also became the first black woman to reach the rank of captain. She became a corporal in 1982, a sergeant in 1986, and a lieutenant in 1990. Since 1992 Smith has served as the department's affirmative action officer and will remain in that post to oversee the department's equal opportunity program in hiring, training, and promotion. Smith is a native of Ross Township in Allegheny County. She enrolled in the University of Pittsburgh's College of General Studies.

Sources: *Jet* 87 (16 January 1995): 24.

1998 • Leonard Washington Jr. (1945–) became the first black Pennsylvania state police officer to be elevated to major. He commanded the force in the western part of Pennsylvania. The Pittsburgh native received his bachelor's degree from California University of Pennsylvania in 1980. He was experienced in law enforcement, having served as a state trooper, corporal, sergeant, lieutenant, captain, and now as major.

Sources: *Jet* 93 (9 February 1998): 13; *Who's Who among African Americans*, 26th ed., p. 1291.

2000 • John Sherwin Shropshire (1938–) became the first black county commissioner in northern Pennsylvania. Born in Pittsburgh, he graduated from Clarion University of Pennsylvania and Shippensburg University. He was the first black head coach at Central Dauphin East High School, where he remained from 1961 to 1972. He has held a number of positions at his alma mater, Clarion University, including director of admissions and dean of enrollment management and academic records.

Sources: *Jet* 97 (27 December 1999–3 January 2000): 10; *Who's Who among African Americans*, 14th ed., p. 1171.

Rhode Island

1885 • Mahlon Van Horne (1840–1910), a leading black figure in the state, became the state's first black legislator, an office he held for three terms. He later became one of the nation's first black diplomats. He was also an influential clergyman and community leader. Van Horne was born in Princeton, New Jersey, on March 30, 1840, to free parents. He graduated from Lincoln University in Pennsylvania, was ordained, and moved to Newport first as acting pastor and then as permanent pastor of the Colored Union Congregational Church. The historic church, known as the "Old Salt Box," had served its members since former slave Newport Gardner (1746?–1826) founded it sixty years earlier. It was demolished around 1871 and a new church structure erected that would be known as the Union Congregational Church. Like many other early black churches, Van Horne made it a center of activity for the black community. Van Horne ran for the Newport School Committee in 1873 and drew enough votes from blacks and whites to become the first black member. He used his position to fight for school integration and to improve education for black youth, well before the modern Civil Rights Movement. He won three one-year consecutive terms in the state house of representatives, serving from 1885 through 1887, becoming the first black legislator. Van Horne was a member of the National Colored Labor Union League, an organization that worked to see that blacks were accepted into labor unions. In 1896 President William McKinley named Van Horne general consul to the Danish West Indies (now the U.S. Virgin Islands), where he served for twelve years. Van Horne resigned the post in 1908 and became a missionary pastor in Antigua's Moravian Church. He died two years later, about a month after he returned to Newport.

Sources: "Van Home, Mahlon." http://www.BlackPast.org. Accessed October 9, 2012.

1959 • A lifelong Republican, Joseph G. LeCount (1887–1981) was appointed legal counsel to the state Milk Commission, becoming the first black sworn in as counsel to a state administrative unit. He was also one of the state's first black lawyers and a leading civil rights activist who was known by black lawyers throughout the country. In the 1920s he and other prominent blacks forced the Rhode Island Auditorium to integrate its audiences. He was successful in his fight to integrate restaurants, barbershops, and other places of entertainment. He joined Thurgood Marshall in the 1940s in a successful fight to integrate the Boilermakers Union at Providence's shipyard. LeCount was born in Washington, D.C., and moved to Rhode Island with his family when he was two years old. Although he dropped out of high school to help support his family, he became an avid reader and was admitted to Howard University where he received a law degree in 1912. He was admitted to the Rhode Island bar in 1914, becoming one of the state's first black attorneys. LeCount was president of the local NAACP from 1935 to 1939 and later became its legal counsel. A polite and genteel man, he continued to practice law until age ninety-three, becoming the oldest practicing attorney in the state.

Sources: "National Report," *Jet* 16 (April 30, 1959): 8.

South Carolina

1868 • The South Carolina General Assembly was the first state legislative body with a black majority, when it met on July 6, 1868. There were eighty-seven blacks and forty whites in the lower house. The whites, however, had a majority in the state senate, and in 1874 there was again a white majority in the house.

Sources: Bennett, *Before the Mayflower,* p. 629; Hornsby, *Chronology of African-American History,* p. 42.

1868 • Francis L. Cardozo (1837–1903) was the first black South Carolina secretary of state. He served for four years in the position, and became the secretary of the treasury; he was elected to two terms in 1872 and 1874, and claimed the election in 1876, but did not try to maintain his position after the downfall of the Republican regime in 1877. During the last fourteen months of his tenure as secretary of state, Cardozo employed a deputy in South Carolina, while he served as professor of Latin at Howard University. A free-born native of Charleston, he pursued an education in Scotland. From 1884 to 1896 he was principal of the Colored Preparatory High School, Washington, D.C., and its successor, the M Street High School.

Sources: Bennett, *Before the Mayflower,* p. 629; Clayton, *The Negro Politician,* pp. 26–27; Logan and Winston, *Dictionary of American Negro Biography,* pp. 89–90; Smith, *Notable Black American Men,* pp. 171–73.

1870 • Jonathan Jasper Wright (1840–1885) was the first black state supreme court justice in the United States. Born in Pennsylvania, Wright had studied law in that state, where he was the first black admitted to the bar in 1866. He was elected on February 1, 1870, to fill an unexpired term, and re-elected to a full term in November. After the overthrow of the Reconstruction government, Wright resigned December 1, 1877, and died in obscurity of tuberculosis.

Jonathan Jasper Wright

Sources: Bennett, *Before the Mayflower,* pp. 233, 487, 639; Logan and Winston, *Dictionary of American Negro Biography,* pp. 669–70; Hornsby, *Chronology of African-American History,* p. 43; *Negro Almanac,* p. 1425.

1971 • Herbert Ulysses Fielding (1923–) was the first black elected to the state house since Reconstruction. He was re-elected in 1983 and in 1985 he was elected to the state senate. He was vice president and funeral director of Fielding House for Funerals. A native of Charleston, he took a bachelor's degree in business administration at West Virginia State College in 1948.

Sources: *Ebony Success Library,* vol. 1, p. 111; *Who's Who among African Americans,* 26th ed., p. 406.

1978 • Aletha Morgan was the first black woman trooper in the state highway patrol. A graduate of Howard University, Morgan lived in Orangeburg.

Sources: *Jet* 71 (22 December 1986): 8.

1986 • Lucille Simmons Whipper (1928–) was the first black woman member of the state legislature from Charleston County. She took her undergraduate degree at Talladega in 1948 and her master's degree from the University of Chicago in 1955. She worked in the Charleston County Schools, in the county Office of Economic Opportunity, and at the College of Charleston, from which she retired. Whipper was also the first president of the Avery Institute of Afro-American History and Culture.

Sources: *Jet* 70 (8 September 1986): 36; *Who's Who among African American,* 26th ed., p. 1314–15; *Initiative, Paternalism, and Race Relations: Charleston's Avery Normal Institute.*

1994 • By acclamation of the South Carolina legislature, Ernest A. Finney Jr. (1931–) became chief justice of the state's supreme court, the first black to hold that post. When he retired in 1999, after fourteen years on the state's high court, Senator Ernest Hollings praised him on the floor of the United States Senate for his civil rights work. Finney became the first black circuit court judge in the state in 1979. In that year, as well, he was the first black chairman of the South Carolina Commission on Aging. Born in Smithfield, Virginia, he graduated from Claflin College in Orangeburg, South Carolina, in 1952. He is a 1954 graduate of the New York University School of Law. Finney was resident judge in the Sumter County (South Carolina) Courthouse, Third Judicial Court from 1976 to 1985. He became the state's first black associate justice of the South Carolina Supreme Court in 1985.

Sources: *Jet* 68 (22 April 1985): 5; 86 (6 June 1994): 50; 95 (29 March 1999): 10; 97 (10 April 2000): 10; *Who's Who among African Americans,* 26th ed., pp. 409–10.

Tennessee

1873 • When the Tennessee legislature convened on January 6, 1873, Sampson W. Keeble (1833?–1880?) became the first black member of the state house of representatives.

Born a slave in Rutherford County, Tennessee, prior to the Civil War he had worked as roller boy and pressman for newspapers in Murfreesboro, Tennessee. Toward the end of the war he moved to Nashville and around 1866 he established Rock City Barber Shop. He was a member of the Freedman's Savings and Trust Company Bank board and treasurer of the Colored Agricultural and Mechanical Association's board. The Davidson County Republican party was the party of choice for blacks during Reconstruction. Keeble became involved and in 1872 was nominated for a seat in the state house. He won in the November 1872 election by a slim margin and took office on January 6, 1873. While in the legislature Keeble introduced several bills that related to black businesses, the protection of black laborers, and the support of the Tennessee Manual Labor University, but the bills were defeated. Among these bills, the third was vastly important in his political career. Black leaders who were artisans, craftsmen, and small entrepreneurs organized the Colored Agricultural and Mechanical Association. In December 1866 the association's leaders organized the Tennessee Manual Labor University. The association was a strong political base for Keeble and others; it held an annual fair in the fall and attracted national black Republican leaders, such as John Mercer Langston and Frederick Douglass. Keeble held a second political office; he was elected magistrate of Davidson County and served from 1877 to 1882. He lost his bid for a return to the general assembly in 1878.

Sources: Scott, *The Negro in Tennessee Politics,* pp. 28–29; Taylor, *The Negro in Tennessee, 1865–80,* pp. 247–48; *Tennessean* (9 February 1992).

1876 • William Francis Yardley (1844–?) was the first black to run for governor of the state. He was also one of the first black educators in Knox County and later the first black attorney in Knoxville. He may have been the first black attorney in Tennessee. Yardley was a fireman, a justice of the peace, an insurance agent, and an alderman for the Fifth Ward of Knoxville.

Sources: Jones, *Every Day in Tennessee History,* p. 8.

1878 • J. A. Hodge was the first black state legislator from Hamilton County; he served until 1887. He represented the Fourth Ward of Chattanooga on the city council from 1878 to 1887. He was born a slave in North Carolina and lived in Chattanooga for many years. He was a self-employed contractor, stone-cutter, and house-mover. Hodge also became a city jailer in 1882 and was the night mail-transfer agent for the East Tennessee, Virginia & Georgia Railroad.

Sources: Jones, *Everyday in Tennessee History,* p. 235.

1881 • The state of Tennessee passed the first Jim Crow law to require that railroads be segregated. This initiated a period of statutory, rather than customary, segregation in the South. The state laws were buttressed by the U.S. Supreme Court decision in *Plessy v. Ferguson* (1896). The dismantling of legal segregation took a major effort during the second half of the twentieth century.

Sources: Bennett, *Before the Mayflower,* p. 500; *Negro Almanac,* pp. 19, 150–52.

1884 • William C. Hodge was elected to the state legislature and became the first black from Hamilton County in the general assembly.

Sources: Jones, *Every Day in Tennessee,* p. 214.

1952 • Sarah Roberta Church (1914?–1995) became the first black woman elected to the Tennessee Republican State Committee. She was the daughter of Robert R. Church Jr., who organized the first branch of the NAACP in Tennessee. After his death in 1952, she took his place as candidate for the state Republican committee and was successful in the election. In 1953 she joined the Dwight D. Eisenhower administration, in the Department of Labor, as consultant for minority groups. From 1961 until her retirement in 1982, she worked in the Department of Health, Education and Welfare where she monitored joint federal and state programs. In 1970 President Richard M. Nixon appointed her to the President's Advisory Council on Adult Education.

Sources: *Jet* 88 (7 August 1995): 53.

1964 • On November 3, 1964, [Archie W.] A. W. Willis Jr., (1925–1988) was the first black elected to the general assembly since 1889, taking his seat on the first Monday in January 1965. Born in Birmingham, Alabama, and raised in Memphis, Tennessee, he was a practicing attorney in Memphis from 1953 to 1971. Willis had served as chief counsel for James Meredith when Meredith sought to enter the University of Mississippi in 1962. From 1971 until he died, Willis was a real estate broker. He also was director of the Greater Memphis Race Relations Council and secretary of the Tennessee Voters' Council. Willis graduated from Talladega College in Alabama and received his law degree from the University of Wisconsin School of Law.

Sources: Scott, *The Negro in Tennessee Politics,* pp. 195–98; Jones, *Every Day in Tennessee History,* pp. 53, 215.

1965 • Benjamin Lawson Hooks (1925–2010) was the first black criminal court judge in the state since Reconstruction. Governor Frank G. Clement appointed him to complete a judgeship that had become vacant. The next year he was elected for a full term; however, he resigned to become president of the Mahalia Jackson Fried Chicken franchise.

Sources: *Ebony Success Library,* vol. 1, p. 158; *Encyclopedia of Black America,* p. 443–44; Smith, *Notable Black American Men,* pp. 565–68; *Who's Who among African Americans,* 26th ed., p. 581; *Notable Black American Men,* pp. 565–68.

1966 • James O. Patterson Jr. (1935–) of Memphis was the first black elected to the state senate. In 1969 Avon Nyanza Williams Jr. (1921–1994) was elected, becoming the second black elected to the senate. Patterson was a lawyer and a bishop of the Church of God in Christ. With law degrees from the University of Boston in 1947 and 1948, Williams had been a leading Nashville lawyer and was much in the public eye for his major role in the Nashville school desegregation case. Williams was born in Knoxville, Tennessee, and graduated from Johnson C. Smith University in Charlotte, North Carolina, in 1940. His education at Boston University School of Law was interrupted when he joined the army. He practiced law in Knoxville until 1953, and filed a successful suit to desegregate Tennessee's public schools. Williams moved to Nashville and went into general law practice with civil rights lawyer Z. Alexander Looby, remaining there for sixteen years. Looby, Williams, and William's cousin, Thurgood Marshall, then with the NAACP's Legal Defense and Education Fund, filed suit in 1955 that resulted in desegregation of public schools in Nashville in 1971. During the 1950s and 1960s Williams was involved in over twenty-four major civil rights suits. He made his first bid for public office in 1968, when he sought to fill a seat in the newly created Nineteenth Senatorial District. He defeated Dorothy Lavinia "D" Brown and became the second black elected to a seat in the Tennessee Senate.

Sources: *Biographical Dictionary of African-American Holiness Pentecostals 1880–1990,* pp. 210–11 (Patterson); Hornsby, *Chronology of African-American History,* pp. 134, 199; Smith, *Notable Black American Men,* pp. 1224–27; *Tennessean* (9 February 1992); *Who's Who among Black Americans, 1992–93,* p. 1512 (Williams); Smith, *Notable Black American Men,* pp. 1224–27 (Williams).

1967 • Dorothy Lavinia "D" Brown (1919–2004) was the first black woman to serve in the state legislature. Elected from the Fifth District in 1966, she took office the next year and for two years served in the lower house. In 1968 she was unsuccessful in her bid for a seat in the Tennessee senate.

Sources: *Encyclopedia of Black America,* p. 194; Smith, *Notable Black American Women,* pp. 114–16; *Tennessean* (9 February 1992); *Who's Who among Black Americans,* 14th ed., p. 151.

1972 • State Senator James O. Patterson Jr. (1935–), a Democrat, in August became the first black to win a major party congressional nomination in the state's history. He was nominated during the fall primary elections for a seat in the newly established Fourth Congressional District (Memphis) of Tennessee.

Sources: Hornsby, *Milestones in 20th Century African-American History,* p. 164.

1980 • Memphis attorney George Brown was the first black on the Tennessee Supreme Court. Appointed in June this year, he lost to the Democratic nominee in the August election.

Sources: *Tennessean* (22 August 1993).

1982 • Bernice Bouie Donald (1951–) was the first elected black woman judge in the state of Tennessee as general sessions court judge in Shelby County. In 1988 Donald became the first black woman to serve on a U.S. Bankruptcy Court. Donald was born in DeSoto County, Mississippi. She graduated from Memphis State University (now the University of Memphis) in 1974 with a bachelor's degree and from the Memphis State School of Law in 1979 with a law degree.

Sources: *Who's Who among African Americans,* 26th ed., pp. 347.

1987 • Adolpho A. Birch Jr. (1932–) was the first black member of the state court of appeals. Birch was a criminal court judge in Nashville at the time of his appointment. He was also the first black district attorney in Nashville from 1966 to 1969, and the first judge in both the general sessions from 1969 to 1978 and criminal courts from 1978 to 1987. In 1993 Birch became the first black to serve on the Tennessee Supreme Court, when he was appointed and then elected to serve until his term expired in 1998. In 1996 Birch became the state's first black chief justice. He also was lecturer in law at Fisk and Tennessee State universities in Nashville. A native of Washington, D.C., Birch studied at Howard University in Washington and received both his bachelor's and his law degree in 1956. He moved to Nashville and practiced law from 1958 to 1969. During that same time he was adjunct professor of legal medicine at Meharry Medical College in Nashville.

Sources: *Jet* 72 (1 June 1987): 20; 90 (17 June 1996): 36; 90 (17 June 1996): 36; *Tennessean* (12 May 1996); *Who's Who among African Americans,* 26th ed., p. 103.

Thelma Harper

1987 • Lois Marie DeBerry (1945–) was the first black woman speaker *pro tempore* of the house. Deberry was first elected to the house in 1972. She was born in Memphis and educated at LeMoyne-Owen College in that city. She is president emeritus of the National Black Caucus of State Legislators. She is also founder and chair of the Annual Legislative Retreat of the Tennessee Black Caucus. DeBerry has been widely recognized for her work with the Tennessee legislature.

Sources: *Jet* 71 (16 February 1987): 8; 79 (14 January 1991): 12; Smith, *Notable Black American Women,* Book II, pp. 167–70; *Who's Who among African Americans,* 26th ed., p. 328.

1991 • Thelma Marie Harper (1940–) was the first black woman elected to the state senate. She has served continuously since her first election. A graduate of Tennessee State University, Harper was already a noted entrepreneur and leading member of the Nashville City Council at the time of her election. As a council member, she has fought to discontinue a landfill in located in a black section of Bordeaux, a Nashville suburb. Harper was born in Williamson County.

Sources: *Tennessean* (9 February 1992); *Who's Who among African Americans,* 26th ed., p. 533.

Texas

Barbara Jordan

1967 • Barbara Charline Jordan (1936–1996) was the first black to sit in the Texas senate since 1883. In 1972 she became president *pro tempore* of the senate, the first black woman to preside over a legislative body in the United States, and the first acting black governor of the state. Later that year, she was elected to the U.S. House of Representatives. In 2001 the City Council of Austin approved a statue to Jordan to be placed in the Austin–Bergstrom International Airport at the Barbara Jordan Passenger Terminal by 2002. The seven-foot-tall bronze work was crafted by Bruce Leslie Wolfe, a California artist.

Sources: *Encyclopedia of Black America,* p. 480; *Negro Almanac,* p. 449; Smith, *Notable Black American Women,* pp. 609–12; *Who's Who among Black Americans, 1992–93,* p. 800; *Jet* 99 (23 April 2001): 22.

1973 • Albert Hopkins Sr., (1928–) of Houston, was the first black in the South to serve as a member of the Texas State Board of Pharmacy. A 1949 graduate of Xavier University, he served until 1992.

Sources: *Jet* 82 (24 August 1992): 13; *Who's Who among African Americans,* 14th ed., p. 617.

1984 • Donald Joseph Floyd was the first judge and first black appointed to the newly created County Court-at-Law No. 3. Floyd had served as a municipal court judge in Port Arthur.

Sources: *Jet* 65 (9 January 1984): 26.

1984 • El Franco Lee was the first black to win a seat on the Harris County Commissioners Court, the governing body of the county. Harris County was formed in 1836.

Sources: *Jet* 66 (25 June 1984): 5.

1984 • Myra Atwell McDaniel (1932–) was appointed secretary of state, the first black to hold that post. She left the post in 1987. In 1994 Governor Ann Richards named Ron Kirk, who became the second black in that position. The Philadelphia native graduated from the University of Pennsylvania in 1954 and received her law degree from the University of Texas Law School in 1975. She served with the Railroad Commission of Texas and was assistant special counsel and assistant attorney general in charge of the Taxation Division. She was general counsel to Texas Governor Mark White. She was also a partner in two law firms. McDaniel was admitted to practice before the U.S. Supreme Court, the U.S. Fifth Circuit Court of Appeals, and the U.S. District Courts for the Eastern, Western, Southern, and Northern Districts of Texas.

Sources: *Jet* 85 (4 April 1994): 16; *Who's Who among African Americans,* 26th ed., p. 840.

1988 • On September 6, Lee Roy Young (1947–) became the first black Texas Ranger in the 165-year history of the group. A graduate of the University of Texas, he was a Navy veteran and a resident of Del Rio, where he was born. Young studied at several colleges in Texas, graduating from Southwest Texas Junior College with an associate's degree in 1973, and from the University of Texas at Austin, with a bachelor's degree in 1975. He has considerable experience in law enforcement in Texas, including his service as state trooper and criminal intelligence investigator.

Sources: *Jet* 75 (15 August 1988): 8; 75 (26 September 1988): 22; *Negro Almanac,* p. 1432; *Who's Who among African Americans,* 26th ed., p. 1397.

1998 • C. A. "Tony" Sherman became the first and only black and professional artist to serve as a commissioner on the Texas Commission of the Arts. The nationally recognized artist and sculptor, who was appointed by Governor George Bush, is owner of Tony Sherman's Fine Art Gallery in Missouri City, Texas.

Sources: *Jet* 93 (16 February 1998): 38; *Who's Who among African Americans,* 26th ed., p. 1119.

2001 • Wallace B. Jefferson was sworn in office in April and became the first black in Texas history to serve as state supreme court judge. Jefferson, of San Antonio, had been a partner with the firm that he helped to establish, Crofts, Callaway and Jefferson. The state bar named him to the State Commission on Judicial Conduct in 1999. He is also a member of the Supreme Court of Texas Advisory Committee and was president of the San Antonio Bar from 1988 to 1999. Jefferson graduated from Michigan State University in 1985 and the University of Texas School of Law in 1988.

Sources: *Jet* 99 (2 April 2001): 14; *Who's Who among Black Americans,* 26th ed., p. 655.

2007 • The first juvenile inmate ordered freed by a special master appointed to investigate the sentences of many youth held in Texas juvenile prisons was fifteen-year-old Shaquanda Cotton. Texas governor Rick Perry ordered the statewide investigation to determine whether or not the prison terms for many youths might have been unfairly extended. The teen, a ninth-grader when sentenced, was convicted of "assault on a pubic servant" after shoving a school hall monitor at Prison High School. She was sentenced to prison for up to seven years.

Sources: *Jet* 111 (13 April 2007): 9.

2007 • Craig Watkins (1967–) became the first black district attorney for Dallas County and the first Democrat to hold office there in twenty years. Of his appointment, Watkins said that he expected such an appointment to happen someday and that "it's kind of a disgrace that it took this long to happen."

Sources: *Jet* 111 (5 March 2007): 32; *Who's Who among African Americans,* 26th ed., p. 1295.

Utah

1977 • Robert L. Harris became the first black elected to the Utah House of Representatives. He was elected in a predominantly white district. Harris is a minister in the Church of God in Christ church.

Sources: *African-American Holiness Pentecostal Movement,* p. 91.

1984 • Tyrone E. Medley was the first black judge in the state, serving on the Fifth Circuit Court. He is a 1977 graduate of the University of Utah Law School.

Sources: *Jet* 66 (2 July 1984): 31.

Virgin Islands

1970 • Melvin H. Evans (1918–1984) became the first popularly-elected governor of the Virgin Islands—a U.S. territory on the eastern Caribbean. In mid-1969, President Richard M. Nixon appointed him governor, but it was not until August 1968 that Congress passed the Virgin Islands Elective Governor Act, giving residents the right to elect their governor. A Republican, Evans served from 1970 until 1975. He was a Howard University-educated physician who had served as assistant commissioner of health of the islands.

Sources: Alford, *Famous First Blacks,* p. 39; *Black Americans in Congress, 1870–2007,* pp. 494–87; *Ebony* 26 (March 1971): 105–8; 34 (March 1979): 26; *Negro Almanac,* p. 1556.

Virginia

1968 • William Ferguson Reid (1925–) was the first black in the House of Delegates in this century. Reid obtained his medical degree from Howard University School of Medicine in 1948 and was a staff surgeon in Richmond hospitals.

Sources: *Encyclopedia of Black America,* p. 730.

1978 • Jean Louise Harris (1931–) became the first black secretary of human resources for the state of Virginia; she held the cabinet position until 1982. The Richmond native graduated from Virginia Union University in that city. In 1955 she received her medical degree from the Medical College of Virginia, where she was the first black graduate. At the time of the appointment to the state post, she was professor of family practice at the Medical College of Virginia. From 1969 to 1973 she served as executive director of the National Medical Association Foundation and later as senior associate director and director of medical affairs at the University of Minnesota Hospital. In 1994, Harris became mayor of Eden Prairie, Minnesota.

Sources: *Crisis* 57 (April 1950): 228; *Ebony* 10 (July 1955), cover, pp. 76–81; *Jet* 53 (19 January 1978): 16; *Who's Who among African Americans,* 14th ed., p. 551.

1983 • John Charles Thomas was the first black member of the state supreme court. Thomas is a native of Norfolk.

Sources: *Jet* 64 (2 May 1983): 30.

1984 • Yvonne Bond Miller (1934–) was the first black woman member of the general assembly. In 1988 Miller became a member of the state senate. She became a professor at Norfolk State University in 1976.

Sources: *Jet* 65 (27 February 1984): 20; *Who's Who among African Americans,* 26th ed., p. 989.

1986 • L. [Lawrence] Douglas Wilder (1931–) was the first black lieutenant governor of Virginia. In 1990 Wilder became the nation's first black elected governor. In a hard-fought race, he defeated his Republican opponent and was elected to office on November 7, 1998. (In 1872 Pinckney Benton Stewart Pinchback [1837–1921] became the country's first black governor, but he was appointed to the short-term post.) Wilder was born in segregated Richmond, a mere two miles from the Governor's Mansion where he would live later on. He took his bachelor's degree at Virginia Union University in 1951 and his law degree at the Howard University School of Law in 1959. Wilder served in the U.S. Army and was sent to Korea. He became a sergeant and was awarded the Bronze Star. After his discharge, he entered Howard University's law school and graduated in May 1959. Wilder joined his father's law firm in Richmond and became known as a very effective trial lawyer. He made a successful bid for the Virginia State Senate in 1969, becoming the first black to hold that position. In his first address before the senate, he criticized the state song, "Carry Me Back to Old Virginia," stating that some of the lyrics glorified slavery and were offensive to blacks. Nonetheless, Virginia retained its song. Wilder continued to enjoy political success as was seen in 1989 when he ran for governor. On September 13, 1991, he announced that he would seek the 1992 Democratic nomination for president, but later withdrew his name and devoted his efforts to solving the state's financial problems. In 1997 Virginia Union named its new library and learning center in his honor. From 2005 to 2009, he was mayor of Richmond, the first black to hold that post.

Sources: *Contemporary Black Biography,* vol. 3, pp. 255–59; Hornsby, *Chronology of African-American History,* pp. 412, 420–21; Smith, *Notable Black American Men,* pp. 1217–20; *Who's Who among African Americans,* 26th ed., p. 1327.

1987 • Marcus Doyle Williams (1952–) was the first black state judge in Fairfax County, and also the youngest at age thirty-four. The Nashville, Tennessee, native is a 1973 Fisk University graduate. Williams took his law degree at the Catholic University of America School of Law in 1977. He has served as assistant commonwealth attorney from 1978 to 1980, lecturer in business legal studies at George Mason University from 1980 to 1985, assistant county attorney from 1980 to 1987, and judge in the General District Court from 1987 to 1990. In 1990 he became a circuit court judge. In 1992 he served on the National Judicial College faculty.

Sources: *Jet* 72 (17 August 1987): 36; *Who's Who among African Americans,* 26th ed., p. 1347.

1993 • Michelle Burton Mitchell (1963–) became the first black woman to serve as sheriff in Virginia. The Richmond native graduated from Virginia Commonwealth University in 1984. Since 1986 she has held several posts in the Virginia Department of Corrections.

Sources: *Jet* 85 (22 November 1993): 9; *Who's Who among African Americans,* 26th ed., p. 886.

1994 • Upon the nomination of President Bill Clinton, John W. Marshall became the first black U.S. marshal for the eastern district of Virginia. He is the youngest son of U.S. Supreme Court Justice Thurgood Marshall. He left the post to become director of the U.S. Marshal's Service.

Sources: *Jet* 86 (16 May 1994): 18; *Who's Who among African Americans,* 26th ed., p. 814.

1997 • Paul Clinton Harris Sr. (1964–), who was elected in Albermarle County, became the first black Republican in the state legislature in more than a century. He received 72 percent of the vote in the Republican primary on June 10 this year. He won the general election on November 4 with 63 percent of the vote. Harris stepped down from office in 2001 to become deputy assistant U.S. attorney general in Washington, D.C. Harris grew up in Charlottesville and earned degrees from Hampton University and George Washington University's law school.

Sources: *Jet* 93 (24 November 1997): 4; *Who's Who among African Americans*, 26th ed., p. 542; *New York Times* (4 November 1997).

2000 • Frank J. Thornton became the first black chairman of the Board of Henrico County Supervisors. A professor at Virginia Union University in Richmond, he was appointed to the board in 1996 and subsequently became vice chairman. He was the only Democrat on the five-person board.

Sources: *Jet* 97 (21 February 2000): 36.

2001 • The first foreign-born woman, the first female veteran, and the first black woman elected to Virginia's House of Delegates was Winsome Sears (1964?–). A Republican and former member of the U.S. Marines, she broke the hold that Democrats had on the seat in the predominantly black Norfolk district. While campaigning, she went door to door in housing projects and elsewhere talking to people. Quoted in the *New York Times*, she said, "When I set out in this race, I didn't intend to make history."

Sources: *New York Times* (15 December 2001).

2002 • Earle Sears became the first GOP woman delegate to Virginia's Black Legislative Caucus.

Sources: *Jet* 102 (25 February 2002): 10.

2002 • Belle Smith Wheelan (1951–) was sworn in office as Secretary of Education to Virginia Governor Mark Warner's cabinet on January 13, making her the first black woman to serve in this capacity.

Sources: *Who's Who among African Americans*, 26, ed., pp. 1314.

Washington

1889 • After Washington achieved statehood this year, William Owen Bush (1832–1907) was the first black elected to the state legislature. The son of the pioneer George Washington Bush (1790?–1863), William Owen Bush was a master farmer, who won a gold medal for his wheat in the 1876 Centennial Exposition in Philadelphia. While in office, Bush pushed for bills related to agriculture, especially those that called for the establishment of an agricultural college in the state. He was elected to a second term in the legislature.

Sources: *Black World* 19 (July 1970): 90–98; Logan and Winston, *Dictionary of American Negro Biography*, p. 83; Katz, *The Black West*, pp. 74, 75, 77; Salzman, *Encyclopedia of African-American Culture and History*, vol. 5, p. 2785.

1950 • Charles M. Stokes (1904?–1997) became the first black in this century to be elected to the state house of representatives. Ten years later he became the first black in the state to run for lieutenant governor.

Sources: *Jet* 91 (13 January 1997): 18.

1989 • The first black elected mayor of Seattle was Norman Blann Rice (1943–), who had spent eleven years on the City Council. He took office in 1990 and was re-elected in 1993. Rice left office in 1997; a year earlier he launched a campaign for governor but was unsuccessful in his bid. Born in Denver, he received his bachelor's degree from the University of Washington in 1972 and his master's degree in public administration from that institution in 1974.

Sources: *Jet* 89 (1 April 1996): 24; *Who's Who among African Americans*, 26th ed., p. 1045; Salzman, *Encyclopedia of African-American Culture and History*, Supplement, pp. 232–33.

2001 • Rosa Franklin, a Democrat from Tacoma, became the first black president *pro tempore* of the state senate. Her responsibilities require her to preside over the forty-nine member senate in the absence of the lieutenant governor. A retired nurse, she has served in the senate since 1993. From 1998 to 2000 Franklin was senate majority whip. She advocated health and public safety.

Sources: *Jet* 99 (19 March 2001): 19.

West Virginia

1962 • Mildred Mitchell-Bateman (1922–2012) was the first woman in the United States to head a state Mental Health Department; she was also the first black to have cabinet rank in West Virginia government. Mitchell-Bateman is a native of Cordele, Georgia. She graduated from Johnson C. Smith University in Charlotte, North Carolina, and later from the Women's Medical College of Pennsylvania. After interning at Harlem Hospital in New York, she completed a psychiatric residency at Winter Veterans Administration Hospital in Topeka, Kansas. She served as physician, clinical director, and superintendent at Lakin State Hospital in West Virginia, in the late 1950s. Then she became supervisor and acting director of the West Virginia State Department of Mental Health in the early 1960s. From 1962 to 1977 she was the department's fulltime director. Mitchell-Bateman has been prominently featured in a number of publications, including *Vogue* and several state textbooks.

Sources: *Ebony Success Library,* vol. 1, p. 224; *Negro Almanac,* pp. 1387–88; *Who's Who among African Americans,* 26th ed., p. 887; Smith, *Notable Black American Women, Book II,* pp. 479–80.

1992 • The first black executive director of the West Virginia Commission for the Deaf and Hard of Hearing was Hubert Anderson Jr. He became hearing disabled as a result of spinal meningitis when he was six years old. He is a staunch advocate and spokesperson for hearing and speech disabled in the state.

Sources: *Jet* 92 (14 July 1997): 18.

Wisconsin

1978 • Vel R. Phillips (1924–) was the first woman, and the first black, to be elected to a statewide constitutional office, secretary of state. Her law degree from the University of Wisconsin in 1951 was also a first. She was the first black elected to the Milwaukee Common Council (1956–71), the first black elected to serve on the National Convention Committee of either party in 1958, and the first black woman judge in the state in 1972.

Sources: Clayton, *The Negro Politician,* pp. 132–37; *Ebony Success Library,* vol. 1, p. 246; Lee, *Interesting People,* p. 136; Smith, *Notable Black American Women,* pp. 848–51; *Who's Who among Black Americans, 1992–93,* p. 1122.

GOVERNMENT: FEDERAL

District of Columbia Bar

1872 • The first black woman lawyer in the United States, and the third woman admitted to law practice in this country, was Charlotte E. Ray (1850–1911). As a graduate of Howard Law School (Washington, D.C.), she was automatically admitted to practice in the lower courts of the district, and on April 23, 1872, she became the first black woman admitted to practice before the Supreme Court. Ray was born in New York City. Hampered by her gender, she eventually became a teacher in the Brooklyn schools. She attended the National Women's Suffrage Association held in New York City in 1876 and she was active in the National Association of Colored Women. Ray's father, Charles Bennett Ray (1807–1886), was a notable abolitionist, minister, and editor. Her sister, Florence T. Ray (1849–1916), was an accomplished poet.

Sources: Hine, *Black Women in America,* pp. 965–66; *Encyclopedia of Black America,* p. 500; Smith, *Notable Black American Women,* pp. 922–24.

Federal Appointees

1861 • William Cooper Nell (1816–1874), historian and anti-slavery leader, was the first black to hold a federal position as a Boston postal clerk. In 1855 Nell published *The Colored Patriots of the American Revolution,* which was the first substantial historical work by a black man in America. After studying law for a brief period, he joined local abolitionists in their efforts to desegregate Boston's schools. He was associated with the *Liberator* during the early 1840s as a writer and supervisor of its Negro Employment Office. He also worked with William Lloyd Garrison, representing him at anti-slavery functions. He was unsuccessful in his bid for the state legislature in 1850. Nell continued his anti-slavery efforts by working in the Underground Railroad and by becoming a founder of a Committee on Vigilance that worked to undermine the Fugitive Slave Act. He served as postal clerk until his death.

Sources: Logan and Winston, *Dictionary of American Negro Biography,* pp. 472–73; Jackson, *A History of Afro-American Literature,* pp. 201–2; Robinson, *Historical Negro Biographies,* p. 104; Smith, *Notable Black American Men,* pp. 871–74.

William Cooper Nell

1865 • James Lewis (1832–1914) was the first black to receive an appointment from the federal government as inspector of customs for the Port of New Orleans. When the Union troops occupied New Orleans in 1862, Lewis abandoned the Confederate ship on which he was serving as a steward, raised two companies of black soldiers, and led the 1st Regiment of the Louisiana National Guard during the battle for Port Hudson. He was active in Reconstruction politics and received several federal appointments.

Sources: Baskin, *Dictionary of Black Culture,* p. 270.

Ebenezer Bassett

1869 • Ebenezer Don Carlos Bassett (1833–1908) became the first black diplomat when he was appointed minister resident to Haiti. Prior to the appointment, he served as principal of Philadelphia's Institute for Colored Youth. After completing his Haitian assignment in 1877, he served for ten years as a general consul from Haiti to the United States.

Sources: Logan and Winston, *Dictionary of American Negro Biography,* p. 32; Garrett, *Famous First Facts about Negroes,* pp. 46, 158; Robinson, *Historical Negro Biographies,* p. 49.

1869 • Henry McNeal Turner (1833–1915) was the first black to serve as a United States postmaster. He served as postmaster for Macon, Georgia. Turner resigned after serving for only a few months, because racism prevented him from performing his duties.

Sources: Logan and Winston, *Dictionary of American Negro Biography,* pp. 608–10; Robinson, *Historical Negro Biographies,* p. 132; Smith, *Notable Black American Men,* pp. 1133–37.

1871 • Daniel Alexander Payne Murray (1852–1925), librarian, bibliographer and bibliophile, was the first black to hold a professional position at the Library of Congress. Under the mentorship of the librarian of Congress, Ainsworth R. Spofford, Murray became proficient in several languages and acquired invaluable research skills. In 1881 he was advanced to assistant librarian, a position he held until his retirement in 1923. He was asked to prepare an exhibit on black achievements for the 1900 Paris Exposition, and an accompanying bibliography was a cornerstone for future black bibliographies by him and others. He was a builder as well and became involved in several fine residences in Washington and in the Anacostia section of the District of Columbia. His interest in industrial education led him to agitate for industrial training in the local black schools. As a result, the city established the Armstrong Manual Training Building for such training and as "a monument to his energy." Murray was born in Baltimore, Maryland, and studied in local schools, then entered the Unitarian Seminary in Baltimore.

Daniel Murray

Sources: Logan and Winston, *Dictionary of American Negro Biography,* pp. 463–56; Garrett, *Famous First Facts about Negroes,* p. 97; Smith, *Notable Black American Men,* pp. 860–61.

1871 • James Milton Turner (1840–1915), educator and diplomat, was the first black minister to Liberia. In 1866 he was appointed to teach in Missouri's first tax supported school for blacks. His support of Ulysses S. Grant resulted in his appointment as minister resident and consul-general to Liberia on March 1, 1871. He was actually the second black named, since James W. Mason, nominated in March 1870, never took his post.

Sources: Bennett, *Before the Mayflower,* pp. 489, 625; Logan and Winston, *Dictionary of American Negro Biography,* p. 611; Baskin, *Dictionary of Black Culture,* p. 441.

1875 • Bass Reeves (1838–1910) was sworn in as a federal deputy marshal in Fort Smith, Arkansas, and became the first black federal law enforcement officer on the early Western frontier. For thirty-two years he was a deputy U.S. marshal in Indian Territory and also served with the Muskogee Police Department. Reeves worked as deputy marshal with Judge Isaac C. Parker, known as the "hanging judge." For twenty-one years, Reeves and Parker worked in the federal territory that later became Oklahoma. Born in slavery on a Texas cotton plantation, Reeves fled his master who allowed him to demonstrate his skill as a marksman but refused to teach him to read. Reeves was a fugitive in the Oklahoma territory until the Civil War ended. As a free black, he became a farmer until Parker was named federal judge for the Western District of Arkansas, the early name for the Oklahoma territory. When Parker dedicated himself to rounding up the fearless bands of desperados, murders and outlaws, he sought equally fearless men to enforce the law. Reeves, a crack shot and one who knew the territory, befriended the local Native Americans and was said to fear "nothing that moves or breathes." He trailed and ended the life of notorious Bob Dozier and later captured his own son, a fugitive charged with killing his wife. Rather than retire in 1907, when other law enforcement agencies took over the marshal's duties, Reeves worked for two years with the Muskogee police force. In 1994 the Bass Reeves Foundation was formed in Muskogee, Oklahoma, to perpetuate the legacy of the legendary lawman. A memorial was placed in city hall at Muskogee, Oklahoma, in his honor.

Sources: *Jet* 87 (5 December 1995): 6; Clayton, *I've Been Marching All the Time,* pp. 222–26.

1877 • In March President Rutherford B. Hayes appointed Frederick Douglass (1818–1895) U.S. marshal for the District of Columbia, a first for an African American. This was his reward for service to the Republican Party. In March 1881 newly-elected President James A. Garfield appointed Frederick Douglass recorder of deeds for the District of Columbia. He held the post for five years and was the first black to hold this position.

Sources: Smith, *Notable Black American Men,* pp. 326–31.

1891 • Minnie M. Geddings Cox (1869–1933) was the first black postmistress in the United States. Cox was appointed to serve in the town of Indianola, Mississippi. President Benjamin Harrison appointed her to the post. President William McKinley reappointed her on May 22, 1897, and the appointment drew controversy from whites who wanted blacks removed from leadership positions. In 1902 she offered to resign; however, President Theodore Roosevelt refused her resignation. In 1903 Cox left Indianola but returned the next year after the controversy had waned. Born to former slaves from Lexington, Mississippi, Cox graduated from Fisk University with a teacher's certificate. She taught public school in Lexington and later in Indianola. She later moved to Rockford, Illinois, where she supported the Republican party, founded a number of businesses, and became an advocate of racial pride and progress.

Sources: Garrett, *Famous First Facts about Negroes,* p. 156; Hine, *Black Women in America,* vol. 1, pp. 289–90.

1893 • C. H. J. Taylor (?–1898) was the first black appointed to serve as a diplomat to a European country. President Grover Cleveland appointed him to serve as minister to Bolivia; however, the Senate refused to confirm his nomination. He later accepted the post of recorder of deeds for the District of Columbia.

Sources: Garrett, *Famous First Facts about Negroes,* p. 161.

1905 • Charles W. Anderson (1866–1938) was the first black person in the twentieth century appointed by a president to hold office north of the Mason-Dixon line. He was appointed Collector of Internal Revenue for the Second District of New York. An Ohio native, Anderson received his business training in Cleveland, Ohio. In the late 1880s he received his first appointment in New York City as United States gauger in the Second District, where he inspected bulk goods subject to duty. He received other presidential appointments until his retirement in 1934.

Sources: *Alexander's Magazine* 2 (15 September 1906): 19–20; Logan and Winston, *Dictionary of American Negro Biography,* pp. 14–15.

1911 • William Henry Lewis (1868–1949), football player and coach, lawyer, and public official, was the first black appointed to a sub-cabinet post. President William Howard Taft appointed him an assistant attorney general of the United States on November 26, 1911.

Sources: Bennett, *Before the Mayflower,* pp. 266, 515; Logan and Winston, *Dictionary of American Negro Biography,* pp. 396–97; Garrett, *Famous First Facts about Negroes,* p. 161.

1924 • Clifton Reginald Wharton Sr. (1899–1990) was the first black American to pass the foreign service examination. Wharton received his law degree from Boston University in 1923. He entered the United States Foreign Service in 1925, functioning as third secretary to Monrovia, Liberia. Over the next thirty years he held posts in the Malagasy Republic, Portugal, and Rumania. In 1958 Wharton became the first black to head a United States diplomatic mission, when he became minister to Romania under the Eisenhower

Administration. In 1961 Wharton was sworn in as ambassador to Norway and became the first black ambassador to that country.

Sources: *Jet* 91 (10 March 1997): 19; *Current Biography, 1990*, p. 665; Garrett, *Famous First Facts about Negroes*, p. 7; Robinson, *Historical Negro Biographies*, p. 259.

1936 • Mary Jane McLeod Bethune (1875–1955), educator, civil rights leader, advisor to presidents, and government official, was the first black woman to head a federal office. On June 24 President Franklin D. Roosevelt appointed Bethune to serve as director of the Division of Minority Affairs of the New Deal's National Youth Administration (NYA). The NYA was founded in 1935 to provide job-training for unemployed youths, and part-time work for needy students.

Sources: Logan and Winston, *Dictionary of American Negro Biography*, pp. 41–43; Smith, *Notable Black American Women*, pp. 86–92; Robinson, *Historical Negro Biographies*, p. 163.

George Crockett

1939 • George W. Crockett Jr. (1909–1997) was the first black lawyer with the Department of Labor. In 1943 he was named senior attorney with the Fair Labor Standards Act Administration, hearing examiner for Fair Employment Practices Commission. He left that post and became founder and director of the International United Auto Workers, Fair Employment Practices Department in Detroit. He became well known for his work with fair labor practices and as a civil rights activist. In 1946 he became a founding partner with the Goodman, Crockett, Eden, and Robb legal firm, one of the first integrated firms in the nation. In the 1960s Crockett became a key player in the Civil Rights Movement. He left his law office and, at the request of the National Lawyer's Guild, he became director of Project Mississippi, an organized effort to halt white institutions' illegal practices against black residents in Mississippi. He later returned to Detroit and was elected to the Recorder's Court and for a brief time was a visiting judge on the Michigan Court of Appeals. He became a member of the U.S. House of Representatives in 1972. Born in Jacksonville, Florida, Crockett was educated at Morehouse College in 1931 and the University of Michigan in 1934. He was senior attorney, U.S. Department of Labor, from 1939 to 1943.

Sources: *Negro Almanac, 1976*, p. 1024; *Who's Who in Colored America, 1950*, p. 127; Smith, *Notable Black American Men*, pp. 236–38; *Jet* 92 (22 September 1997): 56–57; *Contemporary Black Biography*, vol. 10, pp. 36–40.

1944 • Ralph Johnson Bunche (1904–1971) became the first black non-diplomatic official in the Department of State, when he was made divisional assistant, Division of Political Studies. In 1947 he transferred to the United Nations. He headed various divisions of the United Nations and mediated the end of the Arab-Israeli War in 1949—he was the highest-ranking American at the United Nations. In 1950 he became the first black American to win the Nobel Peace Prize.

Sources: Baskin and Runes, *Dictionary of Black Culture*, p. 74; Garrett, *Famous First Facts about Negroes*, p. 185; Robinson, *Historical Negro Biographies*, p. 170; Smith, *Notable Black American Men*, pp. 152–56; *Contemporary Black Biography*, vol. 5, pp. 41–45.

1948 • Edward R. Dudley (1911–2005) was the first black diplomat to receive the formal designation of ambassador. President Harry S. Truman appointed him ambassador to Liberia, where he served from 1949 until 1953. (It was not until 1948 that the post in Liberia was raised from a ministership to an ambassadorship—the policy of the State Department until this period was to limit the appointment of blacks in the foreign service to ministerships, consulates, and vice-consulates.) Truman was responsible for elevating Liberia to full diplomatic status, making it the first black nation to hold that designation. After returning to the United States, in October 1955 Dudley was named judge on the Domestic Relations Court. In 1961 he was elected borough president of Manhattan. In 1962 became the first black to be nominated for attorney general of New York, but lost the election. On November 3, 1966, he was elected to the state supreme court. Born in Virginia, he studied at Johnson C. Smith and Howard universities and earned his law degree at St. John's University in Brooklyn.

Sources: Baskin and Runes, *Dictionary of Black Culture,* p. 144; Garrett, *Famous First Facts about Negroes,* p. 7; Robinson, *Historical Negro Biographies,* p. 186; Smith, *Notable Black American Men,* pp. 341–44.

1950 • Edith S. Sampson (1901–1979) was named a delegate to the United Nations and became the first black woman to hold the designation. President Harry S. Truman appointed her to the post; she continued her term under the Eisenhower Administration until 1953.

Sources: *Jet* 96 (18 October 1999): 19; Smith, *Notable Black American Women,* pp. 969–73.

1954 • On March 4, 1954, Jesse Ernest Wilkins Sr. (1894–1959) was appointed as the first black assistant secretary of labor. President Dwight D. Eisenhower appointed him to this sub-cabinet post. Wilkins was the top-ranking black in the executive branch at the time. He was also the first black leader of a U.S. delegation to the International Labor Organization meetings held in Cuba and in Europe. The son of a Baptist minister, Wilkins was born in Farmington, Missouri, and graduated from the University of Illinois in 1918. He worked his way through the University of Chicago law school and received his law degree in 1921. His son James Ernest Wilkins Jr. (1923–2011) had the distinction of obtaining a doctorate in mathematics from the University of Chicago at age nineteen, in 1942.

Sources: Bennett, *Before the Mayflower,* p. 549; Baskin and Runes, *Dictionary of Black Culture,* p. 471; Hornsby, *Milestones in Twentieth-Century African-American History,* p. 55; Smith, *Notable Black American Men,* pp. 1220–22.

1954 • On August 7, 1954, Charles H. Mahoney (1886–1966), lawyer, was nominated by President Dwight Eisenhower and confirmed by the Senate as the first black permanent member of the delegation to the United Nations. Born in Michigan, Mahoney was educated at Fisk University and the University of Michigan. In 1928 he helped form the Great Lakes Mutual Insurance Company and later became its president and chairman of the board.

Sources: Bennett, *Before the Mayflower,* pp. 550, 625; Garrett, *Famous First Facts about Negroes,* p. 192; *Who's Who in Colored America, 1950,* p. 350.

1955 • Jewel Stradford Lafontant (1928–1997) was the first black woman named assistant U.S. attorney for the Northern Illinois district. President Dwight D. Eisenhower appointed her to the post. A Chicago native, Lafontant was the daughter of renowned attorney C. Francis Stradford. She received her education at Oberlin College and the University of Chicago, and was a trial lawyer with the Legal Aid Bureau. She served in the Illinois office until 1958. In 1973 Lafontant became the first black woman deputy United States solicitor general. In 1983 she became a partner in the firm Vedder, Price, Kaufman and Kammholz. In 1989 she was appointed by President George Bush as an ambassador-at-large and coordinator for refugee affairs.

Sources: *Contemporary Black Biography,* vol. 3, pp. 139–41; Hine, *Black Women in America,* pp. 689–90; Smith, *Notable Black American Women,* p. 644.

1955 • E. Frederic Morrow (1909–1994) was the first black man to serve as White House aide. President Dwight D. Eisenhower appointed him administrative assistant on July 9. A New Jersey native and son of a minister, Morrow was educated at Bowdoin College and received his law degree from Rutgers University. He worked with the public affairs division of Columbia Broadcasting System and took a leave in 1952 to join Eisenhower's election campaign. Morrow resigned his position with CBS, expecting to be named to a post in Eisenhower's administration. He remained unemployed until he accepted a position as advisor on business affairs in the Department of Commerce. Two years later he was named an administrative officer for the Special Projects Group. In 1957 he was named a White House aide to Arthur Larson, the President's chief speechwriter. A year later he returned to the Special Projects Group and was sworn in on January 25, 1958. In 1963 he wrote *Black Man in the White House.*

Sources: *Who's Who among Black Americans, 1977,* p. 651; *Who's Who in Colored America, 1950,* p. 385; Smith, *Notable Black American Men,* pp. 833–34; *Jet* 86 (8 August 1994): 16–17.

1957 • Archibald J. Carey Jr. (1908–1981), clergyman and public official, was the first black American to head the President's Committee on Government Employment Policy. Appointed by President Dwight D. Eisenhower on August 3, Carey was a lawyer and two-term Chicago alderman. He received his law degree from John Marshall Law School. From 1953 to 1956 he served as an alternate delegate to the United Nations.

Sources: Baskin and Runes, *Dictionary of Black Culture,* p. 82; Garrett, *Famous First Facts about Negroes,* p. 162; *Jet* 84 (9 August 1993): 24; 86 (8 August 1994): 20.

1957 • Clinton Everett Knox (1908–?) was the first black secretary to the United States Mission to the North Atlantic Treaty Organization (NATO). Born in Massachusetts, Knox was educated at Williams College, and Brown and Harvard universities. A career foreign service officer, he held posts in Haiti, Dahomey, Honduras, and France.

Sources: Baskin and Runes, *Dictionary of Black Culture,* p. 258; *Who's Who among Black Americans, 1977,* p. 530.

1960 • Andrew T. Hatcher (1923–1992) was the first black presidential press secretary. President John Kennedy named Hatcher as associate press secretary, on November 10, 1960, and for a time he was the highest-ranking black appointee in the executive branch of the federal government. Hatcher, the father of seven children, was mentioned in the press without reference to his race; little has been written about him in the scholarly publications on Kennedy and his administration. Hatcher joined Kennedy's campaign and worked with Pierre Salinger, whom he had known during Adlai Stevenson's unsuccessful campaign. After the elections, Salinger was named press secretary, and he asked that Hatcher become his associate. Hatcher helped to coordinate press activities and fielded requests from hundreds of correspondents and photographers assigned to the White House. In Salinger's absence, Hatcher conducted news conferences and briefed the press. On Kennedy's inauguration day, television cameras caught two men seated behind him; they were Salinger and Hatcher. Hatcher at one time was managing editor of San Francisco's *Sun Reporter*. Toward the end the 1950s he was assistant labor commissioner of California, under the administration of Democratic governor Edmund Brown.

Sources: Hornsby, *Chronology of African-American History,* p. 111; Hornsby, *Milestones in Twentieth-Century African-American History,* p. 67; Giglio, "Kennedy," *American Visions* (February–March 1995), pp. 40–41.

1960 • Frank D. Reeves (1916–1973), who was active in local politics in Washington, D.C., became the first black special assistant to the President, John F. Kennedy. A native of Montreal, Quebec, Canada, he graduated from Howard University law school in 1939. He was an assistant NAACP counsel and served on Thurgood Marshall's staff. Known for his great legal mind, he was a pioneer in civil rights case, including *Brown vs. Board of Education* that led to school integration in 1954. Reeves was the Washington representative for the NAACP Legal Defense and Educational Fund between 1946 and 1961. He was also active in national Democratic politics and became the Democratic Party's first black national committeeman from the District of Columbia; in 1960 he seconded the nomination of Kennedy for president. During Kennedy's campaign, it was Reeves who introduced him to black America's leading figures, including Roy Wilkins and A. Philip Randolph, and encouraged black leaders to support Kennedy during the elections. After Kennedy was elected, he considered Reeves for a district judgeship; instead, he was named special assistant to the president. Reeves was largely responsible for furthering desegregation of government facilities. He aided in the appointment of blacks to federal posts, in particular the Internal Revenue Service. Kennedy nominated Reeves to membership on the district's board of commissioners. However, before the Senate confirmed the nomination, Reeves was accused of failure to pay income and property taxes. Kennedy responded by withdrawing his nomination; Reeves acknowledged his malfeasance, left his post, and became a law professor at Howard University. In 1969 Reeves was a fellow at the Metropolitan Applied Research Center. Later he helped to establish the Joint Center for Political Studies and until 1972 he headed the center. He remained active in civil rights activities. Now forgotten by the public, Reeves was an important figure in the history of civil rights; his life reflects the racial progress and the enduring legacy of the Kennedy era. He died in Freedmen's Hospital in Washington, D.C., on April 8, 1973, from the effects of a stroke.

Sources: *American Visions* (February–March 1995): 40–41; *Crisis* 80 (August/September 1973): 250; *Jet* 44 (26 April 1973): 33.

1961 • Mercer Cook (1903–1987), scholar, author and diplomat, was the first black American ambassador to Nigeria. Born in Washington, D.C., Cook was educated at Amherst College, the Sorbonne, and Brown University. He had a distinguished teaching career at Howard and Atlanta universities. He published a number of books and edited several scholarly journals. His diplomatic career included appointments in Nigeria (1961–64) and Senegal and Gambia (1964–66).

Sources: Baskin and Runes, *Dictionary of Black Culture,* p. 117; Robinson, *Historical Negro Biographies,* p. 175; *Who's Who in Colored America, 1950,* p. 119.

1961 • Cecil Francis Poole (1907–1997) was the first black federal attorney in the continental United States. Until his appointment, black attorneys for the United States served only in the U.S. Virgin Islands. Poole was appointed to the San Francisco office. The Alabama-born attorney received his legal training at the University of Michigan and Harvard University. He was a practicing lawyer in California and taught at the University of California, Berkeley. In 1976 he became a U.S. district judge.

Sources: Baskin and Runes, *Dictionary of Black Culture,* p. 354; Kane, *Famous First Facts,* p. 49; *Who's Who among Black Americans, 1992–93,* p. 1135; *New York Times* (16 November 1997); *Jet* 93 (8 December 1997): 55.

1961 • Robert Clifton Weaver (1907–1997) was the first black administrator of the Federal Housing and Home Finance Administration, the highest federal post ever held by an African American at the time. While in office, Weaver coordinated activities of five subordinate agencies. In 1961 President Kennedy was unsuccessful in his attempt to make the agency a cabinet department.

Sources: Hornsby, *Chronology of African-American History,* pp. 111, 126; Garrett, *Famous First Facts about Negroes,* p. 113; Robinson, *Historical Negro Biographies,* pp. 257–58; Smith, *Notable Black American Men,* pp. 1195–98.

1962 • Henry M. Michaux Jr. (1930–) was the first black federal assistant district attorney in the South. Born in Durham, North Carolina, Michaux was educated at North Carolina Central University and Rutgers University. He joined the firm Michaux and Michaux as senior partner and real estate broker. From 1962 to 1972 Michaux was chief assistant district attorney for Durham County. He was U.S. attorney for the Middle Judicial District, North Carolina, from 1977 to 1981. Since 1985 he has been a member of the North Carolina General Assembly.

Sources: *Paths Toward Freedom,* p. 65; *Who's Who among African Americans,* 26th ed., p. 870.

1963 • Howard Jenkins Jr. (1915–2003) was the first black to serve on the National Labor Relations Board. A native of Denver, Colorado, Jenkins was a law professor, when he was first appointed by President John F. Kennedy. He was reappointed in 1968 by President Lyndon B. Johnson, in 1973 by President Richard M. Nixon, and in 1978 by President Jimmy Carter.

Sources: Christmas, *Negroes in Public Affairs and Government,* p. 323; *Ebony Success Library,* vol. 1, p. 174; *Who's Who among Black Americans, 1992–1993,* p. 742.

1963 • Leslie N. Shaw (1922–1985) was the first black postmaster to head a postal unit of a major city. An Ohio native, Shaw was appointed postmaster of Los Angeles, California—the world's third largest postal operation. He supervised over ten thousand employees and handled more than eighty-four million dollars in stamps and services. He was educated at Ohio State University, and the University of California, Los Angeles. He began his career in the post office as a janitor.

Sources: Baskin and Runes, *Dictionary of Black Culture,* p. 400; Garrett, *Famous First Facts about Negroes,* p. 156; *Who's Who among Black Americans, 1977,* p. 804.

1963 • Thomas Young became regional director of the Department of Labor's Bureau of Veteran's Reemployment Rights for the states of New York and New Jersey. He was the first black to head a regional office for the department. During World War II he was captain of an artillery unit in the Pacific Theater. A federal government employee since 1945, Young brought to the office experience in veterans' programs. In 1946 he joined the New York Veterans Administration office and assisted veterans in receiving benefits that various acts of Congress provided.

Sources: *Sepia* 12 (December 1963), p. 34.

1964 • Charlotte Moton Hubbard (1913?–1995) was the first black woman deputy assistant secretary of state for public affairs. President Lyndon Johnson named her to the post—the highest permanent position held by a woman at that time. She helped eliminate racial discrimination against black soldiers in the Vietnam War, supervised the Vietnam Coordination Staff, the Office of Media Services, and the Office of Public Services. Before her appointment, she had devoted almost thirty years to education and public relations. Hubbard was later the first black appointed to an important position with a television station. The daughter of Tuskegee Institute president Robert Russa Moton (1867–1940), she was born in Hampton, Virginia, and grew up on the Tuskegee campus. She was educated at Tuskegee, Boston University, and Bennington College.

Sources: *Negro Almanac, 1976,* p. 1008; *Jet* 88 (9 January 1995): 18.

Carl Rowan

1964 • Carl Thomas Rowan (1925–2000) was the first black to head the United States Information Agency, where he served until 1965. From 1961 to 1963 he was deputy assistant secretary of state for public affairs, and from 1963 to 1964 he was ambassador to Finland. He began his career in journalism in 1948 as a copy editor for the *Minneapolis Tribune.* From 1950 to 1961 he was a staff reporter for that newspaper. In 1965 he became columnist for the *Chicago Daily News.* Rowan was political commentator for radio and television stations and frequently served as a panelist for *Agronsky and Company* and for *Meet the Press.* He was the first black to ever attend a meeting of the National Security Council. The U.S. Department of State recognized Rowan in 2001 when it dedicated the department's Carl T. Rowan Briefing Room in his honor. Rowan was born in Ravenscroft, Tennessee, and received his bachelor's degree from Oberlin College in 1947, and a master's degree in journalism from the University of Minnesota in 1948.

Sources: *Contemporary Black Biography,* vol. 1, pp. 208–12; Baskin and Runes, *Dictionary of Black Culture,* p. 385; Robinson, *Historical Negro Biographies,* p. 246; Obituary, *Who's Who among African Americans,* 14th ed., p. 1476.

1965 • Andrew Felton Brimmer (1926–), economist and educator, became the first black member of the governing body of the Federal Reserve System. Brimmer was born in Newellton, Louisiana, the son of a sharecropper and warehouseman. He was educated at the University of Washington, received his doctorate from Harvard University, and taught at Michigan State University. He joined government service as an assistant secretary for economic affairs at the Commerce Department. In 1976 he formed and became president of Brimmer and Company, an economic consulting firm, and serves on numerous boards of financial institutions and other agencies.

Sources: *Contemporary Black Biography,* vol. 2, pp. 37–39; *Negro Almanac, 1976,* pp. 345–46; Smith, *Notable Black American Men,* pp. 116–18.

Andrew Brimmer

1965 • Patricia Roberts Harris (1924–1985), lawyer and diplomat, was the first black woman ambassador appointed to an overseas post and the first black woman to hold diplomatic rank. A graduate of Howard and George Washington universities, Illinois-born Harris was appointed ambassador to Luxembourg by President Lyndon B. Johnson. Two years later she was named an alternate delegate to the United Nations. In 1971 she was elected to the boards of directors of International Business Machines and Chase National Bank.

The same year she was also elected to head the credentials committee at a meeting of the Democratic National Committee—the first black to chair the committee.

Sources: Garrett, *Famous First Facts about Negroes,* p. 7; Hornsby, *Chronology of African-American History,* p. 280; Kane, *Famous First Facts,* pp. 31, 50; Smith, *Notable Black American Women,* pp. 468–72; *Contemporary Black Biography,* vol. 2, pp. 99–101.

1965 • James Madison Nabrit Jr. (1900–1997) educator and civil rights lawyer, was the first black American ambassador to the United Nations. Atlanta-born Nabrit was educated at Morehouse College and Northwestern University. President Lyndon B. Johnson appointed him deputy representative to the United Nations Security Council, where he served from 1965 to 1967.

Sources: Bennett, *Before the Mayflower,* p. 574; Hornsby, *Chronology of African-American History,* p. 105; *Who's Who among Black Americans, 1992–93,* p. 1045.

Patricia Roberts Harris

1965 • Robert B. Pitts (1909–1982), business executive, was the first black appointed to a federal regional administrative post with the United States Department of Housing and Urban Development, in Region VI (San Francisco). Born in Georgia, he was educated at Howard University and the University of Washington.

Sources: *Who's Who among Black Americans, 1977,* p. 718; *Contemporary Black Biography,* vol. 13, pp. 87–91.

1965 • President Lyndon B. Johnson appointed Aileen Clarke Hernandez (1926–) to the Equal Employment Opportunities Commission, making her the first woman commissioner and one of the five minorities on the board.

Sources: Smith, *Notable Black American Women,* pp. 491–94.

1966 • Robert Clifton Weaver (1907–1997) was named secretary of housing and urban development by President Lyndon B. Johnson, becoming the first black to serve in the cabinet of a president. His innovative ideas for urban development resulted in easing of loan requirements, government loan guarantees, and other evidences of government intervention. Weaver was born in Washington, D.C. He received his bachelor's, master's, and doctorate degrees from Harvard University. He was an influential member of President Franklin D. Roosevelt's "Black Cabinet," a group that Mary McLeod Bethune called together in August 1936 to pressure for important advances for blacks. He continued to advise Roosevelt during the 1940s on housing, education, and employment issues. In 1960 and again in 1962, he was national chairman of the NAACP. Weaver held a number of government positions interspersed with teaching assignments at several universities, including Northwestern, Columbia, and New York. A productive scholar, he wrote four books and 185 articles on housing and urban issues. The Department of Housing and Urban Development headquarters building in Washington, D.C., was renamed to honor the country's first black cabinet member.

Robert Weaver

Sources: Hornsby, *Chronology of African-American History,* pp. 111, 126; Garrett, *Famous First Facts about Negroes,* p. 113; Robinson, *Historical Negro Biographies,* pp. 257–58; Smith, *Notable Black American Men,* pp. 1195–98.

1966 • Gertrude Sims Campbell was the first black woman hired in the post office in Greenville, Mississippi.

Sources: *Jet* 93 (12 January 1998): 19.

1967 • President Lyndon B. Johnson named Thurgood Marshall (1908–1993) the first black associate justice of the Supreme Court. In 1965 he became the first black American U.S. solicitor general. Baltimore-born Marshall graduated from Lincoln University in Pennsylvania and Howard University, and became one of the nation's foremost civil rights lawyers. From 1938 to 1961 he served for many years as NAACP counsel. Marshall represented the plaintiff in *Brown v. Board of Education* before the Supreme Court, which ruled in 1954 that racial segregation in public schools was unconstitutional. In 1962 President John F. Kennedy appointed Marshall judge of the Second Circuit Court of Appeals. President Lyndon B. Johnson appointed him solicitor general—the highest law enforcement position held by an African American at the time. He was the recipient of the coveted NAACP Spingarn Medal in 1946.

Sources: Kane, *Famous First Facts,* p. 624; Robinson, *Historical Negro Biographies,* p. 226; Hornsby, *Chronology of African-American History,* pp. 101, 112, 125; Smith, *Notable Black American Men,* pp. 762–67; Gates and Higginbotham, *African American National Biography,* vol. 1, p. 3; Finkelman, *Encyclopedia of African American History,* vol. 3, pp. 263–66.

1968 • Barbara M. Watson (1918–1983), administrator, was the first black and the first woman to serve as an assistant secretary of state. Born in New York City, Watson received her education at Barnard College and New York Law School. She began her career in the State Department in 1966. Under President Lyndon B. Johnson, she served as administrator of the Bureau of Security and Consular Affairs from 1977 to 1980, and from 1980 to 1981, under President Jimmy Carter's administration, she was ambassador to Malaysia. In the latter post she was the ranking American official in Malaysia with responsibility for all U.S. mission operations. She retired in 1981.

Sources: Garrett, *Famous First Facts about Negroes,* pp. 163, 197; *Jet* 63 (7 March 1983): 12; Smith, *Notable Black American Women,* Book II, pp. 691–93.

1970 • Samuel Riley Pierce Jr. (1922–2000) was the first black to serve as a general counsel to the Treasury Department. He was a member of the legal team that defended civil rights leaders including Martin Luther King Jr. against the *New York Times.* In 1980 President-elect Ronald Reagan named Pierce secretary of the Department of Housing and Urban Development; he was sworn in on January 23, 1981. He was the first and only black cabinet member in the Reagan administration. His office became under intense scrutiny during the late 1980s and Pierce was forced to resign in 1989. Some of his associates were indicted for fraud, bribery, and other wrongdoing, but Pierce was never charged. Pierce was born in Glen Clove, Long Island, New York, and educated at Cornell University. He held a number of governmental offices in New York prior to his entry into federal service.

Sources: Hornsby, *Chronology of African-American History,* p. 307; Hornsby, *Milestones in Twentieth-Century African-American History,* pp. 182, 307, 418; Obituary, *Who's Who among African Americans,* 14th ed., p. 1475; Smith, *Notable Black American Men,* pp. 936–38.

1970 • As human resources development officer for the Bureau of Latin America, Gloria Gaston was the first black to hold a major post in the Agency for International Development.

Sources: *Negro Almanac, 1976,* p. 1005.

1972 • As economic and commercial officer, James Estes Baker (1935–2001) was the first black assigned to serve in South Africa during apartheid. Baker was born in Suffolk, Virginia, and educated at the Haverford College and at Fletcher School of Law and Diplomacy at Tufts University. He entered the State Department in 1961. From 1973 to 1975 he served as an economics specialist at the U.S. Embassy in Pretoria. From 1980 to 1995, Baker directed economic and emergency relief programs at the United Nations. He later served as an adjunct professor at Long Island University and taught courses on diplomacy and disaster relief. At the time of his death from lung disease on April 15, 2001, he was living in Sag Harbor, New York, and Greenwich Village.

Sources: Alford, *Famous First Blacks,* pp. 29–30; Hornsby, *Milestones in Twentieth-Century African-American History,* p. 164; *Who's Who among African Americans,* 14th ed., pp. 55–56; *New York Times* Obituaries (25 April 2001).

1972 • Benjamin Lawson Hooks (1925–2010) was the first black commissioner of the Federal Communications Commission. Born in Memphis, Tennessee, Hooks was the grandson of Julia Hooks (1852–1942), the first black woman in the country to graduate from Berea College in Kentucky. He received his law degree from DePaul University in 1948, after studying at Le Moyne College and Howard University. He was a Baptist minister and a founding member of the Southern Christian Leadership Council. He was named executive secretary of the National Association for the Advancement of Colored People on

November 6, 1976, and held the post until 1992. Hooks returned to Memphis and became pastor of the Greater Middle Baptist Church. He was the 1986 NAACP Spingarn medalist.

Sources: *Contemporary Black Biography*, vol. 2, pp. 109–12; Hornsby, *Milestones in Twentieth-Century African-American History,* pp. 215, 489; Smith, *Notable Black American Men,* pp. 565–68; *Contemporary Black Biography,* vol. 2, pp. 109–12.

1973 • Henry Minton Frances (1922–) was the first black deputy assistant secretary of defense. Born in Washington, D.C., Frances was educated at the University of Pennsylvania, the U.S. Military Academy, and Syracuse University. He was deputy assistant secretary from 1973 to 1977. He served with the Department of Housing and Urban Development as executive assistant to the first secretary. He held several posts at Howard University and was president of the Black Revolutionary War Patriot Foundation.

Sources: *Who's Who among African Americans,* 26th ed., p. 430.

1976 • The first black to serve as chief delegate to the United Nations was Andrew J. Young Jr. (1932–). President Jimmy Carter appointed the then-congressman to the position. In August 1979, when Young met with the U.N. observer for the Palestine Liberation Organization, Zehdi Labib Terzi, he caused a stir in the State Department for violating rules that forbad contact with the PLO and was forced to resign his post.

Sources: Smith, *Notable Black American Men,* pp. 1280–83; *Contemporary Black Biography,* vol. 3, pp. 263–67.

1977 • On February 11, 1977, Clifford Alexander Jr. (1933–) was confirmed as the first black secretary of the U.S. Army, a post he held until 1980. Born in New York City, Clifford graduated from Harvard University in 1955 and took a law degree from Yale in 1958. He served in the U.S. National Guard from 1958 to 1959. He held posts in New York City, including that of assistant district attorney in 1959, executive director of the Manhattan-Hamilton-Grange Neighborhood agency from 1961 to 1963, and executive director of HARYOU youth agency from 1962 to 1963. Throughout the 1960s and 70s he served in a succession of presidential administrations, including chair of the Equal Opportunity Commission. At present he heads his own law firm, Alexander and Associates, in Washington, D.C.

Sources: Bennett, *Before the Mayflower,* p. 603; Hornsby, *Milestones in Twentieth-Century African-American History,* pp. 276–77; *Who's Who among African Americans,* 26th ed., p. 14; Smith, *Notable Black American Men,* pp. 15–17.

1977 • Drew Saunders Days III (1941–) was the first black director of the Justice Department's Civil Rights Division. Days, an Atlanta native, is a graduate of Hamilton College (1963) and Yale University Law School (1966). He was a Peace Corps volunteer as well as a volunteer attorney for the Civil Liberties Union. He has held a number of other positions, such as associate professor of law at Temple University and attorney with the NAACP Legal Defense Fund. Days is Alfred M. Ranking Professor at Yale Law School.

Sources: Hornsby, *Chronology of African-American History,* p. 281; *Who's Who among African Americans,* 26th ed., p. 326.

1977 • Emma Daniels McFarlin (1921–) was the first black woman to head the western region of the U.S. Department of Housing and Urban Development. Born in Camden, Arkansas, she graduated from Philander Smith College in 1950, the University of Wisconsin in 1961, and the U.S. International University, where she received her doctorate in 1976. Her career includes special assistant in the mayor's office in Los Angeles, teacher in San Francisco schools, and manager of the Low Rent Housing Project, Little Rock Redevelopment and Housing Authority.

Sources: *Who's Who among African Americans,* 26th ed., p. 845.

1977 • Terence A. Todman (1926–) was the first black named assistant secretary of state for Latin America. Todman was born in the United States Virgin Islands and educated in Puerto Rico and at Syracuse University. He began his diplomatic career in 1952 and held positions in India, Africa, Costa Rica, Spain, the United Nations, and Latin America. When he retired in 1994, he was honored at a reception in Capitol Hill's Statuary Hall; this was the first time such a ceremony was held there.

Sources: *Who's Who among African Americans,* 26th ed., p. 1238; Salzman, *Encyclopedia of African-American Culture and History,* vol.1, p. 105.

1977 • Azie B. Taylor Morton (1936–) was the first black American treasurer of the United States. Texas-born, Morton was educated at Huston-Tillotson College.

Sources: Kane, *Famous First Facts,* p. 675; *Who's Who among Black Americans, 1992–93,* p. 1030.

1977 • Joan Scott Wallace (1930–), educator, was the first black and the third woman to serve as assistant secretary for administration in the Department of Agriculture. Among her significant accomplishments while in office were programs designed to address the plight of black farmers. She helped recruit blacks to serve the USDA and held national forums to inform black farmers of assistance programs that were available to them. Born in Chicago, she is closely affiliated with the National Urban League, Howard University, and social work organizations, and has contributed articles to the *Howard Law Review, Focus, Diversity, Journal of Sociology and Social Work,* and *Atlantic Economic Journal.*

Sources: Smith, *Notable Black American Women,* pp. 1195–97; *Who's Who among Black Americans, 1977,* p. 922.

1977 • Togo Dennis West Jr. (1942–), business executive and attorney, was the first black U.S. Navy general counsel. His experience includes associate deputy attorney general for the Department of Justice; and special assistant to the secretary, deputy secretary, and general counsel for the Department of Defense. He was secretary of the U.S. Army from 1993 to 1998. After that, he became acting secretary for Veterans Affairs. Born in Winston-Salem, North Carolina, West received his bachelor's and his law degrees from Howard University.

Sources: *Contemporary Black Biography,* vol. 16, pp. 226–29; *Who's Who among African Americans,* 26th ed., pp. 1311.

1977 • Patricia Roberts Harris (1924–1985) became the first black woman to serve as a Cabinet secretary. Appointed by President Jimmy Carter, she was secretary of Housing and Urban Development. In 1980 she was named secretary of Health, Education and Welfare, later known as the Department of Health and Human Services. Before accepting the federal posts, Harris rose through the ranks at Howard University as law school lecturer and associate dean of students from 1961 to 1965 and 1967 to 1969, and later dean of the law school in 1969. She was the first black woman dean of the law school. After President Carter left office in 1980, Harris made an unsuccessful run for mayor of Washington, D.C., and became law professor at George Washington University.

Sources: *Contemporary Black Biography* vol. 2, pp. 99–101; Smith, *Notable Black American Women,* pp. 468–72; Hornsby, *Chronology of African-American History,* p. 280.

1977 • Veteran geophysicist and seismologist Waverly Person (1927–) became the first black director of the U.S. Geological Survey's National Earthquake Information Center (NEIC) in Colorado. He was assigned to locate earthquakes, compute their size, and disseminate his findings quickly and efficiently to specific sites throughout the world. Born in Blackridge, Virginia, he graduated from St. Paul's College in Lawrenceville, Virginia, and completed graduate work at American and George Washington universities.

Sources: *Contemporary Black Biography,* vol. 9, pp. 168–71.

1978 • Carolyn Robertson Payton (1925–2001), educator and psychologist, was the first woman and black to head the Peace Corps. She held the post from September 1977 to November 1978. Payton was born in Norfolk, Virginia. A graduate of Bennett College, the University of Wisconsin, Madison, and Columbia University, Payton was prominent in the field of education. She taught at Livingstone College, Elizabeth City State University (both in North Carolina), and Virginia State University. Payton joined the Peace Corps in 1964 as a field assessment officer and later supervised the selection of officers. She supervised 130 volunteers who worked on eight islands in the eastern Caribbean. While with the Peace Corps, Payton worked to attract more blacks and Hispanics to the Peace Corps, a volunteer oversees service organization. She accused Action, the agency that oversaw the corps, of trying to make the corps an "arrogant, elitist" political organization, and claimed that the corps had strayed from its mission. She retired from the Peace Corps due to differences over policy.

Sources: Smith, *Notable Black American Women*, pp. 833–34; Obituary, *Who's Who among African Americans*, 14th ed., p. 1474; *New York Times* Obituaries (14 April 2001; 22 April 2001).

1978 • Jack Tanner (1919–2006) became the first black federal judge in the state of Washington. From 1955 to 1978 he was in private practice. He was lauded in the *Congressional Record* in 2000 for completing thirty-two years on the bench and as one of the "Great Native Sons."

Sources: *Jet* 98 (10 July 2000): 8; *Who's Who among African Americans,* 14th ed., p. 1254.

1979 • Marcus Alexis (1932–), bank official, was the first black American to chair the United States Interstate Commerce Commission. Born in Brooklyn, he received his education at Brooklyn College and Michigan State University, and the University of Minnesota, where he received his doctorate. He has taught at Northwestern University and the University of Illinois at Chicago. He was also deputy chairman of the Federal Reserve Bank of Chicago.

Sources: *Who's Who among African Americans,* 14th ed., p. 17.

1979 • John D. Glover was the first black Federal Bureau of Investigations field office chief and headed the FBI's operations in Milwaukee, Wisconsin. He was also the first African American inspector at FBI headquarters. In 1986 Glover became the highest-ranking black in the bureau, as the first black executive assistant director in charge of administration.

Sources: *Negro Almanac,* p. 1432.

1979 • President Jimmy Carter named Cecil Francis Poole (1907–1997) to the Ninth Circuit Court of Appeals this year, making him the first black to serve on that court and only the second black in the nation to serve on any federal circuit court of appeals.

Sources: *New York Times* (16 November 1997); *Jet* 93 (8 December 1997): 55.

1980 • George Albert Dalley (1941–), attorney, was the first black member of the United States Civil Aeronautics Board. Born in Havana, Cuba, Dalley received his education at Columbus College, Columbia University Graduate School of Business, and Columbia University School of Law. He worked for Congressman Charles Rangel, the State Department, and was a campaign manager for the "Mondale for President" effort. He has been law partner in two firms.

Sources: *Who's Who among African Americans,* 26th ed., p. 298; *Who's Who in American Politics, 1987–88,* p. 251.

1980 • Norma Holloway Johnson (1932–) was named chief federal judge for the District of Columbia, becoming the first black woman to lead the federal court in the nation's capital.

Sources: *Jet* 92 (18 August 1997): 39; *Who's Who among African Americans,* 26th ed., pp. 676; Smith, *Notable Black American Women*, pp. 591–93.

1981 • Clarence M. Pendleton Jr. (1930–1988) was the first African American to chair the United States Civil Rights Commission. He led the commission toward a "colorblind" approach to matters of civil rights. Pendleton was born in Louisville, Kentucky, but grew up in Washington, D.C. He was educated at Howard University and after a stint in the U.S. Army, he taught physical education at that school. He held positions with the National Recreation and Parks Association and, after he moved to San Diego, he was director of the local Model Cities program. By 1975 he had been named head of the San Diego Urban League. He also supported California governor Ronald Reagan in his bid for the presidency.

Sources: Hornsby, *Chronology of African-American History,* p. 369; Hornsby, *Milestones in African-American History,* pp. 308, 379; *Negro Almanac,* p. 101; *Who's Who in American Politics, 1987–88,* p. 136.

1981 • Lennie-Marie Pickens Tolliver (1928–) was appointed as the first black to head the Commission on Aging. Born in Cleveland, Ohio, she was educated at Hampton University, the University of Chicago, and Union Graduate School, receiving her doctorate from the latter institution. Tolliver had a long and distinguished career in social services prior to her appointment by President Ronald Reagan. She resigned in 1984 and became professor of social work at the University of Oklahoma.

Sources: *Who's Who among African Americans,* 14th ed., p. 1295–96.

1981 • Carlos Cardozo Campbell (1937–), banking executive, writer, and actor, was the first black assistant secretary of commerce. Born in New York City, Campbell was educated at Michigan State University and the Catholic University of America. He was the assistant secretary for economic development and affiliated with the Inter-American Development Bank. Since 1885 he has headed the C. C. Campbell and Company management consulting firm.

Sources: *Who's Who in American Politics, 1987–88,* p. 1524; *Who's Who among African Americans,* 26th ed., p. 202.

1981 • Gloria E. A. Toote (1931–), attorney and entrepreneur, was the first black chair of the Merit System Protection Board (formerly the Civil Service Commission). Born in New York City, Toote received her law degree in 1954 from Howard University School of Law and became the youngest graduate in the school's history at that time. She received her master of law degree from Columbia University Graduate School of Law in 1956. After working with the law firm Greenbaum, Woolf, and Ernest, Toote joined Governor Nelson Rockefeller's staff, and then entered private practice. She also worked for the National Affairs section of *Time* and for the Department of Housing and Urban Development.

Sources: Smith, *Notable Black American Women,* Book II, pp. 653–55; *Who's Who among African Americans,* 26th ed., p. 1240–41.

1982 • Harold E. Doley Jr. (1947–) was the first person of any race to serve as director of the Mineral Management Service of the United States Department of the Interior. Born in New Orleans, Doley was educated at Xavier and Harvard universities. He is an investment counselor with a long career in minority and African counseling. Doley, in 1983, was the first black United States executive director for the African Development Bank and Fund.

Sources: *Who's Who among African Americans,* 14th ed., p. 351; *Who's Who in American Politics, 1987–88,* p. 586; *Contemporary Black Biography,* vol. 26, pp. 58–59.

1983 • Barbara J. Mahone, automobile executive, was the first black woman to chair the United States Federal Labor Relations Authority. Born in Alabama, Mahone was educated at Ohio State University, the University of Michigan, and Harvard University. She has held a variety of positions in the automotive industry.

Sources: *Who's Who among African* Americans, 26th ed., p. 803.

1984 • Aulana Louise Peters (1941–), attorney, was the first black woman appointed to the Securities and Exchange Commission. Born in Louisiana, Peters was educated at the College of New Rochelle and the University of Southern California.

Sources: *Who's Who among African Americans,* 26th ed., p. 986.

1985 • Julius Wesley Becton Jr. (1926–) was the first black director of the Federal Emergency Management Agency. A retired army officer, Becton was born in Bryn Mawr, Pennsylvania, and educated at Prairie View Agricultural and Mechanical College, the University of Maryland, and the National War College. He was commanding general of several divisions in the military, including the 1st Cavalry Division, U.S. Army Operations Test and Evaluation Agency, and the VII U.S. Corps. From 1989 to 1994 Becton was president of Prairie View Agricultural and Mechanical University in Texas. He was superintendent of schools in Washington, D.C., from 1996 to 1998.

Sources: *Negro Almanac,* pp. 892–93; *Who's Who among African Americans,* 26th ed., p. 83.

1986 • Edward Joseph Perkins (1928–), diplomat, was the first black American ambassador to South Africa—a class A post. A veteran foreign service professional, Perkins was serving as ambassador to Liberia, when President Ronald Reagan made the appointment; he was confirmed on October 15. Perkins was born in Sterlington, Louisiana, and attended a segregated, two-room school. Forty years later he continued his education at Lewis and Clark College and then the University of Maryland, where he received a bachelor's degree. He later earned a master's and a doctoral degree from the University of Southern California. His experiences in government service were wide. In 1985 President Ronald Reagan appointed him ambassador to Liberia; the next year he was appointed ambassador to South Africa. While in the latter post, he mandated that representatives of all races be included in all embassy functions. When this assignment ended, Perkins was sworn in as director general of the Foreign Service and director of personnel. President George Bush in 1992 named him ambassador to the United Nations. The next year President Bill Clinton named Perkins ambassador to Australia, a position he held until retiring in 1996.

Julius Becton

Sources: Hornsby, *Chronology of African-American History,* p. 342; Hornsby, *Milestones in Twentieth-Century African-American History,* p. 349; *Who's Who among African Americans,* 26th ed., pp. 981; *Contemporary Black Biography,* vol. 5, pp. 227–30; Smith, *Notable Black American Men,* pp. 925–27.

1989 • Gwendolyn Stewart King (1941–) was the first black woman to serve as commissioner of social security. She held that post until 1992. King was first employed by the U.S. Department of Health and Human Services in 1971. After holding other posts, she was deputy assistant to the President from 1986 to 1988. In 2001 she was appointed to the Social Security Panel. King was born in East Orange, New Jersey, graduated from Howard University in 1962, and did graduate work at George Washington University from 1972 to 1974.

Sources: *Who's Who among African Americans,* 26th ed., p. 725.

1989 • Audrey Forbes Manley (1934–), was the first black female assistant secretary in the U.S. Health and Human Services Department. Born in Jackson, Mississippi, Manley was educated at Spelman College, Meharry Medical College, and Johns Hopkins University, where she received a master's degree in public health. After graduating from Meharry and completing a residency at Cook County Children's Hospital in Chicago, she became the first black woman appointed chief resident. From 1966 to 1976 she held various appointments in pediatrics and medical education at the Chicago Medical College, the University of Illinois, the University of Chicago, Emory University, Howard University, and elsewhere. She also held a number of health-related administrative offices in Georgia and Washington, D.C. On July 1, 1997, Manley accepted the presidency of Spelman College in Atlanta, becoming the college's first alumna president. In 2001 she announced her pending retirement.

Sources: *Contemporary Black Biography,* vol. 16, pp. 147–49; *Who's Who among African Americans,* 26th ed., p. 807.

1989 • Roscoe Michael Moore Jr. (1944–) was the first chief veterinary officer for the U.S. Public Health Service. The Richmond, Virginia, native graduated from Tuskegee Institute (now Tuskegee University) with a bachelor's degree in 1968 and a veterinary medicine degree in 1969. In 1970 he received a degree in public health from the University of Michigan. He studied at Johns Hopkins University, graduating in 1982 with a master's degree in health services and in 1985 with a doctorate. His career has been mostly with federal government health organizations, such as veterinarian for the National Institutes of Health (1970–71), epidemic intelligence service officer for the Centers of Disease Control, and senior veterinarian for the Center for Veterinary Medicine (1973–74). He was associate professor at the University of Washington in Seattle beginning 1989, and chief veterinary medical officer for the Public Health Service (1989–93). In 1992 he became associate director of the Public Health Service's Office of International and Refugee Health. He has been highly recognized for his contributions to veterinary science, receiving, among other honors, the Surgeon General's Exemplary Service Medal in 1990.

Sources: *Jet* 77 (30 October 1989): 20; *Who's Who among African Americans,* 14th ed., p. 935.

1989 • Constance Berry Newman (1935–), government official, was the first black administrator of the Office of Personnel Management. Newman was born in Chicago and grew up in Tuskegee, Alabama. She was educated at Bates College and the University of Minnesota School of Law. Active in Republican politics, she was part of President Bush's transition team. In 1992 Newman was named under secretary of the Smithsonian Institution. The post put her in charge of the fifteen museums and galleries, the National Zoological Park, and research facilities in eight states and the Republic of Panama. In 1999 she was named "Washingtonian of the Year."

Sources: *Who's Who among African Americans,* 26th ed., p. 932; Smith, *Notable Black American Women,* Book II, pp. 498–500.

1989 • Louis Wade Sullivan (1933–), physician, was the first black cabinet member in President George Bush's administration, as secretary of the Department of Health and Human Services. Sullivan was born in Atlanta, Georgia, and educated at Morehouse College and Boston University. He was engaged in medical education at Harvard University, New Jersey College of Medicine, and Boston University. He was the first dean and president of the Morehouse School of Medicine (1974–89). After leaving his federal post in 1993, he returned to Morehouse until stepping down in June 2002. Sullivan's activities have included membership on the medical school's board of trustees and fundraising.

Sources: Hornsby, *Chronology of African-American History,* p. 385; *Who's Who among African Americans,* 14th ed., p. 1245; Smith, *Notable Black American Men,* pp. 1092–94; *Contemporary Black Biography,* vol. 8, pp. 241–44; *Jet* 100 (3 September 2001): 14–15.

1989 • Edward J. Perkins (1928–) became the first black Foreign Service officer to be named director general. He held the post from 1989 to 1992. In 1993 Perkins was named ambassador to Australia, the first black to hold the post.

Sources: *Contemporary Black Biography,* vol. 5, pp. 227–30; *Jet* 96 (4 October 1999): 19; Smith, *Notable Black American Men,* pp. 925–27.

1989 • President George Bush appointed Condoleezza "Condi" Rice (1954–) as director of Soviet and East European Affairs on the National Security Council, making her the first black woman to hold that post. Her post required her to analyze and explain to the President items of international importance and to prepare him for his summit meetings with the Soviet president, Mikhail Gorbachev.

Sources: *Contemporary Black Biography,* vol, 3, pp. 206–8; Smith, *Notable Black American Women,* Book II, pp. 552–54; *Tennessean* (18 December 2000).

1990 • George Williford Boyce Haley (1925–), attorney, was the first black American to chair the United States Postal Rate Commission. Born in Henning, Tennessee, and the brother of writer Alex Haley, George Haley was educated at Morehouse College and the University of Arkansas. He was active in legal circles in Kansas and served as a state senator before entering the federal service.

Sources: *Who's Who among African Americans,* 26th ed., p. 513.

1993 • Ron [Ronald Harmon] Brown (1941–1996) was confirmed as the first black secretary of the Department of Commerce. Born in Washington, D.C., Brown and his family soon moved to New York City and settled in Harlem next door to the Apollo Theatre. Brown received his bachelor's degree in 1962 from Middlebury College and his law degree in 1970 from St. John's University Law School. He joined the army immediately after graduating from Middlebury and became the only black officer at a U.S. Army post in West Germany. He later was transferred to Korea and promoted to captain. After discharge, he returned to New York City. He entered politics, becoming district leader of the Democratic Party in Mount Vernon in 1971. He relocated to Washington, D.C., where he was spokesperson and deputy director of the Urban League's Washington operations, and worked in the offices of Senator Edward Kennedy. His growing promise was noticeable, and Senator Edward Kennedy appointed Brown deputy manager of his presidential campaign in 1979. Now in national spotlight, he became chief counsel, then deputy chairman for the Democratic National Committee. In 1989 he was named chairman of the National Democratic Party—the first black to hold this office. An expert at political maneuvering, he worked behind the scenes to help Bill Clinton win the 1992 nomination and election. When he took office, President Clinton appointed Brown Secretary of Commerce. The Senate confirmed the nomination on January 14, 1993, making Brown the first black to hold that post. He died April 3, 1996, with his staff in an airplane crash off the coast of Croatia.

Ron Brown

Sources: *Who's Who among Black Americans, 1996–97*, p. 191; *Jet* 89 (22 April 1996): 4–18; 51–56; *Contemporary Black Biography,* vol. 5, pp. 32–35; Smith, *Notable Black American Men,* pp. 131–33.

1993 • Jesse Brown (1944–) was the first black confirmed to the cabinet as head of Veterans Affairs. Brown, executive director of the Disabled American Veterans, for more than twenty-five years, had been an advocate for those who served in America's armed forces. He began his career with the DAV in the Chicago bureau, where he was a national service officer. He was promoted in 1973, becoming supervisor of appeals in the Washington office. He was a member of the legislative staff from 1982 to 1988 and executive director from 1988 to 1993. Brown was born in Detroit and educated at Chicago City College, after serving as a marine in the Vietnam conflict, where he lost the use of his right arm.

Sources: *Atlanta Constitution* (18 December 1992); *Crisis* 100 (March 1993): 16; *Ebony* 48 (May 1993): 64; *Contemporary Black Biography,* vol. 6, pp. 50–52; *Who's Who among African Americans,* 14th ed., p. 155.

Jesse Brown

1993 • Mike [Alphonso Michael] Espy (1953–) became the first black secretary of the Department of Agriculture in January. He was born in Yazoo City, Mississippi, to a former county agent for the USDA. He graduated from Howard University in Washington, D.C. (B.A. 1975) and from the University of Santa Clara (LL.B., 1978). After receiving his law degree, he returned to his home state and became managing attorney at Central Mississippi legal Services. From 1980 to 1984 Espy was assistant secretary of state for the Public Lands Division. He became politically active during this period and served as Second Congressional District coordinator for Ed Pittman who ran for state attorney general. In 1984 he became a member of the Rules Committee of the Democratic National Committee. From 1984 to 1985 he was assistant attorney general for consumer protection. He was elected to Congress in 1987 and held that post until 1993. Espy became one of the first blacks in Congress to endorse Bill Clinton for the presidency. In January 1993 Espy became the first black to head the Department of Agriculture. He became extremely adept in discharging the duties of his office and in making operations more efficient. He cut staff size and modernized the department's meat inspection system. He established aid initiatives and agricultural and multilateral trade treaties with other countries. In spite of his achievements, allegations of ethics violations and other improprieties emerged, damaging his reputation. He was accused of accepting free travel, meals, and tickets to sports events from Tyson Foods, of asking the Environmental Protection Agency to delay a ban on a pesticide that one of his campaign contributors used, of accepting a bribe from Sun Diamond Growers of California, and other improprieties. Although Espy partially reimbursed Tyson, other companies, and the federal government, the damage had been done and he resigned from office. Later, trials cleared Espy of all charges. When Espy's portrait was unveiled at USDA in 1998, President Bill Clinton noted that the jury had redeemed him.

Sources: *Contemporary Black Biography,* vol. 6, pp. 87–90; Smith, *Notable Black American Men,* pp. 378–81; *Jet* 99 (1 January 2001): 19.

Mike Espy

1993 • Myrick Bismarck was the first black to serve as consul general in Durban, South Africa. He was consul general in Capetown from 1993 to 1995, and in 1996 was appointed ambassador to Lesotho, a position he held until 1998. He was inducted into the U.S. Army's Hall of Fame at Fort Benning's Officers Candidate School, Fort Benning, Georgia, in 1997.

Sources: *Jet* 91 (13 January 1997): 20; 93 (22 June 1998): 23.

1993 • Kenneth R. Kimbrough, a Chicago executive, was named commissioner of the General Services Administration's Public Buildings Service in Washington, D.C., becoming the first black to hold the post. The Oklahoma native was educated at Oklahoma State University and the University of Rochester. He worked with International Paper Company and later became general manager for real estate services with Ameritech-Bell Telephone.

Sources: *Jet* 84 (9 August 1993): 26; *Who's Who among African Americans,* 26th ed., p. 722.

Joycelyn Elders

1993 • M. Joycelyn Elders (1933–) became the first black and the second woman named United States Surgeon General, in August. (Antonia Novello was the first woman surgeon general.) Elders, an outspoken advocate of the immunization of children, quality health care for all American citizens, and the elimination of diseases, had been opposed by politicians for her liberal views on health care issues. She was also the first woman and the first black to hold the position of Arkansas health director. Now in office, her outspoken views on drugs, guns, human sexuality, birth control, and similar issues stirred controversy with conservatives. In 1994 her solution to curbing sexual activities among school children drew President Clinton's ire; he demanded and received her resignation on December 10, 1994. Elders returned to the faculty at the University of Arkansas Medical School in 1995. Subsequently she retired. The Schaal, Arkansas, native graduated from Philander Smith College in Little Rock and received a medical degree from the University of Arkansas Medical School.

Sources: Smith, *Notable Black American Women,* Book II, pp. 200–203; *Tennessean* (8 September 1993); *Who's Who among African Americans,* 26th ed., p. 381.

1993 • Sharon Farmer (1951–) was one of four and the first black woman to serve as White House photographer, covering President Bill Clinton and the first family. Her assignments took her throughout the United States and foreign countries. Farmer had a staff of five photographers. When on assignment, Farmer carried five cameras around her neck.

Sources: *Jet* 84 (20 September 1993): 10; 99 (23 January 2001): 12; *Who's Who among African Americans,* 26th ed., p. 399.

1993 • Jeanette L. Brown left her post as director of the Office of Procurement and Grants Management, U.S. Small Business Administration in Washington, D.C., to become director of the Office of Acquisition Management, U.S. Environmental Protection Agency. She was the first black and the first woman to hold the position.

Sources: *Jet* 85 (15 November 1993): 20.

1993 • Alexis M. Herman (1947–) became the first black woman to direct a White House liaison program. From 1993 to 1997 Herman was director of the White House Office of Public Liaison as well as assistant to President Bill Clinton.

Sources: *New York Times* (24 February 1997); Smith, *Notable Black American Women,* Book II, pp. 287–89; *Who's Who among African Americans,* 26th ed., p. 572.

Hazel O'Leary

1993 • Hazel Rollins O'Leary (1938–) was the first black and the first woman secretary of energy. Born in Newport News, Virginia, to parents who were physicians, she graduated from Fisk University, and Rutgers Law School. After receiving her law degree, she was named assistant prosecutor in Essex County, New Jersey, and later named assistant attorney general for New Jersey. She moved to Washington, D.C., and joined the accounting firm of Coopers and Lybrand. She acquired governmental experience in President Gerald Ford's administration, joining the Federal Energy Administration and later becoming director of the Office of Consumer Affairs/Special Impact. Her office managed the antipoverty programs and she became known as an advocate for the poor. During President Jimmy

Carter's administration, O'Leary became chief of the Department of Energy's Economic Regulatory Administration. She regulated petroleum under both the Ford and Carter administrations. O'Leary left the government and set up an energy consulting firm with her husband, John F. O'Leary. After her husband died in 1987, she held other posts until she was named executive vice-president of Northern States Power Company of Minnesota, the post she held at the time of her appointment as Secretary of Energy. President Bill Clinton nominated her for office, the Senate confirmed, and O'Leary was sworn in office on January 22, 1992. In office she called for action in the environment, natural gas, and cleanup. When she opened documents related to the government's human radiation treatments during the 1940s and 1950s, she caused a stir among many women who had received the treatments. O'Leary returned to her alma mater, Fisk University, as president from 2004 to 2012.

Sources: *Ebony 48* (May 1993): 64; *Contemporary Black Biography,* vol. 6, pp. 203–5; Smith, *Notable Black American Women,* Book II, pp. 506–9.

1993 • Rodney Earl Slater (1955–) was the first black to head the Federal Highway Administration. Born in Marianna, Arkansas, Slater received his bachelor's degree at Eastern Michigan University and took his law degree at the University of Arkansas in 1980. He was assistant state attorney general of Arkansas from 1980 to 1982, assistant to Bill Clinton from 1983 to 1987 when Clinton was governor of the state, director of governmental relations at Arkansas State University (1987–1993), and member of the Arkansas State Highway Commission from 1987 to 1993. After moving to the federal post, Slater was charged with planning the future of the nation's highways. He responded by creating the National Highway System and projecting a network of new roads to link the lower forty-eight states. His plan also aimed to improve transportation in Alaska and Hawaii. He was closely associated with the Bill Clinton state administration, where he was one of Clinton's closest advisors, and with the presidential campaign.

Sources: *Who's Who among African Americans,* 26th ed., p. 1135; *Contemporary Black Biography,* vol. 15; *Jet* 84 (11 July 1993): 26–27.

Rodney Slater

1993 • Clifton Reginald Wharton Jr. (1926–), was the first black named deputy secretary of state.

Sources: *Ebony 48* (May 1993): 62; *Contemporary Black Biography,* vol. 7, pp. 289–93; *Who's Who among African Americans,* 26th ed., p. 1313.

1993 • Anthony A. Williams (1951–) became the first chief financial officer for the U.S. Department of Agriculture, managing funds for twenty-nine agencies throughout the United States and abroad. In 1998 he was elected mayor of Washington, D.C., succeeding Marion Barry. Williams was born in Los Angeles and educated at Yale (B.A.) and Harvard Law School (J.D.). He was head of the neighborhood housing and development for the Boston Redevelopment Authority (1988–90), executive director of the St. Louis Community Development Agency (1990–91), and then deputy controller for the State of Connecticut (1991–93).

Sources: *Contemporary Black Biography,* vol. 21, pp. 191–94; *Who's Who among African Americans,* 26th ed., p. 1332.

1994 • The first black regional administrator for the Federal Aviation Administration was named this year. Garromme P. Franklin, a twenty-five-year veteran of the FAA, was named to head the eight-state Great Lakes section, with 6,750 employees.

Sources: *Jet* 86 (5 September 1994): 10.

1994 • Evelyn M. White was named director of personnel for the U.S. Department of Agriculture, the first black woman to hold the post. In 1993 she received the USDA's Distinguished Service Award. Born in Kansas City, Missouri, White was educated at Central Missouri University.

Sources: *Jet* 85 (30 May 1994): 40; *Who's Who among African Americans,* 26th ed., p. 1317.

1994 • The first black person nominated as director of the U.S. Bureau of Mines in its eighty-four-year history was Rhea L. Graham, a senior geologist with a private engineering firm in Albuquerque, New Mexico. Action on her nomination was blocked in the closing hours of the Senate. Graham is senior scientist with Science Applications International Corporation in Albuquerque, New Mexico.

Sources: *Jet* 86 (24 October 1994):46; 89 (8 January 1996): 10; *Who's Who among African Americans,* 26th ed., p. 483.

1994 • Al Mauldin became the first black to direct the White House military office. His position included coordinating the chief executive's travels and providing necessary security.

Sources: *Jet* 85 (31 January 1994): 10.

1994 • Ronald K. Noble was sworn in as U.S. Treasury undersecretary for enforcement, becoming the highest ranking black in the history of federal law enforcement. He was also the first American to lead Interpol. He resigned, effective February 5, 1996, to resume teaching at New York University School of Law. Noble was born in Fort Dix, New Jersey. He received his bachelor's degree from the University of New Hampshire and his law degree from Stanford Law School.

Sources: *Jet* 86 (1 August 1994): 36; *Who's Who among African Americans,* 26th ed., p. 938.

1994 • William Benjamin Gould IV (1936–), noted labor attorney, was confirmed by the U.S. Senate and became chairman of the National Labor Relations Board (NLRB) in Washington, D.C., the first black to hold the post. Although he worked behind the scenes, he played a pivotal role in resolving the seven-month-old baseball strike. Under his leadership, the department charged the baseball owners with unfair labor practice that resulted in uniting the opposing sides. Gould left the position in 1998. The Boston-born Gould received his bachelor's degree from the University of Rhode Island in 1958. He received his law degree in 1975 from Cornell Law School. He did graduate study at the London School of Economics and took a master's degree in 1975 from the University of Cambridge, in Massachusetts. Gould has taught in several law schools, including those at Stanford and Harvard. His career includes the position of assistant general counsel for the United Auto Workers and as attorney for the National Labor Relations Board.

Sources: *Jet* 85 (28 March 1994): 22–23; 87 (24 April 1994): 10; 89 (29 January 1996): 10; *Who's Who among African Americans,* 26th ed., p. 481.

1994 • Loretta Collins Argrett (1937–) became the first black woman in the history of the Justice Department to hold a position that required Senate confirmation. She was the first black member of the Joint Committee on Taxation of the U.S. Congress. Argrette graduated from Howard University in Washington, D.C. (B.S. 1958) and the Harvard Law School (J.D. 1976). She was partner in the law firm Wald, Harkrader and Ross, and law professor at Howard University.

Sources: *Jet* 85 (31 January 1994): 8; *Who's Who among African Americans,* 14th ed., p. 38.

1994 • Laura Fitz Pelgado was approved as assistant secretary of Commerce and director general of the Foreign Commercial Service. She is the first black to hold the post.

Sources: *Jet* 86 (13 June 1994): 10.

1994 • The first black to become inspector general for the United States Information Agency was lawyer Marian C. Bennett. She was educated at Radcliffe College and the University of Pennsylvania Law School. In her career she has served as investigator and staff attorney for the National Labor Relations Board, and she has held various positions with the Department of Energy.

Sources: *Jet* 85 (24 January 1994): 15; 88 (9 October 1995): 10; *Who's Who among African Americans,* 14th ed., p. 90.

1994 • Upon the nomination of President Bill Clinton, John W. Marshall became the first black U.S. marshal for the eastern district of Virginia. For fourteen years Marshall served the nation's oldest federal law enforcement agency as a trooper. He rose in rank in the Uniform Patrol Division and was also a special agent in the agency's Bureau of Criminal Investigation, Narcotics. He is the youngest son of late U.S. Supreme Court Justice Thurgood Marshall. He left the post in 1999 to direct the U.S. Marshals Service, becoming the first black to hold that post.

Sources: *Jet* 97 (27 December 1999–3 January 2000): 9; *Who's Who among African Americans,* 26th ed., p. 814.

1995 • Renetta Smith (1960?–2007), a former trial attorney for the U.S. Immigration and Naturalization Service in Chicago, became the first black and the only woman judge with the INS in that city.

Sources: *Jet* 87 (1 May 1995): 20; *Who's Who among African Americans,* 14th ed., p. 1205.

1995 • Christopher Alvin Hart (1947–) was named assistant administrator for system safety with the Federal Aviation Administration, becoming the highest-ranking black in the FAA. Hart is great-nephew of James Herman Banning, who in 1926 became the first black to receive a pilot's license in the United States. Born in Denver, Hart graduated from Princeton University (B.S.E. 1969, M.S.E 1971) and Harvard Law School (J.D. 1973). His various positions include deputy assistant general counsel for the Department of Transportation (1977–79), managing partner with the firm Hart and Chavers (1981–90), and deputy administrator for the National Highway Traffic Safety Administration.

Sources: *Jet* 89 (19 February 1996): 48; *Who's Who among African Americans,* 26th ed., p. 549.

1995 • Jacquelyn L. Williams-Bridgers (1956–) became the first black and the first woman inspector general of the State Department. She received both the bachelor's and master's degrees from Syracuse University. Before assuming her post, Williams-Bridgers held several positions in the General Accounting Office, including associate director for housing and community development, and management analyst.

Sources: *Jet* 87 (10 April 1995): 32; *Who's Who among African Americans,* 14th ed., p. 1418.

1995 • J. Terry Edmonds (1940–) was the first black presidential speechwriter in history and the first black director of speechwriting to work in the White House for the President of the United States. From 1995 to 1997 Edmonds was special assistant to the president and later deputy director of speechwriting. He has held a number of positions in the field of public relations and has worked for such companies as Blue Cross Blue Shield of Maryland and Macro Systems. Edmonds was press secretary in the Office of Kweisi Mfume and senior speechwriter then director of speechwriting in the Office of Donna Shalala, when she was secretary of Health and Human Services. After leaving the White House staff, Edmunds took a communications position with the Merck pharmaceutical company. Edmonds was born in Baltimore and received his bachelor's degree from Morgan State University in that city.

Sources: *Contemporary Black Biography,* vol. 17, pp. 74–76; *Jet* 96 (30 August 1999): 17; 97 (14 February 2000): 18; *New York Times* (24 January 2000); *Who's Who among African Americans,* 26th ed., p. 374.

1995 • The first woman director of the Minority Business Development Agency at the Department of Commerce was Joan Parrott-Fonseca. A graduate of Georgetown University Law School, she has served as associate administrator of the General Services Administration, Office of Enterprise Development.

Sources: *Jet* 87 (1 May 1995): 10; 88 (3 July 1995): 21; *Who's Who among African Americans,* 26th ed., p. 996.

1995 • Bob J. Nash, who was appointed associate director and personnel chief for White House Personnel, became the first black male policymaker appointed during the Clinton administration. Born in Texarkana, Arkansas, he was educated at the University of Arkansas at Pine Bluff (B.A. 1969) and Howard University (M.A. 1972). His previous positions included assistant to the deputy mayor of Fairfax, Virginia; vice president of the Winthrop Rockefeller Foundation; senior executive assistant for economic development for the office of Bill Clinton when he was governor of Arkansas; and president of the Arkansas State Development Finance Authority.

Sources: *Jet* 87 (27 February 1995): 22; *Who's Who among African Americans,* 26th ed., p. 924.

1995 • The first black woman to chair the Nuclear Regulatory Commission (NRC) was Shirley Ann Jackson (1946–). She was placed in charge of regulating the safety of the country's 110 nuclear power plants. Once in office, she called for a review of all plants to determine how many had violated the standards by moving fuel. After that, the NRC shut down three Millstone plants.

Sources: *Contemporary Black Biography,* vol. 12, pp. 92–95; *Jet* 87 (1 May 1995): 10; *Who's Who among African Americans,* 26th ed., p. 644.

1995 • Carolyn G. Morris (1939?–) was promoted to assistant director of information resources for the FBI, becoming the highest-ranking black woman in the bureau's history. Morris was educated at North Carolina Central University and Harvard University.

Sources: *Jet* 89 (13 November 1995): 4; *Who's Who among African Americans,* 26th ed., p. 905.

1996 • Franklin Delano Raines (1949–) was named director of the Office of Management and Budget under the Clinton administration, the first black to hold the post. He served there from April 1996 to May 1998 and was the first director in a generation to balance the federal budget.

Sources: *Contemporary Black Biography,* vol. 14, pp. 178–80; *Jet* 90 (9 October 1996): 33; 93 (4 May 1998): 46; Salzman, *Encyclopedia of African-American Culture and History,* Supplement, pp. 178–80.

1996 • Hubert Thomas Bell Jr. (1942–) became the first black inspector general of the Nuclear Regulatory Commission. He was assistant director, Office of Protective Operations and executive director for diversity management with the U.S. Secret Service. Bell was born in Mobile, Alabama, and graduated from Alabama State University in Montgomery in 1965, with a bachelor's degree. He joined the U.S. Secret Service in Washington, D.C., as assistant director of the office of protective operations and then became executive director for diversity management. He has served as national president of the National Organization of Black Law Enforcement executives (1994–95), president of the Virginia Chapter, Fraternal Order of Police (1991), and vice president of Region II, of the FOP (1977).

Sources: *Jet* 90 (8 July 1996):10; *Who's Who among African Americans,* 26th ed., p. 85.

1996 • Carol Jenifer was the first black woman to direct operations of an Immigration and Naturalization Service office. Her position required oversight of a $14 million annual budget, a staff of 254, and traffic at a checkpoint where forty-five million people pass each year. Jenifer is a former police officer in the District of Columbia.

Sources: *Jet* 89 (1 April 1996): 10.

1996 • Leonard Harrison Robinson (1943–) was named U.S. consul for Sao Tome and Principe, becoming the first black to hold the position. Born in Winston-Salem, North Carolina, Robinson received his bachelor's degree from Ohio State in 1964, and studied for both his master's and doctorate degrees at American University (1982–89). He has held positions with the Peace Corps, the Inner City Community Program, the Department of State, African Development Foundation, and the Washington Strategic Group. Robinson has published widely.

Sources: *Jet* 90 (30 September 1996): 13; *Who's Who among African Americans,* 14th ed., p. 1112.

1996 • The first black special agent in charge of the St. Louis Division of the Federal Bureau of Investigation was Wiley Thompson III (1952?–). The St. Louis native left his position as deputy assistant director of the Inspection Division of the FBI at its headquarters in Washington, D.C.; he had held a variety of positions with the FBI in Denver, Chicago, Baltimore, and elsewhere. Thompson received his bachelor's degree from Lincoln University in Missouri.

Sources: *Jet* 89 (29 April 1996): 9.

1997 • Thurgood Marshall Jr. (1956–), son of Supreme Court Justice Thurgood Marshall, became the first black to serve as Cabinet secretary. He was named assistant to President Bill Clinton and was the highest-ranking black in the White House. Previously, Marshall was deputy counsel and director of legislative affairs in the Office of the Vice President. Marshall was born in New York City and educated at the University of Virginia (B.A., 1978) and the University of Virginia School of Law (J.D., 1981). He was law clerk for Judge Barrington D. Parker, counsel and staff director for Senator Albert Gore Jr., senior policy advisor for the Clinton-Gore campaign, and director of legislative affairs for the Office of the Vice President.

Sources: *Jet* 91 (3 March 1997): 4; *Who's Who among African Americans,* 26th ed., p. 842.

1997 • William Earl Kennard (1957–) was sworn in as chairman of the Federal Communications Commission (FCC), becoming the first black to hold this post. Born in Hollywood, California, Kennard was a Phi Beta Kappa graduate of Stanford University (B.A., 1976) and a graduate of Yale Law School (J.D., 1981). He had a one-year fellowship with the National Association of Broadcasters (NAB) in 1981. He joined the law firm of Verner, Liipfert, Bernard, Pherson, and Hand, located in Washington, D.C., and in 1983 became assistant general counsel for NAB. In 1984 he returned to his previous law firm and provided legal services to media staff personnel. Vice President Al Gore swore him into office on November 7, 1997.

William Kennard

Sources: *Jet* 93 (24 November 1997): 9; *Contemporary Black Biography,* vol. 18, pp. 95–97; *Who's Who among African Americans,* 26th ed., p. 717.

1997 • The first black postmaster in the state of Idaho was Marcus E. Spigner. After holding a variety of positions for nineteen years with the postal service, he was named postmaster of the United States Postal Service in Eagle, Idaho. He was previously acting postmaster in Meridian, Indiana. The Tyler, Texas, native served in the U.S. Air Force and the Idaho National Guard.

Sources: *Jet* 92 (27 October 1997): 19.

1997 • The first black legal attaché in Cairo, Egypt, was Alfred J. Finch. He served as the FBI's representative to Egypt, Ethiopia, and other African countries.

Sources: *Jet* 92 (8 September 1997): 39.

1997 • Harriet L. Elam-Thomas became the first black agency counselor of the U.S. Information Agency, and the highest-ranking American woman in all three of the U.S. diplomatic missions in Belgium. She is a graduate of Simmons College and from Fletcher School of Law and Diplomacy at Tufts University.

Sources: *Jet* 92 (16 June 1997): 10; *Who's Who among African Americans,* 26th ed., pp. 380–81.

1997 • The first black food-stamp chief was Shirley Robinson Watkins (1938–), who was named undersecretary for Agriculture's Food, Nutrition and Consumer Services agency. The Hope, Arkansas, native was educated at the University of Arkansas, Pine Bluff (B.S., 1960) and the University of Memphis (M.Ed., 1970). She has teaching experience in the Memphis schools and has also held several positions with the Department of Agriculture.

Sources: *Jet* 92 (9 September 1997): 10; *Who's Who among African Americans,* 26th ed., pp. 1296–97.

1997 • Ambassador Ruth A. Davis (1943–) became the first director of the Foreign Service Institute, the top training facility for U.S. diplomats. Later this year she was promoted to career minister, becoming the first black woman to hold the top rank. She also became one of the three women ambassadors among the twenty-six career ministers in the program. Davis was born in Phoenix, Arizona, and educated at Spelman College in Atlanta and the University of California, Berkeley. She has served the Foreign Service Institute as principal assistant secretary for consular affairs and as ambassador to the Republic of Benin.

Sources: *Jet* 92 (4 August 1997): 10; 92 (13 October 1997): 12; 101 (21 January 2002): 10; *Who's Who among African Americans,* 26th ed., p. 320.

1997 • Jerry Belson (1949–), the former deputy regional director for the southeast region of the National Park Service in Atlanta, was named regional director for that area, the first black to hold that post. Sixty-two parks in nine southeastern states, Puerto Rico, and the U.S. Virgin Islands make up the southeast region. Born in Lafayette, Louisiana, Belson graduated from Southern University in Baton Rouge (B.A., 1970) and Sulross State University (B.S., 1983). In his career he has served as district ranger for the Amistad National Recreation Area, superintendent of the National Park Service's Ft. Frederica National Monument, superintendent of the Martin Luther King National Historic Site, deputy superintendent of the Yosemite National Park, and general superintendent of the Southern Arizona Group.

Sources: *Jet* 92 (21 July 1997): 24; *Who's Who among African Americans,* 26th ed., p. 90.

Alexis M. Herman

1997 • Alexis M. Herman (1947–) became the first black secretary of the Department of Labor. President Bill Clinton nominated Herman, who was already serving as his director of public liaison. She endured a bitter four-month confirmation battle and then received Senate confirmation by a vote of 85 to 13. Herman was born in Mobile, Alabama, and educated at Xavier University (B.A., 1969) and studied at other academic institutions. She has served in a number of recruitment and training programs in such positions as director of the Southern Regional Council's Black Women Employment Program (1972–74) and consulting supervisor of the Department of Labor Recruitment Training Program (1973–74). She was director of the Women's Bureau, U.S. Department of Labor (1977–81). In 1981 she became president and chief executive officer of her own company, A. M. Herman and Associates. Herman has served the Democratic National Convention as chief executive officer (1991–92) and was deputy director of the Clinton-Gore Presidential Transition Office (1992–93). Herman brought to her new post several years of experience as a public servant, including her work during the Carter Administration.

Sources: *Contemporary Black Biography,* vol. 15, pp. 109–11; Smith, *Notable Black American Women,* Book II, pp. 287–89; *Who's Who among African Americans,* 26th ed., p. 572.

1997 • Rodney E. Slater (1955–) became the first black U.S. Secretary of Transportation. From 1993 to 1996 he was the first black federal highway administrator.

Sources: *Contemporary Black Biography,* vol. 15, pp. 194–95; *Who's Who among African Americans,* 26th ed., p. 1135.

1997 • Ann Dibble Jordan (1935–) became the first black woman to serve in the command role as co-chair for the inauguration of a U.S. President. As she prepared for the second-term inauguration of President Bill Clinton, she spearheaded the theme of diversity utilizing minorities and women in each activity that was planned.

Sources: *Jet* 91 (27 January 1997): 7.

1997 • Robert G. Stanton (1940–) became the first black director of the National Park Service in August this year. He was charged with overseeing 15,000 employees and some 375 monuments, national parks, and park police. A native of Fort Worth, Texas, he had no association with parks in the segregated South where he lived. After hearing a speech by Secretary of the Interior Stewart Udall, Stanton was persuaded to seek a career in a nontraditional area. His summer job in 1962, which was as park ranger in Grand Teton National Park, gave him an experience that would influence his career choice. Stanton graduated from Huston-Tillotson College in 1963 and continued his studies at Boston University and George Washington University. After a brief stint at his undergraduate college, he began what would become a long line of service to the national parks. Among the posts he held were management assistant for the National Capital Parks; supervisor of the U.S. Virgin Islands National Parks; associate director of operations, National Parks Service, national office; regional director of the park's Capital Region; and since 1997 director of the National Park Service. Among his accomplishments, Stanton has worked to make the parks financially stable, to increase the involvement of youth in the park's programs, and to increase minority involvement in the National Park Service.

Sources: *Contemporary Black Biography*, vol. 20, pp. 199–202; *Jet* 92 (21 July 1997): 38; 92 (8 September 1997): 38; *Who's Who among African Americans*, 26th ed., p. 1171.

1997 • Patricia "Patti" G. Smith (1947–) was named head of the Commercial Space Transportation section of the Federal Aviation Administration, becoming the first black woman to lead a line of business in FAA history. She manages private space launches, including private communication satellites and private scientific space research experiments. Smith was born in Tuskegee, Alabama, and graduated from Tuskegee Institute (now Tuskegee University). She has studied at a number of other universities, sometimes as an exchange student. Smith has held a number of positions in broadcasting and marketing, including service with the National Association of Broadcasters and Group W Westinghouse Broadcasting Company, WJZ Television, and the Federal Commerce Commission. She was acting associate administrator, then associate administrator before she was promoted to her present post.

Sources: *Jet* 94 (13 July 1998): 32; *Who's Who among African Americans*, 26th ed., p. 1152.

1997 • President Bill Clinton nominated Calvin D. "Buck" Buchanan (1958?–) as U.S. Attorney in the Northern District of Mississippi. He was confirmed and took office this year, becoming the first black to hold that post. Buchanan was educated at the University of Mississippi, where he received both the B.A. and J.D. degrees. He was a judge advocate in the army from 1983 to 1990, and then became assistant U.S. attorney for the Northern District of Mississippi.

Sources: *Jet* 89 (15 April 1996): 4; *Who's Who among African Americans*, 26th ed., p. 175.

1998 • Gertrude Sims Campbell moved up in positions she held in the Greenville, Mississippi, post office and in 1998 the former supervisor in customer services was named the new postmaster in Starkville. With the promotion she became the highest-ranking woman postmaster in the state.

Sources: *Jet* 93 (12 January 1998): 19.

1998 • Thomasina Venese Rogers became the first black commissioner for the Occupational Safety and Health Review Commission. Until it was dissolved in 1995, Rogers chaired the Administrative Conference of the United States. She was also a member of the federal government's Senior Executive Service.

Sources: *Jet* 94 (23 November 1998): 38.

1998 • Carolyn D. Jordan (1941–) became the first black executive director of the National Credit Union Administration, an independent federal agency that supervises and insures 97 percent of the 12,000 federally-insured credit unions. Previously, Jordan was counsel for the Senate Banking, Housing and Urban Affairs committee. Jordan received a bachelor of arts degree from Fisk University and a law degree from Howard University in Washington, D.C.

Sources: *Jet* 94 (28 September 1998): 6.

1999 • Franklin D. Raines (1949–) resigned his position in the Clinton Administration to become chairman and chief executive officer of Fannie Mae Corporation, on January 1.

The Washington-based company was the nation's largest provider of home mortgage financing. The position made Raines the first black CEO of a Fortune 500 company.

Sources: *Jet* 93 (4 May 1998): 46; Salzman, *Encyclopedia of African-American Culture and History*, Supplement, pp. 229–30.

1999 • In May, Rear Admiral Evelyn Juanita Fields (1949–) became the first woman and the first black director of the National Oceanic and Atmospheric Administration (NOAA), located in Washington, D.C. Fields was born in Norfolk, Virginia, and graduated from Norfolk State College (now University) in 1971. She rose through the ranks at NOAA and has served in a number of positions such as cartographer. Then she became operations officer, for NOAA vessels *Mt. Mitchell* and *Peirce,* and later commander of the *McArthur* vessel. She was administrative officer for the National Geodetic Survey and chief of the Hydrographic Surveys. Fields served as deputy administrative assistant for National Oceanic Service until she obtained her present post. In 1999 the Congressional Black Caucus awarded her the Ralph H. Metcalf Health, Medicine, and Science Award.

Sources: *Jet* 96 (2 August 1999): 4–5; *Who's Who among African Americans,* 26th ed., p. 407; *Contemporary Black Biography,* vol. 27, pp. 60–62.

1999 • Broadine M. Brown was named management chief at the U.S. Marshal Service in Arlington, Virginia, becoming the first black to reach the executive level. Previously she was senior budget analyst at the law enforcement agency. Among other assignments, the marshals, whose budget she oversees, protect judges, transport prisoners, and run the witness protection program.

Sources: *Jet* 96 (16 August 1999): 20.

1999 • The first black vice chair of the Federal Reserve Board was banking executive Roger W. Ferguson Jr. (1951–), whom President Bill Clinton nominated for the post. He took office in October of this year. He had served as a Federal Reserve governor for two years, the third black to hold that post. Born in Washington, D.C., Ferguson graduated from Harvard University, receiving a bachelor's degree in 1973, a law degree in 1979, and a doctorate in 1981. He practiced law in New York City, then became director of research and information and partner with the management consulting firm McKinsey and Company in New York City. He has served on the Federal Reserve Board from 1997 to 1999, and then was named vice chairman.

Sources: *Jet* 96 (23 August 1999): 4; *Contemporary Black Biography,* vol. 25, pp. 61–63; *Who's Who among African Americans,* 26th ed., p. 404.

1999 • Sylvia Stanfield became the first black woman ambassador to Brunei. She also became one of the highest-ranking blacks in the diplomatic service. Stanfield is one of the country's few Chinese language specialists. She graduated from Western College for Women in Oxford, Ohio, and studied at the University of Hawaii and the University of Hong Kong.

Sources: *Jet* 96 (15 November 1999): 8.

2000 • Darrell L. Davis was named laboratory director for the Drug Enforcement Administration's Office of Forensic Sciences, becoming the first black to hold that post. He is a graduate of Prairie View Agricultural and Mechanical University in Texas and in 1979 became a forensic chemist.

Sources: *Jet* 97 (7 January 2000): 38.

2000 • A retired deputy superintendent for the Chicago Police Department, James L. Whigman became the first black marshal in the Northern District of Illinois. Before his new appointment, Whigman had spent thirty-three years with the police department.

Sources: *Jet* 98 (14 August 2000): 16.

2000 • Carl Wendell Turnipseed (1947–), a banker, was named executive vice president and head of the financial services group of the New York Federal Reserve Bank, Buffalo

Branch, becoming the first black to hold the senior executive-level post. His responsibilities include oversight of business development, fiscal services, and electronic payment services. He has more than twenty years of management experience with the Federal Reserve Bank of New York, serving in accounting, government bonds, personnel, and elsewhere. Turnipseed was born in Baltimore, Maryland, and educated at Morgan State College (B.S., 1969) and New York University Graduate School of Business (M.B.A., 1974).

Sources: *Jet* 98 (3 July 2000): 3; *Who's Who among African Americans,* 26th ed., pp. 1254–55.

2000 • Quenton White (1960?–) became the first black chief federal prosecutor for the thirty-three-county Middle District of Tennessee, on August 7. President Bill Clinton appointed him to the post. White grew up in a farming family in Louisiana. He received both undergraduate and law degrees from Southern University in Baton Rouge. For three years he served in the U.S. Army, where he was an army lawyer. After that, he was a business consultant in Maryland and later an assistant public defender in Nashville. Before taking the new office, White had served as executive director of 100 Black Men of Middle Tennessee, a civic organization that aims to enhance opportunities for young black males. White left office and opened a law practice in Nashville in January 2002.

Sources: *Tennessean* (29 September 1999); (8 August 2000); (20 January 2002).

2001 • In January Roderick Radnor Paige (1933–) was sworn in as U.S. secretary of education, the first black to hold that post. In this year as well, the American Association of School Administrators named him Superintendent of the Year. Paige was born in Monticello, Mississippi, and grew up when racial segregation was still rigidly practiced. He worked his way through college, Jackson State University, and received his bachelor's degree in 1955. He obtained his master's and his doctorate from Indiana University. Paige was first a football coach serving at Utica Junior College (1955–62) and then Jackson State University (1962–69). He moved to Houston, where he was head football coach, athletic director, and a faculty member at Texas Southern University (1971–84). In 1984 Paige became dean of the school of education. He was elected to the Houston school board in 1989 and district superintendent in 1994—the position he held when President-elect George W. Bush tapped him to head the Department of Education. Paige supported Bush's call for school choice vouchers that would allow parents to send their children to select private schools rather than remain in public schools. Paige streamlined the Department of Education and spoke out on a variety of issues, such as the rash of shootings in several of the nation's schools.

Sources: *Contemporary Black Biography,* vol. 29, pp. 127–29; *Jet* 99 (22 January 2001): 8–10; *New York Times* (30 December 2000).

2001 • James L. Dunlap was named special agent in charge of the U.S. Secret Service, Detroit Field Office, becoming the first black to head the Secret Service in Michigan. He was previously assistant special agent in charge of the Forensic Services Division of the Secret Service in Washington, D.C. He joined the Secret Service in 1983, serving on President Ronald Reagan's detail and the presidential protective division.

Sources: *Jet* 99 (4 June 2001): 36.

2001 • Condoleezza "Condi" Rice (1954–) was named head of the National Security Council in the George W. Bush administration. She took office this year, becoming the first woman to hold that post, which does not require confirmation. An expert on the Soviet Union, Rice served in the administration of the senior Bush. Rice was born in segregated Birmingham, Alabama, but moved to Colorado with her family when she was in middle school. She skipped two grades in school, and at age fifteen she began to study at the University of Denver with the idea of becoming a top pianist. Instead, she developed an interest in international studies and graduated from the university in 1974. In 1975 she received her master's degree from the University of Notre Dame and in 1981 received her Ph.D. from the University of Denver's Graduate School of International Studies. Rice completed an internship with the U.S. Department of State in 1977, and an-

The First Black Secretary of State

In 2001 Colin Powell became the first black Secretary of State. President-elect George W. Bush tapped him for the post in December, as he began to select members of his cabinet. A retired four-star general in the U.S. Army, Powell had held other top-level posts in the federal government. He was the first black national security advisor in 1987 and the first black to head the Joint Chiefs of Staff in 1989. The son of Jamaican immigrants, Powell was born in the Harlem section of New York City. He graduated from City College of the City University of New York (B.S. 1958), George Washington University (M.B.A., 1971), and the National War College (1976). A member of the ROTC while in college, he entered the army after graduation as a second lieutenant. He had wide experience in the military, serving as military adviser in Vietnam, battalion executive officer and division operations officer, battalion commander in South Korea, and in various other positions in Colorado, Kansas, and West Germany. By 1989 he had become commander-in-chief of the U.S. Forces Command at Fort McPherson, Georgia. In 1989 he was promoted to general and he was also named chairman of the Joint Chiefs of Staff in Washington, D.C. In the latter position, Powell successfully oversaw operations Desert Storm and Desert Shield. In 1993 he retired from the military and was given a colorful send-off at Fort Meyer, Virginia, that was broadcast nationally. At that time he was presented the Presidential Medal of Freedom with Distinction, the nation's highest civilian award. After retirement Powell joined the lecture circuit, served on a number of boards, and also chaired President Bill Clinton's volunteer program, Summit for America's Future. The program aimed to improve children's lives. He returned to government service in 2001, when he became secretary of state.

Sources: *Contemporary Black Biography,* vol. 1, pp. 195–98; Smith, *Notable Black American Men,* pp. 958–61; *Tennessean* (18 December 2000).

Condoleezza Rice

other with the Rand Corporation in 1980. She taught political science at Stanford University from 1981 to 1989, where she was also a member of the Center for International Security and Arms Control. From 1985 to 1986 Rice was a fellow at Stanford's internationally known think tank, the Hoover Institute. Another fellowship in 1987 enabled her to serve a special assistant to the Joint Chiefs of Staff; she was assigned to Strategic Nuclear Policy. After serving President George Bush's administration as director of Soviet and European Affairs on the National Security Council in 1989–91, she returned to Stanford and became provost—the number two job at Stanford. She was the youngest and the first black chief academic and budget officer at the school. Rice became national security consultant in the George W. Bush campaign, and then took her new position when Bush became president.

Sources: Smith, *Notable Black American Women,* Book II, pp. 552–54; *Tennessean* (18 December 2000).

2001 • When Ruth A. Davis (1943–) was sworn in as director general of the United States Foreign Services and director of human services for the U.S. Department of State, Secretary of State Colin Powell read the oath of office. This was the first time in history that a black secretary of state administered the oath to a black foreign services officer. Davis also became the first black woman to reach that high level in the Department of State. Davis was born in Phoenix, Arizona, and graduated from Spelman College in Atlanta and the University of California at Berkeley. She held several teaching positions and appointments in academia before she was named to her post.

Sources: *Jet* 99 (2 April 2001): 19; 100 (6 August 2001): 4; *Who's Who among African Americans,* 26th ed., p. 320.

2001 • On June 11, the U.S. Secret Services named Larry Cockell (1951?–) to the position of deputy director, minority agent, making him the first black to hold that post. He also became the highest-ranking black in the organization. Before the promotion, Cockell was assistant director of the Office of Human Resources and Training. He began his career in law enforcement with the St. Louis police department. After that he spent twenty years with the Secret Service, the oldest federal law enforcement agency. Cockell held several positions within the Presidential Protective Division and rose to special agent in charge. He was in charge of daily security for President Bill Clinton, the First Family, and the White House complex as a whole.

Sources: *Crisis* 108 (July/August 2001): 12.

2001 • Pierre-Richard Prosper (1963–) was confirmed as ambassador-at-large for war crimes, becoming the first minority attorney ever promoted to this rank in the Department of State. He was previously special counsel and policy advisor to the Office of War Crimes Issues. He is also experienced in tracking drug cartels and prosecuting war criminals. Prosper was a special assistant to the assistant attorney general of the Criminal Division before he was detailed to the Department of State. When he acted as war crimes prosecutor for the U.N. tribunal in Rwanda, he handled the first known trial for genocide. As an assistant U.S. attorney, he has also investigated and prosecuted gang-related homicides for the Central District of California. Prosper is a native of Denver and grew up in New York state. He was educated at Boston University and the law school of Pepperdine University.

Sources: *Jet* 100 (24 September 2001): 34–35.

2001 • The first black to head the Department of Labor's regional statistics office is Sheila Watkins, a career employee for eighteen years.

Sources: *Jet* 100 (3 September 2001): 13.

2001 • Kelvin Mack became the first black postmaster for the city of Baltimore. He led a staff of 2,500 members and directed a $375 million budget.

Sources: *Jet* 100 (24 September 2001): 10.

2005 • Condoleeza Rice (1954–) was named secretary of state under the George W. Bush Administration, becoming the first black woman to hold that post.

Sources: *Who's Who among African Americans,* vol. 24, p. 1014.

2009 • The first black woman to become a Federal Communications Commissioner was Mignon Clyburn (1962–). She was nominated to the position on June 25 and sworn into office on August 3, to a term that expired on June 30, 2012. The daughter of U.S. Representative Jim Clyburn (D. SC), she has a long history of public service in South Carolina, having served on the South Carolina Public Service Commission. She graduated from the University of South Carolina.

Sources: *Link to Link* 11 (Fall 2009): 21.

Federal Employees

1866 • William Slade was hired as steward to President Andrew Johnson, becoming the first black American to serve in that position (now known as chief usher of the White House). He was also the first person hired under a new law of 1866, providing him a federal salary. Slade was highly respected in Washington's free black community. He was in charge of the property and grounds and for managing the budget that Congress appropriated for the White House. Following the president's request, he reorganized the White House along more practical lines. He assigned private caterers on a per-plate fee to provide for the large dinners, thus effecting savings in cost. Those White House staffers who were paid by the federal government were under Slade's supervision. These included doormen, a coachman, and others. The basement contained servants halls; however, one was for blacks servants and the other for whites.

Sources: *American Visions* (February–March 1995): 16–20.

1941 • Oscar Wayman Holmes (1916–2001) was assigned to the New York airway traffic control center as assistant controller, becoming the Civil Aeronautics Administration's (CAA) first black air traffic controller. Born in Dunbar, West Virginia, Holmes attended the segregated public schools in nearby Charleston. He received a bachelor's degree from West Virginia State College (now University) and a master's degree from The Ohio State University. He taught at Claflin College in Orangeburg, South Carolina, and then moved to Erie, Pennsylvania. Holmes participated in the civilian Pilot Training Program made available under the Franklin D. Roosevelt Administration. After that, he trained as an air traffic controller through CAA. Upon completing the program, he was assigned to New York's La Guardia Airport. He joined the U.S. Navy in 1942 and in 1944. He was assigned to the Aviation Cadet Selection Board in New York City. He managed to secure a flying assignment with the Naval Air Transport Service, Air Ferry Squadron II, at Terminal Island, California. In January 1946 he returned to his former post at La Guardia. Holmes returned to school and earned a law degree in 1954 from the Brooklyn Law School, having studied through its night program. For a while he maintained a part-time law practice but left to join the FAA at its Washington, D.C., headquarters. He rose in rank, retiring in 1973 as a federal hearing officer. Holmes died on November 5, 2001.

Sources: *Washington Post* (2 December 2001).

1976 • Johnnie Mae M. Gibson (1949–) was the first black woman agent with the Federal Bureau of Investigation. Born in Caryville, Florida and educated in Georgia and Florida, Gibson graduated from Albany State University in Georgia in 1971 and Georgia State University in 1976. In the course of her career, she was a high school teacher from 1971 to 1972 and then moved into law enforcement. She was a police officer in Georgia from 1972 to 1976, then became a special agent for the FBI in Florida in 1976. She joined the FBI in Washington, D.C., in 1979 as a special agent. Other positions were at the supervisory or special agent level with different divisions of the FBI. Finally, she became head of applicant investigations of the FBIs Unit Chief Bureau.

Sources: *Who's Who among African* Americans, 14th ed., p. 470; *Contemporary Black Biography,* vol. 23, pp. 84–87.

1989 • Kristin Clark Taylor (1959–) became the first black director of media relations for President George Bush's White House staff. The youngest of seven, Taylor was born in Detroit and graduated from Michigan State University in 1982 with a B.A. degree. Her experiences include an internship with the *Detroit Free Press* in 1982; news writer, editor, and public affairs officer for *USA Today* from 1982 to 1987; assistant press secretary for Vice President George Bush from 1987 to 1988; and director of media relations for the White House from 1989 to 1990. She joined BellSouth Corporation in 1990, serving as director of communications until 1994. In 1994 she became vice president of external affairs for the Student Loan Marketing Association.

Sources: *Contemporary Black Biography,* vol. 8, pp. 245–47; *Black Enterprise* 24 (November 1993): 135; *Ebony* 45 (October 1990): 76.

1989 • The first black to serve as secretary for a First Lady of the United States was Anna Perez (1951–). She provided assistance to Barbara Bush from 1989 to 1993; her duties included arranging interviews, coordinating the First Lady's appointment schedule, and traveling with the President and Mrs. Bush (Perez accompanied the Bushes to China in 1989). The New York City native attended Hunter College in New York. With her husband, Ted Sims, she became co-owner of a community newspaper in Tacoma, Washington. She was named press aid to senator Slade Gorton in the late 1970s, then press secretary to U.S. representative John Miller. After leaving her position as press secretary, Perez held top positions at Creative Artists and the Walt Disney Company, then became general manager of corporate communications and programs for the Chevron Corporation.

Sources: *Contemporary Black Biography,* vol. 1, pp. 193–94; *Essence* 20 (August 1989): 48.

1992 • Vernon E. Jordan Jr. (1935–) chaired the transition team for President-elect Bill Clinton, becoming the first and only black to serve in that capacity. Although Jordan refused to accept the position of U.S. attorney general in Clinton's administration, he helped Clinton select cabinet officers. During Clinton's tenure, Jordan remained an advisor to the President on domestic and foreign policies and became one of the most influential voices in the Clinton administration. Since the 1960s Jordan has been a high-profile figure in America. The Atlanta-born Jordan received his bachelor's degree from DePauw University in Greencastle, Indiana, and his law degree from Howard University's law school. He moved into civil rights work immediately, serving as law clerk in the office of civil rights attorney David Hollowell in Atlanta. He was a member of Hollowell's legal team that worked with Charlayne Hunter-Gault and Hamilton Holmes in their efforts to enroll in the all-white University of Georgia. When Hunter-Gault was finally admitted, Jordan used his body as a shield and forced a path through an angry white mob that tried to prevent her entering the campus. From 1961 to 1963 Jordan was field secretary of the NAACP's Georgia branch. In 1964 he joined civil rights attorney Wiley A. Branton in Little Rock, who was counsel for the "Little Rock Nine" who integrated Central High School. Jordan was director of the Southern Regional Council's Voter Registration Project for four years. After a stint with the U.S. Office of Equal Opportunity in Atlanta and a year as fellow at Harvard University's John F. Kennedy School of Government, he became executive director of the United Negro College Fund (now the College Fund/UNCF). In 1972 he became executive director of the National Urban League until the end of 1981. Then he became partner in the law firm of Akin, Gump, Strauss, Hauer, and Feld, in its Washington, D.C. office. His book, *Vernon Can Read* (2001), is a memoir of his life from his early years through winter 2001, when he received the NAACP's Spingarn Medal.

Sources: Jordan, *Vernon Can Read: A Memoir,* p. 328; Smith, *Notable Black American Men,* pp. 667–70.

1994 • The first black woman to serve as the assistant attorney general of the Justice Department's Tax Division was Loretta Collins-Agrett (1937–). She graduated from the Harvard Law School in 1976 and later became the first black lawyer for the Joint Committee on Taxation for the U. S. Congress.

Sources: *Jet* 86 (12 September 1994): 10.

2000 • Flora Murphy Shaffer was promoted from regional director of information technology for the U.S. General Services Administration (GSA), located in Chicago, to grade 15, reaching the highest level in the government's pay system. She was the first black in the Great Lakes region to reach that rank.

Sources: *Jet* 97 (21 February 2000): 24.

2000 • Cassandra M. Chandler (1958?–) was named assistant director for training for the FBI, becoming the first black woman at the agency to hold the rank of assistant director. She also became the agency's top black woman. A seventeen-year veteran with the FBI, Chandler became responsible for all training programs for new hires and continuing education for those already on the FBI force. Each year the Training Division conducts advanced training for state and local officers.

Sources: *Jet* 101 (25 February 2002): 5–6.

2002 • Kenton Keith was the first black man to serve in the strategic role as director of the Coalition Information Services, a joint combine of the United States and Britain set up in Islamabad, Pakistan, that works to eliminate terrorism. On the war scene Keith determines how to move forward socially, culturally, and in political circles of Muslim countries. The retired foreign diplomat was senior vice president for the Meridian International Center, a private non-profit organization that promotes international understanding located in Washington, D.C. In 1961 Keith was the first black to graduate from the University of

Kansas Naval Training Program. He spent over thirty years in the U.S. State Department with assignments in Lebanon, Iraq, Saudi Arabia, Turkey, Morocco, and Syria.

Sources: *Jet* 101 (4 February 2002): 26.

Judiciary

John Sweat Rock

1865 • John Sweat Rock (1825–1866), lawyer, was the first black man admitted to practice before the Supreme Court, but not the first to argue a case. Following his admission to the court, he may have been the first black lawyer received on the floor of the House of Representatives. Born to free parents in Salem, New Jersey, Rock received a medical degree in 1852; the American Medical College in Philadelphia may have awarded him the degree. Later he was admitted into the Massachusetts Medical Society. Rock gained prominence first as an abolitionist. In 1858 he went to France where he spent eight months studying French literature and language. Since Rock experienced problems with his throat, he also use that time to give his voice relief from his many speaking engagements. Although he practiced both dentistry and medicine, when he returned from Paris he curtailed his medical practice. His health forced him to give up his practice and study law.

Sources: Logan and Winston, *Dictionary of American Negro Biography,* pp. 529–31; Garrett, *Famous First Facts about Negroes,* p. 23, 93; *Journal of Negro History* 52 (July 1967): 169–75; Kane, *Famous First Facts,* p. 345.

1942 • Lawrence Bailey Sr. (1918?–1998) was named deputy clerk of the U.S. District Court in Washington, becoming the first black deputy of such a court.

Sources: *New York Times* (28 April 1998).

Irving Mollison

1945 • Irving Charles Mollison (1899–1962) was the first black judge of a U.S. Customs Court in New York. This was the first time that a black served as a federal judge in the United States. The Vicksburg, Mississippi-born jurist was educated at the University of Chicago, where he received his undergraduate degree in 1920. He was admitted to the University of Chicago Law School and graduated in 1923. Mollison practiced law in Chicago for twenty years and became known for his work as lead attorney in the Hansberry case of 1940. In that case, playwright Lorraine Hansberry's father challenged Chicago's restrictive housing covenants that kept blacks from receiving fair housing opportunities. Mollison successfully argued the case *Hansberry v. Lee* before the Supreme Court. After Mollison was named to the Customs Court, he and his family moved to New York. The Irvin C. Mollison School located on South King Drive in Chicago, was named in his honor in 1955.

Sources: Garrett, *Famous First Facts about Negroes,* p. 87; *Negro Almanac, 1976,* p. 1045; *Negro Year Book, 1941–46,* p. 285; Smith, *Notable Black American Men,* pp. 828–29.

1949 • William Henry Hastie (1904–1976) became a federal appeals judge, the first black appointed to the federal bench. He presided over Delaware, New Jersey, Pennsylvania, and the Virgin Islands. In his new position Hastie frequently spoke out against racism and segregation. He was appointed district judge in the Virgin Islands. He was also the first black governor of the Virgin Islands in 1944. Hastie served as civilian aide to the Secretary of War (1941–43). He resigned to protest the lack of a positive commitment to recruit black pilots. Hastie was born in Knoxville, Tennessee. He graduated from Amherst College (B.A., 1925) and Harvard University (LL.B., 1930 and S.J.D., 1933). He was in private law practice, then became assistant solicitor of the Department of Interior (1933–37). He was the dean of Howard University's law school (1939–40), and civilian aid to the Secretary of War (1940–43). He was governor of the Virgin Islands before being named appeals judge.

Sources: *Contemporary Black Biography,* vol. 8, pp. 107–10; *Negro Almanac, 1976,* p. 281; Robinson, *Historical Negro Biographies,* p. 199; Smith, *Notable Black American Men,* pp. 519–22.

1961 • James Benton Parsons (1911–1993) was the first black appointed judge of a district court in the continental United States. Chicago attorney Parsons was appointed judge of the U.S. District Court of Northern Illinois. He received a lifetime appointment, becoming the first black to receive this status. Parsons was born in Kansas City, Missouri, the son of a Disciples of Christ minister. Later the family moved to Decatur, Illinois. Parsons graduated from Milliken University and Conservatory of Music (B.A. 1934) and the University of Chicago (M.A., 1946, LL.D., 1949). For a while he taught music, but volunteered for the U.S. Navy, serving from 1942 to 1945. In 1949 Parsons began a career in law by teaching law at John Marshall Law School, working as corporate counsel for the city of Chicago, and by entering law practice with the firm Gassaway, Crosson, Turner and Parsons. For nine years he was U.S. district attorney before becoming superior court judge in Cook County in 1960. He served the district court from 1961 to 1992, when he retired. Among his notable achievements was the role that he played settling the air traffic controllers' dispute in 1970 and in upholding the Tenant's Bill of Rights in Chicago in 1987.

Sources: Hornsby, *Chronology of African-American History*, p. 112; Kane, *Famous First Facts*, p. 333; *Negro Almanac, 1976*, p. 284; *Contemporary Black Biography*, vol. 14, pp. 175–77; *Jet* 86 (15 August 1994): 20.

1962 • Thelton Eugene Henderson (1933–) became the first black to join the U.S. Justice Department's Civil Rights Division. He was born in Shreveport, Louisiana, and graduated from the University of California, Berkeley (B.A., 1956 and J.D., 1962). After his stint with the Department of Justice, he held several posts in California, including that as assistant dean of the Stanford University Law School (1968–76). Later Henderson became chief judge of the Ninth Circuit Court in San Francisco.

Sources: *Jet* 91 (16 December 1996): 4; *Who's Who among African Americans*, 26th ed., pp. 567–68.

1965 • The first black solicitor general was Thurgood Marshall (1908–1993). The Senate confirmed his nomination on August 11. He held office until 1967, when he was appointed to the Supreme Court. Although he held a lifetime appointment on the court of appeals, Marshall resigned that post, took a pay cut, and accepted the post as solicitor general. This prepared Marshall for his selection to the nation's highest court. As solicitor general, Marshall held the third-highest post in the department of justice. He argued nineteen cases before the Supreme Court and won fifteen, including a case that challenged the Voting Rights Act of 1965.

Sources: Smith, *Notable Black American Men*, pp. 762–67; *Jet* 92 (11 August 1997): 19.

1966 • James Lopez Watson (1922?–2001), who sat on the federal bench, was the first judge to be given assignments in the Deep South. He heard and decided customs court cases in Atlanta, Tampa, Houston, San Antonio, Dallas, and other southern cities. In 1991 Watson became senior judge on the Court of International Trade, previously known as the Customs Court. Watson was born in Harlem and graduated from New York University in 1947 and from Brooklyn Law School in 1951. He entered private practice with his father, James S. Watson, who for eighteen years was a municipal court justice. The younger Watson served with the Buffalo Soldiers of World War II. He was elected to the state senate in 1954 and to the civil court in 1963.

Sources: *New York Times* (6 September 2001).

1968 • Charles M. Stokes (1904?–1997) became the first black appointed a district court judge in Seattle. He served on the bench until he retired in 1978. Stokes was a native of Fredonia, Kansas.

Sources: *Jet* 91 (13 January 1997): 18.

1975 • The first black woman appointed judge of the District of Columbia Appellate Court was Julia P. Cooper (1921–). She was the highest ranking woman in the federal courts.

Sources: *Negro Almanac*, p. 71.

The Court of Appeals' First Black Judge

In 1966 Spottswood Robinson (1916–1998) became the first black judge of the U.S. Court of Appeals in Washington, D.C. Robinson was born in Richmond, Virginia. He attended Virginia Union University in Richmond for a while, but entered Howard University School of Law, graduating *magna cum laude* in 1939 with a law degree. He taught at Howard in Washington, D.C., for eight years, moving from teaching fellow to become associate professor. Robinson was admitted to the Virginia bar and practiced in Richmond during the struggle for civil rights. Immediately his work catapulted him to national prominence. He left Howard and became an attorney for the Legal Defense Fund of Virginia's NAACP. He joined his former mentor, Charles Hamilton Houston, in a successful Supreme Court case that outlawed restrictive covenants that prevented the sale of real estate to blacks. He was named southeast regional counsel for the NAACP's defense fund in 1951. He was successful in his argument before the Supreme Court, resulting in the court's historic decision in the *Brown v. Board of Education* to strike down the "separate but equal" doctrine in public education in the South. Other civil rights cases that Robinson won related to desegregation in interstate buses and in public parks. Robinson left his practice in 1960 and became dean of the law school at Howard University until 1963. President John F. Kennedy in 1961 named him to the U.S. Commission on Civil Rights. In 1964, Robinson became the first black to serve as a judge of the U.S. District Court in Washington, D.C. He was named to the Court of Appeals in 1966, becoming chief judge of that court from 1981 to 1986. Robinson retired in 1992 and returned to Richmond where he died.

Sources: *Contemporary Black Biography,* vol. 22, pp. 167–69; *Jet* 94 (2 November 1998): 57.

1975 • James Benton Parsons (1911–1993) became the first black to serve as chief judge of a U.S. district court. He served the Court for the Northern District of Illinois.

Sources: Hornsby, *Chronology of African-American History,* p. 112; Kane, *Famous First Facts,* p. 333; *Contemporary Black Biography,* vol. 14, pp. 175–77; *Jet* 99 (23 April 2001): 33.

1977 • George Howard Jr. (1924–2007) was the first black U.S. District Court judge in Arkansas. He was assigned to the Pine Bluff area. In 2011 a federal building and U.S. courthouse in Pine Bluff was renamed in his honor.

Sources: *Jet* 111 (14 May 2007): 18.

1978 • Robert Frederick Collins (1931–) was the first black federal judge in the Deep South in modern times. Active in legal services in Louisiana, Collins was appointed a U.S. District Court judge in 1978. In 1991 he was also the first federal judge to be found guilty of taking a bribe. The New Orleans native received his undergraduate degree from Dillard University in New Orleans and his law degree from the Louisiana State University. He also completed a program at the University of Nevada National Judge College in 1973. In the course of his career he has been a law school instructor, partner in a law firm, assistant city attorney and legal advisor for the New Orleans Police Department, judge on the Criminal District Court for Orleans Parish, and then U.S. District Court judge.

Sources: *Negro Almanac,* p. 341; *Who's Who among African Americans,* 26th ed., p. 262.

1979 • Joyce London Alexander (1949–) was the first black American federal judge in the District of Massachusetts. She subsequently was named chief judge of that court. She was also the first African American woman chief judge in any court in Massachusetts. Alexander was educated at Howard University and the New England Law School. She held a law fellowship with the Boston Legal Assistance Project from 1972 to 1974. From 1974 to 1975 she was Youth Activities Commission's legal counsel. After teaching at Tufts Uni-

The First Black Woman Federal Judge

I n 1966 Constance Baker Motley (1921–2005), who received national acclaim for her civil rights work, became the first black woman federal judge on January 25. After receiving President Lyndon B. Johnson's nomination and Senate confirmation, she became judge on the United States District Court, the Southern District of New York. She was elected to the New York state senate in 1964, and in 1965 she became president of the Borough of Manhattan. Her appointment as a judge of the Circuit Court of the Southern District of New York made her the highest paid black woman in government. The Connecticut-born jurist received her education at New York and Columbia universities. Motley worked with the NAACP as legal assistant and associate counsel and won many difficult civil rights cases—her most famous victory was the case of James Meredith against the University of Mississippi. Working with the NAACP Legal Defense Fund, she and other attorneys represented the demonstrators in the sit-in movement, Martin Luther King Jr., Fred Shuttlesworth, and others in protest. Her numerous writings have been published in legal and professional journals.

Sources: Hine, *Black Women in America*, vol. 2, pp. 822–24; Smith, *Notable Black American Women*, pp. 779–82; Robinson, *Historical Negro Biographies*, p. 230; *Contemporary Black Biography*, vol. 10, pp. 180–83.

versity from 1975 to 1976, she served as general counsel for the Massachusetts Board of Higher Education from 1976 to 1979. From 1978 to 1979 Alexander was on-camera legal editor for station WBZ-TV.

Sources: *Contemporary Black Biography*, vol. 18, pp. 4–6; *Who's Who among African Americans*, 26th ed., p. 15.

1979 • Amalya Lyle Kearse (1937–) became the first woman justice in the Second Circuit Court. President Jimmy Carter appointed her to the Court of Appeals for New York City on June 21 this year. (Thurgood Marshall was the first black in that post.) Kearse was also the first black woman partner in a Wall Street law form, Hughes, Hubbard, and Reed. Kearse was born in Vauxhall, New Jersey, and graduated from Wellesley College in 1959 with a bachelor's degree. In 1962 she received her law degree from the University of Michigan, graduating near the top of her class. She was admitted to the New York Bar in 1963 and was admitted to practice before the Supreme Court in 1967. Kearse also became known as one of the country's most talented bridge players. In 1975 she wrote *Bridge Conventions Complete* and in 1976 she edited the third edition of the *Official Encyclopedia of Bridge*. She translated and edited *Bridge Analysis* in 1979. In addition to winning two major national titles in 1971 and 1972, she was the National Women's Team Bridge Champion in 1987. Kearse has been active in legal circles, the National Urban League, and the NAACP Legal Defense Fund.

Sources: Smith, *Notable Black American Women*, Book II, pp. 374–76; *Contemporary Black Biography*, vol. 12, pp. 101–4; *Who's Who among African Americans*, 26th ed., p. 713; *Black New Yorkers*, p. 366.

1979 • Benjamin F. Gibson (1931–) became the first black federal judge in the Western District of Michigan, on October 2. On February 15, 1991, he was named chief judge of that same court, the first black to hold that post. In 1963 Gibson was named assistant prosecuting attorney for Ingham County, Michigan, the first black to serve in that capacity. He was born in Saffold, Alabama, and relocated to Detroit with his family when he was four years old. The first in his family to attend or graduate from college, he completed his bachelor's degree at Wayne University (now Wayne State University) in Detroit in 1955. From 1955 to 1956 the Detroit Edison Company hired him as an attorney, making him the first black employed in a professional position with that company. He became interested in law and completed a law degree at Detroit College of Law. After practicing law for a while, he became the first black to teach in the Thomas M. Cooley Law School in Lansing, Michigan. Gibson continued his teaching position until 1984. He became a federal district judge in 1979.

Sources: Smith, *Notable Black American Men*, pp. 452–56; *Who's Who among African Americans*, 26th ed., p. 459.

1979 • In October President Jimmy Carter appointed Anna Diggs-Taylor (1932–) to the federal court for the Eastern District of Michigan (based in Detroit). She was sworn in on November 15, becoming the first black woman in the state to receive such a post. Taylor was born in Washington, D.C., and graduated from Barnard College in 1954. In 1967 she graduated from Yale University law school with the LL.B. degree. With the assistance of J. Ernest Wilkins, she became an assistant solicitor in the Solicitor's Office, U.S. Department of Labor, where she remained from 1957 to 1960. She was assistant Wayne County prosecutor from 1961 to 1962, assistant U.S. attorney for the Eastern District of Michigan, 1966–67, and held a number of other posts until 1979, when she was named a federal judge.

Sources: *Contemporary Black Biography*, vol. 20, pp. 59–61; Hine, *Black Women in America*, pp. 1142–43.

1979 • Matthew J. Perry Jr. (1921?–2011) became the first black federal judge in South Carolina, on September 20. President Jimmy Carter appointed him to the post. A civil rights lawyer, he argued hundreds of cases that helped desegregate schools, hospitals, and other public places. The state honored the long-ignored civil rights hero in mid-2002, when the new federal courthouse building bearing his name opened.

Sources: *Ebony* 35 (November 1979): 156; *Jet* 98 (16 October 2000): 36.

1980 • Odell Horton (1929–) was the first black federal judge in the state of Tennessee. A native of Tennessee, Horton was educated at Morehouse College and Howard University. He was president of Le Moyne-Owen College (1970–74) before his appointment to the U.S. District Court in Tennessee.

Sources: *Who's Who among African Americans*, 14th ed., p. 622.

1980 • U. W. Clemon (1943–) became the first black federal district judge in Alabama. Born in Fairfield, Alabama, he graduated from Miles College in Birmingham and Columbia University School of Law. He was a law clerk with the NAACP Legal Defense Fund, partner in law practice, and served in the state senate from 1974 to 1980.

Sources: Bailey, *They Too Call Alabama Home*, pp. 78–79; *Who's Who among African Americans*, 26th ed., p. 246.

1982 • Reginald Walker Gibson (1927–) was the first African American to sit on the bench of the U.S. Claims Court (now the U.S. Court of Federal Claims.). Born in Lynchburg, Virginia, Gibson was educated at Virginia Union University, Howard University, and the University of Pennsylvania. In his career he has served as agent for the Internal Revenue Service; trial attorney for the Department of Justice, Tax Division; and senior, then general tax attorney for International Harvester. Since 1995 he has been senior judge on the U.S. Court of Federal Claims.

Sources: *Who's Who among African Americans*, vol. 26, p. 460.

1984 • Ann Claire Williams (1949–), judge, was the first black woman nominated to the federal bench in Chicago. Born in Michigan, Williams was educated at Wayne State University, the University of Michigan, and Notre Dame University. Prior to her appointment to the U.S. District Court, Williams was an attorney and adjunct professor at Northwestern University.

Sources: *Who's Who among African Americans*, 26th ed., p. 1332.

1990 • Thelton Eugene Henderson (1933–) was the first black chief judge of the Northern California U.S. District Court. Henderson is a member of the Charles Hamilton Houston Law Association and the National Bar Association.

Sources: *Who's Who among African Americans*, 26th ed., pp. 567–68.

1993 • Eric H. Holder Jr. (1951–) became the first black U.S. attorney for the District of Columbia. President Bill Clinton nominated him for the position. When he took office he faced a major case involving Democratic congressman Dan Rostenkowski from Illinois, who was indicted on charges of misusing House accounts. During his tenure, Holder worked to bridge the communications divide between racial communities.

Sources: Smith, *Notable Black American Men,* pp. 556–47; *Contemporary Black Biography,* vol. 9, pp. 118–20; *Who's Who among African Americans,* 26th ed., p. 592.

1994 • The first black U.S. attorney for Delaware was Gregory M. Sleet (1951–), who was sworn in office in Wilmington. He is the son of *Ebony-Jet* photographer Moneta Sleet and Mary Sleet. Sleet belongs to the New York State, American, and National bar associations.

Sources: *Jet* 93 (16 February 1998): 12; 86 (11 July 1994): 33; *Who's Who among African Americans,* 26th ed., p. 1136.

1994 • Vanessa D. Gilmore (1956–) was sworn in as a federal district judge in Texas, becoming the only black and the youngest sitting judge in that post in the state.

Sources: *Jet* 86 (18 July 1994): 20; *Who's Who among African Americans,* 26th ed., p. 465.

1995 • The first woman and the first black federal administrative law judge in Mississippi was Covette Rooney. A graduate of Temple University's law school, she was assigned to Hattiesburg to handle backlogs in Social Security cases. In 1996 Rooney became the first black woman administrative law judge at the Occupational Safety and Health Review Commission (OSHA). The independent federal agency handles disputes between employers and OSHA that relate to work place safety and health violations.

Sources: *Jet* 87 (30 January 1995): 13; 91 (16 December 1996): 10.

1996 • The first black woman to become special master for the District Court in the U.S. Virgin Islands was Darlene Grant. Previously, Grant was general counsel/prison litigation for the National Council on Crime and Delinquency in Washington, D.C.

Sources: *Jet* 90 (22 July 1996): 40.

1996 • Joyce London Alexander became the first black woman chief judge in Massachusetts and the first black chief federal magistrate in the nation. In 1997 she received the C. Francis Stradford Award from the National Bar Association, named for one of the association's founders.

Sources: *Jet* 89 (12 February 1996): 20; *Contemporary Black Biography,* vol. 18, pp. 4–6; *Who's Who among African Americans,* 26th ed., p. 15.

1997 • Norma Holloway Johnson (1932–) became the first black woman chief federal district judge for the District of Columbia. She became known worldwide when she presided over the grand jury that considered allegations against President Bill Clinton tied to his relationship with White House intern Monica Lewinsky. The Lake Charles, Louisiana, native graduated from Miner's Teachers College in Washington, D.C., (1955) and Georgetown University Law Center (1962). She worked first as a trial attorney in the Department of Justice.

Sources: Smith, *Notable Black American Women,* pp. 591–93; *Jet* 92 (18 August 1997): 39; 94 (31 August 1998): 5; *Contemporary Black Biography,* vol. 17, pp. 106–9; *Who's Who among African Americans,* 26th ed., pp. 676.

1998 • Susan D. Davis (1963?–) became the first black federal magistrate for New Jersey as well as the state's youngest judge on the federal bench. She was the second woman to become U.S. magistrate and one of eleven magistrates in the district. Davis is a graduate of Norfolk State University and the Marshall Wythe School of Law at William and Mary. She has been a law partner and public defender for the state of New Jersey.

Sources: *Jet* 93 (19 January 1998): 38; *Who's Who among African Americans,* 14th ed., p. 326.

1999 • The first black federal district judge in Middle Tennessee was William J. "Joe" Haynes Jr. (1949–). He was sworn in office on December 7. Born in Memphis, Haynes graduated from the College of St. Thomas and the Vanderbilt Law School. Haynes has served as assistant attorney general for the state of Tennessee and was deputy attorney general for the Tennessee State Antitrust and Consumer Protection. He was special deputy attorney general for special litigation for one year; since 1984 he had been a federal magistrate for Middle Tennessee.

Sources: *Tennessean* (11 November 1999); (8 December 1999); *Who's Who among African Americans,* 26th ed., p. 560.

1999 • For the first time, three black federal appellate judges formed a panel for the Sixth Circuit Court of Appeals in Cincinnati. They heard cases from Ohio, Michigan, Tennessee, and Kentucky. The three jurists were R. Guy Cole Jr. of Columbus, Ohio; Nathaniel R. Jones (1926–) of Cincinnati; and Eric Lee Clay (1948–) of Detroit. More black judges serve on the Sixth Circuit than any other circuit in the federal judiciary.

Sources: *Jet* 96 (23 August 1999): 4; *Who's Who among African Americans,* 26th ed., p. 244 (Clay), p. 698 (Jones).

2000 • Former Common Pleas Court judge Petrese B. Tucker (1951–) was confirmed by the Senate, becoming the first black woman federal judge in Philadelphia.

Sources: *Jet* 98 (19 June 2000): 12.

2000 • The first black woman judge for the Court of Appeals, ninth circuit, was confirmed, making Johnnie Rawlinson (1952?–) the first black woman ever to serve on the court. The ninth circuit covers nine states in the West and includes Hawaii and Alaska. President Clinton in 1998 named her to the District Court. Before that, she served in the Clark County, Nevada, district attorney's office for eighteen years, spending the last few years as assistant district attorney.

Sources: *Jet* 98 (14 August 2000): 36–37.

2001 • The Senate confirmed Roger Lee Gregory (1953–) as a judge on the Court of Appeals serving Virginia, Maryland, South Carolina, North Carolina, and West Virginia. His court serves the highest percentage of minorities in the nation. In December 2000 President Bill Clinton gave him a temporary appointment to the court. President George W. Bush nominated Gregory for a permanent seat in May 2001. When he was confirmed in July, with lifetime appointment, he became the first black to hold that post. He was also President Bush's first nominee to receive a hearing. Gregory was born in Philadelphia and educated at Virginia State University in Petersburg, and the University of Michigan's law school. He has served as associate attorney for several law firms and as managing attorney in the firm Wilder and Gregory in Richmond.

Sources: *Jet* 99 (28 May 2001): 13; *Tennessean* (21 July 1992); *Washington Post* (21 July 2001); *Who's Who among African Americans,* 26th ed., p. 499.

2006 • Jerome Holmes (1962?–) became the first black American on the U.S. Court of Appeals for the 10th Circuit. His circuit includes Colorado, Oklahoma, Kansas, New Mexico, Utah, and Wyoming. Holmes has served as Oklahoma City attorney and previously practiced law with a prominent firm with offices in Oklahoma City, Tulsa, and Norman. A native of Washington, he received his law degree from Georgetown University and was a federal prosecutor in Oklahoma City for eleven years. Holmes also worked on the Oklahoma City bombing case.

Sources: *Jet* 110 (14 August 2006): 12.

2007 • Gregory Sleet (1951?–) became the first black chief judge of the U.S. District Court in Wilmington, Delaware. "I'm glad to be able to add my voice in this capacity and position of leadership," he said. Sleet has worked in civil and corporate law, became the first black federal judge in the state, and served as Deputy Attorney General for Delaware.

A native of New York, Sleet graduated from Hampton University and Rutgers University School of Law. At Rutgers he was the Earl Warren legal scholar.

Sources: *Jet* 112 (16 July 2007): 11; *Who's Who among African Americans,* 26th ed., p. 1136.

2009 • Eric Holder (1951–) was appointed U.S. Attorney General, becoming the first African American to hold that post. He became the highest-ranking black American law enforcement officer in history in 1997, when he was confirmed as deputy attorney general. He held the number-two post at the Justice Department. He resigned in 2001 and became a partner in the law firm of Covington & Burling in Washington, D.C. Holder was born in New York City and educated at Columbia University earning a bachelor's degree in 1973 and a law degree in 1976. Holder was previously a trial attorney for the U.S. Department of Justice, Public Integrity Section and associate justice of the Superior Court in Washington.

Eric Holder

Sources: *Contemporary Black Biography,* vol. 9, pp. 118–20; Smith, *Notable Black American Men,* pp. 556–47; *Who's Who among African Americans,* 26th ed., p. 592.

2010 • The U.S. Senate, on June 15, confirmed Marion Superior Court Judge Tanya Walton Pratt (1959–) to a lifetime appointment as a federal judge of the Southern District of Indiana. This action made Pratt the first black federal judge in Indiana. Senator Evan Bayh called the move "a step toward realizing equal justice under the law." Pratt had served the Marion Supreme Court since 1997.

Sources: *Jet* 118 (5 July 2010): 18.

Political Parties

1843 • Henry Highland Garnet, Samuel Ringgold Ward, and Charles B. Ray were the first blacks to participate in a national political gathering, the convention of the Liberty Party. Garnet (1815–1882) pastored a New York Presbyterian church and preached a social gospel. At a Lincoln's birthday memorial, February 12, 1865, he became the first black man to preach in the rotunda of the Capitol to the House of Representatives. In 1843, at the Convention of Free Men in Buffalo, New York, he outlined a brilliant plan for a general slave strike. Ray (1807–1886), one of the convention's secretaries, was a minister best known for his work as publisher of *The Colored American,* and president of the New York Society for the Promotion of Education among Colored Children. Ward (1817–1866), who led a prayer at the convention, was the leading black abolitionist before Frederick Douglass. His autobiography, *Autobiography of a Fugitive Slave,* was published in 1855.

Henry Highland Garnet

Sources: Logan and Winston, *Dictionary of American Negro Biography,* pp. 252–53 (Garnet), 515–16 (Ray), 631–632 (Ward); Baskin and Runes, *Dictionary of Black Culture,* pp. 181, 370, 460; Robinson, *Historical Negro Biographies,* pp. 82, 140; Smith, *Notable Black American Men,* pp. 437–41 (Garnet); pp. 1177–79 (Ward).

1866 • Frederick Douglass (1817–1895) was the first black delegate to a national political convention, that of the National Loyalists' Union party. Born a slave in Talbot County on Maryland's Eastern Shore, and named Frederick Augustus Washington Bailey, Douglass's talent as an orator won him employment as a lecturer by the Anti-Slavery Society. His freedom was bought while he was on a lecture tour in England. From 1847 until his death, he was a fearless leader of his race. When he returned from England, Douglass founded a newspaper in 1847, the *North Star* which he co-edited with Martin R. Delany. The editors used the paper to speak out against slavery and oppression. Later, Douglass changed the name of the publication to *Frederick Douglass' Paper.* Douglass found all forms of oppression intolerable and maintained a close relationship with reformers throughout the country. Therefore, he easily supported the woman's rights movement, attended the Woman's Rights Convention held at Seneca Falls, New York, in July 1848, and remained committed to woman's rights throughout his life. On July 4, 1852, Douglass delivered one of his most stirring speeches, "What to the Slave Is the Fourth of July?" In 1872 Douglass was the first black to be nominated as a vice-presidential candidate, by the Woman Suffrage Association convention. During Reconstruction he demanded the vote

Frederick Douglass

for the freedman. He moved to the nation's capital and became the first black to serve as recorder of deeds in 1881. He was named minister-resident and counsel general to Haiti in 1889. He published his classic autobiography in 1845, a second version appeared in 1855, and this work was again revised and enlarged under the title *The Life and Times of Frederick Douglass* in 1882.

Sources: Logan and Winston, *Dictionary of American Negro Biography,* p. 181; Garrett, *Famous First Facts about Negroes,* p. 160; *Negro Almanac,* p. 290; Smith, *Notable Black American Men,* pp. 326–31.

1952 • Charlotta A. Spears Bass (1880–1961), journalist and political activist, was the first black woman to run for vice-president. She was the nominee of the Progressive Party. Bass, born in South Carolina, moved to New England and began a career as a journalist. In 1912, she became editor of the *California Eagle* in Los Angeles. She was educated at Brown and Columbia universities and the University of California.

Sources: Hine, *Black Women in America,* vol. 1, p. 93; Smith, *Notable Black American Women,* p. 61–64; *Who's Who in Colored America, 1928,* p. 23.

Channing E. Phillips

1968 • Julian Bond (1940–) and Channing E. Phillips (1928–1987), civil rights leaders, were the first blacks proposed for president and vice-president at the same convention. Bond was an early member of the Student Nonviolent Coordinating Committee (SNCC) and communications director of the organization. At the Democratic convention he was the first black to be nominated from the floor of a major convention for the office of vice-president. After a few states voted, he withdrew, as he was too young to accept the nomination. Phillips was the first black nominated for president at a major political convention in modern times. Born in Brooklyn, New York, Phillips was educated at Virginia Union University, and Colgate Rochester Divinity School. He was a Congregationalist minister and active in Democratic politics. As favorite son of the Washington, D.C., delegation, he received 67 ½ votes.

Sources: *Contemporary Black Biography,* vol. 2, pp. 22–27 (Bond); Baskin and Runes, *Dictionary of Black Culture,* p. 59 (Bond); Baskin and Runes, *Dictionary of Black Culture,* p. 351 (Phillips); Garrett, *Famous First Facts about Negroes,* p. 163 (Phillips); Kane, *Famous First Facts,* p. 479 (Bond); *Who's Who among Black Americans, 1977* (Phillips); 26th ed, p. 118 (Bond); Smith, *Notable Black American Men,* pp. 91–93 (Bond).

1976 • Aris T. Allen (1910–1991), at Detroit, Michigan, was the first black man to call the roll at a Republican National Convention. In 1977 Allen was the first black to serve as Republican state chairman in Maryland. The Texas-born physician was educated at Howard University.

Sources: *Who's Who among Black Americans, 1977,* p. 12.

1976 • Barbara Charline Jordan (1936–1996) delivered a powerful keynote address at the Democratic National Convention in New York City, becoming the first black woman selected to present the keynote address.

Sources: Smith, *Notable Black American Women,* pp. 609–12; *Jet* 89 (5 February 1996): 54–55; *The Black New Yorkers,* p. 361.

1976 • Ben Brown (1940?–1999) became the first black deputy chairman of the Democratic National Committee. In this year also he was deputy campaign director for President Jimmy Carter. Brown graduated from Clark College in Atlanta (now Clark Atlanta University) and received his law degree from Howard University. While at Clark he was president of the student body. He and actor Charles Black helped to organize the first civil rights lunch-counter sit-ins in Atlanta. The two organized more than 200 students who occupied eleven segregated lunch counters on March 15, 1960. In 1966 Brown became a member of the Georgia House of Representatives, where he served for eleven years.

Sources: *New York Times* Obituaries (5 February 1999).

The First Black Chairman of the Republican National Convention

John Roy Lynch (1847–1939) was elected chairman of the Republican National Convention on September 10, 1884, the first black to be elected to that post. An eloquent speaker, he was also the first black to deliver the keynote address to the convention. In 1869, when Lynch was only twenty-two years old, he was elected a member of the Mississippi State House of Representatives and in 1871 he was elected Speaker of the House.

Sources: Logan and Winston, *Dictionary of American Negro Biography,* pp. 407–9; *Jet* 88 (11 September 1995): 19; Smith, *Notable Black American Men,* pp. 748–49.

1984 • Julian Carey Dixon (1934–2000), public official, was the first black to chair the rules committee for the Democratic National Convention. Born in Washington, D.C., Dixon was educated at California State University at Los Angeles and Southwestern University. Elected to Congress in 1978, Dixon was the first black member to chair an appropriations subcommittee in the District of Columbia. He introduced the first economic sanctions against apartheid in South Africa to be signed into law. He was author of the resolutions passed in the House of Representatives calling for the awarding of the Presidential Medal of Freedom to the renowned educator Benjamin E. Mays. Dixon also chaired the Congressional Black Caucus from 1983 to 1984 and later became president of the Black Caucus Foundation. He was a member of the board of visitors for the U.S. Military Academy.

Sources: *Negro Almanac,* 387–88; *Who's Who in American Politics, 1987–88,* p. 103; *Contemporary Black Biography,* vol. 24, pp. 56–58; Obituary, *Who's Who among African Americans,* 14th ed., p. 1470.

Julian Dixon

1984 • Jesse Louis Jackson (1941–) was the first black American to be a viable candidate for the presidential nomination. Founder of Operation PUSH (People United to Serve Humanity), Jackson was born in South Carolina and educated at the University of Illinois and North Carolina Agricultural and Technical College (later University). He was ordained a Baptist minister in 1968, after studying at the Chicago Theological Seminary. He was a field director for the Congress of Racial Equality (CORE), and in 1967 was named by the Southern Christian Leadership Conference (SCLC) to head its Operation Breadbasket, which he had helped found. A close associate of Martin Luther King Jr., Jackson left the SCLC in 1971 and in Chicago founded Operation PUSH. In 1983 Jackson launched a major voter-registration drive among black Americans and toward the end of the year declared his candidacy for the Democratic presidential nomination. Jackson ran in a large number of Democratic primary elections in 1984, finishing a strong third to former Vice-President Walter Mondale and Senator Gary Hart. In 1987 Jackson again entered the race for the Democratic presidential nomination.

Sources: *Contemporary Black Biography,* vol. 1, pp. 108–12; Hornsby, *Milestones in Twentieth-Century African-American History,* pp. 122, 185, 247; *Negro Almanac,* 278–79; Smith, *Notable Black American Men,* pp. 598–602; *Who's Who among African* Americans, 26th ed., p. 639.

Jesse Jackson

1985 • Sharon Pratt Dixon [Sharon Pratt Kelly] (1944–) was the first black (and woman) treasurer of the Democratic National Committee. Born and educated in the nation's capital, Dixon is active in political affairs.

Sources: Hine, *Black Women in America,* vol. 1, pp. 675–76; Hornsby, *Milestones in Twentieth-Century African-American History,* p. 456; Smith, *Notable Black American Women,* p. 278; *Contemporary Black Biography,* vol. 1, pp. 58–59.

1995 • Minyon Moore (1958–) became the first black woman to serve as political director for the National Democratic Committee. In 1997 she became the first black deputy political director in the White House. From 1988 to 1999 she was assistant to the president and director of public liaison. In the course of her career, Moore held positions with Encyclopedia Brittanica Educational Corporation, and Operation PUSH, Inc., was national deputy field director for Jesse Jackson's 1988 presidential campaign, the National Rainbow Coalition, and also held various posts with the Democratic National Committee.

Sources: *Jet* 87 (13 March 1995): 10; *Who's Who among African Americans*, 26th ed., p. 898.

1996 • The Democratic National Committee hired media consultant Delmarie Cobb as press secretary, making her the first black in that post. She was assigned to handle the Chicago media for the 1996 convention and to serve as spokesperson for Debra DeLee, the convention's chief executive officer. Previously, Cobb was director of communications and press secretary for Jesse Jackson Jr., who held a successful campaign in Illinois' 2nd Congressional District. She has also served as general assignment reporter for ABC and NBC television. Cobb was born in Chicago and educated at Purdue University and Indiana University.

Sources: *Jet* 89 (19 February 1996): 46–47; *Who's Who among African Americans*, 26th ed., p. 250.

1997 • J[ulius] C[aesar] Watts Jr. (1957–), Republican representative from Oklahoma and then the only black Republican in the House of Representatives, became the first black to give his party's national response to a president's State of the Union address. His response followed the speech of President Bill Clinton. Although Watts commented on the Republican agenda, he pushed for bipartianship. In 1998 Watts, the only black without membership in the Congressional Black Caucus, became the first black Republican elected to a leadership post in modern times. On November 19, he was elected chair of the Republican Conference, the Number four position in the House of Representatives.

Sources: *Contemporary Black Biography*, vol. 14, pp. 220–23; *Jet* 91 (24 February 1997): 8; *New York Times* (19 November 2001); *Tennessean* (23 November 1998).

1999 • Donna L. Brazile (1959–) was placed in charge of day-to-day operations for presidential candidate Al Gore, becoming the first black woman to manage a major presidential campaign. She was second in command in the Gore operation, working out of his campaign headquarters in Nashville, Tennessee. She has managed four presidential campaigns, working for Jesse Jackson in 1984 in his unsuccessful bid for the Democratic nomination, and in 1988 for Jackson, Richard Gephardt, and Michael Dukakis. In 1984 Brazile was national director of the twentieth anniversary of the March on Washington. She is known for her sharp mind and tongue; often this is what made her noticed. Brazile was born in New Orleans, Louisiana, and graduated from Louisiana State University. In 2002 she was named chair of the Democratic Voting Rights Institute in Atlanta, succeeding former Atlanta Mayor Maynard Jackson.

Sources: *Jet* 101 (1 April 2002): 10; *New York Times* (23 May 2000); *Tennessean* (10 October 1999); *Who's Who among African Americans*, 26th ed., p. 139.

2000 • Patrick J. Buchanan, representing the Reform Party in the U.S. presidential elections, picked Ezola Foster (1938–) to become his vice presidential running mate. She became the first black candidate to seek the vice presidency for that party. Buchanan also named her as co-chairperson of his campaign. The former Democrat and former Republican followed Buchanan into the Reform Party in 1999. Foster taught public school in South Central Los Angeles for thirty-three years. Twice she was unsuccessful in her bid for a seat in the California Assembly. She founded Americans for Family Values, a local organization.

Sources: *New York Times* (12 August 2000); (14 August 2000).

2009 • The first black to head the Republican National Committee was Michael S. Steele (1958–). A controversial figure, he was frequently at odds with members of his party. In January 2011, he announced that he would not seek reelection and left office. Steele was also the first African American to serve in a Maryland state-wide office and as the state's first Republican lieutenant governor—a post created in 1970.

Sources: "WhoRunsGov," http://www.washingtonpost.com/whorunsgov, accessed September 21, 2012; *Who's Who among African Americans,* 26th ed., p. 1174.

U.S. House of Representatives

1868 • John Willis Menard (1839–1893), public official, was the first black elected to Congress. He was awarded his full salary but never seated. The committee on elections ruled that it was too early to admit a black to Congress. He was appointed inspector of customs of the Port of New Orleans. Born of French creole parents living in Illinois, Menard moved to Louisiana after the Civil War to work for the Republican party. When he was allowed to plead his own case on February 27, 1969, he became the first black to speak on the floor of the House.

Sources: Bennett, *Before the Mayflower,* p. 626; Garrett, *Famous First Facts about Negroes,* p. 29; Robinson, *Historical Negro Biographies,* pp. 99–100.

1870 • Joseph Hayne Rainey (1831–1887) was the first black elected to Congress to represent South Carolina. He was sworn in on December 12, 1870, to fill an unexpired term. After serving as a delegate to the state constitutional convention in 1868 and to the state senate in 1870, in 1874 Rainey was the first black ever to preside over the House. He served in Washington, D.C., for four consecutive terms until 1879. After that, he became a special agent of the Treasury Department where he remained until 1881. Then he ran a note brokerage and banking business in Washington until his business failed. By 1886 he was co-owner of a coal and wood yard until he returned to his hometown, Georgetown, South Carolina, in 1887. Born of slave parents, Rainey purchased his freedom as well as that of his parents sometime between 1840 and 1850. He became a prosperous barber in his hometown. After leaving South Carolina for a while, he returned at the end of the Civil War and began his work with the Republican party.

Joseph Hayne Rainey

Sources: Bennett, *Before the Mayflower,* p. 488; Christopher, *America's Black Congressmen,* p. 33; Logan and Winston, *Dictionary of American Negro Biography,* p. 510; Garrett, *Famous First Facts about Negroes,* p. 32; Robinson, *Historical Negro Biographies,* p. 112.

1870 • On February 1, 1871, Jefferson Franklin Long (1836–1900) was the first black to speak in the House of Representatives as a congressman. Long was the second black member of Congress and the first and only one from Georgia during Reconstruction. He served from January 1871 to the end of the session on March 3, 1871.

Sources: Bennett, *Before the Mayflower,* p. 489; Logan and Winston, *Dictionary of American Negro Biography,* p. 405.

1871 • Josiah Thomas Walls (1842–1905?) was the first black congressman elected from the state of Florida, taking office on March 4, 1871. Born in Winchester, Virginia, Walls had limited education and became a prosperous farmer in Florida after serving as a soldier during the Civil War. He was elected a Republican congressman-at-large in 1870 and reelected twice, serving until 1876, when he was unseated. He served for a while in the post of superintendent of a farm on the campus of Tallahassee State College (later Florida Agricultural and Mechanical University).

Sources: Garrett, *Famous First Facts about Negroes,* p. 33; Robinson, *Historical Negro Biographies,* p. 139; Logan and Winston, *Dictionary of American Negro Biography,* pp. 629–30.

1873 • John Roy Lynch (1847–1939) was the first black congressman from Mississippi. Son of a slave mother and a white Louisiana planter, Lynch attended night school, worked as a photographer's assistant, began to dabble in politics, and at the age of twenty-four became speaker of the Mississippi House. He was elected U.S. congressman three times, and served with distinction from 1873 to 1877. He served the Republican Party as state chairman of the executive committee (1881–89) and received federal appointments (1898–1911) as a reward. In 1884 Lynch was the first black to preside over a national nominating convention held by a major political party. He was named temporary chairman of the Re-

John Lynch

Blacks Elected to the House of Representatives
in the Nineteenth Century

Representative	State	Years of Service
John Willis Menard*	Louisiana	
Joseph H. Rainey	South Carolina	1869–79
Jefferson F. Long	Georgia	1870–71
Robert C. Delarge	South Carolina	1871–73
Benjamin S. Turner	Alabama	1871–73
Robert B. Elliott	South Carolina	1871–75
Josiah T. Walls	Florida	1871–77
Alonzo J. Ransier	South Carolina	1873–75
James T. Rapier	Alabama	1873–75
Richard H. Cain	South Carolina	1873–75, 1877–79
John R. Lynch	Mississippi	1873–77, 1881–83
Jeremiah Haralson	Alabama	1875–77
John A. Hyman	North Carolina	1875–77
Charles E. Nash	Louisiana	1875–77
Robert Smalls	South Carolina	1875–79, 1881–87
James E. O'Hara	North Carolina	1883–87
John Mercer Langston	Virginia	1889–91
Thomas E. Miller	South Carolina	1889–91
Henry P. Cheatham	North Carolina	1889–93
George Washington Murray	South Carolina	1893–97
George H. White	North Carolina	1897–1901

*Although Menard was the first black elected to Congress, in 1868, he was never seated.

Sources: *Negro Almanac, 1976,* pp. 318–31.

publican party meeting in Chicago. He wrote an authoritative account of post Civil War period, *The Facts of Reconstruction,* in 1913.

Sources: Logan and Winston, *Dictionary of American Negro Biography,* pp. 407–9; Robinson, *Historical Negro Biographies,* p. 98; Smith, *Notable Black American Men,* pp. 748–49.

1875 • John A. Hyman (1840–1891) was the first black to serve the state of North Carolina as a U.S. congressman. He was born a slave in North Carolina, and was sold and sent to Alabama where he remained until after the Civil War. He was self-educated. He was elected to the Forty-fourth Congress. During his term, he served on the Committee of Manufacturers. He held several federal appointments in North Carolina.

Sources: Garrett, *Famous First Facts about Negroes,* p. 35; *Paths Toward Freedom,* p. 160.

1888 • John Mercer Langston (1829–1897), educator and public official, was the first black Virginian elected to the House of Representatives. Langston was also the first black to win an elective office, as a member of the city council of Brownhelm, Ohio, in 1855. An active leader in the convention movement before the Civil War, he helped to organize the freedmen in the Negro National Labor Union. In 1868 President Andrew Johnson appointed him Inspector General of the Freedmen's Bureau. From 1869 to 1876, he was associated with Howard University. President Rutherford B. Hayes appointed him minister to Haiti in 1877. Later, Langston served as president of Virginia Normal and Collegiate Institute at Petersburg, Virginia (now Virginia State University). Elected to Congress as a Republican in 1888, he was not seated until 1890 because the election was contested. He published a collection of addresses, *Freedom and Citizenship* in 1883, and his autobiography, *From the Virginia Plantation to the National Capitol* in 1894. In 1996 Virginia recognized him as one of its distinguished sons—the first black to represent the state in Congress—by erecting a historic marker near his birthplace in Louisa County.

Sources: Christopher, *America's Black Congressmen,* p. 139; Logan and Winston, *Dictionary of American Negro Biography,* pp. 382–84; Hornsby, *Chronology of African-American History,* pp. 27–28, 55; *Jet* 90 (1 July 1996): 10.

1929 • Oscar Stanton DePriest (1871–1951) was the first black congressman elected in the twentieth century and also the first from a northern state. He served three terms representing the Twenty-first Congressional District of Illinois. Born in Florence, Alabama, and reared in Kansas, he moved to Chicago and became active in real estate before entering politics. He also became Chicago's first black alderman in 1915. He blazed the trail for the return of blacks to Congress.

Sources: Logan and Winston, *Dictionary of American Negro Biography,* pp. 173–74; Garrett, *Famous First Facts about Negroes,* p. 37; Hornsby, *Chronology of African-American History,* p. 76; Smith, *Notable Black American Men,* pp. 294–97.

1934 • Arthur W. Mitchell (1883–1968) was the first black Democratic congressman. He defeated Republican congressman Oscar DePriest of Illinois. He was born in Alabama and attended Tuskegee Institute (Alabama), Columbia (New York), and Harvard (Massachusetts) universities. Mitchell was active in rural industrial education in Alabama, before studying law and moving to Washington, D.C., and Chicago to practice as a lawyer and real estate broker. He served from the Seventy-fourth to the Seventy-seventh Congress. He was an ardent civil rights advocate and won a significant Supreme Court case in 1941 involving interstate travel.

Sources: Clayton, *The Negro Politician,* pp. 54–55; Garrett, *Famous First Facts about Negroes,* p. 37; Gosnell, *Negro Politicians,* pp. 90–91; Hornsby, *Chronology of African-American History,* p. 89.

Arthur W. Mitchell

1944 • Adam Clayton Powell Jr., (1908–1972) was elected to Congress from Harlem on August 1, becoming the first black member of the House of Representatives from the East. For ten years Powell and William L. Dawson of Chicago were the only blacks in Congress. With his good looks, loud mouth, and willingness to confront racism, Powell was one of the most flamboyant and controversial politicians of the twentieth century. In 1961 Powell was the first black to chair the powerful Education and Labor Committee. By 1963 Powell became the target of criticism for personal misconduct and misuse of government funds. In 1967 a House subcommittee reported that its probe into Powell's life revealed several serious allegations. He was stripped of his chairmanship of his committee. Congress later voted to exclude him from membership. In 1968, however, the Supreme Curt ruled in his favor; his seniority was restored in 1969. Powell was born in New Haven, Connecticut, and relocated to New York City when he was six years old. His father had become pastor of New York's Abyssinian Baptist Church and moved his family to the city. After Powell Jr. graduated from Colgate University, the board of deacons of Abyssinian church licensed him to preach. He enrolled at Union Theological Seminary but later transferred to Columbia University, graduating in 1933 with a master's degree. Already heir apparent to the leadership of Abyssinian church, he became pastor when his father retired in 1937. Before he was elected to Congress, Powell was elected to the New York City Council. After winning a seat in Congress, he began a long and controversial twenty-three-year career.

Adam Powell

Sources: Hornsby, *Chronology of African-American History,* pp. 92, 194, 224; Robinson, *Historical Negro Biographies,* pp. 238–39; Smith, *Notable Black American Men,* pp. 954–58.

1949 • On January 18, 1949, William L. Dawson (1886–1970) became the first black to head a congressional standing committee in recent times, as chair of the House Expenditures Committee. Born in Albany, Georgia, he studied at Fisk University, Kent College of Law, and Northwestern University. Dawson won election to Congress in 1942 and took office on January 4, 1943—the third northern black and the second black Democrat in Congress. He served longer than any other black (1941–70). In 1944 he was the first black to be the vice-president of a major political party.

William L. Dawson

Charles Diggs

Sources: Bennett, *Before the Mayflower,* p. 627; Clayton, *The Negro Politician,* pp. 67–85; Hornsby, *Chronology of African-American History,* p. 91; Smith, *Notable Black American Men,* pp. 269–72.

1954 • Charles C. Diggs Jr. (1922–1998) was elected to the House, becoming the first black federal legislator from Michigan. His election marked the first time in the twentieth century that as many as three blacks served in the House. Detroit-born, Diggs was educated at Wayne State University (1946) and Detroit College of Law (1952). Diggs was a founder and first head of the Congressional Black Caucus. In 1969 Diggs was the first black to chair the Foreign Relations Subcommittee on Africa. In 1973 he became the first black congressman to head the Committee for the District of Columbia. He resigned his seat in 1980, after being convicted of mail and payroll fraud in 1978.

Sources: Garrett, *Famous First Facts about Negroes,* p. 40; Hornsby, *Chronology of African-American History,* p. 102; *Negro Almanac,* pp. 74, 77; *Contemporary Black Biography,* vol. 21, pp. 52–54.

1958 • Robert Nelson C. Nix Sr. (1898–1987) was the first black congressman from Pennsylvania. Elected congressman from the state's Second District to fill an unexpired term, he won re-election to each subsequent Congress. He held membership on the foreign affairs, post office, and civil service committees. Born in South Carolina, Nix studied in New York and Pennsylvania (Lincoln University and University of Pennsylvania Law School). He was one of the first congressmen to speak out in support of the Montgomery Bus Boycott. Nix's son, Robert N. C. Nix Jr., was the first black to sit on a state supreme court bench since Reconstruction; he was inaugurated as chief justice of the Pennsylvania supreme court in 1984.

Sources: Baskin and Runes, *Dictionary of Black Culture,* p. 331; Finkelman, *Encyclopedia of African American History,* vol. 3, p. 502; Garrett, *Famous First Facts about Negroes,* p. 40; Hornsby, *Chronology of African-American History,* p. 327.

Augustus Hawkins

1962 • Augustus Freeman Hawkins (1907–2007) was the first black elected to the House from California and from a western state. Born in Shreveport, Louisiana, and educated in California, Hawkins was active in real estate and youth work before entering state politics. He ran for Congress from the Twenty-first District and won by an overwhelming majority. He chaired the House Rules Committee and he sponsored a number of important bills, including the Humphrey-Hawkins Full Employment and Balanced Growth Act and the Equal Employment Opportunity Section of the landmark 1963 Civil Rights Act. During his fifty-six years of public service, Hawkins sponsored over three hundred state and federal laws. Representative Carolyn C. Kilpatrick (D-MI) characterized him as "a champion of civil rights, servant of the people and guardian of the American dream." Hawkins retired from office in 1990. In 1996 he gave his congressional papers to the UCLA library.

Sources: Garrett, *Famous First Facts about Negroes,* p. 41; Robinson, *Historical Black Biographies,* pp. 200–201; *Negro Almanac,* pp. 391–92; *Who's Who among African Americans,* 14th ed., p. 566; *Jet* 112 (3 December 2007): 24; Gates and Higginbotham, *African American National Biography,* vol. 4, pp. 117–18.

Shirley Chisholm

1968 • Shirley Anita St. Hill Chisholm (1924–2005) was the first African-American woman elected to the House of Representatives. Born in Brooklyn, New York, Chisholm was six years old when she and her two younger sisters were sent to Barbados to live with their grandmother. They returned to Brooklyn seven years later. Chisholm graduated from Brooklyn College and Columbia University. In 1964 she was elected to the New York state legislature, and upon her entry into national politics, she won a committee assignment on the veterans affairs committee. As she remained in Congress and moved up in seniority, she became a member of the powerful House Rules Committee. After leaving office in 1983, she was named Purington Professor at Mt. Holyoke College until 1987. In 1993 she served as U.S. ambassador to Jamaica. Chisholm chronicled her early life and her rise in politics in the book *Unbought and Unbossed* (1970).

Sources: Hine, *Black Women in America,* vol. 1, pp. 236–38; Garrett, *Famous First Facts about Negroes,* p. 42; Hornsby, *Chronology of African-American History,* p. 133; Smith, *Notable Black American Women,* pp. 185–89; *Who's Who among African Americans,* 14th ed., p. 233.

1968 • Louis Stokes (1925–) became the first black elected to Congress from Ohio. While in office, he became chair of the Select Committee on Assassinations, known for its probe into the killings of President John F. Kennedy and Martin Luther King Jr. Stokes was the first black to head such a committee. He criticized the Warren Commission Report that detailed the Kennedy assassination in 1963. Stokes chaired the House Intelligence Committee and became a member of the Iran-Contra Investigating Committee. Early in 1991 he headed the House Ethics Committee. After thirty years in Congress, he retired in 1998. By then, a host of facilities were named in his honor, including a school auditorium, a library, a bridge, and a telecommunications center. He had also received twenty-four honorary degrees, and many scholarships and programs now bear his name.

Louis Stokes

Sources: *Contemporary Black Biography,* vol. 3, pp. 237–39; *Jet* 94 (5 October 1998): 36; 94 (2 November 1998): 8; *Who's Who among African Americans,* 14th ed., p. 1237.

1970 • William L. Clay (1931–) was the first black elected to represent Missouri in Congress. Born in Saint Louis, Missouri, Clay was the firebrand of black demonstrations in Saint Louis, while he served as alderman. In 1968 Clay defeated his Republican opponent and assumed his place in Congress. He was educated at Saint Louis University and worked as a real estate broker and manager of Industrial Life Insurance Company. Clay retired from Congress, announcing in 1999 that he would not seek reelection when his term expired.

Sources: Garrett, *Famous First Facts about Negroes,* p. 41; *Negro Almanac,* pp. 383–84; *Who's Who among African Americans,* 26th ed., p. 244.

1970 • Walter E. Fauntroy (1933–), public official, was the first black nonvoting delegate to Congress from the District of Columbia. Before he took office, the district had no representation in Congress. He worked long with Martin Luther King Jr. and was a coordinator of the 1963 civil rights march on Washington, and the Poor People's Campaign of 1968. Fauntroy fought for home rule and statehood for the District of Columbia. The Washington, D.C., native is a graduate of Virginia Union University and the Yale Divinity School. He pastors New Bethel Baptist Church in Washington, D.C. He continues to work on behalf of the district's citizens, often lobbying before Congress on their behalf.

Sources: *Encyclopedia of Black America,* p. 384; *Negro Almanac,* p. 389; *Who's Who among African Americans,* 26th ed., p. 401; *Contemporary Black Biography,* vol. 11, pp. 77–79.

1970 • Parren James Mitchell (1922–2007) became the first black congressman from Maryland, serving from 1970 to 1986. He was also the first black since 1898 elected to Congress from a state before the Mason-Dixon line. Kweisi Mfume succeeded him in office. His work to promote economic empowerment in the black community and his support of legislation that benefited minorities inspired Congress to call him "Mr. Minority Enterprise." During his eight terms in Congress, Mitchell was whip-at-large, chair of the House Small Business Committee, chair of the Task Force on Minority Enterprise, and chair or member of other important committees. He was also a founding member of the Congressional Black Caucus. Born in Baltimore the ninth of ten children, Mitchell graduated from Morgan State College (as it was known then) in 1950. He sued the University of Maryland that same year for refusing to enroll him as its first black graduate student. He won the case and graduated from Maryland in 1952. He taught at Morgan State, was assistant director of the school's Urban Affairs Institute, and held several other posts in the community. He entered the political arena, winning a seat in Congress.

Parren Mitchell

Sources: Smith, *Notable Black American Men,* pp. 824–26; *Who's Who among African Americans,* 14th ed., p. 921.

1971 • Louis Stokes (1925–) was the first black member of the Appropriations Committee. Elected U.S. congressman from Ohio in 1968, Stokes received his legal training at

John Marshall School of Law in Cleveland, and had a private practice until his entry into politics. In 1983 Stokes became the first black member of the House Select Committee on Intelligence and in 1985 the first black congressman to head the Program and Budget Authorization subcommittee of the House Permanent Select Committee on Intelligence. The latter assignment made him the first black lawmaker to chair a permanent select committee on intelligence. He also chaired the Assassination Committee that investigated the murders of Martin Luther King Jr. and President John F. Kennedy.

Sources: *Contemporary Black Biography*, vol. 3, pp. 237–39; Hornsby, *Milestones in African-American History*, pp. 103, 493; *Negro Almanac*, p. 395.

1971 • The Congressional Black Caucus of the House of Representatives was the first concerted effort on the part of black representatives to influence congressional party politics. An affiliation of black members of Congress, the all-Democratic group, representing mainly Northern big-city districts, was permanently headquartered on Capitol Hill with a director and staff. It maintained political liaison with other black groups and projected a black agenda to influence and promote economic, social, and political goals favored by black Americans. It was formally organized in 1971, and later included Republican members. Michigan congressman Charles C. Diggs Jr. was founder and first head of the caucus. The first woman to chair the CBC was Representative Yvonne Braithwaite Burke of California (installed 1976), followed by Representative Cardiss Collins of Illinois (elected 1979), and then Representative Maxine Waters of California (installed 1996).

Sources: Baskin and Runes, *Dictionary of Black Culture*, p. 46; Hornsby, *Milestones in Twentieth-Century African-American History*, pp. 360, 404; *Negro Almanac*, pp. 380–82; *Jet* 91 (9 December 1996), p. 5.

1972 • Yvonne Watson Braithwaite Burke (1932–) was the first black congresswoman from the West. Born in Los Angeles, she was educated in the University of California system, taking her bachelor's degree from the University of California, Los Angeles, and her law degree from the University of Southern California. She was victorious in a 1966 campaign to become the first black California assemblywoman. She was the first black woman vice-chair of the Democratic National Convention in 1972. A Democrat, she entered national congressional politics and went to Washington in 1972. In 1973 she became the first member of Congress to give birth while serving in office. She resigned in 1978 to run for a local office in California.

Sources: Hine, *Black Women in America*, vol. 1, p. 195; Hornsby, *Chronology of African-American History*, p. 211; Smith, *Notable Black American Women*, pp. 130–32.

Yvonne Burke

1972 • Barbara Charline Jordan (1936–1996) was the first southern black woman elected to the House. Houston-born Jordan gained recognition from a nationwide television audience as the House Judiciary committee considered articles of impeachment against President Richard Nixon. She received her education at Texas Southern University and Boston University Law School. She was elected to the Texas legislature in 1965. Her reputation as one of the twentieth century's great orators was sustained by her keynote address to the 1976 Democratic Convention. Jordan decided in 1978 to retire from Congress. She became the Lyndon B. Johnson Centennial Chair in National Policy professor at the University of Texas at Austin.

Sources: Hine, *Black Women in America*, pp. 658–59; *Negro Almanac, 1976*, p. 313–14; Smith, *Notable Black American Women*, pp. 609–12.

1972 • Andrew Jackson Young Jr. (1932–) was the first black member of the House from Georgia since 1870. Born in New Orleans, Young was educated at Howard University and the Hartford Theological Seminary. He was a leader in the Civil Rights Movement and a close associate of Martin Luther King Jr. Young won re-election to Congress in 1974 and 1976. In 1977 President Jimmy Carter announced the nomination of Young as U.S. ambassador to the United Nations—marking the first time an African American led the American delegation (the position carried cabinet-level status). He later served as mayor of

Andrew Young Jr.

Atlanta (1982–90) and ran unsuccessfully for governor of the state of Georgia. He was co-chair of the Atlanta Committee for the Olympic Games in 1996.

Sources: *Contemporary Black Biography,* vol. 3, pp. 263–67; Hornsby, *Chronology of African-American History,* pp. 280, 282, 290, 305, 349, 409, 428; Smith, *Notable Black American Men,* pp. 1280–83; *Who's Who among African Americans,* 26th ed., p. 1395.

1973 • Cardiss Hortense Robertson Collins (1932–) was the first black congresswoman from Illinois and the fourth black woman to serve in Congress. In 1975 she became the first black to chair the House Government Operations Subcommittee on Manpower and Housing. Born in St. Louis, Missouri, and educated in Michigan and Illinois, Collins was elected to the House of Representatives to fill the seat left vacant by the death of her husband. She was the first black whip-at-large (1975). After serving twenty-three years in the House and becoming the longest-serving black woman in the House of Representatives, Collins announced in 1995 that she would not seek reelection at the end of her term.

Sources: Hine, *Black Women in America,* vol. 1, pp. 264–65; Smith, *Notable Black American Women,* p. 204; *Who's Who among Black Americans,* 26th ed., p. 260.

Cardiss Collins

1974 • Harold Eugene Ford Sr. (1945–) was the first black congressman from the state of Tennessee. He served in the Tennessee state legislature from 1970 to 1974 before being chosen to represent his state in Congress for the Ninth Congressional District. Born in Memphis, he was educated at John Gupton [Mortuary] College, Tennessee State University, and Howard University. Since 1969, he has been vice president and manager of Ford and Sons Funeral Home in Memphis.

Sources: Hornsby, *Milestones in Twentieth-Century African-American History,* pp. 221, 405; *Negro Almanac,* p. 390; *Who's Who among African Americans,* 26th ed., p. 421.

1974 • Charles Bernard Rangel (1930–) was the first black member of the House Ways and Means Committee. This is an important committee that makes key decisions regarding tax and welfare legislation. A native of New York City, Rangel was educated at New York University and St. John's University Law School. In 1983 Rangel was the first black deputy whip in the House. This was a prestigious role in floor leadership. Rangel had been elected to Congress in 1970, after a successful legislative career in New York. He had also defeated Adam Clayton Powell Jr. as representative of the state's Sixteenth Congressional District.

Sources: Hornsby, *Milestones in Twentieth-Century African-American History,* pp. 44, 103; *Who's Who among African Americans,* 26th ed., pp. 1025–26; Salzman, *Encyclopedia of African-American Culture and History,* vol. 4, pp. 2263–64.

1979 • Carrie Meek (1926–) was the first black woman to represent Florida in Congress. Meek was born in Tallahasee, Florida, the granddaughter of a slave. She came under the influence of Mary McLeod Bethune of Bethune-Cookman College, a school at which she served as physical education director, after graduating from Florida Agricultural and Mechanical University—where she was a legend in athletics. She was a Florida state senator, and as a legislator sponsored more than thirty major bills and programs—ranging from education to small business to women's rights.

Sources: *Who's Who in American Politics, 1987–88,* p. 318; *Ebony* 48 (January 1993): 32; *Jet* 82 (28 September 1992): 34; 83 (23 November 1992): 15, 52; *Contemporary Black Biography,* vol. 6, pp. 192–95; Smith, *Notable Black American Women,* Book II, pp. 467–70.

1979 • Melvin Herbert Evans (1918–1984) became the first black delegate representing the Virgin Islands in the U.S. Congress. He was sworn in to the Ninety-sixth Congress on January 3, 1979, and served until 1981, losing his re-election bid in 1980. The entirely Democratic Congressional Black Caucus also welcomed him into its fold, despite his Republican affiliation, making him the first-ever Republican caucus member. Evans supported efforts to establish a national holiday for civil rights leader Martin Luther King Jr.

Sources: *Black Americans in Congress, 1870–2007,* pp. 494–87.

Melvin Evans

1983 • Major Owens (1936–) became the first and only librarian in the U.S. House of Representatives. Owens was born in Memphis, Tennessee, and graduated from Morehouse College in 1956 and Atlanta University in 1957. The next year he accepted a position in the Brooklyn public library and soon became deeply involved in the Civil Rights Movement. Soon he chaired the Brooklyn Congress of Racial Equality and joined the Democratic Party. His appointment as Commissioner of Community Development for the City of New York put him in touch with antipoverty and self-help programs. In 1974 he was elected to the New York state senate. After he was elected to the U.S. House, he became a national spokesperson for libraries.

Sources: *Contemporary Black Biography,* vol. 6, pp. 207–09; Salzman, *Encyclopedia of African-American Culture and History,* Supplement, p. 212.

1984 • William H. Gray III (1941–) was the first black congressman to chair the House Budget Committee. Born in Baton Rouge, Louisiana, Gray was an ordained Baptist minister and was elected to Congress from 1978 to 1991. He served on the Democratic Congressional Steering Committee, the Congressional Black Caucus, and the House Committees on Foreign Affairs, Budget and District of Columbia. In 1989 Gray was the first black to serve as a majority whip in the House. In 1991 he gave up his congressional career to head the nation's most influential fund-raising organization for black colleges, United Negro College Fund (now called the College Fund/UNCF).

Sources: *Contemporary Black Biography,* vol. 3, pp. 77–80; Hornsby, *Milestones in African-American History,* p. 501; *Who's Who among African Americans,* 26th ed., p. 498; Smith, *Notable Black American Men,* pp. 478–81.

1986 • Mike [Alphonso Michael] Espy (1953–) was the first black congressman elected from Mississippi since Reconstruction. Born in Mississippi, Espy was educated at Howard University and Santa Clara Law School. He was active in legal services in Mississippi. In 1993 he was confirmed as the first black Secretary of Agriculture.

Sources: *Crisis* 100 (March 1993): 16; *Ebony* 48 (May 1993): 62; *Negro Almanac,* 388–89; *Who's Who among African Americans,* 26th ed., pp. 389–90; Smith, *Notable Black American Men,* pp. 378–81; *Contemporary Black Biography,* vol. 6, pp. 87–90.

1986 • The first black Methodist minister in the House of Representatives since Reconstruction was Floyd H. Flake (1945–), who represented the Sixth Congressional District in New York as a Democrat. He served on the banking and finance committees and the small business committee. He was elected to the House six times, but resigned mid-term in 1997 to devote more time to his AME ministry at Allen AME Church in Queens, New York. Flake was born in Los Angeles and educated at Wilberforce University and United Theological Seminary. In the course of his career he has been a social worker in Dayton Ohio, and a marketing analyst for Xerox Corporation. Then he moved to academia, holding administrative positions at Lincoln University in Pennsylvania. He moved to Boston University as dean of students, university chaplain, and director of the Martin Luther King Jr. Afro-American Center.

Sources: *Contemporary Black Biography,* vol. 18, pp. 49–52.

Floyd Flake

1988 • Donald Milford Payne (1934–2012), teacher and businessman, was the first black congressman elected from the state of New Jersey. Born in Newark, New Jersey, he grew up in a working-class neighborhood. He was educated at Seton Hall University, and taught school in the urban areas of New Jersey. He was a local legislator prior to his election to the U.S. Congress. He taught in the Newark school district for a while and later became manager for the National Council of the YMCA. He became national president of the YMCA in 1970, the first black to hold that post. His membership on the YMCA's World Refugee and Rehabilitation Committee took him to over eighty countries. Payne chaired the South Ward Democratic organization in Newark, for eighteen years. He was vice president of the Urban Data Systems in Newark

Sources: *Negro Almanac,* p. 393; *Who's Who among African Americans,* 26th ed., p. 972; *Contemporary Black Biography,* vol. 2, pp. 188–90.

1990 • Gary A. Franks (1953–) became the first black Republican elected to the House of Representatives in nearly fifty years and the first black congressman elected from Connecticut. With the victory he became a rising star in the Republican party; he often criticized black liberals in his predominantly white conservative district. He ran for reelection in 1996 and was beaten handily after a bitter race. He also became the first Republican member of the traditionally-liberal Congressional Black Caucus since 1979, when Melvin Herbert Evans, R-Virgin Islands, joined. Franks's membership in the CBC, however, made him the first black member representing the Continental United States. Republicans, Edwards Brooks, senator from 1967–79, refused to join, and J. C. Watts, representative from Oklahoma from 1995 to 2003, declined membership in the CBC.

Sources: *Black Americans in Congress,* 1870–2007, p. 586; *Contemporary Black Biography,* vol. 2, pp. 83–84; *New York Times* (8 November 1996); Salzman, *Encyclopedia of African-American Culture and History,* Supplement, pp. 100–101; *Who's Who among African Americans,* 26th ed., p. 433.

Gary A. Franks

1990 • Louisiana's first black representative in the U.S. Congress since Reconstruction was William Jennings Jefferson (1947–). Born in Lake Providence, Louisiana, Jefferson received his B.A. degree from Southern University in Baton Rouge, his M.A. and J.D. degrees from Harvard University, and LL.M. degree from Georgetown Law Center. He was a judicial clerk for the U.S. Court of Appeals, a legislative assistant for Senator J. Bennett Johnson, and founding partner in the law firm Jefferson, Bryan and Gray, in New Orleans. After serving in the Louisiana State Senate from 1980 to 1990, he was elected to the U.S. House.

Sources: *Contemporary Black Biography,* vol. 25, pp. 105–7; *Who's Who among African Americans,* 26th ed., p. 655; Salzman, *Encyclopedia of African-American Culture and History,* Supplement, pp. 143–44.

1992 • Alcee Lamar Hastings (1936–) was the first impeached federal officer to be elected to another federal post. In 1979 Hastings was the first black federal judge in Florida. Hastings was born in Altamonte, Florida, and educated at Fisk, Howard, and Florida Agricultural and Mechanical universities. He was impeached by a committee of the U.S. Senate in 1989—the impeachment was nullified by a Supreme Court decision, because according to constitutional procedures the whole Senate must rule in an impeachment. He was elected in 1992 to the House of Representatives.

Sources: *Atlanta Constitution* (5 November 1992); Hornsby, *Milestones in Twentieth-Century African-American History,* pp. 400, 424; *Who's Who among African Americans,* 26th ed., pp. 552–53.

1992 • Cynthia Ann McKinney (1955–) was the first black woman elected to the U.S. House from Georgia. Atlanta-born and a two-term state representative, McKinney was victorious in a new congressional district mandated by the 1990 census. McKinney was educated at the University of Southern California, and Fletcher School of Law and Diplomacy at Tufts University. She taught at Agnes Scott College in Atlanta, Georgia. She is a member of the Congressional Black Caucus, the Women's Caucus, and a member of the Progressive Caucus. During her second term in Congress, the U.S. Supreme Court ruled that the boundaries for the new district in Georgia that she represented were drawn solely on the basis of race. That meant that the boundaries for the Eleventh District were unconstitutional. Although that district was subsequently redrawn and eliminated many black voters, she won reelection in the white majority district.

Sources: *Jet* 88 (17 July 1995): 4–5; 91 (25 November 1996): 4–5; *Contemporary Black Biography,* vol. 11, pp.160–63; Salzman, *Encyclopedia of African-American Culture and History,* Supplement, pp. 180–81; *Who's Who among African Americans,* 26th ed., p. 853.

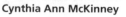

Cynthia Ann McKinney

1992 • Eva M. Clayton (1934–) and Melvin Watt (1945–) were the first black representatives from North Carolina in the twentieth century. Clayton was also the first black woman. She is the owner of her own development company in North Carolina, and a former county official. She took office in November immediately after the election to fill an unexpired term, and so had two month's seniority over other freshman congress members. A Phi Beta Kappa graduate of the University of North Carolina, Watt received his legal training from the Yale University Law School. He was active in local politics and part owner of an elder-care facility. His Twelfth Congressional District, which stretches 170 miles from Gastonia to Durham (and at one place includes only the northbound lanes of Interstate 85) might have been challenged as the result of a historic Supreme Court decision—*Shaw v. Reno*—in the closing days of the term that ended June 23, 1993.

Sources: *Atlanta Constitution* (4 November 1992); *Contemporary Black Biography*, vol. 26, pp. 180–82 (Watt), vol. 20, pp. 42–44 (Clayton); *Ebony* 48 (January 1993): 34, 52; *Jet* 83 (23 November 1992): 15, 52; *Washington Post National Weekly Edition* (19-25 July 1993): 14. *Who's Who in American Politics, 1987–88*, p. 1127 (Watts).

1992 • Jim [James] Clyburn (1940–), activist, was South Carolina's first and only black congressman in modern times. In 1998 he became the first Southerner to head the Congressional Black Caucus. Involved in the Civil Rights Movement, Clyburn was a student activist at South Carolina State College where he was educated. He is a former schoolteacher and community leader.

Sources: *Contemporary Black Biography*, vol. 21, pp. 40–42; *Ebony* 48 (January 1993): 52; *Jet* 83 (23 November 1992), pp. 40–42.

1992 • Earl Frederick Hilliard (1942–) was the first black elected to represent Alabama in the House since Reconstruction. Born in Birmingham, Hilliard was educated at Morehouse College and Atlanta and Howard universities. After that he was a fellow with the Birmingham Legal Aid Society from 1970 to 1972. Hilliard served as assistant to the president at Alabama State from 1968 to 1970 and from 1972 to 1973 he was a partner in the law firm Pearson and Hilliard. Hilliard was a state representative in Alabama from 1970 to 1972. He was a civil rights activist and worked in voter-registration drives and protest marches in the 1960s, thus becoming well known in the black community and gaining access to blacks across the South. In 1980 he was elected a state senator and he was in his fourth term at the time of his election to the U.S. Congress.

Jim Clyburn

Sources: *Atlanta Constitution* (4 November 1992); *Ebony* 48 (January 1993): 27; *Jet* 83 (23 November 1992): 15, 52; *Contemporary Black Biography*, vol. 24, pp. 82–84; *Who's Who among African Americans*, 26th ed., p. 585; Salzman, *Encyclopedia of African-American Culture and History*, Supplement, pp. 130–31.

1992 • Bobby [Robert C.] Scott (1947–), attorney, became the first black Virginian elected to Congress in the twentieth century. Scott was born in Washington, D.C., and grew up in Newport News, Virginia. He is a graduate of Harvard University and Boston College of Law School. From 1973 to 1991, Scott was a practicing attorney in Newport News. He served in the state house of delegates from 1978 to 1983 and in the state senate from 1983 to 1993, when he was elected to Congress from the Third District in Virginia. He had at the top of his agenda in Congress jobs, health care, and crime prevention. He served on the Education and Workforce Committee and the Judiciary Committee, becoming the ranking Democrat on the latter committee in 1998.

Sources: *Ebony* 48 (January 1993): 54; *Jet* 83 (23 November 1992): 15, 52; *Contemporary Black Biography*, vol. 23, pp. 178–81.

Bobby Scott

1992 • Corinne Brown (1946–), representing the Third Congressional District and Carrie Meek (1926–), representing the Seventeenth Congressional District, became the first black women elected to Congress from Florida since Reconstruction. Although the boundaries of the Third District were redrawn in 1995, when she ran for a third term in 1996, Brown won a convincing victory. Both women had also served in the Florida state assembly. Brown served in the House of Representatives from 1982 to 1990. After Meek served in the House from 1979 to 1983, she was elected to the Florida Senate where she remained until elected to Congress. Brown was born in Jacksonville and graduated from Florida Agricultural and Mechanical University (FAMU) in Tallahassee (B.S., 1969) and the University of Florida (Ed.S., 1974). She taught at the University of Florida and at Florida

Community College. A Tallahassee native, Meek also graduated from FAMU, later receiving her master's degree from the University of Michigan.

Sources: *Contemporary Black Biography,* vol. 24, pp. 18–20 (Brown); *Contemporary Black Biography,* vol. 6, pp. 192–95 (Meek); Smith, *Notable Black American Women,* Book II, pp. 467–70 (Meek).

1993 • Ronald V. Dellums (1935–) was the first black chair of the House Armed Services Committee; in 1977 he had been the first black member. A native of Oakland, California, he represented a district which includes Oakland and Berkeley, the starting places for both the student movement and the Black Panther party of the 1960s. When he was elected to the House in 1970, the district was only twenty-two percent black, but he forged a firm coalition by 1974, and his length of service has underpinned his leadership role in Congress. A notable opponent of major military spending, he is nonetheless respected by the military establishment, and by more conservative members of the committee.

Sources: *Who's Who in American Politics, 1987–88,* p. 102; *Ebony* 48 (May 1993): 66; *Negro Almanac,* pp. 386–87; *Contemporary Black Biography,* vol. 2, pp. 54–57; *Who's Who among African Americans,* 26th ed., p. 331.

1993 • The first black and the first woman elected to Congress from North Texas was Eddie Bernice Johnson (1935–). Johnson was born and raised in Waco, Texas, and received a bachelor's degree in nursing from Texas Christian University. She holds a master's degree in politics from Southern Methodist University. She was a psychiatric nurse at the Dallas Veterans Administration Hospital for sixteen years, and then decided to enter politics. Johnson ran for a seat in the Texas house in 1972 and won in a landslide to become the first black woman from Dallas elected to public office. In 1977 she became regional director for the Department of Health, Education, and Welfare, but left that appointed position when Ronald Reagan replaced Jimmy Carter as president of the United States. She opened Eddie Bernice Johnson and Associates in Dallas and in 1986 she reentered politics, becoming a state senator until 1992.

Sources: *Contemporary Black Biography,* vol. 8, pp. 142–44. Smith, *Notable Black American Women,* Book II, pp. 340–41; *Who's Who among African Americans,* 26th ed., pp. 667–68.

1994 • The first black elected an Oklahoma congressman was J[ulius] C[aesar] Watts Jr. (1957–). He was easily re-elected in 1996, 1998, and 2000, continuing as the sole black Republican in Congress. Born in the farming community of Eufaula, Oklahoma, Watts was the first black quarterback on his high school football team. He entered the University of Oklahoma in 1981, on a football scholarship and became starting quarterback. He led the team to two consecutive Orange Bowl spots, in 1980 and 1981. He played with the Canadian Football League for six years. After deciding to enter politics, he switched from the Democratic party to the Republican party and in 1990 won one of the three seats on Oklahoma's Corporation Commission, the regulatory body for the telephone, gas, and oil industries. He was then the first black elected to a statewide office on Oklahoma. He overcame accusations of improper activities while serving on the commission and in 1994 won a seat in the U.S. Congress, representing Oklahoma's nearly all-white Fourth District. He was featured at the Republican National Convention in 1996.

Sources: *Jet* 88 (12 June 1995): 7; *Contemporary Black Biography,* vol. 14, pp. 229–23; Salzman, *Encyclopedia of African-American Culture and History,* Supplement, pp. 276–77.

1996 • Julia M. Carson (1938–2008) was the first woman of any race elected to Congress from Indianapolis, Indiana. Born in Louisville, Carson studied at Indiana University and St. Mary of the Woods. After serving as secretary to the United Auto Workers local office and serving as director of the area office for Congressman Andrew Jacobs, she made a successful run for office and was elected a state representative in 1992. She was elected to the state senate in 1976 and held that office until 1990. She was owner of the firm J. Carsons.

Sources: *Contemporary Black Biography,* vol. 23, pp. 37–39; vol. 69, pp. 24–26; *Jet* 91 (27 January 1997): 10; *Who's Who among African Americans,* 14th ed., pp. 210–11.

Julia M. Carson

1996 • Donna M. Christian-Green (1945–) became the first woman physician elected to Congress. Although she represented the Virgin Islands and was a non-voting member of Congress, she was the first woman to represent a U.S. possession in Congress. Born in Teaneck, New Jersey, Christian-Green graduated from St. Mary's College in South Bend, Indiana, and George Washington University Medical School. She established private practice in the Virgin Islands, where she also served in the Department of Health. She was twice president of the Virgin Islands Medical Society, and was territorial assistant commissioner of health and acting commissioner of health. After a stint in local politics, she was unsuccessful in her bid for Congress. In 1996 however, she unseated incumbent Victor O. Frazer in a run-off election. Christian-Green joined the Resources Committee and such subcommittees as National Parks and Public Lands. She was a member of the Congressional Black Caucus as well as the Congressional Caucus for Women.

Sources: *Contemporary Black Biography,* vol. 17, pp. 27–29; *Who's Who among African Americans,* 26th ed., p. 237.

1997 • Harold Ford Jr. (1970–), son of retired U.S. Representative Harold Ford Sr., was elected to the House in 1996, becoming the youngest member elected to the 105th Congress and the second youngest member to date. (William Claiborne, sworn in office in 1997 at the age of twenty-two and below the Constitutional requirement of twenty-five, was the youngest.) Ford represented the Ninth Congressional District in Tennessee. The election marked the first time in Congressional Black Caucus history that a son had succeeded a father. Ford was born in Memphis and graduated from the prestigious St. Albans School in Washington, D.C. He took his college degree from the University of Pennsylvania and his law degree from the University of Michigan Law School. He was a special assistant for the Justice/Civil Rights Cluster of Bill Clinton's 1992 Transition Team. Ford worked under the leadership of U.S. Secretary Ron Brown, who was a friend of the Ford family; Ford served as special assistant to the Economic Development Administration. Ford drew the national spotlight when he addressed delegates at the Democratic National Convention in 2000.

Sources: *Jet* 91 (25 November 1996); 6; 91 (27 January 1997): 4; *Contemporary Black Biography,* vol. 16, pp. 60–63.

2007 • U.S. House Majority Whip James Clyburn (1940–), Democrat from South Carolina, was the first black person to address a joint session of the South Carolina General Assembly. The assembly praised Clyburn for his "high position in the legislative branch of government." Clyburn graduated from South Carolina State University.

Sources: CBB 21, 71; *Jet* 111 (23 April 2007): 11.

2007 • The first black Muslim elected to Congress was Keith Maurice Ellison (1963–), Democrat from Minnesota. When taking the oath of office, Ellison caused controversy when he refused to use the Bible and instead used Thomas Jefferson's copy of the Koran, published in 1764 and kept in the Rare Book and Special Collections Division of the Library of Congress. Ellison is also the first black elected to Congress from Minnesota.

Sources: *Jet* 110 (22 June 2007): 9.

2007? • The first black to serve as clerk of the House of Representatives was Lorraine C. Miller. Of her appointment, Miller said that she was "proud to undertake this new challenge to serve Congress and the American people." She was also president of the Washington branch of the NAACP and senior advisor to Speaker of the House Nancy Pelosi. Miller also served as bureau chief for Consumer Information at the Federal Communications Commission and was the FCC's director of government relations. The Fort Worth, Texas, native holds an executive master's degree from Georgetown University.

Sources: *Jet* 111 (19 February 2007): 12.

2008 • The first black woman elected to represent Maryland in Congress was Donna Edwards (1959?–), who won a special election in the state's 4th congressional District. She held the seat until the end of the year. She lost he run for the congressional seat in 2006. She ran for a full term in November 2008 and won.

Sources: *Jet* 113 (7 July 2008): 7.

2010 • Allen West (1961–) became Florida's first black Republican Congressman since 1876, when Josiah T. Walls left the seat. Walls was first seated on March 4, 1871 and twice re-elected. West was born in Atlanta when the Civil Rights Movement was at its peak. His father served in World War II and one of his brothers in Vietnam. The family taught their children to love their country, their family, and to give service to people. West followed this advice and served as a Lieutenant Colonel in the U.S. Army. He served in several combat zones, including Operation Desert Storm and Operation Iraqi Freedom. Now retired from the military, he is married and has two daughters. He focuses on restoring the nation's fiscal health and rebuilding the black community. "I do not believe there is necessarily going to be a shift to Republicanism in the Black community," he said after his election in fall 2010, but he does recognize a move toward "conservative ideology." West was practically unknown in state and national politics until 2010 but "surged to star status in the ranks of the Tea Party."

Allen West

Sources: "About: Allen West for Congress," http://allenwestforcongress.com/about; *Jet* 118 (27 December 2010–3 January 2011): 12–14.

2010 • Terri A. Sewell (1965–) became the first black woman Alabama has sent to Congress. She was elected to fill the 7th District congressional seat. The Huntsville native is an attorney and a partner in the firm Maynard Cooper & Gale in Birmingham. Sewell graduated from Princeton and Oxford Universities, and holds a law degree from Harvard Law School.

Sources: *Jet* 118 (22 November 2010): 24–25, 28, 31; *Linked 1* (Winter/Spring 2011), p 54; "Congresswoman Terri A. Sewell," http://sewell.house.gov/, accessed September 22, 2012.

2010 • Representative-elected Tim Scott defeated the son of Strom Thurmond in the primary and went on to win his run for Congress. He became the first black Republican elected to the House since Reconstruction (1865–77). He owns an insurance company.

Sources: *Jet* 118 (27 December 2010–3 January 2011): 1214.

U.S. Senate

1870 • Hiram Rhoades [Rhodes] Revels (1822–1901), was the first black U.S. senator. He was elected to fill the vacated seat of Confederate President Jefferson Davis on January 20, 1870. He was born of free parents in North Carolina, and educated by Quakers in North Carolina, and at Knox College in Illinois. He became a minister in the African Methodist Episcopal Church, a teacher, and a Freedman's Bureau worker in Mississippi. He was elected to the Mississippi state senate in 1869, and elected U.S. senator by the legislature. He served from February 21, 1870, to March 3, 1871. After serving in the Senate, he served as the first president of the newly founded Alcorn College for Negroes. He remained active in the powerful circles of his church.

Hiram Revels

Sources: Bennett, *Before the Mayflower,* p. 487; Logan and Winston, *Dictionary of American Negro Biography,* pp. 523–24; Robinson, *Historical Negro Biographies,* p. 116; Smith, *Notable Black American Men,* pp. 1005–8.

1874 • Blanche Kelso Bruce (1841–1898) was the first black elected to a full term in the U.S. Senate. Mississippi's second black senator, Bruce took his seat in 1875. He is the only black senator to serve a full term, until the mid-twentieth century. He was born a slave in Farmville, Prince Edward County, Virginia, and later obtained an education at Oberlin College in Ohio. He was a wealthy Mississippi farmer and a successful banker. In 1878 Bruce presided over the Senate, the first black to do so. In 1881 President Ulysses S. Grant appointed him register of the treasury.

Blacks Elected to the Senate in the Nineteenth Century

Senator	State	Years Served
Hiram Rhoades Revels	Mississippi	1870–71
Blanche K. Bruce	Mississippi	1875–81

Sources: *Negro Almanac, 1976,* pp. 318–31.

Blanche Bruce

Sources: Logan and Winston, *Dictionary of American Negro Biography,* pp. 74–76; Hornsby, *Chronology of African-American History,* p. 45, 50, 56; Robinson, *Historical Negro Biographies,* pp. 56–57; Smith, *Notable Black American Men,* pp. 143–46.

1966 • Edward William Brooke III (b. 1919), attorney, was the first black to be elected to the U.S. Senate since Reconstruction, and the first ever elected by popular vote. He was elected on November 8 and was seated on January 10, 1967, in the 90th Congress. He remained in office until 1979 and then went into private law practice. Born in Washington, D.C., Brooke was a graduate of Howard University and Boston University. He served in World War II as a captain. He moved to Massachusetts, where he served as attorney general for the state. He was elected to the U.S. Senate on the Republican ticket. Brooke was awarded the Presidential Medal of Freedom in 2004. He published his autobiography, *Bridging the Divide: My Life,* in 2007.

Sources: *Contemporary Biography,* 1967, pp. 40–43; Hornsby, *Chronology of African-American History,* pp. 113, 129, 264; Robinson, *Historic Negro Biographies,* p. 166; Smith, *Notable Black American Men,* pp. 121–24; Gates and Higginbotham, *African American National Biography,* vol. 1, pages 372–74.

1972 • John L. LeFlore Sr. (1911–1976) was officially certified in August 26 as the first black candidate for the United States Senate in Alabama since Reconstruction. The Alabama Secretary of State certified him under the predominantly black National Democratic Party of Alabama (NDPA). LeFlore was a civil rights leader and journalist in Mobile.

Sources: *Crisis* (April 1976): 141–42; Hornsby, *Milestones in 20th Century African-American History,* pp. 165–66.

1980 • Ron [Ronald] H. Brown (1941–1996), political party executive, was the first black American chief counsel of the Senate Judiciary Committee. He was spokesperson and deputy director of the Urban League's Washington operations, and worked in the offices of Senator Edward Kennedy. In 1989 he was named chairman of the National Democratic Party—the first black to hold this office.

Sources: *Atlanta Constitution* (18 December 1992); *Crisis* 100 (March 1993): 16; *Ebony* 48 (May 1993): 62; *Who's Who among African Americans, 1996–97,* pp. 191; Smith, *Notable Black American Men,* pp. 131–33.

1983 • Trudi Michelle Morrison (1950–), attorney and presidential aide, was the first black woman deputy sergeant-at-arms of the Senate. Born in Denver, Colorado, Morrison took her undergraduate degree from Colorado State University, and her law degree from George Washington University. She studied for her doctorate at the University of Colorado, Denver. She held a variety of positions, including that of attorney for the Denver District Attorney's Office, criminal justice administrator for the Colorado Division of Criminal Justice, and regional deputy director for the Department of Health and Human Services.

Sources: *Who's Who among African Americans,* 26th ed., p. 909.

1992 • Carol E. Moseley Braun (1947–) was the nation's first black woman senator. She was elected on November 3 and served one term beginning in the 103rd Congress, representing Illinois. She was also Illinois's first black senator. In 1995 she became the first woman named to a full term on the powerful Senate Finance Committee. The Chicago-born attorney was educated at the University of Illinois, Chicago (B.A., 1969) and the University of Chicago (J.D., 1972). She was active in Chicago legal circles and the state legislature, and served as Cook County (Illinois) recorder of deeds/registrar of titles. In 2000 she became ambassador to New Zealand and to the tiny South Pacific state of Samoa, formerly Western Samoa. In fall 2001, she became professor of politics at Morris Brown College in Atlanta.

Sources: Hine, *Black Women in America,* vol. 1, pp. 162–64; *Crisis* 100 (March 1993): 7; *Jet* 83 (23 November 1992): 8; *Contemporary Black Biography,* vol. 4, pp. 26–29; *Who's Who among African Americans,* 14th ed., pp. 947–48.

Carol Braun

2002 • Ron Kirk (1954–), former mayor of Dallas, won the Democratic nomination for the U.S. Senate, the first black Texan to do so. He lost in the general election to John Cornyn.

Sources: *Jet* 101 (29 April 2002): 20–21; *Who's Who among African Americans,* 26th ed., p. 730.

2003 • The first black to serve as chaplain of the United States Senate was Navy Rear Admiral Barry Black (1948–); he was elected the sixty-second chaplain. As spiritual advisor and counselor, the chaplain serves as one of the Senate's officers and is nonpartisan, nonpolitical, and nonsectarian in his services to the senators, their families, and staff. Black is also the first Seventh-Day Adventist to serve in this role. For over twenty years Black served in the U.S. Navy and was named chief of Navy chaplains. The Baltimore native graduated from Oakwood College, Andrews University, North Carolina Central University, Eastern Baptist Seminary, Salve Regina University, and United States International University. He is the author of *From the Hood to the Hill.*

Sources: *Contemporary Black Biography,* vol. 47, pp. 6–8; *Jet* 113 (30 June 2008): 21.

U.S. Supreme Court

1880 • Samuel R. Lowery (1832–1900?) on February 2, 1880, was the first black lawyer to argue a case before the Supreme Court. This first is distinct from John Sweat Rock's first in 1865—Rock was admitted to practice before the court, a recognition of standing as a lawyer obtained by many more lawyers than ever actually appear before the court to argue a case. Lowery became a Christian Church minister in 1848. By 1856 the lives of free blacks in Nashville, where Lowery lived, had changed dramatically, and city officials and white vigilantes ordered free black schools that had operated since 1839 closed. Lowery moved to Ohio and became pastor of Harrison Street Christian Church in Cincinnati. He returned to Nashville and became a Christian Church missionary and chaplain for the 9th U.S. Colored Artillery Battalion. He also became teacher for the 2nd U.S. Colored Light Artillery, Battery A troops. Lowery and his father founded Tennessee Manual Labor University in 1867 but questions concerning financial impropriety later closed the school around 1872. Lowery studied law under a white attorney and set up law practice. He moved to Huntsville, Alabama, in 1875, establishing Lowery's Industrial Academy; later he founded the S. R. and R. M. Lowery Industrial Silk Culture and Manufacturing Company. Lowery was admitted to the bar of the Supreme Court on February 2, 1880. In the 1880s he established Loweryvale, a cooperative community in Jefferson County, Alabama, and died there around 1900.

Sources: *Encyclopedia of Black America,* p. 499; *Leaders of Afro-American Nashville*; Simmons, *Men of Mark,* pp. 144–48.

1948 • William Thaddeus Coleman Jr. (1920–) was the first black clerk in the Supreme Court. Born in the Germantown district of Philadelphia, Coleman was educated at the University of Pennsylvania and Harvard University. He was an honor graduate, the first black to serve on the board of editors for the *Harvard Law Review,* and recipient of a number of academic honors. He was selected to serve as law secretary to Justice Felix Frankfurter. At the end of his clerkship, he became an associate at the New York law firm Paul, Weiss, Rifkind, Wharton, and Garrison. At the same time he became a volunteer with

The Supreme Court's First Black Justice

In 1967 Thurgood Marshall (1908–1993) became the first black U.S. Supreme Court justice. For twenty-three years, Marshall was chief attorney for the NAACP. While there, he distinguished himself for using the legal system to break racially discriminatory practices in voting, housing, transportation, and other areas. He left the NAACP and was confirmed on September 11, 1962, as judge on the U.S. Court of Appeals, Third Circuit. On August 11, 1965, he was confirmed as solicitor general. He served the courts with distinction, and then took a seat on the U.S. Supreme Court on August 2, 1967. When President Lyndon B. Johnson nominated him to the post, four senators from the South vehemently opposed his confirmation; he was confirmed by a vote of 69 to 11. He served on that court until 1991, when he retired due to advancing age and health problems. Marshall was an outspoken member of the court who never hesitated to make his opinions known, especially when the subject had to do with civil rights. Born in Baltimore, Marshall graduated from Lincoln University in June 1930. Denied admission to the University of Maryland Law School because of his race, Marshall enrolled in Howard University Law School in Washington, D.C. There he established a good relationship with Charles Hamilton Houston, then vice-dean of the law school and later the first black lawyer to win a case before the U.S. Supreme Court. Marshall graduated *magna cum laude* and first in his class in 1933. He was admitted to the Maryland bar in 1933 and maintained a private law practice in Baltimore from 1933 to 1936. In 1934 he was appointed counsel for the Baltimore chapter of the NAACP while continuing his practice. Still incensed over the University of Maryland's rejection of his application, with the assistance of Charles Hamilton Houston he successfully sued the university in 1935 to admit Donald Murray, another black student. Marshall's devoted his entire legal career to find a working solution to the problems of civil rights and individual liberties.

Sources: *Contemporary Black Biography,* vol. 1, pp. 146–49; Smith, *Notable Black American Men,* pp. 762–67; Williams, *Thurgood Marshall.*

Thurgood Marshall

Thurgood Marshall and the NAACP Legal Defense and Education Fund. He and Marshall became friends, and Coleman became his personal lawyer when Marshall was on the Supreme Court. He returned to Philadelphia and became the first black lawyer to join the white law firm of Dilworth, Paxon, Kalish, Levy, and Green. Later he became a partner in the firm. He continued to work with the NAACP. Five of the cases in which he was involved led to the Supreme Court's decision in *Brown v. Board of Education.* Coleman held important positions in the federal government. He was senior consultant and assistant counsel to the Warren Commission that investigated the assassination of President John F. Kennedy. After Marshall was elevated to the Supreme Court, Coleman became president of the NAACP Legal Defense and Education Fund. In 1975 President Gerald Ford appointed him as secretary of the Department of Transportation. In 1995 President Bill Clinton awarded him a Presidential Medal of Freedom.

Sources: Kane, *Famous First Facts,* p. 625; *Who's Who in Colored America, 1950,* p. 116; Smith, *Notable Black American Men,* pp. 217–20.

1954 • Charles Vernon Bush (1939–) was the first black Supreme Court page. Bush was born in Tallahassee, Florida, and was educated at the U.S. Air Force Academy, Georgetown University, and Harvard Business School. After serving in the U.S. Air Force as an intelligence officer, he held various management positions with White Weld and Company, Celanese Corporation, Max Factor, ICN Pharmaceuticals, and other companies. He was president of Marnel Investment Corporation, and the Nostalgia Television Network and then became vice president of G. M. Hughes Electronics Corporation.

Sources: Alford, *Famous First Blacks,* p. 56; Kane, *Famous First Facts,* p. 626; *Who's Who among African Americans,* 26th ed., p. 187–88.

U.S. Presidency

1888 • Frederick Douglass (1817–1895) was the first black to be nominated as a presidential candidate, at the Republican convention. He received one vote.

Sources: Logan and Winston, *Dictionary of American Negro Biography,* p. 181; Garrett, *Famous First Facts about Negroes,* p. 160; *Negro Almanac,* p. 290;

1904 • The first black to run for president of the United States on a minor party ticket was George Edwin Taylor (1857–1925). He represented the National Liberal Party.

Sources: Martin, *The Almanac of Women and Minorities in American Politics,* p. 120.

1972 • Shirley Chisholm (1924–2005) became the first black to seek to run for U.S. president, representing one of the major parties. She sought to become the nominee of the Democratic Party. Chisholm pulled together a coalition of blacks, feminists, and other minorities. During the campaign, Hubert H. Humphrey and other candidates released 151 votes to Chisholm, but this was insufficient for her to win the nomination.

Sources: *The Black New Yorkers,* p. 352; *Contemporary Black* Biography, vol. 50, pp. 36–38; Hine, *Black Women in America,* vol. 1, pp. 236–38; Smith, *Notable Black American Women,* pp. 185–89.

1988 • Lenora Fulani (1950–) was the first black American woman to qualify for federal matching funds in a presidential election—and the first African American (and woman) to appear on the presidential ballot in all fifty states. She was also the only black woman Marxist psychologist to run for president. Fulani, a social psychologist, was running on the National Alliance Party ticket. She was on the ballot in forty-five states in 1992. Born Lenora Branch in Chester, Pennsylvania, she received her bachelor's degree from Hofstra University; master's degree from Teachers College, Columbia University; and received her doctorate degree from City University of New York, Graduate Center.

Sources: *Emerge* 4 (October 1992): 59; *Contemporary Black Biography,* vol. 11, pp. 100–3.

2008 • Barack Hussein Obama (1961–) won the nomination for the U.S. Presidency and became the first African American elected to the highest office in the nation. He was sworn in on January 20, 2009, and took the oath of office using the Bible that President Abraham Lincoln used when sworn in during his first inauguration in 1861, making Obama the first president sworn in using that Bible since its initial use. When the Democratic primary season for the Presidency ended on June 3, 2008, Obama became the first African American to secure the nomination of any major national political party. His stirring keynote address before the Democratic National Convention in July 2004 catapulted Obama onto the national political scene. With a landslide victory in November, he was also elected U.S. Senator from Illinois, becoming the third African American elected to the U.S. Senate since Reconstruction. In February 2007 he announced his intent to seek the Democratic Party's nomination for the U.S. Presidency. During his campaign, Obama garnered financial support from small donations solicited over the Internet and went on to amass a record-breaking $745 million. His use of the Internet, 24-hour cable television programming, blogs, and other nontraditional media changed the way political campaigns are conducted. During his campaign, Obama frequently drew enormous crowds and was placed under Secret Service protection nine months before the election and earlier than any other candidate who ever ran for president. He defeated Senator John McCain (R-AZ) in the November 4 election, and was sworn into office on January 20, 2009, as the forty-fourth president. His first one hundred days in office were consumed by a range of activities, including passage of a massive stimulus bill to help jumpstart the sagging economy, interventions in the housing and credit markets, a plan to bail out the automobile industry, strict regulations proposed for Wall Street, an overhaul of foreign policy, and a push for a national health insurance plan. Obama was born in Honolulu, Hawaii, the son of Barack Obama Sr., a native of Kenya, and Ann

President Barack Obama

Dunham, a white woman and a native of Kansas; they divorced in 1964. Obama lived in Jakarta, Indonesia, with his mother and stepfather before resettling in Hawaii, where he lived with his grandparents and attended an elite college preparatory school. In 1983 Obama graduated from Columbia University in New York City, and then worked as a researcher. Two years later he moved to Chicago and became a community organizer in several low-income neighborhoods. He entered Harvard Law School in 1988 and in 1990 was elected president of the prestigious and competitive *Harvard Law Review*—the first African American to hold that honor. While he is articulate, serious, and challenging, Obama's initial popularity at home and abroad, and, for a time his continuing high approval rating among the American public, led him to be regarded as a celebrity president.

Sources: *Black Americans in Congress, 1870–2007,* pp. 724–25; *Encyclopedia of African American History 1896 to the Present,* pp. 1–95; Ifill, *Breakthrough: Politics and Race in the Age of Obama,* 2009.

First Lady Michelle Obama

2009 • When Barack Obama took office as President of the United States, Michelle Robinson Obama (1964–) became the first black "First Lady" of the United States. She filled her new role by extending her interests far beyond that of attending official ceremonies and dinner parties. Her special concerns include the plight of military families, childhood obesity, and promoting healthier eating habits. Michelle Obama quickly became a fashion trendsetter as she selected styles from affordable dress lines to the high-end fashion designers. The Chicago native and former community organizer graduated from Princeton University and Harvard Law School. The Obamas have two daughters: Malia and Sasha.

Sources: Smith, *Encyclopedia of African American Popular Culture,* vol. 3, pp. 1045–47.

GOVERNMENT: INTERNATIONAL

Belize

2008? • After ten years of scandal and economic troubles, the small Central American nation of Belize swore in Dean Oliver Barrow (1951–) as prime minister, making him the first black to hold that post. Barrow led the United Democratic Party (UDP) and previously served as foreign affairs minister. A native of Belize, Barrow is the father of Jamal "Shyne" Barrow, a rapper now known as Moses Michael Levi who went to jail for a 1999 New York nightclub shooting.

Sources: *Contemporary Black Biography,* vol. 69, pp. 1–8.

Bermuda

1997 • The first woman and the youngest prime minister in Bermuda's 400-year history was Pamela Gordon (1956?–). The ruling United Bermuda Party selected her to succeed fifty-seven-year-old David Saul. In eighteen months she would meet another black woman in the general election, Progressive Labour Party leader and respected parliamentarian Jennifer Smith (1947–). Gordon is the daughter of E. F. Gordon, a civil rights leader and a physician who was born in Trinidad and was a founder of the Bermuda Industrial Union.

Sources: *Jet* 91 (14 April 1997): 6.

1998 • Jennifer Smith (1947–) was elected premier of Bermuda in November, becoming the first elected woman premier. In 1991 Smith also became the first woman senator in Bermuda's upper house and was elected deputy chair of the Progressive Labor Party (PLP). Smith was appointed to the Bermuda senate in 1980 and reappointed in 1983 and 1985. During her first term in the senate, she attended the John F. Kennedy School of Government's program for senior executives in government. In 1989 she was elected to the senate, then re-elected in 1993. After two terms as shadow minister of education and culture, 1989–93 and 1993–98, she became premier and minister of education. She had defeated United Bermuda Party leader Pamela Gordon. In 1996 she became head of the PLP. Born in Bermuda, Smith studied art at the Art Institute of Pittsburgh and returned home after she received an associate's degree in 1970. From 1970 to 1974 she served as a political reporter and editor of the *Bermuda Recorder,* where she called attention to her country's list of banned books and became an instant celebrity. From 1974 to 1976 she was writer and assistant editor with *Fame* magazine. In 1993 she was made assistant editor of the *Bermuda Times*.

Sources: *Contemporary Black Biography,* vol. 21, pp. 169–71.

Brazil

Celso Pitta

1996 • Celso [Roberto] Pitta [do Nascimento] became the first black mayor of Sao Paolo, Brazil's largest city and economic powerhouse, in November. He won in a runoff election, defeating former mayor Luiza Erundina by an overwhelming margin, becoming Sao Paolo's first black elected leader. An accountant and political novice, Pitta was educated in the United States. After serving as an accountant on an estate farm, he was Sao Paolo's budget director and finance secretary before being elected as mayor. His plans to develop the city included implementation of a new health care system for the poor, completion of a housing project to replace some of the city's worst slums, and maintenance of financial order.

Sources: *Jet* 91 (9 December 1996): 35; *Contemporary Black Biography,* vol.17, pp. 149–51.

Burundi

1993 • The first president of Burundi to be elected to office was Melchior Ndadaye (1953–1993). He held office for only three months before he was assassinated on October 21, 1993, at the presidential palace during a military coup. Ndadaye was born and educated in Burundi. When his country was beset by a civil war and coup attempts, he went into exile in Rwanda where the Burundian political dissidents knew him well. There he founded a worker's party. He returned to Burundi in 1983 and worked in a private bank until 1992, actively participating in nonviolent underground political activities. In 1986 he founded the Front for Democracy in Burundi (FRODEBU) and was elected president of his country on the FRODEBU ticket.

Sources: *Contemporary Black Biography,* vol. 7, pp. 207–10.

Canada

1972 • Rosemary Brown (1930–2003), social activist, educator, and politician, was elected to the provincial legislature of British Columbia, becoming the first black woman to serve in a Canadian parliament. She served until 1986 and then taught women's studies at Simon Fraser University, where she held an endowed professorship. She taught at other universities as well. Brown was born in Kingston, Jamaica, and moved to Canada in 1951. After studying at McGill University and the University of British Columbia, she began a career in social work. She spent her life promoting equality and human rights, particularly for women and minorities, and won a multitude of honors for her efforts, including her selection as an officer of the Order of Canada. Her autobiography, *Being Brown: A Very Public Life,* was published in 1989.

Sources: *Contemporary Black Biography,* vol. 62, pp. 23–25; *heroines.ca: A Guide to Women in Canadian History,* www.heroines.ca/people/brown.html.

1994 • Emery Oakland Barnes (1930?–1998) became the first black speaker of the provincial parliament of British Columbia. He won a seat in 1972 and was appointed deputy speaker in 1991. Three years later he was elected speaker and served until he retired from politics in 1996. Born in the United States, Barnes was a standout athlete at the University of Oregon and played professional football for the Green Bay Packers in 1956. He left the Packers a year later to play in the Canadian Football League. He retired from the sport in 1964 after the British Columbia Lions won the Grey Cup. In 1986 he was inducted into the Oregon Sports Hall of Fame and the British Columbia Sports Hall of Fame.

Sources: AP Online (8 July 1998).

Dominica

1980 • The first woman to come to power in the Caribbean was Mary Eugenia Charles (1919–2005), who became prime minister of Dominica. By the late 1990s she was the only black woman to lead an independent nation. For her determination to serve her people well and for her longevity, she was affectionately called "The Iron Lady of the Caribbean." Charles was born in Pointe Michel, Dominica, near the capital of Roseau, to a homemaker and a well-known entrepreneur and land-speculator who founded Penny Bank on the island. Charles received her law degree from the University of Toronto and continued her studies in law at the London School of Economics. She was admitted to the bar in England in 1947. Returning to Dominica, she practiced law from 1949 to 1968 and handled legal cases in several islands in the West Indies. From 1968 to 1970 Charles was a lecturer. In 1970 she was appointed to the Dominica House of Assembly and in 1975 elected member and political leader of the House of Assembly. In addition to her service as prime minister, she was minister of finance, foreign affairs, defense, and economic affairs. In 1991 Queen Elizabeth II of England knighted Charles, making her Dame Eugenia.

Sources: *Current Biography,* October 1986, pp. 9–12; *Contemporary Black Biography,* vol. 10, pp. 28–31.

France

1945 • Madame E. T. Eboue was elected to the French assembly on November 10. She was the first black to win a seat.

Sources: *Chicago Defender,* 15 September 1945; 3 November 1945.

Ghana

1957 • The first African-born prime minister of a sub-Saharan British dependency was Kwame Nkrumah (1909–1972). He became head of state when the Gold Coast gained independence and became known as Ghana. Born in Nkroful, British West Africa, he graduated from the Government Training College in Accra. He also earned a bachelor's degree from Lincoln University in Missouri (1939), a bachelor's degree from Lincoln Theological Seminary (1942), and masters of art and science from the University of Pennsylvania. He returned to the Gold Coast in 1947 and became secretary of a political party known as the United Gold Coast Convention. In 1949 he founded the Convention People's Party. His rise to the top leadership of his country was swift. In 1951 he was elected prime minister of the Gold Coast, then re-elected in 1954 and 1956. After serving as head of state of Ghana from 1957 to 1966, a military coup ousted him from office. He made his last speech before the national assembly on February 1, 1966, and then left the country. Meanwhile, Sekou Toure, leader from Guinea, appointed him joint head of state of Guinea. Nkrumah was well known as a leading philosopher of Pan-Africanism. His first exposure to Pan-Africanism came as early as the 1930s, when he was exposed to the Pan-African ideas of W. E. B. Du Bois and Marcus Garvey. Nkrumah was also well known as a writer. In time his works became highly revolutionary. In 1968 he established a publishing company to publish his works. Included in his writings are *The Autobiography of Kwame Nkrumah* (1957), *Towards Colonial Freedom* (1962), *Africa Must Unite* (1964), and *Revolutionary Path* (1973). He died of cancer in Bucharest, Romania, on April 27, 1972.

Sources: *Contemporary Black Biography,* vol. 3, pp. 175–78.

Haiti

1995 • The first woman prime minister of Haiti was Claudette Werleigh (1946–). She was inducted in a ceremony held at the national palace in Port-au-Prince and held office from November 7, 1995 to February 8, 1996.

Sources: *Jet* 89 (27 November 1995): 89.

Ireland

2007? • Rotini Adebari (1964–), a native Nigerian, became the first black mayor in Ireland, in the commuter town of Portlaoise, located west of Dublin. An independent politician, he had served on the town council since 2004 and ran unopposed in the election. Adebari, his wife, and two boys traveled to Ireland in 2000, claiming asylum due to religious persecution. Beyond the political arena, he earned a master's degree in intercultural studies, established a consulting agency, and became host of a weekly radio show.

Sources: *Jet* 112 (15 July 2007): 11.

Israel

1996 • Belaynesh Zevadia (1967?–) became the first Ethiopian member of Israel's Foreign Ministry. She was appointed vice consul to the Consulate General of Israel to the Midwest in Chicago. Her position made her accountable for academic and community relations. Zevadia is the daughter of a former grand rabbi of the Ethiopian Jews. She grew up in the Gondhar province, where most Ethiopian Jews lived, and left for Israel in December 1983. She earned degrees from Hebrew University and ten years later joined the Israeli Foreign Ministry.

Sources: *Jet* 90 (30 September 1996): 18.

1996 • The first black elected to the Israeli parliament was Addisu Messele. In 1980 he had been airlifted to Israel from Ethiopia. He proposed to use his position to enhance the lives of some 60,000 Ethiopian Jews then living in Israel. A leading Ethiopian political activist, in 1989 the Israeli government sent him on a return visit to Ethiopia to arrange for other Ethiopian Jews, including his parents and siblings, to be released. After he moved to Israel, Messele earned degrees in mechanical engineering and social work. He also founded the United Ethiopian Jewish Organization.

Sources: *Jet* 90 (3 June 1996): 23.

Ivory Coast (Côte d'Ivoire)

Felix Houphouet-Boigny

1960 • Félix Houphouët-Boigny (1905–1993) became the first president of Côté d'Ivoire (the Ivory Coast), when it gained its independence from France. He was also the first West African minister in the French government in 1956, while also serving as mayor of Abidjan. The son of a wealthy cocoa planter and his wife, Houphouët-Boigny completed a degree in primary school teaching in Dakar, Senegal, in 1919 and received a medical degree from Dakar Medical School, graduating in 1925 at the head of his class. Although lacking in the education needed to become a medical doctor, he was called "African Doctor," making him a member of the intellectual elite in the Ivory Coast. In 1940 he became a district chief, having inherited the title at age five when his maternal uncle was assassinated; however, he could accept that responsibility only when he was mature enough to understand its responsibilities. At age thirty-five he left the colonial service where he had worked to become *chef de canton,* or district chief. He held that post until 1960. In the meantime, Houphouët-Boigny held a number of political positions. In 1945 he was elected to the Abidjan Municipal Council and also represented the Ivory Coast to the French Constituent Assembly. He was a co-founder of the Democratic party of the Ivory Coast in 1946 and was representative to the French Constituent Assembly. He co-founded and became president of the African Democratic Rally that same year. He was a member of the French National Assembly from 1946 to 1958, and in 1956 he became the first West African minister in French government and simultaneously became mayor of Abidjan. He was president of the Ivory Coast Territorial Assembly and Grand Council of French West Africa in Dakar, Senegal in 1957–58. After serving as prime minister of the Ivory Coast from 1958 to 1960, he became its president in 1960, making him head of government, state, and the military.

Sources: *Contemporary Black Biography,* vol. 4, pp. 118–23.

Jamaica

1993 • P. J. [Percival Noel James] Patterson (1935–) became the first prime minister of Jamaica to have been born of two black parents. In 1992 his predecessor, Michael Manley, appointed him to office; he was elected to office in March 1993. Patterson was born in St. Andrew, Jamaica, and graduated from the University of the West Indies in 1959 with an honors degree in English. In 1963 he earned his bachelor of law degree from the London School of Economics; he passed the bar in Britain and in Jamaica. From 1970 to 1992 he worked for the People's National Party, serving in a number of posts, including foreign minister, minister for foreign trade, and deputy prime minister. He became known as the "Fresh Prince" and was successful in stabilizing Jamaica's economy. Patterson broke the "third term barrier" and served as prime minister until 2006.

Sources: *Contemporary Black Biography*, vol. 20, pp. 171–73; *Black Enterpise* 23 (December 1992), p. 22.

Kenya

1964 • The first president of Kenya was Jomo Kenyatta (1891?–1978). A Pan-Africanist, he was an astute politician who gave great importance to black African rule. He was born Kamau wa Ngengi, in Ngenda, Kiambu District of British East Africa Protectorate (now Kenya); his name was changed to Johnstone Kamu in 1914 and later on he became known as Jomo Kenyattta. He was the son of a farmer and herdsman. Kenyatta attended University College in London, studied in Moscow in 1932, and did postgraduate study in anthropology at London School of Economics in 1937. Earlier in his career he held a number of positions, including that of educator and educational administrator. After serving as vice principal of Independent Teachers' College in Githunguri beginning 1946, he was named principal. He served as president of the Kenya African Union political party from 1947 to 1952. In October 1952 the British government arrested Kenyatta and several members of a Mau Mau Committee as terrorists; Kenyatta was jailed from 1953 to 1961. After his release, he became president of the Kenya African National Union again. He served as minister for Internal Security, Defense, and Foreign Affairs in from 1963 to 1964, as prime minister in from 1963 to 1964, and then held the presidency from 1964 to 1968. He died in his sleep on August 22, 1978.

Jomo Kenyatta

Sources: *Contemporary Black Biography*, vol. 5, pp. 156–61.

Liberia

1848 • Joseph Jenkins Roberts (1809–1876) became the first president of Liberia. Born in Petersburg, Virginia, he was the son of free blacks. At age twenty he, his mother, and his younger brothers immigrated to Liberia. Roberts became a wealthy merchant and an unofficial aide to Thomas H. Buchanan, governor and member of the American Colonization Society. After Buchanan died in 1842, Roberts was appointed to take his place, becoming the colony's first black governor. Roberts and other colonists declared Liberia a republic on July 26, 1847; he was elected president the next year. Roberts became president of the new Liberia College in 1856. Following the country's prolonged financial crisis, Roberts returned to served as president from 1872 to 1876.

Sources: "Liberia: African-American Mosaic Exhibition" (Library of Congress). http://www.loc.gov/exhibits/african/afam003.html. Accessed February 28, 2002; *New Encyclopedia Brittanica*, vol. 10, p. 107.

Joseph Roberts

1953 • Angie Elizabeth Brooks (1928–2007) became the first woman to practice law in her country. Born in Virginia, Montserrado County, Liberia, on August 24, 1928, she was one of nine children of an African Methodist Episcopal Zion minister. Because her parents were unable to care for their large family, Brooks was raised in a foster home. She was also a product of three indigenous tribes in West Africa. Brooks grew up in Monrovia, the capital of Liberia, and by age eleven, having taught herself to type, earned money by copying

Africa's First Independent Republic

When Liberia declared its independence on July 26, 1847, it became the first independent Republic in Africa. While Haiti is the oldest independent nation with a predominantly black population, Liberia is the second. It was settled in 1822 to become a homeland for freed slaves. It is also a great producer of iron ore. Monrovia was its first city, settled in 1822. Located at the foot of West Africa, Liberia is 43,000 squares miles in geographic area.

Sources: *Jet* 94 (27 July 1998): 19.

legal documents. This work inspired Brooks to become a lawyer. Although a poor, back-country girl, she paid her expenses through high school by working as a part-time typist for the Treasury Department. After that she was a stenotypist for the Justice Department. Dissatisfied with her country's laws, she reasoned that she might enter the legislature and help improve them. Since Liberia had no law school and legal training for women was hard to find, Brooks took the only option available to her: she studied with Clarence L. Simpson, later Liberia's foreign minister. Her male associates ridiculed her and opposed her when she tried her first case in the courtroom, causing Brooks to walk out and never return. Still determined to become a lawyer, Brooks obtained the assistance of Liberia's president, William V. S. Tubman, and raised enough money to go to Shaw University in Raleigh, North Carolina. There she earned her way by cleaning, cooking, and washing dishes. She also met racial segregation for the first time, when she was remanded to the back of a public bus. Graduating from Shaw in 1949, Brooks began studying law at the University of Wisconsin. She graduated in 1952 with two degrees, a law degree and a master's degree in political science and international relations. She continued graduate study in 1952 and 1953 at the University College Law School at London University. Soon after she returned to Liberia, in August 1953 she was admitted as counselor-at-law to the Supreme Court of Liberia, becoming the first woman to practice law in her country. She joined the Justice Department where, from August 1953 to March 1958, she was assistant attorney general of Liberia. She also encouraged women to enter the field and she helped dismantle permanently the all-male domination of the legal profession in Liberia. She helped organize the department of law at Liberia University and taught law part-time there from 1954 to 1958. President Tubman appointed her assistant secretary of state in 1958. She was also elected the first African woman president of the United Nations. In Africa, she continued to champion the cause for women and was successful in her bid to liberate women.

Sources: *Current Biography,* 1970, pp. 48–50; *Crisis* 76 (November 1969): 372, 381; *Ebony* 17 (December 1961): 122–28.

Ellen Johnson-Sirleaf

2006 • Ellen Johnson-Sirleaf (1938–), president of Liberia, took office and became the first democratically-elected female president in postcolonial Africa. She survived a run-off election on November 8, 2005, handily defeating her opponent, George Weah. When she took office the following February, she immediately faced $3.7 billion in international debt as well as the aftermath of a devastating civil war that lasted from 1989 to 2003. Sirleaf moved quickly to address these problems, notably to persuade debtors to forgive at least some of the debt. The United States forgave $358 million that was owed to them. Sirleaf was born in Monrovia, married while a teenager but divorced around 1961, and began her college education at Monrovia's College of West Africa. She soon moved to the United States and enrolled in Madison Business College in Wisconsin, graduating in 1964 with a bachelor's degree in business administration. She earned a second bachelor's degree (in economics) from the University of Colorado in 1970 and in 1971 received a master's degree in public administration from Harvard. While completing her education, she regularly returned to Liberia and in 1965 began working as a financial specialist for the Liberian government. She had become minister of finance by 1979 and president of the Liberian Bank for Development and Investment for a brief period. She held other posts, becoming a candidate for president of Liberia as early as 1996. Despite her efforts as president and the country's rich resources, Liberia continued to suffer from questionable economic policies and an unstable environment. In 2007, President George W. Bush awarded her the Presidential Medal of Freedom, the highest civilian honor that a president can award. In 2011, Sirleaf joined two other women from Africa and the Middle East in receiving the Nobel Peace Prize for improving their nations and advancing the role of women's rights.

Sources: *Contemporary Black Biography,* vol. 71, pp. 142–44; *Essence* 36 (March 2006): 94, 96; *Jet* 112 (5 November 2007): 10.

Malawi

1994 • Bakili Muluzi (1943–) won in the country's first free presidential election in thirty years and began a new phase in Malawi's history. He was born Elson Bakili Muluzi in Nyasaland (now Malawi) and educated at Boston College of Education in England and Thisted College of Further Education in Denmark. He rose through the ranks in his political party, the Malawi Congress Party. He was elected to parliament in 1975 and held several ministerial posts of increasing power. By 1982 he was promoted from Minister without Portfolio to Minister of Transport and Communications. From 1977 to 1981 he was secretary-general and administrative secretary of the Malawe Congress Party. In 1992 he founded the United Democratic Front. Malawi held its first general election in the new, multi-party era in 1994, and Muluzi was victorious in his bid to become president.

Sources: *Contemporary Black Biography,* vol. 14, pp. 172–74.

Mexico

1829 • Vincente Guerrero (? –1831) was elected president, becoming the first black Indian president. While in office he issued the decree abolishing slavery. He also worked to abolish the death penalty, taxed the rich, protected small businesses, and established the village council movement that enabled peasants to elect representatives without qualifications of race, property ownership, or literacy. He signed his correspondence "Citizen Guerrero." Since childhood Guerrero had been an activist; by trade he was a mule driver. Toward the end of Mexico's war for independence from Spain (1810–1821), he led a coalition of blacks and indigenous peoples. Guerrero's political opponents kidnapped and killed him in 1831.

Sources: Vincent, *The Legacy of Vincente Guerrero, Mexico's First Black Indian President.*

Mozambique

1975 • The first president of Mozambique after it gained independence from 470 years of Portuguese colonial rule was Samora Moises Machel (1933–1986). Born in Chilembene, the Chokwe District of the Gaza Province in Mozambique, Machel was the son of a farmer. He attended nursing school at Miguel Bombarda Hospital in Mozambique from 1954 to 1959. After serving as a nurse in that hospital from 1954 to 1963, he served as a member of the Mozambique Liberation Front and was its secretary of defense from 1966 to 1969, then president from 1970 to 1975. On a return trip from Zambia on October 19, 1986, he died in a plane crash in South Africa.

Sources: *Contemporary Black Biography,* vol. 8, pp. 161–63.

Nigeria

1963 • The first president and a champion for African independence was Nnamdi Azikiwe (1904–1996), a lawyer, political scientist, journalist, and political activist. For many years he was Nigeria's elder statesman. He agitated for nationhood for Nigeria and in 1960 became

Samora Moises Machel

governor general of the Nigerian Federation when Nigeria gained independence from Britain. He ran for reelection in 1979 and 1983, between military governments. It was Azikiwe who introduced universal adult suffrage and worked to extend schooling nationwide. Azikiwe, an Ibo, was born November 16, 1904, in Zungeru (northern Nigeria) and attended an English-run missionary school. He continued his education in the United States, at Storer College in West Virginia, Howard University in Washington, D.C., Lincoln University in Pennsylvania, and Columbia University in New York City. After teaching at Lincoln University in the early 1930s, he returned to Africa and in Accra, Ghana, he founded in 1934 the *African Morning Post*, the first of five newspapers that he would establish. While in Ghana, he was mentor to Kwame Nkrumah (1909–1972), who in 1957 became that country's president. In 1937 Azikiwe returned to Nigeria, worked as an editor and essayist, and then entered politics. He became a member of the Legislative Council in 1948 and in 1954, and now an outspoken advocate of independence, became premier of the Eastern Region. His death was announced erroneously in 1989, following his disappearance from public life. After a long illness, he died in a hospital in Nigeria in 1996, at the age of ninety-one.

Sources: Times News Service (14 May 1996).

Norway

2007? • Prime Minister Jens Stottenberg appointed Manuela Ramin-Osmundsen (1963–) minister of children and equality, making her the first black member of the Norwegian government. The Martinique native relocated to Oslo in 1991, accompanied by her husband who is Norwegian and a former government adviser. In hew new country, Ramin-Osmundsen founded the Center Against Ethnic Discrimination and held top positions in the Norway Directorate of Immigration.

Sources: *Jet* 112 (19 November 2007): 50.

Manuela Ramin-Osmundsen

Russia

1934 • Robert Robinson (1904?–1994) became the first black councilman in Moscow. The first black toolmaker at Ford Motor Company in Detroit, Michigan, Robinson signed a one-year contract to teach toolmaking in Russia in 1930. Later on he renounced his citizenship and decided to live in Moscow, becoming a citizen of the Soviet Union in 1937. He also became senior engineer at Moscow's First State Ball Bearing Plant and invented at least twenty-seven industrial tools. During his years in Moscow, Robinson learned to speak Russian, French, and Spanish. Russia used him during the Cold War to show that the country was active in civil rights. Robinson later wanted to return to the United States but was refused permission to leave Russia. U.S. diplomat William B. Davis and Mathias Lubega, who was Uganda's ambassador to Russia, facilitated his escape to Kampala, Uganda, and later to the United States.

Sources: *Ebony* 15 (January 1960): 66–67; *Jet* 86 (4 July 1996): 58; Robinson, *Black on Red*.

Senegal

1960 • Léopold Sédar Senghor (1907?–2002), who led his country to independence from France in 1960, was also elected Senegal's first president. He was re-elected in 1963, 1968, and 1973 and held office until he retired in 1980. In that year Senghor became the first African president to resign power voluntarily; he selected his successor, Abdiu Diouf. In 1984 Senghor became the first black member of the French Academy. Born in the south of Senegal in the coastal region of Joal, he studied in a convent school in Senegal. There he was awarded a scholarship to Paris' Louis-Le-Grand College, where he became a classmate and lifetime friend of Georges Pompidou, later the president of France. Senghor studied classical languages and literature and from 1935 to 1948 he taught in several French cities. After receiving French citizenship in World War II, he became a volunteer in the French army. While imprisoned in a German prison camp for eighteen months, Senghor

Léopold Senghor

devoted his time to writing. It was here that he produced some of his most poignant poems. His poems—written in French and in his native Serere dialect—and later his politics reflected his passion for African nationalism.

Sources: *Jet* 101 (14 January 2002): 17.

2001 • Madior Boye was named prime minister of Senegal, becoming the first woman to hold that post and one of a few women in Africa to hold such a senior post. A well-respected lawyer and politician, she was appointed after Senegal President Abdoulaye Wade fired prime minister Moustapha Niasse, whose party acted contrary to the wishes of the governing coalition in that country.

Sources: *Jet* 99 (26 March 2001): 12.

South Africa

1994 • The first all-race election was held in South Africa on April 26. The last vestiges of apartheid were legally dissolved on this historic day, ending decades of struggle by the African National Congress (ANC) and other black organizations that sought liberation. For 300 years, a white minority had ruled South Africa. Polling extended over a four-day period and an estimated 22.7 million eligible voters participated in the elections. In the end, a new South African flag replaced the existing 1928 flag and was raised at 12:01 A.M. on April 26. At that time as well, the country's new constitution and bill of rights took effect. Nine new all-race provinces were created as the old racist government was dissolved.

Sources: *Jet* 99 (30 April 2001): 20.

1994 • Nelson Rolihlahla Mandela (1918–), once one of the most famous political prisoners in the world, became the first black president of South Africa on April 27 and served under its first multiracial democratic constitution. He defeated the incumbent president, F. W. deKlerk, in a landslide victory. In his inaugural address on May 10 in Pretoria, Mandela proposed a government that would be one of national unity. He said, "We enter into a covenant that we shall build the society in which all South Africans, both Black and White, will be able to walk tall, without any fear in their hearts, assured of their inalienable right to human dignity—a rainbow nation at peace with itself and the world." A forty-four-member official delegation from the United States, including government officials, poet Maya Angelou, and a number of other luminaries, attended the inauguration. A nameless African and African American bonding ceremony of Calling the Spirits was held at Johannesburg's Market Theatre. Angelou lifted the names of black ancestors, including W.E.B. Du Bois and Patrice Lumumba, who made that moment possible. Martin Luther King Jr., Marcus Garvey, and Steve Biko were among the other names lifted up and praised. Mandela was freed on February 11, 1990, after spending twenty-seven years in jail as a political prisoner and becoming legendary among South Africa's black majority. On the evening of his release, Mandela gave his first public address in Cape Town. In June the next year, at age seventy-one, he toured thirteen nations around the world denouncing the evils of apartheid. Mandela was born in Umtata, Transkei, South Africa, the son of a tribal chief. His tribal name is Rolihlahla, or "one who brings trouble upon himself." Although he was in line to become a tribal chief, he renounced his right and attended the University College of Fort Hare and Witwatersrand University, and in 1942 received his law degree from the University of South Africa. He joined the African National Congress at age twenty-four. He was also a founder of a sub-group called the Congress Youth League, an activist group that supported civil disobedience. As group leader, he supported labor strikes; his work with the group and the ANC led to his arrest several times. In 1956 his arrest along with other anti-apartheid leaders led to his infamous "Treason Trial." After the trial ended and the ANC was declared illegal, Mandela founded a new underground guerrilla organization known as Umkonto we Sizwe ("Spear of the Nation"). The group fought against all symbols of apartheid. As mass protests continued and the group claimed responsibility for over seventy acts of sabotage, Mandela was arrested on August 4, 1962, and charged with organizing illegal demonstrations. He was tried and sentenced to five years in prison,

Nelson Mandela

then charged with treason and sabotage, and in June 1964 was sentenced to life in prison. Despite the length of his jail term and his time in solitary confinement, Mandela never lost sight of his goal. He also refused to accept then-president P. W. Botha's offer of freedom in exchange for his renunciation of violence, unless the government granted blacks full political rights. On February 11, 1990, Mandela was released from prison as the entire world watched, marking one of the most notable events of that year. In 1993, Mandela and F. W. deKlerk became co-recipients of the Nobel Peace Prize, for their combined efforts to bring apartheid to a peaceful end. Mandela received the Tshwane/Pretoria "Freedom of the City" Award in Johannesburg in 2008.

Sources: *Contemporary Black Biography,* vol. 14, pp. 161–66; *Jet* 84 (1 November 1993): 4; 85 (30 May 1994): 4 –19, 52–55; 99 (12 February 2001): 20.

1995 • Franklin Sonn became South Africa's first non-white ambassador to the United Nations. President Nelson Mandela named him to the post. A respected educator, Sonn was rector of the Peninsular Technikon, a technical school in Cape Town, with an enrollment of 8,000 in 1985.

Sources: *Jet* 87 (27 February 1995): 6–7.

1998 • Siphiwe Nyanda (1950–) became the first black to head the armed forces for his country. When he took that post, he headed a force of 98,000 troops. He was born in the Soweto area of Moroka and studied at the University of Zululand until he was expelled for political reasons. In the 1970s he was a sports reporter for *The World.* From 1974 to 1976 he was a recruiting officer for South Africa's African National Congress. He held a number of positions, including commander of trainees for the commissar of Transvaal urban operations, commander for border operations for Swaziland, chief of defense force staff, deputy chief for the Gauteng Command, and finally chief. In that position he headed the entire army, air force, navy, and intelligence service. President Nelson Mandela presided over the swearing-in ceremony, parade, and other activities held in Pretoria on May 29, 1998.

Sources: *Contemporary Black Biography,* vol. 21, pp. 128–30.

1999 • South African President Nelson Mandela appointed Sheila Violet Makate Sisulu (1948?–) ambassador to the United States, making her the first black person and the first woman to hold that post. Born in Soweto, near Johannesburg, she began her education in the racially segregated schools. Her parents later transferred her to St. Michael's School for Girls, a boarding school in neighboring Swaziland. She received a bachelor's degree in English and philosophy in 1974 from the University of Lesotho (Botswana and Swaziland) as well as a bachelor's degree in education from the University of the Witwatersrand. In 1974 Sisulu became a teacher for the South African Committee for Higher Education. After the South African government declared that all classes were to be taught in Afrikaans, the spoken language of white South Africans, blacks rioted; Sisulu then taught a class to help blacks pass the examinations required to graduate from high school and to enter college. She also headed a local distance learning college for blacks. She joined the South African Council of Churches in 1998, an anti-apartheid organization that, among other activities, exposed the horrors of local conditions to the outside world. In 1992 Sisulu accepted a post with the Joint Enrichment Project, an organization that concerned itself with the future of young black South Africans. Nelson Mandela's election to the presidency of South Africa gave Sisulu an advantage. Since her husband Walter Sisulu and Mandela had been friends since the 1940s and both husband and wife supported Mandela, in 1997 she was named consul-general in Washington, D.C. Her charge was to secure foreign investment in her country's economy. Her next appointment was as ambassador to the United States, in 1999.

Sources: *Contemporary Black Biography,* vol. 24, pp. 148–51; *Ebony* 54 (October 1999: 190.

Switzerland

2007? • The first black elected to serve on the Swiss parliament was Ricardo Lumengo (1962?–), an attorney. A native of Angola, in 1982 he sought asylum in the country and worked as a dishwasher to support himself through law school. Circulars distributed by his opposition, the Swiss People's Party, had racial and anti-immigration overtones; they showed a black sheet being kicked out of the country by white sheet.

Sources: *Jet* 112 (19 November 2007): 50.

Tanzania

1964 • Julius Nyerere (1922–1999) became the first president of the United Republic of Tanzania. He was re-elected in 1970, 1975, and 1980, and was recognized as one of his country's greatest leaders. He was one of a few African leaders to step down peacefully from office. Nyerere was also the first chancellor of the University of East Africa from 1963 to 1970. Born Kambarage Nyerere in Butiama-Musoma, Lake Victoria, Tanganyika, he was the son of a village chief of the Zanaki tribe. He graduated from Makerere College in Uganda in 1945 and received his master's degree in 1952 from Edinburgh University in Scotland. Nyerere held several teaching positions before becoming president of the University of East Africa. After leaving that post in 1970, he was chancellor of the University of Dar-es-Salaam from 1970 to 1985. He held posts on the Tanganyika Legislative Council and then, in 1961–62, he became prime minister of his country. After his election to the presidency, Nyerere continued to be highly recognized in Tanzania and throughout Africa.

Sources: *Contemporary Black Biography,* vol. 5, pp. 215–19.

Julius Nyerere

United Kingdom

1966 • David Thomas Pitt (1913–1994) was the first black West Indian to run for a seat in the British House of Commons. The Labour Party candidate for north London's well-to-do Hampstead area, he lost that election. In 1966 he became London's first black magistrate. He was elected to the London County Council, representing Hackney, a mixed-race area in London's East End. After serving as deputy chairman in 1969–70, in 1974 he became the first black chairman of the Greater London Council and held that post until 1977. Prime Minister Harold Wilson elevated Pitt to the peerage in 1975, giving him the title Lord Pitt of Hampstead and making him the second black elevated to the peerage. (The first was cricket player Learie Constantine, who received the honor in 1969.) Born in St. David's, Grenada, in the West Indies, Pitt immigrated to Britain in 1947. He graduated with honors from Scotland's Edinburgh University, one of Britain's top medical schools. He was district medical officer in St. Vincent, West Indies, for two years, and then moved to San Fernando in Trinidad. He worked as a physician at San Fernando Hospital from 1939 to 1941, and also established a general practice in the city. Pitt became interested in politics, joining in Trinidad's fight for independence by serving as a council member and as deputy mayor. He was a founding member and later president of the West Indian National Party. Pitt became disillusioned over Trinidad's slow political development and moved to Euston, in north London. He continued his medical practice, treating patients of all races for thirty years. Pitt was elected president of the British Medical Association in 1984, an honor usually given to doctors other than general practitioners. In addition to his activities in medicine and in London's political arena, Pitt was a tireless worker for racial equality. He spoke out for the newly arrived black immigrants in the 1950s and 1960s and became the first and only chairperson of the Campaign Against Racial Discrimination (CARD), an organization that Martin Luther King promoted. He also belonged to national and local committees that were concerned with immigrants and race relations. Despite his many accomplishments, Pitt never achieved his ambition to become a member of the House of Commons.

Sources: *Contemporary Black Biography,* vol. 10, pp. 209–12.

1969 • Learie Constantine [Lord Constantine] (1801–1971) was the first black to become a British peer. He was knighted in 1962, and from 1962 to 1964 he was high commissioner from Trinidad. He was also a member of the West Indies Cricket touring team from 1922 to the 1940s.

Sources: File, *Black Settlers in Britain,* pp. 82–83; *Jet* 68 (8 July 1985): 4.

Diane Abbott

1987 • Diane Julie Abbott (1953–) became the first black woman elected to the British House of Commons, representing Hackney North and Stoke Newington (London). She also founded the Black Women Mean Business Convention. The convention held its third annual meeting in London in 1996 and hosted over 200 black businesswomen leaders from the United Kingdom and the United States. Born in Paddington, London, she is the daughter of a welder and a nurse who immigrated from Jamaica. Abbott was the only black in the Harrow County School for Girls and graduated with top marks. She graduated from Newnham College, Cambridge University, with a bachelor's degree in history. She had been one of the three black women students at the college and the only one with a working-class background. After college, Abbott was a trainee for the Home Office, a ministry with no U.S. equivalent but including a variety of responsibilities. She was a race relations officer for the National Council for Civil Liberties, and in the early 1980s became a researcher for Thames Television. After several positions in public relations, she became councilor of Westminster City Council (1982–86). Abbott had been active with the Labour Party since 1971; this was her first political election. She represented the ward of her birth and then set her sights on parliament. Although Abbott lost the opportunity to serve as her party's candidate in 1985, which almost certainly guaranteed her a seat in parliament, she was her party's candidate in the next election. She became known in parliament for her frank opinions, controversial views, and strong language.

Sources: *Contemporary Black Biography,* vol. 9, pp. 1–3; *Jet* 89 (15 April 1996): 16–17; "Black in Britain: Diane Julie Abbott," http://www.blackinbritain.com/DianeJulieAbbott .htm, accessed September 23, 2012.

1996 • The first black to take a seat in the British House of Lords was John Taylor (1952–). When he became a baron (life peer), he became Baron Taylor of Warwick, County Warwickshire and was one of the youngest members in the House of Lords and its only black member. Taylor, who refers to himself as Afro-Saxon, had a long been active in Conservative Party politics. He was born in Birmingham to Jamaican immigrants; his father was a professional cricket player and his mother a nurse. Taylor received his bachelor's degree from the University of Keele. He began law practice in 1978, and from 1978 to 1990 he was exclusively a barrister (attorney) who practiced in the upper courts. In 1990–91 he was appointed special advisor to Home Secretary and Home Office Ministers. In 1991–92 he was consultant for Lowe Belle Communications. Beginning 1994, Taylor has been producer and presenter for the British Broadcasting Corporation (BBC). As barrister, he appears on BBC radio and television, thereby helping to keep public consciousness focused on specific issues of importance. Taylor also became involved in charity work for minority youth.

Sources: *Contemporary Black Biography,* vol. 16, pp. 206–8; *Ebony* 52 (May 1997): 96–100.

1998 • Prince Charles named Colleen Harris deputy press secretary, making her the first black member of the British royal household staff.

Sources: *Jet* 93 (23 March 1998): 10.

2002 • Paul Boateng (1952?–) was named chief secretary to the Treasurer and became the first black Cabinet minister in Great Britain. Prime Minister Tony Blair shuffled his government after the transport minister resigned and named Boateng to the second highest post in the Treasury, below Gordon Brown, Chancellor of the Exchequer. Boateng was born in London to a Ghanaian father and a Scottish mother. He was trained as a lawyer and in 1987 he was elected to Parliament. Earlier he was a political activist and agitated for a section in the Labor Party to address the needs of minorities.

Sources: *New York Times* (30 May 2002).

2003 • In May, Baroness Valerie Amos (1954–) was appointed Secretary of State for International Development and became the first black woman in the British Cabinet. She was also appointed head of the House of Lords on October 6, becoming the first black woman to hold this post. She remained in her post until 2007. The House of Lords is the highest chamber in the British parliament. Amos was born in Guyana and educated in the United Kingdom at the Universities of Warwick, Birmingham, and East Anglia. Before joining the Cabinet, she was the government's international development representative for the House of Lords and as well as Foreign Office Minister for Africa. She was rewarded for her political service to the Labor Party in August 1997, when she became a life peer or baroness

Sources: *Contemporary Black Biography,* vol. 41, pp. 8–10; *Jet* 114 (13 October 2008): 26.

2007? • The first black and the first woman attorney general in Great Britain was Baroness Patricia Scotland, whom Prime Minister Gordon Brown appointed early in his tenure. With this appointment, the Dominican-born Scotland became the second black woman to serve as a member of the Cabinet. She also served under Tony Blair's government as parliamentary secretary under office. She was also parliamentary secretary at the Lord Chancellor's Department and as Home Office Minister of the State for the Criminal Justice System and Law Reform, all under Blair's leadership.

Sources: *Jet* 112 (23 July 2007): 13.

Patricia Scotland

United Nations

1964 • The first black and the first diplomat from a black African nation to preside over the General Assembly of the United Nations was Ghana's Alex Quaison-Sackey (1924?–1992). He served as president from December of this year through September 1, 1965. He had served as diplomatic trouble-shooter for Kwame Nkrumah (1909–1972), the first president of Ghana after its independence in 1957. From 1957 to 1959 Quaison-Sackey was First Secretary at the Ghana High Commission. He was ambassador to the United States from 1978 to 1980. Born into a politically active family in the coastal town of Winneba, he studied at Achimota College and graduated in 1948. In 1952 he received an honors degree from Oxford University.

Sources: *Jet* 85 (6 December 1993): 59; *New York Times* (31 December 1992).

1969 • Angie Elizabeth Brooks (1928–2007), a Liberian woman, was elected president of the twenty-fourth United Nations General Assembly in September, becoming the first black, the first African woman, and the third African to serve in that post. The only other woman elected to the presidency up to that time was India's Madame Vijaya Lakshmi Pandit, who served in 1953. Brooks held a number of posts at the United Nations since 1954, including vice chairperson of the assembly's Fourth Committee (for trust and non-self-governing territories) in 1956, vice president of the committee on information from non-self-governing territories in 1961, chair of the Fourth Committee in the 1961 session, and vice president of the Trusteeship Council in 1966. She was the first woman and the first African to serve as president of the Trusteeship Council, which is the United Nations' watchdog over its trust territories. Although the presidency of the General Assembly was slated to go to Africa in 1969, Brooks still found it necessary to campaign for the post, for her elevation to the presidency was uncertain. She won the election on September 16, 1969.

Sources: *Current Biography,* 1970, pp. 48–50; *Crisis* 76 (November 1969): 372, 381; *Ebony* 17 (December 1961): 122–28.

1976 • The United Nations Day of Solidarity with South Africa was first declared on October 11 by U.N. membership. United Nations General Assembly Resolution 31/6C issued a proclamation on November 9, 1976, calling for the immediate and unconditional release for all South African prisoners who had been jailed for their struggle for liberation. Those held in prison in South Africa joined in the observance.

Sources: *Jet* 94 (12 October 1998): 19.

1996 • The first black African to become secretary general of the United Nations was Kofi Atta Annan (1938–). Annan grew up in the Gold Coast (now Ghana). He received his

Kofi Annan

bachelor's degree from Macalester College in St. Paul, Minnesota, in 1961 and his master's degree in management from Massachusetts Institute of Technology. He was a Sloan Fellow while at M.I.T. Annan became an activist early on and took an interest in public service before he studied at Macalester. After graduating, he became administrative and budget officer for the World Health Organization in 1962. He returned to Ghana for two years and became managing director of the Ghana Tourism Control Board. Annan held various positions with the United Nations, including deputy chief of staff services (1976–80), deputy director of administration and head of personnel for the United Nations High Commissioner for Civil Rights (1980–83), director of budget in the Office of Finance (1984–87), and undersecretary for peacekeeping (1993–96). In the last position, he had authority over 80,000 troops and sent them to the appropriate sites to maintain order when needed. Annan became the natural choice to fill the secretary general's post when United Nations Secretary-General Boutros-Ghali left office.

Sources: *Contemporary Black Biography*, vol. 15, pp. 9–13.

Zaire (Congo)

1994 • Iyombe Botumbe Akerele became the first black woman to seek the presidency of an African country. She worked to overthrow Marshal Mobutu of Zaire in the December election. Akerele founded and became president of the grassroots Congress Lokole party. She also founded the Friends of Zaire Association, an organization that develops programs in health, education, and economics. Well-educated and a feminist, Akerele is a member of one of her country's royal families and the mother of three children. She was a political aide to one of Zaire's former prime ministers and cabinet secretary.

Sources: *Jet* 85 (11 April 1994): 5.

Zambia

1964 • Kenneth David Kaunda (1924–) was elected the first president of Zambia on October 24. He held that post until 1991, when he was ousted from office following multi-party elections. In 1960 Kaunda founded the United National Independence Party and worked to bring independence to his country in 1964. He was a member of the African National Congress, and then joined the Zambia African National Congress. He was born in Nyasaland (now Malawi), the son of an African missionary teacher. Kaunda graduated from college, and became a teacher.

Sources: *Contemporary Black Biography*, vol. 2, pp. 129–32.

Kenneth Kaunda

Zimbabwe

1947 • Joshua [Mqabuko Nyongolo] Nkomo (1917–1999) became a social worker for the Rhodesian Railways, the first black to hold this important job on the nation's railroads. He was born in the Matopo district of Southern Rhodesia (now Zimbabwe), the son of a cattle farmer. He studied at Jan Hofmeyer School of Social Work in Johannesburg and received his bachelor's degree from the University of South Africa. On returning to his native land in 1947, he took his position at the Rhodesian Railways. Concern for the inequities that his people faced led Nkomo to become politically active. His political activities began after he became general-secretary of the Rhodesian Railways African Employees' Association. He made the organization into a power, establishing twenty-two branches and recruiting more than 2,500 members. Then considered a political moderate, he was invited to represent black opinion at a planning session for three British colonies held in London in 1952. Still a moderate, Nkomo rejected all proposals that left control of Rhodesia in white hands. He was elected president of the African National Congress (ANC), a national political group that worked to end white minority rule, and held that office until 1958 when the ANC was banned. Nkomo continued his political activities and in 1980–81 and again in 1990 he was one of two vice presidents of Zimbabwe. For his efforts to assure black majority rule, Nkomo has been called affectionately the "father of Zimbabwean nationalism," "Father Zimbabwe," and "The Old Lion."

Sources: *Contemporary Black Biography,* vol. 4, pp. 180–83.

1979 • Black people in Rhodesia voted in national elections for the first time in April. Abel Tendekayi Muzorewa (1925–2010), a candidate on the sole black party on the ballot, was elected prime minister—the first black to head the country. He succeeded Prime Minister Ian Smith as head of the Republic of Zimbabwe Rhodesia. Muzorewa held his seat briefly and during a period of intense turmoil, civil war, and transition from white to black leadership. For concessions from the international community to take place, and for economic sanctions against Rhodesia to be removed, he resigned his office in December 1979. A candidate from the United African National Council (UANC), he won a seat in the House of Assembly. Zimbabwe became an independent, major, or black-ruled nation in April 1980.

Sources: *Contemporary Black Biography,* vol. 85, pp. 124–27; *New York Times* (9 April, 2010).

Government: Local

Alabama

1964 Tuskegee • Kenneth L. Buford (1917–) and Stanley Hugh Smith were the first blacks elected with white opponents in the state of Alabama in this century, when they won election to the city council. Buford was a minister; and Smith a professor at Tuskegee Institute.

Sources: *Jet* 59 (18 September 1980): 18; *Who's Who among Black Americans, 1992–93,* p. 193 (Buford).

1968 Birmingham • Arthur D[avis] Shores (1904–1996), prominent in the civil rights struggle in Alabama in the 1950s and 1960s, became the first black member of the Birmingham City Council. In December 1968 he was appointed to replace a white councilman who had died, and later he was elected to the post. He retired from the council in 1977. Shores was also one of Alabama's first black lawyers and, after two black attorneys died, for a time the state's only practicing black lawyer. In the 1950s he worked for Autherine Lucy in her effort to desegregate the University of Alabama, and he was involved in the lawsuit that led to the admission of Vivian Malone and James Hood to the university in 1963. During his civil rights activities, Shores' home was bombed on August 15, 1963, presumably because he built in a section that whites had occupied. A second bombing occurred on September 4 that year and was followed by rioting. Other efforts to bomb his home were unsuccessful. Shores practiced for over fifty years, working mainly on probate cases in later years. He was born in Bessemer, Alabama, and grew up in an area later known as Wenonah. He walked ten miles round trip to attend the county's only black high school, Industrial High School (later Parker High). He graduated from Talladega College in Alabama (B.S., 1927) and from Chicago's LaSalle Extension University, where he received his law degree in 1935. After a long illness, Shores died at home in Birmingham on December 15, 1996.

Sources: Bailey, *They Too Call Alabama Home,* pp. 345–50; *New York* Times (18 December 1996).

1972 Prichard • Algernon J. Cooper (1944–) was the first black to defeat a white incumbent in a sizable Alabama city since Reconstruction, when he won the race for mayor in September, 1972. A 1969 graduate of the New York University School of Law, Cooper had returned to Mobile, Alabama, his native city, as an NAACP Legal Defense Fund lawyer.

Sources: *Ebony* (December 1972): 163–68; *Ebony Success Library,* vol. 2, pp. 52–55; *Negro Almanac,* 1976, p. 73.

1976 Montgomery • John L. Baker (1946–) became the first black head of a department in municipal government. He became city clerk in January, with the responsibility of maintaining official city records, compiling and maintaining council minutes, and handling other city-related business activities of the council. He was also manager for municipal elections.

Sources: Bailey, *They Too Call Alabama Home*, pp. 26–28.

1979 Birmingham • Richard Arrington Jr. (1934–), became this city's first black mayor. He was elected to the Birmingham City Council in 1971 and served two terms— until 1979—when he decided to run for the city's highest position, that of mayor. He was re-elected four times but resigned in 1999 before his fifth term ended. He wanted his hand-picked successor, William Bell, to run as incumbent in the next elections. While in office, Arrington made a noticeable difference in this Southern industrial city that had been known earlier for its deep racial divide. He had regional and national influence as well. Despite his accomplishments, law enforcement agencies kept him under close scrutiny, and he was accused of corruption—actions that he called racial targeting. Arrington was born into a sharecropper family in Livingston, Alabama. He graduated from Miles College in 1955 and received his master's degree from the University of Detroit. In 1966 he received his doctorate from the University of Oklahoma. Arrington returned to Miles where he was a teacher, later a counselor, and then academic dean. He left in 1970 to become executive director of the Alabama Center for Higher Education. Later, he became a visiting professor in the Center for Urban Affairs at the University of Birmingham.

Sources: Bailey, *They Too Call Alabama Home*, pp. 20–23; *Contemporary Black Biography*, vol. 24, pp. 7–9; *Who's Who among Black Americans*, 26th ed, p. 42.

1980 Birmingham • James Baker became the first black city attorney.

Sources: Bailey, *They Too Call Alabama Home*, p. 8.

1984 Union Springs • John McGowan was the first black mayor of Union Springs. The same election day also saw Nathanial Torian, of Hillsboro, and Mary Stoval, of Hurtsboro, as the first black mayors of their towns.

Sources: *Jet* 66 (20 August 1984): 34.

1986 Birmingham • Johnny Johnson was the first black lieutenant in the Birmingham Police Department.

Sources: *Jet* 70 (5 May 1986): 20.

1997 Decatur • The first black police chief of Decatur was Joel Gilliam, a retired commander of the Detroit Police Department. Earlier he was public services supervisor at the Von Braun Civic Center in Alabama.

Sources: *Jet* 91 (17 March 1997: 19.

1997 Gadsen • Jack Lowe Jr. was promoted to chief of the Etowah County Sheriff's Department in Gadsden, becoming the highest-ranking black in the county and the first black chief. He also became the first black to run for sheriff in Etowah County.

Sources: *Jet* 91 (17 February 1997): 19.

1997 Selma • Assistant chief Earnest L. Tate (1938?–), who had served the department for thirty years and was the third black to join the force, became the first black chief of police in November. Mayor Joseph T. Smitherman appointed him to succeed Randy Lewellen, who was fired during a corruption investigation.

Sources: *Jet* 93 (22 December 1997): 22.

1998 Pritchard • The first black woman police chief in Pritchard and one of three women police chiefs in the state was Gwendolyn Boyd. She was a member of the police force in Miami for twenty-four years. After moving to Pritchard, she became a major, then moved up in command.

Sources: *Jet* 93 (12 January 1998): 39.

1999 Decatur • Lorenzo "Sonny" Jackson Jr. was promoted to lieutenant with the Decatur Fire and Rescue Services, becoming the first black to receive that rank. He previously served two years as a driver for the services.

Sources: *Jet* 96 (21 June 1999): 30.

2000 Birmingham • A twenty-year veteran with the Birmingham Police Department, Annetta W. Nunn became the first black woman deputy chief and the second woman to hold that title. She commanded the patrol division. Before her promotion, she was a captain with the department's training academy.

Sources: *Jet* 97 (15 May 2000): 22.

2001 Birmingham • Anthony L. Barnes was appointed chairman of the Birmingham Water Works and Sewer Board, making him the first black to hold that post. The Birmingham system is one of the largest water systems in the nation, serving nearly one million people who live in a five-county service area. Previously, Barnes was real estate commissioner for Alabama.

Sources: *Jet* 100 (10 December 2001): 20.

Arizona

1965 Phoenix • Hayzel Burton Daniels (1907–1992) was the first black judge in Arizona when he was appointed one of the ten city magistrates. Daniels' entire education was at the University of Arizona (B.A. 1939, J.D. 1948). He served in the U.S. Air Force, in the Far East, between 1943 and 1945.

Sources: *Ebony Success Library*, vol. 1, p. 85.

Arkansas

1873 Little Rock • Mifflin Wistar Gibbs (1823–1915) was the first black elected municipal court judge. However, earlier, on November 26, 1872, Macon B. Allen (1816–1894) was chosen as a judge of the inferior court of Charleston, South Carolina, by the state General Assembly. Gibbs was also an owner and the editor of the first black newspaper in California, *Mirror of the Times*, in 1855. In 1866 Gibbs was elected to the city council of Victoria, British Columbia. Gibbs began to complete his law studies at Oberlin (Ohio) in 1869, and after his service as municipal judge, he held several offices in the federal government, including that of United States consul in Madagascar. In 1902 he published a biography, *Shadow and Light*.

Mifflin Gibbs

Sources: Bennett, *Before the Mayflower*, p. 639; Logan and Winston, *Dictionary of American Negro Biography*, pp. 258–59; *Negro Almanac*, p. 1425; *Encyclopedia of Black America*, p. 403; Katz, *The Black West*, pp. 139–42; Smith, *Notable Black American Men*, pp. 450–52.

1986 Little Rock • Lottie H. Shackelford (1941–) was the first woman mayor of Little Rock. Shackelford had served for eight years on the city's board of directors.

Sources: *Jet* 71 (9 February 1987): 57; *Who's Who among African Americans*, 14th ed., pp. 1159.

1994 Jonesboro • Grover Evans became the first black chair of the Spinal Cord Commission for the state. Previously, he was the first black elected to the city council.

Sources: *Jet* 86 (5 September 1994): 20.

Selma's First Black Mayor

In 2000 businessman James Perkins (1953?–) defeated the seventy-year-old white incumbent Joe Smitherman to become the first black mayor elected in Selma. Smitherman was mayor during the violence in Selma in March 1965, on what was called the Bloody Sunday march across the Edmund Pettus Bridge. The eruption caused national spotlight on Selma and led lawmakers to pass the Voting Rights Act of 1965. Perkins, a Selma native, graduated from Alabama Agricultural and Mechanical University in Huntsville and studied further at Auburn University.

Sources: *Jet* 99 (2 October 2000): 4–8; 98 (23 October 2000): 32–33.

California

1781 Los Angeles • Los Angeles is the first major city founded with a majority black population. Of the eleven founding families, more than half the adults were black, two were white, and the rest Native Americans.

Sources: Davis, *The History of Black Catholics in the United States,* pp. 33–34.

1953 Bakersfield • Henry Holton Collins was the first black elected to a city council in California, when he won his election in Bakersfield, California. Collins was pastor of Saint Paul Christian Methodist Episcopal Church. He easily won re-election in 1957.

Sources: *Jet* (16 April 1970): 11; *Sepia* 8 (May 1960): 23.

1961 Los Angeles • Vaino Hassen Spencer (1920–) was the first black municipal court judge in California. She served on the Los Angeles Municipal Court. She was also the first black president of the National Association of Women Judges. Spencer was born in Los Angeles and graduated from Los Angeles City College with a bachelor's degree. She had an active real estate business for a while, and then completed her law degree at Southwestern School of Law in Los Angeles in 1952. Spencer practiced law from 1952 to 1961, while also serving on various appointive commissions and boards. She became active in politics, particularly in 1958 when she supported Edmund G. "Pat" Brown for governor. Once elected to office, Brown appointed Spencer to the California Law Revision Committee in 1960. In 1961 he named her to the newly created position of municipal court judge for the Los Angeles Judicial District. She then ran for re-election in 1964.

Sources: Clayton, *The Negro Politician,* p. 125; *Ebony* 20 (August 1966): 97; *Jet* 77 (4 December 1989): 6; *Sepia* (January 1963): 52–55; Smith, *Notable Black American Women, Book II,* pp. 612–14.

1961 Los Angeles • Henri O'Bryant became the first black fire commissioner in the United States. Mayor Sam Yorty appointed him to the five-member board on July 1. He later became president of the commission, the first black to achieve this title.

Sources: *Sepia* 12 (November 1963): 41.

1963 Los Angeles • Thomas Bradley (1917–1998) was the first black elected official in the city upon his election to the Los Angeles city council. Between 1940 and 1961 he was a member of the police department, becoming the first black to hold the rank of lieutenant. Bradley studied law at night, and was admitted to the bar in 1956.

Sources: *Contemporary Black Biography,* vol. 2, pp. 33–36; *Encyclopedia of Black America,* p. 189; *Negro Almanac,* p. 478; Smith, *Notable Black American Men,* pp. 104–8; *Who's Who among Black Americans, 1992–93,* p. 144.

1963 Los Angeles • Leslie Shaw (1923?–) became the first black postmaster in Los Angeles on April 15 and headed a staff of 10,488 employees. He was also the first black appointed postmaster in a major city in the United States. He finished among the top three candidates who took the Civil Service examination. The Columbus, Ohio, native moved to Los Angeles in 1949 and took a job with the Watts Savings and Loan Association. He moved up in rank from janitor to vice president, and director. Shaw left that position to become postmaster.

Sources: *Sepia* 12 (June 1963): 11–15.

1971 Berkeley • Warren Hamilton Widener (1938–) was the first black elected mayor of Berkeley, in a very close election in April 1971. Widener was perceived to be part of the radical coalition that was trying to take control of the city. He held the office until 1979. A native of Oroville, California, he was educated at the University of California, Berkeley (A.B., 1960) and Boalt Hall, the University of California (J.S.D., 1967). Widener was an attorney for Safeway Stores from 1968 to 1970. From 1969 to 1971 he was a member of the Berkeley City Council. He was an attorney for the Housing and Economic Development Law Project at the University of California, Berkeley, from 1970 to 1972, and then was elected mayor in 1971. He later became president of the Urban Housing Institute. Widener entered politics again, serving as Alameda County Supervisor from 1982 to 1992.

Sources: *Ebony* 26 (October 1971): 74–82; Hornsby, *Chronology of African-American History,* p. 168; *Who's Who among African Americans,* 14th ed., p. 1385.

1973 Compton • The first black woman to govern a metropolitan city as mayor was Doris Ann Davis, who was elected to office on June 5. She was one of several black woman mayors in the United States around this time. In 1972 Ellen Walker Craig-Jones (1906–2000) became mayor of the municipality of Urbancrest, Ohio, and in 1973 Lelia Smith Foley (1942–), became mayor of the small town of Taft, Oklahoma, both with less than 800 people. The city council of Sophia Mitchell's village of Rendville, Ohio, with less than one hundred people, appointed her mayor.

Sources: *Jet* 99 (11 June 2001): 19; *Who's Who among African Americans,* 26th ed., p. 313; Cummings, "Black Women in Public Life," *Black Enterprise* 5 (August 1974): 33–35.

1974 San Francisco • Curtis Emile Green (1923–2002) was the first African American to head a major transit system, San Francisco's Municipal Railway, or Muni. A native of Franklin, Louisiana, in 1942–45 Green was a platoon sergeant in the U.S. Marine Corps. He joined Muni in 1945 as a ninety-cent-an-hour bus driver. Between 1969 and 1973, he held several higher posts, including chief of inspections, and director of Operations and Administrations. When he reached the top position, becoming a pioneer in American public transit, he directed his drivers to distribute thousands of little buttons that red "Muni Loves You." Sometime during his Muni career, he received a B.S. degree from San Francisco State. After a thirty-seven-career with Muni, Green retired in 1982. In 1987, the railway's principal rail base, where cars are housed and repaired, was named the Curtis E. Green Light Rail Center, in his honor.

Sources: "Curtis E. Green—Rose from Bus Driver to Head of S.F. Muni," http://www.sfgate.com/bayarea/article/Curtis-E-Green-rose-from-bus-driver-to-head-2816575.php; *Who's Who among African Americans,* 10th ed., 1997, p. 582.

1977 Berkeley • Odell Howard Sylvester Jr. (1924–) was the first black police chief in the city. Sylvester began as a patrolman in the department in 1947, and moved up in rank. He retired in 1981. Born in Dallas, Texas, he graduated from the University of California (B.D., 1948) and the University of Southern California (M.P. A., 1974). He also did postgraduate work at Harvard University.

Sources: *Jet* 53 (6 October 1977) 4; *Who's Who among African Americans,* 26th ed., pp. 1198–99.

1977 Oakland • Lionel J. Wilson (1915–1998) was the first black mayor of Oakland, California. He served three terms during a period of racial, cultural, economic, and polit-

First Black Mayor of Los Angeles

In 1973 Thomas Bradley (1917–1998) became the first black mayor of Los Angeles, at a time when only fifteen percent of the voters were black. Bradley first ran for mayor in 1969 against incumbent Sam Yorty. The election was beset by bitter racial overtones, coming on the heels of the riots in the city's Watts section. He lost in a run-off election. Bradley won handily in 1973, having garnered the support of civil rights liberals and young anti-war protesters. Among the accomplishments seen during his leadership, a rapid transit system was developed, the 1984 Summer Olympics came to the city, there was an increase in international businesses, and the downtown area was revitalized. The infamous Rodney King case involving alleged police brutality brought national spotlight to the city and to Bradley's authority. In 1982 and again in 1986 Bradley ran for governor of California, but in both races he was narrowly defeated. He was the first black candidate to receive statewide support of the Democratic party, which was composed primarily of whites. He announced his retirement as mayor in 1992. Bradley was born in Calvert, Texas, and moved to Los Angeles with his family when he was seven years old. He studied at the University of California at Los Angeles where he was a track star, but left school to join the Los Angeles Police Department. He enrolled in law school, graduating in 1956 from Southwestern. He left the force in 1961 and established a law practice.

Sources: *Encyclopedia of Black America*, p. 189; *Contemporary Black Biography*, vol. 2, pp. 33–36; *Jet* 82 (12 October 1992): 4–5; *Negro Almanac*, p. 478; *Who's Who among Black Americans, 1992–93*, p. 144; Smith, *Notable Black American Men*, pp. 104–8.

---

ical unrest, but suffered a defeat in 1990 when he ran for a fourth term. In 1960, Wilson had also been the first black judge in Alameda County. He had a distinguished career as a Superior Court judge before he stepped aside to run for mayor. A native of New Orleans, Wilson graduated from the University of California, Berkeley, and Hastings College of Law. He practiced law until becoming a Superior Court Judge. Wilson died at home on January 23, 1998.

Sources: *Black Enterprise* 8 (August 1977): 37; *Negro Almanac*, p. 433; *New York Times* (31 January 1998); *Who's Who among Black Americans, 1992–93*, p. 1549.

1978 Los Angeles • Yvonne Braithwaite Burke (1932–) was the first black member of the Los Angeles County Board of Supervisors.

Sources: *Jet* 56 (5 July 1979): 9; Smith, *Notable Black American Women*, pp. 130–32.

1982 Pasadena • On May 6, 1982, Loretta Thompson Glickman became the first woman mayor of a city of more than 100,000. She was elected by the city's board of directors.

Sources: Hornsby, *Chronology of African–American History*, p. 311; *Jet* 62 (24 May 1982): 13; 63 (31 January 1983): 38.

1986 Los Angeles • Paul A. Orduna was the first black assistant chief in the Los Angeles City Fire Department. Orduna joined the department in 1957.

Sources: *Jet* 70 (5 May 1986): 20.

1986 Los Angeles • Maxine F. Thomas (1947–) was the first black woman presiding judge in the Los Angeles Municipal Court. She had been a member of the court since 1980.

Sources: *Jet* 70 (14 July 1986): 14; *Who's Who among Black Americans, 1992–93*, p. 1385.

1986 Oakland • Jayne Williams (1948?–) was the first black woman city attorney in the state of California when she was appointed to the post in Oakland. Williams was thirty–

eight years old at the time, and held a law degree from the University of California Hastings College of Law.

Sources: *Jet* 72 (15 June 1987): 36.

1988 Los Angeles • Jesse A. Brewer was the first black assistant chief in the Los Angeles Police Department. In 1981 Brewer had also been the first black deputy chief.

Sources: *Jet* 73 (11 January 1988): 30.

1990 Carson City • Juanita Millender-McDonald (1938–) was elected to the city council, becoming the first black woman to sit on the council. She was appointed mayor *pro tempore* during her second year in office. She was born in Birmingham, Alabama, and relocated to Los Angeles with her father and siblings after her mother died. She received her bachelor's degree from the University of Redlands and her master's degree from California State University in Los Angeles. After teaching for a while, Millender-McDonald became a writer for the Los Angeles Unified School District, where she edited a textbook called *Images*; it was designed for young women and girls. In 1984 she took her daughter to the Democratic National Convention as a delegate; they were the first mother–daughter team to serve as delegates to a political party's national convention. Millender-McDonald was director of gender equity programs for the Los Angeles School District for a while. Already interested in politics, in 1990 she was elected to the Carson City Council. Two years later she was elected to the California state legislature representing the 55th Assembly District, the first woman to represent that district. In 1996 she was elected to the U.S. House of Representatives, filling the unexpired term of a former representative who resigned from office. She won the seat in the full election seven months later, defeating her Republican challenger with 85 percent of the vote.

Sources: *Contemporary Black Biography*, vol. 21, pp. 102–4.

1991 Los Angeles • Rita Walters was the first black woman to serve on the Los Angeles City Council.

Sources: *Jet* 80 (8 July 1991): 23.

1992 Los Angeles • Willie Lawrence Williams (1943–) was the first black to head the police force in Los Angeles. He took the post in the midst of the allegations of police department brutality against blacks. Brutality charges emerged during the nationally-televised account of attacks on Rodney G. King, who was accused of resisting arrest. The incident and accusations of racism discredited the existing chief of police, Darryl F. Gates, and a created need to replace him. Williams was known for his success in leading a big-city police force and in improving community relations. He left his post as police commissioner in Philadelphia to accept the new position. Born in Philadelphia, Williams graduated from Philadelphia College of Textiles and Science, studied for a graduate degree at St. Joseph's University, and attended Harvard University.

Sources: *Contemporary Black Biography*, vol. 4, pp. 278–81.

1994 San Jose • Kathy Cole (1947?–) became the first council member to be voted out of office for racial remarks and gestures that Latinos, Asians, and gays considered offensive. She made the remarks at an African American leadership conference in May. Cole represented the Evergreen District whose residents were one-third Asian American and one-quarter Hispanic.

Sources: *Jet* 86 (16 May 1994): 15.

1995 Los Angeles • Helena Ashby was appointed chief of detectives for the Los Angeles Sheriff's Department, becoming the highest-ranking woman and the first woman to hold the position. The department was the nation's third largest police agency. When she became a rookie deputy assigned to the Sybil Brand Women's Institute in East Los Angeles thirty years earlier, this was the only entry point for women deputies. Ashby graduated from the University of Southern California intent on entering the Foreign Service. She later received a master's degree in public administration from Harvard University's Kennedy

School of Government. She completed a three-month training program at the Federal Bureau of Investigation's National Academy in Quantico, Virginia.

Sources: *Modern Maturity* 38 (September–October 1995): 12.

1995 San Francisco • Doris M. Ward was sworn in as assessor of the city and county, becoming the first black elected to that post in California. Previously, Ward was president of the San Francisco Board of Supervisors.

Sources: *Jet* 87 (6 February 1995): 25.

1996 San Francisco • Former speaker of the California Assembly Willie L. Brown Jr. (1934–) was elected mayor of San Francisco, winning in a landslide victory in a runoff election on December 12, 1995. He was sworn into office on January 8, 1996. Brown was born in Mineola, Texas, a railroad town about eighty miles east of Dallas. He worked his way through school and graduated from San Francisco State College in 1955. In 1958 he received his law degree from Hastings College of Law and the University of California. Brown became known as a capable defender in legal cases. His reputation helped him to succeed in the political arena, which he entered in the mid-1960s. By then he was also a civil rights advocate. On June 2, 1964, Brown was elected to the California State Assembly representing San Francisco, the first black to hold that post. He also became the first black speaker of the house and the longest-serving speaker in California, serving from 1980 to 1995. Brown stepped down from office on June 5, 1995, to run for mayor of San Francisco.

Sources: *Jet* 89 (29 January 1996): 34–36; Smith, *Notable Black American Men,* pp. 141–43.

1997 Garden City • Steve Bradford (1960?–) became the first new councilman in fifteen years and the first black elected to the post. The thirty-seven-year-old councilman is also the youngest to hold that position. Bradford was district director for Juanita Millender-McDonald, congresswoman from Carson.

Sources: *Jet* 91 (7 April 1997): 19.

1997 Los Angeles • The first black elected president of the West Basin Municipal Water District in Los Angeles was R. Keith McDonald, son of California Congresswoman Juanita Millender-McDonald.

Sources: *Jet* 92 (13 October 1997): 38.

1998 Long Beach • Wilma D. Powell became the first woman president of the Marine Exchange of Los Angeles–Long Beach Harbor. The exchange is a mutual benefit trade organization that documents the tonnage of ship movement through the two harbors. Powell is chief wharfinger of the Port of Long Beach.

Sources: *Jet* 93 (4 May 1998): 17.

1999 San Diego • The first black woman to chair the Port of San Diego Board was Patricia A. McQuater. A self-supporting public benefit company, the Port of San Diego monitors the protection and development of public tidelands around the San Diego Bay.

Sources: *Jet* 95 (1 March 1999): 32.

2000 Los Angeles • A thirteen-year veteran of the Los Angeles County Fire Department, Veronica Steele-Small became the first black woman in the department to be promoted to captain. She was a part of the Emergency Operations Center team that handles disasters. Steele-Small had served as a paramedic and a primary Emergency Medical Technician teacher for the recruitment classes.

Sources: *Jet* 99 (4 June 2001): 36.

2000 San Francisco • Karen V. Clopton became chief of operations for the Port of San Francisco, the first black woman to hold the position. She was the first black woman president of the San Francisco Civil Service Commission. Among her responsibilities, she directs daily business operations and supervises the Operations Division, including human resources, legislative affairs, and workers' compensation.

Sources: *Jet* 98 (27 November 2000): 40.

2001 Los Angeles • The first black woman to become captain with the Los Angeles Police Department was Ann E. Young, a nineteen-year veteran with the department. The commanding officer of the Van Nuys Operations Support Division has held several ranks within the LAPD, including lieutenant, sergeant, and detective. She graduated from the FBI National Academy for Law Enforcement.

Sources: *Jet* 99 (28 May 2001): 24.

2001 Los Angeles • Valerie L. Shaw was elected president of the Los Angeles Board of Public Works, the city's only full-time policy-making commission. Shaw was the first black woman to hold that post. She is jointly employed as general manager for the Public Works Department.

Sources: *Jet* 100 (10 December 2001): 20.

2007 Inglewood • Jacqueline Seabrooks (1981?–), a veteran in law enforcement, and former captain of the Santa Monica Police Department, became this city's first women chief of police. The police force consisted of 300 members.

Sources: *Jet* 112 (1 October 2007): 22.

2008 Sacramento • Retired NBA star Kevin Johnson (1966?–) defeated a two-term incumbent and became the first black elected major of Sacramento. He ran on the theme of "change" and "No more business as usual." While campaigning, Johnson called on Magic Johnson, Charles Barkley, and Shaquille O'Neal, fellow NBA greats, for support. He also had the support of billionnaire entrepreneur Warren Buffet. He graduated from the University of California at Berkeley. After twelve seasons with the Phoenix Suns, he retired from the NBA in May 2000.

Sources: *Contemporary Black Biography,* vol 70, pp. 87–89; *Jet* 114 (8 December 2008): 10.

Colorado

1983 Denver • Norman S. Early Jr. was the first black district attorney in Denver. A native of Washington, D.C., Early took his law degree at the Illinois University College of Law, and was thirty-seven at the time of his appointment.

Sources: *Jet* 63 (28 February 1983): 15.

Kevin Johnson

1995 Denver • Lieutenant Armedia Gordon became the first black division chief of special operations for the Denver Police Department. Previously, she was supervisor of the homicide unit.

Sources: *Jet* 89 (20 November 1995): 20.

Connecticut

1978 New London • Leo Edwin Jackson (1925–2009) was the first black mayor of the city. He was elected by the City Council. This also made him the first black mayor in New England. In 1975 Jackson had become the first black elected to the council. The Springfield, Massachusetts, native attended Tuskegee Institute (now University) in Alabama (1944–45) and Mitchell College in New London, Connecticut (1970–72).

Sources: *Jet* 57 (27 December 1979): 5; *Who's Who among African Americans,* 14th ed., p. 659.

1981 Hartford • Thirman L. Milner (1933–) was the first popularly elected black mayor in any of the six New England states. The Hartford-born Milner held the position until

Denver's First Black Mayor

In 1991 Wellington Edward Webb (1941–) became the first black mayor of Denver. He took office on June 30 that year. Active in both local and national politics, Webb was a state representative from 1973 to 1977, and was auditor of the city at the time of his election. Born in Chicago, he moved to Denver to live with his grandmother and to seek relief for a severe asthmatic condition. Webb graduated from Colorado State College and the University of Northern Colorado. He worked in social service and also taught emotionally disturbed children. He entered politics in 1972 when he ran successfully for state representative from northeast Denver. Webb remained in the legislature until 1977. In 1976 he headed the state's campaign to elect Jimmy Carter president. After his election, Carter named Webb regional director of the Department of Health, Education, and Welfare. After Carter's administration left office, Colorado governor Richard Lamm appointed Webb executive director of the state Department of Regulatory Agencies, the only black in the state cabinet. In his position he oversaw the Civil Rights Commission, the Public Utilities Commission, and the Division of Banking. He lost his first bid to become Denver's mayor in 1983 and in 1987 he became Denver's city auditor. In the 1980s Webb and his wife Wilma, who was a state representative, became known as "the political couple." She helped to pass one of her husband's proposals to make Martin Luther King Jr.'s birthday a state holiday. In a runoff election with another black candidate, Norm Early, in 1991 Webb won Denver's mayoral election with 58 percent of the vote. Among his accomplishments while in office were the erection of a new international airport, a new convention center, and the renovation of the main library.

Sources: Salzman, *Encyclopedia of African-American Culture and History,* Supplement, p. 277; *Contemporary Black Biography,* vol. 3, pp. 251–54.

1987. At the time of his election, he had served two terms in the state legislature. He returned to the senate in 1993 and was assistant minority leader. After leaving office, Milner became director of government affairs for First National Supermarkets, Inc.

Sources: *Jet* 61 (26 November 1981): 9; 69 (13 January 1986): 7; *Who's Who among African Americans,* 26th ed., p. 881.

1987 Hartford • As mayor of Hartford, Carrie Saxon Perry (1931–) was the first black woman mayor and the second black mayor of a major northeastern city. She was elected on November 3, 1987, and inaugurated on December 1 that year as the city's sixteenth mayor. Perry had been an administrator in health care and government agencies and knew well the poverty, racism, and sexism that existed. Now mayor, she sought ways to change society so that new ideas and directions might be set. She established Operation Bridge, a program that targeted potential school dropouts and provided interaction between young, middle-class Hartford residents and the targeted group. Perry won re-election in 1989. She also ran successfully in 1980 for a seat in the state legislature. She was reelected three additional times. She was born into poverty in Hartford but managed to attend Howard University in Washington, D.C., in 1949. She spent two years at Howard's law school and then returned to Hartford.

Sources: *Jet* 77 (27 November 1989): 15, 18; Smith, *Notable Black American Women,* pp. 837–40; *Who's Who among African Americans,* 12th ed. p. 1037.

1997 New Haven • The first black police chief was Melvin Wearing (1944?–), who was sworn in office on February 24. He moved up from assistant chief to fill the vacancy created when the previous chief was forced to resign due to a scandal. Previously, the twenty-eight-year veteran with the department held a number of positions: he was the first black chief of detectives (1991–93) and the first black assistant chief of police for the city (1993–97). When he became chief, Wearing was a fellow of Yale University's Child Study Center. Wearing received a degree in criminal justice and law enforcement from the University of New Haven.

Sources: *Jet* 91 (10 March 1997): 46; *Who's Who among African Americans,* 26th ed., p. 1302.

Delaware

1901 Wilmington • Thomas Postles was elected to the Wilmington City Council, becoming the first black to win public office in the state.

Sources: Salzman, *Encyclopedia of African-American Culture and History,* vol. 2, p. 741.

1984 Smyrna • George C. Wright Jr. (1932–) was the first black mayor of the town of Smyrna, and the first black mayor in the state. He held office until 1995. Wright was also chief of staffing for civilian personnel at Dover Air Force Base from 1956 to 1989. Over twenty-five percent of the small town's population is black. Wright was born in Chesapeake City, Maryland, and in 1953 received his bachelor's degree from Maryland State College at Princess Ann (now the University of Maryland, Eastern Shore).

Sources: *Jet* 60 (6 August 1981): 21; *Who's Who among African Americans,* 26th ed., p. 1385.

1992 Wilmington • James H. Sills (1932?–), former legislator and college educator, became the first black mayor of Wilmington.

Sources: *Jet* 90 (30 September 1996): 34.

District of Columbia

1902 Washington • Robert Herenton Terrell (1857–1925) was the first black justice of the peace, as judges of the municipal court were then called. He held this position until his death. He was born in Charlottesville, Virginia. An 1884 *magna cum laude* graduate of Harvard, Terrell took his two law degrees from Howard University Law School in Washington, D.C., the LL.B. 1889 and the LL.M. in 1893. He taught in the District of Columbia's public schools from 1884 to 1989 and left to become chief clerk in the office of the auditor for the U.S. Treasury. While serving as judge, he also taught in the law school at Howard University. Terrell married Mary Church (1863–1954), who became a teacher, author, and noted civil rights leader in Washington.

Sources: Logan and Winston, *Dictionary of American Negro Biography,* pp. 585–86; *Encyclopedia of Black America,* p. 815; *Negro Almanac,* p. 338.

1967 Washington • Walter E. Washington (1915–2003) was sworn in office on September 28, becoming the first black mayor named as head of a major American city. Born in Dawson, Georgia, he graduated from Howard University and in 1948 received his law degree from Howard Law School. Between 1941 and 1961 he held various posts related to housing in the capital city. In 1961 President John F. Kennedy named him executive of the National Capital Housing Authority; he was the first black to hold this post. He worked with NCHA for five years, concentrating on housing for the poor. New York mayor John V. Lindsay invited him to join his cabinet; on November 22, 1966, Washington became chair of the New York Housing Authority. He left the next year when President Lyndon B. Johnson named him commissioner of Washington, D.C.; previously, a three-person commission headed the city. He took office on September 28, 1967. President Richard M. Nixon twice re-appointed him to office, in 1969 and 1973. In 1975 local residents elected him to a four-year-term in office, making him the city's first black elected mayor. While in office, Washington concentrated on crime, unemployment, and welfare. After leaving office, he became a partner in the Washington office of the New York law firm Burns, Jackson, Miller, and Summit.

Sources: *Jet* 100 (1 October 2001): 19; Smith, *Notable Black American Men,* pp. 1191–93.

1976 Washington • Theodore Roosevelt Newman Jr. (1934–) was named the chief judge of the Washington Court of Appeals; he was the first black in the United States to head a court at this level. At the time of his appointment, there were fewer than a dozen black judges on appeals courts in the various states. Newman was born in Birmingham and completed undergraduate work at Brown University. He also graduated from Harvard Law School with the J.D. degree. He held several judiciary posts, including associate judge of the District of Columbia superior court (1970–76). After serving as chief judge of the Court of Appeals from 1976 to 1991, he became senior judge in 1991.

Sources: *Jet* 51 (9 December 1976): 20; *Who's Who among African Americans,* 26th ed., p. 933.

1978 Washington • Burtell Jefferson (1926?–) was the first black chief of police in the District of Columbia. A native Washingtonian, Jefferson was fifty-two years old and a twenty-year veteran on the force. He was named second-in-command of the department in 1974 by Mayor Walter Washington.

Sources: *Jet* 53 (19 January 1978): 5.

1983 Washington • Carmen Elizabeth Pawley Turner (1931–1992) was the first black woman to head a major public transportation network. Turner was named as general manager of the Washington, D.C., transit authority, and served until 1990. Under her administration, Washington's Metropolitan Area Transit Authority grew from forty-two miles and forty-seven stations, to seventy miles and sixty-three stations. In mid-December 1990, Turner became the first black undersecretary at the Smithsonian Institution. The institution had suffered from poor management and financial problems, yet Turner had the management style and insight needed to turn the Smithsonian around. Her tenure was brief, however. In 1991 she was diagnosed with cancer that caused her death on April 9, 1992. Born in Teaneck, New Jersey, she and her family relocated to Washington, D.C. She graduated from Howard University with a bachelor's degree. She received her master's degree from American University and completed course work for her doctorate there as well. In 1995 a memorial to Turner was dedicated in the Smithsonian's metro rail station in Washington.

Sources: *Ebony* 39 (March 1984): 93–94, 98; *Jet* 79 (29 October 1990): 10; Smith, *Notable Black American Women,* Book II, pp. 659–61; *Washington Post* (3 October 1990); *Who's Who among Black Americans,* 1992–93, p. 1419.

1985 Washington • Joyce F. Leland (1941–) was the first woman deputy police chief in the city. The Washington, D.C., native graduated from Howard University (B.A., 1965) and the Union Institute (Ph.D., 1998). Leland had been on the force for twenty years and rose through the ranks to become deputy chief.

Sources: *Jet* 67 (28 January 1985): 24; *Who's Who among African Americans,* 26th ed., p. 762.

1990 Washington • Zinora M. Mitchell (1957–) and Michael L. Rankin were the first husband and wife to serve together on the Superior Court of the District of Columbia. Rankin was appointed in 1985, and Mitchell in 1990. A graduate of Spelman College, Mitchell took her law degree at the University of Georgetown Law School. She has served as a trial attorney for the Department of Justice, and assistant attorney for Washington, D.C. Rankin took his law degree at Howard University School of Law. He has served as deputy chief in the U.S. Attorney's Office, Felony Trial Division. After serving in Washington's superior court, he became presiding judge of the criminal division.

Sources: *Jet* 77 (5 February 1990): 32; *Who's Who among Black Americans,* 14th ed., p. 922 (Mitchell); p. 1070 (Rankin).

1997 Washington • Sonya T. Proctor (1954?–) became the first black woman acting chief of police for the District of Columbia. She held the post until the D.C. financial control board completed its national search for a replacement. The Washington, D.C., native joined the force in 1974 and moved up in rank from assistant chief. She gained national attention for ordering 2,000 bulletproof vests for the police force.

Sources: *Jet* 93 (22 December 1997): 23; 93 (29 December–5 January 1998): 10; *Who's Who among African Americans,* 26th ed., p. 1071.

1998 Washington • Cathey L. Ranier was placed in the command slot in the Fourth District, becoming the first black woman commander of any of the seven police districts in the city. She was charged with addressing the most crime-ridden sections of the city.

Sources: *Jet* 98 (18 September 2000): 12.

2007 Washington • Burton W. Johnson (1918?–2007), who served the District of Columbia as fire chief from 1973 to 1978, was the first black to hold that position.

Sources: *Jet* 112 (September 24, 2007): 17.

Florida

1565 St. Augustine • This city, the center of the Spanish Florida colony, is the first permanent dwelling place for blacks in the present territory of the United States. It had both slaves and free blacks from its beginning.

Sources: Davis, *The History of Black Catholics in the United States,* p. 30.

1738 St. Augustine • Gracia Real de Santa Teresa de Mose, also known as Fort Mose, was legally sanctioned by the Spanish government and became the first free African settlement. It was established by Colonial Spanish Florida's governor Manuel Montiano and provided sanctuary to Africans who challenged enslavement in the English Colony of Carolina. Located two miles north of St. Augustine, the community was comprised of more than twenty households. Their frontier community drew on a range of African backgrounds mixed with Spanish, American Indian, and English cultural traditions.

Sources: Fort Mose Historical Society, http://www.fortmose.org. Accessed September 24, 2012.

1887 Eatonville • Eatonville became the first all-black incorporated township in Florida. The town later became known as the birthplace of folklorist and writer Zora Neale Hurston.

Sources: Garrett, *Famous First Facts about Negroes,* p. 191; Smith, *Notable Black American Women,* p. 543.

1958 Miami • Blanche Calloway (1902–1973) was the first black woman to vote in the city.

Sources: *Encyclopedia of Black America,* p. 212; Smith, *Notable Black American Women,* pp. 152–53.

1981 Miami • Howard Gary was the first black city manager of Miami. Gary was ousted in 1984.

Sources: *Jet* 67 (12 November 1984): 6.

1982 Opa-Locka • Helen Miller (1925?–1996) became the first black woman mayor of this city. At the time of her death, she was vice mayor.

Sources: *Jet* 90 (21 October 1996): 59.

1985 Miami • In January 1985, Clarence Dickson was the first black police chief of Miami. He resigned in 1988, citing mistreatment by the city commissioners. At the time of his resignation, Dickson was fifty-four, and a twenty-nine-year veteran on the police force.

Sources: *Jet* 75 (8 August 1988): 33.

1995 Miami • The first black city clerk was Walter Foeman, who had been a city employee for several years. After completing a three-year program at Syracuse University in 1990, he became a certified municipal clerk.

Sources: *Jet* 88 (11 September 1995): 27.

Washington's First Black Woman Mayor

The first black woman to be elected mayor of a major American city was Sharon Pratt Dixon [Kelly] (1944–) in 1990. The Washington, D.C., native was educated at Howard University where she received her bachelor's degree in 1965 and her law degree from the university's law school in 1968. She held a number of positions before becoming mayor. From 1970 to 1971 she worked with the Joint Center for Political Studies as house counsel and the next year became an associate with Pratt and Queen law firm. From 1972 to 1976 she was attorney and professor at Antioch School of Law in Washington. Dixon joined Potomac Electric Power Company, serving as associate general counsel (1976–79), director of the office of consumer affairs (1979–83), vice president (1983–86), and vice president of public policy (1986–89). While serving as mayor, she continued her involvement with the Democratic National Committee, where she has held such positions as acting general counsel, co-chair of the rules committee, and treasurer.

Sources: *Marketing* (14 April 1992), p. 47; *Contemporary Black Biography*, vol. 1, pp. 58–59; Smith, *Notable Black American Women*, pp. 278–80; *Who's Who among African Americans*, 14th ed., p. 742.

1996 Opa-Locka • Robert B. Ingram (1936–) became the only person elected to six consecutive terms as mayor of this city when he was re-elected in 1996. That same year, Ingram was immediate past president of the National Conference of Black Mayors. He had served as a police officer in the city from 1959 to 1980. From 1980 to 1985 he was chief of police for the City of Opa-Locka. In addition to teaching at Florida Memorial College, he was pastor of Allen Chapel African Methodist Episcopal Church beginning 1994. The Miami native graduated from Florida International University in Miami (B.S., 1974 and M.S., 1975) and Union Experimental College and University in Cincinnati (Ph.D., 1978).

Sources: *Jet* 91 (9 December 1996): 54; *Who's Who among African Americans*, 14th ed., p. 645.

1996 Palm Beach • The first black commissioner elected to the Port of Palm Beach was Michael D. Brown, an attorney and head of the Business Economic Development Corporation of Riviera Beach.

Sources: *Jet* 89 (29 January 1996): 10.

1997 St. Petersburg • Goliath J. Davis III was appointed chief of police, becoming the first black to hold that post. Up to then, he was assistant chief of the administrative services bureau of the Police Department. He was also adjunct professor of criminology at the University of South Florida in St. Petersburg.

Sources: *Jet* 92 (21 July 1997): 24; *Who's Who among African Americans*, 26th ed., p. 315.

1997 Tallahassee • Anita R. Favors (1951–) was named city manager, becoming the first woman and the first black to hold the post. With her appointment, she became one of only three black women who managed cities with populations of over 100,000. She was deputy city manager from 1990 to 1995 and senior assistant city manager from 1995 to 1997. Beginning 1983 she was commissioner of the Kansas State Department of Social and Rehabilitation Services and Adult Services. Born in Kansas City, Kansas, Favors graduated from Park College in Parkville, Missouri (B.A., 1977) and Central Michigan University (M.A., 1981).

Sources: *Jet* 92 (26 May 1997): 20; *Who's Who among African Americans*, 14th ed., p. 408.

2000 Tallahassee • Phillip Brutus, a Democrat, was elected a state representative and became the first Haitian-American in the Florida legislature.

Sources: *New York Times* (19 May 2001).

2001 North Miami • Joseph Celestin was elected mayor, becoming the first Haitian-American mayor of a sizeable city in this country. Celestin arrived in the United States in 1979 and soon recognized a need for Haitian-American representation in politics. In the 1990s he and other Haitian-Americans conducted voter registration drives and ran for positions on school boards, city councils, and in other public offices. Celestin's first bid for public office was in 1999, but he lost the race.

Sources: *New York Times* (19 May 2001).

2008 Fort Lauderdale • The first black chief of police for Fort Lauderdale was Frank Adderley. He had served the department since 1980 and rose in rank to become assistant chief of investigation.

Sources: *Jet* 113 (30 June 2008): 26.

2011 Jacksonville • An historic win in his native Jacksonville, Florida's largest city, made Alvin Brown (1963?–) the first black mayor of that city. Although the race was a close call, Brown, a Democrat, had the support of business leaders and Republicans. Brown holds bachelor's and master's degrees from Jacksonville University. He is a former senior urban affairs advisor for both President Bill Clinton and Vice President Albert Gore.

Sources: *Jet* 119 (20–27 June 2011): 14; *Tennessee Tribune* (30 June–6 July 2011); *Who's Who among African Americans,* 26th ed., p. 151.

Alvin Brown

Georgia

1947 Savannah • In April, 1947, John White was named the first black police officer in the state of Georgia. He retired from the force on November 1, 1984, at the age of fifty-nine, with the rank of sergeant.

Sources: *Jet* 67 (8 October 1984): 5.

1970 Savannah • Bowles C. Ford (1911–1993) was the first black elected to the Savannah city council. At the time of his election he was executive vice president and secretary of the Guaranty Life Insurance Company.

Sources: *Ebony Success Library,* vol. 1, p. 114; *Who's Who among Black Americans, 1992–93,* p. 469.

1973 Atlanta • On October 16, 1973, Maynard Holbrook Jackson Jr. (1938–2003) was elected the first black mayor of the city; he was inaugurated the following year. Jackson was admitted to the Georgia bar in 1965, and ran for the United States Senate against Herman Talmadge in 1968. He lost by a small margin. Not only was Jackson the first black mayor of a major southeastern city, he was also the youngest person ever elected mayor of Atlanta. He led the city through precarious times, when the white leadership changed to provide a more equitable racial balance. He became known as an aggressive and outspoken leader who insisted that blacks were involved in community building projects, such as the new international airport. He served as mayor for two consecutive four-year terms, from 1974 to 1982, and was re-elected on October 3, 1989. Jackson was born in Dallas, the son of Baptist minister Maynard Holbrook Sr. and Irene Dobbs Jackson. The senior Jackson became the first black candidate in Texas to seek a seat on the board of education. Irene Dobbs Jackson was a member of the prominent John Wesley Dobbs family in Atlanta. Maynard Jackson Jr. graduated from Morehouse College in Atlanta (B.A., 1956) and North Carolina Central School of Law (J.D., 1964). He was admitted to the Bar of Georgia in 1965. He also held other positions until he was elected vice-mayor of Atlanta from 1970 to 1973 and became cofounder and senior partner of the law firm Jackson, Patterson and Parks.

Sources: *Current Biography Yearbook,* 1976, pp. 193–96; *Ebony Success Library,* vol. 1, p. 169; *Encyclopedia of Black America,* p. 467; Hornsby, *Chronology of African-American History,* p. 209; *Who's Who among African Americans,* 14th ed., p. 660; Smith, *Notable Black American Men,* pp. 602–5.

Georgia's First Black Judge

On February 23, 1964, Austin Thomas Walden (1885–1965) became the first black judge in Georgia since Reconstruction, when he was named an alternate municipal judge in Atlanta. Walden was born in Fort Valley, Georgia, to former slaves. He graduated from Fort Valley Industrial School (B.A., 1902), Atlanta University (M.A., 1907), and the University of Michigan (LL.B., 1911). After serving in the U.S. Army where he was a trial judge advocate, he practiced law in Atlanta, becoming one of the country's leading civil rights attorneys. In 1949 he founded the Atlanta Negro Voters League.

Sources: Hornsby, *Chronology of African-American History,* p. 117; Salzman, *Encyclopedia of African-American Culture and History,* Supplement, pp. 269–70.

1975 Atlanta • Edward L. Baety (1944–) became the first black full-time municipal traffic judge, and Mary Welcome became the first black municipal court solicitor. Baety was born in Jacksonville and educated at Morris Brown College (B.S., 1965) and Howard University School of Law (J.D., 1968). He held several posts in Atlanta, including staff attorney and associate counsel for law firms. He was also associate judge for the City of Atlanta Court beginning in 1976.

Sources: Hornsby, *Chronology of African-American History,* p. 249; *Who's Who among African Americans,* 26th ed., p. 52.

1976 Atlanta • Mary Hall was the first woman of any race on the Special Weapons and Tactics Team of the Atlanta Police Department. At the time, she was twenty-two years old and mother of a two-year-old son.

Sources: *Jet* 50 (15 April 1976): 28–29.

1981 Augusta • Edward M. McIntyre (1932?–) was elected the first black mayor of Augusta on October 28, 1981, when he was forty-nine years old. He won in a run-off election with 53.7 percent of the vote. A native of Augusta, McIntyre was a graduate of Morehouse College (Atlanta, Georgia), a teacher, and an insurance executive. He served on the Richmond County Commission and later headed the Augusta African American Historical Community.

Sources: *Jet* 61 (19 November 1981): 9; 62 (22 March 1982): 32; (30 August 1982): 30; 81 (18 November 1991): 50; Logan and Winston, *Dictionary of American Negro Biography,* pp. 620–21.

1992 Fulton County • Jacquelyn H. Barrett (1950–) broke racial and gender barriers when she was elected sheriff on November 3. She was the first black women sheriff in the United States. Born in Charlotte, North Carolina, Barrett graduated from Beaver College and Clark Atlanta University. She worked with the Georgia Peace Officers Standards and Training Council from 1976 to 1985 and served as chief administrative officer for the Fulton County Sheriff's Office from 1985 to 1987. After serving as director of the Fulton County Public Safety Training Center from 1987 to 1992, she was elected sheriff.

Sources: *Who's Who among African Americans,* 26th ed., p. 71; *Contemporary Black Biography,* vol. 28, pp. 11–13; *Ebony* 50 (August 1995): 94–98, 136.

1994 Atlanta • The first black woman to lead the police force in a major metropolitan city in the United States was Beverly Joyce Bailey Harvard (1950–). Mayor Bill Campbell named her chief of the Atlanta Police Department on October 26. She had joined the force during a period of social and political turmoil in Atlanta, when claims of police brutality in the black community bore merit. She became known as a gifted administrator who moved up in ranks to become chief. Harvard was an officer with the Atlanta Police Department from 1973 to 1979, and then worked with the Department of Public Safety as affirmative action specialist (1979–80) and as director of public affairs (1980–82). She had served as deputy chief of police from 1982 to 1994 and as acting chief from April to October 1994. As police chief, she worked to prepare for the annual Freaknik in Atlanta, when some 100,000 students from black colleges came together for fun and excitement during spring break. She was challenged also to rid the police force of its poor image. She developed a plan to unite the police force and the community in combating crime. Born in Macon, she graduated from Morris Brown College in Atlanta (B.A., 1972) and Georgia State University (M.S., 1980). In 1983 she also graduated from the Federal Bureau of Investigation's National Academy.

Sources: *Contemporary Black Biography,* vol. 11, pp. 121–23; *Who's Who among African Americans,* 14th ed., p. 562; Salzman, *Encyclopedia of African-American Culture and History,* Supplement, p. 125; *Jet* 87 (14 November 1994): 22.

1995 Savannah • Floyd Adams Jr. (1945–), publisher of the black newspaper, the *Savannah Herald,* was elected mayor in November, becoming the first black to hold the post. The Savannah native graduated from Armstrong College with a bachelor's degree in business. He was one of the first black students to attend the institution. After graduating, he joined the staff of the *Herald,* a newspaper that his parents had founded on May 11, 1945. After his father died in 1983, he became chief officer of the newspaper. A year earlier, in 1982, Adams defeated a bitter rival to become a member of the city council as alderman, representing the west side-downtown first district. He was alderman until 1995 when he was elected mayor. After his claim that black artists were overlooked in the city, in 1989 he seated himself on the Savannah Arts Council. Both through his newspaper and his office as mayor, Adams has been an outspoken advocate of the rights of the black community.

Sources: *Jet* 89 (8 January 1996): 12; 89 (22 January 1989): 32; *Who's Who among African Americans,* 26th ed., p. 6; *Contemporary Black Biography,* vol. 12, pp. 1–3.

1996 East Point • The city's first black police chief was Frank Lewis Brown (1945–), a twenty-nine-year veteran with the department. He was selected from a pool of ninety-four applicants.

Sources: *Jet* 90 (10 June 1996): 24; *Who's Who among African Americans,* 26th ed., p. 156.

1996 Washington • A. J. White Sr. was promoted to chief of police, becoming the first black to hold that post.

Sources: *Jet* 93 (24 November 1997): 24.

1997 Augusta • Ronnie Few became the first black fire chief for the city of Augusta.

Sources: *Jet* 93 (24 November 1997): 40.

1997 Stone Mountain • City councilman Chuck Burris (1951?–) defeated a six-year incumbent for mayor on November 4 and was elected as the first black mayor of the city. Burris was born in New Orleans to parents who were educators; they taught him survival skills for living in a racially segregated community. He was admitted to Morehouse College in Atlanta when he was sixteen years old, where Martin Luther King Jr. was one of his teachers. While in college Burris became active in politics, serving on the vice mayoral campaign of Maynard Jackson Jr. in 1968 and later on Andrew Young's campaign for Congress in 1970 and his re-election in 1972 and 1981. Burris graduated from Morehouse in 1971 with a bachelor's degree and in 1975 received his law degree from John Marshall Law School in Atlanta. Before becoming mayor, he held a number of posts in Atlanta, including that as research analyst for the Crime Analyst Team for the City of Atlanta (1975–77) and supervisor of the evaluation division for the budget office and other agencies (1977–81). He co-founded Strategic Targeting and Research Computer Consulting firm in 1981 and left the firm in 1986. He worked for the Office of Secretary of State of Georgia (1991–94) as consultant for computer projects. In 1994 he became president of MountainWare, Ltd. From 1991 to 1996 Burris was a member of the Stone Mountain city council and was later elected mayor of the predominantly white town in 1997. (Ironically, Stone

Mountain is the headquarters for the National Knights of the Klan.) Under his leadership economic and social opportunities for the town's residents improved, as has the perception of Stone Mountain as a bastion of hate. When Burris and his wife, Marcia Baird Burris, were asked to the White House in 1998 to be present during President Bill Clinton's State of the Union speech, this marked the first time that a mayor of the city received such an invitation.

Sources: *Contemporary Black Biography,* vol. 21, pp. 26–29; *Jet* 93 (8 December 1997): 25; *Tennessean* (17 November 1997); *Who's Who among African Americans,* 14th ed., p. 182.

1998 Brunswick • Roosevelt Harris Jr. became the first black city manager. The former executive director of community development for Brunswick oversees and implements plans for growth and development of the city.

Sources: *Jet* 94 (5 October 1998): 20.

2001 Atlanta • The first black to head the Metropolitan Atlanta Rapid Transit Authority (MARTA) was Nathaniel P. Ford Sr. He was promoted from executive vice president of operations and development to general manager and chief executive officer of MARTA, the seventh-largest transit system in North America. Over 4,800 people comprise his staff.

Sources: *Jet* 99 (26 February 2001): 25.

2001 Atlanta • A first-time candidate, Shirley Clarke Franklin (1954–), won the mayoral election on November 6 to become the first woman to be elected mayor of Atlanta and the only black woman then leading a major southern city. She narrowly defeated her closest rival and avoided a run-off election. Georgia Supreme Court Justice Leah Ward Sears administered the oath of office to Franklin on January 7, 2002. Franklin's election brought to nine the number of women mayors then leading the nation's fifty largest cities. For eight years Franklin served as the city's top appointed official and worked with former mayors Maynard Jackson and Andrew Young. She succeeded Bill Campbell in office. After leaving office, she became a distinguished professor at Spelman College.

Sources: *Jet* 10 (28 January 2001): 4–5; *New York Times* (8 November 2001); (8 January 2002); *Tennessean* (8 January 2002).

Illinois

1819 Edwardsville • Edward Coles purchased land near this town to settle seventeen slaves he had manumitted. This is the first known example of slave owner's freeing slaves and resettling them on land in free territory. Unfortunately, the community failed and lost the land to whites because of lack of capital to farm successfully.

Sources: Cha-Jua, *America's First Black Town.*

1827 Lovejoy (Brooklyn) • Eleven families fled Missouri to establish a community in St. Clair County, Illinois. The group put down roots and later became the all-black community of Brooklyn. In 1891 the post office was designated Lovejoy to distinguish it from another Brooklyn in Illinois, and the town adopted the changed name. It is the first known all-black community in Illinois and perhaps the first in the United States.

Sources: Cha-Jua, *America's First Black Town.*

1872 Chicago • Mayor Joseph Medill appointed the first black fire company of nine men. This is believed to be a first in northern cities. The first black police officer was also appointed in this year; he served for three years.

Sources: Cantor, *Historic Landmarks of Black America,* p. 5; Gosnell, *Negro Politicians,* pp. 198, 247.

1891 Chicago • The first black appointed to Chicago's law department was Franklin A. Denison (1862–?), who served for six years under two mayors as assistant city prosecuting attorney. Neither Denison nor his law partner, S. A. T. Watkins, would receive ap-

Chicago's First Woman Judge

In 1962 Edith Spurlock Sampson (1901–1979) became the first black woman elected judge on the municipal court. After graduating from New York School of Social Work, she moved to Chicago and became a full-time social worker. In 1925, having attended its night school program, she graduated from John Marshall Law School in Chicago with an LL.B. degree. Continuing her studies, in 1927, Sampson was the first woman to receive an LL.M. degree from Loyola University. In 1934 she was admitted to practice before the Supreme Court. Sampson was also the first black appointed to serve on the United States delegation to the United Nations in 1950. President Harry S. Truman appointed her as an alternate delegate. Born in Pittsburgh, she grew up poor and in a family of seven brothers and sisters. Sampson died in Chicago on October 8, 1979, after distinguishing herself as a public servant and one who worked for equality for black people.

Edith Sampson

Sources: Hine, *Black Women in America*, pp. 1002–3; *Encyclopedia of Black America*, p. 740; Smith, *Notable Black American Women*, pp. 969–72.

pointments to the city government until 1911. In 1915 Denison would become commander of the 8th Illinois Infantry, which he led in a Mexican expedition in 1916 and in France during the American intervention in World War I.

Sources: Barbeau, *Unknown Soldiers of World War I*, pp. 75–77; Gosnell, *Negro Politicians*, pp. 112, 198–99.

1915 Chicago • Oscar S. DePriest (1871–1951) was the first black alderman in Chicago. Although he encountered several political misfortunes, he became a significant figure in Chicago politics.

Sources: Clayton, *The Negro Politician*, p. 45; Gosnell, *Negro Politicians*, pp. 170–72; Logan and Winston, *Dictionary of American Negro Biography*, pp. 173–74; Smith, *Notable Black American Men*, pp. 294–97.

1950 Chicago • Robert Raylor was the first African American to chair the Chicago Housing Authority.

Sources: Gloria Hamilton, email to Jessie Carney Smith, November 8, 2011.

1966 Chicago • Henry W. McGee (1910?–2000) was appointed postmaster of the largest postal district in the United States, becoming the first black in the city to hold that post. He held the position until 1972. In 2000 the new post office building was named in his honor. A native of Texas, he graduated from the Illinois Institute of Technology in 1949 and from the University of Chicago in 1961. McGee became a charter member of the Joint Negro Appeal, a local self-help organization.

Sources: *Jet* 97 (7 August 2000): 52; 98 (7 August 2000): 10.

1968 Chicago • Winston E. Moore (1929–) was the first black to head a major jail, the Cook County Jail. Moore was born in New Orleans and graduated from West Virginia State College and the University of Louisiana. Among other positions, he was staff psychologist for the Illinois State Employment Service from 1966 to 1968. After serving as head of the Cook County Jail, he became executive director of the Cook County Department of Corrections in 1970.

Sources: *Ebony* 24 (July 1969): 60–68.; *Ebony Success Library,* vol. 2, pp. 170–73; *Who's Who among African Americans,* 14th ed., p. 935.

1971 Chicago • Joseph G. Bertrand (1931–) was the first black elected to a major city office when he was made city treasurer in April 1971. At the University of Notre Dame, where he took a bachelor's in economics in 1954, Bertrand was the school's first black basketball All-American. He had been engaged in banking before his election to city treasurer.

Sources: *Ebony Success Library,* vol. 1, p. 26.

1971 Chicago • Anna Riggs Langford (1910–2011) was the first black woman elected alderman in Chicago. She lost her bid for reelection in 1975 but continued in politics from 1983 to 1991, when she served two terms on the Chicago City Council. A native of Springfield, Ohio, Langford attended Roosevelt University (1946–48). She received her law degree from John Marshall Law School in 1956 and then began her extensive career, becoming prominent in criminal and civil rights cases. In the turbulent 1960s, Langford defended civil rights workers and also participated in civil rights marches that Martin Luther King Jr. and his staff held in Chicago.

Sources: *Ebony* 24 (March 1969): 57–64; *Ebony Success Library,* vol. 1, p. 196; *Chicago Defender* (15 March 1997); *Who's Who among African Americans,* 14th ed., p. 770;

1971 East St. Louis • On April 6, 1971, James E. Williams Sr. became the first black mayor of East St. Louis.

Sources: Hornsby, *Chronology of African-American History,* p. 168.

1978 Rock Island • Jim Davis was the first black mayor of this city. Davis was an elementary school principal in the city and served as acting mayor before his election to a four-year term.

Sources: *Jet* 56 (10 May 1979): 14.

1983 Chicago • Fred Rice (1926–2011) was the first black police superintendent and was chosen to permanently lead the force. His career with the Chicago Police Department began in 1955 and he rose through the ranks until 1983, when he was named superintendent. He took over a racially polarized police force and drew the ire of some when he racially integrated police teams. In protest, the officers called his action "forced integration." The Chicago native graduated from Roosevelt University in Chicago with a BS in 1970 and an MS in public administration in 1977.

Sources: *Chicago Tribune* (26 February 2011); *Jet* 65 (12 September 1983): 8; *Who's Who among African Americans,* 14th ed., p. 1089.

Harold Washington

1983 Chicago • Harold Washington (1922–1987) was elected the first black mayor of Chicago on April 12 and was sworn in office on April 29. As mayor, he reduced the city's budget deficit and placed more minorities in visible positions. He also hired the city's first black chief of police. His administration, however, was beset with political infighting. He was re-elected in 1987, but died of a massive heart attack on November 25. Washington had been a member of the House of Representatives since 1980 before becoming mayor. The Chicago native graduated from high school and joined the army. In 1949 he enrolled in Roosevelt University and later Northwestern University Law School, where he was an undergraduate and later a law school student. He had been the only black admitted in his class. After graduating, he was assistant city prosecutor from 1954 to 1958. Between 1958 and 1964, he was the only black arbitrator for the Illinois Industrial Commission. He had a flourishing law practice until he gave full-time attention to politics. An astute politician and a major figure in state and local politics, Washington died before he could accomplish more than he did. To honor his work, the main public library building in Chicago is named in his honor.

Sources: Bennett, *Before the Mayflower,* pp. 613, 618–19; Hornsby, *Chronology of African-American History,* p. 318–19, 354; *Who's Who among Black Americans, 1988,* p. 721; Smith, *Notable Black American Men,* pp. 1189–91.

1988 Chicago • Jacqueline Murray was the first black woman commander on the Chicago police force. She had served on the force for twenty-one years.

Sources: *Jet* 75 (10 October 1988): 20.

1992 Cairo • Harold E. Nelson was the first black chief of police of Cairo, Illinois. The sixty-year-old Nelson was a thirty-two-year veteran of the Illinois State Police, retiring in 1987.

Sources: *Jet* 82 (17 August 1992): 38; *Who's Who among African Americans,* 26th ed., p. 928.

1993 Evanston • Lorraine H. Morton (1919?–) was the first black, and the first Democrat, elected mayor of this Illinois city. Previously, she had served as an alderman, representing the Fifth Ward. Evanston, an upscale suburb of Chicago, had a population of 73,000, of whom twenty-three percent are black. Morton was born in North Carolina and graduated from Winston-Salem State University (B.S.Ed.) and Northwestern University (M.S.Ed.). She taught in various schools in Evanston from 1953 to 1977 and she was principal of Haven Middle School from1977 to 1989.

Sources: *Ebony* 48 (July 1993): 39, 42; *Who's Who among African Americans,* 26th ed., p. 910.

1995 Chicago • Terry Hilliard was promoted from Area 2 deputy chief of patrol to chief of detectives of the Chicago Police Department, the first black to hold that post.

Sources: *Jet* 88 (7 August 1995): 22.

1996 Chicago • The first woman commission of the Department of Water was Judith Carol Rice (1957–), an executive assistant to Mayor Richard Daley. The Chicago native graduated from Loyola University (B.A., 1981) and John Marshall Law School (J.D., 1988). She held a number of posts including assistant state's attorney (1988–89), director of administrative adjudication for the City of Chicago (1990–92), and revenue director (1993–95).

Sources: *Jet* 90 (15 July 1996): 18; *Who's Who among African Americans,* 26th ed., p. 1044.

1996 Peoria • The first black city manager was Michael D. McKnight, a twenty-three-year city employee.

Sources: *Jet* 90 (9 September 1996): 25.

1997 Chicago • The city's first black woman to serve as a mounted police officer was Dawn Peter (1966?–). A native of Chicago, she had become a regular patrol officer six years earlier. She also worked as a plainclothes officer before becoming a mounted officer.

Sources: *Jet* 92 (30 June 1997): 36.

1997 Decatur • Betsy Stockard became the first black woman to serve on the city council. A childcare counselor for Kemmerer Village in Assumption, Illinois, she founded and served as director for the Youth Empowerment Agency. The agency addressed violence and gang prevention.

Sources: *Jet* 91 (5 May 1997): 20; *Who's Who among African Americans,* 26th ed., p. 1183.

1998 Chicago • Carolyn Williams Meza became the first woman to hold the top job at the Chicago Park District. She was promoted from chief operating officer to general superintendent, supervising 3,300 employees. A graduate of Coe College in Iowa, she also held an M.B.A. from Kellogg School of Management at Northwestern University.

Sources: *Jet* 93 (16 February 1998): 38.

1999 East St. Louis • The first black woman mayor of East St. Louis, Illinois, and the second-youngest mayor of the city was Debra A. Powell (1964–). She was elected to office on April 13, when she was thirty-five years old. Once in office, she worked to improve entry points to the city, remove the city's long history of corruption, improve streets, and renovate school buildings, among other enhancements. The East St. Louis native was a prominent track athlete and basketball player while in high school. She graduated from the University of Nebraska in 1985 with a degree in communications. Powell was news anchor and news director of Gateway East Metropolitan Ministries, on cable station Channel 17 in East St. Louis from 1990 to 1998. She lived in Pasadena, California, for awhile, and was a municipal public relations professional from 1986 to 1990. From 1993 to 1998 Powell was a member of the East St. Louis city council.

Sources: *Contemporary Black Biography,* vol. 23, pp. 161–63; *Who's Who among African Americans,* 26th ed., p. 1008.

Indiana

1994 Gary • Karen Marie Freeman-Wilson (1960–) became the first black woman judge of the Gary City Court. Previously, she was in private practice and a public defender. For three-and-one-half years the Gary native directed the Indiana Civil Rights Commission. Born in Gary, she received an M.A. and A.B. in 1982 from Harvard University in Cambridge, Massachusetts. She graduated from the Harvard Law School in 1985 with M.A. and J.D. degrees. Before becoming judge she had held a number of posts including public defender for the Lake County Defender's Office in Crown Point, Indiana (1989) and director of the Indiana Civil Rights Commission in Indianapolis (1989–92). She had also established a private practice and handled civil and criminal litigation.

Sources: *Jet* 87 (21 November 1994): 37; *Who's Who among African Americans,* 26th ed., p. 438.

Iowa

1995 Clinton • LaMetta K. Wynn (1933?–) was elected mayor, becoming the first black mayor of that city and of the state. She took office on January 1996. Wynn graduated from St. Luke's Hospital School of Nursing in Cedar Rapids. She had been active in a number of organizations, including the American Nurses Association and the Iowa Nurses Association. She served on the Clinton Community School Board for twelve years, three years as president. She also chaired the Iowa Commission on the Status of African-Americans. Wynn received several honorary doctoral degrees, and *Newsweek* magazine named her one of twenty-five Most Dynamic Mayors in America.

Sources: *Jet* 89 (27 November 1995): 4; 89 (22 January 1996): 38; *Who's Who among African Americans,* 26th ed., p. 1391.

1997 Des Moines • Preston Daniels became the first black mayor of Iowa's largest city. At the time, Daniels was director of Court and Community Relations for Employee and Family Resources. He has been active in various organizations, including the National Conference of Mayors and the National Conference of Black Mayors. He has been active with the University of Iowa Advisory Board for Addiction Technology and the Iowa Democratic Party.

Sources: *Jet* 93 (24 November 1997): 4; *New York Times* (4 November 1997); *Who's Who among African Americans,* 26th ed., p. 302.

Kentucky

1945 Louisville • Eugene S. Clayton was the first black elected to a seat on a city council since Reconstruction.

Sources: Clayton, *The Negro Politician,* p. 119.

Louisiana

1867 St. Martin • Monroe Baker was elected mayor of this small town and may have been the first black mayor popularly elected in the United States.

Sources: *African Americans in American Politics,* p. 119.

1970 New Orleans • Ernest Nathan "Dutch" Morial (1929–1989) was the first black judge on the Juvenile Court of the city. In 1972, he was the first black elected to the

New Orleans's First Black Mayor

On November 12, 1977, Ernest Nathan "Dutch" Morial (1929–1989) was elected the first black mayor of New Orleans and served two terms, until 1986. His election was important and attracted national attention because New Orleans ranked fourth among cities with the largest number of blacks and the city was the nation's second largest port city. He became nationally known for creating the first Office of Economic Development, an agency that coordinated the city's efforts to attract and retain businesses. Morial also employed the first minority business enterprise counselor to work with small and minority-owned businesses.

Sources: *Contemporary Black Biography,* vol. 26, pp. 104–6; Smith, *Notable Black American Men,* pp. 831–32; *Jet* 100 (19 November 2001): 26.

Ernest Morial

Louisiana Fourth Circuit Court of Appeals. The New Orleans native graduated from the historically black Catholic institution, Xavier University, in New Orleans in 1951. In 1954, Morial became the first black graduate of the Louisiana State University School of Law, and in 1965 he was the first black lawyer to work in the United States Attorney's office in Louisiana. In 1967 he became the first black elected to the state legislature in the twentieth century, and the first ever elected as a Democrat.

Sources: *Ebony Success Library,* vol. 1, p. 228; *Encyclopedia of Black America,* p. 568; Hornsby, *Chronology of African-American History,* p. 418; *Contemporary Black Biography,* vol. 26, pp. 104–6; Smith, *Notable Black American Men,* pp. 831–32.

1975 New Orleans • Abraham Lincoln Davis (1915?–1978) became the first black member of the New Orleans City Council in January 1975. Davis was one of the founders, and the first vice-president, of the Southern Christian Leadership Conference.

Sources: Hornsby, *Chronology of African-American History,* p. 301.

1983 Baton Rouge • Freddie Pitcher was the first black municipal judge in Baton Rouge. A native of the city, Pitcher was thirty-eight years old.

Sources: *Jet* 64 (30 May 1983): 6.

1985 New Orleans • Warren G. Woodfork Sr. was the first black police superintendent of New Orleans. Woodfork had been named deputy police chief in 1981. In 1985, he was forty-seven years old, and a twenty-year veteran of the force.

Sources: *Jet* 67 (21 January 1985): 30.

1993 New Orleans • Warren E. McDaniels became the first black fire department superintendent in the New Orleans Fire Department. McDaniels had served in the department for twenty-four years.

Sources: *Jet* 84 (3 May 1993): 52.

1996 Monroe • The first black mayor of Monroe elected since the Reconstruction was Abe Pierce III (1935?–). He became the first new mayor in seventeen years for a town of 62,000 whose population was 52 percent black. Pierce retired as assistant superintendent of the Ouachita Parish School System on June 30 and was sworn in as mayor on July 1.

Sources: *Jet* 90 (20 May 1996): 23.

1997 New Orleans • Keith B. Pittman (1971–) became the youngest person and the first black to serve as director of the New Orleans Metropolitan Convention and Visitors Bureau.

Sources: *Jet* 91 (12 May 1997): 20; *Who's Who among African Americans,* 26th ed., p. 997.

2003 New Orleans • The first black district attorney for New Orleans, the top prosecutor, was Eddie Jordan. Later he was accused of discriminating against forty-three white staff members, firing them en mass, and replacing them with blacks. Under the weight of a $3.7 million bias judgment against his office, dating back to 2005, Jordan resigned in 2007.

Sources: *Jet* 112 (19 November 2007): 12.

2006 Westlake • Gerald Washington (1950–) was sworn in office on December 19 as the city's first black elected mayor and the first new mayor of the predominantly white town in twenty-four years. A few days before he was to take office, he was shot to death. Confusion surrounded the circumstances of his death. A retired oil-refinery worker, Washington had served on Westlake's city county before running for mayor.

Sources: *Jet* 110 (22 January 2007): 33–34.

Maine

1988 Augusta • William D. Burney Jr. (1951–) was the first black mayor of Augusta, and the first in the state. A native of Augusta, Burney graduated from Boston University with both the B.S. and M.A. degrees. He received M.E. and J.D. degrees from the University of Maine in 1977, and worked for the Maine State Housing Authority in Augusta beginning in 1981. He has been active on numerous boards, including the board of directors for the Holocaust Human Rights Center of Maine and Yankee Healthcare in Augusta.

Sources: *Negro Almanac,* p. 428; *Who's Who among African Americans,* 26th ed, p. 183.

1993 Lewistown • John T. Jenkins was elected mayor, becoming the first black to hold that position; he served until 1997. Jenkins was also a state senator, from 1996 to 1998, one of the few officials who held two elective offices. He was president of Dirigo Corporation from 1988 to 1997 and from 1970 to 1997 he was owner of the John Jenkins Academy of Personal Development. He was World Martial Arts Champion five times and was also inducted into the World Martial Arts Hall of Fame.

Sources: *Jet* 91 (24 March 1997): 10; *Who's Who among African Americans,* 26th ed., p. 658.

Maryland

1885 Baltimore • Everett J. Waring (1859–1915) presented himself to the supreme bench of Baltimore city on October 10 and became the first black lawyer admitted to the Maryland courts. Waring was born in Springfield, Ohio. He was the son of a school principal and upon graduation in 1887, he became an assistant to his father; he later succeeded his father as principal. In 1882 he became editor of a small newspaper; that same year he was appointed examiner of pensions in the District of Columbia. While there he studied at Howard University, graduating in 1885. In 1893 he received a master's degree and for a while practiced law in the District. He later moved to Ohio and then to Philadelphia.

Sources: Koger, *The Negro Lawyer in Maryland,* p. 7.

1967 Baltimore • Victorine Quille Adams (1912-2006), owner of a charm school in Baltimore, began a movement fifty years earlier to elect blacks to public office. She became the first black woman on the city council this year, representing the Fourth District. Later she was a member of the House of Delegates for the Fourth District, Maryland General Assembly. Born in Baltimore, she was educated at Morgan State University and Coppin State Teachers College.

Sources: *Jet* 91 (18 November 1996): 12; *Who's Who among African Americans,* 14th ed., p. 8.

1970 Baltimore • Milton B. Allen (1917–2003) was the first black elected state's attorney for the city of Baltimore. He was the first black to be public prosecutor in any major American city. A member of the Maryland bar since 1948, and a 1949 graduate of the University of Maryland Law School, Allen had tried more than seven thousand cases and built a very prosperous law practice before he ran for elected office. He became a judge of the supreme bench of Baltimore in 1976.

Sources: *Ebony Success Library,* vol. 2, pp. 2–5; *The Negro Almanac,* p. 1397; *Who's Who among Black Americans, 1992–93,* p. 23.

1973 College Park • Dervey Lomax (1924?–2008) was the first black mayor of College Park; he served from 1973 to 1975

Sources: *Jet* 113 (7 July 2008): 9; Obituary, *Who's Who among African Americans,* 26th ed., p. 141.

1984 Baltimore • Bishop Robinson was the first black commissioner of the Baltimore police. Robinson was fifty-seven, and a thirty-two-year veteran of the force at the time of his appointment. Born in Baltimore, Robinson received a bachelor's degree in police administration from Coppin State College. He is a founder, and a past president, of the National Organization of Black Law Enforcement Executives.

Sources: *Jet* 66 (9 July 1984): 37.

1987 Baltimore • On December 8, 1987, Kurt Lidell Schmoke (1949–) became the first elected black mayor of Baltimore. The first black mayor was Clarence Du Burns (1918?–2003), president of the City Council, who was not an elected mayor; in January 1987, Du Burns succeeded Mayor William Donald Schaeffer, who had been elected governor of the state. Du Burns had been a high school locker attendant until his election to the city council in 1971. Schmoke was born in Baltimore; he was a Rhodes scholar at Oxford after his graduation from Yale; he earned a law degree at Harvard in 1976. Schmoke worked as an assistant United States attorney, and as state's attorney for Baltimore City, before his election. In the year of his election Schmoke gained international attention with his statement that drugs should be legalized and drug addiction treated as an illness. He was mayor for two terms but decided against seeking a third term.

Kurt Schmoke

Sources: *Contemporary Black* Biography, vol. 1, pp. 215–18; *Jet* 71 (9 February 1987): 54; *Negro Almanac,* pp. 431–32; *Who's Who among Black Americans, 1992–93,* p. 201 (Du Burns); *Who's Who among African Americans,* 26th ed., p. 1099 (Schmoke).

1992 Baltimore • Herman Williams Jr. became the first black fire chief of a major city in the United States. In 1954 he became one of the first blacks to join the firefighting team. In 2002 he published the book *Firefighter* (with James Hall) detailing his experiences battling flames and racism in Baltimore to become city's first black fire chief. Williams is the father of famed talk show host Montel Williams.

Sources: *Jet* 101 (25 March 2002): 37–38; 101 (22 April 2002): 10.

1995 Baltimore • Kathy [Kathryn] Waters became the first black and the first woman in Maryland to manage a commuter rail service. After serving as acting manager of Maryland's MARC commuter rail system's Office of Transit Operation, she was named manager.

Sources: *Jet* 88 (2 October 1995): 19; *Who's Who among African Americans,* 26th ed., p. 1294.

1995 Baltimore • The first senior director of marketing for the National Aquarium was Denise London. Earlier she was the first woman patrol officer in Camden County, New Jersey. London graduated from Glassboro State College and did further study at Texas Agricultural and Mechanical University and the University of Cambridge. After serving as a broadcast station account executive, she was zone manager for Ford Motor Company. She was director of marketing for the Texas State Aquarium before moving to the National Aquarium. Later she was promoted to vice president for marketing for the aquarium.

Sources: *Jet* 88 (23 October 1995): 16; *Who's Who among African Americans,* 26th ed., p. 786.

Sheila Dixon

2008 Baltimore • The first black woman to be elected mayor of Baltimore was Sheila Dixon (1953–). She had served as interim mayor since January 2007 and won the mayoral election with 88 percent of the vote. Her predecessor, Martin O'Malley, left the office when he was elected governor. Fighting crime became one of her signature issues. She also aimed to establish a jobs program, focus on recycling, and make the city greener. Dixon resigned from office on February 4, 2010, amid charges that she used or kept gift cards donated for the poor. In a plea deal, she was also fined, placed on probation, and ordered to perform public service. Later, she will be eligible to run for office again.

Sources: *Contemporary Black Biography,* vol. 68, pp.59–61; *Jet* 110 (5 February 2007): 12; *Who's Who among African Americans,* 26th ed., p. 344.

Massachusetts

1969 Boston • Thomas I. Atkins (1939–) was the first black elected to the Boston City Council. Atkins received a law degree from Harvard University (1969) and served in the governor's cabinet from 1971 to 1975. He left public service to work in private law practice.

Sources: *Ebony Success Library,* vol. 1, p. 14; *Who's Who among African Americans,* 14th ed., p. 45.

1986 Boston • Bruce C. Bolling was the first black president of the Boston City Council. The council had been in existence for 166 years, being established in 1820.

Sources: *Jet* 69 (27 January 1986): 4; *Who's Who among Black Americans,* 26th ed., p. 117.

1994 Oak Bluffs • Barbara Houtman, the justice of the peace for Boston, became the first black member of the board of selectmen.

Sources: *Jet* 86 (22 August 1994): 10.

1996 Essex County • Frank Cousins Jr. (1960?–) became the first black sheriff in the county and in the state of Massachusetts. Cousins was a member of the state legislature from 1993 to 1996. While in the legislature, he sponsored a number of crime bills, including legislation to impose stiff penalties for assaulting a police officer and another for stronger drunk driving laws. Earlier, he served on the Newburyport City Council.

Sources: *Jet* 90 (21 October 1996): 25; *Who's Who among African Americans,* 26th ed., p. 279.

1998 Somerville • Kevin Tarpley was elected to the Board of Aldermen, becoming the first black elected to the eleven-member board. He represented Ward 2.

Sources: *Jet* 93 (16 February 1998): 38.

Michigan

1945 Ypsilanti • Frank M. Seymour (1916–) was the first black official elected in Washtenaw County when he won a seat on the Ypsilanti City Council. In 1965, he founded Seymour and Lundy Associates, a public relations firm in Detroit.

Sources: *Ebony Success Library,* vol. 1, p. 278.

1967 Flint • Floyd McCree was elected the first black mayor of Flint.

Sources: Hornsby, *Chronology of African-American History,* p. 131.

1974 Pontiac • The city commissioners elected Wallace E. Holland (1926–1998), a member of the commission since 1970, as mayor for the term 1974–78, making him the first black to hold the post. At that time the position was basically part-time. He was re-

Detroit's First Black Mayor

In 1973 Coleman Alexander Young (1918–1997) was elected the first black mayor of Detroit. He served an unprecedented five terms. Young and Thomas Bradley, elected at the same time, were the first black mayors of cities with populations over one million. In 1968 Young was the first black to serve on the Democratic National Committee. Young was born in Tuscaloosa, Alabama. His family relocated to Detroit in search of better economic opportunities. Unable to attend college for financial reasons, he went to work as an apprentice electrician for the Ford Motor Company in the 1930s. In the early 1940s Young joined the Ford assembly line and organized an underground union; he also became a civil rights activist. He became a member of the Tuskegee Airmen during World War II and as a second lieutenant flew missions as a bombardier navigator. He later joined other black officers in integrating a segregated officer's club. After the war he returned to Detroit and spent his time primarily in union organizing. After Young campaigned for the Progressive Party in the 1950s and founded the National Negro Labor Council, he was called to testify before the House Un-American Activities Committee. Rather than surrender his list of members to the attorney general, he disbanded the labor council. His reputation in civil rights and union organizing made it difficult for Young to find or keep employment. He became a delegate to the Michigan Constitutional Convention in 1960; his work with the Democratic Party led to his election in 1964 to the state senate. There he fought for open housing legislation as well as busing for school integration. In his first bid to become mayor, Young won the election and promised to turn the city around. Thereafter he won each election by a wide margin. Among his accomplishments in office, Young revitalized the downtown area and expanded the riverfront, bringing conventions and tourists to the city. He also strengthened police-community relations.

Sources: *Encyclopedia of Black America*, p. 873; *Negro Almanac*, pp. 434–35; Hornsby, *Chronology of African-American History*, p. 211; *Who's Who among Black Americans, 1994–95*, p. 1647; Smith, *Notable Black American Men*, pp. 1285–89.

elected to the position in 1982 and again in 1990, serving until 1993. Holland retired from his position at General Motors in 1982 to run for the post.

Sources: *Jet* 93 (23 March 1998): 56; *New York Times* Obituaries (4 March 1998); *Who's Who among African Americans*, 9th ed., p. 713.

1981 Detroit • Billie Ann Willis was the first woman of any race to become a police precinct commander in Detroit. A graduate of West Virginia State College, Willis had served on the force for twenty-three years.

Sources: *Jet* 60 (21 May 1981): 13; 61 (17 September 1981): 21.

1982 Detroit • Real estate executive Bella Marshall (1950–) became the first woman to head the finance department for the city of Detroit. She headed a staff of 500 and took charge of all of the city's baking and investments. After leaving her post in 1993, she became president and chief executive officer for the Waycor Development Company which she and her husband, Don Barden, owned. Marshall was born in Windsor, Ontario, Canada, and grew up in Detroit. She graduated from Wayne State University and the University of Michigan Law School.

Sources: *Contemporary Black Biography*, vol. 22, pp. 140–41.

1996 Jackson • J. Gregory Love was named fire chief, the first black to hold that post. He was fire chief of Royal Oak Township from 1995 to 1996 and captain of the Detroit Fire Academy. He had served the Detroit Fire Department for twenty-four years, where he was also firefighter and instructor. Love graduated from the University of Detroit and received his M.E. degree from Wayne State University.

Sources: *Jet* 91 (13 January 1997): 20; *Who's Who among African Americans,* 26th ed., p. 789.

Minnesota

1992 St. Paul • William K. Finney was the first black police chief in St. Paul, Minnesota. The forty-three-year-old Finney was a native of St. Paul, and a twenty-one-year veteran of the force.

Sources: *Jet* 82 (3 August 1992): 56.

1994 Eden Prairie • Jean Louise Harris (1931–) was elected mayor, becoming the first black and the first woman mayor of this suburban town. Born in Richmond, Virginia, Harris was educated at Virginia Union University (B.S., 1951) and the Medical College of Virginia (M.D., 1955). After a two-year period with the District of Columbia Department of Health (1967–69), she became executive director of the National Medical Association Foundation (1969–73). She taught at the Medical College of Virginia (1973–78), and then took a post in Virginia state government. She was vice president of Control Data Corporation (1982–88) and president and chief executive officer for the Ramsey Foundation in St. Paul, Minnesota. She continued her service in health care, serving as senior associate director and director of medical affairs at the University of Minnesota Hospital. She became mayor of Eden Prairie in 1994.

Sources: *Jet* 87 (12 December 1994): 6; *Who's Who among African Americans,* 14th ed., p. 551.

1994 Minneapolis • The first black and the first woman mayor of Minneapolis took office this year. Sharon Sayles Belton (1951–), the former welfare mother and women's rights advocate, was elected in 1993 and won a second term in 1997, capturing 55 percent of the vote of a largely white population. Many of her advisors and colleagues were women, who focused on neglected issues such as sexual assault and domestic violence. Belton was born in St. Paul, Minnesota, and studied for two years at Macalester College in that city. In 1986 she attended a program for senior executives at the John F. Kennedy School of Government at Harvard University. While in college she became involved in civil rights and voter-registration activities; she registered blacks to vote in Jackson, Mississippi. She later was a parole officer for the Department of Corrections in Minnesota (1972–83). The next year she was associate director of the Minnesota Program for Victims of Sexual Assault; she helped to build twenty-six centers to help rape victims throughout the state. She also helped to establish one of the nation's first shelters for abused women, the Harriet Tubman Shelter. Her work led to her election to the City Council from 1984 to 1993, representing the Eighth Ward of Minneapolis. From 1989 to 1993 Belton was president of the council until she was elected mayor in 1994. She lost her bid for re-election in November 2001.

Sources: *Ebony* 49 (February 1994): 98; *Jet* 85 (22 November 1993): 5; 85 (24 January 1994): 22–23; *Contemporary Black Biography,* 16, pp. 12–14.

Mississippi

1870 Natchez • In December 1870 Robert H. Wood was elected mayor, one of the earliest black mayors in the United States.

Sources: Bennett, *Before the Mayflower,* pp. 489, 629; *Ebony* (March 1982), p. 130.

1887 Mound Bayou • Sam Bass was the first black mayor of Mound Bayou, an all-black town incorporated in 1887.

Sources: Alford, *Famous First Blacks,* pp. 47, 71.

1964 Laurel • Simon Shanks Sr. (?–1982) was the first black patrolman in the police department. Shanks eventually became a captain.

Sources: *Jet* 62 (14 June 1982), p. 9.

1969 Fayette • On May 13, 1969, James Charles Evers (1922–) was elected the first black mayor of a racially mixed Mississippi town. Fayette is the county seat of Jefferson County and had a population of about two thousand. In June 1971, he became the first black in the twentieth century to seek the governor's office. Later he was unsuccessful in his bid for a seat in the state senate and for a seat in the U.S. House of Representatives. Born in Decatur, he received his bachelor's degree from Alcorn State University in Alcorn, Mississippi, in 1951. From 1963 to 1969 Evers was field secretary for the NAACP. Since 1969 he has served as president of the Medgar Evers Fund, named in honor of his brother, a slain civil rights leader. In 1997 he published his autobiography, *Have No Fear: The Charles Evers Story*.

Sources: *Ebony Success Library*, vol. 1, p. 109; *Encyclopedia of Black America*, p. 378; Hornsby, *Chronology of African American History*, pp. 137, 176, 191, 262; *Negro Almanac*, p. 51; *Who's Who among African Americans*, 26th ed., p. 396.

1976 Meyersville • Unita Blackwell (1933–) was the first black woman mayor in Mississippi. She was a leading figure in the civil rights struggle, and in the organization of the Mississippi Freedom Democratic Party in 1964. She became the first woman president of the National Conference of Black Mayors in 1990. The Lula, Mississippi, native received her master's degree from the University of Massachusetts in 1983. She had been active in civil rights activities earlier, serving as key organizer for the Mississippi Freedom Democratic Party in 1964. From 1977 to 1983 she was national president of the U.S.-China People's Friendship Association. After she was elected mayor, that same year she had her town incorporated. Blackwell was awarded a MacArthur Fellowship in 1992.

Sources: *Contemporary Black Biography*, vol. 17, pp. 11–15; *Jet* 82 (6 July 1992): 34–35; Lanker, *I Dream a World*, p. 50; *Tennessean* (16 June 1992).

1986 Greenville • Malcolm Wynn (1940–) was the first black chief of police, a position he held until his retirement from police work in 1989. In 1977 Wynn had been the first black captain on the force. The Greenville, Mississippi, native received a certificate from the Mississippi Law Enforcement Training Academy (1969), the Louisiana State University Law Enforcement Institute (1972), and the FBI National Academy in Quantico, Virginia.

Unita Blackwell

Sources: *Who's Who among African American*, 26th ed., p. 1391.

1988 Natchez • Eddie Jones was the first black chief of the police department of Natchez. Jones was forty-five years old, and had served on the police force for nineteen years.

Sources: *Jet* 75 (17 October 1988): 28.

1989 Tchula • Jessie Banks was the first black mayor of Tchula. Banks had been elected the first black alderman of the city in 1977.

Sources: *Jet* 76 (7 August 1989): 8.

1992 Greenwood • David Lee Jordan (1933–) became the only political candidate in the country to hold two elective posts concurrently. He was elected to the City Council in Greenwood, the first black to sit on the council. Later the council became predominantly black in membership and in 1985 he was elected president. He was successful in his bid for the state senate in 1992 and now held two elective jobs. Jordan began his efforts as early as 1970; he sued the city of Greenwood, bringing about a change in its government resulting in the election of blacks to the city council. He also sued the state of Mississippi, resulting in a redistricting the second congressional district and the election of blacks to the U.S. Congress. Jordan was born in Greenwood and graduated from Mississippi Valley State University (B.S., 1959) and the University of Wyoming (M.S., 1979).

Sources: *Jet* 97 (3 April 1995): 39; *Who's Who among African Americans,* 26th ed., p. 705.

1996 Itta Bena • Thelma Collins (1945?–), a ninth-grade school teacher, was elected mayor, becoming the first black and the first woman to hold the post. She received 51 percent of the vote in a town of three thousand.

Sources: *Jet* 90 (2 September 1996): 58.

1996 Jackson • The first black fire chief was Joseph "Joe" Graham (1939?–), a twenty-four-year veteran of the Fire Department. He led a 410-member staff. Previously, Graham was assistant fire chief for almost five years.

Sources: *Jet* 90 (29 July 1996): 12.

Harvey Johnson Jr.

1997 Jackson • Harvey Johnson Jr. (1947?–) was sworn in office, becoming the first black mayor of this city, the capitol of Mississippi with approximately 200,000 residents. Sixty percent of the residents were black. The Vicksburg native was educated at Tennessee State University in Nashville and the University of Cincinnati. He served as community planner in the office of Mississippi's governor, and taught political science at Jackson State University. Entering the political arena, Johnson became a state tax commissioner as well as a commissioner on the Mississippi Gaming Board, a powerful organization in the state. For a while he was a political commentator on a local television station. After an unsuccessful bid to become mayor, four years later Johnson upset incumbent Kane Ditto and became the Democrat's candidate for mayor. Then he defeated Republican candidate Charlotte Reeves and in June 1997 received 70 percent of the vote to become mayor of Jackson. He went on to serve two consecutive terms (1997–2005) and was re-elected to a third term in 2009. To acknowledge the important activities in Jackson during the Civil Rights Movement of the 1960s, he supported the establishment of a Civil Rights Driving Tour, Jackson's first "millennium activity."

Sources: *Contemporary Black Biography,* vol. 24, pp. 98–99; *Jet* 92 (23 June 1997): 8; *Ebony* 52 (August 1997): 76.

1999 Hattiesburg • James R. Davis, who had been superintendent of the Plano, Texas, Independent Schools and an educator for forty-two years, became the first black superintendent of the Hattiesburg School District. In the late 1970s he became the first black mayor of Rock Island, Illinois.

Sources: *Jet* 96 (7 June 1999): 32.

2000 Jackson • Wanda Collier-Wilson became the first person to head the Convention and Visitor's Bureau and the first person promoted to the top position within the bureau. She joined the staff in 1983.

Sources: *Jet* 97 (7 January 2000): 38.

2000 Tchula • Yvonne Brown was elected mayor of Tchula, becoming the first black Republican woman mayor in the state. She was born in Toledo, Ohio, and spent her summers in Tchula, with her grandmother. After she married Robert Brown, the couple settled in Tchula, a town that was devastated early on by slavery and the Ku Klux Klan. She spent seven years in Tchula, and then was elected mayor; she also received a grant of $500,000 from the U.S. Department of Agriculture's rural Development Authority to develop a town complex.

Sources: *Jet* 101 (3 June 2002): 6.

2001 Hattiesburg • Johnnie DuPree (1954?–) defeated a white incumbent and took the oath of office at City Hall, becoming the first black mayor of the mostly white city of nearly 45,000. Previously, DuPree served on the Forrest County Board of Supervisors.

Sources: *Jet* 100 (23 July 2001): 27.

2001 Jackson • For the first time, two blacks ran against each other in a general election. Democratic incumbent Harvey Johnson Jr. (1947?–) won re-election, defeating black Republican candidate C. Daryl Neely, a city councilman.

Sources: *Jet* 100 (25 June 2001): 32.

Missouri

1982 Pagedale • As mayor, Mary Hall headed the first all-black, and all-woman, city administration.

Sources: *Jet* 82 (24 May 1982): 13.

1991 Kansas City • Emanuel Cleaver II (1944–) became the first black mayor of Kansas City, Missouri, on March 26, and was sworn in office on April 10. He had served as mayor *pro tempore* from 1987 to 1991. Cleaver was an experienced politician, having served on the city council from 1979 to 1991 as a representative of the Fifth District. From 1984 to 1987 he was chair of the City Council Plans and Zoning Committee of Kansas City. He chaired the council's Policy and Rules Committee from 1987 to 1991. A native of Waxahachie, Texas, Cleaver was pastor of St. James United Methodist Church (now St. James Paseo United Methodist Church) at the time of his election. He graduated from Prairie View Agricultural and Mechanical College (now University) in 1968 and received his master's degree from St. Paul School of Theology, where he also studied for his doctorate in social ethics.

Sources: *Jet* 81 (18 November 1991): 66; *Heritage and Hope*, p. 284; *Who's Who among African Americans*, 26th ed., pp. 245–46; *National Black Review* 6 (July/August 1993): 9; *Contemporary Black Biography*, vol. 4, pp. 42–44.

Emanuel Cleaver II

1993 St. Louis • Freeman Robertson Bosley Jr. (1954–) was elected the first black mayor of St. Louis. He was clerk of the circuit court from 1983 to 1993. His father, Freeman Bosley Sr., a longtime city alderman, had run for mayor twice. A St. Louis native, Bosley was born into a family that pressed for civil rights. He graduated from the University of St. Louis (B.A., 1976) and the University of St. Louis School of Law (J.D., 1979). After completing his law degree, he worked as an attorney for Legal Services of Eastern Missouri in St. Louis from 1979 until 1981. After that, he was an associate in the law firm of Bussey and Jordan in 1982.

Sources: *Ebony* 48 (July 1993): 38, 40; *Jet* 83 (26 April 1993): 8; *Who's Who among African American*, 26th ed., p. 123.

1996 St. Louis • The first woman elected comptroller in St. Louis was Darlene Green, the city's former budget director. She was also the first woman elected to the city's Board of Estimate and Apportionment, which controls the city's budget.

Sources: *Jet* 90 (9 September 1996): 25; *Who's Who among African Americans*, 26th ed., p. 492.

1998 St. Louis • Alice F. Pollard became the first woman commissioner of corrections. Previously, Pollard was executive assistant to the director of public safety. Her new position placed her in charge of the city jail, probation and parole, medium security institutions, alternative sentencing, and the training academy for correctional officers.

Sources: *Jet* 93 (25 May 1998): 20.

2000 Kansas City • Gregory B. Gillis became the first black drug court commissioner. He previously served as prosecutor for Jackson County.

Sources: *Jet* 98 (26 June 2000): 10.

2000 Kansas City • The first black chief of the fire department was Sherman George (1945?–). Since 1990 he had been deputy chief. He received a degree in fire science from Central Missouri State University and later completed the public executives' program at

John F. Kennedy School of Government, Harvard University. He also graduated from the Carl Homes Executive Development Institute. He became an adjunct instructor of fire fighting at Dillard University in New Orleans.

Sources: *Jet* 97 (27 December 1999–3 January 2000): 33.

2001 St. Louis • For the first time a Catholic priest became president of the Board of Police Commissioners. Maurice Joseph Nutt (1962–), the first black pastor of historic St. Alphonsus Ligouri "Rock" Church in St. Louis, was elected to that post. The St. Louis native graduated from Holy Redeemer College (B.A., 1985), Catholic Theological Union (1989), Xavier University of Louisiana (1989) and continued study at Acquinas Institute of Theology. Nutt has served on the faculty of St. Louis University and as pastor of St. Alphonsus Rock Church. His professional and community affiliations include being a member of the St. Louis Civil Rights Commission and president of the National Black Catholic Seminarians Association.

Sources: *Jet* 100 (8 October 2001): 20; *Who's Who among African Americans*, 26th ed., pp. 943–44.

2007 Wichita • Carl Brewer, the new mayor of Wichita, was sworn in office, becoming the first elected black mayor of the city. With 62 percent of the vote, Brewer defeated the incumbent; he promised to develop the downtown area and make government efficient. He was re-elected to a four-year term in April 2011.

Sources: *Jet* 111 (30 April 2007): 11.

Nevada

1997 North Las Vegas • Joe Tillman was appointed chief of police, becoming the first black to hold that post in the state's history. Before his promotion, Tillman was interim deputy chief. The seventeen-year-veteran of the department had served as patrol officer, supervisor, and undercover narcotics officer.

Sources: *Jet* 92 (22 September 1997): 19.

1999 Las Vegas • Lynette Boggs McDonald was sworn in as a member of the city council, becoming the first woman and the first black to serve on the council. The representative for Ward 2, she was director of marketing and community relations at the University of Nevada, Las Vegas. McDonald graduated from the University of Notre Dame and received a Master's of Public Administration from the University of Nevada, Las Vegas. She is a former Miss Oregon.

Sources: *Jet* 96 (2 August 1999): 7.

2001 Las Vegas • David L. Washington became the first black chief of the Fire and Rescue Department. The Delhi, Louisiana, native began his career with the city as a firefighter in 1974. He was deputy chief/fire marshal and then was promoted to interim fire chief.

Sources: *Jet* 100 (15 October 2001): 25.

New Jersey

1966 Paterson • William H. Hicks (1925–) was the first black alderman in Paterson. Hicks was a very successful car salesman. In 1971, he was elected to the New Jersey legislature. Born in Littleton, North Carolina, Hicks was educated at William Patterson College. Hicks also served as director of State County Housing, an alderman for Paterson's Fourth Ward (1966–71), and a New Jersey assemblyman (1971–75).

Sources: *Ebony Success Library*, vol. 1, p. 151; *Who's Who among African Americans*, 26th ed., p. 5977.

Newark's First Black Mayor

On June 16, 1970, Kenneth Allen Gibson (1932–) was elected mayor of Newark, becoming the first black mayor of a major eastern city. While in office, Gibson focused on a number of areas: he worked to improve the city's economy, to reduce serious crime, and to provide better health care. He held office until 1986, when he was defeated in the mayoral election. Gibson was born in Enterprise, Alabama, and relocated to Newark with his family when he was eight years old. A 1963 graduate of the Newark College of Engineering, he had worked part-time for ten years before receiving his degree. He also worked on Urban Renewal projects for the Newark Housing Authority before his election as mayor. He was also the first black president of the United States Conference of Mayors in July 1976.

Sources: *Current Biography Yearbook*, 1971, pp. 149–52; *Ebony Success Library*, vol. 1, p. 125; *Encyclopedia of Black America*, p. 404; Hornsby, *Chronology of African-American History*, p. 145; *Who's Who among Black Americans*, 26th ed., p. 460; *Contemporary Black Biography*, vol. 6, pp. 96–99.

1970 Princeton • James A. "Jim" Floyd was elected the first black mayor of Princeton Township by the five-member township committee. He took office on January 1, 1971. Floyd was born in Trenton and moved to Princeton in 1946.

Sources: Historical Society of Princeton; Hornsby, *Chronology of African-American History*, p. 158; *Negro Almanac*, p. 61; *New York Times* (3 September 2001).

1971 Princeton • In December 1971 Frederick M. Porter became the first black police chief.

1972 Englewood • Walter Scott Taylor (1916–1984) was the first black mayor of Englewood. Born in Jackson, Mississippi, this United Methodist minister held the office until 1975. He was educated in Atlanta, at Clark College (A.B., 1943) and Gammon Theological Seminary (B.D., 1946). He has pastored several churches.

Sources: *Jet* 66 (30 July 1984): 33; "Rev. Walter Taylor, Ex-Mayor in Jersey Led Drive for Rights," *New York Times* (18 June 1984).

1984 Atlantic City • James Leroy Usry (1922–2002) was the first black mayor of Atlantic City. While in office, he was an advocate for programs aimed to benefit the poorer residents, such as housing, education, affirmative action, and redevelopment of the blighted northeast Inlet neighborhood. Other residents, however, protested what they called lukewarm interest in the city's economic base, the casino and hotel industry. Usry was mayor until 1990, when he was defeated in the middle of a municipal corruption scandal. Although indicted on charges of conspiracy, official misconduct, and bribery, the case against him appeared to collapse. He later pleaded guilty to violating the campaign finance law and worked with the Salvation Army to meet his sentence of sixty hours' community service. Municipal corruption had existed in Atlantic City since the 1960s; three of his five predecessors were convicted of or pleaded guilty to crimes. Born in Athens, Georgia, Usry moved with his family to Atlantic City when he was a small child. He served in World War II with the 92nd Infantry Division. For a while he played professional basketball with the Harlem Globetrotters and the New York Renaissance. Usry graduated from Lincoln University in Pennsylvania and Glassboro State College (now Rowan University). He was a teacher and school administrator before entering politics at age sixty. Suffering from diabetes and cancer, he died in a nursing home in Galloway Township.

Sources: *Who's Who among African Americans*, 14th ed., p. 1315; *Contemporary Black Biography*, vol. 23, pp. 208–10; *New York Times* Obituaries (28 January 2002).

1990 Trenton • Douglas Harold Palmer (1951–) was elected mayor, the first black to hold that post. He was re-elected in 1994 after receiving 73 percent of the vote. Born in Trenton, New Jersey, Palmer graduated from Hampton Institute (now University) in Virginia in 1973. He was a senior account for the Trenton Board of Education from 1976 to 1988, coordinator of communication from 1981 to 1982, and assistant secretary of purchasing in 1982. He entered the political arena, becoming Mercer County Legislator before he was elected mayor.

Sources: *Jet* 86 (20 June 1994): 37; *Who's Who among African Americans,* 26th ed., p. 959.

1994 Englewood • James Earl Mosley Sr. (1939–) was promoted to chief of police, becoming the first black to hold that post. The twenty-nine-year veteran of the department was deputy police chief before his promotion. Mosley was born in Hackensack, New Jersey, and received an associate's degree in 1975 from Bergen Community College. He had been active in professional and civic organizations, including the National Organization of Black Law Enforcement Executives, heading the organization since 1990.

Sources: *Jet* 86 (20 June 1994): 20; *Who's Who among African Americans,* 26th ed., p. 913.

1996 Fairfield • Viola Thomas became the city's first black mayor.

Sources: *Jet* 91 (25 November 1996): 10.

1997 Paterson • The first black mayor of Paterson, New Jersey, was Martin G. Barnes (1948–); he was appointed mayor in January 1997 and won the post in the November election. In 1988 he ran unopposed. In 2002 Barnes pleaded innocent to federal charges of routinely accepting cash and gifts from companies that did business with the city. He also faced a forty-count indictment on various charges, including extortion.

Sources: *Jet* 102 (25 March 2002): 19; *Who's Who among African Americans,* 26th ed., p. 69.

1998 Newark • Barbara George was sworn in office, becoming the first black woman police captain. The Newark native joined the force in 1981. She has also headed the department's Sexual Assault and Rape Analysis Unit.

Sources: *Jet* 93 (9 March 1998): 38; *Who's Who among African Americans,* 14th ed., p. 466.

2001 Camden • Gwendolyn A. Faison (1924?–) became the first woman mayor and the forty-fifth person to hold that office. She held the post in an acting position since December 2000, when the mayor in office was imprisoned for corruption. For sixteen years Faison had served on the city council.

Sources: *Jet* 100 (6 August 2001): 18.

2007 Atlantic City • Firefighter brothers Keith, Edward, and Harold Coursey became the first three black siblings promoted to captain on the same day. After they lost two sisters in a house fire in 1959, they were motivated to become firefighters and hoped it would "never happen to anyone else, if we can prevent it." They work at Deputy Chiec Pierre Hollingsworth Station # 3, which is named in honor of one of the city's pioneering black firefighters, now retired.

Sources: *Jet* 111 (23 April 2007): 31.

New York

1626 New York City • There were eleven blacks in New Amsterdam, now New York City, in the year of its founding, 1626. Four are the first named blacks there: Paul d'Angola, Simon Congo, Anthony Portuguese, and John Francisco.

Sources: Johnson, *Black Manhattan,* p. 4.

1917 New York City • The first black representative elected to the Board of Aldermen was James C. Thomas, who was elected in November.

Sources: *The Black New Yorkers,* p. 158.

1929 New York City • The first black district leader in the Republican Party was Charles W. Fillmore.

Sources: *The Black New Yorkers*, p. 206.

1935 New York City • Businessman Herbert L. Bruce became the first black district leader in the Democratic Party.

Sources: *The Black New Yorkers*, p. 231.

1935 New York City • Dorothy Irene Height (1912–2010) became the first black personnel supervisor for the Department of Welfare. Previously, she was a caseworker for the department. She was promoted to the advisory position after the Harlem riots of 1935; her charge was to examine the unrest. She also became concerned with the plight of black women who worked as domestics. Serving as an advocate for them, she testified before the New York City Council in 1938 concerning the "slave market" for black domestics who were paid substandard wages. After leaving her post in New York, in 1939 Height became executive secretary of the YMCA's Phyllis Wheatley Home in Washington, D.C. Around this time as well, she met Mary McLeod Bethune, founder and president of the National Council of Negro Women (NCNW). In 1957 Height became president of the NCNW, an organization that aimed to unite and uplift black women in humanitarian and social action programs. While still discharging her duties at NCNW, Height remained active in civil rights activities. During the 1960s, she led the organization to become active in voter registration drives in the North and South. She saw that the YWCA remained involved in civil rights activities as well. During her tenure with the NCNW, she brought substantial financial support to the organization, guided the NCNW through phenomenal growth, and ensured that it remained diligent in effecting change in black women and their position in society. She retired from NCNW in 1988 and Jane E. Smith became her successor. Height was born in Richmond, Virginia, and relocated with her family to Rankin, Pennsylvania. She graduated from New York University with a bachelor's and master's degree; later she did postgraduate work at New York University. At her death on April 20, 2010, President Barack Obama called her "godmother of the Civil Rights Movement."

Dorothy Height

Sources: *African American Almanac*, 11th ed., pp. 510–11; The *Black New Yorkers*, p. 230; Smith, *Notable Black American Women*, pp. 485–89.

1935 New York City • Eunice Hunton Carter (1900–1970) was the first black woman assistant district attorney. She held the post for ten years, also serving as the only black on Thomas E. Dewey's staff in his investigation of the rackets. Carter was born in Atlanta to Alphaeus Hunton and Addie [Waites] Hunton, who figured prominently in the development of the YMCA and the YWCA. The Hunton family relocated to Brooklyn, New York, in 1906, after the race riots of that year. Carter graduated from Smith College in 1921, with both the A.B. and A.M. degrees. In October 1932 she received her LL.D. degree from Fordham University and was admitted to the New York Bar in October 1932. She established a private practice and remained active as a lawyer, civic worker, and political worker in the Republican politics. After the 1935 New York riots, Mayor Fiorella La Guardia named her secretary of the Committee on Conditions in Harlem. Thomas E. Dewey in 1935 named her special prosecutor for an extraordinary grand jury probe into organized crime. She was the only woman and the only black on his ten-member staff. Carter was a charter member of the National Council of Negro Women; she was also the organization's legal advisor and chair of its board of trustees. She retired from active law practice in 1952 and devoted her time to the work of various organizations until her death.

Sources: *Jet* 84 (19 July 1993): 39; Lerner, *Black Women in White America*, p. 322; Smith, *Notable Black American Women*, pp. 165–66.

1941 New York City • Adam Clayton Powell Jr. (1908–1972) was the first black to serve as a member of the City Council in 1941.

Sources: Cantor, *Historic Landmarks of Black America*, p. 93; Hamilton, *Adam Clayton Powell Jr.*, p. 116.

The First Black Woman Judge

In 1939 Jane M. Bolin (1908–2007) became the first black woman judge in the United States when she was appointed to the Domestic Relations Court of New York City. Bolin was born in Poughkeepsie, New York. Her father, Gaius C. Bolin, had been the first black graduate of Williams College in 1889. Jane Bolin graduated from Wellesley College and Yale University School of Law. She was a clerk in her father's law practice and later established her own practice in Poughkeepsie for a brief period. From 1937 to 1939 she was assistant corporation counsel for New York City. Mayor Fiorello La Guardia then appointed her to the Domestic Relations Court on June 22, 1939. Later that court was renamed Family Court of the State of New York. Subsequent mayors reappointed Bolin to that court, enabling her to serve successive ten-year terms. Bolin retired on January 1, 1979, after forty years of service on the bench.

Sources: *Encyclopedia of Black America*, p. 185; *Negro Almanac*, p. 1426; Smith, *Notable Black American Women*, pp. 94–95; *Contemporary Black Biography*, vol. 22, pp. 38–40.

1943 Buffalo • Robert Berry Howard Jr. (1916–) was the first black firefighter in Buffalo. A native of Barnesville, Georgia, Howard became commissioner of the department in 1966. He was a lieutenant with the Buffalo Fire Department from 1943 to 1951. From 1951 to 1960 he was captain, and then was named fire commissioner until he retired.

Sources: *Ebony Success Library*, vol. 1, p. 160; *Who's Who among African Americans*, 14th ed., pp. 626–27.

1951 New York City • William Leon Rowe (1915–1997) became the city's first black deputy chief commissioner in August. Rowe was also a nationally syndicated newspaper columnist for the *Pittsburgh Courier*. He was born in St. Matthews, South Carolina, and educated at Southern University, where he received his Ph.D. Most of Rowe's experience, however, was in the media. He was senior war correspondent in World War II, theatre editor for the *Interstate Tattler/Harlem News/Pittsburgh Courier*; and press agent and consultant for MGM and 20th Century Fox. Other positions include host and producer of "Conversation Rowe," a radio show.

Sources: *Jet* 92 (13 October 1997): 18; *Who's Who among African Americans*, 10th ed., p. 1303.

1953 New York City • On December 31, 1953, Hulan Jack (1905–1986) became the first black borough president of Manhattan. At the time, he was this country's most powerful, highest paid, and highest-ranking black elected official. When elected, he had integrated New York's Democratic political machine known as Tammany Hall. A native of Saint Lucia, in the British West Indies, Jack was the son of a bishop of the African Orthodox Church. He came to New York City as a very young man, and soon was active in politics. He also supported the Marcus Garvey movement that focused on equality and racial pride. Jack had served in the state assembly for thirteen years when he became head of Manhattan. After being charged with accepting an illegal gift, he resigned his position in 1959 during his second term. His constituency, however, considered the charges discriminatory. After resigning, Jack continued to work for the Democratic party and sought to clear his name as well. Although he cleared his name with his constituency, the conviction was never overturned.

Sources: Clayton, *The Negro Politician*, pp. 57–61; Hornsby, *Chronology of African-American History*, p. 99; *Encyclopedia of Black America*, p. 465; *Negro Almanac*, p. 28; Smith, *Notable Black American Men*, pp. 594–96.

1954 New York City • Anna Arnold Hedgeman (1899–1990) was the first black woman member of the cabinet of a mayor, Robert F. Wagner. In 1922 she was the first African-

American graduate of Hamline University (St. Paul, Minnesota). After working at Rust College in Mississippi, she went to work for the Young Women's Christian Association in Springfield, Ohio (1924), eventually moving to the Harlem branch in New York City. She worked for local and federal governments, and for religious and civic organizations throughout her life. She was a major organizer of the March on Washington in 1963. She also helped to create the interfaith leadership of Catholics, Protestants, and Jewish people that successfully worked to pass the 1964 Civil Rights Act.

Sources: *Encyclopedia of Black America*, p. 435; *Negro Almanac*, pp. 1381–82; Smith, *Notable Black American Women*, pp. 483–89.

1957 Brooklyn • The first black city councilman was J. Daniel Diggs.

Sources: *The Black New Yorkers*, p. 283.

1959 New York City • The first black to head a department of public welfare in a major American city was James Dumpson. He advocated city programs to help black families and young people.

Sources: *The Black New Yorkers*, p. 289.

1965 New York City • James A. Thomas was promoted to the rank of warden for the House of Detention for Men on Rikers Island, becoming the first black to hold that post in the city's Department of Corrections. He joined the Department of Corrections in 1946. Although his appointment was provisional, it came three years before that of James C. Harrison, the first black warden at the Brooklyn House of Detention. Harrison is sometimes credited with being the department's first black warden. The provisional status for both men was removed when each was sworn in on April 29, 1965. In honor of Thomas, on April 28, 1989, the House of Detention for Men on Rikers Island was renamed the James A. Thomas Center.

Sources: Jail Exchange: Rikers Island - James A. Thomas Center, http://www.jailexchange .com/CountyJails/New_York/New_York/Rikers_Island_James_A_Thomas_Ctr.aspx, accessed September 25, 2012. "Black History Month Notes: Firsts and Facility Names," http://www.correctionhistory.org/html/chronicl/nycdoc/html/blackhst. html, accessed September 25, 2012.

1965 New York City • The first black appointed executive deputy superintendent of schools was John B. King. In 1967 he became a faculty member on the school of education at Fordham University.

Sources: *The Black New Yorkers*, p. 316.

1966 New York City • On January 1, 1966, Robert O. Lowery (1916–2001) was the first black fire commissioner of a major city and was also the first commissioner that Mayor John V. Lindsay appointed after his election that year. Lowery had joined the department as a fireman in 1941. Born in Buffalo, he attended the College of the City of New York and Michigan State University. He also trained at the National Institute on Police and Community Relations.

Sources: *The Black New Yorkers*, p. 319; *Ebony Success Library*, vol. 2, pp. 154–57; *Negro Almanac*, p. 1412; *New York Times* (27 July 2001); *Who's Who among African Americans*, 14th ed., p. 820.

1966 New York City • Constance Baker Motley (1921–2005) was the first black woman president of the Borough of Manhattan.

Sources: *Negro Almanac*, pp. 344–45; *Ebony Success Library*, vol. 2, pp. 174–77; *Encyclopedia of Black America*, p. 582; Smith, *Notable Black American Women*, pp. 779–82; *Who's Who among African Americans*, 14th ed, p. 951.

1969 New York City • Ivan Michael, a Harlem lawyer, became the first black appointed to the Planning Commission. The general counsel for the United Block Association, he also served as a board member of the New York Urban League.

Sources: *The Black New Yorkers*, p. 337.

1969 New York City • The nation's first black superintendent of a woman's prison was Jessie L. Behagan, who was appointed to that post. She took charge of Rikers Island, where over 500 inmates were housed. Behagan graduated from City College of New York and, during thirty-one years of service, rose through the ranks in the city's Department of Corrections.

Sources: *The Black New Yorkers*, p. 337.

1970 New York City • Governor Nelson Rockefeller appointed Lawrence Bailey Sr. (1918–1998) to the Metropolitan Transportation Authority board, making him the first black to hold that post. He remained on the board for twenty years, and in 1975 became vice chair, the first black to hold office on MTA. He retired in 1990.

Sources: *New York Times* (28 April 1998); *Who's Who among African Americans*, 10th ed., p. 60.

1970 Staten Island • The first black appointed as assistant district attorney was Arthur Lewis.

Sources: *The Black New Yorkers*, p. 346.

1972 New York City • Benjamin J. Malcolm (1919–2001) was the first black appointed commissioner of corrections. New York was then the third major city in America to have a black in charge of its prison system. Malcolm held the post until 1977. Previously, he was a parole and corrections officer. He resigned as commissioner in November 1977 to become a member of President Jimmy Carter's nine-member United States Parole Commission. In 1984 he turned down the opportunity to chair the State Parole Board; instead, he founded the private company, Parole Services of America, which provides parole data to inmates seeking a parole. Born in Philadelphia, Malcolm graduated from Morehouse College in Atlanta in 1940 and received his master's degree from New York University in 1970.

Sources: *Encyclopedia of Black America*, p. 544; *The Black New Yorkers*, p 353; *New York Times* Obituaries (30 May 2001).

1974 New York City • Paul Gibson Jr. (1927–) was the first black deputy mayor for New York. Gibson was in charge of city planning.

Sources: *Black Enterprise* 2 (September 1971): 15–18; *Encyclopedia of Black America*, p. 404; *Who's Who among African Americans*, 26th ed., p. 460.

1977 New York City • Percy E. Sutton (1920–2009), pioneering civil rights attorney, political power broker, and media mogul, was the first seriously regarded black candidate for mayor. In 1965 he was elected to the New York State Assembly. When he was borough president of Manhattan from 1966 to 1977, at first he completed the term of Constance Baker Motley who became a federal judge, then he was regularly re-elected and became New York City's highest-ranking African American elected official. In 1971, Sutton co-founded Inner City Broadcasting Corporation, the first radio chain aimed at black listeners, and purchased radio stations WLIB (the city's first black-owned radio station), WBLS-FM, and other radio stations across the country. He also headed a group that owned *The Amsterdam News*, the nation's second largest black weekly. He led the revitalization of Harlem, including the restoration of the historic Apollo Theater in 1981, and also produced its syndicated music television show, *Showtime at the Apollo*. Sutton was born in San Antonio, the last of fifteen children, and grew up on a farm near Prairie View, Texas. He attended Prairie View A & M College, Tuskegee Institute, and Hampton Institute (all now universities) without graduating. His solid academic record enabled him to enter Columbia Law School; he transferred to Brooklyn Law School and graduated with the J.D. degree in 1950. Meanwhile, in his younger years he was a stunt pilot for country fairs. He joined the Tuskegee Airmen in World War II, became an intelligence officer with its 99th Pursuit Squadron, and flew sorties over the Italian and Mediterranean theaters. He was also an air force intelligence officer in Washington, D.C., later becoming the first black trial judge advocate in that branch of service. Sutton was a valued adviser to David Paterson, who in 2008 became governor of New York. Sutton was active in civil rights. After establishing his law firm in Harlem with two partners, including his brother, the Sutton firm defended the arrests of over 200 defendants during the 1963–64 civil rights marches. He was legal representative for Malcolm X. He was known among his associates as "the chairman." He was so well groomed, with a beard and mustache well-trimmed, and impeccably dressed in tailored suits that he also bore the moniker "wizard of ooze." Among his numerous awards was the NAACP's Spingarn Medal, in 1987. At Sutton's death, President Barack Obama called him "a true hero to African-Americans in New York City and around the country." and said that Sutton's "life-long dedication to the fight for civil rights and his career as an entrepreneur and public servant made the rise of countless young African-Americans possible."

Sources: *Contemporary Black Biography,* vol. 42, pp. 170–73. vol. 84, pp. 147–50; *New York Times Obituary* (27 December 2009); "Percy Sutton, Attorney for Malcolm X, Dies At 89." http://www.msnbc.com/id/34599259/ns/us_news-life/; *Who's Who among African Americans,* vol. 26, p. 1194.

1977 New York City • Lucille Mason Rose (1918–1987) was the first black woman named deputy mayor of the city. Her first efforts were devoted to providing jobs for teenagers. A native of Richmond, Virginia, Rose and her family relocated to the largely black Bedford-Stuyvesant section of Brooklyn when she was seven years old. She graduated from Brooklyn College (B.A., 1951) and later attended the college's night program and received a degree in economics. She received a master's degree in manpower planning and development from the New School of Social Work. In 1963 Rose became director of the Brooklyn Field Office of the New York City Department of Labor. Mayor John Lindsay in 1966 named her assistant commissioner and later first deputy commissioner for the Manpower and Career Development Agency. In 1972 Mayor Abraham Beame named Rose commissioner of the New York City Department of Employment. In 1977 Beame named her deputy mayor for planning and manpower, making her the first woman to be appointed deputy mayor. Rose had served on the National Democratic Executive Committee and, at the time of her death, was a member of the Democratic National Committee. She was a founding director of the Bedford-Stuyvesant Restoration Corporation. Active with religious organizations as well, from 1981 to 1985 she was the first woman president of the Catholic Interracial Council.

Sources: *Jet* 52 (24 March 1977): 6; 72 (7 September 1987): 52; *The Negro Almanac,* pp. 1390–91; Smith, *Notable Black American Women,* Book II, pp. 573–74.

1982 New York City • JoAnn M. Jacobs was the first black woman firefighter in the city. At the time, Jacobs was thirty-one years old and a physical education instructor.

Sources: *Jet* 63 (13 December 1982): 44.

1984 New York City • Benjamin Ward (1926–2002) was the first black police commissioner of New York City. He served until 1989, when he resigned for health reasons. He had joined the department in 1951 and had served in several posts, including that of police chief in 1979. Born in Brooklyn, Ward graduated from Brooklyn College (B.A., 1960) and the Brooklyn Law School (LL.B., 1965).

Sources: *Jet* 77 (16 October 1989): 38; *Who's Who among African Americans,* 14th ed., p. 1340.

1985 Mount Vernon • As mayor of Mount Vernon, Ronald A. Blackwood (1926–) was the first black elected mayor in the state of New York, serving until 1995. He was chosen in a special election to replace a mayor who died in office. Blackwood also served on the Westchester County Board of Supervisors and was active in various community organizations. A native of Kingston, Jamaica, Blackwood graduated from Iona College in New Rochelle, New York, with a bachelor's degree in management. He had lived in the city for thirty years.

Sources: *Jet* 67 (4 March 1985); *Who's Who among African Americans,* 26th ed., p. 108.

David Dinkins

1989 New York City • On November 7, 1989, David Norman Dinkins (1927–) was elected the first black mayor of New York; he took office in 1990 as the 106th mayor. He had defeated Republican district attorney Rudolph Giuliani, who later defeated Dinkins in his bid for re-election in 1993. Among his accomplishments while in office, Dinkins practiced sound financial management that resulted in a budget surplus in 1992. He also deactivated a racial time bomb that was set to ignite after cases of police brutality emerged in Los Angeles and elsewhere. Beginning in 1956, he was active in Democratic Party politics, and was elected to the New York State Assembly in 1966. He held office as president of the city Board of Elections (1972–73), city clerk (1975–85), and Manhattan borough president (1986–90) before he became mayor. Dinkins was born in Trenton, New Jersey, and was drafted into the U.S. Army after graduating from high school. He later transferred from the Army into the Marines. After he was discharged in 1946, he enrolled in Howard University and graduated in 1950. He received his law degree from Brooklyn Law School in 1956. After graduation, he entered law practice with Basil Paterson, who was vice-chairman of the Democratic National Committee. There he handled cases involving banking, probate, and real estate, and at the same time became known as a skilled mediator. He became associated with J. Raymond Jones, called the "Harlem Fox;" Jones headed the Carver Democratic Club which provided a training ground for black business and political leaders. While Dinkins ran errands for the organization and performed many tasks related to a political campaign, he also became the protégé of Jones, who recognized in Dinkins a political ambition. It was Jones who helped him win his first election in 1966. After leaving office as mayor, Dinkins remained involved in a call-in radio show, held office on numerous corporate boards, and taught at Columbia University's School of International and Public Affairs.

Sources: Hornsby, *Chronology of African-American History,* pp. 411–12; *Jet* 79 (22 January 1990): 4; 81 (18 November 1991): 62; Smith, *Notable Black American Men,* pp. 304–7; *Who's Who among African Americans,* 26th ed., p. 342.

1989 New York City • Janice White was first woman warden of the Manhattan House of Corrections, often called the "Tombs," and at the time the only woman warden in the New York penal system. Born in Philadelphia, the forty-nine-year-old White had worked for the state corrections department for some twenty years.

Sources: *Jet* 76 (17 April 1989): 28–31.

1989 New York City • C. Virginia Fields became the first black woman elected to the city council from Manhattan. She served for two terms (eight years). In 1997 she was elected Manhattan Borough president, and then inaugurated president for her second term in January 2002. New York Supreme Court Justice Leland DeGrase swore her in office at a ceremony at the Metropolitan Museum of Art. Fields vowed to help rebuild lower Manhattan; she also supported plans for a memorial to those who lost their lives in the terrorist attacks on September 11, 2001. Fields graduated from Knoxville College in Tennessee and received her master's degree from Indiana University.

Sources: *Contemporary Black Biography,* vol. 25, pp. 64–66; *Who's Who among Black Americans,* 26th ed., p. 407.

1994 New York City • Joyce Stephens was promoted from lieutenant to captain on the police force, becoming the first black woman to attain that rank. She was a thirteen-year veteran of the Police Department.

Sources: *Jet* 86 (20 June 1994): 20.

1996 New York City • Stephanie Palmer (1952–) became the first woman executive director of the New York City Mission Society. Previously, she was executive director of the city's Human Services Council. Palmer was born in Philadelphia and educated at Middlebury College (B.A, 1974) and Temple University (M.A., 1978).

Sources: *Jet* 91 (16 October 1996): 22; *Who's Who among African Americans,* 26th ed., p. 959.

New York's First Black District Attorney

In 1989 Robert T. Johnson (1948–) became district attorney for New York City, the first black to hold that post. Born in the Bronx section of New York City, he watched his father serve as a court officer and later hold a ranking spot on the court police force. He decided then that law could be his mission in life. Johnson graduated from City College of New York (B.A., 1972) and New York University (J.D., 1975). After graduating from law school, Johnson served as criminal defense attorney for the New York Legal Aid Society from 1975 to 1978. He was Bronx assistant district attorney from 1978 to 1986. He was also deputy chief of the Major Offense Bureau in 1984 and chief of the Narcotics Bureau from 1984 to 1986. In August 1986 he was appointed a judge of the New York Criminal Court, and then in 1987 he was promoted to acting justice of the New York State Supreme Court. He was elected district attorney of Bronx County on November 8, 1988, and took office on January 1 the following year. He continues to serve as district attorney as of 2012.

Sources: *Contemporary Black Biography*, vol. 17, pp. 110–13; *Who's Who among African Americans*, 26th ed., p. 679.

2002 New York City • Firefighter Ella McNair was promoted to lieutenant in a ceremony at the Fire Department's Brooklyn headquarters on January 29, becoming the first black woman to hold that rank in the department. In 1982 she was a member of the first class of firefighters to include women. McNair, now in her mid-forties, grew up in Bedford-Stuyvesant and became a firefighter while in her early twenties. Early in her tenure, she found a news clipping on the firehouse wall that she considered derogatory to women firefighters. As she attempted to remove it with a knife, a male colleague took the knife from her, resulting in a badly cut finger for McNair and a $15,000 fine, suspension, and transfer for the colleague. McNair resigned in 1988 but returned two years later. Since 1992 she worked at Engine Company 283 in Brownsville, Brooklyn.

Sources: *New York Times* (30 January 2002).

2002 New York City • The first black comptroller for New York City was William C. Thompson Jr., former president of the New York City Board of Education. Thompson was elected the 108th comptroller by an overwhelming majority vote.

Sources: *Jet* 102 (4 March 2002): 19.

2002 New York City • Helen M. Marshall took office on January 1, becoming the first black woman elected as Queens Borough president. Previously, Marshall served on the city council.

Sources: *Jet* 100 (3 December 2001): 10.

2007 Rochester • Theresa Everett became the first black woman to be named deputy fire chief for the Rochester Fire Department. An experienced fire fighting administrator, she served as director of training for the department. Earlier, she was a firefighter and fire official in Florida. Everett was also executive director of the International Association of Black Professional Firefighters.

Sources: *Jet* 111 (16 April 2007): 31.

North Carolina

1885 Princeville • Toward the end of the Civil War, blacks settled along the banks of the Tar River community called "Freedom Hill." Sometime after the war ended, the town was renamed to become Princeville. In 1885 it became the first town in North Carolina chartered by blacks. Located sixty-two miles east of Raleigh, Princeville was home to 2,100 people. Until recent years, when continuous floods damaged the area, the town thrived. Princeville reached national public attention in 2000, after Hurricane Floyd dropped as much as twenty inches of rain on the area on September 16, 1999, devastating the area. Some 1,183 homes, apartments, and mobile homes were destroyed or damaged; flood insurance covered only seven of the houses. President Bill Clinton in 2000 directed twelve federal agencies and several Cabinet members to take action to repair and rebuild the town. U.S. representatives Eva Clayton of North Carolina and Charles Rangel of New York spearheaded the president's efforts.

Sources: *Jet* 97 (20 March 2000): 9; *New York Times* (10 September 2000).

1959 Kinston • Alice Priscilla Stateman Hannibal (1917?–1994) became the first woman and the first black elected to the Board of Aldermen.

Sources: *Jet* 87 (28 November 1994): 60.

1966 Fairmont • Joy Joseph Johnson (1921–1996) was the first black elected to the town board. The pastor of the First Baptist Church, Johnson would become the second black elected to the state House since Reconstruction in 1970. In 1989 he became the first black mayor of Fairmont. Born in Laurel Hill, North Carolina, Johnson graduated from Shaw University in Raleigh with A.B. and LL.D. degrees. He was pastor of First Baptist Church in Fairmont. In 1978 he became state parole commissioner and from 1972 to 1973 he was a member of the state legislature.

Sources: *Ebony Success Library,* vol. 1, p. 179; *Who's Who among African Americans,* 14th ed., p. 694.

1969 Chapel Hill • Howard N. Lee (1934–) was elected mayor of Chapel Hill, becoming the first black elected mayor in a predominantly white southern city. Lee would hold this office until 1975. Born in Lithonia, Georgia, Lee graduated from Ft. Valley State College (now University) in Georgia (B.A., 1959), the University of North Carolina (M.S.W., 1966), and Shaw University (LL.D., 1971). His wide experiences include positions as probation officer with the Juvenile Domestic Relations Court in Savannah (1961–64), youth program director at Duke University (1966–68), visiting assistant professor at North Carolina Central University (1961–64), president and chairman of the board for Plastiwood Products, and director of the office of human development at Duke.

Sources: *Ebony Success Library,* vol. 1, p. 199; *Encyclopedia of Black America,* p. 503; *Negro Almanac,* p. 51; *Who's Who among African Americans,* 26th ed., p. 756.

1983 Charlotte • Harvey Bernard Gantt (1943–) was the first black elected mayor of Charlotte. This Charleston, South Carolina, native and architect holds a degree from Clemson in South Carolina (1965), in which he was the first black to enroll, and an M.A. from the Massachusetts Institute of Technology (1970). Gantt had served as mayor pro tempore of Charlotte from 1981 to 1983. On June 6, 1990, he was the first black to win the Democratic nomination for United States Senator.

Sources: Hornsby, *Chronology of African-American History,* p. 431; *Jet* 65 (20 February 1984): 40; *Who's Who among African Americans,* 26th ed., 447; *Contemporary Black Biography,* vol. 1, pp. 72–74.

1999 Trenton • The Trenton Town Council, by unanimous vote, elected Sylvia Willis as mayor, making her the first black to hold office. She completed the term of Joffree Leggett, who resigned in March after saying that blacks were unfit to govern, that they were not leaders, and they preferred white leaders. He supported the town's refusal to annex three black neighborhoods; after that, a black boycott of Trenton's businesses spurred the council to annex the communities. At that time, Trenton had fifty blacks among its 200 residents. Willis had retired from management positions in post offices in New York and North Carolina.

Sources: *Jet* 95 (10 May 1999): 34; *New York Times* (2 November 1999).

2001 Fayetteville • Marshall Pitts Jr. (1964?–) became the first black major of Fayetteville. A first-term council member, Pitts won the election with 56 percent of the vote.

Sources: *Jet* 100 (3 December 2001): 5.

2002 Charlotte • The first black woman appointed captain of the Charlotte Fire Department was Sylvia Smith-Phifer (1969?–). She was one of the few women to apply for a position with the fire department within the last ten years. She was successful in the strenuous physical portion of the department's qualifying battery of tests that included dragging a 200-foot hose and wearing a 50-pound vest while climbing stairs. Of the 280,000 firefighters nationwide, approximately 2 percent are women. In Charlotte, however, 4 percent of the 872 firefighters are women. Smith-Phifer joined the department in 1992, the last black woman to be hired. She is also married to a firefighter.

Sources: *Jet* 101 (18 February 2002): 39.

Ohio

1942 Cleveland • Perry B. Jackson (1896–1986) was the first black judge in Ohio when he was appointed to the Municipal Court of Cleveland. In 1960 Jackson became judge in the Court of Common Pleas of Cuyahoga County, a position from which he retired in 1972.

Sources: *Ebony* (April 1947): 17; 6 (September 1950): 45–49; *Ebony Success Library,* vol. 1, p. 170; *Encyclopedia of Black America,* p. 468.

1949 Cleveland • Jean Murrell Capers (1913–) was the first black woman elected to the city council.

Sources: Clayton, *The Negro Politician,* pp. 137–38; *Ebony* 6 (September 1950): 45–49; 6 (November 1950): 48–49; 11 (August 1956): 82; 21 (August 1966): 97.

1966 Springfield • On January 3, 1966, Robert Clayton Henry (1923–) was the first black mayor of an integrated Ohio city. Born in Springfield, Ohio, Henry, director of Robert C. Henry and Son Funeral Home, was a commissioner for the City of Springfield from 1963 to 1966.

Sources: Alford, *Famous First Blacks,* p. 46; *Jet* 61 (7 January 1982): 24; *Who's Who among African Americans,* 14th ed., p. 584.

1969 Cleveland • Lillian W. Burke (1917–2012) was the first black woman elected to the Ohio bench. She was a judge in the municipal court. A native of Thomaston, Georgia, Burke took her law degree at the Cleveland Marshall Law School in 1951. She practiced law from 1952 to 1962 and then became a school teacher. From 1962 to 1966 she was assistant general attorney. Burke was member and vice chair of the Ohio Industrial Commission from 1966 to 1969 and then returned to teaching, this time at Cleveland Community College, Western Campus. She was first appointed judge in 1969 and elected a full term judge beginning that same year.

Sources: *Ebony Success Library,* vol. 1, p. 51; *Encyclopedia of Black America,* p. 199; *Who's Who among African Americans,* 26th ed., p. 180.

1972 Cincinnati • Theodore Moody Berry (1905–2000) was the first black mayor of the city. He was chosen by the city council, rather than by popular election. He held the office until 1975. Berry had been the first black elected to the city council in 1949. While he served as acting mayor in December 1955, he was long denied the title he had earned through his competence and vote-getting abilities. Born in Maysville, Kentucky, Berry graduated from the University of Cincinnati (A.B., 1928, LL.B., 1931). He was a member of the Cincinnati City Council from 1950 to 1957 and assistant director of the Office of Economic opportunity from 1965 to 1969. Berry was an attorney with Tobias and Kraus,

The First Black Elected Mayors of Major Cities

On November 13, 1967, Carl Burton Stokes (1927–1996) was elected mayor of Cleveland, becoming the first black elected mayor of a major American city. (Although Walter E. Washington took office on September 28 that year, becoming the first black to head the District of Columbia, he was appointed to the post.) Stokes and Richard G. Hatcher (1933–) were elected on the same day, but Hatcher was not sworn in until January 1, 1968, when he became the first black mayor of Gary, Indiana. Stokes was born in Cleveland and graduated from the University of Minnesota (B.S., 1954) and Cleveland Marshall Law School (J.D., 1956). He held a number of posts, including partner in the law firm Minor McCurty Stokes and Stokes from 1956 to 1958. He was Cleveland's assistant city prosecutor from 1958 to 1962. He was a state representative in the Ohio State Assembly from 1962 to 1967. After serving as mayor of Cleveland from 1967 to 1972, he became a correspondent and anchorman for WNBC-TV in New York City and was partner in several law firms. He was presiding administrative judge for the Cleveland Municipal Court from 1983 to 1986 and chief judge from 1986 to 1994. He was named U.S. ambassador to the Republic of the Seychelles in 1994.

Sources: *Ebony Success Library,* vol. 1, p. 145 (Hatcher); p. 293 (Stokes); *Encyclopedia of Black America,* pp. 422–23 (Hatcher); p. 810 (Stokes); *Who's Who among Black Americans, 1992–93,* p. 622 (Hatcher); p. 1343 (Stokes); Smith, *Notable Black American Men,* pp. 1086–88 (Stokes); *Contemporary Black Biography,* vol. 10, pp. 230–34 (Stokes).

and adjunct professor from 1976 to 1978 at the University of Cincinnati College of Law. He served as interim general counsel from 1979 to 1980.

Sources: Clayton, *The Negro Politician,* pp. 62–66; *Ebony Success Library,* vol. 1, p. 26; *Encyclopedia of Black America,* p. 173; Obituary, *Who's Who among African Americans,* p. 1467.

1972 Urbancrest • Ellen Walker Craig-Jones (1906?–2000) was the first black woman elected mayor of a U.S. municipality, serving as mayor from 1972 to 1975. Those who know her well affectionately called Craig-Jones "Aunt Dolly" or "Mother Craig." Previously, she had served twelve years as a member of the village Council. In recognition of her accomplishments, Craig-Jones was inducted into the Ohio Women's Hall of Fame in 1994. Born in Franklin County, Ohio, she was one of eleven children. Her mother died when Craig-Jones was eleven years old. After her father remarried, three more children were added to the family. She was educated in Urbancrest and Columbus, and followed the Christian principles that her parents had taught her. She was in her thirties when she completed her high school education. Although Craig-Jones worked as a domestic for a while, she had developed strong leadership skills and was committed to her community. In addition to her service as mayor, she served on various boards, commissions, and councils and became the first president of the Columbus Metropolitan Area Community Action Organization Federal Credit Union. She was honored widely for her humanitarian efforts in the community; the most noticeable of these came in 1974 when Ohio governor John Gilligan proclaimed Ellen Walker Craig Day and again in 1975 when Springfield, Ohio, also proclaimed an Ellen Walker Craig Day.

Sources: Cummings, "Black Women in Public Life," *Black Enterprise* 5 (August 1974): 33–35; *New York Times* (26 January 2000); Salem, *African American Women,* pp. 133–34.

1982 Akron • Janet Purnell was the first black, and the first woman, executive director of the Metropolitan Housing Authority. Purnell was an elementary school principal in the city at the time of her appointment.

Sources: *Jet* 63 (15 November 1982): 6.

First Black Women* Elected Mayors of
Selected Cities, Municipalities, and Towns

Date	Name	City, Municipality, Town
1972	Ellen Walker Craig-Jones	Urbancrest, Ohio
1973	Doris A. Davis	Compton, California
1973	Lelia Smith Foley	Taft, Oklahoma
1974	Carrie Kent	Walthouville, Georgia
1977	Unita Blackwell	Mayersville, Mississippi
1982	Loretta Thompson Glickman	Pasadena, California
1982	Mary Hall	Pageville, Missouri
1984	Mary Stoval	Hurtsboro, Alabama
1986	Helen Miller	Opa-Locka, Florida
1986	Carrie Saxon Perry	Hartford, Connecticut
1986	Jessie M. Rattley	Newport News, Virginia
1986	Lottie H. Shackelford	Little Rock, Arkansas
1989	Jessie Banks	Tchula, Mississippi
1990	Sharon Pratt Dixon Kelly	District of Columbia
1992	Patsy Jo Hilliard	East Point, Georgia
1993	Lorraine H. Morton	Evanston, Illinois
1994	Sharon Sales Belton	Minneapolis, Minnesota
1994	Sarah Brockington Bost	Irvington, New Jersey
1994	Jean Louise Harris	Eden Prairie, Minnesota
1995	LaMetta K. Wynn	Clinton, Iowa
1996	Thelma Collins	Itta Bena, Mississippi
1996	Viola Thomas	Fairfield, New Jersey
1999	Debra A. Powell	East St. Louis, Illinois
1999	Sylvia Willis	Trinton, North Carolina
2000	Mamie Evelyn Locke	Hampton, Virginia
2001	Gwendolyn A. Faison	Camden, New Jersey
2001	Rhine McLin	Dayton, Ohio
2002	Shirley Clarke Franklin	Atlanta, Georgia
2003	Yvonne Beals	Pittsburg, California
2007	Yvonne J. Johnson	Greensboro, North Carolina
2007	Sheila Dixon	Baltimore, Maryland
2009	Mia Love	Saratoga Springs, Utah
2009	Linda Thompson	Harrisburg, Pennsylvania

*Some are the first black person or the first woman of any race.

1982 Cleveland • George James was the first black director of the Cuyahoga Metropolitan Housing Authority. James had been director of the Los Angeles County Housing Authority.

Sources: *Jet* 63 (20 December 1982): 21.

1982 Cleveland • As deputy police chief, Lloyd Patterson (1931–) was the first black to hold an executive position in the Cleveland police department. Born in Cleveland, Patterson attended the Federal Bureau of Investigation's National Academy, graduating in 1975. He also graduated from the National Training Center of Polygraph Sciences in New York City. He served in several positions, including lieutenant, with the police department from 1957 to 1982. He also taught in Case Western Reserve University Law Medicine Center from 1978 to 1983.

Sources: *Who's Who among African Americans*, 26th ed., p. 969.

1992 Cincinnati • Dwight Tillery was the first black popularly elected mayor of Cincinnati. The two blacks who held the office previously had been selected by the city council.

Sources: *Ebony* 47 (March 1992): 107, 110; *Who's Who among African Americans,* 26th ed., p. 1235.

1995 Columbus • The first black woman executive director of the Equal Business Opportunity Commission in Columbus, Ohio, was Gwendolyn H. Rogers. She has served as legislative analyst for the Columbus City Council.

Sources: *Jet* 88 (11 September 1995): 27; *Who's Who among African Americans,* 26th ed., p. 1072.

1997 Akron • The first black fire chief in the city was Charles R. Gladman (1948?–). In 1973 he was one of seven blacks who integrated the department. He rose through the ranks from lieutenant/company officer to become captain, district fire chief, deputy chief, and then chief.

Sources: *Jet* 91 (19 May 1997): 39; *Who's Who among African Americans,* 26th ed., p. 468.

1997 Bexley • Jawama Smith became the first black police officer in the sixty-four-year history of the department. A graduate of Grambling State University in Louisiana, she continued her studies after joining the department, graduating from the Ohio State Highway Patrol Academy.

Sources: *Jet* 91 (3 March 1997): 20.

1997 Columbus • The first woman superintendent of the 63,000-student district of the Columbus Public Schools was Rosa A. Smith, beginning September. In this year as well, the former superintendent of the Beloit, Wisconsin, school district was named Superintendent of the Year in Wisconsin.

Sources: *Jet* 92 (22 September 1997): 19.

Michael B. Coleman

1999 Columbus • Michael Bennett Coleman (1954–) was elected mayor on November 2, becoming the first black to hold the post. He won the race with about sixty percent of the vote. He was also the first Democrat in that office since 1972. Coleman had served on the city council for eight years, becoming the council's president in 1997. Inaugurated on December 30, 1999, he took office in 2000. Born in Indianapolis, Coleman and his family moved to Toledo when he was three years old. He graduated from the University of Cincinnati in 1977 and received his law degree from the University of Dayton in 1980. In 1982 Coleman was legislative aid to Columbus City Councilman Ben Espy. He practiced law in Columbus with the firm Schottenstein and Zox, later becoming a partner in the firm.

Sources: *Contemporary Black Biography,* vol. 28, pp. 53–54; *New York Times* (2 November 1999); *Who's Who among African Americans,* 26th ed., p. 256;.

2001 Cleveland • Police department veteran Mary Bounds was sworn in as police chief, becoming the city's first woman and second black to hold that post. Since 1999 Bounds was deputy chief of administrative operations.

Sources: *Jet* 100 (17 September 2001): 35.

2001 Dayton • Former state majority leader, Rhine McLin (1948–) was elected mayor, becoming the first woman of any race to win that position. Although she was considered the "super-underdog," she defeated two-term incumbent Mike Turner, a Republican. She was also the first African American woman elected to the Ohio State senate and the first African American woman to serve as Ohio Senate minority leader. In late 2005, she became the first African American woman to serve as head of the Ohio Democratic Party.

Sources: "City Mayors: Rhine McLin—Mayor of Dayton, Ohio," www.citymayors.com/mayors/dayton-mayor.html, accessed September 25, 2012; *Jet* 100 (26 November 2001): 4–8.

2001 Toledo • State representative Jack Ford was elected mayor of Toledo, the first black to win election. Ford entered the race a year after his opponent and won the election with 61 percent of the vote.

Sources: *Jet* 100 (26 November 2001): 4–8.

2007 Columbus • The first black to serve as assistant director of tourism for the state of Ohio was Alicia Reece. Previously she served as vice mayor of Cincinnati and senior president of Communiplex Promotional Services. Reece's responsibilities included promoting tourism in the state through the use of the radio, print media, and online.

Sources: *Jet* 112 (30 July 2007): 20.

Oklahoma

1973 Taft • On April 16, 1973, Lelia Smith Foley (1942–) was elected mayor of this town of about 500 and has been called the first black woman mayor in the United States. In reality, she was the first black woman mayor in Oklahoma, holding office for thirteen years. (Ellen Walker Craig-Jones [1907?–2000] became mayor of Urbancrest, Ohio, a town of less than 800, in 1972, the first black woman in the nation to hold that post.) Foley, the mother of five children, was thirty-one years old when she was elected mayor. She was a former welfare mother who later married, then was divorced. She became a teacher's aide for about one year, and in 1969 became assistant staff director of Taft's Office of Economic opportunity community action center. She was promoted to director of the center in 1970 but her post was cut in 1972 due to fiscal problems. She was unsuccessful in her 1973 bid for a post on the local school board but continued in her determination to become a leader. After reading the book *The Making of a Black Mayor,* Foley was determined that she would run for mayor. Her children embarked on a door-to-door campaign and she won over the male incumbent by only thirty votes. Although the position was part-time and paid a token annual salary of $100, Foley gave the position full-time attention. To this she added her monthly unemployment compensation of $232 that she used to support herself and her family.

Sources: *Essence* 4 (October 1973): 8; *Jet* 60 (23 April 1981): 61–62; Lee, *Interesting People,* p. 93; *Negro Almanac,* p. 429.

Pennsylvania

1971 Philadelphia • Ethel D. Allen (1929–1981), a physician, politician, and civil rights activist, became the first black woman Republican council member. A native of Philadelphia, she graduated from West Virginia State College (now University). She wanted to fulfill her lifelong ambition to become a physician; however, for seven years after graduation she was unable to gain admission. Finally, she enrolled in the Philadelphia College of Osteopathic Medicine where she fought racism as well as sexism. She graduated in 1963 and served an internship in Grand Rapids, Michigan. Allen returned to Philadelphia and began community medicine, literally attending to some of her patients on the city streets. In the 1960s she became medical director at the Spring Garden Community Center on a federally-funded model cities program. She also taught community medicine at Hahnemann Medical College in the 1970s. Allen was successful in her run for a seat on the city council in 1971 representing the fifth council district; she was re-elected in 1975, this time filling an at-large seat. In the 1975 election she became the first black councilwoman elected to an at-large seat on the council and was the top vote-getter for the Republican party. In 1979 Allen was named secretary of commerce for Pennsylvania but was dismissed from office in the early 1980s for violating procedures. She was charged with accepting honoraria for speeches that state employees prepared and for absenteeism. After leaving that post, Allen became a clinician for the Philadelphia School District. She died on December 16, 1981, about two months after undergoing open heart surgery.

Sources: *Contemporary Black Biography,* vol. 13, pp. 13–17; Smith, *Notable Black American Women,* pp. 2–5.

1984 Philadelphia • On January 2, 1984, W[oodrow] Wilson Goode (1938–) became the first black mayor of Philadelphia. He won a second term in 1987. His term of service was marked by controversy over the firebombing of a house occupied by a cult group the police were trying to remove. In 1988 a two-year investigation cleared him of criminal responsibility. Goode became deputy assistant secretary of the U.S. Department of Education, but stepped down from the post in 2000. On December 12, 1999, he was ordained at the First Baptist Church of Paschall, where he had held membership since 1950. He also taught at Muhlenberg College in Allentown, Pennsylvania. In 1999 Philadelphia elected its second black mayor, John F. Street (1943?–), a nineteen-year veteran lawmaker. Goode was born outside Seabord, North Carolina, to parents who were sharecroppers. He graduated from Morgan State University (B.A., 1961) and Wharton School (M.P.A., 1968).

Sources: Hornsby, *Chronology of African-American History,* p. 326; *The Negro Almanac,* pp. 86, 88, 430; *Who's Who among African Americans,* 26th ed., p. 474; *Contemporary Black Biography,* vol. 4, pp. 107–10.

1986 Pittsburgh • William "Mugsy" Moore was the first black police chief in Pittsburgh. The sixty-year-old Moore had joined the force in 1951, become a detective in 1960, and been promoted to inspector in 1969. He resigned in 1987, calling his appointment "window dressing" and saying, "this city will have to find someone else to play the role of token." He was sixty-one years old at the time of his resignation.

Sources: *Jet* 70 (12 May 1986): *Jet* 72 (1 June 1987): 8.

1988 Philadelphia • Willie L. Williams (1943–) was the first black commissioner of police in Philadelphia. Williams was forty-four years old, and a twenty-four-year veteran of the police force. In 1992 Williams became the first black chief of police in Los Angeles, California.

Sources: *Contemporary Black Biography,* vol. 4, pp. 278–81; *Ebony* 48 (December 1992): 71–74, 132; *Jet* 74 (20 June 1988): 8; *Tennessean* (1 July 1992); *Who's Who among African Americans,* 26th ed., p. 1356.

1994 Philadelphia • Harold B. Hairston (1940?–) became the first black fire commissioner. He had been a twenty-nine-year veteran of the Fire Department.

Sources: *Jet* 86 (4 July 1994): 20; *Who's Who among African Americans,* 26th ed., p. 511.

1996 Philadelphia • Lauretha Vaird (1953?–1996) became the first black woman police officer killed in the line of duty, when she responded to a silent alarm at PNC Bank's Feltonville Branch. She joined the force in 1986, after serving as a teacher's aide.

Sources: *Jet* 89 (29 January 1996): 16–17.

1996 Philadelphia • Janet Pennick (1946–) became the first woman promoted to lieutenant in the Sheriff's Department. Previously she was the first woman promoted to sergeant. Since 1977 she had been a master sergeant with the U.S. Army Reserves and in 1991 received the Bronze Star for service in Operation Desert Storm. Pennick had served the city of Philadelphia for twenty-three years, spending twelve of these years in the Sheriff's Department.

Sources: *Jet* 91 (9 December 1996): 54; 91 (20 January 1997): 23; *Who's Who among African Americans,* 26th ed., p. 979.

Rhode Island

1981 Newport • Paul Laurence Gaines Sr. (1932–) was the first black mayor of the city. In 1977 he had also been the first black member of the City Council. The mayor of Newport is designated by the council. Gaines was a forty-eight-year-old administrator at Bridgewater State College in Massachusetts. Born in Newport, Gaines graduated from Xavier University in New Orleans (B.Ed., 1955) and Bridgewater State College (M.E., 1968). His career includes serving as teacher in the Newport, Rhode Island, public schools (1959–68), basketball coach at Rogers High School in Newport (1959–68), counselor for the Newport Youth Corps (1960–66), and various positions at Bridgewater State College (1968–96).

Sources: *Jet* 61 (15 October 1981): 16; *Who's Who among African Americans,* 26th ed., p. 444.

South Carolina

1982 Charleston • Reuben M. Greenberg (1943–) became the first black chief of police in Charleston on March 17, 1982; this also made him the first black police chief in South Carolina in modern times. Born in Houston, Greenberg graduated from San Francisco State University (B.A., 1967) and the University of California (M.P.A., 1969 and M.C.P., 1975). He was undersheriff in San Francisco from 1971 to 1973, the first black to hold that post. He taught at California State University at Hayward and the University of North Carolina at Chapel Hill.

Sources: Hornsby, *Chronology of African-American History,* p. 310; *Who's Who among African Americans,* 26th ed., p. 495.

1996 Charlestown County • Lisa A. Green, a juvenile detective, was promoted to lieutenant in the Sheriff's Office, becoming the first black officer to receive that rank. The Charleston-born Green graduated from Claflin University in Orangeburg in 1986. She was named training coordinator for the Charleston City Sheriff's Office in 1997.

Sources: *Jet* 90 (30 September 1996): 20; *Who's Who among African Americans,* 26th ed., p. 493.

1996 Ninety Six • Charles Harts (1931?–), a retired electrical engineer, returned to South Carolina from Buffalo, New York and was elected the town's first black mayor.

Sources: *Jet* 89 (22 January 1996): 10.

2010 Columbia • The first African American mayor of Columbia, South Carolina, is Steve Benjamin, who also became the city's first new leader in twenty years. A lawyer and lobbyist, he is also former head of the State Department of Probation, Pardon, and Parole. He is a graduate of the University of South Carolina and its school of law.

Sources: "Steve Benjamin Elected As Columbia, SC Mayor," *WLTX News,* www.wltx.com, accessed February 9, 2012. "Steve Benjamin Elected First African American Mayor of Columbia, S.C.," http://www.naacp.org/news/entry/steve-benjamin-elected-first-african-american-mayor-of-columbia-sc, accessed September 25, 2012.

Tennessee

1780 Fort Nashborough (now Nashville) • The small party of men who explored and settled the Fort Nashborough site in the winter of this year included a free black man, Jack Civil. Fort Nashborough (Nashville), was settled about this year. The population was approximately 20 percent black, most of whom were slaves. Free blacks, however, were among the original settlers.

Sources: Lovett, *The African-American History of Nashville,* p. 1–4, 9.

1867 Nashville • In March, blacks held their first political meetings to organize the black vote. In September that year blacks voted for the first time in the city elections. Two black councilmen were elected. One of them, Daniel Wadkins, was not seated for unknown reasons. Instead, a white man was appointed to fill his seat.

Sources: Lovett, *The African-American History of Nashville,* p. 212.

1868 Nashville • For the first time since 1832, blacks voted in the November elections. For the most part, they voted for General Ulysses S. Grant for U.S. President.

Sources: Lovett, *The African-American History of Nashville,* p. 209.

1872 Knoxville • William Francis Yardley (1844–1924) became the first black lawyer in Knoxville, when he was only twenty-eight years old. Yardley was born in Knox County to a white mother and a black father. He was left on the doorstep of the Yardleys, a white family. The family accepted him and gave him their name. He taught black children at Knox County's Ebenezer School around 1869. He also studied law with a white lawyer, passed the bar, and opened a law practice. In time he became known as the dean of black lawyers in the county; he was known as well for the Prince Albert coats and derby hats that he wore. He also taught other prospective lawyers. A member of the city's first fire department from 1876 to 1877 he was its second assistant chief. In 1878 he was publisher and editor of the Knoxville *Examiner,* the city's first black newspaper. In 1882 he began another newspaper, the Knoxville *Bulletin.* Yardley entered politics a well. He was elected to the Knoxville Board of Aldermen in 1872 and served on the Knox County Court from 1876 to 1882. In 1876 he became a Republican candidate for governor of Tennessee.

Sources: Lovett and Wynn, *Profiles of African Americans in Tennessee,* pp. 149–50.

1911 Nashville • Solomon Parker Harris, an attorney, was elected to the city council, becoming the first black member since 1885.

Sources: Lovett, *The African-American History of Nashville,* p. 230.

1913 Knoxville • James Garfield Beck (1881–1969) was hired by the Knoxville Post Office, becoming the first black postal clerk in Tennessee.

Sources: Lovett and Wynn, *Profiles of African Americans in Tennessee,* pp. 7–8.

1951 Nashville • Z. Alexander Looby (1899–1972) and fellow attorney Robert Emmitt Lillard (1907–1991) became the first two blacks elected to the city council since 1911. Looby in 1963 became a member of the local Metropolitan Charter Commission. He served on the old and new Metropolitan Council a total of twenty years. Lillard, who won in a run-off election, also served on the council for twenty years and never missed a regular meeting.

Sources: Lovett and Wynn, *Profiles of African Americans in Tennessee,* pp. 78–79 (Looby); pp. 75–77 (Lillard).

1967 Nashville • Robert Emmitt Lillard (1907–1991) became the first black vice mayor *pro tempore.* Born in Nashville, Lillard graduated from Kent College of Law in 1935. He passed the bar examination in 1936 and worked for the Nashville Fire Engine Company No. 11, in the black community, until he retired on a disability pension in 1950. After that, he practiced law full-time, later gaining admission to the federal district court, the U.S. Court of Appeals (Sixth Circuit Court), and the U.S. Supreme Court. Through his efforts, the city established a second high school for local blacks, Cameron Junior High School. Lillard also gained an ordinance to desegregate the Parthenon building located in the then-segregated Centennial Park. Although he had a successful tenure as vice mayor *pro tempore*, he was unsuccessful in his bid to become vice mayor and council member at large.

Sources: Lovett and Wynn, *Profiles of African Americans in Tennessee,* pp. 75–77.

1982 Nashville • A[dolpho] A. Birch Jr. was the first black presiding judge of Nashville-Davidson County's twelve courts.

Sources: *Jet* 62 (12 April 1982): 21.

1989 Chattanooga • The first black police chief was Ralph Cothran (?–1995). Cothran graduated from Cleveland State College and the FBI National Academy.

Sources: NAACP, "Black History Month: Unsung Heroes Project," http://naacp-unsung-heroes.tumblr.com/post/380198087/ralph-h-big-ralph-cothran-became-the-first, accessed September 25, 2012.

1992 Memphis • Willie W. Herenton (1940–) was elected the first black mayor of Memphis; he took office in 1992. Herenton had begun his teaching career in the elementary schools of the Memphis City School System, and had become the first black superintend-

Nashville's First Black Police Chief

In 1996 Emmett Turner (1943?–) became the highest-ranking black official and the first black police chief of Nashville. Turner grew up in racially segregated Brownsville, Tennessee, about fifty miles east of Memphis. His father was an electrical contractor and his mother an educator. In August 1966, during the Vietnam War, he was called into the U. S. Army and joined the 52nd Aviation Battalion in the jungles of Southeast Asia. After his discharge, he was an automobile salesman and also worked on an assembly line. Turner moved to Nashville where he worked as a patrolman beginning in 1969 and studied part-time at Tennessee State University. In 1972 he graduated with a bachelor's degree in sociology and later received his master's degree in psychology. He was youth enforcement officer from 1970 to 1972, and from 1971 to 1978 he was a school resource officer. From then on Turner rose through the ranks in the police department, becoming sergeant in the Sexual Abuse Unit from 1979 to 1984, lieutenant with the Patrol Unit from 1986 to 1988, captain of the Patrol Unit from 1988 to 1991, and major with that unit from 1991 to 1993. Turner was appointed assistant chief of police in 1993 and promoted in 1996 to chief of police. In 1996 he was named "Nashvillian of the Year."

Sources: *Nashville Scene* (26 December 1996); *Tennessean* (11 January 1996); (12 January 1996).

ent of the system in 1979. His program to feed children in Memphis during the summer operated for forty-four days in 1997 and served over a million meals.

Sources: *Ebony* 47 (March 1992): 106, 108; *State of Black America 1992*, pp. 383–84; *Who's Who among African Americans*, 14th ed., 585; *Contemporary Black Biography*, vol. 24, pp. 76–78.

1997 Memphis • Herman Morris Jr. became the first black president and chief executive officer of the Memphis Light, Gas and Water Division. He was the first black to lead the largest three-service municipally owned utility company in the nation. Previously, Morris was interim president and CEO, and former general counsel at the division.

Sources: *Jet* 93 (15 December 1997): 20.

2007 Nashville • The first black woman named to a three-year term on the Tennessee Regulatory Authority Board was Mary W. Freeman. Her term began in July. Her panel sets rates and service standards of private telephone systems, natural gas, electric, and water utilities. She has served as chief legislative liaison for Tennessee governor Phil Bredesen.

Sources: *Jet* 113 (31 March 2008): 19.

2011 Knoxville • Daniel T. Brown became the interim mayor of Knoxville and the first black to hold that post. He replaced Mayor Bill Haslam, the elected governor of Tennessee, who took office in January. Brown had served Knoxville's city council for thirteen months. Following the city charter, the council is required to select one of its members to serve until the next mayor can be elected in fall 2011. A native of Knoxville, Brown is a graduate of Tennessee State University and served in the Vietnam War. He is also retired from the U.S. Postal Service.

Sources: *Tennessean* (11 January 2011).

Texas

1900 Bryan • Levi Neal (1851?–1900), a deputy marshal, was probably the first local black peace officer killed in the line of duty. After he arrested a man for public drunkenness in "Rats Row," a downtown saloon, he took the man to jail. The man pulled a pistol from his coat and fatally shot the deputy. Though Neal's memory initially faded into ob-

The First Black Mayor of Dallas

On May 6, 1995, Ron Kirk (1954–) won the Dallas mayoral race with 62 percent of the vote, becoming the first black mayor of a major Texas city. Kirk was born in Austin and graduated from Austin College (B.A., 1976) and the University of Texas School of Law (J.D., 1979). He was in private law practice from 1979 to 1981. From 1981 to 1983 he was legislative assistant in Washington, D.C., for Senator Lloyd Bentson. Kirk was assistant city attorney and chief lobbyist for the City of Dallas from 1983 to 1989. In 1994 he filled the unexpired term of Texas Secretary of State John Hannah, who resigned to become a federal judge. After becoming a partner in the law firm Gardere and Wynne, Kirk was elected mayor. In 2009 he was selected as U.S. trade representative by the Obama administration.

Ron Kirk

Sources: *Ebony* 50 (September 1995): 32–34; *Contemporary Black Biography,* vol. 11, pp. 148–51; *Jet* 88 (22 May 1995): 4–5.

scurity, the Bryan Police Officers Association and other groups honored the fallen officer one hundred years later, after the Combined Law Enforcement Associations of Texas and its president, Ronald Delord, unearthed the story while conducting research for a book about Texas police officers who were killed in the line of duty.

Sources: *New York Times* (9 August 2000).

1964 Houston • The first black judge in Texas was Harold Gordon Tillman Sr. (1925?–1998), who was also an ordained minister and an actor. He was appointed a municipal judge. Tillman was admitted to the Texas bar in 1962. Two years later, Mayor Louie Welch named him to the municipal court. He was general counsel for the Texas Joint Legislative Committee in Prison Reform and a delegate to the state Democratic Party convention. In 1978 and again in 1982 he was unsuccessful in his bid for a seat in Congress. A native of Philadelphia, Tillman graduated from Livingstone College in North Carolina and then enjoyed a brief career in New York as a repertory stage actor. In 1947, when he was in his twenties, he appeared in several films produced by blacks and with all-black casts. The films included *That Man of Mine* (in which he shared top billing with Ruby Dee), and *Love in Syncopation*. He left his film career and became an ordained minister in the African Methodist Episcopal Zion Church in the early 1950s. Tillman served first as assistant pastor of Harlem's Church on the Hill AME Zion but was transferred to Houston. There he pastored Walls Chapel AME Church for fifteen years, broadcasting on local radio, leading a gospel music program, and hosting a talk show. After practicing law for thirty years, he was named a municipal court judge in Houston.

Sources: *New York Times* (22 June 1998); (28 June 1998).

1982 Houston • Lee Patrick Brown (1937–) became Houston's first black chief of police on March 23, 1982. A native of Oklahoma, Brown received a Ph.D. in criminology from the University of California at Berkeley (1970). His career included both university teaching and law enforcement, beginning as sheriff of Multnomah County, Oregon. In 1990 he became police commissioner of New York City, a position from which he soon resigned due to illness in the family. On April 28, 1993, President Clinton announced Brown's nomination as director of the Office of National Drug Policy, a position to which Clinton gave cabinet rank.

Sources: *Contemporary Black Biography,* vol. 24, pp. 21–24; Hornsby, *Chronology of African-American History,* p. 311; *Tennessean* (29 April 1993); *US News and World Report* 109 (31

December 1990): 73; *Washington Post* (2 December 2001); *Who's Who among African Americans,* 26th ed., p. 161.

1986 Dallas • Richard Knight Jr. (1945–) was the first black city manager of Dallas. Knight had served as assistant city manager from 1982 to 1986, and held the position of city manager until 1990.

Sources: *Jet* 75 (17 October 1988): 40; 78 (30 April 1990): 6; *Who's Who among Black Americans,* 26th ed., p. 733.

1990 Austin • Iris J. Jones became the first black woman city attorney of Austin. Jones graduated from the Thurgood Marshall School of Law at Texas Southern University, and had been serving as acting city attorney.

Sources: *Jet* 78 (2 July 1990): 20.

1995 Dallas • The first black chairman of the Dallas Area Rapid Transit was Billy Ratcliff. He joined the agency in 1993.

Sources: *Jet* 88 (9 October 1995): 19.

1995 Gonzales • The first black woman officer on the police force was Joyce Patterson, who previously had served as a reserve officer.

Sources: *Jet* 88 (23 October 1995): 22.

1997 Houston • Lee Patrick Brown (1937–), who had a long and distinguished career in law enforcement, became the first black mayor. He received 53 percent of the vote in a run-off election, defeating Rob Mosbacher. He was sworn in office on January 2, 1998, for a two-year term. Brown was re-elected in 1999. During a runoff election in 2001, Brown won a third and final two-year term handily, defeating City Council member Orlando Sanchez, who made a bid to become the city's first Hispanic mayor.

Lee Patrick Brown

Sources: *Contemporary Black Biography,* vol. 24, pp. 21–24; *New York Times* (8 December 1997); *USA Today* (8 December 1997).

1998 Dallas • Malcolm Robinson served as chairman of the Dallas Convention and Visitors Bureau from 1998 to 2000, becoming the first black to hold that post. Robinson co-founded and was partner in the Dallas law firm Robinson, West and Gooden. In 1998 he was also vice president of the National Bar Association.

Sources: *Jet* 94 (21 September 1998): 20; *Who's Who among African Americans,* 26th ed., p. 1065.

1999 Dallas • Terrell D. Bolton (1959?–) was promoted from assistant chief to chief of police, becoming the first black to hold that post. He took office on September 30 when the current chief retired. Bolton joined the force in 1980 and rose in rank from patrol officer. He pioneered in the Police Mobile Storefront Program and assisted in implementing a community policing program. After becoming police chief, Bolton began a crime-fighting plan called Initiative 2000. Officers were assigned to specific beats and targeted teen curfew violation, prostitution, drug transactions, gangs, and other problems. Born in Richton, Mississippi, Bolton received a bachelor's degree in criminal justice from Jackson State University in 1980. He also graduated from the FBI National Academy in Quantico, Virginia.

Sources: *Contemporary Black Biography,* vol. 25, pp. 19–21; *Ebony* 55 (November 1999): 12; *New York Times* (20 August 1999).

Utah

2001 South Ogden • George Garwood Jr. was elected mayor, becoming the first black to win that election in the entire state. He defeated perennial candidate Dent Mason. For six years, Garwood had served on the City Council. He also served as president of the Utah League of Cities and Towns.

Sources: *Jet* 100 (26 November 2001): 4–8.

Virginia

1948 Richmond • On June 9, 1948, Oliver White Hill (1907–2007) was the first black elected to the city council since Reconstruction. Born in Richmond, Hill received his A.B. degree from Howard University in 1931. In 1933 he received his J.D. degree from Howard University School of Law. He practiced law in Roanoke and in Richmond before he was elected to the council. In 1947 Hill was unsuccessful in his bid for a seat in the Virginia House of Delegates. Of the eighteen candidates running for seven seats, he was the only black. From 1951 to 1954, Hill was the leading attorney on the case *Davis v. County School Board of Prince Edward County* (Virginia), one of the five cases that the U.S. Supreme Court combined into the landmark court case *Brown v. Board of Education*. That decision overturned the early *Plessy v. Ferguson*. After this ruling Hill was hard at work ensuring that the state followed law rather than dismantle its public school system, as it attempted to do. After the schools were integrated, Hill returned to private practice and in 1966 established the firm Hill, Tucker and Marsh.

Sources: Hornsby, *Chronology of African-American History,* p. 96; *Who's Who among African Americans,* 14th ed., p. 597; *Contemporary Black Biography,* vol. 24, pp. 79–81 .

1977 Richmond • On March 8, 1977, Henry L. Marsh III (1933–), a civil rights lawyer, was the first black mayor of Richmond, Virginia. He had served on the city council and for seven years was vice mayor. The council had a 5–4 black majority that selected him to run for mayor; he later ran unopposed. After three consecutive terms in office, he left his seat in 1982. Hill became a partner in the firm Hill, Tucker and Marsh.

Sources: Bennett, *Before the Mayflower,* pp. 604, 630; *Jet* 99 (19 March 2001), p. 38; *Who's Who among African Americans,* 26th ed., p. 913.

1986 Newport News • Jessie M. Rattley (1929–2001) was the first black and first woman mayor of Newport News. Rattley had served on the city council for sixteen years. Born in Newport News, she graduated from Hampton Institute (now University). She established the Business Department at Huntington High School, the first black high school in Newport News to offer business training for its students. In 1970 Rattley was the first black and the first woman elected to the city council; Rattley held the seat until 1986. After serving as vice mayor in 1986, she was elected mayor that same year and remained in office until 1990. In 1990 she was a fellow in Harvard University's institute of politics. Rattley returned to her alma mater, Hampton University and served as senior lecturer from 1991 to 2001.

Sources: *Jet* 70 (28 July 1986): 33; Obituary, *Who's Who among African Americans,* 14th ed., p. 1475.

Mamie Locke

2000 Hampton • Mamie Evelyn Locke (1954–) was elected mayor, becoming the first black to hold the position. A native of Jackson, Mississippi, she was educated at Tougaloo College in Mississippi (B.A., 1976) and Atlanta University (now Clark-Atlanta), (M.A., 1978, Ph.D., 1984.) Locke was archivist for the Department of Archives and History in Jackson (1977–79) and for the Atlanta Historical Society (1979–81). She later moved to Hampton University, where she served as assistant dean of the School of Liberal Arts from 1991 to 1996 and dean in 1996. Locke, however, had been politically active since high school and had a political office in mind when she moved to the Hampton area. In 1994 Locke won a two-year term on the city council and, after running at-large, she was reelected in 1998. In that year as well, the council selected Locke to be vice-mayor and supported her campaign to be elected mayor. She became one of the estimated 200 black elected officials who are also in academia.

Sources: *Jet* 98 (12 June 2000): 29–30; *Who's Who among African Americans,* 26th ed., p. 782; *Black Issues in Higher Education,* pp. 26–27.

2008 Roanoke • Anita Price was elected to the Roanoke City Council and became the city's first black woman to hold that post. Previously, she was president of the Roanoke Education Association. When elected to the council, she was a guidance counselor at Roanoke's Round Hill Montessori Primary School.

Sources: *Jet* 113 (21 July 2008): 22.

Washington

1871 Centralia • George Washington (1817–1905) was the first black to found a large integrated city in the United States. Born in Virginia, his white mother gave him up for adoption to a white family, which moved to the frontier. In 1850 Washington settled in the Oregon Territory, and homesteaded in present-day Washington. He established Centralia in 1872, when the Northern Pacific Railroad crossed his land. A city park bears his name.

Sources: Cantor, *Historic Landmarks of Black America,* p. 336; Logan and Winston, *Dictionary of American Negro Biography,* p. 638; Katz, *The Black West,* pp. 72–73.

1981 Spokane • James Chase (1987–1992) was the first black mayor of this western city of 172,000, of which 1.6 percent were black. Chase had spent forty years as the manager of an auto body shop, and held the position of mayor until 1985.

Sources: *Jet* 61 (26 November 1981): 8; Obituary, *Who's Who among Black Americans,* 1994/95, p. 1658.

1988 Olympia • Cora Pinson was the first black city council member, and the first black woman elected to any city post in the state. A native of Memphis and a graduate of Hammond Business College, Indiana, the fifty-three-year-old Pinson had moved to the city from Chicago thirteen years earlier, and had served two terms as commissioner of the Housing Authority of Thurston County.

Sources: *Jet* 73 (25 January 1988): 12–14.

1989 Seattle • Norman Blann Rice (1943–) was the first black elected mayor of Seattle. A native of Denver, Colorado, he earned a B.A. and an M.A. degree from the University of Washington (1972, 1974). He was manager of corporate contributions and social policy coordinator for Ranier National Bank at the time of his election to the City Council in 1978. From 1983 to 1990 he was president of the council. Nicknamed "Mayor Nice," he established a reputation for consensus-building and sought the public's views on such issues as the local schools. Although race was an issue in Rice's first campaign, when he ran for re-election in 1993, it was no longer an issue; instead, he was concerned with the usual big-city problems: drug abuse, crime, and homelessness. Rice left office in 1997 and became president and chief executive office of the Federal Home Loan Bank of Seattle.

Sources: *Contemporary Black Biography,* vol. 8, pp. 208–10; *Fortune* 126 (2 November 1992): cover and p. 43; *Jet* 77 (22 January 1990): 4; Salzman, *Encyclopedia of African-American Culture and History,* Supplement, pp, 232–33; *Who's Who among African Americans,* 26th ed., p. 1045.

West Virginia

1995 Clarksburg • The first black member of the City Council was David Kates. He has served as pastor of Mt. Zion Baptist Church in Clarksburg.

Sources: *Jet* 87 (20 March 1995): 22.

1996 Dunbar • Irvin B. Lee (1939?–), a trailblazer in law enforcement, became the first woman and the first black chief of police. Earlier, she was the first black woman officer, a sergeant, in the city of Charleston, and then became the first woman detective. Lee retired from the Charleston force after twenty-one years, then joined the force in Dunbar. She also continued to serve as executive director of Charleston's Human Rights Commission. Lee was born in Bear's Fork, West Virginia, and earned a bachelor's degree in criminal justice.

Sources: *Jet* 89 (15 January 1996): 25–26; *Who's Who among African Americans,* 26th ed., pp.756–57.

JOURNALISM

Newspapers

1855 • Mifflin Wistar Gibbs (1823–1915) was owner and editor of the *Mirror of the Times,* an abolitionist newspaper, and California's first black newspaper.

Sources: Logan and Winston, *Dictionary of American Negro Biography,* pp. 258–59; *Encyclopedia of Black America,* p. 403; Penn, *The Afro-American Press,* p. 77.

1862 • *L'Union* was Louisiana's first black newspaper and the first black biweekly. The paper was published from September 27 until December 20, 1862, and became a tri-weekly beginning December 23, 1862. Publication was suspended on May 31, 1864, but the paper continued to struggle until it was disbanded on July 19, 1864. From early July 1863, the paper was published in both English and French. Its chief editor was Paul Trevigne, a black man who was born and reared in New Orleans. In 1864 Louis Charles Roudanez and his associates bought the defunct newspaper, revived it, and published it irregularly until 1871.

Sources: Houzeau, *My Passage at the New Orleans Tribune,* pp. 71–72.

1864 • Thomas Morris Chester (1834–1892), was the first and only black correspondent for a major daily, the *Philadelphia Press,* during the Civil War. His dispatches cover the period from August 1864 through June 1865. He was previously editor of the *Star of Liberia.* For eight months he reported on black troop activity around Petersburg, Florida, and the Confederate capital, both before and after Richmond, Virginia, was taken. Chester was born in Harrisburg, Pennsylvania, to abolitionist parents. He studied first at Alexander High School in Monrovia, Liberia, and later at the Thetford Academy in Vermont. He read law under a Liberian lawyer, then spent three years at Middle Temple in London, England. In April 1870 he became the first black American barrister admitted to practice before English courts.

Sources: Simmons, *Men of Mark,* pp. 671–76; Spradling, *In Black and White,* vol. 1, p. 182; Blackett, *Thomas Morris Chester*; Smith, *Notable Black American Men,* pp. 197–200.

1864 • *La Tribune de la Nouvelle Orléans* was the first black daily published in the United States. Louis C. Roudanez founded the paper on October 4, 1864, and published it in both French and English. Although it was published triweekly at first, it soon became an influential daily newspaper.

Sources: Logan and Winston, *Dictionary of American Negro Biography,* p. 534; *Jet* 94 (27 July 1998): 19.

1865 • The first black owned and managed newspaper in Alabama was the weekly Mobile *Nationalist.* It was published for four years, from December 1865 to October 1869 and functioned as a mouthpiece for the Republican Party. Henry Europe, a Baptist minister and the father of musician James Reese Europe, had a short career as a reporter for the paper.

Sources: Badger, *A Life in Ragtime,* p. 13.

1865 • The first black newspaper in Tennessee was *The Colored Tennessean,* founded in Nashville by William Bennett Scott (?–1917). Scott was a free black who migrated from North Carolina to Knoxville. To prevent Confederate imprisonment of his son, he left Knoxville for nearby Friendsville, and on to Nashville, which Union soldiers now occupied.

Sources: *Negro Yearbook, 1918–1919,* p. 428.

1878 • *The Conservator* was the first black newspaper published in Chicago. Richard H. De Baptiste (1831–?), pastor of Chicago's Olivet Baptist Church, assumed editorial control later this year. In the year that he headed the paper, he expanded circulation to reach the masses. He also became corresponding editor of the *Western Herald,* the short-lived *Saint Louis Monitor,* and the *Brooklyn Monitor.* De Baptiste was born into a prominent family in Fredericksburg, Virginia. Before joining the ministry, he was a bricklayer and plasterer. He moved to Detroit and later taught in Ohio. He was ordained in Mount Pleasant Baptist Church in Ohio in the late 1850s. From 1863 to 1882 he headed Olivet Baptist Church in Chicago. He later was elected president of the American Baptist Association, the first national black Baptist association in the country. He was elected president of the white Baptist Free Mission Society in 1870.

Sources: Penn, *The Afro-American Press,* p. 262; Smith, *Notable Black American Women,* Book II, p. 165.

1878 • William Lewis Eagleson (1835–1899) published the first black newspaper in Kansas in January, 1878.

Sources: Logan and Winston, *Dictionary of American Negro Biography,* p. 207.

1885 • Editor, journalist, and feminist Gertrude Bustill Mossell (1855–1948) began the first black woman's weekly column in the *New York Freemen.* The column was known as "Our Women's Department" it appeared in the first issue of the *Freeman,* in December. Mossell introduced her first column, on the subject "Woman's Suffrage," saying that it was to be "devoted to the interest of women" and that she would continue to "promote true womanhood especially that of the African race." An educator and feminist, Mossell was born in Philadelphia into an elite free black family. She campaigned for equal rights and women's rights. For seven years she taught at various places in New Jersey and in Delaware, but left teaching after she married because married women were not allowed to teach. After that she developed her career in journalism and became active in women's rights and in social reform movements.

Sources: Smith, *Notable Black American Women,* pp. 775–77; Mossell, "Our Women's Department," *(New York) Freeman* (9 January 1886); (25 December 1886); Penn, *The Afro-American Press and Its Editors,* pp. 405–7.

1885 • The *Philadelphia Tribune,* the oldest continually published non-church newspaper, was first published.

Sources: *Encyclopedia of Black America,* p. 647.

1888 • Edward Elder Cooper (1859–?), journalist and editor, established *The Freeman,* in Indianapolis, Indiana. This was the first black illustrated newspaper, the first to make a feature of portraits and cartoons. First published July 14, 1888, the newspaper reached national prominence and made a fortune for its owner. It also was a part of an exchange list with white newspapers and periodicals, something that no other black newspaper enjoyed at the time. Cooper was born in Smyrna, Tennessee, but moved to Philadelphia and then to Indianapolis. He enrolled in school in Indianapolis, graduating first in his class of sixty-

First Black Newspapers by State[1]

State	Founded	Title of Newspaper	Founder(s)/ Editor(s)	Date Publication Ceased
Alaska	1952	*Alaska Spotlight*	George C. Anderson	1970?
Arizona	1918	*Tribune*		1941
Arkansas	1869	*Arkansas Freeman*		
California	1855	*Mirror of the Times*	Mifflin Wistar Gibbs	1862 (merged with *Pacific Appeal*)
Colorado	1880	*Denver Star*		
Florida	1873	*New Era*	Josiah T. Walls	
Georgia	1865	*Colored American*	John T. Shuften	1866
Indiana	1878	*Our Age*	Edwin F. Horn	
Iowa	1883	*Rising Sun*		
Kansas	1855	*Kansas Herald of Freedom*		
Kentucky	1870	*American Baptist*		
Louisiana	1862	*L'Union (The Union)*	Louis C. Roudanez and others	1864
Maryland	1865	*True Communicator*		
Montana	1894	*Colored Citizen*		1894
Minnesota	1885	*Western Appeal*	John Q. Adams and Cyrus Field Adams	
Mississippi	1867	*Colored Citizen*		
Missouri	1870?	*Welcome Friend*		
	1875	*Negro World*		
Nebraska	1889	*Progress*		1905
Nevada	1962	*Las Vegas Voice*	Charles I. West	
New Mexico	1913?	*New Age*		
New York	1827	*Freedom's Journal*	Samuel Eli Cornish and John B. Russwurm	1829
North Carolina	1872	*Light-House*[2]		
Ohio	1843	*Palladium of Liberty*	David Jenkins	1844
Oregon	1896	*New Age*	A. D. Griffin	1907
Pennsylvania	1843	*Mystery*[3]	Martin Robinson Delany	
South Carolina	1865	*Nationalist*	John Silsby October	1869
Tennessee	1865	*Colored Tennessean*	William B. Scott Jr.	
Texas	1868	*Freedman's Press*		
Utah	1895	*The Broad Ax*	Julius F. Taylor	1899 (moved to Chicago)
Virginia	1865?	*True Southerner*	Joseph T. Wilson	
Washington	1894	*Republican*	Horace R. Cayton, Sr.	1915
Wisconsin	1892	*Afro-American*	George Brown March	1893

[1]Compiled from Amistad S. Pride and Clinton C. Wilson II, *A History of the Black Press.*

[2]There are undocumented claims that the first black newspaper published in the state was the *Statesman,* founded in 1873.

[3]Some sources cite 1845 as the founding date.

five. He was the only black in the class. By 1882 he was working with the U.S. railway mail service. In 1883 Cooper joined Edwin F. Horn and others in publishing, in Indianapolis, *The Colored World.* Although the paper was an immediate success, Cooper severed his connection with it. In 1886 he returned to the paper, now known as the *Indianapolis World.*

He sold out his interest a year later and began publishing *The Freeman*. The quality of the paper, coupled with his business skills, led I. Garland Penn in *The Afro-American* Press to call Cooper the greatest black journalist. Cooper's friend and neighbor W. Allison Sweeney noted in his sketch of Cooper in the *New York Age*, "I am glad that Edward Elder Cooper belongs to the negro [sic] race."

Sources: *Alexander's Magazine* 6 (15 August 1908), editorial; Penn, *The Afro-American Press*, pp. 334–39.

The Oldest Continually Published Newspapers

Name	Established
Christian Recorder (African Methodist Episcopal)	1846
Star of Zion (AME Zion)	1867
American Baptist	1880
Philadelphia Tribune	1885
Houston Informer	1892
Baltimore Afro-American	1892
Des Moines, Iowa, *Bystander*	1894
Indianapolis Recorder	1895

Sources: *Encyclopedia of Black America*, p. 642; *Gale Directory of Publication and Broadcast Media*, 1993.

1894 • The first newspaper written for and by women was the *Woman's Era*; it published news and activities of women's clubs throughout the country. The official organ of the National Association of Colored Women, *Woman's Era* had Josephine St. Pierre Ruffin (1842–1924) and her daughter, Florida Ruffin Ridley (1861–1943), as editors until 1900. Josephine Ruffin, a clubwoman, civic leader, and reformer, was born in Boston. She became a founding member of the Women's Era Club (which she, Florida Ridley, and Maria Baldwin organized), the National Federation of Afro-American Women, the National Association of Colored Women, and the Northeastern Federation of Women's Clubs. Florida Ridley was also a clubwoman as well as a writer, educator, and social worker. She was born in Boston and educated at Boston Teachers College and Boston University. Ruffin became a teacher in Boston's public schools. In 1890 she founded the Society for the Collection of Negro Folklore, one of the earliest groups of black folklorists. She also aided her mother in promoting a national organization of black clubwomen.

Sources: Smith, *Notable Black American Women*, pp. 941–42 (Ridley), pp. 961–66 (Ruffin); Hine, *Black Women in America*, vol. 1, p. 982 (Ridley), pp. 994–97 (Ruffin).

1895 • *The Daily American* was the first known black daily newspaper published in Florida. James Weldon Johnson formed a partnership with M. J. Christopher and founded the afternoon daily, with Johnson as editor and Christopher as the business manager. At the time, Johnson thought that they had founded the country's first black daily. During this time, Johnson taught at the Stanton School in Jacksonville, Florida. A printing firm in Atlanta furnished the new business an electrotyped dispatch service. During the eight months of its existence, blacks enthusiastically endorsed the paper; they had found a medium of self-expression and could make themselves heard across racial boundaries. Johnson called the paper's failure his "first taste of defeat in public life."

Sources: Johnson, *Along This Way*, p. 137.

1905 • Robert Sengstacke Abbott (1868–1940) first published the *Chicago Defender*. On May 6, 1905, he established what he called "The World's Greatest Weekly." The *Defender* reached national prominence during the great black migration from the South during World War I, and by Abbott's death, he had made it into the most widely circulated black weekly. Abbott was born in St. Simon's Island, Georgia; his father was of fully African heritage, while his mother was born in Savannah, Georgia. Abbott's father died in 1869, and when his mother remarried, he added his stepfather's name and became known as Robert Sengstacke. He studied at Claflin University in Orangeburg, South Carolina, Hampton Institute, and Kent College of Law in Chicago. At Hampton, he focused on learning the printing trade, having worked earlier as an apprentice at the *Savannah Echo*. When he graduated from law school, as Robert Sengstacke Abbott, he was the only African American in his class. At both Claflin and Hampton, Abbott, who was dark-skinned, was looked down upon by his lighter-skinned schoolmates; he was told by a prominent African American lawyer that his complexion would be a disadvantage to him in the practice of law. These experiences influenced his decision to turn to printing. After he launched the *Defender*, the paper grew slowly, and Abbott had difficult financial years before the paper became a success. It became a full-size newspaper in 1915, the first black newspaper to achieve this feat. In the beginning, Abbott's paper was focused on the black masses. As time passed, he came to favor gradualism as the approach to racial progress and became more entrenched in the Chicago establishment. In 1929, he was the first to attempt publication of a well-financed black magazine, *Abbott's Monthly*; the magazine survived until 1933. Abbott's news and columns as published in the *Defender* established him as a major spokesman for blacks during his lifetime.

Sources: Logan and Winston, *Dictionary of American Negro Biography*, pp. 1–2; Hornsby, *Milestones in Twentieth-Century African-American History*, pp. 5–6; Smith, *Notable Black American Men*, pp. 3–6.

1909 • The New York *Amsterdam News* was first published by James H. Anderson on December 4, 1909. The four-page newspaper sold for a penny a copy. At the peak of its popularity—during and just following the Second World War—the paper claimed a circulation of more than a hundred thousand copies; the *Amsterdam News* began to decline in 1971.

Sources: *Encyclopedia of Black America*, p. 647; *Jet* 67 (10 December 1984): 37; Dates and Barlow, *Split Image*, p. 362.

1918 • Ralph Waldo Tyler (1859–1921), reporter and government official, was the first, and only, black official war correspondent during World War I. Tyler worked in a variety of jobs on the way to becoming a well-known journalist. His job as a stenographer at the *Columbus Dispatch* in Columbus, Ohio, gave him his start in 1888. While working there Tyler gained journalistic skills and also developed and strengthened his interest in politics. He stayed with the *Dispatch* for seventeen years, serving for a while as society editor. After working for the *Ohio State Journal* from 1901 to 1904, Tyler's political activities and a friendship with Booker T. Washington led to his being appointed by President Theodore Roosevelt as auditor in the Navy Department, where he served for nine years. Tyler lost this position in 1913 when the Woodrow Wilson administration removed black officeholders from their positions. While working as an organizer for the National Negro Business League, he wrote columns that discussed the position of blacks in the South. In 1914 his columns were syndicated by the American Press Association. By 1917 he was back in Washington as secretary of the National Colored Soldiers Comfort Committee. When both a representative of the government and black newspaper editors agreed that a first-class journalist was needed to document the experiences of black soldiers in France during wartime, Tyler was a logical choice. He continued to write on this subject after the war ended, for the remainder of his life.

Ralph Waldo Tyler

Sources: Logan and Winston, *Dictionary of American Negro Biography*, pp. 613–14; *Jet* 78 (2 July 1990): 23; Scott, *The American Negro in the World War*, pp. 284–99; Smith, *Notable Black American Men*, pp. 1142–44

1920s • Lester A. Walton (1882–1965), became the first black American to hold a full-time job as journalist for a white newspaper when he was hired by the *New York World* as a staff writer and columnist. Born in St. Louis, Missouri, Walton moved to New York in 1908, where he worked both as a journalist and in the theater. His theater work included producing and directing musicals. His journalistic activities included his work as manager and dramatic editor of *The New York Age*. Walton later wrote for the *New York Her-*

The First Black Woman Newspaper Editor

Publisher Charlotta Bass (1880–1969) is thought to be the first woman to own and publish a newspaper n this country. She bought the *California Owl* in 1912 and ran it for some forty years. Bass was the Progressive Party's vice-presidential candidate in 1952, another first for a black woman. Through her journalistic and political interests, she worked tirelessly in behalf of the elimination of racism and sexism. Bass was born in Sumter, South Carolina, and moved to Providence, Rhode Island, at age twenty, to work for a local newspaper. After ten years, health reasons prompted her to move from Providence to Los Angeles, where she took a part-time job with the *Eagle*. This paper was suffering from both poor management and its editor's ill health. When Bass assumed control of the paper in 1912, she renamed it the *California Eagle*. She was married to John Bass in the same year, and they combined their efforts toward combating racial discrimination. The film *Birth of a Nation,* injustice in the military during World War I, the 1919 Pan-African Conference, the 1931 alleged rape case in Scottsboro, Alabama, and discrimination in employment were among the concerns that came under their scrutiny. In her lifetime, Bass ran for three political offices, but was successful in no case. She was, however, the first black grand jury member for the Los Angeles County Court. Her memoirs, published in 1960 as *Forty Years: Memoirs from the Pages of a Newspaper,* reveal the part that black people played in the development of Los Angeles.

Sources: Hine, *Black Women in America,* vol. 1, pp. 93, 664; Smith, *Notable Black American Women,* pp. 61–64.

ald Tribune and was publicity director for the National Negro Business League. He was appointed Envoy and Plenipotentiary to Liberia by President Franklin Roosevelt in 1935 and stayed involved with politics for over twenty years. When he returned to the United States in 1953, he revived his activities in the arts by working with other black performers as a co-founder of the Coordinating Council for Negro Performers, which had as its purpose increasing the number of African Americans employed in television.

Sources: Salzman, *Encyclopedia of African-American Culture and History,* vol. 3, p. 1502; Salzman, *Encyclopedia of African-American Culture and History,* Supplement, p. 271.

1921 • Harlem Renaissance writer, poet, and editor Claude McKay (1890?–1948) became associate editor of *The Liberator,* a radical literary journal. He was the first black hired in an editorial position. McKay's name remained on the masthead until the journal ceased publication in October 1924. He was born Festus Claudius McKay in Sunny Ville, Jamaica, immigrated to America in 1912, and settled in Harlem in 1914. He became a leading spokesman of the Harlem Renaissance. His writings include *Home to Harlem* (1928), *A Long Way from Home* (1927), and *Banana Bottom* (1933).

Sources: *The Black New Yorkers,* p. 178.

1930 • The *New York Times* adopted the capitalized spelling of "Negro" and "Negress," becoming the first major newspaper to recognize this proper spelling.

Sources: Menken, *The American Language,* p. 379.

1935 • Joel Augustus Rogers (1883–1965) is generally recognized as the first black foreign correspondent. From October 1935 through April 21, 1936, he covered the Italian-Ethiopian War in Addis Ababa, Ethiopia, for the *Pittsburgh Couriere.* (There were other black journalists who preceded him as war correspondents during the Civil War and World War I; some consider Ralph Tyler's World War I coverage to qualify him for the title of first black foreign war correspondent.) Born in Jamaica, Rogers came to the United States in 1906 and was largely self-educated. During his lifetime, he traveled extensively in Europe

The First Black Daily Newspaper

The first black daily newspaper in the twentieth century was the *Atlanta Daily World*, founded on August 3, 1928, by William A. Scott III (1903–1934). In spring 1930 it became a bi-weekly, and on March 13, 1932, it became a daily. After Scott's death, his brother, Cornelius Adolphus ["C.A.," "Pops"] Scott (1908–2000) took over as editor and publisher until 1997, when he retired. In 1997 Alexis Scott Reeves was named publisher of the newspaper founded by her grandfather, William A. Scott. She was with the *Atlanta Journal Constitution* and Cox Enterprises for twenty-two years, moving from reporter and editor to director of human resources and later director of diversity at Cox. Now published two days a week, the paper is run by second- and third-generation family members.

Sources: Alford, *Famous First Blacks*, p. 75; Mason, *Going Against the Wind*, pp. 79, 101; *Jet* (3 March 1992): 29; 92 (29 September 1997): 39; *Negro Yearbook, 1947*, p. 386.

and Africa and became a journalist, historian, and prolific writer. He devoted most of his life to research and scholarship aimed at presenting an accurate account of the black African historical presence. His lack of formal credentials and his race contributed to difficulty in getting his work published as well as questions about the accuracy of his work by some of his scholarly contemporaries. Despite this, Rogers has an impressive list of publications, accomplished with practically no funds. His first book was published in 1917, with a self-published fifth edition released in 1941.

Sources: Logan and Winston, *Dictionary of American Biography*, pp. 531–32; *Encyclopedia of Black America*, p. 735; Kane, *Famous First Facts*, p. 425; Smith, *Notable Black American Men*, pp. 1029–30.

1944 • Harry S. McAlpin (1906–1985) became the first black correspondent to be admitted to a White House press conference. A correspondent for the National Negro Press Association and the Atlanta *Daily World*, he first attended a White House press conference on February 8, 1944. In 1947 the Negro Newspaper Publishers Association and individual newspaper correspondents were accredited to the Congressional Press Galleries and to the State Department. The early journalists accredited at this time were James L. Hicks, accredited to the State Department; and Percival L. Prattis and Louis Lautier, House and Senate press galleries.

Sources: *Jet* 53 (9 February 1978): 58; Kane, *Famous First Facts*, p. 425; *Negro Almanac*, p. 1427; *Negro Year Book, 1952*, pp. 46–48.

1944 • Elizabeth B. Murphy Moss [Phillips] (1917–1998) was the first black woman certified as a war correspondent during World War II. However, due to illness, she returned without filing a report. Moss later became vice-president and treasurer of the Afro-American Company, and publisher of the largest black chain of weekly newspapers in the United States, the Baltimore *Afro-American* group.

Sources: *Encyclopedia of Black America*, p. 570; Hine, *Black Women in America*, vol. 1, p. 664; *Negro Yearbook, 1947*, p. 387.

1947 • On March 18, 1947, the Senate Rules Committee ordered that Louis Lautier (1896–1962) be granted access to the congressional press galleries, making him the first black newspaperman to have such a privilege since 1871. Lautier was bureau chief of the Negro Newspapers Publishers Association and had been denied accreditation on the grounds that he did not represent a daily newspaper. He based his appeal of the original decision that barred him in 1946, on the grounds that he did indeed represent a daily, the *Atlanta Daily World*. Percival L. Prattis (1895–1980) was allowed access to the periodical gallery of both the House and Senate, as part owner of *Our World* magazine. On February

5, 1956, Prattis, as executive editor of the *Pittsburgh Courier,* became the first black admitted to the National Press Club.

Sources: *Negro Year Book, 1952,* pp. 46–47.

1947 • Alice Dunnigan (1906–1983) of the Associated Negro Press was the first black woman accredited to the White House and the State Department, and the first to gain access to the House of Representatives and Senate press galleries. At the State Department, she joined James L. Hicks, assistant chief of the Negro Newspapers Publishers Association, who had been the first black accredited to the department shortly before. Dunnigan was also the first black elected to the Women's National Press Club. In 1948 she became the first black news correspondent to cover a presidential campaign, when she covered Harry S. Truman's whistle-stop trip. She was chief of the Washington bureau of the Associated Negro Press for fourteen years. Dunnigan was born on April 27, 1906, near Russellville, Kentucky. She attended Kentucky State College (now University), earning a teaching certificate in elementary education, and later graduated from West Virginia Industrial College (now West Virginia State University) after teaching and attending school at the same time. Poor salaries for teachers and the need to do menial jobs when the schools were not open led her to seek a government job. In 1942 Dunnigan obtained a job with the War Department in Washington, D.C., and by the end of the war she had risen to the level of economist in the Office of Price Administration. Her interest in writing had begun in her childhood; she wrote a local news column for the *Owenborough Enterprise,* a black-run publication, and continued to write in a variety of formats during her years in Kentucky. It was this background that led to her appointment as chief of the Associated Negro Press in Washington. Dunnigan served in a variety of government positions until 1970, when her Democratic Party allegiance proved to be a disadvantage. She continued to write after leaving government service, publishing her autobiography in 1974 and a second book in 1979. Dunnigan received numerous awards during her career, including induction into the Journalism Hall of Fame at the University of Kentucky in 1982.

Sources: Hine, *Black Women in America,* vol. 1, pp. 368–70; *Jet* 64 (30 May 1983): 42; Smith, *Notable Black American Women,* pp. 301–3; *Negro Year Book, 1952,* p. 47.

1949 • The first black full-time reporter for the *Mirror-News,* owned by the *Los Angeles Times,* was Chester Lloyd Washington (1902–1983). He specialized in superior court cases. Originally a reporter for the *Los Angeles Sentinel,* he became its editor in 1961 and editor-in-chief in 1965. Through purchases and mergers of existing weekly newspapers and the creation of others, he established Central News-Wave Publications in Los Angeles, the largest black-owned newspaper operation in the country. Washington was born in Pittsburgh, Pennsylvania, and graduated from Virginia Union University. He served on the Los Angeles County Parks and Recreation Commission. In 1982 Western Golf Course, in Los Angeles, was renamed the Chester L. Washington Golf Course.

Sources: *Encyclopedia of Black America,* pp. 845–46; *Negro Almanac, 1989,* pp. 1256, 1263–64; *Who's Who among Black Americans, 1988,* p. 721.

1950 • Marvel Jackson Cooke (1903–2000) was the first full-time black woman reporter on a mainstream newspaper, the *Daily Compass,* where she was a colleague of the well-known journalist, I. F. Stone. Cooke was also a trade unionist and rights advocate. Born in Mankato, Minnesota, she graduated from the University of Minnesota. In 1926, during the middle of the Harlem Renaissance, she moved to New York City and began her career as an editorial assistant to W. E. B. Du Bois in 1926 at the *Crisis,* which positioned Cooke to meet many of the artistic and literary figures of the era. She left the *Crisis* in 1928 and joined the *Amsterdam News,* where she helped to organize a unit of the American Newspaper Guild. Cooke became assistant managing editor of Adam Clayton Powell's *People's Voice* in 1935. In 1949 she moved to the *Daily Compass* and, because she was black, she had access to news events about blacks that she wrote about in the paper. This included a series of articles about the exploitation of black domestic workers in the Bronx. She went undercover in the Bronx and gained first-hand knowledge of what she called "The Bronx Slave Market." When the paper closed on November 3, 1952, Cooke worked for the Committee for the Arts, Science and Professions, the Angela Davis Defense Fund, and other leftist organizations. Her affiliation with these organizations and the Communist party led Senator Joseph McCarthy to call her to testify on Capitol Hill; however, she pleaded the Fifth Amendment.

Sources: *Crisis* 108 (January/February 2001): 14; *Contemporary Black Biography,* vol. 31, pp. 40–42; Hine, *Black Women in America,* vol. 1, p. 664; *New York Times* (10 December 2000).

1950 • Albert L. Hinton (1904–1950), representing the Negro Newspaper Association, and James L. Hicks, representing the *Afro-American* group, were the first black war correspondents in the Korean conflict. Hinton died when his plane went down between Japan and Korea, but Hicks carried out his assignment.

Sources: *Negro Year Book, 1952,* p. 46; Spradling, *In Black and White,* Supplement, p. 189.

1952 • Journalist Simeon S. Booker (1918–) was the first full-time black reporter for the *Washington Post,* from 1952 to 1954. In 1982 he was the first black to be awarded the Fourth Estate Award by the National Press Club in Washington, D.C. Booker began his career as a reporter for the Baltimore *Afro-American.* During the 1950s he was a reporter for the *Cleveland Call and Post.* He left the *Post* in 1955 to work for the Johnson Publishing Company; he later became their Washington bureau chief. His reports of civil rights activities were highlighted in 1955, when he covered the trials of two men who lynched Emmett Till in Mississippi. He rode with the Freedom Riders in May 1961—the only journalist to do so—to protest segregated facilities on interstate bus travel. Although he was not harmed when the riders were attacked in Anniston, Alabama, he witnessed the beatings first-hand, reported the attacks to Attorney General Robert Kennedy, and later wrote about the experiences in *Ebony* magazine. He continued to write about the civil rights struggle of the 1960s and early 1970s. Booker interviewed presidents, a number of senators, and other Washington leaders and wrote about the interviews in his column "Ticker Tape U.S.A." Born in Baltimore, he and his family moved to Youngstown, Ohio, when he was five years old. He graduated from Virginia Union University in Richmond and did graduate study at Cleveland College. In 1992 Booker became the second black journalist to receive the Nieman Foundation fellowship for study at Harvard University. The next year the Washington Association of Black Journalists presented him the Career Achievement Award for groundbreaking service in the field of journalism. The National Black Media Coalition in 1998 awarded him the Master Communicator's Award.

Sources: Rush, *Black American Writers,* vol. 1, p. 84; *Who's Who among African Americans,* 26th, p. 121; *Contemporary Black Biography,* vol. 23, pp. 20–23; *Jet* 84 (1 November 1993): 22.

1957 • The first black reporter for the Providence, Rhode Island, *Journal Bulletin* was James N. Rhea (1918?–1989). Around this time the newspaper dispatched two of its top reporters, Rhea and Ben H. Bagdikian—one black and the other white—to the South to examine racial attitudes that followed the Supreme Court's ban on racially segregated public schools. Their articles caused a stir in Providence. However, the National Conference of Christians and Jews (as it was known then) gave them an award for their work. After Rhea died, the press noted his professional work but disregarded the racial barriers that he had broken in Providence and elsewhere. Rhea grew up in Johnson City, Tennessee, and graduated from the University of Michigan. During World War II he served in the army. He later joined the staff of the *Norfolk Journal and Guide.* Rhea retired in 1983 and died in 1989 at the age of seventy-one.

Sources: Rea, James A. "Reporting Civil Rights: Reporters and Writers," http://reporting civilrights.loa.org/authors/bio.jsp?authorId=65. Accessed September 26, 2012.

1962 • William C. Matney (1924–2001) was the first black writer for the *Detroit News.* Matney was born in West Virginia and graduated from the University of Michigan. He spent over thirty years in print and broadcast journalism. He was especially interested in reporting on stories about race and at times produced them himself. He left the paper in 1963 to join

NBC News and was based in Chicago. From 1973 to 1978 he served as correspondent for both NBC and ABC, where his assignments included Capitol Hill and the White House. After retiring in 1978, he worked as a public affairs official for the U.S. Census Bureau.

Sources: *Who's Who among African Americans*, 14th ed., p. 854.

1963 • Robert G. McGruder (1942–2002) became the first black reporter for the *Cleveland Plain Dealer* and in 1971 he was named managing editor. After serving in the U.S. Army, he returned to the *Plain Dealer* in 1966 and covered city government and politics. During his tenure with the paper he was a union member and negotiator. McGruder's work covered the Civil Rights Movement while he was with the *Plain Dealer*. He was a member of the Pulitzer Prize nominating jury in 1986, 1987, 1990, 1991, and 1999. He was a board member of the American Society of Newspaper Editors. In 1984 he received the William Taylor Distinguished Alumni Award from Kent State's journalism school. Born in Louisville, Kentucky, he grew up in Dayton, Ohio. In 1963 he graduated from Kent State University in Ohio and worked with the *Dayton Journal Herald*. He died of cancer on April 12, when he was sixty years old.

Sources: *New York Times* Obituaries, (12 April, 2002); (14 April 2002); *Washington Post* (14 April 2002).

1963 • Thomas Aldrige Johnson (1929–2008) was the first black reporter at *Newsday*. He moved to the *New York Times* in 1966 and became one of the first black journalists hired as a foreign correspondent for a major daily.

Sources: *Jet* 113 (23 June 2008): 27; Martin, Douglas. "Thomas A. Johnson, Pioneering Black Journalist, Dies at 79." *New York Times*. http://www.nytimes.com/2008/06/05/nyregion/05johnson.html?pagewanted=print&_r=0. Accessed October 9, 2012.

1964 • Stanley S. Scott (1933–1992) became the first black full-time general assignment reporter for United Press International (UPI). In 1965 he was nominated for a Pulitzer Prize for his eyewitness account of the assassination of Malcolm X. In 1967 he became the first full-time black news announcer for WINS, an all-news radio station in New York City. Scott won the Russwurm Award for Excellence in Radio News Reporting, as well as the New York Silurians Award.

Sources: *Ebony Success Library*, vol. 1, p. 277; *Who's Who among Black Americans, 1992–93*, p. 1254.

1968 • Kenneth Chow (1947–) founded the *Black Progressive Shopper-News* in Kansas City, Kansas, the first paper of its kind in the Kansas and Missouri area. He received his high school diploma in 1965, while in Terre Haute Federal Penitentiary in Indiana.

Sources: *Encyclopedia of Black America*, pp. 225–26.

1968 • The first black reporter for the *Star-Ledger* of Newark, New Jersey, was Ernest Johnston (1932?–2000). The veteran writer interviewed Martin Luther King Jr. in King's final interview in the North. His ten-minute interview occurred while King's car was stopped at a drawbridge in Newark; King was assassinated a few days later. Johnston worked as a reporter for the *New York Post,* a freelance copy editor and columnist for the *Journal of Jersey City,* and managing editor of the *New York Amsterdam News*. Johnston later served as a communications specialist for the National League. He retired in 1995.

Sources: *Obituaries in the News* (2 February 2000).

1968 • The first black Washington, D.C., correspondent for *Newsweek* was Samuel F. Yette (1929–2011). The journalist, author, and educator "became an influential and sometimes incendiary voice on civil rights." The Harriman, Tennessee, native was the twelfth of thirteen children and the grandson of a slave. He graduated from Tennessee Agricultural and Industrial State University (now Tennessee State University) in 1951 and earned his master's degree in journalism from Indiana University. His career mushroomed after he accompanied Gordon Parks, photographer for *Life* magazine, on a tour of the South in the mid-1950s. Yette worked at Tuskegee Institute (now University) and in the mid-1960s with Sargent Shriver as executive director of the Peace Corps. Then he became assistant to the director of the Office of Economic Opportunity in Washington, D.C., which administered anti-poverty programs. He also taught journalism at Howard University. While a young reporter, he covered the Civil Rights Movement for the black press, including the *Afro-American* newspaper beginning in 1956, and *Jet* magazine. He covered a number of major civil rights events, such as the 1957 March on Washington and other activities that Martin Luther King Jr.'s Southern Christian Leadership Conference organized. His spent a rocky three-year period with *Newsweek* and was fired in 1971. While Yette claimed that his book, *The Choice: The Issue of Black Survival in America,* was the cause of his firing three months after the work was published, *Newsweek,* then owned by the *Washington Post,* said that the reason was based "purely on professional grounds." Yette sued, won an initial court ruling but a federal appeals court reversed the decision later on. Yette spent the last years of his career teaching journalism at Howard University.

Sources: *Tennessean* (21 January 2011); *Washington* Post *(24 January, 2011).*

1968 • Eleanora Elaine Tate (1948–) became the first black woman journalist to work at the *Des Moines Register and Tribune.* Born in Canton, Missouri, Tate was raised by her grandmother. She graduated from Drake University in 1973 with a bachelor's degree in journalism. Her work as a journalist began in 1966, when she was news editor for the *Iowa Bystander.* That paper had awarded her a full scholarship to Drake. In 1968 she moved to the *Des Moines Register and Tribune;* her work brought her in touch with a number of high-profile figures, such as Martin Luther King Jr., whom she interviewed. She relocated to Tennessee in 1976 and joined the *Jackson Sun* for one year. In 1977 she became freelance writer for the *Memphis Tri-State Defender* and later established a public relations company and a media consultant firm. The interest in writing that Tate recognized when she was in the sixth grade had now been brought full circle. She moved from journalism and began to write stories, poems, articles, and books. Tate published her first novel, *Just an Overnight Guest,* in 1980. Since then she has published three installments of her highly-acclaimed *South Carolina* trilogy, and another novel, *Don't Split the Pole: Tales of Down-Home Folk* Wisdom.

Sources: *Contemporary Black Biography,* vol. 20, pp. 206–9; *Who's Who among African Americans,* 26th ed., p. 1202.

1971 • William A. Hilliard (1927–) was the first black city editor on a mainstream paper, the *Portland Oregonian.* He joined the newspaper in 1952 as a copy aide, and on April 5, 1982, he became the first black executive editor of the news department. In 1993 the American Society of Newspaper Editors elected Hilliard its first black president.

Sources: *Jet* 62 (5 April 1982): 29; *Negro Almanac,* p. 1258; *Who's Who among African Americans,* 26th ed., p. 586.

1971 • The *Atlanta Constitution* hired Tina McElroy Ansa (1949–) for its copy desk for the morning edition, making her the first black woman to hold that position. Ansa went on to become an acclaimed novelist whose work broke new ground in black American literature. Born in Macon, Georgia, she graduated from Spelman College in Atlanta in 1971 and began work with the *Constitution.* She moved into several positions with the paper during her eight years of employment. She later moved to the *Charlotte Observer,* first as copy editor then as editor, from the late 1970s to 1981, after spending a year as free-lance journalist. Since 1982 she has been a writing workshop instructor at Brunswick College, Emory University, and Spelman College. Six years after she married filmmaker Jonee Ansa, she and her husband settled in the Sea Islands of South Carolina, where she found fertile ground for the stories that she would write. Ansa found inspiring the first-hand accounts of the older black women, who had worked as midwives or who had other beliefs, rituals, and real-life experiences to relate. Her novels *Baby of the Family* (1989), *Ugly Ways* (1993), and *The Hand I Fan With* (1996) reflect these experiences as well as those of her own family. In 2008 she published *Taking after Mudear,* a sequel to *Ugly Ways.*

Sources: *Contemporary Black Biography,* vol. 14, pp. 11–13; *Who's Who among African Americans,* 26th ed., p. 36.

1972 • Hazel B. Garland (1913–1988) editor-in-chief of the *Pittsburgh Courier*, was the first woman head of a nationally circulated black newspaper in the United States. For more than fifty years her columns were published in various editions of the *Courier*. Some sources say that her greatest contributions were made behind the scenes, as she determined newspaper policy, made staff assignments to reflect social needs, and prepared those who would carry on her work. Hazel Barbara Maxine Hill Garland was born outside Terre Haute, Indiana, and died in McKeesport, Pennsylvania, where she had lived for over fifty years. She worked as a maid and at night spent her time dancing, singing, and playing the drums. Her plan was to become an entertainer. Her contact with the *Pittsburgh Courier* in 1943, when she was a reporter for the local YWCA in Pittsburgh, led to her appointment in 1946 as a full-time staff member. She wrote the column "Things to Talk About." In 1966 John Sengstacke purchased the paper and renamed it the *New Pittsburgh Courier*, and Garland became women's and entertainment editor. She was named editor-in-chief in 1972. The National Newspaper Publisher's Association named her "Editor of the Year" in 1974, the year in which Garland stepped down from her post.

Sources: Hine, *Black Women in America*, vol. 1, p. 664; *Jet* 74 (25 April 1988): 59; Smith, *Notable Black American Women*, Book II, pp. 240–43; *New York Daily News*, 6 April 1988.

1974 • Audrey T. Weaver (1908–1996) was named managing editor of the *Chicago Defender*, making her the first woman to hold this position with a major newspaper. She was previously city editor and had been associate editor for *Jet* magazine. In 1973 and 1974 Weaver was a juror on the Pulitzer Prize Committee. She died in Chicago at age eighty-eight.

Sources: *Jet* 89 (1 April 1996): 64.

Robert C. Maynard

1979 • Robert C. Maynard (1937–1993) was the first black to direct the editorial operations of a major American daily, the *Oakland Tribune* in California. In 1983 he became owner and publisher of the *Oakland Tribune* and the first black to become a majority shareholder in a major metropolitan daily newspaper. Maynard spent ten years at the *Washington Post* as its first black national correspondent, and later as ombudsman and editorial writer. On October 15, 1992, the name and certain assets of the *Oakland Tribune* then the nation's only black-owned major daily newspaper, were sold to the Alameda Newspaper Group. Maynard was a high school dropout whose interest in writing surfaced when he was eight years old. While in high school in Brooklyn he chose to spend time at the offices of the *New York Age*, a black weekly newspaper at the time, instead of attending class. His involvement with the newspaper, which published some of his articles, led to his dropping out of school. Maynard's first big journalistic break came when he was hired as a police and urban affairs reporter for the *York, Pennsylvania, Gazette and Daily* in 1961; he later covered the Civil Rights Movement as well. Maynard added to his formal journalistic training when he was awarded a one-year Neiman Fellowship for journalists at Harvard University. His work at the *Post* led to national visibility: He was one of the only three journalists chosen as questioners for the final debate between Gerald Ford and Jimmy Carter. He was hired by the Gannett newspaper chain while on leave from the *Post* to pursue his strong interest in provision of training programs for aspiring minority journalists. When Gannett made him editor of the *Oakland Tribune*, Maynard made many improvements, but the paper ran into financial difficulties. After putting together sufficient funding, he purchased the *Tribune* when Gannett put it up for sale in 1983.The paper was financially unsuccessful, but it became a symbol of racial pride, and it won a Pulitzer Prize for its photographic coverage of the 1989 Bay Area earthquake. The *Tribune* was sold in 1992 after Maynard became terminally ill.

Sources: *Atlanta Journal and Constitution* (19 August 1993); *Who's Who among Black Americans 1992–93*, p. 935; Smith, *Notable Black American Men*, pp. 778–80; Maynard, *Letters to My Children*.

1982 • Pamela McAllister Johnson (1945–) became the first black woman publisher of a mainstream paper, the *Ithaca Journal* on December 10, 1982. The paper has a circulation of 20,000 and is a part of the Gannett chain. In 1987 Johnson received the Candace Award from the National Coalition of 100 Black Women.

The First Black Columnist to Win a Pulitzer Prize

In 1989 Clarence Page (1947–) became the first black columnist to be awarded a Pulitzer Prize. He joined the *Chicago Tribune* staff in 1969 and later became a syndicated columnist and editorial writer for the paper. His interest in journalism began in high school, and while there he won an award from the Southeast Ohio High School Newspaper Association for best feature article. He received a bachelor's degree in journalism from Ohio University in Athens in 1969 and went to work for the *Tribune* soon after. After a brief tour of duty in the military interrupted his employment, he returned to the *Tribune* and made rapid progress. Page's column is nationally syndicated, and his freelance writings have appeared in a variety of sources. He is also an author of longer works, having written his first book in 1996; a regular analyst for ABC News; and an occasional participant on several television news shows and PBS documentaries.

Sources: *Contemporary Black Biography,* vol. 4, pp. 187–90; *Jet* 76 (17 April 1989): 23; *Who's Who among African Americans,* 26th ed., p. 957.

Sources: Hine, *Black Women in America,* vol. 2, p. 1450; Dates and Barlow, *Split Image,* p. 367; *Negro Almanac,* p. 1432; *Who's Who among Black Americans, 1989,* pp. 766–67.

1987 • Yelena Khanga (1962–) received an award from the Soviet Union that allowed her to work several years as exchange journalist with the *Christian Science Monitor*. She was the first woman to receive the honor. Khanga, whose roots are in Poland, Tanzania, Mississippi, and several other American cities, is the granddaughter of Polish immigrants (who were Jewish) and a black Mississippian. Her mother was a tennis star and scholar in the Soviet Union, and her father an African nationalist. Khanga was born in the former Soviet Union and graduated from Moscow State University, where she majored in journalism. Her book, *Soul to Soul: The Story of a Black Russian American Family, 1865–1992* (1992), along with others news articles she has written, tell of her ancestry and racism as she imagined or experienced it. For several years Khanga worked with the *Moscow World News* and then was selected to participate in an exchange program with the *Christian Science Monitor*. Khanga was profiled on the television program *20/20* after her story became known in the American press. In 1992 she received a fellowship to the John F. Kennedy Institute of Politics at Harvard University.

Sources: *Contemporary Black Biography,* vol. 6, pp. 164–67.

1987 • Roger Wood Wilkins (1932–) was the first black chair of the National Pulitzer Prize Board (1987–88), and served on the Board from 1980 to 1989. In 1973 he shared a Pulitzer Prize with the *Washington Post* for his reports on Watergate. His autobiography, *A Man's Life,* was published in 1982. The Kansas City, Missouri, native is the nephew of former NAACP director Roy Wilkins.

Sources: *Contemporary Black Biography,* vol. 2, pp. 250–53; *Jet* 72 (18 May 1987): 10; *Who's Who among African Americans,* 26th ed., p. 1330.

1990 • The first black chief of the *Detroit Free Press* city-county bureau was Constance C. Prater (1963–). A graduate of the Medill School of Journalism at Northwestern University, she became a reporter for the newspaper in 1989. In 1990 Prater was local president of the National Association of Black Journalists.

Sources: *Jet* 78 (24 September 1990): 29.

1990 • Cynthia Anne Tucker (1955–) was the first black woman to edit the editorial page a major daily newspaper, the *Atlanta Constitution,* with a circulation of over 300,000. She joined the newspaper in 1976, serving then as reporter. She left the paper in 1980 and until

1982 was a reporter for the *Philadelphia Inquirer*. Tucker served as editorial writer and later columnist for the *Atlanta Journal* from 1983 to 1986. She was associate editorial page editor from 1986 to 1991, before being appointed editorial page editor of the *Atlanta Constitution*. Tucker has served as panelist or commentator on Jim Lehrer's *News Hour* and on *CNN and Company*. In 1993 the National Women's Political Caucus named Tucker the nation's top columnist. Born in Monroeville, Alabama, she graduated from Auburn University in 1976.

Sources: *Jet* 81 (27 January 1992): 9; *Contemporary Black Biography*, vol. 15, pp. 205–7; *Who's Who among African Americans*, 26th ed., p. 1247–48.

1990 • Keith Woods (1958–) was named the first black city editor of the (New Orleans) *Times Picayune*. The New Orleans native began his career in the sports department of the newspaper in 1978, became a full-time sports writer for the paper in 1988, and was named assistant city editor in 1989. He graduated from Dillard and Tulane universities.

Sources: Hornsby, *Milestones in Twentieth-Century African-American History*, p. 465; *Jet* 79 (7 January 1991): 37.

1992 • On December 1, 1992, Pearl Stewart (1951–) became the first black woman editor of a major United States daily, the *Oakland Tribune*, with a circulation of over 100,000. Under a Freedom Forum grant, Stewart became journalist-in-residence at Howard University for 1994–95. Stewart graduated from Howard University and received a master's degree from American University. She worked for United Press International and the *Chronicle*, and then joined the *Oakland Tribune*.

Sources: *Jet* 82 (5 October 1992): 36; 86 (29 August 1994): 37; Salzman, *Encyclopedia of African-American Culture and History*, vol. 5, pp. 2389, 2573–74; *Who's Who among African Americans*, 26th ed., pp. 1180–81.

1995 • Robert G. McGruder (1942–2002) became the first black president of the Associated Press Managing Editors. The next year he was promoted from his post as managing editor of the *Detroit Free Press* to become the first black executive editor of that paper, on January 1, 1996. At that time the paper was in the midst of a strike that lasted nearly five and a half years. He joined the *Detroit Free Press* in 1986, serving as deputy managing editor. In 1987 he was named managing editor-news, and then managing editor in 1993. In 2001 he was awarded the John S. Knight Gold Medal, the highest honor awarded to an employee of Knight Ridder, the *Free Press*' parent company. He became known as a champion of diversity. When accepting the award, McGruder said "I stand for diversity.... I represent African Americans, Latinos, Arab Americans, Asians, Native Americans, gays and lesbians, women and all the others we must see represented in our business offices, newsrooms, and our newspapers if we truly want to meet the challenge of serving our communities."

Sources: *New York Times* Obituaries, (12 April 2002); (14 April 2002); *Washington Post* (14 April 2002).

1996 • Lorraine Branham became executive editor of the *Tallahassee Democrat*. She was the first black and the first woman to hold the position. Branham was previously associate managing editor of the *Philadelphia Inquirer.*

Sources: *Jet* 90 (24 June 1996): 10.

1997 • Jacqueline Marie Thomas (1952–) became the first woman and the first black director of the 160-year-old *Baltimore Sun*. Thomas was born in Nashville, Tennessee, and received her bachelor's degree from Briarcliff College in 1972 and her master's degree from Columbia University in 1974. Thomas began her career as reporter for the *Chicago Sun-Times* in 1974 and became associate editor of the *Louisville Courier Journal and Times* in 1986. She left the next year to become associate editor of the *Detroit Free Press*. From 1992 to 1997 she was Washington bureau chief for the *Detroit News*.

Sources: *Jet* 92 (9 June 1997): 12; *Who's Who among African Americans*, 26th ed., p. 1219.

1998 • The first woman of color to become a vice president at the *Daily News* of New York was C. Adrienne Rhodes (1961–). She was promoted from her position as director of communications and media relations for the nation's fourth largest newspaper. She chaired the 1999 World of Women Leaders Conference on "Power of Diversity: An American Legacy" sponsored by the 21st Century Women's Leadership Center. Rhodes was born in Richmond, Indiana, and received her bachelor's degree from Whittier College in 1957 and her master's degree in social work from Fresno State College in 1968.

Sources: *Jet* 94 (5 October 1998): 20; (30 August 1999): 23; *Who's Who among African Americans,* 26th ed., pp. 1042–43.

2000 • Donald V. Adderton became the first black editor of a major daily newspaper in Mississippi, the *Delta Democrat-Times* in Greenville. The paper has a circulation of 12,000. Adderton joined the *Sun Herald* in Gulfport in 1994 as an editor and columnist. He was assistant metro editor for the *Savannah Morning News,* managing editor of *Jet* magazine, and a production assistant for Walter Cronkite at CBS News. Adderton, a New York native, graduated from Shaw University in Raleigh with a degree in radio, television, and film.

Sources: *Jet* 97 (1 May 2000): 15.

2001 • Eleanor Dixson-Hobbs became the first woman and the first black publisher of the 165-year-old daily newspaper, *American Banker,* the banking and financial industry's premiere source of daily information, news, and analysis. Her responsibilities included managing all aspects of the newspaper as well as a monthly magazine, *Future-Banker,* a technology journal for *American Banker* subscribers.

Sources: *Jet* 99 (23 January 2001): 56.

2001 • The *New York Times* promoted Gerald M. Boyd (1950–2006) from deputy managing editor to managing editor, making him the first black to hold one of the two top editing jobs at the newspaper. Boyd was the second highest-ranking member of the 1,200-member news staff. He joined the newspaper in 1983 as national political reporter and later became a White House correspondent. In 1991 he became a senior editor and later held editing posts in the Washington bureau and in national and metropolitan news departments. While he was managing editor, Boyd directed the *New York Times*' account of the World Trade Center bombing in 1993. The next year the paper received a Pulitzer Prize for that coverage. The staff also won a Pulitzer Prize for national reporting in 2000 of the series "How Race Is Lived in America," when Boyd was senior editor. In 1997 he was promoted to deputy managing editor. Boyd graduated from the University of Missouri in 1973. He founded the St. Louis Association of Black Journalists in 1977 and became its first president. On 1980 he was a Neiman Fellow at Harvard University. In addition to teaching at Howard University, he taught in journalism workshops for minority students at the University of Missouri.

Sources: *New York Times* (27 July 2001); 100 (10 September 2001): 25.

2005 • The first black journalist to lead a top newspaper in the United States was Dean P. Baquet (1956–). In October, Baquet, who had already made a name for himself with the *Chicago Tribune* and the *New York Times,* took the number two spot at the *Los Angeles Times*—that of managing editor. In 2005 he was appointed editor of the paper and the first black to head a major mainstream newspaper. He left that post in November 2006 and returned to the *New York Times* as chief of the Washington bureau and assistant editor. A native of New Orleans, Baquet studied at Columbia University and Tulane University but gave up formal training without completing a degree. For seven years he did investigative reporting with the *States-Item* (later subsumed by the *Times Picayune*) but left the New Orleans press in 1984 to join the *Chicago Tribune.* Later he became associate metropolitan editor for investigations. In 1988, Baquet shared a Pulitzer Prize for investigative reporting with fellow journalist Ann Marie Lipinski. He also helped the paper receive thirteen Pulitzer prizes. He left the *Tribune* in 1990 and began investigative reporting for the *New York Times,* becoming deputy metro editor later on, and in 1995 national editor.

Sources: *Contemporary Black Biography,* vol. 63, pp. 30–32; *Jet* 111 (19 February 2007): 58; Smith, *Notable Black American Men,* Book II, pp. 29–31.

Periodicals

1820 • *The Emancipator,* the first anti-slavery magazine, was issued monthly from April 30 to October 31, 1820. It was edited and published by Elihu Embree.

Sources: Kane, *Famous First Facts,* p. 456.

1838 • The first black periodical, *The Mirror of Liberty,* was published in June, 1838, by David Ruggles (1810–1849). The sixteen-page quarterly strongly protested colonization, segregation, disfranchisement, and slavery. It was published in New York City from 1838 to 1841.

Sources: Kane, *Famous First Facts,* p. 456; Logan and Winston, *Dictionary of American Negro Biography,* pp. 536–38.

1910 • The first issue of *Crisis* magazine, the official organ of the National Association for the Advancement of Colored People and the vehicle for the dissemination of educational and social programs for blacks, was published in April 1910. Edited by W.E.B. Du Bois, *Crisis* was first printed in one thousand copies, but by 1920 circulation had increased one-hundredfold.

Sources: Hornsby, *Milestones in Twentieth-Century African-American History,* p. 9; Joyce, *Gatekeepers of Black Culture,* pp. 37, 84; *Negro Almanac,* pp. 21, 260.

1940 • Sue Bailey Thurman (1903–1997) was the founder-editor of *Aframerican Women's Journal* the first published organ of the National Council of Negro Women. (In 1949 the title of the journal was changed to *Women United.*) Its purpose was to inform black women about major women's issues, legislation that affected them and blacks in general, to highlight women's accomplishments, and to report the projected work of the council. Thurman also founded and was first chairperson of the council's library, archives, and museum department. The pioneering activist and wife of theologion Howard Thurman died in her sleep at a hospice in San Francisco, at age ninety-three.

Sources: Hine, *Black Women in America,* vol. 2, p. 858; *Jet* 91 (20 January 1997): 17; Smith, *Notable Black American Women,* pp. 1139–42.

1942 • John H. Johnson (1918–2005) published the *Negro Digest,* the first magazine devoted to summarizing and excerpting articles and news about blacks published in mainstream publications. Immediately successful, the magazine laid the foundation for Johnson Publishing Company's success, which was only increased by magazines like *Ebony* and *Jet. Negro Digest,* was renamed *Black World* before ceasing publication in 1976.

Sources: *Contemporary Black Biography,* vol. 3, pp. 102–4; Dates and Barlow, *Split Image,* pp. 372–74; Smith, *Notable Black American Men,* pp. 630–34; Johnson, *Succeeding Against the Odds.*

1944 • The first issue of *Ebony* was published in November 1944, by Johnson Publishing Company of Chicago, with John H. Johnson (1918–2005), company founder, as editor. In 1945 the magazine was the first advertising medium owned by blacks to attract advertising from white-owned companies.

Sources: *Contemporary Black Biography,* vol. 3, pp. 102–4; Joyce, *Gatekeepers of Black Culture,* p. 63; *Encyclopedia of Black America,* p. 331.

1963 • Ariel Perry Strong became the first woman to head *Tan* (later *Black Stars*) magazine as managing editor. She was a proofreader for *Tan, Ebony,* and *Jet* magazines.

Sources: *Ebony Success Library,* vol. 1, p. 295.

1963 • *Time* magazine's first black national correspondent was Wallace Houston Terry II (1938–2003), whose many assignments included coverage of the Vietnam War. He was named 1993 holder of the John Seigenthaler Chair of Excellence in First Amendment Studies at Middle Tennessee State University. His bestselling book *Bloods: An Oral History of the Vietnam War by Black Veterans* (1984) was nominated for a Pulitzer Prize.

Wallace Terry II

The Oldest Continuously Published Periodical

The first issue of the oldest continuously published periodical, now known as the *Christian Recorder,* was published by the African Methodist Episcopal Church in 1841. Issued first as the *A.M.E. Church Magazine,* and intended as a weekly, it became a quarterly in its first year. Renamed the *Christian Herald* in 1848, it became a weekly again and was published by Martin Robinson Delany, an author, physician, abolitionist, Black Nationalist, and army officer. In 1852 it was renamed the *Christian Recorder.*

Sources: *Encyclopedia of Black America,* p. 33; Penn, *The Afro-American Press,* pp. 78–81.

Sources: *Tennessean* (15 October 1992); *Who's Who among Black Americans, 1992–93,* p. 1237.

1973 • The first black editor-in-chief of the national journal *Nursing Research* was Mary Elizabeth Carnegie (1916–2008), whose career in nursing spanned more than fifty years. Her route to prominence in nursing began in 1934, after graduation from Dunbar High School in Washington, D.C., when a relative encouraged her to consider nursing. Carnegie entered Lincoln School for Nurses, one of few schools in the city that accepted black students. While at Lincoln, she was privileged to hear Mabel Staupers, an executive with the National Association of Colored Graduate Nurses, talk about the association and the struggle of black nurses to gain recognition in the profession. The concern for equality of black women and women of all races in nursing remained a theme for Carnegie. When she graduated from Lincoln in 1937, Carnegie found a job at Veterans Administration Hospital in Tuskegee, Alabama, one of only two U.S. federal hospitals that employed black nurses. She later left Tuskegee to attend West Virginia State College (later University) full-time, graduating in 1942 with a Bachelor of Arts degree. She received a job offer as clinical director of nursing at the hospital that was the black wing of the Medical College of Virginia. However, she received a release from this appointment in order to serve, beginning in 1943, as assistant director of Hampton Institute's proposed new collegiate nursing program. As Carnegie was recognized as being the person primarily responsible for developing the program, her career flourished. She obtained training in nursing administration at the University of Toronto in 1944 and became dean of the nursing program at Florida Agricultural and Mechanical College (now University) in Tallahassee, Florida. Racial discrimination was apparent in Florida, and Carnegie dedicated herself to integrating the state nursing association, which she eventually accomplished. She added to her personal credentials by earning the degree of Master of Arts in Administration in Higher Education from Syracuse University in 1952, and in 1953 began a career in nursing journalism when she became assistant editor of the *American Journal of Nursing.* After three years, Carnegie became associate editor and later senior editor of *Nursing Outlook.* Once more showing her quest for learning, she earned a doctorate in public administration from New York University in 1972, after which she became editor of *Nursing Research,* a position she held until she retired in 1978. Carnegie remained an active professional, serving higher education and the nursing profession, after her retirement.

Sources: Hine, *Black Women in America,* vol. I, pp. 218–19; Smith, *Notable Black American Women,* pp. 156–60.

1990 • Connie Briscoe (1952–) became the managing editor of the *American Annals of the Deaf,* the first black and the first deaf person to hold the position at Gallaudet University. The Washington, D.C., native graduated from American University, after which she became editorial assistant for the Joint Center for Political and Economic Studies in Washington. The difficulties in hearing that she had experienced as a child grew worse and affected her ability to use the telephone at work. Briscoe's condition soon led to total hearing loss. She already knew lip-reading and used a hearing aid in school. She learned sign language, became involved in deaf culture, and chose a career that would accommodate her impairment. Briscoe moved to Gallaudet University in Washington, an institution for the hearing impaired; there she was editorial assistant and by 1990 was managing editor for the school's journal. By 1991 she had written several chapters for a novel. Her eventual book *Sisters and Lovers,* published in 1994, was well received and made it possible for her to become a full-time writer. CBS purchased the paperback edition for a television miniseries. In 1996 she published her second novel, *Big Girls Don't Cry*.

Sources: *Contemporary Black Biography,* vol. 15, pp. 30–32; *Jet* 86 (5 September 1994): 24; *Essence* 26 (July 1994): 32.

1994 • The first woman editor of *Crisis,* the national magazine of the NAACP, was Denise Crittendon (1954?–). The Detroit native completed her studies at Cuernavaca, Mexico, and the University of Zimbabwe. She has taught at Wayne State University, Central Michigan University, and Olivet College in Michigan. For fourteen years she was a reporter for the *Detroit News*.

Sources: *Jet* 85 (7 February 1994): 39.

1998 • The first black editor of a major news weekly in the United States, *Newsweek,* was Mark Whitaker (1957–). Whitaker, a Norton, Massachusetts, native, graduated from Harvard University in 1979. During the early 1980s he attended Balliol College at Oxford University as a Marshall Scholar. As early as 1977 he became associated with *Newsweek,* working as a reporting intern in the San Francisco office. In 1981 Whitaker became a stringer for the bureaus in Boston, Washington, and Paris. He became a fulltime staff member in 1981, and worked with the New York City office. Whitaker became business editor for *Newsweek* in 1987, just in time to report on the stock market crash of that year. Then he reported on such scandals as insider trading and the savings-and-loan crisis. Whitaker was promoted again in 1991 when he was named assistant managing editor; he oversaw the publication of special issues, such as those devoted to the Olympics and the first inauguration of Bill Clinton as President of the United States. Whitaker was named editor of the magazine on November 10, 1998, and was the first black to hold such an influential position with a national weekly news magazine. Although he is interested in racial matters in this country, he has downplayed the issue of race in his selection and his work. He left that post in 2006 and became vice president and editor-in-chief of New Ventures at the online Washingtonpost.Newsweek Interactive. In 2007 he was named senior vice president of NBC News and Washington Bureau Chief for NBC News, succeeding Tim Russert who died. Whitaker became one of its two highest-ranking black executives. In February 2011, he became executive vice president and managing editor for CNN Worldwide.

Sources: *Contemporary Black Biography,* vol. 21, pp. 188–90, 47, pp. 165–67; *New York Times* (11 November 1998); *Washington Post* (11 November 1998).

Gordon A. Parks Sr.

Photojournalism

1949 • Gordon A. Parks Sr. (1912–2006) became the first black photojournalist on the staff of *Life* magazine. Born Gordon Roger Alexander Buchanan Parks in Fort Scott, Kansas, he was the youngest of fifteen children. After his mother died when he was sixteen, Parks moved to St. Paul, Minnesota, to live with his sister and her family. He moved back and forth from St. Paul to Minneapolis, and Chicago. While working as a waiter on the North Coast Limited, he was inspired to become a photographer. He began his career in 1937 with a camera purchased in a pawnshop; it became what he called his "weapon against poverty and racism." He returned to Chicago where he captured much of the South Side slums on his camera. Parks was the first black to receive a Rosenwald Fellowship for photography; in 1942 he was the first black to work for the United States Farm Security Administration (as a photographer); and in 1943, the first to work for the United States Office of War Information (as a photojournalist and a war correspondent). Parks was named the Magazine Photographer of the Year in 1961. A gifted film director, he was the first black to direct movies for a major studio, including the feature film *Shaft*. He also gained fame for his autobiographical books, *A Choice of Weapons* and *The Learning Tree*.

Sources: *Contemporary Black Biography,* vol. 1, pp. 184–88; Lee, *Interesting People,* p. 88; Dates and Barlow, *Split Image,* pp. 161, 163, 376; Smith, *Notable Black American Men,* pp. 907–11.

Press Secretary

1990 • Lynette Moten (1954–) became the first black woman press secretary for a U.S. senator. She worked with Thad Cochran, a Republican from Mississippi, in his Washington, D.C., office. She is a graduate of Tougaloo College and Columbia University's Graduate School of Journalism.

Sources: *Jet* 78 (13 August 1990): 4.

1998 • Great Britain's Prince Charles named Colleen Harris deputy press secretary, making her the first black member of the English royal household.

Sources: *Jet* 93 (23 March 1998): 10.

Radio

1927 • Floyd Joseph Calvin (1902–1939), a journalist, had the first radio talk show, which focused on black journalism. Broadcast on WGBS, it was the first show of its kind sponsored by a black newspaper, the *Pittsburgh Courier*.

Sources: *Encyclopedia of Black America,* p. 213; Dates and Barlow, *Split Image,* p. 184.

1960 • Edmund Stanley Dorsey (1930–) became the first black White House broadcast correspondent with radio station WWDC. Three years later, while he was news director with radio-television station WOOK, he became the first black television news reporter in Washington, D.C. In 1964 he joined station WIND and was sent to Saigon (South Vietnam) in 1966, where he became the first black bureau chief for the Washington Broadcasting Network. While serving with the United States Army in Tokyo, Japan, in 1949, he had become the first black managing editor of the military publication *Stars and Stripes*.

Sources: *Ebony Success Library,* vol. 1, p. 98.

1965 • The first black radio announcer at the United Nations was Beatrice "Bea" Moten-Foster. Foster broadcast her show called "African Profiles" from 1965 to 1969, interviewing over one hundred ambassadors, presidents, and foreign ministers. She also visited the homes of her guests and was served African dishes. She obtained recipes from the officials' wives or their cooks. While living in Indianapolis in 1976, she formed a cookbook committee and later published a book of her own—*200 Years of Black Cookery*—that incorporated African recipes and her own as well. In October 1989 she became host of her own television show, "The Bea Moten-Foster Show," that aired in Indianapolis on weekdays. This also made her the first black woman television announcer in Indianapolis; already she was the city's first woman radio announcer. She had a daily radio cooking program on WGRT Gospel Radio. Moten-Foster appeared on other television shows, including the "Sally Jessy Raphael Show." A resident of Muncie, Foster had a career in business as marketing director and was owner of the Bea Moten Charm and Modeling School. She has been active also in many local organizations.

Sources: *St. Louis Globe-Democrat* (28 September 1983); *Indianapolis Recorder* (June 1979); (26 August 1989).

1987 • Adam Clayton Powell III (1946–) was the first black to direct a major national radio news network, National Public Radio. He has held a number of positions in the communications industry, including that as manager and producer for CBS News in New York City (1976–81). From 1985 to 1994 he was fellow, lecturer, and consultant for the Gannett Center for Media Studies at Columbia University. Powell also became a New York City Councilman. After leaving NPR in 1990, he was producer for Quincy Jones Entertainment, and then became vice president of technology and programs. The New York City native is the son of Adam Clayton Powell Jr. and pianist Hazel Dorothy Scott.

Sources: *Jet* 73 (26 October 1987): 22; Dates and Barlow, *Split Image,* p. 214; *Who's Who among African Americans,* 26th ed., p. 1007.

Television

1958 • The first black newscaster, for WNTA-TV in New York City, was Louis Emanuel Lomax (1922–1970). Lomax, an author and educator, was born in Valdosta, Georgia, and graduated from Paine College in Augusta, Georgia. He began his career in journalism in 1941, when he was a newspaperman. From 1958 to 1970 he was a freelance writer. For two years he was also a news commentator on WNTA-TV in New York City and from 1964 to 1968 for Metromedia Broadcasting. Around this time as well, Lomax was news analyst for KTTV in Los Angeles, news director for WNEW-TV in New York City, and news writer for the *Mike Wallace Show.* He was also a syndicated columnist for North American Newspaper Alliance. For a while Lomax hosted his own television program in Los Angeles called *Louis Lomax.* In addition to teaching at Georgia State University and Hofstra University, he wrote a number of books and contributed articles to *Life, Look,* and *Saturday Evening Post.*

Sources: Baskin and Runes, *Dictionary of Black Culture,* p. 275; *Encyclopedia of Black America,* pp. 539–40; *Black Writers,* p. 363; *Contemporary Authors,* vols. 25–28, pp. 454–55.

1962 • Mal [Malvin] Russell Goode (1908–1995) became the first black network news correspondent for any major television network when he was hired by ABC. Following that, CBS hired George Foster and Lee Thornton as White House correspondents. Born in White Plains, Virginia, Goode became the first black member of the National Association of Radio and Television News Directors in 1971. He was well-known for his coverage of civil rights and human rights activities during the 1960s. From his parents, Goode received the dual message of the importance of both work and education. During his youth, and after his family moved to Homestead, Pennsylvania, he worked in the local steel mills to earn enough money to attend the University of Pennsylvania. After graduating from college, Goode had a number of jobs, including serving as manager of a Pittsburgh housing development, which was at the time one of the country's few racially integrated housing units. He began his career in radio journalism as a commentator for station KQV in Pittsburgh in 1949, moving soon after to station WHOD in Homestead to join his sister, who was a disc jockey there. During this same year, he began work in print journalism by working in the circulation department of the *Pittsburgh Courier.* His duties and responsibilities expanded at both WHOD and the *Courier,* and in 1952 he became the station's news director. When the station closed in 1956, he went to work at a McKeesport, Pennsylvania, station and also sought work at major stations in Pittsburgh, but was unsuccessful. Ten years later he was hired by ABC, based on a recommendation from baseball legend Jackie Robinson and his years of experience. He became nationally known for his coverage of the Cuban missile crisis, when he had major responsibility for reporting United Nations activities. He was one of three journalists chosen by ABC to conduct seminars for African students in 1963. He retired from ABC after twenty years, but remained an ABC consultant. He was a mentor to George Strait and to Bernard Shaw, who followed him as black television journalists.

Sources: *Ebony Success Library,* vol. 1, p. 127; *Negro Almanac,* p. 1280; Dates and Barlow, *Split Image,* p. 389; *Who's Who among Black Americans, 1992–93,* p. 534; Smith, *Notable Black American Men,* pp. 466–68; Senna, *The Black Press and the Struggle for Civil Rights,* p. 134.

1965 • The first major black woman general-assignment, on-camera newscaster for CBS-TV's New York affiliate, WCBS-TV, was Joan Murray (1941–). The *New York Times* called her the first accredited black woman television news correspondent in the country. From 1963 to 1964 she was an on-air interviewer for NBC-TV; a hostess, writer, and production assistant with Kitty Carlisle's *Women on the Move;* and in April 1965 joined WCBS-TV News. A pilot as well, Murray learned to fly when she filmed the New York documentary, *The Small Plane Boom.* In 1966 she was co-pilot and official WCBS-TV's news reporter for the Power Puff Derby, officially the cross-country Trans-Continental Women's Air Race. Murray held several other positions on television. In 1969 she founded and became executive vice president of Zebra Associates, the first integrated advertising agency with black principals and then the largest black-owned and managed advertising agency. Her autobiography, *The News,* was published in 1968. Murray was born in Ithaca, New York, attended Ithaca College, and later Hunter College, the New School for Social Research, the French Institute, and the Alfred Dixon School of Speech.

Sources: *Ebony* 21 (October 1966): 50; *Encyclopedia of Black America,* 584; Smith, *Notable Black American Women,* pp. 782–83; Joan Murray File, Franklin Library, Fisk University.

1969 • Mal Johnson (1924–2007) was the first black woman television reporter to cover the White House. In 1970 she became the first woman national correspondent for Cox Broadcasting Corporation, on WKBS-TV. She hosted *Coffee Break* and *Let's Talk About It.* She was senior correspondent from 1969 to 1972 and director of community relations for Cox Enterprises from 1973 to 1992. Johnson became president of Media Linx International in Washington, D.C. In 1975 she founded the National Association of Black Journalists. She was also a member of various professional journalism organizations and has been honored widely for her achievements in the field. The Philadelphia native was educated at Temple University.

Sources: *Jet* 80 (10 June 1991): 10; Klever, *Women in Television,* pp. 134–38; *Who's Who among African Americans,* 14th ed., pp. 696–97.

1970 • Tony Brown (1933–) became host of the first and longest-running minority affairs show on television, *Black Journal.* He also became a leading voice on black issues. He was also founding dean of the School of Communications at Howard University in Washington, D.C., providing blacks a better change of success in the field of communications. Brown was born in Charleston, West Virginia, and raised by a family friend. He graduated from Wayne State University in Detroit in 1959 and received his master's degree in social work from that school in 1961. He left the social work field to become drama critic for the *Detroit Courier.* After working his way up to city editor, Brown moved to WTVS, Detroit's public television station, where he worked in public affairs programming. He went on to produce *C.P.T.* (Colored People's Time), which was the station's first program aimed toward a black audience. He later produced and hosted another community-oriented program, *Free Play.* In 1968 the Corporation for Public Broadcasting (CPB) funded a new program, *Black Journal;* it was produced in New York at WNET-TV and broadcast nationally on public television. Brown was hired as executive producer and host of the show in 1970. His concern, however, was that its content failed to represent the national black community. First an hour show aired once a month, he changed it to become a thirty-minute weekly. He hired a predominantly black staff to run the show. CPB cut off funding from 1973 to 1974. In 1977 Brown received funding from Pepsi Cola Company, changed its name to become *Tony Brown's Journal,* and moved to commercial stations. Another program of equal success, *Tony Brown at Daybreak,* later aired on WRC-TV in Washington, D.C. In 1982 he returned *Journal* to public television. Continuing his efforts to enhance black people in 1980 he initiated Black College Day, aimed to help save and support black colleges. Brown has been widely honored for his achievements. Among his awards was the 1995 Ambassador of Free Enterprise Award; he was the first black so honored. He also received an NAACP Image Award in 1991. The National Urban League honored him with its Public Service Award.

Sources: *Contemporary Black Biography,* vol. 3, pp. 18–22; Smith, *Notable Black American Men,* pp. 136–38; *Who's Who among African Americans,* 14th ed., p. 164.

1971 • Larry William McCormick (1933–) became the first black news anchorman in Los Angeles. After joining Tribune Broadcasting's KTLA, he became a mainstay in local broadcast journalism. In 1994 the Academy of Television Arts and Sciences awarded him its highest annual honor, the Governor's Award. Before anchoring the news, McCormick hosted musical programs, television talk shows, play-by-play football, and game shows. He was also a radio personality.

Sources: *Jet* 100 (23 July 2001): 29; *Who's Who among African Americans,* 14th ed., p. 868.

1978 • Charlayne Hunter-Gault (1942–) was the first black woman to anchor a national newscast, *The MacNeil/Lehrer Report.* She left that post in 1997 when she moved to South Africa. In 1999 she joined CNN in Johannesburg, South Africa, as bureau chief. She was born in Due West, South Carolina, and moved to Atlanta with her parents and siblings in 1954. In January 1961 she and Hamilton Holmes were the first two black students to attend the University of Georgia, where they were confronted with a student riot protesting their admission. She started college at Detroit's Wayne State University while waiting for a federal court order that would allow her to attend the University of Georgia. She graduated with a bachelor's degree in journalism in 1963. Hunter-Gault's first job after graduation was as a secretary for *The New Yorker* magazine. While there she contributed articles to a feature section and wrote short stories. A Russell Sage Fellowship allowed her to study social science at Washington University in St. Louis, Missouri, in 1967. She edited articles for *Trans-Action* while there and covered the Poor People's Campaign in Washington, D.C. This coverage led to her first television job: investigative reporter and anchorwoman of the evening local news at WRC-TV in Washington. A ten-year position at the *New York Times* followed, after which she went on to *MacNeil/Lehrer.* Hunter-Gault says her interest in journalism began at age twelve, with the comic strip reporter Brenda Starr as her idol. She gives the University of Georgia credit for her style of reporting. The university awarded her the prestigious George Foster Peabody Award in 1986. She also won two Emmys for her work with PBS.

Sources: Hine, *Black Women in America,* vol. 1, pp. 595–96; *Jet* 7 (26 March 1990); 33; 92 (26 May 1997): 33; 101 (14 January 2002): 32; *Current Biography, 1987,* pp. 261–64; Smith, *Notable Black American Women,* pp. 535–36.

1978 • Max Robinson (1939–1988) was the first black network news anchor, with ABC-TV on April 19, broadcasting from Chicago, Illinois. He had been the first co-anchor and the first black on the midday newscast with WTOP, Washington, D.C., in 1969. Robinson left ABC in 1983 to become the first black anchor for WMAQ-TV in Chicago and won an Emmy Award in 1980 for coverage of the national election. Born in Richmond, Virginia, he attended Oberlin College, Virginia Union University, and Indiana University.

Sources: *Contemporary Black Biography,* vol. 3, pp. 209–12; Hornsby, *Milestones in Twentieth-Century African-American History,* p. 390; *Jet* 76 (1 May 1989): 25.

1980 • Bernard Shaw (1940–) was appointed chief Washington correspondent and became the first black anchor at Cable News Network in 1980. In 1987 Shaw joined the major television networks in a nationally televised interview with President Ronald Reagan. The next year he moderated the second presidential debate in Los Angeles. Born in Chicago, Shaw attended the University of Illinois-Chicago. He received an early push toward a career in news when his father routinely brought four Chicago daily newspapers with him every day when he returned home from work. Edward R. Murrow, whose reporting was prominent on CBS, became his role model, and Shaw decided to become a broadcaster. He bought the *New York Times* regularly, visited Chicago commentator Clifton Utley, and frequented newsrooms as he sought to become familiar with the profession. Shaw was in the Marine Corps and stationed in Hawaii in 1961 when, after repeated attempts, he was able to get an appointment with Walter Cronkite to talk about a news career. The persistence shown by Shaw in his preparations came to be noted as one of the characteristics of his approach to reporting. While attending college after leaving the service, he worked without pay in the wire room of a Chicago radio station and became a paid reporter for the station when its format was changed to all-news. Before joining CNN, Shaw worked at other stations, both radio and television, until he decided to leave college when he was offered a job as White House correspondent for WIND in Washington, D.C., a position he held from 1968 to 1971. He worked for CBS for the next three years and in Miami for ABC from 1974 until 1979 as chief of the Latin American bureau. His move to CNN the next year resulted in the position he held until his retirement on February 28, 2001. During his tenure at CNN, Shaw was able to break a number of important news stories, including almost a full day's continuous coverage on the Persian Gulf War. Shaw's work has resulted in numerous awards, including an Emmy in 1989 in the News and Documentaries category, the Award for Cable Excellence as best news anchor in 1990, and the Cable Ace Award from the National Academy of Cable Programming for best newscaster of the year in 1991.

Sources: *Contemporary Black Biography,* vol. 2, pp. 217–21; *Essence* 21 (November 1990): 42; *Negro Almanac,* p. 1285–86; *New York Times* (1 March 2001); Smith, *Notable Black American Men,* pp. 1059–60.

1981 • Ed [Edward R.] Bradley (1941–2006) became the first black co-editor of *Sixty Minutes,* a CBS television network weekly news program in 1981. He replaced Dan Rather in 1980, but his first story aired in 1981. His previous assignments included serving as principal correspondent for *CBS Reports,* CBS News White House correspondent, anchor of the *CBS Sunday Night News,* and reports shown on *CBS Evening News with Walter Cronkite.* The Pennsylvania native graduated from Cheyney State College (now University). Bradley's first job after his 1964 college graduation was teaching sixth grade in Philadelphia. He had become a friend of a Philadelphia radio disc jockey while in college and continued to visit him at the station and to work as a volunteer jazz disc jockey and sometimes newscaster. After he covered personally the breaking story of a riot in Philadelphia, he was offered and took a paying job with the station in 1965. Bradley taught school by day and did his station work, which included music, news, and sports reporting, by night. His first CBS job came when he was hired at New York's WCBS Radio, an all-news station, in 1967. The stress of this job led him to move to Paris to live a less constrained and more artistic life, but his money soon ran out. CBS was able to lure him back in 1971 as a stringer for the Paris bureau. This was part-time work with payment by the story, and Bradley went back to work full-time as a CBS war correspondent. He was wounded while covering Vietnam and Cambodia and returned to the United States after the fall of Saigon, where his first assignment was coverage of Jimmy Carter's presidential campaign; he was assigned to cover the White House after the election. He remained a fixture at CBS. He had additional CBS assignments other than *60 Minutes* since joining that program, but it is *60 Minutes* that made him a familiar and respected face on the television screen. Bradley earned an Emmy in 1981 for his interview of Lena Horne. He earned eleven Emmys and numerous other awards.

Ed Bradley

Sources: *Contemporary Black Biography,* vol. 2, pp. 28–32; *Negro Almanac,* pp. 1278–79; *Who's Who among African Americans,* 14th ed., pp. 129–30; Smith, *Notable Black American Men,* pp. 102–04.

1982 • The first black co-host of *The Today Show* was Bryant Charles Gumbel (1948–). He had been co-host of NBC's Rose Bowl Parade since 1975, worked as chief anchor of NBC's televised football games, and in 1977 was co-host for Super Bowl XI. In 1988 he was NBC's host for the Olympics in Seoul, South Korea. When he replaced Tom Brokaw as co-host of *Today,* after sitting in for him for a few months before being officially named co-host, most of his previous broadcast experience had been in sports, which he acknowledges as his true love. Gumbel was born in New Orleans, Louisiana, but the family moved to Chicago when Bryant and his older brother Greg were infants. He is a 1970 graduate of Bates College, where he played both baseball and football. He wrote an article about Harvard's first black athletic director for *Black Sports,* which led to a contract with the magazine and to his becoming its editor nine months later. He became a weekly sportscaster for Los Angeles' KNBC-TV in 1972, moved to sportscaster on the evening news, and to sports director in a span of just eight months. For a time he worked for both KNBC and as co-host of the NFL pre-game show, commuting back and forth from Los Angeles to New York. He began to do more shows for NBC, and in 1980 was assigned to do three sports features a week for *Today*. When he took over the plum job of co-host of the show, it was in second place in the ratings. By spring 1985, it was in first place, where it remained for most of the Gumbel years. His stay on *Today* was not without controversy. Gumbel is regarded as a hard taskmaster and was given to expressing his opinions about aspects of the show and its cast members in sometimes unflattering terms. This and other instances of creative differences between Gumbel and the producers played a part in his decision to leave the show in 1997. He soon accepted a CBS offer to host *Public Eye,* a prime-time, magazine format, weekly interview show. This show lacked *Today's* longevity, and in 1999 Gumbel returned to the morning show beat as cohost of CBS's *The Early Show;* he left in 2002. He maintained multiple projects and, for awhile, continued his HBO sports show, *Real Sports.* Over the years he earned three Emmys and numerous other awards and honors, including two Image awards from the NAACP and being named Journalist of the Year by the Association of Black Journalists in 1993. He has also become known for his philanthropies, particularly his work on behalf of the UNCF.

Sources: *Jet* 61 (12 November 1981): 15; 91 (31 March 1997): 32; Dates and Barlow, *Split Image,* p. 389; *Contemporary Black Biography,* vol.14, pp. 109–12; Smith, *Notable Black American Men,* pp. 492–95; *Who's Who among African Americans,* 26th ed., p. 507.

1986 • Valerie Coleman-Morris (1946–) veteran television reporter in Los Angeles, was named weekday anchor for KCBS-TV in Los Angeles, becoming the first black in that time slot. Between 1975 and 1988, she received three Emmy awards.

Sources: *Jet* 70 (8 September 1986): 20; *Who's Who among African Americans,* 26th ed., p. 907.

1989 • Carole Simpson (1950–) substituted for Peter Jennings on Wednesday, August 9 this year and again on Thursday night, becoming the first black woman to anchor a major network newscast during weekdays. She was also the first black woman television newsperson in Chicago. Born in Miami, Simpson graduated from the University of Michigan and did graduate study at the University of Iowa. Her career in broadcast journalism began in 1965, when she was news reporter for Chicago's WCFL Radio. After becoming the first black reporter on WMAQ-TV in Chicago in 1970, she was promoted to a weekend anchor post. Simpson moved to Washington, D.C., and from 1974 to 1982 she was a reporter for NBC News. She left in 1982 to become a general assignment correspondent for ABC News, still based in Washington. She was promoted to weekend anchor of *World News Saturday,* in 1988. Simpson covered George Bush when he was vice-president and president. She has also covered many breaking news stories, including Nelson Mandela's release from prison in South Africa in 1990.

Sources: *Contemporary Black Biography,* vol. 6, pp. 244–46; Smith, *Notable Black American Women,* pp. 1022–24; Hine, *Black Women in America,* vol. 2, pp. 1037–38.

1990 • Dana Tyler and Reggie Harris formed the first black anchor team in a major metropolitan city for WCBS-TV, in New York City. Tyler, who graduated from Boston University, is the great-granddaughter of Ralph Waldo Tyler, the first black war correspondent during World War I. Harris, former weekend anchor at the station, graduated from Florida State University.

Sources: *Jet* 78 (2 July 1990): 23.

1999 • The first black woman to introduce herself to the sound of a television show's trademark stopwatch was Vicki L. Mabrey (1956–). She appears with a team of well-respected journalists on CBS's *60 Minutes II,* a spin-off of the network's show *60 Minutes.* The St. Louis native graduated from Howard University in Washington, D.C., in 1977. After a stint as real estate marketer in Baltimore, she became a production assistant with WBAL-TV in Baltimore. In 1984 she was promoted to general assignment reporter for that station. From 1992 to 1995 Mabry was a Dallas-based correspondent for CBS News, and was later reassigned to CBS News in London, England, where she remained from 1995 to 1998. During the London assignment, she covered the fatal car crash in Paris involving Princess Diana and was awarded two Emmy awards for her work.

Sources: *Who's Who among African Americans*, 14th ed., p. 827; *Contemporary Black Biography*, vol. 26, pp. 90–91; *Essence* 30 (April 2000): 80.

1999 • Gwen Ifill (1955–) was hired as moderator of Public Broadcast System's *Washington Week in Review*, becoming the first black woman to host a prominent political talk show on national television. The veteran news reporter began her work in journalism in 1977, when she was a reporter for the *Boston Herald-American*. She left that post in 1989 and from 1981 to 1984 she was a reporter for the *Baltimore Evening Sun*. She joined the *Washington Post* in 1984 as political reporter. From 1991 to 1994 Ifill was first Congressional correspondent for the *New York Times*' Washington, D.C., bureau, then became White House correspondent. Her first assignment as Congressional correspondent was to join other reporters on a bus that trailed presidential candidate Bill Clinton. She served as panelist and occasional moderator from 1992 to 1999, before becoming moderator and managing editor of *Washington Week in Review*. When she made her debut on the show in fall 1999, producers began an advertising campaign for it called "TV's Voice of Reason Has a New Face." Ifill is also senior political correspondent for *The News Hour with Jim Lehrer*.

Gwen Ifill

She received widespread public attention when she moderated the vice-presidential debate between Alaska Governor Sarah Palin and Senator Joe Biden on October 2, 2008. Born in New York City, Ifill was educated at Simmons College. In 2009 her book *The Breakthrough: Politics and Race in the Age of Obama*, was published. Her memberships include the National Association of Black Journalists.

Sources: *Contemporary Black Biography*, vol. 28, pp. 101–3; *Essence* 30 (April 2000): 80; Smith, *Encyclopedia of African American Popular Culture*, vol.2, pp. 729–30.

MILITARY

Air Force

1954 • Benjamin Oliver Davis Jr. (1912–2002) became the first black U.S. Air Force general on October 27. He also became the first black air force officer to complete a solo flight in 1941 and the first black man to command an airbase. During World War II Davis received two promotions in one day in 1943, when he was promoted first to major and then to lieutenant colonel. President Bill Clinton elevated Davis to the rank of four-star general, and in 1994, President Clinton named him to the Board of Visitors of the U.S. Military Academy. Davis' career paralleled that of his father, U.S. Army General Benjamin O. Davis Sr., in rising to the rank of general, albeit in another branch of the armed forces. Davis was born in Washington, D.C., and began his college education in 1929 at Western Reserve University (now known as Case Western Reserve University) in Ohio. He attended the University of Chicago from 1930 to 1932, after which he was able to enter the U.S. Military Academy when he passed the qualifying examinations on his second try. Davis faced racial bias just as his father had during his army experience. It has been reported that none of Davis' West Point classmates spoke to him during his years at the academy, except when absolutely necessary. With a class rank of 35 out of 276, he graduated from West Point in 1936 as the first black to achieve this feat in the twentieth century. He was commissioned a second lieutenant and elected to serve in the U.S. Air Force. He was informed that blacks were not eligible and was assigned to Fort Benning, Georgia, where he was excluded from membership in the officers' club. In 1941, after a tour of duty at Fort Riley, Kansas, Davis was chosen to command the 99th Pursuit Squadron, an all-black flying unit authorized by President Franklin Roosevelt. The squadron trained at Tuskegee Army Air Base in Alabama and went on to fame as the "Tuskegee Airmen," despite the fact they were subjected to tremendous racial bias. Davis went on to command the 332nd Fighter Group, comprised of four black squadrons. This group saw action in Europe and achieved an enviable escort duty and combat record. When they flew escort duty, the group never lost a bomber to the enemy. The exploits of the 332nd are considered to have been instrumental in the 1948 decision of the U.S. Armed Forces to become integrated. In 1951 Davis became the commander of the integrated Fifty-first Fighter Wing in Korea and the Thirteenth Air Force in Vietnam. He became a lieutenant general in 1965. Davis retired from the Air Force in 1970 and took a position as director of public safety in Cleveland, Ohio. From 1971 to 1975 he served as the director of civil aviation security, assistant secretary of environment, safety, and consumer affairs for the U.S. Department of Transportation. Davis was inducted into the Aviation Hall of Fame in 1944. He received numerous military awards, including

Benjamin Oliver Davis Jr.

433

The First Black U-2 Pilot

I n 1966 James T. Whitehead Jr. became the first black U-2 pilot, and until recent years, he remained the only black to pilot the plane. In 1967 he became a flight engineer for TWA at John F. Kennedy International Airport in New York.

Sources: *The Black New Yorkers,* p. 324; *Who's Who among African Americans,* 14th ed., p.1381.

the Distinguished Flying Cross. When the White House Ceremony at which he was promoted to four-star general was held, twenty of the original Tuskegee Airmen were in attendance to give praise to his courageous leadership of the 332nd unit. President Clinton was given an honorary signature Tuskegee Airman jacket at the time. Davis published his book, *Autobiography: Benjamin O. Davis Jr.: American,* in 1991.

Sources: *Contemporary Black Biography,* vol. 2, pp. 51–53; Hornsby, *Milestones in Twentieth-Century African-American History,* p. 55; *Jet* 86 (13 June 1994): 23; 86 (13 October 1994): 27; 94 (26 October 1998): 39; Smith, *Notable Black American Men,* pp. 255–59.

1968 • The first black woman colonel in the U.S. Air Force was Ruth Lucas, who was promoted to that rank on November 25. When Lucas graduated from Tuskegee Institute (now University) in 1942, the limited opportunities available for her to pursue her interest in education led her to enlist in the Women's Army Corps. After completing officer training and receiving her commission, she was assigned to several posts during the course of World War II. Lucas elected to remain in the army and had progressed through the ranks to become a temporary lieutenant colonel in 1962 and a regular lieutenant colonel in 1963. Some five years later she was made a full colonel. A career officer, she took leave in 1957 to continue her interest in education by pursuing and earning a master's degree from Columbia University.

Sources: *Sepia,* 18 (April 1969): 73.

1974 • Juanita Bell (1952–) became the first black woman from Alabama to be commissioned by any armed service. She received her commission as a second lieutenant after being enrolled in the Air Force Reserve Officers Training Corps (AFROTC) program. Born in Birmingham, Bell graduated from Alabama State University in 1974. She had a leadership role in her AFROTC program while in college, coordinating corps activities and giving oversight to cadet training in the General Military course, while maintaining almost a perfect average in her academic work.

Sources: Bailey, *They Too Call Alabama Home,* p. 36.

Lloyd W. Newton

1974 • U.S. Air Force General Lloyd W. "Fig" Newton (1942–) became the first black pilot to join the Thunderbirds, the Aerial Demonstration Squadron for the air force. Newton, a career officer, was born in Ridgeland, South Carolina. He joined the air force in 1966, after graduating from Tennessee State University, where he completed the Air Force ROTC program. Newton pursued additional training at armed service institutions and at George Washington University, where he was awarded a master's degree in 1985. In 1995 he was promoted to the rank of three-star general and named air force assistant vice chief of staff. Two years later he was promoted to the rank of four-star general. Newton was the third black in the air force to achieve this rank, and one of only twelve four-star generals of any race at the time. He assumed command of the air force's Air Education and Training Command at Randolph Air Force Base, Texas, following his promotion. The Distinguished Flying Cross is one of the awards he has received, and he is recognized as a command pilot who accumulated more than 4,000 flying hours.

Sources: *Jet* 88 (21 August 1995): 25; 91 (28 April 1997): 4–5; *Who's Who among African Americans,* 26th ed., p. 934.

1975 • Daniel H. "Chappie" James Jr. (1920–1978) became the first black four-star general in the U.S. Air Force and was named commander-in-chief of the North American Air Defense Command (NORAD). He was not only the first black air force four-star general, but also the first to be promoted to that rank in any of the U.S. armed forces. James was born in Pensacola, Florida. He was educated at Tuskegee University but was expelled for fighting in his senior year; he was not actually awarded his degree until twenty-seven years later. He enrolled in the Army Air Corps program, part of the government's Civilian Pilot Training Program, while a student at Tuskegee and was commissioned as a Second Lieutenant in 1943. James earned renown as a military pilot and one of the original members of the famed "Tuskegee Airmen," the all-black flying unit that faced tremendous racial bias during its training days and its initial flying engagements. Although his military career began in 1944, he was still flying combat missions during the Korean and Vietnam wars. In 1970 James was promoted to the rank of brigadier general, to major general in 1972, and to lieutenant general in 1974. His career spanned thirty-four years, ending with his retirement in 1978. He died of a heart attack less than a month after retirement. James's many civilian and military awards included the Distinguished Flying Cross, a Distinguished Service Medal for Valor, and the George Washington Freedom Foundation Honor Medal, given to him in 1967 for his essay "Freedom—My Heritage, My Responsibility," which he had written for a contest in the *Stars and Stripes*. James, who was the first black to command an integrated combat unit in the U.S. Army, endured much and achieved much. His career almost ended in 1950 when he was in a serious crash while flying in a two-seater plane. He is remembered as a patriotic American, a courageous and dedicated airman, and an advocate of racial equality in the armed forces.

Daniel H. James Jr.

Sources: *Encyclopedia of Black America*, pp. 468–69; *Jet* 92 (8 September 1997): 22; Smith, *Notable Black American Men*, pp. 610–12; *Who's Who among Black Americans, 1977*, p. 466.

1990 • Marcelite Jordan Harris (1943–) became the first black woman brigadier general in the U.S. Air Force. In 1995 she became the first black woman major general. Born in Houston, Texas, Harris' ancestry can be traced back to slavery and reveals the achievements of her forebears. Her maternal great-great-grandfather was the mayor of Donaldsonville, Texas, and served in both houses of the state legislature. Her maternal great-grandfather founded the first school for blacks in Fort Worth, Texas. Harris was educated at Spelman College, Central Michigan University, Chapman College, the University of Maryland, and Harvard University. She entered the air force in 1965 through Officer Training School, and in 1971 she became the first black woman to become an aircraft maintenance officer. (She had to apply three times before her application for training in aircraft maintenance was accepted.) In 1978, as commander of a cadet squadron at the U.S. Air Force Academy, Harris became one of the first two female air officer commanders. She retired from the air force in 1997. While in the service, she was the highest-ranking woman on active duty in the air force and the highest-ranking black woman in the Department of Defense. She also served for a time as social aide to President Jimmy Carter. Her many military honors include the Bronze Star, the Presidential Unit Citation, and the Vietnam Service Medal. President Barack Obama appointed her to the Board of Visitors to the United States Air Force Academy.

Marcelite Harris

Sources: *Contemporary Black Biography*, vol. 16, pp. 79–82; Hine, *Black Women in America*, vol. 1, pp. 538–39; *Jet* 91 (18 November 1996): 16–17; 91 (10 February 1997): 64; Smith, *Notable Black American Women*, pp. 467–68; *Spelman Messenger* 121 (Fall 2010): 11; *Who's Who among African Americans*, 26th ed., p. 540–41.

1994 • Virgil A. Starkes (1948?–) and Sheldon D. Starkes (1947?–) were promoted to U.S. Air Force colonel in what is believed to be the first time black brothers have been simultaneously elevated to that rank. The brothers have a history of following similar paths. Born in Columbia, South Carolina, both graduated from Benedict College in South Carolina with degrees in business and both enlisted in the air force after graduating. They were also commissioned simultaneously as second lieutenants and then promoted at each grade through the rank of colonel. When promoted to colonel, Virgil Starkes was chief of the Personnel Program in the Directorate of Personnel at Wright-Patterson Air Force Base,

Ohio. Sheldon Starkes was the associate dean for operations at the Armed Forces Staff College in Virginia.

Sources: *Jet* 87 (5 December 1994): 32–33.

1996 • The first woman to be named the commanding officer of the Air Force ROTC program at North Carolina Agricultural and Technical State University in Greensboro was Carlette "C.J." Jones, a lieutenant colonel. Her new duties included service as a personnel officer at the institution. She was previously the regional director of admissions for the Southeastern United States and Central America at the U.S. Air Force Academy.

Sources: *Jet* 91 (18 November 1996): 32.

American Revolution

Crispus Attucks

1770 • The first black casualty in the American Revolution was Crispus Attucks (1723?–70). He was not enlisted in an army but instead was part of a Boston group protesting the Townshend acts. Tensions in Boston were already high when Attucks and his companions, who are said to have come from the Boston docks, approached the British garrison. While protesting at the garrison housing the British soldiers who were to enforce the acts, Attucks and several others were shot. This event came to be known as the Boston Massacre and is considered to have triggered the American Revolution. The details of Attucks' early years are not well known. It is believed that he was of African and Native American ancestry, that his father was a slave, and that the family lived in Framingham, Massachusetts. He is also identified as a merchant seaman. Further speculation, based on a 1750 advertisement in the *Boston Gazette,* identifies Attucks as a runaway slave. However, historians are more definite about placing him in Boston in 1770. The Crispus Attucks Monument, in honor of the victims, was dedicated in the Boston Commons in 1888.

Sources: *Jet* 91 (10 March 1997):19; 95 (8 March 1999): 19; *Smith, Notable Black American Men,* pp. 40–42.

1775 • The Earl of Dunmore's Ethiopian Regiment was the first regiment made up of slave soldiers. John Murray, Earl of Dunmore (1732–1809), British Royal Governor of Virginia, issued a proclamation promising freedom to slaves who joined the British forces.

Sources: *Encyclopedia Americana, 1988,* vol. 9, p. 475; Hornsby, *Chronology of African-American History,* p. 7.

1775 • On April 19, 1775, Lemuel Haynes, Peter Salem, Pomp Blackman, Prince Estabrook, Samuel Craft, and Caesar John Ferrit and his son, John, were the blacks known to have participated in the defense of Concord Bridge, the first armed encounter of the American Revolution.

Sources: *Negro Almanac,* p. 803.

1775 • Salem Poor (1747?–?) was the first black soldier to win a battle commendation. The recommendation for his acknowledgement was made on December 5, 1775, to the General Court of Massachusetts Bay. It commended Poor for his bravery at the Battle at Charlestown, describing him as "a Brave & gallant Soldier." The recommendation was signed by fourteen colonial army officers and was entered into court records twice. There is no record as to when or if he received notice of the commendation. The earliest record of Poor appears when he was baptized in Andover, Massachusetts, in 1747. He was an indentured servant until he purchased his freedom in 1769. Poor enlisted in a Massachusetts militia company in April 1775, and on June 17, 1775, fought valiantly at the battle of Bunker Hill, where he wounded a British officer. Other blacks at the battle were Barzillai Law, Cuff Whittemore, Titus Coburn, Charlestown Eads, Peter Salem, Sampson Taylor, and Caesar Brown. Poor's military record extends from 1775 to 1780, with only brief absences for no more than a few months at a time. He was with George Washington at Valley Forge, but he is not listed among the 5,000 blacks who lost their lives during the Revolutionary War and for whom there is a memorial in Pennsylvania's Valley Forge National Historical Park. He fought in a number of other crucial battles, and was finally given recognition for his contributions to the colonial army in March 25, 1975, when the U.S. Postal Service issued a series of stamps during its Revolutionary War Centennial. The stamp series was entitled "Contributors to the Cause." A ten-cent stamp recognized "Salem Poor—Gallant Soldier." The date of Poor's death is not recorded.

Sources: Logan and Winston, *Dictionary of American Negro Biography*, p. 500; *Encyclopedia of Black America*, p. 684; Smith, *Notable Black American Men*, pp. 947–49.

1778 • The First Rhode Island Regiment was the first and only all-black unit to fight in the American Revolution. On February 2, 1778, Rhode Island passed the first slave enlistment act. In August the regiment of 125 blacks—95 among them slaves—successfully sustained three attacks by the British, allowing the rest of the American Army to make a successful retreat at the Battle of Rhode Island.

Sources: Cantor, *Historic Landmarks of Black America*, p. xvii; *Negro Almanac*, pp. 806–7.

Army

1861 • James Stone (?–1862), was the first black to fight with the Union forces during the Civil War. He was a very light-complexioned fugitive slave who enlisted in the First Fight Artillery of Ohio on August 23, 1861, and fought with the unit in Kentucky, the state in which he had been a slave. His racial identity was revealed only after his death from a service-related illness.

Sources: Hornsby, *Chronology of African-American History*, p. 33.

1862 • The First South Carolina Volunteers was the first regiment of black soldiers raised in the Civil War. They were quickly followed by the First and Second Kansas Colored Volunteers, a group who fought the first skirmish by black troops in the Civil War, in Clay County, Missouri. The First Regiment Louisiana Native Guards were mustered into the army on September 27, 1862. For political reasons, all of the groups were disavowed by the central government, and officially disbanded. It was not until the late summer of 1862 that the federal government officially enrolled black soldiers.

Sources: *Encyclopedia of Black America*, p. 63; *Negro Almanac*, p. 833.

1863 • On May 27, 1863, two black Louisiana regiments made charges against the Confederate fortification at Port Hudson, Louisiana. On July 9, 1863, eight black regiments had a prominent part in the siege of Port Hudson, a city whose fall was an important step in the eventual Union control of the Mississippi. These two engagements were the first battles to fully demonstrate the worth of black troops.

Sources: *Encyclopedia of Black America*, p. 63; Hornsby, *Chronology of African-American History*, p. 35.

1863 • The 9th Regiment, U.S. Colored Troops composed the first known battle hymn by black soldiers, "They Look Like Men of War."

Sources: "A Chronology of African American Military Service," http://www.army.mil/africanamericans/timeline.html.

1863 • The 54th Massachusetts Regiment was the first regiment raised in the North during the Civil War. Black leaders helped to recruit blacks from free states, slave states, and Canada. The regiment fought valiantly at Fort Wagner in July; the regiment commander, Colonel Robert Gould Shaw, was killed and buried with his black soldiers. The attack at Fort Wagner was the first major engagement seen by black troops. The regiment objected to the pay differential between black and white enlisted men and served a year without pay rather than accept discriminatory wages.

Sources: Hughes and Meltzer, *Pictorial History of Black Americans, 1972*, p. 180; Cantor, *Historic Landmarks in Black America*, pp. 73–74; Hornsby, *Chronology of African-American History*, p. 35.

1863 • Alexander T. Augusta (1825–1890) was the first black commissioned medical officer.

Sources: Logan and Winston, *Dictionary of American Negro Biography,* pp. 19–20.

1863 • William Harvey Carney (1840–1908), sergeant of Company C, 54th Massachusetts Colored Infantry, was the first black in the Civil War to earn the Medal of Honor, on July 18. Born in Norfolk, Virginia, he was educated privately and later settled in New Bedford, Massachusetts, where he became a seaman. Carney enlisted on February 17, 1863, and earned his Medal of Honor five months later at Fort Wagner, South Carolina. When the color bearer was wounded in the battle, Carney, also hurt, sprang forward and seized the flag before it slipped from the bearer's grasp. By doing so, he prevented the flag from touching the ground. Carney was discharged from the infantry with disabilities caused by the wounds he had received. His Medal of Honor was not issued until May 23, 1900. Upon Carney's death, the flag on the Massachusetts state house was flown at half mast—an honor formerly restricted to presidents, senators, and governors.

William Harvey Carney

Sources: *Alexander's Magazine* 7 (15 January 1909): 109; Logan and Winston, *Dictionary of American Negro Biography,* pp. 90–91; *Encyclopedia of Black America,* p. 835; Lee, *Negro Medal of Honor Men,* pp. 24–26.

1863 • Henry McNeal Turner (1834–1915), clergyman and legislator, was the first black chaplain in the U.S. Army and the first black commissioned army officer. A minister in the African Methodist Episcopal Church, he was a leader of the post-Civil War expansion of the church in the South. Turner was also a Georgia legislator and a member of the Georgia Constitutional Convention from 1867 to 1868. Active in church, he was elected bishop in 1880. Always active in politics, Turner urged blacks to return to Africa where they could realize their manhood and their human rights.

Sources: Logan and Winston, *Dictionary of American Negro Biography,* p. 608; *Encyclopedia of Black America,* p. 820; Kane, *Famous First Facts,* p. 33.

Martin Delany

1865 • Upon the order of President Abraham Lincoln, Martin Robinson Delany (1812–1885) was the first black commissioned as a field officer with the rank of major in the regular infantry. Assigned to Charleston, South Carolina, he recruited two regiments of blacks. Delany was born in what is now Charles Town, West Virginia, the son of a slave father and a free mother. He is reputed to have believed that he was descended from African royalty, and this may have influenced his later activities as a founder of Black Nationalism and advocate of emigration to Africa. The family relocated to Chambersburg, Pennsylvania, after facing racial problems in Charles Town, and Delany was educated in Chambersburg until 1827, when he had to go to work. Four years later he left for Pittsburgh, which was his home for the next twenty-five years. In Pittsburgh he established his leadership as an advocate for blacks and continued his education. In or around 1843, Delany began publishing *The Mystery,* said to be the first black newspaper west of the Alleghenies. In 1850 he entered Harvard Medical School, but left after one semester because of the protests of white students; he gave himself the title of "doctor" and did indeed practice medicine in Pittsburgh. Delany moved to Wilberforce, Ohio, in 1864. It was at this time that he advanced a plan to recruit black troops commanded by black officers to fight on the side of the Union in the Civil War. It was after an interview with Lincoln with regard to the plan that Delany became an army officer. The war ended before his plan could be put into effect. He was assigned to the Freedmen's Bureau in Beaufort, South Carolina. He remained there until he ended his army career in 1868. He transferred his attention to politics and served as a judge briefly, but was removed after being charged with fraud. Some considered Delany a radical, but he was for a time a recognized leader among blacks. He returned to Wilberforce shortly before his death.

Sources: Logan and Winston, *Dictionary of American Negro Biography,* pp. 169–72; *Encyclopedia of Black America,* pp. 306–7; Smith, *Notable Black American Men,* pp. 282–86.

1867 • Congress approved the first all-black units in the regular army. These soldiers, known as "buffalo soldiers" or the U.S. Colored Troops, served in the West and comprised the 9th and 10th Cavalry Regiments as well as the 24th and 25th Infantry Regiments.

The First Black Army Chaplain

In 1884 Henry Vinson Plummer (1844–1905) became the first black chaplain in the regular army. Appointed on July 6, 1884, he held the rank of captain and was assigned to the 9th Cavalry, which was one of the regiments called "buffalo soldiers" by Native Americans. Born a slave in Maryland, Plummer escaped during the Civil War and taught himself to read while serving in the U.S. Navy. A strong advocate for temperance, he was court-martialed and dismissed from the army on a charge of drunkenness. Only one witness, who had a ten-year grudge against him, supported the charge.

Sources: Logan and Winston, *Dictionary of American Negro Biography*, pp. 498–99; Foner, *Blacks and the Military in American History*, p. 65; Nebraska State Historical Society, "Buffalo Soldiers at Fort Robinson," http://www.nebraskahistory.org/sites/fortrob/bufftext.htm. Accessed September 27, 2012.

Their nickname came from Native Americans, who believed their short curly hair was similar to that on the buffalo's neck, and that their brave and fierce fighting matched the buffalo. Eleven black soldiers earned the Congressional Medal of Honor in combat against Utes, Apaches, and Comanches. Soldiers served in black regiments until the integration of U.S. forces in 1952. A monument honoring the buffalo soldiers was unveiled at Fort Leavenworth in 1992.

Sources: *Black Americans in Defense of Our Nation*, pp. 25–27; *Jet* 82 (7 September 1992): 34; Katz, *Black Indians*, p. 174.

1870 • Emanuel Stance (1848?–87), a sergeant of Company F, Ninth United Calvary, Fort Kavett, Texas, was the first black in the Indian Campaigns to earn the Medal of Honor. As a "buffalo soldier," he and a small group of soldiers dispersed a band of Native Americans. It is believed that he was murdered by one of his own men.

Sources: *Black Americans in Defense of Our Nation*, pp. 26–27; Logan and Winston, *Dictionary of American Negro Biography*, pp. 568–69; Lee, *Negro Medal of Honor Men*, p. 59.

1898 • Dennis Bell, Fitz Lee, William H. Thompkins, and George H. Wanton, privates in the Tenth Cavalry, were the first black soldiers honored with Medals of Honor in the Spanish-American War. They selflessly rescued a stranded group of soldiers in the Cuban province of Puerto Principle—a maneuver that had been thwarted on three previous attempts.

Sources: *Black Americans in Defense of Our Nation*, pp. 60–61; Lee, *Negro Medal of Honor Men*, p. 90.

1904 • Charles Young (1864–1922) was the first black military attaché in the history of the United States; he was accredited to Haiti. In 1889 Young was the third man of color to graduate from the U.S. Military Academy, entering the academy after his graduation from Wilberforce University in Ohio. He was a five-year graduate, having dropped out for a year because of deficiencies in mathematics, and had to cope with racial unpleasantries during his experience at West Point. When he graduated, he was commissioned as a second lieutenant in the U.S. Cavalry. During the Spanish-American War, Young served as a major in charge of the 9th Ohio Regiment, an all-black volunteer unit. He served in Haiti, the Philippines, and Mexico, and by 1916 he had attained the rank of lieutenant colonel. Young was the second person and the first military person to be honored with the NAACP's Spingarn Medal in 1916. In 1917 at the advent of World War I, Young was forced to retire for reasons of "physical unfitness for duty." (He was suffering from extremely high blood pressure and Bright's disease.) He held the rank of full colonel at the time. In response, Young mounted his favorite horse at Wilberforce, Ohio, and rode 500 miles to Washington, D.C., to prove that he was indeed fit for service. The army reinstated him in 1918, and he was assigned to train black troops at Fort Grant, Illinois. In 1919 Colonel Young was sent as military attaché to Liberia on a second tour of duty. He died in Lagos, Nigeria, during an

Charles Young

The First Black Lieutenant Colonel

In 1906 Allen Allensworth (1842–1914) became the first black American to hold the rank of lieutenant colonel. Born a slave, he taught under the auspices of the Freedmen's Bureau, operated a number of businesses, and served as a chaplain during the Spanish-American War. At the time of his retirement, he was the senior chaplain in the army. He founded an all–black town named Allensworth in Tulare County, California, in 1908. A town resident named Oscar Over became California's first black justice of the peace in 1914.

Sources: "Biography of Col. Allensworth." Friends of Allensworth, http://www.friendsofallensworth.org/allensworth/allensworthlegacy.html. Accessed October 12, 2012.

Allen Allensworth

inspection tour. He was given a funeral there with full military honors, but was later exhumed at the request of his widow, and is buried in Arlington Cemetery. Black schools in the nation's capital were closed to honor him on the day of his burial. Born the son of slaves in Mayslick, Kentucky, Young grew up in Ripley, Ohio. During the early part of his army career, he taught military science and other subjects at Wilberforce. As a diplomat in foreign countries, he used his cartography skills to draw new maps and revise existing ones. In May 1974 his home in Xenia, Ohio, was declared a National Historic Landmark by the Department of the Interior.

Sources: Logan and Winston, *Dictionary of American Negro Biography*, pp. 679–80; Foner, *Blacks and the Military*, pp. 64, 113; *Integration and the Negro Officer in the Armed Forces of the United States of America*, p. 3; Robinson, *Historical Negro Biographies*, p. 268; Smith, *Notable Black American Men*, pp. 1283–85.

1909 • Wade Hammond, Alfred Jack Thomas, William Polk, and Egbert Thompson were promoted to the rank of chief musician and became the first black bandmasters in the U.S. Army. Previously, the bands attached to black regiments had been headed by whites.

Sources: Southern, *The Music of Black Americans*, p. 301.

1917 • Fort Des Moines, Iowa, was the first U.S. Army camp for training black officers in World War I. About half (639) of the black officers commissioned during the war were trained there.

Sources: Baskin and Runes, *Dictionary of Black Culture*, p. 166; Kane, *Famous First Facts*, p. 31.

1917 • The first black American drafted in World War I was Leo Pinckney.

Sources: Cantor, *Historic Landmarks of Black America*, p. 290; Logan and Winston, *Dictionary of American Negro Biography*, pp. 13–14; Foner, *Blacks and the Military in American History*, p. 65, 70.

1918 • In December 1917 the 369th Infantry Regiment was the first group of black combat soldiers to arrive in Europe. Cited for bravery eleven times, the regiment was awarded the *Croix de Guerre* by the French government.

1918 • James Reese Europe (1880–1919), while serving as an officer of a machine gun company with the 369th Infantry Regiment in Europe, marched into line on April 23. He became the first black officer to lead troops into combat during World War I and may have been the first to lead a raid on enemy lines. Combat action in Europe could not have been anticipated from his life history prior to World War I. The Mobile, Alabama, native grew up in Washington, D.C., after his father received a job there with the postal service. Music dominated the lives of the three youngest Europe children, of which James was the second youngest. He took lessons in Washington and performed in musical programs at his church. The sudden death of his father in 1899 led Europe to move to New York in search of work three or four years later. He was successful after he switched musical instruments, going from the violin to the mandolin and piano. By the time the war broke out, Europe was said to be one of the most influential musicians and orchestra leaders in New York. He also directed musical performances and composed popular music. He was the first president of the Clef Club, a union and a booking agency for black musicians. The Clef Club Orchestra performed at Carnegie Hall in 1912 and toured in several cities in 1913. Europe formed a new group, the Tempo Club, late in 1913, but urged black musicians to join the previously all-white musicians' union when it dropped its racial bars in 1914. He joined the 15th Infantry Regiment of the New York State National Guard in 1916, with the rank of private. He was asked to form a band, and after setbacks—including two operations to address Europe's hyperthyroidism, and racial flare-ups in Spartanburg, South Carolina, where the band had been sent for training—it was sent to France. The band regiment was now the 369th Regiment, and Europe was its bandmaster. They were the first troops to reach the Rhine River. When they returned to New York in 1919, Europe was the representative of the regiment's five black officers in the homecoming parade that greeted the 15th Infantry Regiment. The precise date of his commission as an officer is not noted. Europe assumed presidency of the Clef Club again. While in Boston for a concert, Europe was stabbed in the throat during intermission; he died the same night. It is conjectured that the attack came from a band member who believed Europe had criticized him unjustly. Europe has been credited with introducing American jazz to France.

Sources: Badger, *A Life in Ragtime: A Biography of James Reese Europe*, p. 8; Logan and Winston, *Dictionary of American Biography*, pp. 214–15; Smith, *Notable Black American Men*, pp. 382–86.

1918 • Henry Johnson (1897–1929) and Needham Roberts were the first black soldiers to be awarded the French *Croix de Guerre* as individuals. As privates with the 369th Infantry, they were injured on May 14, 1918, in an assault by German soldiers but succeeded in routing their attackers. During World War I, Johnson, of Albany, New York, joined the Army National Guard's "Harlem Hellfighter" unit. The segregated unit fought under the French in Europe. After France awarded him its highest honor for his bravery, President Theodore Roosevelt also cited him as one of the five bravest Americans during the war. The U.S. military, however, failed to decorate him. When Johnson died, he was buried at Arlington National Cemetery with full military honors. In 1996, efforts were made to award him the Medal of Honor. Errors in military records prevented him from receiving the medal posthumously; since then, he was awarded the Distinguished Service Cross in 2003.

Sources: Baskin and Runes, *Dictionary of Black Culture*, p. 240; *Jet* 101 (28 January 2001): 10 (Johnson); Kane, *Famous First Facts*, p. 367; Logan and Winston, *Dictionary of American Negro Biography*, p. 351; *New York Times* (11 January 2002); (Johnson).

1918 • On an experimental basis, the Army Nurses Corps accepted eighteen black nurses into service for the first time. About half of them were sent to Camp Grant in Illinois and the others to Camp Sherman in Ohio. They lived in segregated quarters but served in an integrated hospital. They were released from service in August 1919, due to postwar reduction in force.

Sources: "Timeline," http://www.army.mil/africanamericans/timeline.html.

1940 • Benjamin Oliver Davis Sr. (1877–1970) was the first black American general in The U.S. Army and the highest-ranking black in the armed forces when he was promoted to brigadier general on October 25. Born and educated in Washington, D.C., he graduated from Howard University in 1898. He entered the army after graduation. Davis served as a temporary lieutenant in the 8th U.S. Volunteers Infantry (an all-black unit) from 1898 to

Benjamin Davis Sr.

1899, fighting in the Spanish-American War. In 1899 he enlisted as a private in the Ninth Cavalry, a unit of the regular army, and soon rose to the highest rank held by any black soldier at the time: sergeant-major. Determined to become an officer, he passed the examinations in 1901, and was promoted to second lieutenant, assigned to the 10th Cavalry. Davis was sent to Wilberforce University in Ohio in 1905 to teach military science, where he remained for four years, after which he served as a military attaché in Liberia. He returned to active duty in the Philippines in 1917 after an assignment in Mexico and a repeat tour of duty at Wilberforce. He was by this time a captain. After a teaching assignment at the Tuskegee Institute, during which he was promoted to lieutenant colonel, he became an instructor to the Ohio National Guard in 1924. Davis was given his own regiment to command, the 369th Cavalry New York National Guard in 1937; he held the rank of colonel at the time. Throughout his army career, Davis was confronted by and fought against segregation and discrimination in the armed forces. His value to the country as a symbol of the army's somewhat belated good intentions is perhaps indicated by the fact that he was past the official age for military promotions when he was promoted to brigadier general. He retired from the army in 1948, having served in the U.S. armed forces for half a century; his career dated from the Spanish-American War to World War II. Davis was a highly decorated soldier, including the French *Croix de Guerre* and the Bronze Star among his awards. He also served as a mentor to the troops during World War II, and was noted as a diplomatic negotiator on racial problems and an advisor to then-General Dwight Eisenhower (who did not fully accept Davis's advice) on integration in the army. Davis continued to be active in public life until poor eyesight and other health problems forced him to cease much of his activity in 1960. He was in a hospital in North Chicago, Illinois, when he died of leukemia. His son, Benjamin O. Davis Jr., followed in his father's footsteps and grew up to become the first black general in the U.S. Air Force. It is of note that Davis Sr. was denied admission to the U.S. Military Academy when he applied after graduating from high school.

Sources: *Black Americans in Defense of Our Nation*, pp. 106–7; *Contemporary Black Biography*, vol. 4, pp. 57–60; Hornsby, *Milestones in Twentieth-Century African-American History*, p. 36; *Jet* 88 (30 October 1995): 19; Smith, *Notable Black American Men*, pp. 259–62.

1941 • Private Robert S. Brooks became the first member of the "Armored Forces" to lose his life at Fort Stotenberg, in the Phillipines.

Sources: Furr, *Democracy's Negroes*, p. 101.

1941 • The U.S. Army established the 78th Tank Battalion on January 13, forming the first black armor unit. In March the first black tankers reported to Fort Knox, Kentucky, to begin armored warfare training. On May 8, the battalion was re-designated as the 758th Tank (or Light) Battalion, and was the first of three such groups comprising the 5th Tank Group.

Sources: Wilson, *The 784th Tank Battalion in World War II*.

1941 • The first and only black air training facility for black airmen, known as the Tuskegee Airmen, was located at Tuskegee Institute, Alabama, in World War II. The military was racially segregated until 1948 and integrated by President Harry Truman's Executive Order 9981. The U.S. Congress in 1941 established the first combat unit for blacks in the Army Air Corps. In 1942 the U.S. Army founded a school for black pilots, in spite of black opposition to the establishment of segregated U.S. Air Force facilities. The War Department provided funds to purchase land some six miles from Tuskegee Institute and to build the training facility. Hangars, repair shops, dormitories, and other facilities were to be erected. Prominent black architects of the day were employed to undertake the project; they included Hilyard Robinson of Washington, D.C., McKissack & McKissack of Nashville, and landscape architect David Augustus Williston also from Washington. While pilots began their training at Tuskegee, ground crews were prepared at Chanute Field in Illinois. The training facility was dedicated in July 1941.

Sources: Smith, *Encyclopedia of African American Popular Culture*, vol. 4, pp. 1416–19; Smith and Wynn, *Freedom Facts and Firsts*, pp. 191–92; *Black Americans in Defense of Our Nation*, p. 35; Cantor, *Historic Landmarks of Black America*, p. 352; Hornsby, *Chronology of African-American History*, p. 90; *Negro Almanac*, pp. 847–48;

1942 • President Franklin D. Roosevelt signed the act that created the Women's Auxiliary Army Corps (WAAC) on May 15. The voluntary unit consisted of both black and white recruits. Charity Adams Earley (1918–2002) completed basic training in the WAAC that year, and two weeks later became the first black woman commissioned in that organization. When she retired from the corps after the end of World War II, she was the highest-ranking black officer in the service. Earley grew up in Columbia, South Carolina, the daughter of a Methodist minister and a former schoolteacher. The influence of segregation was apparent in Columbia, and Earley went on to become a vigorous opponent of racial segregation. She worked her way through Wilberforce University and graduated in 1938. She taught mathematics in Columbia, until she was influenced by the recruitment efforts of Mary McLeod Bethune to enlist in the WAAC. Bethune, a noted educator and influential leader, served as an assistant to the secretary of war and was the black representative on the Advisory Council to the Women's Interests Section, a group organized by the War Department in 1941 to attract women to the armed services. Commissioned as a lieutenant, Earley was named company commander of the women's Basic Training Company on her post. She faced several problems as she sought to expand opportunities for black WAACs. The organization became known as the Women's Army Corps (WAC) when "Auxiliary" was dropped from the unit's name. The name change, made under the guidance of WAAC director Oveta Culp Hobby, was designed to make the unit a direct branch of the military and attract more women with better educational backgrounds. By 1943 Earley was a major, and she was proposed to head a special Negro training regiment. She refused this position, and the segregated unit was never formed. In 1944 she became the first black WAC given overseas duty and commanded a unit in Birmingham, England. She was made a lieutenant colonel in December 1945. When Earley left the army, she resumed graduate studies in psychology at The Ohio State University. She was recognized as a highly effective administrator during her period of military service. She died in her hometown on January 13, 2002.

Sources: *Contemporary Black Biography*, vol. 13, pp. 1–5; *New York Times* Obituaries (22 January 2002).

1942 • Black soldiers were included in the first contingent of American troops to arrive at Ledo in India on December 1, to construct Ledo (later Stillwell) Road. Men used bulldozers and a fleet of worn British trucks, while the black engineers pushed the road far into enemy territory.

Sources: Furr, *Democracy's Negroes,* p. 102.

1942 • The first all-black combat unit to face the Japanese was the 24th Infantry Regiment. The regiment encountered the Japanese at the New Georgia Islands, two days before the battle of Coral Sea on May 4–7.

Sources: Furr, *Democracy's Negroes,* p. 101.

1943 • Lieutenant Charles B. Hall of Brazil, Indiana, shot down the first German plane officially credited to the 99th Pursuit Squadron on July 2, 1943. He was awarded the Distinguished Flying Cross.

Sources: Kane, *Famous First Facts,* p. 65; Lee, *Negro Medal of Honor Men,* p. 112.

1943 • On December 19 the Army Ground Forces Headquarters called for the activation of the 555th Parachute Infantry Battalion, an all-black volunteer unit with officers and enlisted men. The unit was officially activated on December 30 at Fort Benning, Georgia. The first black enlisted paratrooper was Walter Morris. The unit trained for several weeks and then on November 25, 1944, moved to Camp Machall, North Carolina, when it was reorganized as Company A, 555th Parachute Infantry Battallion, formally becoming the world's first black paratroopers. The unit became popularly known as the Triple Nickels. The battalion was never sent overseas during the war; it was instead sent to the west coast of the United States to remain alert for possible Japanese attacks. Its mission there was also to fight forest fires, and the battalion responded by assisting with a number of dangerous fire fighting missions. The men made over one thousand jumps as they fought fires

Tuskegee Airmen

The 100th Squadron of four fighter squadrons comprised solely of black men was activated on October 13, 1942, at the Tuskegee Army Air Field in Alabama; it was the first black American military aviation group. Later three other black fighter squadrons was combined and became known as the Tuskegee Airmen. By the end of the year, the 99th Pursuit Squadron, the first black air unit in the history of the United States, was ready for action. In April 1943 the unit was in French Morocco for training under experienced combat pilots. The following month the leader of the squadron, Captain Benjamin Oliver Davis Jr., was promoted to major, then lieutenant colonel—all in one day. About six hundred black pilots received their wings during World War II. In April 2007, President George W. Bush awarded the legendary airmen the Congressional Gold Medal, the highest honor Congress can award to civilians. President Bush told the men, "You helped win a war, and you helped change our nation for the better." He continued, "And the medal that we confer today means that we are doing a small part to ensure that your story is told and honored for generations to come." Public Law 105–355, which President Bill Clinton approved on November 6, 1998, established the Tuskegee Airmen National Historic Site at Moton Field in Tuskegee, Alabama.

Sources: *Jet* 111 (16 April 2007): 7; 111 (4 June 2007): 21; Smith, *Encyclopedia of African American Popular Culture,* vol. 4, pp. 1416–19; Smith and Wynn, *Freedom Facts and Firsts,* pp. 191–92; *Black Americans in Defense of Our Nation,* p. 35; Cantor, *Historic Landmarks of Black America,* p. 352; Hornsby, *Chronology of African-American History,* p. 90; *Negro Almanac,* pp. 847–48.

in Oregon and California, which earned them a second nickname, "Smoke Jumpers." After the war the group organized as the 555th Parachute Infantry Association, using the motto "Before them there weren't many, after them there weren't any." Three buffalo nickels stacked in pyramid form became their logo.

Sources: 555th Parachute Infantry, http://www.triplenickle.com. Accessed September 27, 2012.

1943 • Nine doctors and thirty nurses comprised the first black medical group sent overseas. The group was sent to Liberia.

Sources: *Black Americans in Defense of Our Nation,* p. 95.

1943 • On August 21 Harriet M. Waddy [West] (1904–1999) became the first black woman major in the Women's Army Auxiliary Corps (WAAC), which later became the Women's Army Corps (WAC). She was at the time chief of planning in the Bureau of Control Division at WAAC Headquarters in Washington, D.C. Waddy was born in Jefferson City, Missouri, and was a graduate of Kansas State College of Agriculture and Applied Science. During the Great Depression, she worked as an aide to noted educator and civic leader Mary McLeod Bethune, who no doubt influenced Waddy's decision to join the WAAC. She entered officer candidate school in 1942. During World War II, Waddy was one of the two highest-ranking black officers in the WAAC, and served as its wartime advisor on racial issues. She was promoted to lieutenant colonel in 1948 and served on active duty until she retired in 1952; she remained in the Reserves until 1969. During her time after retirement from active military duty, she worked for the Federal Aviation Administration and also served as a counselor for girls at a Job Corps Center in Oregon. Waddy was an active recruiter of black women for the WAAC and served for a time as an aide to its director, Oveta Culp Hobby. She also campaigned against the existing racial discrimination in the military. She moved to Las Vegas in 1998 and was in residence there at the time of her death.

Sources: Foner, *Blacks and the Military in American History,* p. 165; *Jet* 98 (21 August 2000): 22; 100 (27 August 2001): 20; Obituary, *New York Times* (1 March 1999); Salzman, *Encyclopedia of African-American Culture and History,* Supplement, p. 269.

The First Black Army Nurse

In 1948 Nancy Leftenant-Colon (1920?–) became the first black member of the Regular Army Nurse Corps in March of this year. She was a graduate of Lincoln Hospital School for Nurses, in the Bronx, New York, which enrolled primarily minority students. She joined the army reserve nurse corps in February 1945. At the time of her enlistment, black nurses were not highly regarded and were not given the status of regular nurse, but in eleven months she was promoted from second to first lieutenant. Her performance as a nurse was no doubt a factor in the acceptance of her 1948 application for admission into the Regular Army Nurse Corps. During her service career, she was a U.S. Air Force flight nurse. Leftenant-Colon retired from the army, with the rank of major, in 1965. She worked from 1971 to 1984 as a nurse at Amityville High School in New York, having moved to Long Island when she left the army. She achieved another "first" as the only woman to be president of the Tuskegee Airmen. She was president of the group from 1989 to 1991.

Sources: Alford, *Famous First Blacks*, p. 65; Hine, *Black Women in America*, vol. 1, p. 795; *Jet* 93 (15 December 1997): 26–27.

1944 • The defense against the attempted German breakthrough in the Ardennes included platoons of blacks assigned to white units—the first and only example of integrated units in World War II.

Sources: *Black Americans in Defense of Our Nation*, p. 35.

1946 • Osborne E. Scott (1916–1997) became the first black appointed to the faculty of the Army Chaplain School. He was a Virginia native, born in Gloucester, and graduated from Hampton Institute (now Hampton University) in Virginia. His later educational training included a degree in divinity from Oberlin College in Ohio and a master's degree from Columbia University Teachers College in New York. Scott was one of the first black army chaplains, serving from 1941 to 1964. He retired from the army in 1964, having reached the rank of lieutenant colonel. While serving in the army, he had supervisor and administrator posts in Asia, Europe, and the Pacific. When Scott left the army, he worked as an executive with the American Leprosy Foundation in Greenville, South Carolina, until he moved to a faculty position at City College in New York in 1969. There he was charged with organizing the college's urban and ethnic studies. He created several courses in response to student protests that occurred in 1969. Scott taught in the black studies department until 1986, retiring with emeritus status. He had been a long-time resident of Mount Vernon, New York, when he died.

Sources: *New York Times* (11 November 1997); *Who's Who among African Americans,* 13th ed., pp. 1183–84.

1951 • William Henry Thompson (1928–1950), private first class, Company M, 24th Infantry Regiment, became the first black to earn the Medal of Honor in the Korean conflict. He was mortally wounded on August 2, 1951, while manning his machine gun during a surprise attack on his platoon. His actions allowed the unit to withdraw to a more defensible position.

Sources: *Black Americans in Defense of Our Nation*, p. 62; Kane, *Famous First Facts*, p. 371; Lee, *Negro Medal of Honor Men*, p. 9–12.

1955 • Clotilde Dent Bowen (1923–2011), who was commissioned in the U.S. Army this year with the rank of captain, became the first black woman medical officer in the army. When she was promoted to colonel, she was the first black woman to receive this rank. Bowen began accumulating "firsts" before she entered the army. When she graduated from The Ohio State University Medical School in 1947, she was the first black woman to receive a medical degree from the institution. Bowen's medical specialty was neuropsychiatry. During the Vietnam War, she served in that country, and was awarded the Bronze Star and the Legion of Merit in 1971, in recognition of her service; the Meritorious Service Medal was given to her in 1974. Several awards from Ohio State, including The Ohio State University Professional Achievement Award in 1998, also recognized her achievements. Bowen was born in Chicago, Illinois, and did both her undergraduate and professional study at Ohio State. Before she entered the army, she practiced in New York City and was associated for a time with Harlem Hospital. Before going to Vietnam, Bowen was assigned to Veterans' Administration hospitals. Her last post before entering private practice was a position as staff psychiatrist at the Veterans Affairs Medical Center in Denver, Colorado, from 1990 to 1996. Bowen's professional skills resulted a certificate in psychiatry from the American Board of Psychiatry and Neurology in 1966, and designation as a Fellow of the American Psychiatric Association. She served in the army for thirty years.

Sources: *Who's Who among African Americans,* 26th ed., p. 126.

1961 • Fred Moore was the first black guard at the Tomb of the Unknown Soldier in Arlington National Cemetery.

Sources: Garrett, *Famous First Facts About Negroes,* p. 16.

1964 • Margaret F. Bailey became the first black colonel in the Army Nurse Corps. After twenty years in the army, she was made a lieutenant colonel. In 1970 she was promoted to full colonel. A native of Selma, Alabama, Bailey attended nursing school in Montgomery and was a student at San Francisco State University. She enlisted in the army in 1944 and served in bases in the United States and abroad in France, Germany, and Japan.

Sources: Bailey, *They Too Call Alabama Home,* p. 26; *Black Defenders of America, 1775–1973.*

1965 • Milton L. Olive III (1946–1965) was the first black Medal of Honor winner in the Vietnam War. First Class Private Olive was a member of the 3rd Platoon of Company B, 2nd Battalion (Airborne), 503rd Infantry on duty in Vietnam. On October 22, 1965, he caught an exploding grenade and died to save his comrades.

Sources: *Black Americans in Defense of Our Country,* p. 76; Cantor, *Historic Landmarks of Black America,* p. 8; Lee, *Negro Medal of Honor Men,* p. 123.

1971 • Benjamin L. Hunton (1919–1981) was the first black army officer to receive a commission as brigadier general in the reserves. Hunton was employed for twenty-two years in the public schools of Washington, D.C., and served at the Departments of Interior and Health, Education, and Welfare.

Sources: *Encyclopedia of Black America,* p. 457.

1972 • Frederick E. Davidson, a major general, was the top-ranked black in the U.S. Army. He commanded the 8th Infantry Division in Europe on April 19, becoming the first black officer to lead an army division.

Sources: *Jet* 95 (26 April 1999): 19.

1976 • Clara Leach Adams-Ender (1939–) was the first black, first woman, and first nurse to graduate with a master's degree from the U.S. Army Command and General Staff College. In July 1967 she was the first woman in the army to be awarded the Expert Field Medical Badge, and in 1982 she was the first black Army Nurse Corps officer to graduate from the Army War College. Adams-Ender became the first black nurse appointed chief of the nursing department at Walter Reed Army Medical Center in Washington, D.C. in 1984. Adams-Ender was born in Willow Springs, North Carolina. Her parents were not highly educated, but they stressed education for their children. She worked on her parents' farm until she entered college at North Carolina Agricultural and Technical State University School of Nursing when she was sixteen years old. She joined the army while in college, in order to help finance her junior and senior years. Shortly before her 1961 graduation, Adams-Ender was commissioned as a second lieutenant. Early posts in the army included Korea, where she

The First Black Woman General in the U.S. Army

Army General In 1979 Hazel Winifred Johnson (1929–2011) climbed the ranks in the military and became the first black woman general in the U.S. Army. She was born in Malvern, Pennsylvania, one of seven children raised on the family farm in West Chester. She knew early that she wanted to be a nurse, and took her first step in this direction when she entered Harlem University School of Nursing in 1950. After receiving her bachelor's degree, she took a job at a veterans' hospital in Philadelphia. She was working there when she joined the army in 1955. In 1960 Johnson achieved the rank of second lieutenant. She found no problems because of her race, and was able to continue her education while in the army, going on to earn degrees from Villanova University (bachelor's in nursing), Columbia University (master's in nursing education) and Catholic University (doctorate in educational administration). Johnson progressed steadily in the army, and by the 1970s her rank of colonel made her the highest-ranking black woman in the armed forces. On her way to becoming a general, Johnson held many responsible positions, including serving as assistant dean of the School of Nursing at the University of Maryland and as chief nurse of the U.S. Army Military Command in Korea. She remained chief of the Army Nurse Corps until 1983, when she retired from military service. Johnson turned her attention to teaching after retirement, holding faculty posts first at George Washington University (while also working with the American Nursing Association), and then at George Mason University. Johnson was named Army Nurse of the Year in 1972, and was awarded several honorary doctorate degrees and military awards.

Sources: Hine, *Black Women in America,* vol. 1, p. 644; *Contemporary Black Biography,* vol. 22, pp. 108–10; Salzman, *Encyclopedia of African-American Culture and History,* Supplement, pp. 144–45.

gained experience in teaching and administration, and she later spent two years at Fort Sam Houston, Texas, as a nursing instructor. She left that assignment in 1967 to do graduate study at the University of Minnesota, where she earned the master's degree in nursing in 1969. When Adams-Ender began her tour of duty in Germany in 1978, she was the assistant chief of nursing, but became chief in less than a year. She was also promoted to colonel while there. When she was appointed in 1987 to the Office of the Attorney General as chief of the Army Nurse Corps, she had been promoted to brigadier general. Thus, Brigadier General Adams-Ender became the first black chief of the Army Nurse Corps.

Sources: Hine, *Black Women in America,* vol. 1, pp. 10–11; *Jet* 63 (15 November 1982): 16; Smith, *Notable Black American Women,* pp. 1–2.

1982 • Roscoe Robinson Jr. (1928–1993) was the first black four-star general in the U.S. Army. He was also the first black representative on the NATO military committee. The Saint Louis-born soldier was educated at West Point Military Academy, the University of Pittsburgh, and the National War College. Robinson was in the army for thirty-four years, retiring in 1985. He served at posts in the United States and abroad, including assignments as commanding general of the U.S. Army in Japan and as commander of a battalion of the 1st Cavalry Division during the Vietnam conflict. Robinson was considered a war hero, and his decorations include the Distinguished Flying Cross and the Master Parachutist Badge. He remained active after his retirement by serving on several corporate boards. He was hospitalized at the Walter Reed Army Hospital in Washington, D.C., at the time of his death.

Sources: *Jet* 84 (9 August 1993): 15; *Negro Almanac, 1976,* p. 656; *Who's Who among Black Americans, 1992–93,* p. 1214.

1985 • Sherian Grace Cadoria (1940–) was the first black woman to be given the rank of brigadier general in the regular U.S. Army and the first black woman to command a male

Roscoe Robinson Jr.

Sherian Cadoria

battalion. In 1985 she also became the first black woman director of manpower and personnel for the Joint Chiefs of Staff. Cadoria served as one of four women army generals. Her tours of duty included service in Vietnam. She held key posts with the Law Enforcement Division and the Criminal Investigation Command. She retired from the army in 1990. Cadoria's route to advancement in the army was unlike that of many of her women colleagues, who were able to advance through the nursing corps; she advanced through her involvement with the military police. She was born in Marksville, Louisiana, where in the 1940s she had to walk five miles to school rather than run the risk of riding the bus. She graduated from Southern University in Louisiana in 1961 and enlisted in the Women's Army Corps (WAC). This led to another "first" for her: She was the first black woman to attend the army's Command and General Staff College, from which she received a diploma in 1971. She also earned a master's degree from the University of Oklahoma and a diploma from the U.S. War College (where she was again the first black woman to attend); she also studied at the National Defense University Institute of Higher Defense Studies. Cadoria's rise through the ranks was accompanied by the frustrations encountered because of her race and her gender—white racism in the South and the army's stereotypical belief that there were army jobs women could not do. Her last army assignment, which began in 1987, was as Deputy Commanding General and Director for the U.S. Total Army Personnel Command in Alexandria, Virginia. During her almost thirty-year army career, Cadoria received many medals and commendations, including three Bronze Stars. She returned to Louisiana when she retired, where she organized the Cadoria Speaker Service.

Sources: Lanker, *I Dream a World,* p. 150; Hine, *Black Women in America,* vol. 1, p. 214; *Contemporary Black Biography,* vol. 14, pp. 34–36; *Who's Who among African Americans,* 26th ed., p. 195.

Colin Powell

1987 • Colin L. Powell (1937–) was the first black National Security Advisor. Born in Harlem in New York City to Jamaican immigrants, Powell received his bachelor's degree from City College of New York in 1958 and his master's in business administration from George Washington University in 1971. He graduated from the National War College in 1976. Powell joined the Reserve Officers Training Corps while at City College and was commissioned as a second lieutenant when he graduated. He made his best grades in the ROTC courses and graduated as a Distinguished Military Student. His first assignment after basic training was to Germany, where he was made a first lieutenant. An assignment to Boston completed his ROTC-required three years of military service in 1961, but he chose to remain active in the military. Powell was trained as a military advisor in 1962 and saw his first tour of war duty in Vietnam. An injury there resulted in his being given first the Purple Heart and later the Bronze Star. He was assigned to the Pentagon in 1971, after another tour of duty in Vietnam. Powell was sent to South Korea in 1973. By 1976 he was a full colonel. In 1979 Powell was promoted to brigadier general and worked for a brief time as assistant to the Department of Energy. For the 1980 presidential election, he switched his political allegiance from the Democratic to the Republican party. He was offered an administrative position with the army after the election, but chose to return to more traditional army duty as he had many times previously when similar opportunities were presented to him. Between 1983 and 1986 Powell rose from major general to three-star general. As such, he commanded the Fifth Corps in Frankfort, Germany. He was back in the United States serving as assistant national security advisor when President Ronald Reagan named him National Security Advisor. Just short of a year later, he became the first National Security Advisor to be given the Secretary's Award, for distinguished contributions.

Sources: *Contemporary Black Biography,* vol. 1, pp. 195–98; Hornsby, *Milestones in Twentieth-Century African-American History,* pp. 412, 419, 460; Smith, *Notable Black American Men,* pp. 958–61; *Who's Who among African Americans,* 26th ed., p. 1008.

1989 • Henry Doctor Jr. was the first black inspector general of the army. A native of Oakley, South Carolina, he received his bachelor's degree in general agriculture from South Carolina State College (now University) in 1954 and entered the army through the ROTC program.

Sources: *Jet* 76 (21 August 89): 10; *Negro Almanac,* p. 898.

1989 • Colin L. Powell (1937–) became the first black chairman of the Joint Chiefs of Staff, which made him the highest-ranking military advisor to the president of the United States. He was the youngest person ever to hold this position and was promoted to four-star general when the appointment was made. Powell was especially prominent in this position because of his highly visible role in the Persian Gulf War. He was the overseer of the successful Operation Desert Storm in 1990 and the equally successful Operation Desert Shield. He retired from the military in 1993, after a stellar career, but remained in the public eye. He became an active lecturer and served on a number of corporate boards. His autobiography, *My American Journey*, was coauthored with Joseph E. Persico and published in 1995. In 1996, Powell was courted by the Republican Party to be the running mate of presidential candidate Bob Dole, but he declined. In 1997 Powell chaired the President's Summit for America's Future, President Bill Clinton's volunteer program aimed at the improvement of children's lives. The kickoff of the summit was held in Philadelphia. Powell stood with President Clinton and former presidents Bush and Carter on the steps of Independence Hall. The sight of these four Americans served to recall to mind the invaluable service Powell provided to both Democratic and Republican administrations. The highest civilian honor in the United States is the Medal of Honor. Powell was in 1996 the only person to have received two of these prestigious awards. President George Bush presented the first of his two medals in 1991; President Bill Clinton presented the second in 1993. In 1997 a poll conducted by the *Wall Street Journal* and NBC News identified Powell as the most popular American, and *Time* magazine called him one of the most influential people in America.

Sources: *Contemporary Black Biography*, vol. 1, pp. 195–198; Hornsby, *Milestones in Twentieth-Century African-American History*, pp. 412, 419, 460; Smith, *Notable Black American Men*, pp. 958–61; *Who's Who among African Americans*, 26th ed., p. 1008.

1991 • The Medal of Honor was awarded posthumously to Corporal Freddie Stowers, a World War I hero. Corporal Stowers had been recommended for the medal during World War I, but it was awarded seventy-two years later, following an army investigation of prejudice in the bestowing of awards. On September 28, 1918, Stowers was a squad leader whose company was trying to capture a hill in the Champagne-Marne section in France. The Germans feigned surrender to lure the Americans into a trap that killed more than half of the company, including those in command. Stowers took charge, leading a squad that destroyed the German guns. He was mortally wounded, but the company pressed on and captured the hill.

Sources: *Atlanta Constitution* (8 April 1993); *Jet* 80 (13 May 91): 9.

1993 • Brigadier General Larry Jordan (1946?–) became the first black general post commander at Fort Knox, Kentucky. A West Point graduate and career military officer, Jordan is a native of Kansas City, Kansas. The appointment of Jordan to the Fort Knox post is seen as an example of opportunities available to all who enter military service. Fort Knox was home to a regular population of 30,000 and provided training for more than 10,000 soldiers per year. Jordan holds a master's degree in history from Indiana University. He had been in the army twenty-five years when appointed to the command post at Fort Knox.

Sources: *Jet* 85 (22 November 1993): 36.

1994 • Imam Abdul-Rasheed Muhammad became the first Muslim chaplain in the armed forces. He had previously served as prison chaplain at two prisons near Buffalo, New York. Appointment by the army of a Muslim chaplain had been the subject of discussion and negotiation between the military and Muslim leaders for ten years. Muhammad has a master's degree in counseling and social work and had served in the army from 1982 to 1985 as a behavioral scientist specialist.

Sources: *Jet* 85 (27 December 1993): 37.

1995 • The first black sergeant major of the U.S. Army and its highest-ranking enlisted soldier was Gene C. McKinney (1950–). Promoted from his rank as command sergeant

Gene C. McKinney

major of the U.S. Army Europe, McKinney's new title ranked him above all other army sergeant majors. A native of Arlington, Virginia, he is a graduate of Park College. He was in the army for twenty-six years when he achieved the top enlisted soldier rank. Less than two years after his promotion, McKinney was suspended from the army while charges that he sexually harassed a white female soldier were investigated. McKinney denied the charges. He served in Vietnam and is the recipient of the Bronze Star and the Meritorious Service Medal.

Sources: *Jet* 88 (31 July 1995): 32; 91 (3 March 1997): 47; *Who's Who among African Americans,* 26th ed., p. 853.

1996 • The first woman director of the Georgetown University Army Reserve Officer Training Corps (ROTC) program was Paulette Francine Ruffin (1956–), a lieutenant colonel. (The Georgetown program had been in existence since 1918.) Ruffin was born in Alexandria, Virginia, and received a bachelor's degree in marketing from Lehigh University in Pennsylvania in 1978 and a master's degree in social psychology from the University of North Carolina-Chapel Hill in 1987. A career officer, Ruffin began her career in the army in 1978 by attending the U.S. Army Ordinance School. She has held several posts during the course of her service, with a number of years spent at the U.S. Military Academy. For part of her time at West Point, she was on the faculty. Her experience also includes having served as a speechwriter for General Johnnie E. Wilson.

Sources: *Jet* 91 (23 December 1996): 19; *Who's Who among African Americans,* 26th ed., p. 1082.

1996 • Voneree [Von] Deloatch was promoted to brigadier general and commanding officer of Civil Affairs Forces in Bosnia, becoming the first U.S. General Officer to be promoted in Bosnia and Herzegovina. He was commanding officer of the 352nd Civil Affairs Command in Riverdale, Maryland, at the time of his promotion. Born in Tarboro, North Carolina, Deloatch graduated from North Carolina Agricultural and Technical State University, and was commissioned a second lieutenant in the army after completing the ROTC program with distinction. In 1973 he earned a master's degree in public administration and city management from Howard University, and went on to complete course work for the doctorate in public administration at the University of Southern California. He has been awarded several medals because of his service in the army, including the Bronze Star.

Sources: *Jet* 90 (2 September 1996): 37.

1997 • The first and only living black to receive the United States' highest battlefield honor, the Medal of Honor, for service in World War II was Vernon Baker. In January 1997, Baker was given the award, along with posthumous awards to six other black soldiers. The seven men had previously been denied the medal because they were black. Baker, a second lieutenant who was later promoted to first lieutenant, was a career army officer. He received the award because of his heroic service in Italy. He was also awarded the United States' second-highest battlefield honor, the Distinguished Service Cross, as well as a Bronze Star and a Purple Heart. During the war he was a member of the all-black 92nd Infantry, known as the Buffalo Division. He spent twenty-eight years in the army and worked for the Red Cross after retiring from the service. The posthumous awards went to Edward A. Carter Jr., John R. Fox, Willy F. James Jr., Ruben Rivers, Charles L. Thomas, and George Watson. Most of the men died in combat. Fox, a first lieutenant, was killed in Italy in 1944. Staff Sergeant Rivers was killed in France. Private First Class James was killed in 1945; he died while leading a squad during an enemy assault.

Sources: Geranios, "Black Soldiers Finally Get Medal of Honor," Associated Press (11 January 1997); *Jet* 91 (3 February 1997): 36; *New York Times* (14 January 1997).

1999 • Shawna Kimbrell fought racial and gender stereotypes to become the first black woman to complete fighter pilot training in the U.S. Army. After receiving her wings this year, the F16 pilot flew her first combat sortie in 2001.

Sources: *African American Almanac,* 11th ed., p. 99; *Ebony* 65 (December 2009/January 2010): 110.

2003 • One month after she joined Operation Iraqi Freedom, Shoshana Nyree Johnson's convoy was ambushed, she was taken captive in Nasiriyah, and became the first black female prisoner of war in U.S. military history. A Specialist of the U.S. Amy's 507th Maintenance Company, 11th ADA, Johnson, a Panamanian, was on her second military assignment when deployed to Iraq. She was a prisoner for twenty-two days and held along with five other members of her unit, including PFC Jessica Lynch, a white woman who was held in a different location. Johnson was freed on April 13, 2003, after a gunfight that led to her capture and a bullet wound in both ankles. She received a temporary disability honorary discharge and was awarded the Bronze Star, Purple Heart, and Prisoner of War Medal for her service in Iraq.

Sources: "Authors: Shoshana Johnson." Simon & Schuster, http://authors.simonand schuster.com/Shoshana-Johnson/46047911. Accessed October 12, 2012.

2009 • Iraq veteran and U.S. Army warrant officer Jonathan Holsey became the first army amputee to attend warrant officer school.

Shoshana Johnson

Sources: *Ebony* 65 (December 2009/January 2010): 110; U.S. Department of Defense, "Soldier Becomes First Amputee Accepted to Warrant Officer School," http://www.defense.gov/news/newsarticle.aspx?id=53247. Accessed September 27, 2012.

2009 • Command Sergeant Major Teresa King (1961–) was the first woman to serve as commandant of the school for U.S. Army drill sergeants. She did so in Fort Jackson, South Carolina, at the U.S. Army Drill Sergeant School, the army's largest training installation. Born in Clinton, North Carolina, the military veteran and sharecropper's daughter said that she was experienced in dismantling racial and gender barriers in the military. Her battalion commander said that she was selected because she knew "the business of taking civilians and making them into soldiers." During her career, she worked for Dick Cheney at the Pentagon, when he was U.S. secretary of defense. She became the first female sergeant to serve in the 18th Airborne Corps in 1997–2001 and also commanded other battalions. King has a master's degree in business management and is pursuing a second master's in theology.

Sources: *Contemporary Black Biography,* vol. 18, pp. 74–76. ; *Jet* 116 (5–12 October 2009): 12.

2011 • When promoted from brigadier general to major general in the U.S. Army, Marcia Anderson became the army's first black female two-star general. The ceremony took place at Fort Knox, Kentucky. A native of East St. Louis, Illinois, Anderson studied at Creighton University in Nebraska. After her promotion, she moved to the office of the chief of the U.S. Army Reserve in Washington, D.C.

Sources: Outside the Beltway, "Marcia Anderson Army's First Black Femail 2-Star General," http://www.outsidethebeltway.com/?s=marcia+anderson. Accessed September 27, 2012.

Civil War

1861 • Nicholas Biddle was the first black wounded in the Civil War. The sixty-five-year-old former slave shed blood from an injury while he accompanied the first Pennsylvania troops through Baltimore on April 18, 1861.

Sources: *Encyclopedia of Black America,* p. 62; Garrett, *Famous First Facts about Negroes,* p. 9.

1863 • Harriet Ross "Moses" Tubman (1821?–1913), known for her work as conductor on the Underground Railroad, was a nurse, cook, and laundress for Union troops in South Carolina. She led Union troops in a raid along the Combahee River in June of 1863, becoming the only woman during the Civil War to plan and carry out an armed expedition against enemy forces.

Sources: Hine, *Black Women in America,* vol. 2, pp. 1176–80; Smith, *Notable Black American Women,* pp. 1151–55.

Harriet Tubman

Arlington Cemetery's First Black Woman Guard

The first black woman to guard the Tomb of the Unknowns at Arlington National Cemetery was Danyell Elaine Wilson (1974–), a sergeant in the U.S. Army. She made her first walk as a tomb sentinel in January 1997. Wilson was also the first black woman and the second woman of any race to receive the "Tomb Guard Identification Badge." The award, created by the army in 1958, has been awarded to only four hundred soldiers. A native of Montgomery, Alabama, Wilson joined the army in 1993, with the rank of sergeant in the military police. She moved to Walter Reed Army Medical Center as a medical supply specialist in 1998.

Sources: *Jet* 89 (15 April 1996): 46; 91 (17 February 1997): 21; *Who's Who among African Americans,* 26th ed., p. 1362.

1863 • For three weeks in September the Black Brigade of Cincinnati, Ohio, was the first black unit from the North to be used for military purposes in the war. The brigade was formed when Confederate General John Hunt Morgan, who had won other regional victories, established plans to attack Cincinnati.

Sources: "The Black Brigade of Cincinnati: Stories of Courage, Stories of Freedom," http://freedomcenter.org/freedom-forum/index.php/2011/05/black-brigade-cincinnati-stories-courage-stories-freedom. Accessed September 27, 2012.

1865 • The first black Confederate troops were mustered into service for the Southern cause. On March 13, 1865, Confederate President Jefferson Davis signed a bill authorizing the employment of blacks as soldiers, settling an issue long disputed in the South. General Robert E. Lee recommended the enlistment as "not only expedient but necessary." The action was taken at very end of the war; Lee surrendered at Appamatox Courthouse on April 9, 1865, and the remaining Confederate forces soon followed his example.

Sources: Hornsby, *Chronology of African-American History,* p. 38.

Coast Guard

1865 • Michael Augustine Healy (1839–1904) was the first black appointed to the coast guard. In 1865 he entered the U.S. Revenue Service, the forerunner of the U.S. Coast Guard. In 1886 he was assigned to command the famous cutter *Bear* and became the chief federal law enforcement officer in the northern waters around Alaska, making him the first officer. The Healy family also produced the first black Roman Catholic American bishop, James Augustine (1830–1900), and the first black American Jesuit and president of Georgetown University, Patrick Francis (1834–1910).

Sources: Logan and Winston, *Dictionary of American Negro Biography,* p. 303–04.

1880 • The Pea Island, North Carolina, Lifesaving Station was the first and only all-black coast guard facility. Richard Etheridge, a former slave, established it. All traces of the station have now been washed away, but the North Carolina Aquarium on Roanoke Island has an exhibit dedicated to the original station.

Sources: *Black Americans in Defense of Our Nation,* pp. 159–60; Cantor, *Historic Landmarks of Black America,* p. 232.

1943 • The USS *Sea Cloud* was the first U.S. warship to be fully integrated. The experiment was held during World War II to determine the feasibility of integrating the crews. Clarence Samuels and Joseph C. Jenkins became the first black coast guard officers a year before the U.S. Navy commissioned blacks. The completely integrated operation had four black officers and about fifty black petty officers and seamen who served the 173-man complement. Although the experiment was successful, it failed to spur widespread racial integration in Coast Guard vessels. The navy chartered the 2,323-ton weather patrol vessel in 1942 and converted it to use in collecting weather data off the coasts of Greenland, Newfoundland, and France. When the vessel was transferred to the navy in April 1943, it was reclassified and later decommissioned in November 1944. It was returned to the owner, who in 1931 had it built in Keil, Germany, as a civilian yacht named *Hussar*. After that, it had a long post-war career both as a yacht and a cruise ship. Joseph C. Jenkins was an instructor at the Manhattan Beach Training Station in New York. In April 1943 he graduated from the Coast Guard Academy as an ensign in the Coast Guard Reserve, a full year before the navy commissioned blacks. Clarence Samuels, a warrant officer and also an instructor at Manhattan Beach, became a lieutenant and was assigned to the *Sea Cloud* in 1943. Jenkins, Samuels, and another instructor, Harvey C. Russell, were declared eligible to apply for commissions, yet the officer training school rejected them at first. Russell later became an ensign and was assigned to the *Sea Cloud*. Samuels became the first black in the twentieth century to command a U.S. Coast Guard vessel in wartime. At first he was captain of Lightship No. 115 and later the U.S. Coast Guard's *Sweetgum* in the Panama Sea. Frontier. Russell was transferred from the *Hoquim* and became executive officer on a cutter, assuming command of the integrated crew soon after the war.

Sources: U.S. Coast Guard, "U.S.S. Sea Cloud, 1942," http://www.uscg.mil/history/web cutters/Sea_Cloud_IX99.asp. Accessed September 27, 2012.

1944 • The Coast Guard's Women's Reserve was created on November 23, 1942, when President Franklin D. Roosevelt signed Public Law 772. The Women's Reserve became known by an acronym based on the Coast Guard's motto: "Semer Paratus— Always Ready," or SPAR. Black women were initially denied admission into the organization. In October this year, the first black SPAR was Yeoman Second Class Olivia Hooker (1922?–). A twenty-two-year-old high school graduate, Hooker had worked in a clerical or sales position before joining the SPARs. Most SPARs enlisted for six years; thus, by December 1944 SPAR recruiting virtually ended. Altogether, only five black women were recruited for SPARs, representing tokenism; they were trained at Manhattan Beach Training Station in New York and were assigned to district offices of the Coast Guard without regard to race.

Sources: Tilley, *A History of Women in the Coast Guard*, p. 6; Thompson, *The Coast Guard & the Women's Reserve in World War II*, p. 3.

1945 • More than seven hundred enlisted members of the Women's Army Corps' 6888th Battalion were sent to England, becoming the only battalion of black women to serve overseas during World War II. The battalion was formed after civil rights organizations and black newspapers accused the military of denying black women meaningful jobs. The women arrived in Britain, where they sorted mail, some of which had been stored for months. There were many letters sent to soldiers who had been transferred, who had died, or who had been scattered about. The commander, Charity Adams [Earley], noted that white women who served in Europe at that time were assigned to tasks equivalent to their male counterparts.

Sources: Hine, *Black Women in America*, pp. 791–97.

1966 • Merle J. Smith Jr. was the first black graduate of the Coast Guard Academy.

Sources: *Black Americans in Defense of Our Nation*, p. 163; Kane, *Famous First Facts*, p. 64.

1989 • Alex Haley (1921–1992) was the first person of any race to receive an honorary degree from the Coast Guard Academy.

Sources: *Jet* 76 (12 June 89): 17.

1995 • Sea captain Michael Augustine "Mike" Healy (1839–1904) became the first black to have a U.S. Coast Guard vessel, a polar-class icebreaker, named in his honor. Over one hundred years ago Healy served in the Revenue Cutter Service, which later became the coast guard. Because of his fearless exploits including prowling the Artic, combat with poachers, and dispensing justice, he was nicknamed "Hell-roaring" Mike Healy.

Sources: *Jet* 87 (20 March 1995): 21.

1998 • Master Chief Petty Officer (MCPOCG) Vincent Patton III was appointed this year and became the first black to hold that rank in the U.S. Coast Guard. The MCPOCG is the most senior enlisted member of the coast guard and serves the commandant as a personal advisor and assistant in matters relating to the enlisted members of the guard, whether they are on active duty or in the reserves. This service also covers their families.

Sources: U.S. Coast Guard, "Vincent Patton," http://www.uscg.mil/history/people/Vincent _Patton.asp, accessed September 27, 2012.

1998 • Erroll M. Brown (1950?–) became the first black to hold the flag rank of rear admiral in the U.S. Coast Guard. A career coast guard officer, Brown grew up during the decades of racial unrest but was not directly involved. He attended high school in St. Petersburg, Florida, where he excelled as a football player. A flyer from the coast guard awakened his interest in the military as a possible career. Despite the fact that he was almost denied admission because of his poor dental health, he graduated from the U.S. Coast Guard Academy in Connecticut with a degree in marine engineering in 1972 and the rank of ensign. He had several assignments during his early years, with each one increasing his leadership responsibilities. He also continued his education. By 1986 he had earned two master's degrees from the University of Michigan, a master's degree from the Naval War College, and a fourth master's degree from Rensselear Polytechnic Institute. Brown became commander of the Coast Guard Integrated Support Command in 1997. He served well in this demanding position, but left the post when he was promoted to rear admiral. After his promotion, he assumed command of the Coast Guard Maintenance and Logistics Command Atlantic in Norfolk, Virginia. Both military and civilian personnel fell under his command.

Sources: *Contemporary Black Biography,* vol. 23, pp. 27–29.

2001 • The first black woman to graduate with an engineering degree from the U.S. Coast Guard Academy in New London, Connecticut, was cadet first class Andrea Parker. The Augusta, Georgia, native received her bachelor's degree in civil engineering. She was to be stationed onboard the *CGC Tahoma* in New Bedford, Massachusetts, as the ship's intelligence officer.

Sources: *Jet* 100 (30 July 2001): 19.

2005 • The first African American female aviator in the U.S. Coast Guard's 215-year history was Jeanine McIntosh-Menze, who received her wings on June 24 at Naval Air Station in Corpus Christi, Texas. She was assigned to fly a C-130 Hercules aircraft out of Air Station Barbers Point in Hawaii. Born in Kingston, Jamaica, she graduated from Florida International University in 2001 and was a flight instructor at Opa Locka Airport in North Miami. She joined the coast guard in 2003.

Sources: *Spelman* Messenger 21 (Fall 2010): 23; Jeanine McIntosy-Menze, USCG. www .uscg.mil/history/people/McIntosh_Menze_Jeanine.asp.

2009 • Cadet Jacqueline Fitch (1987?–) became the U.S. Coast Guard Academy's first black female regimental commander, the highest-ranking cadet in the academy. On September 26 the Catonsville, Maryland, native made her debut when she led the Corps of Cadets in a parade at the academy, on its Washington Parade field. In her post, Fitch acts as a liaison between the commandant of the cadets and the cadet corps. Her responsibilities also included "maintaining good order and discipline, overseeing welfare of the student body and ensuring cadets comply to the regulations and policies" that the superintendent and commandant of cadets established. Fitch's experience as a leader emerged while she attended high school at Western School of Technology and Environmental Sciences in Baltimore.

Sources: *Nashville Pride* (9 October 2009).

2010 • The first African American woman helicopter pilot in the U.S. Coast Guard was La'Shanda Holmes. Lieutenant Jeanine Menze, the first black woman aviator in U.S. Coast

Guard history, pinned her at a ceremony held at Naval Air Station Whiting Field, located in Milton, Florida. Holmes, a Spelman College graduate, was scheduled to go to her next duty station, the Coast Guard Air Station, located in Los Angeles.

Sources: *Spelman Messenger* 121 (Fall 2010): 23.

Court of Military Appeals

1971 • Robert Morton Duncan (1927–) was the first black appointed to the U.S. Court of Military Appeals. Born in Urbana, Ohio, he was educated at The Ohio State University, receiving B.S. (1948), J.D. (1952), and LL.D. (1979) degrees. Duncan spent his first few years after receipt of the J.D. in general law practice in Columbus, Ohio. From 1957 to 1965 he held several municipal government positions. He was named attorney general for Ohio in 1965, served as Franklin County Municipal Court judge from 1966 to 1969, and was named to the state supreme court in 1969. He held the latter position until his appointment to the Court of Military Appeals, where he served until 1985. He was chief justice of the court in 1974. When he left the military court, he returned to the practice of law until 1992, when he became vice president and general counsel at Ohio State. He was named vice president emeritus when he left this position in 1996. Duncan has received a number of awards, including one from the American Civil Liberties Union in 1986.

Sources: *Who's Who among African Americans*, 26th ed., p. 362.

Marines

1942 • Black Marines were first enlisted on June 1, but were placed on inactive status as reservists until the Marines could build a training-size unit in segregated facilities at Montford Point, a training reservation at Marine Barracks, New River, North Carolina. The base was later named Camp Lejeune. On August 26 training for the first black contingent, the 51st Defense Battalion, began at Montford Point. Howard P. Perry was the first black to report on that day. Colonel Samuel A. Woods Jr. was in command. During World War II nearly 20,000 blacks were trained at the segregated facility.

Sources: "The Men of Montford Point: The First Black Marines," http://www.geocities.com/nubiansong/montford.htm. Accessed September 27, 2012.

1944 • James E. Johnson (1926–) was the first black warrant officer in the Marines.

Sources: *Encyclopedia of Black America*, p. 474.

1945 • Frederick C. Branch became the first black commissioned officer in the Marine Corps on November 10. More than fifty years later, he returned to Camp Lejeune, North Carolina, where a base building named in his honor was dedicated. Branch received his army training in 1943 at an all-black training site in Montford Point, which had no black officers. He left with the rank of corporal and served in the South Pacific during World War II. He was later chosen to participate in the U.S. Navy's V–12 program at Purdue University. He was the only black in the class of 250 officer candidates, graduated in 1945 after being a Dean's List student, and received his commission. During his subsequent service, he once commanded an all-white platoon. He left the service in 1952 with the rank of captain. He went on to earn a master's degree from Temple University and to teach in the Philadelphia public schools for thirty-five years. The naming of a building for him at Camp Lejeune recognized his focus on achievement.

Sources: *Jet* 92 (4 August 1997): 18.

1952 • Frank E. Petersen Jr. (1932–) was the first black marine pilot and the first black to win U.S. Marine Corps wings. He was designated a navy aviator and received additional flight training at several training facilities. In 1979 he became the first black general in the marines, and in 1986 he was named the first black commander of the Quantico, Virginia facility, a major Marine base. Petersen, who was born in Topeka, Kansas, earned his bach-

The First Black West Point Graduate

Henry Flipper

In 1877 Henry Ossian Flipper (1856–1940) became the first black to graduate from the U.S. Military Academy at West Point, New York. (Another student, James W. Smith, was the first black to enter the academy in 1870.) A native of Georgia and a student at Atlanta University at the time of his appointment, Flipper graduated fiftieth out of a class of seventy-six after suffering four years of exclusion and ostracism by white cadets. He joined the 10th Calvary in 1878, one of the all-black cavalry regiments making up what became known as the "buffalo soldiers." He served in Oklahoma and Texas. The only black officer in the U.S. Army, Flipper was cleared of an embezzlement charge in 1882, but was convicted of conduct unbecoming an officer and dishonorably discharged. He remained in the West and, for the next fifty years, engaged in engineering, mining, and survey work. He also lived in Atlanta for a number of years with his equally renowned brother, Josephus Flipper, a bishop in the African Methodist Episcopal Church. In 1976 the U.S. Army exonerated Flipper posthumously and granted him a retroactive discharge. On May 3, 1977—the centennial of his graduation—a bust by black sculptor Helene Hemmans was unveiled in Flipper's honor at West Point. Buried at first in a family plot in Atlanta, his remains were moved to his hometown, Thomasville, where he was reburied with full military honors. His *Colored Cadet at West Point* (1878) gives a penetrating insight into his early life. In 1999, 117 years after his wrongful discharge, President Bill Clinton granted him a posthumous pardon at a ceremony held in the White House.

Sources: *Black Americans in Defense of Our Nation*, p. 27; Logan and Winston, *Dictionary of American Negro Biography*, pp. 227–28; Garrett, *Famous First Facts About Negroes*, p. 12.

elor's and master's degrees from George Washington University well after he joined the military; he also graduated from the Army War College. He joined the U.S. Navy in 1950 as a seaman apprentice, but soon entered the Naval Aviation Cadet Corps. He completed that program in 1952 and was commissioned as a second lieutenant in the marine corps. Petersen spent thirty-eight years in the navy, with thirty-six as a marine. He was serving at Quantico with the rank of lieutenant general when he retired from the service in 1988. Petersen was an accomplished fighter pilot, flying sixty-four combat missions in Korea in 1953. For his deeds, he was given six air medals and the Distinguished Flying Cross. Later, in 1968, he served in Vietnam, where he was the first black to command a tactical air squadron in the navy or marine corps; he flew almost three hundred missions in Vietnam. When he retired, Petersen had been given twenty individual medals for bravery in combat and had been the senior ranking pilot in both the navy and the marine corps from 1985 to 1988. He also can boast an affiliation with the Tuskegee Airmen, the celebrated all-black flying unit. Active after his retirement, Petersen is a member of several boards. He was chairman-elect of the board of directors of the national Marrow Donor Program at the beginning of 2001. His autobiography, *Into the Tiger's Jaw: America's First Black Marine Aviator*, was published in 1999.

Sources: *Jet* 70 (14 July 1986): 28; 95 (1 March 1999): 32; 99 (26 February 2001): 26; *Negro Almanac*, p. 905; Smith, *Notable Black American Men*, pp. 930–31.

1967 • Private First Class James Anderson Jr. (1947–1967) was the first black marine to receive the Medal of Honor. On January 22, 1967, in Vietnam, he threw himself on a grenade to save his comrades. Anderson was acknowledged by the naming of a military supply ship in his honor.

Sources: *Black Americans in Defense of Our Nation,* p. 63.

1968 • Paul Stewart Green, a physician, was the first black captain in the U.S. Navy Medical Corps.

Sources: Kane, *Famous First Facts,* p. 467.

1981 • Charles Frank Bolden Jr. (1946–) was the first black U.S. Marine to become an astronaut in August this year. He was selected to become an astronaut in May 1980. Bolden participated in the deployment of NASA's Hubble Space Telescope and also commanded space shuttles *Atlantis* and *Discovery.*

Sources: *Contemporary Black Biography,* vol 7, pp. 16–18; vol 78, pp. 19–21.

1990 • Alford McMichael became the fourteenth person and the first black to be named sergeant major in the U.S. Marine Corps, the senior enlisted advisor to the Commandant. McMichael is a native of Hot Springs, Arkansas.

Sources: *Jet* 96 (26 July 1999): 32.

1992 • Denise H. Hoover became the first woman to graduate from the U.S. Marine Corps Security Force Training Company in Chesapeake, Virginia. She served in the unit from April 1990 through September 1992. Hoover was the first woman permanently assigned to the training company's staff.

Sources: *Jet* 88 (5 June 1995): 26.

1997 • The first black woman colonel in the U.S. Marine Corps was Gilda Jackson, who received the honor in a ceremony at Marine Corps Air Station, Cherry Point, North Carolina. Jackson was an enlisted U.S. Marine before reaching the rank of sergeant. She later attended Ohio Dominican College where she enrolled in the Marine Officer Candidate Platoon Leader Course, becoming commissioned as a second lieutenant.

Sources: *Jet* 92 (20 October 1997): 16.

1999 • Walter E. Gaskin Sr. took command of the 22nd Marine Expeditionary Unit (MEU) at Camp Lejeune, North Carolina, becoming the first black to command the Marines and sailors in MEU. A native of Savannah, Georgia, and a colonel, Gaskin is a twenty-eight-year member of the U.S. Marines. His commands were at the platoon, company, and battalion level.

Sources: *Jet* 95 (1 March 1999): 14.

2001 • Vernice "Fly Girl" Armor (1973–) became the first African American female combat pilot. She earned her wings in July 2001 and ranked No. 1 in her class. Being "first" was not new to Armor. She worked for the Metro Nashville (Tennessee) Police Department from 1996 to 1998, starting as a beat cop and became the department's first female African American motorcycle officer. In 1998, she moved to the police department in Tempe, Arizona, and became its first female African American officer. She was the first woman in any branch of service to see combat, serving two tours in Iraq in 2003–04. Armor served in the marines from 1998 to 2007. While stationed at Camp Pendleton, she played women's professional football in San Diego.

Sources: *Tennessean* (11 July 2010).

2002 • Sergeant Jeannette Winters (1977?–2001) became the first U.S. servicewoman of any race to die during the "war on terrorism," Operation Enduring Freedom. She was also the first woman in the U.S. Marines to die in a combat zone. Winters had worked as a radio operator before joining the marines in 1997. Thirty-six-year-old Stephen L. Bryson, also a sergeant, was the only black man in the marines to die with five other American Marines in the Afghanistan conflict. Their KC–130 Hercules refueling plane crashed into a mountain near southwestern Pakistan. The fallen Marines were members of aerial refueler-transport Squadron 352, part of the Marine Aircraft Group 11, 32d Marine Aircraft Wing called the "Raiders."

Sources: *Jet* 101 (28 January 2002): 9–10.

Military Academy (West Point)

1870 • James Webster Smith was the first black admitted to the U.S. Military Academy at West Point. Nearly four years later, he left the academy; after being subjected to unbearable hazing and ostracism, he was dismissed for failing an examination in his junior year. Smith was court-martialed twice while at West Point and also had to repeat a year. He became supervisor of cadets at South Carolina Agricultural Institute in Orangeburg, South Carolina (now South Carolina State University). Smith was born a slave in Columbia, South Carolina. In 1997 the president of South Carolina State University was presented the gold bars and commission as a second lieutenant that were awarded to Smith posthumously. U.S. Army Secretary Togo West Jr., who made the presentation, declared that the posthumous award was made to correct the wrong that was done to Smith when he failed to receive the support of his cadet classmates and the academy.

Sources: *Integration and the Negro Officer in the Armed Forces of the United States of America*, p. 2; *Jet* 92 (13 October 1997): 22–23.

1976 • James H. Stith was the first black faculty member to become a tenured professor at West Point. He was an associate professor of physics.

Sources: *Jet* 50 (1 April 76): 50.

1979 • Vincent K. Brooks was the first black to serve as first captain and brigade commander of the Corp of Cadets.

Sources: *Black Americans in Defense of Our Nation*, p. 139.

1996 • Tausha Coleman (1973?–) and her niece, Lynyetta Blackshear (1974–), both of Crestview, Florida, are believed to be the first aunt and niece to be graduated together from the U.S. Military Academy at West Point. Coleman would train at Officers Basic Course at Fort Eustis, Virginia, later to be stationed at Fort Stewart, Georgia. Blackshear would be stationed in Korea.

Sources: *Jet* 90 (26 August 1996): 38.

Militia

1994 • Brigadier General John H. Bailey became the first black to command the Texas militia. He was sworn in during Black History Month in a special ceremony in Austin, Texas. The militia, formally known as State Defense Forces, was 159 years old when he took office. Bailey brought to the office his experience on active duty in Vietnam and as a teacher of military science in the Clear Creek Independent School District (Texas). He was given the Lone Star Distinguished Service Medal, Texas' highest military honor, when he became head of the militia.

Sources: *Jet* 85 (7 March 1994): 5.

National Guard

1869 • Robert Brown Elliott (1842–1884) was the first black commanding general of the South Carolina National Guard. Few facts are certain about Elliott's early life. It is speculated that he was born in Liverpool, England, of West Indian parents and educated in England. However, the first undisputed information makes clear that by 1867 he was in the United

States serving as associate editor of the *South Carolina Leader,* a weekly paper that was one of the first Southern papers published and edited by blacks. Elliott, a brilliant lawyer, was elected to the South Carolina legislature in 1868, and in March 1869 he was appointed assistant adjutant general of the state. In this position, he was charged with formation and maintenance of a state militia—often called the Black Militia—to protect white and black citizens from the murderous, fast-growing Ku Klux Klan. Elliott served as a U.S. congressman in 1871 and 1874 and was by this time recognized as a leader in the Republican Party. He resigned from Congress near the end of his second term and returned to South Carolina, where he was once again elected to the state legislature. Democrats took over in South Carolina in 1876, and Elliott's political power was lessened. The law practice he established was not profitable, and in 1879 he was appointed a customs inspector with the Treasury Department in Charleston, South Carolina. He lost this position in 1882, after having first been moved in 1880 from Charleston to New Orleans, Louisiana. The law practice Elliott opened in New Orleans provided minimal support. During his travels as a customs inspector, he had contracted malaria in Florida. He died in New Orleans as a result of the disease.

Robert Brown Elliott

Sources: Eric Foner, *Freedom's Lawmakers,* pp. 69–70; Logan and Winston, *Dictionary of American Negro Biography,* pp. 210–11; *Encyclopedia of Black America,* p. 354; Smith, *Notable Black American Men,* pp. 367–69.

1917 • Vertner Woodson Tandy (1885–1949) was the first black officer in the New York National Guard. During World War I, he was commissioned first lieutenant, later promoted to captain, and then promoted to major in command of a separate unit in the New York National Guard 15th Infantry. Also a prominent architect, Tandy designed Villa Lewaro, the home of Madame C. J. Walker.

Sources: *Encyclopedia of Black America,* p. 813; *Who's Who in Colored America, 1929,* p. 352; Wilson, *African American Architects,* pp. 389–92.

1994 • Irene Trowell-Harris became the first black woman brigadier general and the highest-ranking black in the National Guard. She was also the first woman, first member of a minority group, and first nurse to head a medical clinic in the National Guard. At the time of her promotion, she was serving as nursing assistant to the director of the Directorate of Nursing, Office of the Inspector General, Office of the Air Force Surgeon General at Bolling Air Force Base, Washington, D.C. She also held an appointment with the Department of Veterans' Affairs, serving as director of the Patient Care Inspection and Evaluation Division. Trowell-Harris is an alumna of Columbia University. She holds an honorary doctorate degree from the University of South Carolina.

Sources: *Jet* 85 (11 April 1994): 6; *Who's Who among African Americans,* 26th ed., p. 1247.

2007 • Major General Joseph C. Carter, who in 1974 joined the Massachusetts Army National Guard (MANG) became the first black commander of MANG. Governor Deval Patrick swore him into office. Carter, also adjutant general, became the governor's senior military advisor overseeing MANG preparedness. He also held the post as chief of police for Massachusetts Bay Transportation Authority Transit Police Department.

Sources: *Jet* 112 (19 November 2007): 26.

2008 • A colonel in the Maryland National Guard, Allyson Solomon was promoted to brigadier general and the Air Guard's assistant adjunct general. With the promotion, she became the first black to the post. From her Baltimore base, Solomon leads over 1,500 Air Guard members in the state.

Sources: *Jet* 113 (30 June 2008): 26.

Naval Academy

Joseph C. Carter

1872 • James Henry Conyers was the first black appointed to the U.S. Naval Academy at Annapolis, Maryland, although he did not graduate. He was a native of South Carolina.

Sources: *Black Americans in Defense of Our Nation,* p. 141; Lee, *Negro Medal of Honor Men,* p. 50.

1949 • Wesley A. Brown was the first black graduate of the U.S. Naval Academy at Annapolis.

Sources: *Black Americans in Defense of Our Nation,* p. 142; Baskin and Runes, *Dictionary of Black Culture,* p. 70.

Samuel P. Massie

1966 • Samuel Proctor Massie Jr. (1919–2005) was the first black faculty member of the U.S. Naval Academy at Annapolis. A former president of North Carolina Central University in Durham, he became a member of the chemistry department and remained on the academy faculty for over twenty-five years. A native of Little Rock, Arkansas, Massie, whose parents were schoolteachers, showed early evidence of intellectual precocity. He began to read when he was only two years old and graduated from high school at age thirteen. His enrollment in college was postponed for a year because of his youth. Only eighteen when he graduated from all-black Arkansas Agricultural, Mechanical, and Normal College (now the University of Arkansas at Pine Bluff), he earned a master's degree in chemistry from Fisk University in 1940. He taught for a year at his undergraduate alma mater before leaving for doctoral study at Iowa State University. He withdrew from graduate study temporarily in 1943, but worked at Iowa State as a chemistry research associate until 1946, when he was able to complete his dissertation and receive his doctorate. Massie then taught at his first graduate alma mater, Fisk, for one year, before working at Langston University in Oklahoma until 1953. During his last year at Langston, Massie achieved one of his most notable honors: He was elected president of the Oklahoma Academy of Science. He returned to Fisk in 1953, and it was there that he continued his research on phenothiazine and published a paper in 1954 that is regarded as a classic by chemistry researchers. Massie made two more moves before joining the faculty at Annapolis. He was associate program director for special projects in science education at the National Science Foundation from 1960 to 1963, while working part-time at Howard University. While in Washington, he was named one of the country's six best college-level chemistry teachers in 1961 by the Manufacturing Chemists Association. His move to North Carolina Central came in 1963, and he was serving as its president when he accepted the Annapolis position. Once again, he encountered racism when he had difficulty finding suitable housing and also was faced with students who had never had a black teacher. He went on to become one of the academy's most popular teachers. Appropriately, much of Massie's research at Annapolis focused on health among military personnel. In 1985 he and his research team were awarded a patent for an antibiotic to treat gonorrhea, and he also worked in the area of environmental science. Massie chaired the Maryland State Board of Community Colleges for ten of the twenty-one years that he was a member. In 1989 the Board established the Massie Science Prize, to be given to a student at one of its colleges. He was given a faculty achievement award in 1990 and made professor emeritus when he retired from Annapolis in 1994. His honors continued after retirement and so did his busy schedule. In 1993 Massie became the first black and only the second civilian to be made an honorary member of the National Naval Officers Association. He began work with the Bingwa Software Company, which uses multicultural models in the software it produces. He also continued to lecture and to publish. Many awards have recognized his achievements. The Department of Energy established its Chair of Excellence in his name in 1994 at ten colleges, nine of which are historically black and one that serves primarily students of Hispanic heritage. In 1998 he became one of the three blacks on the list of the world's seventy-five most distinguished chemists, identified by the *Chemical and Engineering News.* Perhaps the most ironic award was his honorary doctorate degree from the University of Arkansas in 1970, which once denied him admission because of his race. He was also honored by Iowa State, which gave him a Distinguished Achievement Citation in 1981.

Sources: *Black Americans in Defense of Our Nation,* p. 142; *Contemporary Black Biography,* vol. 29, pp. 101–04; Smith, *Notable Black American Men,* pp. 775–76; *Who's Who among African Americans,* 14th ed., p. 852.

1980 • Janie L. Mines was the first black woman student at the U.S. Naval Academy at Annapolis. In 1980 she became the first black woman to graduate from the academy.

Sources: *Black Americans in Defense of Our Nation,* p. 142; *Jet* 50 (27 June 76): 16.

1981 • Walter Nobles was the U.S. Naval Academy's first black brigade commander, the highest ranking midshipman at the academy, showing impressive leadership skills. He was born and raised in New York and majored in physical science.

Sources: *Black Americans in Defense of Our Nation*, p. 146.

Navy

1861 • In September the Secretary of the Navy authorized the enlistment of blacks into the U.S. Navy.

Sources: Anthony Powell, 'Portraits in Black: Buffalo Soldiers and Sailors." http://portraitsinblack.com/Navy.htm. Accessed September 27, 2012.

1863 • Robert Smalls (1839–1915) was the first and only black to attain the rank of captain in the U.S. Navy during the Civil War. He was a skilled pilot who took control of the armed Confederate dispatch boat, *The Planter,* in Charleston, South Carolina. With the help of eight black crewmen, Smalls put his family and other fugitives on board, and sailed it out of the harbor to turn it over as a prize of war to the Union Navy on May 13, 1862. The boat was eventually refitted as a gunboat, and Smalls was made a captain in the Union Navy. At the time of his heroic deed, Smalls was a slave. He was born in slave quarters in Beaufort, South Carolina, and his father is believed to have been a European. He was sold in 1851 to a slave owner who lived in Charleston, South Carolina. The owner allowed Smalls to work for pay outside of the plantation, and it was on his job for a ship rigger that he learned about sailing and became a superior sailor. He was employed on *The Planter* in 1861 and began hatching his plan to escape. He was initially commissioned as a second lieutenant in Company B, 33rd Regiment, U.S. Colored Troops; he was denied enlistment in the Federal Navy because he was not a graduate of the naval academy. His promotion to captain came as a result of his actions at the battle at Folly Creek, South Carolina. He was serving on *The Planter* when Confederate troops opened fire on it. Smalls took over after the white commander panicked, and he was able to bring the ship safely back to port. He left the navy at the end of the Civil War, but went on to a career as a politician. As a Republican congressman from South Carolina, he served longer than any other black during Reconstruction, although not in consecutive terms. When he left the House of Representatives in 1887, he became a customs collector, with his last post in his hometown of Beaufort. He held that position until his death.

Robert Smalls

Sources: Logan and Winston, *Dictionary of American Negro Biography,* pp. 56–61; Hornsby, *Chronology of African-American History,* p. 34; *Negro Almanac,* p. 833; Smith, *Notable Black American Men,* pp. 1071–73.

1864 • Robert Blake, powder boy aboard the USS *Marblehead,* was the first black awarded the Naval Medal of Honor "for conspicuous gallantry, extraordinary heroism, and intrepidity at the risk of his own life." The heroic action occurred during a victorious battle off the coast of South Carolina on December 23, 1863.

Sources: Bergman, *The Chronological History of the Negro in America,* p. 233; *Black Americans in Defense of Our Nation,* p. 54; Lee, *Negro Medal of Honor Men,* p. 35; *Negro Almanac,* p. 875.

1898 • Robert Penn (1872–?) was the only black seaman during the Spanish-American War period to receive the Naval Medal of Honor. On July 20, 1898, the USS *Iowa* was anchored off Santiago, Cuba, when an explosion occurred in the boiler room. Penn saved a coal handler, single-handedly averting an explosion that could have destroyed the *Iowa* and taken the lives of many crewmen. The medal was issued to Penn on December 14, 1898. Born in Virginia, Penn enlisted in the Navy and by early 1898 had progressed to Fireman Second Class.

Robert Penn

Sources: Lee, *Negro Medal of Honor Men,* p. 53; *Negro Almanac,* p. 876.

1917 • Alton Augustus Adams (1889–1987), bandmaster, was the first black bandleader in the U.S. Navy. Born in the Virgin Islands, he began music study at the age of nine (by correspondence) with Hugh A. Clarke of the University of Pennsylvania. Adams served as assistant director of the municipal band of St. Thomas, bandmaster of the U.S. Navy band at St. Thomas (the first and only black band in the navy), and supervisor of music of the Virgin Islands' public schools.

Sources: *Encyclopedia of Black America*, pp. 2–3; *Who's Who in Colored America, 1929*, p. 1.

Dorie Miller

1941 • Dorie Miller [Doris Miller] (1919–1943) was the first national black hero during World War II. He was honored with the Navy Cross in 1942, after pressure from newspapers and civil rights groups. Miller was a navy messman first class on the battleship *Arizona* at Pearl Harbor when the Japanese attacked on December 7, 1941. He manned a machine gun and shot down at least four Japanese planes despite the fact that, as a messman, he had not been trained in the use of a weapon. He moved his wounded commander to a safe place before going into action and did not stop firing until he ran out of ammunition and was ordered to abandon ship. His career in the navy was cut short by wartime tragedy. He was among the crew of the carrier *Liscome Bay* when it sank at sea after being struck by a torpedo on November 24, 1943. Thirty years later, in June 1973, the navy commissioned the USS *Miller* (a destroyer escort) in his honor. Born in Waco, Texas, to parents who were sharecroppers, Miller joined the U.S. Navy when he was nineteen, thinking that he would be eligible for fighting service. He, like all other black sailors, was assigned to a menial job in the only rank that was then open to blacks in the navy. Miller was denied promotion after his heroic deeds, and returned to his old navy duties after receiving the Navy Cross medal for gallantry, becoming the first black so honored.

Sources: Logan and Winston, *Dictionary of American Negro Biography*, pp. 434–35; *Encyclopedia of Black America*, p. 837; Lee, *Negro Medal of Honor Men*, p. 107; Smith, *Notable Black American Men*, pp. 814–15.

1942 • Bernard Whitfield Robinson (1918?–1972) became the first black commissioned officer in the U.S. Naval Reserve on June 18. The navy sought to increase the number of doctors in service and then offered commissions to medical students who, upon graduation, began tours of duty. After graduating from Harvard University, Robinson became the first black commissioned through the program, eventually serving as a doctor in the U.S. Naval Reserve. The Bureau of Naval Personnel, however, claimed that his commission had been a "slip." Robinson reported for duty after the "Golden Thirteen" were commissioned in March 1944.

Sources: *Jet* 100 (25 June 2001): 20.

1942 • Oscar Wayman Holmes (1916–2001) was commissioned in the U.S. Navy and reported to duty on September 28. When the navy received his birth certificate some time later, officials realized that they had commissioned their first black officer. (Until June this year, blacks were not officially enlisted except in the messman's branch.) After discovering that the navy had commissioned a black man, officials decided to let him remain, but in a rather unlikely location. Officials assigned Holmes to a seat on the Aviation Cadet Selection Board in New York City. Two years later, after he had learned to fly, he ferried aircraft with the Naval Air Transport Service, Air Ferry Squadron II located at Terminal Island, California. He remained there until he left the navy in 1945, when he became a lieutenant in the Naval Reserve.

Sources: *Washington Post* (2 December 2001).

1943 • William Baldwin became the first black recruit for the U.S. Navy's general service. Blacks were admitted to the navy according to their numbers (ten percent) of the total population.

Sources: "The History Place: African-Americans in World War II," http://www.historyplace .com/unitedstates/aframerwar/index.html. Accessed September 27, 2012.

1944 • The USS *Harmon* was the first U.S. Navy fighting ship named after a black. Leonard Roy Harmon (1916–1942) was a World War II naval hero who "deliberately exposed himself to hostile gunfire in order to protect a shipmate and as a result … was killed in action." He was awarded the Navy Cross.

Sources: *Black Americans in Defense of Our Nation,* p. 37; Baskin and Runes, *Dictionary of Black Culture,* p. 201.

Samuel Lee Gravely Jr.

1944 • Samuel Lee Gravely Jr. (1922–2004) was the first black ensign commissioned during World War II. He was released from active service after the war, but was recalled in 1949. In January 1962 Gravely was given command of the destroyer USS *Falgout.* This was the first time a black officer had been given command of a ship in the modern U.S. Navy. In 1963 Gravely and George I. Thompson were the first two blacks chosen to attend the Naval War College. Three years later, he entered the history books again as the first black commander to lead a ship—the USS *Taussig*—into offensive action. Gravely became the first black admiral in the U.S. Navy in 1971; he had earlier been the first black to achieve the rank of captain. His contributions to the navy continued when he became commander of the 3rd fleet in 1976. He was transferred from Hawaii to Virginia in 1978, when he became director of the Defense Communications Agency. Gravely retired from the navy in 1980 as a three-star admiral. He was born in Richmond, Virginia, into a family committed to government service. Gravely interrupted his college studies at Virginia Union University to enlist in the U.S. Naval Reserve in 1942. By the time he was assigned to his first ship in 1945, he had risen to the rank of captain; he was the first black officer on the ship. During his brief hiatus from the navy, Gravely completed his college work, graduating in 1948. He returned to active duty in the navy in 1952. After his retirement from the navy, he remained active as a consultant and a speaker. During the mid-1980s, he served as executive director of education and training for the Educational Foundation of the Armed Forces Communications and Electronics Association. His thirty-four years in the navy included service in three wars: World War II, the Korean War, and the Vietnam War. Gravely held numerous medals commemorating his service, including the Defense Distinguished Service Medal and the Bronze Star. On November 20, 2010, Gravely was honored posthumously when a guided-missile destroyer, the USS *Gravely* was commissioned in Wilmington, North Carolina. The vessel was hailed as "one of the most advanced ships ever developed." It is over 508 feet long and draws 31 feet of water. Over 380 officers and enlisted personnel serve aboard.

Sources: *Contemporary Black Biography,* vol. 5, pp. 102–4; vol. 49, pp. 48–50; *Jet* 92 (2 June 1997), p. 22; Lee, *Negro Medal of Honor Men,* p. 118; Salzman, *Encyclopedia of African-American Culture and History,* Supplement, p. 118; Smith, *Notable Black American Men,* pp. 473–75.

1944 • The first black women were sworn into the WAVEs. The U.S. Navy accepted only seventy-two enlisted women and two officers. Bessie Garrett became the first black woman admitted. Lieutenant Harriet Ida Pickens and Ensign Frances Willis were the first black women that the WAVEs commissioned; they completed their training on December 13 this year. The WAVEs were incorporated into the regular navy in 1948, thirty years before the WACs were incorporated into the regular army.

Sources: *Black Americans in Defense of Our Nation,* p. 93; Hine, *Black Women in America,* pp. 794–95.

1944 • In March the U.S. Navy knowingly commissioned its first black officers. There were thirteen blacks, including twelve ensigns and one warrant officer. The men later dubbed themselves the "Golden Thirteen." The navy subsequently accepted their designation in recognition of their pioneering efforts to integrate that branch of the military. During World War II, the U.S. Navy commissioned about sixty black Americans.

Sources: *The Golden 13.*

1944 • The USS *Mason,* commissioned at Boston Naval Yard on March 20, was the U.S. Navy's first warship with a predominantly black crew and at least one black officer. The destroyer escort was sometimes called "Eleanor's Folly," in recognition of Eleanor Roosevelt, who had pushed for desegregation of the armed forces. Skipper William M. Blackford provided superior leadership and had the support of the committed men. The ship was sold for scrap in 1947 and its history has been preserved at the Boston National Historical Park.

Sources: "Proudly We Served: The Story of USS Mason and Her Crew," http://www.ussmason.org. Accessed September 27, 2012.

1944 • The first submarine chaser with an all-black crew was the *PC 1264*. Initially, the ship was commissioned by white officers and petty officers, but later the blacks replaced the petty officers. The next year, Ensign Samuel L. Gravely Jr., was assigned to the ship.

Sources: *Black Americans in Defense of Our Nation,* p. 35.

1945 • Phyllis Mae Dailey was the first black woman to serve as a nurse in the U.S. Navy.

Sources: Baskin and Runes, *Dictionary of Black Culture,* p. 125; Hine, *Black Women in America,* vol. 1, pp. 795–96.

1949 • Jesse Leroy Brown (1926–1950) was the first black pilot in the Naval Reserve, and on December 4, 1950, was the first black aviator to die in combat, losing his life in Korea. He received the Distinguished Flying Cross, Air Medal, and Purple Heart posthumously. In 1973 he was the first black officer to have a Knox-class ocean escort ship, the USS *Jesse L. Brown,* named after him. The ship was commissioned at the Boston Naval Yard. He was honored again in 1997, when the Jesse L. Brown Memorial Combined Bachelor Quarters were dedicated at the Naval Air Station in Meridian, Mississippi. Another honor came to him in 2000, when a $2.6 million county tax building in Hattiesburg, Mississippi, was named for him. Brown was a native of Hattiesburg. He earned his pilot wings in 1948 and became a member of the 32nd Fighter Squad, where he soon became a section leader, pointing the way toward his courageous acts during wartime.

Sources: *Black Americans in Defense of Our Nation,* pp. 48–49; Kane, *Famous First Facts,* pp. 90, 561; *Jet* 92 (10 November 1997): 17; 99 (19 March 2001): 20; Lee, *Negro Medal of Honor Men,* p. 14.

Carl Brashear

1965 • Carl Maxie Brashear (1931–2006) became the U.S. Navy's first black diver. He also became the navy's first black master diver, and later the first amputee to earn a master diver certificate. He went on to become a master chief, the highest navy's rank for an enlisted man. Brashear, one of eight children, was born in Tonieville, Kentucky, into a family that he is said to have described as poor but happy. He left high school without graduating, and when he was seventeen years old he enlisted in the navy, where he developed an interest in diving. This was not an activity that was usually open to blacks, and he had to endure racial bias and threats in his quest to become a diver. His determination prevailed, enabling Brashear to progress through the ranks to acting master diver and in-port duty chief. Tragedy struck in 1966, when an accident occurred off the coast of Palomares, Spain, while Brashear and his crew were recovering a nuclear bomb that had been lost. While trying to load the recovered bomb into a crate, the boat moorings broke, and Brashear suffered multiple leg fractures. He encountered delays in getting medical attention, and after being transferred to an Air Force base in New Jersey, he gave permission to amputate his lower left leg, with full expectations of returning to diving. To everyone's astonishment except his own, he entered diving school, fitted with a plastic leg. He achieved the rank of master diver in 1977, and retired in 1979 as a master diver and master chief petty officer. He worked for the government as an engineering technician until 1993. The film *Men of Honor,* which opened in 2000, tells the Brashear story. Brashear served as a military consultant for the movie. In 1998 he became one of only seven enlisted men and the second black enlisted man to be placed in naval archives. (Dorie Miller, a hero at Pearl Harbor, was the first.) In 2000 Brashear received the Secretary of Defense Award for public service when *Men of Honor* was shown at a private screening in Washington, D.C. In 2001 he was given the keys to the city of Newark, New Jersey, when the city opened the twenty-seventh year of the Newark Black Film Festival. His medals and awards are numerous, including not only achievement medals for service in China and Korea, but also eight Good Conduct medals. In 2009 a U.S. Navy ship was named in his honor.

Sources: *Contemporary Black Biography,* vol. 29, pp. 23–25; *Jet* 86 (18 July 1994): 37; 98 (13 November 2000): 60–64; 100 (30 July 2001): 12.

1966 • Thomas David Parham Jr. (1920–2007) was the first black chaplain in the U.S. Navy to attain the rank of captain. A native of Newport News, Virginia, Parham was a chaplain assigned to the Naval Air Station at Quonset Point, Rhode Island. He graduated *magna cum laude* from North Carolina Central University in Durham in 1941, and went on to earn bachelor's and master's degrees in sacred theology with honors from Pittsburgh Theological Seminary. He later earned a master's degree and doctorate from American University in Washington, D.C. Parham was in the U.S. Navy from 1944 to 1982, and holds life membership in the Military Chaplains Association. He received the Legion of Merit award in 1982. His career as a minister has included the pastorate of city churches and service as a university chaplain at Duke University and North Carolina Central Univerity, in addition to his work in the military.

Thomas Parham Jr.

Sources: Kane, *Famous First Facts,* p. 418; Lee, *Negro Medal of Honor Men,* p. 121; *Who's Who among African Americans,* 14th ed., p. 999.

1971 • Samuel L. Gravely Jr. (1922–2004), a veteran of three wars, became the first black admiral in U.S. history. He received two stars, advancing him to rear admiral. The Senate confirmed his promotion on May 15, 1971. After thirty-eight years in the Navy, Gravely retired in 1980 as a three-star vice admiral.

Sources: *Jet* 92 (2 June 1997): 22; Smith, *Notable Black American Men,* pp. 473–75.

1972 • Richard E. Williams (1934–) was the first black to command a naval unit in the deep South.

Sources: *Encyclopedia of Black America,* p. 859.

1974 • Vivian McFadden was the first black woman U.S. Navy chaplain.

Sources: Kane, *Famous First Facts,* p. 419.

1975 • Donna P. Davis became the first black woman physician in the Naval Medical Corps.

Sources: Hine, *Black Women in America,* vol. 1, p. 795.

1993 • The first woman executive officer on an American warship, the USS *Tortuga,* was Michelle Howard (1960–). As its executive officer in 1996, she was the first woman to serve in the number-two position on an American warship. In March 1999 Howard was named commander of the USS *Rushmore,* becoming the first woman captain of the ship and the first black woman to command a U.S. Navy combat vessel. Howard, who grew up in Aurora, Colorado, was the daughter of an air force master sergeant, with a brother who was in the navy. She decided at age twelve that she wanted to go to the U.S. Naval Academy, even though the academy still denied women admission at the time. The restrictions were lifted by the time she graduated from high school in 1978, and when she graduated from the academy in 1982, she was a member of one of the first coeducational classes. She went on to earn a master's degree in military arts and sciences from the U.S. Army's Command and General Staff College in 1998. Like some other blacks in the navy, Howard faced gender and racial bias, but also found opportunities for advancement and fair compensation. She has been given assignments at home and abroad, including serving as tactical action officer during Operation Desert Shield/Desert Storm from 1990 to 1992. In 1992, she became the first black woman to reach the rank of rear admiral. She was transferred to a position in 2002 in which she worked with the Joint Chiefs of Staff. Howard's awards have come throughout her career, beginning with the Secretary of the Navy/Navy League Captain Winifred Collins Award, which she received in 1987. The award is presented each year to one female officer who has demonstrated leadership abilities. She has also been awarded the Kuwaiti Liberation Medal and the Saudi-Arabia Defense Medal.

Michelle Howard

Sources: *Contemporary Black Biography,* vol. 28, pp. 98–100; *Ebony* 54 (September 1999): 102; *Essence* 31 (May 2000): 130.

The First Black Four-Star Admiral

J. Paul Reason

In 1996 J. Paul Reason (1941–) became the first black four-star admiral in the U.S. Navy. With promotion came his assignment as commander-in-chief of the U.S. Atlantic Fleet in Norfolk, Virginia. At the time of his promotion, he was assigned to the Pentagon, serving as deputy chief of naval operations for plans, policy, and operations. Earlier in his naval career, Reason had commanded surface ships in the Atlantic and had served as a naval aide to President Jimmy Carter. (His promotion left the U.S. Marine Corps the only branch of armed services without a black four-star officer.) Born in Washington, D.C., he graduated from the U.S. Naval Academy at Annapolis. Reason held the commander-in-chief post until 1999, after which he established Reason and Associates in Chesapeake Bay, Maryland. His career in the navy spanned three decades; he saw action in the Vietnam War, and received three medals for his service there.

Sources: *Jet* 90 (3 June 1996): 20; *Who's Who among African Americans,* 26th ed., p. 1030.

1994 • Brigitte Lott (1973?–) was named ROTC battalion commander at Norfolk State University, becoming the first black woman in the nation to hold such a post. She was the number-one midshipman and would lead the 285-member battalion during the 1994–95 academic year. Lott was a senior at the school, majoring in English.

Sources: *Jet* 86 (19 September 1994): 10.

1994 • Commander Donnie Cochran (1954–) became the first black to head the U.S. Navy's Blue Angel precision flying team in November. He was at the time the only black pilot in the Blue Angels, who were based at the Naval Air Station in Pensacola, Florida. Cochran stepped down from his position in 1996 and retired from the navy, fearing that his flying was not as safe as it should be and thus might have a negative impact on the flying team. A native of Pelham, Georgia, he is a graduate of Savannah State College, with a degree in civil engineering. Cochran entered the U.S. Navy after graduation in 1976, commissioned as a lieutenant commander. He joined the Blue Angels in 1985, becoming the first black member of the team.

Sources: *Jet* 87 (5 December 1994): 32; 90 (17 June 1996): 46; *Who's Who among African Americans,* 13th ed., p. 257.

1996 • Monje Malak Abd al-Muta Ali Noel Jr. became the first Islamic chaplain to serve in the U.S. Navy. The lieutenant junior-grade was the second Islamic chaplain to serve in the U.S. armed forces, following Imam Abdul-Rasheed Muhammad, who was appointed an army chaplain. Noel, who was born in Salem, New Jersey, saw duty at several U.S. Navy posts before he was commissioned. He did his undergraduate work at Wilmington College in Delaware and earned a master's degree in business administration from New Hampshire College Graduate School for Business. Noel later earned a Master of Divinity degree from a program offered jointly by the Lutheran School of Theology and the American Islamic College in Chicago. He spent twelve years in the navy as an enlisted man before he was honorably discharged, which preceded his being commissioned as an officer. He was the recipient of several navy medals during his years of active duty.

Sources: *Jet* 90 (17 June 1996): 36–37; *Who's Who among African Americans,* 14th ed., p. 977.

1998 • The first black active-duty admiral in the Navy Medical Corps was James A. Johnson. He had served in the U.S. Navy for thirty-two years when he was promoted to admiral. When he entered the service in 1966, he held the rank of ensign, and served as senior medical officer aboard the USS *New Orleans* on his first assignment. Johnson did his undergraduate work at Oberlin College, received his medical degree from the University of Rochester, and did his internship and residency at the University of California at Los Angeles. In July 1998, he held the position of principal director for Clinical Services in the office of the Assistant Secretary of Defense for Health Affairs, in Washington, D.C.

Sources: *Jet* 94 (6 July 1998): 4.

2000 • Rear Admiral Lillian Elaine Fishburne became the first black woman admiral in the U.S. Navy. She became deputy director of fleet liaison at the Space, Information Warfare, Command and Control Directorate. A native of Rockville, Fishburne graduated from Lincoln University in Pennsylvania and received a master's degree from Webster College in St. Louis and a second master's, in telecommunication systems management, from the Naval Postgraduate School. She became a naval computer and telecommunications expert.

Sources: *Ebony* 50 (October 2000): 15.

Lillian Fishburne

2001 • Carroll Antoine was named deputy audit general for the National Audit Service in the U.S. Navy, becoming the first black civilian to hold that post. He would be based in Washington, D.C.

Sources: *Jet* 99 (16 April 2001): 18.

2001 • The first black woman member of the U.S. Navy's search-and-rescue team was Lieutenant Shelly Frank.

Sources: *Jet* 99 (6 February 2001): 19.

Persian Gulf War (Operation Desert Storm)

1991 • Adrienne Mitchell was the first black woman to die in combat in the Persian Gulf War.

Sources: Blackfacts.com, http://www.blackfacts.com/fact/75cf5713-ddcf-4169-9bfd-6f5c21 071352. Accessed September 27, 2012.

World War I

1917 • Eugene Bullard (1894–1961) became the first black combat pilot on August 27, and was the only black pilot to fly during World War I. When the United States entered the war in April 1917, Americans who flew for France were eligible for a U.S. Army commission. Bullard, who had been a member of the French Foreign Legion and the French Army, presented himself to the army, but his application was rejected. He flew for the French air service. Pressure from the American forces led to his being grounded; an injured leg was one of the several possible reasons offered for this action. Bullard flew more than twenty combat missions. For his daring flights Bullard was nicknamed the "Black Swallow of Death." He also became a highly decorated combat pilot, including receipt of the *Croix de Guerre*. Bullard was born in Columbus, Georgia. While growing up, he was witness to racial atrocities, including the murder of his brother by a gang of whites. At age eight, he ran away from home and eventually made his way to France, after spending some time in Scotland and England. He went to Paris with a musical troupe called "Freedmen's Pickaninnies." Bullard led a colorful life: he once boxed professionally, owned a jazz club in Paris, and carried his pet monkey with him on combat flights. He fought briefly with the French at the beginning of World War II. His last job was as an elevator operator in the Empire State Building. The *Today* show featured a segment on him in 1954, and the Smithsonian Institution's National Air and Space Museum honored him in 1994. He was residing in Harlem when he died.

Eugene Bullard

Sources: Carisella, *The Black Swallow of Death*; Cockfield, "All Blood Runs Red," *American Legacy* (February/March 1955), pp. 7–15; *Contemporary Black Biography*, vol. 12, pp. 24–26; Smith, *Notable Black American Men*, pp. 148–50.

MISCELLANEOUS

Aviation

1921 • Bessie Coleman (1893–1926) was the first black woman to become an aviator and to gain an international pilot's license from the Fédération Aéronautique Internationale. Coleman, who envisioned opening a flight school, was also the first black woman "barnstormer," or stunt pilot. In May 1922 she went to Europe for advanced training in stunt flying and parachute jumping, receiving training in France, Holland, Germany, and Switzerland. When she returned to Chicago, the *Chicago Defender* became her sponsor. On Labor Day 1922, Coleman gave her first exhibition in the United States, at Garden City, Long Island, New York. In October that year she performed in the Chicago region and gave successful exhibitions throughout the Midwest. From 1922 to 1926 she lectured in Texas, Florida, and elsewhere, refusing to perform if the audiences were segregated. She prepared for a barnstorming show in Jacksonville, Florida, to be held on April 30, 1926, as a fundraiser for the Negro Welfare League. When Coleman and her co-pilot, William D. Wills, tried out their open-air plane in preparation for the exhibition, the equipment malfunctioned and both died as a result. Coleman was born in Atlanta, Texas, one of thirteen children. While Coleman was still a young child, the family relocated to Waxahachie,

Bessie Coleman

Texas. She loved to read biographies of black achievers. She spent one year at the Teacher's College in Langston, Oklahoma, but dropped out due to financial reasons. Sometime between 1915 and 1917 Coleman moved to Chicago where her brothers John and Walter lived. There she studied at Burham's School of Beauty Culture where she learned the beauty trade. She worked as a manicurist at a barbershop near Comiskey Park, where the White Sox played baseball. She earned enough income to relocate her mother and other family members to Chicago in 1917. Coleman heard stories from the men in the barbershop about black aviators in the armed services and those serving with French units. She became so curious about their activities that she read as many articles about black aviators as she could find. After learning that there were women pilots in France and that some American women were pilots a well, she developed an interest in learning to fly. She was encouraged to study in France and entered the most famous flight school in that country. In 1995 the U.S. Postal Service issued a stamp in the Black Heritage Series honoring Coleman.

Sources: Gubert, Sawyer, and Fanning, *Distinguished African Americans in Aviation and Space Science,* pp. 77–80; Hine, *Black Women in America,* pp. 262–63; Schultz and Hart, *Women Building Chicago, 1790–1990,* pp. 178–80; Smith, *Notable Black American Women,* pp. 202–203.

1932 • The first black aviator to be licensed by the U.S. Department of Commerce was James Herman Banning (1879–1933). An army officer, a friend of his family in Iowa, taught him to fly in 1924. Banning and his mechanic, Thomas Allen, flew across the United States on September 19, 1932, becoming the first blacks to do so. They completed their pioneering journey from Los Angeles to New York on October 9, after spending twenty-two hours in flight over a twenty-day period. They financed the flight with the only money they had (twenty-five dollars) and with contributions from supporters. On February 5, 1933, Banning died in San Diego in an airplane crash—in an aircraft that he did not pilot.

Sources: *Jet* 89 (12 February 1996): 14; Powell, *Black Wings,* p. 92.

1933 • Albert Ernest Forsythe and Charles Alfred Anderson were the first black pilots to make a round-trip transcontinental flight. They left Atlantic City on July 17, 1933, in their Fairchild 24 plane called *The Pride of Atlantic City,* arrived safely in Los Angeles, and completed their round trip on July 28.

Sources: Powell, *Black Wings,* pp. 181–88.

1934 • Willa Brown-Chappell (1906–1992) was the first black woman in the United States to hold a commercial pilot's license, and the first black woman to gain officer rank (lieutenant) in the Civil Air Patrol Squadron. In 1937 Brown and Cornelius R. Coffee, who was her flight instructor and also became her husband, formed the National Airmen's Association of America, the first black aviators' group. Its mission was to promote black aviation. In 1972, Brown-Chappell was the first black member of the Federal Aviation Agency's Women's Advisory Commission. Brown-Chappell was born in Glasgow, Kentucky, and relocated to Indianapolis with her family when she was about six years old. Still later the family moved to Terre Haute, Indiana. In 1927 she graduated from Indiana State Teachers College and then taught school in Gary, Indiana. Five years later she moved to Chicago and taught in the local schools. She began graduate study at Northwestern University in 1934, graduating three years later. While at Northwestern Brown-Chappell developed an interest in aviation and began to take flying lessons. Her friend, aviator Bessie Coleman, had inspired her. In 1935 she received a master mechanic's certificate from the Aeronautical University located in the Chicago Loop. After obtaining her private pilot's license, she became affiliated with a flight service at Harlem Airport and gave short entertainment jaunts for those who would pay one dollar for the ride. After Brown-Chappell, her husband Cornelius R. Coffee, and journalist Enoc P. Waters, Jr. founded the National Airmen's Association of America in 1939, she was elected national secretary of the organization. She also began to teach aviation in the Works Progress Administration's Adult Education Program and worked to stimulate blacks to prepare for careers in aviation through the children's flight clubs that she founded. In the early 1940s Brown-Chappell taught aviation mechanics in the Chicago schools. In 1946 she was the first black woman to run for a congressional seat, but was unsuccessful in her bid.

Sources: *Atlanta Constitution* (22 July 1992); Gubert, Sawyer, and Fanning, *Distinguished African Americans in Aviation and Space Science,* pp. 47–52 (Brown-Chappell); pp. 73–77 (Coffey); *Nashville Banner,* 21 July 1992; Smith, *Notable Black American Women,* Book II, pp. 69–71.

1940 • Willa Brown-Chappell and Cornelius R. Coffey (1903–1944), then a husband and wife team, established the first black-owned flying school, the Coffey School of Aeronautics at Harlem Airport in southwest Chicago. (Some sources say that the school was founded in 1938 or 1939.) This was the first black-owned school certified by the Civil Aviation Authority. The school trained approximately two hundred pilots within the next seven years, and Coffey helped to establish standards that affect aviation today. Pilots flying into Chicago who make their final course correction do so at a point over Lake Calumet. This action was called the Cofey Fix, named for Coffey but shortened due to Federal Aviation Administration regulations. Coffey's first career was in the automotive industry, but in 1927 Charles Lindbergh's trans-Atlantic flight spurred him to become a pilot. He later became the first black to hold both a pilot's and a master mechanic's license. Some of the students who graduated from his school went on to become part of the 99th

Pursuit Squadron, also known as the Tuskegee Airmen—the first black fighter squadron, located at Tuskegee Institute in Alabama. Coffey's aviation school closed in 1945.

Sources: Gubert, Sawyer, and Fanning, *Distinguished African Americans in Aviation and Space Science,* pp. 47–52 (Brown-Chappell); pp. 73–77 (Coffey); *Jet 85* (21 March 1994): 14.

1942 • The first black American hired as a design engineer by Republic Aviation was O. S. "Ozzie" Williams (1921–). He was co-developer of small rocket engines that saved the lives of the *Apollo 13* astronauts in 1970, when the main rocket exploded. Williams was born in Washington, D.C., and in 1943 became the second black American to receive a degree in aeronautical engineering. In 1947 he received his master's degree in the field from New York University. Around the time he graduated from college Williams joined the technical staff for Republic Aviation as a design engineer. He was promoted through the ranks quickly and four years later became a senior aerodynamicist. He helped to design the P47 *Thunderbird,* an escort plane used during World War II to protect high-altitude bombers. The aircraft was pivotal in this country's war efforts. After receiving his master's degree, Williams joined Babcock and Wilcox company as a design draftsman. He was a technical writer for the U.S. Naval Material Catalog Office from 1948 to 1950, and then joined Greer Hydraulics, Inc., in an engineering position. He led a group project that developed the first experimental airborne radio beacon that determined where crashed planes were located. Williams, a pioneer in the area of small rocket design, moved to the Reaction Motors Division of Thiokol Chemical Corporation in 1956. He left that position in 1961 to become propulsion engineer with Grumman Aerospace Corporation and there managed the development of the *Apollo* lunar module control system. He managed projects that enabled crew members of *Apollo 13* to re-enter the earth's atmosphere. He joined the marketing department of Grumman International in 1973 and conducted a market survey mission in West Africa. The next year was named as vice president. In the 1980s he served as a marketing professor at St. John's University.

Sources: *Contemporary Black Biography,* vol. 13, pp. 237–39; Smith, *The African American Almanac,* 8th ed., pp. 1143, 1167.

1957 • Perry H. Young (1919–1998) became the first black captain (pilot) on a scheduled commercial airline, New York airways. His historic flight took place on February 5, when he co-piloted a twelve-passenger helicopter. Ironically, Young took his first airplane ride in July 1937, in Oberlin, Ohio, a few days after Amelia Earhart disappeared on her flight around the world. His career as an aviator spanned over fifty years. In World War II he was one of the first black flight instructors in the U.S. Army Air Corps, assigned to the 99th Pursuit Squadron, later highly decorated and known as the Tuskegee Airmen. Young taught more than 150 pilots, many who went on to fight in the war. One of his students, Lee A. Archer (1921?–) became the only black fighter ace; during combat he shot down five enemy planes. When the war ended and no commercial airline would hire him, for ten years Williams operated his own commercial flight service as a contract pilot and flight mechanic in Haiti, Puerto Rico, and the U.S. Virgin Islands. He became a licensed helicopter and airplane pilot. Seventeen years later he broke the color barrier at New York airways, a firm that now aggressively sought to integrate its professional staff. Young was born in Orangeburg, South Carolina, and grew up in Oberlin, Ohio. He was educated at Oberlin College, Howard University, Spartan School of Aeronautics, and at the American Flyers School in Fort Worth, Texas. Young was a member of the Airline Pilots Association, the American Helicopter Society, the Organization of Black Airline Pilots, and a founding member of Negro Airmen International. He received the outstanding achievement award from the Organization of Black Airline Pilots in 1979. He died of cancer on November 8, 1998, at Horton Medical Center in Middletown, New York.

Sources: *Who's Who among African Americans,* 10th ed., p. 1687; *New York Times* (18 November 1998).

1963 • Former Air Force captain and Korean War pilot Marlon Green, who challenged the airlines' hiring policies, won a landmark judgment against Continental Airlines in the U.S. Supreme Court this year, thus opening interstate commercial airlines to black pilots.

Sources: *New York Times* (18 November 1998).

The First Black Flight Attendant

In 1958 Ruth Carol Taylor (1931–) became the first black flight attendant. She broke the color barrier as a means of fighting discrimination rather than due to her interest in becoming a flight attendant. For more than a year major airlines had rejected her application; then at age twenty-five, Mohawk Airlines hired her and assigned her to travel between New York and other points such as Massachusetts and Michigan. Taylor is a native of Trumansburg, New York. She studied at the Bellevue Hospital Nursing School and became a private nurse. In later life, she continued her fight against injustice. She also wrote *The Little Black Book,* a survival guide for young black men in a racist society.

Sources: Gubert, Sawyer, and Fannin, *Distinguished African Americans in Aviation and Space Science,* pp. 268–71; *Jet* 91 (12 May 1997): 40; 13 (6 February 1958), cover, 22–23.

1970 • Otis B. Young Jr. was the first black pilot of a 740 jumbo jet.

Sources: Alford, *Famous First Blacks,* p. 70; Lee, *Interesting People,* p. 202.

1971 • James O. Plinton Jr. (1914–1996) was the first black top executive of a major airline, Eastern Airlines. A graduate of Lincoln University in Pennsylvania, Plinton became a pilot instructor for the United States Army Air Corps in 1935 and was the first black to complete the Air Corps' Central Instructors School in 1944. He was one of the first black flight instructors in the famed 99th Pursuit Squadron. Plinton was the first black to co-organize an airline outside the United States; Quisqueya, Lte. in Port-au-Prince, Haiti, was established in 1948. He joined Trans World Airlines in 1950 and became vice president for marketing affairs for Eastern in 1971.

Sources: *Black Enterprise* 10 (September 1979): 59–60; *Ebony Success Library,* vol. 1, p. 250; *Encyclopedia of Black America,* pp. 146, 678; *Who's Who among Black Americans, 1992–93,* pp. 1130–31; Smith, *Notable Black American Men,* pp. 943–44.

1978 • Jill Brown (1950–) became the first black female pilot for a major commercial airline, Texas International Airlines. Born in Millersville, Maryland, she began flying at age seventeen. Her father, a U.S. Air Force instrument mechanic and building contractor, had purchased a single-engine Piper Cherokee. They used the plane to travel the United States and the Caribbean, referring to themselves as Brown's United Airline. Brown first soloed in 1967 and later earned her private pilot license. She graduated from the University of Maryland at College Park in 1973 and continued to fly, earning her instrument, commercial, and instructor licenses. Encouraged to pursue a career in military aviation, she contacted a U.S. Navy recruiter and became the first black woman accepted for pilot training in the military. After attending officers' candidate school at Newport, Rhode Island, and naval flying school in Pensacola, Florida, she had a short career in the military. Her primary aim was to become a pilot for a major airline. After six months, she left and taught in the Baltimore schools. Brown later worked for a commuter airline in North Carolina, performing odd jobs such as selling tickets, serving airplanes, and serving as copilot. She flew for Wheeler Airlines, accumulating eight hundred hours. Then Texas International Airlines hired her. Brown and five other women graduated from officer training in 1978 when she was made a first officer. Still her goal was to become the first black woman captain. She flew from Albuquerque, New Mexico, to small towns within that state. The airline later underwent a series of mergers.

Sources: Salem, *African American Women,* pp. 70–71; *Jet* 47 (24 October 1974): 19; Lowe and Clift, *Encyclopedia of Black America,* p. 146.

1984 • Air Atlanta became the first major black-owned airline and was considered a major success for black business. Its founder, Michael Hollis (1955?–), then age twenty-nine, raised over $45 million to launch the airline. The company had four hundred employees and a fleet of five rebuilt Boeing 727–100 jets. It severed Atlanta, New York, Miami, and Memphis. A lack of capital led to the airline filing for bankruptcy in 1987. Hollis grew up in Atlanta and graduated from Dartmouth College. He received his law degree from the University of Virginia and became vice president for public financing at the New York investment banking firm, Oppenheimer & Co. He held several positions in the area of transportation before starting his own low-fare airline.

Sources: "Air Atlanta Works Toward Strengthening its Position," *Air Transport World* 22 (June 1985): 14; "Where Are They Now," *Black Enterprise* 31 (August 2000): 163; *Jet* 98 (12 June 2000): 36–37.

1987 • Erma Chansler Johnson (1942–) was the first black and the first woman to chair the Dallas/Fort Worth International Airport Board of Directors. Born in Leggett, Texas, Johnson was educated at Prairie View Agricultural and Mechanical University (B.S., 1963) and Bowling Green State University (M.Ed., 1968). She taught at Tarrant County Junior College in Fort Worth, Texas, and later became director of personnel and then vice chancellor for human resources at the college. She was also active in numerous civic activities in Fort Worth and Tarrant County.

Sources: *Who's Who among Black Americans,* 26th ed., p. 668.

1995 • Airline pioneer Patrice Clarke Washington (1961–) flew United Parcel Service's DC–8 from Miami to Atlanta and became the first black woman captain to fly for the company. She joined UPS in May 1988 as a DC–8 flight engineer. In 2000 she was among the Trumpet Award honorees recognized in ceremonies in Atlanta. Washington was born in Nassau, Bahamas, and took her first flight, a trip to Miami at age five. She attended Embry-Riddle Aeronautical University in Daytona Beach, Florida, graduating in April 1982 with a commercial pilot's certificate and a Bachelor of Science degree in aeronautical science. She was the first black woman to graduate from the school with a commercial pilot's license. She was a pilot for Trans Island Airways, a charter company in the Bahamas, from 1982 to 1984. Washington then served as a first officer and the first black woman pilot with BahamasAir from 1984 to 1988, flying Boeing 748s and 737s. Racism and sexism followed her. She recalls a passenger who refused to fly on planes that she piloted. United Parcel Services hired her as a flight engineer in May 1988; she worked on three-crew member flights from UPS's home base in Louisville to Anchorage, Alaska, Australia, and Cologne, Germany. In January 1990 UPS promoted her to first officer. She was promoted to captain in November 1994. At that time there were only eleven black women pilots working for top airlines in the United States. Washington is married to Ray Washington, a pilot for a major airline, and lives in Chicago.

Sources: *Jet* 87 (6 March 1995): 34; 97 (31 January 2000): 15; *Contemporary Black Biography,* vol. 12, pp. 219–22; *Ebony* 50 (July 1995): 74–78.

1999 • Hansel Tookes was named president and chief operating officer of Raytheon Aircraft Company and became the first black to hold the position. Raytheon manufactures aircraft for commercial, military, and regional use. Since 1996 Tookes served as president of Pratt & Whitney's Large Military Engines group based in West Palm Beach, Florida. Tookes graduated from the University of West Florida with a master's degree in aeronautical systems.

Sources: *Jet* 96 (18 October 1999): 20.

2000 • When Southwest Airlines named Ellen Torbert (1958?–) to the office of vice president of reservations, she became the company's first black officer. Her responsibilities included guiding and directing over 6,000 reservations employees and ensuring effective operations in the firm's nine reservations centers. Born in Toledo, Ohio, Torbert graduated from Western Michigan University and in March 1987 joined Southwest as a reservations sales agent in the Dallas center. She was promoted in May 1991 to reservations supervisor; later she became manager of reservations training, and in September 1993 she was promoted to director.

Sources: *Tennessee Tribune* (13–19 July 2000); *Ebony* 56 (November 2000): 10.

2000 • Gustavus "Gus" McLeod (1955–), an amateur aviator, took off in a 1939 Boeing Stearman open-cockpit biplane on April 17 and flew a 3,500-mile odyssey over the North Pole. He became the first person to fly over the pole in such aircraft. His achievement was included in the *Congressional Record* on May 3. McLeod was born in Corinth, Mississippi, and graduated from Catholic University in Washington, D.C., in 1976, with a degree in chemical engineering. His interest in flying developed early. He flew his first airplane, an open-cockpit aircraft used in a crop-dusting business, at age thirteen. While the pilot had allowed McLeod to take the controls when the two took flights, McLeod's first solo flight actually came when took the aircraft without the pilot's permission. In an effort to remove his son from what he saw as potential danger, McLeod's father moved the family to Washington, D.C. After graduating from college, McLeod became a chemical engineer for the Central Intelligence Agency and later for the Raytheon Corporation. He bought a surgical supply company in Gaithersberg, Maryland, and also received a beer distributorship. Still interested in flying, in 1995 he bought an open-cockpit aircraft similar to the one that he took in his solo flight. He spent $75,000 to refurbish the aircraft. A television documentary about the failed efforts of pilots who tried to reach the North Pole in two closed-cockpit planes fascinated McLeod. When McLeod took the historic trip, a film crew from the National Geographic Society trailed him in a chase plane. The National Geographic Society provided partial funding for McLeod's trip. The two planes reached the North Pole on April 17, 2000. McLeod's Stearman broke down on the return flight and later the New York Air National Guard retrieved it. McLeod donated the plane to the College Park Aviation Museum.

Sources: *Contemporary Black Biography,* vol. 27, pp. 138–41; *Jet* 97 (15 May 2000): 20–21.

2006 • At age fourteen, Jonathan Strickland became the youngest solo pilot to fly a helicopter and airplane on the same day.

Sources: *Jet* 110 (14 August 2006): 20–21; 23–24; 113 (7 April 2008): 42.

2007 • Young Miami pilot Barrington Irving (1984–) ended a 97-day 27,000-mile flight at Opa-locka Executive Airport outside Miami and became the first black and youngest pilot to fly solo around the globe. The twenty-three-year-old pilot named his single-engine piston plane *Inspiration,* saying "that's what he wanted to be to young people." He aimed to lure young people away from the streets and encourage them to exceed his record-setting feat. After he was introduced to aviation at age fifteen, he became licensed as a commercial, private pilot and as flight instructor. His plane, a Columbia 400 aircraft, was built from donated parts at a cost of $300,000. Irving's solo trip took him across the Atlantic to Europe, the Middle East, and Asia. Born in Jamaica, he grew up in Miami and graduated from historically black Florida Memorial University. He founded a non-profit organization, Experience Aviation Inc., which aimed to expose youth to careers in aviation.

Sources: *Jet* 112 (16 July 2007): 30, 32.

2008 • Flying ace Kelly Anyadiki, then sixteen years old, set a world record as the youngest black female to solo in four different aircraft. Anyadiki and another flying ace, Jonathan Strickland, were part of a program of the Tomorrow's Aeronautical Museum which was designed to attract inner city and minority youths to flight training.

Sources: *Jet* 113 (7 April 2008): 42.

Beauty Industry and Models

1937 • Adrienne Fidelin became the first black model to appear in a mainstream fashion magazine when her photograph was published in *Harper's Bazaar.* The spread containing the picture was captioned "The Bushongo of Africa Sends His Hats to Paris." Three white models appeared as well; however, Fidelin's picture was not integrated into their shoot. Instead, she appeared on one side with their image on the other; she wore a headdress and African jewelry.

1947 • The Brandford Modeling Agency, founded by Edward Brandford (1908?–), was the first licensed black modeling agency in the country. Their models were known as "Brandford Lovelies." Brandford was born in Jamaica, British West Indies, and was apprenticed to a British academician to study painting. He entered Cooper Union Art School in New York City and graduated in 1930. When he moved to America, Brandford envisioned becoming a purely creative artist. After graduating from art school, he worked with Burland Printing Company as an apprentice artist. He was one of the artists who designed the catalog of advertisers for the New York World's Fair in 1939. He became a freelance artist and designed the original copy of *People's Voice*. As his business grew, he opened an office on 42nd Street where he designed book jackets for a number of works, including *The Great Short Novels of Henry James,* edited by Philip Rahr. Brandford's art also appeared in the *New York Herald Tribune*'s book review section and in *American Home* magazine. He saw a need for a black model agency and on July 30, 1947, he opened the Brandford Model Agency. There were 250 black women registered with the agency and 75 on the active list.

Sources: *Opportunity* 25 (Spring 1947): 108–9; 127; Smith, *Notable Black American Women, Book II,* p. 86.

1940s–50s • Sara Lou Harris Carter (1926–), later known as Lady Sarah Lou, broke the stereotype of the black woman by being featured as a glamour girl on Lucky Strike (American Tobacco Company) cigarette posters. Around this time she also became the first black woman to model in the New York buyers' fashion show. Carter was born in Wilkesboro, North Carolina, and graduated from Bennett College for Women in Greensboro. While studying for her master's degree at Columbia University in New York City, she helped support her studies by working as a model, dancer, actress, and in radio and television. In 1946 she toured Europe with the Noble Sissle United Service Organizations troupe. She also was a member of a girl's quartet and had a solo part in *Shuffle Along*. She appeared with singer and actress Juanita Hall (1901–1968) in the radio soap opera *The Story of Ruby Valentine*. After she traveled to British Guiana as a part of a fashion show, she met barrister John Carter; they married in 1959. During her career Harris broadened career options for black women, and she saw them enter such areas as high-fashion modeling.

Sources: Smith, *Notable Black American Women,* Book II, pp. 85–88; Hine, *Black Women in America,* vol. 1, p. 408.

1950s • Dorothea Towles (Church) (1922–2006) became the first black woman to earn a living entirely as a professional model. She was also the first black woman to build a thriving career modeling in Paris. Her career began in Christian Dior's showroom in Europe, and in the early 1950s she walked the runways of the haute couture houses, such as those of Christian Dior, Pierre Balmain, and Italian designer Elsa Schiaparelli. She became prominent in post–World War II European fashion trends and paved the way for early black supermodels. A native of Texarkana, Texas, Towles graduated from Wiley College in Marshall, Texas, and received a master's degree from the University of California, Los Angeles. She also attended a charm school in Los Angeles.

Sources: *Ebony* (9 June 1953): 37; 17 (April 1962): 97; Hine, *Black Women in America,* vol. 1, pp. 407, 408.

1959 • Hal DeWindt (1933?–1997), actor, producer, director, and model, was the first male model in the Ebony Fashion Fair. From 1959 through 1961 he traveled with the fashion troupe and became a hit with audiences. Born in New York City; DeWindt dedicated his career to creating opportunities for blacks in entertainment; for example, he helped locate black musicians for the New York Philharmonic. He assisted Arthur Mitchell in his Dance Theatre of Harlem by helping to bring the dance company to Broadway. DeWindt was founder and artistic director of the American Theatre of Harlem, and also artistic director for the Inner City Repertory Company located in Los Angeles. He acted in a number of productions on stage and on television.

Sources: *Jet* 92 (14 July 1997): 65.

1965 • *Playboy* magazine featured its first black Playmate of the Month, Jennifer Jackson, in the March issue. Although controversy stirred, Hugh Hefner continued to have black playmates and black bunnies. Black model Darine Stern graced the cover of the October 1971 issue of *Playboy,* forging the magazine ahead of many fashion magazines in featuring a black model.

Sources: http://www.oxfordaasc.com/article/print/opr/t0005/w0817?image_size=inline

1966 • The first black model to appear on the cover of a Western magazine was Donyale Luna (1945–), whose image appeared on the cover of British *Vogue,* in March. She was called eccentric and difficult, and had a short career as a fashion model.

Sources: http://www.oxfordaasc. com/article/print/opr/t0005/w0817?image_size=inline

1968 • Fashion model Naomi Sims (1949–) became the first black woman to appear on the cover of *Ladies' Home Journal,* when the magazine featured an article on black models. Sims became the first black model on the cover of *Life* magazine the next year. In both years International Mannequins voted her top model of the year. Two years after she began a modeling career, she appeared in practically every fashion magazine around the world. Around 1969 Sims became the nation's first black supermodel. Five years after becoming a top model, Sims gave up her career and started a wig business, the Naomi Sims Collection. For her wigs she developed and patented a lightweight fiber that resembled black hair much more so than the traditional wigs designed for the masses. She later expanded the business to include perfume and cosmetics designed for black women, and formed the company Naomi Sims Beauty Products. Sims also became an author, writing such books as *All About Health and Beauty for the Black Woman* in 1976, *How to Be a Top Model* in 1979, and *All About Hair Care for the Black Woman* in 1982. Born in Oxford, Mississippi, Sims moved with her family to Pittsburgh, Pennsylvania. After graduating from high school, she moved to New York City and studied merchandising and textile design at the Fashion Institute of Technology. The five-feet-ten-inch Sims approached modeling agencies in New York hoping to find employment. At first she was denied a modeling job on the grounds that there was no work for black models. Then she met the fashion editor for the *New York Times,* had a modeling session, and immediately appeared on the cover of the Sunday edition of the *Times.* While modeling agencies still rejected her after that, Sims joined former top model Wilhelmina Cooper in search of a modeling contract and her career took off. Her dark skin color was newsworthy.

Sources: *Black Enterprise* (March 1989): 42; *Contemporary Black Biography,* vol. 29, pp. 143–46; Hine, *Black Women in America,* vol. 2, p. 1328.

1970 • The first black contestant in a Miss America Pageant was Cheryl Adrenne Brown, Miss Iowa.

Sources: Alford, *Famous First Facts,* p. 68.

1970 • Legendary actress and sportscaster Jayne Kennedy was the first black woman crowned "Miss Ohio." In 1978, she became one of the first women to join the all-male contingency of television sports announcers. Around 1980, she became the first celebrity to have a sex tape leaked.

Sources: Rollingout.com: Digital Urban Voice, "Legendary Actress and Sportscaster Jayne Kennedy Reveals Her True Destiny on TV One." Accessed September 28, 2012.

1970 • The first black Miss World was Jennifer Josephine Hosten, who won the honor on December 3, 1970. The Grenada native was then an airline flight attendant.

Sources: Garrett, *Famous First Facts about Negroes,* p. 23.

1974 • The first black supermodel to appear on the cover of the American version of a major fashion magazine was Beverly Johnson (1952–). The model, actress, and singer appeared on the August issue of American *Vogue* this year. Born in Buffalo, New York, she studied at Northeastern University in Boston. In the early 1970s she was the first black woman to appear on the cover of the French magazine *Elle*. When she appeared on the cover of *Glamour* magazine during the mid–1970s, that magazine's circulation doubled and set a record. By 1992 Johnson had appeared on the covers of some five hundred magazines. Although she was a highly successful model, she left that work to pursue her interest in singing and acting. Around 1977 she teamed with rock singer Phil Anastasia for two single releases. She also worked on an album and made her film debut in *Ashanti*. Johnson later launched a skin care line known as Farabee.

Sources: *Contemporary Black Biography,* vol. 2, pp. 123–24; *Ebony* 47 (September 1992): 32; Hornsby, *Milestones in Twentieth Century African-American History,* pp. 222–23; Smith, *Notable Black American Women,* pp. 575–76.

1977 • Janelle Penny Commissiong (1954–) became the first black Miss Universe. She was also Miss Trinidad and Tobago. The former fashion buyer and fashion institute graduate was born in Trinidad. By 1999, two other blacks had held the title of Miss Universe— Wendy Fitzwilliam of Trinidad and Tobago in 1998 and Mpule Kwelagobe of Botswana in 1999.

Beverly Johnson

Sources: *Essence* 8 (April 1978): 32; *Jet* 53 (10 November 1977): 30.

1982 • The first blacks to be featured on the cover of *GQ* magazine were Sheila Johnson and Charles Williamson, in October.

Sources: *Jet* 90 (28 October 1996):12.

1983 • Vanessa Lynn Williams (1963–), representing New York, became the first black Miss America. She also was the first to resign the title, in 1984. Suzette Charles, the first black Miss New Jersey and the first black runner-up in the Miss America contest, took Williams's place. Williams, whose parents were public school music teachers, was born in the Bronx borough of New York City. The family relocated to the upscale community of Millwood, New York, when Williams was one year old. By age ten, Williams had become deeply involved in music and dance. She studied the French horn, piano, and violin, and classical and jazz dance. She attended Syracuse University from 1981 to 1983, where she excelled in theater and music. While appearing in a college musical, Williams was asked to become a contestant in the Miss Greater Syracuse contest. She won the pageant and in 1983 went on to be crowned Miss New York. On September 14 that year, she won the national pageant and was crowned Miss America. In July 1984, the middle of her reign, a number of provocative photographs of Williams that had been taken in summer 1982 surfaced. Williams then relinquished her crown. Her career in acting and singing, however, took off, and in 1988 her first album, *The Right Stuff,* went gold. She also had three singles in the Top Ten on the rhythm and blues chart. In 1991 one single, "Save the Best for Last," from her hit album *The Comfort Zone,* was number one on the pop and rhythm and blues charts for five weeks. She was nominated for nine Grammy Awards. Williams's film credits include *New Jack City* (1991), *Candy Man* (1992), *Eraser* (1996), and *The Odyssey* (1997). In the 2009 season, she became a regular on ABC's soap, *Desperate Housewives*.

Vanessa Williams

Sources: Hine, *Black Women in America,* pp. 409, 1266–68; 71 *Jet* 71 (2 February 1987): 56; 76 (18 September 1989): 27; *Who's Who among Black Americans,* 26th ed., p. 1354–55; *Contemporary Black Biography,* vol. 17, pp. 202–6.

1989 • Josephine Gentry-Huyghe (1928?–) beat out fifty contestants in Atlantic City on April 12 to become the first black Ms. Senior America. The pageant began fifteen years earlier and honors outstanding women who are at least sixty years old. The talented "Josie," as she was affectionately called, performed disco dances on roller skates. She had a quiet victory, receiving no money, prizes, or media blitz. The era of her reign was significant also because, from March 30, 1990, until April 1990, black women held the titles and crowns of Ms. Senior America, Miss America (Debbye Turner, 1989), and Miss U.S.A. (Carole Gist, 1990). Gentry-Huyghe, a mother of four and grandmother of eight, retired from her position as public health nurse in Detroit, Michigan.

Sources: Josephine Gentry-Huyghe, letter to Jessie Carney Smith, 4 February 1994; *Detroit Free Press* (26 April 1990); *Detroit News* (12 March 1990).

1990 • The first black Miss USA was Carole Anne-Marie Gist (1970?–), who was crowned in Wichita, Kansas, on March 3, 1990. The six-foot tall, twenty-year-old queen from Detroit entered the contest as Miss Michigan—USA, the title she won in 1989. She was also first runner-up in the Miss Universe pageant in April 1990. Gist worked part-time as a singer in a club in Midland, Michigan. She graduated from Cass Technical High School in Detroit and attended Northwood Institute in Midland.

Sources: Hornsby, *Milestones in 20th Century African-American History*, p. 441; *Jet* 77 (19 March 1990): 59; 77 (26 March 1990): 58–60; *Contemporary Black Biography*, vol. 1, pp. 84–85.

1991 • The first black woman to be crowned Miss America by the reigning black queen was Marjorie Judith Vincent (1964–). Vincent was the fourth black Miss America and received her crown from Debbye Turner, who was Miss America for 1990. The five-foot-six, 110-pound Vincent was born in Chicago to Haitian immigrants. Her vision was to become a concert pianist, and she enrolled in De Paul University in Chicago as a music major. She later changed her major to business and graduated in 1988. She became a law student at Duke University.

Sources: *Contemporary Black Biography*, vol. 2, pp. 242–43; *Who's Who among African Americans*, 26th ed., p. 1255

1992 • Doors continued to open for black models, when Veronica Webb (1965–), who appeared in *Jungle Fever* and *Malcolm X*, was the first black model to win an exclusive modeling contract with Revlon. In this year as well, Lana Oglivie, a Canadian and popular print model, was the first black to obtain an exclusive contract with CoverGirl.

Sources: http://www.oxfordaasc. com/article/print/opr/t0005/w0817?image_size=inline

1993 • Jacqui Mofokeng was the first black and the second non-white to win the crown of Miss South Africa in the history of the thirty-seven-year contest. Amy Keinhans, who preceded her as winner, is of mixed-race heritage. Mofokeng received prizes worth $210,000 and represented South Africa at the Miss World Pageant held later in the year.

Sources: *Jet* 84 (23 August 1993): 11.

1993 • Donetta McCullum (1972?–) became the first black homecoming queen at Mississippi College—a majority white, Baptist school located in Clinton. She credited both her white and black friends for electing her in a run-off contest. The Laurel, Mississippi, native was a biology pre-med student.

Sources: *Jet* 85 (6 December 1993): 16.

1994 • Stacey Lynn Fielder was crowned Mrs. Michigan America in Detroit, becoming the first black to win the title. She is the wife of former pro baseball player Cecil Fielder.

Sources: *Jet* 85 (28 March 1994): 45.

1995 • Tyson Beckford (1970–) became the first black man to model in advertisements for Ralph Lauren and the first black to sign an exclusive contract with the company. He became the world's first black male supermodel. Born in New York City to Jamaican parents, he left for Jamaica soon after he was born. When he was seven years old, the family returned to New York and settled in Harlem. His mother's experience as a part-time model helped him to get his start. She realized his extraordinary charisma and took him along on runway shows. Around 1993 a reporter for an influential journal in New York City photographed him. He soon came to the attention of Bethann Hardison, who had her own modeling agency and also took the lead in demanding more work for black models. Beckford's career took off in 1993, when he posed for *Source* magazine and appeared in such publications as *British GQ, EM, Essence,* and *Vibe*. He appeared in fashion shows for Tommy Hilfiger, Nautica, Calvin Klein, Donna Karan, and others.

Sources: *Contemporary Black Biography*, vol. 11, pp. 15–17.

Sports Illustrated's First Black Cover Model

Tyra Banks

The first black woman to appear on the cover of *Sports Illustrated*'s high-profile swimsuit issue was supermodel Tyra Banks (1973–) in 1997. Banks was born on Los Angeles and began her modeling career in Paris, France, in 1991. She left Loyola Marymount University in Los Angeles two days before classes started to accept an offer to model in the Fall haute couture shows in Paris. There she was booked for twenty-five shows, then a record for a newcomer. Banks later landed several lucrative deals, including the *Sports Illustrated* assignment and a multipage advertising campaign for American designer Ralph Lauren. Cosmetics giant CoverGirl hired her, making her the second black to receive a long-term contract with that company. Banks appeared in a number of television shows, including the NBC sitcom *The Fresh Prince of Bel-Air*. Her film credits include *Higher Learning*. Banks later promoted a line of greeting cards for Children+Families. Another line, Cards From the Heart, was created by young children; she uses them to promote literacy among children in troubled environments.

Sources: *Contemporary Black Biography*, vol.11, pp. 9–11.

1995 • Chelsi Smith (1974?–) is the first biracial to be crowned Miss USA. Her prize money totaled $207,000 in cash, and she represented the United States in the Miss Universe pageant held in Windhoek, Namibia, in the spring. At the time of her win, Smith was a sophomore at San Jacinto Junior College in Texas. She planned to draw on her biracial background to teach youth of all races about the perils of racism and the importance of self-esteem.

Sources: *Jet* 87 (27 February 1995): 5.

1996 • The first black crowned Miss Italy was Denny Mendez (1978?–). She was born in the Dominican Republic to a naturalized Italian mother and an Italian father. Her election came in spite of disapproval from two judges who claimed that she did not belong, and that "A black girl can't be Miss Italy." She later competed in the Miss Universe pageant.

Sources: *Jet* 90 (23 September 1996): 14; 90 (30 September 1996): 44.

1996 • Chanté Laree Griffin (1978?–) was elected Miss Teen of America for 1996–97, becoming the first black to hold that title. The pageant, held that year at the U.S. Grant Hotel in San Diego, recognized America's young women and their achievements. She was crowned Miss Teen of California in 1995. At the time of her election, the Fresno, California, native was a student at Pomona College in Claremont.

Sources: *Jet* 90 (28 October 1996): 39.

1997 • The first black to be named Miss University at the University of Mississippi was Carissa Wells (1975?–). She had been named first runner-up in the Miss University pageant at the school when the election results were certified; however, officials realized that she was the overall winner in all of the competitions and awarded her the crown. The Hamilton, Mississippi, native went on to compete in the Miss Mississippi pageant.

Sources: *Jet* 91 (28 April 1997): 23.

1998 • Nita Booth became the first black to be named Miss Virginia. Nicole Johnson, who held the title, was named Miss America, leaving Booth to inherit the title. The Hampton University student received a $13,000 scholarship, an apartment, and an automobile.

Sources: *Jet* 94 (26 October 1998): 10.

2002 • For the first time in the history of the Miss USA pageant, four of the five finalists were black. The winner was twenty-three-year-old Shauntah Hinton, Miss District of Columbia. The other finalists were twenty-five-year-old Kelly Lord, Miss Indiana, second runner-up; twenty-six-year-old Lanore VanBuren, Miss Minnesota, third runner-up; and twenty-two-year-old Alita Hawaah Dawson, Miss Connecticut, fourth runner-up. Deion Sanders, star of the NFL and of baseball, and actress Ali Landry, Miss USA in 1996, co-hosted the show.

Sources: *Jet* 101 (18 March 2002): 6.

2007 • Beyoncé (1981–) became the first non-model and non-athlete to appear on the cover of *Sports Illustrated*'s Swimsuit Issue.

Sources: *Contemporary Black Biography,* vol. 70, pp. 18–22; *Jet* 111 (5 March 2007): 30.

2007 • The first black singer to appear on the cover of the fashion magazine *Vogue* was Jennifer Hudson (1981–). Her image was published on the cover of *Vogue*'s March Power Issue. Previously, talk show phenom Oprah Winfrey and the Oscar-winning actress Halle Berry graced that cover.

Sources: *Contemporary Black* Biography, vol. 63, pp. 94–96; vol. 83, pp. 18–22; *Jet* 111 (5 March 2007): 30.

2007 • Elisabeth Senghor (1989?–) a Senegal native, became the first African to participate in the Crillon Ball, a prestigious and annual celebration held in Paris. Twenty-three new debutantes between ages seventeen and twenty-one, representing such countries as China, Russia, Japan, England, Lebanon, and the United States were introduced. The ball, sponsored by Swiss jeweler Adler, is held annually at the Crillon Hotel. Senghor was then a student at the American University of Paris. She is the granddaughter of former president of Senegal Abdou Diouf, and her great-great uncle, Leopold Sedar Senghor, was Senegal's first president.

Sources: *Jet* 111 (8 January 2007): 36.

Black Winners of the Miss USA Title

Year	Winner
1990	Carole Gist
1992	Shannon Marketic
1993	Kenya Moore
1994	Frances Louise "Lu" Parker
1995	Chelsi Smith (first biracial; later crowed Miss Universe)
2000	Lynette Cole
2002	Shauntay Hinton
2007	Rachel Smith
2008	Chrystle Stewart

Sources: *African American Almanac,* 11th ed., p. 1520; *Jet* 111 (9 April 2007): 7; 115 (9 March 2009): 18; 113 (28 April 2008): 8.

2008 • The first black model featured in *Sports Illustrated Swimsuit* Issue for the fifth year was Jessica White (1985?–). "It's about being different every year, changing up my hair color, changing poses," she said. When she was sixteen, she also became the first black model to hold two cosmetics contracts simultaneously—with Maybelline and CoverGirl. As a model, White landed campaigns with brands Chloé and the Gap. She walked runways with top designers such as Ralph Lauren, Oscar de la Renta, and others. In 2007 she made her first appearance on the catwalk of Victoria's Secret Fashion Show, and remarked that she has been casting for the show since age sixteen. White also founded a charity called "Angel Wings," based in Buffalo, which aids young girls who have been abused, and women who experienced bad situations. She also formed her own production company, White House Productions, to produce her own films and perhaps star in them as well.

Sources: *Jet* 113 (31 March 2008): 58.

2009 • Jacqui Rice (1989?–) became the first black to hold the title Queen Shenandoah LXXXI (also known as the Apple Blossom Queen) of the 81st Shenandoah Apple Blossom. The new queen, an aspiring singer, became the official hostess of the annual Apple Blossom Festival and presides over several events associated with the festival. The festival is also affiliated with the Miss America Pageant and requires candidates to participate in competitions such as talent and gown. Rice is the daughter of NFL Hall of Famer Jerry Rice, who assisted in crowning his daughter at the official ceremony held at the John Handley High School in Winchester, Virginia.

Sources: *Jet* 113 (26 May 2009): 36.

2009 • The first black woman to be crowned Miss England was Rachel Christie, a track-and-field athlete and the niece of Linford Christie, an Olympian. The ceremony was held at London's Metropole Hilton Hotel.

Sources: *Jet* 116 (10–17 August 2009): 32.

Celebrations

1964 • The first African Day Parade was held in Harlem.

Sources: *The Black New Yorkers*, p. 301.

1966 • Maulana Karenga (1941–) founded Kwanzaa to restore and reaffirm African heritage and culture. Kwanzaa originated from the Kiswahili phrase "Matunda Ya Kwanza" and is interpreted as "First Fruits." The additional "a" was added to indicate that the holiday has its roots in African American culture. Many regard the celebration as the most important holiday on the African American calendar. Although the celebration coincides with Christmas season, it was not intended as a religious celebration or one that promotes ideologies; instead it focuses on family values. Each night for seven nights one particular family value is celebrated. These are Umojo (Unity); Kujichagulai (Self-Determination); Ujima (Collective Work and Responsibility); Ujamaa (Cooperative Economics); Nia (Purpose); Kuumba (Creativity); and Imani (Faith). Karenga, a writer, educator, and advocate of black culturalism, was born Ronald McKinley Everett in Parsonsburg, Maryland, the son of a Baptist minister. In the late 1950s he moved to California and studied at Los Angeles City College where he was the first black elected president of the student body. He graduated with the bachelor's degree and later received a master's and doctorate from the University of California. After completing his education, he embraced the Black Power movement and supported Malcolm X. To help restore order in Los Angeles after the 1965 riots, he helped to establish the Black Congress for the residents of Watts. By the mid–1960s Everett changed his name to Maulana Karenga. He also started a group known as US that had as its goal national liberation of blacks. The holiday, Kwanzaa, has been called his most important legacy.

Sources: *The African American Holiday of Kwanzaa*.

Chess

1800s • Theophilus Thompson (1855–?) was the earliest documented black American chess expert. He was born in Frederick, Maryland, and, when he was seventeen, he observed local chess matches, thereby learning about the game. He also began to play chess and to work on chess problems. He published articles on chess in the *Dubuque* (Iowa)

Theophilus Thompson

Chess Journal and in 1873 published a book on chess strategy entitled *Chess Problems.* Little is known of Thompson after 1873.

Sources: Salzman, *Encyclopedia of African-American Culture and History,* vol. 1, p. 528.

1960 • Walter Harris (1942?–) became the first black American to be rated as a master by the United States Chess Federation (USCF). The eighteen-year-old defeated several masters and placed fifth in a junior championship held in Omaha, Nebraska.

Sources: Salzman, *Encyclopedia of African-American Culture and History,* vol. 1, p. 528.

1999 • Maurice Ashley (1966–) became the world's first black grandmaster (or international grandmaster), the game's highest rank, on March 15. He also became one of nearly eight hundred grandmasters worldwide. His rank is the highest that the International Chess Federation bestows. Ashley's addiction to chess began when he was fourteen years old. A Jamaican immigrant who lives in Brooklyn, he graduated from New York City College and began playing chess with the Black Bears School of Chess, an informal black group. As a director of the Harlem Educational Activities Fund, he coached several chess teams; one of them, the Mott Hall Dark Knights, won a national championship in 1994. Ashley decided to make chess his sole pursuit in 1997.

Sources: *Contemporary Black Biography,* vol. 15, pp. 18–20; Smith, *Encyclopedia of African American Popular Culture,* vol. 1, pp. 69–70.

Commemoratives and Monuments

1876 • A monument to Richard Allen (1760–1831), dedicated June 12, 1876, in Philadelphia's Freemont Park, may have been the first erected to a black by blacks.

Sources: Logan and Winston, *Dictionary of American Negro Biography,* p. 13.

1936 • The Dunbar House, the final residence of poet Paul Laurence Dunbar, became the first state memorial to honor a black American. The house, located at 219 Paul Lawrence Dunbar Street in Dayton, Ohio, contains many of Dunbar's personal and literary artifacts. Dunbar's mother, Matilda Dunbar, lived there from the time of Dunbar's death until 1934. The memorial was dedicated on July 23 this year, and later came under the care of the Ohio Historical Society.

Sources: Cantor, *Historic Black Landmarks of America,* pp. 38–40.

1946 • The first coin honoring a black and designed by a black was issued. The fifty-cent piece, which became available on December 16, 1946, featured the bust of Booker T. Washington, the founder of Tuskegee Institute in Alabama. It was designed by Isaac S. Hathaway (1894–?), who later designed the George Washington Carver half-dollar. Hathaway was born in Lexington, Kentucky, and studied art at the New England Conservatory of Music; he also studied in the ceramics department at Pittsburgh Normal College. He spent some time at Alabama State University in Montgomery, where he was head of the ceramics department. Hathaway produced over one hundred busts of prominent blacks; his works are located throughout the country and at the Sorbonne University in Paris.

Sources: Alford, *Famous First Blacks,* p. 68; *Jet* 81 (30 March 1992): 32; 95 (5 April 1999): 19; *Negro Year Book,* 1947, p. 33.

George Washington Carver

1960 • George Washington Carver (1864–1943), an agronomist, scientist, and educator who produced more than four hundred different products from the peanut, potato, and pecan, became the first black scientist memorialized by a federal monument in the United States. On July 14, 1953, the United States Congress authorized the establishment of the George Washington Carver National Monument. It was erected on his birth site near Diamond, Missouri, and dedicated July 17, 1960. His scientific work improved the quality of life for millions of people and enhanced agriculture in the South. He took his mule-drawn "movable school" on weekend visits to impoverished farmlands to teach poor farmers to raise, improve, and preserve foods. Carver was born a slave. In 1894, he became the

Blacks Commemorated on Postage Stamps

The first black American depicted on a U.S. postage stamp was Booker Taliaferro Washington (1856–1915) in 1940. His photograph was reproduced on the ten-cent brown stamp, which became available on April 7, 1940, at Tuskegee Institute in Alabama. The stamp was part of the Famous American Commemorative series issued in 1940. He was honored again on a stamp in 1956, marking the one-hundredth anniversary of his birth. Perhaps the two most important black-related stamps are the Thirteenth Amendment issue of 1940, which celebrated the seventy-fifth anniversary of the Constitutional abolition of slavery in the United States, and the Emancipation Proclamation stamp of 1963, which honored the one-hundredth anniversary of the freeing of slaves in federally controlled areas during the Civil War.

Sources: *Jet* 84 (28 June 1993): 48–51; Kane, *Famous First Facts,* p. 482; National Postal Museum Online, "Booker T. Washington Postal Stamp," http://www.postalmuseum.si.edu/museum/1d_BTW_Stamp.html. Accessed September 28, 2012; ESPER, "African Americans on U.S. Stamps," http://esperstamps.org/history1.htm, accessed September 28, 2012.

Selected List of Blacks Commemorated on Postage Stamps

Date	Honoree	Area of Citation
April 7, 1940	Booker T. Washington	Education
January 5, 1948	George Washington Carver	Science
February 14, 1967	Frederick Augustus Douglass	Civil Rights
May 17, 1969	W. C. Handy	Blues
April 29, 1986	Duke Ellington	Jazz
September 10, 1973	Henry O. Tanner	Painting
May 1, 1975	Paul Laurence Dunbar	Poetry
February 1, 1978	Harriet Tubman	Civil rights; first black woman honored on a stamp
January 13, 1979	Martin Luther King Jr.	Civil rights
February 15, 1980	Benjamin Banneker	Science, Inventions
August 2, 1982	Jackie Robinson	Sports
February 1, 1984	Carter G. Woodson	History
March 5, 1985	Mary McLeod Bethune	Education
May 28, 1986	Matthew Henson	Exploration
February 20, 1987	Jean Baptiste Pointe Du Sable	Exploration
February 2, 1988	James Weldon Johnson	Creative writing
February 1, 1990	Ida B. Wells (Barnett)	Journalism
July 6, 1990. September 10, 1998*	Jesse Owens	Sports
September 15, 1991	Jan E. Matzeliger	Inventions
January 31, 1992	W.E.B. Du Bois	Civil rights
June 22, 1993	Joe Louis Barrow	Boxing
April 27, 1995	Bessie Coleman	Aviation
January 28, 1997	Benjamin O. Davis Sr.	Military
January 28, 1998	Madame C. J. Walker	Business
January 20, 1999	Malcolm X	Civil rights
January 27, 2000	Patricia Roberts Harris	Politics
February 1, 2002	Langston Hughes	Poetry
January 7, 2003	Thurgood Marshall	Law
January 7, 2005	Marian Anderson	Music
January 10, 2007	Ella Fitzgerald	Jazz
July 15, 2010	Negro Leagues Baseball/Rube Foster	Baseball

*A 25 cent stamp was issued in 1990 and a 32 cent stamp in 1998.

first black to graduate from Iowa State College. He joined the faculty of Tuskegee Institute (now Tuskegee University) in 1896, where he developed a program of research in soil conservation and crop diversification.

Sources: *Current Biography, 1940,* pp. 148–50; Logan and Winston, *Dictionary of American Negro Biography,* pp. 92–95; Hornsby, *Milestones in 20th-Century African-American History,* pp. 21, 202; Smith, *Notable Black American Men,* pp. 177–80.

1963 • Georg [George] Olden (1921–), internationally known graphic designer, was the first black artist to design a U.S. postage stamp. The stamp featured a broken link in a large black chain against a blue backdrop and was designed to commemorate the one hundredth anniversary of the Emancipation Proclamation. It went on sale August 16, 1963. Olden attended public schools in Washington, D.C., and studied at Virginia State College (now Virginia State University) in Petersburg. He later became an employee in graphics for the U.S. Department of the Interior and for the Office of Strategic Services. When he was just twenty-four years old, he became director of graphic arts for CBS Television. In 1954 *Idea,* the Japanese art magazine, named Olden one of the fifteen leading graphic designers in the United States. Olden's work is included in the permanent collection of the Amsterdam Museum in Harlem.

Sources: Alford, *Famous First Blacks,* p. 9; *I Have a Dream,* p. 60; *Jet* 32 (17 August 1967): 11

1974 • A monument honoring the life and contribution of Mary McLeod Bethune (1875–1955) was built in Washington, D.C., becoming the first statue of a black erected on public land in the District. A noted educator, in 1939 she was named director of the National Youth Administration's Division of Negro Affairs and thus became the highest ranking black woman in government.

Sources: Cantor, *Historic Landmarks of Black America,* p. 275; Smith, *Notable Black American Women,* pp. 86–92; Robinson, *Historical Negro Biographies,* p. 163.

1984 • President Ronald Reagan signed a bill on November this year designating the third Monday of January each year as a federal holiday. The holiday honors Dr. Martin Luther King Jr., who then became the first black American and the third American after George Washington and Abraham Lincoln to be honored by a federal holiday.

Sources: *Jet* 92 (20 October 1997): 19; 93 (2 November 1998): 19.

1987 • The first state-owned and -operated historic site honoring a black in North Carolina was the Charlotte Hawkins Brown Memorial State Historic Site in Sedalia. In 1983 the Charlotte Hawkins Brown Historical Foundation was incorporated to assist the state in establishing the site—the forty-acre former campus and fourteen buildings of Palmer Memorial Institute, which Brown founded.

Sources: *Greensboro News and Record* (3 November 1991); *Jet* 73 (12 October 1987): 34; Smith, *Notable Black American Women,* p. 113.

1998 • On February 13 the U.S. Mint issued a commemorative silver dollar honoring more than 5,000 blacks who served in and supported the Revolutionary War. In addition to a design on the front side, the back of the coin features black patriot Crispus Attucks, the first person killed in the Boston Massacre. The incident figured prominently in beginning the American Revolutionary War. The Black Patriots Foundation unveiled a design for the coin on October 22, 1997; Treasury Secretary Robert E. Rubin endorsed the design on October 1.

Sources: *Washington Post* (22 October 1997).

1998 • The African American Civil War Memorial in the Shaw neighborhood of the District of Columbia was dedicated in July. The memorial was designed by Ed Hamilton, of Louisville, Kentucky, and ground was broken in 1994 for its erection. It was the first major piece by a black sculptor placed on federal land anywhere in the Nation's Capitol. This was also the first memorial in the District to honor the 178,000 black Union soldiers who fought in the Civil War. There are 209,145 names listed on the Wall of Honor; they are for United

States Colored Troops (USCT) who served in the Civil War as well as 7,000 white officers who served with them. The Shaw neighborhood was named in honor of Colonel Robert Gould Shaw, who commanded the 54th Massachusetts Volunteer Infantry. The infantry group was recognized in the film *Glory,* starring Denzel Washington and Morgan Freeman.

Sources: *Jet* 86 (26 September 1994): 20–21; 113 (7 July 2008): 13.

2000 • West Point Academy dedicated a memorial to four-star general Roscoe Robinson Jr. (1928–1993) of St. Louis. Robinson was the academy's first black graduate.

Sources: *Jet* 97 (1 May 2000): 10.

2000 • This was the first year that the Martin Luther King Jr. national holiday was observed in some form in all fifty states; the national holiday was declared fifteen years earlier. The holiday is observed on the third Monday in January and is usually celebrated with marches, speeches, and efforts to bring national commitment to King's principles and his vision of racial harmony and equality. The drive to commemorate the work of King began shortly after he was assassinated on April 4, 1968. Representative John Conyers Jr. (D-Michigan) introduced a bill in the U.S. House of Representatives to establish the national holiday on January 15; however, his efforts, as well as those of others, failed to move the bill forward. President Jimmy Carter's efforts in 1979 were fruitless as well. Finally, on November 2, 1983, President Ronald Reagan signed the bill into law. Even then the law was disregarded and it was not until January 1986 that the first national holiday for King was observed in only seventeen states, including those states that had already commemorated King's life and work. In 1994, President Bill Clinton signed the King Holiday Service Act into law; the law asks all Americans to use that day as a time to give back to their communities.

Sources: *Jet* 97 (7 January 2000): 5–14.; Smith, *Encyclopedia of African American Popular Culture,* vol. 3, pp. 812–13.

2011 • The first memorial to a black hero to be erected on the capital mall in Washington, D.C., was completed and dedicated this year. It is surrounded by memorials to Thomas Jefferson, Abraham Lincoln, and Franklin Delano Roosevelt. The memorial honoring Martin Luther King Jr. was completed and announced in August, the date on which King gave his historic "I Have a Dream" speech at the Lincoln Memorial in 1963. "In the midst of presidents and memorials that honor war, you have a man of peace now," Martin Luther King III said. Dedication of the monument was scheduled for August 28, following a week of lectures and celebrations but delayed until October 2011 due to extreme weather. President Bill Clinton authorized the memorial, a mission of the Alpha Phi Alpha fraternity. Donors throughout the nation and worldwide contributed to the project. Chinese sculptor Lei Yixin designed the 28-foot-high granite statue which was inspired by a line from King's famous 1963 speech. A crescent wall at the site includes fourteen quotations from King. During the dedication, President Barack Obama said that "King did not quit when the Civil Rights Act and Voting Rights Act did not end poverty and discrimination," nor did he say "This is too hard." Instead, he said, "Let's take those victories and broaden our mission ... to achieve civil and political equality ... and economic justice."

Sources: "Alpha Phi Alpha Brother Brings Dream of King Memorial to Life," To be Equal # 34, National Urban League, August 25, 2011; *Jet* 119 (17 January 2011): 10–11; *Tennessean* (23 August 2011); (17 October 2011).

Exploration

1536 • Estevanico [Estevan] (1500?–1539), probably a native of Azamor, Morocco, was the first black man to traverse the southern portion of the United States. He travelled from Florida to Texas in a journey that lasted eight years. In 1539 he was the first black to explore what is now Arizona and New Mexico. "Little Stephen" also guided the expedition that searched for the fabled cities of Cibola, and was leading an advance scouting party when he was killed at Hawikuh Pueblo, New Mexico. Controversies arose about Estevanico's ethnicity and some writers suggest that he was of "Hamiti" stock and therefore not black. Others writers claim that he was black indeed, and that he was arrogant and wore bracelets and anklets. Native American tribes accepted him well, and he was reported to be a healer or some type of medicine man. His lust for Indian women was said to have led to his death.

Sources: Cantor, *Historic Landmarks of Black America*, pp. 286, 320–21; Logan and Winston, *Dictionary of American Negro Biography*, p. 213; Garrett, *Famous First Facts about Negroes*, p. 68; *Negro Almanac*, p. 2.

1804 • York (1770?–1832?) was the first black to reach the mouth of the Columbia River overland. He was a member of the Lewis and Clark Expedition that explored the Missouri River and continued on to the mouth of the Columbia in the Pacific Northwest. He had been William Clark's slave since the two were boys and was said to be a key member of Lewis and Clark's expedition. York excited the admiration of Native Americans because of his size, strength, and color, and helped smooth relations with the tribes encountered during the journey. He became a valued member of the expedition, both for his skills and his public relations value. At the end of the expedition, York may have remained a slave for nearly a decade until Clark granted him his freedom. He returned to Kentucky, where he eventually gained his freedom, but he ran into difficulties in his attempts to establish a business. York remained in obscurity for a long time. A statue of him was later erected at the University of Portland, overlooking the Columbia River that flows into the Pacific Ocean.

Sources: Cantor, *Historic Landmarks of Black America*, pp. 313–14, 326–27; Logan and Winston, *Dictionary of American Negro Biography*, pp. 676–77; *New York Times* (26 February 2000).

1859 • Martin Robinson Delany (1812–1885) was the first American black explorer in Africa. In the spring of 1859, Delany sailed to Africa and traveled in Liberia and the Niger Valley for nine months. Delany's *Official Report of the Niger Valley Exploring Party* appeared in 1861.

Sources: Logan and Winston, *Dictionary of American Negro Biography*, pp. 169–73; Simmons, *Men of Mark*, pp. 1007–15; Jackson, *A History of Afro-American Literature*, vol. 1, pp. 364–69; Smith, *Notable Black American Men*, pp. 282–86.

Matthew Henson

1909 • Matthew Alexander Henson (1866–1955) was the first person to reach the North Pole, of which he was co-discoverer with Robert E. Peary. There is some debate as to whether Peary was accurate in his claim to have reached the pole, but Henson went ahead to blaze the trail while Peary, whose toes were frozen, was pulled on the sledge. Henson planted the flag at the location Peary determined to be the pole, since Peary was unable to stand. Henson was born in Charles County, Maryland, just at the close of the Civil War. He ran away from home when he was around eleven years old and ended up in Washington, D.C., where he lived with his aunt. He became excited by sea stories that he heard from a man called Baltimore Jack, and walked to Baltimore, where he hung around the waterfront. He became a cabin boy on the *Katie Hines* that sailed to China and around the world under the command of Captain Childs, who took an interest in Henson. He was only twelve years old when his adventures in sailing began. After the captain died, Henson worked at odd jobs in Baltimore until he met Robert Peary. Peary hired Henson in 1887 to accompany him to Nicaragua to survey a canal route. Peary soon learned that Henson was an experienced seaman who also knew how to prepare a survey chart. In 1891 Peary and Henson prepared for what would be a failed trip to reach the North Pole. On their seventh expedition, they reached the Pole on April 6, 1909. Conflicting reports of their discovery have been published. Henson recounted his experiences in his book, *A Negro Explorer at the North Pole*, in 1912. In 1961 Maryland erected a monument to honor Henson on the grounds of the state capitol.

Sources: Cantor, *Historic Landmarks of Black America*, pp. 62–64; Logan and Winston, *Dictionary of American Negro*, p. 308.

1939 • George Gibbs (1916?–2000) became the first black to set foot on Antarctica about this time. One of forty U.S. Navy men selected from two thousand applicants, he was a member of Admiral Richard Byrd's third expedition to the South Pole from 1939 to 1941. The men sailed on the USS *Bear*. Later, Gibbs became a civil rights leader in Rochester, New York, and helped to organize the local chapter of the NAACP. In 1974 he was denied membership in the Rochester Elks Club, bringing national attention to the club and its action. Gibbs had been the first black to apply for membership. He also helped to break the color barrier at local service clubs.

Sources: *New York Times* Obituaries (9 November 2000).

Honors and Awards

1915 • The first black to receive the Spingarn Medal was Ernest Everett Just (1883–1941). The National Association for the Advancement of Colored People annually awards the medal for the highest or most noble achievement by a black American. Ernest Just, a biologist and educator, was born in Charleston, South Carolina, and graduated from Dartmouth College and the University of Chicago. He began teaching at Howard University in Washington, D.C., before he earned his doctorate at the University of Chicago in 1916. He pioneered in medical education at Howard by incorporating research methods into medical school courses. He received numerous grants from the Rockefeller Foundation, the General Education Board and other groups to support his research. He spent six months or more each year away from his work at Howard University engaged in research at Woods Hole. Just found teaching burdensome and quarreled with the officials at Howard University, who claimed that his fellowships were to strengthen the department of zoology and to support black scientists at the graduate level. His career as a distinguished biologist was hampered by racial prejudice, and he increasingly turned to Europe as a base, where he found richer opportunities for research. In 1940 he was interned in France by the Germans, but managed to return to the United States where he died of pancreatic cancer on October 27, 1941.

Ernest Just

Sources: *Contemporary Black Biography,* vol. 3, pp. 123–25; Logan and Winston, *Dictionary of American Negro Biography,* pp. 372–75; Smith, *Notable Black American Men,* 675–78.

1922 • Mary Morris Burnett Talbert (1866–1923) was the first black woman to receive the NAACP's Spingarn Medal, for her efforts to preserve the home of Frederick Douglass in Anacostia, Virginia. In 1922 the home was dedicated as the Frederick Douglass Museum. In 1920 Talbert had become the first black delegate to be seated at the International Council of Women. Talbert, an educator, civil rights activist, and activist in the black women's club movement, was born in Oberlin, Ohio, where she attended the local public schools. She graduated from the literary program at Oberlin College in 1886, receiving the S.P. degree. In 1894 she received the B.A. degree from Oberlin. She taught algebra, geometry, Latin, and history in the segregated school system in Little Rock, Arkansas, and won praise for her teaching ability from educators nationwide. She married William Talbert, who was an organizer of the Niagara Movement of 1905, the forerunner of the NAACP. After the Talberts moved to Buffalo, New York, Mary Talbert became an activist for women's rights and an important force in the black women's club movement. She held several posts in the National Association of Colored Women and rose in rank to become president of the group. She also became a national vice president of the NAACP and held the post until she died. Talbert was known for her interest in children, black history and culture, penal reform, the eradication of racism, and other issues; she worked through various reform movements to help achieve what she thought was right for black people.

Mary Burnett Talbert

Sources: Brown, *Homespun Heroines,* pp. 217–19; Dannett, *Profiles of Negro Womanhood,* vol. 1, pp. 316–17; *Encyclopedia of Black America,* p. 807; *Negro Yearbook, 1921–22,* p. 18; Smith, *Notable Black American Women,* pp. 1095–1100.

1927 • Laura Wheeler Waring (1887–1948) was the first black woman to receive the Harmon Award for her painting. She painted prominent persons in the struggle for black culture and taught for more than thirty years at Cheyney Training School for Teachers in Philadelphia. In 1946 she began a series of religious paintings that included *Jacob's Lad-*

The First Black Academy Award Winner

Hattie McDaniel

In 1940 Hattie McDaniel (1895–1952), singer, vaudeville performer, and actress, was the first black to win an Academy Award for her supporting role Mammy in *Gone with the Wind.* McDaniel made her radio debut in 1915, and is said to be the first black American woman to sing on radio. Often called "Hi-Hat Hattie," she was born in Wichita, Kansas, and moved to Hollywood in 1931. She made her movie debut in *The Golden West* in 1932, and appeared in more than three hundred films during the next two decades. Her career was built on the "Mammy" image, a role she played with dignity. She appeared on radio with Eddie Cantor and the "Amos 'n Andy" shows. She was entered into the Black Filmmakers Hall of Fame posthumously in 1975.

Sources: Logan and Winston, *Dictionary of American Negro Biography,* pp. 414–15; Hornsby, *Milestones in Twentieth-Century African-American History,* p. 35; *Negro Almanac,* p. 1426; Smith, *Notable Black American Women,* pp. 703–05.

der, *The Coming of the Lord,* and *Heaven, Heaven.* Waring was born in Hartford, Connecticut and for six years studied at the Pennsylvania Academy of Fine Arts.

Sources: Hine, *Black Women in America,* pp. 1124–25; Logan and Winston, *Dictionary of American Negro Biography,* p. 632; *Jet* 65 (6 February l984): 67; Smith, *Notable Black American Women,* pp. 1205–06.

1930 • Nella Larsen (1891–1964) became the first black American woman to receive a Guggenheim Fellowship in creative writing and the fourth black to receive the honor. Although Larsen was a librarian and nurse, she was also a highly acclaimed writer who was recognized for her work during the Harlem Renaissance of the 1920s. She was born in Chicago to a Danish mother and West Indian father. She studied in the high school division of Fisk University in Nashville, Tennessee, from 1909 to 1910, and then at the University of Copenhagen in Denmark. From 1912 to 1915 she studied nursing and spent the year 1915–16 at Tuskegee Institute in Alabama. She lived most of her remaining years in New York City. From 1916 to 1921 Larsen was a nurse at Lincoln Hospital and then for the New York City Health Department. She received a certificate from the New York Public Library and by 1924 she was a children's librarian at the Library's 135th Street Branch, where the Schomburg Collection began. Larsen's access to the social circles in Harlem enabled her to cultivate friendships with such luminaries as Walter White of the NAACP and Carl Van Vechten, a white writer who embraced the Harlem Renaissance. Larsen left her post as children's librarian and became a full-time novelist. Her works *Quicksand* (1928) and *Passing* (1929) received critical attention. She also won the Harmon Foundation's bronze medal for literature in 1928. After her Guggenheim Fellowship year in Europe, Larson returned to Nashville, Tennessee, to join her husband at Fisk University. Subsequently the marriage failed and Larsen returned to New York and resumed her nursing career in 1941. She worked at various hospitals in Manhattan. Her works were rediscovered in the 1960s and 1970s, subjected to critical scrutiny, and came to be considered important works of black American literature.

Sources: *Contemporary Black Biography,* vol. 10, pp. 138–42; Smith, *Notable Black American Women,* pp. 652–57.

1942 • The North Carolina Society of Mayflower descendants awarded J. Saunders Redding (1906–1988) the Mayflower Cup on December 3, making him the first black to receive the award.

Sources: Smith, *Notable Black American Men,* pp. 1000–1002; *Jet* 85 (6 December 1993): 59; *Contemporary Black Biography,* vol.26, pp. 122–25.

The First Black Tony Award Winner

In 1949 Juanita Hall (1901–1968), singer, actress, and choral director, became the first black American to win a Tony Award for her performance as Bloody Mary in the 1949 Broadway production of *South Pacific.* Hall was born in Keyport, New Jersey, and sang in church choirs in her community. In 1928 she appeared in the chorus of the Ziegfield production of *Show Boat.* From 1931 to 1936, Hall was soloist and assistant director of the Hall Johnson Choir. For more than twenty years she devoted her life to the performing arts, working as choral conductor, actress, and singer on stage and screen.

Sources: Logan and Winston, *Dictionary of American Negro Biography,* pp. 277–78; Smith, *Notable Black American Women,* pp. 439–40; Southern, *Biographical Dictionary of Afro-American and African Musicians,* pp. 161–62.

1946 • Emma Clarissa [Williams] Clement (1874–1952) of Louisville, Kentucky, was the first black woman named "American Mother of the Year." The Golden Rule Foundation gave her the honor on May 1, 1946. At the time, Clement's son, Rufus, was president of Atlanta University. Clement, a church leader, clubwoman, and social and civil rights activist, was born in Providence, Rhode Island, and studied at Livingston College in Salisbury, North Carolina, graduating in 1898. She moved to Louisville, Kentucky, when her husband, George Clement, was named bishop in the African Methodist Episcopal Zion Church's third district. She was named "American Mother of the Year" in recognition of her qualities as the mother of children who served their country and their people, for her partnership with her husband, and for her work as a social and community worker. She embodied "the great spirit of America." After winning the award she spent considerable time speaking at sites from New York to California.

Sources: *Chronology of African-American History,* p. 93; Logan and Winston, *Dictionary of American Negro Biography,* p. 117; Hornsby, *Milestones in Twentieth-Century African-American History,* p. 44; *Negro Year Book, 1947,* p. 33; Smith, *Notable Black American Women,* Book II, pp. 103–5.

Emma Clarissa Clement

1950 • The first black to win a Pulitzer Prize was poet Gwendolyn Brooks (1917–2000). Brooks' book of poetry, *Annie Allen,* won the award on May 1 for the best book of poetry in the United States.

Sources: *Jet* 88 (12 June 1995): 20; *Contemporary Black Biography,* vol. 28, pp. 33–37; Smith, *Notable Black American Women,* pp. 105–09

1955 • Dorothy Dandridge (1922–1965) was the first black woman nominated for an Academy Award in a leading role for her portrayal of Carmen in *Carmen Jones,* a role she acted while someone else sang for her. She was born on November 9, 1922, in Cleveland. She and her sister Vivian were child stars, performing with their mother in various events in Cleveland. In search of a career in film, the mother and daughters moved to Los Angeles. "The Wonder Kids," as the sisters were known, had small roles in films. They later added Etta Jones as their third member and became known as the Dandridge Sisters, working regularly in New York at the Cotton Club. It was there that the fourteen-year-old Dandridge was noticed for her talent and beauty. She studied at the Actors' Laboratory in Los Angeles, and entered a career in film through her singing talent. Between 1937 and 1964, Dandridge appeared in a number of films, often typecast in the stereotypical roles commonly given to black actresses—in her case, she was cast as the "tragic mulatto." In 1951 she was the first black to perform in the Empire Room of New York's Waldorf Astoria. She conquered international audiences, integrated many previously "whites only" night spots, and, when performing at hotels, broke attendance records. *Island in the Sun,* a 1957 film in which she appeared opposite white actor John Justin, marked the first time the theme of interracial love was explored in the movies. Harry Belafonte and Joan Fontaine were also

The First Black Nobel Peace Prize Winner

The first black awarded the Nobel Peace Prize was Ralph Bunche (1904–1971). The award was presented on September 22, 1950, for his peace efforts in the Middle East. Born in the slums of Detroit, Bunche received his doctorate in political science from Harvard University in 1934, becoming the first black to be awarded the degree. In 1968 he became undersecretary general of the United Nations and was the highest ranking black in the U.N. at that time. Other blacks who have received Nobel Prizes are Martin Luther King Jr. (the youngest black so honored) in 1964, Albert J. Luthuli of South Africa in 1960, Desmond Tutu in 1984, and Nelson Mandela in 1993.

Sources: *Encyclopedia of Black America*, pp. 198–99; Hornsby, *Milestones in Twentieth-Century African-American History*, pp. 47, 49, 73, 158; *Contemporary Black Biography*, vol. 4, pp. 41–45; Smith, *Notable Black American Men*, 152–56.

paired in this film. In 1959 Dandridge appeared in the film version of the black opera *Porgy and Bess* and won a Golden Globe Award as best actress in a musical. When her film career faltered, she returned to nightclub performances. Dandridge suffered from severe nervous disorders, and later in life she was accused of being a drug and alcohol abuser. Reportedly, the cause of her death was an overdose of a drug prescribed for her depression, Tofranil.

Sources: Logan and Winston, *Dictionary of American Negro Biography*, pp. 157–58; Lee, *Interesting People*, p. 129; Smith, *Notable Black American Women*, pp. 248–49; *Ebony* 54 (August 1999), pp. 102–06; Bogle, *Dorothy Dandridge, A Biography*.

1956 • Writer, actress, and director Alice Childress (1920–1994) became the first black woman to win an Obie Award, for her off-Broadway play *Trouble in Mind*. The play dealt with stereotypes of black actors in white plays. Due to disagreements over its theme and interpretation, the play was never produced on Broadway. Childress was born into a poor, uneducated family in Charleston, South Carolina, and was reared in Harlem. She began her career as an actress in New York in 1940. She worked with the American Negro Theater and also performed on Broadway and on television. Her first novel, *A Hero Ain't Nothin' but a Sandwich*, was published in 1973. In addition to her theatrical and literary contributions, she taught at several colleges and universities.

Sources: Smith, *Notable Black American Women*, pp. 181–82; *The Black New Yorkers*, p. 281; Salzman, *Encyclopedia of African-American Culture and History*, vol. 1, pp. 537–38.

1959 • Playwright and activist Lorraine Hansberry (1930–1965) was the first to win the New York Drama Critics Award, for *A Raisin in the Sun*, in May 1959. The play, whose title she took from Langton Hughes' poem "Harlem," premiered in March 11 this year. It was the first on Broadway written by a black woman, and the first serious black drama to impact the dominant culture.

Sources: Abramson, *Negro Playwrights in the American Theatre*, pp. 239–54; Hine, *Black Women in America*, pp. 524–29; *Encyclopedia of Black America*, vol. 1, p. 425; Smith, *Notable Black American Women*, pp. 452–57.

1963 • William Leo Hansberry (1894–1964) was the first recipient of the Hailie Selassie I prize, which he received for his pioneering work in African history and anthropology. Hansberry was born in Gloster, Mississippi, and educated at Harvard University (B.A., 1921; M.A., 1932). He did further study at the University of Chicago's American Oriental Institute from 1936 to 1937, Oxford University from 1937 to 1938, and Cairo University in 1953. He taught at Howard University in Washington, D.C., from 1922 to 1959. In 1963 he was visiting professor at the University of Nigeria. His knowledge of Africa and African history, especially during the dawning of the Civil Rights Movement in the 1950s, helped him to become known as the "Father of African Students" at Howard University.

Sources: Logan and Winston, *Dictionary of American Negro Biography,* p. 386; *Contemporary Black Biography,* vol. 11, pp. 111–15.

1964 • On April 13, Sidney Poitier (1924–) became the first black actor to win an Oscar, for a starring role—best actor in the film *Lilies of the Field.* He was born on February 20, 1924, in Miami, and later moved to the Bahamas with his family. At age fifteen, Poitier returned to Miami and then moved to New York City. He made his Hollywood debut in 1950 and from then throughout the 1960s he made his greatest impact in film. In 1967 Poitier became the first black to have his hand and footprints placed in front of Grauman's Chinese Theater. His most controversial film was *Guess Who's Coming to Dinner?* (1967). Although he has many other acting credits, Poitier became a producer and director as well, working to provide more positive images of blacks. The first major film that he directed was *Buck and the Preacher* (1972), with Harry Belafonte as co-producer and co-star. With Bill Cosby, he had a highly successful series of comedies in the 1970s, including *Uptown Saturday Night* and *A Piece of the Action.* He appeared in numerous television episodes, programs, and specials that included *The New Bill Cosby Show* (1972), *The Night of 100 Stars II* (1985), and *The Kennedy Center Honors: A Celebration of the Performing Arts* (1989). Among his various honors, Queen Elizabeth II knighted him in 1968. In 1992 he became the first black to win a Lifetime Achievement Award at the Academy Award ceremony.

Sidney Poitier

Sources: *Encyclopedia of Black America,* p. 697; Kane, *Famous First Facts,* p. 405; *Negro Almanac,* pp. 191, 1153; Smith, *Notable Black American Men,* pp. 944–47.

1966 • Actor and comedian Bill Cosby became the first black to win an Emmy Award for continued performance as Outstanding Lead in a Dramatic Series, *I Spy.* In the show he played an undercover agent but disguised himself as trainer-companion to an international tennis player.

Sources: *Jet* 113 (26 May 2008): 20.

1969 • The first black male and the first black journalist to win a Pulitzer Prize for a feature photograph was Moneta J. Sleet Jr. (1926–1996). On May 5 he won the award for his photograph of Coretta Scott King and her daughter at the funeral of Martin Luther King Jr. Sleet was born in Owensboro, Kentucky. A box camera given to him by his parents when he was a child marked the beginning of his enchantment with photography. He continued his training and graduated from Kentucky State College, after which he obtained his master's degree in journalism from New York University. He joined the staff of *Ebony* magazine in 1955. Sleet also covered the Montgomery movement and the Selma to Montgomery March. He was the staff photographer for Johnson Publishing Company for over four decades. He was the official photographer for his high school and for Kentucky State College. Sleet covered many historical moments and was with Martin Luther King Jr. in Norway when King accepted the Nobel Peace Prize. The first exhibition of his photographs took place at a one-man show sponsored by Alpha Kappa Alpha Sorority in 1970. Sixteen years went by before his second exhibition, sponsored jointly by the Johnson and Phillip Morris companies, was mounted. Sleet's photographs always reflected the care and sensitivity of approach that came to be his trademark. In 2000, Sleet was honored with an historical marker, the Moneta Sleet Historical marker, located in Owensboro, Kentucky, across the street from his childhood home.

Sources: *Ebony Success Library,* vol. 1, p. 283; *Encyclopedia of Black America,* p. 796; Smith, *Notable Black American Men,* pp. 1069–70.

1969 • Learie Constantine [Lord Constantine] (1901–1971) was the first black to become a British peer. He was a member of the West Indies Cricket touring team from 1922 to the 1940s. He was knighted in 1962, and from 1962 to 1964 he was high commissioner from Trinidad.

Sources: File, *Black Settlers in Britain,* pp. 82–83; *Jet* 68 (8 July 1985), p. 4.

1970 • Jacob Lawrence Jr., (1917–2000) was the first black artist to receive the NAACP's Spingarn Award. Considered one of America's premier artists, he is represented in many

Emmy Award Firsts

The first black actress to receive an Emmy Award was Gail Fisher (1935–2000). She won the award in 1969 for her portrayal of secretary Peggy Fair on the CBS television show *Mannix*. In 1961 Fisher was also the first black to have a speaking part in a nationally televised commercial and is the only black woman to receive the Duse Award from the Lee Strasberg Actors Studio. She was one of America's most recognized television personalities in the 1960s and 1970s. Born in Orange, New Jersey, Fisher studied at the American Academy of Dramatic Arts, Lincoln Arts Center (where she was the first black accepted to the repertory theater), and the Actors Studio. In the 1950s she was a successful model with the Grace Del Marco organization and became well known in the black press for her work.

Sources: Bogle, *Primetime Blues,* pp. 137, 139, 153; *Ebony* (November 1974): 77; (November 1975): 158; (October 1978): 40; *Negro Almanac,* pp. 1137–38; *New York Times* (18 February 2001); Smith, *Notable Black American Women,* Book II, pp. 223–24.

museum collections. Lawrence's depictions include Toussaint L'Ouverture, John Brown, Harriet Tubman, the struggles of the Revolutionary heroes, and Harlem.

Sources: *Encyclopedia of Black America,* p. 498; *Negro Almanac,* pp. 1050–51; Robinson, *Historic Negro Biographies,* p. 222; Smith, *Notable Black American Men,* pp. 702–05.

1970 • Charles Gordone (1925–1995) was the first black playwright to win the Pulitzer Prize for drama. The play was *No Place to be Somebody*; it is the story of a black petty hustler and saloon owner who tried to elude local white Mafia. His first play and the most favorably received of all of his works, it was first presented on May 4, 1969 at the Joseph Papp Public Theater. Gordone was born in Cleveland and raised in Elkhart, Indiana. For nine years before his death, he taught English and theater at Texas Agricultural and Mechanical University.

Sources: Baskin, *Dictionary of Black Culture,* p. 187; *Black Writers,* pp. 224–26; *Jet* 89 (11 December 1995): 56; Salzman, *Encyclopedia of African-American Culture and History,* Supplement, pp. 113–14.

1970 • Charlemae Hill Rollins (1897–1979) was the first black winner of the Contance Lindsay Skinner Award (now the WNBA Award) of the Women's National Book Association. She was born in Holly Springs, Mississippi, on June 20, 1897. The family moved to the Oklahoma Territory in 1904 and settled in the small town of Beggs. A graduate of the University of Chicago, she became the first children's librarian at the George Cleveland Hall Branch in Chicago in 1932. She retired from that post thirty-one years later. Rollins had a regular storytelling hour, wrote book reviews, selected books for children, and held workshops for parents and teachers. Since she was a member of the book selection committee of the Children's Department, she made certain that her colleagues knew the detrimental effects of stereotypical images on black children. Therefore, she worked to dispel negative images of blacks in books for children and young adults and became an expert on intercultural relations and children's literature. In 1941 at the request of the National Council of Teachers of English, she published *We Build Together: A Reader's Guide to Negro Life and Literature for Elementary and High School Use.* From 1957 to 1958 Rollins was the first black president of the American Library Association's Children's Services Division. After she retired in 1963, Rollins wrote full-time and produced the type of books that she had recommended to black children. Her works included *Christmas Gif'* (1963) *They Showed the Way* (1964), *Famous American Negro Poets* (1965) and *Famous Negro Entertainers of Stage, Screen, and TV* (1967).

Sources: *Black Writers,* p. 494; Josey, *The Black Librarian in America,* pp. 153–54; Smith, *Notable Black American Women,* pp. 949–53; Schultz and Hast, *Women Building Chicago, 1790–1990,* pp. 764–66.

1972 • The first black woman nominated for an Academy Award for costume design was Elizabeth Courtney, for *Lady Sings the Blues.*

Sources: Hine, *Black Women in America,* p. 1328.

1979 • Sir Arthur Lewis [W. Arthur Lewis] (1915–1991) was the first black to win a Nobel Prize in a category other than peace, and the first to win in economics. Born in the West Indies, he received his bachelor's degree from the University of London in 1937 and his doctorate in 1940. He taught at that university and also at the University of Manchester. In 1959 Lewis was named vice chancellor of the University of the West Indies in Kingston, Jamaica. In 1963 Queen Elizabeth knighted him; in that year he also moved to Princeton University and remained there for twenty years, until he retired in 1983. During his career, Lewis wrote twelve books and numerous articles. He died on June 15, 1991.

Sources: *Jet* 57 (1 November 1979): 5; 98 (20 November 2000): 19; Scobie, *Black Britannia,* p. 149.

1979 • The first black recipient of the AMC Cancer Research Center Humanitarian Award was Kenneth Gamble (1943–). Born in Philadelphia, Gamble became a businessman and songwriter, and co-founded Philadelphia International Records. He and his partner, Leon Huff, wrote and produced chart-topping songs and records for such artists as Lou Rawls, Teddy Pendergrass, and the O'Jays. He received a Grammy Award in 1976.

Sources: 59 (15 January 1981): 29; *Who's Who among Black* Americans, 26th ed., p. 446.

1989 • The first recipient of the Actors' Equity award for broadening participation in the theater was Rosetta LeNoire (1911–2002). The award was later named in honor of LeNoire and presented annually. LeNoire, a theatrical producer, created nontraditional casting before the phrase itself was created. She was born Rosetta Borton in the Hell's Kitchen section of Manhattan. At age fifteen she became a chorus girl with the Time Steppers, her godfather's troupe. She studied at the Works Progress Administration program at a theater on the Lower East Side and earned an entry into the all-black version of *Macbeth.* She later joined the Robert Earl Jones Theater Group. In 1939 LeNoire made her Broadway debut in the all-black *The Hot Mikado.* Other theater credits include *A Streetcar Named Desire, Cabin in the Sky,* and *Lost in the Stars.* In 1944 she played Stella in *Anna Lucasta,* and starred in the 1958 film version. She played Mother Winslow on the television show *Family Matters* and acted in other shows, such as *Search for Tomorrow, The Guiding Light,* and *Gimme a Break.* In 1968 LeNoire founded the nonprofit theater group Amas, and later added a children's theatrical course to the program.

Sources: *New York Times* Obituaries (20 March 2002).

1992 • John Singleton (1968–) was the first black film director nominated for an Academy Award for the box office hit *Boyz N the Hood,* starring rap artist Ice Cube, Cuba Gooding Jr., Larry Fishburne, and Morris Chestnut. The film also earned him the New York Critics Circle Best New Director Award in 1991 and the MTV Movie Award for Best New Filmmaker in 1992. Although the film presents an anti-drug and anti-violence message, it sparked violence when it opened in several cities in the United States on July 12, 1991.

Sources: Hornsby, *Milestones in Twentieth Century African-American History,* p. 479; *Time* 139 (23 March 1992); Salzman, *Encyclopedia of African-American Culture and History,* Supplement, pp. 248–49.

1993 • Woody Strode (1915?–1995), known for his groundbreaking roles in films, was the first black inducted into the Walk of Western Stars at a ceremony held at the California Institute of the Arts in Valencia, California. He played villains and heroic figures in classic westerns and costume epics. Strode acted in a number of films, including *Sergeant Rutledge, Posse, Spartacus,* and *The Ten Commandments.* He played roles in John Wayne films as well, including *The Man Who Shot Liberty Valance,* in which he had a prominent part. Strode had been an outstanding football player—a 220-pound end, along with Kenny Washington, who starred for UCLA from 1937 to 1940. When professional football lifted its racial barrier, the Los Angeles Rams of the National Football League signed on Strode and Washington. While active in football, Strode started his acting career in 1941.

Sources: *Jet* 84 (3 May 1993): 34; 87 (23 January 1995): 61; Salzman, *Encyclopedia of African-American Culture and History,* vol. 2, pp. 1012–15.

1994 • Georgia Stribling became the first woman to earn the highest award for a suggestion from the U.S. Postal Service's St. Louis, Missouri, Accounting Center. She was award $35,000. After spending twenty-one years with the service, nineteen of her ideas were implemented, and she received bonuses for sixteen of her ideas. Among her ideas was a process to eliminate duplicate payments on replacement money orders, resulting in a savings of more than $2 million; projections were that the amount would continue to increase.

Sources: *Jet* 85 (11 April 1994):14.

1994 • The first black recipient of the American Culinary Federation Chef Professional Award was Johnny Rivers. Rivers was executive chef at Disney Village Marketplace in Lake Buena Vista, Florida.

Sources: *Jet* 86 (10 October 1994): 20.

1995 • Radio pioneer Herg Ken, known as the "King of Dusties," became the first black disk jockey inducted into the Radio Hall of Fame. Now broadcasting for over sixty years, he is believed to one of the oldest active disc jockeys on the air. He taught radio broadcasting part-time. His autobiography, *The Cool Gent: The Nine Lives of Radio Legend Herb Kent,* was published in 2009.

Sources: *Jet* 114 (4 August 2008): 30.

1996 • Composer and pianist George Theophilus Walker (1922–) won a Pulitzer Prize in music for his composition *Lilacs* for tenor or soprano and orchestra. He became the first living black American composer to win the prize. Composer Scott Joplin won the award posthumously in 1976 for *Treemonisha.*

Sources: *CBMR Digest* 9 (Fall 1996): 3.

1997 • The first jazz musician to win a Pulitzer Prize was Wynton Marsalis (1961–). He was honored for his epic jazz opera, *Blood on the Fields.*

Sources: *Contemporary Black Biography,* vol. 16, pp. 150–55; *Jet* 91 (28 April 1997), pp. 60–63; Smith, *Notable Black American Men,* pp. 758–62.

1997 • Civil rights pioneer Rosa Parks (1913–2005) received the first Lifetime Achievement Award from the Federal Transit Administration. During the awards ceremony held in Washington, D.C., she was honored for refusing to give up her seat to a white passenger on a segregated bus in Montgomery, Alabama, on December 1, 1955; this landmark act spurred the modern Civil Rights Movement. In 1998 Parks received the first International Freedom Conductor Award. The award honors people who were courageous in public or private actions and who have made significant contributions to freedom and human rights worldwide.

Sources: *Jet* 91 (31 March 1997): 32; 94 (2 November 1998): 20–22.

1998 • The first jazz musician to receive a MacArthur Fellowship was Maxwell "Max" Roach (1925–2007). Among other contributions, he teamed with songwriter Oscar Brown Jr. and vocalist Abbey Lincoln to create the album *We Insist: The Freedom Now Suite.*

Sources: *Jet* 93 (12 January 1998): 20; *Contemporary Black Biography,* vol. 21, pp. 150–55.

1998 • The first black recipient of the Edward J. Devitt Distinguished Service to Justice Award was Detroit judge Damon J. Keith (1922–), judge for the U.S. Sixth Circuit of Appeals. The award recognizes the best federal judges and is perhaps the most prestigious honor for a federal judge. Other judges nominate candidates, and a special committee selects the winner.

Sources: *Jet* 94 (29 June 1998): 46; *Contemporary Black Biography,* vol. 16, pp. 107–11.

1998 • Comedian Richard [Franklin Lennox Thomas] Pryor (1940–2005) was awarded the first Mark Twain Prize for American humor. The Peoria, Illinois, native was the first black comic to successfully draw on the inner life of the black community and its relationship to the broader society in his humor. The albums that he made in the 1970s and 1980s, filled with adult language and humor, sold millions. He entered television in 1964 when he appeared on the series *On Broadway Tonight*; he also appeared on the *Ed Sullivan Show* and the *Merv Griffin Show*. Pryor relocated from New York to Los Angeles and had bit parts in several movies, including *The Green Berets*. Toward the end of the 1960s he developed an addiction to cocaine. Other troubles followed, but by 1972 he had a new standup act and also appeared in the film *Lady Sings the Blues*. Pryor wrote for a number of television shows, including *The Flip Wilson Show* and *Sanford and Son*. He wrote and starred in the 1976 film *Bingo Long Traveling All Stars and Motor Kings*. On June 9, 1980, Pryor nearly burned to death from a fire that some writers claim he set, or that resulted from the process of freebasing cocaine. After recovery, he returned to writing, directing films, and starring in such films as *Jo Jo Dancer, Stir Crazy,* and *Bustin' Loose* before being slowed by multiple sclerosis.

Sources: *Jet* 94 (9 November 1998): 16–18; *Contemporary Black Biography,* vol. 24, pp. 136–40.

1999 • Oliver S. C. Franklin, who was educated at Lincoln and Oxford universities, became the first black British honorary consul in Philadelphia.

Sources: *Jet* 95 (18 January 1999): 10.

1999 • Actor-playwright John Amos (1941–) became the first honorary ambassador from the United States for the Legion of Goodwill, a Brazilian nonprofit group that offers social services to underprivileged children in North and South America. Amos was born in Newark, New Jersey, and attended Colorado State University and Long Beach City College. Between 1962 and 1965 he played for the American, Continental, and Canadian professional football leagues, then turned actor, producer, director, and writer. Although best known for his featured appearance on the television show *Good Times,* he also appeared on the *Mary Tyler Moore Show, Maude,* and *Roots.* Among his film appearances were *American Flyers, Coming to America,* and *Die Hard 2.* Amos appeared in a number of stage productions as well, including *The Emperor Jones* and *Split Second.*

Sources: *Jet* 95 (12 April 1999): 21; *Contemporary Black Biography,* vol. 8, pp. 10–13.

2001 • The first building in downtown Washington, D.C., to be named for a black man—the first black Cabinet member—was the Robert C. Weaver Federal Building. The structure was first dedicated in 1968 when Robert C. Weaver (1907–1997) was the first black secretary of Housing and Urban Development (HUD); it was rededicated in 2001. It houses the headquarters of HUD.

Sources: *Jet* 98 (17 July 2000): 17; 98 (31 July 2000): 20–22; Smith, *Notable Black American Men,* pp. 1195–98.

2001 • French President Jacques Chirac named composer Quincy Delight Jones (1933–) commander of the French Legion of Honor during a ceremony at the Elysee Palace in Paris. Jones became the first musician born in the United States to achieve this status. He was named to the Legion of Honor in 1990, becoming the thirty-second American so honored.

Sources: *Jet* 99 (16 April 2001): 27; Smith, *Notable Black American Men,* pp. 656–60.

2002 • Suzann-Lori Parks (1964?–) became the first black woman to win a Pulitzer Prize for drama, for her play *Topdog/Underdog.* The play premiered in July 2001 at the nonprofit Public Theater off Broadway. *Topdog/Underdog* is a dark comedy with only two characters—brothers Lincoln and Booth. A native of Fort Knox, Kentucky, Parks attended mount Holyoke College in Massachusetts and studied with James Baldwin at Hampshire College. It was Baldwin who encouraged her to write plays. Parks received a $500,000 MacArthur Fellows grant in 2001 to support her work. Now a resident of Brooklyn, New York, and

Academy Award Firsts

In 2002 when Halle Maria Berry (1967? –) won an Oscar for her lead role in *Monster's Ball,* she became the first black actress to win the award in that category in Academy Award history. Presented in Hollywood ceremonies on March 24, 2002, the Oscar was awarded for her portrayal of a Death Row widow who forged a relationship with a white prison guard. Oscar night was a momentous one for black actors in Hollywood. For the first time in almost four decades, a black actor won an Oscar for a lead role. Denzel Washington (1954–) won for his portrayal of a corrupt police office in *Training Day.* In 1989 he won a supporting Oscar for *Glory.* Sidney Poitier (1927–), who in 1963 was the first black actor to win the award for a starring role, in *Lilies of the Field,* won an honorary career-achievement award. He accepted the honor, he said, "in memory of all of the African-American actors who went before me, on whose shoulders I stand." Actress Whoopi Goldberg helped to make the occasion an historic one by continuing to serve as master of ceremonies.

Sources: *Jet* 101 (8 April 2002): 14–15; *New York Times* (25 March 2002); *Tennessean* (25 March 2002).

Venice Beach, California, she heads the dramatic writing program at the California Institute of Arts.

Sources: *Atlanta Journal/Constitution* (9 April 2002); *USA Today* (9 April 2002); *Jet* 101 (29 April 2002): 25; *New York Times* (8 April 2002).

2007 • Grandmaster Flash and the Furious Five, rap pioneers, became the first hip-hop artists inducted into the Rock and Roll Hall of Fame, in March. D.J. Grandmaster Flash (1948–) was born Joseph Saddler and served as musical director/house DJ on *The Chris Rock Show.* The Furious Five include Melle Mel and his brother, Kid Creole, or Nathaniel "Danny" Glover; Cowboy, or Keith Wiggins; Mr. Ness aka Scorpio, or Ed Morris; and Raheim, or Guy Todd Williams.

Sources: *Jet* 110 (29 January 2007): 52–53

2007 • The first rap artist to receive a star on the Hollywood Walk of Fame was Queen Latifah.

Sources: *Jet* 112 (23 July 2007): 60–61.

2007 • The Academy Awards this year was one of the most diverse ever, when eight blacks received nominations, making the show a historic first. Those nominated were Bob Beemer, Willie Burton, Jennifer Hudson, Michael Minkler, Will Smith, Forest Whitaker, Djimon Hounsou, and Eddie Murphy.

Sources: *Jet* 111 (12 March 2007): 8–10, 62, 64

2009 • An anchor on CNN, Soledad O'Brien became the first recipient of the Soledad O'Brien Freedom's Voice Award, presented in Atlanta in April. An author, anchor, and special correspondent for CNN's *In America,* O'Brien is known for her award-winning documentaries, such as *Black in America* 1 and 2, *The King Assassination,* and others. The daughter of mixed-race marriage of immigrants, she grew up in Smithtown, Long Island, and studied at Harvard.

Sources: *Jet* 113 (28 June 2008): 18; O'Brien, *The Next Big Story: My Journey Through the Land of Possibilities.*

2010 • Notre Dame University had its first black valedictorian in its 161-year-history this year. Katie Washington (1989–), who earned the honor, presented the valedictory address during Commencement exercises on Sunday, May 16, in the school's stadium. The Gary, Indiana, native majored in biology with a view toward following her father's footsteps into medicine.

Sources: *Jet* 117 (3 May 2010): 10.

2010 • Lester N. Coney (of Mesirow Financial) and Peter C. B. Bynoe (of Loop Capital) received the first-ever August Wilson Award for their commitment to increase diversity at the Goodman Theater in Chicago.

Sources: *Jet* 118 (13 December 2010): 41.

2010 • Geoffrey Fletcher became the first African American to win an Oscar for an adapted screenplay. The Oscar was presented at the 82nd Annual Academy Awards on March 7. The play *Precious* was based on the novel *Push* by Sapphire.

Sources: *Tennessean* (8 March 2010).

2011 • Alberra Mogessie, president of the Geological Society of Africa and a fellow of the African Scientific Institute, is the first African to hold this position. He received the Nigerian Mining and Geosciences Society Award at the Annual Conference of the NMGS held in Minna, Niger State, Nigeria, March 6–11 this year. The award is given to any hard rock geologist regardless of nationality who has made significant contributions to hard rock geology of the African continent.

Sources: Email from Lee O. Cherry to Jessie Carney Smith, 18 April 2011.

Miscellaneous Topics

1806 • A child named Thomas was the first black child born at the White House. He was born to slave parents Fanny and Eddy, the property of President Thomas Jefferson. The child died two days later. Jefferson's grandson, also named Thomas, was the first child born there.

Sources: Seale, "Upstairs and Downstairs," *American Visions* (February–March 1995), pp. 16–20.

1850? • A black chef, possibly Hyram S. Thomas Bennett, was reputed to have introduced potato chips in America. It has also been claimed that an American Indian, George Crum, first made potato chips in 1853; they were called Saratoga Potato Chips. Another claim is made on behalf of a locally famous black cook, Catherine A. Wicks (1814–1917). She is said to have introduced them at Moon's Clubhouse in Saratoga Lake, New York.

Sources: Bennett, *Before the Mayflower,* p. 650; Kane, *Famous First Facts,* p. 493; *Negro Year Book, 1921–22,* p. 6.

1862 • The first time a United States president addressed an exclusively black audience was on August 14, when Abraham Lincoln invited a committee of blacks to come to the White House. Later, Lincoln was criticized for offering as a solution to the U.S. racial problem the immigration of blacks to Africa or Central America.

Sources: *Jet* 94 (17 August 1998): 19.

1866 • James Mason (1840–?) bought a house and lot on West Cumberland Avenue in Knoxville, Tennessee, and became the city's first black property owner and taxpayer. Mason participated in a variety of civic and charitable causes. Born in Knoxville, he had been a slave, the property of Major James Swan who taught him and the other slaves that he owned to read. He was permitted to hire himself out for extra money. After he was freed, he continued to work to buy his wife's freedom. After Emancipation, his slave wife was freed and he used his money to buy a house and a lot, becoming the city's first black to own property. He became a charter member of Shiloh Presbyterian Church in 1865. Mason was especially concerned about the black hearing-impaired in Tennessee, and in 1879 he founded a school for such children that the Tennessee School for the Deaf would not serve. The state legislature passed a bill on April 4, 1881, establishing a school for the black hearing-impaired and the first session was held in Mason's home. Ten children attended. In summer 1883 the students were transferred to a site on Dandridge Avenue. To support himself during this endeavor, from 1884 to 1902 Mason worked as a police officer.

Sources: Lovett and Wynn, *Profiles of African Americans in Tennessee*, pp. 84–85.

1889 • "Nigger Add" [Old Add, Old Negro Ad] (fl. 1889–1906?) was the first known range boss in the Southwest. He was also a rider and roper. With his strong, stocky build and powerful hands, he always rode horses that others feared. He worked most of his active life with cattleman George W. Littlefield or his outfits in the Texas Panhandle and Eastern Mexico. He never found the horses too rough to ride nor was the trip too long to handle. By the end of the century he was no longer a range boss, as by then white cowboys resented him. By the early twentieth century he was too old and crippled to break in young horses, but he maintained a concern for the young, neophyte riders. Among other recognitions, he was remembered as "the most famous Negro cowpuncher in the Old West."

Sources: Logan and Winston, *Dictionary of American Negro Biography,* pp. 5–6.

1892 • Hotel Berry in Athens, Ohio, was the first to provide needles, thread, buttons, and cologne in its guest rooms. Owned by Edwin C. Berry (1854–1931), the hotel had twenty rooms, all of which were restricted to white patrons. Berry was born in Oberlin, Ohio, and moved with his family to Athens County, Ohio, in 1856. He became active in the Republican party and ran unsuccessfully for a clerkship in state government in 1899. In 1892 he built Hotel Berry on property next to a restaurant that he owned; it soon prospered and by 1921, when Berry retired, he had expanded the hotel to fifty rooms. He was said to be the most successful black hotel operator in any small city in the country.

Sources: Logan and Winston, *Dictionary of American Negro Biography,* p. 40–41.

1901 • President Theodore Roosevelt invited Tuskegee Institute's president Booker T. Washington (1956–1915) to dinner at the White House on October 16, 8:00 P.M., marking the first time a black American had been entertained there. Blacks had previously visited the White House as a spokesperson or as a political symbol. After dinner, Washington and Roosevelt discussed the president's plans for the South.

Sources: Chase, "Memorable Meetings," *American Visions* (February–March, 1995): 26–33.

1905 • George McJunkin (1851–1922), cowboy, bronco buster, Native American arrowhead collector, and explorer, was the first person to recognize the bones of extinct bison near Folsom, New Mexico, and try to call them to the attention of other people. The bones themselves were less significant than the spear points found with them: He had discovered the first site that proved people lived in North America over 10,000 years ago. Born in rural Texas, he grew up on a horse ranch. As a child he worked as a freighter's helper and a buffalo skinner. He knew how to handle horses and cows well, and when he was twenty-one he helped drive several hundred horses through Texas to the border of Colorado and Mexico. McJunkin died in Folsom, New Mexico, in January 1922.

Sources: Logan and Winston, *Dictionary of American Negro Biography,* pp. 417–18; Durham, *The Negro Cowboys,* pp.159–60; Salzman, *Encyclopedia of African-American History and Culture,* Supplement, p. 180.

1914 • The first black to be buried (with military honors) in the Rosedale Cemetery in Los Angeles was Colonel Allen Allensworth (1842–1914). He was a businessman, chaplain, educator, and town founder. He was born to slave parents in Louisville, Kentucky, and, after three attempts escaped from his master. Allensworth joined the 44th Illinois Infantry as a civilian nurse in the hospital corps in 1862. He also worked on a hospital ship until he joined the navy in April 1863 and later became a chief petty officer. He studied at a Freedmen's Bureau school in Louisville and in 1868 taught at one of the bureau's schools in Christmasville, Kentucky. Allensworth was ordained a Baptist minister in Louisville and served several congregations in the state. In 1886 President Grover Cleveland commissioned him as a chaplain of the all-black 24th Infantry, and he was a part of the Philippine Insurrection during the Spanish American War. After retiring from the military in 1906, when he was the senior chaplain in the army, Allensworth moved to Los Angeles and organized a company to assist blacks in migrating to California. The company set up a new town in Tulare County called Allensworth; they sold lots to the new residents. Soon nearly 200 families had settled there, establishing farms and businesses. After he died on September 14, the town began to decline. The site of the town is now the Allensworth State Historical Park.

Sources: *American Visions* 15 (August–September 2000): Logan and Winston, *Dictionary of American Negro Biography,* pp. 13–14.

1919 • Southside Settlement House, the first for blacks with a black staff, was founded in 1918–19 by Ada Sophia Dennison McKinley (1868–1952), who recognized such a need among the thousands of blacks who migrated to Chicago during World War I in search of work. The Works Progress Administration (WPA) supported the settlement house in the mid–1930s and early 1940s. On April 1, 1949, with the help of the community, a new home was founded and renamed the Ada S. McKinley Community House in her honor. Although she had retired, McKinley continued to contribute to the program by mentoring graduate social work students. The home continued to exist at the beginning of the twenty-first century. McKinley was born in Galveston, Texas, and relocated with her family to Corpus Christi. She graduated from Prairie View College in Prairie View, Texas, as well as Tillotson Missionary College in San Antonio. She taught school in Austin and later married and moved to Chicago's South Side. McKinley was a volunteer hostess to black soldiers at War Camp Community Services, organized by the Chicago Urban League. She organized the Soldiers and Sailors Club in 1919 at the facility on South Wabash that housed the program. After the war she assisted returning soldiers and blacks who had migrated from the South to find shelter, jobs, food, and to meet other needs. McKinley aided in settling the racial unrest that occurred on July 27, 1919 (the Chicago riots). She worked with the Chicago Commission on Race Relations to help restore order and provide other needed relief. She revitalized the South Side Community Services program and with the help of black banker Jesse Binga and others, she renamed the facility the South Side Settlement House. At the same time, she became president, head resident, teacher, and office worker at the center.

Sources: Lee, *Interesting People,* p. 25; Schultz and Hast, *Women Building Chicago, 1790–1990,* pp. 571–73.

1920 • The Katy Ferguson Home for black unwed mothers opened, the only such home at that time. Catherine "Katy" Williams Ferguson (1779?–1854), for whom the home was named, was a social worker and a pioneer in the Sunday school movement. Her mother, a house slave, gave birth to Ferguson as she traveled by schooner from Virginia to New York. Although the Sunday school movement began in Gloucester, England, in 1770, it spread to the United States. Since state law required slave masters to teach the Scripture to black children, many in the area took the children to the New York African Free School for this instruction. Ferguson became involved by teaching children in her home.

Sources: *The Black New Yorkers,* p. 172; Smith, *Notable Black American Women,* pp. 342–43.

1947 • Kenneth Bancroft Clark (1914–2005) and Mamie Phipps Clark (1917–1983) established the Northside Center for Child Development. This was the first comprehensive agency that addressed the psychological and social needs of black children. Kenneth Bancroft Clark was born in the Panama Canal Zone and received his bachelor's and master's degrees from Howard University in 1935 and 1936, and his doctorate from Columbia University in 1942. He taught at Howard University, Hampton Institute (now Hampton University), and City College of New York. His interest in the nature of racism led him and his wife, Mamie, to publish the results of their research on the effects of segregation on Washington, D.C., kindergarten students. He also had a long involvement in the case *Brown v. Board of Education* that resulted in the desegregation of public schools in 1954.

Mamie Phipps Clark was born in Hot Springs, Arkansas, and received her bachelor's and master's degrees from Howard University in 1938 and 1939. She and her research partner and husband Kenneth Clark received fellowships from the Rosenwald Foundation to continue their study. She received her doctorate in psychology from Columbia University in 1943; she and Kenneth Clark were Columbia's first two black students to be awarded doctorates in psychology. Her work in psychological testing at a shelter for homeless girls in New York City pointed up the need for psychological services for minorities, and led the Clark team to establish the Northside Center.

Sources: *The Black New Yorkers*, p. 265; Salzman, *Encyclopedia of African-American Culture and History*, vol. 2, p. 577 (Kenneth Bancroft Clark); Supplement, pp. 43–54 (Mamie Phipps Clark).

Sammy Davis Jr.

1969 • Sammy Davis Jr. (1926–1990) became the first black entertainer to sleep in the White House. Known as America's "Ambassador of Goodwill," he began his career at age three, performing in vaudeville with his father, Sam Sr., and his uncle, Will Mastin. This singer, dancer, and actor appeared on almost every variety show and comedy series on network television between 1956 and 1980. Davis also appeared in cabarets, night clubs, Broadway musicals, and motion pictures. He had a number of pop hits as well, including "What Kind of Fool am I" in 1962 and "The Candy Man" in 1972. In 1973 he won a Grammy Award for "The Candy Man" and he had two Emmy Award nominations early on in his career. While Davis often worked with his friends Frank Sinatra and Dean Martin and others in what was called "The Rat Pack," he made his last film appearance in 1989 with Gregory Hines in *Tap*. Davis was born in the Harlem section of New York City. He received no formal education but spent his life in entertainment.

Sources: Hornsby, *Milestones in Twentieth-Century African-American History*, p. 447; *Jet* 78 (4 June 1990), pp. 32, 34; Southern, *Biographical Dictionary of Afro-American and African Musicians*, p. 96.

1969 • Harlem-Dowling Children's Services was established, becoming New York City's first black-staffed agency that addressed the needs of black and Latino children and their families. It was a satellite of Spence-Chapin Services to Children.

Sources: *The Black New Yorkers*, pp. 339–40.

1969 • The Metropolitan Applied Research Center became the first black think-tank established in the United States. Located in Manhattan, its mission was to analyze and advocate solutions to problems of black people, especially those related to education. Psychologist Kenneth Bancroft Clark (1914–2005) was in charge of the center.

Sources: *The Black New Yorkers*, pp. 338–39.

1996 • The first black-owned building on Washington, D.C.'s historic Pennsylvania Avenue, between Capitol Hill and the White House, was dedicated in 1996. The building was the new headquarters for the National Council of Negro Women. President Bill Clinton wrote to NCNW leaders, "Welcome neighbors."

Sources: *Jet* 90 (23 September 1996), p. 13.

1999 • Nathaniel Abraham was the first child charged as an adult for murder, when he was age eleven. He was convicted in an Oakland County Court in Michigan for shooting a man with a rifle and was released from prison in 2007, just before his twenty-first birthday.

Sources: *Jet* 119 (5 February 2007): 16.

2006 • The world's oldest woman this year was Lizzie Bolden (1890–2006), according to the *Guinness Book of World Records*. When she died in Memphis in December, she was 116 years old. Earlier, the daughter of former slaves was a farmworker in Fayette County, Tennessee. Only two of her seven children survived her. Other survivors included 40 grandchildren, 75 great grandchildren, 150 great-great grandchildren, 220 great-great-great grandchildren and 75 great-great-great-great grandchildren.

Sources: *Jet* 111 (8 January 2007): 55.

2007 • George Bell, a sheriff's deputy, stands 7 feet 8 inches, and, according to Guinness World Records, he is the tallest person in the United States. His medical condition, called gigantism, led to a severe growth spurt at age nine, when he was 5 feet 4 inches tall. The Portsmouth resident is a former college basketball player and later played with the Harlem Wizards and the Harlem Globetrotters.

Sources: *Jet* 112 (26 November 2007): 56.

2007 • William "Kip" Ward, who served as Commander U.S. Africa Command from 2007 to 2011, was chosen as the first to hold the AFRICOM post. The post was designed to aid Africa in handling its security issues.

Sources: *Ebony* 65 (January 2010): 110.

2008 • The first black woman to win a world championship in public speaking was LaShunda Rundles. When she delivered a speech called "Speak" at the Toastmasters International Speech Contest, she became the first black woman to win the title World Champion of Public Speaking. The Dallas native won her trophy at the finals held in Calgary, Alberta, Canada.

Sources: *Jet* 114 (3 November 2008): 18.

2008 • Kimberly McInnis Shelton was the first black to be named National Young Mother of the Year. She won the title at the American Mothers, Inc. convention held in Lincoln, Nebraska. The wife and full-time mother of two lives in New Hampshire.

Sources: *Jet* 113 (21 July 2007): 220.

Pioneers

1811 • Paul Cuffe (1759–1818) led the first group of blacks to investigate resettlement in Sierra Leone. He transported thirty-eight blacks there in the first systematic attempt to repatriate blacks from the United States.

Sources: Logan and Winston, *Dictionary of American Biography,* vol. 2, no. 2, p. 585; Robinson, *Historical Negro Biographies,* pp. 12–13; Simmons, *Men of Mark,* pp. 336–39; Smith, *Notable Black American Men,* pp. 241–43.

1816 • Bob, baptized as Juan Crisobal (1819), was the first black English-speaking settler in California.

Sources: *Encyclopedia of Black America,* p. 78.

1826 • Peter Ranne [Ranee] was the first black to reach California via overland travel.

Sources: *Encyclopedia of Black America,* p. 78.

1847 • Green Flake, Oscar Crosby, and Hank Lay were the first blacks to settle in Salt Lake Valley, Utah.

Sources: Cantor, *Historic Landmarks of Black America,* p. 334.

Transportation

1840s • A. F. Boston was the first known black to command an American whaling ship, the *Loper*. The officers and most of the ship's crew were black, and the ship made at least one successful trip.

Sources: *The Real McCoy,* p. 35.

1860 • The first black Pony Express riders were stagecoach driver and gold miner George Monroe (1843–1886) and William Robinson. Little else is known about their activities, although Monroe became a noted stage driver in whose honor Monroe Meadows in Yosemite National Park is named.

Sources: Katz, *Black West,* pp. 128–29; *Negro Almanac,* p. 213; Reasons, *They Had a Dream,* vol. 2, p. 41.

Hugh Mulzac

1942 • Hugh Mulzac (1886–1971) was the first black captain of an American merchant marine ship. In 1920 he became the first black to earn a ship master's license, but he was unable to find a position as captain because of racial prejudice. In 1942 he was granted the right to man the liberty ship *Booker T. Washington*. His ship saw antiaircraft action on a number of occasions.

Sources: Baskin and Runes, *Dictionary of Black Culture*, p. 311; Hornsby, *Chronology of African-American History*, p. 91; *Negro Almanac*, p. 1426.

1942 • The first Liberty ship named for an African American was the S.S. *Booker T. Washington*. Singer Marian Anderson christened the ship and it was launched from a New Jersey shipyard. It carried war cargo to Europe during World War II.

Sources: *African American Almanac*, 11th ed., p. 82.

1969 • A nuclear-powered submarine named in honor of George Washington Carver was launched and commissioned, becoming the first submarine to honor a black.

Sources: Garrett, *Famous First Facts about Negroes*, p. 122; Kane, *Famous First Facts*, p. 562.

1978 • Vallorie Harris O'Neil was the first black woman engineer for the Burlington-Northern Railroad. Harris worked in the Cicero, Illinois, yard.

Sources: Jet 53 (5 January 1978): 28.

1979 • Audrey Neal was the first woman of any ethnic group to become a longshoreman on the Eastern seaboard.

Sources: *Negro Almanac*, p. 1432.

1992 • William "Bill" Pinkney became the first black American and the fourth American to navigate a sailboat single-handedly around the world. He grew up in Chicago, raised by his mother on the South Side. His interest in sailing developed out of a fictional work that he read as a child; it dealt with a Polynesian boy who lost his fear of water by sailing his own boat. A former marketing executive for Johnson Products and other cosmetic companies, and a navy veteran, he had been licensed to sail by the U.S. Coast Guard. He spent five years preparing for the trip. He bought a forty-seven-foot cutter that he named *Commitment* and set sail from Boston in August 1990. He sailed 32,000 nautical miles, stopping in Brazil, Australia, and elsewhere; he encountered tropical storms along the way. In June 1992 he ended his twenty-two-month solo journey in Boston's harbor.

Sources: James, "Dream Voyage: Captain Pinkney Spans the Globe," *American Visions* 10 (December/January 1996): 21–24.

1995 • Trooper Mark Campbell (1967–) became the first black soldier to join the Sovereign's escort of the Household Cavalry in London and, on state occasions, ride next to the Queen. After years of persuasion, led by Prince Charles, to remove racial barriers and recruit minorities, Campbell joined the elite Household Cavalry. Previously he was a postal worker.

Sources: *Jet* 88 (28 August 1995): 65.

1996 • Beatrice Vormawah of Ghana became the only woman to captain a ship in Africa, and one of about a dozen female captains in the world. Growing up in Ghana, she was unable to swim and was forbidden from going near the water.

1999 • In the U.S. Coast Guard commissioned a cutter in honor of Pulitzer Prize winner Alex Haley (1921–1992), marking the first time a military vessel was named for a journalist (U.S. Coast Guard honorees John H. Murphy and Robert L. Vann were publishers as well as journalists.) The vessel is the 282-foot cutter formerly known as the USS *Edenton,* once a rescue and salvage vessel for the U.S. Navy and now reentered into the Coast Guard's fleet. It was based at Kodiak, Alaska, and used for law enforcement and search and rescue missions in the Bering Sea, Gulf of Alaska, and the northern Pacific Ocean. Haley spent twenty years in the Coast Guard and became the first head of its office of public affairs.

Sources: *Jet* 96 (2 August 1999): 22–23.

Ships Named in Honor of African Americans, 1943–2011: A Selected List

	Date	Name of Ship	Type	In Honor of
U.S. Navy Ships				
	1943	USS Harmon*	destroyer escort	Mess Attendant First Class Leonard Roy Harmon
	1972	USS Jesse L. Brown	Knox-class frigate	Ensign Jesse L. Brown, Naval aviator
	1973	USS Miller	DE 1091, later FF1091	Cook Third Class Doris ("Dorie") Miller
	1979	USNS PFC James Anderson	T-AK-3002	Pfc James Anderson Jr., USMC
	1987	USS Rodney M. Davis	FFG-60	Sergeant Rodney M. Davis, USMC Vietnam War hero
	1998	USNS Henson	T-AGS-63	Matthew Alexander Henson, Ship's Cook 3rd class
	2004	USS Pinckney	DDG 91	William Pinckney, Navy Cross recipient
	2009	USNS Carl Brasher	T-AKE 7	Master Chief Boatswain's Mate (master diver) Carl M. Brasher
	2010	USNS Charles S. Dre	warship (cargo/ammunition)	Dr. Charles S. Drew, founder of first blood bank
	2010	USS Gravely	DDG 107	Vice Adm. Samuel L. Gravely Jr., War ship commander
	2011	USNS Medgar Evers*	Cargo/ammunition T-AKE 10	Medgar Evers, civil rights leader, War ship commander
Liberty Ships				
	1943	SS George Washington Carver	Cargo	Scientist, educator
	1943	SS Frederick Douglass	Cargo	Abolitionist
	1943	SS Paul Laurence Dunbar	Cargo	Poet
	1943	SS James Weldon Johnson	Cargo	Author, civil rights activist
	1943	SS John Merrick	Cargo	Insurance company executive
	1944	SS John H. Murphy	Cargo	Newspaper publisher
	1944	SS Harriet Tubman	Cargo	Abolitionist
	1942	SS Booker T. Washington	Cargo	College founder
	1944	SS Bert William	Cargo	Minstrel show actor
Victory Ships				
	1945	SS Fisk Victory	Cargo	Fisk University
	1945	SS Lane Victory	Cargo	Lane College
	1945	SS Howard Victory	Cargo	Howard University
	1945	SS Tuskegee Victory	Cargo	Tuskegee Institute

* Initially, ships were named after kings, heroes, ideals, institutions, American places, and small insects with a potent sting, such as Hornet and Wasp. The Merchant Marine Act of 1936 called for America's shipbuilding program. World War II provided the impetus to intensify efforts to replace the obsolete and declining numbers of ships. Some 2,710 mass-produced ships, known as Liberty ships, were built. The Liberty ships proved to be too slow and too small to serve the needs of the U.S. and her Allies during wartime. Then larger and faster vessels were built and were known as Victory ships. The first Victory Ship named in honor of a black college was the SS Fisk Victory, on April 25, 1945. Of the 2,700 Liberty Ships built, 17 were named for outstanding African Americans. The first and perhaps the only U.S. Liberty ship named in honor of a black woman was the SS Harriet Tubman, launched on June 3, 1944. By 2011, twelve U.S. Navy ships were named honoring blacks.

Sources: "Liberty Ships and Victory Ships, America's Lifeline in War," http://www.nps.gov/nr/twhp/wwwlps/lessons/116liberty_victory_ships/116liberty_victory_ships.htm; "Ships Named after Black Americans, *Black Americans in Defense of Our Nation*, p. 37.

ORGANIZATIONS

Academic and Intellectual Societies

1786 • On August 23, 1786, Jean-Baptiste Lislet-Geoffrey was the first black correspondent of the French Academy of Sciences. Lislet was an artillery officer and in charge of maps on the Isle de France (now Mauritius). He made contributions in cartography and natural science.

Sources: *Jet* 56 (23 August 1979): 18; 70 (25 August 1986): 24; Simmons, *Men of Mark,* pp. 991–92.

1877 • George Washington Henderson was the first black elected to Phi Beta Kappa. (Edward Alexander Bouchet [1825–1918] was elected on the basis of his work as a member of the Yale class of 1874, but not until 1884.) Phi Beta Kappa was founded in 1776 and became the most prestigious humanities honors society. Henderson was elected by the Alpha chapter at the University of Vermont, from which he graduated. The Yale chapter, Alpha of Connecticut, ceased to function in 1871 but was revived in 1884. Henderson was born in slavery; he served in the Vermont regiment of the Union Army from 1861 to 1865. After the war Henderson, who was illiterate, enrolled in courses at the University of Vermont, graduating in 1877 at the top of his class. He later attended Yale Divinity School and chose an academic career as a theologian.

Sources: *Black Issues in Higher Education* (27 September 1990): 20; Logan and Winston, *Dictionary of American Negro Biography,* pp. 50–51; Current, *Phi Beta Kappa in American Life,* p. 233; Smith, *Notable Black American Men,* pp. 97–99. (Bouchet); Phi Beta Kappa, *Membership Directory,* 2000, vol. 1, p. ix.

1897 • The American Negro Academy, founded on March 5, 1897, with the purpose of studying various aspects of black life and establishing a black intellectual tradition, was the first national black learned society. Papers appeared in print until 1924. A leading figure in the establishment of the academy was Alexander Crummell (1819–1898). Its membership of forty included W. E. B. Du Bois (1868–1963), Kelly Miller (1863–1939), and Paul Laurence Dunbar (1872–1906). Noted contributors to its publications were Du Bois and Theophylus G. Steward.

Sources: Bennett, *Before the Mayflower,* p. 507; Logan and Winston, *Dictionary of American Negro Biography,* pp. 145–47; Moses, *Alexander Crummell,* pp. 258–75, 365–66.

The Association for the Study of Negro Life and History

Carter G. Woodson

In 1915, the Association for the Study of Negro Life and History was organized by Carter G. Woodson (1875–1950) as the first learned society specifically devoted to the professional study of black history. Its first meeting was on September 9, 1915, in the office of the Wabash Avenue YMCA in Chicago. Woodson was born in New Canton, Virginia, and educated at Berea College in Kentucky (Litt.B., 1907), the University of Chicago (B.A., 1907; M.A., 1908) and Harvard (Ph.D., 1912). The first issue of the *Journal of Negro History* appeared in 1916. This organization first sponsored Negro History Week (now Black History Month) in 1926. That same year Woodson, who is known as the "Father of Black History," received the NAACP's Spingarn Medal for his contributions to the advancement of black people.

Sources: *Cantor, Historic Landmarks of Black America*, p. xxvi; Logan and Winston, *Dictionary of American Negro Biography*, pp. 665–67; *Ebony* 48 (February 1993): 23–24, 28; Smith, *Notable Black American Men*, pp. 1256–59.

1937 • Hugh Morris Gloster (1911–2002) was the founder and first president of the College Language Association. A native of Brownsville, Tennessee, Gloster graduated from Morehouse College in Atlanta in 1931 and received a master's degree from Atlanta University in 1933. After teaching at LeMoyne-Owen College in Memphis, he returned to Morehouse where he taught until 1943. In that year he also received a doctorate from New York University. Gloster worked for the United Service Organizations in Arizona and Atlanta. Later he moved to Hampton Institute (now Hampton University) in Virginia and rose to become dean of the faculty. He was a Fulbright professor of English at Japan's Hiroshima University and became a part of the international educational exchange program at the University of Warsaw in Poland. Gloster's distinguished career in education was capped with his presidency of Morehouse College from 1967 to 1987. While there he strengthened the college's endowment, doubled the size of the campus as well as the faculty, doubled faculty salaries, increased to sixty-five percent the total the number of faculty with Ph.D. degrees, and quadrupled the enrollment. He was the school's seventh president and its first alumnus to lead the institution. Among Gloster's publications were *Negro Voices in American Fiction* (1948) and *My Life—My Country—My World* (1952). He died in Decatur, Georgia, on February 16, 2002, at age ninety.

Sources: *New York Times* (7 March 2002); Shockley and Chandler, *Living Black American Authors*, pp. 56–57; *Who's Who among Black Americans*, 14th ed., p. 480.

1943 • On December 22, 1943, W[illiam] E[dward] B[urghardt] Du Bois (1868–1963) was the first black elected to the National Institute of Arts and Letters. Founded in 1989, the institute was chartered by an act of Congress to honor "notable achievement in art, music or literature." It was modeled after the National Institute of France and limited membership to two hundred and fifty.

Sources: Logan and Winston, *Dictionary of American Negro Biography*, pp. 193–99; *New York Times* (23 December 1943).

1946 • Charles Spurgeon Johnson (1893–1956) was the first black to head the Southern Sociological Society. A distinguished sociologist and founder of the National Urban League's magazine, *Opportunity*, he also became the first black president of Fisk University in Nashville, in 1946.

Sources: Logan and Winston, *Dictionary of American Negro Biography*, pp. 347–49; *Encyclopedia of Black America*, pp. 471–72; Smith, *Notable Black American Men*, pp. 616–19.

1948 • E. Franklin Frazier (1894–1962), sociologist, educator, writer, and activist, was the first black president of the American Sociological Society. Born in Baltimore, Frazier received his bachelor's degree from Howard University in 1916, his master's degree at Clark University in Worchester, Massachusetts, in 1920, and his doctorate from the University of Chicago in 1931. From 1916 to 1917 he taught at Tuskegee Institute (now Tuskegee University) in Alabama but left because he rejected the school's vocational emphasis at the time. He taught at other black colleges, including St. Paul's Normal and Industrial School in Lawrenceville, Virginia, and Atlanta University, where he was acting director of the School of Social Work while also serving as professor of sociology at Morehouse College. Frazier spent most of his teaching career, which spanned from 1934 to 1959, at Howard University in Washington, D.C. A prolific author, his most famous work is *Black Bourgeoisie* (1957).

E. Franklin Frazier

Sources: Logan and Winston, *Dictionary of American Negro Biography,* pp. 241–44; Robinson, *Historical Negro Biographies,* pp. 192–93; Smith, *Notable Black American Men,* pp. 428–31.

1953 • Ralph Johnson Bunche (1904–1971) was the first black president of the American Political Science Association.

Sources: *Encyclopedia of Black America,* pp. 1298–99; *Who's Who in America, 1960–61,* p. 407.

1953 • The first chapter of Phi Beta Kappa at a black university was established at Fisk University in Nashville on April 4, 1953. The chapter at Howard University was formed four days later. The only other black colleges with a Phi Beta Kappa chapter were Morehouse and Spelman colleges. Phi Beta Kappa, founded in 1775, is the most prestigious honorary society for undergraduate achievement in the humanities.

Sources: Delta of Tennessee, Phi Beta Kappa, Charter; *Famous First Blacks,* p. 35; Current, *Phi Beta Kappa in American Life,* p. 231.

1957 • W. Montague Cobb (1904–1990) was the first black president of the American Association of Physical Anthropologists (1957–59). A native of Washington, D.C., Cobb received his doctorate at Western Reserve University (now Case Western Reserve University) in 1932. He spent most of his career as professor of anatomy at Howard University. In 1957 he presided over the first Imhotep Conference held March 8–9. The organization's purpose was to eliminate segregation in the field of hospitalization and health care.

Sources: Morais, *The History of the Negro in Medicine,* pp. 142–144; Robinson, *Historical Negro Biographies,* pp. 174–75; *Who's Who among Black Americans, 1992–93,* p. 1596.

1962 • John Hope Franklin (1915–2009) was elected to membership in the Cosmos Club, an exclusive organization in Washington, D.C. The club has been called "the closest thing to a social headquarters for Washington's socially elite"; many of Washington's public policy intellectuals have gathered there. Founded in 1878, the Cosmos Club has as its objectives "the advancement of its members in science, literature, and art" and "their mutual improvement by social intercourse."

Sources: Cosmos Club https://www.cosmosclub.org/default.aspx, accessed September 28, 2012. *Contemporary Black Biography,* vol. 5, pp. 96–101; Smith, *Notable Black American Men,* pp. 421–27.

1965 • David Harold Blackwell (1919–2010) was the first black member of the National Academy of Sciences. A mathematician specializing in statistics, he took three degrees at the University of Illinois (A.B., A.M., 1938; and Ph.D., 1941). Blackwell taught at several institutions, including Southern University, Clark College, Howard University, and the University of California, Berkeley. In 1955 he became president of the Institute of Mathematical Statistics. Blackwell was born in Centralia, Illinois.

David Blackwell

Sources: *A Common Destiny: Blacks and American Society,* p. 68; *Encyclopedia of Black America,* pp. 183, 744; *Who's Who among African Americans,* 14th ed., p. 103.

1969 • Kenneth Bancroft Clark (1914–2005) was the first black president of the American Psychological Association. The achievements of this distinguished psychologist were recognized by the award of the NAACP's Spingarn Medal in 1961.

Sources: *Encyclopedia of Black America*, p.273; *Negro Almanac*, p. 1403; *Who's Who among African Americans*, 26th ed., p. 107.

1973 • John Hope Franklin (1915–2009) became the first black president of Phi Beta Kappa. He held office until 1976 and presided over the two-hundredth anniversary celebrations of this honorary society for the humanities. He was also the first black president of the Southern Historical Association (1970) as well as the American Historical Association (1978). Born in Rentiesville, Oklahoma, Franklin received his bachelor's degree from Fisk University in 1935 and his master's degree and doctorate from Harvard University in 1936 and 1941. He returned to Fisk to teach from 1936 to 1937. He later moved to North Carolina, where he taught first at St. Augustine's College from 1939 to 1943 and then at North Carolina College from 1943 to 1947. After teaching at Howard University from 1947 to 1956, he moved to Brooklyn College as chairman of the history department, becoming the first black historian to hold a full-time position on the faculty at a white institution. He left in 1964 to join the faculty at the University of Chicago. There he was chair of the history department from 1967 to 1970 and John Matthews Manly Distinguished Service Professor from 1969 to 1982. He was named professor emeritus in 1982, before moving to Duke University as James B. Duke Professor of History. Franklin held several posts at Duke before he was named professor emeritus in 1985. During his stellar career he became involved in a number of activities that had far-reaching effects. For example, in 1953 he provided historical research for the *Brown v. Board of Education* case that attacked racial segregation in the schools. In 1997 he headed President Bill Clinton's advisory panel to address the American racial divide. Among his numerous awards, in 1995 he received the nation's highest civilian honor, the Presidential Medal of Freedom for "extraordinary work … in American History and … studies of the South." He published widely but perhaps his most popular work was *From Slavery to Freedom,* first issued in 1947 (the 9th edition was published in 2011) and often adopted as a textbook in African American history. He spent forty years in research on early black historian George Washington Williams, resulting in a biography published in 1985. Duke University named the John Hope Franklin Center for Interdisciplinary and International Studies in his honor. The newly renovated historic structure opened in fall 2000. Franklin's autobiography, *Mirror to America,* was published in 2005

Sources: *Black Issues in Higher Education*, vol. 17 (18 January 2001), p. 31; *Current Biography*, 1963, pp. 139–41; Gates and Higginbotham, *African American National Biography*, vol. 3, pp. 361–63; Smith, *Encyclopedia of African American Popular Culture*, vol. 2, pp. 548–50; Smith, *Notable Black American Men*, pp. 421–26.

1977 • Henry Aaron Hill (1915–1979) was the first black president of the American Chemical Association. Hill was born in St. Joseph, Missouri, and graduated from Johnson C. Smith University in Charlotte, North Carolina, in 1936. He received his doctorate from Massachusetts Institute of Technology in 1942. After serving as a Rosenwald Fellow, he became a research chemist for Atlantic Research Associates. Later he was vice president for research. He also served as president of Riverside Research Laboratories.

Sources: *Encyclopedia of Black America*, p. 437; *Who's Who in America, 1978–79*, vol. 1, p. 1494.

1980 • James E. Blackwell (1926–) was the first black president of the Society for the Study of Social Problems. Blackwell, a sociologist, was born in Anniston, Alabama. He received his bachelor's and master's degrees from Western Reserve University (now Case Western Reserve University) in 1948 and 1949 and his doctorate from Wayne State University in 1959. Blackwell has taught at Grambling State College (now Grambling State University), Wayne State University, San Jose State, Case Western Reserve, and the University of Boston. He has also served in the Peace Corp.

Sources: *Jet* 57 (18 October 1979): 29; *Who's Who among Black Americans, 1992–93*, p. 115.

1986 • Reginald Bess was the first black to chair a session of the International Courtly Literature Society. Bess was professor of German and English at Grambling State University in Louisiana.

Sources: *Jet* 70 (8 September 1986): 20.

1986 • J. Russell George was the first black president of the Harvard Ripon Society. George was a twenty-five-year-old member of the first-year law school class.

Sources: *Jet* 70 (12 May 1986): 8.

1996 • The College Fund/UNCF established the Frederick D. Patterson Research Institute, named for the UNCF's founder. This was the nation's first major black-led research institute in education. Its mission is "to design, conduct, and disseminate research to policy makers, educators, and the public with the goal of improving educational opportunities and outcomes for African Americans." While the College Fund/UNCF focuses on fundraising for its member colleges, the institute concentrates on maximizing the benefits of education in the African American community. *The African American Education Databook* (1997) was one of the institute's first publications.

Sources: *Jet* 89 (11 March 1996): 8; Foreword, *The African American Education Databook.*

1998 • Spelman College in Atlanta was awarded a chapter of Phi Beta Kappa, becoming the first black woman's college to receive this honor.

Sources: *Jet* 93 (2 March 1998): 22.

2005 • Belle S. Wheelan is the first black and first woman to serve as president of the Southern Association of Colleges and Schools, the accrediting agency for schools and colleges located in the south. She has spent over thirty years in education and served in various capacities. In several of her positions she was the first African American and/or woman to hold those posts.

Sources: "Belle S. Wheelan, Ph.D," http://www.sacscoc.org/docs/Belle%Wheelan's%20Bio .doc, accessed September 28, 2012.

2007 • Patricia Hill Collins (1948–) made history at the American Sociological Association's annual meeting this year by becoming the first black women elected president of that organization. The ASA was founded in 1905 and represents 14,000 sociologists worldwide. A distinguished professor in the University of Maryland's Department of Sociology, Hill served the organization for three years, first as president-elect, then as president, and past-president. Collins graduated from Brandeis University, received a master's degree in teaching from Harvard University, and a Ph.D. degree from Brandeis. Her writings include *Black Sexual Politics, Black Feminist Thought* (both award-winning works), *Fighting Words: Black Women and the Search for Justice,* and *From Black Power to Hip Hop.*

Sources: *Contemporary Black Biography,* vol. 67, pp. 24–27; *Jet* 112 (1 October 2007): 26.

Business and Professional Organizations

1900 • Booker T. Washington (1856–1915) organized the National Negro Business League in Boston on August 23 and was elected its first president. He completely dominated the league and served as its president until his death. The league concentrated on encouraging black-owned and black-operated businesses.

Sources: *Jet* 94 (24 August 1998): 19; Logan and Winston, *Dictionary of American Negro Biography*, pp. 633–38.

1904 • John Robert Edward Lee (1870–1944), director of the Academic Department of Tuskegee Institute, was the first president of the National Association of Teachers in Colored Schools. Lee later served as president of Florida Agricultural and Mechanical College (1924–28).

Sources: *Encyclopedia of Black America,* p. 503; *Negro Year Book,* 1921–22, p. 410.

1904 • John R. Mitchell Jr. (1863–1929) was the first black member of the American Bankers Association. A native of the outskirts of Richmond, Virginia, Mitchell first won fame as the crusading and militant editor of the *Richmond Planet*, which he took over in 1884. He turned the *Planet* into one of America's leading black newspapers. Mitchell vehemently opposed racial discrimination and lynching of blacks that was prevalent at that time. He urged blacks to arm themselves for self-defense. He served on the Richmond City Council from 1888 to 1896 but lost his bid for reelection due to open fraud by white Democrats who stuffed the ballot box. Mitchell then turned to business enterprises. As chancellor of the Virginia Knights of Pythias, he used funds available to him to invest in real estate. He also bought a movie theater, a cemetery, and other local business property. In 1902 he founded the Mechanics Saving Bank. After his bank failed in 1922, Mitchell was indicted for mismanagement but never convicted. He died at home on December 3, 1929, virtually a poor man.

Sources: Logan and Winston, *Dictionary of American Negro Biography,* pp. 444–45; Penn, *The Afro-American Press,* pp. 183–87; Simmons, *Men of Mark,* pp. 314–32.

1911 • Selena Sloan Butler (1872–1964) founded the first black Parent-Teacher Association at Yonge Street School in Atlanta. It was the first such association in the country. She also founded similar associations at the state and national levels. In 1919 she developed the Georgia Colored Parent-Teacher Association and for a number years was acting president. On May 7, 1926, she founded the National Congress of Colored Parents and Teachers, served as founding president, and established a successful working link with the white National Congress. When the national organizations merged sometime after her death, Butler was named a national founder. Butler was born in Thomasville, Georgia, and was educated at Spelman Seminary (later Spelman College), graduating with a high school diploma. She taught elocution and English in Atlanta and taught in the kindergarten program that she founded at Morris Brown College in Atlanta.

Sources: Smith, *Notable Black American Women,* pp. 147–50; Hine, *Black Women in America,* vol. 1, pp. 210–11.

1923 • Paul Revere Williams (1894–1980), renowned architect in Los Angeles, became the first black member of the American Institute of Architects (AIA). He joined after one year of private practice. In 1957 he became the first black fellow of the AIA. The association also awarded him a gold medal for "excellence of design."

Sources: *Jet* 92 (30 June 1997): 19; Smith, *Notable Black American Men,* pp. 1238–41; Hudson, *Paul R. Williams, Architect,* p. 19.

1925 • George H. Woodson of Des Moines, Iowa, became the first president of the Negro Bar Association (now the National Bar Association), an organization formed to forward the concerns of black lawyers. Woodson was one of the five black lawyers who founded the NBA; the others were Joe Brown, James Morris, Charles Howard Sr., and Gertrude E. Durden Rush (the only woman in the group). The group founded the professional organization for black lawyers primarily because the American Bar Association refused to admit blacks at that time.

Sources: *Encyclopedia of Black America,* pp. 129–30; *Negro Almanac,* p. 1358; Smith, *Notable Black American Women,* pp. 575–76.

1940 • The National Negro Newspapers Association (now the National Newspaper Association) was founded in 1940. The association was co-founded by Frank L. Stanley Sr. (1906?–1974) and Carter Walker Wesley (1892–1969). In 1989 the association had 148 members. The word "Negro" was dropped from the organization's title in 1956.

Sources: *Ebony Success Library,* vol. 1, p. 292 (Stanley); *Encyclopedia of Black America,* p. 850 (Wesley); Hornsby, *Chronology of Black America,* pp. 237–38; *Negro Almanac,* pp. 305, 1288; Dates and Barlow, *Split Image,* p. 355.

1955 • Lloyd Augustus Hall (1894–1971) became the first black to serve on the Board of Directors of the American Institute of Chemists. At the time of his election to the board, he was also elected councilor-at-large. Hall was born in Elgin, Illinois, and received his bachelor's degree in 1916. He also attended the University of Chicago. His experiences in the field of chemistry include that of senior chemist with the Chicago Board of Health from 1916 to 1917. He was chief chemist for the John Morrell Company from 1919 to 1921 and for the Boyer Chemical Laboratory from 1921 to 1922. From 1922 to 1925 Hall was president and chemical director of Chemical Products Corporation. He became chief chemist and director of research for Griffith Laboratories from 1925 to 1946, then technical director from 1946 to 1959. He was consultant for the George Washington Carver Foundation from 1946 to 1948 and for the United Nations Food and Agricultural Organization. Hall had wide service on professional boards and also wrote some fifty scientific papers.

Sources: *Contemporary Black Biography,* vol. 8, pp. 99–102.

1961 • Maurice Sorrell (1914?–1998) became the first black member of the White House News Photographers Association. On the basis of this thirty-two-year record with the association, in 1995 he was voted a life member. He became known for capturing on film the history of the Civil Rights Movement.

Sources: *Jet* 87 (8 May 1995): 8; *New York Times* Obituaries (24 June 1998).

1962 • Herman Jerome Russell (1930–) was the first black member of the Atlanta Chamber of Commerce. Russell was an Atlanta builder and land developer, who served on many business, civic, and religious boards. In 1981 he became the second black president of the chamber. Born in Atlanta, Russell graduated from Tuskegee Institute (now Tuskegee University) with a bachelor's degree. He joined his father's plastering business after graduation; the business specialized in small residential projects, including renovations. After the elder Russell died, he assumed charge of the company and renamed it H. J. Russell and Company and expanded its focus to include duplexes and larger apartment building. Among the public projects that the company handled were the City Hall Complex, the Martin Luther King Community Center, and renovation of Grady Memorial Hospital. The firm assisted in building the Hartsfield International Airport, the Georgia Power Company's headquarters building, the Coca-Cola Company's world headquarters, and the Georgia Dome Stadium. Russell donated $1 million to his alma mater, Tuskegee University.

Sources: *Ebony Success Library,* vol. 1, p. 270; *Jet* 59 (25 January 1981): 39; *Who's Who among African Americans,* 26th ed., p. 1083; *Contemporary Black Biography,* vol. 17, pp. 166–69.

1968 • Elizabeth Duncan Koontz (1919–1989) was the first black president of the National Education Association (NEA). Koontz was a classroom teacher in North Carolina and an active member of the NEA until she became president of the department of classroom teachers in the NEA in 1965. After installation as president at the annual meeting in Dallas on July 6, 1968, Koontz called for statesmanship as the hallmark of teaching and saw the school as a way for Americans to transform their dreams into reality. From 1969 to 1972 she was director of the Women's Bureau of the United States Department of Labor. Born in Salisbury, North Carolina, Koontz graduated from Livingstone College in her hometown in 1938 and received her master's degree from Atlanta University in 1941.

Sources: Hine, *Black Women in America,* vol. 1, pp. 683–84; *Encyclopedia of Black America,* p. 490; Smith, *Notable Black American Women,* pp. 638–43.

1969 • The first black woman inducted into the National Professional Journalism Society was Charlayne Hunter-Gault (1942–).

Sources: *The Black New Yorkers,* p. 342.

1970 • Edward S. Lewis (1901–1986) was the first black president of the National Cooperative Education Association. A native of Platte City, Missouri, Lewis received his bachelor's degree from the University of Chicago in 1925 and his doctorate from New York University in 1961.

Sources: *Ebony Success Library,* vol. 1, p. 201.

1971 • Cleo W. Blackburn (1909–1978) was the first black director of the United States Chamber of Commerce. Blackburn was an educator who was president of Jarvis Christian College, Hawkins, Texas, from 1953 to 1964.

Sources: *Encyclopedia of Black America,* p. 181.

1971 • Effie Lee Morris (1921–), lecturer and librarian, became the first black president of the Public Library Association. The Richmond, Virginia, native holds the BA, BLS, and ML. degrees from Case Western University.

Sources: *Who's Who among African Americans,* 26th ed., p. 905.

1972 • Fred McClellen Crosby (1928–) was the first black elected to the board of the Ohio Council of Retail Merchants Association. In 1963 Crosby became president and chief officer of the Crosby Furniture Company, one of Cleveland's most successful black businesses. Active in numerous civic activities, Crosby has been widely recognized for his work.

Sources: *Ebony Success Library,* vol. 2, p. 82; *Who's Who among African Americans,* 26th ed., p. 288.

1972 • Carl T. Rowan (1925–2000) was the first black member of the Gridiron Club, an organization of Washington journalists founded in 1885.

Sources: *Ebony Success Library,* vol. 2, pp. 228–31; Hornsby, *Milestones in 20th-Century African-American History,* p. 167.

1972 • The first and only black executive director of the American Library Association was Robert Wedgeworth Jr. (1937–). Wedgeworth was born in Ennix, Texas, and graduated from Wabash College in Crawfordsville, Indiana, in 1959. In 1961 he received his master's degree in library and information science from the University of Illinois. He served on the library staff at several sites in Missouri, including the Kansas City Public Library, Park College, and Meranac Community College. He later joined the library staff at Brown University, where he introduced automation to the library system. He became a fellow of the Council on Library Resources, studying the Western European book trade in summer 1963. He studied for his doctorate at Rutgers University and also taught in the Graduate School of Library Science before leaving in 1972 to head the ALA.

Sources: *American Libraries* 41 (July/August 1980): 458; Josey and Shockley, *Handbook of Black Librarianship,* p. 22; Smith, *Notable Black American Men,* pp. 1198–1200.

1972 • Allen E. Broussard (1929–1996) became the first black president of the Conference of California Judges (now the California Judges Association). He held the post from 1972 to 1973. Broussard, who became a justice on the California Supreme Court in San Francisco in 1981, wrote key opinions on the death penalty and the environment. Born in Lake Charles, Louisiana, Broussard received his bachelor's and law degrees from the University of California, Berkeley in 1950 and 1953. After he was in private practice and later was a research attorney for a presiding judge of the District Court of Appeals, First Appellate District, he joined the firm Metoyer Sweeney and Broussard. He was judge in the Oakland-Piedmont District Municipal Court and later judge in the Alameda Superior Court in Oakland. He later became a partner in the firm Coblentz, Cahen, McCabe and Breyer.

Sources: *Jet* 91 (25 November 1996): 18; *Who's Who among African Americans,* 9th ed., p. 173.

1973 • Celestine Strode Cook (1924–) was the first black woman to serve on the National Business Committee for the Arts. Strode was a businesswoman in Galveston, Texas, until 1958, when she moved to New Orleans, Louisiana. In 1974 she became the first black woman selected as one of the ten most outstanding women of New Orleans.

Sources: *Encyclopedia of Black America,* p. 286.

1974 • Lewis Carnegie Dowdy (1917–2000), president of North Carolina Agricultural and Technical State University, was the first black president of the National Association of Universities and Land Grant Colleges. Born in Eastover, South Carolina, he received his bachelor's degree from Allen University in 1939, his master's degree from Indiana State University in 1949, and his doctorate in education from Indiana University in 1965. Dowdy was a school principal in his hometown from 1939 to 1951. After teaching at North Carolina A and T and later serving as dean and dean of instruction, he served as president and chancellor of the school from 1964 to 1980.

Sources: *Encyclopedia of Black America*, p. 325; *Famous First Blacks*, p. 33–34; *Who's Who among African Americans*, 14th ed., p. 358.

1975 • Opera singer Dorothy Maynor (1910–1996), who founded the Harlem School of the Arts in New York, became the first black member of the Metropolitan Opera Board.

Sources: *Jet* 89 (25 March 1996): 52; Smith, *Notable Black American Women*, pp. 739–40; *Contemporary Black Biography*, vol. 19, pp. 155–58.

1975 • The first president of the National Association of Black Journalists was Charles Sumner "Chuck" Stone (1924–). He also was a cofounder of that organization. Chuck Stone, as he is generally known, was born in St. Louis. During World War II he was trained in Tuskegee, Alabama, where he took U.S. Air Corps navigator training. He received his bachelor's degree from Wesleyan University in 1948 and his master's degree from the University of Chicago in 1951. He became an experienced journalist and worked with the *Washington Afro-American,* the *Chicago Daily Defender,* and the *Philadelphia Daily News.* Stone was special assistant to U.S. Representative Adam Clayton Powell Jr. from 1965 to 1967. He hosted radio talk shows, including the PBS-TV's *Black Perspective on the News* (later *Another Voice*). Stone was a fellow in Harvard University's John F. Kennedy School of Government in 1982 and in 1981 became Walter Spearman Professor at the University of North Carolina at Chapel Hill. He also became nationally syndicated columnist for United Media. His writings include *Black Political Power in America* (1968), *Tell It Like It Is* (1968), and *King Strut* (1970).

Sources: *Contemporary Black Biography*, vol. 9, pp. 218–23.

1976 • Joe Booker became the first black vice president of the National Association of Intercollegiate Athletics Sports Information Directors. At the time of his selection, he was sports publicity director at Prairie View Agricultural and Mechanical University in Texas. He was the only black officer of the association.

Sources: *Jet* 50 (6 May 1976): 20.

1976 • Mary Hatwood Futrell (1940–) was the first black president of the Virginia Education Association. She would go on to serve as president of the National Education Association from 1980 to 1989. Born in Alta Vista, Virginia, Futrell received a bachelor's degree from Virginia State College (now Virginia State University) in Petersburg and master's and doctoral degrees from George Washington University. During her tenure as NEA president, she saw a sizeable growth in membership. She also called on educators and politicians to reform America's schools.

Sources: *Negro Almanac*, pp. 1379–80; Smith, *Notable Black American Women*, pp. 376–80; *Who's Who among African Americans*, 26th ed., p. 442.

1976 • Clara Stanton Jones (1913–2012) was the first black president of the American Library Association. A graduate of Spelman College, Jones spent most of her professional career with the Detroit Public Libraries, of which she became the first black, and the first woman, director in 1970. Born in St. Louis, Jones received here bachelor's degree from Spelman College in Atlanta in 1934 and received a undergraduate library science degree from the University of Michigan in 1938. After holding professional library posts at Atlanta, Dillard, and Southern universities, she joined the Detroit Public Library staff. She was a pioneer in the development of branch libraries in Detroit.

Sources: *Encyclopedia of Black America*, p. 476; *Jet* 50 (12 August 1976): 29; Smith, *Notable Black American Women*, pp. 593–97.

1976 • As president of the New York City Housing Patrolmen's Benevolent Association, Jack Jordan was the first black to head a police union in the state.

Sources: *Jet* 51 (30 December 1976): 46.

1976 • Black Agency Executives was founded to support black managers of social service agencies in New York City that served primarily black constituencies. Previously, whites had headed these agencies.

Sources: *The Black New Yorkers*, p. 360.

1977 • Roslyn Maria [Roz] Abrams (1948–) became the first black vice president of the Atlanta Press Club. Abrams was a news reporter for WXIA-TV at the time.

Sources: *Ebony* 34 (January 1979): 115; *Jet* 52 (2 June 1977): 20; *Who's Who among Black Americans, 1992–93*, p. 3.

1977 • Samuel L. Williams was the first black president of the Los Angeles Bar Association. In 1981 Williams was the first black president of the State Bar of California. A Los Angeles attorney, Williams had turned down an offer of an appointment to the state supreme court in 1977.

Sources: *Jet* 61 (12 November 1981): 28.

1977 • Jesse Hill Jr. (1926–) was the first black president of the Atlanta Chamber of Commerce and the first black to head a major metropolitan Chamber of Commerce in the nation. Hill was president and chief executive officer of the Atlanta Life Insurance Company.

Sources: *Contemporary Black Biography*, vol. 13, pp. 103–5; Smith, *Notable Black American Men*, pp. 549–52; *Who's Who among African Americans*, 14th ed., p. 596.

1977 • Marilyn French Hubbard (1946–) was the founder and first president of the National Association of Black Women Entrepreneurs. Born in Lansing, Michigan, Hubbard received a bachelor of business administration from the University of Detroit in 1974. She also received certificates for her training at University Associates in La Jolla, California, and the Chrysler Corporation in Troy, Michigan, from 1978 to 1979. Hubbard was official court reporter for the Wayne County Common Pleas Court from 1969 to 1976. She founded her own company in Detroit, Marilyn Hubbard Seminars, in 1976, becoming also its president.

Sources: *Jet* 77 (16 October 1989): 40; *Who's Who among African Americans*, 14th ed., p. 629.

1977 • Milton L. Reynolds (1924–) was the first black president of the New York State School Boards Association. Reynolds was a systems programming manager for International Business Machines (IBM).

Sources: *Jet* 53 (17 November 1977): 29; *Who's Who among Black Americans, 1992–93*, p. 1182.

1979 • Jack Bell was the first black president of the Texas Restaurant Association. Bell was a restaurant operator and caterer in Corpus Christi, Texas.

Sources: *Jet* 56 (26 July 1979): 22.

1979 • Curtis J. Moret was the first black president of the Municipal Court Clerks Association of California. Moret was division chief of the Oakland-Piedmont municipal court.

Sources: *Jet* 57 (27 December 1979): 21.

1979 • Mack Sewell was the first black president of the Georgia Association of Independent Juvenile Courts. Sewell was a probation officer in Clarke County.

Sources: *Jet* 57 (25 October 1979): 21.

1980 • J. Clay Smith Jr. (1942–) was the first black president of the Federal Bar Association, an organization for federal lawyers. After working for the U.S. Army and the government, Smith became a law professor at the Howard University School of Law (1982) and then became dean of the school in 1986. Born in Omaha, Nebraska, Smith graduated from Creighton University in Omaha (A.B., 1964), Howard University Law School (J.D., 1967), and George Washington Law School (LL.M., 1970; S.J.D., 1977).

Sources: *Jet* 59 (9 October 1980): 6; 61 (17 September 1981): 6; 61 (26 November 1981): 11; *Who's Who among Black Americans,* 26th ed., p. 1146.

1980 • Larry W. Whiteside (1937–) was the first black chair of the board of directors of the Baseball Writers Association of America. A journalist, he was a sportswriter for the *Boston Globe* newspaper. Whiteside was born in Chicago and received his bachelor's degree at Drake University in 1959. He became a John Knight Fellow from 1987 to 1988 at Stanford University. After serving as researcher for Johnson Publishing Company from 1958 to 1959, he became a sports reporter and assistant editor for the *Kansas City Kansan.* He served as sports reporter or columnist for the *Milwaukee Sporting News, Boston Sporting News,* and *Boston Globe.* Whiteside became a member of the U.S. Basketball Writers, the NBA Basketball Writers, Boston Baseball Writers, and the Baseball Writers Association of America.

Sources: *Jet* 57 (10 January 1980): 21; *Who's Who among African Americans,* 14th ed., p. 1382.

1981 • Arnette Rhinehart Hubbard was the first woman president of the National Bar Association, the national association for black lawyers. She was elected on July 31 as its thirty-ninth president. The Stephens, Arkansas, native received her bachelor's degree from the University of Southern Illinois. A Chicago attorney, Hubbard took her law degree at John Marshall Law School in 1969. She had also been the first woman president of the Cook County (Illinois) Bar Association. In 1994 Hubbard was official monitor of the first all-race elections of South Africa.

Sources: *Ebony* 37 (January 1982): 32; *Jet* 60 (20 August 1981): 21; *Who's Who among African Americans,* 26th ed., p. 613.

1982 • Samuel Fredrick Lambert (1928–2010) was the first black president of the National Association of Power Engineers. A native of Monroeville, Alabama, Lambert received his marine engineers license in 1953 from Armstrong School of Engineering. In 1978 he received his bachelor's degree from Pace University. He served as supervisor of custodians and engineers for the New York City Board of Education.

Sources: *Jet* 62 (19 July 1982): 21; Obituary, *Who's Who among African Americans,* 26th ed., p. 1413.

1982 • Scott C. Westbrook III (1939–) was the first black president of the Michigan Occupational Education Association. Westbrook became supervisor of Vocational Specialist Needs for the Pontiac, Michigan, School District.

Sources: *Jet* 62 (9 August 1982): 21; *Who's Who among Black Americans, 1992–93,* p. 1487.

1983 • Charles R. Smith was the first black president of the North Carolina Watchmakers Association. Smith was a member of the Cape Fear Watchmakers Guild.

Sources: *Jet* 64 (1 August 1983): 21.

1983 • Betty Lou Thompson (1939–) was the first black president of Women in Municipal Government. Thompson was a councilwoman in University City, Missouri. Born in Helm, Mississippi, she received her bachelor's degree from Harris Teachers College in 1962. In 1963 she became a talk show host for KATZ Radio.

Sources: *Jet* 64 (21 March 1983): 24; *Who's Who among African Americans,* 26th ed., p. 1227.

1983 • Betty Anne Williams (1952–) was the first black president of the Washington Press Club. Williams worked for the Associated Press and left that position to work for the *Democrat and Chronicle* newspaper in Rochester, New York.

Sources: *Crisis* 90 (November 1983): 38; *Jet* 64 (9 May 1983): 13; 65 (13 February 1984): 13; 67 (17 December 1984): 10.

1984 • Maxine Young was the first woman of any race to hold the position of executive director of the Gary, Indiana, Chamber of Commerce.

Sources: *Jet* 66 (9 July 1984): 21.

1985 • I. S. Leevy Johnson (1942–) was the first black president of the South Carolina Bar Association. This lawyer and funeral director is also one of the first three blacks elected to the South Carolina legislature in this century. In 1999 he received the Order of the Palmetto Award as one of the "state's strongest advocates for the rights of all South Carolinians," the highest honor that the governor gives. Born in Richland County, South Carolina, Johnson graduated from Benedict College in South Carolina. He received a law degree from the University of South Carolina in 1968. He taught at his alma mater, Benedict College, and also became a licensed embalmer and owner of the firm Leevy's Funeral Home in Columbia, South Carolina.

Sources: *Jet* 68 (22 July 1985): 6; *Who's Who among African Americans*, 26th ed., p. 670.

1985 • Sharon McPhail (1948–) became the first woman president of the Wolverine Bar Association, an affiliate of the National Bar Association. She was president of the National Bar Association from 1991 to 1992. Born in Cambridge, Massachusetts, McPhail graduated from Northeastern University (B.A., 1972; J.D., 1976). From 1976 to 1980 she worked as a staff attorney for Ford Motor Company in Dearborn, Michigan, and in 1982 was named assistant U.S. attorney for the Eastern District of Michigan. McPhail later became an associate with two law firms and was named principal attorney for Wayne County Corporation Counsel in Detroit from 1986 to 1987. She served as chief of screening and districts court for the Wayne County Prosecutor's Office and on the Detroit City Council.

Sources: *Contemporary Black Biography*, vol. 2, pp. 158–60.

1986 • As president of the Saint Louis chapter of the National Academy of Television Arts and Sciences, Ava L. Brown was the first black woman to hold a presidential post on either the local or national level. She was public access director for City Cable Television, a black-owned firm.

Sources: *Jet* 70 (8 September 1986): 20.

1986 • Montez Cornelius Martin Jr. (1940–) was the first black president of the Trident Chamber of Commerce (Charleston, Dorchester, and Berkeley Counties, South Carolina). Martin was born in Columbia, South Carolina, and is a construction engineer and a real estate agent.

Sources: *Jet* 70 (4 August 1986): 6; *Who's Who among African Americans*, 26th ed., p. 819.

1987 • Barbara Rudd Gross was the first black president of the Women's Advertising Club, Chicago.

Sources: *Jet* 72 (15 June 1987): 30.

1987 • Sharon B. Hartley was the first black, and the first woman, elected president of the Niagara Frontier Corporate Counsel Association. Hartley was counsel for Delaware North Companies, Buffalo, New York.

Sources: *Jet* 71 (26 January 1987): 20.

1987 • Elnor B. G. Hickman (1930–) was the first black president of Professional Secretaries International, Illinois Division. Hickman was executive secretary to the executive director of the Legal Foundation Assistance of Chicago. She was born in Jackson, Mississippi.

Sources: *Jet* 72 (15 June 1987): 30; *Who's Who among African Americans*, 26th ed., p. 575.

1987 • Ira Jackson was the first black president of the Georgia Municipal Association. Jackson became an Atlanta city councilman.

Sources: *Jet* 72 (3 August 1987): 26.

1987 • Dolores G. McGhee was the first black president of the Georgia School Boards Association. She was also the first black elected to the Fulton County Board of Education.

Sources: *Jet* 73 (12 October 1987): 20.

1987 • Bert Norman Mitchell (1938–) was the first black president of the New York State Society of Certified Public Accountants, a first in the United States. In addition to his work as an accountant and an administrator for various organizations, Mitchell has published more than fifty professional articles. Mitchell graduated from City College of New York (B.B.A., 1963; M.B.A., 1968) and studied at the Harvard Graduate School of Business. After serving as assistant controller for the Ford Foundation from 1967 to 1969, he served as a partner in the law firm Lucas Tucker and Company, CPAs from 1969 to 1973. He became chief executive officer for Mitchell/Titus and Company in 1973.

Sources: *Jet* 72 (11 May 1987): 20; *Who's Who among African Americans,* 26th ed., p. 883.

1987 • Alan Herbert Peterson (1948–) was the first black member of the national executive board of the National Police Officers' Association of America. Born in New York City, Peterson worked as a police officer in Newark, New Jersey. An on-duty explosion in 1983 permanently disabled him.

Sources: *Jet* 73 (7 December 1987): 20; *Who's Who among African Americans,* 26th ed., p. 987.

1987 • Gregory J. Reed (1948–) was the first black chairman of the Arts, Communication, Entertainment, and Sports Section of the Michigan State Bar Association, the first black to hold such a position in the United States. Reed's specializations as an attorney are corporate, taxation, and entertainment law. He is the author of several books on entertainment and sports law. The Michigan native was educated at Michigan State University (B.S., 1970; M.S., 1971) and Wayne State University (J.D., 1974, LL.M., 1978).

Sources: *Jet* 72 (11 May 1987): 22; *Who's Who among African Americans,* 14th ed., p. 1078.

1987 • Shirley Street was the first black to head Women in Real Estate, Chicago.

Sources: *Jet* 72 (3 August 1987): 20.

1988 • Albert Abrams was the first black general manager and vice president for organizational development of the Greater Macon (Georgia) Chamber of Commerce. He is believed to be the only black to hold such a position in the South.

Sources: *Jet* 75 (21 November 1988): 20.

1988 • Donald DeHart was the first black state president of the New Jersey Jaycees. DeHart was a probation officer with the Passaic County Probation Department in Paterson, New Jersey.

Sources: *Jet* 75 (31 October 1988): 20.

1988 • Richard Knight Jr. (1945–), the first black city manager of Dallas, Texas, was the first black member of the Salesmanship Club. In 1990 he became the first black to hold the position of director of total quality management with Caltex Petroleum Corporation, Irving, Texas. He served as town manager of Carboro, North Carolina, from 1976 to 1980; deputy city manager of Gainesville, Florida, from 1980 to 1982; Dallas assistant city manager from 1982 to 1986 and city manager from 1986 to 1990. Born in Fort Valley, Georgia, Knight graduated from Fort Valley State College (B.A., 1968) and the University of North Carolina (M.P.A., 1976).

Sources: *Jet* 75 (17 October 1988): 40; 78 (30 April 1990): 6; *Who's Who among African Americans,* 26th ed., p. 733.

1989 • LaVerne Collins-Reid (1946–) was the first black president of Business and Professional Women/USA. Collins was a human resource specialist for the Federal Aviation Administration in Seattle, Washington. Her experiences with the FAA were extensive and included airports program instructor in 1992. Born in San Angelo, Texas, she graduated from the University of Alaska (B.S., 1977) and the University of Southern California (M.P.A., 1980).

Sources: *Jet* 76 (4 September 1989): 30; *Who's Who among African Americans,* 14th ed., p. 263.

1989 • Sandra Cavanaugh Holley (1943–) was the first black president of the American Speech-Language-Hearing Association. Holley was professor of communications disorders at Southern Connecticut State University. Born in Washington, D.C., she received her bachelor's and master's degrees at George Washington University in 1965 and 1966, and her doctorate from the University of Connecticut in 1979.

Sources: *Jet* 75 (19 December 1988): 22; *Who's Who among African Americans,* 14th ed., p. 608.

1989 • Elaine R. Jones (1944–) was elected to the American Bar Association Board of Governors, the first black to hold that post. Jones became well known as a leader in the fight to combat racism and discrimination.

Sources: *Jet* 99 (1 January 2001): 25; Smith, *Notable Black American Women,* Book II, pp. 348–50; *Who's Who among African Americans,* 26th ed., p. 593.

1990 • Lee Patrick Brown (1937–), New York City police commissioner (1990–1992), was the first black president of the International Association of Chiefs of Police.

Sources: *Who's Who among African Americans,* 26th ed., p. 161.

1990 • Blanton Thandreus Canady (1948–) was the first black president of McDonald's Owners of Chicago and Northwest Indiana. A native of West Point, Georgia, and Chicago businessman, Canady is a 1970 graduate of the University of Illinois. He received his master's degree in business administration from the University of Chicago in 1975.

Sources: *Jet* 78 (3 September 1990): 20; *Who's Who among African Americans,* 26th ed., p. 205.

1990 • Conrad Kenneth Harper (1940–) was the first black to head 120-year-old Association of the Bar of the City of New York. He was law clerk for the NAACP Legal Defense Fund from 1965 to 1966, and then staff lawyer from 1966 to 1970. An associate with the firm from 1971 to 1974, in 1974 Harper became a partner at Simpson, Thacher, and Bartlett, one of the first black partners in a major law firm. The Detroit native received his bachelor's degree from Howard University in 1962 and his law degree from Harvard Law School in 1965.

Sources: *Jet* 78 (11 June 1990): 18; *Who's Who among African Americans,* 26th ed., p. 532; *The Black New Yorkers,* p. 397.

1991 • Lois Terrell Mills (1958–) was the first black national president of the American Business Women's Association. With a degree from Stanford in 1980, Mills became an industrial engineer with the Ethicon division of Johnson and Johnson in Albuquerque, New Mexico.

Sources: *Jet* 79 (21 January 1991): 20; *Who's Who among African Americans,* 26th ed., p. 880.

1992 • Edwyna G. Anderson (1930–), general counsel of the Duquesne Light Company, was the first black, and the first woman, president of the Pennsylvania Electric Association. The Tulsa, Oklahoma, native received her bachelor's degree from Fisk University in 1950. She did further study at the University of Michigan and later received her law degree from the Detroit College of Law in 1974. Her various positions include assistant prosecuting attorney (1974–80) and chief (1978–80) of the Genesee County Prosecuting Attorney's Office, Consumer Protection and Economic Crime Division; commissioner for the Michigan Public Service Commission (1980–88), and special counsel to the president of Dusquesne Light Company (1994–95).

Sources: *Jet* 82 (12 October 1992): 20; *Who's Who among African Americans,* 14th ed., p. 29.

1992 • Hubert Anderson was the first black elected to the board of the National Association of the Deaf. Anderson, who was serving as outreach chair for the organization, had also been a basketball coach at Gallaudet University, from which he graduated. He was coach of the gold-medal winning basketball team in the World Games for the Deaf in 1985.

Sources: *Jet* 83 (21 December 1992): 26.

1992 • Andre L. Dennis (1943–) was the first black chancellor of the Philadelphia Bar Association, which has some twelve thousand members. Dennis is a 1969 graduate of Howard University School of Law. He was born in Burton-On-Trent, England, and received his bachelor's degree from Cheyney State College (now Cheyney State University) in 1966 and his law degree from Howard University School of Law in 1969. He became an associate (1969–76) and partner (1976) with the firm Stradley, Ronson, Stevens and Young, L.L.P.

Sources: *Jet* 83 (21 December 1992): 29; *Who's Who among African Americans*, 26th ed., p. 333.

1992 • M. David Lee Jr. (1943–), architect and educator, was the first black president of the Boston Society of Architects. The Chicago native received his bachelor's degree from the University of Illinois in 1967 and his master's degree from Harvard University in 1971. Lee served several architectural firms as planning draftsman, draftsman, and urban design draftsman and then became a partner in the Boston firm Stull and Lee Architects. He has served as adjunct professor at Harvard University. He was a fellow in the Institute for Urban Design and a faculty member in the Mayor's Institute of the National Endowment for the Arts.

Sources: *Jet* 81 (16 March 1992): 36; *Who's Who among African Americans*, 26th ed., p. 757.

1992 • Ben Miles was the first black president of the Virginia Association of Broadcasters. Miles was general manager of WCDX, Richmond, Virginia.

Sources: *Jet* 82 (3 August 1992): 35.

1992 • Leslie Seymore was the first woman chair of the National Black Police Association. Seymore had served on the Philadelphia police force since 1973.

Sources: *Jet* 81 (16 March 1992): 36.

1992 • Arnette Rinehart Hubbard, an attorney, became the first black commissioner elected president of the Association of Election Commissioners of Illinois. She later became a Circuit Court judge in Chicago.

Sources: *Jet* 94 (3 August 1998): 19; 98 (7 August 2000): 19.

1993 • Cornelia [Connie] Whitener Perdreau was the first black elected to head Administrators and Teachers of English as a Second Language. Perdreau became a faculty member at Ohio University in Athens. She also headed the Education Abroad program beginning in 1998. Born in Beacon, New York, she received her bachelor's degree from Potsdam College in New York in 1969 and master's degrees from Ohio University in Athens in 1971 and 1972.

Sources: *Jet* 83 (26 April 1993): 20; *Who's Who among African Americans*, 26th ed., p. 581.

1993 • Deirdre Hughes Hill was elected president of the Los Angeles Police Commission, becoming the youngest person and the first black woman to hold the post. She held the position until 1996. The Loyola Law School graduate became senior associate attorney with the firm Saltzburg, Ray and Berman. She was previously vice president of the commission.

Sources: *Jet* 88 (9 October 1995): 19; *Who's Who among African Americans*, 14th ed., p. 594

1994 • Coren D. Flournoy (1974?–) of Chicago was elected president of the National Future Farmers of America, becoming the first black to head the 400,000-member organization. He was elected at the FFA's sixty-seventh national convention held in Kansas City, Missouri. When elected, Flournoy was a student at the University of Illinois, majoring in agricultural and economics.

Sources: *Jet* 87 (5 December 1944): 36.

The New York Bar Association's First Black President

The first black president of the New York Bar Association was Archibald R. Murray (1933–2001), elected in 1993. Murray was also the second black chairperson of the New York City Bar Association's executive committee, where he headed a staff of approximately 1,000 lawyers. From 1974 to 1994 Murray headed the Legal Aid Society. Born in Barbados, Murray came to the United States in 1950. He studied at Howard University and later Fordham University School of Law, graduating in 1960. He was assistant district attorney in New York County in 1960 and later became assistant counsel to Governor Nelson A. Rockefeller in 1962. Murray worked in private practice from 1965 to 1967, as counsel to the New York State Crime Control Council until 1971, and commissioner in the Division of Criminal Justice from 1971 to 1974.

Sources: *New York Times* Obituaries (21 September 2001); *Who's Who among African Americans,* 14th ed., p. 955.

1994 • Cornelia W. Fairfax became the first black woman president of the International Association of Financial Planners. Fairfax became a financial planner in Riverside, California.

Sources: *Jet* 86 (25 July 1994): 20.

Herman Cain

1994 • Herman Cain (1945–) became the first black president of the National Restaurant Association, the leading trade organization for the food service industry. The Memphis-born Cain received his bachelor's degree from Morehouse College in 1967 and his master's degree from Purdue University in 1971. He served as vice president for corporate systems and services of the Pillsbury Company from 1977 to 1982 and regional vice president of Burger King Corporation, Philadelphia, from 1982 to 1986. He also served as president of Godfather's Pizza in Omaha, Nebraska, from 1986 to 1988, and president and chef executive officer of Burger King in 1988. He ran unsuccessfully for U.S. president in 2012.

Sources: *Contemporary Black Biography,* vol. 15, pp. 43–45; *American Visions* 10 (April/May 199): 41.

1994 • The first black president of the Professional Secretaries International was Elnor Hickman of Chicago. She was elected during the forty-ninth convention in Orlando to head the world's premiere professional organization for secretaries, executive assistants, administrative assistants, and similar office professionals.

Sources: *Jet* 86 (22 August 1994): 16.

1994 • William S. Norman (1938–) became the first black president of the Travel Industry of America, representing the $397 billion industry. Norman was born in Roper, North Carolina. He received his bachelor's degree from West Virginia Wesleyan University in 1960 and his master's degree from American University in 1967. He also participated in Stanford University's executive program in 1976. After teaching briefly in Norfolk, Virginia, Norman moved into the corporate world. His experiences include various administrative positions with Cummins Engine Company in Columbus, Indiana, and vice president of sales and marketing for Amtrak's National Railroad Passenger Corporation in Washington, D.C.

Sources: *Jet* 87 (21 November 1994): 10; *Who's Who among African Americans,* 26th ed., p. 940.

1994 • The first black national secretary of the Public Relations Society of America, in New York, was Debra W. Miller. This is the world's largest group of public relations professionals.

Sources: *Jet* 85 (15 March 1994): 20.

1994 • Louis Stout was named commissioner of the Kentucky High School Athletic Association to become the first black head of a full state athletic association. He was the fifth commissioner in the association's history. He was named assistant commissioner in 1971 and executive assistant in 1992. Stout was born in Cynthiana, Kentucky, and graduated from Regis College.

Sources: *Jet* 86 (25 July 1994): 49; *Who's Who among African Americans,* 26th ed., p. 1186.

1994 • Raymond C. Marshall became the first black president of the Bar Association of San Francisco. He was a partner in the law firm McCutchen, Doyle, Brown and Enersen. The association has taken a leadership role in minority group recruiting.

Sources: *Journal of Blacks in Higher Education* (Summer 1994): 60.

1995 • Robert G. McGruder (1942–2002) became the first black president of the Associated Press Managing Editors group. He was a member of the Pulitzer Prize nominating jury in 1986, 1987, 1990, 1991, and 1999. The late executive editor of the *Detroit Free Press* held positions with the *Dayton Journal Herald* and the *Cleveland Plain Dealer,* becoming managing editor of the latter newspaper. He rose in rank at the *Detroit Free Press,* from deputy managing editor to the top post. Born in Louisville, Kentucky, McGruder received his bachelor's degree from Kent State University in 1963.

Sources: *Contemporary Black Biography,* vol. 22, pp. 142–44; *Who's Who among African Americans,* 14th ed., p. 880.

1995 • The first black president of the Association of Teacher Educators is Rose Duhon-Sells. An educator at Southern University in Baton Rouge, she became dean of education and superintendent of the laboratory school.

Sources: *Jet* 87 (17 April 1995): 40.

1995 • Clarence E. Fitch became the first black president of the National Council of Professors of Educational Administration. He is professor of educational administration at Chicago State University.

Sources: *Jet* 88 (9 October 1995): 19.

1995 • Marie V. McDemmond (1946–), then vice president and chief operating officer at Florida Atlanta University, became the first black woman president of the Southern Association of College and University Business Officers.

Sources: *Jet* 99 (16 October 1995): 22; *Who's Who among African Americans,* 26th ed., p. 841.

1995 • The first black woman to become president of the California Teachers Association was Lois Tinson, a high school teacher in Baldwin Park.

Sources: *Jet* 89 (4 December 1995): 19.

1995 • Cheryl Bradley was named chair of the Chicago Chapter of the American Chemical Society, becoming the first black woman to hold that post. She is senior research chemist at Amoco Corporation's Naperville Technical Center.

Sources: *Jet* 88 (16 October 1995): 22.

1995 • William R. Jenkins, a special assistant to the attorney general of Georgia and head of his own law firm, became the first black elected to the Georgia State Bar's executive committee.

Sources: *Jet* 88 (17 July 1995): 20.

1995 • Naomi Bryson became the first woman to head the National Brotherhood of Skiers Inc., headquartered in Chicago. The Detroit resident has also served as national membership director.

Sources: *American Visions* 10 (April/May 1995): 10.

1995 • Percy Edward Pollard Sr. (1943–) became the first black chairperson of the Board of the Environmental Careers Organization in Boston. He also held several posts with the IBM Corporation, including executive assistant. Pollard was born in King and Queen Courthouse, Virginia. He received his bachelor's and master's degrees from Virginia State University in 1966 and 1977.

Sources: *Jet* 88 (2 October 1995): 19; *Who's Who among African Americans,* 26th ed., p. 1102.

1995 • H. Len Henderson became the first black president of the State Employees Association of North Carolina, based in Dudley. Henderson served as administrative assistant to the director of Cherry Hospital in Goldsboro.

Sources: *Jet* 88 (2 October 1995): 19.

1995 • The first black president of the Richland County (South Carolina) Bar Association was Luther H. Battiste III, an attorney in Columbia. This was one of the nation's largest local bar associations.

Sources: *Jet* 87 (20 February 1995): 19.

1995 • Frank N. Green became president of the Connecticut Association of Realtors, the first black to head the state's professional real estate organization. Green, a commercial broker in Stamford, Connecticut, was born in a Beauford, South Carolina.

Sources: *Ebony* 50 (August 1995): 11.

1995 • Annelle Lewis, who was director of development at Piney Woods Country Life boarding school in Mississippi, became the first woman president of the Urban League of Metropolitan Denver.

Sources: *Jet* 89 (4 December 1995): 19.

1995 • Carolyn Kennedy Worford (1949–) became the first black woman to chair NATPE (National Association of Television Program Executives) International, the largest trade association of television programming executives in the world. She had served as station manager and vice president of program development at Detroit's WJBK-TV. She was born in Kansas City, Missouri.

Sources: *Ebony* 50 (July 1995): 8; *Who's Who among African Americans,* 26th ed., p. 1382.

1995 • Franklyn Green Jenifer (1939–) became the first black chair of the American Council on Education, an umbrella for the nation's colleges and universities. He was the first Howard alumnus president of Howard University in Washington, D.C., serving from 1990 to 1994. Jenifer was born in Washington and received his bachelor's and master's degrees from Howard in 1962 and 1965. He received his doctorate from the University of Maryland in 1970. With background in higher education, Jenifer taught at Livingstone College of Rutgers University and then held several administrative posts at Rutgers, becoming associate provost. He was chancellor of the New Jersey Department of Higher Education from 1986 to 1990 and then left to accept the presidency of Howard University. He left Howard in 1994 and to serve as president of the University of Dallas.

Sources: *Jet* 85 (14 March 1994): 23; *Contemporary Black Biography,* vol. 2, pp. 121–22; *Who's Who among African Americans,* 26th ed., p. 656.

1995 • The first black president of the Society of Automotive Engineers International was Claude A. Verbal (1942–), plant manager for General Motors Service Parts Operations in Lansing, Michigan. He held a number of posts with General Motors, working in research and development, chassis design, and quality control. The Durham, North Carolina, native graduated from North Carolina State University in 1964 with a bachelor's degree in mechanical engineering.

Sources: *Jet* 89 (11 March 1996): 19; *Who's Who among African Americans,* 26th ed., pp. 263–64.

1995 • *Library Journal* named Carla Diane Hayden Librarian of the Year, making her the first black to receive the honor. She was also the first librarian from Enoch Pratt Free Library in Baltimore to receive the award. Hayden was born in Tallahassee, Florida, and received her bachelor's degree from Roosevelt University in 1973 and her master's and doctorate from the University of Chicago in 1977 and 1987. She joined the Chicago Public Library staff as children's librarian in 1973. Hayden served as young adult services coordinator from 1979 to 1981. From 1982 to 1987 she served as library services coordinator at Chicago's Museum of Science and Industry. After a stint as assistant professor at the University of Pittsburgh from 1987 to 1991, she was named chief librarian and deputy commissioner of the Chicago Public Library. In 1993 Hayden became executive director of the Enoch Pratt Free Library in Baltimore.

Sources: *Jet* 89 (4 March 1996): 22; *Who's Who among African Americans,* 26th ed., p. 556.

1996 • Margaret A. Dixon (1923?–) was installed in May of this year as national president of the American Association of Retired Persons (AARP), becoming the first black to hold the post. Although AARP provided a special office in its headquarters building in downtown Washington, D.C., Dixon's extensive schedule led her to use her suburban Maryland home for much of her work as well. A native of Columbia, South Carolina, Dixon graduated from Allen University in Columbia, Hunter College, Fordham University, and Nova Southeastern University, where she received her doctorate. She taught physically challenged students and directed an early learning program in New York City. She was also principal of a large urban school there before she took her first retirement. Dixon later returned to Columbia where she taught adults at her alma mater, Allen University, and engaged in volunteer work for the Meals on Wheels program. After Dixon and her husband, Octavius, moved to Washington, D.C., to be nearer to their children, she was elected vice president of AARP. She held the presidency for two years and then retired but continued her volunteer activities.

Sources: *Jet* 89 (6 May 1996): 36; "The Different Faces of Contemporary Black Women," *Ebony* 53 (March 1998): 84–100; *Who's Who among African Americans,* 26th ed., p. 344.

1996 • A trial lawyer in Washington, D.C., Sandra Hawkins Robinson (1951–) became the first woman and the third black president-elect of the Trial Lawyers Association of Metropolitan Washington, D.C. Born in Lynchburg, Virginia, Robinson received her bachelor's degree from Oberlin College in 1973 and her law degree from Catholic University School of Law in 1982. She was a partner in the firm Robinson and Robinson from 1985 to 1987. She served the Federal Elections Commission as senior attorney from 1987 to 1990, before becoming an attorney for Jack H. Olender and Associates.

Sources: *Jet* 91 (12 May 1997): 20; *Who's Who among African Americans,* 26th ed., p. 1067.

1996 • Joyce J. Bolden became the first woman and the first minority chairperson of the Commission on Accreditation for the National Association of Schools of Music. Bolden became professor of music and chairperson of the fine arts department at Alcorn State University in Lorman, Mississippi.

Sources: *Jet* 89 (22 January 1996): 20.

1996 • When the National Intramural Recreational Sports Association held its forty-seventh annual conference, Juliette R. Moore (1953–) was elected president, becoming the first black woman elected to lead the association. Moore became director of campus recreation at Northern Illinois University in DeKalb. She held positions in sports and recreation at several institutions, including the University of West Florida, Arizona State University, and James Madison University. New Orleans-born Moore received her bachelor's degree from Xavier University in 1975 and her master's degree from the University of West Florida in 1977.

Sources: *Jet* 90 (1 July 1996): 20; *Who's Who among African Americans,* 26th ed., p. 897.

1996 • Niara Sudarkasa (1938–) became the first black chair of the Pennsylvania Association of Colleges and Universities, an organization of 117 institutions.

Sources: *Jet* 91 (16 December 1996): 22; *Who's Who among African Americans,* 26th ed., p. 1191.

1996 • The first black president of Vanderbilt University's Bar Association was Richard H. Harris II. He became an attorney with Weil Gotshal and Manges LLP in Houston, Texas.

Sources: *Jet* 90 (14 October 1996): 22.

1996 • The first black chairperson of the Council of Independent Colleges was John L. Henderson (1932–). Henderson was born in Evergreen, Alabama, and received his bachelor's degree from Hampton Institute (now Hampton University) in 1955, and his master's and doctorate from the University of Cincinnati in 1966 and 1976. He held positions at several academic institutions, including Xavier University in Cincinnati, the University of Cincinnati, and Sinclair Community College in Dayton. Later he was named president of Wilberforce University in Ohio.

Sources: *Jet* 89 (4 March 1996): 22; *Who's Who among African Americans,* 26th ed., p. 566.

1996 • The first black attorney to become president-elect of the Young Lawyers Division of the Pennsylvania Bar Association was Steven B. Nesmith, an associate at Philadelphia's law firm, Saul, Ewing, Remick and Saul.

Sources: *Jet* 90 (5 August 1996): 19.

1996 • Gayle Briscoe was installed as president of the Greater Baltimore Board of Realtors, the nation's oldest real estate board. She was the board's first black woman president.

Sources: *Jet* 91 (16 December 1996): 22; *Who's Who among African Americans,* 26th ed., p. 143.

1996 • The first black president of the Association of International Educators, formerly the National Association for Foreign Student Affairs, was Cornelia [Connie] Whitener Perdreau. The association is the world's largest organization devoted to international exchange of students and scholars. Perdreau served as study-abroad coordinator at Ohio University in Athens.

Sources: *Jet* 91 (9 December 1996): 54; *Who's Who among African Americans,* 26th ed., p. 980.

1997 • The Memphis Bar Association installed Prince C. Chambliss Jr. (1948–) as president this year, making him the first black lawyer to hold the post. A partner with the law firm Armstrong Allen Prewitt Gentry Johnston and Holmes, he was also vice president of the Tennessee Board of Examiners and secretary of the Tennessee Bar Association. The Birmingham, Alabama, native received his bachelor's degree from the University of Alabama, Birmingham in 1971 and his law degree from Harvard University School of Law in 1974. Chambliss served as special assistant to the president of the University of Alabama, Birmingham, from 1974 to 1975 and as a law clerk for Judge Sam C. Pointer Jr. from 1975 to 1976. In 1976 he became an attorney with Armstrong Allen in Memphis.

Sources: *Jet* 91 (3 February 1997): 19; *Who's Who among African Americans,* 26th ed., p. 226.

1997 • The first black and the second educator to be named president of the Public Relations Society of America was Debra A. Miller. Miller served as principal and senior consultant for D. Miller and Associates in Plantation, Florida, and was a member of the faculty at Florida International University's School of Journalism and Mass Communications.

Sources: *Jet* 91 (28 April 1997): 20.

1997 • Shirley Strickland Saffold took office in 1997 as president of the American Judges Association, the first black woman to serve in an executive position. Saffold received her bachelor's degree from Central State University and her law degree from John Marshal College of Law. She became judge in the Cayuga County Court of Common Pleas.

Sources: *Jet* 90 (28 October 1996): 46; *Who's Who among African Americans,* 26th ed., p. 1086.

1997 • Israel Tribble Jr. (1940–), president and chief executive officer of the Florida Education Fund, became the first black elected to head the Greater Tampa Chamber of Commerce.

Sources: *Jet* 91 (5 May 1997): 20; *Who's Who among African Americans,* 14th ed., p. 1301.

1997 • Retired banker Fran A. Streets became the first black president of the International Women's Forum, an organization that promotes the exchange of ideas and experiences of women worldwide. Among its members were Hillary Rodham Clinton and Coretta Scott King.

Sources: *Jet* 24 (24 November 1997): 20; *Who's Who among African Americans,* 26th ed., p. 1187.

1997 • For the first time, three black women judges in Michigan headed the three judicial associations in the state. They were Vera Massey Jones (1943–), president of the Michigan Judges Association; Jeanette O'Banner-Owens, president of the Michigan District Judges Association, and Carolyn H. Williams, president of the Michigan Probate Judges Association. Jones received her bachelor's degree from Fisk University in 1965 and her law degree from the University of Denver Law School in 1969. She was a private-practice attorney from 1969 to 1970, deputy defender for the Legal Aid and Defender Association of Detroit from 1970 to 1973, referee for the Detroit Recorder's Court Traffic and Ordinance Division from 1973 to 1979, before becoming chief judge in that division. Born in Detroit, O'Banner-Owens graduated from Wayne State Law School. She became judge in the Thirty-sixth District Court in Detroit. Williams also became a probate judge with the Family Division of Circuit Court in Kalamazoo, Michigan.

Sources: *Jet* 92 (26 May 1997): 8; *Who's Who among African Americans,* 26th ed., p. 702 (Jones); p. 944 (O'Banner-Owens); p. 1334 (Williams).

1997 • Richard D. Hailey, an attorney, became the first black president of the Association of Trial Lawyers of America. Established in 1946, the association's primary goal is to safeguard the civil justice system. It serves 60,000 members throughout the United States and Canada. Hailey was a partner in the firm Ramey and Hailey.

Sources: *Jet* 92 (29 September 1997): 39.

1997 • Lois Jean White (1938–) was elected to office in 1997, becoming the first black president of the National Parent Teacher Association. A native of Nashville, Tennessee, White graduated from Fisk University in 1960. Her career includes teacher at Mills College in Birmingham and member of the community orchestra in Atlanta. She held offices in the Knoxville Council PTA and in the Tennessee State PTA. Continuing her career in music, White was principal flutist for the Oak Ridge, Tennessee, Symphony from 1971 to 1995. She later became a private flute instructor in Oak Ridge.

Sources: *Contemporary Black Biography,* vol. 20, pp. 224–26; *Jet* 90 (22 July 1996): 24–27.

1997 • Walter G. Sellers (1925–2008) was elected president of Kiwanis International, becoming the first black to hold that position. A thirty-one-year member of the local Kiwanis in Xenia, he also served as its president. He became governor of the Ohio Kiwanis District. He also served on the Kiwanis International Board, as member, vice president, and treasurer. Sellers was an administrator at Central State University, becoming director of alumni affairs and public relations by the time he retired. The alumni building at the college was named in his honor.

Sources: *Jet* 92 (28 July 1997): 35; *Contemporary Black Biography,* vol. 1157.

1997 • August Wright Pounds (1936–) became the first black president of the American Association of University Women's Legal Advocacy Fund. Pounds, an experienced educator, taught at Iowa State University, the University of Kentucky, and Anne Arundel Community College. He was also visiting professor at the University of Zambia in 1984. Born in Wadley, Alabama, he received his bachelor's and master's degrees from Oakland University 1973 and 1975, and his doctorate from Iowa State University in 1980.

Sources: *Jet* 92 (1 September 1997): 10; *Who's Who among African Americans,* 26th ed., pp. 1006–07.

1998 • The first full-time president of the New Jersey Cable Telecommunications Association, located in Trenton, New Jersey, was Karen D. Alexander. She left her post as vice president of public affairs for Ogden Energy Group in Fairfield, New Jersey, to accept the new position.

Sources: *Jet* 94 (12 October 1998): 20.

1998 • Deborah Crockett became the first black president of the National Association of School Psychologists, the largest professional association for school psychologists in the world. Crockett was school psychologist with the Atlanta Public Schools.

Sources: *Jet* 94 (27 July 1998): 20.

1998 • The first African-American Male Empowerment Summit was held this year and attracted over five hundred men and women who attended sessions on business, mentoring to the community, family development, and other subjects. Citicorp Center in New York was the meeting site.

Sources: *Jet* 94 (16 November 1998): 12.

1998 • Linda D. Bernard became the first black president of the 191-year-old National Association of Women Lawyers. Bernard has served as president and chief executive officer of Wayne County Neighborhood Legal Services in Michigan, serving the county's indigents.

Sources: *Jet* 94 (14 September 1998): 22; *Who's Who among African Americans,* 26th ed., p. 96.

1999 • Robert L. Mathews became the first black to chair the International Food Service Executives Association (IFSEA), in Margate, Florida. Formed in 1901, IFSEA is this country's first hospitality association.

Sources: *Jet* 95 (3 May 1999): 29.

1999 • The American Management Association named its first black vice president in its seventy-five-year history. Gilbert Green took over as North American Vice President this year.

Sources: *Jet* 95 (15 March 1999): 22.

1999 • Alphonso C. Mance became the first black executive director of the Tennessee Education Association. He had served as assistant executive director for fifteen years and was also manager of the Instruction and Professional Development Division, where he advised the TEA on teacher preparation, evaluation, certification, and other issues. The South Carolina native was a public school teacher, having taught chemistry and biology in Florida and New York.

Sources: *Tennessean* (8 April 1999).

1999 • Sarah N. Hall became the first black woman chair of the National Conference of Bar Examiners. Hall graduated from West Virginia University College of Law and serves the West Virginia Bureau of Employment Programs as administrative judge.

Sources: *Jet* 97 (6 December 1999): 20.

1999 • Michael E. Flowers, the first black chair of the Business Law Section of the American Bar Association was elected this year. He was a law partner in Columbus, Ohio, with Bricker and Eckler LLP. Among the initiatives that Flowers implemented was the Business Law Ambassadors program for minority lawyers.

Sources: *Jet* 96 (13 September 1999): 27; *Who's Who among African Americans,* 26th ed., p. 417.

1999 • Delon Hampton (1933–) became the first black to be named president of the American Society of Civil Engineers. Born in Jefferson, Texas, Hampton received his bachelor's degree from the University of Illinois in 1954 and his master's and doctorate from Purdue University in 1958 and 1961. He taught at Kansas State University and Howard University and held research posts with Eric H. Wang Civil Engineering Research Facility and IIT Research Institute. He was president and later chief executive officer of Gnaedinger, Banker, Hampton and Associates in Washington, D.C.

Sources: *Jet* 97 (1 November 1999): 10; *Who's Who among African Americans*, 26th ed., p. 523.

1999 • The International Criminal Police Organization, or Interpol, named Ronald K. Noble (1957?–) to head the organization, making him its first black chief. In 1994 he was the highest ranking black in the history of law enforcement. He held several positions with the U.S. Department of the Treasurer and taught in New York University's law school, and then became head of Interpol. Born in Fort Dix, New Jersey, Noble took his undergraduate degree at the University of New Hampshire and his law degree from Stanford Law School.

Sources: *Jet* 96 (26 July 1999): 4; *Who's Who among African Americans,* 26th ed., p. 938.

Ronald K. Noble

1999 • The National Association of Schools of Music elected Joyce Bolden an honorary member of its board of directors, making her the first person of color and the second woman to receive the honor. Bolden was professor and chair of the Fine Arts Department at Alcorn State University in Lorman, Mississippi.

Sources: *Jet* 95 (15 March 1999): 20.

2000 • State commissioners nationwide elected George Nichols III (1960–) as president of the National Association of Insurance Commissioners, making him the first black president since its founding in 1871. In 1996 he was named commissioner for the Kentucky Department of Insurance. Born in Bowling Green, Kentucky, Nichols received his bachelor's degree from Western Kentucky University in 1983 and his master's degree from the University of Louisville in 1985.

Sources: *Jet* 97 (14 February 2000): 46; *Who's Who among African Americans*, 26th ed., p. 935.

2000 • Tyrone Means became the first black president of the Alabama Trial Lawyers Association, representing 2,000 attorneys statewide. A managing partner in the law firm Thomas, Means, Gillis, Devlin, Robinson, and Seay in Montgomery and a practicing attorney for twenty-three years, Means served the association as treasurer, secretary, and vice president.

Sources: *Jet* 98 (14 August 2000): 16.

2000 • Clarice Lorraine Chambers (1938–2010), an elected official and clergyman, became the first black woman to head the National School Boards Association. She was elected for the 2000–2001 term. Previously she was the first black president of the Pennsylvania School Boards Association and since 1975 served on the Harrisburg Board of Education. Born in Ossining, New York, she studied in a number of Bible training programs and received her bachelor's degree in biblical studies from Trinity College of the Bible and a master's degree from the International Bible Institute and Seminary. In 1979 she became pastor of Antioch Tabernacle.

Sources: *Jet* 97 (15 May 2000): 22; Obituary, *Who's Who among African Americans,* 26th ed., p. 1406.

2000 • Ronald C. Owens was elected president of the Washington Advertising Club, the first black to head the organization. A veteran in advertising, marketing, and public relations firms, he was account executive with N. W. Ayer in New York and later directed worldwide advertising and public relations for Pitney Bowles. In 1995 he became a partner in the Owens firm and became senior vice president of Laughlin, Marinaccio and

Owens Advertising. The Baltimore native graduated from Morgan State with a bachelor's degree and a master's degree in business administration.

Sources: *Jet* 97 (28 February 2000): 38.

2000 • Frank R. Williams became the first black president of the New Orleans Metropolitan Association of Realtors. The founder and manager of Parkway Realty, Williams continued the association's mission of raising standards in real estate practice, preserving the rights of property ownership, and promoting high ethical standards.

Sources: *Jet* 97 (7 January 2000): 38.

2000 • The first black woman to become executive director of the United States Tennis Association, Eastern Section, was Denise M. Jordan, who had served as executive director and USA Tennis and Regional Programs director.

Sources: *Jet* 98 (13 November 2000): 36.

2001 • State representative Helen Giddings (1943–), of Dallas, Texas, was sworn in as the first black president of the National Order of Women Legislators (NOWL). The organization represents over 1,000 women in government at the local, state, and national level. At the time of her election to NOWL, Giddings had recently won her fifth consecutive term in the Texas House of Representatives.

Sources: *Jet* 99 (23 January 2001): 20.

2002 • Civil rights attorney Fred Gray Sr. became the first black president of the Alabama State Bar Association.

Sources: *New York Times* (30 March 2002).

2002 • Harry S. Johnson became the first black president of the Maryland Bar Association.

Sources: *Jet* 102 (8 April 2002): 12.

2008 • The first black and first male chief executive officer of the National Parent Teacher Association (PTA) was Byron V. Garrett; he took the helm in June and left the office in 2010. Previously, Garrett was a school principal (K–8) and later National Program Leader for the National 4-H Headquarters at the U.S. Department of Agriculture. He became the first black and first male chief of staff for the Office of Public Affairs at the U.S. Customs and Border Protection (an agency of the U.S. Office of Homeland Security). "[T]he PTA family is rich in culture and tradition.... We are the largest child advocacy organization in the country.... we're woven into the fabric of American society," he said. He is a graduate of High Point University and the University of Phoenix and is pursuing a doctorate from Pepperdine University. Garrett was on *Ebony* magazine's "The Most Influential Black Americans" for 2009.

Sources: Byron Garrett's Keynote Remarks, http://www.pta.org/3435.htm; *Jet* 113 (July 7, 2008): 22.

2009 • Richard R. Buery Jr. (1969?–) became the first black chief executive of the Children's Aid Society, a private charitable organization that gives comprehensive services to 150,000 children and their families in New York City. For a decade, Buery masterminded several innovative initiatives to improve the lives of economically advantaged young people in the city. Buery was born in the East New York section of Brooklyn in a neighborhood known for crime and poverty. He graduated from Stuyvesant High School, Harvard University, and Yale Law School. While at Harvard, he and a classmate created a summer program for youth in a Boston housing project. He cofounded iMentor, an e-mail based mentoring service, and was founding director of Groundwork Inc., a social service provider based in East New York.

Sources: Stephen, "Caring for Young People," *Crisis* 116 (Fall 2009): 9.

Charitable and Civic Organizations

1780 • Formed on November 10, 1780, the African Union Society of Newport, Rhode Island, was the first attested black mutual aid society. The second, the Free African Society of Philadelphia, was formed in 1787. The African Society of Boston was formed in 1796, and the New York African Society in 1808.

Sources: Baskin and Runes, *Dictionary of Black Culture,* p. 15; Yee, *Black Women Abolitionists,* p. 74.

1787 • The Free African Society was formed in Philadelphia on April 12, 1787. This society is generally regarded as the first black organization of note in this country because it quickly became the nucleus for two black churches. (The African Union Society of Newport, Rhode Island, was formed in 1780. In Philadelphia, the Female Benevolent Society of Saint Thomas' Episcopal Church was formed in 1793, and the male African Friendly Society of Saint Thomas, in 1795.)

Sources: Bennett, *Before the Mayflower,* pp. 55–56, 80–81, 621–22; *Dictionary of American Negro Biography,* p. 147; Hornsby, *Chronology of African-American History,* p. 9; *Negro Almanac,* pp. 6, 234, 1333; Sterling, *We Are Your Sisters,* p. 105.

1790 • The Brown Fellowship of Charleston, South Carolina, is the first known mutual aid society in South Carolina. Limited to fifty free men of color, one of its principal functions was to manage a cemetery for the black members of Saint Philip's Episcopal Church, since they could not be buried in the church's cemetery. The organization survived well into the twentieth century, by which time it had become an exclusive social organization.

Sources: Gatewood, *Aristocrats of Color,* pp. 14–15.

1828 • In January, twenty-one black women, with the advice of male ministers, met in New York to draw up plans for the African Dorcas Society, which was officially organized in February. This was the first black women's charitable group. Its principal object was to aid young blacks in attending schools by supplying them with clothing, hats, and shoes.

Sources: Yee, *Black Women Abolitionists,* pp. 75–76; *The Black New Yorkers,* p. 61.

1853 • The first Colored Young Men's Christian Association was organized in Washington, D.C. Its first president was Anthony Bowen who worked for the patent office. A second YMCA for blacks was organized, in Charleston, South Carolina, and in 1867 yet another chapter was organized in New York City.

Sources: Ashe, *A Hard Road to Glory,* vol. 1, p. 12; Logan and Winston, *Dictionary of American Negro Biography,* p. 449; Baskin and Runes, *Dictionary of Black Culture,* p. 61; *Negro Year Book,* 1925–26, p. 275.

1867 • The first black delegate to an international convention of the Young Men's Christian Association was Edward V. C. Eato (?–1914). Eato was a prominent figure in New York social life as a member of the Ugly Club, Masons, and Society of the Sons of New York. For twenty-five years, he was the president of the African Society.

Sources: Ashe, *A Hard Road to Glory,* vol. 1, p. 12; Gatewood, *Aristocrats of Color,* pp. 213, 224, 233, 252; *Negro Year Book,* 1925–26, p. 275.

1876 • The first student branch of the Young Men's Christian Association at a black school was organized at Howard University, Washington, D.C. By 1911 the number of black student branches was about one hundred.

Sources: Logan and Winston, *Dictionary of American Negro Biography,* p. 339; *Negro Year Book,* 1921–22, p. 218.

1888 • William Alphaeus Hunton (1863–1916) became probably the first black employed by the Young Men's Christian Association (YMCA) when he went to the Norfolk, Virginia, branch. In 1893 Hunton became the first black secretary of the International Young Men's Christian Association. Born free in Chatham, Ontario, Canada, he devoted his life to work with the association, particularly in the Colored Men's Department. He was active first in the Ottawa YMCA and later accepted the Norfolk post. In January 1890 he visited all of the black YMCAs across the country to assess their needs. Hunton also visited as many black colleges as he could in an effort to identify new leaders for the black branches. During his lifetime he was successful in strengthening the black branches, bringing blacks into administrative posts, building new YMCA buildings, and in increasing black membership.

Sources: Ashe, *A Hard Road to Glory,* vol. 1, p. 12; Logan and Winston, *Dictionary of American Negro Biography,* pp. 338–40; Smith, *Notable Black American Women,* pp. 537–38.

1893 • The first black branch of the Young Women's Christian Association (YWCA) was opened in Dayton, Ohio.

Sources: Ashe, *A Hard Road to Glory,* vol. 1, p. 12.

1897 • Victoria Earl Matthews (1861–1907) and Maritcha Lyons (1848–1929) founded the White Rose Mission, on February 11. Matthews was the organization's first superintendent. Its mission was a home for black girls and women, whose purpose was to train them for "practical self-help and right living." It operated from San Juan Hill district in the Manhattan section of New York City and provided food and living quarters for Southern and West Indian migrants. Matthews was born in Fort Valley, Georgia, one of nine children of a slave mother. Her mother relocated to New York after emancipation, taking with her the only two of her children that she could find. Although she had little formal education, Matthews was an avid reader and took advantage of every opportunity to grow intellectually and culturally. She used the pen name "Victoria Earle" and wrote a number of works. She became founder and first president of the Woman's Loyal Union of New York City. Lyons, an educator, writer, and lecturer, was born a free black in New York City. After graduating from high school, she became a teacher, since such education at that time qualified one to teach. She taught in the Brooklyn schools for forty-eight years and later became assistant principal and teacher trainer. She was also active in the women's club movement.

Sources: *The Black New Yorkers,* p. 117; Smith, *Notable Black American Women,* pp. 736–39 (Matthews); Smith, *Notable Black American Women,* Book II, pp. 417–21 (Lyons).

1899 • The Colored Young Men's Christian Association Building in Norfolk, Virginia, was the first YMCA building constructed for blacks.

Sources: *An Era of Progress and Promise,* p. 533 (photograph).

1899 • The first black YMCA in New York City opened this year, at Mount Olivet Baptist Church in Manhattan.

Sources: *The Black New Yorkers,* p. 119.

1905 • The first black woman on the staff of the Young Women's Christian Association (YWCA) was Eva del Vakia Bowles (1875–1943). Born in Albany, Athens County, Ohio, Bowles came from a family that was well educated and distinguished. She attended The Ohio State and Columbia universities and was prepared to teach music and the blind. She became the first black teacher at Chandler Normal School, an American Missionary Association institution in Lexington, Kentucky. She also taught in Saint Augustine, Florida, Raleigh North Carolina, and in Lawrenceville, Virginia, at Saint Paul's Normal and Industrial Training Institute. Bowles met Addie D. Waites Hunton while in Virginia, and became familiar with the YMCA work of her husband, William Hunton. She was named head of a project for black women that was conducted under the auspices of the YWCA. Soon it became the 137th Street Branch YWCA in New York City, and for a while the nation's largest black branch. With that post Bowles became the first salaried black YWCA secretary. She was an advocate of interracial YWCAs and fought against opponents who wanted a permanent "colored department" as well as those who wanted all decisions made under white leadership. She believed that the YWCA was a "pioneer in interracial experimentation." She spoke at various YWCA conferences, YWCA branches, and at black and white colleges throughout the nation, presenting her views on this matter. Bowles resigned from the YWCA in 1932 when she believed that the national board's recent reorganization made no

The YWCA's First Black Secretary

In 1907 Addie D. Waites Hunton (1875–1943) was the first secretary for colored student affairs for the National Board of the Young Women's Christian Association (YWCA). In addition to her work for the YWCA—in the United States and in France during World War I— Hunton was also very active in the club movement and the women's suffrage movement. In 1889 she became the first black to graduate from the Spencerian College of Commerce in Philadelphia. Hunton was born in Norfolk, Virginia. After graduating from college, she taught school in Portsmouth, Virginia for one year. The next year she became principal at State Normal and Agricultural College in Alabama (now Alabama A & M University). She married William Alphaeus Hunton, who became active in YMCA work in Norfolk and pioneered in establishing black YMCAs around the country.

Sources: Ashe, *A Hard Road to Glory*, vol. 1, p. 12; Logan and Winston, *Dictionary of American Negro Biography*, pp. 337–38; Smith, *Notable Black American Women*, pp. 536–40.

provisions for blacks in policymaking. After that, she was an executive with the National Colored Merchants Association. She returned to work with the YWCA, becoming secretary of the West End Branch of Cincinnati. Later she was a Harlem organizer for the Wendell Willkie Republicans.

Sources: Smith, *Notable Black American Women*, pp. 98–100; *The Black New Yorkers*, p. 127; Hine, *Black Women in America*, vol. 1, pp. 152–53.

1918 • The first rural branch of the National Association for the Advancement of Colored People was founded in Virginia, near Falls Church. Joseph Tinner, a stonemason, was the branch's first president and Edwin Bancroft Henderson was secretary. In 1999 the Tinner Hill Monument, a Gothic arch, was unveiled to recognize the work of the branch and its first officers.

Sources: *Jet* 97 (1 November 1999): 22.

Addie D. Waites Hunton

1940 • Jesse O. Thomas (1883–1972) was the first black to work for the American Red Cross in a professional and policy-making position. Born and raised in Mississippi, Thomas graduated from Tuskegee Institute in 1911, the New York School of Social Work in 1923, and Chicago School of Research in 1925.

Sources: *Who's Who in Colored America, 1929*, p. 361.

1942 • Molly Moon (1912–1990) was the organizer and first president of the National Urban League Guild, a fund-raising organization for the Urban League. She headed the organization until her death. Moon was born in Hattiesburg, Mississippi, and graduated from Meharry Medical College in Nashville, Tennessee, with a degree in pharmacy. She worked as a pharmacist in New Orleans, Gary, Indiana, and New York City. She became interested in social work, however, and left pharmacy to work with the Department of Social Services in New York City. She had wide contacts in New York's social circles and used her connections to help support the National Urban League. Moon and a group of friends held a benefit for the league in early 1942; the Victory Cocktail Party was highly successful and became a New York tradition. The black-tie ball continued to be held each February and was renamed the Beaux-Arts Ball. Moon became the founding president of the Council of Urban League Guilds that functioned to raise money for the league. By the time of her death in 1990, she had been its only president.

Sources: Hine, *Black Women in America*, vol. 2, pp. 810–12; Hornsby, *Chronology of African-American History*, p. 436; Smith, *Notable Black American Women*, pp. 760–61.

Josephine Groves Holloway

1943 • Josephine Groves Holloway (1898–1988) founded the first black Girl Scout Troop in Middle Tennessee; she was also its first executive. Holloway was born in Cowpens, South Carolina. She began her college education at Fisk University in Nashville, Tennessee, but interrupted her training due to illness. She graduated in 1923 with a bachelor's degree. She worked to improve the quality of life for blacks in Cowpens and also searched for employment. Since Holloway wanted to reform the world for black girls, in 1923 she accepted a position at the Bethlehem Center in Nashville. While there she learned about previous attempts to establish scouting at the black branch of the YMCA, Blue Triangle. After training at a local conference, Holloway was commissioned captain and then revived scouting for black girls in Nashville. In 1924 her registered platoon had from 150 to 160 members. It all ended in fall 1925, however, when she was forced to resign her position because she had married. She continued her education and received a second bachelor's degree from Tennessee Agricultural and Industrial College (now Tennessee State University). Her interest in scouting continued and between 1926 and 1933 she established another troop and encouraged others to do so as well. In May 1943 the Girl Scout Council approved its first black troop and made the status retroactive to 1942, when Holloway first attempted to register her troop. Holloway became widely celebrated for her work in addressing the needs of black girls and in breaking down racial barriers in scouting organizations.

Sources: Smith, *Notable Black American Women,* pp. 295–97; *Sunday Tennessean* (20 May 1990).

1946 • Channing Heggie Tobias (1882–1961) was the first black to head the Phelps-Stokes Fund, an organization founded to further black education. A native of Augusta, Georgia, Tobias was an ordained minister of the Colored (now Christian) Methodist Episcopal Church. In 1911 he began to work for the Young Men's Christian Association, where he achieved prominence as senior secretary of the Colored Division of the National Council. In 1950 he was the first black to receive an honorary Doctor of Laws degree from New York University.

Sources: Logan and Winston, *Dictionary of American Negro Biography,* pp. 593–95; Robinson, *Historical Negro Biographies,* pp. 252–53; Smith, *Notable Black American Men,* pp. 1122–25.

1946 • Ella Josephine Baker (1903–1986) was elected president of the New York branch of the National Association for the Advancement of Colored People (NAACP), becoming the first woman to hold the post. Baker was a community organizer, civil rights and domestic activist, and consultant in education. She was born in Norfolk, Virginia, and grew up in a small town in North Carolina. She graduated from Shaw University in Raleigh, North Carolina. She joined George Schuyler, a writer for the *Pittsburgh Courier,* in establishing the Young Negro Cooperative League, a consumer cooperative. Baker began to work with the NAACP in the early 1940s as assistant field secretary. She later became national director of branches. She became disillusioned when she saw that the organization was directed from the top down. She resigned her position but remained active with the New York branch. After the bus boycott began in Montgomery, Alabama, in 1955, Baker concentrated on the movement and the U.S. Supreme Court's decision to end racial segregation in public accommodations, including buses. In 1957 largely through Baker's efforts, the Southern Christian Leadership Conference (SCLC) was formed. Although Martin Luther King Jr. became the SCLC's leader, Baker ran the office and coordinated the organization's programs. She remained coordinator for about two years. She later helped student protesters to organize the Student Nonviolent Coordinating Committee (SNCC) and became its executive secretary. She also assisted the students in voter registration drives. In 1964 she helped to establish the Mississippi Freedom Democratic Party and gave the keynote address at its founding convention. It was well after the Civil Rights Movement ended that Baker and her work began to receive due recognition.

Sources: *The Black New Yorkers,* p. 265; Smith, *Notable Black American Women,* pp. 40–43; Hine, *Black Women in America,* vol. 1, pp. 70–74.

1965 • Lois Towles Caesar (1922–1983), a musician and educator, was the first black to serve on the board of directors of the San Francisco Symphony Foundation. She was also

The United Negro College Fund

The United Negro College Fund was first founded on April 24, 1944, to coordinate the fundraising efforts of forty-one private, accredited, four-year schools. Chartered in New York, it was the first attempt by private black colleges to establish a cooperative fundraising organization. Now called The College Fund/UNCF, its efforts still contribute significantly to the survival of black higher education. The fund's founder was Frederick D. Patterson (1901–1988), a veterinarian, who also founded the nation's first and only black veterinary school at Tuskegee Institute (now Tuskegee University). He served as president of Tuskegee for twenty-five years, until his retirement. Patterson was born in Washington, D.C., and graduated from Iowa State University in 1923 with a degree in veterinary medicine. After teaching at Virginia State College (now Virginia State University), he returned to Iowa and obtained his master's degree in veterinary medicine. He joined Tuskegee's faculty in 1932 and established a friendship with researcher George Washington Carver that lasted until Carver died. Patterson continued his education at Cornell University and returned to Tuskegee with his doctorate in bacteriology, the first Tuskegee faculty member to earn the terminal degree. While president of Tuskegee, he established the Commercial Aviation program and trained Tuskegee students as pilots. The program became well known for training the group of black military pilots known as the Tuskegee Airmen. After he left Tuskegee, Patterson became president of the Phelps Stokes Fund in New York City and remained there until 1970. Patterson was awarded the Medal of Freedom on June 23, 1987.

Frederick Patterson

Sources: *Ebony Success Library,* vol. 1, p. 242; *Encyclopedia of Black America,* p. 823; Hornsby, *Chronology of African-American History,* p. 92; *Jet* 72 (11 May 1987): 24; 72 (27 July 1987): 22; *Negro Almanac,* p. 1329; Smith, *Notable Black American Men,* pp. 914–17.

the first black to serve on the board of directors of the San Francisco Symphony Association in 1969. In 1976 she became the first black and woman to serve on the Mayor's Criminal Justice Commission of San Francisco, California. In 1978 she became the first minority chair of the commission. She was born in Texarkana, Arkansas, and graduated from Wiley College (A.B) and State University of Iowa (M.A.; M.F.A.).

Sources: Handy, *Black Women in American Bands and Orchestras,* pp. 213–14; *Jet* 41 (2 March 1972): 38; *Our World* 8 (May 1953): 28–43; *Who's Who among African Americans,* 26th ed., p. 195.

1967 • Helen Claytor (1907–2005) was the first black president of the national Young Women's Christian Association (YWCA). Claytor was born in Minneapolis, Minnesota, the daughter of a Pullman porter and a cooking instructor. She graduated from the University of Minnesota in 1928. She served with the YWCA in Trenton, New Jersey, and in Kansas City, Missouri. She was secretary for interracial education with the National YWCA in the 1940s and was a member of the YWCA World Council from 1946 to 1952. In 1946 to 1973 she was a member of the National YWCA Board of Directors.

Sources: Garrett, *Famous First Facts about Negroes,* pp. 201–2; *Contemporary Black Biography,* vol. 14, pp. 54–57.

1970 • Donald Milford Payne (1934–) was the first black to head the National Council of the Young Men's Christian Association. In 1989, he was elected as New Jersey's first black congressman.

Sources: *Negro Almanac,* p 104; *Who's Who among African Americans,* 26th ed., p. 972; *Contemporary Black Biography,* vol. 2, pp. 188–90.

1973 • The National Black Feminist Organization was founded to address the concerns of black women. Within a year, ten local chapters had been organized and met in a national conference.

Sources: Rosen, *The World Split Open,* pp. 282–83; Hine, *Black Women in America,* vol. 1, p. 423.

1975 • Gloria Dean Randle Scott (1938–) was the first black president of the Girl Scouts of America. Scott rose in position from first vice president to become national president and held this position until 1978. Early in her presidency she conducted workshop sessions for heads of national organizations for member countries in the Western Hemisphere of the World Association of Girl Scouts and scouts in Rio de Janeiro. Scott was born in Houston, Texas. She received her bachelor's, master's and doctorate from Indiana University and has had extensive experience in teaching and academic administration. Scott became the second woman president of Bennett College for women, in Greensboro, North Carolina, and held the post from 1987 to 2001. While at Bennett, Scott was challenged to plan for black women's colleges to survive in the future. She was distressed that black students lost an important role model when the black teacher was displaced, and she was troubled over national issues that seemed to defy resolution. She called herself a race woman and one who saw importance in giving back to black people.

Sources: Hine, *Black Women in America,* pp. 1018–19; Smith, *Notable Black American Women,* pp. 993–97; *Who's Who among African Americans,* 26th ed., pp. 1101–02.

1975 • Margaret Berenice Bush Wilson (1919–2009), activist, lawyer, and civil rights leader, became the first black woman to chair the National Association for the Advancement of Colored People's Board of Directors, from 1975 to 1984. After she was admitted to the Missouri bar in 1943, real estate law became Wilson's specialty. Her struggle against the racially restrictive covenants in housing contracts ended with the landmark Supreme Court decision in 1948, *Shelley v. Kraemer.* In 1948 she became the first black woman from Missouri to run for a seat in the U.S. Congress but was soundly defeated. Active with the NAACP since 1956, Wilson became the first woman president of the Saint Louis branch in 1962. Wilson was born in St. Louis, Missouri, and received her bachelor's degree from Talladega College in Alabama in 1940 and her law degree from Lincoln University School of Law in 1943.

Sources: Smith, *Notable Black American Women,* pp. 1268–71; *Current Biography Yearbook,* 1975, pp. 443–46; Hine, *Black Women in America,* vol. 2, pp. 1272–73.

1977 • Fredda Witherspoon (1918?–1996) was the first black president of the Metropolitan St. Louis Young Women's Christian Association. She was also one of the first blacks to integrate St. Louis University.

Sources: *Jet* 54 (15 June 1978): 24; *Who's Who among Black Americans, 1992–93,* p. 1559.

1977 • The Black Tennis and Sports Foundation was first set up in 1977. Its founder was Augustus G. Jenkins Jr. (1941–). Born in Brooklyn, New York, Jenkins received his bachelor's degree from Central State University in Ohio in 1965 and his master's degree from The Ohio State University in 1966. The owner of Jenkins Funeral Chapel, he also became a flight instructor.

Sources: *Jet* 72 (10 August 1987): 9; *Who's Who among African Americans,* 26th ed., p. 657.

1978 • Faye Wattleton (1943–) became the first black and the first woman president of the Planned Parenthood Federation. She was often at the forefront of national debates over legal abortion but remained firm in her belief in women's rights and reproductive rights.

A native of Saint Louis, Missouri, Wattleton took her nursing degree from the Ohio University School of Nursing in 1964. She was the first person in her family to earn a college degree. She held the post as president until her resignation in 1992 and then became a television show host for Tribune Entertainment in Chicago. She also served on the boards of several foundations.

Sources: Hine, *Black Women in America,* pp. 1239–40; *Contemporary Black* Biography, vol. 9, pp. 256–59; Smith, *Notable Black American Women,* pp. 1230–32; *Who's Who among African Americans,* 14th ed., p. 1359.

1979 • Raymond W. Fannings was the first black director of the Chicago Child Care Society, Chicago's oldest charitable organization.

Sources: *Jet* 56 (10 May 1979): 21.

1979 • Franklin A. Thomas (1934–) was the first black to head a major foundation, the Ford Foundation. He was born in New York City and received his bachelor's degree from Columbia University in 1956, where he was the first black to serve as captain of the basketball team. He became an attorney and worked both in government positions and in private practice. He stepped down from the position in March 1996.

Sources: *Ebony Success Library,* vol. 1, p. 302; *Current Biography Yearbook,* 1981, pp. 413–16; *Contemporary Black Biography,* vol. 5, pp. 252–55; Smith, *Notable Black American Men,* pp. 1112–13.

1982 • Sherman Jarvis Jones (1935–) was the first black vice president of Optimists International, a community service organization. At the time of the election, Jones was a sergeant on the Kansas City, Missouri, police force. Born in Winston-Salem, North Carolina, he studied at Kansas City Community College. In addition to his police work, Jones was a professional baseball player from 1953 to 1965 and a state senator in Kansas.

Sources: *Jet* 62 (9 August 1982): 21; *Who's Who among African Americans,* 14th ed., p. 726.

1984 • Walter G. Harris, Birmingham, Alabama, city school superintendent, was the first black member of the Birmingham Rotary Club. Two years later he was elected to its board of directors, becoming the first black to hold that post.

Sources: *Jet* 67 (12 November 1984): 29; 70 (4 August 1986): 31.

1984 • Gwendolyn Calvert Baker (1931–) became the first black woman to be named national executive director for the YWCA.

Sources: *Contemporary Black Biography,* vol. 9, pp. 8–10; Smith, *Notable Black American Women,* Book II, pp. 20–24; *Ebony* 44 (October 1989): 40.

1985 • Anna F. Jones was the first black woman to head a major community foundation, the Boston Foundation. Jones is the daughter of the first black president of Howard University, Mordecai W. Johnson.

Sources: *Jet* 67 (4 March 1985): 5.

1985 • Archibald Mosley was the first black president of the Pontiac, Michigan, Kiwanis Club. Mosley became a Pontiac communications coordinator.

Sources: *Jet* 69 (23 December 1985): 20.

1986 • Marie Gadsden (1919–2012) was the first black woman to chair Oxfam America. Gadsden was executive director of the Phelps-Stokes Fund (Washington, D.C.,) and later deputy director of the National Association for Equal Opportunity in Higher Education/ AID Cooperative Agreement. Gadsden was born in Douglas, Georgia, and later relocated to Savannah. She received her bachelor's degree from Savannah State College in 1938, her master's degree from Atlanta University in 1945, and her doctorate from the University of Wisconsin in 1951. She was a Fulbright Scholar and for two years she studied at St. Ann's College, Oxford University and did post-doctoral research at the University of Dublin in Ireland. She held teaching positions at a number of institutions, including Southern University in Baton Rouge, Atlanta University, Georgia State College (now Georgia State University), Morehouse College, Spelman College, Georgetown University, American University, and Columbia University. From 1963 to 1967 Gadsden was a specialist with the Peace Corps and taught English as a foreign language (TEFL). She also served as a TEFL resource person at the British Embassy and elsewhere.

Sources: *Jet* 71 (24 November 1986): 20; Smith, *Notable Black American Women,* pp. 381–83.

1986 • Leria Lowe Jordan was the first black member of the Junior League of Birmingham, Alabama. Jordan was a twenty-nine-year-old auditing analyst.

Sources: *Jet* 72 (18 May 1987): 24.

1987 • The first black president of the Community Service Society of New York was David R. Jones (1948–). Born in Brooklyn, Jones received his bachelor's degree from Wesleyan University in 1970 and his law degree from Yale University School of Law in 1974. He was a senate intern with U.S. Senator Robert Kennedy in 1967 and a law clerk for Federal District Judge Constance Baker Motley from 1974 to 1975. He was special advisor to New York City Mayor Edward I. Koch from 1979 to 1983. From 1983 to 1986 Jones was executive director of the New York City Youth Bureau.

Sources: *The Black New Yorkers,* p. 387; *Who's Who among African Americans,* 26th ed., p. 689.

1988 • Madeline Ford was the first woman vice president and corporate secretary of the Young Men's Christian Association of Greater New York. She was thus the highest ranking woman to date in this organization.

Sources: *Jet* 74 (16 May 1988): 20.

1989 • Herbert Carter was the first black chairman of the board of directors of United Way. Carter was executive vice chancellor at California State University at Los Angeles.

Sources: *Jet* 76 (24 July 1989): 8; 76 (25 September 1989): 20.

1989 • Gabriel S. Lee Jr. (1922–) was the first black president of the Cleveland, Ohio, Host Club/Lions Club International. Lee, a clergyman, became very active in civic and social work.

Sources: *Jet* 77 (18 December 1989): 20; *Who's Who among Black Americans, 1992–93,* p. 857.

1989 • Mahlon Martin was the first black to head the Rockefeller Foundation. A native of Arkansas, Martin was the first black city manager in Little Rock in 1980, and the first black director of the state Finance and Administration Department (1983–86).

Sources: *Jet* 76 (22 May 1989): 24.

1989 • Nancy Leftenant-Colon (1920?–) became the first and only woman to hold the presidency of the Tuskegee Airmen. She had served in the U.S. Air Force as a flight nurse.

Sources: *Jet* 93 (15 December 1997): 26–27.

1990 • As president of the Rotary Club of Cheraw, Elmer D. Brooks was the first black president of the organization in the state of South Carolina. Brooks had been a mortician in Cheraw for ten years.

Sources: *Jet* 77 (19 February 1990): 20.

1990 • Gayleatha Brown, an embassy economic aide in Dar-es-Salaam, was the first and only woman member of the Rotary Club of Tanzania.

Sources: *Jet* 78 (27 August 1990): 11.

1990 • Walter G. Sellers (1925–2008) was the first black trustee of Kiwanis International. This educator had a long association with Central State University, Wilberforce, Ohio, and in 1990 was special assistant to the university's president. Sellers was born in Ann Arbor, Michigan, and received his bachelor's degree from Central State University in Ohio in 1951.

Sources: *Jet* 78 (6 August 1990): 22; *Who's Who among African Americans,* 14th ed., p. 1157.

1992 • Mary Ann Nelson was the first black elected to the national board of the Sierra Club. Nelson was an environmental attorney in Boston.

Sources: *Jet* 82 (13 July 1992): 20.

1992 • Anthony Joseph Polk (1941–) became the first black to hold at senior management post at the American Red Cross when he became director of transformation operations. Born in New Orleans, Polk received his bachelor's degree in 1966 from McNeese State University in Lake Charles, Louisiana, and his master's degree in 1974 from Bowling Green State University in Kentucky. During his stint in the armed services, Polk was blood supply manager at several army installations, including the U.S. Department of Defense Tri-Services Blood program.

Sources: *Who's Who among African Americans,* 26th ed., p. 1000.

1993 • Elaine R. Jones (1944–) became the first woman to head the Legal Defense Fund (LDF), a nonprofit organization that fights discrimination and civil rights violations. At one time the LDF was an arm of the National Association for the Advancement of Colored People but split from the organization in 1957; the relationship between the two organizations continued in name only. Only three leaders preceded Jones: Thurgood Marshall, Jack Greenberg, and Julius L. Chambers.

Sources: Smith, *Notable Black American Women,* Book II, pp. 348–50; *Contemporary Black Biography,* vol. 7, pp. 145–48.

1995 • Annelle Lewis, previously a development officer at Piney Woods Country Life School in Mississippi, became the first woman president of the Urban League of Metropolitan Denver.

Sources: *Jet* 89 (4 December 1995): 19.

1995 • The first black state commander of the Veterans of Foreign Wars in Minnesota was Gordon W. Kirk. He was elected at the seventy-sixth state convention.

Sources: *Jet* 88 (11 September 1995): 27.

1995 • A veteran of the U.S. Air Force, William Alton Bowman (1933–) became the first black male commander of the world's largest American Legion post, Post 3 in Lincoln, Nebraska. He served during the conflicts in Korea and in Vietnam, from 1954 to 1976. Born in Fayetteville, North Carolina, he has held positions with the State Department of Roads, the U.S. Postal Service, and Budget Rent-A-Car.

Sources: *Jet* 88 (21 August 1995): 22; *Who's Who among African Americans,* 26th ed., p. 128.

1996 • The first black state commander of the Veterans of Foreign Wars (VFW), Department of Texas, was Alexander Vernon. Vernon holds a master's degree in criminal justice. He held a number of posts with the VFW, such as all American post commander, all-state post commander, state chief of staff, state safety chair, and national security co-chair.

Sources: *Jet* 90 (1 July 1996): 6; *Who's Who among African Americans,* 26th ed., p. 1264.

1996 • Theresa E. Loveless became the first black executive director of the Girl Scout Council of Greater St. Louis. This was the nation's second largest of 331 councils and served over 43,000 young people in the area.

Sources: *Jet* 90 (16 September 1996): 19; *Who's Who among African Americans,* 26th ed., p. 790.

1997 • The first black woman in South Carolina to become commander of a Veterans of Foreign Wars Post in that state was Margarite Robinson Blakely (1948?–), a native of Columbia. A veteran of the Persian Gulf War, Blakely was elected to head the Gandy-Griffin VFW Post 4262 in Columbia. She was also a member of the U.S. Army reserve and a licensed practical nurse at Columbia's Richland Memorial Hospital.

Sources: *Jet* 92 (18 August 1997): 8.

1999 • The first black to serve as senior vice commander of the Department of California's Veterans of Foreign Wars (VFW) was Arthur L. Harris Sr. (1935–). He represented VFW members at the state and national level. One year later he became VFW state commander.

Sources: *Jet* 96 (23 August 1999): 20; *Who's Who among African Americans,* 26th ed., p. 535.

2000 • The first black president of the YMCA board in Richmond, Virginia, was Kelly C. Harris.

Sources: *Jet* 97 (7 January 2000): 52.

2001 • Roslyn McCallister Brock became the youngest and first woman vice chair of the National Association for the Advancement of Colored People Board of Directors. Since 1996 Brock, who was director of business and community development for Secours Baltimore/ Richmond Health Systems, had served on the board as an at-large member.

Sources: *Jet* 99 (26 March 2001): 10; 99 (16 April 2001): 18.

Civil Rights and Political Organizations

1775 • The Pennsylvania Society for the Abolition of Slavery was the first abolition society. It was organized in Philadelphia on April 14, 1775, and its first president was John Baldwin. After reorganizing and adopting a new constitution, it became incorporated as the Pennsylvania Society for Promoting the Abolition of Slavery, for the Relief of Free Negroes Unlawfully Held in Bondage, and for Improving the Condition of the African Race, on December 8, 1789.

Sources: *Encyclopedia of Black America,* p. 789; Hornsby, *Chronology of African-American History,* p. 7; Kane, *Famous First Facts,* p. 1; *Negro Almanac,* pp. 5, 812.

1788 • The African Union Society of Newport, Rhode Island, was the first black organization to advocate black emigration to Africa. This position was challenged by the Free African Society of Philadelphia.

Sources: Bennett, *Before the Mayflower,* p. 145; *Encyclopedia of Black America,* p. 280; *The Negro Almanac,* p. 6.

1895 • The National Conference of Colored Women met in Boston, Massachusetts, in August, 1895. The leading spirit in organizing the conference was Josephine St. Pierre Ruffin (1842–1924), the founder of the Women's New Era Club. One hundred women from twenty clubs in ten states came together for the session. The meeting led to the formation of the National Federation of Afro-American Women, which was merged into the National Association of Colored Women the following year on July 21, 1896. The new organization was founded as a national coalition of black women's clubs and was the first and foremost national organization of black women at the time. Mary Church Terrell (1863–1954) became the first president of the National Association of Colored Women.

Sources: Bennett, *Before the Mayflower,* p. 507; Logan and Winston, *Dictionary of American Negro Biography,* pp. 535–36; *Encyclopedia of Black America,* pp. 815, 863; Smith, *Notable Black American Women,* pp. 961–66 (Ruffin); pp. 1115–19 (Terrell).

1905 • Twenty-nine black intellectuals and activists from fourteen states met near Niagara Falls, New York, on July 11–13 to establish the Niagara Movement. Led by W.E.B. Du Bois and William Monroe Trotter, the organization rejected the accomodationist views of Booker T. Washington and encouraged blacks to press for immediate civil rights without compromise. In 1909 the movement merged with the National Association for the Advancement of Colored People.

Sources: Alford, *Famous First Blacks*, p. 24; Bennett, *Before the Mayflower*, p. 512; Hornsby, *Chronology of African-American History*, p. 61.

1909 • The organizational meeting of the National Association for the Advancement of Colored People was held in New York City on February 12—Abraham Lincoln's birthday. Among those who signed the original charter were Jane Addams, John Dewey, W. E. B. Du Bois, William Dean Howells, and Oswald Garrison Villard. The permanent organization was created May 12–14, 1910; Moorfield Story, a Boston lawyer, was elected president. The social change organization celebrated its one-hundredth anniversary in 2009.

Sources: Bennett, *Before the Mayflower*, pp. 337–39, 512; Hornsby, *Chronology of African-American History*, p. 64; *Negro Almanac*, p. 21.

1911 • The National Urban League was formed in October from the merger of the Committee for Improving the Industrial Conditions of Negroes in New York (1906), the National League for the Protection of Colored Women (1906), and the Committee on Urban Conditions Among Negroes (1910). George Edmund Haynes and Eugene Kinckle Jones were among the cofounders. Edwin R. A. Seligman was president and Jones was executive secretary. The National Urban League became an early leader among black organizations in research when Charles S. Johnson organized the research department in 1920. In addition, Johnson became editor of *Opportunity: A Journal of Negro Life*, a black periodical founded in 1923.

Sources: Bennett, *Before the Mayflower*, pp. 339, 515; *Encyclopedia of Black America*, p. 635; *Negro Almanac*, pp. 22, 262.

George Edmund Haynes

1925 • The first ladies' auxiliary of the Brotherhood of Sleeping Car Porters was formed as the Hesperus Club of Harlem.

Sources: *The Black New Yorkers*, p. 191; Hine, *Black Women in America*, vol. 2, p. 1320.

1934 • The first and only woman to serve as president general of the University Negro Improvement Association (UNIA) was Henrietta Vinton Davis (1860–1941). Born in Baltimore, Maryland, Vinton became an elocutionist, actress, and political organizer. She taught school in Maryland and Louisiana and then became a copyist in the Office of the Recorder of Deeds in Washington, D.C. During her stay in that office, she came under the supervision of Frederick Douglass, who encouraged her to study drama. She followed his suggestion and studied drama in Washington, and at the Boston School of Oratory. She toured principal cities and gave a range of selections, from Negro dialect to Shakespeare's works. Davis also became an organizer for Marcus Garvey's Negro Improvement Association in 1919 and continued until her death in 1941.She was a strong advocate of racial pride. She embraced the Populist party and later the Socialist party. She was among the UNIA's top leadership in the 1920s and 1930s.

Sources: Smith, *Notable Black American Women*, pp. 255–56; *The Black New Yorkers*, p. 216; Hine, *Black Women in America*, pp. 308–9.

1935 • Mary McLeod Bethune (1875–1955) was instrumental in founding the National Council of Negro Women on December 5, 1935—the first black organization for women and the first national coalition of black women's organizations established in the twentieth century. The organization was founded in New York City when fourteen black women's organizations came together at the 137th St. YWCA. Bethune became its first president, a post she held until 1949. This organization had a centralized direction and purpose that Bethune found lacking in the National Association of Colored Women.

Sources: *Encyclopedia of Black America*, pp. 863–64; *Negro Almanac*, p. 1360; Smith, *Notable Black American Women*, pp. 86–92.

1957 • The Southern Christian Leadership Conference (SCLC) was founded on February 14 this year, with Martin Luther King Jr. becoming its first president and Joseph E. Lowery (1924–) becoming vice president. Originally the organization was called the Southern Negro Leaders Conference, then the Southern Leadership Conference, and eventually became known as the Southern Christian Leadership Conference (SCLC). The organization was formed as result of the Montgomery Bus Boycott and its success. The founders needed a re-gional organization to work through black churches in the South in the interest of civil rights. After King's death, Ralph Abernathy (1926–1990) became SCLC president. Lowery, a cler-gyman and civil rights activist, became head of the organization in 1977, when Abernathy resigned. He had worked with the SCLC full time until July 1997, when he stepped down.

Sources: Smith, *Notable Black American Men,* pp. 686–91 (King); pp. 742–46 (Lowery).

1960 • Marion S. Barry Jr. (1936–) was the first national chairman of the Student Non-violent Coordinating Committee (SNCC). A native of Itta Bena, Mississippi, Barry would become mayor of Washington, D.C., in 1979.

Sources: *Ebony Success Library,* vol. 1, p. 21; Hornsby, *Milestones in Twentieth Century African-American History,* pp. 352, 450–51, 483; *Who's Who among Black Americans,* 14th ed., p. 70; *Contemporary Black Biography,* vol. 7, pp. 6–10.

1965 • Samuel D. Wright (1925?–1998) became the first chairperson of the Black and Puerto Rican Caucus. A native of New York City, he graduated from Brooklyn Law School in 1960. Representing the 39th District in Brooklyn, he was elected to the state assembly in 1965, and then named chair of the Black and Puerto Rican Caucus. He headed the cau-cus in both the state house and senate. In 1976 Wright was unsuccessful in challenging Shirley Chisholm for her Congressional seat as she represented the 39th District. Wright was chairman of the Ocean Hill-Brownsville school district and credited with bringing sta-bility to the schools. He was convicted in 1978 of soliciting a $5,000 payment from a pro-ducer of educational materials in return for his obtaining a contract with that company from the school board; as result, he lost his seat on the city council, a post he had held since 1973. Wright later became the National Association for the Advancement of Colored Peo-ple's national labor director and also established a law practice. He died of Parkinson's dis-ease at his home in Hilton Head, South Carolina, on January 20, 1998.

Sources: *New York Times* (1 February 1998).

1968 • Columnist and political editor for the *Amsterdam News,* James Booker organized the first national conference of black elected officials in Chicago. Booker was also a con-sultant for the National Advisory Committee on Civil Disorders as well as consultant and director of information for the White House Conference on Civil Rights, held in 1966.

Sources: *The Black New Yorkers,* pp. 332–33.

1969 • Steven [Stephen] Biko (1946–1977) founded and became the first president of the South African Students' Organization. His was a spin-off of the multiracial National Union of South African Students (NUSAS) Biko was born in King William's Town in South Africa, and graduated from St. Francis College, Natal, South Africa. After that, he attended Natal University's black medical section, becoming one of the first few blacks in South Africa to attend a major university. Although Biko and other students became involved with the NUSAS, they challenged its growing conservatism; thus, the splinter group was formed. He traveled the country promoting the Black Consciousness movement. In response, the South African government in 1973 moved to stop his work and placed him under house arrest. In 1977 Biko was arrested at a roadblock under the country's Terrorism Act that allowed for the arrest of anyone the state considered dangerous. He died in a Pretoria prison on September 12, 1977, of severe head injuries, that, according to many sources, the government caused. Critics around the world, including U.S. Ambassador to the United Nations Andrew Young, spoke out in protest and predicted a spark in unprecedented racial violence.

Sources: *Contemporary Black Biography,* vol. 4, pp. 22–25.

1972 • Melvin H. Evans, the first popularly elected governor of the Virgin Islands (elected in 1970), was the first black vice chairman of the Southern Governors' Conference.

Sources: Alford, *Famous First Blacks,* p. 39; *Negro Almanac,* p. 1556.

1975 • Elaine Brown (1943–) moved up in ranks to become chairperson of the Black Panther Party, making her the highest ranking woman in the party, the first black woman to hold the post, and second in command only to Huey P. Newton, who founded the party. Born in Philadelphia, Pennsylvania, Brown studied pre-law at Temple University and music at the Philadelphia Conservatory. She dropped out of school and in 1965 moved to Los Angeles in pursuit of a career as songwriter. Brown was soon introduced to leftist ideas as well as the emerging black power movement. She became a member of the Los Angeles Black Congress, an umbrella organization for various black groups, and worked on its newspaper, *Harambee*. Her work brought her in contact with Angela Davis. Brown joined the Black Panther party (BPP) in 1968 and became minister of information for the Los Angeles chapter in 1969. She worked in the party's breakfast program, led voter registration drives, and also became a delegate to the 1976 Democratic National Convention. Brown chaired the BPP from 1974 to 1977 and then left the party.

Sources: Rosen, *The World Split Open,* pp. 283–84; Smith, *Notable Black American Women,* Book II, pp. 65–67; Brown, *A Taste of Power.*

1994 • The first woman to head the Congressional Black Caucus Foundation, Inc., was Illinois Congresswoman Cardiss Collins (1931–).

Sources: *Jet* 85 (25 April 1994): 33.

1994 • The first woman president of the National Black Caucus of State Legislators was Tennessee state representative Lois Marie DeBerry (1945–), who was also Tennessee speaker *pro tempore* for the House of Representatives.

Sources: *Jet* 86 (9 May 1994): 46; *Who's Who among African Americans,* 26th ed., p. 328; Smith, *Notable Black American Women,* Book II, pp. 167–70.

1995 • The first black woman to direct the Washington office of the American Civil Liberties Union was Laura Murphy Lee.

Sources: *Jet* 88 (22 May 1995): 10.

1997 • The first woman to become vice president for research at the Joint Center for Political and Economic Studies, a think tank in Washington, D.C., was economist Margaret Simms (1946–), one of the few black women to hold such a post.

Sources: *Jet* 91 (28 April 1997): 20.

1998 • The National League of Women Voters elected Carolyn Jefferson-Jenkins (1952–) as fifteenth president, the first black to hold that post. She took office in 1998 and in 2001 was in her second two-year term. Born in Cleveland, Ohio, she was educated at Western College (B.A., 1974), John Carroll University (M.Ed., 1981), Kent State University (Ed.S., 1985), and Cleveland State University (Ph.D., 1991). Jefferson-Jenkins was principal of Cleveland Heights-University Heights Schools from 1993 to 1995 and vice president of Junior Achievement from 1996 to 1998.

Sources: *Ebony* 55 (October 1999): 12; *Who's Who among African Americans,* 14th ed., p. 674.

2001 • Sara Bost, mayor of Irvington, New Jersey, became the first black to head the Women Mayors Division of the U.S. Conference on Mayors, at its Detroit conference.

Sources: *Jet* 100 (6 August 2001): 12.

Fraternal, Social, and Religious Groups

1775 • Prince Hall (1735–1807) and fourteen others joined a Masonic lodge sponsored by British Army officers at Castle William near Boston on March 6. These are the first American black Masons and the origin of the Masonic movement among blacks. On September 29, 1784, the British Grand Lodge approved the formation of African Lodge No. 459, but the notification did not arrive until 1787. The African Grand Lodge was established on June 24, 1791; Prince Hall was the grand master. A second black lodge was formed in Philadelphia in 1797. In 1808 the existing black lodges formed the Prince Hall Masons, an organization that declared itself independent from all other Masonic lodges. During the American Revolution, Prince Hall became the most famous black in the Boston area. His work and that of the early lodges set the stage for the Masonic lodges that followed.

Sources: Logan and Winston, *Dictionary of American Negro Biography,* pp. 278–80; *Encyclopedia of Black America,* pp. 394–95, 412–13; *Negro Almanac,* p. 825; Smith, *Notable Black American Men,* pp. 502–4.

1843 • The first black Oddfellows lodge, Philomethian Lodge No. 646, was established in New York City by Peter Ogden. He was a ship's steward, who held a card from a lodge in Liverpool, England.

Sources: Baskin and Runes, *Dictionary of Black Culture,* p. 336; *Encyclopedia of Black America,* p. 395; Woodson, *Negro Makers of History,* p. 80.

1854 • The United Brothers of Friendship and Sisters of the Mysterious Ten was formed in Lexington, Kentucky. In 1861 the state granted the organization a charter, so that it became the first chartered and regularly constituted black organization south of the Ohio River. Its ancestry lay in the Union Benevolent Society of 1843. The whites who knew of this society, and who supported its charitable goals, did not know that it was also very active in assisting fugitive slaves.

Sources: *Encyclopedia of Black America,* p. 395; *Negro Year Book,* 1921–22, pp. 158, 416.

1871 • The first black Masonic lodge recognized by white Masonry in the United States was Alpha Lodge of New Jersey, Number 116, Free and Accepted Masons. The first meeting was held on January 31, 1871, under its first master, Nathan Mingus.

Sources: Kane, *Famous First Facts,* p. 276.

Major Fraternal Organizations

Founded	Name	Location
1864	Knights of Pythias	Washington, D.C.
1865	Grand Order of Galilean Fishermen	Baltimore, Maryland
1866	Grand United Order of J. R. Gidding's and Jolliffe Union	Norfolk, Virginia
1867	Independent Order of Saint Luke	
1868	Grand United Order of Brothers and Sisters, Sons and Daughters of Moses	
1871	Knights and Daughters of Tabor	Independence, Missouri
1881	United Order of True Reformers	Richmond, Virginia
1882	National Order of Mosaic Templers of America	Little Rock, Arkansas
1884	Royal Knights of King David	Durham, North Carolina
1886	Colored Brotherhood and Sisterhood of Honor	Franklin, Kentucky
1894	Ancient Order of Gleaners	Cairo, Michigan
1899	Improved Benevolent and Protective Order of Elks of the World	Cincinnati, Ohio
1900	Grand United Order Sons and Daughters of Peace	Newport News, Virginia
1901	Supreme Camp of American Woodmen	
1909	Royal Circle of Friends of the World	Helena, Arkansas
1915	Woodmen of Union	
1923	African Blood Brotherhood	Louisville, Kentucky
1923	Knights of the Invisible Colored Kingdom	Tennessee

Sources: *Encyclopedia of Black America,* pp. 395–96; *Negro Year Book, 1921–1922,* pp. 414–17.

1904 • The first black Greek letter organization, Sigma Pi Phi, known as the Boulé, was formed at a meeting in the Philadelphia home of physician Henry McKee Minton (1870–1946) on May 4, 1904. Six men were present for the initial meeting. This organization was designed to meet the social needs of black professional and business leaders, and to address social issues. It focused on post-college years of the black elite who provided meaningful service in the community. It was expected that the members would have similar attributes in education, skills, and level of accomplishment. Minton became the first grand sire archon.

Sources: Logan and Winston, *Dictionary of American Negro Biography,* pp. 440–41; Gatewood, *Aristocrats of Color,* pp. 234–36; *Negro Almanac,* pp. 1366–67.

1906 • Alpha Phi Alpha was the first intercollegiate Greek letter fraternity. It was founded at Cornell University, Ithaca, New York, on December 4, 1906. Initially the fraternity was a social study club. The first president was George B. Kelley. The first convention, at Howard University, Washington, D.C., was held in 1908. Other black fraternities include Kappa Alpha Psi (founded in 1911), Omega Psi Phi (1911), and Phi Beta Sigma (1914).

Sources: *Encyclopedia of Black America,* p. 397; Kane, *Famous First Facts,* p. 275.

1908 • The first black Greek letter sorority was Alpha Kappa Alpha, founded at Howard University, Washington, D.C., on January 15, 1908. The prime mover was Ethel Hedgeman Lyle (1887–1950), who became the first vice president. Lucy Slowe (1885–1937) was the first president. Two other early sororities were Delta Sigma Theta (founded in 1913) and Zeta Phi Beta (1920).

Sources: *Encyclopedia of Black America,* p. 397; Kane, *Famous First Facts,* p. 603; Smith, *Notable Black American Women,* pp. 1031–33.

1909 • The Knights of Peter Claver was founded in Mobile, Alabama. This was the first national Catholic black fraternal order. It embraces some one hundred thousand Catholic families in the United States. There is also a junior auxiliary for boys (established in 1917), a ladies' auxiliary (1922), and a girls' auxiliary (1909).

Sources: Davis, *The History of Black Catholics in the United States,* pp. 234–37; *Directory of African American Religious Bodies,* pp. 210–12; Ochs, *Desegregating the Altar,* p. 182.

1911 • The first Greek-letter fraternity formed by blacks on a black college campus was the Omega Psi Phi Fraternity. It was established at Howard University in Washington, D.C., on November 17, 1911.

Sources: *Jet* 93 (24 November 1997): 19; Salzman, *Encyclopedia of African-American History and Culture,* vol. 3, p. 1517.

1926 • Frederick Williams Seymour of Hartford, Connecticut, was the first black member of the Connecticut Society of the Sons of the American Revolution. His greatgrandfather, Dudley Hayes, was wounded in action on October 19, 1777.

Sources: *Opportunity* 4 (March 1926): 107.

Reverdy Ransom

1934 • Reverdy C. Ransom (1861–1959), bishop in the African Methodist Episcopal Church, organized the Fraternal Council of Negro Churches, the first black ecumenical organization. It had an explicit agenda that included social change and racial uplift within a religious context. Concerned that the predominantly white Federal Council of Churches had failed to address black concerns in a substantive way, Ransom and other black church leaders saw the new council as the "authoritative voice" coming from a "united Negro church." Sixteen predominantly black communions and six predominantly white churches formed the council. Two of the thirty-nine members of the executive committee were women: Belle Hendon of Chicago, who represented the National Baptist Convention of America, and Ida Mae Myller of Gary, Indiana, representing the Community Center Church. Ransom was born in Flushing, Ohio, and then moved to a small farm near Old Washington, Ohio. The family later moved to Cambridge, Ohio. He attended a local summer normal school and later enrolled at Wilberforce University, where he came to the attention of Bishop Daniel A. Payne and Benjamin W. Arnett. He attended Oberlin College the next year but returned to Wilberforce later and graduated in 1886 with a bachelor's degree in divinity. Ransom edited the *AME Church* Review from 1912 to 1924. He was elected bishop in the African Methodist Episcopal Church in 1920.

Sources: Joyner, *Down by the Riverside,* p. 307; Smith, *Notable Black American Men,* pp. 990–94 (Ransom).

1972 • William Sterling Cary (1927–) became the first black president of the National Council of Churches in America on December 7, 1972. This distinguished Baptist minister was born in Plainfield, New Jersey, and became a prominent political activist. He graduated from Morehouse College (B.A., 1949; D.D., 1973) and Union Theological Seminary (M.Div., 1952). He has held pastorates at Butler Memorial Presbyterian Church (1953–55), International Church of the Open Door in Brooklyn (1955–58), and Grace Congregational Church in New York City (1958–68). Cary was area minister of Metro and Suffolk Associations, New York Conference of United Church of Christ (1968–75), and conference minister, Illinois conference of United Church of Christ (1974–94).

Sources: *Ebony Success Library,* vol. 1, p. 61; *Encyclopedia of Black America,* p. 219; Hornsby, *Chronology of African-American History,* p. 204; *Negro Almanac,* p. 1326; *Who's Who among African Americans,* 26th ed., p. 222.

1977 • Karen Batchelor Farmer (1951–) was the first known black member of the Daughters of the American Revolution. She traced her ancestry to William Hood, a soldier in the Revolutionary army. Farmer was born in Detroit and received her bachelor's degree from Oakland University in Rochester, Michigan, in 1980 and her law degree from Wayne State University Law School in 1985. After serving as law clerk in Wayne County Probate Court and with Dykhouse Wise and Marsac law firm, she was an associate attorney with the firm from 1985 to 1987. Farmer was vice president and associate counsel of Standard Federal Bank in Troy, Michigan, from 1987 to 1991, and in 1991 became staff attorney for Michigan Consolidated Gas in Detroit. She found passion, however, in tracing her roots and in her membership in the National Society of the Daughters of the American Revolution. She also was a co-founder in 1979 of the Fred Hart Williams Genealogical Society in Detroit.

Sources: *American Libraries* 39 (February 1978): 70; *Negro Almanac,* pp. 73, 1431; *Who's Who among Africans,* 14th ed., p. 405.

1983 • William Watley was the first black national chairman of the National Workshop on Christian Unity. Watley was ordained in the African Methodist Episcopal Church, and he was associate general secretary of the Consultation Church Union, Princeton, New Jersey.

Sources: *Jet* 65 (10 October 1983): 21.

1984 • Philip R. Cousin (1933–) was the first black from a predominantly black denomination to preside over the National Council of Churches. This African Methodist Episcopal (AME) minister served with distinction as bishop and college president. Cousins was born in Pittston, Pennsylvania, and educated at Central State University, Boston University, and Colgate Rochester Divinity School, where he received his doctorate in ministry. After pastoring churches in North Carolina, Virginia, and Florida, he became president of the now-defunct Kittrell College near Raleigh, North Carolina (1960–65). After that, he was named bishop of Alabama. He became college president again, this time of Edward Waters College in Jacksonville, Florida, and was named bishop of the Eleventh Episcopal district

Sources: *Jet* 65 (30 January 1984): 24; *Who's Who among African Americans,* 26th ed., p. 279.

1985 • As department commander of the Louisiana American Legion, Alvin A. Roche Sr. was the first black to head a state unit in the deep South. Only six other blacks in the past ten years had occupied a similar post, none in the South. Roche was sixty-nine years old and a veteran of World War II.

Sources: *Jet* 69 (30 September 1985): 37.

1986 • Alpha Kappa Alpha was the first black sorority to have a house on the campus of the University of Alabama.

Sources: *Jet* 71 (29 September 1986): 31.

1987 • The Eta Beta chapter of Phi Beta Sigma was the first black fraternity to have a house on fraternity row at the University of Mississippi.

Sources: *Jet* 72 (31 August 1987): 24.

1991 • Maryann Coffey was the first black, and the first woman, co-chair of the National Conference of Christians and Jews.

Sources: *Jet* 80 (6 May 1991): 37.

1991 • Vinton Randolph Anderson (1927–) became the first black president of the World Council of Churches. He retired from the post in 1998. Anderson was born in Somerset, Bermuda, and received his bachelor's degree from Wilberforce University in Ohio, his master's degree in divinity from Payne Theological Seminary, and a master's of arts degree from Kansas University. He did further study at Yale Divinity School. Anderson had a stellar career in the ministry, pastoring a number of African Methodist Episcopal churches in Wichita, Kansas, and in St. Louis. He severed as presiding bishop and chief pastor of the Ninth Episcopal District in Alabama from 1972 to 1976, and served the Third Episcopal district of Ohio, West Virginia, and West Pennsylvania from 1976 to 1984. From 1984 to 1988 he was with the Office of Ecumenical Relations and Development and in 1988 he was assigned to the Fifth Episcopal District serving fourteen states and 255 churches west of the Mississippi River. Among his numerous accomplishments, Anderson developed the bicentennial edition of a church hymnal.

Sources: *Jet* 94 (27 July 1998): 10; *Who's Who among African Americans,* 26th ed., p. 34.

1994 • The first black admitted to the eighty-four-year-old Charlotte Country Club in North Carolina was Frank Emory (1957?–). The highly regarded attorney was a litigation partner in the law firm of Robinson, Bradshaw, and Hinson, P.A. He graduated from Duke University and took his law degree at the University of North Carolina, Chapel Hill.

Sources: *Jet* 87 (19 December 1994): 50.

1994 • Belle Meade Country Club in Nashville, Tennessee, broke down racial barriers and elected Richard Sinkfield to membership, making him its first black member. A prominent attorney in Atlanta and longtime member of Vanderbilt University's board of trustees, Sinkfield sought membership as a non-resident of the area. Sinkfield graduated from Tennessee State University in Nashville and received his law degree from Vanderbilt University in 1971. After graduation, he joined the law firm Powell, Goldstein, Frazier and Murphy in Atlanta. He left five years later and joined several young attorneys in forming Rogers and Harding law firm, where he remained.

Sources: *Tennessean* (18 August 1994).

1995 • William and Marsha Jews became the first black members of the Baltimore Country Club in Maryland. William Jews was president and chief executive officer of Blue Cross and Blue Shield of Maryland.

Sources: *Jet* 87 (27 February 1995): 10.

1996 • Hiliary H. Holloway (1928–2000) became the first black president of the National Interfraternity Conference. The banking executive was born in Durham, North Carolina, and educated at North Carolina Central University in Durham (B.S., 1949), Temple University (Ed.M., 1956), and Temple University School of Law (J.D., 1964). His career experiences include business manager of St. Augustine's College in Raleigh (1950–53); executive director of the Kappa Alpha Psi Fraternity (1953–65); private law practice (1955–68); and assistant counsel (1968–72), vice president and general counsel (1972–82), and senior vice president and general counsel (1982–89) of the Federal Reserve Bank of Philadelphia. He was chairman and chief executive officer of the New Atlantic Bank from 1989 to 1993, and partner in the law firm Marshall, Dennehey, Warner, Coleman and Goggin.

Sources: *Jet* 89 (15 January 1996): 20; *Who's Who among African Americans*, 14th ed., p. 610.

1997 • Dionne N. Curbeam became the first woman president of the National Baptist Convention of America Inc., National Youth and Children's Convention in New York City. The graduating senior at Bowie State University in Maryland was immediate past president of the Maryland Baptist Convention, Youth Department.

Sources: *Jet* 92 (11 August 1997): 22.

1997 • Eugene L. Gibson Sr. became president of the Illinois Baptist State Association and its minister's conference, the first black to hold both offices. The organization is an affiliate of the Southern Baptist Convention. Gibson was senior pastor of the Mission Faith Baptist Church in Chicago.

Sources: *Jet* 91 (13 January 1997): 20.

1998 • Catholic bishops in America elected Wilton Gregory (1947–) as vice president of the National Conference of Catholic Bishops and the United States Catholic Conference, making him the first black to hold that post. This put him next in line to become president of the conference. His election also acknowledges the growing presence of blacks in church ranks. The United States Catholic Conference is a support organization for the group and conducts research and prepares position papers on important policies that affect the Catholic church.

Sources: *Jet* 95 (7 December 1998): 20; *Who's Who among African Americans*, 26th ed., p. 499.

2000 • Christina Houston broke the racial barrier in the University of Alabama's Greek system when she became a member of the white sorority, Gamma Phi Beta, in November of her freshman year. Under the assumption that they were still racially segregated, the Faculty Senate passed a resolution in August 2001 calling for fraternities and sororities to accept black members or risk penalties. The Chicago native, who is biracial, left the university after one semester but returned in fall 2001 and became an alumna member of the sorority.

Sources: *Jet* 100 (24 September 2001): 8; *New York Times* (7 September 2001).

2002 • Barbara Hatton (1941–) broke the color barrier at Knoxville, Tennessee's, oldest country club, the private Cherokee Country Club, becoming its first black member. An anonymous donor paid her entrance fee and monthly dues. Hatton, then president of Knoxville College, viewed her membership in the club as a way to build a new legacy for her college. Hatton was born in LaGrange, Georgia. Her degrees include a B.S. (1962), M.A (1966), M.E.A. (1970), and Ph.D. (1970). Before becoming president of Knoxville College, she held posts at Atlanta University, in the Atlanta Public Schools, Federal City College, Stanford University, and was president of South Carolina State University.

Sources: *Who's Who among African Americans*, 26th ed., p. 544; *Jet* 101 (22 April 2002): 24.

Medical and Dental Associations

1854 • John Van Syrly De Grasse (1825–1868) was the first black physician to join a medical society. The Massachusetts Medical Society admitted him on August 24, 1854. Born in New York City, he attended local schools, studied at Oneida Institute in New York, and studied in Paris for two years. He returned to New York City and studied medicine with Samuel R. Childs. De Grasse enrolled at Bowdoin College (Brunswick, Maine) and received his medical degree on May 19, 1849. He studied further in Europe, returned to New York City where he established a medical practice, and eventually set up practice in Boston. De Grasses was a volunteer in the Union Army and was one of the eight blacks commissioned as surgeons in the army during the Civil War.

Sources: Logan and Winston, *Dictionary of American Negro Autobiography,* p. 169; Morais, *The History of the Negro in Medicine,* p. 38.

1884 • The Medico-Chirugical Society of the District of Columbia is the first black medical society. Its formation on April 24 was the result of refusal of the white medical society to admit blacks. It would not be until 1952 that black physicians could join the local American Medical Society branch. A national organization for blacks would be formed in 1895, when the Medico-Chirugical Society was reactivated and incorporated. Although the society originally had white members—three of the eight incorporators were white— by 1920 it was entirely black.

Sources: *Encyclopedia of Black America,* p. 673; Gatewood, *Aristocrats of Color,* p 65; Morais, *The History of the Negro in Medicine,* pp. 57–58; Cobb, *The First Negro Medical Society,* p. 1.

1895 • The National Medical Association was formed in October, 1895, in Atlanta, Georgia, during the Cotton States and International Exposition. The association was formed in reaction to the practices of predominantly white associations. The American Medical Association refused to urge all its local members to remove restrictive provisions until 1950. Founded as the National Association of Colored Physicians, Dentists, and Pharmacists on September 18, 1895, it had a small membership of fewer than fifty in 1904 and that grew to over 500 by 1912. The first president of the black association was R. F. Boyd of Nashville, Tennessee. In 1903 the association changed its name to become the National Medical Association. Its *Journal of the National Medical Association* became the chief means of spotlighting the work of its members. The journal remained the primary source of information on black doctors and dentists until the mainstream press covered their contributions in health care. The NMA continues to serve the black medical community.

Sources: Morais, *The History of the Negro in Medicine,* pp. 68–69; Salzman, *Encyclopedia of African-American Culture and History,* Supplement, p. 204.

1908 • The founding meeting of the National Association of Colored Graduate Nurses (NACGN) was held at St. Marks Methodist Church in New York City. The organization, the first national organization for black nurses, aimed to meet the increasing concern of black nurses to enhance themselves professionally. Few mainstream nursing schools of the North, and none in the South, admitted blacks for training. Fifty people attended the first meeting. Martha Minerva Franklin (1870–1968), who was the force behind the gathering of black nurses, became the founding president. The NACGN soon attacked the practice of setting up separate black and white state boards of nursing; it also promoted legislation to benefit its members as well as the black community as a while. The association established a national headquarters in 1934, with nurse Mabel Keaton Staupers (1890–1989) as executive secretary. After obtaining full participation in the American Nurses' Association, the NACGN board voted the black organization out of existence on January 25, 1951.

Sources: *Jet* 90 (26 August 1996): 19; Hine, *Black Women in America,* vol. 2, pp. 840–42; *The Black New Yorkers,* pp. 129–30.

1913 • Daniel Hale Williams (1856–1931) became the first black elected to the American College of Surgeons on November 13, 1913.

Sources: Logan and Winston, *Dictionary of American Negro Biography,* pp. 654–55; *Encyclopedia of Black America,* p. 857.

1948 • In December the Baltimore County Medical Society was the first American Medical Association affiliate in a Southern state to drop the bars against black membership. Oklahoma and Missouri state societies followed in 1949, and the Delaware and Florida societies in 1950.

Sources: *Encyclopedia of Black America,* p. 674; Morais, *The History of the Negro in Medicine,* p. 133.

1950 • Peter Marshall Murray (1888–1969) was the first black to serve in the American Medical Society's House of Delegates. Murray had graduated from Howard University

School of Medicine in 1914 and immediately joined the school's medical faculty. The next year he established a private practice in Washington, D.C. In 1917 and 1918 he was medical inspector for the District of Columbia public schools. He was also named assistant surgeon-in-chief at the local Freedman's Hospital in 1918. Murray moved to New York City in 1920 in search of greater professional opportunities. He established a practice there and in 1928 he became provisional assistant adjunct visiting staff member in gynecology at Harlem Hospital. This gynecologist from Houma, Louisiana, was also the first black to serve on the New York City Board of Hospitals in 1958. In 1954, as president of the New York County Medical Society, he was the first black to head an organization that was a component of the American Medical Association.

Sources: Logan and Winston, *Dictionary of American Negro Biography*, pp. 465–67; Morais, *The History of the Negro in Medicine*, pp. 119–21, 130, 133–35, 163, 179, 235, 281; *Who's Who in America, 1960–61*, p. 2103; Smith, *Notable Black American Men*, pp. 862–63.

1974 • Richard Caesar was the first black president of the San Francisco Dental Society.

Sources: *Jet* 53 (19 January 1978): 44.

1979 • John Heartwell Holland (1916–1985) was the first black chairman of the board of governors of the American National Red Cross.

Sources: *Encyclopedia of Black America*, p. 443; *Jet* 56 (3 May 1979): 28.

1979 • Mary Runge was the first black and first woman president of the American Pharmaceutical Association. Runge was a pharmacist in Oakland, California.

Sources: *Jet* 56 (30 August 1979): 6.

1980 • Lonnie R. Bristow (1930–) was the first black physician elected to the Council on Medical Services of the American Medical Association. In 1981 he would become the first black president of the American Society of Internal Medicine, and in 1985 the first black physician elected to the board of trustees of the American Medical Society. A graduate of the New York University College of Medicine, Bristow was an internist in San Pablo, California.

Sources: *Jet* 57 (7 February 1980): 21; 61 (5 November 1981): 47; 68 (8 July 1985): 29; Smith, *Notable Black American Men*, pp. 118–21.

1982 • Colonel William Lofton Jr. was the first black man named a fellow of the American Occupational Therapy Association. Lofton was director of occupational therapy at the Fitzsimons Army Medical Center, Aurora, Colorado.

Sources: *Jet* 62 (16 August 1982): 21.

1984 • Charles Warfield Clark (1927–) was the first black president of the Washington, D.C., Urological Society. Clark, a graduate of the Howard University Medical School (1944), became a professor of urology at that school in Washington, D.C. Clark was born in Washington and received his bachelor's degree from the University of Michigan in 1939 and his medical degree from Howard University School of Medicine in 1944. He completed his internship at the local Freedman's Hospital. An experienced urologist, he was chief resident in urology at Freedman's Hospital (1952–53), clinical instructor in urology at Howard University's School of Medicine (1946–52), and then clinical assistant professor of urology in that school (1955–59).

Sources: *Jet* 65 (19 September 1983): 38; *Who's Who among African American*. 14th ed., p. 237.

1984 • Claude H. Organ Jr. (1928–) was the first black surgeon to chair the American Board of Surgery. Since 1960, Organ has taught at Creighton University School of Medicine in Omaha, Nebraska.

Sources: *Jet* 69 (17 February 1986): 12; *Who's Who among Black Americans, 1992–93*, p. 1074.

1987 • Henry Cade was the first black president of the National Association of Boards of Pharmacy. Cade was public affairs and professional relations manager for the Walgreen Company in Deerfield, Illinois.

Sources: *Jet* 72 (13 July 1987): 14.

1987 • Ross M. Miller Jr. (1939–1996) was elected the first black president of the Southern California Chapter of the American College of Surgeons. Miller was also the governor of the American College of Surgeons, the first black to hold this national position. Miller became a general surgeon and professor of surgery at the University of California in Los Angeles and Charles R. Drew medical schools. In 1993 he also became the first black president of the Los Angeles Surgical Society.

Sources: *Jet* 72 (27 April 1987): 26; 89 (13 May 1996): 61; *Who's Who among Black Americans, 1992–93,* p. 992.

1989 • Jerome C. Scales (1942–), a pediatric dentist, was the first black president of the Alabama Society of Pediatric Dentistry and held the post for one year. Scales had a practice in Birmingham and was associate professor of dentistry at the University of Alabama at Birmingham. Scales was born in Birmingham, Alabama, and graduated from Tennessee State University (B.S., 1969) and Meharry Medical College in Nashville (D.D.S., 1973). He received a certificate in pediatric dentistry from the University of Alabama School of Dentistry in 1975.

Sources: *Jet* 76 (18 September 1989): 20; *Who's Who among African Americans,* 26th ed., p. 1098.

1990 • Ezra C. Davidson Jr. (1933–) was the first black president of the American College of Obstetricians and Gynecologists. Davidson took his medical degree at Meharry Medical College in 1958. He became chair of the obstetrics and gynecology department of Charles Drew University of Medicine and Science, Los Angeles, in 1971.

Sources: *Jet* 78 (27 August 1990): 20; *Who's Who among African Americans,* 26th ed., pp. 307–08.

1992 • Juliann Stephanie Bluitt (1938–) became the first woman president of the Chicago Dental Society and held that post for one year. Among her contributions, she focused on the problems affecting the health of women, an area previous overlooked or disregarded. At the time of her selection, Bluitt was an associate dean of the Northwestern University School of Dentistry.

Sources: *Jet* 82 (13 July 1992): 15; Smith, *Notable Black American Women,* Book II, pp. 34–37; *Contemporary Black Biography,* vol. 14, pp. 23–26; *Who's Who among African Americans,* 26th ed., p. 113.

1992 • Paul A. Stephens (1921–) was the first black president of the Academy of General Dentistry, which is the second-largest dental association in the country. The Muskogee, Oklahoma, native graduated from Howard University (B.S., 1942) and from its School of Dentistry (D.D.S., 1945). Since 1946, Stephens has been a long-time practitioner in Gary, Indiana.

Sources: *Jet* 82 (24 August 1992): 36; *Who's Who among African Americans,* 14th ed., p. 1229.

1994 • Anthony Ramsey-Wallace, of San Francisco's Catholic Healthcare West, became the first black president-elect of the Association of Healthcare Internal Auditors.

Sources: *Jet* 86 (24 October 1994): 20.

1995 • The first black elected president of the American College of Surgeons was LaSalle Doheny Leffall Jr. (1930–). He was also president of the Society of Surgical Oncology (1978–79) and of the Society of Surgical Chairman (1988–90). Born in Tallahassee, Florida, Leffall received his bachelor's degree from Florida Agricultural & Mechanical College (now Florida A &M University) in 1948 and his medical degree from Howard University School of Medicine in 1952. He was active in medical education, serving as assistant dean of Howard's medical school from 1964 to 1970 and acting dean in 1970. He was professor and chairman of the Department of Surgery in from 1970 to 1995.

Sources: *Jet* 87 (14 November 1994): 47; *Who's Who among African Americans,* 26th ed., p. 760.

1995 • Regina M. Benjamin (1956–) became the first black woman and only the second black named to the American Medical Association's Board of Trustees. Benjamin was born in Bayou La Batre, Alabama, a small shrimping town. She became a family practitioner and the only doctor in her hometown. She holds a B.S. degree from Xavier University of New Orleans, M.D. from the University of Alabama, and MBA from Tulane University. In 2009, President Barack Obama nominated Benjamin as Surgeon General of the United States. She assumed office on November 3 and became 18th person and the second African American woman to hold that post. "America's Doctor," as she is known, holds numerous honors and awards, including eleven honorary doctorates and the Nelson Mandela Award for Health and Human Rights (1998).

Sources: *Jet* 88 (10 July 1995): 40." Biography of the Surgeon General, www.surgeongen eral.gov/about/biographies/ biosg.html; *Who's Who among African Americans,* 26th ed., p. 91.

1995 • The first black president of the Dallas County Medical Society in its 119-year history was James L. Sweatt III (1937–), a thoracic surgeon in the city of Dallas. Sweatt received his bachelor's degree from Middlebury College in 1958 and his medical degree from Washington University in 1962. A surgeon in private practice, he became active in local and national medical associations and a member of the Texas board of regents for the state university system.

Sources: *Jet* 88 (22 May 1995): 24; *Who's Who among African Americans,* 26th ed., p. 1196.

1995 • The first black elected president of the North Carolina Society of Nuclear Medicine Technologists Inc. was Michael A. Lewis. He became a certified nuclear medicine technologist at the Veterans Association Medical Center in Asheville.

Sources: *Jet* 88 (31 July 1995): 19.

1996 • Audrey B. Rhodes became the first black and the second woman president of the South Carolina Academy of Family Physicians. Rhodes is director of the state project HOPE For Kids in Columbia.

Sources: *Jet* 89 (15 January 1996): 20; *Who's Who among African Americans,* 26th ed., p. 1042.

1996 • Kathryn [Kathy] Garrett (1955–), a radiologist and since 1989 a partner with the Medical Center Radiology Group in Orlando, Florida, was elected chair of the one-hundred-year-old Florida Board of Medicine, the first black to hold that post. The Cincinnati native received her bachelor's degree from Brown University in 1976 and her medical degree from the University of Cincinnati Medical School in 1981. In 1993 and again in 1997 Garrett was named African American Physician of the Year.

Sources: *Jet* 90 (17 June 1996): 20; *Who's Who among African Americans,* 26th ed., p. 450.

1997 • Clayton Marcellus Ramsue became the student board member of the American Academy of Family Physicians, the first black to hold the post. Ramsue, a Morehouse School of medicine student, planned a career in family medicine.

Sources: *Jet* 93 (8 December 1997): 20.

1997 • Karen Allen became the first black president of the National Nurses Society on Addictions. Allen became associate professor in the Department of Psychiatry, Community Health, and Adult Primary Care at the School of Nursing, University of Maryland at Baltimore. In 1995 Allen received the Distinguished Alumna Award from the College of Nursing, University of Illinois at Chicago.

Sources: *Jet* 91 (24 February 1997): 19; *Who's Who among African Americans,* 26th ed., p. 21.

The American Medical Association's First Black President

In 1995 Lonnie Bristow (1930–) became the first black president of the American Medical Association. A New York City native, Bristow was the son of a Baptist minister and a nurse. He grew up in Harlem and spent many hours at the Sydenham Hospital where his mother worked and where he went to escort her home at night. His experiences there stimulated him to become a doctor and to provide quality health care to patients regardless of race. Bristow graduated from City College of New York (B.S., 1953) and New York University College of Medicine (M.D., 1957). He completed several residencies, the last at the University of California's School of Medicine in San Francisco. He established a private practice in San Pablo, California, in 1964, and became highly active in medical societies as well. He became the first black president of the American Society of Internal Medicine in 1982. He served the American Medical Association in a variety of posts, such as alternate delegate to AMA's House of Delegates in 1978, chair of the Council of Medical Service in 1979, and chair of the board of trustees in 1993. In 1985 he was the first black elected to AMA's board.

Sources: Smith, *Notable Black American Men,* pp. 118–21; *Ebony* 50 (August 1995): 82, 85; *Jet* 88 (10 July 1995): 38–40.

1998 • The first black president of the Dade County Medical Association in Miami was James W. Briggs, an obstetrician and gynecologist.

Sources: *Jet* 94 (13 July 1998): 20.

1998 • Donna M. Norris (1943–), a psychiatrist, became the first black and first woman speaker at the assembly of the American Psychiatric Association in the association's 153-year history. Norris was born in Columbus, Ohio, and received her bachelor's degree from Fisk University in 1964 and her medical degree from the Ohio State University College of Medicine in 1969. She completed an internship at Mt. Carmel Medical Center in Columbus, Ohio, in 1970. She later completed a residency at Boston University Medical Center in 1972 and Children's Hospital Judge Baker Guidance Center in 1974. She taught at Harvard Medical School, served as medical director of the Family Services Association of Greater Boston, and returned to the Children's Hospital in 1983 as associate in psychiatry.

Sources: *Jet* 93 (4 May 1998): 17; *Who's Who among African Americans,* 26th ed., pp. 9940–41.

1998 • Terry Reynolds, a resident of Atlanta, became the first black president of the American Academy of Implant Dentistry, the oldest oral implant organization in the country. Reynolds was an international lecturer in implant dentistry and a diplomat of the American Board of Oral Implant Dentistry.

Sources: *Jet* 94 (31 August 1998): 18.

1999 • The first black person to chair the American Hospital Association's (AHA) Board of Trustees was Carolyn B. Lewis. The AHA is the country's largest hospital and health system association. She took office on January 1. Lewis graduated from Hampton University in Virginia. After serving with the U.S. Securities and Exchange Commission as assistant director of investment management, she retired in 1997. From 1989 to 1994 she was a commissioner for the Joint Commission on Accreditation of Healthcare Organizations.

Sources: *Jet* 94 (12 October 1998): 25; *Who's Who among African Americans,* 14th ed., p. 795.

2000 • The first woman president of the Atlanta-based Association of Black Cardiologists, for the 2000–2002 term, was Elizabeth O. Ofili. The association is a non-profit advocacy group dedicated to reducing cardiovascular disease in minorities. Ofili was born in Nigeria and became chief of cardiology for Morehouse School of Medicine.

Sources: *Jet* 97 (10 April 2000): 25.

RELIGION

African Methodist Episcopal (AME) Church

1794 • Richard Allen (1760–1831) was instrumental in the construction of Bethel Church in Philadelphia, founded in 1794. Bethel started as a Methodist Episcopal church, but in 1816 it became the mother church of the African Methodist Episcopal (AME) Church. Allen became known as the founder of the first black-controlled denomination in the United States. Allen was born into slavery in Philadelphia; around 1768 his owner, a prominent Philadelphia attorney, sold Allen and six members of his family to Stokely Surgis, a farmer in Kent County near Dover, Delaware. Allen received no formal education but became literate through his own efforts. He converted to Methodism during his adolescence. In 1780 Surgis allowed Allen and his brothers to hire out and to purchase their freedom over time. Allen preached and worked in New Jersey. He traveled on various circuits with Methodist preachers. In 1786 Allen preached in a Methodist church in Philadelphia before deciding to settle there and evangelize the growing black population. He campaigned for an independent black Methodist church in 1794, when Bishop Francis Asbury presided over the inauguration of his new church. Until that time, blacks attended the predominantly white St. George's Church. After quarrels between St. George's and Bethel Church, Bethel finally won its independence from St. George's. When the church was put up for auction, Allen bought Bethel Church in summer 1815 for $10,125. He was ordained an elder on April 10 and the next day he was ordained bishop. Then he served as pastor of Bethel Church and AME bishop. The AME church grew under Allen's leadership, especially in the Middle Atlantic states. Allen was an early supporter of the woman evangelist Jarena Lee as well as an ardent supporter of anti-slavery. He opposed the American Colonization Society that tried to return free blacks to Africa. In 1830 Allen was elected president of the First National Negro Convention but died before the second was held.

Sources: Logan and Winston, *Dictionary of American Negro Autobiography,* pp. 12–13; Lincoln and Mamiya, *The Black Church in the African American Experience,* pp. 51–52; Smith, *Climbing Jacob's Ladder,* p. 36; Smith, *Notable Black American Men,* pp. 21–24.

1801 • Richard Allen compiled the first black hymnal, *Collection of Spiritual Songs and Hymns, Selected from Various Authors.* There was another edition in 1807, and this in turn was revised in 1818 with the help of Jacob Tapsico. These hymnals contained only texts that were sung to a limited number of traditional tunes.

Sources: *Encyclopedia of Black America,* p. 33; Smith, *Climbing Jacob's Ladder,* p. 60; Southern, *The Music of Black Americans,* pp. 75–79.

1815 • Black Methodists in Charleston, South Carolina, secretly formed their own church, when the separate black quarterly conference was abolished. Morris Brown (1770–1849) was one of two people sent North to be ordained by Richard Allen. Brown became pastor of the first church. The church was suppressed, and the building demolished in 1822, due to the involvement of some of its members in the Denmark Vesey slave uprising. Brown escaped by being smuggled North. He settled in Philadelphia and continued his work in the AME church. In 1826 he took charge of the Bristol Circuit in Bucks County. He became the first to travel west and develop the church in western Pennsylvania and Ohio. In 1828 Brown was elected second bishop of the AME church and shared the burden of the older and weaker Allen. He was consecrated at Bethel Church on May 25, 1828, and became sole bishop after Allen died in 1831. Brown was born free, of mixed parentage, and lived in Charleston, South Carolina. Although he had no schooling, he was successful in strengthening the AME church.

Sources: Logan and Winston, *Dictionary of American Negro Biography,* pp. 69–70; Shockley, *Heritage and Hope,* p. 31; Raboteau, *Slave Religion,* pp. 163, 205–6; Smith, *Notable Black American Men,* pp. 129–31.

1816 • On April 9 representatives of five Methodist congregations assembled at the Bethel Church in Philadelphia. Dissatisfied with the treatment of blacks within the Methodist Episcopal Church, they organized the African Methodist Episcopal Church (AME). The representatives elected Daniel Coker (1780–1846) as their first bishop but he declined. Richard Allen (1760–1831) then became the first AME bishop. This denomination is currently the largest black Methodist group in the United States, with some 2.2 million members.

Sources: Logan and Winston, *Dictionary of American Negro Biography,* pp. 12–13 (Allen); 119–20 (Coker); *Encyclopedia of Black America,* p. 32; Lincoln and Mamiya, *The Black Church in the African American Experience,* p. 52; Smith, *Climbing Jacob's Ladder,* pp. 59–61.

1817 • Jarena Lee (1783–?) was the first woman to preach in the African Methodist Episcopal (AME) Church. Lee was born in Cape May, New Jersey. After hearing Richard Allen preach, she experienced conversion and later felt a call to preach. In 1817 she rose in Bethel Church, Philadelphia, to give a spontaneous talk. Although never formally licensed to speak by the church, Lee began an extraordinary career as an evangelist. She began her work as leader of a predominantly female praying and singing band, later becoming an evangelist. Lee, and other women like Juliann Jane Tillman, made a considerable impact on religious life, as well as the growth of their denomination. Although she had little formal education, Lee published two autobiographies: *The Life and Religious Experience of Jarena Lee* in 1836 and *Religious Experiences and Journal of Jarena Lee* in 1849. Both of these works are extant.

Sources: Hine, *Black Women in America,* p. 707; Smith, *Climbing Jacob's Ladder,* pp. 64–65; Smith, *Notable Black American Women,* pp. 662–63.

1847 • Quinn Chapel was the first African Methodist Episcopal church in Chicago, Illinois. The church was listed on the *National Register of Historic Places* on September 4, 1979

Sources: Baer and Singer, *African-American Religion in the Twentieth Century,* p. 74.

1850 • Saint Andrew's African Methodist Episcopal (AME) Church, Sacramento, California, was the first AME church in California. The original affiliation was with the Methodist Episcopal Church, but after a leadership failure the congregation joined the AME church. Saint Andrew's was established in a private home, but within four years it had its own building, and in the basement, opened the first school for nonwhites in California.

Sources: Cantor, *Historic Landmarks of Black America,* p. 294; Shockley, *Heritage and Hope,* p. 309; *Negro Almanac, 1989,* p. 192.

1888 • The first woman missionary of the African Methodist Episcopal Church appointed to a foreign field was Sarah E. Gorham.

Sources: Hine, *Black Women in America,* vol. II, p. 1315.

The First Black Missionary to Africa

In 1819 Daniel Coker (1780–1846) became the first African missionary associated with the African Methodist Episcopal (AME) Church. On April 9, 1816, Coker had declined to become the church's first bishop. He was expelled from the church in 1818, but restored in 1819. The Maryland Colonization Society sent Coker to Liberia. He set sail on January 31, 1820, accompanying the first ship of free blacks who were repatriated to Africa by the society. However, his group was detained in Sierra Leone because of unfavorable conditions in Liberia. Coker eventually stayed in Freetown, Sierra Leone, where he established a church and spent the rest of his life. Born Isaac Wright to a slave father and white indentured servant in Frederick or Baltimore County, Maryland, he had a white half-brother also named Daniel Coker. He ran away to New York when he was very young and adopted his brother's name, Daniel Coker. Later the runaway slave moved to Baltimore but kept out of public view until his freedom was purchased. He became a Methodist and Francis Asbury, a founding bishop of the Methodist Episcopal church, ordained him a deacon. Around 1800 Coker and George Collins taught in a Baltimore school but Coker gave up teaching in 1816. After then he taught in the African Bethel Church for a time. Coker joined the black Sharp Street Church and was known as "the leading spiritual overseer of the Colored Methodist Episcopal Church of Baltimore." He also established the first choir at the Sharp Street Church.

Daniel Coker

Sources: Logan and Winston, *Dictionary of American Negro Biography*, pp. 119–20; Smith, *Notable Black American Men*, pp. 212–14.

Henry Turner

1898 • Henry McNeal Turner (1834–1915) was the first prominent black churchman to declare that God is black. He said: "We had rather believe in no God, or ... believe that all nature is God than to believe in the personality of a God, and not to believe that He is a Negro." Turner was also the first black chaplain in the United States Army in 1863. As a minister and bishop in the African Methodist Episcopal (AME) Church, Turner later advocated black return to Africa. Born free in Newberry Court House, South Carolina, he worked in cotton fields along with slaves for a while and later on moved to Abbeville where he was a janitor in a lawyer's office and later a beginning carpenter. While working at the lawyer's office, he received instruction in elementary subjects, in violation of state law. Turner converted to Christianity in 1844 and joined the Baptist church. After hearing stirring messages from Methodist preachers at summer camp meetings, he was admitted to the Methodist church in 1848. He was licensed as an exhorter in 1851 and as a preacher in 1853. Turner became an evangelist and preached throughout the South where he attracted blacks and whites with his spellbinding sermons. He rose rapidly within the denomination, pastoring churches in the Baltimore conference while he supplemented his education. He later pastored Union Bethel in Baltimore and Israel Church in Washington, D.C. In 1860 he was ordained a deacon and in 1862 an elder. His work with the AME Book Concern and his writings for the *Christian Recorder* enhanced his reputation in the church. He was a chaplain for the First Regiment of the United States Colored Troops, receiving his commission on November 6, 1863. Turner became involved in Reconstruction politics from 1867 to 1871 and used his church's resources to help organize the Republican Party in Georgia. In 1868 he served as a member of the Georgia legislature. Turner was elected bishop in 1880 and presided over various districts for four-year terms. He had doctrinal differences with the church that gradually led to his having a more liberal position on the Bible. In 1896 he called for a new translation of the Bible by and for blacks, and initiated some of the themes of a black theology. Around this time he declared that "The devil is white and never was black" and by 1895 he proclaimed at a Baptist convention in Atlanta that "God is a Negro." Further, Turner believed that the first humans on earth were black. He advocated increased missionary activity and founded a women's auxiliary, the Woman's Home and Foreign Missionary Society to support his cause. In time be became unpopular for his stance on emigration to Africa and in 1897 when he called for blacks to keep guns in their homes during the rising tide of anti-black violence and lynchings. Turner is remembered, however, for his vigorous and effective leadership of the AME church in the South.

Sources: *Black Apostles,* pp. 227–46; Hornsby, *Chronology of African-American History,* pp. 66–67; Lincoln, *The Black Church Since Frazier,* p. 148; Smith, *Notable Black American Men,* pp. 1133–37; Angell, *Bishop Henry McNeal Turner and the African-American Religion in the South.*

1901 • Anna Hall was commissioned this year, becoming the first black graduate deaconess of the African Methodist Episcopal Church. Only a few black women had been commissioned as deaconesses since 1888, and most were assigned to work with the destitute and in urban areas. Hall started a city mission this year, supervising fieldwork of women students from Clark College. Five years later she went to Liberia where she remained for twenty-four years working as evangelist, dentist, nurse, teacher, and in other capacities. In 1952 the Liberian Church named a mission station in her honor. The Anna E. Hall Apartments for married students at Gammon Theological Seminary in Atlanta were dedicated in 1952.

Sources: Carpenter, "Black Women in Religious Institutions," p. 100.

1988 • The Service and Development Agency was the first international development program sponsored by a black church. The first head of this organization was Jonathan L. Weaver.

Sources: *Jet* 75 (15 August 1988): 12.

Vashti McKenzie

2000 • On July 11 of this year, Vashti Murphy McKenzie (1947–) became the first woman elected bishop in the African Methodist Episcopal (AME) Church. The election came during the church's quadrennial convention held in Cincinnati. McKenzie and the Reverend Carolyn Tyler Guidry, a presiding elder who supervised nineteen AME churches in the Los Angeles area, were the only women among forty-two candidates. McKenzie became bishop of the 18th Episcopal District in southeast Africa that includes Lesotho, Botswana, Swaziland, and Mozambique, where there were 10,000 members and 200 churches. In September McKenzie left for her four-year assignment. The commanding preacher achieved a first in 1990 as well, when she was appointed pastor of Payne Memorial AME Church, a large church in Baltimore. Under her leadership, Payne instituted twenty-five new ministries and increased the size of its membership from 300 to over 1,700. McKenzie is a member of the Murphy family, founders of the *Afro-American* newspaper. The Baltimore native graduated from the University of Maryland at College Park and became a fashion model; she also followed her great-grandfather, John Murphy, into the field of journalism. After working as journalist and as broadcaster on a Christian radio station, she decided to enter the ministry. She received a master of divinity degree from Howard University and a doctor of divinity from the United Theological Seminary in Dayton, Ohio. McKenzie was national chaplain for the Delta Sigma Theta Sorority and granddaughter of one of the sorority's founders, Vashti Turley Murphy. In 1997 *Ebony* magazine named McKenzie one of its "Fifteen Greatest African-American Preachers" and placed her at the top of the list. Among McKenzie's publications are the books *Not without a Struggle: Leadership Development for African American Women in Ministry* (1996) and *Strength in the Struggle: Leadership Development for Women* (2002).

Sources: Brown, *Crisis* 107 (November/December 2000): 29–31; *Christian Science Monitor* (1 February 2001), http://www.csmonitor.com/2001/0201/p14s1.html; *Contemporary Black*

Biography, vol. 29, pp. 105–9; *Ebony* 50 (September 2000): 184–90; *Jet* 98 (32 July 2000): 30–31.

African Methodist Episcopal (AME) Zion Church

1796 • Peter Williams Sr. (?–1823), a former slave and sexton of the John Street Methodist Church in New York City, organized the first African Chapel for Methodists in a cabinet-maker's shop owned by William Miller, a fellow member of the John Street Methodist Episcopal Church. Services were held there until a black church was completed in 1800. The church was called the African Methodist Episcopal Zion Church, which became the mother church of the denomination in 1820. Despite his role in founding the church, Williams remained a member of the John Street Methodist Church, and his son, Peter Jr., became a Protestant Episcopal priest.

Sources: Logan and Winston, *Dictionary of American Negro Biography,* pp. 660–62; Lincoln and Mamiya, *The Black Church in the African American Experience,* pp. 56–57; Smith, *Climbing Jacob's Ladder,* pp. 38–40.

1801 • In New York City the first church of what would become the African Methodist Episcopal Zion Church was incorporated by Peter Williams Sr. and Francis Jacobs. The building was completed in 1800. The church was initially pastored by a white minister, supplied by the parent John Street Methodist Church. Complete independence would be asserted in 1820.

Sources: Logan and Winston, *Dictionary of American Negro Biography,* pp. 660–61; *Encyclopedia of American Religion,* vol. 1, p. 194; Lincoln and Mamiya, *The Black Church in the African American Experience,* pp. 50–52; Smith, *Climbing Jacob's Ladder,* pp. 38–40.

1820 • On August 11 the African Methodist Zion and Asbury African Methodist churches, both of New York City, started their own separate African Methodist Episcopal Conference, still within the Methodist Episcopal Church. The *Book of Discipline* they adopted in September 1820 included an open anti-slavery declaration and required local preachers to free slaves. With four other congregations from Pennsylvania, Connecticut, and New York, the conference held its first annual meeting on June 21, 1821. The denomination uses 1820 as its foundation date, although the breach with the Methodist Episcopal Church did not become complete until 1824. The designation "Zion" was officially added to the name in 1848. It is currently the second largest black Methodist church, with some 1.2 million members in the United States.

Sources: Logan and Winston, *Dictionary of American Negro Biography,* pp. 616–17; *Encyclopedia of Black America,* pp. 35–36; Lincoln and Mamiya, *The Black Church in the African American Experience,* pp. 57–58; Smith, *Climbing Jacob's Ladder,* p. 63.

1822 • James Varick (1750?–1827) became the first bishop—or superintendent as he was originally called—of the African Methodist Episcopal Zion Church. He was consecrated on July 30, 1822. He was known also as one of the leaders in the creation of separate black churches. Born to a slave mother near Newburgh in Orange County, New York, Varick became a shoemaker and later a tobacco cutter. He joined the John Street Methodist Church, was active in the Zion Church, and became a deacon in 1806. In addition to his ministerial duties, Varick ran a school in his home and later in a church building. In 1810 he became the first chaplain of the New York African Society for Mutual Relief and in 1817 he was vice president of the African Bible Society. He was a supporter of the establishment of the first black newspaper in this country, *Freedom's Journal,* which was founded in 1827.

James Varick

Sources: Logan and Winston, *Dictionary of American Negro Biography,* pp. 616–17; Lincoln and Mamiya, *The Black Church in the African American Experience,* pp. 57–58; Smith, *Climbing Jacob's Ladder,* p. 63; Smith, *Notable Black American Men,* pp. 1155–56.

1894 • Julia A. J. Foote (1823–1901), of the African Methodist Episcopal Zion church, became the first woman ordained a deacon on May 20, 1894. Foote became the second black woman elder in 1900. Bishop Alexander Walters, with whose family Foote lived from 1884 to 1901, ordained two black women elders in the AME Zion church—Mary J. Small in 1898 and then Foote in 1900. They became the first women of any race in the Methodist denomination that achieve the full rights that ordination as an elder provided. Born in Schnectady, New York, Foote was the fourth child of former slaves. She went to live with a prominent white family in 1833 where she enrolled in an integrated school. In 1836 she moved with the family to Albany, New York. In 1838, when she was fifteen years old, Foote received a religious conversion. She married in 1839, moved to Boston, and joined the AME Zion Church. Like Foote, all members of the church had left the Methodist Episcopal Church in search of greater religious freedom and affiliated with a black denomination. Until her conversion, Foote made it known that she opposed women in the ministry; however, she said later that she had to preach in response to her call from God. For over fifty years Foote was an evangelist and a pioneering black Methodist holiness preacher. She traveled and lectured widely, speaking at camp meetings, revivals, and churches in several states. Later she wrote about her experiences in her autobiography, *A Brand Plucked from the Fire.*

Sources: Hine, *Black Women in America,* pp. 440–41 (Foote); Lincoln and Mamiya, *The Black Church in the African American Experience,* p. 285; Smith, *Notable Black American Women,* Book II, pp. 227–28; Thomas, *Daughters of Thunder,* pp. 57–68.

African Orthodox Church

1919 • The movement that became the African Orthodox Church was organized on April 9, 1919, by George Alexander McGuire (1866–1934), who was consecrated its first bishop on September 28, 1921. In 1918 McGuire, an ordained Episcopal priest, was appointed the first chaplain-general and a spokesperson of the United Negro Improvement Society by Marcus Garvey. McGuire was disappointed in his hope that the African Orthodox Church would become the official church of the UNIA, but he saw his church spread to Africa and the Caribbean before his death.

Sources: Baer and Singer, *African-American Religion in the Twentieth Century,* pp. 124–25; Logan and Winston, *Dictionary of American Negro Biography,* pp. 416–17; *Directory of African American Religious Bodies,* p. 126; *Encyclopedia of American Religions,* vol. 1, pp. 109–10.

1992 • Samuel Chuka Ekemam was the first non-American black elected to head the Board of Bishops of the African Methodist Episcopal Zion Church. Ekemam, a Nigerian, was educated at Livingstone College, and Yale and Columbia universities.

Sources: *Jet* 81 (13 April 1992): 7.

African Union
American Methodist Episcopal Church

1801 • Blacks in Wilmington, Delaware, withdrew from Asbury Methodist Church and—under the leadership of Peter Spencer and William Anderson—established Ezion Church. Because neither leader was ordained, Asbury Church appointed a white minister in 1812. Unable to keep control of the building in the ensuing legal dispute, the blacks again withdrew and built another church, which was dedicated in 1813. Severing all ties with the Methodist Episcopal Church, they formed the Union Church of Africans. The Union Church of Africans was the first all-black independent Methodist Church, and the mother church of one of the smaller black Methodist denominations, the African Union American Methodist Episcopal Church, which had about 6,500 members in 1988. The first annual conference was held in 1814 with three churches. The denomination refused to join the African Methodist Episcopal church in 1816.

Sources: *Directory of African American Religious Bodies,* p. 241; *Encyclopedia of American Religions,* vol. 1, pp. 194–95; Lincoln and Mamiya, *The Black Church in the African American Experience,* p. 48; Smith, *Climbing Jacob's Ladder,* pp. 58–59.

The First Black Woman Elder

In 1898 Mary J. Small (1850–1945), wife of Bishop John Bryant Small (1845–1905), became the first Methodist woman to be ordained an elder. Earlier in May 19, 1895, Small became the second woman to be ordained a deacon. Her status infuriated some of the male clergy who thought it inappropriate for women to hold such status. There is no indication that Small ever pastored a church but she was active in evangelistic activities. She was an officer in the Women's Home and Foreign Missionary Society and also belonged to the Women's Christian Temperance Union. Small was born in Murfreesboro, Tennessee. She joined her husband in his parish work in Connecticut, North Carolina, Washington, D.C., and elsewhere. She was licensed as an evangelist and missionary in 1892. Small died in McKeesport, Pennsylvania.

Sources: Hine, *Black Women in America*, pp. 440–41 Lincoln and Mamiya, *The Black Church in the African American Experience*, p. 285; Thomas, pp. 91–97.

African-American Catholic Church

1990 • George Augustus Stallings Jr. (1948–) established the African-American Catholic Church on May 13, 1990. He was its first bishop, having been consecrated by Richard Bridges, who broke away from the Independent Old Catholic Church. Stallings broke with the Roman Catholic Church over what he saw as its neglect of the spiritual needs of blacks. Born in New Bern, North Carolina, he received his bachelor's degree from St. Pius X Seminary in 1970. He attended North American College in Rome, Italy, and in 1973 he received the S.T.B. degree from Pontifical University of St. Thomas Aquinas in 1973. In 1974 he received a master's degree in pastoral theology and in 1975 the S.T.L. degree, both from St. Thomas Aquinas.

Sources: Hornsby, *Chronology of African-American History*, p. 429; *Contemporary Black Biography*, vol. 6, pp. 251–53.

Anglican Church

1978 • Desmond Mpilo Tutu (1931–) was named secretary general of the South African Council of Churches, becoming the first black to hold that post. In 1984 Tutu became bishop of Johannesburg and the first black bishop of his church in South Africa. On December 10, 1984 he also was awarded the Nobel Peace Prize for his work as a unifying figure in ending the problems of apartheid in South Africa. Tutu was ordained an Anglican priest in 1960. He received a bachelor of divinity degree in 1965 and a master of theology in 1966, both from King's College in London. His numerous publications include *The Rainbow People: The Making of a Peaceful Revolution*.

Sources: *Jet* 86 (17 October 1994): 22; 67 (3 December 1984): 31; *Contemporary Black Biography*, vol. 6, pp. 269–74.

Antioch Association of Metaphysical Science

1932 • The Antioch Association of Metaphysical Science seems to be the first predominantly black New Thought church. New Thought grows out of a Christian Science background, emphasizes healing through mental power, and should not be confused with the current New Age movement. The Antioch Association was founded in Detroit by Lewis Johnson.

Sources: Baer and Singer, *African-American Religion in the Twentieth Century*, p. 200; *Encyclopedia of American Religions*, vol. 2, p. 886.

Baptism

1623 • The first known black child baptized in the colonies was William, the son of Isabella and Anthony Johnson, at Jamestown, Virginia. It is possible that this father is the same Anthony Johnson who owned five servants and was granted five hundred acres of land in 1651.

Sources: Blockson, *Black Genealogy,* p. 46; Cantor, *Historic Landmarks of Black America,* p. 255; *Negro Almanac* (1976), p. 1041; Smith, *Ethnic Genealogy,* pp. 346–47.

1641 • The first baptism of a black in New England was performed. The name of the woman is unknown, but she was a slave in Dorchester, Massachusetts.

Sources: Raboteau, *Slave Religion,* pp. 108–9; Southern, *The Music of Black Americans,* ed., p. 1.

1664 • The lower house of Maryland asked the upper house to draft an act declaring that baptism of slaves did not lead to their freedom. Maryland was the first to enact such a law. By 1710 at least six of the colonies had laws making this specific declaration.

Sources: Raboteau, *Slave Religion,* p. 99.

Baptists

1743 • The first known black Baptist was Quassey, a member of the Newport, Rhode Island, church.

Sources: Lincoln and Mamiya, *The Black Church in the African American Experience,* p. 23; Gaustad and Barlow, *New Historical Atlas of Religion in America,* p. 13.

1758 • The first known black Baptist congregation was the "Bluestone" African Baptist Church, located on the William Byrd plantation in Mecklenberg, Virginia. The church's nickname comes from its location near the Bluestone River. (A claim for priority is also advanced for a congregation said to exist at Luneberg in 1756. The evidence is not clear cut, but all claims so far refer to Virginia and the decade of the 1750s.)

Sources: Baer and Singer, *African-American Religion in the Twentieth Century,* p. 16; Lincoln and Mamiya, *The Black Church in the African American Experience,* p. 23; Smith, *Climbing Jacob's Ladder,* p. 33; Wilmore, *Black and Presbyterian,* p. 41.

1773 • The first black Baptist church under black leadership seems to have been formed in Silver Bluff, South Carolina. David George, a slave, became its first black pastor. George Liele (1750?–1820) and, less probably, Andrew Bryan (1737?–1812) have also been associated with the church. The congregation seems to have been founded between 1773 and 1775. The present church was remodeled in 1920, and a cornerstone with the founding date of 1750 was put in place. This date appears too early to most historians. In 1793 the congregation of some sixty persons, led by Jesse Galpin, moved to Augusta, Georgia, about twelve miles away.

Sources: Lincoln and Mamiya, *The Black Church in the African American Experience,* pp. 23–24; Raboteau, *Slave Religion,* pp. 139–40.

1775? • George Liele [Leile, Lisle] (1750?–1820), the first known black Baptist missionary, was active before the Revolutionary War. Liele was born a slave in Virginia and became a convert after his master moved to Georgia. He was freed a short while before he began to preach. Liele preached in Savannah, Georgia, during the British occupation of the town from 1779 to 1782. Since British officers had protected him against an attempt to re-enslave him, he accompanied the withdrawal of the British troops to Jamaica. In 1784 he established the first black Baptist church on the island, in Kingston with four other people. A few years later Liele built a church and later a second one at Spanish Town.

Sources: Logan and Winston, *Dictionary of American Negro Biography,* p. 397; Lincoln and Mamiya, *The Black Church in the African American Experience,* p. 23–24; Smith, *Climbing Jacob's Ladder,* pp. 32–33; Smith, *Notable Black American Men,* pp. 723–24.

Early Baptist Churches

Founded	Name	Location
1786	Harrison Street Baptist Church	Petersburg, Virginia
1788	First African Baptist Church	Savannah, Georgia
1790	African Baptist Church	Lexington, Kentucky
1793	First African Baptist Church	Augusta, Georgia
1805	Joy Street Baptist Church	Boston, Massachusetts
1809	African Baptist Church	Philadelphia, Pennsylvania
1809	Abyssinian Baptist Church	New York, New York
1833	First Colored Baptist Church	Washington, D.C.
1835	First Colored Baptist Church	Baltimore, Maryland

Sources: Logan and Winston, *Dictionary of American Negro Biography,* p. 287; *Encyclopedia of Black America,* pp. 159–60; Lincoln and Mamiya, *The Black Church in the African American Experience,* pp. 22–23; Raboteau, *Slave Religion,* pp. 139–40; Smith, *Climbing Jacob's Ladder,* pp. 31–33, 45, 46, 47–48, 51–55, 76–77, 79, 81–84.

1783 • David George (1742?–1810) established the first black Baptist church in Nova Scotia. Born a slave in Virginia, his attempt to flee and seek freedom in Georgia was foiled when he was captured by Creek Indians. He was eventually sold to George Gaufin and sent to a plantation at Silver Bluff, South Carolina, where he became pastor of the first black Baptist congregation in 1773. During the British occupation of Charleston, South Carolina, Gaufin moved there, and George preached in that city. George and his family were among those who accompanied the British troops when they evacuated the city. In 1792 he and almost all his congregation emigrated to Sierra Leone, where he had a church of nearly two hundred members at the time of his death.

Sources: Logan and Winston, *Dictionary of American Negro Biography,* p. 257; Smith, *Climbing Jacob's Ladder,* p. 33.

1791 • The African Baptist Church of Petersburg, Virginia, some five hundred strong, was officially recognized by the Dover Association in 1791. The origin of the church went back to a black man named Moses, who persisted in preaching and holding meetings in spite of whippings. Moses was followed by Gowan Prophet. The church appears to have been in existence before 1786.

Sources: Raboteau, *Slave Religion,* pp. 138–39.

1792 • Josiah [Jacob] Bishop is the first black known to be employed as a preacher by a racially mixed congregation. His congregation in Portsmouth, Virginia, purchased his freedom and that of his family.

Sources: Raboteau, *Slave Religion,* p. 134.

1792 • Andrew Bryan (1737–1812) began to erect the First African Baptist Church building in Savannah, Georgia. The first building built for the purpose of black worship in the city, it was finished in 1794. Bryan was a slave who refused to give up his mission in spite of whipping and imprisonment for preaching. He had formed his church on January 20, 1788. The lot on which the church stood remained in the church's possession until at least 1913. The black Baptist church in Savannah was established before there was a white Baptist church, as was also the case in Petersburg, Virginia. Bryan was born a slave near Charleston, South Carolina, in Goose Creek. Sometime before 1790 Brown purchased his freedom. Around 1773 or 1774 he may have come in contact with George Liele, when Liele preached on the Bramton plantation where Bryan lived last before he became free. Bryan was baptized in 1782 and began preaching about nine months later. He also learned to read around this time. In 1788 a white minister from Georgia, Abraham Marshall, ordained him. Bryan and his supporters preached in cells on plantations, either in the open or clandestine, depending on the disposition of the plantation owners.

Andrew Bryan

The Oldest Surviving Black Church

The African Meeting House, built in 1806 and known as the Joy Street Baptist Church, in Boston, Massachusetts, is the oldest surviving building constructed to serve as a black church. It housed the first black Baptist congregation in Boston, organized in 1805 by Thomas Paul Sr. (1773–1831), who also founded the Abyssinian Baptist Church in New York City in 1809. On January 6, 1832, William Lloyd Garrison organized the Anti-Slavery Society in the church basement with the participation of prominent church members.

Sources: Baer and Singer, *African-American Religion in the Twentieth Century,* p. 26; Logan and Winston, *Dictionary of American Negro Biography,* pp. 482–83; Lincoln and Mamiya, *The Black Church in the African American Experience,* p. 25; Smith, *Climbing Jacob's Ladder,* pp. 48, 51–52.

Sources: Logan and Winston, *Dictionary of American Negro Biography,* p. 77; Lincoln and Mamiya, *The Black Church in the African American Experience,* pp. 23–24; Raboteau, *Slave Religion,* pp. 137, 141–42; Smith, *Climbing Jacob's Ladder,* pp. 33, 76; Smith, *Notable Black American Men,* pp. 146–48.

Lott Carey

1821 • Lott Carey [Cary] (1780–1829) was the first black Baptist missionary to Africa. He established the First Baptist Church in what is now Monrovia, Liberia. Carey was born a slave and an only child in Charles City County, Virginia, about thirty miles from Richmond. Around 1804 his owner hired him out as a laborer, enabling him to work in a tobacco warehouse in Richmond. He underwent conversion in 1807 and then was baptized as a member of the First Baptist Church in Richmond. After that Carey learned to read and write. He continued to work in the warehouse and saved enough money to purchase his own, and his two children's, freedom. However, by 1813 his children had died. Carey began to preach soon after his conversion; he preached on plantations near Richmond and later pastored the African Baptist Church. From his work with the Richmond African Baptist Missionary Society, he was determined to preach the gospel in Africa. On January 23, 1821, Carey, Colin Teague, and twenty-eight others, set sail for Africa. When a group of churches in Virginia, North Carolina, and Washington, D.C., withdrew from the National Baptist Convention, USA, in 1897, they formed the Lott Carey Foreign Mission Convention, which is still in existence today.

Sources: Logan and Winston, *Dictionary of American Negro Biography,* pp. 95–97; Lincoln and Mamiya, *The Black Church in the African American Experience,* pp. 26, 45; Smith, *Climbing Jacob's Ladder,* p. 92; Smith, *Notable Black American Men,* pp. 180–82.

1822 • Nathan Paul (1793?–1893) was the first pastor of the African Baptist Church, Albany, New York, the only black church in the city. Nathan, brother of Thomas Paul of Boston, was a prominent abolitionist, and in 1832 the first American black to go to England to further this cause. Paul went to raise money for a school in Wilberforce, Ohio. He was nearly lynched when he came back without any money, and claimed he was owed $1,600 in back salary. The fact that his second wife was an Englishwoman, and probably white, did not improve his situation.

Sources: Logan and Winston, *Dictionary of American Negro Biography,* p. 482.

1834 • The first all-black Baptist association of churches was the Providence Association, in Ohio.

1846 • By this date the first known black Baptist church in Canada, outside the maritime provinces, was in existence. The precise date of its founding in Toronto is unknown.

Sources: *Encyclopedia of Black America,* p. 161.

1846 • Free blacks in Mobile, Alabama, organized African Street Baptist Church informally about 1815, some two decades before the white First Baptist Church was organized in 1835. This early black, informal church is referred to as the Stone Street Church. On December 20, 1846, the two white Baptist churches in Mobile placed their black members into a separate body, also known as Stone Street Colored Church, formally making it the mother church of black Baptists in Mobile.

Sources: Badger, *A Life in Ragtime,* pp. 11–12.

1853 • Nelson Grover Merry (1824–1884) became the first black pastor of the church formed by the separation of some five hundred black members from the white First Baptist Church of Nashville in 1847. It was not until 1866 that the breakaway church became fully independent of the white First Baptist. Samuel A. Davidson, a white minister, headed the black congregation until Merry took over. On March 9, 1853, by unanimous vote of his church, Merry was licensed to preach and became the first ordained black minister in Nashville. He was pastor of the church, presently known as the First Baptist Church, Capitol Hill, until 1884. The church became the state's largest black church, with a membership of over 2,000. He was a founder of the Tennessee Colored Baptist Association in 1866. He also edited *The Colored Sunday School Standard,* from 1874 to 1875. He went on to organize at least fourteen black Baptist churches. Merry was born a slave in Kentucky and moved to Nashville with his master. After the master died, his widow willed him to the First Baptist Church where he was employed, later baptized, and finally freed on November 1, 1845.

Sources: May, *The First Baptist Church of Nashville 1820–1970,* pp. 76–77; Lovett and Wynn, *Profiles of African Americans in Tennessee,* pp. 92–94; Raboteau, *Slave Religion,* p. 204; *Tennessee Tribune* (3–9 December 1998).

1856 • The first black Baptist church organized in Chicago was Mt. Olivet Baptist Church. It was only the second black church founded in the city.

Sources: Buck, *The Progress of the Race in the United States and Canada,* p. 512.

Early Baptist Associations

Founded	Name	Location
1836	Union Association	Ohio
1839	Colored Baptist Society and Friends to Humanity	Illinois[1]
1840	American Baptist Missionary Convention	New England and Middle Atlantic
1841	Amherstburg Association	Canada and Michigan
1853	Western Colored Baptist Convention	
1864	Northwest and Southern Baptist Convention	
1867	Consolidated American Baptist Missionary Convention	

[1]This organization split in 1849 to become the Mount Olive Association and the Colored Baptist Association; the latter became the Wood River Colored Baptist Association in 1856.

Sources: *Directory of African American Religious Bodies,* pp. 228–29; *Encyclopedia of Black America,* pp. 161–62; Lincoln and Mamiya, *The Black Church in the African American Experience,* pp. 26–27; Smith, *Climbing Jacob's Ladder,* pp. 63–65.

1867 • The Consolidated American Baptist Missionary Convention was the first national organization of black Baptists. It was organized in Nashville, Tennessee, in August, 1867, and held its final meeting in 1879.

Sources: *Directory of African American Religious Bodies,* p. 229; *Encyclopedia of Black America,* p. 162; Lincoln and Mamiya, *The Black Church in the African American Experience,* p. 27.

1878 • John Jasper (1812–1901) preached for the first time his famous sermon "De Sun Do Move." He would deliver this sermon 253 times before his death. Born a slave on a plantation in Fluvanna County, Virginia, and converted in 1837, Jasper became a powerful and very popular preacher. He retained the language of the uneducated, rural black, but

John Jasper

his evident sincerity and the power of his oratory impressed even those among his large audiences who came to scoff.

Sources: Logan and Winston, *Dictionary of American Negro Biography,* pp. 343–44; *Encyclopedia of Black America,* pp. 160, 511; Smith, *Climbing Jacob's Ladder,* pp. 110–11.

1880 • The Baptist Foreign Mission Convention of the United States of America was formed at a meeting in Montgomery, Alabama, on November 24, 1880, with W. W. Colley as its first corresponding secretary. Not only did the convention support African missions abroad, at home it was an anti-liquor and anti-tobacco organization. Colley was a missionary sponsored by the Southern Baptist Convention in Africa from 1875 to 1879 and did not agree with that convention's treatment of Africans.

Sources: *Directory of African American Religious Bodies,* p. 229; *Encyclopedia of Black America,* pp. 162–63; Lincoln and Mamiya, *The Black Church in the African American Experience,* pp. 27–28.

1886 • The first meeting of the American National Baptist Convention was held on August 25, 1886, in St. Louis, Missouri. Its first president was William J. Simmons (1849–1890). This convention was the largest component of the three bodies that joined to form the National Baptist Convention, USA, in 1895. Simmons had a varied and productive career as a religious and educational leader, but he is most remembered as author of the collection of biographies, *Men of Mark, Eminent, Progressive,* and *Rising* (1887).

Sources: Logan and Winston, *Dictionary of American Negro Biography,* pp. 556–57; *Directory of African American Religious Bodies,* p. 229; *Encyclopedia of Black America,* p. 163; Lincoln and Mamiya, *The Black Church in the African American Experience,* p. 28; Smith, *Notable Black American Men,* pp. 1066–67.

1895 • The National Baptist Convention, USA, held its first meeting in Atlanta, Georgia, on September 28, 1895. E. C. Morris was its first president. This remains the largest Baptist organization under the title National Baptist Convention, USA, Inc. The second largest is the National Baptist Convention of America, which split from the parent organization in 1915 in a dispute primarily about the control of the American Baptist Publication Society. The third largest is the Progressive National Baptist Convention, which broke away from the parent organization in 1961 over the issue of the churches' posture on civil rights.

Sources: *Directory of African American Religious Bodies,* pp. 229–32; *Encyclopedia of Black America,* pp. 163–64; Lincoln and Mamiya, *The Black Church in the African American Experience,* p. 28.

Nannie Burroughs

1907 • Nannie Burroughs (1879–1961) first proposed Women's Day celebrations in churches in Memphis, Tennessee, in September this year. When she gave her report as corresponding secretary of the Woman's Convention Auxiliary to the National Baptist Convention, Burroughs presented the idea, purpose, and plan for the special day. When she presented a resolution for Woman's Day (as it was first called), she was dubbed as "upstart" and the day was criticized as only tokenism for women. The convention, however, voted to accept the resolution. The purpose of this national observance day was to stimulate women's interest in local churches to raise money for Foreign Missions—then the primary interest of the Woman's Convention. Rather than raise money, some claimed that the focus was on "raising women." In fact, when women were first allowed in the pulpit, the occasion was Women's Day celebrations, when they moved from church to church to speak. Women's Day observation in churches continues to provide women an opportunity to lead the worship service and deliver sermons. It is a highly respected day in the black church and an important time to promote expressions of black Christian women. In time Women's Day activities became successful fundraisers and have become important in expanding the ranks of black women, particularly in leadership roles.

Sources: Smith, *Notable Black American Women,* pp. 137–40; Hine, *Black Women in America,* vol. 2, p. 968; Murphy, *Down by the Riverside,* p. 102.

1915 • E. P. Jones was the first president of the National Baptist Convention, Unincorporated (now the National Baptist Convention of America). The split with the National Baptist Convention, Inc., over control of the Baptist Publishing Board, became official on September 9, 1915. The second largest Baptist convention, it now has some 2.4 million members.

Sources: *Encyclopedia of American Religions,* vol. 2, pp. 89–90; *Encyclopedia of Black America,* pp. 164–65; Lincoln and Mamiya, *The Black Church in the African American Experience,* pp. 33–35.

1962 • L. Venhael Booth was the first president of the Progressive National Baptist Convention, USA. The split in the Baptist convention began in 1957, with a challenge to the renewal of the mandate of J. H. Jackson, the long-standing president of the National Baptist Convention, USA, Inc. It grew to encompass ministers who were ready to follow Martin Luther King Jr. and undertake activist efforts to secure civil rights. The smallest of the three major Baptist organizations, it had some 1.2 million members in 1989.

Sources: *Directory of African American Religious Bodies,* pp. 231–32; *Encyclopedia of American Religions,* vol. 2, p. 91; *Encyclopedia of Black America,* pp. 165–66; Lincoln and Mamiya, *The Black Church in the African American Experience,* pp. 36–37.

1965 • The first black to serve as dean of March Chapel at Boston University was Howard Thurman (1900–1981), theologian, clergyman, mystic, and civil rights advisor. He was also professor of spiritual disciplines and resources. After he retired from Boston, he headed the Howard Thurman Educational Trust that was devoted to the education of black youth. Born in Daytona Beach, Florida, Thurman received a Bachelor of Arts degree from Morehouse College in 1923 and a Bachelor of Divinity degree Colgate-Rochester Divinity School in 1926. His first church appointment was at Mt. Zion Baptist Church, a black church in Oberlin, Ohio. The inspiring and effective preacher soon attracted whites and blacks from the surrounding area, thus making the church integrated. He also met the Quaker philosopher and mystic Rufus Jones, who would become his spiritual mentor. Thurman did post-professional work at Oberlin and at Haverford College, where he studied with Jones, and then returned to Morehouse where he taught and became chaplain. In 1931 he moved to Howard University's School of Religion and quickly was appointed dean of the school's Rankin Chapel. He established what would become a lifelong friendship with Benjamin E. Mays, dean of the School of Religion at Howard. Together the men developed the School of Religion into a highly reputable divinity school. Thurman chaired a delegation of black Americans who went to India, Burma, and Ceylon (now Sri Lanka) in 1935 on a "pilgrimage of friendship," sponsored by the YWCA. There he addressed many crucial issues related to Christianity and racial oppression and strengthened his commitment to pacifism and nonviolence in settling disputes. Both the visit to India and a meeting with Mahatma Gandhi in 1936 helped him to seal his philosophy on nonviolence. He left Howard for San Francisco, where he co-founded and served as co-pastor of the Church for the Fellowship of All Peoples. So impressive and effective was his work there that Boston University asked Thurman to establish a similar minister there while serving as dean of the chapel. He left his San Francisco church in 1953 when he became the first black dean of the chapel as well as the first to conduct non-traditional chapel services. Thurman's chapel services used liturgical dance and artistic liturgies, mixed with long meditations and silence—his mystic trademark. Toward the end of his tenure, *Life* magazine named him one of the nation's twelve greatest preachers. He wrote more than twenty books on spirituality and social consciousness and also published his autobiography, *With Head and Heart.* Thurman died in his San Francisco home and left a legacy as one of the greatest mystics and theologians of the twentieth century.

Howard Thurman

Sources: Thurman, *With Head and Heart;* Smith, *Notable Black American Men,* pp. 1114–118; *Contemporary Black Biography,* vol. 3, pp. 243–47.

1969 • Thomas Kilgore Jr. (1913–1998) was the first black to serve as head of the predominantly white American Baptist Convention. For twenty-two years Kilgore was senior pastor of Second Baptist Church in Los Angeles, California, which is the oldest black Baptist church in the city. At one time he was pastor of Friendship Baptist Church in New

York City. Kilgore was a native of Woodruff, South Carolina, and graduated from Morehouse College.

Sources: Alford, *Famous First Blacks,* p. 21; *Ebony* (25 August 1970): 106; 37 (March 1982): 129; *Ebony Success Library,* vol. 1, p. 191; *Who's Who among Black Americans, 1992–93,* p. 818; *Jet* 93 (23 February 1998): 17.

1983 • As pastor of Mariner's Temple Baptist Church in New York City, Suzanne Denise Johnson (1957–) was the first black, and the first female, pastor in the American Baptist Churches USA.

Sources: *Essence* 14 (September 1983): 42; *Jet* 64 (13 June 1983): 25.

1983 • Deborah Cannon Partridge Wolfe (1916–2004) was the first woman Baptist to be president of the Clergy Council of Cranford, New Jersey. Wolfe was a professor of education at Queens College, New York, as well as being a minister. Wolfe was born in Cranford, New Jersey. Both of her parents held theological degrees and were active in religious and educational affairs. Wolfe graduated from New Jersey Teachers College in Jersey City. Before graduating, she directed a community center for migrant workers in Hardlock, Maryland, and also taught at a local high school under the Works Progress Administration adult education project. In 1938 she received her master's degree from Teachers College of Columbia University. Wolfe taught at Tuskegee Institute (now Tuskegee University) from 1938 to 1950, becoming principal and teacher-trainer at its laboratory schools. In 1945 Wolfe received her doctorate in education from Columbia. Later on she taught at Queens College and directed City University's Center for African and Afro-Studies. She was ordained in the Baptist church in 1970, as an associate minister at First Baptist Church in Cranford. She also held several posts in the Progressive National Baptist Convention.

Sources: *Current Biography, 1962,* pp. 469–71; *Jet* 64 (4 July 1983): 21; Smith, *Notable Black American Women,* pp. 1276–78; *Who's Who among African Americans,* 14th ed., p. 1437.

1983 • The South Carolina Baptist Educational and Missionary Convention authorized the ordination of women. This was the first state organization in the National Baptist Convention to do so.

Sources: *Jet* 64 (30 May 1983): 26.

1987 • Leroy Gainey was the first black trustee-elected professor at a Southern Baptist institution, Golden Gate Theological Seminary, Mill Valley, California.

Sources: *Jet* 73 (19 October 1987): 20.

1989 • Rodney S. Patterson founded the first all-black church in Vermont, the New Alpha Missionary Baptist Church, located in Burlington.

Sources: *Negro Almanac,* p. 1432.

1989 • Frederick J. Streets became the first black and the first Baptist to become university chaplain at Yale University. Streets, age forty-two at the time of his appointment, graduated from Yale Divinity School in 1975. He received his bachelor's degree from Ottawa University in 1972, and his master's and doctorate in social work from Yeshiva University in 1981 and 1997. He also was involved in independent research in London, England, in 1970, received a certificate from Harvard University's Graduate School of Education in 1982, and attended a second graduate program in Harvard's School of Education in 1989. Streets has published numerous articles in his field.

Sources: *Jet* 82 (11 May 1992): 6; "Profile," www.Jerrystreets.org. Accessed September 29, 2012.

1995 • G. Elaine Smith was elected president of the American Baptist Churches USA, becoming the first black woman to hold that position. She assumed office in January 1996. Smith holds membership in the bar association in Tennessee, Pennsylvania, and New Jersey.

Sources: *Jet* 88 (31 July 1995): 19; *Who's Who among African Americans,* 26th ed., p. 1144.

1998 • The Florida Baptist Convention elected its first black leader this year, when it named Elroy Barber (1945?–) to head the group. This marked progress toward racial reconciliation that the Southern Baptist Convention had discussed three years earlier. The convention in 1995 as well passed a resolution on racial reconciliation and apologized for the denomination's failure to oppose slavery before the Civil War. A native of Mississippi, Barker graduated from New Orleans Baptist Seminary. Since 1993 he has served as pastor of West Side Baptist Church in Hollywood, Florida.

Sources: *Jet* 95 (14 December 1998): 19.

Black Christian Nationalist Church

1966 • Albert B. Cleage Jr. [Jaramogi Abebe Agyeman] (1913–2000) preached a famous sermon at his independent, and very activist, Detroit church, and became the first proponent of Black Theology to attract national attention. He subsequently published two books presenting his position, *The Black Messiah* in 1968 and *Black Christian Nationalism* in 1972. In 1970 Cleage changed his name to Jaramogi Abebe Agyeman. He graduated from Wayne State University in 1937 and received his divinity degree from Oberlin College in 1943. The church maintains that Jesus was a black Messiah and revolutionary sent to liberate blacks. The church building became known as the Shrine of the Black Madonna and the name was added to that of the church, which became Shrines of the Black Madonna Pan-African Orthodox Christian Church. By 1972 another name for the group was also in use—the Black Nationalist Church.

Sources: Baer and Singer, *African-American Religion in the Twentieth Century,* pp. 60–61, 126; *Ebony Success Library,* vol. 1, p. 70; *Directory of African American Religious Bodies,* pp. 128–29; *Encyclopedia of American Religions,* vol. 3, p. 156.

Catholics

186? • Saint Victor I was the first pope identified as an African; his racial identity is not clearly established. What was rare then, and now, is that he was a deacon when he became pope. It was Saint Victor who established a set date for the annual celebration of Easter. He reigned until 197? and died in 199, a martyr for the faith. He was buried on Vatican Hill near St. Peter's tomb. Two other early popes, who, like Saint Victor I, became saints, are also of African origin—Saint Miltiades (311–14) and Saint Gelasius I (492–96). Saint Miltiades ended persecutions by signing the emperor Constantine's famous Edict of Milan in 313. Christianity then became the empire's established and legal religion. Highly regarded as pope, according to Saint Augustine, Saint Miltiades was called "a son of peace and father of Christians." He was the last pope to be buried in a catacomb. Saint Gelasius I was born in Rome and became well known for holiness, kindness, and scholarship. Although he upheld old traditions, he also made exceptions and modifications, including "his decree obliging the reception of the Holy Eucharist under both kinds." He is credited with saving Rome from famine and he also was recognized for his concern for the poor. He composed a book of hymns for use in the church and also clarified the church's teaching on the Eucharist. He was ranked high as a writer. Many of his decrees were incorporated into the Canon Law.

Sources: Davis, *The History of Black Catholics in the United States,* p. 13; "Pope St. Gelasius I," www.newadvent.org/cathen/06406a.htm.

410 • Saint Moses the Black is the first saint whose black identity is well established. A rebellious former slave who had become an outlaw in the Egyptian desert, he became a monk and priest and left writings on monastic life. Moses was martyred in 410.

Sources: Davis, *The History of Black Catholics in the United States,* pp. 9–10.

1730 • The Ursuline nuns of New Orleans, Louisiana, undertook efforts to instruct black Catholics; their efforts persisted until 1824. Catholic instruction for blacks was practically nonexistent in most places, and white Catholics were only somewhat better served.

Sources: Raboteau, *Slave Religion,* p. 114.

1794 • The first known Sunday catechism classes for blacks in Baltimore, Maryland, were established in 1794. Louisiana was the only other area with a substantial number of black Catholics. Intermittent efforts to instruct blacks had been made there, with the Ursuline nuns giving instruction to black girls since the 1720s.

Sources: Ochs, *Desegregating the Altar,* p. 22.

1824 • The first attempt to build a community of black nuns was the formation of an auxiliary group to the Sisters of Loretto in Loretto, Kentucky. This group consisted of three free black women whose names were not recorded. The attempt did not outlive the stay of the sponsoring priest, who soon left for Missouri.

Sources: Davis, *The History of Black Catholics in the United States,* p. 98.

1829 • On July 2, 1829, the first permanent order of black Catholic nuns, the Oblate Sisters of Providence, was founded in Baltimore, Maryland. The order was founded through the efforts of a French priest, James Joubert, and four women of Caribbean origin—Elizabeth Lange, Rosine Boegues, Mary Frances Balas, and Mary Theresa Duchemin. This teaching order was formally recognized October 2, 1831. The sisters opened the first Catholic school for girls in 1843. The school survives today as Mount Providence Junior College, established in 1952. The second order founded was the Sisters of the Holy Family. Henriette Delille and Juliette Gaudin founded the order in New Orleans in 1842; that order was not officially recognized until after the Civil War. The third predominantly black order was the Franciscan Handmaids of the Most Pure Heart of Mary, founded in Savannah, Georgia, in 1916. At the invitation of Cardinal Patrick Hayes, the Handmaids moved to Harlem in 1924; at the time that many blacks were relocating there. The cardinal saw a need for a day nursery for working parents' children and the Handmaids responded by opening the St. Benedict Day Nursery, now their primary charity. They also operate a summer sleep-away camp in Staten Island. The order is located on West 124th street between Lenox and Fifth avenues. In its heyday, over eighty Handmaids of Mary were members of the order. By 2001 the oldest member of the order was Sister Mary Joseph who was 101 years old. In October 2001 the Handmaids celebrated their eighty-fifth anniversary.

Sources: Davis,*The History of Black Catholics in the United States,* pp. 99–105; *Encyclopedia of Black America,* p. 220; *New York Times* (31 October 2001); Ochs, *Desegregating the Altar,* pp. 24–25; Smith, *Notable Black American Women,* pp. 813–14; Smith, *Climbing Jacob's Ladder,* pp. 97–100.

1836 • George Paddington was the first black to be ordained by an American bishop, on May 21, 1836, in Port-au-Prince, Haiti. Bishop John England was a representative of the Holy See at the time. Little is known about Paddington, who was from Dublin, Ireland.

Sources: Davis, *The History of Black Catholics in the United States,* pp. 93–94.

1843 • The Society of Colored People of Baltimore is the first black Catholic association whose documentation has been preserved. Their notebook began on December 3, 1843, and continued until September 7, 1845, when the society wound up. Besides meeting for worship, the society maintained a library.

Sources: Davis, *The History of Black Catholics in the United States,* pp. 86–88.

1854 • On June 10, 1854, James Augustine Healy (1830–1900) was ordained a priest in Paris, France. He was the first American black to be ordained in the Catholic church. Two brothers followed him; for a while they were the first three black Catholic priests in the United States. The next black Catholic priest, Augustus Tolton (1854–1897) would not be named until 1886. All three Healy brothers had to study abroad. James Healy became the first black bishop, of Portland, Maine, in February 1875. Alexander Sherwood was ordained for the Diocese of Massachusetts. Patrick Francis (1834–1910) became a Jesuit; he obtained the first Ph.D. earned by a black, from Louvain University in Belgium, and became the first black Jesuit, as well as the first black president of Georgetown University. The three brothers were the sons of an Irish plantation owner in Georgia and a mulatto slave woman. Their sister Eliza (Sister Mary Magdalen, 1846–1918) became a nun and notable school head. Another brother, Michael Alexander (1839–1904), became a captain in the U.S. Revenue Cutter Service (now the U.S. Coast Guard) and the first black to become de facto chief law enforcement officer in Alaskan waters. While the racial identity of the Healys had not been entirely concealed, it was not widely broadcast; many were able to pass as white.

Sources: Davis,*The History of Black Catholics in the United States,* pp. 147–51; Logan and Winston, *Dictionary of American Negro Biography,* pp. 301–2 (Eliza); 302–3 (James); 303–4 (Michael); 304–5 (Patrick); Smith, *Notable Black American Women,* pp. 479–81 (Eliza); Ochs, *Desegregating the Altar,* pp. 26–29; *Notable Black American Men,* pp. 533–36 (James).

1863 • Saint Francis Xavier Church in Baltimore, Maryland, became the first exclusively black parish in the United States. The Sulpician order of priests had maintained a chapel for blacks earlier in the century, until 1836. Saint Francis Xavier Church grew out of the Chapel of Blessed Peter Claver, which had been established by the Jesuits in 1857. The church was purchased by the Jesuit Fathers on October 10, 1863, and dedicated on February 21, 1864.

Sources: Kane, *Famous First Facts,* p. 156; Smith, *Climbing Jacob's Ladder,* pp. 97–100.

1875 • James Augustine Healy (1830–1900) became the first black Catholic bishop. He presided in Portland, Maine, over a predominantly white ministry and encountered racism. He held the position, with distinction, until his death in 1900.

Sources: Davis, *The History of Black Catholics in the United States,* pp. 149–51; Logan and Winston, *Dictionary of American Negro Biography,* pp. 302–3; *Encyclopedia of Black America,* p. 433; Ochs, *Desegregating the Altar,* pp. 26–28.

1883 • The first black Catholic church in New York City opened in the Greenwich Village section. It was named in honor of the black saint who lived in Sicily in late 1500s—St. Benedict the Moor, patron saint of black Catholics.

Sources: *The Black New Yorkers,* p. 107; Delaney, *Dictionary of Saints,* p. 98.

1886 • Augustus Tolton (1854–1897) celebrated his first mass in the United States at Saint Mary's Hospital in Hoboken, New Jersey, on July 7, 1886. Although Tolton was not the first black priest, he was the first to be widely known and publicized. He seems to have believed himself that he was the first, preceding the Healy brothers. Tolton became a priest on August 24, 1886, and served principally in Quincy, Illinois, and Chicago, Illinois.

Sources: Davis, *The History of Black Catholics in the United States,* pp. 152–62; Logan and Winston, *Dictionary of American Negro Biography,* pp. 596–97; Ochs, *Desegregating the Altar,* pp. 77–79, 94–95.

1889 • The first meeting of the Catholic Afro-American Lay Congress (now the National Black Catholic Conference or NBCC) began on January 1, 1889, at St. Augustine Catholic Church in Washington, D.C., under the presidency of William H. Smith. The historic event included distinguished black men from all over the United States. President Grover Cleveland recognized the men by inviting them to the White House for a meeting. There were five congresses from 1889 to 1894; after that, congresses were held in 1987, 1992, and 1997. The most pressing problem for many delegates was the lack of black priests. Only one black priest had been ordained since the Healy brothers earlier in the century. This priest was Augustus Tolton (1854–1897), who took his vows in 1886; he was present for the conference and celebrated High Mass. (Tolton has sometimes been identified as the first American-born black priest; he was the fourth, as the three Healy brothers were all born in Georgia.) Daniel Rudd (1854–?), the NBCC founder, was probably born in Bardstown, Kentucky, where both parents were slaves, but on separate estates. He was one of twelve children. After the Civil War, Rudd moved to Springfield, Ohio, to obtain a secondary-school education. After he founded the NBCC in 1889, he orchestrated five of the conferences. The first was held at St. Augustine Catholic Church in Washington, D.C., and the 1894 conference was held at St. Peter Claver Church in Baltimore. For his work with the congresses and the black Catholic newspaper that he founded in 1886 and later named the

American Catholic Tribune, Rudd has been called one of the most important figures of the nineteenth and twentieth centuries.

Sources: Cantor, *Historic Landmarks of Black America,* p. 11; Davis,*The History of Black Catholics in the United States,* pp. 171–94; Logan and Winston, *Dictionary of American Negro Biography,* pp. 596–97; *Directory of African American Religious Bodies,* pp. 258–60; Ochs, *Desegregating the Altar,* pp. 27–28.

1891 • Charles Randolph Uncles (1859–1933) became the first black priest ordained in the United States, on December 19, 1891, in Baltimore, Maryland. (The four previous American blacks had all been ordained in Europe.) Uncles was ordained at the Cathedral of the Assumption, as it was known then. He attended Baltimore Normal School for Teachers and taught in Baltimore County public schools, but mainly at Epiphany College. He died on July 21, 1933, at the age of seventy-four. He had been a priest for forty-two years.

Sources: Ochs, *Desegregating the Altar,* pp. 81–82, 456.

1902 • The first Roman Catholic church in Nashville, Tennessee, with a black congregation was the Church of the Holy Family, located on North College Street. It was dedicated on June 30.

Sources: Jones, *Every Day in Tennessee History,* p. 128.

1923 • Saint Augustine's Seminary was established in Bay Saint Louis, Louisiana, by the Society of the Divine Word. This was the first separate and segregated seminary to train black priests. The work of the seminary had begun two years earlier in Greenville, Mississippi. The seminary had a six-year combined high school and college course, a year's novitiate, and a six-year seminary course. The first four missionary priests from the seminary were ordained in 1934.

Sources: Cantor, *Historic Landmarks of Black America,* p. 169; Davis, *The History of Black Catholics in the United States,* pp. 234–35; Ochs, *Desegregating the Altar,* pp. 5–6, 271–72.

1953 • On April 22, 1953, Joseph Oliver Bowers (1910–) became the first black bishop consecrated in the United States since James A. Healy in 1875, as bishop of Accra in the soon-to-be independent Ghana. He was from the West Indies, forty-six years old, and a graduate of Saint Augustine's Seminary. He became a priest in 1939. In 1953 he became the first black bishop to ordain black priests in the United States.

Sources: *Ebony* 13 (December 1957): 18; 9 (August 1953): 25–33; Ochs, *Desegregating the Altar,* pp. 422–23.

1960 • On March 31, 1960, Laurean Rugambwa (1921–1997) became the first African cardinal in the Catholic church in modern times. Rugambwa was born near the Lake Victoria town of Bukoba in what was then called Tanganyika, East Africa. He came from a noble tribe, the Nsiba, and was baptized by missionaries when he was eight years old. After attending seminary in Uganda, he was ordained in 1943. He became the first bishop of the new Diocese of Rutaboa in 1951. In 1960 he became Bishop of Bukowa, and in that same year he was elevated to the Sacred College of Cardinals. In 1968 Rugambwa became Archbishop of Dar-es-Salaam. He was active in the Second Vatican Council early on and also was a strong voice for ecumenism, calling for collaboration with other Christian denominations.

Sources: *Contemporary Black Biography,* vol. 20, pp. 188–90; *Current Biography, 1960,* pp. 350–52; *Jet* 70 (31 March 1986): 18; *New York Times* (11 December 1997).

1962 • Martin de Porres (1579–1639) was the first black in the Americas to be canonized a saint by the Catholic church in the twentieth century. He was born in Peru, the illegitimate son of a Spanish knight and Anna, a freedwoman from Panama. In 1594 he became a Dominican lay brother, and won an exceptional reputation both for his work with the sick and poor and for his holiness.

Sources: Davis, *The History of Black Catholics in the United States,* pp. 25–27; Delaney, *Dictionary of Saints,* p. 477.

1966 • On January 6, 1966, Harold Robert Perry (1916–1991) became the first black Catholic bishop to serve in the United States in the twentieth century. He was the first since James A. Healy in 1875. He was named auxiliary bishop of New Orleans, Louisiana. The son of a rice mill worker and a cook, he was born in Lake Charles, Louisiana, the oldest of six children in a family of devout Catholics. He was ordained in 1944 after completing the course of the Divine Word Seminary in Louisiana. In 1938 Perry began major theological study at St. Mary's Seminary in Techny, Illinois, and then completed his studies at St. Augustine's Seminary in Bay St. Louis, Mississippi. He spent fourteen years in parish work, and then became rector of the seminary in 1958. Perry was active in secular as well as religious organizations. In 1963 President John F. Kennedy invited a group of 150 religious leaders of various faiths to discuss peaceful desegregation of public accommodations with him at the White House; Perry was a member of that group.

Sources: *Current Biography 1966*, pp. 311–12; *Ebony* 21(February 1966): 62–70; *Negro Almanac, 1989,* p. 1330; Ochs, *Desegregating the Altar,* p. 446; Smith, *Notable Black American Men,* pp. 927–30.

1968 • James P. Lyke (1939–1992) was the first black priest in Tennessee, when he served in the predominantly black Saint Thomas Parish in Memphis. At the time of his death from cancer, he was the second black archbishop of Northern Georgia. He was installed as archbishop of Atlanta on June 24, 1991, and became the highest-ranking black bishop in the U.S. Catholic church. He was leader in the creation of *Lead Me, Guide Me,* an African American Catholic hymnal. Lyke was born in Chicago, the youngest of seven children. He was raised poor in a housing project by his mother. Although his mother was Baptist, she sent him to a Catholic school when he was in the fourth grade, hoping to keep him out of trouble. He was ordained as a Franciscan priest in 1966. Lyke asked for an assignment in Tennessee in 1968 and became the first black Catholic priest regularly assigned to the state. He was ordained as bishop in 1979. In 1990 Lyke was sent to Atlanta as apostolic administrator and then as archbishop. The move was deliberate, to help the community overcome the trauma surrounding Archbishop Eugene A. Marino's improprieties and subsequent resignation.

Sources: The Georgia Bulletin, "Bishop Lyke Apponted As Archbishop," http://www.georgia bulletin.org/local/1991/05/02/a/?s=archbishop%20james%20lyke%20installed, accessed September 29, 2012. *Jet* 83 (18 January 1993): 54; Spencer, *Black Hymnody,* pp. 188–89; *The Tennessee Register* (4 January 1993): 1.

1968 • The first black Roman Catholic priest in the New York City Archdiocese, Harold A. Salmon, was installed on July 3 as vicar delegate for Harlem.

Sources: *The Black New Yorkers,* p. 196.

1977 • Joseph Lawson Howze (1925–) became the first black to head a diocese in the Catholic church in this century, when he became diocesan bishop of Biloxi, Mississippi. Howze was born in Daphne, Alabama, and received his bachelor's degree from Alabama State University in 1948. After teaching in the public schools of Mobile for some years, he felt a vocation to become a priest. He entered Epiphany Apostolic College in Newburgh, New York. On his graduation from Saint Bonaventure University in New York in 1959, he was ordained a priest for the Diocese of Raleigh on May 7 that year. He was consecrated Titular Bishop of Massita and Auxiliary Bishop of Natchez-Jackson on January 28, 1973. Howze became first Bishop of Biloxi on March 8, 1977, and was installed as Bishop of Biloxi on June 6, 1977.

Sources: *Crisis* 80 (April 1973): 141; *Ebony Success Library,* vol. 1, p. 160; *Negro Almanac,* p. 1328; The National Black Catholic Congress, NBCC Directory, "Most Reverend Joseph Lawson Howze, D.D.," http://www.nbccongress.org/aboutus/congress-directory/african-american-catholic-bishop-james-lawson-howze.asp, accessed September 29, 2012.

1981 • Carl Anthony Fisher (1945–1993) was named national coordinator of the Junior Catholic Daughters of the Americas, the first black to hold this position. Ordained in 1974, he became director of vocations for Saint Joseph's Society, and in 1982, the first black parish priest of Saint Francis Xavier Church in Baltimore, Maryland. Saint Francis Xavier was the first black parish, created in 1863. On December 19, 1986, Pope John Paul named him auxiliary bishop of Los Angeles, the first black Catholic bishop in the western United States.

Sources: Ochs, *Desegregating the Altar,* pp. 450–51; *Jet* 61 (22 October 1981): 24; 63 (6 December 1982): 24; 84 (27 September 1993): 12.

1982 • Sergio Carrillo was the first black priest ordained in the Archdiocese of Miami. Carrillo was a member of the failed Bay of Pigs invasion of Cuba in 1960.

Sources: *Jet* 62 (10 May 1982): 43.

1982 • Emerson J. Moore Jr. became the first black auxiliary bishop in the Archdiocese of New York. Earlier in 1982, he had been named the first black Episcopal vicar of Central Harlem. Moore had been named pastor of Saint Charles Borromeo in Harlem, in 1975, and had served in the archdiocese for eighteen years when he became bishop.

Sources: *Negro Almanac,* pp. 1431–32; *Jet* 62 (2 August 1982): 23.

1982 • Moses B. Anderson (1928–) was the first Catholic auxiliary bishop in the Archdiocese of Detroit. Anderson was fifty-four years old and had been a priest for twenty-four years. He graduated from Saint Edmond Seminary in Burlington, Vermont, and did graduate work at Xavier University and the University of Legion, Ghana.

Sources: *Jet* 63 (17 January 1983): 53; 63 (14 February 1983): 8; *Who's Who among Black Americans,* 26th ed., p. 32.

1987 • The first National Black Catholic Congress (NBCC) since 1894 met in Washington, D.C. The congress is comprised of member organizations that represent black American Roman Catholics who work with National Roman Catholic organizations. The black bishops elect one of its members to serve as president of the NBCC's Board of Trustees; two other members are elected to serve as trustees. Daniel Rudd founded the congress in 1899.

Sources: *Jet* 72 (15 June 1987): 7; The National Black Catholic Congress, www.nbccongress.org/aboutus/default.htm.

1988 • L. Warren Harvey was the first black priest in the Diocese of Little Rock, thus becoming the first in Arkansas.

Sources: *Jet* 74 (27 June 1988): 38.

1988 • Charles and Chester Smith were the first black identical twins ordained priests in the Catholic church.

Sources: *Jet* 74 (9 May 1988): 20.

1990 • The first black nun to head a parish in the United States was Cora Billings, in Richmond, Virginia. In 1999 she was Diocesan Director for Black Catholics.

Sources: Hine, *Black Women in America,* vol. II, p. 1332.

1993 • On May 5, J. Terry Steib (1940–) became the first black bishop in the state of Tennessee, when he was installed as fourth bishop of the Diocese of Memphis. Steib was born in Vacherie, Louisiana, and attended St. Augustine Divine Word Seminary in Bay St. Louis, Mississippi, from 1953 to 1957. He completed college at Divine Word Seminary in Conesus, New York, in 1961. In 1963 he completed philosophical studies at Divine Word Seminary in Techny, Illinois. Steib did post-graduate study at Divine Word Seminary from 1963 to 1967 and in 1973 received a master of arts degree from Xavier University in New Orleans. He became a priest on January 6, 1967, in Bay St. Louis. Then he was ordained auxiliary bishop for the Archdiocese of St. Louis and Titular Bishop of Sallaba in St. Louis on February 10, 1984. He was the third black to head a Catholic diocese.

Sources: "The Most Reverend J. Terry Steib, S.V.D.," http://www.cdom.org/bishop/bishop-home.htm. Accessed September 29, 2012.

1994 • George H. Clements (1932–), a Catholic priest who became known worldwide for founding his "One Church—One Child" adoption program in the 1980s, established

The First Black Catholic Archbishop

In 1988 Eugene Antonio Marino (1934–2000) became the first black archbishop in the United States, and so only the second ordinary bishop (a bishop who heads a diocese). Marino was a native of Biloxi, Mississippi, and educated at Saint Joseph's Seminary in Washington, D.C. He was ordained to the priesthood on June 9, 1962. Marino taught at Epiphany College from 1962 to 1968. From 1968 to 1971 he was spiritual director of St. Joseph's Seminary. He was elected vicar of the Josephites in 1971 and assisted the society further by serving as director of spiritual and educational formation. In September 1974 he became auxiliary bishop in Washington, D.C. He became archbishop of the Diocese of Atlanta from 1988 to May 1990 and was the ranking black member of the Catholic hierarchy when he stepped aside due to exhaustion and stress. In August, however, his inappropriate relationship with Vicki Long, a single mother, became public knowledge. He went into seclusion after he resigned and received spiritual direction as well as psychiatric and medical care for stress. Before his death, he spent his last five years as spiritual director in an outpatient program for clergy at St. Vincent's Hospital in Harrison, New York, while he lived at a Salesian Fathers home in New Rochelle.

Sources: Hornsby, *Chronology of African-American History*, p. 364; *Jet* 81 (18 November 1991): 57; 83 (5 April 1993): 32–37; Obituary, *Who's Who among African Americans*, 14th ed., p. 1473; Smith, *Notable Black American Men*, pp. 756–57; "Archbishop Marino Dies at New York Retreat Center," http://www.archatl.com/ministries/obcm/memoriam/marino.htm, accessed September 29, 2012.

the "One Church—One Addict" program this year. Clements saw the program was as an example of a private, community-based leadership needed to defeat drug use. He called for community institutions, religious congregations, schools, health care and treatment facilities, law enforcement agencies, and coalitions to come together and stay involved in the program. Clements was born in Chicago and received his bachelor's and master's degrees from St. Mary of the Lake Seminary. In 1957 he became the first black ordained in Quigley Seminary. In addition to serving as pastor of Holy Angels Roman Catholic Church in Chicago, he has been active in a number of community organizations, including the Afro-American Firemen's League and Operation Breadbasket. He also organized the Black Clergy Caucus.

Sources: *Jet* 85 (14 March 1994): 35; *Who's Who among African Americans,* 14th ed., p. 245.

1996 • John H. Ricard (1940–) became the first black to head the Catholic Relief Services, the second largest aid provider in the world, giving aid to over eighty countries. He was born in Baton Rouge, Louisiana, and raised in a family of eight children. He attended the Josephite College Seminary in Newburgh, New York, and completed his theological training at St. Joseph's Seminary in Washington, D.C. He was ordained to the priesthood on May 25, 1968. After that, he received his master's degree from Tulane University in 1970 and his doctorate from the Catholic University of America in 1983. After Richard's Episcopal ordination on July 2, 1984, he was Auxiliary Bishop for the Archdiocese of Baltimore, and one of Baltimore's three auxiliary bishops. He remained in Baltimore for twelve years, serving as Urban Vicar and Regional Bishop. He had responsibility for parishes in Baltimore. Richard moved to Florida and was installed as the fourth bishop of the Diocese of Pensacola-Tallahassee, on March 13, 1997.

Sources: *Jet* 89 (5 February 1996): 12; "Most Reverend John H. Ricard, SSJ." http://www .nbccongress.org/aboutus/congress-directory/african-american-catholic-bishop-john-ricard.asp, accessed September 29, 2012.

2001 • Bishop Wilton D. Gregory (1947–) became the first black president of the United States Conference of Catholic Bishops, at the fall meeting in Washington, D.C. He became the public voice of the bishops and presided over their meetings. He serves a three-year term. For the past three years he was vice president of the conference. Gregory hoped to change the church's image and to project a new image of an inclusive and multicultural church. According to the *Chicago Tribune,* quoted in *Jet* magazine, he said "It is my fondest prayer that my election is an expression of the love of the Catholic church for people of color." Gregory was born on Chicago's South Side and graduated from Niles College of Loyola University (B.A., 1969), St. Mary of the Lake Seminary (S.T.B., 1971; M.Div., 1973; S.T.L., 1974), and the Pontifical Liturgical Institute of Saint Anselmo in Rome, Italy (S.L.D., 1980). He was ordained in 1973. He later taught at St. Mary of the Lake Seminary. He was Titular Bishop of Oliva. In 1983 he became the first black auxiliary bishop of the Archdiocese of Chicago. He held that post until 1993, when Pope John Paul II named him Bishop of Belleville, located in Southern Illinois.

Sources: *Jet* 100 (3 December 2001): 35; "The Most Reverend Wilton D. Gregory," http://www.archatl.com/archbishops/gregory/; *Who's Who among African Americans,* 26th ed., p. 499.

Christian Church (Disciples of Christ)

1853 • Alexander Cross, a former slave from Kentucky, was the first missionary of any race sent to Africa by this denomination. After the Christian Missionary Society called for a qualified person to serve Liberia as a missionary, the society chose Cross. He was a pious man and a gifted public speaker; first, however, he needed to be freed from his slave master. Although he could have been sold for $1,200, the church bought Cross's freedom for $530. The church also helped him prepare for the missionary assignment by providing him books and tutelage to help improve his education. Cross arrived in Africa in winter 1853. He over-exerted himself soon after his arrival and quickly fell victim to the climate and died.

Sources: *Encyclopedia of Black America,* p. 226.

1867 • The ministries of the National Convocation of the Christian Church, or the black disciple conventions of the Disciples of Christ, were organized beginning this year.

Sources: Jordan, *Two Races in One Fellowship,* p. 51.

1874 • The first black state group of Disciples of Christ was organized in Missouri in 1874. Ten years later, the "colored" Disciples organized its first state group in Mississippi, ten years before other states established such groups. States that followed were Arkansas, Alabama, Georgia, Illinois, Indiana, Kentucky, North Carolina, Ohio, South Carolina, Tennessee, Texas, Virginia, and West Virginia.

Sources: Jordan, *Two Races in One Fellowship,* p. 51.

1982 • Cynthia Lynette Hale (1952–) became the first woman president of the predominantly black National Convocation of the Christian Church (Disciples of Christ). She held that post until 1988. Hale was chaplain at the Federal Correctional Institute at Butner, Alabama, and others in Colorado and North Carolina, becoming the first female chaplain to serve in all-male correctional institutions. Since 1986 she has been pastor of the Ray of Home Christian Church in Decatur, Georgia. Born in Roanoke, Virginia, Hale received her Bachelor of Arts degree in 1975 from Hollins College (now Hollins University) in Virginia, her Masters of Divinity in 1979 from Duke Divinity School in North Carolina, and Doctor of Divinity in 1991 from Union Theological Seminary in Dayton.

Sources: *Jet* 62 (30 August 1982): 24; *Who's Who among African Americans,* 26th ed., p. 512.

Church of England

1704 • Elias Neau (?–1722), an agent of the Anglican Society for the Propagation of the Gospel in Foreign Parts, opened a catechism school for blacks in New York City. In 1720

Black Disciples of Christ Conventions

Date Founded	Location
1867	Southern District of Churches of Christ (Disciples of Christ)
1867	National Convention of Disciples (colored), Rufus Conrad, founder
1871	South Carolina Christian Missionary Convention
1872	Western District of Churches of Christ (Disciples of Christ)
1872	Kentucky Christian Missionary Convention
1880	Alabama Christian Missionary Convention
1881	Texas Christian Missionary Convention
1882	Goldsboro/Raleigh Assembly, Goldsboro, West of Tar River
1882	Piedmont Tri-State District Convention
1887	Mississippi Christian Missionary Convention
1892	Western District of Churches of Christ (Disciples of Christ)
1910	Washington and Norfolk District of Churches of Christ (Disciples of Christ), East of Tar River

Sources: "National Convocation of the Christian Church (Disciples of Christ), "History," http://www .nationalconvocation.org/History/tabid/916/Default.aspx, accessed September 29, 2012.

the school had thirty-five women and forty-nine men; all but four women were slaves. It survived after Neau's death until the American Revolution.

Sources: *Negro Almanac*, p. 3; Raboteau, *Slave Religion*, pp. 117–18; Smith, *Climbing Jacob's Ladder*, pp. 26, 28.

1743 • The Society for the Propagation of the Gospel in Foreign Parts established in Charleston, South Carolina, was the first known school to train black missionaries. Two blacks, Harry and Andrew, were in charge and the school lasted until 1764, when Harry, who was the teacher, died. Andrew had "proved a profligate" some time earlier and been dismissed.

Sources: Raboteau, *Slave Religion*, pp. 116–17; Smith, *Climbing Jacob's Ladder*, p. 28.

1968 • Coretta Scott King (1927–2006) was the first woman of any race to preach at Saint Paul's Cathedral, London, England.

Sources: Alford, *Famous First Blacks*, p. 21; Hine, *Notable Black American Women*, pp. 631–34; Smith, *Notable Black American Women*, pp. 631–34.

Colored (Christian) Methodist Episcopal Church

1870 • W. H. Miles and Richard H. Vanderhorst were the first bishops of the Colored (now Christian) Methodist Episcopal Church. This denomination was formed by blacks leaving the Methodist Episcopal Church (South).

Sources: *Encyclopedia of American Religions*, vol. 1, pp. 195–96; Lincoln and Mamiya, *The Black Church in the African American Experience*, p. 62; Smith, *Climbing Jacob's Ladder*, pp. 123–24.

Coretta Scott King

Congregationalists

1693 • Cotton Mather (1663–1728), the Boston cleric, drew up "Rules for the Society of Negroes" for a group of blacks who were seeking to hold their own prayer meetings on Sunday evenings. These rules are the first known example of this kind of ethnic religious association, which would not, at this date, be a separate church solely under black direction.

Sources: Smith, *Climbing Jacob's Ladder*, pp. 26–27.

Lemuel Haynes

1785 • Lemuel Haynes (1753–1833) was the first black Congregational minister. Haynes was born in Connecticut. He never knew his black father, and his white mother refused to recognize him. Haynes was very well educated by the man to whom he was bound as a servant. Haynes, who served in the Revolutionary army, was ordained in 1785 and became the pastor of a white congregation in Torrington, Connecticut. In 1788 he became pastor in Rutland, Vermont, moving to Manchester, Vermont, in 1819 and to Granville, New York, in 1822. He was the first black to receive an honorary degree, in 1804, when Middlebury College in Vermont gave him an honorary Master of Arts degree. In April 1841 the abolitionist Samuel Ringgold Ward (1817–1866?) would also become minister of a white Congregationalist congregation located in South Butler, New York—a position he held until 1843, when he resigned because of ill health.

Sources: Logan and Winston, *Dictionary of American Negro Biography,* pp. 300–1 (Haynes); pp. 631–32 (Ward); *Negro Year Book,* 1913, p. 115; Smith, *Climbing Jacob's Ladder,* p. 31; Smith, *Notable Black American Men,* pp. 532–33; Cooley, *Sketches of the Life and Character of the Rev. Lemuel Hayes.*

1820 • The Dixwell Congregational Church in New Haven, Connecticut, was the first all-black Congregational church. Francis L. Cardozo, who made a mark in South Carolina politics during Reconstruction, was one of its pastors. The number of black Congregationalists was quite small, but the influence of the denomination as a whole on black life is immense. Through the American Missionary Association, Congregationalists founded or supported some five hundred schools in the South after the Civil War. These include surviving black schools (most now renamed) of such eminence as Fisk University in Tennessee, Atlanta Christian College in Georgia, Hampton Institute in Virginia, Tougaloo College in Mississippi, and Dillard College in Louisiana.

Sources: *Encyclopedia of Black America,* p. 286; Gatewood, *Aristocrats of Color,* p. 288.

1967 • Joseph H. Evans became the first black national secretary of the United Church of Christ.

Sources: Garrett, *Famous First Facts about Negroes,* pp. 191–92.

1973 • Margaret Austin Haywood (1912–2004) became the first woman to head the United Church of Christ and the first black woman to lead a major religious denomination in the United States. Haywood held the post at the same time that she was senior judge of the superior court of the District of Columbia. Born in Knoxville, Tennessee, she moved with her family to Washington, D.C., while she was a young child. She graduated from Terrell Law School in Washington. She was in general law practice from 1940 to 1972 and a member of the District of Columbia city council from 1967 to 1972. She was associate judge of the superior court from 1972 to 1982 and then was elevated to senior judge.

Sources: *Contemporary Black Biography,* vol. 24, pp. 73–75.

1987 • Kwame Osei was the first black to head the Potomac Association Conference of the United Church of Christ in Washington, D.C.

Sources: *Jet* 72 (27 July 1987): 38.

1991 • Denise Page Hood became the first black woman to chair the Executive Council of the United Church of Christ.

Sources: *Jet* 80 (5 August 1991): 10.

Early Christians

35? C. E. • The first person identified as a black convert to Christianity was the unnamed Nubian eunuch, who was the treasurer of the Candace, either the queen-mother or a queen ruling in her own right. This man was converted by Philip the Deacon.

Sources: Acts 8: 26–40.

Episcopalians

1794 • On October 12, 1794, the original African Free Society building in Philadelphia was dedicated as Saint Thomas' African Episcopal Church, the first black Protestant Episcopal church. Absalom Jones (1746–1818) was unofficial leader of the church and became lay reader in this year. He was ordained as the first black deacon in the denomination on August 6, 1795, and became pastor of Saint Thomas. He became the first black American priest in the denomination in 1804. He was also the first black minister of any denomination to be ordained in the United States. Jones was born a slave in Sussex, Delaware. A house servant, he received tips that enabled him to buy a primer, a spelling book, and a copy of the New Testament. He begged reading instructions from anyone who would help him. Jones moved to Philadelphia in 1762, along with his mother and six siblings who were sold. For a brief period he was allowed to attend school at night where he learned enough mathematics to help him in trade. After trying to purchase his freedom beginning in 1778, on October 1, 1784, he was finally manumitted but remained with his former master as a wage worker. Around 1786 Jones became a licensed Methodist lay preacher and in the following May he joined Richard Allen and African American religious leaders in forming the Free African Society. During the smallpox epidemic of 1793, Jones and Allen worked together to collect and bury those who had died from the disease.

Sources: Logan and Winston, *Dictionary of American Negro Biography,* pp. 262–364; Lincoln and Mamiya, *The Black Church in the African American Experience,* pp. 51–52; Smith, *Climbing Jacob's Ladder,* pp. 36–37; Smith, *Notable Black American Men,* pp. 644–45.

1819 • On July 3, 1819, Saint Phillip's African Church became the first black Protestant Episcopal church in New York City. Its leader was Peter Williams Jr. (1780–1840), who became the second black American priest on July 10, 1826.

Sources: Baer and Singer, *African-American Religion in the Twentieth Century,* p. 104; Logan and Winston, *Dictionary of American Negro Biography,* 660–61; *Encyclopedia of Black America,* p. 375; Smith, *Climbing Jacob's Ladder,* pp. 47–48, 50.

1828 • The Protestant Episcopal Church of Saint Thomas in Philadelphia was the first black church to own an organ. This church also introduced the trained choir into services, placing it among the leaders in the development of new musical styles of worship taking place in Protestant churches at the time. The introduction of a trained choir in the African Methodist Episcopal mother church in Philadelphia, in 1841–42, caused a struggle that split the congregation.

Sources: Smith, *Climbing Jacob's Ladder,* p. 43; Southern, *The Music of Black Americans,* pp. 127–28.

1829 • William Levingston was the first black priest to do missionary work in the South. He established Saint James' Church in Baltimore, Maryland.

Sources: *Encyclopedia of Black America,* p. 375.

1854 • After determining that a separate parish for blacks should be organized, the Church of the Good Shepherd was formed, becoming the first Episcopal congregation in the Diocese of Alabama.

Sources: Badger, *A Life in Ragtime,* p. 12.

1863 • Peter Williams Cassey (1831–1927), a free-black and son of a prominent Philadelphia family, became the first person ordained on the West Coast, at the infant Trinity Church in San Jose in September. He was confirmed at the church on April 26, 1863. He had moved to the Bay Area with the idea of improving the condition of blacks in that area. He established himself quickly as an industrious missionary. Perhaps in that same year Cassey founded a Sunday school for black youth and then moved swiftly to expand the school. At that time the San Jose School District denied blacks admission to local schools. Realizing the need for a high school for poor black youth, Cassey founded St. Philip's Mission School for Negroes in December 1862. At first the Diocese of California funded the school and later the San Jose School District provided appropriations. Cassey also added $3,000 of his own money. Although the school was never a financial success, it enjoyed a high reputation and continued to attract students from as far away as Portland, Oregon. An average of twenty-two students a year for both the day and night programs attended. Cassey's wife, Anna, supported his efforts, especially the Sunday School. Cassey's commitment to blacks continued and by 1868 he had founded St. Philips Mission. This was the first Episcopal house of worship for blacks in the Diocese. Although financial obligations mounted, the mission remained open. Cassey aided other black congregations such as St. Cyprian's Mission and Christ Mission in San Francisco. After Cassey was called to St. Cyprian's in New Bern, North Carolina, to become the first black priest there, the missions and schools that he had founded soon closed. By then local schools were integrated and parishioners migrated elsewhere.

Sources: Blackpast.org, "Cassey, Peter William (1831-?)," http://www.blackpast.org/?q= aaw/cassey-peter-william-1831, accessed September 29, 2012.

James Holly

1874 • James Theodore Holly (1829–1911) became the founder and first bishop of the Protestant Episcopal Church in Haiti, a position he held until his death in 1911. As rector of Saint Luke's in New Haven, Connecticut, he baptized W.E.B. DuBois in 1868. He was consecrated on November 8, 1874. Holly championed black emigration and dreamed of establishing a colony in Haiti. His consecration made him the first black bishop in any Episcopal church. His church was absorbed into the Episcopal Missionary Diocese in 1913. In more recent years, Lafond Lapointe tried to re-establish the church after the fall of the Duvalier regime.

Sources: Logan and Winston, *Dictionary of American Negro Biography*, pp. 319–20; *Encyclopedia of American Religions*, vol. 1, p. 70; *Encyclopedia of Black America*, pp. 282, 284, 375–76; Smith, *Notable Black American Men*, pp. 560–63.

1883 • The Conference of Churchworkers Among Colored People was the first black caucus in the Protestant Episcopal Church. The leader in its foundation was Alexander Crummell (1819–1898). The modern successor organization is the Union of Black Episcopalians, formed in 1968.

Sources: Baer and Singer, *African-American Religion in the Twentieth Century*, p. 104; Logan and Winston, *Dictionary of American Negro Biography*, pp. 145–47.

1885 • Samuel David Ferguson (1842–1916) became the first missionary bishop of the Protestant Episcopal Church and the first black to sit in the American House of Bishops. He served the House of Bishops until his death in August 1916. He was also the first black bishop of Liberia this year. The first suffragan bishops (auxiliary bishops who are given special missions) would not be elected until 1918, and the first diocesan bishop until 1970. Ferguson also founded Cutting College.

Sources: *Encyclopedia of Black America*, pp. 376–77; *Negro Almanac, 1989*, p. 1425.

1918 • Edward T. Demby (1869–1957) and Henry Beard Delany (1858–1928) were the first black suffragan bishops (auxiliary bishops who are given special missions) of the Protestant Episcopal Church. Delany was the father of Sadie and Bessie Delany, who became prominent in 1993 with the publication of their autobiography, *Having Our Say*. In 1885 Samuel David Ferguson became a missionary bishop, but the first diocesan bishop would not be consecrated until 1970. American blacks had earlier been named bishops of foreign dioceses: James Theodore Holly, bishop of Haiti (1874); and Samuel David Ferguson, bishop of Liberia (1885). Samuel Crowther, a native African, was made bishop of Nigeria in 1864.

Sources: *Encyclopedia of Black America*, p. 377; *Negro Year Book*, 1918–19, p. 23; Smith, *Notable Black American Women*, Book II, pp. 170–73.

1969 • Dillard Robinson, with his position as dean of the cathedral in Newark, New Jersey, became the first black dean in an Episcopal cathedral.

Sources: *Encyclopedia of Black America*, p. 377.

The First Black Episcopal Bishop

In 1969 John M. Burgess (1909–2003) was elected presiding bishop of the Protestant Episcopal Church. He was also elected bishop of the Diocese of Massachusetts. With these accomplishments, he was the first black priest elected, consecrated, and instituted as a diocesan bishop in the entire Episcopal church. He was presiding bishop from 1970 until his retirement in 1976. While other black priests were consecrated as Episcopal bishops before his appointment, their activities were restricted to blacks in America and the jurisdiction in Haiti and Liberia. Burgess was born in Grand Rapids, Michigan, and received his bachelor's and master's degrees from the University of Michigan in 1930 and 1931. His summer job as a social worker led him into the ministry. In 1934 he graduated from the Episcopal Seminary with a bachelor's degree in divinity. Burgess was ordained to the priesthood and then assigned to St. Philip's church in Grand Rapids. There he was active in the Conference of Church Work among Colored People and in 1937 attended the Cincinnati meeting of the conference. The next year he became vicar of the Mission of St. Simon the Cyrene in Lincoln Heights, Ohio. Burgess relocated to Washington, D.C., in 1946, when he became the first denominational chaplain at Howard University and directed the Canterbury House on campus. He became the first black canon of Washington Cathedral in 1951. His elevation in the church continued and on December 8, 1962, Burgess was consecrated suffragan bishop of Massachusetts. He was elected bishop coadjutor in 1969 and became diocesan bishop the following year, securing his place in the church's history as the first black diocesan bishop. After retiring, Burgess joined the faculty of Yale University's Berkeley Divinity School.

Sources: Toppin, *Biographical History of Blacks,* pp. 261–62; Wormley, *Many Shades of Black,* p. 331; *Negro Almanac,* p. 1326; Smith, *Notable Black American Men,* pp. 156–58.

1970 • George Daniel Browne (1933–1993) was consecrated on August 6 this year and became the first native diocesan bishop of Liberia. He was also the first missionary bishop directly elected by a diocese. Browne was born in Garroway, Liberia, and graduated from Cuttington College and Virginia Theological Seminary. He became known for leading the church in Liberia toward becoming self-sufficient and to gain independence from the American Church and membership in the Province of West Africa.

Sources: "The Right Reverend George Daniel Browne, 1933–1993," http://www.episcopal archives.org/Afro-Anglican_history/exhibit/leadership/browne.php

1971 • The first indigenous bishop of Haiti was Luc Anatole Jacques Garnier (1928–1999). Born in Maissade, Haiti, he served several rural parishes. He was rector of the Church of the Epiphany in Port-au-Prince and Holy Trinity Catholic. He was also executive administrator of the diocese. He was consecrated on April 20, 1971.

Sources: "Luc Anatole Jacques Garnier 1928–1999," http://www.ecusa.anglican.org/black/ 109403_58981_ENG_HTM.htm. Accessed September 29, 2012.

1972 • Lemuel Barnett Shirley (1916–1999) became the first native Panamanian ordained priest and the first indigenous bishop. The fourth bishop of Panama and the Canal Zone, Shirley was consecrated archdeacon of Panama on February 19, 1972.

Sources: Episcopal Church Archives, "Lemuel Barnett Shirley," http://archive.episcopal church.org/black/109403_58987_ENG_HTM.htm. Accessed September 29, 2012.

1972 • The first indigenous bishop of the Dominican Republic was Teseforo Alexander Isaac (1929–), who was consecrated on March 9 this year. He was born in San Pedro de Macoris, Dominican Republic, and became a school chaplain and rural priest. After that, he was called to San Andres Church in Santo Domingo.

Sources: "Black Bishops of the Episcopal Church," http://archive.episcopalchurch.org/black/109403_111315_ENG_HTM.htm.

1976 • H. Irving Mayson (1926–) was the first Episcopal suffragan bishop (an auxiliary bishop who is given a special mission) in Michigan.

Sources: *Ebony* 11 (March 1956): 23; *Jet* 51 (4 November 1976): 20.

1977 • On January 8, 1977, Pauli Murray (1910–1985) became the first woman ordained a priest in the Protestant Episcopal Church. She was also a lawyer, poet, scholar, author, educator, administrator, and civil rights and women's movement activist. Murray was born in Baltimore, Maryland, and christened Anna Pauline Murray. After her mother died in 1914, Murray moved to Durham, North Carolina, and lived with her aunt and maternal grandparents. Ill with the effects of typhoid fever, her father was unable to care for his five children. Murray graduated from Hunter College in New York City in 1933, one of four blacks students in a class of 247 women. She worked for the Works Progress Administration (WPA) in the 1930s, serving as a teacher in the Remedial Reading Project in New York City's public schools. She later was employed in the WPA's Workers' Educational Project and honed her skills as a writer. The friendship that she developed with Stephen Vincent Benêt around this time was beneficial, for he guided and encouraged her as a writer and urged her to write about her family. Her family's history was published in 1956 as *Proud Shoes.* As early as the 1930s, Murray was active in movements to foster racial and gender equality in the United States. In fall 1938, for example, she sought admission to the graduate school at the University of North Carolina but was denied admission due to her race. Her efforts became public news nationwide and were the first of its kind to receive wide attention. Ironically, her material grandmother, Cornelia Smith Fitzgerald, was born as a result of a racially mixed relationship in the Chapel Hill area, and her white great-grandfather, Hames S. Smith, had served on the University of North Carolina's board of trustees. In addition, early on the Smith family created a permanent trust for students at the university. In 1978 the university offered to award Murray an honorary degree; she refused the degree because the university system refused to implement an appropriate plan to desegregate its sixteen campuses. Murray's interest in civil rights was demonstrated also in March 1940, when she and a friend, Adelene Mcbean, were arrested in Virginia for refusing to move to the back of a Greyhound bus, into a broken seat. While in jail for three days, the women drafted a "Statement of Fact." In 1946 vindication came for the two women in the *Morgan v. Virginia* case that declared the state's Jim Crow statute invalid. In 1941 Murray entered the law school at Howard University and graduated in 1944. Her senior thesis that analyzed the "separate but equal" doctrine in American education was used to help win the *Brown v. Board of Education of Topeka* case that broke down racial barriers in America's public schools. In 1945 Murray received her Master of Law degree from the Balt Hall of Law at the University of California and was admitted to the California bar. In January 1946 she became the first black deputy attorney general of California. Continuing her education, in 1965 Murray received the Doctor of Juridical Science from Yale University's law school, the first person to receive this degree from Yale. Murray became active in women's rights and in October 1966 she was one of the thirty-two women who founded the National Organization for Women (NOW). She left the church in 1966, because it refused to include women in active roles in worship services. However, she returned to the church the next year and after serving in administrative and teaching positions in academia, she enrolled in divinity school. In 1976 Murray received the Master of Divinity degree from the General Theological Seminary and was ordained a deacon of the Episcopal Church. She was ordained an Episcopal priest on January 8, 1977, at the National Cathedral in Washington, D.C., the first black woman ordained a priest in the church's two-hundred-year history. Murray's life is captured in her book *Song in a Weary Throat: An American Pilgrimage,* published posthumously in 1987.

Sources: *Encyclopedia of Black America,* p. 584; Smith, *Notable Black American Women,* pp. 783–88; Hine, *Black Women in America,* vol. 2, pp. 825–26.

1977 • John T. Walker (1925–1989) was the first black bishop of the Episcopal Church in the Diocese of Washington, installed on September 24, 1977. He had been named coadjutor in 1971. In 1977 a statue of Walker was set to be established at the Washington National Cathedral. Born in Barnesville, Georgia, he became a priest in 1955, after taking a Bachelor of Divinity degree from Virginia Theological Seminary, where he had been the first black graduate in 1954. Walker's great-grandfather had founded the African Methodist Episcopal Church in Barnesville.

Sources: *Ebony Success Library,* vol. 1, p. 316; *Encyclopedia of Black America,* p. 830; *Jet* 77 (16 October 1989): 7; 96 (4 October 1999): 10; *Negro Almanac,* p. 1418.

1982 • Winnie McKenzie Bolle was the first black, and the first woman, priest in the Diocese of Southeast Florida. A fifty-seven-year-old native of Jamaica, Bolle is a graduate of the Divinity School of the Pacific, Berkeley, California.

Sources: *Jet* 62 (12 July 1982): 30.

1982 • Gayle Elizabeth Harris was the first black woman priest in the Diocese of Newark, New Jersey. The fifth woman ordained in the Episcopal Church, Harris is an early black graduate of the Divinity School of the Pacific, Berkeley, California.

Sources: *Jet* 62 (14 June 1982): 38.

1982 • Sandra Antoinette Wilson became the first woman priest of the Protestant Episcopal Church in the New York City Archdiocese on January 25, 1982.

Sources: *Jet* 61 (15 February 1982): 32; *Negro Almanac,* p. 43.

1985 • The first indigenous bishop of Nicaragua was Sturdie Wyman Downs (1947–). Born on Corn Island, Nicaragua, he became rector of All Saints' church in Managua. He was consecrated bishop on February 9 this year.

Sources: "Black Bishops of the Episcopal Church," http://archive.episcopalchurch.org/black/109403_111315_ENG_HTM.htm.

1989 • Barbara Clementine Harris (1930–) became the first woman Anglican bishop in the world. Although she was elected on September 24, 1988, she took office the next year. On February 12, 1989, she was consecrated suffragan bishop (an auxiliary bishop who is given a special mission) in the Diocese of Massachusetts. As a woman, her election to a post held only by men from the time of Saint Peter, aroused the same controversy as the ordination of eleven women priests did in 1974. This earlier event encouraged Harris to prepare for the priesthood to which she herself was ordained in 1980. Harris felt a call to the church while she was a young child growing up in Philadelphia. While a teenager, she was baptized and confirmed at St. Barnabas Church in the Germantown section of Philadelphia. She completed college courses and special training for mid-career clergy recruits at Villanova University from 1977 to 1979 and received a Doctor of Sacred Theology degree from Hobart and Smith College in 1981. She was ordained to the diaconate in 1979, and from 1979 to 1980 she served as deacon-in-training at the Church of the Advocate. She was ordained to the priesthood in 1980. From 1980 to 1984 Harris was priest-in-charge at St. Augustine-of-Hippo in Norristown, Pennsylvania, and interim rector at the Church of the Advocate, the position she held when she was elected as suffragan bishop of the Massachusetts diocese. Harris's election stirred controversy—she was divorced, female, an advocate of women's rights, and had a different educational background than suffragan bishops usually possessed. Harris survived the controversy, however, and became an effective religious leader and catalyst for social justice.

Sources: Hine, *Black Women in America,* p. 537–38; Hornsby, *Chronology of African-American History,* p. 382; *Negro Almanac,* pp. 105–6; Smith, *Notable Black American Women,* pp. 462–66; *Contemporary Black Biography,* vol. 12, pp. 79–81.

1991 • As suffragan bishop of the Diocese of Los Angeles, Chester Lovelle Talton became the first black Protestant Episcopal bishop in the West on January 26, 1991.

Sources: *State of Black America 1992,* p. 362.

1992 • Nathan Dwight Baxter (1948–) became the first black dean of Washington National Cathedral in Washington, D.C. Baxter graduated from Lancaster Theological Seminary in 1976 and received the Doctor of Ministry degree from that seminary in 1984. He received a Doctor of Sacred Theology degree from Dickenson College and a Doctor of Divinity degree from St. Paul's College. He served as chaplain and professor of religious studies at St. Paul's College and then became dean and associate professor of church ministry at Lancaster Theological Seminary. After that, Baxter was administrative dean and associate professor of Pastoral Theology at Episcopal Divinity School.

Sources: *Jet* 81 (2 March 1992): 8; *Who's Who among African Americans,* 14th ed., p. 76.

1997 • Anna Martin Henderson (1943?–) was named vicar at St. Anselm's Episcopal Church in Nashville, Tennessee, becoming the first black woman priest at the church and the only black priest among eighty in the Middle Tennessee diocese. She was also the only black woman and the fifth black among more than two hundred Episcopal priests in the state. St. Anselm's is one of Nashville's two black Episcopal churches. During her life in the clergy, Henderson faced racism from white congregations and sexism from black congregations. As circuit priest at the all-white blue-collar Episcopal church in Red Bank, New Jersey, where she served before moving to Nashville, she experienced resistance from some members who left the church rather than remain under her leadership. She knew as well that many black Episcopal churches resisted women as leaders, having never worked with women as priests. Henderson graduated from St. Augustine's College, an historically black Episcopal school located in Raleigh, North Carolina. While there she vaguely considered entering the Episcopal ministry and in 1964 she felt her call to the church. She served in the Peace Corps in San Juan, Puerto Rico. Henderson became a third-generation Episcopal priest.

Sources: *Tennessean* (26 March 1997).

2000 • The first black elected to lead an Episcopal diocese in Michigan was Wendell N. Gibbs Jr. (1954–). He succeeded the former bishop in October 2000. The Michigan diocese is comprised of ninety-seven churches. Gibbs was born in Washington, D.C., and received a Bachelor of Arts degree from Towson State University in 1977 and a Master of Divinity degree from Seabury-Western Theological Seminary in 1987. He served Episcopal ministries in Rockford, Illinois; Utica, New York; and Four Point Parish in New York State. Before he moved to Michigan, he was rector of St. Andrew's Church in Cincinnati. He was ordained a deacon in June 1987 and as priest in December that year. A former Roman Catholic monk, he was consecrated as Bishop Coadjutor of the Diocese of Michigan on February 5, 2000, and seated as the tenth bishop on November 4.

Sources: *Jet* 97 (1 November 1999): 31; The Episcopal Diocese of Michigan, "The Rt. Rev. Wendell N. Gibbs, Jr." http://www.edomi.org/home20/governance/the-rt-rev-wendell-n-gibbs-jr.html. Accessed September 29, 2012.

2000 • The first Episcopalian diocese in the South to elect a black bishop was in North Carolina. Michael Bruce Curry (1953–), a Baltimore minister, was chosen to oversee 250 pastors and 33,000 members; he was installed on June 17. Although blacks in the South have served as suffragan bishops (auxiliary bishops who are given special missions), never before had a black served as bishop. Curry spent twelve years as rector of St. James Episcopal Church in Baltimore, where he helped to rebuild the church leveled by fire. Curry was born in Chicago and received a Bachelor of Arts degree from Hobart College in 1975 and a Master of Divinity from Yale University Divinity School in 1978. He was rector of St. Stephen's Episcopal Church from 1978 to 1982 and served on the racism staff of the Diocese of Southern Ohio from 1982 to 1987. He was also rector and pastor of St. Simon of Cyrene Church from 1982 to 1988, before moving to St. James Episcopal Church.

Sources: *New York Times* (12 February 2000); *Who's Who among African Americans,* 26th ed., p. 295.

2008 • Eugene T. Sutton was elected the fifteenth bishop of the Episcopal Diocese of Maryland, becoming the first black to hold that post. He was elected on the first ballot during a special convention of the diocese. In his role, Sutton leads 116 parishes and 50,000 members located in Baltimore and in ten area counties. For the past eight years, he was canon pastor and director of the Cathedral Center for Prayer and Pilgrimage at the National Cathedral.

Sources: *Jet* 113 (21 July 2008): 22.

Ethiopians

1920 • The militant claim that blacks were Ethiopians who would fulfill a Biblical prophecy to return to their homeland, first received national attention when Grover Cleveland Redding set an American flag afire during a parade by his movement in Chicago. Whites tried to intervene and the ensuing struggle left two persons dead. Redding's associate in founding the group was R. D. Jonas.

Sources: Baer and Singer, *African-American Religion in the Twentieth Century,* p. 113.

Faith Healing

1860s–70s • Elizabeth Mix [Mrs. Edward Mix], who had been healed of tuberculosis, became the nation's first black healing evangelist around this time. Mix was so well respected for her accomplishments that doctors sent their patients to her for prayer. She had been healed under the ministry of Ethan O. Allen who, in 1846, became the first American to associate Christian perfection with divine healing. He, too, had been healed of tuberculosis while in his late twenties, and later became the first American to practice faith healing ministry full time. On February 27, 1879, Mix offered prayer to Carrie Judd [Montgomery] (1858–1946), an invalid white woman from Buffalo, New York. Within a few months Judd was healed and told her story in the *Buffalo Commercial Advertiser* on October 20, 1880. Judd became a prominent Pentecostal as a minister-teacher, writer, and social worker in Oakland, California. Mix, who was a Baptist, married a Baptist minister and lived in Wolcottville (later called Torrington), Connecticut.

Sources: Burgess and McGee, *Dictionary of Pentecostal and Charismatic Movements,* pp. 357–58; *The Life and Teachings of Carrie Judd Montgomery, The Prayer of Faith,* pp. 12–17, 118–19; Montgomery, *"Under His Wings:" The Story of My Life,* pp. 54–60.

Faithful Central Bible Church

2001 • One of the largest churches in California, Faithful Central Bible Church of Inglewood, bought Great Western Forum, the former home of the Los Angeles Lakers, making the facility the only black-owned venue of its kind. It is also the first entertainment venue to be owned by a faith-based organization. The church was created in 1983 and since then has seen dramatic growth. Membership in the mega-church reached 11,000 in 1998 and continued to grow. The church has used the 17,600-seat Forum from 2000 until this printing, but in 2012 it was sold to Madison Square Garden, Inc., which plans to renovate it and use it again as a venue for concerts. On Easter Sunday 2002 the service lasted three-and-one-half hours and drew 13,000 worshippers. Headed by Bishop Kenneth C. Ulmer, the church reaches out to a constituency that is diverse and multiracial. Ulmer has been prominent on the local black political scene and was closely associated with Tom Bradley when the latter was major of Los Angeles. Ulmer also served on the board of Rebuild Los Angeles to restore the city after the civil unrest. When he arrived in 1982 the church was Baptist and had less than 200 members. Since then it affiliated with the Macedonia International Bible Fellowship and offered three Sunday services. Some 2,500 people attend each service. Ulmer, a prolific and widely sought speaker, graduated from the University of Illinois in June 1969. He received his Ph.D. from Grace Graduate School of Theology in Long Beach (June 1986) and his D.Min. from United Theological Seminary (May 1999). He was ordained at Mount Moriah Missionary Baptist Church in Los Angeles in 1977. Two years later Ulmer founded the Macedonia Bible Baptist Church in San Pedro. He has served as instructor at several seminaries in the area.

Sources: Faithful Central Bible Church, https://www.faithfulcentral.com, accessed October 12, 2012. *Jet* 99 (16 April 2001): 16–18, 54; *New York Times* (21 April 2002).

First Church of the Women's E. W. of A. (Queen Esther Mission)

1904 • Mary Lark Hill sought to bridge the gap between women in all denominations and to encourage and advance women preachers. About 1904 she founded an organization known as the First Church of the Women's E. W. of A., or Queen Esther Mission, located on Dearborn Street in Chicago. Most of the officers and members were women preachers who were now united in their efforts to spread the gospel. Hill, a native of Tennessee, was converted in Nashville. She was a member of Seay's Chapel M. E. Church when she was called to the ministry. Hill worked as an evangelist and conducted large revival meetings in Louisville, Kentucky; Evansville, Indiana; Chicago, Illinois; and in many other large cities. Until she began her own ministry, Hill was a member of St. Mark's M. E. Church in Chicago.

Sources: Faithful Central Bible Church, https://www.faithfulcentral.com. Buck, *The Progression of the Race in the United States and Canada,* pp. 312–13.

Holiness

1886 • A congregation established in Method, North Carolina, became known as the first black holiness church. It grew out of a revival conducted by Isaac Cheshier on the first Sunday in May. Around this church grew a holiness movement that became the United Holy Church of America in 1916. The present United Holy Church could be placed in either the Pentecostal or the Holiness Movement.

Sources: Baer and Singer, *African-American Religion in the Twentieth Century,* p. 149; *Directory of African American Religious Bodies,* pp. 114, 250; *Encyclopedia of American Religions,* vol. 1, p. 443; Burgess and Moore, *Dictionary of Pentecostal and Charismatic Movements,* p. 857.

1929 • Known as the "Happy Am I Evangelist," Solomon Lightfoot Michaux (1885–1968) of the Gospel Spreading Church, Washington, D.C., began radio broadcasts in 1929. After the purchase of a local station by the CBS network, he was the first black to have a national and international audience on a regular basis. In 1934 he broadcast on Saturdays on the CBS radio network and internationally on shortwave radio, to reach an estimated audience of twenty-five million people. He preached a mixture of holiness themes and positive thinking, and his church was related to the Church of God, Holiness. By 1941 his radio broadcasts were heard only in a few cities where he had congregations, but the broadcasts continued until his death. Michaux once sold fish on the streets of Newport News, Virginia. A shrewd businessman, he became chief local purveyor of fish to the U.S. Navy during World War I. This brought him a fortune and he used his money to support needy black and white people. The Solomon Lightfoot Michaux Temple was located at the corner of Jefferson Avenue and Nineteenth Street in Newport News. He had large congregations in New York, Philadelphia, and Washington, D.C., as well.

Sources: Baer and Singer, *African-American Religion in the Twentieth Century,* pp. 155–57; Logan and Winston, *Dictionary of American Negro Biography,* pp. 432–33; *Encyclopedia of American Religions,* vol. 1, p. 223.

Interchurch Organizations

1986 • Christine E. Trigg was the first woman president of the New Jersey Council of Churches. Trigg was a member of the Clinton Memorial African Methodist Episcopal Zion Church in Newark, New Jersey.

Sources: *Jet* 70 (9 June 1986): 20.

1991 • Vinton Randolph Anderson (1927–) became the first black president of the World Council of Churches. He retired from the post in 1998. Anderson was born in Somerset, Bermuda, and received his Bachelor of Arts from Wilberforce University in Ohio, his Master of Divinity from Payne Theological Seminary, and his Master of Arts from Kansas University. He did further study at Yale Divinity School. Anderson had a stellar career in the ministry, pastoring a number of African Methodist Episcopal churches in Wichita, Kansas, and in St. Louis. He was named presiding bishop and chief pastor of the 9th Episcopal District in Alabama (1972–76), moving to the Third Episcopal district of Ohio, West Virginia, and West Pennsylvania from 1976 to 1984. From 1984 to 1988 he was with the Office of Ecumenical Relations and Development, then in 1988 he was assigned to the Fifth Episcopal District involving fourteen states and 255 churches west of the Mississippi River. Among his numerous accomplishments, Anderson developed the bicentennial edition of a church hymnal.

Sources: *Jet* 94 (27 July 1998): 10; *Who's Who among African Americans,* 26th ed., p. 34.

Islam

622 • Bilal (?–641?) was the first muezzin of Islam. He was a slave of Ethiopian origin and reputed to be the second adult convert, after Abu Bakr. He suffered much for his faith, but was eventually secured and freed by Abu Bakr. Bilal emigrated to Medina with the Prophet, who appointed him to call the faithful to prayer. The first to issue the call to prayer from the roof of the Kaaba after the return, he attained high prestige during his lifetime.

Sources: *Encyclopaedia of Islam,* p. 1215; *Shorter Encyclopaedia of Islam,* pp. 62–63.

Bilal

1913 • Noble Drew Ali, a name adopted by Timothy Drew (1886–1929), formed the Moorish Science Temple in Newark, New Jersey. This is the first step to the appearance, or the reappearance, of various forms of black Islam. (There is a debate about the survival in the nineteenth century of remnants of Islam coming from Africa.) Noble Drew Ali taught that blacks were not Ethiopians, but the descendants of the Moabites of the Bible, whose homeland was said to be Morocco. He also saw Marcus Garvey as a precursor to his organization. W. D. Fard, the founder of the Nation of Islam in the early 1930s, was originally a member of the Moorish Science Temple.

Sources: Baer and Singer, *African-American Religion in the Twentieth Century,* pp. 51, 60, 118–19; *Directory of African American Religious Bodies,* pp. 141–42; *Encyclopedia of American Religions,* vol. 3, p. 178.

1930 • W. D. Fard (1891–?) organized the group that became Temple No. 1 of the Nation of Islam in Detroit. Accounts of his life vary widely. He used several names, including Fred Dodd and Wallace Ford; by the time he arrived in Detroit, however, he had become W. D. Fard. He was known to his followers as Fard Muhammad. He was born to a white mother and a black father, or may have had Polynesian ancestry. Whatever his ethnic heritage, he was known to have passed for white when he was jailed later on. His birthplace was either New Zealand or Portland, Oregon. In the 1920s Fard operated a café in Los Angeles. After various encounters with the law, he was jailed and spent three years in San Quentin Prison for selling narcotics. He was released from prison on May 27, 1929 and then settled in Detroit where he worked as a retail salesman in the black community. He began to organize the Nation of Islam in 1930. By some account, Fard thought of himself as the deity. "My name is Mahdi; I am God, I came to guide you into the right path that you may be successful and see the hereafter," he told Elijah Muhammad when asked who he was and what was his real name. The Nation of Islam was considered radical and therefore a target for police harassment. In November 1932 Fard was arrested only because the police tied a murderer to the Nation of Islam. When it became known that Fard's persecution made him a martyr, he was ordered to leave Detroit. Fard instead went into hiding and prepared Elijah Karriem to head the organization, giving him the surname of Muhammad and making him chief minister of Islam. The fragile unity of the Nation of Islam was shattered and fierce fighting followed. The police also accelerated its harassment. Meanwhile, Elijah Muhammad avoided the struggles and finally relocated the headquarters to Chicago. He met with Fard in June 1934 and after that, Fard disappeared.

Sources: Smith, *Notable Black American Men*, p. 854.

Elijah Muhammad

1932 • Elijah Muhammad [Elijah Poole] (1897–1975) established the Nation of Islam's Temple Number Two, the first temple in Chicago. Upon the 1934 disappearance of W. D. Fard, who had founded the movement, Elijah Muhammad became the leader of the movement. Muhammad was born in Sandersville, Georgia, the sixth of thirteen children. The family relocated to Cordele, Georgia, in 1900. While in Cordele, he had the traumatic experience of witnessing the aftermath of a lynching. He moved to Macon when he was sixteen and worked at odd jobs. In April 1924, during the mass black migration, Elijah Muhammad moved to Detroit but found economic and social conditions no better for blacks there than they were in Georgia. The Nation of Islam movement grew under his leadership, especially in the late fifties and the sixties, in part due to the charismatic leadership of his principal lieutenant, Malcolm X (1925–1965). Malcolm X's suspension from the movement in 1963 marked the first major split in the organization. By 1965 Elijah Muhammad suffered from a number of ailments but remained active in the movement. His health failed completely on February 25, and he died in Mercy Hospital in Chicago. After Elijah Muhammad's death, Louis Farrakhan formed a new Nation of Islam in 1978. The group led by Wallace J. Muhammad moved closer to orthodox Islam and renamed itself the American Muslim Mission.

Sources: *Directory of African American Religious Bodies*, pp. 139–40; *Encyclopedia of American Religions*, pp. 175–76, 179–80; *Negro Almanac, 1989*, pp. 1304–5, 1319; Smith, *Notable Black American Men*, pp. 853–56.

1991 • On June 25 Siraj Wahaj, the black Imam of Brooklyn, New York, was the first Muslim to give the invocation in the U. S. House of Representatives. The forty-one-year-old Wahaj was from the Bedford-Stuyvesant area of New York City. A former member of the Nation of Islam, he became vice president of the Islamic Society of North America. Siraj Wahhaj lost his interest in Christianity when Martin Luther King Jr. was assassinated and decided that, in response to the death of his hero, he would become either a Black Muslim or Black Panther. He became a Muslim in 1969, when he was nineteen and a student at New York University. After Elijah Mohammed died in 1975, he began to read books and the Qu'ran, and attended conferences to learn more about Islam.

Sources: *Jet* 80 (15 July 1991): 30–31; DiscoverTheNetworks.org: A Guide to the Political Left, "Siraj Wahhaj," http://www.discoverthenetworks.org/individualProfile.asp?indid=716. Accessed September 20, 2012.

Judaism and Black Judaism

1886 • F. S. Cherry, a widely traveled seaman and railroad worker founded in Chattanooga, Tennessee, the Church of the Living God, the Pillar Ground of Truth of All Nations (Black Jews). It is the oldest known black Jewish sect. Although little is known about the church, it is known that Cherry moved the group to Philadelphia. According to Cherry, God called him to found a church and let the world know that blacks were the true descendants of the biblical Hebrews. In his view, God, Jesus, Adam, and Eve were black. He believed that whites descended from the servant Gehazi, whom the prophet Elisa cursed with skin "as white as snow" (II Kings 5:27). He preached that white Jews were interlopers and frauds. In 1896 William S. Crowdy, a cook on the Santa Fe Railroad, founded a church with similar views, the Church of God and Saints of Christ in Lawrence, Kansas. The church mixes Judaism, Christianity, and Black Nationalism and is sometimes called the first black Jewish group. Crowdy claimed also that God called him to lead his people to the identity and historic religion that were truly theirs. A principal belief is that blacks are the direct descendants of the lost tribes of Israel. Like Cherry, Crowdy also moved his church to Philadelphia but relocated in 1905 to Belleville, Virginia, in Nansemond County near Portsmouth. After that, braches of the church were established in cities throughout

The Original Hebrew Israelite Nation

In 1968 the Original Hebrew Israelite Nation (also known as the Abeta Hebrew Cultural Center) became the first black American Jewish group to migrate to Israel. Formed in the 1960s by Ammi Carter [born G. Parker], the group was at first unsuccessful in establishing itself in Liberia and changed its goal to Israel. Some 1,500 members now live communally in Israel.

Sources: Baer and Singer, *African-American Religion in the Twentieth Century,* pp. 117–18; *Directory of African American Religious Bodies,* p. 133; *Encyclopedia of American Religions,* pp. 1291–92.

the country and overseas. Crowdy's church used rituals and symbols adopted from Jewish practices. Like the Jewish church, the Crowdy's church circumcised newborn boys, adopted the Jewish calendar, required men to wear skullcaps, observed Saturday as the Sabbath, and celebrated Passover. They blended these rituals with Christian practices, such as foot washing and consecration of bread and water as Christ's blood. The first black Jewish sect in New York City arose in 1899, when Leon Richelieu (?–1964) established the Moorish Zionist Temple in Brooklyn. This group emphasized a Jewish ideology rather than nationalism and seems to have included some white Jewish members.

Sources: Baer and Singer, *African-American Religions in the Twentieth Century,* pp. 50–51, 114–15; *Directory of African American Religious Bodies,* p. 131; *Encyclopedia of American Religions,* vol. 3, pp. 27, 152–53; Chireau and Deutsch, *Black Zion,* pp. 57–58

2009 • Alysa Stanton became the first African American woman ordained a rabbi in Jewish history. She was formally ordained on June 6 by rabbi David Ellenson, president of Hebrew Union College–Jewish Institute of Religion in Cincinnati, where Stanton completed seven years of rabbinical training. She began her new post at Congregation Bayt Shalom in Greeneville, North Carolina, on August 1. Her synagogue, is affiliated with the Reform and Conservative movements. Her appointment made her the first black woman rabbi to lead a majority white congregation; about sixty families comprise the congregation. Of the seminaries in mainstream Judaism, there were 994 women rabbis ordained by the end of 2009, and one ordained black male rabbi. A Cleveland, Ohio, native, Stanton grew up in a Pentecostal family and had an early interest in Judaism. Her mother encouraged her to explore different religions when she was a child, and she received her first Hebrew grammar book at age ten. Meanwhile, she moved to Colorado when she was eleven years old and graduated from Colorado State University. She studied Judaism on her own and later drove from Fort Collins to Denver to study with an Orthodox rabbi. Her uncle, a devout Christian, frequently attended Jewish ceremonies and by her early twenties, Stanton decided to convert. "I did so because it was the path for me," she said, "from a religious standpoint" as well as "from an ethical and social and communal standpoint, it was important to me." She said also that "Judaism is the language of my soul, and it's what resonates with me." Stanton worked as a licensed psychotherapist with a specialty in grief, loss and trauma. She began her rabbinical training at age thirty-eight. A divorcee, Stanton is the mother of a sixteen-year-old adopted daughter.

Sources: Cornwell, Lisa, " Rabbi Persevered along Spiritual Path," *Tennessean* (20 June 2009); Friedman, "Alysa Stanton Becomes First Female Black Rabbi," http://abcnews.go .com/US/story?id=7639090&page=1; Hoffman, "1st Black Woman Rabbi's Journey to History," *Jet* 116 (6–13 June, 2009): 16–18.

Lutherans

1983 • Nelson W. Trout (1920–1996) was the first black elected bishop of the Evangelical Lutheran Church in America on June 17, 1983. He was elected to serve the South Pacific District of the former American Lutheran Church. Trout was a professor at Trinity

Lutheran Seminary, Columbus, Ohio, when he was named bishop of the South Pacific District in California. He was a graduate of Trinity Lutheran Seminary and of Capital University in Columbus and received a doctor of divinity degree from Wartburg College in Waverly, Iowa. He served congregations in Eau Claire, Wisconsin; Mobile, Alabama; and Los Angeles. Before joining the faculty at Trinity, Trout was executive director of Lutheran Social Services in Dayton. In 1991 the seminary established in his honor the Nelson W. Trout Lectureship in Preaching.

Sources: Hornsby, *Chronology of African-American History,* pp. 320–21; *Who's Who among African Americans,* 14th ed., p. 1302.

1988 • Sherman G. Hicks (1996–) became the first black bishop of the Metropolitan Chicago Synod of the Evangelical Lutheran Church in America. He left that post and by 2001 had become pastor of a church in Washington, D.C. Hicks was active with the National Aids Fund and the AIDS National Interfaith Network, serving on the board of directors for both organizations. Other board memberships included the Community Family Life Services as well as Lifeline, a Mental Retardation Partnership.

Sources: *Jet* 74 (23 May 1988): 12; *Who's Who among African Americans,* 26th ed., p. 577.

Methodists

1758 • On November 29, in England, John Wesley baptized the first two known black converts (one being a woman) to the Methodism movement. At this time, Methodism had not broken away from the Anglican Church. In the United States the split between the Protestant Episcopal Church and the Methodist Episcopal Church would not be complete until 1784.

Sources: Shockley, *Heritage and Hope,* p. 27; Lincoln and Mamiya, *The Black Church in the African American Experience,* p. 50.

1764 • A slave named Anne Sweitzer [Aunt Annie] was one of the founding members of the first Methodist society in the colonies, organized in Frederick County, Maryland. Blacks were members of Methodist groups from the beginning; for example, they belonged to Saint George's Methodist Church in Philadelphia, which dates to 1767 and in 1776, a black servant called Betty would be a charter member of the John Street meeting, the first society in New York City.

Sources: Shockley, *Heritage and Hope,* p. 24; Lincoln and Mamiya, *The Black Church in the African American Experience,* p. 50; Smith, *Climbing Jacob's Ladder,* pp. 33–35, 39.

1781 • The first known black Methodist preacher was Harry "Black Harry" Hosier [also spelled Hoosier, Hoshur, and Hossier] (1750?–1806). He was so nicknamed because he was very black. His sermon, "Barren Fig Tree," was delivered at Adams Chapel, Fairfax County, Virginia, in 1781, and was the first preached by a black to a congregation of Methodists. His sermon in 1784 at Thomas Chapel in Chapeltown, Delaware, was the first preached by a black to a white congregation. Hosier was a circuit-riding preacher who traveled from the Carolinas to New England where he brought the gospel to slaves, free blacks, and poor and affluent whites. Although he was uneducated, Hosier had a remarkable talent and was unusually intelligent. He had a great ability to retain information; since he was unable to read, he memorized the Bible, and he became highly creative in his sermons. Some sources call him the most eloquent preacher of his time. Hosier was born a slave near Fayetteville, North Carolina. Except that they came from Africa and were enslaved nothing is known about his parents. Hosier became a free man and was converted to Methodism either before or after he was freed. He met Francis Asbury, the founder of American Methodism, around 1780, a meeting that Asbury called "providentially arranged." When Asbury went to Todd, North Carolina, near that time, he may have encountered Hosier. Hosier became servant and guide to Asbury, while at the same time becoming a circuit-riding preacher. In 1784 and again in 1786, Asbury arranged a preaching tour through Delaware, Maryland, and Virginia, to introduce Thomas Coke to the work of

The First Black Methodist Church

Richard Allen (1760–1831) and Absalom Jones (1746–1818) organized the Free African Society in Philadelphia on April 12, 1787. This society was originally a mutual aid society. When black members withdrew from Saint George's Methodist Episcopal Church in Philadelphia, in protest against increased segregation in seating (apparently in November 1787), the Free African Society became the nucleus for the first black Episcopal church, Saint Thomas, in 1794. In the same year, those blacks who wished to remain Methodists formed the Bethel Church, which became the mother church of the African Methodist Episcopal Church in 1816. (The incident in Saint George's is also assigned to the date of 1792. It is possible that the Cumberland Street Methodist Episcopal Church in Charleston, South Carolina, was in fact the first to install a segregated gallery, in 1787, which became a traditional way to separate congregations.)

Sources: Logan and Winston, *Dictionary of American Negro Biography,* pp. 12–13 (Allen); 362–64 (Jones); Shockley, *Heritage and Hope,* p. 29; Lincoln and Mamiya, *The Black Church in the African American Experience,* pp. 50–51; Smith, *Climbing Jacob's Ladder,* pp. 36–37.

the Methodists. Coke came to America as John Wesley's representative. After hearing Hosier preach, Coke wrote in his journal that he believed Hosier was one of the best preachers in the world and that he was also one of the humblest people he ever saw. The first tour ended in time for the Christmas Conference in Baltimore's Lovely Lane Chapel on December 24 to January 2, 1785. It was here that the Methodist Episcopal church was formally established in America. This also established a permanent relationship between black and white Methodists. Hosier was present at the historic conference. After being cleared of an erroneous charge against him in 1791, Hosier fell from grace in the church. He was then excluded from that group of black Methodist preachers, including Richard Allen, who were ordained around 1799.

Sources: *Encyclopedia of Black America,* pp. 511, 555; Shockley, *Heritage and Hope,* pp. 50–51, 307; Lincoln and Mamiya, *The Black Church in the African American Experience,* p. 66; Smith, *Climbing Jacob's Ladder,* pp. 34–35; Smith, *Notable Black American Men,* pp. 573–75.

1784 • Richard Allen (1760–1831) and Absalom Jones (1746–1818) were granted licenses to preach, at the Old St. George's Methodist Episcopal Church in Philadelphia, making them the first black men to be so licensed.

Sources: Southern, *The Music of Black Americans,* 2nd ed., p. 61.

1785 • The first Methodists in Baltimore met in Lovely Lane and Strawberry Alley beginning in 1772. Blacks began to form their own Colored Methodist Society between 1785 and 1787. This is the origin of the first black Methodist churches in Baltimore, Sharp Street Church (1802), and Bethel African Methodist Episcopal Church.

Sources: Shockley, *Heritage and Hope,* p. 43; Smith, *Climbing Jacob's Ladder,* p. 35.

1794 • African Zoar Church was organized as a mission church in Philadelphia. This was the first all-black church for persons who eventually stayed in the Methodist Episcopal church. Zoar was incorporated in 1835.

Sources: *Encyclopedia of Black America,* pp. 32, 555; *Heritage and Hope,* p. 43; Smith, *Climbing Jacob's Ladder,* pp. 36, 44.

1799 • Richard Allen (1760–1831) became the first black ordained deacon in the Methodist Episcopal church in 1799. Born a slave, he became a member of a Methodist society in Delaware about 1780, and by 1783 he was a licensed preacher in New Jersey and Pennsylvania. In 1786 he established prayer meetings for blacks in Philadelphia. Resent-

Richard Allen

ing an effort by the white members of Saint George's Methodist Episcopal Church to further segregate black members of the congregation, Allen and Absalom Jones led a walkout of blacks in 1787. The African Free Society, which seems to have been already organized as a mutual aid society, became the center of the congregation's worship. Jones entered the Protestant Episcopal ministry in 1794, but Allen remained a Methodist. When five black churches broke from the parent Methodist organization in 1816, Allen became the first bishop of the new African Methodist Episcopal (AME) Church. He is also one of the first black authors of a biography, *The Life Experiences and Gospel Labors of the Right Reverend Richard Allen*.

Sources: Logan and Winston, *Dictionary of American Negro Biography*, pp. 12–13; *Directory of African American Religious Bodies*, p. 242; Smith, *Climbing Jacob's Ladder*, pp. 35–37; Smith, *Notable Black American Men*, pp. 21–24.

1800 • Henry Evans (?–1810), a free–born shoemaker, established the first Methodist church in Fayetteville, North Carolina. Evans Chapel was dedicated in 1802 and Francis Asbury, the founding bishop of American Methodism, visited it in 1805. The church originally had white members and the numbers increased so that blacks were displaced from their original seating. Evans himself was displaced as minister before his death. The white members withdrew before the Methodist Episcopal Church split into northern and southern parts in 1844. Evans Chapel joined the African Methodist Episcopal Zion Church in 1866.

Sources: Shockley, *Heritage and Hope*, p. 44; Lincoln and Mamiya, *The Black Church in the African American Experience*, p. 66; *Negro Almanac*, p. 1301; Raboteau, *Slave Religion*, p. 135.

1816 • John Stewart (1786–1823) was the first black missionary to the Wyandotte Indians. Jonathan Poynter, a black who had been raised by the Wyandottes, assisted him. Stewart died one year before his church was completed. In 1960 his grave and missionary church in Upper Sandusky, Ohio, were designated as one of ten official shrines of American Methodism. A monument to him had been established previously on October 19, 1916.

Sources: Logan and Winston, *Dictionary of American Negro Biography*, p. 371; Shockley, *Heritage and Hope*, pp. 36, 307; *Negro Almanac, 1989*, p. 223; *Negro Year Book, 1918–1919*, pp. 23–24.

Early Black Methodist Churches

Founded	Name	Location
1800?	Evans Chapel	Fayetteville, North Carolina
1801	Mount Hope	Salem, New Jersey
1802	Sharp Street	Baltimore, Maryland
1805	Ezion	Wilmington, Delaware
1814	Mount Zion	Washington, D.C.
1823	Union	Massachusetts
1824?	Calvary	Cincinnati, Ohio
1838	Wesley Chapel	New Orleans, Louisiana
1840	Newnan Station	Newnan, Georgia
1844	Asbury	Lexington, Kentucky
1846	Union Memorial	St. Louis, Missouri
1850	*First Colored Methodist	Sacramento, California
1863	Wesley	Little Rock, Arkansas
1866	Clark Memorial	Nashville, Tennessee

*Joined the African Methodist Episcopal Church in 1851.

1858 • Francis Burns (1809–1863) was the first black Methodist Episcopal missionary bishop. A native of Albany, New York, he served in Liberia for twenty-four years. In 1849 he had been the first black to be designated a presiding elder for his work in Liberia. A second missionary bishop, John W. Roberts, was elected in 1866; a third, Isaiah B. Scott, in 1904; and a fourth, Alexander P. Camphor, in 1916. Only in 1920 would a regular bishop be elected. The lack of leadership roles for blacks in the denomination was one of the factors leading to black annual conferences, held officially from 1864 to 1939, and, in effect, dividing the denomination along racial lines.

Sources: *Encyclopedia of Black America,* pp. 555–57; Shockley *Heritage and Hope,* pp. 54, 67.

1884 • Marshall W. Taylor (1847–1887) became the first black editor of the *Southwestern Christian Advocate* of the Methodist Episcopal Church. The periodical was established in 1876 and became the center for both dissemination of news and debate on issues of concern for blacks in the denomination. In 1941 this periodical became the *Central Christian Advocate,* and continued publication until 1968.

Sources: Shockley, *Heritage and Hope,* pp. 67, 148–49; *Encyclopedia of Black America,* p. 558.

1920 • Robert E. Jones (1872–1960) and Matthew W. Clair Sr. (1865–1943) were the first bishops elected by the United Methodist Church for service in the United States. The denomination had elected its first black missionary bishop for service in Liberia in 1858.

Sources: *Encyclopedia of Black America,* p. 557; Shockley, *Heritage and Hope,* pp. 87–88, 308, 314; *Negro Year Book,* 1921–22, p. 16.

1936 • Laura J. Lange was the first woman ordained a local elder in Methodist Episcopal Church, by the Lexington Conference. Lange had been made a deacon in 1926. It would not be until 1956 that a black woman would be ordained an elder and admitted into full connection in an Annual Conference. This woman was Sallie A. Crenshaw.

Sources: Shockley, *Heritage and Hope,* pp. 53, 155.

1955 • Simon Peter Montgomery was the first Methodist minister assigned to an all-white congregation, in Old Mystic, Connecticut.

Sources: *Negro Almanac, 1989,* p. 1429.

1958 • Joseph Reed Washington was the first Methodist minister with two all-white churches, the Methodist church in Newfield, Maine, and the Congregational church in West Newfield, Maine. These places are some three miles apart.

Sources: *Negro Almanac, 1989,* p. 1429.

1964 • Prince Albert Taylor Jr. (1907–2001) and James Samuel Thomas Jr. (1919–2010) were the first black bishops of the United Methodist Church appointed to predominantly white jurisdictions. Taylor, a bishop since 1956, became the first when he was appointed to the New Jersey area on June 25, 1964, and the second was Thomas, who was appointed to Iowa, on July 10, 1964. In 1965 Taylor was also the first black president of the Council of Bishops, a post he held for two years. Taylor was born in Oklahoma in 1907, the same year that Oklahoma became a state. One of fourteen children, his father was a clergyman as well. Taylor grew up to pastor churches in North Carolina and New York; he taught at Bennett College for Women in Greensboro, North Carolina, and at Gammon Theological Seminary in Atlanta. He edited the news magazine for the Central Jurisdiction, the Central *Christian Advocate,* from 1948 to 1956. For eight years he was bishop in Monrovia, Liberia, and then was assigned to the New Jersey Area where he served until he retired in 1976. He was president of the Methodist Press Association, now the United Methodist Association of Communicators, and in 1983 he was inducted into its Hall of Fame. The Government of Liberia gave him "The Venerable Knighthood of the Pioneers." Taylor received his B.A. degree from Houston-Tillotson College in Texas, his B.D. from Gammon, his M.A. from Union Theological Seminary and Columbia University, and his Ed.D. from New York University. He died from cancer on August 15, 2001, at Shore Memorial Hospital in Somers Point, New Jersey, when he was ninety-four years old. James Samuel Thomas was born in

Orangeburg, South Carolina, and educated at Claflin College in Orangeburg (A.B., 1939), Gammon Theological Seminary (B.D., 1943), Drew University (M.A., 1944), and Cornell University (Ph.D., 1953). He was ordained in 1942 and from 1942 to 1943 he was pastor for the Orangeburg Circuit. He served as pastor in York, South Carolina, from 1946 to 1947, chaplain at South Carolina State College (now South Carolina State University) from 1944 to 1946, and professor at Gammon Theological Seminary from 1947 to 1953. He later moved to Nashville, Tennessee, and served as associate director of the Methodist Board of Education from 1953 to 1964. In 1958 he was visiting professor in the Perkins School of Theology at Southern Methodist University. Thomas was named bishop for the Iowa Area Methodist Conference in 1964. After retirement, he returned to Atlanta to serve on the board of trustees for Gammon.

Sources: *Ebony* (February 1965): 54–60; (March 1982): 129; *Ebony Success Library*, vol. 1, p. 302 (Thomas); *New York Times* (18 August 200) (Thomas); Shockley, *Heritage and Hope*, pp. 161–63; *Who's Who among African Americans*, 14th ed., p. 1274 (Thomas); Wormley and Fenderson, *Many Shades of Black*, pp. 349–50 (Thomas).

1968 • In Cincinnati, Ohio, the First National Conference of Negro Methodists organized a black caucus for the denomination, Black Methodists for Church Renewal.

Sources: Baer and Singer, *African-American Religion in the Twentieth Century*, p. 106; *Directory of African American Religious Bodies*, pp. 204–5, 245; Shockley, *Heritage and Hope*, pp. 209–10.

1968 • Abel Tendekayi Muzorewa (1925–2010) was consecrated Bishop of Rhodesia, becoming the first black to head the Rhodesian branch of the United Methodist Church. He attended a missionary school operated by the Methodists and also followed his father, a teacher and lay preacher in the church, into the ministry. Muzorewa was ordained a United Methodist minister in August 1953, pastored a church in Chiduku, and then studied in the United States where he earned degrees from Scarritt College in Nashville and Central Methodist College in Missouri. After serving as secretary of Rhodesia's Student Christian Movement, he became a bishop. He joined other United Methodist ministers in political activities and helped to establish the African National Council (ANC) and successfully protested the white-ruled government of Rhodesia.

Sources: *Contemporary Black Biography*, vol. 85, pp. 124–27.

1969 • The Washington Square United Methodist Church in New York City was the first white church to give money in response to James Forman's demand for reparations from white churches. James Forman (1928–2005), then leader of the Student Non-Violent Coordinating Committee, had demanded reparations of $500 million from white churches on May 4, 1969, in a surprise appearance in the pulpit of the interracial and interdenominational Riverside Church in New York City. The National Black Economic Development Conference had chosen that date to interrupt service in white churches nationwide. Foreman unveiled the *Black Manifesto* that he wrote that year to set forth demands from whites. He demanded $500 million from white churches and from synagogues to serve as reparations to blacks for the abuses they endured during slavery.

Sources: Baer and Singer, *African-American Religion in the Twentieth Century*, p. 238; *Negro Almanac*, pp. 1304, 1305; Smith, *Notable Black American Men*, pp. 406–8.

1971 • Claire Collins Harvey (1916–1989) became the first black to head Church Women United. Harvey was a Mississippi businesswoman, a civil rights activist, and a church worker. Harvey was born in Meridian, Mississippi, and educated at Spelman College in Atlanta (B.A., 1937), Indiana College of Mortuary Science (1942), Columbia University (M.A., 1951), and the School of Metaphysics in Jackson, Mississippi (1937–39). She worked as a freelance bookkeeper in Jackson from 1937 to 1937. Collins was general manager from 1940 to 1970 and president since 1970 of the Collins Funeral Home and Insurance Company in Jackson. Since 1980 she had been board chair and chief executive officer of Unity Life Insurance Company.

Sources: *Encyclopedia of Black America,* p. 560; Shockley, *Heritage and Hope,* p. 268; *Who's Who among African Americans,* 14th ed., p. 562.

1981 • William M. Smith was the first black head of the Ecumenical Committee of the World Methodist Conference. Presiding bishop of the First Episcopal District of the African Methodist Episcopal Zion Church, he lived in Mobile, Alabama.

Sources: *Jet* 61 (22 October 1981): 24.

1984 • Leontine Turpeau Current Kelly (1920–2012) became the first woman bishop of a major denomination, the United Methodist Church. She was consecrated on July 20, 1984. In addition, she was the first woman of any race to preach on the program National Radio Pulpit of the National Council of Churches. Born in Washington, D.C., Kelly's call to the ministry came after the death of her third husband. Made an elder in 1977, she had experience at both the local and the national level. Upon the retirement of the first, and only, woman bishop in the church, she was elected and supervised the California and Nevada conferences until her retirement in 1988. Kelly was born in the parsonage of the church that her father pastored, Mount Zion Methodist Episcopal Church in Washington, D.C. She was the seventh of eight children. Later the family relocated to Pittsburgh and settled in Cincinnati by the late 1920s. The basement of their Cincinnati parsonage had been used as a station on the Underground Railroad and connected the house to the church. Leontine Kelly interrupted her college education when she married and had children. She later remarried and returned to school, receiving her bachelor's degree in 1960 from Virginia Union University in Richmond. After her second husband died, the congregation of Galilee United Methodist Church in Edwardsville, Virginia, where James Kelly was pastor, asked her to succeed him. Already she was active in the church and a popular speaker whose style the parishioners called "preaching" and not speaking. By now she also felt a divine calling and served as layperson in charge of the church. She began theological study at Wesley Theological Seminary in Washington, D.C., and graduated in 1976 with a Master of Divinity degree. She was ordained as a minister and became a deacon in 1972. In 1977 she was ordained an elder. After holding several posts, she joined the national staff of the United Methodist Church, located in Nashville, from 1983 to 1984 and received the prominence she needed to become a candidate for bishop.

Sources: Hine, *Black Women in America,* pp. 675; Shockley, *Heritage and Hope,* p. 280; Smith, *Notable Black American Women,* pp. 621–26; *Who's Who among African Americans,* 26th ed., p. 716.

1987 • J. D. Phillips was the first black to head a predominantly white United Methodist church in the Central Texas Conference: Saint Andrew's United Methodist Church in Killeen, Texas.

Sources: *Jet* 72 (13 July 1987): 22.

1996 • The first black bishop of the Florida Conference was Cornelius L. Henderson (1934?–2000). Henderson left the office of president-dean of Gammon Theological Seminary in Atlanta to serve the conference, where he raised membership for the first time in eight years. By the time of his death, the Florida Conference had nearly 743 United Methodist churches and 340,000 members. Henderson had served the United Methodist Church for forty-five years. Among the positions he held during this was that of senior pastor of Ben Hill United Methodist Church in Atlanta, one of the world's largest black churches in terms of membership. He led the congregation from four hundred to over forty-five hundred members.

Sources: *New York Times* (8 December 2000).

1999 • James King (1948?–), became the first black pastor of the overwhelmingly white Brentwood United Methodist Church in Brentwood, Tennessee, near Nashville. Brentwood is one of the largest and richest churches of the denomination. Cross-racial appointments, fairly common in the United Methodist churches in mid-state Tennessee, reflect the church's official commitment to ethnic diversity both in administrative offices and in local churches. An Alabama native, for ten years King pastored Clark Memorial United Methodist Church, a black church in Nashville. He also held various positions in the Tennessee Conference, most recently the superintendent for the Murfreesboro area. In 2000 King left the post when was elected bishop for the Louisville, Kentucky, area. Later, he was reassigned to an area in Georgia.

Sources: *Tennessean* (27 April 1999).

2000 • Bettye Lewis was named a district superintendent for the Tennessee Conference, becoming the first black woman to hold this position. She oversees churches in the Pulaski District, which includes the counties of Giles, Lawrence, Lincoln, Wayne, and part of Hardin. Lewis is a 1988 graduate of Vanderbilt Divinity School in Nashville. In 1995 she was named director of the Wesleyan Foundation at Austin Peay University in Clarksville, Tennessee. After that, in 1988, she was assistant chaplain at Meharry Medical College and Hubbard Hospital; she also served as pastor in Tennessee Conference churches.

Sources: *Tennessean* (18 March 2000).

2001 • Charles Lee (1957?–) became the first black pastor at Huffman United Methodist Church, a predominantly white church in Birmingham, Alabama, with about 1,500 members. Of those members, there were twelve black families. Alabama's Methodist officials concluded that an exceptional pastor was needed to attract new black members and, at the same, hold on to the tightly knit white members. Huffman, a sensitive and experienced pastor, emerged as the obvious choice. The community surrounding the church is rapidly gaining black residents. The Georgia native in 1994 became senior pastor of Christ Church United Methodist in Birmingham's suburbs, where the congregation was all-white.

Sources: *New York Times* (23 June 2001).

Mormons

Elijah Abel

1836 • Elijah Abel (?–1884) was the first black to become an elder (priest) in the Mormon church, while the Mormons were headquartered in Nauvoo, Illinois. Abel was an undertaker and had been converted in 1832. He moved with the Mormons to Salt Lake City, Utah, where he became a hotel manager. He was active in the church until his death. After the very early years of the church, a long-standing ban prevented blacks from advancing to the priesthood. This ban was abolished in 1978, and the church has since attracted a number of black members.

Sources: Cantor, *Historic Landmarks of Black America*, p. 334; *Encyclopedia of Black America*, pp. 1–2.

1978 • Joseph Freeman Jr. became the first black priest (elder) in the twentieth century. Advancement to this rank is normal for all male members of the church, but it had been denied to blacks until a revelation to the presiding elder changed the church's policy in 1978.

Sources: Cantor, *Historic Landmarks of Black America*, p. 334; Kane, *Famous First Facts*, p. 167; *Negro Almanac*, p. 1325.

Peace Mission

1914 • It was about this year that M. J. "Father" Divine [George Baker] (1879–1965) first proclaimed himself God as he established his movement, Father Divine's "Kingdom" and Peace Mission. His initials stood for Major Jealous, which was taken from Exodus 34:14, "for the Lord, whose name is Jealous, is a jealous god." His followers also believed that he was God. He was tried on a charge of insanity in a Valdosta, Georgia, court on February 27, 1914, on the grounds that his claim to be God was clearly aberrant. He was convicted but not incarcerated. Born in Rockville, Maryland, into a poor family, Baker learned the skills of a gardener and yard worker. He moved to Baltimore in 1899 and became interested in the storefront churches that were popular at that time. He became a preacher who developed his own ideas about religion, drawing on Methodist, Catholic, and popular black traditions; he was also influenced by the New Thought movement that preceded the Christian Science and modern New Age movements. Baker went South in 1902 where he sought to save souls. Then he moved to the West Coast where William J. Seymour and his Azuza Street revival meetings and the traditions of the Pentecostal movements influenced him. As he heard blacks and white "speak in tongues" and did so himself, he began to reshape his religious thoughts. Baker met the preacher Samuel Morris in 1907 and the two united in a ministry. After that, Morris called himself Father Jehovia, and Baker became the Messenger and the Son. Reverend Bishop Saint John the Vine, or John A. Hickerson, joined them and the three built up a following at their residence. They went their separate ways in 1912. The Messenger, or Father Divine, returned to the South and spread his message as he traveled. His pattern of worship consisted of preaching, singing, and lavish Holy Communion banquets. His following then was predominantly black women who found him liberating, as he denounced male chauvinism. Baker drew the ire of black ministers and a confrontation in Savannah in 1913 led to his imprisonment and sixty days on the chain gang. By 1917 he had married a woman named Peninnah, who became known as Mother Devine, and spread his gospel to the North as well. He settled in Sayville, Long Island, New York and widened his support to attract middle- and upper-class whites. Then he shifted his base to New York City where he held a series of successful meetings at Harlem's Rockville Palace. Father Divine established a Peace Mission that included restaurants and other businesses that became the source of much of his revenue. His mission grew rapidly in 1937, but his entire institution declined after that. He moved his Peace Mission to Philadelphia around 1942, but the aging and frail Divine ceased public appearances in 1963 and died two years later.

Sources: *Directory of African American Religious Bodies,* pp. 122–24; Logan and Winston, *Dictionary of American Negro Biography,* pp. 178–80; Smith, *Notable Black American Men,* pp. 307–10; Watts, *God, Harlem U.S.A.,* pp. 31–43.

Pentecostals

1906 • From April 14, 1906, the preaching of William Joseph Seymour (1870–1922) at the Azusa Street Mission in Los Angeles began one major strand in the diffusion of the Pentecostal movement among both blacks and whites. The first widely influential revival to emphasize the centrality of speaking in tongues as evidence of baptism in the Holy Spirit, it drew both blacks and whites. C. H. Mason's experiences at the Azusa Street Mission in 1907 led him to make the practice central in Church of God in Christ. In 1908 G. B. Cashwell introduced the practice he had learned from Seymour to the predominantly white Church of God, USA. Pentecostalists soon split along racial lines. C. H. Mason's church was incorporated, however, and some white leaders of segregated congregations continued to be ordained by Mason for a few years so that they would legally be recognized as ministers. Seymour was born in Centerville, Louisiana; little is known about his early life, but early on he claimed to have had several visions of God. He became a waiter in an Indianapolis hotel about 1880 and attended the local predominantly white Methodist Episcopal Church. He moved to Cincinnati in 1900 where he was induced to join a revivalist Holiness group known as the Evening Lights Saints, a predominantly black offshoot of the Church of God in Anderson, Indiana. Seymour had an attack of smallpox that blinded him in one eye, and after that he decided to become an itinerant preacher. The Church of God ordained him in 1902. He wandered as an evangelist from 1903 forward, traveling in Chicago, Georgia, Mississippi, Louisiana, and Texas. He settled in Houston and in summer 1905 and during her absence, he replaced the female Holiness preacher Lucy Farrow. On her return, Farrow, who had experienced speaking in tongues, convinced Seymour of its importance. In 1906 he relocated to Los Angeles where he led a prayer group in a house on Bonnie Brae Avenue. Members of the group began speaking in tongues in the spring of 1906. On April 14 Seymour held his first service at the Azusa Street Mission. The revival at the mission was at its height between 1906 and 1909, attracting wide-spread attention in the United States and abroad and serving as a catalyst for the Pentecostal movement.

William Seymour

Sources: Baer and Singer, *African-American Religion in the Twentieth Century*, pp. 180–81; *Black Apostles*, pp. 213–25; *Directory of African American Religious Bodies*, pp. 250–51; *Encyclopedia of American Religions*, vol. 1, pp. xxxvii, 43, 45, 226, 231, 243–44; Lincoln and Mamiya, *The Black Church in the African American Experience*, p.79; Smith, *Notable Black American Men*, pp. 1056–59.

1915 • In January, Indianapolis Pentecostal minister Garfield Thomas Haywood (1880–1931) was rebaptized in Jesus' name by Glenn A. Cook, a white adherent of the "New Issue," which triggered a major fissure among Pentecostals. Garfield led the Pentecostal Assemblies of the Word to become the first major oneness church. (Oneness teaches that God, Christ, and the Holy Spirit are not distinct persons, thus denying the existence of the Trinity—the alternate designation, "Jesus Only," is used mainly by outsiders.) Haywood was a major influence on the widespread popularity of the oneness position among black American Pentecostals. The church was not originally segregated. Although many white congregations broke away, leaving the church predominantly black, it is still integrated at every level. Haywood became the first bishop of the church in 1925.

Sources: Burgess and McGee, *Dictionary of Pentecostal and Charismatic Movements*, pp. 349–50, 700–701; Synan, *The Century of the Holy Spirit*, p. 279.

Lucy Smith

1916 • Lucy Madden Smith (1875–1952) founded the interracial All Nations Pentecostal Church in Chicago, becoming the first woman in the city to transform the roving congregation into an established church. She was said to be known as the "preacher to the disinherited class." In 1925 Elder Smith, as she became known, first broadcast her Sunday night services over radio station WSBC; later station WIND aired her services on Sundays and Wednesdays. She was the first black religious leader to broadcast services on the air. In 1933 she became a pioneer in black gospel radio, exposing her ministry to wider audiences. She was the first in the city to mix gospel programming with appeals for the poor. Smith was born on a plantation in Oglethorpe County, Georgia. Although she had little education, she learned to read later in life. She married in 1896 and by 1910 and had nine children. After a move to Athens, Georgia, William Smith abandoned the family and Lucy Smith struggled to support their children on her own. She moved to Atlanta and then to Chicago, arriving in spring 1910 during the black migration. There she joined Olivet Baptist Church, became dissatisfied, and left in 1912 to join Ebenezer Baptist Church. Then she became curious about the Pentecostal faith and attended Stone Church, where the Pentecostal congregation was white. Two years later she was baptized into that faith, continued to attend Stone, and then received her calling as "divine healer." She offered solace to the socially disinherited in Chicago, held prayer meetings in her one-room house, and then founded All Nations Pentecostal Church in 1916.

Sources: Schultz and Hast, *Women Building Chicago, 1790–1990*, pp. 814–17; Smith, *Notable Black American Women*, Book II, pp. 601–3.

1924 • Ida Bell Robinson (1891–1946) founded what became the first sizeable black Pentecostal denomination headed by a woman. The new body, Mount Sinai Holy Church of America, was chartered in Philadelphia this year. Born in Hazelhurst, Georgia, Robinson spent most of her childhood in Florida. She had been fervently religious early on and began her ministry while a teenager. She held prayer services in homes in Pensacola. After she married in 1917, she moved to Philadelphia where she became pastor of Mount Olive Holy Church in 1919. The affiliate of the United Holy Church was fertile ground for Robinson, who began to attract people to her small congregation. Women found her ministry especially appealing and by the early 1920s women worshippers outnumbered the men two to one. Robinson was concerned about the church's restriction on female ordination, especially since she had so many women parishioners and they demanded a more active role in the church. She left the United Holy church and established a denomination to "loosen [women] from the bondage of male domination." Mount Sinai was chartered in Philadelphia in 1924, and Robinson soon filled her church to capacity. She was known as a great preacher who sometimes gave two- to three-hour sermons. Within her sermons she would intersperse such hymns as "What a Beautiful City" and "Oh I Want to See Him." Her

The First COGIC Women's Department

In 1911 Mother Lizzie Woods Roberson (1860–1945) was the first to organize a women's department in the Church of God in Christ. She was born a slave in Phillips County, Arkansas and learned to read the Bible by the time she was eight years old. She grew up Baptist and completed her education at the Baptist Academy in Dermott. Arkansas. Roberson left the Baptist church in 1911 and joined the Church of God in Christ (COGIC) which became the largest black Pentecostal denomination. Bishop Charles Harrison Mason (1866–1961), who founded the church, saw women as vital to the church and could use their spirituality to guide others. Thus, he recognized and respected Roberson as a strong woman and used her in an important post. She headed the Women's Department until she died. Women of the church were not allowed to become pastors and could only give lectures from a subordinate rostrum rather a sermon from the pulpit. Under her guidance, the Women's Department was exceptionally well organized. Roberson also developed prayer and Bible bands for women. She had married Elder Roberson in 1881 and they helped build the COGIC church as they traveled as evangelists and established churches. Other notable women in the church were Lillian B. Coffey (1896–1964), who succeeded Roberson, and Arenia Conelia Mallory (1905–1977), who headed the Saints Industrial School and Academy in Mississippi.

Sources: Salem, *African American Women*, pp. 423–24; Smith, *Notable Black American Women*, p. 770.

church spread to Florida and as far away as England and included eighty-four affiliates. She ensured that women were placed in the pulpit as she ordained 125 women out of a total of 163 ministers.

Sources: Salem, *African American Women*, pp. 25–26; Thomas, *Daughters of Thunder,* pp. 194–207.

Presbyterians

1757 • Samuel Davis, a white minister in Hanover County, Virginia, reported that he had baptized about 150 blacks after eighteen months of preaching to them. He had begun his activity in 1748. This is the first organized activity of Presbyterians among blacks. Davis would in time become the president of the College of New Jersey (later Princeton University).

Sources: Raboteau, *Slave Religion*, p. 129–30; Wilmore, *Black and Presbyterian*, p. 40.

1800 • Blacks participated in the Gasper River and Cane Ridge, Kentucky, camp meetings, which were the first to inaugurate the Great Western Revival. The lead given by the Presbyterians was followed by other denominations, and camp meetings became important in the conversion of slaves. Many scholars maintain that the majority of blacks were not converted to Christianity until this second wave of revivalism was taken up by other denominations, principally the Baptists and Methodists, along with new denominations, such as the Campbellites (Disciples of Christ).

Sources: Baer and Singer, *African-American Religion in the Twentieth Century*, p. 6; *Directory of African American Religious Bodies*, pp. 5–6; *Encyclopedia of American Religions*, pp. xxix–xxxi; Raboteau, *Slave Religion*, p. 132.

1801 • John Chavis (1763–1838) became the first black Presbyterian missionary in the South. Chavis was born free in North Carolina; the exact place of his birth is disputed. After fighting in the Revolutionary War, he received an education at Washington Academy (now Washington and Lee University) in Virginia and at Princeton. Chavis became a communicant in the Presbyterian Church in October 1799. The Presbytery of Lexington, Vir-

The First Black Presbyterian Church

In 1807 the first black Presbyterian church, First African, was organized in Philadelphia. It grew out of the work of John Gloucester Sr. (1776?–1822), a freed slave from Tennessee. The second church, in New York City, would not follow until fifteen years later. Little is known about Gloucester's early life; however, it is known that he was ordained a Presbyterian minister in 1792 and pastored a church that his owner Gideon Blackburn established in 1804 as a mission for the Cherokee Indians. Gloucester also preached in private homes and after his congregation became too large to meet in a house, he took his congregations to the street. This led to the founding in May or early June 1807 of his church. He had substantial powers both as a preacher and religious worker.

Sources: *Encyclopedia of Black America*, p. 704; Smith, *Climbing Jacob's Ladder*, p. 44; Smith, *Notable Black American Men*, pp. 462–64.

ginia, met on November 18–19, 1800, and licensed him to preach. He returned to North Carolina after being appointed a Presbyterian missionary to blacks. Between 1802 and 1832 he was active in the Presbyterian ministry intermittently; when he was active, however, he rode his horse through the countryside and preached to slaves, free blacks, and whites in North Carolina, Virginia, and Maryland. In North Carolina, he also preached to all-white churches in Granville, Wake, and Orange Counties. By 1808, he set up a school where he taught Latin and Greek to both black and white students. The first known black to have taught both races in the South, Chavis taught the children of free blacks as well as students from many aristocratic white families in the state. Many of his white students enrolled at the University of North Carolina at Chapel Hill; they entered such professions as medicine, law, the ministry, and politics. One became governor of the state. Chavis was forced to give up his school and pulpit in 1831, after the Nat Turner revolt resulted in laws that barred blacks from teaching and preaching in North Carolina.

Sources: Logan and Winston, *Dictionary of American Negro Biography*, pp. 101–2; Raboteau, *Slave Religion*, p. 135; Wilmore, *Black and Presbyterian*, p. 64; Smith, *Notable Black American Men*, pp. 190–91; Othow, *John Chavis*, 2001.

1818 • George M. Erskine was the first slave in Tennessee to be licensed as a preacher by the Presbyterians. After buying his freedom, and that of his wife and seven children, he went to Africa as a missionary. Only one other southern black is known to have been ordained by the church before the civil war—Harrison W. Ellis in 1846. He was sent to Liberia as a missionary.

Sources: Raboteau, *Slave Religion*, p. 207.

1821 • Samuel E. Cornish (1795–1858) established the first black Presbyterian church in New York City: the First Colored Presbyterian Church on New Demeter Street. It was the second in the country. A notable abolitionist, Cornish was also coeditor, with John B. Russworm, of the first black newspaper, *Freedom's Journal*, in 1827.

Sources: Logan and Winston, *Dictionary of American Negro Biography*, pp. 134–35; *Encyclopedia of Black America*, pp. 288–89; Smith, *Climbing Jacob's Ladder*, pp. 48, 51–52; Wilmore, *Black and Presbyterian*, pp. 65–66; Smith, *Notable Black American Men*, pp. 229–30.

1828 • Theodore Sedgewick Wright (1797–1847) was the first black graduate of Princeton Theological Seminary. Educated at the New York City African Free School and at Princeton, he succeeded Samuel Cornish at the First Colored Presbyterian Church in New York City, and became a noted abolitionist and supporter of rights for blacks.

Sources: Logan and Winston, *Dictionary of American Negro Biography*, pp. 675–76; *Encyclopedia of Black America*, p. 704; Wilmore, *Black and Presbyterian*, pp. 65–66.

Theodore Wright

Representative Black Churches Founded since 1865

Founded	Name	Founder
1865	Colored Primitive Baptists	
1867	United Free Will Baptist Church	
1869	Reformed Zion Union Apostolic Church	James R. Howell
1869	Second Cumberland Presbyterian Church	
1870	Colored Methodist Episcopal Church[1]	
1886	United Holy Church of America	
1889	Church of the Living God (Christian Workers for Fellowship)	William Christian
1894	Church of Christ Holiness, USA/Church of God in Christ[2]	C. P. Jones and C. H. Mason
1896	Church of God and Saints of Christ	William S. Crowdy
1896	Church of Christ, Holiness, USA	C. P. Jones
1902	Triumph the Church and Kingdom of God in Christ	E. D. Smith
1903	Christ's Sanctified Holy Church	
1905	Free Christian Zion Church of Christ	E. D. Brown
1907	National Primitive Baptist Convention of the USA	
1908	Church of the Living God, the Pillar and Ground of the Truth	Mary L. Tate
1908	Fire Baptized Holiness Church	W. E. Fuller
1920	Apostolic Overcoming Holy Church of God	William Thomas Phillips
1920	National Baptist Evangelical Life and Soul Saving Assembly of USA	A. A. Banks
1921	African Orthodox Church	George Alexander McGuire
1929	Kodesh Church of Immanuel	Frank Russell Killingsworth
1930	Lost-Found Nation of Islam in the West (Black Muslims)	W. D. Fard
1932	The National David Spiritual Temple of Christ Church Union (Inc.), USA	David William Short
1957	Bible Way Church of Our Lord Jesus Christ World Wide	Smallwood E. Williams
1961	Bible Church of Christ	Roy Bryant Sr.

[1]Now called the Christian Methodist Episcopal Church. [2]The two churches do not agree about their history, particularly about the date of the adoption of the name Church of God in Christ. See the *Encyclopedia of American Religions,* vol. 1, pp. 222, 272.

Sources: *Directory of African American Religious Bodies; Encyclopedia of American Religions; Negro Almanac,* pp. 1306–25.

1869 • The Colored Cumberland Presbyterian Church was founded in 1869. This church was one of the first to split away from white denomination, as separate black churches became legally possible after the Civil War. Some contact with the parent denomination was maintained, and the separation of the churches was not absolute until 1874. This denomination is now known as the Second Cumberland Presbyterian Church and has some 15,000 communicants.

Sources: *Directory of African American Religious Bodies,* p. 129; *Encyclopedia of American Religions,* vol. 1, p. 170.

1893 • The Afro-Presbyterian Council was the first formal organization for black Presbyterians in the North and West. (Southern Presbyterians were already in segregated synods.) The organization became the Council of the North and West in 1947, and was formally dissolved in 1957. The realization that the dissolution had been premature led to the formation of the Black Presbyterians United in 1968.

Sources: Wilmore, *Black and Presbyterian,* pp. 69–71.

1938 • Albert B. McCoy was the first black secretary of the Presbyterian Division of Work with Colored People.

Sources: Wilmore, *Black and Presbyterian,* p. 69.

1964 • Edler Garnet Hawkins (1908–1977) was elected the first black moderator of the United Presbyterian Church on May 21, 1964. Born in New York City on June 13, 1908, he received his Bachelor of Divinity from Union Theological Seminary in 1938. Hawkins built his church from nine black members to an integrated congregation of more than one thousand. He was also the first moderator of the church to visit the Roman Catholic pope.

Sources: *Current Biography 1965,* pp. 193–95; *Ebony* (September 1968): 66; *Encyclopedia of Black America,* p. 706.

1974 • Katie Geneva Cannon (1950–) was ordained on April 23, becoming the first black woman ordained in the Presbyterian church. In that same year, Jacqueline Alexander was also ordained. Cannon was born in Kannapolis, North Carolina, and graduated from Barber-Scotia College in nearby Concord (B.S., 1971), Johnson C. Smith Seminary of the Interdenominational Theological Center in Atlanta (M.Div., 1974), and Union Theological Seminary in New York City (M.Phil., Ph.D., 1983). She was pastor of New York City's Ascension Presbyterian Church from 1977 to 1980, visiting lecturer at Yale Divinity School in 1987, visiting scholar at Harvard Divinity School from 1983 to 1994, visiting professor at Wellesley College, 1991, and assistant professor in the Episcopal Divinity School in Cambridge, Massachusetts. She became associate professor of Christian ethics at Temple University's Department of Religion in 1993

Sources: Brown and Felton, *African American Presbyterian Clergywomen: The First Twenty-Five Years,* pp. 16, 93; *Contemporary Black Biography,* vol. 10, pp. 24–27.

1975 • Lawrence Wendell Bottoms (1908–1994) was the first black to become moderator of the Presbyterian Church (Southern Division). After his ordination in 1936, Bottoms was pastor of a Louisville, Kentucky, church until 1949. He served on many church boards and commissions.

Sources: *Encyclopedia of Black America,* p. 187; Hornsby, *Chronology of African-American History,* p. 226; *Jet* (4 July 1974): 44.

1976 • Thelma Davidson Adair (1921–) became the first black woman moderator of the United Presbyterian Church. Adair was a fifty-five year-old professor who specialized in early childhood and elementary education at Queens College in New York. The first black moderator was Edler G. Hawkins.

Sources: *Afro-American* (25 May 1976): 1; *Encore* 8 (6 July 1979): 41; *Jet* 50 (1 July 1976): 9.

1989 • Joan Salmon Campbell was the first black woman and only the sixth woman to head the Presbyterian Church, USA. A trained singer, Campbell has a degree from the Eastman School of Music.

Sources: Hornsby, *Chronology of African-American History,* p. 392; *Ebony* (November 1989): 100, 102, 104; *Jet* 77 (26 June 1989): 17; (20 November 1989): 38.

1989 • Sara Brown Cordery (1920–2007) was the first black woman moderator of the Presbytery of Baltimore. From 1991 to 1994 she was moderator of the Presbyterian Women Churchwide, becoming the first black woman to hold that post. She has been an elder in the Presbyterian Church, USA, since 1978. Born in Chester, South Carolina, Cordery graduated from South Carolina State College (now University) in Orangeburg (B.S., 1942), and Columbia University in New York City (Ed.D., 1955). In the course of her career, she was statistical analyst from 1942 to 1945 for the U.S. Government in Washington, D.C. Between 1946 and 1974 she held various posts at Barber-Scotia, serving as teacher, department chair, division chair, director of institutional research, special assistant to the president, and finally vice president for academic affairs. After that she moved to Morgan State University in Baltimore and from 1975 to 1985 she was professor and dean of the school of business and management.

Sources: *Jet* 77 (27 November 1989): 20; *Who's Who among African Americans,* 14th ed., p. 277.

Rastafarians

1935 • Haile Selassie (1892–1975) was crowned emperor of Ethiopia in 1935, the approximate date of the founding of the Rastafarian movement in Jamaica. The coronation of Selassie seemed to fulfill a 1927 prophecy by Marcus Garvey that the crowning of a king in Africa would be a sign that the end of black oppression by whites was near. Since about 1960 the group in the United States has grown to an estimated three to five thousand.

Sources: *Directory of African American Religious Bodies,* pp. 133–36; *Encyclopedia of American Religions,* vol. 3, pp. 156–57; *Negro Almanac, 1989,* p. 1319.

Reformed Dutch Church

1954 • James Joshua Thomas became the first black pastor in this denomination. He was given a church in the Bronx, New York City.

Sources: *Negro Almanac, 1989,* p. 1429.

Haile Selassie

Salvation Army

1970 • B. Barton McIntyre was the first black lieutenant colonel in the Salvation Army in the United States.

Sources: Garrett, *Famous First Facts about Negroes,* pp. 171–72; Romero, *In Black America,* p. 140.

Southern Baptists

1992 • Freedom Baptist Church of Selma, Alabama, was the first black church to be admitted to the Selma Baptist Association, made up of twenty-five white churches affiliated with the Alabama Southern Baptist Convention.

Sources: *Jet* 83 (9 November 1992): 33; *Time* 140 (2 November 1992): 22.

1996 • Harriet Tucker Watkins (1946?–) was ordained in the Peachtree Baptist Church in Atlanta; this was the first time the church had ordained a woman. This year she also became assistant pastor of the church—a predominantly white church. A dozen Confederate soldiers are buried in the church cemetery. Tucker holds membership in the Southern Baptist Convention—an organization that is overwhelmingly white in membership. Watkins grew up in Albany, New York, and was baptized in the Hudson River. She regularly attended the Church of God in Christ, a black Pentecostal church. While in high school, Watkins felt a call to the ministry but dismissed ordination as a choice because women did not preach in her church. Instead, she taught Sunday school and worked with youth groups. Watkins saw a need to become a lawyer to help people defend their rights. She graduated from law school in 1970 and for fifteen years worked for the U.S. Justice Department and other organizations in Washington, D.C. She moved to San Diego where, in defiance of denominational policy, a local bishop in the Church of God in Christ ordained her as a minister. Her ordination may have been only ceremonial, however, for Watkins was never allowed to function in a ministerial role. After she moved to Atlanta, she found a church that welcomed her gifts—a white Baptist congregation. She gave up a lucrative law career for the ministry.

Sources: *Atlanta Journal/The Atlanta Constitution* (17 August 1996).

2012 • Fred Luter Jr., pastor of Franklin Avenue Baptist Church in New Orleans, became the first black president of the Southern Baptist Convention on June 19. The SBC is the largest Protestant denomination in the nation. Seeking to diversify its leadership and membership, in June 2011 the SBC elected Luter as its first vice president and the number two officer, making him the first black to hold that post. He was the first black to give the convention sermon at the SBC convention held in New Orleans. Luter also gave one of the keynote addresses at the 2011 convention. This followed the Southern Baptists' statement issued six years earlier apologizing for the denomination's support of slavery and for the failure of many of its members to embrace the Civil Rights Movement.

Sources: *New York Times* (14 June 2011); *Tennessean* (15 June 2011); *Los Angeles Times* (19 June 2012).

Spiritual

1915 • The first verifiable black spiritual (formerly referred to as spiritualist) congregation is the Church of the Redemption in Chicago. It is possible that Mother Leafy Anderson had established an earlier one in Chicago before she moved to New Orleans and established the first in that city, Eternal Life Spiritual Church, sometime between 1918 and 1921.

Sources: Baer, *The Black Spiritual Movement*, p. 2.

1922 • The first black spiritual denomination was the National Colored Spiritualist Association of Churches, formed in 1922 by a breakaway of blacks from the predominantly white National Spiritualist Association. William Frank Taylor and Leviticus Lee Boswell founded the largest present-day association of black spiritual churches, Metropolitan Spiritual Churches of Christ, in 1925.

Sources: *Directory of African American Religious Bodies,* p. 130; *Encyclopedia of American Religions,* vol. 2, pp. 270–71.

Unitarian-Universalists

1982? • Yvonne Reed Chappelle (1936?–), also known as Yvonne Seon and "Mama Inga," was the first black woman ordained in the Unitarian-Universalist Church. In 1959, she graduated from Allegheny College and the following year studied at American University on a Woodrow Wilson Fellowship and received her master's degree. She holds a Ph.D. in African and African American Humanities and studied for her divinity degree at Howard University. During the 1960s, she spent two years in the Congo, on invitation from Patrice Lumumba, who became prime minister in 1960. While there she was secretary to the High Commission on the Inga Dam, one of the first positions as a foreign affairs officer in the Office of International Conferences. When the Fourteenth General Assembly of UNESCO met in Paris, she was the first African American selected as secretary of the delegation, the chief administrative officer. She returned to the United States and settled in Yellow Springs, Ohio, in late 1960s and later became founding director of Bolinga Black Cultural Resources Center at Wright State University, one of the first African American Studies Programs in the country. Seon is the mother of William S., entertainer Dave Chappelle, and daughter Felicia Chappelle Jones.

Sources: *Black Scholar* 1 (January 1970) 36–39; *Jet* 61 (11 February 1982): 32.

2001 • During its annual convention in Cleveland, Ohio, William G. Sinkford (1946?–) was elected president of the Unitarian-Universalist Association, becoming the first black president in the church's history. He won by a two-to-one margin over the only other candidate, a woman—the Reverend Diane M. W. Miller. The church is a liberal body with a predominately white membership. Sinkford grew up in Cincinnati and had a corporate career primarily in marketing. After that, he entered divinity school and was ordained in

1995. Now a resident of Cambridge, Massachusetts, he has served as director of congregational, district, and extension services for the Boston-based denomination.

Sources: *Jet* 100 (9 July 2001): 16; *New York Times* (23 June 2001).

United Church and Science of Living Institute

1966 • Frederick J. Eikerenkoetter II [The Rev. Ike] (1935?–2009) first founded his church in 1966. He had begun his ministry in the late 1950s as a Pentecostal, but was shifting away towards a New Thought position, a transition that would be complete by 1968. He rejected sin, taught that salvation must be achieved here and now, and praised monetary and material acquisitiveness.

Sources: Baer and Singer, *African-American Religion in the Twentieth Century,* pp. 64, 200–202; *Directory of African American Religious Bodies,* pp. 124–25; *Encyclopedia of American Religions,* vol. 2, p. 255.

United Society of Believers in Christ's Second Coming (Shakers)

1859 • Rebecca Cox Jackson (1795–1871) established the first largely black Shaker family in Philadelphia. Its existence in Philadelphia can be traced until at least 1908. A religious visionary, Jackson became an itinerant preacher and spiritual autobiographer. She was free-born and lived in Philadelphia early on. Around 1830, when she was thirty-nine years old, she challenged the African Methodist Church that had nourished her until then. Jackson joined praying bands that the Holiness movement within the Methodist church influenced. Throughout the late 1830s and early 1840s she traveled in Pennsylvania, northern Delaware, New Jersey, southern New England, and New York state and recounted her own experiences while also urging people to live free and celibate. In June 1847, Jackson and her friend and disciple, Rebecca Perot, joined the Shaker society; they lived in the Watervliet community, located near Albany, until June 1851 when they returned to Philadelphia. Jackson returned to Watervliet from 1858 to 1959 and negotiated with the Shakers about her right to establish a separate mission in Philadelphia. Jackson was known in the Shaker community as a very unusual speaker and one with impressive performance. Her spiritual writing survived; it traces her inner life and gives examples of her visionary dreams and various accounts of Shakerism.

Sources: Hine, *Black Women in America,* pp. 626–27; Smith, *Notable Black American Women,* pp. 561–65.

SCIENCE & MEDICINE

Federal Employees

1864 • Solomon G. Brown (1829–1903?) became the first black museum assistant at the Smithsonian Institution. Brown was born in Washington, D.C., near Boundary and 14th streets, NW, the fourth of six children. With no formal education, he worked for Samuel F. B. Morse when the inventor was developing the telegraph system in the 1840s. In 1852 Brown followed Joseph Henry, an associate of Morse, who became first secretary to the Smithsonian. Brown was an indispensable worker who prepared almost all of the illustrations for the Smithsonian's scientific lectures until 1887. His work at the Smithsonian enabled him to acquire a vast knowledge about natural history. He used that knowledge to lecture before adult groups and scientific societies. In 1855 he may have been the first American black to deliver a public lecture on science, when he gave a lecture on insects to the Young People's Club of the Israel A.M.E. Church in Washington, D.C.

Sources: Logan and Winston, *Dictionary of American Biography,* pp. 70–71; Simmons, *Men of Mark,* pp. 320–23.

1966 • Samuel Milton Nabrit (1905–2003) was the first black member of the Atomic Energy Commission. A zoologist born in Macon, Georgia, Nabrit received his master's degree in 1928 and his doctorate in 1932 from Brown University. (He was the first black to receive a doctorate in biology from that school.) While enrolled in graduate school, Nabrit taught biology at Morehouse College in Atlanta and conducted research at the Marine Biological Laboratory in Woods Hole, Massachusetts. From 1932 to 1947 he chaired the biology department at Atlanta University. Nabrit became dean of Atlanta University's School of Fine Arts in 1947 but left that same year when he was appointed the second president of Texas Southern University. He was a founder of Upward Bound, a student retention program. President Lyndon Johnson appointed him to the Atomic Energy Commission in 1966.

Sources: *Current Biography Yearbook,* 1963, pp. 295–97; *Encyclopedia of Black America,* pp. 611–12, 745; *Who's Who among African Americans,* 14th ed., p. 960; Salzman, *Encyclopedia of African-American Culture and History,* Supplement, p. 201.

Hospitals

1832 • The Georgia Infirmary in Savannah, Georgia, founded by whites, was the first hospital and asylum established for the relief and protection of aged and afflicted blacks.

The First Black Chief Surgeon

I n 1881 Charles Burleigh Purvis (1842–1929), physician, medical educator, and hospital administrator, became the first black surgeon-in-chief to head a hospital under civilian auspices. He received the appointment to the Freedmen's Hospital in the nation's capital. (Alexander Thomas
Augusta's appointment in 1865 was to Freedmen's when it was a military hospital.) Purvis was the
son of the prosperous abolitionists, Robert Purvis and Harriet Forten Purvis (a founder of the Female Anti-Slavery Society). He attended Oberlin College in Ohio and, wishing to pursue medical
training, transferred to Wooster Medical College (later Western Reserve Medical School) in Cleveland, Ohio, graduating in 1865. He served in the army until 1869, when he became the assistant surgeon at Freedmen's and a faculty member at Howard University in Washington, D.C. Purvis figured
prominently in the development of Howard University and its medical school. When President
James A. Garfield was felled by an assassin's bullet in 1881, Purvis was one of the doctors called to
care for the fatally wounded chief executive—the first and only black physician to serve a president
of the United States.

Sources: Logan and Winston, *Dictionary of American Negro Biography,* p. 507; Morais, *The History of the Negro in Medicine,* p. 51.

It was chartered in 1832, and the first organizational meeting was held on January 15,
1833.

Sources: Garrett, *Famous First Facts about Negroes,* p. 111; Kane, *Famous First Facts,* p.
309.

1863 • The nation's first hospital for black soldiers opened in Beaufort, South Carolina,
in April. The first patients were from the 1st South Carolina Volunteers, the nation's first
officially sanctioned black regiment. They mustered in on November 7, 1862, with colonel
Thomas Wentworth in command. While the wounded were hospitalized, Civil War nurse
Susie King Taylor (1848–1912) visited them often.

Sources: *Contemporary Black Biography,* vol. 13, pp. 208–9.

1881 • Good Samaritan Hospital, established in Charlotte, North Carolina, was the first
privately run hospital exclusively for blacks in the United States.

Sources: Randolph, *An African-American Album,* p. 84.

1891 • Provident Hospital in Chicago, Illinois, was the first American hospital operated
by blacks. Founded by Daniel Hale Williams (1856–1931), it spurred blacks to organize
comparable hospitals in other cities. Williams's aim was to create a hospital where black
doctors and nurses could be prepared, and black patients receive decorous care without
fear of racial bias.

Sources: Baskin and Runes, *Dictionary of Black Culture,* p. 362; Morais, *The History of the
Negro in Medicine,* p. 75.

1895 • Nathan Francis Mossell (1856–1946) founded Philadelphia's first hospital primarily for blacks, the Frederick Douglass Memorial Hospital and Training School for
Nurses. Although the hospital attracted a fine staff of black physicians—and white doctors who aided in their training—it was in constant conflict with Mercy Hospital, founded
by Henry McKee Minton and others in Philadelphia in 1907. After hospital officials agreed
that the black population's needs could be served better by one hospital, the two facilities
merged around 1948 and moved into a modern building in 1954. Mossell was born in
Hamilton, Ontario, Canada, to free-black parents who fled to Canada in search of a better
life. In 1873 he enrolled in Lincoln University and graduated in 1879 with a bachelor's de-

gree. He enrolled in medical school in 1872 and became the first black graduate of the University of Pennsylvania when he received his medical degree in 1882. After a bitter struggle, Mossell was the first black admitted to the Philadelphia Medical Society in 1885. He studied at prestigious hospitals in London, England, before he attacked the problem of founding a hospital. An ardent civil rights activist, Mossell went to Niagara Falls in 1905 with W.E.B. Du Bois as one of the organizers of the Niagara Movement, a forerunner of the NAACP. Paul Robeson, singer, actor, and activist, was his nephew.

Sources: Logan and Winston, *Dictionary of American Negro Biography,* pp. 457–58; *Dictionary of Black Culture,* p. 308; Morais, *The History of the Negro in Medicine,* p. 79.

1915 • Walden Hospital, the first and only black-owned and operated hospital in Chattanooga, Tennessee, was dedicated on July 30. Emma Rochelle Wheeler (1882–1957), a trailblazing physician, was founder and operator. The building held thirty-nine beds; there were nine private rooms and a twelve-bed ward. The hospital closed on June 30, 1953. Wheeler was born near Gainesville, Florida, and developed an interest in medicine when she was six years old and treated for an eye infection. She graduated from Cookman Institute in Jacksonville when she was seventeen. She married, but her husband died of typhoid fever the next year. She relocated to Nashville, Tennessee, to pursue her interest in medicine. Wheeler graduated from Walden University's Meharry Medical, Dental, and Pharmaceutical College in 1905 and then married a physician. After graduation, the Wheelers moved to Chattanooga and established a medical practice on Main Street. Ten years later, with money she had saved, she opened Walden Hospital. The facility included surgical, maternity, and nursery departments and had two staff doctors. Seventeen other physicians and surgeons used the facility and admitted their patients. Wheeler managed the hospital until 1953, when declining health led her to retire.

Sources: Smith, *Notable Black American Women,* Book II, pp. 702–4 (Wheeler); Jones, *Every Day in Tennessee History,* p. 139.

1925 • The first black-owned hospital in New York City, the Edgecombe Sanitarium, opened in Harlem. Louis Tompkins Wright was among the surgeons who practiced there.

Sources: *The Black New Yorkers,* p. 193.

Inventions and Patents

1781 • The first known black clockmaker in America, and the only black clockmaker known to have worked in the late eighteenth and early nineteenth centuries, was Peter Hill (1767–1820). He was one of the few blacks who opened a small business. Other black entrepreneurs of this period were barbers, restaurateurs, caterers, merchants, and tailors. Since Hill was not an inventor, his contribution to the art of clock-making was minor yet his historic achievement as America's first black clockmaker is significant. Born on July 19, 1767, probably on the property of Quaker clockmaker Joseph Hollinshead Jr., Peter Hill was the son of Hollinshead's slaves. To provide assistance in his shop, Hollinshead trained Hill in the craft of clockmaking. Hollingshead followed the custom of local Quakers, who dedicated themselves to enhancing the lives of blacks by teaching them certain skills. From the time he was fourteen until he was twenty-one, Hill served a form of an apprenticeship with his master. After that Hill may have been a salaried skilled shop assistant or a journeyman clockmaker. Since Hill was paid for his work, he earned enough money to buy his freedom, and in 1794 the master freed his twenty-seven-year-old mulatto slave. Hill married Tina Lewis on September 9, 1795, four months after he was manumitted; he purchased her freedom as well. While the date on which he opened his first shop is unclear, it is known that Hill opened a shop before he was freed, sometime before 1795. Records locating Hill's shop in different locations lead to confusion; however, he lived and worked in Burlington Township, New Jersey, and later in Mount Holly. He operated a clockmaking business in Burlington Township for twenty-three years. He bought land at various times between 1801 and 1811, and his prosperity increased during these years. By 1814, however, he and his wife may not have fared as well and sold some of their land. By 1820

The First Black Patent Recipient

Thomas L. Jennings (1791–1859) is believed to be the first black to receive a patent, for a drycleaning process, on March 3, 1821. He was a tailor and dry cleaner in New York City and an active abolitionist; he was the founder and president of the Legal Rights Association.

Sources: Haskins, Jim, *Outward Dreams*, pp. 4–5; James, *The Real McCoy*, p. 31; Katz, Eyewitness: *The Negro in American History*, pp. 98, 99, 139.

the Hills had purchased a new house and several buildings, suggesting that the family prospered again. Hill enjoyed his new home and surroundings briefly before he died in December 1820. His wife may have died around the same time. Hill was buried in the Society of Friends' Burial-Ground near the Friend Meeting House in Burlingtown Township, across the street from one of Hill's residences and shops. Five of Peter Hill's clocks are known to be extant; they contain eight-day striking movements. Hill's work and skill demonstrate a rare accomplishment for blacks in early American history.

Sources: Hine and Jenkins, *A Question of Manhood*, vol. 1, pp. 19–20, 252–73.

1798? • James Forten Sr. (1766–1842) was the inventor of a novel sail-handling device, an invention that brought him considerable affluence. He became owner of a sail loft in 1798, and by 1832 was a wealthy man, employing about forty workers. His fortune enabled him to become one of the leading figures in the abolition movement.

Sources: Logan and Winston, *Dictionary of American Negro Biography*, pp. 234–35; Baskin and Runes, *Dictionary of Black Culture*, pp. 166–67; James, *The Real McCoy*, pp. 33–35.

1832? • Augustus Jackson (1808–?), an African American chef, was head chef in the White House during the first quarter of the nineteenth century and the inventor of modern ice cream manufacture. Although he did not invent ice cream, some claim that he did; he greatly improved ice cream, however, and created several new flavors and improved the methods of manufacturing the product. He is sometimes called "the Father of Ice Cream." The hazy sketches of Jackson's life indicate that Jackson resigned his White House post in the late 1820s and returned to his native Philadelphia. There he opened a successful catering business, creating several popular ice cream flavors. Jackson developed techniques to control the custard while it was freezing. He distributed his ice cream in packaged tin cans to various ice cream parlors in the area. Around that time Philadelphia was known for its fine caterers, and many blacks in the Philadelphia area owned ice cream parlors or became ice cream makers. Jackson, an accomplished entrepreneur, is said to have been "the most successful and his cream flavors were well loved." He was also a candy confectioner. He became one of the city's wealthiest residents.

Sources: Bellis, "Augustus Jackson," http://inventors.about.com/od/ijstartinventors/a/Augustus Jackson.htm; Rossant, "Augustus Jackson: African American White House Chef," http://www.superchefblog.com/2005/07/augustus-jackson-african-american.html. Accessed October 10, 2012.

1834 • Henry Blair (1804?–1860) of Glenross, Maryland, was long believed to be the first black to obtain a patent, for a corn planter, on October 14, 1834. The device was easier to operate than the crude planters that existed, and permitted seeds to be dropped in the soil in a checkerboard fashion.

Sources: *Negro Almanac*, pp. 1079–1424; *Jet* 96 (6 September 1999): 19.

1843 • Norbert Rillieux (1806–1894) was the first person to apply a multiple vacuum evaporation system to the production of sugar, and by so doing, revolutionized production. This invention helped change the food consumption patterns of the world and determined the nature of colonial dependency for a substantial part of the Third World. Born a free

Norbert Rillieux

Elijah McCoy's First Patent

On July 2, 1872, Elijah McCoy (1843–1929) patented the first version of his lubricator for steam engines. This was the first in a series of forty-two patents, most of which were designed to facilitate machine lubrication. Numerous continuous industrial devices flooded the market soon after McCoy's. According to folk etymology, his devices were sought after and those in the know wanted "the real McCoy," nothing else. The claim that the phrase "the real McCoy" originated with his devices is not fully substantiated. Around 1920 McCoy opened his own business, the Elijah McCoy Manufacturing Company, where he made and sold a number of his inventions. McCoy was born in Colchester, Ontario, Canada, and after an apprenticeship in mechanical engineering in Edinburgh, Scotland, moved to Michigan where his family had relocated after the Civil War erupted. His last patent was granted in 1920 for a graphite lubrication device.

Sources: Logan and Winston, *Dictionary of American Negro Biography*, pp. 413–14; *Contemporary Black Biography*, vol. 8, pp. 167–70; Haskins, *Outward Dreams*, pp. 40–44; James, *The Real McCoy*, pp. 73–75; Smith, *Notable Black American Men*, pp. 787–89.

black in New Orleans, Rillieux received a thorough education in mechanical engineering at the École Centrale in Paris. After demonstrating the practical effects of his invention in New Orleans and making a good deal of money, Rillieux returned to France in 1854 because of the increasing restrictions on free blacks in Louisiana.

Sources: Logan and Winston, *Dictionary of American Negro Biography*, pp. 525–26; Haskins, *Outward Dreams*, pp. 26–33; James, *The Real McCoy*, pp. 41–43.

1848 • Lewis Temple (1800–1854), born in Richmond, Virginia, was the inventor of an improved model of the whaling harpoon used in the nineteenth century. (In 1845 Temple was running a blacksmith shop in New Bedford, Massachusetts, having moved there in 1829.) He did not patent his new model, which was quickly adopted in the whaling business, but he did enjoy a modest affluence. He was active in the abolitionist movement and divided his time between the movement and the whaling industry. Unfortunately, his widow and children were left destitute at his death.

Elijah McCoy

Sources: Logan and Winston, *Dictionary of American Negro Biography*, pp. 582–83; Haskins, *Outward Dreams*, pp. 20–21; James, *The Real McCoy*, pp. 35–37; *Negro Almanac*, p. 1090.

1878 • Inventor J. R. Winters patented the first fire escape ladder, on May 7. He improved the wooden ladder in existence at the time and used a metal frame with parallel steps. The escape ladder was attached to the side of buildings and used to enable people to safely escape from fire or other perils.

Sources: *Jet* 99 (14 May 2001): 32.

1882 • Lewis Howard Latimer (1848–1928) patented the first cost-efficient method for producing carbon filaments for electric lights on June 17, 1882. Born in Chelsea, Massachusetts, his father, George, was an escaped slave whose capture precipitated the first of the highly publicized fugitive slave trials in 1842, and provoked Frederick Douglass's first appearance in print. During the Civil War, Lewis Latimer enlisted in the U.S. Navy as soon as he was old enough. He then became an office boy in a patent office and soon became a patent draftsman. Latimer made drawings for many of Alexander Graham Bell's telephone patents. He also worked for the United States Electric Lighting Company, where he made many significant innovations in the development of electric lighting, and supervised the installation of electric light plants in New York and Philadelphia. In 1884 he began to work for the Edison Electric Light Company and entered its legal department in 1890. From 1896 to 1911 he was head draftsman for the Board of Patent Control and later worked as a patent consultant.

Lewis Latimer

Sources: Logan and Winston, *Dictionary of American Negro Biography,* pp. 385–86; Haskins, *Outward Dreams,* pp. 49–52; James, *The Real McCoy,* pp. 96–99; Smith, *Notable Black American Men,* pp. 698–700.

1882 • W. B. Purvis of Philadelphia, Pennsylvania, obtained his first patent on a paper bag device on April 25, 1882. On February 27, 1883, he patented the hand stamp. This was a wooden device to which rubber letters are attached. Of the sixteen patents he obtained by 1897, eleven were connected with the manufacture of paper bags. Most of the patents were sold to the Union Paper Bag Company of New York.

Sources: *Jet* 91 (3 March 1997): 19; *Journal of Negro History* 2 (January 1917): 33; Culp, *Twentieth Century Negro Literature,* pp. 403, 410; Work, *Negro Year Book, 1925–26,* pp. 366–67.

1883 • On March 20, 1883, Jan Matzeliger (1852–1889) patented the first successful shoe-lasting machine. Matzeliger was born in Surinam of a Dutch father who was an engineer and a black mother who was Surinamese and probably came from West Africa. He left Suriname in 1871 and became a sailor on an East Indian ship. Matzeliger settled in Philadelphia for a while, holding odd jobs until he moved to Boston in 1876. The next year he settled in nearby Lynn, Massachusetts. There he developed his device while working in a shoe factory. The machine increased productivity as much as fourteen times over hand methods and led to concentration in the industry. Matzelinger continued to work on the machine to improve its quality, and received a patent for a third and improved model on September 22, 1891. He invented a number of other devices, including a mechanism for distributing tacks and nails.

Sources: Logan and Winston, *Dictionary of American Negro Biography,* pp. 429–30; James, *The Real McCoy,* p. 70–72; Smith, *Notable Black American Men,* pp. 776–78.

1883 • On April 3, 1883, Humphrey H. Reynolds was the first black to patent an improved window ventilator for railroad cars. The device was adopted on all Pullman cars. Since he received no compensation from the company, Reynolds quit his job as a railroad porter and sued. He won $10,000.

Sources: James, *The Real McCoy,* p. 72.

1883 • S. E. Thomas was the inventor of a waste trap, patented on October 16. The curved, elbow-shaped metal pipe connected to a plumbing fixture to form a seal, preventing air from escaping through the pipe either from the back or below. The waste trap used today is based on this design.

Sources: *Jet* 90 (21 October 1996): 20.

Granville T. Woods

1884 • Granville T. Woods (1856–1910) patented his first electric device, an improved telephone transmitter on December 2, 1884. By 1900 Woods—often called the "Black Edison"—had received twenty-two patents, most dealing with electricity used in railway telegraphy systems and electric railways. He was born free in Columbus, Ohio, where he completed only three years of schooling. Woods was self-educated, however, and spent considerable time in public libraries reading about electricity. After an apprenticeship as a machinist and blacksmith, Woods worked principally on railroads, becoming a locomotive engineer before founding the Woods Electric Company in Cincinnati, Ohio, around 1884. On January 3 that year he patented a steam boiler furnace, and on December 2 he patented a telephone transmitter. Perhaps the most advanced devices among his inventions was the Synchronous Multiplex Railway Telegraph that he patented in 1887, allowing moving trains to communicate with each other and with railroad stations to avoid accidents. Woods moved to New York in 1890 and patented an automatic air brake purchased by George Westinghouse in 1902. His inventions paved the way for the development of the electric streetcar.

Sources: Logan and Winston, *Dictionary of American Negro Biography,* pp. 663–65; Haskins, *Outward Dreams,* pp. 47–49, 95–96; James, *The Real McCoy,* pp. 94–95; Smith, *Notable Black American Men,* pp. 1250–52.

1885 • The first known black woman inventor is Sarah E. Goode, who patented a folding cabinet bed on July 14, 1885. Since ethnic identity is not part of a patent application, it is impossible to be sure of absolute priority. Another black woman might be the first, since Ellen F. Eglin of Washington, D.C., invented a clothes wringer before April 1890. While no patent was issued in her name, Eglin sold the idea to an agent for eighteen dollars since she believed that it would be impossible for a black woman to exploit the device successfully. At the beginning of the twentieth century, Miriam E. Benjamin of Massachusetts, who patented a gong signal systems for summoning attendants on July 17, 1888, was believed to be the first; her invention was adopted by the U.S. House of Representatives to summon pages.

Sources: James, *The Real McCoy,* p. 67; Macdonald, *Feminine Ingenuity,* p. 172; Culp, *Twentieth Century Negro Literature,* p. 407.

1889 • On July 23, inventor W. A. Martin patented a lock that could be locked or unlocked from either side—an improvement over the old bolt that the Chinese invented four thousand years earlier. The Martin lock included a cylinder and spiral coiled around a metal pin; it became the forerunner of modern door locks.

Sources: *Jet* 96 (26 July 1999): 19.

1892 • Sarah Boone was the first person to receive a patent for an ironing board. Her invention was a narrow board with a padded cover and collapsible legs, an improvement over the existing boards that were placed across chairs for support.

Sources: Potter and Claytor, *African American Firsts,* p. 242.

1893 • Inventor E. R. Robinson was the first person to receive a patent for an electric railway trolley on September 19. To propel the car, he used electricity that flowed from an overhead wire through a pole attached to the roof of the vehicle. It became the forerunner of the electric street railways and buses that continue to operate in some sections of the country.

Sources: *Jet* 96 (20 September 1999): 19.

1895 • The U.S. Patent Office advertised its first special exhibit of the inventions of blacks.

Sources: James, *The Real McCoy,* p. 57.

1897 • Andrew Jackson Beard (1849–1941), of Alabama, was the first black to patent a coupling device for railroad cars, called Janney (sometimes misspelled "Jenny") Coupler, on November 23. A coupler consisted of a knuckle joined to the end of a drawbar which fastened to a mechanism on the car. The knuckled end was also designed to prevent moving cars from derailing on curved track. To engage the coupler, it was necessary for a railroader to stand between the cars and drop a pin in place when the cars came together. This was a dangerous maneuver, because misalignment in the knuckles when the cars came together could lead to the loss of an arm, hand, or even death. In 1873 Eli H. Janney, a dry good clerk and former Confederate Army officer from Alexander, Virginia, patented a knuckle-style coupler that became the standard for freight cars aid is still used today. Although the coupler devices were among the most popular subjects for patents—there were some 6,500 patents by this 1897—Beard was able to sell his invention for some $50,000. Beard's invention was adopted nationally in 1916; his work was so impressive that he was elected an honorary member of the Master Car Builders Association. Beard's invention made him Alabama's first black millionaire. He was a prolific inventor, receiving patents for such items as a plow and a steam engine. Beard was born a slave in Mount Pinson (now Pinson) in Jefferson County, Alabama, and was freed at age fifteen. He never learned to read or write, or to recognize his name in print. After marrying, he became a farmer near Birmingham. He built a school on his farm for his tenants, and he later built a flour mill near Hardwick. After he became a millionaire, he organized Beard's Jitney (taxi) Line in Birmingham, and made his fleet one of the best that existed. He was a poor financial manager who, with failing health in later years, ruined his own career.

Sources: James, *The Real McCoy,* pp. 72–73; *Journal of Negro History* 2 (January 1917): 34; Bailey, *They Too Call Alabama Home,* pp. 33–34.

1899 • George F. Grant invented the wooden golf tee, receiving a patent on February 16 this year. An avid golfer, he was the first person known to invent the device. His invention would revolutionize the way golfers swing at the ball. Grant was a Boston native and became the second black to graduate from the Dental School at Harvard University. He became the first black member of Harvard's faculty, where he was a "demonstrator" and instructor from 1878 to 1889. He became known for his bridgework. One of Grant's personal patients was Harvard University president Charles William Eliot.

Sources: "George Grant—Improved Golf Tee," http://inventors.about.com/od/blackinventors/a/George_Grant.htm; Sollors, Titcomb, and Underwood, *Blacks at Harvard,* p. 6.

1904 • Granville T. Woods (1856–1910) and his brother Lyates patented the first of two improvements on railroad brakes on March 29, 1904. The second patent was issued on July 18, 1905. Both were of sufficient importance that the Westinghouse Electric Company purchased them.

Sources: *Journal of Negro History* 2 (January 1917): 32.

Garrett A. Morgan

1912 • Garrett A. Morgan (1875–1963) was the first black to receive a patent for a safety hood and smoke protector. He demonstrated its worth in 1916 by rescuing workers trapped in a smoke-filled tunnel of the Cleveland, Ohio, waterworks. Born on a farm near Paris, Kentucky, Morgan was one of eleven children born to a part-Indian slave mother who was freed by the Emancipation Proclamation, and a father who was the son of a Confederate colonel. Morgan moved to Cincinnati and worked for a prosperous landowner as a handyman. He hired a tutor to help him improve his grammar. In 1895 he moved to Cleveland and worked for a clothing manufacturer, adjusting sewing machines. This led to one of several businesses that he began. First Morgan sold and repaired sewing machines, and in 1909 he established the Morgan Skirt Factory, a tailoring plant with thirty-two employees. In 1913 he founded the G. A. Morgan Hair Refining Company that offered a complete line of hair-care products bearing the Morgan label. Morgan was also the first to patent a three-way automatic traffic signal, in 1923; he sold the patent to General Electric. He became known as a very astute businessman and inventor.

Sources: Cantor, *Historic Landmarks of Black America,* p. 352; Logan and Winston, *Dictionary of American Negro Biography,* p. 453; James, *The Real McCoy,* pp. 91–93; Smith, *Notable Black American Men,* pp. 829–31.

1913 • Henry Edwin Baker (1859–1928), a black assistant examiner in the U.S. Patent Office, published the first separate list of black inventors, *The Negro Inventor.* Baker used his position in the patent office to discover and publicize the inventions of blacks. This was quite a formidable task since race is not recorded on applications. Despite this obstacle, Baker was able to reveal the names of some four hundred blacks.

Sources: James, *The Real McCoy,* pp. 77–78.

1928 • Marjorie Stewart Joyner (1896–1994) was the first black to patent a permanent waving machine for hairstyling and became one of the first black woman to receive a patent for an invention. She later developed a hair straightening comb. Joyner was an employee of Madame C. J. Walker, to whose company the patent was assigned. She eventually became national supervisor of the Walker organization's chain of beauty schools. In 1916 Joyner, the first black graduate of A. B. Molar Beauty School in Chicago, opened her own salon. In 1945 she was a cofounder of the United Beauty School Owners and Teachers Association. (The graduates of these schools comprise the Alpha Phi Omega sorority and fraternity.) She organized the first Bud Billiken Parade in 1929—a benefit for delivery carriers of the black newspaper, the *Chicago Defender.* The granddaughter of slaves, Joyner was born in the Blue Ridge Mountains near the town of Monterey, Virginia. She was one of thirteen children, only four of whom lived beyond infancy. The family relocated to Dayton, Ohio, in 1904 and soon the parents divorced. She lived with one family member and then another, finally settling in Chicago with her mother. Her high school education was interrupted until 1935, when finally she graduated. In the meantime, she received a music school certificate in 1924. It was not until 1973, when she was seventy-seven years old, that she received her bachelor's degree from Bethune-Cookman College in Florida. There she was often called the "Godmother of Bethune-Cookman College." She was also called the "Grand Dame of Black Beauty Culture." Among her various honors, in 1990 the city of Chicago honored her by naming her birthday Marjorie Stewart Joyner Day.

Sources: Macdonald, *Feminine Ingenuity,* pp. 297–301; *Who's Who among Black Americans,* 1992–93, p. 806; Smith, *Notable Black American Women,* Book II, pp. 366–70.

1936 • Percy Lavon Julian (1899–1975) was the first black to be hired as a director of research by a major chemical manufacturing company, the Glidden Company of Chicago. He received 105 patents, 66 of which were assigned to this company. In 1954 he established his own company, Julian Laboratories. His name is linked with the synthesis of physostigmine in 1935 (used in treating glaucoma) and the precursors of cortisone (for the treatment of arthritis), among many other achievements in chemistry. Julian was born in Montgomery, Alabama, and developed an interest in science early on. Influenced by the work of chemist St. Elmo Brady, he enrolled in DePauw University in Greencastle, Indiana, in 1916 as a "sub-freshman." He graduated in 1920 with a bachelor's degree and was class valedictorian and elected to Phi Beta Kappa. After teaching chemistry for two years at Fisk University in Nashville, Tennessee, he enrolled in Harvard University and received a master's degree in organic chemistry in 1923. He held other teaching posts, including one at Howard University in Washington, D.C., studied abroad, and in 1931 received his doctorate degree from the University of Vienna. Julian returned to Howard that year to head the chemistry department; he returned to DePauw the following year. He left the university in 1936 and became director of research for the Glidden Company in Chicago.

Sources: *Ebony Success Library,* vol. 2, pp. 150–53; Haber, *Black Pioneers of Science and Invention,* pp. 87–101; Smith, *Notable Black American Men,* pp. 672–75; *Contemporary Black Biography,* vol. 6, pp. 159–63.

1940 • Frederick McKinley Jones (1892–1961) was the inventor of a practical refrigeration system for trucks and railroad cars. He received the patent on July 12, 1940. Born in Cincinnati, Ohio, his parents died early on, and then he lived in Covington, Kentucky, with a Catholic priest, Father Ryan. His formal education ended in the sixth grade. His keen interest in machines and his obsession with automobiles led him to convert ordinary cars into mint-condition racers. Jones worked as an automobile mechanic and an automobile shop foreman, and later moved to hotel maintenance. While working in a hotel, Jones met a guest from Minnesota who recognized his skills and offered him a position repairing farm equipment and cars in Hallock, Minnesota. Jones became an automobile racer as well, racing on the dirt track circuit until 1925. He also became movie projectionist in Hallock. By 1930 his self-teaching was so effective that he was manufacturing movie sound equipment and later invented and patented a movie ticket dispensing machine. The development of the refrigerating device marked a new direction for his efforts, and its success revolutionized the transportation and marketing of fresh foods. In 1991 he was the first black to receive the National Medal of Technology (posthumously).

Sources: Logan and Winston, *Dictionary of American Negro Biography,* p. 366; *Negro Almanac,* p. 1084; Smith, *Notable Black American Men,* pp. 647–48.

1961? • Otis F. Boykin (1920–1982) invented the implantable heart pacemaker—a medical contraption used to prevent heart failures, the most popular item of the twenty-eight different electronic and mechanical devices that he invented. The pacemaker "has helped to save and lengthen the lives of thousands of men and women around the world," and helped to make him one of the greatest inventors of his time. Variations of his resistor models are used worldwide in televisions, computers, guided missiles, and radios. He received his first patent in 1959—a wire precision resistor, followed by the 1961 inexpensive electrical resistor, U.S. patent No. 2,972,726, with the ability to withstand great temperature changes, extreme accelerations, and shocks. Not all of his works were patented; however eleven of his inventions were patented. His achievements attracted wide attention and led to his work as electronic consultant in the United States and abroad. Boykin was born in Dallas and attended Fisk University in Nashville. He worked for several electronic firms in Chicago and did graduate study at Illinois Institute of Technology. He died of heart failure in Chicago.

Sources: "Bio of Inventor Otis Boykin: African-American Invented the Pacemaker," http://www.associatedcontent.com/article/18087/bio_of_inventor_otis_boykin_africananme; "Biography of Otis F. Boykin," http://profiles.incredible-people.com/otis-f-boykin/; "Inventor of the Week Archives," http://web.mit.edu/invent/iow/boykin.html.

1969 • George Robert Carruthers (1939–) was the first black to patent an image converter for detecting electromagnetic radiation, on November 11, 1969. Born in Cincinnati, Carruthers graduated from the University of Illinois with a bachelor's degree in 1961 and a master's in 1962. After earning a doctorate in physics from that university in 1964, Carruthers began working as a researcher for the U.S. Navy and later for the National Aeronautics and Space Agency. He received the NASA Exceptional Scientific Achievement medal for his work as one of the two people responsible for the development of the lunar surface ultraviolet camera/spectrograph placed on the moon in April 1972 during the Apollo 16 mission.

Sources: *Ebony* 28 (October 1973): 61–63; Haskins, *Outward Dreams*, pp. 83–84, 88; *Negro Almanac,* p. 1080; *Who's Who among African* Americans, 26th ed., p. 212.

1986 • Patricia E. Bath (1942–) discovered and invented laserphaco, a new device for cataract surgery. She is also the first black woman doctor to receive a patent for a medical purpose. An ophthalmologist and laser scientist, Bath advocates for blindness prevention, treatment, and cure. She now holds four patents. In 1974 Bath became the first woman opthalmologist to be appointed to the faculty of the University of California at Los Angeles School of Medicine Jules Stein Eye Institute. In 1983, she was the first woman to chair an ophthalmology residency program in the United States. Born in Harlem, she graduated from Hunter College and received her MD from Howard University.

Sources: "Dr. Patricia E. Bath," Changing the Face of Medicine, www.nlm.nih.gov/changing thefaceofmedicine/physicians/biography_26.html, accessed March 4, 2012; "Patricia Bath," www.info.please.com/biography/patricia-bath.html, accessed March 4, 2012.

1988 • Los Angeles aerospace engineer Lonnie Johnson unveiled an air-powered water gun called the "Power Drencher" on February 24. It became highly popular as the "Super Soaker" and was the first known gun of its type.

Sources: "Post-Gazette, Black History Month: Special Reports," www.post-gazette.com/newslinks/Facts2000.asp. Accessed September 30, 2012.

2008 • Cleveland native Phil Davis (1960?–) invented the world's smallest patented, personal-sized and portable microwave, called the iWave Cube. Although the microwave was invented in 1947, its size required that it be placed on a kitchen counter, over the range, or on a cart or table. The iWave Cube was manufactured in China by Midea, weighs 12 pounds, and measures 10" × 10.5" × 12". It can be used to cook popcorn, heat meals, warm beverages, cook small pizzas or small frozen entrees, and cook any small or single-sized food item. When invented, the iWaveCube used 600 watts and was relatively quiet when in operation. Davis expected to have an 800-watt version with a dual power supply by December that year; an American, European, or Asian plug could accommodate the machine. Early on, Phil Davis invented a deodorant for children. He is a graduate of Stanford University and holds an MBA from the University of Virginia.

Sources: *Jet* 113 (14 April 2008): 38.

Medical Agencies and Schools

1882 • Leonard Medical School, established at Shaw University in Raleigh, North Carolina, this year, became the South's first four-year medical school for blacks. Although the medical college no longer exists, the Leonard Building still stands, having endured a fire in 1988. In 1996 Shaw received a grant from the U.S. Department of Interior and the Philip

The Oldest Surviving Black Medical School in the South

Meharry Medical College was the first medical school founded solely for the education of blacks. Situated in Nashville, Tennessee, Meharry was a department of the Central Tennessee College (later known as Walden University), founded in 1866, and maintained by the Freedmen's Aid Society. The school opened in October 1876 with fewer than a dozen students. Meharry Medical College received a separate charter in October 1915. The driving spirit behind the school for forty-five years was George Whipple Hubbard (1844–1924), a white Civil War missionary to the freedmen of the South who organized the school, taught on the faculty, served as dean, and was elected president of the school on January 7, 1916. From 1900 to 1901 he was also president of Central Tennessee College. Hubbard had graduated from the Medical Department of the University of Nashville in 1876 and received a medical diploma in 1879 from Vanderbilt University.

Sources: Baskin and Runes, *Dictionary of Black Culture*, p. 294; Morais, *The History of the Negro in Medicine*, p. 44; Roman, *Meharry Medical College: A History*.

Morris Companies Inc. to save the building, one of the historically important buildings on the campus.

Sources: *American Visions,* Advertising Travel Supplement, 1994: 19; *Jet* 90 (28 October 1996): 38; Salzman, *Encyclopedia of African-American Culture and History,* vol. 3, p. 1250.

1945 • The first and only school of veterinary medicine in a black college or university was established at Tuskegee Institute in Alabama. Instruction began September 1, 1945. Frederick D. Patterson (1901–1988), veterinarian and then president of Tuskegee, founded the school.

Sources: Bowles and DeCosta, *Between Two Worlds,* p. 131; *Jet* 72 (29 June 1987): 22; Tuskegee Institute, *Sixty-Fifth Annual Catalog, 1946–47,* p. 31.

1980 • Maurice C. Clifford (1920–2002) was inaugurated as the first black president of the Medical College of Pennsylvania—the first black president of at a predominantly white college. Born in Washington, D.C., Clifford received his bachelor's degree in 1941 from Hamilton College in Clinton, New York, and his master's degree in 1942 from the University of Chicago. He went on to study medicine and received his medical degree from Meharry Medical College in 1947. Clifford was in private practice in obstetrics and gynecology from 1951 to 1978. At the Medical College of Pennsylvania, Clifford was vice president for medical affairs from 1978 to 1979 and acting president from 1979 to 1980. He held the presidency of that college from 1980 to 1986. He also served as commissioner of Philadelphia's Department of Public Health from 1986 to 1992. Clifford was also executive president from 1993 to 1996 and president and chief executive officer from 1996 to 1999 for the Lomax Companies.

Sources: *Who's Who among African Americans,* 14th ed., p. 2247.

1993 • David Satcher (1941–) was the first black appointed director of the Centers for Disease Control and Prevention (CDC) in Atlanta, Georgia, on August 20. A native of Anniston, Alabama, he graduated from Morehouse College in Atlanta in 1963 with a bachelor's degree and as a member of Phi Beta Kappa. He enrolled in Case Western Reserve University, and in 1970 Satcher became the first black to earn both a master's degree and doctorate simultaneously in cytogenetics, or the study of chromosomes, from that school. After serving in administrative and teaching positions at King-Drew Sickle Cell Center in Los Angeles, he returned to Atlanta in 1979, where he chaired the community medicine department at the Morehouse School of Medicine. In 1982 Satcher was named president of Meharry Medical College and executive officer of its Hubbard Hospital in Nashville,

David Satcher

Tennessee. To ease the financial burden that the hospital faced—due to its extensive care for Nashville's indigent patients and inadequate funding from the city to bear the costs—he developed a plan to merge Meharry and the city-owned Nashville General Hospital. The plan was approved after he left in 1993 to head the CDC. In 1997 President Bill Clinton nominated Satcher to become the U.S. surgeon general, the nation's top doctor. Various issues prevented his immediate approval, and it was not until 1998 that he was confirmed for the post. He was sworn in on February 13 as surgeon general and assistant secretary for health at the Department of Health and Human Services. He was the first black man and only the second black person to become surgeon general. He resigned his post in 2002 and returned to Morehouse School of Medicine.

Sources: *Atlanta Journal and Constitution* (21 August 1993); *Who's Who among African American,* 26th ed., p. 1095; *Contemporary Black Biography,* vol. 7, pp. 241–44; Smith, *Notable Black American Men,* pp. 1044–46.

Medicine

1667 • Lucas Santomee was the first trained black physician in New Amsterdam.

Sources: *Encyclopedia of Black America,* p. 670.

1706 • Onesimus was the first black to introduce inoculation against smallpox to the American colonies. He taught the practice to his master, Cotton Mather, the Massachusetts Puritan minister, who promoted inoculation during the epidemic of 1721. There was considerable resistance to this life-saving procedure, and several proponents, including Mather, were threatened with mob violence. Inoculation was generally accepted by 1777.

Sources: James, *The Real McCoy,* p. 25; Morais, *The History of the Negro in Medicine,* p. 11.

James McCune Smith

1837 • James McCune Smith (1811–1865) was the first black to obtain an medical degree. Born in New York City, he studied at the African Free School in New York, where he was so gifted a student that when Lafayette visited the United States in 1824, the young Smith delivered the welcome address. Unable to pursue his education in the United States because no college was open to him, Smith studied at the University of Glasgow in Scotland, where he received his bachelor's, master's, and medical degrees. He was a very successful physician in New York, with a busy practice and two pharmacies, where he trained several black pharmacists. Sometimes Smith was accused of elitism and snobbery because of his wealth and his mansion on Sixth Avenue. He served on the staff of the Free Negro Orphan Asylum for twenty years. An avid abolitionist, he supported the Underground Railroad and was especially involved in the movement for black manhood suffrage in the state. Smith and Henry Highland Garnet (1815–1882) argued before the state legislature in 1841, demanding the removal of restrictions to black manhood suffrage. Smith also supported women's suffrage, calling for a state women's rights convention to be held in Rochester. Prominent in education and journalism as well, in 1838 he assumed editorial responsibility for the *Colored American.* He resigned in June 1839 and became an unpaid columnist for Frederick Douglass's paper. In 1859 he launched the *Weekly Anglo-American,* a short-lived publication.

Sources: Garrity and Carnes, *American National Biography,* pp. 216–17; Morais, *The History of the Negro in Medicine,* p. 31; Smith, *Notable Black American Men,* pp. 1073–75.

1846 • David Ruggles (1810–1849), hydropathist, journalist, abolitionist, and businessman, erected the first building constructed for hydropathic treatments in the United States. He was a free man of color born in Connecticut. Known as the "water cure doctor," Ruggles operated his successful center in Northampton, Massachusetts, until his death. He was an active abolitionist, supporter of the Underground Railroad movement, and editor and publisher of *The Mirror of Liberty* (1838).

Sources: Logan and Winston, *Dictionary of American Negro Biography,* pp. 536–37; Morais, *The History of the Negro in Medicine,* p. 23; Smith, *Notable Black American Men,* pp. 1034–35.

The First Black Physician

James Durham [Derham] (1762?–?) was the first regularly recognized black physician in the United States, by the 1780s. Born a slave in Philadelphia, his early masters taught him the fundamentals of reading and writing. He was owned by a number of physicians, ending up in New Orleans with a Scottish physician, who hired him to perform many medical services. He bought his freedom in 1783. Durham moved to Philadelphia and was lauded by prominent local doctors. He returned to New Orleans and had a flourishing practice. There he treated patients with diphtheria and was instrumental on helping to contain the yellow fever epidemic that ravaged New Orleans in 1796. In 1801 the city council restricted him because he was unlicensed and untrained.

Sources: Logan and Winston, *Dictionary of American Negro Biography*, pp. 205–6; Morais, *The History of the Negro in Medicine*, pp. 5, 7–10; *Encyclopedia of African-American Culture and History*, Supplement, pp. 77–78.

1847 • David J. Peck was the first black to graduate from an American medical school, Rush Medical College in Chicago.

Sources: *Encyclopedia of Black America*, p. 671; Morais, *The History of the Negro in Medicine*, p. 30.

1862 • John H. Rapier (1835–1865) enrolled in the department of medicine and surgery at the University of Michigan, becoming the first black to gain admittance. Rapier caused an uproar because he "dared to present himself as a candidate for admission." He withdrew from the program a few months later and in autumn 1863 he enrolled in the medical school of Iowa University at Keokuk, graduating in June 1864. He later became an assistant to a surgeon in the United States Army, reporting to the Freedmen's Contraband Hospital in Washington. D.C. He was the brother of James T. Rapier (1837–1883), congressman from Alabama during Reconstruction.

Sources: Schweninger, *James T. Rapier and Reconstruction*, pp. 24–29.

1863 • Alexander Thomas Augusta (1825–1890) became the first black surgeon in the U.S. Army. A free-born black from Norfolk, Virgina, Augusta was apprenticed in a local barbershop when he was a young boy. Since blacks and slaves were forbidden to read, he secretly learned to read on his own. He moved to Baltimore in the mid–1840s and studied medicine under private tutors. He married in 1847 and relocated to Philadelphia. There he continued to study medicine, this time under the respected physician William Gibson, who also taught on the medical faculty at the University of Pennsylvania. Gibson took an interest in Augusta, especially since he knew that the university twice denied him admission because of his race. Augusta served his medical apprenticeship in Philadelphia and graduated from Trinity Medical College in Toronto, Canada, in 1856, with the bachelor of medicine degree. For a while he was director of the university's hospital. He joined the Union forces in 1863 with the rank of major. He was honorably discharged from the army on October 13, 1866. Augusta became the first black to head any hospital in the United States when the newly created Freedmen Bureau erected buildings on the grounds of Howard University, and established the Freedmen's Hospital with Augusta in charge. (Formerly, freedmen were treated at Camp Barker.) In 1868 Howard University opened its own medical school, with Augusta as demonstrator of anatomy. He was the first black to receive an honorary degree from Howard University in 1869.

Alexander Augusta

Sources: Logan and Winston, *Dictionary of American Negro Biography*, pp. 19–20; Garrett, *Famous First Facts about Negroes*, pp. 112–13; Morais, *The History of the Negro in Medicine*, p. 50.

1864 • Rebecca Davis Lee Crumpler (1831–1895) was the first black woman awarded a medical degree in the United States. Born in Richmond, Virginia, she was raised in Philadelphia by an aunt. By 1852 she had moved to Charlestown, Massachusetts, and worked as a nurse until 1860. She completed the four-year medical program at the New England Female Medical College in Boston, and on March 11, 1864, she was awarded the Doctress of Medicine degree. She married, and at the end of the Civil War Crumpler returned to Richmond to work with the Freedmen's Bureau providing health care and treatment to newly freed blacks who had no medical provisions. After returning to Boston in 1869, she may have continued her practice; whatever the case, there is no indication that she was in active practice after 1883. Crumpler's interest in women and children led her to publish a two-part work of advice, *Book of Medical Discourses* in 1883. In honor of her pioneer work in the medical profession, the first medical society for black women was founded and named the Rebecca Lee Society.

Sources: Hine, *Black Women in America,* vol. 1, pp. 290–91; Gates and Higginbotham, *African American National Biography,* vol. 2, pp. 499–500; Kane, *Famous First Facts,* p. 467; Morais, *The History of the Negro in Medicine,* p. 43; Salzman, *Encyclopedia of African-American Culture and History,* Supplement, pp. 65–66.

1867 • Robert Tanner Freeman (1847–1873) graduated from Harvard University on March 6 of this year, becoming the first black to receive a doctoral degree in dentistry from that school. He was born in North Carolina to parents who had escaped from slavery, and died on June 14, 1873.

Sources: *Ebony* 15 (April 1960): 92; Sammons, *Blacks in Science and Medicine,* 1990, p. 96; *The Black Collegian* (March/April 1978): 30.

1870 • Susan Maria Smith McKinney Steward (1848–1918) was the first black woman to graduate from a New York state medical school. Born in Brooklyn, she became only the third black woman doctor in the country. After graduating from New York Medical College for Women on March 23, 1870, she practiced in Brooklyn for more than twenty years. In 1873 she became the first black woman doctor to be formally certified. Steward undertook postgraduate work at the Long Island Medical School Hospital in 1888, the only woman in the entire college. Steward worked to enhance the cause of women in medicine and was a founder of the Women's Loyal Union of New York and Brooklyn. In 1881 she co-founded the Women's Hospital and Dispensary in Brooklyn. In 1882 she served on the medical staff of the New York Hospital for Women. Steward married a prominent African Methodist Episcopal minister, Theophilus Gould Steward, in 1896, and became the resident physician at Wilberforce University in Ohio.

Sources: Hine, *Black Women in America,* vol. 2, pp. 1109–12; Logan and Winston, *Dictionary of American Negro Biography,* pp. 569–70; Smith, *Notable Black American Women,* pp. 1077–79.

1871 • J. T. Newman became the first black physician appointed surgeon and visiting physician at New Orleans Charity Hospital. Later he became a member of the Louisiana Board of Health. Newman was born in New Orleans but later lived in Chicago. In October 1871 he became resident physician at Straight University in New Orleans (before it merged with Leland and New Orleans universities to become Dillard). While there, he organized sewing and homemaking classes for destitute girls and gave free public lectures on a variety of topics.

Sources: Blassingame, *Black New Orleans,* p. 129.

1872 • Rebecca J. Cole (1846–1922) was the first black woman to establish a medical practice in Pennsylvania. Born in Philadelphia, she completed her secondary education at the Institute for Colored Youth (now Cheney University) in 1863. Cole became the first black graduate of the Female Medical College of Pennsylvania in 1867 and only the second black woman physician in the United States. From 1872 to 1881 she was resident physician at New York Infirmary for Women and Children, a health care facility that women physicians owned and operated. She and another woman physician, Charlotte Abbey, began Women's Directory Center in Philadelphia, providing medical and legal services to Philadelphia's destitute women and children. Cole practiced medicine for half a

The First Black Woman Dentist

In 1890 Ida Gray Nelson Rollins (1867–1953) became the first black woman to earn a doctor of dental surgery degree in the United States. She graduated from the University of Michigan in June. Nelson Rollins was born in Clarksville, Tennessee. Her family arranged for her to live in Cincinnati with a relative, Caroline Gray. Around 1860 she worked in the office of Jonathan Taft, a local dentist of prominence. He had supported women in the dental profession. When he became dean of the Dental Department at the University of Michigan, he maintained his office in Cincinnati and thus kept in touch with Nelson Rollins. He encouraged her to apply to the dental school, knowing that her experience in his office would help her to pass the entrance examinations. She enrolled in October 1887 and graduated in June 1890, then returned to Cincinnati where she established a dental practice. There she served all races and ages and women and men. After she married in 1895, she moved to Chicago and opened an office there. Although sources give conflicting information, she appears to be the first black woman to establish a dental practice in Chicago.

Sources: Smith, *Notable Black American Women*, Book II, pp. 496–97; Schultz and Hast, *Women Building Chicago 1790–1990*, pp. 622–23; Salem, *African American Women: Biographical Dictionary*, pp. 210–11.

century in Philadelphia, Pennsylvania; Columbia, South Carolina; and Washington, D.C. For a while she was superintendent of the Government House for Children and Old Women, located in Washington.

Sources: Hine, *Black Women in America*, vol. 1, pp. 261–62; Morais, *The History of the Negro in Medicine*, p. 43; Smith, *Notable Black American Women*, pp. 201–2.

1872 • Henry Fitzbutler (1842–1901) was the first black graduate of the Medical School of the University of Michigan. The Canadian-born doctor moved to Louisville, Kentucky, and became the first black to enter the profession in the state. He was devoted to the cause of black medical education, and in 1888 the Kentucky legislature granted him and his associates permission to establish a school of medicine, the Louisville National Medical College. The school closed in 1911.

Sources: Baskin and Runes, *Dictionary of Black Culture*, p. 162; Morais, *The History of the Negro in Medicine*, pp. 65–66.

Ida Gray Nelson Rollins

1889 • Monroe Alpheus Majors (1864–1960) was the first black physician to pass the California state boards. Majors had begun practice in Texas, but he was forced to leave the state by segregationist pressures. Majors was born in Waco, Texas, and moved with his parents to Austin as the parents sought better educational opportunities for their children. He attended Tillotson College and Normal School in Austin (now Huston-Tillotson College) from 1881 to 1883. He later moved to Nashville to pursue medical training. Majors enrolled in the literary course at Central Tennessee College and then enrolled at Meharry Medical College, graduating in 1886 with a medical degree. He returned to Texas in 1886, established a medical practice, and joined thirteen other physicians in founding the Lone Star Medical Association, later known as the Lone Star State Medical, Dental, and Pharmaceutical Association. This was second black medical association in the country. After his life was threatened, Majors left Brenham, where he was living, and moved to Calvert, then Dallas, and finally to California, where he became the first black to practice medicine on the Pacific Coast and west of the Rockies. He also became editor of the *Los Angeles Western News*. Majors returned to Waco in 1890 and began to compile what became an indispensable biographical dictionary, *Noted Negro Women: Their Triumphs and Activities*, published in 1893. He established a drugstore in Waco, becoming the first black to estab-

M. A. Majors

lish a drugstore in the Southwest. A remarkably versatile man, he was also a politician, poet, and hospital administrator.

Sources: Logan and Winston, *Dictionary of American Negro Biography*, pp. 421–22; Morais, *The History of the Negro in Medicine*, p. 58; Smith, *Notable Black American Men*, pp. 753–56.

1891 • Halle Tanner Dillon Johnson (1864–1901) became the first black woman to practice medicine in Alabama and also the first woman ever admitted on examination to practice medicine in that state. Johnson was born in Pittsburgh, one of nine children born to Benjamin Tucker Tanner and Sarah Elizabeth Miller Tanner. Benjamin Tanner was a successful minister, a bishop in the African Methodist Episcopal Church, and editor of the *Christian Recorder* and later the *AME Church Review*. The Tanners encouraged a wholesome cultural development of their children; as result, one of them, the gifted Henry Ossawa Tanner, became a celebrated landscape painter. Halle Tanner Johnson became known in the field of medicine. When she was twenty-four years old, she began study at the Women's Medical College in Pennsylvania, graduating on May 7, 1891. Booker T. Washington, founding president of Tuskegee Institute (now Tuskegee University) in Alabama, wrote to the Women's Medical College for a black graduate to become the first resident physician at Tuskegee. Johnson accepted the post and began her work on in August 1891. When she passed the strenuous state examinations that year, she became the first black physician and the first woman to do so. She established a Nurses' Training School and Lafayette Dispensary at Tuskegee. After Johnson married, she moved first to Columbia, South Carolina, and later to Nashville, Tennessee, where she died at home on April 26, 1901.

Halle Johnson

Sources: Smith, *Notable Black American Women*, pp. 584–87; Dannett, *Profiles of Negro Womanhood*, vol. 1, p. 277; Hine, *Black Women in America*, vol. 1, pp. 642–44.

1892 • Miles Vandahurst Lynk (1871–?) was the first editor of the first black medical journal in the nation. *The Medical and Surgical Observer* was published in Jackson, Tennessee. The first issue, dated December 1892, was thirty-two pages long. It was published regularly for eighteen months. An 1891 graduate of Meharry Medical College, Lynk organized the Medical Department of the University of West Tennessee, in Memphis, in 1900.

Sources: Baskin and Runes, *Dictionary of Black Culture*, p. 279; Garrett, *Famous First Facts about Negroes*, p. 113; Morais, *The History of the Negro in Medicine*, p. 64.

1893 • Daniel Hale Williams (1856–1931) performed the world's first successful heart operation on July 9, 1893. The open-heart surgery was executed at Provident Hospital in Chicago, Illinois, a hospital that Williams founded. He opened the chest of James Cornish, a laborer who had been stabbed, found the pericardial sac, emptied it of blood, and successfully sutured it. "Doctor Dan" was a founder and first vice president of the National Medical Association, and the first and only black invited to become a charter member of the American College of Surgeons in 1913. Born in Hollidaysburg, Pennsylvania, Williams graduated in 1883 from the Chicago Medical College. He founded Provident Hospital, the nation's first interracial hospital, in 1891. He was the first black on the Illinois State Board of Health in 1889, and in 1893 he was appointed surgeon-in-chief of Freedmen's Hospital, where he reorganized the services and established a nursing school. Williams had two main interests: the NAACP and the construction of hospitals and training schools for African American doctors and nurses.

Daniel Williams

Sources: Logan and Winston, *Dictionary of American Negro Biography*, p. 654; Morais, *The History of the Negro in Medicine*, p. 75; Smith, *Notable Black American Men*, pp. 1230–32.

1896 • Austin Maurice Curtis (1868–1939) was the first black on the medical staff of Chicago's Cook County Hospital, and the first black to receive such an appointment in a non-segregated hospital. An 1891 graduate from Northwestern University, he was the first physician to intern with Daniel Hale Williams. He later succeeded Williams as head of Freedmen's Hospital in Washington, D.C., and taught at Howard University College of Medicine.

Sources: Logan and Winston, *Dictionary of American Negro Biography*, pp. 153–54; Baskin and Runes, *Dictionary of Black Culture*, p. 123; *Journal of Negro History* 25 (October 1940): 502; Morais, *The History of the Negro in Medicine*, p. 78.

1897 • Charles Burleigh Purvis (1842–1929) was the first black physician to serve on the Board of Medical Examiners in Washington, D.C.

Sources: Logan and Winston, *Dictionary of American Negro Biography*, p. 507; Morais, *The History of the Negro in Medicine*, p. 51.

1897 • Augustus Nathaniel Lushington (1869–1939), a native of Trinidad, became the first black to earn a Doctor of Veterinary Medicine degree from the University of Pennsylvania. After practicing in Philadelphia for two years, he became an instructor in veterinary sanitation and hygiene at Bell Mead Industrial and Agricultural College in Rock Castle, Virginia. He later resigned and returned to private practice in Lynchburg, Virginia, were he became known for the proficient and high-class service that he offered.

Sources: Sammons, *Blacks in Science and Medicine*, p. 157; Waddell, *The Black Man in Veterinary Medicine*, p. 28.

1897 • Solomon Carter Fuller Jr. (1872–1953) became the nation's first black psychiatrist. He was also one of the first black physicians to teach on the faculty of a multiracial medical school in the United States, the University of Boston School of Medicine. Fuller was born in Monrovia, Liberia, and received his bachelor's degree in 1893 from Livingstone College in Salisbury, North Carolina. He earned his medical degree from Boston University Medical School in 1897. That same year he worked in the Westborough State Hospital for the Insane, where he was an intern in the pathology laboratory. He was named head of pathology in 1899 and served in that position until 1919. Still with the hospital, he became a faculty member in the pathology department at Boston University's medical school in 1899, and in 1904 he took a sabbatical for one year of study at the University of Munich in Germany. There he studied psychiatry with influential neuropsychiatrist Emil Kraepelin. In 1919 Fuller taught full-time at the medical school but later retired due to racism. He was denied status as a full professor and, although he was the functioning head of the Department of Neurology, that title was never assigned to him. When the school promoted a white assistant professor to full professor and department head as well, Fuller had had enough. He retired in 1933 and worked in a succession of part-time posts. He had suffered from diabetes for some time, and beginning 1942 his eyesight began to fail. Still he accepted psychiatric patients and gave up all else except a positive attitude on life. In 1909 Fuller married Meta Vaux Warrick, a talented sculptor who had studied with Paul Rodin in Paris.

Solomon Fuller Jr.

Sources: *Contemporary Black Biography*, vol. 15, pp. 95–98; *Who's Who in Colored America*, 1927, p. 20; *Negro History Bulletin* (March/April 1977): 679–81.

1902 • Justina L. Ford (1871–1952) became the first black woman licensed to practice medicine in Colorado. Affectionately known as "The Baby Doctor" and "The Lady Doctor," she was also the first black woman physician to practice in the Rocky Mountain West. Ford was born in Knoxville, Illinois, grew up in Galesburg, and in 1899 graduated from Hering Medical College in Chicago. For two years she was hospital director in Normal, Alabama, and physician at a state school there. Ford decided to move from Alabama to a place that was friendlier to blacks and their work. She moved to Denver around 1902, received her state license, and established a medical practice. At first neither Ford nor black patients had access to the Denver General Hospital; consequently, Ford delivered health care to homes in Denver and the surrounding area. Only fifteen percent of her patients were black. Because she delivered over 7,000 babies, she became known as the "Baby Doctor." After a distinguished practice that spanned over fifty years, she died at home on October 14, 1952.

Sources: Smith, *Notable Black American Women*, Book II, pp. 229–31; Potter and Claytor, *African American Firsts*, pp. 243–24.

1906 • Henry McKee Minton (1870–1946) received a medical degree this year from Jefferson Medical College in Pennsylvania, becoming the first black graduate of that institution. He had been inspired by his association with medicine earlier; in fall 1897 he opened what may have been the state's first pharmacy owned by blacks. In summer 1906 Minton joined Eugene T. Hinson and Algernon B. Jackson in founding Mercy Hospital in Philadelphia. It followed Douglass Hospital, established by Nathan Francis Mossell in 1895. He was superintendent of Mercy until 1910. Minton was born in Columbia, South Carolina, and studied at Phillips Exeter Academy in New Hampshire in 1891. He later entered the University of Pennsylvania Law School, but lost interest and withdrew. In 1895 he graduated from the Philadelphia College of Pharmacy and Science and two years later opened what may have been the first black-owned pharmacy in Pennsylvania. Still interested in medicine, he completed his medical studies at the Jefferson Medical College in 1906.

Sources: Logan and Winston, *Dictionary of American Negro Biography*, pp. 440–41; *Journal of the National Medical Association* (July 1955): 285–86.

1909 • Gertrude Elizabeth Curtis McPherson (1880?–?) became the first black woman to pass the New York State Board of Dentistry. She began practice this year. The second black woman licensed to practice dentistry in New York was Bessie Delany (1891–1995). McPherson studied at the New York College of Dental and Oral Surgery from 1905 to 1909, and received the Doctor of Dental Surgery degree this year.

Sources: *Who's Who in Colored America*, 1928–29, p. 252; Smith, *Notable Black American Women*, Book III, p. 172.

1911 • The first black admitted to Cornell University Medical School was Roscoe Conklin Giles (1890–1970). Although racial discrimination restricted him to an internship at Provident Hospital in Chicago, he benefited from his experiences there by establishing a lifetime relationship with such renowned black physicians of that time as George Cleveland Hall, Daniel Hale Williams, and U. Grant Dailey. Denied many early appointments because of his race, in 1917 he was appointed supervisor of the Chicago Health Department. He also became assistant attending physician at Provident Hospital in that year. In 1937 Giles was elected president of the National Medical Association. His reputation gained in stature as he published a number of papers in the *Journal of the Negro Medical Association*. Giles was also an educator, librarian and book collector, and an athlete. He was born in Albany, New York.

Sources: *Who's Who in Colored America*, 1933–37, p. 206; Organ and Kosiba, *A Century of Black Surgeons*, vol. 1, p. 298.

1912 • Lydia Ashburne Evans (1887?–1992) became the first black woman to graduate from Howard University Medical School and the first black woman licensed to practice general medicine in Virginia. Evans was the daughter of former slaves. She grew up in Bowers Hill, Virginia, and in 1908 graduated from Norfolk Mission College. She practiced in Virginia for a while and moved to Chicago in 1916, where she opened another office and practiced medicine until 1977. She died in Chicago at age 105.

Sources: *Jet* 85 (17 January 1994): 14.

1916 • Ella P. Stewart (1893–1987) was the first black woman graduate of the University of Pittsburgh School of Pharmacy. She was also the first black woman to pass the Pennsylvania State Board of Pharmacy. She and William Wyatt Stewart, whom she married in 1920, opened a drugstore in Toledo, Ohio, in 1922, where they hosted a number of black luminaries. Stewart was active in numerous organizations, especially the National Association of Colored Women. She was national chair of NACW's Department of Negro Women in Industry and later national treasurer for the organization. Born in Stringtown, a village near Berryville, Virginia, to sharecroppers, she received her undergraduate degree from Storer College in Harpers Ferry, West Virginia, and graduated in 1910. She moved to Pittsburgh that year and became bookkeeper and cashier in Lincoln Drug Company. It was there that she developed an interest in pharmacy as a profession.

Sources: Salem, *African American Women*, pp. 479–81; Smith, *Notable Black American Women*, pp. 1079–83.

1919 • Louis Tompkins Wright (1891–1952) became the first black to be appointed to a New York City municipal hospital when he was named clinical assistant in the outpatient department of Harlem Hospital. He served with distinction at that hospital for more than thirty years. Wright was born in LaGrange, Georgia, and graduated from Clark University (now Clark Atlanta University) in 1911. Determined to become a medical researcher, he enrolled in Harvard Medical School and graduated cum laude in 1915. Because he was black, he was placed last in the graduation procession. Wright was an officer in the Army Medical Corps during World War I. In 1945 he was the only black member of the American College of Surgeons. Wright was a militant civil rights advocate and a prominent member of the NAACP. As chair of the board of the civil rights organization (1935–52), he was responsible for the establishment of a board committee on health. The association named him its Spingarn Medalist in 1940 for his work as a champion of human rights.

Sources: Logan and Winston, *Dictionary of American Negro Biography,* pp. 670–71; *Journal of the National Medical Association* 45 (March 1953): 130; Morais, *The History of the Negro in Medicine,* p. 106; Smith, *Notable Black American Men,* pp. 1266–68.

1920 • Harold Ellis was the first black to obtain a degree in neurology. He eventually held an appointment as chief-of-service in neurology at Harlem Hospital.

Sources: Morais, *The History of the Negro in Medicine,* p. 120.

1922 • Clilan Bethany Powell (1894–?) was the first black roentgenologist in New York City. A Virginia native, Powell was educated at Virginia State College (now University) and Howard University College of Medicine. An x-ray specialist, he opened the first laboratory for x-ray diagnosis and treatment in a black community. He served on many government commissions and operated a finance company, insurance company, and the *New York Amsterdam News.*

Sources: *Who's Who in Colored America,* 1950, p. 423; *The Black New Yorkers,* p. 180.

1922 • Joseph H. Ward (1870–1956) was the first black appointed to head a Veterans Administration hospital. In 1922 he was named medical officer-chief of the Veterans Hospital in Tuskegee, Alabama, and had a distinguished twelve-year tenure.

Sources: Garrett, *Famous First Facts about Negroes,* p. 115; Morais, *The History of the Negro in Medicine,* p. 111.

1926 • May Edward Chinn (1896–1980) was the first black woman to intern at Harlem Hospital. She was also the first black woman to practice medicine in Harlem, the first to receive admitting privileges at Harlem Hospital, the first woman physician to ride with Harlem Hospital's ambulance crews on emergency calls, and the first black woman to graduate from the University of Bellevue Medical Center. Chinn was born an only child in Great Barrington, Massachusetts. On the basis of tests that she passed without a high school degree, she was admitted to Teachers College of Columbia University. In 1926 she received her doctor of medicine degree from the University of Bellevue Medical Center (now University Medical College, New York University). Chinn received a master of science degree in public health from Columbia in 1933. She later studied with specialists in the field of cytology and also attended postgraduate seminars in medicine and related fields in the United States, Europe, and Japan. She held a number of posts as she practiced medicine and worked in the field of cancer research.

Sources: Hine, *Black Women in America,* vol. 1, pp. 235–36; Smith, *Notable Black American Women,* pp. 183–85; *Contemporary Black Biography,* vol. 26, pp. 43–45.

1929 • Numa Pompilius Garfield Adams (1885–1940) was the first black dean at the Howard University School of Medicine. Born in Virginia, he moved to Pennsylvania, where he received his early education. A graduate of Howard University and Columbia University, he taught at Howard (1912–19) before entering Chicago's Rush Medical College, where he received his medical degree in 1924. In June 1929 Adams was appointed dean at Howard University College of Medicine. There he reorganized the curriculum on a more

The First Black American College of Surgeons Fellow

▌n 1934 Louis Tompkins Wright (1891–1952) was admitted as a fellow of the American College of
▌Surgeons, becoming the first black to hold that distinction since the organization's early days.

Sources: Logan and Winston, *Dictionary of American Negro Biography*, pp. 670–71; *Journal of the National Medical Association* 45 (March 1953): 130; Morais, *The History of the Negro in Medicine*, p. 106; Smith, *Notable Black American Men*, pp. 1266–68.

rational basis, establishing the primacy of the school in the teaching functions of Freedmen's Hospital, and recruiting capable young men to study.

Sources: Logan and Winston, *Dictionary of American Negro Biography*, p. 5; Baskin and Runes, *Dictionary of Black Culture*, p. 13; Morais, *The History of the Negro in Medicine*, pp. 90–92.

1934 • Leonidas H. Berry (1902–1995) was the first black specialist in the field of digestive diseases and endoscopy. In 1946 he became the first black physician on the staff of Chicago's Michael Reese Hospital. That year he also became the first black internist at Cook County Hospital. Berry was born in Woodsdale, North Carolina, and grew up in Norfolk, Virginia. He received his bachelor's degree from Wilberforce University in 1924 and received his medical training at Rush Medical College in Chicago and at the University of Illinois. He was a diplomat of the American Board of Internal Medicine. Berry developed one of the early gastroscopes, known as the Elder-Berry gastrobiopsy scope, and was at the forefront in the movement to increase communications between the black and white medical associations. He was author of several books, including *Gastrointestinal Pan-Endoscopy*. He also wrote a genealogical history of his family, *I Wouldn't Take Nothin' for My Journey: Two Centuries of an Afro-American Minister's Family* (1981).

Sources: Berry, *I Wouldn't Take Nothin' for My Journey*, p. 243; *Jet* 82 (24 August 1992): 32; Obituary, *Who's Who among African Americans*, 10th ed., p. 1694.

Charles Drew

1940 • Charles Richard Drew (1904–1950) was the first person to set up a blood bank. His work made him internationally prominent and earned him the title "Father of Blood Plasma." Born in Washington, D.C., Drew graduated from Amherst College in 1926. He also coached and taught at Morgan State College (later University), received his medical degree from McGill University in 1933, and taught pathology at Howard University in 1935. Drew's research at the Columbia Medical Center in New York City led to the discovery that blood plasma could supplant whole blood in transfusions. He set up and administered the British blood bank from 1940 to 1941, then the American Red Cross project to collect and store blood. Drew was dropped from the American Red Cross project because he objected to the policy of refusing the blood of black donors. He asserted that there was no scientific difference between the blood of blacks and whites. His research was responsible for saving numerous lives during World War II. He was accorded the NAACP's Spingarn Medal, as well as other tributes. While accounts vary concerning his care after an automobile accident near Burlington, North Carolina, according to the *New York Times,* he died at a segregated hospital "that had no blood plasma that might have saved his life."

Sources: Logan and Winston, *Dictionary of American Negro Biography*, pp. 190–92; Morais, *The History of the Negro in Medicine*, pp. 107–9; Smith, *Notable Black American Men*, pp. 331–33.

1948 • Dorothy Lavinia "D" Brown (1919–2004) was the first black woman appointed to a residency as a general surgeon in the South. After completing her residency, in 1954 she became the first black woman surgeon in the South. Born in Philadelphia to a young unwed mother, Brown lived in an orphanage from age five months to age thirteen. Reunited with her mother for a brief period, she was then hired out as a domestic. With the support of the Women's Division of Christian Service of the Methodist Church in Troy,

New York, Brown received a scholarship for study at the Methodist-affiliated Bennett College for Women in Greensboro, North Carolina. Graduating in 1941, Brown worked in a defense plant in Troy and saved money to support her medical study at Meharry Medical College. She graduated in 1948 with an M.D. and interned at Harlem Hospital in New York City. Brown then took a residency in general surgery at George Hubbard Hospital in Nashville, Tennessee, from 1949 to 1954. Later, when she was forty years old and unmarried, she became the first single black woman in Tennessee to adopt a child.

Sources: Hine, *Black Women in America,* vol. 1, pp. 174–75; Smith, *Notable Black American Women,* pp. 114–16; *Who's Who among African Americans,* 14th ed., p. 151.

Dorothy Brown

1949 • William Augustus Hinton (1883–1959) was the first black professor at Harvard Medical School. A world-renowned bacteriologist, he developed the Hinton test for syphilis and the Davis-Hinton tests for blood and spinal fluid. His book *Syphilis and Its Treatment* (1936) became an authoritative reference work. Born in Chicago, the son of former slaves, he grew up in Kansas and later taught school in Nashville, Tennessee, and Langston, Oklahoma. He received his bachelor's degree in 1905 from Harvard College and his medical degree in 1912 from Harvard Medical School. He became an instructor of preventive medicine at Harvard in 1912, and continued there until his retirement in 1950. He was promoted to the rank of clinical professor in 1949. Hinton directed the Massachusetts Department of Public Health's Wassermann Laboratory from its establishment in 1915 until 1954.

Sources: Logan and Winston, *Dictionary of American Negro Biography,* p. 315–16; Garrett, *Famous First Facts about Negroes,* p. 114; Morais, *The History of the Negro in Medicine,* pp. 103–4.

1949 • Jack E. White (1921–1988) was the first black trained as a cancer surgeon at Sloan Kettering Hospital. A graduate of Florida Agricultural and Mechanical University in 1941 and the Howard University School of Medicine in 1944, White held the directorship of the Howard University Cancer Research Center of Freedman's Hospital in Washington, D.C.

Sources: *Who's Who among Black Americans,* 26th ed., p. 1318.

1949 • The first two black women to graduate from veterinary school and to receive the doctorate in veterinary medicine degree were Jane Hinton (1920?–) and Alfreda Johnson Webb (1923–1992). Hinton received her degree from the University of Pennsylvania School of Veterinary Medicine. Her father was William Augustus Hinton, a medical researcher who invented the Hinton Test, an accurate test for syphilis, at Harvard. After serving as a technician in Arizona during World War II, Jane Hinton pursued her degree in veterinary medicine. She graduated and returned to her home in Canton, Massachusetts, and worked in Framingham as a practitioner for small animals. She later became an inspector for the federal government, working in Framingham Center, Massachusetts. Alfreda Johnson Webb was born in Mobile, Alabama, and received her bachelor's degree from Tuskegee Institute (now Tuskegee University) in 1943. Tuskegee established its veterinary school that same year; it remains the only such school on a black college campus. The school was established specifically to train black veterinarians. After receiving her veterinary degree from Tuskegee, Webb completed her master's degree at Michigan State University in 1951 and went on to teach and conduct research. She moved to Greensboro, North Carolina and taught at North Carolina Agricultural and Technical State College (now University). She also became a renowned anatomist.

Sources: Salem, *African American Women,* pp. 250–51 (Hinton); 551–52 (Webb).

1950 • Helen Octavia Dickens (1909–2002) became the first black woman admitted as a fellow of the American College of Surgeons. Dickens was long recognized in the medical profession and in academia for her research on intensive medical, psychological, educational, and social services intervention with socially-deprived pregnant teenagers and their families. Dickens was born in Dayton, Ohio, and received her bachelor's degree in 1932 from the University of Illinois. She became one of five women in a class of 137 students at the University of Illinois College of Medicine and graduated in 1934 with her medical degree. She completed an internship and residency in obstetrics at Provident Hospital in

Chicago. For approximately six years, she was a general practitioner and obstetrician in Philadelphia. While in Philadelphia, in 1941 she enrolled in the University of Pennsylvania School of medicine where she studied for a year toward a master's in medical science, specializing in obstetrics and gynecology. In 1946 she completed a residency at Harlem Hospital in New York City and was certified by the American Board of Obstetrics and Gynecology. She directed the Department of Obstetrics and Gynecology at Philadelphia's Mercy Douglass Hospital, and in 1953 Dickens became a fellow of the American College of Surgeons. She held faculty appointments at the Medical College of Pennsylvania as well as the University of Pennsylvania School of Medicine. Dickens specialized in women's illnesses and the treatment of pregnant teenagers.

Sources: *Contemporary Black Biography,* vol. 14, pp. 76–80; Smith, *Notable Black American Women,* Book II, pp. 179–82.

1951 • The first black woman to graduate from Harvard University's Medical School was Mildred Fay Jefferson. She later became president of the National Right to Life Committee.

Sources: Hine, *Black Women in America,* p. 1324.

1952 • The first black president of Meharry Medical College in Nashville, Tennessee, was Harold Dadford West (1904–1974). West was born in Flemington, New Jersey and educated at the University of Illinois (B.A., 1925; M.S., 1930; Ph.D., 1930). He held teaching positions at Morris Brown College in Atlanta from 1925 to 1927 and at Meharry Medical College from 1927 to 1952. He served as president of Meharry from 1952 to 1966, before returning to a teaching post as professor of biochemistry from 1966 to 1973. He served on the Board of Trustees until he retired.

Sources: Sammons, *Blacks in Science and Medicine,* p. 246; *Who's Who among Black Americans,* 1992–93, p. 1485.

1955 • Dolores Cooper Shockley (1930–) became the first black woman to receive a doctorate in pharmacology from Purdue University. Born in Clarksdale, Mississippi, she decided early on to become a licensed pharmacist and to open a pharmacy in her hometown. She received her bachelor's degree from Louisiana State University in 1951 and received a two-year assistant instructorship at Purdue University, where she earned a master's degree in 1953 and a doctorate in 1955. In addition to becoming a licensed pharmacist, she developed a keen interest in research. Shockley joined the faculty at Meharry Medical College in 1955 but interrupted her new post in 1955–56 to accept a Fulbright fellowship for postdoctoral study at the University of Copenhagen in Denmark. While on leave in 1959, she taught at Einstein College of Medicine in New York.

Sources: Warren, *Black Women Scientists in the United States,* pp. 253–54; Sammons, *Blacks in Science and Medicine,* p. 213; Smith, interview with Dolores Shockley, April 5, 2002.

1956 • Julius Hill (1917–1983) was the first black orthopedic surgeon in California. An Atlanta native, Hill graduated from Johnson C. Smith University in 1933, the University of Illinois in 1937, and Meharry Medical College in 1951. He completed his orthopedic surgery work at the University of Southern California in 1956. Hill was president of the National Medical Association in 1969–70 and the Golden State Medical Association from 1960 to 1972.

Sources: *Who's Who among African Americans,* 14th ed., p. 596.

1961 • Samuel L. Kountz (1930–1981), along with another transplant specialist, performed the first successful transplant between humans who were not identical twins. While receiving surgical training at the Stanford University School of Medicine, he worked with Roy Cohn, a pioneer in organ transplantation. The two made medical history, performing the surgery at the Stanford Medical Center. He later joined a medical team at the University of California, San Francisco, where he helped develop the prototype for the Belzer kidney perfusion machine. Kountz was born in Lexa, Arkansas, and became interested in medicine early on. He received his bachelor's degree from Arkansas Agricultural, Mechanical, and Normal College in 1952 and his master's degree from the University of

Arkansas in 1956. He later enrolled in the University of Arkansas Medical School and became one of the first black students to graduate.

Sources: *Contemporary Black Biography*, vol. 10, pp. 130–33; *Ebony* 20 (November 1964): 119–24; 29 (July 1974): 61.

1966 • The first black admitted to the Vanderbilt University Medical School was Levi Watkins Jr. (1945–). He learned of his acceptance when he read the headline in the local newspaper, the *Tennessean*. He also became the medical school's first black to graduate in 1970. From 1977 to 1978 he became the first black physician to serve as chief resident in cardiac surgery at Johns Hopkins University. Watkins was a research fellow at Harvard University Medical School from 1973 to 1975 and served on the medical faculty at Johns Hopkins from 1978 to 1984. In 1984 he became the first black doctor to establish the surgical implantation of an automatic defibrillator in the human heart. Born in Parsons, Kansas, Watkins and his family moved to Montgomery, Alabama, while he was still an infant. While he was in high school, he became a member of Dexter Avenue Baptist Church, where Martin Luther King Jr. was the pastor. He found King's sermons inspiring and his call for racial equality and peaceful protest appealing, and he was active in the Montgomery bus boycotts of 1950. Watkins graduated from Tennessee State University in Nashville in 1966 and then entered medical school.

Sources: *Contemporary Black Biography*, vol. 9, pp. 252–55; *Who's Who among African Americans*, 26th ed. p, 1296.

1967 • Jane Cooke Wright (1919–) was America's first black woman associate dean of a major medical school, New York Medical College. Wright grew up in New York City and came from a distinguished medical tradition. Her father, Louis Tompkins Wright, one of Harvard University's first black graduates, was a prominent surgeon and researcher. Jane Wright received her bachelor's degree from Smith College in 1942 and her medical degree from New York Medical College in 1945. She had appointments at Harlem Hospital and its Cancer Research Foundation, and began teaching at New York Medical School in 1955. In July 1967 she became associate dean and professor of surgery at her alma mater, retiring in 1987. In 1971 she became the first woman elected president of the New York Cancer Society.

Sources: Smith, *Notable Black American Women*, pp. 1283–85; *Who's Who among African Americans*, 14th ed., p. 1449; *Current Biography*, 1968, p. 443.

1967 • Julianne Stephanie Bluitt (1928–) became the first black to teach full-time in Northwestern University's Dental School. She accepted that post at a time when the dental school decided to upgrade its dental hygiene program to departmental status and needed to strengthen its faculty.

Sources: *Contemporary Black Biography*, vol. 14, pp. 23–25; Smith, *Notable Black American Women*, Book II, pp. 34–37.

1967 • James E. Bowman (1923–2011) became the first tenured African American professor in the University of Chicago's Biological Sciences Division. He directed the University of Chicago's Sickle Cell Center and also the school's blood bank. Bowman was an internationally recognized expert on pathology, inherited blood diseases, and population genetics. He was a fierce advocate for minority students.

Sources: "Father of White House Adviser Valerie Jarrett Dies," http://thegrio.com/2011/09/29/father-of-white-house-adviser-valerie-jarrett-dies. Accessed October 10, 2012; Gloria Hamilton, email to Jessie Carney Smith, November 8, 2011.

1971 • The first black woman to head a major teaching hospital was Florence Small Gaynor (1920–1993). She became the new executive director of the Sydenham Hospital in the Harlem section of New York City, taking over when the hospital experienced a financial crisis. She stabilized the hospital's finances and developed a new neighborhood Family Care Center that included a sickle cell anemia clinic. Gaynor later headed Martland Hospital in New Jersey, and joined the staff at Meharry Medical College in Nashville.

She ended her administrative career at the West Philadelphia Community and Medical Community and Mental Health Consortium. Gaynor graduated from the nursing school of Lincoln Hospital in the Bronx, earned a bachelor's degree in 1964 and a master's degree in 1966 from New York University. She prepared for a career in health care administration by studying further at the University of Oslo in Norway.

Sources: Potter and Claytor, *African American Firsts,* pp. 249–50; Salzman, *Encyclopedia of African-American History and Culture,* Supplement, p. 110.

1973 • John Lawrence Sullivan Holloman (1919–2002) was the first black president of the New York City Health and Hospital Corporation. In 1963 Holloman led a physicians' picket line protesting racism within the medical profession. A Washingtonian, Holloman graduated from Virginia Union University and received his medical degree from the University of Michigan. He operated a private practice n New York City from 1947 to 1996. He also taught, worked as regional medical officer for the U.S. Federal Drug Administration, and served as assistant attending physician at St. Lukes/Roosevelt Hospital.

Sources: Morais, The *History of the Negro in Medicine,* p. 162; *Who's Who among African Americans,* 14th ed., p. 609.

1973 • Clive Orville Callender (1936–) established the only transplant center at a black medical school when he founded the center at Howard University. One of the nation's foremost transplant surgeons, he was also the only top-rated black transplant surgeon in the country. Calendar was born in New York City, received his bachelor's degree from Hunter College in 1959, and earned his medical degree from Meharry Medical College in 1963. He received a transplant fellowship for further study and spent two years in training with Samuel Kountz, the first black transplant surgeon in the United States.

Sources: *Contemporary Black Biography,* vol. 3, pp. 25–27; *Who's Who among African Americans,* 26th ed., p. 199.

1973 • Rosalie A. Reed (1945–) became the first woman veterinarian employed by the Los Angeles Zoo—the nation's third largest zoo. She was also the first woman veterinarian at a major American zoo. She was born in Mount Vernon, New York, and developed an interest in animals early on. She brought stray animals home and kept them under her care. Reed graduated from Tuskegee Institute (now Tuskegee University) in 1972 with a degree in veterinary science. After that she applied for the post at the Los Angeles Zoo, passed the required written and oral examinations, and was hired in 1973. Her responsibilities included maintaining healthy animals, performing surgery, determining the animals' dietary needs, and quarantining new arrivals. She also aided in the rehabilitation of a California condor at the site.

Sources: Salem, *African American Women,* pp. 417–18.

1975 • The first woman to become dean of a dental school in the United States was Jeanne Frances Craig Sinkford (1933–). Sinkford was born in Washington, D.C., and graduated from Howard University B.S., 1953) and Northwestern University School of Dentistry (M.S., 1962; Ph.D., 1963). She entered dental training when women comprised only 1.2 percent of the students in dental school. In the course of her career she chaired the prosthodontics department at Howard, becoming the first woman in the country to administer such a unit. Sinkford served as associate dean from 1967 to 1974 and on July 1, 1975, she broke racial and gender barriers when she was appointed dean. Her induction into the International College of Dentists made her the first American woman dentist to receive this honor.

Sources: *Contemporary Black Biography,* vol. 13, pp. 187–90; Smith, *Notable Black American Women,* Book II, pp. 597–601.

1978 • The first black woman optometrist in Mississippi was Linda Dianne Johnson (1954–), director of optometry for the Jackson-Hinds Comprehensive Health Center in Jackson. In 1997 she was elected for a two-year term as president of the National Optometric Association. Johnson was born in Richland, Mississippi, and graduated from

Jackson State University (B.A., 1974) and Indiana University School of Optometry (O.D., 1978).

Sources: *Jet* 92 (6 October 1997): 20; *Who's Who among African Americans,* 26th ed., p. 674.

1982 • The National Black Women's Health Project (NBWHP) held the first national conference on black women's health issues. The NBWHP was founded under the leadership of Byllye Y. Avery (1937–). It aimed to mobilize black women to take charge of their lives and also improve their health. Avery also co-founded the Women's Health Center in Gainesville, Florida, to provide an alternative birthing place for women in the city. Avery graduated from Talladega College with a bachelor's degree and received her master's degree from the University of Florida. Her publications include *An Altar of Words: Wisdom, Comfort, and Inspiration for African American Women.*

Sources: Hine, *Black Women in America,* pp. 60–61; *Who's Who among African Americans,* 26th ed., p. 49.

1984 • The nation's first known black quintuplets were born. The Gaithers quintuplets— Joshua Frank Johnson, Brandon Burrus, Ashlee Charlene, Renee Brooks, and Rhealy Frances—were born four weeks premature to Sidney and Suzanne Gaither. The Gaithers had been married for more than twenty years and had a two-year-old son; the quintuplets were conceived without the use of fertility drugs. Though rarely in public view, in 1993 they made a commercial for McDonald's.

Sources: *Jet* 99 (7 May 2001): 12–17; 114 (1 September 2008): 24–25, 45.

1984 • Alexia Irene Canada (1950–) was the first black woman neurosurgeon in the United States. The Lansing, Michigan-born Canada completed her bachelor's degree in 1971 and her medical education in 1974 at the University of Michigan, with a specialty in pediatric neurosurgery. Canada was certified by the American Board of Neurological Surgery in 1984. She has taught at the University of Pennsylvania, the Henry Ford Hospital in Detroit, and at Wayne State University in Detroit. In 1977 she became the first woman, and the first black, neurosurgical resident at the University of Minnesota. Among her various honors, in 1993 the American Women's Medical Association named Canada Woman of the Year. She was also inducted into the Michigan Women's Hall of Fame in that year.

Sources: Lanker, *I Dream A World,* p. 128; Smith, *Notable Black American Women,* pp. 155–56; *Who's Who among African Americans,* 26th ed., p. 205; *Contemporary Black Biography,* vol. 28, pp. 41–43.

1984 • Jane Morgan Lyons was the first black woman to serve as chief executive officer of Sea View Hospital Rehabilitation Center and Home in Staten Island, New York. The facility contained 304 beds and adult day care and respite programs.

Sources: *The Black New Yorkers,* p. 380.

1987 • Benjamin Solomon Carson (1951–) gained international acclaim when he separated seven-month-old West German twins who were conjoined at the backs of their heads. On September 6, Carson led a seventy-member surgical team in a twenty-two-hour operation at Johns Hopkins Hospital in Baltimore to perform the first successful operation of this kind. Carson was born in Detroit and raised in an inner city neighborhood. He received his bachelor's degree from Yale University in 1973 and his medical degree from the University of Michigan in 1977. After completing an internship at Johns Hopkins Hospital, Carson moved to Western Australia and became senior neurosurgical resident at the Sir Charles Gairdner Hospital, a leading center for brain surgery. In 1985 he returned to Johns Hopkins, became one of its leading surgeons, and at age thirty-four he was promoted to director of pediatric neurosurgery, becoming one of the youngest such directors in the country. He became especially successful in performing high-risk operations. The life story of Carson, based on the best-selling book *Gifted Hands: The Ben Carson Story,* was made into a television movie and aired on TNT on February 7, 2009. President George W.

Bush awarded Carson the Presidential Medal of Freedom in 2008 "for his skills as a surgeon, high moral standards and dedication to helping others."

Sources: *Contemporary Black Biography,* vol. 1, pp. 48–49; vol. 35, pp. 24–26; vol. 76, pp. 20–23; *Jet* 92 (8 September 1987): 22; Smith, *Encyclopedia of African American Popular Culture,* vol. 1, pp. 252–54; Who's *Who among African Americans,* 26th ed., p. 212.

1993 • Barbara Ross-Lee (1942?–), a practicing family physician, naval officer, and medical educator, was named dean of Michigan State University College of Osteopathic Medicine in East Lansing, Michigan. She took the position on August 1, to become the first black woman to head a medical school in the United States. (Osteopathic physicians focus on primary care, such as family practice, general internal medicine, and general pediatrics.) Ross-Lee holds a bachelor's degree from Wayne State University. In 1973 she graduated from Michigan State University College of Osteopathic Medicine and for ten years had a private practice. She became president of the National Osteopathic Medical Association in 1992. In 1994 she was inducted into the Ohio Women's Hall of Fame. Ross-Lee is the sister of the late singer and actress Diana Ross.

Sources: *Jet* 84 (31 May 1993): 20; 84 (8 November 1993): 18; *Tennessean* (28 September 1993); Who's *Who among African Americans,* 26th ed., p. 1078.

1994 • Valerie Walker became a member of the Missouri Board of Registration for the Healing Arts, the first black woman to serve in this capacity. The board regulates and licenses physicians and surgeons. Walker is medical director of West End Medical Center in St. Louis.

Sources: *Jet* 85 (10 January 1994): 20.

1995 • Michael A. Rashid, president and chief executive officer of Mercy Health Plan in Trenton, became the first black to head a health maintenance organization in New Jersey.

Sources: *Jet* 89 (November 20, 1995): 10.

1995 • The first black dentist in Maryland to receive master status from the Maryland Academy of Dentistry was Bruce Yuille. He maintained offices for practicing family dentistry in Randallstown and Catonsville.

Sources: *Jet* 88 (21 August 1995): 35; Who's *Who among African Americans,* 26th ed., p. 1399.

1996 • The first black dean of the dental school at Tufts University in Boston was Lonnie H. Norris. He also became one of only a few black deans at the fifty-four dental schools in the country. The Houston native is a graduate of Fisk University in Nashville, Tennessee. Before completing a postgraduate residency in oral and maxillofacial surgery at Tufts, he received his doctor of dental medicine, master of arts, and master of public health from Harvard University. He has been a fellow of the American College of Dentistry and of the International College of Dentistry. The National Academies of Practice also named him Distinguished Practitioner.

Sources: *Jet* 89 (11 March 1996): 22; Who's *Who among African Americans,* 26th ed., p. 941.

1997 • The first woman dean of the School of Medicine at Meharry Medical College in Nashville, Tennessee, was Anna Cherrie Epps (1930–). She assumed the post on July 1. In 1999 she became senior vice president of academic affairs, the first woman to hold that post as well. Epps was born in New Orleans and graduated from Howard University (B.S., 1951; Ph.D., 1966) and Loyola University (M.S., 1959). Epps was blood bank specialist at the National Institutes of Health in 1959. From 1960 to 1969 she was program director and assistant professor of microbiology at Howard University School of Medicine. She relocated to Tulane University School of Medicine in 1969, becoming a faculty fellow. Epps was promoted in rank at Tulane, becoming associate professor of medicine, full professor, and associate dean. She ended her tenure there as director and medical representative for student academic support services.

Sources: *Jet* 92 (27 October 1997): 19; 96 (15 November 1999): 24; Smith, *Notable Black American Women,* Book III, pp. 86–89; *Who's Who among African Americans,* 26th ed., p. 387.

1997 • Jacqueline and Linden Thompson, of Washington, D.C., gave birth to the first black sextuplets in the United States. Although one daughter was stillborn, there were five girls and one boy. Born at Georgetown University Medical Center, they were delivered by Caesarean section and each weighed between two pounds and two pounds, six ounces. The surviving children—Octavia Daniela, Stella Kimerly, Ann Marie, Amanda, and Richard Linden—had no health problems. To aid the family, a number of businesses and organizations donated goods and services to the family. These included Freddie Mac Corporation's donation of a five-bedroom home and the Chevrolet Division of General Motors' gift of new Astro minivan.

Sources: *Jet* 92 (2 June 1997): 32; *Ebony* 50 (February 1998): 38, 40–46.

1997 • Adewale Troutman was named public health director of the Fulton County Health Department in Atlanta, becoming the first black to hold that post. Previously Troutman was director of Emergency Medical Services at United Hospitals Medical Center in Newark, New Jersey. He was also assistant clinical professor at the University of Medicine and Dentistry of New Jersey.

Sources: *Jet* 92 (13 October 1997): 19.

1997 • Doctors Paula R. Mahone and Karen L. Drake made medical history when they delivered the first septuplets born alive in the United States, at the Iowa Methodist Medical Center in Des Moines. Highly respected in the field of perinatology, the women were concerned that some of the embryos might not survive and were excited when they did. The babies were also in much better health than expected. The parents, Kenny and Bobbi McCaughey, who had experienced infertility, sought healthcare from Paula Mahone; they decided against "selective reduction" when they realized that the pregnancy involved seven embryos.

Sources: *Ebony* 53 (February 1998): 39, 44, 47; *Jet* (8 December 1997): 93; *Time* (1 December 1997): 150.

1998 • Reginald P. Dickerson, a cardiologist, became the first black to serve as chief of medical staff at Meridia Huron Hospital. The hospital is a part of the Cleveland Clinic Health System located in East Cleveland, Ohio.

Sources: *Jet* 94 (22 June 1998): 57.

1998 • The first black chief resident of the Johns Hopkins Hospital Department of Radiology in Baltimore was Gregory Johnson (1958?–). Johnson graduated from State University of New York, Health Science Center of the Brooklyn Medical School.

Sources: *Jet* 95 (5 April 1998): 18.

1998 • Aubrey W. Lee became the first black chairman of the William Beaumont Hospital Board of Directors, in Royal Oak, Michigan. He was senior vice president of the municipal banking group at NBD, which was a subsidiary of Bank One, Inc., based in Detroit.

Sources: *Jet* 95 (21 December 1998): 53.

2000 • David E. Gay Jr. became the first black director of Bryce Hospital, Alabama's largest state-run mental health facility, and its two nursing homes in Tuscaloosa, Alabama. Gay had been involved in mental healthcare since 1974.

Sources: *Jet* 98 (13 November 2000): 36.

2007 • When the historic Hip-Hop 4 HIV Know Your Status concert was held in Houston's Reliant Stadium, a record 7,500 teenagers and young adults showed up. The event became the largest single HIV testing event in U.S. history. To be admitted, attendees were required to be tested and to receive an immediate report. Included at the event were Rapper Bun B, Kelly Rowland of Destiny's Child, Lil' Wayne, David Banner, and other visiting and local artists. First-term Texas state representative Borris L. Miles (District 146) spearheaded the event; it was one of many that TexStars Foundation sponsored. TexStars promotes, sponsors, and assists inner-city communities in promoting tolerance in racial and sexual orientation, and in education and leadership development.

Sources: *Jet* 112 (27 August 2007): 58.

Museums

Neil deGrasse Tyson

1977 • Margaret Santiago was the first black to become registrar of a major scientific museum, the Smithsonian's National Museum of Natural History.

Sources: *State of Black America 1992*, p. 357.

1996 • Neil deGrasse Tyson (1958–), an astrophysicist, was named Frederick P. Rose Director of the American Museum of Natural History's Hayden Planetarium, in New York City. He was the first black to hold the post. Tyson was born in New York City and demonstrated an early interest in astronomy. When he was in the sixth grade he took the course Astronomy for Young People, and his decision to study the universe was firmly set. Tyson attended the Bronx High School of Science and in 1980 received his bachelor's degree from Harvard University. Continuing his studies, in 1983 Tyson received his master's degree from the University of Texas, and in 1991 he earned his doctorate from Columbia University. He has published several research papers on astronomy and has contributed to a Macmillan/McGraw-Hill science text series for high schools. Tyson has served as science expert on a number of television shows, including *Good Morning America*, *Today Show*, and *ABC Nightline*.

Sources: *Contemporary Black Biography*, vol. 15, pp. 208–10; *New York Times* (29 January 2000); *Scientific American* 282 (February 2000): 28–30.

National Science Foundation

Walter Massey

1990 • Walter Eugene Massey (1938–) was the first black to head the National Science Foundation. Born in Hattiesburg, Mississippi, Massey graduated from Morehouse College and earned his doctorate at Washington University in Saint Louis, Missouri. A physicist, he has had a distinguished career, including being the first black president of the American Association for the Advancement of Science. He became the first black dean of the undergraduate college at Brown University in 1970. From 1979 to 1993 he was professor at the University of Chicago as well as director of the Argonne National Laboratory. In 1993 Massey was designated vice-president for academic affairs and provost of the University of California system. He returned to Atlanta in 1995 to become the ninth president of his alma mater, Morehouse College.

Sources: *Negro Almanac*, pp. 1086–87; *Scientific American* 266 (June 1992): 40–41; *Who's Who among African Americans*, 26th ed., p. 823; Smith, *Notable Black American Men*, pp. 773–75.

Nursing

Susie Taylor

1863 • Susie King Taylor (1848–1912) was the first black army nurse in United States history, serving with the First Regiment of the South Carolina Volunteers. While at first she served as a laundress who cared for uniforms, bandages, and other supplies, she began assisting military surgeons as well by caring for the sick. One of Taylor's fondest memories was her meeting with Clara Barton, founder of the American Red Cross, in summer 1863. Taylor's Civil War memoirs, *Reminiscences of My Life in Camp* (1902), constitute the first and only continuous written record of activities of black nurses during the war. Taylor was born a slave on a plantation located on the Isle of Wight in Liberty County, near Savannah, Georgia. Although forbidden by law, Taylor learned to read and write as early as age seven. She

The First Black Graduate Nurse

In 1879 Mary Elizabeth Mahoney (1845–1926) became the first black graduate nurse in the United States. She was thirty-three years old in 1878, when she entered the New England Hospital for Women and Children to begin a sixteen-month course in nursing. Of the forty applicants in her class, only three remained to receive their diplomas, two white women and Mary Mahoney. Boston-born, Mahoney began as a maid in the hospital, and was later admitted to the nursing program. She moved to New York in 1911 to head the Howard Orphan Asylum for Black Children in Kings Park, Long Island. In addition to her work as a nurse, Mahoney was a strong supporter of the women's suffrage movement and became one of the first women in her city to register to vote in 1921, at the age of seventy-six. The Mary Mahoney Medal was named in her honor by the American Nurses' Association; the award is given biennially to the person making the most progress toward opening opportunities in nursing for all, regardless of race, creed, color, or national origin. Mahoney was born in the Dorchester section of Boston and grew up in Roxbury.

Sources: Hine, *Black Women in America,* vol. 2, pp. 743–44; Garrett, *Famous First Facts about Negroes,* p. 148; Morais, *The History of the Negro in Medicine,* p. 70; Smith, *Notable Black American Women,* pp. 720–21.

received her schooling from a free black woman and later from the woman's daughter, until she outgrew her teachers. After that she used white children in the area as tutors.

Sources: Logan and Winston, *Dictionary of American Negro Biography,* p. 581; Garrett, *Famous First Facts about Negroes,* p. 147; Smith, *Notable Black American Women,* pp. 1108–13.

1886 • Spelman Seminary (now Spelman College) in Atlanta, Georgia, began the first nursing school for black women. Blacks were forced to organize schools of their own for the training of nurses, and the number of African American graduate nurses steadily rose. Spelman's nursing school flourished until 1921.

Sources: Kane, *Famous First Facts,* p. 436; Morais, *The History of the Negro in Medicine,* p. 71.

1891 • The first three schools of nursing for blacks attached to hospitals were established in 1891 at Dixie Hospital in Hampton, Virginia; MacVicar Hospital, in connection with Spelman College in Atlanta, Georgia; and Provident Hospital Training School in Chicago. Alice M. Bacon, founder of the Dixie Hospital, was connected with Hampton Institute, although her hospital was independent.

Sources: Morais, *The History of the Negro in Medicine,* p. 71; *Negro Education,* vol. 1, p. 176.

1916 • The first black nurse to enroll officially in the Red Cross nursing service was Frances Elliott Davis.

Sources: Hine, *Black Women in America,* vol. 2, p. 1319.

1936 • Estelle Massey Osborne (1901–1981) was the first black director of nursing at City Hospital No. 2 (now the Homer G. Phillips Hospital Training School). She had been the first black nursing instructor at Harlem Hospital School of Nursing and later the first educational director of nursing at Freedmen's Hospital School of Nursing (now the Howard University College of Nursing). In 1943 as the first black consultant on the staff of any national organization (in this case the National Nursing Council for War Service), she more than doubled the number of white nursing schools to admit blacks. Osborne attended Prairie View State College in Texas, but sought more education by attending Columbia University, graduating with a bachelor's degree in 1931. In 1948 Osborne was the first recipient of a master's degree in nursing education from Teachers College of Columbia University. She was the first black member of the nursing faculty at New York University, and also became the first black to hold office in the American Nurses Association. Osborne was born in Palestine, Texas, the eighth of eleven children.

Sources: Hine, *Black Women in America,* pp. 903–5; *Encyclopedia of Black America,* p. 90; Morais, *The History of the Negro in Medicine,* p. 255; *Who's Who in Colored America,* 1950, p. 402.

1969 • Anna Bailey Coles (1925–) became the founding dean of Howard University's College of Nursing. The school was formed when a 1967 act of Congress called for the transfer of Freedmen's Hospital School of Nursing to Howard. Freedmen's admitted its last class in 1970 and graduated its last class in 1973. Altogether, seventeen hundred nurses had graduated from the school. Born in Kansas City, Kansas, Coles graduated from Avila College in Missouri (B.S., 1958) and Catholic University of America (M.S., 1960; Ph.D., 1967). She was supervisor of the Veterans' Administration Hospital in Topeka, Kansas, from 1950 to 1958 and then moved to Freedman's Hospital where she was director of nursing from 1961 to 1968.

Sources: *Jet* 87 (21 November 1994): 20; *Who's Who among African Americans,* 26th ed., p. 258.

1973 • The first black nurse to become chief of the Nursing Department at the National Institutes of Health in Washington, D.C., was Vernice Ferguson.

Sources: Hine, *Black Women in America,* vol. 2, p. 1329.

1998 • Fannie Gaston-Johansson became the first black female full professor with tenure at Johns Hopkins University School of Nursing. Gaston-Johansson holds the Elsie M. Lawler Endowed Chair and directs International and Extramural Affairs at the nursing school.

Sources: *Jet* 95 (30 November 1998): 20.

Publications

Benjamin Banneker

1792 • Benjamin Banneker (1731–1806) was the first black man to issue an almanac. (The series continued until 1797.) Banneker was born free in Maryland, where he became a tobacco farmer. As a result of his interest in mathematics and mechanics, he constructed a successful striking clock around 1752. His model for the clock was the mechanism of a watch someone lent to him. The clock was still running at the time of his death. In 1787 a Quaker neighbor lent Banneker some texts on astronomy and instruments, and he taught himself the skills necessary to produce his almanac. Banneker also helped in surveying the national capital. Although Banneker was unwell and could not work in the field, he did function as an assistant to George Ellicot in the survey of the ten-mile square District of Columbia from early February to the end of April 1791, when he returned to his farm.

Sources: Bedini, *The Life of Benjamin Banneker,* pp. 42–46, 103–36, 137–95; Logan and Winston, *Dictionary of American Negro Biography,* pp. 22–25; Smith, *Notable Black American Men,* pp. 49–52.

1909 • Charles Victor Roman (1864–1934) was the first editor of the *Journal of the National Medical Association.* The physician, teacher, historian, and author favored support of black institutions, and believed black history should be written by blacks. Born in Williamsport, Pennsylvania, Roman studied at Fisk University and Meharry Medical College, both in Nashville, Tennessee. He later directed the health service at Fisk and taught at Meharry. In 1934 Roman published *Meharry Medical College: A History.*

Sources: Logan and Winston, *Dictionary of American Negro Biography,* p. 532; *Encyclopedia of Black America,* pp. 735–36; Morais, *The History of the Negro in Medicine,* pp. 69–70.

Tuskegee University

Tuskegee University in Alabama opened the National Center for Bioethics in Research and Health Care. The center is the first in the nation devoted to exploration of the moral issues that underlie research and the medical treatment of blacks and others who are underserved. In 1997 President Bill Clinton gave a public apology for the U.S. Public Health Service's "Tuskegee Study," which tracked the progression of syphilis in black men in Macon County, Alabama, from 1932 to 1972. The men never knew that they had the disease or that there were treatment options after penicillin was determined to be a cure. The study was done surreptitiously and caused outrage among blacks when it became known. Tuskegee received a $200,000 grant to begin its center, followed by over $20 million in grants and pledges.

Sources: *Jet* 96 (7 June 1999): 23.

Research and Development

1942 • W. Lincoln Hawkins (1911–1992) was the first black researcher hired by Bell Telephone Systems, a company from which he retired in 1976. He earned a doctorate from McGill University in 1938. In 1992, he became the second black to receive the National Medal of Technology.

Sources: *Jet* 82 (20 July 1992): 24; *Who's Who among Black Americans*, 1992–93, pp. 626–25.

1971 • Walter S. McAfee (1914–1995), ranking scientist at the Army Electronics Research and Development Command, was the first black to attain the civil service rank of GS 16 while working for the army. McAfee was involved in the first radar contact with the moon in 1946.

Sources: *Ebony* 13 (May 1958): 20; *Negro Almanac*, p. 1088; Obituary, *Who's Who among African Americans*, 10th ed., p. 1705.

1997 • The first person in the United States to undergo experimental laser heart surgery was Dorothy Walker (1940?–). Cardiothoracic surgeon Keith Howard performed the surgery at Northwestern Memorial Hospital. The procedure is less painful and requires a shorter recovery time than previous methods. A Chicago native, Walker is the mother of three and a retired postal clerk.

Sources: *Jet* 92 (18 August 1997): 54–55.

1997 • J. Theodore Brown Jr., who for twenty years had worked in the field of drug abuse, created the first over-the-counter home drug test approved by the Federal Drug Administration. The system was initially marketed to parents who wanted to test their children's use of illicit drugs. President and chief officer of the Baltimore-based Personal Health and Hygiene, Brown established a state-of-the-art laboratory to develop his kit and received requests from around the world for the product. Brown graduated from State University of New York at Stony Brook.

Sources: *Jet* 91 (17 February 1997): 10–11.

2000 • Kimberly Briggs made medical history after a robot removed her gallbladder, at Henrico Doctors Hospital in Richmond, Virginia. This was the first operation in the United States performed by the daVinci Surgical System, a recently approved system.

Sources: *Jet* 98 (31 July 2000): 39–40.

2000 • The first person to have a new type of miniature heart pump successfully implanted temporarily was Lois Spiller (1948?–), a Houston native. On approval of the U.S.

Food and Drug Administration, her physicians inserted the battery-operated heart pump, the Jarvik 2000 left ventricular device. It was used to maintain blood flow until doctors could locate a replacement heart. Three months before the implant, Spiller had become extremely weak and struggled to talk.

Sources: *Jet* 98 (7 August 2000): 8.

2001 • Robert Tools (1942–2001) became the first person to receive a fully implantable artificial heart on July 2. He underwent seven hours of surgery and it was not until August that he appeared in public view. After his surgery, he remained in the Jewish Hospital in Louisville, Kentucky, for nearly five months. He had received a self-contained AbioCor mechanical heart that beat flawlessly over twenty million times. In 1997 Tools was treated for heart failure at St. Thomas Hospital in Nashville, Tennessee. There the cardiologist attempted to salvage his failing heart; the doctor considered tools for a heart transplant, but determined that he was too ill for the procedure. Without a transplant, Tools, who was almost bedridden, had an 80 percent chance of dying within thirty days. He had lost over fifty pounds, primarily muscle, and could barely raise his head. After reading a magazine article about an artificial heart, Tools elected to take a chance with the surgery rather than "stay home and die." His surgery took place in Jewish Hospital; his response was greater than doctors expected. By September he had gained weight as well as muscle tissue and appeared before television cameras several times. He also took trips outside the hospital to ice cream parlors, a local club, and a park. His recovery proceeded so well that in November the hospital worked with the Food and Drug Administration to prepare for his hospital discharge. His doctors hoped to release him in time to return home for Christmas. Tools had been warned, however, that unexpected complications could arise, and they did on several occasions, as soon as a few hours after his surgery. As the nation cheered Tools's survival and wished him well, his health began to fail. He had several setbacks within three weeks, in late October and early November. On November 11 he suffered a major stroke that left his right side paralyzed and impaired his speech. After living with the implant for 151 days, he suffered from bleeding and organ failure and died on Friday, November 30, 2001, at age fifty-nine. Tools was born in Mobile, Alabama, and graduated from high school in Tampa, Florida. He served in the Vietnam War as a member of the U.S. Marine Special Forces. Before he retired, Tools was employed with U.S. West Communications in Denver. He lived in Franklin, Kentucky.

Sources: *Jet* 100 (10 September 2001): 22–23; *New York Times* (1 December 2001); *Tennessean* (24 August 2001); (30 November 2001).

Space

1963 • On March 31, 1963, Edward Joseph Dwight Jr. became the first black astronaut candidate. He was dropped from the program in 1965.

Sources: *Ebony* 18 (June 1963): 74–81; 20 (June 1965): 29–36; *Jet* 68 (1 April 1985): 20.

1967 • Robert H. Lawrence Jr. (1935–1967), who had been named the first black astronaut in 1966 and assigned to the Manned Orbiting Laboratory, died in a plane crash on December 8 before the start of the mission. Lawrence was a native of Chicago, Illinois, having grown up on the South Side. He received his U.S. Air Force commission and a bachelor's degree in chemistry from Bradley University in 1956. He completed a doctorate in physical chemistry at Ohio State University. Lawrence was officially recognized as an astronaut thirty years after his death. After a long bureaucratic dispute over the definition of an astronaut, in December 1997, his name was added to the astronaut's memorial at Kennedy Space Center. The Robert H. Lawrence School in the Jeffrey Manor neighborhood in Chicago was named in his memory.

Sources: *Ebony* 23 (February 1968): 90–94; *Jet* 69 (17 February 1986): 17; *Negro Almanac*, pp. 1085–86; *New York Times* (9 December 1997).

1976 • The first woman scientist trained to be an astronaut was Patricia Suzanne Cowings (1948–). An alternate in the early astronaut period, she preceded Sally Ride's appointment but never had a chance to fly. The Spacelab Mission Development-3 was a joint effort between Johnson Space Center and the Ames Research Center. It was the first simulation of a life-sciences-dedicated space shuttle mission. Cowings and Dick Grindland were the back-up payload specialists for the program; they were in intense training for nearly two years. Cowings was born in New York City and grew up in the Bronx. She graduated from State University of New York at Stony Brook in 1970 and enrolled in the doctoral program in psychology at the University of California at Davis, graduating in 1973 with both master's and doctorate degrees in psychology. She became a research psychologist with the National Aeronautical and Space Administration (NASA), marking the beginning of a long relationship with that agency. She also was a guest investigator at Rockefeller University, where she worked in the area of biofeedback. Her work brought her in collaboration with international space agencies, engineers, astronauts, and other scientists. With NASA, Cowings worked on flight experiments on Spacelab missions and made important contributions to the space program.

Sources: Smith, *Notable Black American Women,* Book II, pp. 150–52; "Patricia S. Cowings, Ph.D.," *Women of NASA*; Warren, *Black Women Scientists in the United States.*

1980 • Arnaldo Tamayo Mendez was the first black astronaut. A Cuban, he participated in a mission launched by the Soviets.

Sources: *Class* (December 1983): 8; *Jet* 59 (9 October 1980): 8.

1983 • On August 30, 1983, Guion [Guy] Stewart Bluford Jr. (1942–) was the first black American astronaut to make a space flight. He made his maiden voyage into space on the STS–8, the shuttle's eighth mission. He worked the remote manipulator system, Spacelab–3 experiments, shuttle systems, Shuttle Avionics Integration Laboratory, and the Flight Systems Laboratory. He went on to make two more flights and spent 314 hours in space before retiring from the program in 1993. A native of Philadelphia, Pennsylvania, Bluford received his doctorate in aerospace engineering from the Air Force Institute of Technology in 1978. He had earned his wings in 1965. He was the second black in space: a black Cuban had previously flown on a Soviet mission.

Guy Bluford Jr.

Sources: *Contemporary Black Biography,* vol. 2, pp. 19–21; *Ebony* 34 (March 1979): 54–62; *Who's Who among African Americans,* 26th ed., p. 113; Smith, *Notable Black American Men,* pp. 86–88.

1985 • Frederick D. Gregory (1941–) led the *Challenger* on a seven-day mission, becoming the first black to pilot a space shuttle. A nephew of the developer of blood plasma storage, Dr. Charles Drew, Gregory spent over 455 hours in outer space and from 1985 to 1991 he commanded three major space missions. Gregory grew up in an integrated neighborhood in Washington, D.C. and, until the eighth grade, was bused across town to an all-black school. He graduated from the United States Air Force Academy in 1964 with a bachelor's degree, and earned a master's degree from George Washington University in 1977. Gregory was a research test pilot for the National Aeronautics and Space Administration from 1974 to 1978, and in 1978 he was selected for the astronaut training program. He worked in the Shuttle Avionics Integration Laboratory from 1979 to 1983, piloted the *Challenger* in 1985, commanded the crew of the orbiter *Discovery* in 1989, and commanded the crew of the orbiter *Atlantis* in 1991. In 1992 Gregory was appointed associate administrator for the Office of Safety and Mission Quality. He has published a number of papers on cockpit designs and aircraft handling qualities.

Frederick Gregory

Sources: *Jet* 77 (20 November 1989): 23; 80 (15 July 1991): 26; Gubert, Sawyer, and Fannin, *Distinguished African Americans in Aviation and Space*, pp. 142–45; *Who's Who among African Americans,* 26th ed., p. 499; *Contemporary Black Biography,* vol. 84, pp. 82–84.

1986 • On January 20, 1986, Ronald McNair (1950–1986) was the first black astronaut killed during a space mission, when the space shuttle *Challenger* met disaster, exploding shortly after liftoff. He was also the nation's second black astronaut to travel in space. McNair was born in Lake City, South Carolina, and was able to read and write by age three. He received his bachelor's degree from North Carolina Agricultural and Technical State

Ronald McNair

University in Greensboro in 1971 and received a scholarship to Massachusetts Institute of Technology where he received his doctorate magna cum laude in 1976. McNair then joined Hughes Research Laboratories in Malibu, California, as a researcher. He joined the space program on invitation from the National Aeronautics and Space Administration in 1978. McNair completed training and evaluation for shuttle mission specialist and then worked at the Shuttle Avionics Integration Laboratory. He made three space flights in 1984. While these were rather routine flights, the mission flight scheduled for January 28, 1986, was a high-profile event—it would carry the first private citizen, teacher Christa McAuliffe. McNair was mission specialist. As millions of television viewers watched the rocket bearing the shuttle liftoff at 11:38 A.M. and climb nearly nine miles, the sudden explosion seventy-three seconds later killed all seven on board, devastated witnesses, and challenged the U.S. space program. Later, Morton Thiokol, manufacturer of the O-rings used in the shuttle, was charged with negligence for knowingly using a defective design and failing to advise astronauts of the problem.

Sources: *Contemporary Black Biography,* vol. 3, pp. 164–66; Gubert, Sawyer, and Fannin, *Distinguished African Americans in Aviation and Space,* pp. 210–14; Hornsby, *Chronology of African-American History,* p. 340; *Negro Almanac,* p. 1094; Smith, *Notable Black American Men,* pp. 798–800.

1987 • Mae C. Jemison (1956–) was named the first black woman astronaut. On September 12, 1992, she boarded the space shuttle *Endeavor* as science mission specialist on the historic eight-day flight. Jemison left the National Aeronautic and Space Administration in 1993 and founded a private firm, the Jemison Group. The firm specializes in projects that integrate science issues into the design, development, and implementation of technologies. She also became professor of environmental studies at Dartmouth College and directs the Jemison Institute for Advancing Technology in Developing Countries. Jemison was born in Decatur, Alabama, and moved to Chicago with her family when she was three years old. She graduated from Stanford University in 1977 with a degree in chemical engineering and Afro-American Studies. Jemison received her medical degree from Cornell Medical School in 1981. She worked as a staff physician for the Peace Corps for two and a half years in Sierra Leone.

Mae Jemison

Sources: *Contemporary Black Biography,* vol. 1, pp. 113–14; Gubert, Sawyer, and Fannin, *Distinguished African Americans in Aviation and* Space, pp. 176–79; *Jet* 82 (14 September 1992): cover, 34–38; *Negro Almanac,* p. 1064; Smith, *Notable Black American Women,* pp. 571–73; *Who's Who among African Americans,* 14th ed., p. 675.

1994 • The first in a series of joint ventures between the United States and Russian space programs began on February 3 and ended on April 11. Black commander Charles Frank Bolden Jr. (1946–) was the first black to lead the National Aeronautics and Space Administration's shuttle *Discovery* mission on such a joint venture. Born in Columbia, South Carolina, Bolden graduated from the U.S. Naval Academy in 1968, became a second lieutenant in the Marine Corps, and fought in Vietnam where he flew over one hundred combat missions. He received his master's degree from the University of Southern California in 1977. He was a candidate for the National Aeronautic and Space Administration (NASA) from 1980 to 1981 and did systems development group work for NASA. Bolden held several positions with NASA; he served as special assistant to the director and pilot on the STS 61-C for Johnson Space Administration. He was commander for STS–60, the Russian/American Space Shuttle Mission. In May 2006 he was inducted into the Astronaut Hall of Fame.

Sources: *Contemporary Black Biography,* vol. 78, pp. 19–21; Gubert, Sawyer, and Fannin, *Distinguished African Americans in Aviation and Space,* pp. 30–33; *Jet* 85 (21 February 1994): 9, 12; *Who's Who among African Americans,* 14th ed., p. 112.

1995 • Bernard Anthony Harris Jr. (1956–), a physician as well as an astronaut, became the first black astronaut to walk in space. During this trip, his second flight in space, he walked five hours in *Discovery's* cargo bay. The eight-day flight included a rendezvous with Russia's space station Mir. In August 1992 Harris was a mission specialist on STS-55, Spacelab D–2. He flew aboard *Columbia* for ten days while on that mission and altogether logged over 239 hours in space. Harris trained as a flight surgeon at the Aerospace School of Medicine at Brooks Air Force Base in San Antonio, Texas. Harris was born in Temple, Texas, and graduated from the University of Houston (B.S., 1978), the Texas Tech University Health Science Center (M.D., 1982), the University of Texas Medical Branch (M.S., 1996), and the University of Houston (M.B.A., 1999). He was in private practice with various medical groups and also taught at the University of Texas Medical School, Baylor College of Medicine, and elsewhere. He became an astronaut in 1991 and remained in the program until 1996. Harris was awarded a NASA space flight medal, a NASA Award of Merit. In 2000 he became a fellow of the American College of Physicians and received the Horatio Alger Award.

Sources: Gubert, Sawyer, and Fannin, *Distinguished African Americans in Aviation and Space,* pp. 149–53; *Jet* 87 (20 February 1995): 4–5; (27 February 1995): 46; 88 (28 August 1995): 25; *Who's Who among African Americans,* 26th ed., p. 535.

Bernard Harris Jr.

2007 • A record-making mission occurred in 2007 when NASA astronaut and space mission specialist Robert L. Curbean Jr. made a spacewalk to repair a jammed solar energy panel on the Quest Airlock. He "set a new record for the most spacewalks completed during a shuttle mission by a single crew member," at the International Space Station. This was Curbean's fourth spacewalk and lasted six hours and thirty-eight minutes.

Sources: Gubert, Sawyer, and Fannin, *Distinguished African Americans in Aviation and Space,* pp. 86–88; *Jet* 111 (8 January 2007): 4.

2009 • Charles Frank Bolden Jr. (1946–?) became the first African American to lead the NASA space program. With that appointment, Bolden became "America's leading voice for space exploration." He also became the twelfth administrator of the agency and bears responsibility for managing NASA's resources as well as advancing its mission and goals. President Barack Obama appointed the highly decorated and highly regarded Bolden to the position and on July 15 the Senate confirmed his appointment. Of his experiences in space, Bolden said "I never dreamed of being an astronaut" but admitted that astronaut Ronald McNair encouraged him to apply for the space program. "And had it not been for him, who knows what I would have been doing now, but I wouldn't have been sitting here as NASA administrator." NASA's manned space program ended in July 2011.

Charles Bolden Jr.

Sources: *Contemporary Black Biography,* vol. 7, pp. 16–18; vol. 78, pp. 19–21; Joiner, "Bold Moves: Charles Bolden is the First African American to Lead the NASA Space Program," *Crisis* 116 (Fall 2009): 23–27.

SPORTS

Administration

1859 • On October 16 the first black director of physical culture at Harvard University was Abraham Molineaux Hewlitt.

Sources: Ashe, *A Hard Road to Glory,* vol. 1, pp. 11–12.

1986 • Harriet Hamilton of Fisk University became the first black woman athletic director in the Southern Intercollegiate Athletic Conference.

Sources: *Jet* 70 (14 July 1986): 16.

1992 • Vivian L. Fuller (1954–) was named athletic director at Northeastern Illinois University (NIU), becoming the first black woman to hold that post in Division I of the National Collegiate Athletic Association. In October 1997, Tennessee State University in Nashville named Fuller athletic director, making her the only black woman in charge of a top division NCAA sports program. Her appointment made her one of only nineteen women athletic directors in the NCAA who control both men's and women's programs, and one of only seven such women to control programs that include football. After a dispute with the school, she left to become athletic director for the University of Maryland, Eastern Shore. Born in Chapel Hill, North Carolina, she graduated from Fayetteville State University in 1977 with a bachelor's degree in physical education and earned a master's degree from the University of Idaho and a doctorate from Iowa State University. Fuller had served as an assistant or associate athletic director at Bennett College for Women, North Carolina Agricultural and Technical University, Indiana University, and the University of Pennsylvania before moving to NIU

Sources: Hine, *Black Women in America,* vol. 2, p. 1332; *Tennessean* (October 11, 1997); *Who's Who among African Americans,* 26th ed., p. 442.

1992 • Anita Luceete DeFrantz (1952–), president of the Athletic Foundation of Los Angeles and elected to the International Olympic Committee in 1987, was the first black elected to its executive board. She served as vice-president of the board in 1997, the first woman accorded this honor. In 2001 she became the first woman and the first black to run for the presidency of the International Olympic Committee (IOC). Counting her years on Olympic teams and her years of service to the organization, by this time she spent twenty-four years (half her life) with an Olympic connection. DeFrantz won a bronze medal for Rowing Eights in the Montreal Olympics in 1976, where she was the first black American to compete for the United States in Olympic rowing. An outspoken critic of the Olympian movement during the 1980 boycott, DeFrantz became only the second American athlete to receive the International Olympic Committee's Bronze Medal of the Olympic Order. She was born in Philadelphia, Pennsylvania, and did her undergraduate work at Connecticut College, graduating with honors in 1974. In 1977 she received the J.D. degree from the University of Pennsylvania. She worked for the U.S. Olympics organization in some capacity from 1981 to 1997, beginning as vice president of the Los Angeles Olympic Coordinating Committee. She continued her career in sports administration when she became president of the Amateur Athletic Foundation of Los Angeles. Her long list of honors and awards includes recognition for athletic, administrative, and legal skills; public service, and honorary degrees. In addition to her 1976 Olympic bronze medal, she won a silver medal at the 1978 World Championships, was on six national championship teams, and won another Olympic bronze medal in 1990.

Sources: Ashe, *A Hard Road to Glory,* vol. 3, pp. 215–16; *Jet* 71 (9 February 1987): 51; 72 (27 July 1987): 48; 82 (17 August 1992): 48; 99 (26 February 2001): 50; Page, *Black Olympian Medalists,* pp. 30–31; *Tennessean* (5 February 2001); *Who's Who among African Americans,* 26th ed., p. 329.

1992 • Leroy Tashreau Walker (1918–2012) was the first black to hold the four-year post of president of the United States Olympic Committee. The retired coach, who in 1976 was head coach of the United States Track and Field team at the Olympic Games in Montreal, became chancellor emeritus of North Carolina Central University. In 1994, acting as USOC president, Walker announced plans to form two separate task forces to resolve the lack of minority representation on USOC executive boards, with one task force to deal with women's representation and the other to handle representation of ethnic minorities. A survey by *USA Today* had revealed the disproportion between team membership and Olympic executive positions. Walker was a pioneer Olympic coach when he served as head track coach for teams from Ethiopia, Israel, Trinidad and Tobago, and Kenya. He had a prior history of front-office involvement with the U.S. Olympic Committee, serving on committees and as treasurer from 1988 to 1992. Walker was serving as the vice president and director of sports for the Atlanta Committee for the Olympic Games when he became president of the U.S. Olympic Committee. His career as a college administrator and his experience as a coach gave him a wealth of experience on which he could call. Walker was born in Atlanta, Georgia, but grew up living with an older brother in Harlem after his father died. He entered Benedict College (South Carolina) in 1936 on an athletic scholarship and went on to Columbia University after his graduation from Benedict in 1940. Armed with a graduate degree, Walker returned to Benedict as chairman of the physical education department and coach for four major sports in 1941. Between 1942 and 1945 he held similar positions at Bishop and Prairie View College (both in Texas). He started out the same way at North Carolina College (now North Carolina Central College). He was a particularly successful track coach, sending many of his players to the Olympics between 1956 and 1980. By 1957 Walker had obtained his doctorate in biomechanics from New York University, and in 1974 he stepped up to the position of vice chancellor in university relations. He held this position until 1983 and moved to the position of chancellor in 1983. When he retired as chancellor in 1986, he had been in service to North Carolina Central for more than forty years, while also being involved with the Olympics and other global causes and publishing three books between 1960 and 1969. He continued a broad pattern of activity after he left his long-time home base. A host of organizations, institutions, and societies have recognized Walker's leadership qualities. He has received awards as a distinguished alumnus and a distinguished teacher; distinguished service and role model awards; and achievement awards. He is a member of several halls of fame, including the U.S. Olympics Hall of Fame.

Sources: *Ebony* 47 (August 1992): 7; *Jet* 83 (26 October 1992): 46; *Who's Who among African Americans,* 26th ed., p. 1273; Smith, *Notable Black American Men,* pp. 1166–67.

1994 • Louis Stout was named commissioner of Kentucky's High School Athletic Association to become the first black head of a full-state athletic association. He was the fifth commissioner in the association's history. He was named assistant commissioner in 1971 and executive assistant in 1992. Stout was born in Cynthiana, Kentucky, and graduated from Regis College.

Sources: *Jet* 86 (25 July 1994): 49; *Who's Who among African Americans,* 26th ed., p. 1186.

1995 • Wendy Hilliard, director of amateur sports for New York City Sports Commission, became the first black elected president of the Women's Sports Foundation in that city.

Sources: *Jet* 87 (1 May 1995): 20.

1997 • Tom A. Goss became the Ronald R. Shepherd Director of Intercollegiate Athletics at the University of Michigan. Until his resignation in 2000, he oversaw twenty-three varsity coaches and teams as well as the university's athletic fields and facilities. He was previously managing partner of The Goss Group, Inc., located in Oakland, California. When he was a student at the university, Goss was All-Big Ten defensive tackle. In returning to his alma mater as athletic director, he became the university's first black person to hold that position.

Sources: *Who's Who among African Americans,* 14th ed., p. 490; *Jet* 92 (6 October 1997): 20.

2001 • Craig Littlepage (1951?–) was named athletic director for the University of Virginia, becoming the first black in the history of the Atlantic Coast Conference to hold that post and the sixth currently in NCAA Division I-A. He had served as an administrator in Virginia's athletic department since 1990 and was the senior associate director when named director.

Sources: *Jet* 100 (10 September 2001): 56.

2012 • The first black vice chancellor for athletics and university affairs and athletics director at Vanderbilt University is David Williams II. He also continues his position as general counsel, university secretary, and professor of law. Since 2003, athletics was put under his charge along with other responsibilities. The Detroit native received bachelor's and master's degrees from Northern Michigan University, a Master of Business Administration and Doctor of Jurisprudence from the University of Detroit. His LL.M. (Taxation) degree is from New York University. He came to Vanderbilt in 2002.

Sources: "David Williams, II," Office of the General Council, Vanderbilt University, www.vanderbilt.edu/generalcounsel/williams.html, accessed 17 July 2012; *Tennessean* (13 July 2012).

Associations

1906 • The first black athletic association, the Interscholastic Athletic Association, was organized with the purpose of fostering sports in the Baltimore/Washington, D.C., area. Comprised of colleges and high schools, the first meet—a track and field event— was held on May 30 at Howard University.

Sources: Ashe, *A Hard Road to Glory,* vol. 1, pp. 13–14, 61, 105; Young, *Negro Firsts in Sports,* pp. 91–92.

1924 • William "Pres" Rucker led a group of black business leaders in Indianapolis to form a racing league known as the Colored Speedway Association. The league held the first Colored Speed Championships that year. Later the contest was known as the Gold and Glory Sweepstakes Series; it was part of a professional auto racing circuit for black drivers and mechanics. The race spread throughout the Midwest in the 1920s and to Pennsylvania, Atlanta, Los Angeles, and Fort Worth by the 1930s, and was last run in the mid-1930s.

Sources: Smith, *Encyclopedia of African American Popular Culture,* vol. 1, p. 238.

The United States Olympic Committee's First Black CEO

In 2001 Lloyd David Ward (1949–) was unanimously elected chief executive officer of the United States Olympic Committee (USOC) on October 21, becoming the first black to hold that post. Also in the running for the post were former Baltimore mayor Kurt Schmoke and acting USOC chief executive officer Scott Blackburn. The USOC is based in Colorado Springs, Colorado, and every four years has a budget of almost $500 million. Previously Ward was chairman and chief executive officer of Maytag Corporation and later chairman and chief executive office of iMotors.

Sources: *Jet* 100 (3 December 2001): 48; *Crisis* 109 (January/February 2002): 12.

Automobile Racing

1923 • Rojo Jack became the first black to participate in automobile racing, albeit on a restricted basis. Jack was the only black participant in the two Honolulu Chamber of Commerce-sponsored races in early 1954, and drove his 275-horsepower car to victory. Although he lost an eye in a 1938 racing accident, the California resident continued to race beyond the age of sixty.

Sources: *Encyclopedia of Black America*, p. 139; Young, *Negro Firsts in Sports*, pp. 176–77.

1954 • Berton Groves became the first black to enter the Pikes Peak Hill Climb automobile race.

Sources: Jones and Washington, *Black Champions Challenge American Sports*, p. 114; Young, *Negro Firsts in Sports*, p. 281.

Wendell Scott

1963 • Wendell Oliver Scott (1921–1990), was the first and only black driver to win a NASCAR Winston Cup (then the Grand National) race. He was the first black driver since Rojo Jack (1923) to earn a national following. Scott began racing at Danville Fairgrounds Speedway in his hometown of Danville, Virginia, and won more than one hundred short-track Sportsman races, as well as several state and track titles. He moved to NASCAR's premier division in 1961 where he made almost five hundred starts. In the summer of 1964 Scott won a short-track race at Jacksonville, Florida. Injuries in a race at Talladega ended his career in 1973. The 1977 film *Greased Lightning*, starring Richard Pryor, was based on his life. Scott was subjected to many instances of discrimination during his racing career—from not being allowed to compete, to slashed tires, or not receiving points he should have been awarded. His driving skills eventually led to a degree of recognition. From 1949 until his death in 1990, Scott owned and operated Scott's Garage, where his skills as an auto mechanic were in great demand. A street in Danville was named for him in 1997. In 1999 he was one of five drivers, and the only black, inducted into the International Motorsports Hall of Fame, in Talladega, Alabama.

Sources: Ashe, *A Hard Road to Glory*, vol. 2, pp. 231–32; *Autoweek* 41 (7 January 1991): 55; *Contemporary Black Biography*, vol. 19, pp. 197–200; *Jet* 79 (14 January 1990): 51; 93 (26 January 1998): 54; Smith, *Notable Black American Men*, pp. 1054–56; *Tennessean* (22 October 1998).

1972 • The first black to enter a team in the Indianapolis 500, with Vanguard Racing, was Leonard W. Miller, president of the Miller Racing Group, Inc. By the mid-1990s, MRG primarily fielded black drivers in races such as NASCAR, ARCA, and Formula BMW Americas. Miller and his son, Leonard T., navigated around hostile officials and promoters and a host of bigoted competitors to break the racial and class barrier and "become an enduring presence in NASCAR racing." In addition, corporations that sponsored white drivers were unwilling to do the same for blacks. The elder Miller was born in Philadelphia and spent some time tinkering with the family's 1937 Ford when he was a teenager. While serving in the Third Army's 45th Ordinance Battalion, Direct Automotive Support Company, he learned to repair jeeps and trucks. For fifteen years he directed an auto-racing organization known as Black American Racers Association (BARA), which helped to create opportunities for black drivers in NASCAR. For his pioneering work in motorsport history, the senior Miller is in the Black Athletes Hall of Fame. The Lawrenceville, New Jersey, native Leonard T. Miller is a graduate of Morehouse College. He is a licensed airline pilot who recognized his passion for flying at age fourteen. He became a pilot for Allegheny Airlines and Business Express in 1987 and 1988, and in 1989 United Airlines hired him as a DC-10 flight engineer. He has flown a number of aircraft, including the Boeing 737, 757, 767, and 777 through the Americas, the Caribbean, Europe, the Middle East, and Asia. He is the currently president of the Miller Racing Group.

Sources: Smith, *Encyclopedia of African American Popular Culture,* vol. 1, p. 239.

Leonard W. Miller

1991 • Willy [Willie] T. Ribbs (1956–) became the first black ever to qualify for the Indianapolis 500. He attended the Jim Russell Driving School and began racing in and around San Jose, California. Ribbs has participated in various forms of racing, from Indy cars to IMSA, including a season in NASCAR Winston Cup competition. He has had difficulty in finding sponsors, a perennial problem for unestablished drivers, compounded by his reputation for being outspoken and aggressive. He entered the race again in 1993, but in spite of entertainer Bill Cosby's advice, support, and offers to make free personal endorsements to any major sponsor, no one would share the commitment. A NASCAR driver for Bobby Hamilton of Nashville, Tennessee, in 2001 Ribbs became the first black driver to launch a full season in any top NASCAR division in the modern era, which dates from post–1971. He also became the first black driver in NASCAR's Craftsman Truck Series. He had been trying to become a NASCAR driver for several years when given the opportunity to qualify for the Florida Dodge Dealers 250 truck race. In 1987 Ribbs was the first driver ever suspended by IMSA for hitting another driver; he was sidelined for thirty days. Ribbs, who was born in San Jose, California, was exposed to racing early: His father was an amateur race driver. He went to England at age twenty-one to further enhance his skills as a driver. Although his career has had its ups and downs, he has received several awards, including one as Trans-Am Rookie of the Year and two as Norelco GTO Driver of the Year.

Willy T. Ribbs

Sources: Ashe, *A Hard Road to Glory,* vol. 3, pp. 232–33, 258; *Contemporary Black Biography,* vol. 2, pp. 196–99; *Jet* 95 (31 May 1999): 19; *Road and Track* 44 (August 1993) 130–32; Smith, *Notable Black American Men,* pp. 1008–10; *Tennessean* (13 February 2001).

1995 • Walter Payton (1954–1999) became the first black team owner in the Indy Car series. A former star running back with the Chicago Bears football team, Payton became a partner with Dale Coyne to race on the Indy Circuit in preparation for the race in Florida in March. The car driven in the race, number 34, bore the number of Payton's retired jersey. Payton, who was born in Columbia, Mississippi, graduated from historically black Jackson State College (now University). After his retirement from the Bears in 1986, he became a successful businessman, including co-ownership of CART racing team. He was a resident of Barrington, Illinois, at the time of his death.

Sources: *Jet* 88 (26 December–2 January 1995): 48; *Who's Who among African Americans,* 13th ed., p. 1514.

2005 • The first African American team owners to win a track championship in National Association for Stock Car Auto Racing (NASCAR) history was the Miller Racing Group (MRG). The team won in NASCAR's Weekly Racing Series held at Old Dominion Speedway held in Manassas, Virginia. Racer Franklin Butler piloted the Millers' Chevrolet late model stock.

Sources: Smith, *Encyclopedia of African American Popular Culture,* vol. 1, pp. 239–40.

2007 • Rookie driver Lewis Hamilton (1985?–) drove a McLaren-Mercedes and won the Canadian Grand Prix Formula One (F1) auto race held in Montreal, becoming the first black driver to win an F1 race. He was also the first black driver in Formula One racing; he had six straight top three finishes in six starts. At that time, no other first-year F1 driver

Lewis Hamilton

matched his record. For some time Hamilton, a British driver, anticipated the win with confidence; he said, "The team gave me the best car and I had no problems during the race at all."

Sources: *Jet* 111 (35 June 2007): 10.

Baseball

1867 • In October 1867 the Brooklyn Uniques were hosts to the Excelsiors of Philadelphia in a contest called "the championship of colored clubs." These two teams are among the first known black baseball clubs, and this is the first known intercity contest. The Excelsiors won 37–24.

Sources: *Total Baseball,* p. 548.

1869 • The Philadelphia Pythons were the first black team to play an all-white club. They defeated the Philadelphia City Items, 27–17.

Sources: *Total Baseball,* p. 548.

1878 • The first known black professional player—predating the present league organization—was pitcher John W. "Bud" Fowler [John W. Jackson] (1858?–?). In April 1878 he played for a team from Chelsea, Massachusetts that defeated the Boston club of the National League in an exhibition game. Fowler later became also a second baseman, and his career as a semi-professional can be traced at least as late as 1891. He was the first of more than seventy black players on interracial teams in organized baseball during the nineteenth century until the last, Bert Jones, of Atchison in the Kansas State League, was forced out in 1899.

Sources: Chalk, *Pioneers of Black Sport,* pp. 5, 25–27; *Total Baseball,* pp. 548, 550; Young, *Negro Firsts in Sports,* pp. 16, 55–56, 206.

Moses Walker

1881 • Moses Fleetwood Walker (1857–1924) was the first black college varsity baseball player and a member of the first Oberlin College varsity baseball team. In 1883 the bare-handed catcher signed for the Northwestern League Toledo team. He became the first black in major league baseball when the team entered the American Association in 1884. There was not another black player in major league baseball for more than fifty years. Walker was born in Mount Pleasant, Ohio, of mixed racial heritage. When he was three years old, the family moved to Steubenville, Ohio, where his father became the only black physician in the city. Walker's father later became a minister, and the family moved twice again before returning to Steubenville by 1880. Walker was admitted to Oberlin in 1878 as a college student after attending the institution's preparatory program. In 1882 his baseball talent led to his enrollment at the University of Michigan, with plans to study law and play baseball. His studies ceased when he joined the Toledo club. Walker faced great hostility from both his teammates and fans in the stands. He did have a smoother course on the field when he was teamed with a black pitcher, George Washington Stavey, when he joined the Newark team in the International League (IL) in 1887. Anti-black sentiment in baseball did not, however, disappear. Walker moved to the Syracuse team in the IL in 1888, where he remained for two seasons. He stayed in Syracuse when he left baseball. In 1891 he was arrested and charged with murder after a street brawl; he was later acquitted. Walker worked with the post office, where he established a poor record. He served a year in prison after being convicted of taking money from the mail. When released, he returned to Steubenville, where he at times ran the family billiard parlor and published a newspaper. He also traveled, giving kinescope exhibitions; opened the Cadiz opera house in 1904; and published a booklet in 1908 urging blacks to return to Africa. Walker was working as a clerk in a billiards parlor at the time of his death.

Sources: Ashe, *A Hard Road to Glory,* vol. 1, pp. 70–72; Kane, *Famous First Facts,* p. 104; *Total Baseball,* pp. 548–49; Young, *Negro Firsts in Sports,* pp. 16, 55, 73; Smith, *Notable Black American Men,* pp. 1168–71.

1889 • In 1885 Frank P. Thompson organized a group of waiters and bellmen at the Argyle Hotel on Long Island, New York, to form the Cuban Giants. Four years later the team joined the Middle States League and became the first black professional baseball team, finishing the season with a 55–17 record. The Cuban Giants made a final minor league appearance in 1891. The last black team in organized interracial baseball of this period was the Acme Colored Giants of the Pennsylvania Iron and Oil League in 1898.

Sources: Ashe, *A Hard Road to Glory,* vol. 1, pp. 72, 73; Kane, *Famous First Blacks,* p. 105; *Total Baseball,* p. 550; Young, *Negro Firsts in Sports,* pp. 55–58, 206.

1901 • Charles Grant, a second baseman, became the first black player in the American League (not yet a major league). He was a member of the black Columbia Giants and played for the Baltimore Orioles. He used the name Charles Tokahama and claimed to be of Cherokee decent until the deception was exposed.

Sources: *Encyclopedia of Black America,* p. 125; Kane, *Famous First Facts,* p. 104; *Total Baseball,* p. 550; Young, *Negro Firsts in Sports,* pp. 56–57, 61, 72, 149.

1920 • Andrew "Rube" Foster (1879–1930), a former pitcher, organized the first successful black professional baseball league, the National Association of Professional Baseball Clubs, usually called the Negro National League, on February 13. He was known as the father of the Negro Leagues. (The International League of Independent Baseball Clubs, with four black and two white teams, lasted one season in 1906, and in 1910 the National Negro Baseball League collapsed before a single game had been played.) The Indianapolis ABC played the Chicago Giants in the league's first game. Foster insisted that all teams in the league should be black-controlled with the one exception being the Kansas City Monarchs. The league ran into difficulties in 1926 when Foster became ill, and it collapsed in 1931, a year after his death. A new Negro National League was organized in 1933 controlled by men in the numbers racket. Donn Rogosin wrote, "The Negro National League meetings were enclaves of the most powerful black gangsters in the nation." Foster, who was born in Calvert, Texas, the son of a minister. He showed promise as a baseball organizer early, managing a team while in grade school. He left for Fort Worth, Texas, when he was in the eighth grade, to go further in baseball. His personal playing days included stints with several Negro teams, including the American Giants (so named by Foster) who have been called one of the greatest Negro baseball teams. Foster was a businessman as well as a baseball phenomenon; he owned a barbershop and an automobile service shop. An accident with a gas leak in his home in 1925 preceded declining health for Foster, both physically and mentally. He was in the state asylum in Illinois at the time of his death. He was elected to the National Baseball Hall of Fame in 1981. In 2001, a set of two U.S. postage stamps bearing the image of Negro Leagues Baseball and Rube Foster was issued .

Andrew "Rube" Foster

Sources: Ashe, *A Hard Road to Glory,* vol. 1, pp. 83–84; *Encyclopedia of Black America,* p. 125; *Jet* 90 (23 September 1996): 19; *Total Baseball,* p. 552; Young, *Black Firsts in Sports,* pp. 58–62; Smith, *Notable Black American Men,* pp. 417–20.

1920 • The New York Lincoln Giants played the Atlantic City Bacharach Giants at Ebbets Field in Brooklyn on July 17. Six thousand fans attended the game and witnessed the historic event—the first time two Negro League teams would play at a major league stadium.

Sources: *The Black New Yorkers,* p. 168.

1924 • The first world series between Negro league clubs was held this year. Leagues from this period included the National Negro Baseball League, the American Association League, the Mid-Western Baseball League, and the Negro International League.

Sources: Chalk, *Pioneers of Black Sport,* p. 66–67; *Encyclopedia of Black America,* p. 125; Young, *Negro Firsts in Sports,* p. 158.

1933 • Gus Greenlee organized the first annual East-West All-Star Game in Chicago. The event came to overshadow the black World Series, and by 1939 leading players were attracting 500,000 votes.

Sources: *Total Baseball,* p. 552.

Players from Negro Leagues in Baseball Hall of Fame

Year Inducted	Player
1971	Satchel Paige
1972	Josh Gibson
1972	Walter "Buck" Leonard
1973	Monfors "Monte" Irvin
1974	James "Cool Papa" Bell
1975	William "Judy" Johnson
1976	Oscar Charleston
1977	Martin Dihigo
1977	John Henry "Pop" Lloyd
1981	Andrew "Rube" Foster
1987	Ray Dandridge
1995	Leon Day
1996	Bill Foster
1997	Willie Wells
1998	Bullet Rogan
1999	Joe Williams
2000	Turkey Stearnes
2001	Hilton Smith

Sources: *Total Baseball,* pp. 311–12, 322, 329, 331, 338, 341, 352, 354, 361–62, 376–77, 517–23; National Baseball Hall of Fame and Museum, http://baseballhall.org/hall-famers. Accessed September 30, 2012.

Jackie Robinson

1947 • Jackie [John Roosevelt] Robinson (1919–1972) joined the Brooklyn Dodgers as a third baseman to become the first black in major leagues of the modern era. Other blacks who began playing this year included Larry Doby for Cleveland, Dan Bankhead for Brooklyn, and Hank [Henry Curtis] Thompson and Willard Jessie Brown for Saint Louis. Robinson played his first game in this capacity against the Boston Braves at Ebbetts field in Brooklyn on April 15, 1947, and in 1948 shifted to second base. He was named Rookie of the Year in 1947. Robinson probably received more racial insults in his career than any other person in history. In 1949 he became the first black batting champion and the first black to receive the National League's Most Valuable Player Award. Robinson was the first black enshrined in the Baseball Hall of Fame in 1962. Robinson was actually the first black to play at any level in the major leagues. He played with the Montreal Royals, the Dodgers' top minor league farm club, in 1946, and proceeded to hit .800 with 4 runs batted in, 4 runs scored, and 2 stolen bases in his debut game. Born in Cairo, Georgia, Robinson's mother moved the family to Pasadena, California, after her husband left them, when Robinson was thirteen months old. There he became active in sports while in grade school, playing competitively for the first time in a fourth grade soccer game. In high school and Pasadena Junior College, he lettered in football, baseball, basketball, and track. His excellence in athletics continued at UCLA (California), but Robinson left there because of financial pressures in 1941, just shy of a degree. He was drafted in 1942, and after boxing champion Joe Louis and other notables protested, he was allowed to enter Officers Candidate School and was commissioned as a lieutenant in the U.S. Army in 1943. Threatened with a court martial while in the army, because he defied bus segregation law in Fort Hood, Texas, he was exonerated. His first professional baseball team, which he joined in 1945, was the Kansas City Monarchs of the Negro American League. He was with this team when he came to the attention of the Dodgers. Robinson's impact on baseball goes far beyond his baseball statistics. He had to excel not only athletically but to comport himself well in the face of the opposition to him because of his race. He is recognized for the extent to which he succeeded in both regards, and is widely credited with opening the door for other black aspirants to a career in major league baseball. Facing a trade in 1956, Robinson retired from baseball and became an executive with the New York-based Chock Full O' Nuts restaurant chain. He combined this position with active community involvement on be-half of African American businesses, but he was often at odds with other black leaders of the day. New York's Governor Nelson Rockefeller named him special assistant for com-munity affairs in 1946. Independent throughout his life, Robinson refused participation in a 1969 Old-timers' Game to protest baseball's lack of African American involvement in baseball management and front office positions. An ailing Robinson threw out the first ball at the 1972 World Series. He died in Stamford, Connecticut, nine days later. In 1997, fifty years after Robinson burst upon the baseball scene, major league baseball officials dedicated the 1997 season to the pioneer, honoring the fiftieth anniversary of his break-ing the color barrier and entering major league baseball.

Sources: Jones and Washington, *Black Champions Challenge American Sports,* pp. 96–101; *Total Baseball,* pp. 383–84, 503, 1412; Smith, *Notable Black American Men,* pp. 1022–25; Rampersad, *Jackie Robinson: A Biography; Jet* 89 (6 May 1996): 51; 91 (17 March 1997): 48–49.

1947 • Dan [Daniel Robert] Bankhead (1920–1976), a member of the Brooklyn Dodgers, became the first black pitcher in the major leagues on August 26. A native of Empire, Al-abama, he played in the majors until 1951. Baseball was a family affair for Bankhead and four of his brothers, all of whom played in the Negro Leagues. Bankhead began his career with the Negro League's Birmingham Black Barons and went on to play with the Memphis Red Sox and Canadian and Mexican League teams before signing with the Dodgers. He pitched in all-star games in 1941, 1946, and 1947. Also in 1947, he and his teammate Jackie Robinson were the first black players to compete in the World Series. He was a res-ident of Houston, Texas, at the time of his death.

Sources: *The Black New Yorkers,* p. 267; *Ebony* (May 1969): 110; *Negro Almanac,* pp. 1427–28; *Total Baseball,* p. 1586; Young, *Negro Firsts in Sports,* p. 207.

1947 • The first black player in the American League was Larry [Lawrence Eugene] Doby (1923–2003), who joined the Cleveland Indians on July 5. In 1948 he hit the winning home run in Game 4 (or 5) of the World Series; sources disagree on which game it was. He was the first black player to hit a home run in the World Series. The first black home run cham-pion in 1952, with thirty-two homers for the Indians, Doby spent thirteen seasons in major league ball and was an All-star in each season from 1949 through 1955. In 1954 he led the American League in both homers and runs batted in. In the middle of the 1978 season, he became manager of the Chicago White Sox, for whom he had earlier held a two-year coach-ing position after leaving Cleveland. Over the years Doby held several coaching positions, but he also served in administrative positions, first for the NBA's New Jersey Nets (1977 and from 1980 to 1989), and most recently in the licensing department of Major League Base-ball Properties, beginning in 1990. His birthplace, Camden, South Carolina, honored Doby in 1997 with a key to the city and announced plans for a monument and a baseball field as additional recognition of his achievements. An additional honor came his way in 1998, when Paterson, New Jersey, which became his hometown as a teenager, named its post of-fice for him. Doby's father, who died when Doby was eight years old, had been a semi-pro-fessional baseball player, giving him early exposure to the game. He was, however, an all-around athlete in high school, lettering in baseball, basketball, and football. He played with the Newark Eagles of the Negro Leagues when he was seventeen, using an assumed name to protect his standing as an amateur. The next season he played basketball with the Paterson Panthers in the American Basketball League, but after a tour of duty in the U. S. Navy, he returned to the Newark Eagles until signed by Cleveland. Segregation was ram-pant when Doby entered the major league; he endured personal affronts as well. He survived to earn recognition by baseball halls of fame at several levels, culminating with his election to the National Baseball Hall of Fame on July 26, 1998.

Larry Doby

Sources: Bennett, *Before the Mayflower,* p. 633, 636; *Encyclopedia of Black America,* p. 127; *Total Baseball,* pp. 332, 1072; Salzman, *Encyclopedia of African-American Culture and His-tory,* pp. 775–76; *Contemporary Black Biography,* vol. 16, pp. 38–41; *Jet* 92 (16 June 1997): 50; 93 (23 March 1998): 8, 47.

1947 • The first black players in a World Series were Brooklyn Dodgers players Dan Bankhead and Jackie Robinson, in October this year. Robinson participated in all seven games against the New York Yankees; Bankhead played in only one.

Sources: Bennett, *Before the Mayflower,* p. 633; *Total Baseball,* p. 157.

Satchel Paige

1948 • Satchel [Leroy Robert] Paige (1900–1982) was the first black pitcher in the American League and the first black to actually pitch in a World Series game. One of the best-known players in black baseball, he became the first black elected to the Baseball Hall of Fame for his career in the Negro Leagues, in 1971. During five seasons in the majors, 1948–53, he won twenty-eight games and lost thirty-two. He appeared in one game in 1965 to pitch three innings for the Kansas City Athletics. At fifty-nine, the oldest man ever to pitch in the majors, Paige allowed one hit. A native of Mobile, Alabama, Paige grew up in a family with eleven children. He began work at the Mobile Train Depot at age seven and often skipped school, although he pitched for the school baseball team when he was ten years old. He further developed his baseball skills and also added to his formal education during the five and one-half years he spent while serving time in a juvenile correctional facility after a shoplifting offense at age twelve. When Paige was released, he joined the all-black semiprofessional team of the Mobile Tigers, and his career was launched. In 1926 he became a professional baseball player when the Chattanooga Black Lookouts, a Negro Southern League team, signed him. He continued to play with Negro League teams, and while he was with the Pittsburgh Crawfords in the 1930s, his teammates included five future Hall of Fame stars. In between his two stints with the Crawfords, Paige took a step back to semiprofessional baseball, when he played with the Bismarck (North Dakota) team. This marked his first experience with white teammates. He also played with an all-star team he formed, and once faced famed pitcher Dizzy Dean's exhibition team on a series of six games; Paige's team won four of the six. A few more moves led him to the Kansas City Monarchs, where he was their ace pitcher in the early 1940s. He was with the Monarchs when he became a major league pitcher for the Cleveland Indians. He later played with other teams, and continued to have a role as coach, pitcher, or in public relations until shortly before his death. He died three days after he threw out the first pitch in a Kansas City Royals game. Paige's name is legend in the baseball world. *Sporting News* included him in their 1998 list of the 100 greatest baseball players of the twentieth century.

Sources: Ashe, *A Hard Road to Glory,* vol. 2, p. 31, 38, 40; *Jet* 99 (12 February 2001): 20; *Total Baseball,* pp. 158, 376–77, 1871; Young, *Negro Firsts in Sports,* p. 207; Smith, *Notable Black American Men,* pp. 901–4; Rubin, *Satchel Paige: All-Time Baseball Great.*

1949 • Henry Thompson signed on with the New York Giants, becoming the team's first black player. Source: *The Black New Yorkers,* p. 272.

Don Newcombe

1949 • The only man in baseball history to win all three of baseball's major sports awards was Don Newcombe (1926–). In this year he was named Rookie of the Year, and in 1956 he was named Most Valuable Player and recipient of the Cy Young Award. Like many of the early black players in the major leagues, Newcombe's route ran through the Negro Leagues. Born in Madison, New Jersey, he had a brother who managed a semiprofessional baseball team, and at age nine, Newcombe got an early start in batting and pitching practice. He played both football and baseball in junior high, but had to forgo baseball in high school, because the school had no baseball team. Newcombe's youth kept him out of the armed forces when he tried to enlist in 1942 and resulted in an early discharge in 1943. Despite the fact that he had not really considered a baseball career, he tried out for and was hired by the Newark Eagles of the Negro Leagues in 1943. Newcombe pitched so well in a 1945 outing at Brooklyn's Ebbets Field, during which he faced white major league players for the first time, that the Dodgers gave him a tryout, signed him, and sent him to training camp in 1946, along with future Dodger star catcher Roy Campanella. Frustrated by the belief that he would never get to pitch for the Dodgers, Newcombe walked out on Dodgers' Montreal team for three days in 1948. When he joined the Dodgers in 1949, he compiled an enviable first-season record. The armed services experience Newcombe had sought in the 1940s caught up with him during the early 1950s, and he was absent from baseball until 1955, when he returned to the Dodgers and resumed his winning ways until he began to struggle on the mound during the 1957 season. During the peak of his career, Newcombe was also feared as a hitter.

Sources: *Contemporary Black Biography,* vol. 24, pp. 115–19; *The Black New Yorkers,* p. 272.

1950 • Sam Jethroe (1918?–2001), who joined the Boston Braves in April this year, became the first black major leaguer with the team. A center fielder, he was named National League Rookie of the Year, becoming the oldest player ever to receive the award. Jethroe was a native of East St. Louis, Illinois. He played for the Cincinnati and Cleveland Buckeyes in the Negro Leagues from 1942 to 1948. His first major league tryout came with the Boston Red Sox in 1945; he was never contacted afterward. His record in the Negro Leagues included a league batting title and four all-star appearances. Speed was one of Jethroe's hallmarks: While playing on the Dodgers' Montreal farm team before being sold to Boston, he stole eighty-nine bases one year, and led the major league in steals during his first two seasons of play. In one instance of poetic justice, Jethroe hit a home run for the Braves when they played an exhibition game against the Boston Red Sox in Fenway Park in 1952. Before leaving baseball, he played briefly for the Pittsburgh Pirates. In the middle 1990s, Jethroe sued major league baseball for pension payments former Negro leaguers had been denied. Although the suit was dismissed, payments began to be given to Jethroe and other former players from the Negro Leagues in 1997.

Sam Jethroe

Sources: *New York Times* (19 June 2001).

1950 • Lorenzo "Piper" Davis (1918?–1997) became the first black player to sign with the Boston Red Sox.

Sources: *Jet* 92 (16 June 1997): 17.

1951 • Monte [Monford Merrill] Irvin (1919–), of the New York Giants, was the first black runs-batted-in champion of the National League. Born in Columbia, Alabama, Irvin attended Lincoln University (Pennsylvania) for two years and played baseball in the Cuban Winter League and for the New York Giants from 1949 to 1955. He played for the Chicago Cubs in 1956, and then moved to an administrative baseball position, serving in the Office of the Baseball Commission, as special assistant to the Commissioner. He also served outside baseball as a vice president of the Diversified Capital Corporation. Irvin was elected to the Baseball Hall of Fame in 1973.

Sources: Ashe, *A Hard Road to Glory,* pp. 14–15, 266; Jones and Washington, *Black Champions Challenge American Sports,* p. 107; *Who's Who among African Americans,* 14th ed., p. 647; Young, *Negro Firsts in Sports,* pp. 209–10.

1951 • Don [Donald] "Newk" Newcombe (1926–) was the first black pitcher to win twenty games in a major league. In 1956 he became the first black winner of the Cy Young Award, with a season record of 27–7. Newcombe's remarkable on-the-field achievements began to slump in 1957, while he was with the Brooklyn Dodgers, and he was traded to the Cincinnati Reds. He was traded to the Cleveland Indians in 1959 and retired from baseball in 1960. A recovered alcoholic, Newcombe counsels other baseball alcoholics as Director of Community Relations for the Dodgers and is an active participant on behalf of other worthy causes.

Sources: *Contemporary Black Biography,* vol. 24, pp. 115–119; *Current Biography,* 1957, pp. 399–401; Jones and Washington, *Black Champions Challenge American Sports,* p. 104; *Total Baseball,* p. 374.

1951 • The first American-born black player with the Chicago White Sox was Sam Hairston (1920?–1997), who played his first game on July 21. (Minnie Minoso actually was the first player of color with the White Sox, signing almost three months before Hairston. Minoso, who hit the first pitch thrown to him for a home run just one day after his May 1 signing date, was considered Cuban and not black American.) Hairston spent more than fifty years in professional baseball, but most of his time was spent outside the major leagues. He played in the Negro Leagues during the 1940s, on teams with some of the biggest black stars in the game. His stay with the White Sox was brief—four games in which he was a substitute catcher and pinch hitter. Hairston spent the greater part of the next thirty years as a scout and coach. His last position was with the Birmingham (Alabama) Barons of the Negro League, where he was a coach until a few months before he died. Hairston was in a Birmingham nursing home at the time of his death.

Sources: *New York Times* (9 November 1997).

Roy Campanella

1953 • Roy "Campy" Campanella (1921–1993) became the first black catcher to hit twenty or more homers in five successive seasons (22–31–33–22–41). He also had the most put-outs (807) and the most runs batted in (856) by a catcher. The first black to be named the Most Valuable Player three times (1951, 1953, and 1955), Campanella was inducted into the Hall of Fame in Cooperstown, New York, in 1969. A 1958 automobile accident left the Philadelphia, Pennsylvania, native confined to a wheelchair, effectively curtailing his baseball career. Campanella, with Italian acestry on his father's side, was born in Philadelphia, but the family moved to North Philadelphia when he was a child, and he grew up there. His affinity for sports was amply demonstrated during his high school years, when he earned letters in football, baseball, basketball, and track. During his junior year, he accepted a token sum to catch for the Philadelphia Bacharach Giants, a Negro Leagues team and later caught a double-header game for the Baltimore Elite Giants, also a Negro Leagues team. Protests from the coach of a rival high school baseball team led to his being disqualified from high school baseball. Campanella left school and returned to the Elites, where he remained from 1937 to 1945. While with them, his power hitting skills helped the Elites win a Negro League championship in 1939. It is said that Campanella was offered a contract with the Brooklyn Dodgers in 1945 before one was offered to Jackie Robinson, but turned it down because he thought the offer was to play on a Brooklyn all-black team. He did later sign with the Dodgers and entered a new phase in his career with their Nashua (New Hampshire) team. After a 1947 season with the Dodgers' team in Montreal, Campanella entered training camp with the Brooklyn Dodgers in 1948. Rather than beginning the season with them, he was called up in June from the minor league team in St. Paul (Minnesota) when the Dodgers floundered somewhat early in the season. In 1949 the Dodgers won the National League pennant. Their success that year and in several subsequent years is attributed to Campanella's skill as a catcher, fielder behind the plate, and hitter. Although confined to a wheelchair after his accident, he continued an active life. He managed the liquor store he owned and hosted a radio show on CBS until that network bought the Yankees and cancelled "Campy's Corner." He also did sports commentary and coached young catchers during spring training for almost twenty years. The transplanted Los Angeles Dodgers held a benefit game in his honor in 1959, and in 1975 he was elected to the Black Athletes Hall of Fame. Campanella was residing in Woodland Hills, California, at the time of his death from an apparent heart attack.

Sources: *Jet* 84 (12 July 1993): 14–17; 91 (25 November 1996): 22; *Negro Almanac,* p. 1428; *Total Baseball,* pp. 318–19, 1005; Young, *Negro Firsts in Sports,* pp. 213–14; Smith, *Notable Black American Men,* pp. 166–68.

1953 • "Gene" [Eugene Walter] Baker (1925–1999) became the first black to play with the Chicago Cubs. His first team affiliation was with the Kansas City Monarchs, a Negro League team, in 1948, after his return from service in the U. S. Navy. His solid high–200 batting averages attracted the attention of the Cubs. During his years with Cubs farm teams, Baker became a stellar shortstop. The Cubs moved him to second base in 1954, where he and Ernie Banks were noted as super double-play artists. After playing for the Pittsburgh Pirates from 1957 to 1961, he moved to the management echelon when he was named manager of Pittsburgh's Batavia (New York) farm club.

Sources: *Sepia* 12 (August 1963): 63–67.

1953 • Second baseman Toni Stone [Marcenia Lyle] (1921–1996) joined the Negro League's Indianapolis Clowns as the first woman to play as a regular on a big-league professional baseball team. Her refusal to be limited by her gender was exhibited early. Born in St. Paul, Minnesota, she described herself as a "tomboy" and showed very early a wish

The First World Series Winning Black Pitcher

In 1952 a member of the Brooklyn Dodgers and the 1952 Rookie of the Year, Joe Black (1924–2002), became the first black pitcher to win a World Series game. The Dodgers beat the New York Yankees on October 1 by a score of 4 to 2. Black later became a vice president of Greyhound Corporation. In 1995 he was inducted into the Brooklyn Dodgers Hall of Fame at the Brooklyn Museum.

Sources: Alford, *Famous First Blacks*, p. 85; *Jet* 88 (17 July 1995): 20; *Negro Almanac*, pp. 1400–1401; *Total Baseball*, pp. 162, 508, 1600.

to play baseball. She began playing in a children's Wheaties league when she was ten years old. By age fifteen Stone had progressed to playing with the St. Paul Giants, a semi-professional club. When she moved to Oakland, California, after her high school graduation, she got a job as a centerfielder with an American Legion team, after which she moved to a black barnstorming team, the San Francisco Sea Lions. Stone made more moves before and after signing with the Clowns. Her last team was the Kansas City Monarchs, with whom she played in 1954. She retired from baseball after that season. It has been suggested that Stone's hiring by the Clowns was a ploy to draw attention back to the Negro Leagues, which was suffering from a player drain to major league baseball's integration efforts. Her play, however, was serious, allowing her to maintain a respectable batting average and play the difficult second-base position. It is unclear when Marcenia Lyle became Toni Stone, but she is said to have chosen the name "Toni" because it sounded like the "tomboy" nickname she had as a child. By whatever name, she eventually came to be recognized for her contributions to baseball. She was inducted into the International Women's Sports Hall of Fame in 1985, the Baseball Hall of Fame in 1991, and both the Women's Sports Hall of Fame and the Sudafed International Women's Sports Hall of Fame in 1993. Stone is said to have stated that her most memorable moment in baseball was a hit off of Satchel Paige on Easter Sunday 1953—the only hit that he gave up in that game. She was in a nursing home in Alameda, California, at the time of her death, after having been an Oakland resident for many years.

Sources: *Contemporary Black Biography*, vol. 15, pp. 199–201; *New York Times* (7 November 1996); *Tennessean* (7 November 1996).

1954 • Thomas Alston became the first black player for the St. Louis Cardinals. He signed on as a first baseman until 1957 and had a batting average of .244, four home runs, and 36 RBIs in 91 games.

Sources: *Jet* 85 (24 January 1994): 50.

1955 • Elston Gene "Ellie" Howard (1929–1980) became the first black player for the New York Yankees. First an outfielder and later a catcher, he became the Yankee's first black coach—and the first in the American League—in 1969. He held this position until 1979. In the 1958 World Series he became the first black to win the Babe Ruth Award, and on November 7, 1963 he was named Most Valuable Player in the American League, the first black so honored. Howard, who was born in St. Louis, Missouri, started his career in baseball playing with the Negro League's Kansas City Monarchs. When he became the starting catcher for the Yankees, his immediate predecessor was the legendary Yogi Berra. He stayed with the Yankees for thirteen years and appeared in ten World Series while there. He spent a season with the Boston Red Sox (who won a pennant that year) after being traded to them in 1967, but soon returned to new, non-player positions with the Yankees. He was a resident of New York when he died.

Sources: Ashe, *A Hard Road to Glory*, vol. 2, p. 17; *Jet* 98 (November 13, 2000): 19; Jones and Washington, *Black Champions Challenge American Sports*, pp. 107, 149; *The Black New Yorkers*, pp. 280, 298; *Total Baseball*, pp. 1193, 2155.

The American League's First Black Batting Champion

The first black batting champion in the American League was Tony [Pedro] Oliva [Lopez] of the Minnesota Twins in 1954.

Sources: Alford, *Famous First Blacks,* p. 80; Jones and Washington, *Black Champions Challenge American Sports,* p. 148; *Total Baseball,* p. 1356.

1955 • The first black to pitch a no-hitter, and the first pitcher to have a no-hit game in forty years, was Samuel "Toothpick Sam" Jones (1925–1971), a player in the game held in Chicago between the Chicago Cubs and the Pittsburgh Pirates on May 12.

Sources: Clark, *Sports Firsts,* p. 28; *Ebony* 14 (October 1959), p. 46; *Total Baseball,* pp. 495, 1769.

1959 • The first National League player to win the Most Valuable Player award two years in succession was Ernie [Ernest] Banks (1931–), of the Chicago Cubs. Also known as "Mr. Cub," he and second baseman Gene Baker formed the first black double-play combination in the major leagues. A "disaster on base," Banks produced four consecutive years of more than forty home runs between 1957 and 1960. The Jackson, Mississippi, native played in the Negro American League between 1950 and 1953. He was on the roster of the Negro Leagues' Kansas City Monarchs when signed by the Cubs as an infielder. He remained with the Cubs until 1971. During his playing days, Banks was named the National League's Most Valuable Player in 1958 and 1959, was named to all-star teams thirteen times, and set the National League record for the most grand slam homers. Banks became a member of the National Baseball Hall of Fame in 1977. He is a noted motivational speaker and the author of *Mr. Cub.*

Sources: Ashe, *A Hard Road to Glory,* vol. 2, pp. 19, 20, 25, 42, 271; *Encyclopedia of Black America,* p. 12; Jones and Washington, *Black Champions Challenge American Sports,* pp. 106–7, 149; *Total Baseball,* pp. 309–10, 946–47; *Who's Who among African Americans,* 26th ed., p. 63.

1959 • Pumpsie [Elijah Jerry] Green (1933–), of Oakland, California, infielder, was the first black player on the Boston Red Sox, the last major league team to sign a black player.

Sources: Ashe, *A Hard Road to Glory,* vol. 2, pp. 21, 32; *Total Baseball,* p. 1144; Young, *Negro Firsts in Sports,* p. 215.

1961 • Gene [Eugene Walter] Baker (1925–1999) was the first black to manage a club at any level in the major leagues. The Pittsburgh Pirates gave him the position at their Batavia, New York, Class D franchise. In 1963 the Davenport, Iowa, native was serving as coach of another minor league team when he became the second black coach in the history of major league baseball. (The first, Buck O'Neal, became a coach for the Cubs one year earlier).

Sources: Ashe, *A Hard Road to Glory,* vol. 3, pp. 19, 32; *Sepia* 12 (August 1953), pp. 63–67; *Total Baseball,* pp. 561, 944; Young, *Negro Firsts in Sports,* pp. 208, 217.

1962 • The Chicago Cubs signed John Jordan "Buck" O'Neil (1911–2006) as coach, making him the first black coach on a major league baseball team. He served until 1988. A notable first baseman in black baseball, he had served for several years as a scout. O'Neil was born in Carrabelle, Florida, and began his semi-professional career with the Sarasota Tigers when he was only twelve years old. Edward Waters College awarded him baseball and football scholarships. He attended the Florida school for two years and then joined the old Negro Leagues. He played on various teams from 1934 to 1938, including the New York Tigers, the Miami Giants, and the Shreveport Acme Giants. From 1948 to 1955 he managed the Kansas City Monarchs. During this time, racial segregation prevented him from playing in Major League Baseball; however, he became a scout for the Chicago Cubs until 1988 and then returned to Kansas City and became a scout for the Kansas City Royals. He chronicled his life in the Negro Leagues in his book *I Was Right on Time*.

Sources: Ashe, *A Hard Road to Glory,* vol. 1, p. 32; Bennett, *Before the Mayflower,* p. 637; *Contemporary Black Biography,* vol. 19, pp. 165–67, vol. 59, pp. 130–33; Young, *Negro Firsts in Sports,* pp. 208–9.

1966 • The appointment of Emmett Ashford (1914–1980) as an American League umpire made him the first black umpire in the major leagues. This completed the cycle begun by his earlier "first," which occurred in 1951 when he became the first black professional umpire in the minor leagues. Ashford went on to umpire both an all-star game (1967) and a World Series (1970) before the American League's mandatory age retirement policy caught up with him at age fifty-five. A native of Los Angeles, California, he was raised by his mother after his father left when he was only a year old. Ashford credits her with inspiring him to pursue his dreams. He worked after school but still managed to be the first black student body president at his high school, edit the school newspaper, belong to the Scholarship Society, and join the track team. Baseball entered his life path when he made the baseball team at Chapman College. Ironically, he owes his career as an umpire to the fact that he was not a very good baseball player. While playing for a semiprofessional team after graduating from college, a substitute umpire was needed for a game. Ashford drew the assignment since it was unlikely that Ashford would be on the field as a player. He did so well and was so well received by the fans that he was named umpire. He continued to umpire while working at the U.S. Post Office, and after returning from service in the U.S. Navy (1944–46); he progressed from umpiring high school and college games to a tryout with the Southwest International League. Despite the refusal of the other members of the umpiring crew to work with him, he worked for the league for a year. The league collapsed, but he was able to land other umpiring jobs. He was working in the Pacific Coast League when the call came from the American League. He worked his first game in Washington, where the Senators were to play the Cleveland Indians. Vice President Hubert Humphrey was on hand to throw out the first ball. As might have been expected, Ashford and his wife had difficulty getting into the stadium because the security people did not believe he was an umpire. After his retirement, he maintained involvement with baseball by umpiring in Alaska and later by serving as the West Coast representative of Baseball Commissioner Bowie Kuhn. He served in this capacity until incapacitated by illness. In 1982 the Emmett Ashford Memorial Baseball Field was dedicated in Los Angeles.

Sources: Ashe, *A Hard Road to Glory,* vol. 3, p. 32; *Contemporary Black* Biography, vol. 22, pp. 20–22; *Jet* 89 (15 April 1996): 19; 91 (14 April 1997): 19; Young, *Negro Firsts in Sports,* p. 209.

1966 • Frank Robinson (1935–), playing for the National League Cincinnati Reds in 1961 and for the American League Baltimore Orioles in 1966, was the first black named the Most Valuable Player in both leagues. In 1966 he was also was the first black to win the triple crown—the most home runs, most runs batted in, and the highest batting average. Robinson was born in Beaumont, Texas, one of ten children in a family that the father deserted when Robinson was in his infancy. He grew up in Oakland, California, after his mother moved the family there, and it was there that he decided to become a professional baseball player. The Cincinnati Reds organization signed him right after he finished high school. Robinson realized his dream when he became a member of the Reds team in 1956, beginning a playing career that lasted until 1977 and went through Baltimore (Orioles), California (Dodgers and Angels), and Ohio (Cleveland Indians). During his career, he starred as an outfielder and at first base.

Frank Robinson

Sources: Clark, *Sports Firsts,* p. 32; *Encyclopedia of Black America,* p. 128; Jones and Washington, *Black Champions Challenge American Sports,* pp. 107, 137, 148, 149, 151; *Total Baseball,* p. 383, 1411, 2146; Smith, *Notable Black American Men,* pp. 1020–22.

1972 • The first person of any race to hit thirty or more home runs in fourteen seasons was outfielder Hank [Henry Louis] Aaron (1934–). "Hammering Hank" hit forty more in

The Baseball Hall of Fame's First Special-Election

Inductee Roberto Clemente [Walker] (1934–1972), born in Puerto Rico of black and Hispanic heritage, was the first black (and first of any race) to enter the Hall of Fame in a special election (before the five-year waiting period was met) in 1973. He was the first Hispanic to enter the Hall of Fame and the second baseball player to be featured on a stamp, on August 17, 1984. He died in 1972 in a airplane crash.

Sources: *Current Biography 1973*, p. 452; *I Have A Dream*, pp. 50–51; *Negro Almanac 1976*, pp. 696–97; *Total Baseball*, pp. 324, 1025–26.

Hank Aaron

1973. Aaron, who was born in Mobile, Alabama, truly earned his reputation as a slugger. Aaron played sandlot baseball as a child, and is credited with teaching himself the game. There was no baseball team at his high school, but he was able to play in some local and semiprofessional games. The Indiana Clowns, a Negro Leagues team, offered him a contract in 1952, and Aaron was on his way. He was with the Clowns for only a short time when he left to join the Milwaukee Braves organization. After playing with farm clubs in Wisconsin and in Jacksonville, Florida, he joined the Braves in 1954. During his time in Florida, Aaron endured tremendous racial abuse, but excelled on the field nevertheless, being named South Atlantic League Most Valuable Player in 1953. While playing with the Milwaukee Braves (who later became the Atlanta Braves), Aaron became a star, recognized as a huge home run threat and base stealer.

Sources: Alford, *Famous First Blacks*, p. 80; Ashe, *A Hard Road to Glory*, vol. 3, pp. 18–19, 268; *Total Baseball*, pp. 306, 924; Smith, *Notable Black American Men*, pp. 1–3; *Contemporary Black Biography*, vol. 5, pp. 1–4.

1972 • Ferguson [Arthur] Jenkins (1943–), a Canadian, of the Chicago Cubs, was the first pitcher to win twenty games in six consecutive years.

Sources: Alford, *Famous First Blacks*, p. 85; Ashe, *A Hard Road to Glory*, vol. 3, pp. 6, 29; *Total Baseball*, pp. 353, 1763.

1972 • Art Williams (1934–1979) was the first black umpire in the National League. He was a minor league pitcher in the mid 1950s and was the first black player with the Detroit Tigers. He learned the umpiring trade by attending and graduating from baseball's Umpire Development School. After serving as a minor league umpire for four seasons, he made his major league debut in San Diego. He was later fired from the position. His lawsuit with the Equal Employment Opportunity Commission was pending when he died in 1979.

Sources: *Jet* 43 (5 October 1972): 48; 55 (1 March 1979): 48; 100 (24 September 2001): 19.

1974 • Playing for the Atlanta Braves, on April 8, 1974, Hank [Henry Louis] Aaron (1934–) "Hammering Hank" hit his 715th home run in a game with the Los Angeles Dodgers to beat Babe Ruth's major league record. He led the National League in runs batted in four times. He retired in 1976 with 755 regular-season home runs to his credit, and became vice president of player personnel for the Braves. He was named senior vice president in 1989. In 1982 Aaron was elected to the Baseball Hall of Fame. In 1991 he published his autobiography, *I Had a Hammer*, which was on the *New York Times* best-seller list for ten weeks. Aaron's chase for the home run record was one of the most dramatic stories in sports history, made all the more so because Aaron did not revel in his stardom. Many, but not all, cheered as he inched toward dethroning the legendary Ruth; others sent death threats. He set many records, most of which he still holds. Aaron was a National League all-star twenty-three times between 1952 and 1976. His childhood home in Mobile was relocated next to the Hank Aaron Stadium, where the Mobile's minor league, the Mobile BayBears, play. It became a museum.

Sources: *Contemporary Black Biography,* vol. 5, pp. 1–5; *Jet* 87 (10 April 1995): 20; 95 (12 April 1999): 20; 99 (16 April 2000): 20.

1975 • Frank Robinson became the first black manager of a major league baseball team when the Cleveland Indians hired him on October 3, 1975. He was manager of the Rochester Red Wings in 1978, and from 1978 to 1980 he coached the Baltimore Orioles. He was manager of the San Francisco Giants from 1981 to 1984, coached the Orioles again from 1985 to 1987, and later managed the Orioles from 1988 to 1991. He was assistant to the general manager from 1991 to 1997. Robinson moved to another level when he left the Orioles, becoming director of operations for the Arizona Fall League in 1997. Three years later, in 2000, he was appointed to the newly created position of vice president for baseball's on-field operations. The new position centralized former separate American and National League offices. In 2002, he became manager of the Montreal Expos. Robinson was inducted into the Baseball Hall of Fame in 1982.

Sources: Smith, *Notable Black American Men,* pp. 1020–22; *Contemporary Black Biography.* vol. 9, pp. 201–04; *Jet* 92 (2 June 1997): 20; 97 (13 March 2000): 51.

1979 • Outfielder Dave [David Gene] Parker (1951–) was the first person of any race to become a million-dollar-a-year player when he signed a five-year, five-million-dollar contract with the Pittsburgh Pirates. A drug addiction problem led to poor performance, and he won the reputation of the most unpopular player ever to wear the Pittsburgh uniform. In 1984 Parker signed with Cincinnati as a free agent, having overcome his drug problem.

Sources: Ashe, *A Hard Road to Glory,* vol. 3, pp. 39–40, 41; *Jet* 70 (12 May 1968): 46; *Total Baseball,* pp. 377, 1367.

1980 • Sharon Richardson Jones was named director of outreach activities for the Oakland Athletics, becoming the first black woman in major league baseball administration.

Sources: *Jet* 81 (2 March 1992): 20.

1988 • Robert Jose "Bob" Watson (1946–) became baseball's first black assistant general manager and the first black general manager. He was assistant general manager with the Houston Astros from 1988 to 1993, and later became general manager in 1993. He served in that position for two years. Before ascending to the management level, Watson had paid his dues as a player. A native of Los Angeles, California, he enrolled in Los Angeles Harbor College, but left school when the Astros offered him a place with them in 1965. Signed as a catcher, he later played in the outfield and at first base. He worked his way through the southern minor league teams, living through the problems of segregation. When he was sent down to the minor league team in Savannah in 1969, no hotel would give him a room. He booked a flight to Los Angeles, fully intending to quit baseball. By chance, the plane had a stop in Houston. The Astros' manager met the plane and convinced Watson to stay on. He stayed with the Astros for ten years and established his reputation as a strong hitter. In two of those years he batted in more than one hundred runs. The Astros traded him to the Boston Red Sox in 1979. His hitting prowess made him a prime candidate for the role of the designated hitter, and this was his stock in trade while with the Red Sox and later the New York Yankees. He was with the Yankees in 1981 when they played the Los Angeles Dodgers in the World Series; Watson hit a three-run homer in the first game, and the Yankees won the game. He spent a year with the Atlanta Braves, and retired from player status at the end of that season, in 1984, with a near-.300 lifetime batting average. He took his first step toward management when he became a hitting coach for the Oakland Athletics. He was serving in this position when he accepted the offer from the Astros.

Sources: *Contemporary Black Biography,* vol. 25, pp. 175–77; *Jet* 93 (23 February 1998): 46; Salzman, *Encyclopedia of African-American Culture and History,* Supplement, p. 272; *Who's Who among African Americans,* 26th ed., p. 1299.

1989 • Eric Gregg was the first black umpire to officiate in a World Series game. He appeared in the contest between the Oakland Athletics and the San Francisco Giants but was unable to work behind the plate since the series ended before his turn. In 1993 Charlie Williams became the second black umpire to officiate in a World Series game. In his thirteen years as a National League umpire, Williams was the first black to call balls and strikes in a World Series game.

Sources: *Jet* 84 (8 November 1993): 57.

1989 • Bill [William De Kova] White (1934–), a Lakewood, Florida, native, became the first black president of a baseball league, the National League, on April 1. He entered professional baseball in 1956 when he joined the New York Giants. His credentials as a player are well established. During the course of his thirteen-year career, he played with the St. Louis Cardinals after the Giants, moved to the Philadelphia Phillies for a year, and later moved back to the Cardinals for his last year as a player. He won a Gold Glove for his play at first base seven times and was named to the National League all-star team six times. White became a radio and television announcer after his retirement in 1969 and served as a play-by-play television commentator for the Yankees for eighteen seasons, from 1971 until he was named president of the National League. White attended Hiram College for a year before he began his baseball journey. He was a frequent vocal critic of the conditions black baseball players faced during his early playing days. His appointment as National League president made him the top-ranked executive in any of the U.S. professional sports and one of the very few blacks in sports management positions.

Sources: *Contemporary Black Biography,* vol. 1, pp. 243–45; *Total Baseball,* p. 1540; *Who's Who among African Americans,* 26th ed., p. 1316.

Ken Griffey Jr.

1990 • Ken [George Kenneth] Griffey Sr. (1950–) and Ken [George Kenneth] Griffey Jr. (1969–) played for the Seattle Mariners this season, the first time that father and son had played together while serving the same team. Griffey Sr. was born in Donora, Pennsylvania. He was a professional baseball player from 1973 to 1992. He starred as an outfielder for the Cincinnati Reds, New York Yankees, and Seattle Mariners. He played in both the infield and the outfield for the Atlanta Braves and a second outing with the Reds. His last playing season was with the Mariners, but he remained with the Mariner organization. He became a special assistant for player development and a hitting coach for them once he left the playing field. Griffey made several appearances as an all-star and was also named Most Valuable Player in his league and as an all-star during the course of his career. Griffey Jr. was born in the same town as his father but did most of his growing up in the various cities that were home to the teams with which his father played. He graduated from high school in Cincinnati in 1987 and was drafted by the Seattle Mariners that same year. He became a starting outfielder for the Mariners in 1989. He has amply illustrated the "like father, like son" proverb. Griffey Jr. was named to consecutive all-star teams from 1990 to 1999, and was the game's Most Valuable Player in 1992 and 1997. He won ten consecutive Gold Glove awards and seven Silver Slugger awards. He was the Most Valuable Player in the American League in 1997 and the youngest player to be named to Major League Baseball's All Century Team, which was unveiled in 1999. He has also won community service awards and is the author of *Junior: Griffey on Griffey,* published in 1997. The Griffey father-son playing duo was a noted event in baseball history. Griffey Jr. was traded to the Cincinnati Reds in 2000.

Sources: *Contemporary Black Biography,* vol. 12, pp. 68–71; Salzman, *Encyclopedia of African-American Culture and History,* Supplement, pp. 118–119; *Who's Who among African Americans,* 26th ed., p, 500.

1991 • Major League Baseball joined in a reunion of Negro Leagues players for the first time, in a special tribute honoring living legends from the leagues. The Baseball Hall of Fame in Cooperstown, New York, sponsored the event for seventy-five former players.

Sources: *Jet* 94 (17 August 1998): 19.

1991 • Rickey Henderson (1958–) was the first black to steal 939 bases in a career, surpassing Lou Brock. He already shared the record for the most in one season, 130. The first person of any race to steal 130 bases in one season under the present-day way of counting was Maury [Maurice Morning] Wills (1932–), a Los Angeles Dodgers shortstop, who

Baseball's First Black Woman Executive

The first black woman assistant general manager of the Red Sox was Elaine C. Weddington (1963–), on January 26, 1990. She also became the first black woman executive of professional baseball organization. From 1988 to 1990 she was associate counsel for the team, having moved from the post as intern in the Commissioner of Baseball's office. Born in Flushing, New York, she graduated from St. Vincent College of St. John (B.S. 1984) and from St. John's University School of Law (J.D., 1987). In April 1988 she was admitted to the New York State Bar. Weddington became vice president, assistant general manager, and legal counsel for the team.

Sources: *Jet* 77 (26 February 1990): 52; 101 (28 January 2002): 22; *Who's Who among African Americans,* 14th ed., p. 1365.

broke Ty Cobb's 1915 record of ninety-six stolen bases in a single season in 1962. His son Bump Wills was also a proficient base stealer during his six-year career (1977–82). Lou [Louis Clark] Brock (1939–) topped Wills' record in 1974 with 118 and ended his career in 1976 with what was then the all-time record of 938.

Sources: Ashe, *A Hard Road to Glory,* vol. 2, pp. 21, 26–27, 43; vol. 3, pp. 27–28, 43–44, 269; *Current Biography 1975,* pp. 43–44 (Brock); *Encyclopedia of Black America,* p. 129; *Jet* 80 (20 May 1991): 46–47; Jones and Washington, *Black Champions Challenge American Sports,* pp. 149–50, 151; *Total Baseball,* pp. 31, 316, 404, 1547.

1992 • Cito [Clarence Edward] Gaston became the first black manager to lead a major league baseball team to win a World Series title, when the Toronto Blue Jays defeated the Atlanta Braves on October 25. Born in San Antonio, Texas, Gaston began his professional baseball-playing career with the Atlanta Braves in 1967. He played with the San Diego Padres between 1969 and 1974, was in Atlanta again between 1976 and 1978, and briefly in Pittsburgh with the Pirates in 1978. The outfielder and pinch hitter was made a hitting instructor with Atlanta in 1981. Gaston was a member of the National League all-star team in 1970.

Sources: *Jet* 97 (1 November 1999): 19; 100 (29 October 2001): 24; *Who's Who among African Americans,* 13th ed., p. 473.

1993 • Anthony Young of the New York Mets was the first pitcher of any race to lose twenty-seven consecutive decisions, the longest losing streak in major league baseball. The Mets beat the Marlins 5–4 at Shea Stadium on Wednesday, July 28. Young's previous win was April 19, 1992, at Montreal, a span of seventy-four appearances.

Sources: *Tennessean* (29 July 1993).

1993 • Charlie Williams (1944?–) became the first black umpire to call balls and strikes in a World Series game. Although veteran black umpire Eric Gregg had worked an earlier World Series game, he did not work behind the plate because the Series ended before his scheduled turn for plate duty. Williams had a real indoctrination in his first Series game. It lasted over four hours, and twenty-nine runs were scored. No umpire controversies occurred.

Sources: *Jet* 84 (8 November 1993): 57.

1994 • Frank Edward "Big Hurt" Thomas Jr. (1968–) became the only player in recent history to win back-to-back Most Valuable Player citations, in 1993 and 1994. Playing with the Chicago White Sox, he was a leader in several offensive and defensive categories in those years and a member of the All-Star team from 1993 through 1997. A native of Columbus, Georgia, Thomas decided early that he wanted to play professional baseball. At age nine he played tight end in the Pop Warner (football) League, even though the usual age for League players was twelve years old. He also played Little League baseball. His athletic talent won him a scholarship to a private college preparatory institution in Columbus, where he stayed for three years. Thomas returned to public school when he was a sophomore, responding to his yearning for stiffer athletic competition. He excelled in baseball, basketball, and football. Disappointed when he failed to be drafted in 1986, Thomas instead accepted a scholarship to Auburn University (Alabama). As an Auburn freshman he hit .359 and led the team in runs batted in. An injury during his sophomore year forced him to stop playing football. This left baseball as his only sport. He won a Most Valuable Player award in baseball in the Southeastern Conference (SEC) and was an All-SEC Tournament selection. The White Sox drafted him in 1989, and he made his professional baseball debut with the Sarasota, Florida, White Sox farm club. He was with the Birmingham Barons in 1990 when *Baseball America* named him Minor League Player of the Year. He joined the White Sox in August of that year, and the next year he was the regular first baseman for the Chicago White Sox, where his batting average was over .300 and he batted in more than one hundred runs; he also led the major leagues in walks. He led the American League again in several categories in 1992. He was by then considered a superstar. Thomas was on the way to a possible Triple Crown (first in batting average, home runs, and runs batted in) when a strike cut the 1994 season short. He won the American League batting championship in 1997. Off the field, Thomas works actively with many charities, including the Leukemia Foundation, which has a special significance for him because his two-year-old sister died of leukemia in 1977.

Sources: *Contemporary Black Biography,* vol. 12, pp. 211–14; *Who's Who among African Americans,* 26th ed., p. 1218.

1994 • James Thomas "Cool Papa" Bell (1903–1991) became the first baseball star from the Negro Major Leagues to have a street in Mississippi named in his honor. At age ninety-one, the former star, who boasted a .583 batting average when he played with the Negro League Homestead Grays, was present in Jackson, Mississippi, for the occasion. Bell, a Mississippi native, was an outfielder who was known for his speed as well as his hitting. Speed was his weapon when catching and throwing from the outfield and in running bases. He was the first Mississippi native to be elected to the Baseball Hall of Fame.

Sources: Riley, *Biographical Directory of the Negro Baseball Leagues,* pp. 72–74; *Jet* 86 (25 July 1994): 25.

1996 • Robert Jose "Bob" Watson (1946–), who managed the New York Yankees from 1995 to 1997, led that team to the World Series championship in 1996 and became the first black to achieve this victory for the Yankees. This was the Yankees' first series appearance in sixteen years. Watson resigned as Yankee general manager in February 1998. He moved to the world of financial management, joining a firm owned by his son.

Sources: *Contemporary Black Biography,* vol. 25, pp. 175–77; Salzman, *Encyclopedia of African-American Culture and History,* Supplement, p. 272; *Who's Who among African Americans,* 14th ed., p. 1358.

1997 • The first permanent black manager with the Chicago White Sox was Jerry Manuel. Baseball star Larry Doby had at one time served as White Sox manager, but Doby was appointed as an interim manager and held the position for only eighty-seven games. Manuel was one of fourteen candidates considered for the job. He had served previously as bench coach for the Florida Marlins.

Sources: *Jet* 93 (22 December 1997): 53; *Who's Who among African Americans,* 26th ed., p. 809.

1998 • *Sporting News* placed the names of twenty-five blacks on its list of 100 greatest baseball players of the twentieth century.

Sources: *Jet* 94 (16 November 1998): 48.

1999 • Don Edward Baylor (1949–) became the first black manager of the Chicago Cubs. With Baylor's appointment, both Chicago teams (Cubs and White Sox) had black managers. Baylor was serving as hitting coach for the Atlanta Braves when tapped for the Chicago position, after having managed the Colorado Rockies for six years. The Cubs fired him during the 2002 season. Baylor was born in Austin, Texas, and began his nineteen-year career as a baseball player with the Baltimore Orioles. He played for six different teams—all in the American League—between 1970 and 1988. From 1990 through 1992 he was a hitting coach: first for the Milwaukee Brewers and later for the St. Louis Cardinals. He moved to the Colorado Rockies as manager in 1993 and to Atlanta as a hitting coach in 1998. Baylor received many awards as a player, starting when he was in the minor league. He was voted Minor League Player of the Year in 1970. In 1979 he was both the American League Most Valuable Player and the *Sporting News* Player of the Year. Baylor also holds two less enviable records: the American League career record for being hit by a pitch (267 times) and the American League record for being hit by a pitch the most times in a single season (35). A three-time member of the American League Silver Slugger Team, Baylor played in seven league championship series and played in the World Series for each of his last three seasons.

Sources: *Who's Who among African Americans*, 26th ed., pp. 78–79; *Jet* 96 (15 November 1999): 59.

2000 • The first black general manager for the Chicago White Sox is Ken [Kenneth Ray] Williams (1969–). Currently, he is the only black general manager in baseball and one of the youngest of any race. The White Sox are the first team to have both a black general manager and a black manager. Williams's career involvement with baseball began when the White Sox drafted him out of Stanford University in 1982. He retired from baseball as a player in 1992, having played with three other major league teams in Detroit, Montreal, and Toronto. He moved to baseball administration once he left the playing field, serving first as the White Sox Director for Minor League Operations. Williams then became the Sox's vice president for player development and had held that position for five years when named to the managerial post. He is the third black general manager in the history of the major leagues, having been preceded in the position by Bill Lucas (Atlanta Braves, 1976) and Bob Watson (Houston Astros, 1993; and New York Yankees, 1995).

Sources: *Who's Who among African Americans,* 26th ed., p. 1346; *Jet* 98 (13 November 2000): 59.

2001 • The San Diego Padres' leftfielder Rickey Henderson (1958–) broke Babe Ruth's major league all-time walks record on April 25, with 2,063 walks. Later he pushed that total to 2,141. On October 3 he drove in run number 2,246, passing the seventy-three-year record of 2,245 runs that Ty Cobb had set decades earlier. But he was not through for the season. He got his 3,000th hit on the last day of the season, making him the twenty-fifth member of the 3,000-hit club. These records, when added to his record as the king of stolen bases and the big-league record for leadoff homers (79), suggest that the name "Henderson" should be synonymous with the word "record." Henderson was born in Chicago, Illinois, but graduated from high school in Oakland, California. He had an outstanding high school record in baseball, basketball, and football; and made the All-Oakland Athletic League in baseball three times. The Oakland Athletics drafted him in 1976. After moving through the farm club system, he became a member of the team in 1979 and began his march toward the record book. Traded to the New York Yankees in 1985, Henderson began to improve his hitting, but injuries plagued him between 1986 and 1990 and continued to affect his play somewhat throughout the 1990s. He was on the move several times from 1989 on. He went back to Oakland in 1989, to Toronto in 1993, back to Oakland again in 1994, to San Diego in 1996, to Anaheim (for twelve games) in 1997, once more to Oakland in 1998, to the New York Mets in 1999, to the Seattle Mariners in 2000, and finally to the Padres for his phenomenal 2001 season. Henderson was named Most Valuable Player in the American League Championship Series in 1990, has been an all-star eight times, and was named to the Oakland Athletics All-Century Team.

Rickey Henderson

Sources: *Contemporary Black Biography,* vol. 28, pp. 89–92; *Jet* 99 (14 May 2001): 46; *New York Times* (4 October 2001); Baseball-Reference.com, Ricky Henderson, http://www.baseball-reference.com/players/h/henderi01.shtml, accessed September 30, 2012.

Barry Bonds

2001 • San Francisco Giants outfielder Barry Lamar Bonds (1964–) made home run history when he hit number 71 on October 4. Before the season ended, he had hit 73 home runs. He also hit his 400th career home run and became the only major league player to reach that level and to steal 400 bases in his career. The 2001 season was a watershed year for Bonds. When he hit home run number 71, he broke the single-season home run record that had been set by Mark McGwire in 1998. It was the first time in his career that he had hit more than 49 home runs in a season. His 400/400 home runs and steals lifted him from the 300/300 club that had only four members: Andre Dawson; his godfather Willie Mays; and his father Bobby, a former major league all-star. He also broke Babe Ruth's record for walks, with 177, and bested Ruth's record slugging percentage, finishing the season with a percentage of .863. Ruth's comparable figures were 170 (in 1923) and .847 (in 1920). And there is more. Bonds became the first player to win the Most Valuable Player award four times, with previous wins in 1990, 1992, and 1993. Prior to this achievement, he was one of only eight players who had won the award three times. He has been an all-star eight times and won consecutive Gold Glove awards for his fielding between 1990 and 1998. Bonds was born in Riverside, California, and gave every indication of having benefited from his heritage as the son of a former baseball player. He attended Arizona State University, and entered major league baseball with the Pittsburgh Pirates in 1986. He was with the Pirates through 1992. He became a San Francisco Giant in 1993. The hero of the 2001 season became a free agent but Bonds decided to remain with the Giants. In 2002, Bonds and the Giants lost to theAnaheim Angels in an exciting seven-game World Series. While playing against the San Diego Padres at Petch Park in August 2007, Bonds tied Hank Aaron's career record of 755 home runs. Later he was found guilty of making false statements to a grand jury when he said that he never knowingly received steroids and growth hormones from his trainer. He was found guilty of one count of obstruction in April 2011.

Sources: *Jet* 94 (7 September 1998): 52; *Tennessean* (6 October 2001); *Who's Who among African Americans,* 26th ed., p. 119.

Basketball

1900 • Julian Ware was the first black player of a varsity sport at a Big Ten college. He played basketball for the University of Wisconsin from 1900 to 1902.

Sources: *New York Times* (23 March 1900).

1908 • The first intercity competition between black clubs was that between the Smart Set Club of Brooklyn, New York, and the Crescent Athletic Club, Washington, D.C. The Brooklyn club won at home and away.

Sources: Young, *Negro Firsts in Sports,* p. 238.

1909 • Lincoln University (Pennsylvania), Hampton Institute (now University), and Wilberforce University fielded the first black college basketball teams in 1909 and 1910. YMCAs and YWCAs formed the first black teams and introduced the game on campuses through their student associations and the schools eventually embraced it.

Sources: Ashe, *A Hard Road to Glory,* vol. 1, pp. 104–5; Bennett, *Before the Mayflower,* p. 633; Young, *Negro Firsts in Sports,* p. 238.

1923 • The Rens, named after the team's home court, the Renaissance Casino in New York, was the first black professional basketball team. Founded and managed by Robert J. Douglas, the team ran up a record of 1,588 wins to 239 losses. They played from 1923 to 1939 and were the first black team in the Basketball Hall of Fame. On March 28, 1939, the Rens became the first black team on record to win a professional world's championship. The first starting five were Hilton Slocum (captain), Frank Forbes, Hy Monte, Zack Anderson, and Harold Mayers. The Rens had a different, more traditional style of play than the more widely known black Harlem Globetrotters, who blended entertainment via novelty exploits with solid basketball. The Rens won their very first game by a score of 28 to 22, an indicator of how much the game has changed in the ensuing years. The team was initially based in Brooklyn (New York), where they played first as the Spartan Braves and later as the Spartan Five. Relocation to Manhattan gave rise to their new name: the New York Renaissance Big Five. They were reputedly the first black professional basketball players to be paid full salaries.

Sources: Chalk, *Pioneers of Black Sport,* pp. 83, 85–86, 88–89, 90–95; *Encyclopedia of Black America,* p. 129; Henderson, *The Black Athlete,* pp. 65–67; *The Black New Yorkers,* pp. 183–184; Young, *Negro Firsts in Sports,* pp. 80, 238.

1931 • George Gregory, captain of his Columbia University (New York) team, was the first black selected for All-American basketball honors. Gregory, who played in an era when basketball lacked the perfectly designed and equipped gymnasiums and field houses that are commonplace in the modern day, went on to become a Commissioner of Civil Service in New York City.

Sources: Menke, *Encyclopedia of Sports,* 5th ed., p. 187.

1947 • The first basketball game between black and white colleges was played this year. Wilberforce University played Bergen College of New Jersey at Madison Square Garden, winning the game 40–12.

Sources: *The Black New Yorkers,* p. 268.

1947 • The first black to play in the NBA was Earl "The Pearl" Lloyd (1928?–) of West Virginia State College, a forward for the Washington Capitols. Although he was recruited later than Charles Cooper and Nat "Sweetwater" Clifton, he became the first to play (by one day) because of a quirk in NBA scheduling. Though Lloyd played ten seasons with Washington, Syracuse, and Detroit, his NBA statistics were modest. Nevertheless, he and Jim Tucker, a teammate, were the first black players to be on a championship NBA team, when the Syracuse Nationals won the title in 1952. Lloyd's last team was the Detroit Pistons. He played with them from 1958 to 1960. When he retired from play, he was named the Pistons' first black assistant coach; he became the NBA's first black nonplaying coach eleven years later, in 1971 with the Pistons, a position from which he was fired in 1973. He was also the first black chief scout in the NBA. Lloyd was raised in Alexandria, Virginia. He attended West Virginia State College, an all-black institution, and is quoted as saying that until the Capitols drafted him he had never even talked to a white person. He considered playing with the Harlem Globetrotters, but went with the Capitols, where he faced racial prejudice from fans along the way. When Lloyd left basketball, he started a new career with the Detroit public schools. He later worked for the auto parts company owned by Dave Bing, one of the black players he had coached on the Pistons. By 2000 Lloyd was retired and living in Tennessee. On the fiftieth anniversary of their entry into the NBA games, the NBA honored Lloyd, Clifton, and Cooper at Madison Square Garden in November 2000.

Earl Lloyd

Sources: *Detroit Free Press* (14 January 1992); *Encyclopedia of Black America,* p. 131; Jones and Washington, *Black Champions Challenge American Sports,* pp. 89, 100; Young, *Negro Firsts in Sports,* p. 239; *Contemporary Black Biography,* vol. 26, pp. 87–89.

1950 • Junius Kellogg (1917?–1988) was the first black scholarship athlete at Manhattan College in New York City. In his sophomore year, he was offered a bribe by the team's co-captain to fix a score by shaving points. Instead, the tall center reported the offer to his coach and touched off what is reputed to be the widest betting scandal in the history of basketball. He followed the report to his coach with a report to the District Attorney, and when those who sought to fix the game approached him a second time, he was wearing a wire. Kellogg was both praised and vilified for his actions. After an interruption for service in the U.S. Army, he graduated from Manhattan in 1953 with his original class. He then joined the Harlem Globetrotters and was riding with the team to an exhibition game when an automobile accident in 1954 left him paralyzed. He spent four years in the hospital, and was able eventually to regain use of his hands and arms, but his ambulatory playing days were over, and he spent the rest of his life in a wheelchair. His basketball involvement, however, was not over. For nine years (1957–1966) he coached the Pan Am Jets, a wheelchair team, lead-

NBA Firsts

In 1950 Chuck [Charles] Cooper (1908–1984) of Duquesne University became the first black drafted by a National Basketball Association team, the Boston Celtics, on April 15. The New York Knickerbockers purchased Nathaniel "Sweetwater" Clifton, of Xavier University, from the Harlem Globetrotters in 1950, making him the second black player signed by the NBA. Called "Tarzan" because of his long arms, Cooper played center and was known for his ability to block shots. He had played previously with the Rens, a New York black professional basketball team. After he retired from the National Basketball Association in 1956, he spent a year playing with another black team, the Harlem Magicians. Cooper re-entered school, earned a master's degree in social work, and moved to Philadelphia. He was an active member of that community until he succumbed to cancer.

Sources: Bennett, *Before the Mayflower*, p. 634; *Detroit Free Press* (14 January 1992); *Encyclopedia of Black America*, p. 130; *Jet* 65 (20 February 1984) :51; 91 (18 November 1996): 48; Lee, *Interesting People*, p. 131; Young, *Negro Firsts in Sports*, p. 239.

ing them to four international championships in wheelchair basketball. When he left the Jets, he worked for the City of New York until his death. He was the first deputy commissioner and director of strategic planning for the Community Development Agency. Kellogg was born in Portsmouth, Virginia, the oldest of eleven children in a family that often had a difficult time making ends meet. In 1997 his alma mater awarded him an honorary degree. He died of respiratory failure in the same Bronx hospital in which he had recuperated from the tragic accident that had changed the course of his life.

Sources: *New York Times* (18 September 1988).

1953 • Tennessee State University in Nashville became the first all-black team to complete in a national NAIA (National Association of Intercollegiate Athletic) basketball tournament. The next year the team won the NAIA preseason tournament, another benchmark for a black college team. Under the leadership of John B. "Coach Mac" McLendon Jr. (1915–1999), the team won three consecutive national championships between 1957 and 1959, a first for the team and its coach. He was credited with introducing the fast break in basketball, an innovation that continues to have one of the most dramatic impacts on the game. McLendon was a founder of the post-season Central Intercollegiate Athletic Association (CIAA) Tournament.

Sources: "Coach Mac," *Sports View* 4 (Winter 1993): 30–32.

1953 • The first black American woman to make the national Amateur Athletic Union (AAU) women's basketball team was Missouri "Big Mo" Arledge of Philander Smith College in Arkansas. In 1955, she also became the first black woman All-American basketball player. The five-foot, ten-inch player averaged twenty-one points a game.

Sources: Hine, *Black Women in America*, vol. II, p. 132; Young, *Negro Firsts in Sports*, p. 241.

1961 • Wilt [Wilton Norman] "Wilt the Stilt" Chamberlain (1936–1999), then with the Philadelphia 76ers, was the first professional player to score more than 3,000 points in one season. During the 1961–62 season he scored 4,029 points and became the first player to score more than 4,000 points in a single season. Chamberlain was also the first black to score 100 points in a single game. He had a fourteen-year career in basketball, dominating the professional game in the 1960s and 1970s and setting records that may never be broken. Chamberlain was born in Philadelphia, Pennsylvania, one of nine children. His first notable achievement as an athlete occurred when he ran the anchor leg for the 300-yard shuttle in the Penn Relays in 1946. In junior high, he developed a serious interest in basketball, possibly because he was by then six feet three inches tall (at age twelve) and was doing well in both basketball and track. By the time he entered high school Chamberlain had added eight

Wilt Chamberlain

The Harlem Globetrotters

Harlem Globetrotters

In 1952 the Harlem Globetrotters Chicago-based team was founded, owned, and coached by Abe Saperstein of Chicago. While based in Chicago, they were the first basketball club to make complete playing trips around the world, first in 1952 and again in winter 1960–61. They were the first professional basketball team to have their own fall training camp in October 1940. The best known and best-loved team in the world, their finest decade was the 1950s. Mannie Jackson, a former Globetrotter, became the first black to own the team in 1993. The team was founded in Hinckley, Illinois, around 1923–24 and played its first game there on January 7, 1927. Since then there have been 500 team members, who have played in 115 countries. In 1999 based in Phoenix, the Globetrotters received the John W. Bunn Award in recognition of their contribution to the game of basketball. They were the first team in the history of the Basketball Hall of Fame to receive the prestigious award.

Sources: Henderson, *The Black Athlete*, pp. 61, 64–65; *Jet* 84 (9 August 1993): 49–51; 96 (8 November 1999): 49; Jones and Washington, *Black Champions Challenge American Sports*, pp. 57–58, 82, 83, 87–89, 110–11; Young, *Negro Firsts in Sports*, pp. 230–38; Nadel, *Tales from the Past*, 1990.

inches, and by the time he was a senior more than 200 colleges and universities were seeking his basketball services. He chose to enter the University of Kansas, where it became his lot to contribute to integration of the area. He was a consistent high scorer on the basketball team and also won two high-jump titles in track and field competitions. Choosing to leave Kansas before he graduated, he played in 1958–59 with the Harlem Globetrotters, and later joined the Philadelphia Warriors. He was named Rookie of the Year and Most Valuable Player at the end of the season. Chamberlain played with the Globetrotters during the following summer, but returned to the Warriors late in 1960 and played with them for six seasons. After playing with the Lakers from 1968 to 1973, he left the National Basketball Association for a position as player-coach and part owner of the San Diego team in the American Basketball Association. The Lakers, however, were successful in getting a court order that prevented Chamberlain from playing. Without him, the ABA team had a dismal record, and Chamberlain retired when the season was over. He was elected to the Basketball Hall of Fame in 1979, was elected to the NBA's 35th Anniversary Team in 1980, and was given the Living Legend Award by Philadelphia sportswriters in 1991. Basketball and track were not his only activities. Chamberlain became a professional volleyball player when he was in his early thirties and went on to found the International Volleyball Association. He had a career in business and in performing, appearing in a 1984 movie with Arnold Schwarzenegger and Grace Jones. He was an all-around athlete and a man of many talents. Chamberlain was a resident of Bel-Air, California, at the time of his death.

Sources: Ashe, *A Hard Road to Glory*, vol. 2, pp. 67, 70–71, 299–300, 303; Chalk, *Pioneers of Black Sports*, pp. 114, 115, 116, 117; *Current Biography 1960*, pp. 85–86; Young, *Negro Firsts in Sports*, pp. 78–79, 239, 265; Smith, *Notable Black American Men*, pp. 184–86; *Jet* 97 (1 November 1999): 51–56; *Who's Who among African Americans*, 13th ed., p. 1508.

1961 • Johnny [John B.] "Coach Mac" McLendon Jr. (1915–1999) was the first black coach of a predominantly white professional team in the modern era. In the 1961–62 season he coached the Cleveland Pipers of the American Basketball League. He resigned from the Pipers in the second half of the 1961–62 season. McLendon's college coaching career included tours of duty at Tennessee State, North Carolina College (now North Carolina

Central), Hampton, Kentucky State, and Cleveland State. As a college coach his record of .825 in twenty years was the second highest winning percentage behind that of Adolph Rupp of Kentucky. When his 1953 Tennessee State team was the first all-black team to play in the national tournament of the National Association of Intercollegiate Athletics (NAIA), this marked the integration of the national small-college championship tournament. They won the preseason tournament the next year and the regular season title for three consecutive years from 1957 through 1959. In 1966 he became the first black man to coach at a predominantly white school, Cleveland State. He was a member of the U.S. Olympic Basketball Committee in 1966 and of the Olympic coaching staff in 1968 and 1972. After retiring, he became an athletic adviser at Cleveland State, where he also taught an advanced class in coaching basketball. Born in Hiawatha, Kansas, McLendon attended college at the University of Kansas, where his physical education instructor, James Naismith, was the man credited with inventing the game of basketball. McLendon could not play basketball at Kansas because of racial prejudice, but he credits Naismith with exposing him to the philosophy of the game. How gratifying it must have been when he was elected to the Naismith Memorial Basketball Hall of Fame in 1978. McLendon was known as an innovative coach, whose creativity in designing strategy on the court had no equal. He is given credit for starting use of the "fast break" and for using what he called the "two in the corner" offense in the first tournament of the Central Intercollegiate Athletic Association, in 1948. This strategy became known as the "four corners" offense when later used by the University of North Carolina's longtime coaching legend, Dean Smith. History reports that McLendon taught the offense to Smith in 1970, while both were attending a convention of the Fellowship of Christian Athletes in Colorado. He shared his coaching genius in his two books: *Fast Break Basketball* and *The Fast Break Game*. McLendon died of cancer in Cleveland Heights, Ohio. His ability as a player may have been disparaged. His ability as a coach, with a record of 523–162 is beyond challenge.

Sources: Ashe, *A Hard Road to Glory,* vol. 2, pp. 55, 56, 285; Bennett, *Before the Mayflower,* p. 636; Young, *Black Firsts in Sports,* pp. 90, 117, 239–40; *Jet* 96 (18 November 1999): 49–50; Obituary, *Who's Who among African Americans,* 14th ed., p. 1473.

1966 • Bill [William Felton] "Mr. Basketball" Russell (1934–), while still a member of the Boston Celtics basketball team, was signed by the Celtics on April 18 to become the first black coach in the National Basketball Association and the first to coach a major, predominantly white professional team. In his second year as coach, he produced a world championship team in 1968, and produced another in 1969. Called the greatest defensive player ever, Russell led the University of San Francisco to six straight wins and two NCAA championships, won a Gold Medal in men's basketball in the 1960 Olympics, and led the Celtics to eight consecutive world titles. As a college player, he played in one losing game, and at the end of 1955 the NCAA widened the foul lane from six to twelve feet because of his dominance at rebounds. Russell was born in Monroe, Louisiana, at a time when racism was the mode of the day. The Russell family moved to Oakland, California, when Bill was still a child. Raised by his father after his mother died when she was thirty-two, Russell was not the family's first basketball star. His older brother Charlie was a star in high school, while Russell had an inauspicious start in junior high. He was able to make his high school varsity team when he was a senior, and this led to a basketball scholarship from the University of San Francisco, where he began to shine on the court as the team's premier center. Sought by many NBA teams, he was signed by the Celtics in 1956. He remained with them until his retirement in 1969. During his years as a player, Russell became a superstar and the Celtics established a dynasty. When he retired, he had won eleven championship rings, been an NBA all-star each year from 1957 to 1969, and been named Most Valuable Player five times. Russell's retirement was brief. He became a commentator for NBA games in the early 70s, served as Seattle Super Sonics coach and general manager from 1973 to 1977, and later returned to broadcasting until he retired again in 1983. He was lured out of retirement yet another time. In 1987 he was the coach of the Sacramento Kings. He moved to an executive position with them the next year, and left the organization in 1989. Russell was inducted into the Basketball Hall of Fame in 1975. He received the Presidential Medal of Freedom in 2011.

Sources: Ashe, *A Hard Road to Glory,* vol. 3, pp. 68–70; Bennett, *Before the Mayflower,* p. 636; *Contemporary Black Biography,* vol. 8, pp. 215–218; *Encyclopedia of Black America,* pp. 130–31, 737; Jones and Washington, *Black Champions Challenge American Sports,* pp. 108–9, 137, 138; Page, *Black Olympian Medalists,* p. 132; Smith, *Notable Black American Men,* pp. 1035–38.

1967 • Clarence Edward "Bighouse" Gaines Sr. (1923–2005) led the Winston-Salem Rams of Winston-Salem State University in North Carolina to national prominence when they became the first black college and the first in the entire South to win the NCAA (National Collegiate Athletic Association) College Division Basketball championship. Gaines never had a losing season and closed his coaching career with eight CIAA Conference victories, more than any other coach. He was celebrated more recently after winning his eight-hundredth basketball game on January 24, 1990. Gaines retired in 1993, having served the college for forty-seven years as head basketball coach, head football coach, chair of the department of physical education, and athletic director. He was forced to retire when he reached age seventy, thus losing his chance to break Adolph Rupp's record. By the time he retired, Gaines was no longer able to attract top basketball players to Winston-Salem (a Division II school), because of competition from the larger Division I schools, and his teams were not doing well. He was given the title of professor emeritus when he retired. The Paducah, Kentucky, native graduated from Morgan State College (B.S., 1945) and Columbia University (M.A., 1950). His first job was at the Winston-Salem institution, as a teacher and assistant coach. The next year Gaines was made head coach. He won the first of his ten CIAA basketball championships in 1953. The team drew sell-out crowds of both black and white fans when future professional star Earl "The Pearl" Monroe played with them in 1967. Gaines' nickname dates from his days at Morgan State. The manager of the football team gave him the nickname "Bighouse" because of his imposing size (six feet four inches tall and around 250 pounds). He has been recognized with many awards for his stellar achievements as a coach.

Sources: Ashe, *A Hard Road to Glory,* vol. 3, pp. 55, 56; *Ebony* 24 (February 1969): 46, 50, 52; *Pittsburgh Courier* (4 March 1978); *Sports View* 4 (Winter 1993): 34–37; *Who's Who among African Americans,* 14th ed., p. 453.

1972 • The first black general manager in any sport was Wayne Embry (1937–), of the Milwaukee Bucks. He played as a center in the NBA for eleven years (eight of them with the Cincinnati Royals, then the Boston Celtics and finally the Milwaukee Bucks) and was a five-time NBA all-star. The Springfield, Ohio, native graduated from Miami University of Ohio.

Sources: Alford, *Famous First Blacks,* p. 87; *Ebony* 30 (January 1975): 97; 28 (February 1973): 74–80; *Sepia* 23 (December 1974): 62.

1972 • Fred "The Fox" Snowden (1937–) became the first black basketball coach at a major white institution, the University of Arizona. He was born in a sharecropper's shack in Brewton, Alabama, and grew up in Detroit. In his first year as coach, he brought the Arizona Wildcats to a winning season.

Sources: *Ebony* 32 (April 1977): 44–50; *Jet* 76 (4 September 1989): 40; *Sepia* 27 (April 1979): 48–54.

1973 • The first black vice president of the NBA was Simon Peter Gourdine (1940–), who served as vice-president for administration. He held this position until 1974, when he became deputy commissioner, serving in this position until 1981. Gourdine did his undergraduate work at City College of New York and received a law degree from Fordham University. He also completed Harvard University's Graduate School of Business Certificate Program for Management Development. He was general counsel for the NBA Players Association (1990–95) and its executive director (1995–96). He was an assistant U.S. attorney for the Southern District of New York from 1967 to 1969, before becoming assistant to the commissioner of the NBA in 1970. Between 1982 and 1990, when he became NBA general counsel, he held positions with New York governmental agencies and with the

Rockefeller Foundation. The Jersey City, New Jersey, native received the Army Commendation Medal in 1967 for his service in Vietnam.

Sources: Alford, *Famous First Blacks,* p. 87; *Who's Who among African Americans,* 14th ed., p. 491.

1975 • The first two players to go directly from high school to the National Basketball Association were Bill Willoughby (1957–) and Darryl "Dunks" Dawkins (1957–). Willoughby, who was a regular starter for the Houston Rockets, obtained his bachelor's degree in communications from Fairleigh Dickinson University in 2001, at age forty-four. He received the Trustees Distinguished Service Award at the same time. Dawkins, an Orlando, Florida, native played for several teams, beginning with the San Antonio Spurs and ending with the Detroit Pistons. He achieved fame and his nickname because of his spectacular dunk shots. Willoughby and Dawkins were not the first professional basketball players to leave high school and go directly into the pros. Moses Malone was the first, when he went to play with the Utah Stars in the American Basketball Association in 1974.

Sources: *Jet* 99 (11 June 2001): 19; *Who's Who among African Americans,* 26th ed., p. 323–24; (Dawkins).

1977 • Louisa Harris became the first black American woman drafted by a National Basketball Association team. She refused the offers from the New Orleans Jazz and the Milwaukee Bucks.

Sources: Hine, *Black Women in America,* vol. II, pp. 1329–30.

1982 • John Chaney (1932–) became the first black basketball coach at Temple University in Philadelphia. Chaney received his bachelor's degree from Bethune Cookman College (later University) and master's degree from Antioch College. His first coaching assignment was at Cheyney State College (Pennsylvania). Temple, where he coached until 2006, was his second appointment. During his days as a player, Chaney was the Most Valuable Player in the Philadelphia Public League in 1951 and made NAIA All-American while he was in college. In 2001, he was named to the Basketball Hall of Fame.

Sources: Ashe, *A Hard Road to Glory,* vol. 3, p. 253; *Who's Who among African Americans,* 26th ed., p. 227.

1983 • George Henry Raveling (1937–) became the first black head basketball coach at the University of Iowa. The following year he was an assistant coach for the 1984 Olympic squad. Born in Washington, Texas, Raveling held both college coaching jobs and positions in the business world before becoming basketball coach at the University of Southern California in 1986. One of his earlier coaching positions was at his alma mater, Villanova, as an assistant coach. At one time, Raveling was with Conroy Rubber Company, where he was a promotions representative. He also once wrote a syndicated newspaper column and was awarded a Certificate of Merit for Outstanding Sales, Promotion, and Marketing from the *Philadelphia Tribune* newspaper. He was elected Coach of the Year several times, including being named the National College Coach of the Year in 1992. He left USC in 1996 and has since worked as a sports commentator on CBS and as a public speaker.

Sources: Ashe, *A Hard Road to Glory,* vol. 3, pp. 54, 253; *Jet* 65 (20 February 1984): 40; *Who's Who among African Americans,* 26th ed., p. 1028.

1984 • Hubert Anderson was the first black coach at the 1985 World Games for the Deaf.

Sources: *Jet* 66 (28 May 1984): 47.

1984 • Lynette Woodard (1959–) of the University of Kansas was the first woman to become a member of the Harlem Globetrotters. She had earlier been the first woman chosen for the NCAA Top Five award. She was playing guard for the Cleveland Rockers in 1997–98. She moved to the Detroit Shock when she left the Cleveland team.

Sources: Ashe, *A Hard Road to Glory,* vol. 3, pp. 64, 253; Hine, *Black Women in America,* vol. 2, p. 1282–83; *Jet* 73 (16 November 1987): 48; 77 (12 February 1990): 50; Page, *Black Olympian Medalists,* pp. 126, 163; *Who's Who among African Americans,* 26th ed., p. 1378.

The First Black Coach to Win the NCAA Championship

On April 3, 1984, John Robert Thompson Jr. (1941–), the head basketball coach at Georgetown University, became the first black coach to win the NCAA Division I championship. The squad, led by Patrick Ewing, defeated Houston 84–75. A former Boston Celtics player, Thompson began his coaching career at St. Anthony's High School in Washington, D.C., and moved to Georgetown in 1972. Citing personal reasons, he resigned in 1999, midway through his twenty-seventh season at Georgetown. He had a win-loss record of 596–239 when he retired. He had made three appearances in the NCAA Final Four, and in 1984 was the first black coach to win the title. He was also elected Coach of the Year seven times. In 1988 he coached the U.S. Olympic team that won a Bronze Medal and was the assistant coach of the 1976 Gold Medal team. Thompson was born in Washington, D.C., and did his undergraduate college work at Providence College. He holds a master's degree in guidance and counseling from the University of the District of Columbia. One of his enviable statistics as a college coach is that 97 percent of his Georgetown players who stayed four years received degrees. As a player, Thompson was a member of the National Invitational Tournament championship team in 1963 and was made a member of the Providence Hall of Fame. When he graduated from college, he played with the Celtics for only two years before he moved to the coaching ranks. Thompson was inducted into the Naismith Memorial Basketball Hall of Fame in 1999. In 2001 he was an NBA television analyst for Turner Sports.

Sources: Ashe, *A Hard Road to Glory,* vol. 3, pp. 54, 63, 64, 80, 253; *Jet* 66 (16 April 1984): 52; 95 (25 January 1999): 53; 96 (12 July 1999): 46; 99 (2 April 2001): 33; *Time* (16 April 1984): 64; *Who's Who among African Americans,* 24th ed., p. 1229.

1985 • Manute Bol (1962–2010), who joined the National Basketball Association in 1985, became the first player in NBA history to measure nearly seven feet seven inches. He had other unusual distinctions for an NBA player—such as being the only one to have ever killed a lion with a spear—that stem from his experiences in his Sudan birthplace. A member of the Dinka tribe, Bol was born in Turalei, Sudan, the grandson of a chief. Growing up in Sudan, he never learned to read or write in his native tongue. He attributed his basketball career to a cousin in Khartoum, who saw Bol's picture and suggested that he take up the game. Bol played first for a police team in Wau and later with the Catholic Club and Military teams in Khartoum for three years. A coach from Fairleigh Dickinson saw him in Khartoum and convinced him to come to the United States, where a few problems had to be overcome. Bol could not speak, read, or write in English, and the first team that drafted him decided he needed some college experience. The NCAA, however, had some doubt that he was eligible for college basketball under NCAA rules. Bol was eventually able to study at the University of Bridgeport in Connecticut and make his first appearance with an American basketball team. The Rhode Island Gulls of the United States Basketball League signed him after his first college year. He went from the Gulls to the NBA Washington Bullets as a center, and played also for the Golden State Warriors before being traded to the Philadelphia 76ers in 1990. Early in his NBA career he became known for his star defense; in his first season he led the league in blocked shots. He has had an intriguing history, facing trials growing up in Sudan, watching the situation there grow worse, and adjusting to life in the United States while maintaining strong ties to his homeland and the family relatives he left behind. Bol left the NBA in 1995.

Sources: *Contemporary Black Biography,* vol. 1, pp. 27–30; *Who's Who among African Americans,* 14th ed., p. 112.

1986 • The first black coach at the University of Arkansas and the first black coach in the Southwestern Conference was Nolan Richardson (1941–). He was born in El Paso, Texas, and by the time he was twelve years old both of his parents had died. He and his sisters were raised by their grandmother in a predominantly Hispanic section of segregated El Paso. Perhaps Richardson's first "first" occurred when he became the first black student to attend El Paso's Bowie High School in 1955. He played football, basketball, and baseball in high school, despite the fact that he faced racial prejudice and could not stay with the team when they traveled or go to the movies with them. He made Junior College All-American as a first baseman while he was attending Aurora Junior College and was actually offered a minor league contract. Richardson chose instead to go to the University of Texas-El Paso, where he played basketball, and graduated from there in 1974. Once again he received an offer from a professional sports team. The San Diego Chargers football team invited him to try out, but a pulled hamstring kept him out of football and later out of professional basketball. His first coaching job was at his old high school, where he also taught physical education. He was El Paso's first black coach. He concentrated on basketball because the principal told him that he would never make head football coach at the school. During his years at Bowie High School, he was named Texas High School Basketball Coach of the Year three times. Richardson moved to the college ranks in 1979 at West Texas Junior College and then moved to the University of Tulsa three years later. He won championships (junior college and National Invitational) at both institutions. When he won the junior college championship, he was the first black coach to have that distinction. At Tulsa, he was the first black coach at a major Oklahoma college. His first two years at Arkansas were unsuccessful, and fan reaction was vocal. In 1990, however, the Arkansas Razorbacks reached the pinnacle of college basketball's "March Madness": They made it to the Final Four. In 1994 Richardson led his team, the Arkansas Razorbacks, to the NCAA Division I championship, becoming the second black to win the NCAA title. Since he had also won community college championships, he became the first college coach ever to win both titles. Richardson has been outspoken in his belief that black coaches—Richardson included—often do not get the respect they deserve. In his case, at least, respect seemed to come to him at last after the 1994 college season. He was named 1994 Naismith Coach of the Year. Richardson left Arkansas in 2002.

Sources: *Contemporary Black Biography,* vol. 9, pp. 197–200; *Jet* 85 (25 April 1994): 50–54; *Who's Who among African* Americans, 26th ed., p. 1049.

1989 • The first black head coach of a major sport in the Southeast Conference was Wade Houston. He became basketball coach at the University of Tennessee, Knoxville, on April 3, 1989, and resigned in 1994. The Alcoa, Tennessee, native was assistant coach at Louisville for thirteen years.

Sources: *Tennessean* (1 March 1994).

1992 • Robert Oran Evans (1946–) became the first black head coach at the University of Mississippi. He was born in Hobbs, New Mexico, and received his undergraduate degree from New Mexico State University in 1968, after earning an associate degree from Lubbock Christian University in 1966. Evans became assistant basketball coach at New Mexico State after his graduation and remained in that position until 1975. Between 1975 and 1992 he held coaching positions at Texas Tech University and Oklahoma State University. He left the University of Mississippi in 1998 to become the men's basketball head coach at Arizona State University. He has been elected to the basketball halls of fame at both of his alma maters, and was Southeastern Conference Coach of the Year and College Hoops Insider National Coach of the Year in 1996.

Sources: *Tennessean* (31 March 1992); *Who's Who among African Americans,* 26th ed., p. 394.

1993 • Mannie L. Jackson (1939–) became the only black owner in a major professional sport to have controlling interest in his team as owner of the Harlem Globetrotters. Jackson's story has been described as the ultimate rags-to-riches saga. He began life in Illmo, Missouri, born in a boxcar that had been converted to house the temporary labor force working on the Cotton Belt Railroad. The Jackson family moved to Edwardsville, Illinois, when Jackson was three years old. Although the family was frequently in financial difficulty, Jackson credits his family with teaching him to set goals. His ability as a basketball

The First Black NBA Team Owners

The first black NBA team owners were Chicago businessmen Bertram Lee (1939–) and Peter C. B. Bynoe (1951–). On July 10, 1989, they purchased the Denver Nuggets for $65 million. Bynoe was born in Chicago, Illinois, and received bachelor's and master's degrees from Harvard University, a master's degree from Harvard Business School, and a law degree from Harvard Law School. He began his career as an executive intern with Citibank in 1976 and held two executive positions with other organizations before he became involved with sports. Bynoe was executive director of the Illinois Sports Facility from 1988 to 1992, overlapping his time as co-owner of the Nuggets. He moved to partner in a Chicago law firm in 1995. Lee was born in Lynchburg, Virginia. He received his undergraduate degree from North Carolina Central College (now North Carolina Central University) and did graduate work at Roosevelt University in Illinois. He worked at a number of city agencies in Chicago and was holding (and continued to hold) corporate executive positions when he became a Nugget co-owner. He has received several community service awards. Bynoe and Lee retained their co-ownership until 1992.

Sources: Hornsby, *Milestones in Twentieth-Century African-American History,* p. 409; *Jet* 76 (24 July 1989): 51; *Who's Who among African Americans,* 14th ed., p. 783 (Lee); 26th ed., p. 193 (Bynoe).

player helped him along the way. He became a star player in his newly integrated high school. He helped lead the Edwardsville team to the state championship final for its first and only time in 1956. Jackson entered the University of Illinois, on full scholarship, in 1956. Edwardsville teammate Governor Vaughn entered with him, and they were the first black players to start for Illinois' varsity basketball team. Beginning as a forward but later switched to guard, he was the fourth leading scorer in the institution's history when his Illinois career was over. Jackson graduated in 1960 and tried out for the NBA. He did not make the New York Knicks team, but did become a starter for a semi-professional team. In 1962 he joined the Harlem Globetrotters and played with them until 1964. He moved to Detroit, where he entered graduate school and earned a master's degree in marketing and economics from the University of Detroit in 1968. He worked with General Motors from 1964 to 1968 and later moved to the Honeywell Corporation in Minneapolis, Minnesota, where he was often the only black at his executive level. He rose to the position of senior vice president. Jackson's business acumen led him to the Globetrotters, who were no longer enjoying the glory of earlier years. Once he and his team of investors took over, Jackson undertook the task of restoring the team to their previous status, highlighting athleticism and playing serious basketball while retaining some of the comedic elements. The team has thus far thrived under Jackson's management. *Black Enterprise* magazine named Jackson one of the forty most powerful and influential black corporate executives in 1993. He helped found a networking organization for black corporate executives, the Executive Leadership Council, in 1986 and was president of the organization from 1990 to 1992.

Sources: *Contemporary Black Biography,* vol. 14, pp. 134–37; *Who's Who among African Americans,* 26th ed., p. 641.

1993 • C. Vivian Stringer (1948–) became the first woman's basketball coach to advance to the Final Four from two different colleges. While she coached the women's team at Cheyney State in Pennsylvania in 1982, she led the team to the NCAA tournament in Philadelphia. As head coach of the women's basketball team at the University of Iowa, in 1983 she led her Hawkeyes to a place in the NCAA Final Four. Both teams were eliminated after their respective opening games. Stringer was born in Edenborn, Pennsylvania, a town so small that her high school had no girls' basketball team. She achieved her first "first" when she became the first black cheerleader at the school. Stringer made up for the lack of high school sports at Slippery Rock University, where she played basketball, field hockey, softball, and tennis, and was elected to the institution's Athletic Hall of Fame. She graduated from Slippery Rock in 1971 and when her husband took a job at Cheyney, she became the women's basketball coach there because she volunteered for the job; it lasted from 1971 to 1982. She had a record of 251 wins and 51 losses when she left in 1983 to become head coach at Iowa. The team that had struggled before Stringer arrived became a winner in her very first season and continued to excel throughout her stay. At Iowa she had a win/loss record of 520–135 over a twelve-year period, had ten straight twenty-win seasons, won six conference championships, and went to the NCAA tournament nine times. She was named NCAA District V Coach of the Year three times and won two of her three National Coach of the Year awards while there. Her achievements are all the more notable because her personal life has had its share of tragedies: her fourteen-month-old daughter contracted meningitis just as she was involved with her first Final Four, and her husband died suddenly the season before she went to her second Final Four. In 1995 Stringer, who had compiled impressive records as a coach at Cheyney State and Iowa State, signed a multi-year contract with Rutgers University to coach women's basketball and became the country's highest-paid women's coach. Her hiring occurred after an ill-advised 1994 remark by the institution's president concerning the genetic heritage of blacks that prevented them from scoring well on standardized tests. Some thought that Stringer was hired to appease the minority students, who had protested and staged a sit-in at a basketball game after the remark was made. Stringer's prior coaching record and her own statements challenged the notion that she was a token hire.

Sources: *Contemporary Black Biography,* vol. 13, pp. 202–5; *Who's Who among African Americans,* 26th ed., p. 1188.

Michael Jordan

1994 • Michael Jeffrey Jordan (1963–) earned $30.1 million in endorsements of commercial products, becoming the highest paid athlete for the year. Jordan, whose exploits on the basketball court have made him a household name throughout the world, was born in Brooklyn, New York, but grew up in Wilmington, North Carolina. He played Little League baseball as a child and at first participated in almost every sport but basketball when he was in high school. He was cut from the basketball team during his sophomore year but emerged as a promising player as a junior, after growing four inches over the summer. When he entered the University of North Carolina at Chapel Hill in 1981, Jordan was six-feet six-inches tall. He was named Atlantic Coast Rookie of the Year for the 1981–82 season and was a unanimous All-American choice the following season. He was named College Player of the Year twice and was a member of the U.S. Olympic gold medal men's basketball team in 1984. Jordan joined the Chicago Bulls after his junior year in college and continued along the route to superstardom in the pros. The Bulls won three consecutive NBA titles (1991–1993) during the first Jordan years. Jordan himself was piling up statistics and individual championships and awards. He was also on the Olympic teams that won gold medals in basketball in 1992 and 1996. He took a brief respite from basketball in 1993, to try his hand at professional baseball. He announced his retirement shortly after his father was murdered. He returned to the Bulls in 1995 and won his fourth NBA Finals Most Valuable Player award; a fifth such award followed in 1998. In 1997, during the All-Star Weekend, he became the first NBA player to make a triple-double in points, assists, and rebounds. His reputation suffered momentary blemishes in 1991 and 1993 when he was alleged to have an involvement in gambling at cards and on the golf course, but the allegations were not confirmed. It would be difficult to find a basketball honor that Jordan has not received. His sparkling play gave rise to a variety of nicknames: "Superman," "Last Shot," "Air Jordan." He retired again in 1998 after the Bulls won their sixth championship in eight years, but retirement did not signify departure from the world of basketball. In 2000 he became president and a minority owner of the Washington Wizards NBA team. He also became CEO of the special Nike branch that carries Air Jordan shoes. He returned to the NBA in the 2001–2002 season, playing with the Wizards but donating his salary to charities associated with the September 11, 2001, terrorist attacks relief efforts.

Sources: *Jet* 87 (1 May 1995): 52; *Who's Who among African Americans,* 26th ed., p. 707; *Contemporary Black Biography,* vol. 21, pp. 86–91; Salzman, *Encyclopedia of African-Amer-*

ican Culture and History, Supplement, pp. 151–2; Smith, *Notable Black American Men,* pp. 664–67.

1994 • The first black man to oversee the development of an expansion NBA franchise in a foreign country was Isiah Lord Thomas III (1961–), who became vice president of the Toronto Raptors. The year before, he had been playing for the Detroit Pistons when an injury ended his days as a player. During his star-studded career as a player, he was an All-Star thirteen times, the Most Valuable Player twice, and the member of an NBA championship team twice. Thomas was born in Chicago, Illinois, and was attending Indiana University when he entered the draft to begin his professional basketball career with the Pistons in 1981. He is one of relatively few players whose entire playing career was spent with one team. As president, he remained with the Raptors until 1998, and became an NBA TV analyst for NBC. In 2001, he became the head coach of the Indiana Pacers. Thomas, who has a reputation as a skilled businessman, credits his mother, who was for a time a single parent, for the values she instilled in him. The made-for-TV movie *A Mother's Story: The Mary Thomas Story* was released in 1989 starring Alfre Woodard.

Sources: *Jet* 87 (3 April 1995): 48–49; *Who's Who among African Americans,* 26th ed., p. 1219; *Contemporary Black Biography,* vol. 26, pp. 157–62.

1995 • Bernadette Locke-Mattox (1958–) was named head coach of the women's basketball team at the University of Kentucky, the first black woman to hold that post. Previously she was assistant director of athletics at the school. A native of Rockwood, Tennessee, Locke-Mattox earned an associate degree from Roane State Community College in Tennessee and a bachelor's degree in education. Her first job after graduation was as academic advisor at the University of Georgia. She held several other jobs before she took her first job as a coach. She became the assistant coach at the University of Georgia in 1985, and held that position for five years. She moved to the University of Kentucky as assistant coach in 1990 and remained in that position until she was named assistant athletic director in 1994. The move to head coach took place the following year. Locke-Mattox was an Academic All-American at the University of Georgia in 1981.

Sources: *Jet* 88 (22 May 1995): 24; *Who's Who among African Americans,* 126th ed., p. 782.

1995 • Lenny [Leonard R.] Wilkens (1937–), coach for the Atlanta Hawks, became the winningest coach in NBA history, surpassing the record of Red Auerbach, legendary coach of the Boston Celtics, who had 938 career wins. He was in his 22nd season as an NBA coach, when his team beat the Washington Bullets by the score of 112–90. He coached the Hawks for seven years: After the Hawks posted their worst ever record (28–54) during the 1999–2000 season, he resigned his coaching post. He was also the winningest coach in a single season when he coached for the Cleveland Cavaliers during the 1992–93 season. Wilkens was born in Brooklyn, New York. He was a star player at Providence College in Rhode Island, where he graduated with a degree in economics in 1960. In 1960 he won the Most Valuable Player award at the National Invitational Tournament during his senior year in college. After graduation Wilkens entered the professional ranks as a player for the St. Louis Hawks, and remained with them until 1968. He was the Most Valuable Player of the NBA all-star game in 1971 and has won numerous other awards as a basketball player and coach and for his humanitarian service. He went on to serve as either a player or player-coach for the Seattle SuperSonics (1968–72), Cleveland Cavaliers (1972–74), and the Portland Trail Blazers (1974–75). From the 1975–76 season on, all of his appointments were to the head coaching job, beginning with Portland in 1975–76 and proceeding to Seattle (1976–85), Cleveland (1986–93), Atlanta (1993–2000), Toronto (2000-2003), and then the New York Nicks (2004-2005). Along the way, he served as general manager of the SuperSonics for a season. He became a member of the Naismith Memorial Basketball Hall of Fame in 1990, and was the coach of the U.S. men's basketball team in the 1996 Olympics. When he received the monetary award for setting the winning coaching record, he donated the money to a Seattle home for children.

Sources: *Jet* 87 (23 January 1995): 51; 97 (15 May 2000): 46; *Who's Who among African Americans,* 26th ed., p. 1328; *Contemporary Black Biography,* vol. 11, pp. 232–35.

Tubby Smith

1995 • Tubby [Orlando] Smith (1951–) was named head coach at the University of Georgia, Athens, becoming the school's first black coach. He was appointed shortly after his Tulsa Golden Hurricane team had made it to the "Sweet 16" during the NCAA national tournament. The Golden Hurricane had won the Missouri Valley Conference championship during Smith's last two years there. Smith is reputed to have been the only person interviewed for the Georgia post. The Scotland, Maryland, native graduated from High Point College in 1973 and became a head coach for the first time at the University of Tulsa, where he served from 1992 to 1995. During his stay at Georgia, from 1995 to 1997, the team had a win/loss record of 45/19 and was among the NCAA national tournament teams twice.

Sources: *Jet* 87 (17 April 1995): 50; *Contemporary Black Biography,* vol. 18, pp. 164–66; *Tennesseean* (13 May 1997); *Who's Who among African Americans,* 26th ed., p. 1155.

1995 • Harry Miller, who for two months was interim head basketball coach at Baylor University, received permanent status and became the first minority to head any sport at the school.

Sources: *Jet* 87 (13 February 1995): 49.

1996 • While playing for the Charlotte Hornets, Robert Parish (1953–) played his 1,561st game and surpassed the record that Kareem Abdul-Jabbar set for the most games played. He and Abdul-Jabbar were at the time the only NBA players who had played for twenty seasons. Parish, who was born in Shreveport, Louisiana, attended Centenary College. His professional career began with the Golden State Warriors in 1976, for whom he played until 1980. He spent the next fourteen years starring as the center for the Boston Celtics, played two years for the Hornets, and retired after playing his final year for the Chicago Bulls. He scored his 10,000th point playing against Phoenix in 1984. In 1998 the Boston Celtics retired his number.

Sources: *Jet* 89 (29 April 1996): 48; *Who's Who among African Americans,* 26th ed., p. 961.

1996 • The first woman to receive the Most Courageous Award from the United States Basketball Writers Association was Cori Carson (1971–), a junior guard for Marymount University and a Division III All-American. She survived a liver transplant after temporarily losing her eyesight and suffering a coma. Carson was told that without the transplant she would have died.

Sources: *Jet* 89 (29 April 1996): 47.

Sheryl Swoopes

1996 • The first sportswoman to get her own signature line of athletic footwear was Sheryl Swoopes (Swoopes-Jackson) (1971–), when Nike introduced "Air Swoopes" for women. Spike Lee directed a high-profile commercial for Swoopes, who made numerous personal appearances across the country to promote the shoe. A Brownfield, Texas, native, she started on her way to basketball history in high school, where she made All-State and All-American. She entered Texas Tech University after attending South Plains Junior College. By the time she left Texas Tech after the 1992–93 season, Swoopes had been named National Junior College Player of the Year, had scored a phenomenal fifty-three points when Tech played the University of Texas in the Southwest Conference final, and—most notably—became the only college player (male or female) to score forty-seven points in a collegiate national championship game. Tech won this women's NCAA championship, played against Ohio State, by a score of 84–82 in 1993. Swoopes was named National Collegiate Player of the Year and Sportswoman of the Year. Her Tech statistics reveal that in her two seasons there, she scored over thirty points fourteen times and averaged twenty-seven points and 9.3 rebounds. Her Texas Tech jersey was retired in 1994. Swoopes found few opportunities in the United States for women to play professional basketball, so she went to Europe and played for Bari in the Italian women's professional league. She played only ten games there and returned to Tech to complete her degree requirements, graduating in 1994. She tried out and earned a place on the U.S. women's national basketball team; she was with the team when they won a gold medal in the 1996 Olympic games. Swoopes joined the Houston Comets in the newly organized Women's National Basketball Association in 1997. She was the first woman in WNBA history to record a triple-double.

Sources: *Who's Who among African Americans,* 26th ed., p. 1197; *Contemporary Black Biography,* vol. 12, pp. 207–10.

1996 • The first black head basketball coach at the University of Southern Mississippi, Hattiesburg, was James Green (1961?–). He brought to the post the experience gained from his position of assistant coach at Iowa State University.

Sources: *Jet* 90 (20 May 1996): 46; *Who's Who among African Americans,* 26th ed., p. 493.

1996 • At age eighteen, Kobe B. Bryant (1978–) joined the Los Angeles Lakers of the National Basketball Association, becoming the first player of his age ever to play with the NBA. He was at the time one of only twenty-eight in NBA history to bypass college and enter the NBA straight out of high school. He was born in Philadelphia, Pennsylvania, son of professional basketball player Joe Bryant. The Bryants moved frequently during Joe Bryant's sixteen-year playing career, but in 1983, Joe Bryant left the NBA and moved the family to Italy, where he played with the Italian professional league. Kobe Bryant played both basketball and soccer in Italy. When his father retired completely in 1991, the family returned to a comfortable Philadelphia existence. Bryant the son became a starter for his varsity basketball team and soon became a Philadelphia celebrity because of his basketball prowess. His 2,883 points as a high school player made him the leading all-time scorer in the history of Southeastern Pennsylvania basketball, and he was named the Pennsylvania High School Player of the Year as a junior. He won many citations as a senior, including National High School Player of the Year and Naismith Player of the Year. Many colleges sought the young star, but he made the decision to enter the NBA draft. Bryant was drafted by the Charlotte Hornets, who traded him to the Los Angeles Lakers. He was given an endorsement contract from Adidas very soon after he entered the league. He was actually less than eighteen when he signed a contract from the Lakers to play with the Southern California Summer Professional League. Bryant played well until he broke his wrist just before the September start of training camp, and was allowed to play with the Lakers sparingly at first. Nevertheless, he made the Rookie All-Star team, scored thirty-one points, and won the slam-dunk competition. He made the NBA All-Star team in 1998, and was, yet again, the youngest player ever to make a team.

Kobe Bryant

Sources: *Contemporary Black Biography,* vol. 15, pp. 39–42; *Who's Who among African Americans,* 26th ed., p. 173.

1997 • Dallas Mavericks' forward A. C. Green Jr. broke the NBA record for consecutive games played and became the league's new "Iron Man." He played his 907th game in the Reunion Arena in Dallas, against the Golden State Warriors, who won in overtime by the score of 101–97. Green was given the game ball and other memorabilia to commemorate the event. A native of Portland, Oregon, he attended Oregon State University. He came into the NBA in 1986 as a forward with the Los Angeles Lakers. He played with the Lakers twice, first from 1985 to 1993 and returned to them in 1999. Between his Laker turns, he played with the Phoenix Suns from 1994 to 1996 and with the Dallas Mavericks from 1996 to 1999. He was on the NBA All-Star team in 1990.

Sources: *Jet* 93 (8 December 1997): 51; *Who's Who among African Americans,* 26th ed., p. 491.

1997 • Allen Iverson (1975–), a forward for the Philadelphia 76ers, became the first rookie in NBA history to score forty points or more in four consecutive games. Wilt Chamberlain had set the record of forty or more points in three consecutive games during the 1959–60 season. In Iverson's next game after he broke the record, he again scored forty points, raising the new benchmark to five consecutive games. His performance won him the designation of NBA Player of the Week. The Hampton, Virginia, native attended Georgetown University. He was a first-round draft pick in 1996.

Sources: *Jet* 91 (5 May 1997): 30; *Who's Who among African Americans,* 26th ed., p. 631.

1997 • The first black men's basketball coach at the University of Kentucky was Tubby [Orlando] Smith (1951–), whose appointment followed the 1995 hiring of Bernadette

The First Black Woman Referee

The first black woman to serve as referee in the NBA was Violet Palmer in 1997. The only other woman official in the league at this time was Dee Kanter; together they were the first two women officials in any men's professional sports league. Both women were experienced in women's college basketball and in the fledgling Women's National Basketball Association. Both had also worked in NBA summer league and preseason games. Palmer was born in Compton, California. During her years as a point guard at California Polytechnic Institute in Pomona, she was a member of NCAA Division II championship teams in 1985 and 1986. Her officiating career began after her graduation from college. Kanter was a supervisor of officials in the WNBA before jumping to the men's game.

Sources: *Jet* 92 (17 November 1997): 50; *Who's Who among African Americans,* 26th ed., p. 959 (Palmer).

Locke-Mattox as women's basketball coach. Under Smith's leadership, the Kentucky Wildcats won the NCAA championship in 1998. He was the first rookie coach at Kentucky to win a national championship. Smith's previous head coach positions at the Universities of Georgia and Tulsa had provided valuable experience in both regular season and tournament play. Smith had been an assistant coach at Kentucky for two years prior to being named head coach. Just as was the case when he became head coach at Georgia, he was the only person interviewed for the Kentucky post. In his six previous seasons as a head coach, Smith amassed a 124–62 win/loss record. Part of the publicity engendered by Smith's appointment as a Kentucky head coach can be attributed to the fact that the men's basketball team was coached by Adolph Rupp for forty-two years, and for most of those years Rupp's reluctance to sign black players was almost as big a story as his teams' achievements on the basketball court.

Sources: *Jet* 92 (26 May 1997): 51; 92 (26 May 1997): 51; 95 (30 November 1998): 48; *Who's Who among African Americans,* 26th ed., p. 1155.

1997 • Steve Robinson was appointed head basketball coach at Florida State University in Tallahassee, becoming the first black coach of any sport at the school. He also became the only black coach in the Atlantic Coast Conference. He was the head coach at the University of Tulsa when he accepted the Florida position. During his two seasons at Tulsa, he had a record of forty-six wins and eighteen losses. The Tulsa team went to the NCAA national tournament during both of his years as basketball coach. He was named Basketball Coach of the Year for the Western Conference, Mountain Division, for the 1996–97 season. Robinson was on the list of the Outstanding Young Men of America in 1986 and was inducted into the Radford University Sports Hall of Fame in 1997.

Sources: *Jet* 92 (21 July 1997): 46; *Who's Who among African Americans,* 26th ed., p. 1068.

1997 • Minnesota Gopher Bobby Jackson (1973–) became the first member of the team ever chosen Big Ten Player of the Year. Also honored was head basketball coach Clem Smith Haskins (1943–), who was the overwhelming choice for Big Ten Coach of the Year. The Gophers were the regular-season Big Ten conference champions, winning twenty-seven of their thirty games. They entered the NCAA national tournament as the number-one seed in the Midwest Region. Jackson joined the Denver Nuggets as a guard after the 1996–97 season was over. He moved to the Minnesota Timberwolves in 1999. Haskins was born in Campbellsville, Kentucky, and graduated from Western Kentucky University. He was a star basketball player in high school and college, being named to the Kentucky High School Hall of Fame and making First Year All-American in the NCAA in 1967. He entered the NBA in 1967, playing with the Chicago Bulls; he moved several times as a player, ending his playing career with the Washington Bullets in 1977. He began his coaching career at Western Kentucky and won Rookie Coach of the Year and Ohio Valley Conference Coach of the Year awards in his first year (1980) as head coach. Haskins was elected to the Kentucky Hall of Fame in 1990.

Sources: *Jet* 91 (31 March 1997): 49; *Who's Who among African Americans,* 26th ed., p. 634 (Jackson), p. 552 (Haskins).

Dennis Rodman

1997 • Chicago Bulls basketball star Dennis Keith Rodman (1961–) became the first basketball player to top Mr. Blackwell's list of "Worst Dressed Women." Blackwell called Rodman a "unisex wreck." He was known for his brightly colored hair, tattoos, and outrageous costumes. In 1996 Rodman published his tell-all book, *Bad As I Wanna Be.* At a book signing in Chicago, he wore make-up and a hot pink feather boa, had silver-colored hair and silver nails, and rode to the signing on a pink Harley-Davidson motorcycle. Rodman's flair for the unusual in dress and behavior became a part of his basketball image, but he also demonstrated the playing skills that made him so notable. The Trenton, New Jersey, native attended Cooke County Junior College and Southeastern Oklahoma State University. His professional basketball career began as a forward with the Detroit Pistons in 1986. He later played with the San Antonio Spurs and the Chicago Bulls, before moving to the Los Angeles Lakers in 1998. His name appeared several times on the list of NBA awards. He was the Defensive Player of the Year twice (1990 and 1991), was on the NBA All-Defensive Team from 1989 to 1993 and again in 1996, and was on the 1990 and 1997 NBA all-star teams. He holds the NBA record for the most seasons (six) leading the league in rebounds per game. Rodman is also a businessman, owning the Rodman Excavating Company and a shop named "Illusions."

Sources: *Jet* 90 (20 May 1996): 56; *Reuters* 16 (14 January 1997): 11; *Who's Who among African Americans,* 26th ed., p. 1071.

1998 • The first black basketball coach at St. John's University was Mike Jarvis. For the previous eight years he coached at George Washington University, and before then, at Boston College, where he served for five years. He never had a losing team.

Sources: *Jet* 94 (29 June 1998): 50.

1998 • Chamique Holdsclaw (1977–), a member of the University of Tennessee-Knoxville Lady Vols, became the first women's basketball player to win the Sullivan Award, given annually to the top amateur athlete in the nation. She was named Associated Press Player of the Year for 1998 and 1999, becoming the first to repeat the title. She was also the first three-time All-American. She has an impressive list of other awards and honors as a college player, including the award as Female Athlete of the Year for the 1998–99 season. Holdsclaw was a number-one draft pick in the 1999 WNBA draft and joined the Washington Mystics as a combination forward and guard. She continued her award-winning ways by winning the WNBA Rookie of the Year award in 1999.

Sources: *Jet* 95 (22 April 1999): 50; *Who's Who among African Americans,* 26th ed., p. 592; *Contemporary Black Biography,* vol. 24, pp. 88–90.

1999 • Karl A. Malone (1963–), forward with the Utah Jazz, became the first player in league history to be named to eleven All-NBA first teams. Several basketball legends— including Michael Jordan and Kareem Abdul-Jabbar—were tied with ten appearances on All-Star first teams. Malone's professional record also includes being named to the NBA All-Rookie Team in 1986, multiple awards as Most Valuable Player, and membership on the 1997 All-Star Defensive Team. He was on the U.S. men's basketball team in 1992 and 1996, and he was chosen as one of the Fifty Greatest Players in NBA History in 1996. The Summerfield, Louisiana, native attended Louisiana Tech University, and entered the NBA with the Jazz in 1985.

Sources: *Jet* 96 (28 June 1999): 46; *Contemporary Black Biography,* vol. 18, pp. 107–11; *Who's Who among African Americans,* 26th ed., p. 806.

Karl Malone

1999 • The Women's National Basketball Association's first All-Star Game was held at Madison Square Garden before a sell-out crowd. Lisa Deshaun Leslie (1972–) led the Western Conference to victory over the East, becoming the first black woman to do so. She was named the first Most Valuable Player in WNBA all-star history.

Sources: *Jet* 96 (2 August 1999): 46; *Who's Who among African Americans,* 26th ed., p. 764; *Contemporary Black Biography,* vol. 16, pp. 131–34.

1999 • Carolyn Peck (1966–) became the first black woman to coach a team to the women's NCAA national championship. She coached the Purdue Boilermakers to a 62–45 win over Duke University and to its first NCAA championship this year. She was also named Big Ten Conference Coach of the Year and Associated Press Coach of the Year. As Purdue's women's basketball coach, she was the first woman to receive the New York Athletic Club's Winged Foot Award. Peck left Purdue at the end of her second season and became head coach and general manager of the WNBA's Orlando Miracle. A graduate of Vanderbilt University, Peck entered the coaching ranks in 1993, when she became assistant coach at the University of Tennessee. Appointments as assistant coach at Kentucky and at Purdue would follow before she was named Purdue's head coach.

Sources: *Jet* 95 (12 April 1999): 50; *Who's Who among African Americans,* 26th ed., p. 764; *Contemporary Black Biography,* vol. 23, pp. 154–57.

2000 • C. Vivian Stringer (1948–) became the first black woman and the third woman's basketball coach in Division I history to record 600 victories. The head coach of Rutgers University's Scarlet Knights has taken thirteen teams to NCAA tournaments. In 2000 Stringer became the first black woman basketball coach to have 600 career victories. The Rutgers Scarlet Knights defeated a strong Texas team by a score of 68–64.

Sources: *Jet* 97 (17 January 2000): 50; *Contemporary Black Biography,* vol. 13, pp. 202–5; *Who's Who among African Americans,* 26th ed., p. 1188.

2001 • The first woman to coach a men's professional basketball team was Stephanie Ready (1976?–). She helped break ground as an assistant for Coppin State's men's team for the previous two years and later left to become assistant coach of the Greenville, South Carolina, Groove. The Groove is a team in the NBA's then new eight-team developmental league. The league, later known as the NBDL, succeeds the defunct Continental Basketball Association and is essentially an NBA minor league. Ready was an honor graduate from Coppin State and was a four-year starter on the women's basketball team. She also played volleyball, and she was serving as the volleyball coach there when chosen to be men's basketball assistant coach. While at Coppin State, Ready was the only woman on the coaching staff of a Division I men's basketball team and the second one in the history of the game. In her post, Ready refers to herself as "part of the old-boy network. It's like a fraternity."

Sources: *New York Times* (15 August 2001)

Allen Iverson

2001 • Allen Iverson (1975–), NBA's Most Valuable Player for 2001, is the shortest player and the lightest in weight in NBA history ever to win the award. He was also the Most Valuable Player in the NBA All-Star game this year. Iverson had stumbled somewhat during the 1999–2000 season, when he was not on the best of terms with his coach and was criticized for the image he portrayed through his hair, tattoos, and questionable rap lyrics. But during the 2000–2001 season, he led the league in scoring and steals, and was tied for most minutes played. Iverson was the first player to lead in both scoring and steals since Michael Jordan did so in the 1992–93 season.

Sources: *Jet* 99 (4 June 2001): 47; *Who's Who among African Americans,* 26th ed., p. 634.

2001 • Kwame Brown (1982–) was the first high school senior ever selected as first overall pick in the NBA draft. Michael Jordan, part owner and president of basketball operations of the Washington Wizards, picked the nineteen-year-old in the draft. Brown was drafted out of Glynn Academy, a high school in his Brunswick, Georgia, hometown. Of the first four draft picks, three were high school seniors. In previous years no high school senior had been chosen higher than number three.

Sources: *Jet* 100 (16 July 2001): 51–55; *New York Times* (28 June 2001).

2001 • Dikembe Mutombo (1966–), center with the Philadelphia 76ers, was named the 2000–2001 Defensive Player of the Year, becoming the first four-time winner of the award. No other player was even close, since no one had won the award more than twice. Mutombo's feat in this year was all the more impressive since he began the season with the Atlanta Hawks and was traded to Philadelphia in February. After the trade he had a strong season, finishing sixth on the NBA list of most blocked shots in a career. Mutombo came to this country from his birthplace in Zaire and was the number-four, first-round draft pick of the Denver Nuggets in 1991, moving to Atlanta in 1996. He made the All-Rookie first team in 1992 and was on the 1997 and 1998 All-Star teams.

Sources: *Jet* 99 (14 May 2001): 46; *Who's Who among African Americans,* 26th ed., p. 921.

2001 • Utah Jazz forward Karl Malone (1963–) has made more free throws than any other player in NBA history up to this year. In April he was the first player to make 8,534 of 11,576 free throws in his sixteen-year career. He achieved this record just two seasons after he became the new record-holder for most consecutive appearances on NBA all-star first teams.

Sources: *Jet* 99 (16 April 2001): 52; *Who's Who among African Americans,* 26th ed., p. 806.

2002 • Former Chicago Bulls player and assistant coach Bill [James William] Cartwright (1958?–) was named the fourteenth coach of the Chicago Bulls, becoming the first black head coach in the franchise's history. Cartwright entered the NBA in 1979 when he was a first-round draft pick with the New York Knicks. He was the first center on the Knicks' team to start in every game. Cartwright played with the Bulls for six seasons, from 1988 to 1994. He was also a vital part of the team's first NBA championships. He ended his career as a player with the Seattle SuperSonics.

Sources: *Jet* 101 (21 January 2002): 46; *Who's Who among African Americans,* 26th ed., p. 221.

2002 • The first black to become head coach of the Phoenix Suns was Frank Johnson (1958–). He replaced Scott Skiles, who stepped down as coach. Johnson was Skiles's top assistant during his last two seasons with the team. On November 5, 1992, Johnson joined the team, signing on as a reserve guard. He played two seasons and then became assistant coach on February 20, 1997. Since the 1987–88 season, the Suns have made the playoffs every year.

Sources: *Jet* 101 (4 March 2002): 52; *Who's Who among African Americans,* 26th ed., p. 669.

2007 • A forward with the Texas Longhorns, Kevin Durant became the first freshman in history to be named Division I Player of the Year by the National Association of Basketball Coaches. A native of Maryland, the six-foot-nine Durant was key in the Longhorns' 25–10 record and their second trip to the NCAA Tournament. He scored 25.8 points each game, with 11.1 rebounds per game, both ranked fourth nationally. He also had 20 double-doubles for the year, setting Texas and Big 12 records "with eleven 30 point performances."

Sources: *Jet* 111 (9 April 2007): 51.

Kevin Durant

2008 • The first top three picks in the lottery were all black. Memphis guard Derrick Rose, who grew up on Chicago's South Side was chosen No. 1 by the Chicago Bulls; he was known for his speed, athleticism, and poise, and averaged 14.9 points per game. The Miami Heat chose forward Michael Beasley, who led NCAA Division I with 12.4 rebounds per game and 26.2 points per game while a freshman. The Minnesota Timberwolves chose guard O. J. Mayo, the No. 3 pick. A guard at Southern California, Mayo earned the "First Team All-Pac–10 and All-Freshman Team honors."

Sources: *Jet* 114 (14 July 2008): 48–49.

Bodybuilding

1970 • The first black Mr. America winner was Chris Dickerson (1939–). During his career he earned fifteen bodybuilding titles. One of a set of triplets, Dickerson was born in Montgomery, Alabama. He was an outstanding athlete during his school years and gave up his early interest in a singing career in the mid–1960s to become a bodybuilder. Later, he combined his musical talent with his sport.

Sources: *Negro Almanac,* pp. 1430–31; *The African American Almanac,* 8th ed., p. 98; Salzman, *Encyclopedia of African-American Culture and History,* vol. 1, p. 58; Smith, *Encyclopedia of African American Popular Culture,* vol. 2, pp. 410–12.

2001 • The winners of the first open International Federation of Body Builders' Professional Body Building European Championship were Chris Cormier, Dennis Tyrone James, and Dexter Jackson. The contest was held in the Budapest Convention Center in Budapest, Hungary. The three black Americans won the right to compete in the Mister Olympia contest in Las Vegas in October.

Sources: *Jet* 99 (26 March 2001): 52.

Bowling

1939 • Wynston Brown was the first president of the National Negro Bowling Association, organized in Detroit on August 20. In the 1940s the organization dropped the word "Negro" from its title and included white members as well.

Sources: *Negro Almanac,* p. 952; Young, *Negro Firsts in Sports,* pp. 179–80, 183.

1951 • In April a team from Inskter, Michigan, became the first to be entered in the American Bowling Congress (ABC) Bowling Championships. Team member William "Bill" Rhodman (1916–1962) rolled a 719 series in the tournament, becoming the first black bowler to win top rank in ABC competition. He also became the first black member of the Greater Detroit Hall of Fame. Other members of the history-making lineup for the championship tournament were C.W. Williams (the first black to cash in the top five of the annual *Bowlers Journal* tournament), Maurice "Ace" Kilgore (the first black to appear on a televised bowling event), George Williams, and Lavert Griffin.

Sources: Young, *Negro Firsts in Sports,* p. 281; Allen, "Hey, Bowlers Have Contributed to Black History!," "Up Allen's Alley," *Bowlers Digest* (February 20, 1992), p. 13.

1960 • Detroit native Fuller B. Gordy (1918?–1991) became the first black professional bowler in the United States, on February 15. He was also the first black from Michigan to be accepted into the Professional Bowlers Association. He was the older brother of Motown's founder, Berry Gordy.

Sources: "Fuller B. Gordy," http://www.friendsoffuller.org/Fuller_B.html, accessed October 1, 2012.

1986 • George Branham III (1962–) defeated Mark Roth in a final event at Glendale Heights, Illinois, on November 22 and won the Brunswick Memorial World Open, becoming the first black to win a Professional Bowlers Association title. Branham was born in Detroit, Michigan. He joined the Professional Bowlers Association in 1984, the year after he won the Southern California Junior Bowler of the Year award. He followed that win with several others, winning tournaments in 1987 and 1993. Branham was also the first black to win a Triple Crown event. In 1993, he became the first black bowler to win the Firestone Tournament of Champions. He won two championships in less than a month, including the Baltimore Open. The Detroit native learned to bowl when he was six years old and turned professional in 1984

Sources: *Jet* 84 (7 June 1993): 46; 96 (22 November 1999): 19; *Who's Who among African Americans,* 14th ed., p. 134; *Who's Who among African Americans,* 26th ed., p. 158.

2001 • The first black president of the American Bowling Congress was Thomas DeChalus, who took office on May 1.

Sources: *Jet* 99 (19 March 2001): 10.

Boxing

1791 • The first black fighter on record is Joe Lashley, who fought in England. His place of birth is unknown.

Sources: Ashe, *A Hard Road to Glory,* vol. 1, p. 21.

1805 • Bill [William] Richmond (1763–1829), born on Staten Island, New York, was the first black to become a prominent boxer in England. He was active until 1810 and fought again in 1814 and 1818. He was also the first black to seek his living as a boxer, and the first American boxer to achieve a substantial measure of success. As a fifteen-year-old soldier for the British Army during the American Revolution, Richmond was the hangman at Nathan Hale's execution. He accompanied the British troops when they withdrew to England after the American Revolution.

Sources: Ashe, *A Hard Road to Glory,* vol. 1, pp. 17–21, 30; Chalk, *Pioneers of Black Sport,* pp. 121–23; *Encyclopedia of Boxing,* p. 190; *Negro Almanac,* 1976, p. 580; Young, *Negro Firsts in Sports,* pp. 5, 18–20, 49.

1810 • Tom Molineaux (1784–1818) defeated the recently retired white boxer Tom Cribb to become the first black American boxing champion in England. His victory was never acknowledged, however, because Londoners did not want the public to know that Cribb had lost to a black. Instead, they referred to Molineaux as an "unknown." Molineaux astonished everyone, not only by his extraordinary power of hitting and his gigantic strength, but also by his acquaintance with the science, which was far greater than any had given him credit for. The two fought again on September 11, 1811, and Molineaux defeated him for the second time. By then, Molineaux had become a celebrated boxer in England but his success remained unrecorded in the American press—where the institution of slavery flourished and crushed the hope of Africans becoming Americans. Born a slave in the Georgetown section of Maryland (now a part of the District of Columbia), on March 23, 1784, Molineaux came from a family of boxers and "was forged into a pugilist of historical significance and acclaim." He defeated "Black Abe," another slave, and won $100 for his master and his freedom. He moved to New York City, worked as a porter and later a stevedore, turned semi-professional in 1800, and continued his boxing career in England in 1809.

Tom Molineaux

Sources: Smith, *Encyclopedia of African American Popular Culture,* vol. 1, p.184; Smith and Wynn, *Freedom Facts and Firsts,* pp. 329–30.

1886 • On September 25, Peter "The Black Prince" Jackson (1861–1901) became the first black to win a national boxing crown, the Australian heavyweight title. A native of the Virgin Islands, he knocked out Frank Slavin in 1892 to gain the British Empire heavyweight title.

Sources: Ashe, *A Hard Road to Glory,* vol. 1, pp. 25–28; Chalk, *Pioneers of Black Sport,* pp. 141–43, 144, 145; Young, *Negro Firsts in Sports,* pp. 23–24.

1890 • George "Little Chocolate" Dixon (1870–1909), born in Halifax, Nova Scotia, became the first black world champion in boxing when he defeated Nunc Wallace to win the bantamweight title on June 27. On March 31, 1891, he knocked out Cal McCarthy and became the first black man to hold an American title in any sport. In that same year he won the featherweight title when he defeated reigning champion Fred Johnson. Dixon was also the first to regain the title and the first to win the paperweight world championship. When he began boxing professionally, the relatively diminutive Dixon stood five feet three-and-one-half inches tall and weighed eighty-seven pounds. In 1956 Dixon was elected to boxing's Hall of Fame.

George Dixon

Sources: Ashe, *A Hard Road to Glory,* vol. 1, pp. 22–24, 113; Bennett, *Before the Mayflower,* p. 634; *The Black New Yorkers,* p. 110; *Encyclopedia of Boxing,* p. 40; *Jet* 88 (31 July 1995): 20; Young, *Negro Firsts in Sports,* pp. 19, 24–26, 225.

1901 • Joe Walcott (1873–1935), the first black welterweight champion, defeated Rube Ferns and won the title at Fort Erie, Ontario, on December 18. He won the New England lightweight and middleweight wrestling titles in the same night. He also was ranked as the number one all-time welterweight. In 1955 Walcott was elected to the Ring Boxing Hall of Fame and in 1991 to the International Boxing Hall of Fame. Born in Barbados, West Indies, Walcott was sometimes known as the "Barbados Demon." The short, squat fighter had long arms, a strong punch, and throughout his twenty-four-year career he weighed between 133 and 148 pounds.

Sources: Ashe, *A Hard Road to Glory,* vol. 1, pp. 24–25; Bennett, *Before the Mayflower,* p. 634; Chalk, *Pioneers of Black Sport,* pp. 130–34, 136–37; *Encyclopedia of Boxing,* p. 134; *Jet* 101 (24–31 December 2001): 120.

1902 • Joe Gans [Joseph Gaines] (1874–1910) was the first American-born black to win a world crown (the lightweight), defeating Frank Erne in one round at the Fort Erie on May 12. He held the title for six years. Born in Knoxville, Tennessee, he was elected to the Hall of Fame in 1954. Gans retired in 1909 and died of tuberculosis in 1910.

Sources: Ashe, *A Hard Road to Glory,* vol. 1, pp. 28–30; Bennett, *Before the Mayflower,* p. 634; *Encyclopedia of Black America,* p. 132; *Encyclopedia of Boxing,* p. 51; Young, *Negro Firsts in Sports,* p. 225.

1908 • Jack [John Arthur] Johnson (1878–1946) knocked out Tommy Burns on December 26 in Sydney, Australia, in the fourteenth round to become the first black heavyweight boxing champion of the world. He lost only five of his first ninety-seven fights. Born in Galveston, Texas, Johnson was known as "Little Arthur" in his childhood. Because of his fearlessness, flamboyant style, and colorful life, he became one of the most reviled and hated men in America. Some experts called him the greatest fighter of this weight class ever. His professional career, which included more than 125 fights, spanned more than thirty years; forty-four of his wins were by knockouts. Johnson did not have a blissful boxing career. He had difficulty getting a title fight despite an astounding record of 54 and 2 in official bouts. Once he did, and won, there was a hue and cry to find "The Great White Hope," a white boxer who could win the title back. Boxing promoters settled on former champion Jim Jeffries, who retired unbeaten four years earlier. Johnson faced Jeffries on July 4, 1910, at Reno, Nevada, in a scheduled forty-five-rounder called the "Fight of the Century;" the one-sided fight ended in the fifteenth round, when Jeffries went down three times. As the news spread around the country, it hit a racial nerve and ignited riots and unrest. He lost his title in Havana, Cuba, in 1915 and continued to wander until 1920, when he returned to his homeland, where he spent close to a year in prison. Once released, he boxed sporadically, winning some and losing others. He also continued to perform as a vaudevillian, which he had begun years earlier to supplement his boxing income. In 1954 Johnson was elected to the Boxing Hall of Fame. He was made a member of the International Boxing Hall of Fame in 1990. Johnson's story is told in the stage play and movie *The Great White Hope.*

Sources: Bennett, *Before the Mayflower,* p. 634; Chalk, *Pioneers of Black Sport,* 141, 144–48, 152–63; *Contemporary Black Biography,* vol. 8, pp. 145–48; *Encyclopedia of Boxing,* pp. 65–66; *Jet* 91 (31 March 1997): 22; 95 (5 April 1999): 19; Jones and Washington, *Black Champions Challenge American Sports,* pp. 25–27, 36–38; Smith, *Encyclopedia of African American Popular Culture,* vol. 2, pp. 766–68; Smith, *Notable Black American Men,* pp. 624–26.

1926 • Tiger [Theodore] Flowers (1895–1927) became the first black middleweight champion of the world, defeating Harry Greb in fifteen rounds to win the title in New York City on February 26. A religious, honest, and clean-living man, he was knocked out during a fight in 1927 and died of injuries to the brain four days later. Flowers' habit of reading Bible verses earned him the nickname "Georgia Deacon."

Sources: Bennett, *Before the Mayflower*, p. 634; *The Black New Yorkers*, p. 194; *Encyclopedia of Boxing*, p. 48; Jackson and Washington, *Black Champions Challenge American Sports*, pp. 48, 60; *Jet* 95 (1 March 1999): 19; Young, *Negro Firsts in Sports*, pp. 20, 29, 31, 226.

1937 • The sole person to hold three championships and three world titles at once was Henry "Hammering Hank" Armstrong (1912–1988). During a ten-month period between 1937 and 1938, he won the featherweight, welterweight, and lightweight titles and challenged for the middleweight crown, fighting to a draw. Armstrong won twenty-seven fights in 1937 alone, twenty-six by knockout. He lost the last of his three titles, the welterweight, in 1940. Having saved little of his earnings to support himself, Armstrong became an ordained minister in 1951. Born in Columbus, Mississippi, his father was half Irish and half black and his mother was Native American. The family moved to St. Louis, Missouri when Armstrong was three years old. Small in size as a child, he had to fight to defend himself, found out that he was good at it, and decided he wanted to be a boxer. Armstrong worked on his athletic skills while in high school, where he was class president, poet laureate, and valedictorian of his graduating class. He worked on the railroad after graduation, but soon quit to pursue his boxing dream. He had his first amateur fight at the St. Louis Coliseum in 1929, knocking his opponent out in the second round. He fought professionally in Chicago and Pittsburgh, losing his first professional bout. He subsequently moved to Los Angeles, where he operated a shoeshine stand from 1931 to 1934 while waiting for boxing matches. Armstrong began to establish himself as a professional boxer in 1932. Holding three concurrent world championships was a specific goal set by the fighter and his managers, not an accident. During this winning streak he also produced and starred in *Keep Punching,* a movie based on his life. He was named Fighter of the Year in 1938 and was one of the first three inductees into the Boxing Hall of Fame in 1954; Joe Louis and Jack Dempsey were his co-inductees. Armstrong hung up his gloves in 1945, having won 145 of his 174 bouts, with 98 knockouts. He tried several lines of activity after retirement, but settled on the dream his grandmother had had for him: minister of the Gospel. He returned to St. Louis in 1972, staying there until he returned to Los Angeles in 1978. He was a resident of that city when he died. The International Boxing Hall of Fame elected him to membership in 1990. Armstrong's father's name was Henry Jackson Jr., his mother's maiden name was Armstrong. Sources do not reveal his reasons for choosing to fight under the name of Armstrong. The fact that his mother died when he was six years old may have had something to do with the decision.

Henry Armstrong

Sources: *The Black New Yorkers*, p. 240; *Encyclopedia of Black America*, p. 134; *Encyclopedia of Boxing*, p. 12; Jones and Washington, *Black Champions Challenge American Sports*, pp. 71–73; Young, *Negro Firsts in Sports*, p. 226; Smith, *Notable Black American Men*, pp. 26–29.

1938 • Joe Louis [Joseph Louis Barrow] (1914–1981) became the first black of his rank to score a first-round knockout when he defeated Max Schmeling on June 22, immediately becoming the first black national sports hero. He was the first black to hold a boxing title ten years or more, maintaining the title of world champion for almost twelve years. He was also the first black heavyweight champion since Jack Johnson, in 1908. Universally loved, Louis fought Max Baer at New York on September 24, 1935, and became the first black fighter to draw a million-dollar gate. The following year he was the first black to win *Ring* magazine's Fighter of the Year award. By 1949 Louis had become the first black to defend his title successfully twenty-five times, and in 1954 he became the first black heavyweight and one of the first three boxers elected to Boxing's Hall of Fame. Born in Alabama, this son of a sharecropping cotton farmer fought often as a child. At the age of eight he knocked out four boyhood tormentors, and by 1934 he turned professional. A folk hero, his success broke down many barriers to black participation in athletics in other areas. Louis' personal integrity contributed to his popularity, and so did his services to the armed services during World War II. He volunteered for the army in 1942, received the Legion of Merit medal when he was discharged in 1945, and had fought title matches for the benefit of army and navy relief funds. In his later years, problems with the Internal Revenue Service plagued him. He was charged with having an enormous unpaid tax bill but was eventually able to negotiate a settlement. After suffering an aneurysm in 1977, Louis was paralyzed and wheelchair-bound. There are many tributes to Louis' memory: The U.S. Mint struck a coin with his face on one side and victories on the other in 1982, and he was the subject of a Postal Service commemorative stamp in 1993.

Sources: Cantor, *Historic Landmarks of Black America,* pp. 24–25; *The Black New Yorkers,* p. 240; *Encyclopedia of Black America,* p. 133; Young, *Negro Firsts in Sports,* pp. 98–114, 228–29; Smith, *Notable Black American Men,* pp. 740–42.

1947 • The first televised heavyweight boxing championship bout was between Joe Louis and Jersey Joe Walcott (Arnold Raymond Cream, 1914–1994) on December 5 from Madison Square Garden. In 1951 Walcott and Ezzard "Quiet Tiger" Charles (1921–1975) fought in the first heavyweight championship prizefight telecast from coast-to-coast. In the fifteen-round bout held in Philadelphia's Municipal Stadium on June 5, Walcott outpointed Charles. Then thirty-seven years old, Walcott was the oldest person ever to win the heavyweight title. The first prizefight heavyweight championship bout televised on large-screen was the Joe Louis match with Lee Savold. The American Telephone and Telegraph Company telecast the event by microwave to the Empire State Building and later by coaxial cable closed-circuit to movie theaters in six cities. The fight was held in New York City on June 15; Louis won the scheduled fifteen-round fight in the sixth.

Sources: Ashe, *A Hard Road to Glory,* vol. 2, p. 330; Chalk, *Pioneers in Sports,* pp. 191–93; *Encyclopedia of Black America,* p. 133; *Encyclopedia of Boxing,* p. 149; Kane, *Famous First Facts,* p. 652.

1958 • Sugar Ray [Walker Smith] Robinson Jr. (1921–1989) became the first black fighter to hold the middleweight title on five separate occasions. He lived like a champion, drove flashy cars, and enjoyed fun and nightlife, but he was always well prepared for his fights. In 202 professional fights Robinson lost only 19, and was never knocked out. The Detroit, Michigan, native was ten years old when he began to go to a gymnasium to watch amateur boxer Joe Louis. Two years later he and his mother moved to Harlem in New York City. He had several odd jobs, including dancing as a street performer. He began to box at age fourteen and used the American Athletics Union card of a Ray Robinson, because as Walker Smith he was under age. Somehow he became "Sugar Ray." He went to high school for three years. He did not graduate, but his career as an amateur boxer was accelerating. He won the Golden Gloves tournament in 1939 and 1940 in featherweight and lightweight divisions, and the last win marked the end of his amateur career. Robinson won his first professional fight later in 1940, and had fought both champions and contenders by 1942, and won the Fighter of the Year award that year. World War II interrupted Robinson's onslaught on boxing. He was inducted into the U.S. Army and joined Joe Louis' boxing troop in 1943. He won the first of his titles—welterweight—in December 1946. His first middleweight titles came when he defeated the middleweight champions of the Netherlands and Germany. He was named boxer of the year in 1950 by the New York Boxing Writers Association and won the J. Neil Robinson Memorial Plaque. In 1951 he defeated Jake La Motta to win the world middleweight title. He lost the title in July 1951, but regained it two months later. Robinson retired from boxing briefly after losing a fight for the light heavyweight title in June 1952 and took a foray into show business as a tap dancer. He held the title once again when he defeated Carl "Bobo" Olson. Once more he lost the title, regaining it in 1958 by defeating Carmen Basilio. He moved to Los Angeles in 1965, after retiring from boxing. He became a member of the Boxing Hall of Fame in 1967. Robinson is reputed to have been either one of the best or the best prizefighter in history, praised for his footwork and hand speed. In a career that featured 175 victories, he had 110 knockouts. He developed extensive business investments and also opened a foundation for Los Angeles' inner city children. During his boxing career, he sometimes donated his purses to charity. He was in a medical facility in Culver City, California, when he died from Alzheimer's disease.

Sources: *Current Biography 1951,* p. 526; *Encyclopedia of Black America,* pp. 111–12; Robinson, *Historical Negro Biographies,* p. 246; Smith, *Notable Black American Men,* pp. 1027–29.

The Record for Most Knockouts

In 1963 Archie Moore (1913–1998), former light-heavyweight boxing champion, set the record for the most knockouts during his twenty-seven-year career that ended this year. Moore, who was noted for not telling people how old he was, won the light heavyweight title in 1952. He was champion for eleven years. In 228 career fights, he knocked out 141 opponents. He was, according to biographers, forty-nine when he ended his career with a knockout of his opponent in 1963. He fought for the heavyweight title twice, but lost each time. According to Moore, he was born in Collinsville, Illinois, in 1916; Moore's mother is reported to have said the place was Benoit, Illinois, and the year was 1913. Moore had heart surgery a few years before his death and experienced severely declining health in his last few weeks of life. According to the record books, he died at age eighty-four in a San Diego, California, hospice; if he could, Moore would probably say he was eighty-one when he succumbed.

Sources: Salzman, *Encyclopedia of African-American Culture and History,* Supplement, p. ix.

1960 • Floyd Patterson (1935–2006) became the first black to regain the heavyweight title. Born to an extremely poor family in Waco, North Carolina, he developed his famous peek-a-boo defense as an amateur. After winning the championship in 1956, Patterson lost his heavyweight title to Ingemar Johansson on June 26 and regained it nearly a year later when he knocked out Johansson in the fifth round. When he first won the championship, Patterson was the youngest ever at twenty-one years of age. He was also the first man to win the heavyweight championship twice. Patterson won an Olympic medal in 1952 and became the first black Olympic medallist to win a world title. Sonny Liston knocked him out at 2:06 of the first round to win the heavyweight title in 1962; in the rematch Patterson lasted four seconds longer than he did in the first match. After retiring from boxing, he became the owner of the Huguenot Boxing Club.

Sources: Ashe, *A Hard Road to Glory,* vol. 2, pp. 90–92; Chalk, *Pioneers of Black Sports,* pp. 194–95, 198–99; *Encyclopedia of Black America,* p. 133; *Encyclopedia of Boxing,* p. 105; *Contemporary Black Biography,* vol. 19, pp. 171–74; *Who's Who among African Americans,* 14th ed., p. 1008.

1963 • The first and only person to win five championships in boxing was Emile Griffith (1938–), of the Virgin Islands. First a welterweight champion, he later moved into the middleweight division.

Sources: Chalk, *Pioneers of Black Sports,* p. 189; *Encyclopedia of Boxing,* p. 55; Jones and Washington, *Black Champions Challenge American Sports,* pp. 130, 131, 132.

1970 • Joe Frazier (1944–), who won the Olympic gold medal in Japan in 1964, became the first American Olympic heavyweight champion to win the heavyweight title of the world. Frazier has contributed much to the annals of boxing history. As heavyweight champion, he had the highest knockout percentage in history and had been knocked down but never knocked out, although he was the victim of a technical knockout at least once. Frazier grew up on his family's farm in his Beaufort, South Carolina. He was the youngest in his family of twelve living brothers and sisters. The Frazier family was the first in the Laurel Bay section of Beaufort to have a television set, and the family spent considerable time watching boxing, which comprised a large part of the available programming. Frazier was about eight years old when he vowed to fulfill an uncle's prophecy that he, Frazier, could be "the next Joe Louis." He began working toward that end by making his own punching bag out of materials common on the farm and being diligent in its use. School was not high on his list of priorities, and he dropped out at age fourteen. Soon thereafter racial tensions

Joe Frazier with Muhammad Ali

caused him to leave Beaufort for New York. After a short time, Frazier moved to Philadelphia, Pennsylvania, where he had relatives, and where he found work at a slaughterhouse after a while. This job allowed him more unorthodox boxing practice: He used hanging sides of beef as punching bags. He was overweight when he joined the Philadelphia Police Athletic Gym and realized his skills were nowhere near as good as he had thought they were. Hard work helped him trim his weight and improve his skills, and in 1962 he won the Philadelphia Golden Gloves novice heavyweight title. Frazier won the Middle Atlantic Golden Gloves heavyweight championship three years in a row (1962 to 1964). During his entire amateur career, he had only one loss. Originally accepted as an alternate on the Olympics team, an injury to a starter gave Frazier his chance to excel. He won the gold medal despite the fact that he had hurt his left thumb in an earlier contest. Frazier turned professional in 1965. In 1971, in the first of his classic battles with Muhammad Ali, Frazier won by a unanimous decision. Although there was no knockout, both fighters had to go to the hospital. Frazier lost his title to George Foreman in 1973. The title was up for grabs again in Manila in 1975, when Ali and Frazier met for the third time; this time Frazier lost when the towel was thrown in the fifteenth round. He had cataract surgery that same year, and trouble with his vision led to his retirement in 1976. The musical group that had been a part-time venture while he was boxing became "Smokin' Joe and the Knockouts," a full-time group that received favorable reviews as it toured the U.S. He also bought his old training gymnasium, owned a restaurant, and ran a limousine service. He made one attempt to fight again in 1981, but quit for good after that. He received the New York Police Department Award of Honor and the World Boxing Association Living Legend award in 1995.

Sources: *Contemporary Black Biography,* vol. 19, pp. 74–78; *Who's Who among African Americans,* 26th ed., p. 434.

1971 • The first black boxers to draw a multimillion dollar gate were Joe Frazier (1944–) and Muhammad Ali (1942–) in their fight at Madison Square Garden on March 8. After fifteen rounds, Frazier won the match on points. The bout grossed some $20 million, and each fighter received $2.5 million. Frazier and Ali fought each other three times. Two of their bouts, the first and third, are considered classics and examples of endurance and courage.

Sources: Ashe, *A Hard Road to Glory,* vol. 3, p. 345; Chalk, *Pioneers of Black Sports,* pp. 204–8; *Contemporary Black Biography,* vol. 19, p. 74; *Encyclopedia of Boxing,* pp. 49–50, 199; Jones and Washington, *Black Champions Challenge American Sports,* pp. 160–61; Smith, *Notable Black American Men,* pp. 17–21; *Who's Who among African Americans,* 26th ed., p. 18 (Ali), 434 (Frazier).

1978 • The first black prizefight to gross more than a five-million dollar gate was the bout at the Louisiana Superdome in New Orleans on September 15. Muhammad Ali (1942–) won in a thirteen-round unanimous decision over Leon Spinks and became the first to win the heavyweight title three times. He held the title from 1964 to 1967, 1974 to 1978, and 1978 to 1979. Almost all of Ali's fights became events with enormous popular appeal. Ali was born Marcellus Cassius Clay in Louisville, Kentucky. He changed his name in 1963 when he became a Muslim. When he burst upon the boxing scene, he was articulate, outspoken, and given to writing poetry (sometimes in rhyme, sometimes in blank verse). He won an Olympic gold medal in Italy in 1960, six Kentucky Golden Gloves championships, and one National Golden Gloves title. He has, however, suffered both highs and lows in terms of public opinion. His lows became evident after he refused to serve in Vietnam because, as a Muslim, he was a conscientious objector. In 1967 the New York State Athletic Commission and the World Boxing Association suspended Ali's boxing license, and the heavyweight title was taken from him. He was sentenced to prison, but released on appeal. His conviction was overturned three years later. He returned to winning boxing matches in November 1970, and after losing the championship to Joe Frazier in Manila in 1971, he won it back in their 1974 rematch. Personal health became a problem for Ali in 1980 when he was misdiagnosed as having a thyroid condition. He fought his sixty-first and last fight in a losing effort in 1981. In 1982 he began to be treated for Parkinson's Disease. As he neared the end of his boxing career, he became more active in politics, supporting Jimmy Carter for the presidency in 1980. In 1985 he worked with his advisors to secure freedom for four Americans in Lebanon who had been kidnapped, but was unsuccessful. Toward the end of the 1990s he seemed to become a beloved figure once more. He was chosen to light the Olympic torch in Atlanta in 1996. The young Ali became known as "The Greatest." His autobiography, *The Greatest—My Own Story,* was published in 1975.

Sources: Ashe, *A Hard Road to Glory,* vol. 3, p. 100; *Contemporary Black Biography,* vol. 2, pp. 1–4; *Encyclopedia of Boxing,* pp. 7–10; Kane, *Famous First Facts,* p. 508; Salzman, *Encyclopedia of African-American Culture and History,* Supplement, p. 5.

1980 • The first black woman commissioner on the Michigan State Boxing Commission was Hiawatha Knight.

Sources: *Jet* 57 (6 March 1980): 18.

1987 • The first black to win boxing titles in five different weight classes was Thomas "Hit Man" Hearns (1958–). In 1977 he was national NAA light welterweight champion and national Golden Gloves welterweight champion. His titles include the vacant USBA welterwight title (March 2, 1980); the WBA welterweight title (August 2, 1980); the WBC junior middleweight title (December 3, 1982); the world middleweight title (April 15, 1985); and the WBC light heavyweight title (February 1987). Hearns was among the boxers who dominated the middle divisions during the 1980s. He was noteworthy because of the strength that allowed him to stop his opponent and end the fight quickly with an early knockout. Hearns was born in Grand Junction, Tennessee, or Memphis, Tennessee; sources disagree. He grew up, however, in Detroit, Michigan, where he showed an early interest in boxing. At age ten he had a fight in the gymnasium near his home. Later he joined the amateur team at a noted Detroit recreation center and dropped out of the twelfth grade to concentrate on boxing. Hearns won the WBO Super Middleweight title in 1988 and the WBA light-heavyweight title in 1991, bringing the number of titles he had held to seven. He continued to fight during the decade of the nineties and won another title, the IBO cruiserweight title, in England in 1999. When he defended this title in 2000, he sprained his ankle in the second round and was unable to continue. He retired from boxing after this fight. Hearns was named Fighter of the Year by two different boxing-related entities in 1980 (*Ring Magazine* and the New York Boxing Writers Association). *Ring* gave him this honor again in 1985. He developed business interests after his retirement.

Thomas Hearns

Sources: Ashe, *A Hard Road to Glory,* vol. 3, pp. 347–50; *Negro Almanac, 1989,* pp. 980–81; *Contemporary Black Biography,* vol. 29, pp. 74–77; *Current Biography,* 1983, pp. 178–82; Salzman, *Encyclopedia of African-American Culture and History,* Supplement, p. 32; *Who's Who among African Americans,* 26th ed., p. 563.

1994 • In ten rounds, George Edward Foreman (1948–) knocked out Michael Moorer in the heavyweight championship fight in Las Vegas on November 5 and regained the title he had lost to Muhammad Ali twenty years earlier. In doing so, he became the oldest man to hold the world heavyweight championship. The Associated Press named him Male Athlete of the Year in this year. Foreman was born in Davis County, Texas, and began his boxing career while he was working with a Job Corps training program in an Oregon conservation camp. He won the Corps Diamond Belt Tournament while there. He won an Olympic gold medal in the 1968 games held in Mexico. In 1969 he turned professional, leaving the amateur rank with a record of nineteen of his twenty-two bouts, which were held in a two-year period. The World Boxing Association named him Boxer of the Year in 1974. At one point in his professional career he had won thirty-seven consecutive bouts. He retired from boxing in 1997. In recent years, Foreman has become familiar to television viewers who have seen him promote his "Lean Mean Fat Grilling Machine." He sold the rights to his name and image to the company that makes the machine for a reported $137 million in January 2000. Foreman is also a minister. His five sons are all named George: George H., George II, George III, George IV, and George V.

Sources: *Contemporary Black Biography,* vol. 15, pp. 81–84; Salzman, *Encyclopedia of African-American Culture and History,* Supplement, p. 98; *Tennessean* (10 January 1995); *Who's Who among African Americans,* 26th ed., p. 423.

1997 • Former wrestling star Chris [Christopher Lundy] Campbell (1954–) was named executive director of United States Amateur Boxing, Inc., the first black to hold that post. He was on the U.S. Olympic wrestling team in 1980 when the U.S. boycotted the Games. He was on the team again in 1992 and won a bronze medal. His appointment gave Campbell wide jurisdiction over the affairs of amateur boxing. Campbell was born in Westfield, New Jersey, and holds the J.D. degree from Cornell Law School (1987), along with the B.S. from the University of Iowa (1978), and graduate work at Iowa State University (1980–83). He held three positions as assistant wrestling coach between 1979 and 1987, working successively at Iowa State, Iowa University, and Cornell. After 1987, his positions capitalized on his training as a lawyer, serving as a corporate attorney. Campbell was the first American selected as the world's most technically prepared wrestler, in 1981. He also won the prestigious Sullivan Award, given to an amateur athlete, in that same year. He won a silver medal in world competition in 1990, and was a World Cup champion in 1981, 1983, 1984, and 1991. He also won three National Freestyle Championship titles between 1980 and 1991. He is on the USA Wrestling Board of Directors.

Sources: *Jet* 92 (21 July 1997): 52; *Who's Who among African Americans*, 26th ed., p. 203.

Laila Ali

2001 • Laila Ali (1978–) scored a majority decision in a fight with Jacqui Frazier-Lyde on June 8 at the Tuning Stone Casino in Verona, New York. This was the first pay-for-view boxing match between two black women. By all accounts, the fight lived up to hopes and expectations, with both women slugging it out. Although both women are considered highly talented boxers, the pre-fight publicity and anticipation probably was due as much to their lineage as to their talent. Each is the daughter of a legendary boxer—Muhammad Ali and Joe Frazier—and the fathers had their own rivalry and contests. Joe Frazier was there to spur his daughter on; Muhammad Ali was not, but Laila Ali's mother was present. Frazier-Lyde had hoped to run her string of consecutive knockouts to eight.

Sources: *Contemporary Black Biography*, vol. 27, pp. 5–7 (Ali); *Jet* 100 (25 June 2001): 51–54; *Tennessean* (9 June 2001); *Who's Who among African Americans*, 26th ed., p. 18 (Ali), 435 (Frazier-Lyde).

2002 • Jacqui Frazier-Lyde beat Suzette Taylor at the Pennsylvania Convention Center in Philadelphia and won the Women's International Boxing Association (WIBA) light heavyweight belt. Her father, Joe Frazier, also won the bout during his career; thus, Frazier-Lyde's win marks the first time a father and daughter have held boxing championships.

Sources: *Jet* 101 (14 February 2002): 48.

Cricket

1950 • The West Indies cricket team beat the English team for the first time in a test match in England. The teams played in a series of four cricket matches in the Test (or top-level professional) games played between national teams. After playing first at Lord's Cricket Ground, the series stood even. Next, the teams played at Trent Bridge and beat England decisively, setting several individual and team records. In the final Test match played at Oval, Kennington, the West Indies scored 503 runs and held the English batsmen to 274 runs. This victory put the West Indies among the best of the cricketing nations. They remained one of the dominant forces in world cricket after that.

Sources: *Natural History* 104 (May 1995), pp. 58–65.

Cycling

1898 • Marshall W. "Major" Taylor (1878–1932), of Indianapolis, Indiana, was the first native-born black American to win a major bicycle race. He began as a trick rider for a local cycling shop and participated in a few amateur events. Taylor won his first professional start, a half-mile handicap held at Madison Square Garden, in spite of racism in cycling. Taylor was also the first black member of an integrated professional team. Toward the end of the year, he compiled twenty-one first-place victories, thirteen second-place berths, and eleven third-place showings. Taylor was known as the "fastest bicycle rider in the world" until his 1910 retirement. He was born in Indianapolis, where his father worked as a coachman for a wealthy white family. Taylor and the son of the employing family became fast friends and it was through his friend that Taylor was tutored, learning to read and write, and became exposed to riding bicycles. Working for a bicycle shop, he rode in his first race as part of the shop team; he won the first prize gold medal at age thirteen. Taylor won more races but was also barred from the Indianapolis track after he broke a track record. By 1895 he was in Worcester, Massachusetts, having reached there by accompanying retired cyclist Louis "Birdie" Munger when Munger established a bicycle factory there. In Worcester, Taylor raced with a black club. In 1896 he raced against top amateurs in Middletown, Connecticut. Prejudice against him as a black rider did not disappear after his 1898 win. He raced in Europe for a few months in 1901, winning twenty-one of twenty-five races. He became a celebrity after this performance. He had his last European season in 1909 and raced in Salt Lake City in 1910. After retiring, Taylor tried his hand at being an inventor, but his efforts to produce a more efficient wheel for cycling were unsuccessful. Several of his other business ventures also failed to catch fire. He resurfaced to race one more time in a 1917 old-timers' race and won. Taylor fell upon hard financial times and spent his last years in Chicago, where he had gone to push sales of his self-published autobiography. The book had been published in 1929. He was in the charity ward of a Chicago hospital when he died, and he was buried in a pauper's grave. In 1948 the owner of the Schwinn Bicycle Company had Taylor's body reburied in a more desirable section of the cemetery. At the dedication ceremony, a bronze plaque commemorating his importance to cycling was installed.

Marshall W. "Major" Taylor

Sources: Alford, *Famous First Blacks,* p. 97; Ashe, *A Hard Road to Glory,* vol. 1, pp. 54–57; *Encyclopedia of Black America,* p. 143; Young, *Negro Firsts in Sports,* pp. 177–78; Smith, *Notable Black American Men,* pp. 1103–5.

Darts

1972 • Adele Nutter, the only black woman in dart championship play this year, became the first black U.S. dart champion. She was a founder and charter member of the American Dart Foundation.

Sources: *Black Sports* (April 1973), pp. 26–27.

Fencing

1969 • When she was only seventeen year old and still in high school, Ruth Carleton White (1951–) became the youngest woman and the first black American to win a national fencing championship. She held four national titles. In 1972 she was a member of the U.S. Olympic Team.

Sources: U.S. Fencing Hall of Fame, http://usfencinghalloffame.com.

1973 • Peter Westbrook (1952–) became the first black American and one of the youngest people to win the national title in saber fencing. Between 1973 and 1995, Westbrook had an unprecedented reign as the National College Athletics Association's (NCAA) saber champion thirteen times. In 1975 he won a silver team medal and a bronze individual medal at the pan American Games held in Mexico City. He was also a six-time Pan-American Games team member. Westbrook was born in St. Louis, Missouri, to a Japanese mother and African American father. His mother raised him alone in poverty in Newark, New Jersey, where the family had relocated. He learned fencing while enrolled in Essex Catholic High School, a predominantly white, all-boys school in northern Newark. In Westbrook's fencing program his teacher started him out with the saber—a military sword—instead of the foil, the weapon of most beginners. He continued fencing training at New York University, and, on becoming NCAA champmion in his junior year, he was the best college sabrist in the country. After graduating in 1974, Westbrook began his career with IBM. He later became president of the Peter Westbrook Foundation and a member of the board of directors of the U.S. Olympic Committee. The American Library Association's publications *Booklist* and *Choice* listed his memoir, *Harnessing Anger,* in the best African-American Nonfiction and Best Books for Young Adults categories.

Sources: Westbrook, *Harnessing Anger,* 1997.

1994 • Nikki V. Franke, head women's fencing coach at Temple University in Philadelphia, was the only black woman coach at a Division I school. Franke, who is an associate professor of health education at Temple, is a native of New York. She holds both a master's degree and doctorate from Temple.

Sources: *Ebony* 49 (October 1994): 10.

Football

1890 • William Henry Lewis (1868–1949) and teammate William Tecumseh Sherman Jackson became the first recorded black players on a white college football team. Lewis was captain of the Amherst team in 1891–92 and the first black to win this distinction at an Ivy League school. He was the first black All-American and was selected as a center on Walter Camp's All-American teams of 1892 and 1893. Lewis completed his law degree at Harvard and became assistant district attorney in Boston. He wrote *How to Play Football* in 1896, becoming the first black athlete known to write a book. He became line coach at Harvard while he studied law, and later he became an Assistant United States Attorney General. Jackson was also the first black track star as a runner for Amherst; he set a school record of 2 minutes 5.4 seconds for 880 yards.

Sources: Ashe, *A Hard Road to Glory,* vol. 1, pp. 22, 90–91, 97; Bennett, *Before the Mayflower,* p. 635; Logan and Winston, *Dictionary of American Negro Biography,* pp. 396–97; Henderson, *The Black Athlete,* pp. 45–46; Jones and Washington, *Black Champions Challenge American Sports,* pp. 18, 19, 22, 43.

1892 • Biddle University (now Johnson C. Smith University) in Charlotte, North Carolina, played Livingston College, Salisbury, North Carolina, in the first recorded black college football game on Thanksgiving day, winning by a 4–0 score. Two years later, Howard University, Lincoln University (Pennsylvania), and Atlanta University fielded football teams.

Sources: Ashe, *A Hard Road to Glory,* vol. 1, pp. 94–95; Bennett, *Before the Mayflower,* p. 634; Clark, *Sports Firsts,* p. 36.

Frederick "Fritz" Pollard Sr.

1916 • Frederick Douglas "Fritz" Pollard Sr. (1890–1986), a diminutive back of Brown University, became the first black to play in the Rose Bowl. Brown lost to Washington State 14–0. Pollard became the first black quarterback and head coach in professional football in 1919, when he served with the Akron Indians, a team in the American Professional Football Association, which later became the National Football League. He coached the team to a championship in 1920, and was the first black quarterback and head coach in the National Football League in 1923. In 1921 actor-activist Paul Robeson became one of Pollard's players. Pollard's career lasted through 1925. Pollard's son, Frederick Douglas Pollard Jr., continued the family's athletic tradition by playing football for North Dakota and winning a bronze medal for the high hurdles in the 1936 Olympics. Pollard Sr. was born in Chicago, Illinois. He was a star football player in high school, but was at first denied admission to Brown when he was unable to meet the foreign language requirement. He enrolled at Dartmouth, Harvard, and Bates before finally being admitted to Brown in 1915, where he was the first black football player ever at Brown. He dropped out of Brown the next year and joined the U.S. Army. His professional football career began after the end of World War I. Pollard, who was considered one of the best running backs of his day, compiled a number of "firsts," both on and off the football field. He was the first black collegiate All-American. In the business worlds of Chicago and New York, he established the first all-black investment company, published the first black-owned and black-operated tabloid in Harlem, and

The First Black Professional Football Player

In 1904 Charles W. Follis (1879–?) became the first black professional football player, for the Blues of Shelby, Ohio. He was born in Cloverdale, Virginia, and moved to Wooster, Ohio, where he played at Wooster High. One of his high school teammates was Branch Rickey, later president of the Brooklyn Dodgers baseball team. The Blues were part of the American Professional Football League, formed in Ohio in this year, and a forerunner of the National Football League, which was formed in Canton, Ohio, in the summer of 1919, the year usually taken as the date of the beginning of modern professional football.

Sources: Ashe, *A Hard Road to Glory,* vol. 1, pp. 98, 99; Clark, *Sports Firsts,* p. 40; *Encyclopedia of Football,* pp. 18–23.

was actively involved in production of some of the first all-black movies. Pollard's football achievements can perhaps be put in perspective by the reminder that the NFL did not name its second black head coach until 1989, three years after Pollard's death.

Sources: Ashe, *A Hard Road to Glory,* vol. 1, pp. 100–102; Bennett, *Before the Mayflower,* p. 634, 636; Chalk, *Pioneers of Black Sport,* pp. 216–20, 222–23; Jones and Washington, *Black Champions Challenge American Sports,* pp. 40–41; Young, *Negro Firsts in Sports,* pp. 75–76, 146, 147, 250, 251.

1921 • The first black to receive the Most Valuable College Player Award was Frederick "Duke" Slater (1898–1966), tackle with the University of Iowa's undefeated team in 1921. He became a municipal court judge in Chicago in 1948. He was the first black elected to the College Football Hall of Fame at Rutgers in 1951.

Sources: Alford, *Famous First Blacks,* p. 92; Chalk, *Pioneers of Black Sport,* pp. 220–26, 253; Jones and Washington, *Black Champions Challenge American Sports,* pp. 49–50.

1929 • The Prairie View Bowl, played on January 1, was the first black college football bowl game. It was held in Houston, Texas, and Prairie View lost to Atlanta University by a 6–0 score. The bowl was discontinued in 1961.

Sources: *Negro Almanac,* p. 1426; Young, *Negro Firsts in Sports,* p. 254.

1947 • Buddy (Claude Henry Keystone) Young (1926–1983) became the first black to score a Rose Bowl touchdown, in the University of Illinois vs. UCLA New Year's Day game. Young joined the AAFC New York Yankees in 1947 and eventually played for the Cleveland Browns from 1953 to 1955. In 1964 he became the first director of player relations for the NFL, the first black to hold an executive position with the league. His football jersey was retired by the Baltimore Colts in 1965, a first for a team. He later worked as an executive for the NFL before dying in a car accident in 1983.

Sources: Ashe, *A Hard Road to Glory,* vol. 3, p. 129; *Encyclopedia of Football,* p. 607; *Jet* 65 (25 January 1984): 53; Young, *Negro Firsts in Sports,* p. 279.

1947 • Kenny [Kenneth] William Washington (1918–1971) of UCLA became the first black professional player to break the color barrier in existence since 1933, when Joe Lillard of the Chicago Cardinals and Ray Kemp of the Pittsburgh Pirates were the last of the thirteen blacks who played in the National Football League between 1920 and 1933. It is surmised that the barrier in the NFL was broken only because the newly organized All-American Football Conference was signing black players. Washington signed with the NFL's Los Angeles Rams on March 21. Other blacks who signed in that year were Woody Strode, with the Rams on May 7; and in the All-American Conference, Bill Willis on August 6, and Marion Motley on August 9, both with the Cleveland Browns. The last NFL team to be integrated was the Washington Redskins, which signed Bobby Marshall in 1962.

Washington played for the Rams through 1948. Born in Los Angeles, California, he had been a baseball and football star as a high school student and continued to play both sports at the University of California at Los Angeles for three years. When he left UCLA no professional teams were open to him, so he played semi-professional ball and was named All-Pacific Coast halfback four times. Once he became a pro, he was able to play for only two seasons, because of knee injuries. Before he retired in 1949, he set a number of records for the Rams. Washington also had a limited career as a movie actor. He first appeared in *While Thousands Cheer* in 1940. He appeared in several more movies, including *The Jackie Robinson Story* in 1950 and *Tarzan's Dead Silence* in 1970.

Sources: Ashe, *A Hard Road to Glory,* vol. 2, pp. 108–9; vol. 3, pp. 128–30; Bennett, *Before the Mayflower,* p. 635; Salzman, *Encyclopedia of African-American Culture and History,* Supplement, p. 273; *Encyclopedia of Football,* p. 592; Jones and Washington, *Black Champions Challenge American Sports,* pp. 79, 91; Young, *Negro Firsts in Sports,* pp. 144–46.

1948 • On January 1 in New Orleans, Wally Triplett and Dennie Hoggard, members of Pennsylvania State, became the first blacks to play in the Cotton Bowl. This was one sign of the very slow and reluctant acceptance of blacks on football teams by the South. Triplett later played for the Detroit Lions and the Chicago Cardinals.

Sources: Ashe, *A Hard Road to Glory,* vol. 3, p. 121; *Encyclopedia of Football,* p. 586; *Jet* 81 (30 December–January 1992): 32.

1948 • Levi Jackson (1926–2000), a star running back, became the first black football captain at Yale University, in November of this year. Only one other black player had been captain of an Ivy League team, and that was in 1893 when William Lewis was named acting captain at Harvard. Jackson also had the distinction of being Yale's first black football player. As a fullback and punter, he was an outstanding player. When he graduated with a triple major (psychology, economics, and sociology), he had set thirteen modern Yale football records. He also played basketball while there and was the first black student in one of the institution's prestigious senior societies. He had some familiarity with Yale, having played high school football in New Haven. His father was a Yale employee, serving as a chef and steward in the campus dining halls. Jackson did not go the professional route. In 1950 he took a position with the Ford Motor Company in Detroit, and went on to hold major executive positions in labor relations and urban affairs. In 1969 Ford named him Citizen of the Year in recognition of his efforts to create opportunities for Detroit's inner-city residents after the city's 1967 riots. He was a vice president at Ford when he retired in 1983. Jackson was a native of Branford, Connecticut. He was a resident of Detroit at the time of his death.

Sources: *Jet* 99 (23 January 2001): 54; *New York Times* (29 December 2000).

1949 • The first black professional player from an all-black college was Paul "Tank" Younger (1928–2001), of Grambling. His godfather was president of the institution at the time. Younger signed with the Los Angeles Rams as a free agent; he was not drafted. He played for the Rams until 1958, when he moved to the Pittsburgh Steelers for his final season. Before his career was over, he had been a Professional Bowl player five times and had held executive positions with the San Diego Chargers and the Los Angeles Rams. Younger's success in professional ball established Grambling's reputation for nurturing future players. He was inducted into the Hall of Fame in 1993, and retired from his position with the Rams in 1995. Younger began as a tackle in college, but switched to running back. When he ended his ten-year professional playing days, he had averaged 4.6 yards per carry. He was the acknowledged star of the Rams team that won the NFL championship in 1951.

Sources: *Encyclopedia of Football,* p. 608; Jones and Washington, *Black Champions Challenge American Sports,* p. 120; *New York Times* (19 September 2001); *Who's Who among African Americans,* 14th ed., p. 1463; Young, *Negro Firsts in Sports,* p. 131.

1952 • The first black quarterback to play the Big Ten was Willie Thrower (1932–2002). In that year he helped Michigan State to a national championship. Although he was not drafted, he signed with the Chicago Bears for $8,500 as backup quarterback, becoming the first black professional quarterback in the NFL. Since the position was viewed tradition-ally as "white," Thrower played only a few downs and was active only one season, play-ing his first and last game at Soldier Field on October 18 against the San Francisco 49ers. In that game he relieved George Blanda and completed 3 out of 8 passes for 27 yards. He had one interception in the game and the team lost 35–28. The Bears cut him from the team in 1954, and after that he played with the Winnipeg Blue Bombers in the Canadian Football League and also with a semiprofessional team in Toronto. Off the field, Thrower was a social worker in New York City and in his hometown of New Kensington, Pennsyl-vania, where he also opened two taverns. Thrower was recognized in an exhibit about black players mounted in the professional Football Hall of Fame twenty-five years after he broke the color barrier. He died at home of a heart attack in February 2002. The first black quarterback to play professionally with any regularity was Marlin Briscoe in 1968 for the Denver Broncos, then in the American Football League.

Sources: Ashe, *A Hard Road to Glory,* vol. 3, p. 125, 143; Chalk, *Pioneers of Black Sports,* pp. 239–40; Clark, *Sports Firsts,* p. 50; *Encyclopedia of Football,* p. 583; *New York Times* (22 February 2002).

1957 • The first black college coach to reach 200 victories was Arnett W. Mumford (?–1966), of Southern University in Baton Rouge, Louisiana. He reached that mark in Octo-ber, when his team defeated Langston University of Oklahoma. Previously Mumford coached at Bishop College, Jarvis Christian College, and Texas College. Fred "Pop" Long followed him in reaching the 200 victory mark. Both men died in 1966. Although Alonzo Smith "Jake" Gaither (1905–1994) of Florida Agricultural and Mechanical University has been called the first, it was not until 1969 that "the Papa Rattler," as he was known, achieved at that level.

Sources: Fred Whitted, letter to the author, 6 June 1996.

1958 • Jim [James] Nathaniel Brown (1936–) was the first black athlete to win the Jim Thorpe Trophy; he won it again in 1965. He is a football legend at his alma mater, Syra-cuse University, and played nine years with the Cleveland Browns. In the 1960s he also be-came the first player to score 126 career touchdowns. He later became an actor, producer, sports commentator, and marketing executive. Brown, who is still heralded as one of foot-ball's greatest running backs, is also noted for his continuing efforts to help the black com-munity, reflecting his belief in the power of economic development. He was born on St. Simons Island, Georgia, and reared by his great-grandmother until his mother, who had moved to Long Island, New York, sent for him when he was seven years old. His adjust-ment to his new surroundings was facilitated by his aptness for almost all sports. By the time he was a high school senior, more than forty colleges and universities were recruit-ing him. Syracuse did not make good use of Brown until he replaced an injured player in a football game during his sophomore year. After that, he was a starter. Before his Syracuse career was over, he had earned three football letters, three lacrosse letters, two basketball letters, and two track letters. The Cleveland Browns made Brown their first-round draft pick in 1957, the year he graduated from Syracuse. He was the Rookie of the Year in 1958. Unlike many athletes, Brown was still a star player when he retired in 1966. He was also making movies for Hollywood producers, and when his film career stalled, Brown had limited success in producing his own films. He had more success in his business and com-munity activities. He was the founder of Vital Issues, Plus in 1986. The organization was targeted toward improvement of life management skills and personal growth techniques among prison inmates and inner-city gang members. It was renamed Amer-I-Can in 1989 and based in Los Angeles, where Brown himself conducted sessions from his home. The much-honored Brown was inducted into the Professional Football Hall of Fame in 1971 and in 1994 was named one of the most important sports figures of the preceding forty years by *Sports Illustrated.* His career touchdown mark (126) stood for almost thirty years, until it was broken by Jerry Rice in 1994.

Sources: Bontemps, *Famous Negro Athletes,* pp. 119–31; *Contemporary Black Biography,* vol. 11, pp. 21–25; *Current Biography,* 1964, pp. 5–58; Henderson, *The Black Athlete,* pp.

200–204; *Historical Negro Biographies,* pp. 169–90; Toppin, *Biographical History of Blacks,* p. 259; Salzman, *Encyclopedia of African-American Culture and History,* vol. 1, pp. 448–50.

1961 • Ernie [Ernest] Davis (1939–1962), a Syracuse University running back, was cited as the first black player of the year and winner of the Heisman Trophy. Other early black Heisman winners were Mike Garrett in 1965, and O. J. Simpson in 1968. Davis was the first draft pick in both the NFL and the AFL, but he never played a moment of professional football since he was diagnosed with leukemia a few days before the college all-star game against the Green Bay Packers.

Sources: Ashe, *A Hard Road to Glory,* vol. 2, p. 12; Bennett, *Before the Mayflower,* p. 635; Henderson, *The Black Athlete,* pp. 203–4; Young, *Negro Firsts in Sports,* p. 281.

1965 • Emlen "The Gremlin" Tunnel (1925–1975) was the first black coach in the National Football League. Tunnel had played for the New York Giants from 1948 to 1958 and the Green Bay Packers from 1959 to 1961. During his career he played in nine Professional Bowls and was an All-Professional four times. The New York Giants signed him as assistant defensive coach on May 1. In 1967 he became the first black elected to the professional Hall of Fame.

Sources: Ashe, *A Hard Road to Glory,* vol. 3, pp. 130–31, 355–56; Bennett, *Before the Mayflower,* p. 635, 637; *Encyclopedia of Football,* p. 586.

1966 • Lowell Perry (1931–2001) became the first black broadcaster in the National Football League, when CBS hired him as an analyst. A native of Ypsilanti, Michigan, Perry was an All-American receiver at the University of Michigan, he played for the Pittsburgh Steelers in 1956, after a tour of duty in the U.S. Army. Sidelined by an injury in his sixth game, he became the first black assistant coach, coaching receivers, in the NFL's modern history, when transferred by the Steelers from player to coach in 1957. He left this position after a year to complete his studies at the Detroit College of Law. Perry held several positions as an attorney, serving with the National Labor Relations Board in 1962–63 and joining the Chrysler Corporation legal team in 1963. His other positions included a brief stint as chairman of the Equal Employment Opportunity Commission in 1975 and positions in Michigan corporate and government offices. From 1991 to 1996 he was director of Michigan's labor department, and from 1996 until his retirement in 1999, he was director of the Michigan Office of Urban Programs. Perry's short stay in the NFL was not free of bigotry, once being barred (along with other black players) from participating in a pre-game parade. He was a resident of Detroit when he died of complications from cancer.

Sources: *New York Times* (11 January 2001); Obituary, *Who's Who among African Americans,* 14th ed., pp. 1474–75.

1966 • The first black assistant coach in the American Football League was Rommie Loudd (1934–1998), a former star linebacker at UCLA, who coached for the New England Patriots. During the early part of the 1980s, Loudd was a player for the NFL Chicago Bears and the AFL Los Angeles Chargers and Boston Patriots. He moved to the Patriots' front office as personnel director after his coaching turn, and stayed with them until he left in the early 1970s for an executive position with the Florida Blazers, a team in the ill-fated World Football League. When Loudd left football, his life took a temporary wrong turn, and he was convicted and imprisoned for a drug offense. He moved later to Miami, Florida, where he was an associate minister in a Baptist church, served on the Miami-Dade County Correction Department citizens' advisory board, and hosted a sports show that was broadcast on county jail TV.

Sources: *New York Times* (14 May 1988); (18 May 1998).

1971 • Alan Cedric Page (1945–) became the first defensive player in the history of the NFL to receive the Most Valuable Player Award. Known as the NFL's Marathon Man, he was the first active NFL player to complete a full 26.2-mile marathon. Page was also a marathon football player. In fifteen seasons with the Minnesota Vikings and the Chicago Bears, he never missed a game. A practicing attorney, on November 3, 1992, he was elected to the

Minnesota supreme court. Page was born in Canton, Ohio, growing up in a family that emphasized the value of education. He enrolled at the University of Notre Dame and received his B.A. in political science in 1967. He was a star football player at Notre Dame, winning three letters and being named All-America defensive end. He was the first-round draft pick of the Minnesota Vikings in 1967. He played with the Vikings until 1978, moving to the Bears where he played until he retired in 1982. Always a celebrated NFL player, Page was elected to the Pro Football Hall of Fame in 1988. He was at the time the Assistant Attorney General in Minnesota. Page obtained his law degree from the University of Minnesota Law School in 1978.

Sources: *Encyclopedia of Football,* p. 529; Hornsby, *Milestones in Twentieth Century African-American History,* p. 502; Smith, *Notable Black American Men,* pp. 899–901; *Who's Who among African Americans,* 26th ed., p. 957.

1973 • On September 16, O. J. [Orenthal James] Simpson (1947–) of the Buffalo Bills was the first black to rush 250 yards in one game. In his years with the NFL he set records for running the most games in a season with 100 yards or more (11 in 1973), the most rushing attempts in a season (332 in 1975), and the most yards gained rushing in a single game (273 in 1976). He began his professional career with the Bills in 1969 and remained with them for nine years. He played his final season (1978–79) with the San Francisco 49ers. Simpson played in the Pro Bowl in 1972, 1974, 1975, and 1976. The San Francisco native graduated from the University of Southern California, where he ran for 3,295 yards, scored thirty-four touchdowns, and led the Trojans to a national championship. In 1968 he received the Heisman Trophy, was named Rose Bowl Football Player of the Year, and received the Walter Camp Award, the Maxwell Award, and the *Sporting News* college player of the year award. Simpson was named NFL Player of the Decade in 1979, and was named to the College Football Hall of Fame (1983) as well as the Professional Football Hall of Fame (1985). He was a movie actor while playing football and after his retirement from football. He worked for ABC-TV sports from 1969 to 1977, for almost the entire time that he played football. He continued this endeavor after he retired from football, spending four years (1978–82) working for NBC TV Sports, three years (1983–86) as the color commentator on *Monday Night Football,* and serving as the co-host of *NFL Live* in 1989. For a time he was prominent in TV commercials and also owner of his own TV production company. In January 1995, Simpson went on trial charged with the 1994 murder of his ex-wife Nicole and her friend Ronald Goldman. He was acquitted of the murder charges but later lost the wrongful death civil suit filed by the families of the victims. In 2008 he was convicted of armed robbery and kidnapping of sports memorabilia collectors in Las Vegas and sentenced to at least nine years in prison, with a maximum of thirty-three years.

O. J. Simpson

Sources: *Contemporary Black Biography,* vol., 15, pp. 190–93; *Encyclopedia of Football,* p. 327; *Great Athletes,* vol. 16, pp. 2341–43; Salzman, *Encyclopedia of African-American Culture and History,* Supplement, p. 211; *Who's Who among African Americans,* 14th ed. 1179 .

1973 • John Hicks held the position as tackle with the Ohio State University Buckeyes from 1970 to 1973, but missed 1972 due to a knee injury. He went to the Rose Bowl during each of his active seasons, becoming the first person to play in three Rose Bowls. In his last year at Ohio State, Hicks won the Lombardi Award as the most outstanding lineman in the country. He also won the Outland Trophy awarded to the best interior lineman in the country. The New York Giants drafted him in the first round, and he went on to become the NFL's Rookie of the Year. He later played for the Pittsburgh Steelers. Hicks, along with sixteen other players and coaches, were enshrined in the National Football Foundation and College Football Hall of Fame.

Sources: *Jet* 101 (14 January 2002): 46.

1974 • Leo Miles (1931–1995) became the first black to officiate during a Super Bowl game. He was the head linesman. The long-time athletic director at Howard University in Washington, D.C., was a game official for twenty-two years. His connection with the NFL did not end when he stopped officiating. Miles spent the last five years of his life working at NFL New York headquarters, where he served as a supervisor of officials, evaluating on-field performance. His dedicated service to college and professional sports led to his induction into several regional halls of fame. He died of a heart attack while hospitalized in Arlington, Virginia.

Sources: *Jet* 88 (16 October 1995): 48.

1974 • The National Football League's first black starting quarterback was Joe "Jefferson Street" Gilliam Jr. (1951?–2000), who played for the Pittsburgh Steelers. He was an eleventh round draft pick for the Steelers in 1972, but was elevated to starting quarterback during a Players' Association strike. After he joined the team, he played superlatively, but lost his starting job after his third straight win. Shortly after he was benched, Gilliam turned to drugs, and the Steelers waived him the following year. He played briefly after that for the New Orleans Saints, but his problem with drugs was with him well into the 1990s. His circumstances were so desperate that at one time he pawned his two Super Bowl rings. Gilliam was a standout quarterback at Tennessee State University, his alma mater. Despite the briefness of his stay in the NFL, he is given credit for paving the way for other black quarterbacks to enter the league in the modern era.

Sources: *Jet* 89 (29 January 1996): 55; *Tennessean* (22 January 1996).

1979 • Willie Jefferies (1939–) became the head coach at Wichita State, the first at a major white institution. Jefferies had coached at South Carolina State (his alma mater), Wichita State, and Howard University. In 2010 he was elected into the College Football Hall of Fame.

Sources: *Jet* 56 (22 March 1979): 48, 117 (14 June 2010): 47.

1983 • The first major black player to sign with the United States Football League was Herschel Walker (1962–), who signed with the New Jersey Gremlins. When the USFL collapsed in 1986, the Dallas Cowboys signed Walker. In 1989 he went to the Minnesota Vikings. Walker had been an outstanding player at the University of Georgia, where he set a NCAA freshman rushing record of 1,616 yards and was the first freshman to finish in the top ten in votes for the Heisman Trophy, which he won. A native of Wrightsville, Georgia, Walker played with the Philadelphia Eagles and the New York Giants after the Vikings, before returning to the Dallas Cowboys in 1996; and, while playing with the USFL, he was a three-time All-American, the leading rusher twice, and the 1985 Most Valuable Player. Walker was a Pro Bowl player in both the USFL and the NFL.

Sources: *Contemporary Black Biography,* vol. 1, pp. 235–36; *Who's Who among African Americans,* 26th ed., pp. 1271–72.

1986 • Walter Jerry Payton (1954–1999) was the first black player to gain more than 20,000 yards. The number-one draft choice of the Chicago Bears in 1975, he set NFL records for the most rushing touchdowns (110), most all-purpose running yards (21,803), most rushing yards (16,726), most seasons with at least 1,000 rushing yards (10), and set a new NFL record for the most rushing yards in a game (275 in 1977). He led the NFC in rushing five times, and in two games rushed 200 or more yards. He was with the Bears when they won the Super Bowl in 1985, fulfilling one of his goals. His career ended on January 10, 1988, with a total of 16,726 rushing yards. The Columbia, Mississippi, native graduated from Jackson State University, Jackson, Mississippi, where he set an all-time NCAA record of sixty-six touchdowns, scored 464 total points, and set nine school records. He was named College Player of the Year and an All-American. His stature as a professional was recognized when the Bears retired his uniform number, 34. Although he had a serious interest in music while growing up, Payton became a football star in high school and was named to the all-conference team three years in a row. He also played basketball and baseball and played the drum in the school band. When the Bears drafted him, they offered him the highest salary ever paid to a football player from Mississippi. After his retirement from football, he kept active by racing cars and boats and by attending to the affairs of Walter Payton, Inc., his personal investment company. He was inducted into the

Football Hall of Fame in 1993. A public memorial tribute was held at Chicago's Soldier Field after his death from cancer; more than 20,000 people attended.

Sources: *Great Athletes,* vol. 14, pp. 1968–71; *Contemporary Black Biography,* vol. 11, pp. 189–93; *Jet* 71 (27 October 1986): 52; 96 (22 November 1999): 51–56; Salzman, *Encyclopedia of African-American Culture and History,* vol. 2, pp. 1017–18, 2116.

1988 • Johnny Grier (1947–) was the first black referee in the National Football League.

Sources: *Jet* 74 (18 April 1988): 46; *Who's Who Among Black Americans,* 26th ed., p. 500.

1988 • Doug Lee Williams (1955–) was the first black quarterback to start a Super Bowl game. Playing for the Washington Redskins, he was their starting quarterback in Super Bowl XXII. The Redskins defeated the Denver Broncos by the score of 42–10; Williams passed for a record 340 yards, tied the touchdown record with four, and was named the game's Most Valuable Player (a "first" for a black quarterback). A graduate of Grambling State University (Louisiana), he was also the first black quarterback from a black college to be chosen in the first round of the NFL draft. Born in Zachary, Louisiana, Williams had impressive statistics as a high school quarterback, but only Southern and Grambling (both all-black, Louisiana schools) recruited him. His record at Grambling was such that he finished fourth in the running for the Heisman Trophy. Drafted by the Tampa Bay Buccaneers in 1978, he made the NFL All-Rookie Team. He remained with Tampa until 1982, when personal problems, related to his wife's serious illness and subsequent death, and contract negotiations with the Buccaneers led him to return to Zachary. New opportunities became available with the inauguration of the USFL, and Williams signed with the Oklahoma Outlaws in 1983. Concerned about the future of the USFL (which folded in 1986), he took a coaching job at Southern University in 1985, but returned to playing when the Redskins beckoned in 1986. He retired from professional football in 1989. After a few years spent following business ventures, Williams turned back to his love of football and began coaching, first at his old high school, then as an assistant coach at the U.S. Naval Academy, and later as head coach at Morehouse College. He returned home literally in 1998 when he was named head football coach at his alma mater, Grambling. The Doug Williams Foundation, established in 1988, is an example of his concern for education and fight against drugs. In 2001 he was one of five players and two coaches inducted into the College Football Hall of Fame.

Sources: *Contemporary Black Biography,* vol. 22, pp. 196–99; *Jet* 81 (16 April 1990): 51; 93 (2 February 1998): 19; 99 (14 May 2001): 52; *Who's Who among African Americans,* 26th ed., p. 1337.

1990 • Eddie G. Robinson (1919–2007) of Grambling State University (Louisiana) became the first college coach of any race to win 408 games in a career. In 1978 he was the first black coach ever to be considered seriously for the position of head coach of the Los Angles Rams. Robinson has sent more players to the pros than any other black coach: sixty-nine as of 1988. He was born in Jackson, Louisiana, but grew up in Baton Rouge, Louisiana. He attributes his interest in coaching to an early age, when he would watch what coaches did while he was attending games. By the time he was in high school, he was organizing street football leagues for neighborhood children. Robinson played football both in high school and at Leland College (Louisiana), where he was the star quarterback. He also attended his first coaching clinic while there. He took his first coaching job at Grambling in 1941; he would be the head coach there for fifty-four of the next fifty-six years, coaching in high school in 1945 and 1946 when World War II kept Grambling from fielding a team. Robinson's coaching credentials defy comparison. The Grambling Tigers joined the Southwest Conference in 1959, and between 1959 and 1994 they were conference champions or co-champions sixteen times. Robinson's coaching record for the same period was 397 wins in 555 games.

He surpassed Alabama's Bear Bryant's then winning record of 323 games in 1985. In 1988 Robinson had the distinction of having been the college coach of the first black quarterback to play in a Super Bowl. Doug Williams, who was the Most Valuable Player of

The NFL's First Modern Black Head Coach

In 1989 Arthur "Art" Shell Jr. (1946–) became the first black head coach in modern NFL history and only the second in all NFL history when he was appointed coach of the Los Angeles Raiders. The first of all time was Fritz Pollard in 1923. Shell, who was born in Charleston, South Carolina, had an illustrious career in professional football before he became a professional head coach. He graduated from Maryland State (now the University of Maryland-Eastern Shore) in 1968 and was drafted by the Oakland Raiders that same year. He was an offensive lineman with them for fifteen seasons, during which he made the Professional Bowl eight times, played in over 200 games, and earned two Super Bowl rings. He was a Raider assistant coach for seven years before being named to the top coaching job. The franchise had moved to Los Angeles the year before Shell first assumed his position as offensive line coach. In 1995 he was relieved of his position as Raiders head coach. The Raiders had made the playoffs several times during his first five years, but did not make the playoffs for the 1994–95 season. He went immediately to the Kansas City Chiefs as offensive line coach, and by 1997 he was offensive line coach for the Atlanta Falcons. Shell was inducted into the Professional Football Hall of Fame in 1989 and was the Associated Press Coach of the Year in 1991.

Sources: *Contemporary Black Biography,* vol. 1, pp. 219–20; *Sports Illustrated* (23 October 1989); *Jet* 77 (23 October 1989): 48; 87 (20 February 1995): 51; 90 (7 October 1999): 19; 91 (14 April 1997): 47; *Who's Who among African Americans,* 26th ed., p. 1117; *Contemporary Black Biography,* vol. 2, p. 1019.

Super Bowl XXII when the Washington Redskins defeated the Denver Broncos, had been a Grambling Tiger. Robinson has received many awards and honors, including the naming of Grambling's $11 million football stadium and the street it is on after him. He was awarded an honorary doctorate from Yale University in 1993. In 1994 the Eddie Robinson Trophy, which is awarded annually to the best football player at a black college, was initiated. When Robinson retired from coaching in 1997, after fifty-six years, he was the winningest coach in football.

Sources: Alford, *Famous First Blacks,* p. 91; Ashe, *A Hard Road to Glory,* vol. 2, p. 119; vol. 3, p. 119; Jones and Washington, *Black Champions Challenge American Sports,* pp. 120–21; *Contemporary Black Biography,* vol. 10, pp. 218–21; *Jet* 93 (15 December 1997): 53–54; *Who's Who among African Americans,* 14th ed., p. 1108–9.

1991 • The first black vice-president for labor relations of the National Football League was Harold Henderson. This was the league's third-highest post, and Henderson became the highest ranking black in the history of the NFL.

Sources: *Jet* 80 (6 May 1991): 48.

Warren Moon

1994 • Warren Moon (1956–), quarterback for the Minnesota Vikings, opened the season on September 4, the first time in National Football League history that a black quarterback opened the season for a black head coach, Dennis Green. At the time, Moon, who had played for six years in Canada and for ten seasons with the Houston Oilers, had passed for more yards than any other professional quarterback and was in his first season as a Minnesota Viking. In 1995 Moon became the first quarterback to eclipse 60,000 yards in passing. He had begun his journey toward the passing record when he played with Canada's Edmonton Eskimos, passing for over 21,000 yards in six seasons (1978–84) while winning six consecutive Grey Cup championships. Born in Los Angeles, California, he attended the University of Washington and began his professional career with the Edmonton Eskimos in 1978. When Washington played Michigan in the Rose Bowl, Moon was the game's Most Valuable Player. He set a number of records while a collegiate player and was named to several All-Rookie teams after his first season in the NFL. Green

(1949–), a native of Harrisburg, Pennsylvania, had an extensive history as a collegiate college coach before he became Minnesota's head coach in 1992. His tours of duty included service at Iowa State, Dayton, Northwestern, and Stanford. He also served for a time as receivers coach for the San Francisco 49ers. He was voted Big Ten Coach of the Year in 1982, while he was at Northwestern.

Sources: *Jet* 86 (5 September 1994): 52; 88 (9 October 1995): 51 (Moon); *Who's Who among African Americans,* 26th ed., p. 893 (Moon), p. 492 (Green).

1994 • Jerry Lee Rice (1962–), while a wide receiver with the San Francisco 49ers, scored touchdown number 127 and broke the all-time career touchdown record set by Jim Brown (1936–), becoming the first player to reach that level. Rice, who was born in Starkville, Mississippi, was raised in rural Crawford, Mississippi. He began playing football in high school and made All-American while attending Mississippi Valley State University. He was named to the All-American team as a consensus wide receiver, having set eighteen Division IAA records. Rice was a first-round draft pick of the San Francisco 49ers in 1985, and made Rookie of the Year that same year. By the end of the 1999 season, he held fourteen NFL records and had won three Super Bowl rings with the 49ers. He was the Most Valuable Player in the 1988 Super Bowl, in which he set ten Super Bowl records. He has been a Professional Bowl player twelve times since 1986, NFL Player of the Year twice, and NFL Offensive Player of the Year once. ESPN's *Sports Century* named Rice the 27th Greatest Athlete of the Twentieth Century in 1999.

Sources: *Jet* 86 (26 September 1994): 46–47; 89 (15 January 1996): 47; Salzman, *Encyclopedia of African-American Culture and History,* Supplement, p. 232; *Who's Who among African Americans,* 26th ed., p. 1044.

1995 • Oklahoma State University named Bob Simmons (1949?–) as head football coach, making him the first black coach in the Big Eight Conference. He came to the position after serving as assistant football coach at the University of Colorado for seven years.

Sources: *Jet* 88 (9 January 1995): 50; *Who's Who among African Americans,* 26th ed., p. 1124.

1995 • Kwame Clark (1978?–) became the first woman and the first black on the varsity football team at Bishop Rosecrans High School in Zanesville, Ohio. The tailback and linebacker scored two touchdowns her first season. Football, however, was just her way of staying in shape for basketball, and she was MVP of her girls' basketball team the previous year. Her usual pre-basketball preparation activity was cross-country running, but when that program was not offered, she turned to football.

Sources: *Jet* 89 (20 November 1995): 48–49.

1996 • Detroit Lions star running back Barry Sanders (1968–) rushed for 1,000 yards in eight consecutive seasons and became the first black to reach that milestone. During the game in which he set the record, he gained 107 yards; this brought Sanders' total rushing yards to 11,271 and pushed him just ahead of O. J. Simpson on the NFL's rushing list. Sanders retired from professional football in 1999, after having spent his entire playing career (1989–99) with the Lions. When he retired, he was second on the all-time list of leading rushers, with over 15,000 yards. He was born in Wichita, Kansas, where he starred as an athlete during his school days. He was not highly recruited by major colleges, because he lacked the typical sturdy build associated with football players. Nevertheless, his exploits at Oklahoma State University include the thirteen NCAA records he set in a single year, and he was awarded the Heisman Trophy that year. Sanders was Rookie of the Year in his first NFL year and was a Pro Bowl player every year from the 1989 season through 1998. He was named Offensive Player of the Year in 1994 and NFL Player of the Year in 1998.

Sources: *Jet* 91 (16 December 1996): 46; Salzman, *Encyclopedia of African-American Culture and History,* Supplement, pp. 240–241; *Who's Who among African Americans,* 26th ed., p. 1090.

1996 • The first two-time winner of the Lombardi Award was Orlando Pace, junior offensive tackle from Ohio State. Named for NFL coach Vince Lombardi on behalf of the American Cancer Society, the award is given to the nation's top college lineman.

Sources: *Jet* 91 (23 December 1996): 50.

Marcus Allen

1996 • The all-time leader in rushing touchdowns was Marcus Allen (1960–) of the Kansas City Chiefs, who scored his 111th touchdown in a game against the Detroit Lions and surpassed the record of Walter Payton of the Chicago Bears. He was the first player to achieve that number of rushing touchdowns. Allen scored his 112th touchdown in the same game. He is no stranger to the chase for records. When he broke the rushing touchdown record, he had played more games than any NFL running back, ranked second to Jerry Rice in total touchdowns, and ranked second to Walter Payton in combined yardage. Allen retired from football in 1998 and became a CBS sports commentator. Born in San Diego, California, he attended the University of Southern California, where he set twelve NCAA records and won the Heisman Trophy in 1981. Allen was a star running back for the Oakland Raiders from 1982 to 1993, after which he moved to the Chiefs. In 1983 he was the Most Valuable Player of the Super Bowl, in which he set a Super Bowl record with 191 yards. Frequently elected to Pro Bowl teams, he was also named Player of the Year twice during his playing career.

Sources: *Jet* 91 (16 December 1996): 51; *Who's Who among African Americans,* 26th ed., p. 22.

1997 • Charles Woodson (1976–), junior at the University of Michigan, became the first predominantly defensive player to win the Heisman Trophy. No defensive player had been a serious contender for the trophy since 1980. The Fremont, Ohio, native, who is best known for his play as a cornerback, also played a significant role on the Michigan team as a punt returner and wide receiver. He joined the world of professional football when he became a member of the Oakland Raiders team. He was elected to the Pro Bowl in his rookie year.

Sources: *Jet* 93 (29 December 1997–5 January 1998): 52; *Tennessean* (14 December 1997); *Who's Who among African Americans,* 26th ed., p. 1381.

1997 • Tuskegee University in Alabama, after 104 years of football, reached the pinnacle of 500 victories and became the first historically black college or university with that many football wins in history. The Golden Tigers won 21–16 over arch-rival Alabama State in the 74th annual Turkey Day Football Classic, the oldest football classic among black colleges.

Sources: *Jet* 93 (29 December 1997–5 January 1998): 52.

1998 • William "Bill" Myles (1936–) became the first black to win the Ohio Gold Award, given by the Columbus Chapter of the National Football Foundation and Hall of Fame. The award recognizes an individual for contributions to amateur football. Myles, associate athletics director at Ohio State University, was at the time in his twenty-first year as a member of the athletic department. He earned a bachelor's degree from Drake University and a master's degree from Central Missouri State. He began his career in 1962 as an assistant basketball/football coach in a Kansas City, Missouri, high school. He held several other coaching positions, including assistant football coach at Ohio State from 1977 to 1985, before being named associate director of athletics there in 1985. In 1988 he received the Drake National Distinguished Alumnus Award.

Sources: *Jet* 93 (23 February 1998): 22; *Who's Who among African Americans,* 26th ed., p. 923.

1998 • The first National Football League player chosen as a member of the National Urban League's Board of Trustees was Jonathan Philip Ogden (1974–), a tackle with the Baltimore Ravens. The commissioner of the National Football League nominated him for the position. Ogden, who attended UCLA, was born in Washington, D.C. He won the Outland Trophy in 1995 and became a Baltimore Raven in 1996, making the All-Rookie Team in that year.

Sources: *Jet* 93 (16 March 1998): 19; *Who's Who among African Americans,* 26th ed., p. 946.

1998 • Donovan Jamal McNabb (1976–) became a three-time Big East Conference offensive player of the year, and a four-time first-team selection, the first player to earn such honors. McNabb, who was born in Chicago, Illinois, is an alumnus of Syracuse University, with a degree in speech communications. He grew to be a star football player while still in high school, was considered "phenomenal" as a quarterback at Syracuse, and was a first-round draft pick of the Philadelphia Eagles in 1999. In high school he made All-American. At Syracuse he was the Big East Rookie of the Year, foreshadowing things to come; he also played back-up guard on the basketball team during his first two years there, was named Most Valuable Player of the Gator Bowl in 1996, and was captain of the football team and the Big East Player of the Year in 1998. Initially booed by Eagles fans, McNabb became the full-time starting quarterback at the start of the 2000–01 season, and the Eagles made the playoffs that year. Off the field he is a strong worker in support of the elimination of diabetes, which caused the death of his grandmother and with which his father has been diagnosed. His annual summer "Celebrity All-Star Weekend" includes an All-Professional football clinic and a celebrity basketball game among the events.

Sources: *Contemporary Black Biography,* vol. 29, pp. 109–11; *Who's Who among African Americans,* 26th ed., p. 859.

1998 • Tennessee State University in Nashville won the Ohio Valley Conference championship game against Murray State and became the first historically black college to win a conference title in a major conference in which the majority of the member institutions were primarily white institutions. During the 1960s and 1970s, TSU was known among black colleges as a football power. The team's record suffered during the next decade, but began to improve after a change in administration in the early 1990s.

Sources: *Tennessean* (15 November 1998).

1999 • Ray Rhodes (1950–) became the first black head coach for the Green Bay Packers, after having been released as coach of the Philadelphia Eagles. The Packers made even more history at the time of Rhodes' appointment. They became the first NFL franchise to have three black men in the top three coaching positions. Offensive coordinator Sherman Lewis came with Rhodes from Philadelphia, and defensive coordinator Emmitt Thomas was already there. The Packer organization knew Rhodes well: He had served as defensive coordinator there in 1992 and 1993, leaving for a one-year turn in the same position with the San Francisco 49ers, and later becoming Eagles head coach in 1995. Rhodes, who was born in Mexia, Texas, attended Texas Christian University. He was a wide receiver and defensive back for the San Francisco 49ers before he took his first coaching job, as an assistant secondary coach, with the 49ers in 1981. He spent ten years (1982–91) as the defensive backfield coach for the 49ers before taking the coaching position at Green Bay in 1992. In 1996, while with the Philadelphia Eagles, he was named NFL Coach of the Year. Rhodes was fired after only one season as head coach of the Packers.

Sources: *Jet* 95 (25 January 1999): 54; 95 (19 April 1999): 48; *Who's Who among African Americans,* 26th ed., p. 1043.

2000 • Minnesota Vikings receiver Cris Carter (1972–) received the first Walter Payton NFL Man of the Year Award, in Atlanta. The award recognized Carter's work with inner-city schoolchildren and community service. Carter, who is a native of Troy, Ohio, and attended Ohio State University, has also been recognized for his achievements on the football field. The skillful wide receiver played with the Philadelphia Eagles from 1987 to 1990, the Vikings from 1991 to 2001, and the Miami Dolphins in 2002. Between 1993 and 1998, Carter was on each Pro Bowl team. He is also a recipient of the NFL Extra Effort Award (1994), along with other honors.

Sources: *Jet* 97 (21 February 2000): 36; *Who's Who among African Americans,* 26th ed., p. 214.

2002 • Dallas Cowboys running back Emmitt J. Smith III (1969–) passed the 1,000-yard season mark and became the first running back in the NFL to gain 1,000 yards in eleven consecutive seasons. He set the record on thirteen-yard run in the third quarter when the

The First Black First-Round NFL Pick

In 2001 Michael Vick became the first black first-round, first-pick in the NFL draft. The Virginia Tech quarterback went to the Atlanta Falcons. He chose to forego his senior year with Virginia Tech. This year, for the second year in a row, nine black players were among the top ten picks. While Vick was initially described as the "franchise" quarterback the Falcons were said to need, it was suggested that he would spend his first year as the "quarterback-in-waiting."

Sources: *Jet* 99 (7 May 2001): 50; *Tennessean* (22 April 2001).

Emmitt Smith

Cowboys played the Detroit Lions at the Silverdome in Pontiac, Michigan. On October 27, 2002, Smith became the all-time rushing leader when he passed by Walter Payton's record of 16,726 yards.

Sources: *Jet* 102 (21 January 2002): 51; *Who's Who among African Americans,* 26th ed., p. 1143.

2002 • Tyrone Willingham (1953–) was appointed head coach at the University of Notre Dame, becoming the first black head coach of any sport at the university. His job was to return the "Fighting Irish" to dominance in college football—a position the team had lacked since the end of the 1993 season. Willingham left his post as head football coach at Stanford University where he had served for seven seasons and had a 44–36–1 record. He took the Cardinals to a PAC–10 conference title and won four bowl games, including the Rose Bowl in 2000. He signed to a six-year deal, becoming one of four black football coaches in Division I-A. Willingham grew up in Jacksonville, North Carolina, when the town was segregated. He and his friends played table tennis, cards, and danced in his home until his parents sold a plot of land near their home to the city on the condition that the city build a community center there for black children. Willingham played on Little League teams in white neighborhoods after integration came. Apparently an excellent quarterback, it was not until his senior year that he was allowed to place in that position in his high school. He graduated from Michigan State University and later held assistant coaching positions at North Carolina State and Rice universities. He also was assistant coach for the Minnesota Vikings.

Sources: *Jet* 101 (21 January 2002): 51; *New York Times* (2 January 2002); *Who's Who among African Americans,* 26th ed., p. 1359.

2005 • Norries Wilson became the first black head football coach in the Ivy League. Wilson began his Ivy League career at Columbia University and led the school to its winningest season, the best record of any first-year coach in that school's history. The Markam, Illinois, native was also the first football coach at Columbia to lead the school to victories over Princeton in consecutive seasons. In 2011, however, he was fired the day after the Lions beat Brown to avoid a winless season.

Sources: "Columbia Fires Football Coach," http://espn.go.com/new-york/ncf/story/_/id/7261601/columbia-lions-fire-football-coach-norries-wilson-1-9-season. Accessed October 1, 2012.

2007 • The first black coach to lead his team to a Super Bowl championship was Anthony Kevin "Tony" Dungy (1955–), on February 4. Super Bowl XLI was held in Miami, Florida, and Dungy led the Indianapolis Colts, the AFC champions, to the win. Friends since their stint with the Tampa Bay Buccaneers, Dungy and his opponent Lovie Smith (1958–), coach of the Chicago Bears, became temporary foes on that day. They were also the first two black coaches to lead their teams to a Super Bowl. Tony Dungy is also the first coach to lead a team to the playoffs for ten consecutive years and the first NFL head coach to defeat all thirty-two NFL teams. After retiring from the Colts, he became an analyst for NBC's *Sunday Night Football.* His friend, Lovie Smith, continued his head coaching post with the Bears.

Sources: *African American Almanac,* 13th ed., p. 1432; Smith, *Encyclopedia of African American Popular Culture,* vol. 2, pp. 433–35.

2007 • Two black quarterbacks were featured in the historic matchup between the Florida Gators and Ohio State, who played in the BCS national championship football game in Glendale, Arizona. Quarterbacks Chris Leak and Tim Tebow led the Gators to a 41–14 win over Ohio State and its Heisman-winning quarterback Troy Smith. With the Leak-Smith matchup, this was the first time in BCS history that two blacks were starting quarterbacks. The win made the Gators the first Division I school to hold simultaneously national titles in football and basketball.

Sources: *Jet* 110 (29 June 2007): 50–51.

2007 • The first ever black college football game, packaged for showing on personal computers, became available. The Black College Football Experience showcases several historically black colleges and universities that are members of the SWAC, SIAC, CIAA, and MEAC. Their bands, cheerleaders, and dance teams were included in BCFx, a video game available for PCs.

Sources: *Jet* 112 (26 November 2007): 51.

2009 • The Tampa Bay Buccaneers hired thirty-two-year-old Raheem Morris (1977?–) as its new head coach; with the appointment, he became the youngest head coach in the NFL. The seventh black NFL head coach, he had been with the Bucs for six seasons but without head coaching experience.

Sources: *Jet* (9 February 2009): 36.

2009 • When the Pittsburgh Steelers won the Super Bowl in a 27–23 victory over the Arizona Cardinals, held in Tampa, their coach Mike Tomlin (1973?–) became the youngest and only the second black to win a Super Bowl crown. The game, Super Bowl XLIII, was played in Raymond James Stadium on February 1. Smith was named the 2005 NFL Coach of the Year.

Sources: *Crisis* 116 (Spring 2009): 17; *Jet* 115 (16 February 2009): 38, 40.

2009 • Yale University hired Tom Williams (1961–) in January as coach of its football team, making him the first black to hold that post in the institution's history and the second in the history of the Ivy League. Williams was a star player while a student at Stanford, an assistant coach at the school, San Jose State and the University of Washington, and later became a defensive coach with the Jacksonville Jaguars.

Sources: New York Times, "Yale Hires New Coach and Racial Issue Fades for the Ivys," http://www.nytimes.com/2009/01/08/sports/ncaafootball/08yale.html?_r=0, accessed October 1, 2012.

2010 • James Franklin (1972–) became the first black football coach, the first black to head a major sport at Vanderbilt University, and the twenty-seventh football coach in the school's history. He left his post as Maryland's assistant head coach and offensive coordinator, and head coach-in-waiting behind Ralph Friedgen. Franklin is a native of Langhorne, Pennsylvania, and was educated at East Stroudsburg and Washington State.

Sources: *Tennessean* (17 December 2010); Vanderbilt University, Development and Alumni Relations, email, 8 January 2011.

2011• Now under forty years old, Mike Tomlin (1973?–) became the youngest coach to take a team to the Super Bowl twice—in 2009 in Tampa and again this year in Dallas. They lost the game to the Green Bay Packers 31–25.

Sources: *Jet* 115 (16 February 2009): 38, 40.

Golf

1896 • The first black golf professional and the first to play in the U.S. Open was John Shippen (1879–1968). He was tied for second place at Long Island's Shinnecock Hills course after the first round, but ended up in fifth place, which earned him a ten-dollar-purse. He was only sixteen years old at the time. Shippen played in four more Opens between 1899 and 1913; he took fifth place again in the 1902 Open. He was born in Washington, D.C., but was living on the Shinnecock Indian reservation where his minister father headed a mission church. Shippen gave up formal education for the sake of golf. He became a club professional and worked at a number of clubs. His last position was as head professional at the Shady Rest Golf & Country Club, a black-operated club in Scotch Plains, New Jersey.

Sources: "John Shippen," http://www.answers.com/topic/john-shippen. Accessed October 2, 2012.

1924 • The Riverside Golf Club was organized, with prominent real estate broker Victor Daly as president. The organization stimulated interest in golf. In the fall of this year, the club held a golf tournament, the first of its kind to be held by blacks in the country. National Benefit Life Insurance Company and local white firms offered prizes. In spring 1925 about eighty-three golfers participated in another tournament. The club had about forty active members and charged a small membership fee to cover mailings to members and other expenses.

Sources: Jones, *Recreation and Amusement among Negroes in Washington, D.C.*, pp. 31–32.

1926 • The United Golf Association held its first national tournament. The winners were Harry Jackson, of Washington, D.C., and Marie Thompson, Chicago, Illinois. Founded in the 1920s, national tournaments for black golfers continued for a number of years. A few black-owned country clubs existed in such cities as Westfield, New Jersey; Kankakee, Illinois; and Atlanta, Georgia. Tuskegee Institute sponsored the first black intercollegiate championship in 1938 on its nine-hole course.

Sources: Ashe, *A Hard Road to Glory*, vol. 2, pp. 66–68; *Encyclopedia of Black America*, p. 141; Young, *Black Firsts in Sports*, p. 164.

1946 • William J. Powell (1917–1999) became the first and perhaps the only black American to design, build, and own a golf course, Clearview Golf Course in East Canton, Ohio. The course, which Powell maintained for over fifty years, was added to the National Register List of Historic Places in 2000. Powell, who was born in Crenshaw County, Alabama, started out in golf as a nine-year-old caddy. He was a good junior player, but was denied access to many Ohio golf courses because of his race. He decided to build Clearview when he returned to East Canton after serving in the U.S. Army during World War II. He enlisted two black physicians as his partners and worked on the land himself during the day, while holding a night job at a local factory. The course was opened to golfers in 1948, and in 1978 it was expanded from its original nine holes to eighteen holes. Powell's daughter Renee is the club professional. The Powell family was awarded the National Golf Foundation Jack Nicklaus Golf Family of the Year Award in 1992. He earned the PGA Distinguished Service Award in April 2009 just before his death.

Sources: Clearview Golf Club (Flyer), 17 January 2001; *New York Times* (28 January 2001); *Who's Who among African Americans*, 26th ed., p. 1009.

1956 • The first black American to play in an integrated women's amateur golf championship was Ann Gregory.

Sources: Hine, *Black Women in America*, vol. II, p. 1325.

1957 • Charlie [Charles] Sifford (1922–) won the Long Beach Open on November 10 and became the first black to win a major professional golf tournament. He was the first black to gain membership in the PGA and the first to play in a major PGA tournament in the South at Greensboro, North Carolina, in 1961. These "firsts" did not come easily. Sifford was born in Charlotte, North Carolina. He started out as a caddy and played at the Carolina Club on Mondays when the course was closed to members. His game showed so much improvement that members complained that he was too good a player. This was the first attempt to force him off the links; there would be many more attempts. Sifford moved to Philadelphia, lived with a relative, and played for the first time on a public golf course. Drafted into the U.S. Army in 1943, he played on an army golf team in Okinawa, and it was this experience that made him decide to turn professional. Few tournaments were open to black players in the 1950s. Sifford played in the National Negro Open, a United Golf Association mini-tour for black golfers; he won the title six times, with five victories in a row between 1952 and 1956. When black singer Billy Eckstine hired him as an all-around valet, golf instructor, and golf partner, Sifford was finally able to enjoy golf without the usual racial tension and to continue to improve his game. He was with Eckstine from 1947 to 1953. He won his first professional tournament, the all-black Southern Open, in 1951 in Atlanta, Georgia. Sifford continued his fight to break segregation's stranglehold on professional golf. Other black golfing pioneers and former heavyweight champion Joe Louis helped him. But even after winning the Long Beach Open, Sifford still was not allowed to enter every PGA event. Baseball pioneer Jackie Robinson called attention to the situation in his column in 1959. Finally, Sifford was given tentative status as an approved PGA player in 1961; there were a number of stipulations in the tentative approval. In 1964 he received his Class A PGA membership card. When he won the prestigious Los Angeles Open in 1969, it was the first victory by a black PGA member in a major professional tournament. By 1975 he was playing on the PGA Senior Tour; he won the Senior Championship that year. In 1980, Sifford won the Suntree Classic. He joined the PGA Super Senior Tour in 1991. Toward the end of his regular PGA career, he moved to Cleveland, Ohio, where he and his wife ran the golf shop at a country club. Sifford is reported to have disliked being labeled "The Jackie Robinson of Golf," but his long, persistent struggles to integrate professional golf certainly helped pave the way for others to follow.

Sources: Ashe, *A Hard Road to Glory,* pp. 150–51, 154, 157; Jones and Washington, *Black Champions Challenge American Sports,* p. 116; Young, *Negro Firsts in Sports,* pp. 162–75, 281; Smith, *Notable Black American Men,* pp. 1063–66; *Contemporary Black Biography,* vol. 4, pp. 222–25; *Who's Who among African Americans,* 26th ed., p. 1123; *Jet* 94 (16 November 1998): 20.

1959 • The National Public Links Championship was won by William A. Wright (1936–), and the victory made him the first black to win a USGA event. Wright was born in Kansas City, Missouri, and received his B.Ed. in education from Western Washington State in 1961. For part of the time after his graduation he was both a teacher in the Los Angeles (California) School District (1953–68) and a follower of the professional golf tour (1964–77). He became owner of the Pasadena Lincoln-Mercury car dealership thereafter. He has received two Man of the Year awards, one in 1959 from the State of Washington and one in 1960 from the city of Seattle, Washington.

Sources: *Who's Who among African Americans,* 26th ed., p. 1389.

1971 • Lee Elder (1934–) became the first black American to compete against whites in South Africa in the South African PGA Open. In 1974 he became the first black to qualify for the Masters Tournament and on April 10, 1975, teed off in Augusta, Georgia, as the Masters' first black entry. He became black America's first Ryder Cup Team member in 1979. Elder was born in Dallas, Texas, but moved to Los Angeles to live with an older sister after his father died in combat during World War II. Like other early black golfers he began his love affair with golf as a caddy, when he was twelve years old. Elder left high school after two years but had no ready entrée to professional golf because racial segregation ruled in most of the country clubs and public courses. This left Elder with only one way to enhance his golf skills: he became a pool hustler. He returned to Dallas for a while; served two years in the U.S. Army (1959–61), where he was in a special services golf unit; followed the United Golf Association tour in the 1960s; and later stopped off in Nashville, Tennessee, where there were several advantages for black golfers. Cumberland Golf Course was black-designed and black-operated; and Ted Rhodes, who had been Joe Louis' golf instructor, was there. While in the army, Elder won the post championship at Fort Lewis, Washington, twice and was second in the 1960 All-Service Tournament. After he turned professional in 1962, he continued to follow the UGA circuit for ten years, and he won the national UGA title four times between 1963 and 1967. He joined the PGA in 1967. He played on the PGA

The First Black Professional Woman Golfer

In 1964 Althea Gibson (1927–2003) became the first black woman to play on the Ladies' Professional Golf Association tour. She is best known, however, for her achievements in professional tennis. She played in several golf tournaments from 1963 to 1967.

Sources: *Arizona Daily Star* (8–11 March 2001) ; Smith, *Notable Black American Women*, pp. 397–402.

circuit until 1984, winning several tournaments and a total of over a million dollars in purses. Elder did not leave golf; he retired to the Senior PGA Tour, where he continued to win tournaments. During the 1970s he received several awards, including one for humanitarian service. Washington, D.C., proclaimed a day in May 1974 as Lee Elder Day.

Sources: Alford, *Famous First Blacks*, p. 94; Ashe, *A Hard Road to Glory*, vol. 3, pp. 154, 156, 158; Bennett, *Before the Mayflower*, p. 635; Jones and Washington, *Black Champions Challenge American Sports*, pp. 147, 159; Smith, *Notable Black American Men*, pp. 362–64.

1982 • Calvin Peete (1943–), who had captured the Greater Milwaukee Open for the second time, the Anheuser-Busch Classic, the BC Open, and the Pensacola Open, became the first black multiple winner on the PGA tour. Peete, who was born in Detroit, Michigan, joined the PGA tour in 1971. In the beginning he was denied access to the most prestigious tournaments, but it has been reported that at some point during his multiple winning spree, he had won more tournaments and more money than any other golfer at that time. He was the most successful black golfer through most of the 1990s. Before he joined the professional tour, his jobs were generally unskilled labor. An accident when he was born had crippled his left arm and he was at first convinced that any form of athletics was out for him. The fact that he overcame this potential handicap and became a highly successful golfer led to his receipt of the B'nai B'rith Award in 1983. The award recognizes a person who has made significant accomplishments while overcoming illness or a physical handicap. Peete joined the Senior Tour in 1993. He has been a member of the U.S. Ryder Cup team, has received both the Ben Hogan and Jackie Robinson awards, and has twice won the Vardon Award, which goes to the PGA tour player with the lowest stroke average. His career earnings are well past the $1 million mark. His success at golf is combined with his activities as a real estate investor.

Sources: *Jet* 96 (19 July 1999): 19; *Encyclopedia of African-American Culture and History*, vol. 2, pp. 1116–17; Salzman, *Encyclopedia of African-American Culture and History*, Supplement, p. 112; *Who's Who among African Americans*, 26th ed., p. 977.

1991 • At fifteen, Eldrick "Tiger" Woods (1975–), of Cypress, California, was the first black and the youngest person ever to win the U.S. Junior Amateur championship. With his participation in the Los Angeles Open in March 1992, he also became the youngest person ever to play in a Professional Golf Association tour event. He became the first two-time winner of the USGA Junior Amateur crown when he successfully defended his title in 1992 at the championship in Milton, Massachusetts. Woods won his third consecutive U.S. Junior Amateur Golf Championship title in 1993, at the Waverly Golf Course and Country Club, Portland, Oregon. He is the only golfer ever to win three straight junior amateur titles. Woods also won three U.S. Amateur championships, and when he won his first one in 1994, he was the first black and the youngest person ever to do so. He entered Stanford University in 1994, and continued to demonstrate his magic strokes and his overall golf know-how. The interests of Woods the golfer soon became paramount, and in 1996 he left Stanford to join the PGA Tour. It did not take long for him to become a household name. He had been on the professional tour less than a year when he won the crown jewel of golf matches—the Masters, held at Augusta, Georgia. He was the youngest ever to win the prestigious event and the first black to win a major professional tournament, and he did it at 18 under par. He was named PGA Player of the Year in his first year on the tour. That was just the beginning. He kept on winning, putting together seasons that made him the one to beat in almost every match. Woods' dominance of the tour was clearly evident by the year 2000. When he won the Mercedes Championship in Hawaii, it was the fifth consecutive championship he had won that season, the first time that had been done since 1953. In July 2000 he became the youngest player to complete golf's career grand slam: the Masters in 1997, the PGA Championship in 1999, the U.S. Open in 2000, and the British Open in the same year. He is one of only five golfers to have completed the golf grand slam. In winning the British Open at 19 under par, he set a record for strokes under par in a major championship. The Associated Press named him Male Athlete of the Year for the third time in 2000. Twice in 2001 he experienced wins at the same golf course, and he was the first player to have three consecutive victories in the NEC Invitational at the Firestone Country Club (Akron, Ohio). His crowning glory, however, came when he won the Masters championship for the second time in April 2001. This was his fourth major championship in a row, with wins at the U.S. Open (June 19, 2000), the British Open (July 23, 2000), and the PGA championship (August 20, 2000) preceding the victory at the Masters. He became the first golfer ever to hold all four major titles at the same time. On his march to the Masters again he became the youngest golfer with thirty wins on the PGA tour and the first to win three straight titles at three tournaments— the Bay Hill Invitational, the Firestone, and the Memorial Tournament. On April 14, 2002, he won the Master's for a third time; he had back-to-back wins in that tournament as well. He is only the third golfer to reach this milestone. In 2007 he was named Player of the Year for the eighth time. There are very few superlatives that have not been used in describing Woods the golfer, and very few records remaining that he has not set. He made a name for himself when he started hitting golf balls at age two, scoring 48 after 9 holes by the time he was three. He added to that name until late 2009, when he stepped away from golf to try to control his personal life beset by admitted infidelity. Woods returned to golf in 2010, continued to suffer a major slump until March 2012 when he ended his thirty-month losing skid and won the Arnold Palmer Invitational at Bay Hill, and he became the first golfer to win over $100 million after winning the Deutsche Bank Championship on September 3, 2012.

Tiger Woods

Sources: *Ebony* 86 (March 2010): 64; *Jet* 82 (31 August 1992): 47; 84 (30 August 1993): 46; 91 (28 April 1997): 52–59; 92 (10 November 1997): 46; 97 (24 January 2000): 51; 99 (16 April 2001): 27; 99 (23 April 2001): 54–60; 100 (18 June 2001): 51; *Tennessean* (24 August 1994); (18 March 2002); (15 April 2002); *New York Times* (24 July 2000); (15 April 2002); Smith, *Notable Black American Men,* pp. 1252–56; *USA Weekend* (24–26 July 1992).

1996 • The first black college golf team to reach the championship level was Jackson State University in Mississippi. Eddie Payton coached the team to a record seventy wins and nineteen losses in the Southwestern Athletic Conference.

Sources: *Jet* 90 (10 June 1996): 10.

2000 • Renee Powell was the first black woman elected as an honorary member of the Ladies' Professional Golf Association. A native of Canton, Ohio, Powell had won the USGA women's title in 1964 and played on the LPGA tour from 1967 to 1980. She is the only black woman to hold Class A membership in both the LPGA and PGA of America. She was the recipient of the Budget Service Award in 1999, and is recognized for her contributions to teaching the game of golf and development of junior programs, including her own Renee Powell Youth Golf Cadre Program, which she established in 1995. Powell is the only club professional at Clearview Golf Club, at the course designed, built, and owned by her father William Powell in 1946.

Sources: Ashe, *A Hard Road to Glory,* vol. 3, p. 152; golf support.com; Spradling, p. 780; Salzman, *Encyclopedia of African-American Culture and History,* vol. 2, pp. 1115–16.

2001 • Jackson State University women's golf team became the first women's golf team from a historically black college to receive a invitation to the NCAA regional championship. They played in the twenty-one-team NCAA East Regional in Chapel Hill, North Carolina, in March.

Sources: *Jet* 99 (19 March 2001): 49.

2008 • Naomi Mitchell (2000–) became the youngest black golfer to win the U.S. Kids World Championship. This golf tournament is the largest competition for young golfers, ages four through twelve. Cheyenne Woods, niece of golfer Tiger Woods, and Austin S. De-Grate, of Austin, Texas, were the other black winners.

Sources: *Jet* 114 (15 December 2008): 42–43.

Gymnastics

1977 • Donna Lynn Mosley (1964?–) became the first black American to complete in the U.S. Gymnastics Federation Junior Olympic Nations, at age thirteen.

Sources: Hine, *Black Women in America,* p. 1330.

1981 • The first black woman to win the United States Gymnastics Championship was Diane Durham, who won the title for two consecutive years. The first internationally ranked black American female gymnast, she seemed a sure medalist for the 1984 Olympics but injured herself just before the competition.

Sources: Ashe, *A Hard Road to Glory,* vol. 3, p. 221; *Jet* 65 (2 January 1984): 31; Salzman, *Encyclopedia of African-American Culture and History,* vol. 2, p. 1161.

1988 • Charles Lakes became the first black man to be a member of the United States Olympic team for gymnastics.

Sources: *Jet* 75 (5 September 1988): 48.

1992 • The first black women gymnasts to compete on a United States Olympic team were Dominique Margaux Dawes (1976–) and Elizabeth Anna [Betty] Okino (1975–), who were in the games in Barcelona, Spain. Dawes, who is a native of Silver Spring, Maryland, won a bronze medal at the games, and won two silver medals (on the uneven parallel bars and the balance beam) at the World Gymnastics Championships Competition held in Birmingham, England, in 1993. Okino, who was born in Entebbe, Uganda, was a bronze medalist at the 1992 Games, had won a silver team medal and an individual bronze medal on the balance beam at the World Championships held in Indianapolis in 1991. In 1992 she was also the American Cancer Society Bikethon champion and received awards from Chicago State University and the Illinois State House of Representatives. She has done some acting and gymnastic coaching since the Olympics.

Sources: *Jet* 82 (17 August 1992): 48; *Who's Who among African Americans,* 26th ed., p. 323 (Dawes), p. 947 (Okino).

Dominique Dawes

1994 • Dominique Margaux Dawes (1976–) became the first black gymnast to sweep all five events in the National Gymnastics Championships held in Nashville, Tennessee, in August. She was the first black woman gymnast to win a national championship and the first woman to win a sweep since 1969, when Joyce Schroeder claimed the honor. She won four individual gold medals and a fifth for the All-Around title. Dawes returned to the Olympic Games in Atlanta in 1996, where she helped the U.S. women's team win its first Olympic gold medal. Dawes began taking gymnastics classes when she was six years old, and she showed potential in all of the gymnastic specialties. Her seriousness about the sport is reflected in the fact that as a teenager she moved from her home in Silver Spring, Maryland, to Gaithersburg, Maryland. She moved in with her coach in order to have more time to train. In 1996 she made her stage debut in *Grease*.

Sources: *Contemporary Black Biography,* vol. 11, pp. 62–65; *Ebony* 50 (May 1995): 84; *Jet* 86 (12 September 1994): 52; 90 (12 August 1996): 54; *Tennessean* (28 August 1994); *Who's Who among African Americans,* 26th ed., p. 323.

2012 • Gabrielle "Gabby" Christina Victoria Douglas (1995–), sixteen-year-old gymnastic phenomenon and a member of the U.S. Women's Gymnastics team at the 2012 Summer Olympics held in London, became the first African American to win a gold medal in the women's all-around final competition. She is also the third straight American to win gymnasics' biggest prize at the Olympics. Gabby came away with two gold medals as she and her "Fierce Five" teammates won team gold two nights earlier. The "Flying Squirrel," as she is also nicknamed, was allowed to leave her mother, two sisters, and brother in Virginia Beach, Virginia, to live with a host family and train with her new coach, Liang Chow, in Des Moines, Iowa. After winning the competition, she said "I hope that I inspire a people. I want to inspire people. My mother said you can inspire a nation." Gabby is the youngest daughter of divorced parents Natalie and Timothy Hawkins.

Sources: "All-around Champ," *Tennessean* (3 August 2012); "USA's Gabby Douglas Takes Women's Gold in All-around," *USA Today* (2 August 2012).

Gabby Douglas

Hockey

1950 • Arthur Dorrington, a dentist, signed with the Atlantic City Seagulls of the Eastern Amateur League on November 15, becoming the first black to play in organized hockey in the United States. He played in the 1950–51 season and in 1952 with the Johnstown (Pennsylvania) Jets.

Sources: Kane, *Famous First Facts,* p. 301; *Negro Almanac,* p. 1428; Young, *Negro Firsts in Sports,* p. 281; Salzman, *Encyclopedia of African-American Culture and History,* vol. 3, p. 1339.

1958 • The first black professional hockey player in the National Hockey League was Willie [William] Eldon O'Ree (1935–), of the National Hockey League's Boston Bruins. He played with the Bruins in their 3–0 win over the Montreal Canadiens in Montreal on January 18, 1958. He was born in Frederickton, New Brunswick, and, like many Canadians, spent considerable time at the ice rink. He first played professional hockey with the minor league Quebec Aces in 1956. O'Ree was a player in the Western Hockey League after the Bruins sent him back to the minor leagues in 1961. He last played with the San Diego Hawks in 1980. He retired from hockey permanently after that season. All in all, he played professional hockey for twenty-one years with permanent eye damage and other assorted breaks, bruises, and contusions. He played with the Bruins in two non-consecutive seasons, 1957–58 and 1960–61, and spent the rest of his playing years with minor league teams. In 1998 he was appointed director of youth development for the NHL, to serve as NHL/USA Hockey Diversity Task Force ambassador and spokesperson.

Sources: Ashe, *A Hard Road to Glory,* vol. 2, p. 222; Clark, *Sports Firsts,* p. 69; *Jet* 91 (17 March 1997): 51; 93 (16 March 1998): 19; *Contemporary Black Biography,* vol. 5, pp. 224–26; *Who's Who among African Americans,* 26th ed., p. 950.

1981 • The National Hockey League drafted its first black player, Grant Scott Fuhr (1962–). He was picked in the first round and became the goalie for the world champion Edmondton Oilers. Fuhr became the most celebrated of all black hockey players. He led his team to five Stanley Cup victories in 1984, 1985, 1987, 1988, and 1990. In 1988 he was awarded the Venzina trophy, presented to the best goaltender in the league. Born in Alberta, Canada, Fuhr left the Oilers in 1990 and went on to play with the Toronto Maple Leafs, the Buffalo Sabres, the Los Angeles Kings, the St. Louis Blues, and the Calgary Flames. He retired after the 1999–2000 season. He was an All-Star multiple times and was on the NHL All-Star First team in the 1987–88 season.

Sources: Ashe, *A Hard Road to Glory,* vol. 3, p. 222; *Who's Who among African Americans,* 26th ed., p. 440; Salzman, *Encyclopedia of African-American Culture and History,* vol. 3, p. 1339.

1993 • Bryant McBride (1965–) was appointed director of New Business Development and became the highest-ranking minority executive in the National Hockey League. McBride, who was born in Chicago, Illinois, moved with his family to Sault Ste. Marie, Ontario, Canada, when he was five years old. Hockey became his favorite sport. When he

The NHL's Goal-Scoring Title

In 2002 Canadian-born Jarome "Iggy" Iginla (1977–) of the Calgary Flames hockey team became the first black to win the National Hockey League's goal-scoring title. He captured the Maurice "Rocket" Richard Trophy as the league's goal-scoring leader and also the Art Ross Trophy as the league's point-leader. His record this year also put him in the running for the Hart Trophy as MVP. In 2002 he first appeared in the NHL All-Star game during his six-season career. He finished the season after scoring fifty-two goals and ninety-six points. Iginla was also one of the few blacks to receive a medal at the 2002 Winter Olympics in Salt Lake City, Utah, taking the gold with Canada's hockey team. He scored three goals in the tournament. The explosive right wing is one of the thirteen black players in the NHL. He started watching hockey when he was seven years old. Although he saw few blacks in the game, he wanted to play in the NHL and be like his idols. Still with the Calgary Flames, in 2003 he was the first black hockey player to be named team captain. He is the son of Elvis Iginla, a Nigerian, and Susan Schuchard, an American.

Sources: *Jet* 101 (13 May 2002): 51; 112 (15 October 2007): 24.

graduated from high school, his athletic skills attracted the attention of West Point Military Academy. After a year at a United States prep school, he entered West Point in 1984. That year he became the first black class president in the Academy's history, while also playing hockey and singing in the Glee Club. McBride decided, however, against a military career and entered Trinity College (Connecticut) in 1986. He was again a class president, the first minority class president in Trinity's history. The hockey team won three Eastern Collegiate Athletic Conferences while he was there, and he himself was a Division II All-American in 1988. McBride did not go on to professional hockey. Instead of moving to professional hockey, McBride enrolled in Harvard University, where he received a master's degree in public administration in 1990. He worked first with a pension fund company, then with the Pioneer Institute in Boston, Massachusetts, and later as chief of staff for a firm in Bloomfield Hills, Michigan. He was with this organization when he was offered the NHL position. McBride has greatly expanded the outreach of hockey to inner-city youth, and called upon hockey pioneer Willie O'Ree to be a role model and offer hockey clinics. He is active in civic affairs and keeps physically fit by running in marathons.

Sources: *Who's Who among African Americans,* 26th ed., p. 832; *Contemporary Black Biography,* vol. 18, pp. 116–18.

1994 • The first black professional hockey coach was John Paris Jr. (1947?–). Coach of the Atlanta Knights in the International Hockey League, Paris won the Turner Cup, the championship trophy in the IHL, in his first year as the head man. Born in Nova Scotia, Canada, Paris began playing hockey when he was four years old. He was never considered big enough to make the top tier as a player, but he did play professionally in minor leagues and in some NFL exhibition games. Paris is by field a sports psychologist and frequently makes motivational and anti-drug speeches and gives seminars.

Sources: *Jet* 86 (29 August 1994): 50.

Horse Racing

1806? • "Monkey" Simon was the first known black jockey. He has been called the best jockey of his day, and he commanded more than a hundred dollars per ride for himself and his master.

Sources: Ashe, *A Hard Road to Glory,* vol. 1, p. 44–45.

1891 • Isaac Murphy [Isaac Burns] (1861?–1896), the first jockey of any race to win the Kentucky Derby three times, was considered one of the greatest race riders in American history: he won forty-four percent of all the races he rode. His Derby record held until 1930. Murphy won the first in 1884, the second in 1890, and the third in 1891, which made him the first jockey to capture Derby titles two years in a row. In 1884 he became the only jockey to win the Derby, the Kentucky Oaks, and the Clark Stakes in the same Churchill Downs meeting. In 1955 Murphy was the first jockey voted into the Jockey Hall of Fame at the National Museum of Racing, Saratoga Springs, New York. Born on the David Tanner farm in Fayette County, Kentucky, he took the name Murphy to honor his grandfather, Green Murphy, a well-known auctioneer in Lexington. He learned to ride at age fourteen and was one of the dominant figures in thoroughbred racing from the Civil War until 1891. He won forty-nine of fifty-one starts in Saratoga in 1882 and had multiple wins in the Hindoo Stakes and the American Derby during the 1880s. In the latter years of his racing career, he had a weight problem and once was suspended for being drunk while racing when in reality weakness from dieting caused him to fall from his horse. His participation in races declined, and he tried to change gears and become a horse trainer. He was a resident of Lexington, Kentucky, at the time of his death. His body was removed from its grave in a segregated cemetery in 1967, with his remains reburied with a marker at Man O' War Memorial Park in Fayette County, Kentucky.

Isaac Murphy

Sources: Ashe, *A Hard Road to Glory,* vol. 1, pp. 47–49; *Churchill Downs News,* 1980 Black Expo Edition, p. 2; Logan and Winston, *Dictionary of American Negro Biography,* pp. 462–63; Young, *Negro Firsts in Sports,* pp. 49; Smith, *Notable Black American Men,* pp. 858–59.

1899 • The Kentucky Derby distance was trimmed from one and one-half miles to one and one-quarter miles in 1896. Willie [Willy] Simms (1870–?) of Augusta, Georgia, was the first winner of the race at this distance. He won many of the best-known horse races in America, such as the Preakness Stakes (1898), Belmont Stakes (1893 and 1894) and the Champagne Stakes at Belmont in 1895. He was also the first American jockey on an American horse to win on the English track, and he became the first black American jockey to win international fame.

Sources: Ashe, *A Hard Road to Glory,* vol. 1, p. 49; Jones and Washington, *Black Champions Challenge American Sports,* p. 18; Young, *Negro Firsts in Sports,* pp. 52–53.

1971 • Cheryl White (1954–) became the first black woman jockey on June 15, at Thistledown Race Track in Cleveland, Ohio. She was the first black woman to ride on a U.S. commercial track. The Rome, Ohio, native started riding horses on her father's farm when she was four years old. Her father was both a horse owner and a trainer, and as she grew up she graduated to exercising horses for her father and other trainers at Thistledown Park before taking to the track as a jockey.

Sources: *Encyclopedia of Black America,* p. 138; *Afro-American Encyclopedia,* vol. 9, p. 2797; *Jet* 90 (17 June 1996): 19.

1984 • The first black chair of the board of the Kentucky Derby Festival was William E. Summers III. He was also the first black to manage and own a radio station, WLOU, in Louisville. His son, William E. Summers IV became the second chair in 2000, at the time that black jockey Marlon St. Julien was a rider. They became a history-making pair for horse racing.

Sources: *Jet* 97 (22 May 2000): 51–53.

2000 • Marlon St. Julien (1972–) became the first black rider since 1921 to compete in the Kentucky Derby. A native of Lafayette, Louisiana, St. Julien was interested initially in both football and horse racing. He played football during his first two years in high school, and when he made the decision to focus on horse racing, he lost almost thirty pounds so he could make the jockey weight. He won his first race in 1989 at Evangeline Downs when he was a junior in high school and won his first stakes race at the same track in 1992. St. Julien won throughout the 1990s, becoming a top-ranked rider at several tracks. He won his 1,000th race in 1998 and became a full-time rider in 1999 at Keeneland Downs and

Kentucky Derby Firsts

The first jockey of any race to win the Kentucky Derby was Oliver Lewis, who rode three-year-old Aristides in the first race in record time in 1875. Thirteen of the fourteen jockeys in the first race were black. In 1921 Henry King was the last black jockey from the United States to ride in a Derby until Marlon St. Julien in 2000. Other Derby winners were:

Year	Jockey
1877	William "Billy" Walker
1880	George Lewis
1882	Babe Hurd
1884	Isaac Murphy
1885	Erskine Henderson
1887	Isaac Lewis
1890	Isaac Murphy
1891	Isaac Murphy
1892	Alonzo Clayton
1895	James Perkins
1896	Willie Sims
1898	Willie Sims
1901	Jimmie Winkfield
1902	Jimmie Winkfield

Sources: Ashe, *A Hard Road to Glory*, vol. 1, pp. 43–53, 129; Alford, *Famous First Blacks*, p. 95; Garrett, *Famous First Facts about Negroes*, pp. 77, 78–79, 185; *Encyclopedia of Black America*, pp. 138, 949.

Churchill Downs. At Keeneland he once won three races in one day, considered a rare accomplishment. St. Julien won 165 races in 1999 and was ranked fifth among jockeys. During Black History Month in 2000, he was one of the seven athletes featured on the ABC-TV special, *Raising the Roof: Seven Athletes for the 21st Century*. He finished seventh (out of nineteen) in the Derby, riding a horse that was a 50:1 long shot. He failed to make the cut for the Derby in 2001.

Sources: *Contemporary Black Biography*, vol. 29, pp. 153–54; *Jet* 97 (22 May 2000): 53.

Horse Riding (Equestrian)

1990 • Donna Marie Cheek (1963–) became the first black member of the U. S. Equestrian Team. In the same year, she was the first and only equestrian to be inducted into the Women's Sports Hall of Fame. She was born in Philadelphia, Pennsylvania, and attended California Polytechnic State University. In 1984 she starred in the NBCTV production of *One More Hurdle: The Donna Cheek Story* and in the same network's *Profiles in Pride* in 1985. She received an NAACP Image Award for her performance in *One More Hurdle*.

Sources: *Jet* 79 (21 January 1991): 48; *Who's Who among African Americans*, 26th ed., pp. 232–33.

Ice Skating

1966 • Atoy Wilson won the championship in the novice men's figure-skating singles, the first U.S. title ever won by a black American skater. His instructor was Mabel Fairbanks, who has been called "a black woman in a white sport," who trained such renowned skaters as Scott Hamilton and Randy Gardner, and gained international acclaim as an instructor.

Sources: *Tennessean* (14 February 1997).

1984 • Debi (Debra) Thomas (1967–) was the first black skater on a World Team, and in 1986 she was the first black woman to hold United States and world figure skating championships. She was also named *Wide World of Sports* Athlete of the Year in 1986. She first made history in France in 1983 at the Criterium International du Sucre, where she was the first black person to win an international senior-level singles competition. Thomas was the first black woman to make the U.S. Olympic figure-skating team. Her 1988 bronze medal was the first medal won by a black athlete in any Winter Olympics sport. Thomas was born in Poughkeepsie, New York, but grew up in San Jose, California, where she started taking ice skating lessons at age five and won in her first competition when she was nine. She followed a rigorous training program from then on, often at an expense that challenged the family budget. When she entered Stanford University in 1986, she continued her skating activities while also a full-time pre-medical student. She took a leave from Stanford in 1987 to prepare for the 1988 Olympics. After the Olympics, she resumed her studies at Stanford, graduating in 1991. In 1997 Thomas graduated from Northwestern University Medical School, where she earned her medical degree with a specialty is orthopedic surgery. Thomas faced intense competition on her way to the top in the figure skating world and also faced racism and bigotry in the early years. She was inducted in the U.S. Figure Skating Hall of Fame in 2000.

Sources: Ashe, *A Hard Road to Glory,* vol. 3, pp. 224, 257; *Contemporary Black Biography,* vol. 26, pp. 154–56; *Jet* 67 (25 February 1985): 54; 99 (26 March 2001): 28; Smith, *Notable Black American Women,* Book II, pp. 635–38; *Who's Who among African Americans,* 26th ed., p. 1217.

1997 • Andrea Gardiner (1981?–) won the junior women's title at the U.S. Figure Skating Championships on February 13, becoming the first black to hold that title. Her performance included four triple jumps. The competition was held in Nashville, Tennessee. Gardiner is a native of Bay City, Texas.

Sources: *Jet* 91 (10 March 1997): 50; *Tennessean* (14 February 1997); *USA Today* (14 February 1997).

2002 • Speed skater Shani Davis (1982–) became the first black to make a U.S. Olympic speed skating team. He won the 1,000-meter short-track final at the Olympic Trials held in Kearns, Utah, and thus qualified for the Winter Olympics in Salt Lake City this year. When he entered the trials, however, Davis was in eighth place. He trained with the Canadian national team in Calgary for two months in fall 2001, and later qualified for the world junior team that competed in Seoul, South Korea, in early 2002. He won an Olympic title in 2006 (in Turin, Italy) and again in 2010 (inVancouver), becoming the first skater of any race to win two consecutive Olympic titles at the Winter Games, A Chicago native, Davis started skating when he was five years old.

Sources: *Jet* 101 (14 January 2002): 51; Smith, *Encyclopedia of African American Popular Culture,* vol. 2, pp. 403–5; *Who's Who among African Americans,* 26th ed., pp. 320–21.

2010 • The French skating pair Yannick Bonheir and Vanessa James were the first black duo to compete in figure skating in the Olympic Games. They competed in the Winter Games in Vancouver. The skaters teamed up two years previously and moved from France to Indianapolis to train with Russian coach Sergei Zaitsev. James was the 2006 British national champion and 2007 silver medalist, and was the first British figure skating champion of African descent.

Sources: *Contemporary Black Biography,* vol. 84, pp. 62–64; *Essence* 41 (May 2010): 99.

Vanessa James and Yannick Bonheir

Lacrosse

1969 • The first black American women to compete on the U.S. National Lacrosse team was Tina Sloan-Green.

Sources: Hine, *Black Women in America*, vol. II, p. 1328.

1993 • Cherie Greer (1972?–) was named to her first World Cup team in 1993, becoming the first black and the youngest player named to a women's world cup team. The team won the title that year. Greer was named to her second World Cup team in 1997 and led the U.S. women's team to its third straight World Cup title. In a sudden-death victory, the team defeated Australia 3–2. During the tournament, which was held in Japan, the midfielder (defense) player was named Most Valuable Player of the game. The Philadelphia native began to play lacrosse when she was in the ninth grade. She became a star player during her college years at the University of Virginia. She was the first lacrosse player to have her jersey (#18) retired. Greer's father, Hal Greer, was an NBA star with the Philadelphia 76ers as well as one of the NBA's 50 Greatest Players. A resident of the Detroit area, Cherie Greer became an executive for a corporation run by NBA star Grant Hill.

Sources: *Jet* 92 (21 July 1997): 49.

Marathon Walking

1879 • The first known black to set a United States record for marathon walking was Frank Hart, also known as "O'Leary's Smoked Irishman." (O'Leary, his trainer, was the former champion.) The contest was held in New York City; the contestants traveled as far as they could in three or six days, for a purse of several thousand dollars.

Sources: Lane, *William Dorsey's Philadelphia and Ours*, p. 17.

Motorcross

2004 • James "Bubba" Stewart (1985–) became the first African American to dominate in motorcross. He racked up a record-breaking eleven American Motorcyclist Association Amateur National titles, was named Rookie of the Year in his pro season in 2002, and in 2004 won both the AMA 125 East Supercross Championship and the AMA 125 Motorcross National Championships. In 2008 he became only the second rider ever, after Ricky Carmichael, to complete a perfect motorcross season. The Bartow, Florida, native entered his first motorcross race at the age of four.

Sources: "James Stewart Bio," AMA Motorcross and Supercross Rider Profile, http://www .motorcycle-usa.com/533/Motorcycles/James-Stewart.aspx, accessed October 2, 2012; Smith, *Encyclopedia of African American Popular Culture,* vol. 4, pp. 1354–55.

Olympics

1904 • George Coleman Poage (1880–1962) became first black to represent the United States in the Olympic Games. He finished fourth in the 400 meters and third in the 400-meter hurdles at the Saint Louis event. He was born in Hannibal, Missouri and later became an orator and scholar.

Sources: Jones and Washington, *Black Champions Challenge American Sports,* p. 31; Page, *Black Olympian Medalists,* pp. 94–95, 149; Young, *Negro Firsts in Sports,* pp. 83–84.

1908 • John Baxter "Doc" Taylor Jr. (1882–1908), became the first black winner of a gold medal in the Olympics He won for the 4 × 400-meter relay in London. One of the first great black quarter-milers, Taylor was also the first black to win a gold medal as a United States team member. Taylor had been a college champion in his sport, held the world record in the 440-yard dash, and already had a degree in veterinary medicine from the University of Pennsylvania at the time of the Olympics. The path to his gold medal was filled with thorns. The 1908 Games featured much friction between the British and U.S. athletes, and the controversies reached a peak with the 400-meter race, in which Taylor was one of four finalists (three American and one British). The race was run twice, nullified the first time on the charge of an American foul by one of the U.S. runners (not Taylor). When it was rerun, the remaining two American finalists (including Taylor) boycotted the run. When Taylor had another chance to go for the gold, in the 1,600-meter medley, he ran the third leg, passed the baton on to the anchor runner with a fifteen-meter lead, and truly earned his gold medal. Taylor had a triumphant return to Philadelphia, but his days of glory were short. He died five months after winning the gold medal.

Sources: Ashe, *A Hard Road to Glory,* vol. 1, pp. 63–64, 65–66; Page, *Black Olympian Medalists,* pp. 111–12, 149; Young, *Negro Firsts in Sports,* pp. 83–84; *American Vision* 11 (June/July 1996): 20–23.

1920 • Harry Francis Vincent Edwards (1895–1973) was the first black Olympic medalist from Great Britain. He won a bronze medal in the 100-meter run and the bronze for the 200-meter run at Antwerp. Italian coach Mussabini was his trainer.

Sources: Page, *Black Olympian Medalists,* pp. 35, 156.

1924 • William DeHart Hubbard (1903–1976) became the first black in Olympic history to win an individual gold medal when he won the broad jump by leaping 24 feet 5½ inches on July 8. He set a new record on July 13, 1925 in the NCAA championships at Stagg Field. Although best known for his broad-jumps, he was also a sprinter, tying the world record of 9.6 seconds in the 100-yard dash. Born in Cincinnati, Ohio, Hubbard began his track career when opportunities for black participation were few in public facilities. The African American clubs that were formed to try to provide more opportunities for black athletes could lead to quality competition only if sanctioned by authorities. Hubbard was given the first such sanction in 1926. Hubbard was also a track star at the University of Michigan, where he enrolled in 1921, winning national and collegiate titles in the long jump and the hop, skip, and jump. The first of his overall six national championships was won in 1922. After his graduation from Michigan, he was sidelined by injuries, but he did defend his Olympic title in Amsterdam in 1928. Hubbard returned to Cincinnati after graduation from Michigan, and worked there with city agencies in recreation and housing from 1927 to 1941. He moved to Cleveland in 1942, and spent the rest of his life there, working with the Federal Public Housing Authority and becoming a proficient bowler. He was inducted into several track Halls of Fame during the late 1950s. He retired in 1969 and in that same year established a scholarship fund for needy students at Central State University (Ohio). Hubbard suffered a series of strokes before his death. In 1979 he was elected to the National Track and Field Hall of Fame.

Sources: Ashe, *A Hard Road to Glory,* vol. 2, p. 79; Page, *Black Olympian Medalists,* pp. 54, 149; Smith, *Notable Black American Men,* pp. 579–80; Salzman, *Encyclopedia of African-American Culture and History,* vol. 3, p. 1322; *Jet* 90 (22 July 1996): 60–61; 96 (12 July 1999): 22.

1932 • The first black women selected for Olympic competition were Louise Stokes and Tydie Pickett. They qualified in the 100-meter race for showpiece games held in Los Angeles. Two white athletes replaced them, but later on Stokes qualified for the 1936 Olympics.

Sources: Hine, *Black Women in America,* vol. II, p. 1321.

1936 • Cornelius Johnson (1913–1946) won a gold medal in the 1936 Olympics for the high jump and became the first black high-jumper to clear the bar at six feet, nine inches. Born in Los Angeles, he attended Compton Junior College.

Sources: Jones and Washington, *Black Champions Challenge American Sports,* p. 70; Page, *Black Olympian Medalists,* pp. 58–59; Young, *Negro Firsts in Sports,* pp. 86–87, 104–5.

1936 • Jesse [James Cleveland] Owens (1913–1980), son of an Alabama sharecropper, ran with Ralph Metcalfe and won the first gold medal for the 4 × 100-meter relay held in

Jesse Owens

Berlin in 1936 and set both Olympic and world records. When he won a gold for the long jump, he set a record that remained unbroken for twenty-four years. He ran 200 meters in 20.7 seconds at the Berlin Olympics, then the fastest ever around a full turn. He tied the Olympic record for the 100-meter run at Berlin. Altogether he won four gold medals and set three records. Earlier, Owens had run in the Big Ten Championships in Ann Arbor, Michigan, on May 25, 1935, and set five world records and tied a sixth within forty-five minutes. For his athletic achievement, his name was published in the record book for forty years, showing that at the pinnacle of his career he had won nine records in seven events and once held as many as eleven records. The world was stunned and his fame spread when Adolf Hitler refused to acknowledge Owens and the medals he had won in the Berlin Olympics. He was successful in business, as a speaker and youth worker. In 1976 he was the first black appointed by the Department of State as goodwill ambassador to the Olympic games. He was appointed to the United States Olympic Committee and in 1976 won the Presidential Medal of Freedom. The Ohio State University, where he had studied, awarded him an honorary doctorate in 1972. In 1984 the Jesse Owens Memorial Monument was dedicated in his hometown, Oakville, Alabama. Owens' life in Oakville was dominated by family financial difficulties and chronic illnesses. He set his first world record when he won the long jump in the Interscholastic Finals in 1933. His high school (East Technical) won the National Interscholastic Championship Track Meet that year, earning a total of 54 points; Owens contributed 30 of those points. He continued to star in track and field at The Ohio State University, but his academic progress did not match his track achievements and he never received an earned degree from the institution. After the 1936 Olympics, the continued segregation and racism in the United States was frustrating to Owens. He tried a number of business ventures before he decided to use his gift for public speaking on the lecture and speaking circuit. He later opened his own public relations firm. In 1979 President Jimmy Carter presented Owens with the Living Legend Award, and in 1990 his widow was given a Congressional Gold Medal in Owens' honor. Buildings at Ohio State are named after him and the Jesse Owens International Track and Field Meet was inaugurated in New York in 1982. He wrote two books that told his story and his philosophy: *Blackthink* (1970, written with Paul G. Neimark) and *I Have Changed* (1972). Owens was a resident of Tucson, Arizona, at the time of his death. Flags flew at half-mast throughout the state of Arizona.

Sources: *Negro Almanac,* p. 964–65; Page, *Black Olympian Medalists,* pp. 91–92, 149; Young, *Negro Firsts in Sports,* p. 98–105, 280; Smith, *Notable Black American Men,* pp. 893–96; *Jet* 96 (2 August 1999): 19.

1936 • The first black to win the 400-meter race in the Olympics was Archie Williams (1915–1993). His time was 46.1 seconds. The Oakland, California, native won a gold medal for the race at the Berlin Olympics. In 1939 he graduated from the University of California, Berkeley, with a degree in mechanical engineering.

Sources: *Jet* 84 (12 July 1993): 51; Jones and Washington, *Black Champions Challenge American Sports,* p. 70; Young, *Negro Firsts in Sports,* p. 86.

1936 • John Woodruff (1915–2007), first great American black middle-distance runner, was the first black to win the 800-meter race in the Olympics. Since his performance in 1936 and 1937, no athlete has equaled his dominance of the 800 meter and half-mile run. He came to national attention in the 1936 Olympic sectional trials when he won this race. He won a gold medal in Berlin; that year he was also AAU champion. In addition to other titles, in 1940 he broke the American 800 record. Woodruff was born in Connellsville, Pennsylvania.

Sources: Alford, *Famous First Blacks,* p. 100; Jones and Washington, *Black Champions Challenge American Sports,* p. 70; Page, *Black Olympian Medalists,* pp. 126–27.

1948 • Don [Donald Argee] Barksdale (1923–1993) of UCLA was the first black player and the first black captain of the United States Olympic basketball team in 1948. Barksdale won an Olympic Gold medal. He and R. Jackie Robinson were the two blacks in the London games. In 1947 Barksdale, of UCLA, was the first black elected to the Helms All Amateur Basketball Hall of Fame, in Culver City, California. Elected to the National Basketball Association's all-star game in 1953, Barksdale was also the first black to participate in that event.

Sources: Bennett, *Before the Mayflower,* p. 634; Jones and Washington, *Black Champions Challenge American Sports,* p. 89; Page, *Black Olympian Medalists,* pp. 162; Young, *Negro Firsts in Sports,* pp. 240, 279.

1948 • Alice Coachman [Davis] (1923–) was the first black woman Olympic gold medal winner in track and field and the only American woman to win a gold medal in the 1948 Olympics in London. She took the gold for the high jump and set an Olympic record that held until two Olympiads later. Born in Albany, Georgia, she received a trade degree from Tuskegee Institute (now Tuskegee University) and later received a bachelor's degree from Albany State College. She was in elementary school when she began jumping for fun, just to see how high she could jump. Coachman made the track team when she entered high school in 1938. She was soon recruited by Tuskegee and competed for them the next year, before she attended a single class. She won the AAU high jump title in 1939 and formally entered Tuskegee Institute High School in 1940. Coachman was already famous by the time she graduated in 1943, having won AAU national finals in the running high jump and the 50-yard dash. Coachman won more titles while studying for her trade degree in dressmaking. She also played basketball at Tuskegee and became an all-conference guard. She continued to win titles while at Albany State. After the Olympics, she became a high school physical education teacher. During her career as a track and field athlete, she won twenty-five AAU national titles and held the national high jump championship for twelve years. Coachman became a coach and recreation director after the Olympics. She became a member of the National Track and Field Hall of Fame in 1975, and was honored in at the Centennial Olympics in Atlanta in 1996 as one of one hundred famous U.S. athletes.

Sources: *Encyclopedia of Black America,* p. 143; Page, *Black Olympian Medalists,* pp. 23–24; Smith, *Notable Black American Women,* pp. 193–95; Bailey, *They Too Call Alabama Home,* pp. 80–81; *Jet* 96 (9 August 1999): 19; 100 (13 August 2001: 20.

1948 • Audrey "Mickey" Patterson-Tyler (1927–1996) became the first black woman from the United States to win a bronze medal. Competing in the Olympic Games in London, she placed third in the 200-meter race.

Sources: *Jet* 90 (9 September 1996): 53–54.

1948 • The first black heavyweight lifting champion in the Olympics was John Davis, of Brooklyn. He had thoroughly established himself in the field in 1941 when he set a record of 1,005 pounds for three lifts. Davis was Olympic champion again in 1952. Once called "the world's strongest man," he was the first weightlifter known to hoist 400 pounds over his head, a feat he accomplished in the 1951 National AAU senior championship in Los Angeles.

Sources: Alford, *Famous First Blacks,* p. 98; Young, *Negro Firsts in Sports,* pp. 184–85.

1952 • The first black to win the 400-meter hurdles in the Olympics was Charles Moore Jr., with a time of 50.8 seconds.

Sources: Alford, *Famous First Blacks,* p. 99; *Encyclopedia of Sports,* p. 741.

1956 • Lee Quincy Calhoun (1933–1989) won a gold medal in 1956 at the Melbourne Olympics and again in 1960 at the Rome Olympics, both for the 110-meter hurdles, and became the first athlete to win this event twice. He trained at North Carolina Central.

Sources: Ashe, *A Hard Road to Glory,* vol. 3, p. 184; Page, *Black Olympian Medalists,* p. 19.

1956 • Charles Dumas became the first man on U.S. Olympic history to high jump seven feet, one-half inches. He achieved this honor in the U.S. Olympic trials held in Los Angeles.

Sources: *Jet* 90 (1 July 1996): 22.

1956 • Nell Cecilia Jackson was head coach of the U.S. women's track and field team for the Olympic games held in Melbourne, Australia, becoming the first black person to serve

The First Black Decathlon Winner

Milt [Milton] Gray Campbell (1934–), one of the first great black decathletes, won 7,937 points and became the first black to win the Olympic decathlon. He first won a bronze medal for the event in 1952 as a high school student. Campbell concentrated on the hurdles and competed in the decathlon only five times in his career. Campbell has been called the best all-round athlete of the 1950s. During his professional football career, it is alleged that he suffered from serious prejudice on the part of the Cleveland Browns for whom he played in the 1957 season, especially because he had married a white woman. Later, he worked with underprivileged youth in New Jersey, and also became a well-known lecturer.

Sources: Ashe, *A Hard Road to Glory*, vol. 3, pp. 152, 183, 184, 516; *Encyclopedia of Black America*, p. 141; Henderson, *The Black Athlete*, p. 245; Jones and Washington, *Black Champions Challenging American Sports*, p. 115; Page, *Black Olympian Medalists*, p. 19.

as head coach of an Olympic team. In 1972 she was head coach again, for the Olympic Games held in Munich, Germany.

Sources: Ashe, *A Hard Road to Glory*, vol. 3, pp. 152, 183, 184, 516; *Encyclopedia of Black America*, p. 141; Henderson, *The Black Athlete*, p. 245; Jones and Washington, *Black Champions Challenge American Sports*, p. 115; Page, *Black Olympian Medalists*, p. 19.

1960 • Rafer Lewis Johnson (1935–), winner of a silver medal for the decathlon at the 1956 Olympics and a gold medal for the same event at the 1960 Olympics, was the first black to carry the American flag at an Olympic event—the opening ceremony at Rome in 1960. In winning the decathlon, Johnson set a new Olympic record of 8,001 points. Johnson was born in Hillsboro, Texas, but the Johnson family moved to Kingsburg, California, when Johnson was ten years old. In high school he was a four-letter athlete, excelling in baseball, basketball, football, and track and field; he was also an excellent student. Nothing changed after he enrolled in the University of California at Los Angeles in 1954. He won the decathlon championship at the Pan-American Games in 1955, along with the NCAA and AAU decathlon titles. He graduated from UCLA in 1959 and retired as a competing athlete in 1960. Once off the track, Johnson became involved in community activities in California. He was with presidential candidate Robert F. Kennedy in Los Angeles when he was assassinated in 1968. He has been national head coach for Special Olympics, has made several appearances in films, and has served as a corporate executive for his own firm and for Continental Telephone in Bakersfield, California. For the 1984 Olympics in Los Angeles, Johnson brought the Olympic torch into the Coliseum to signal the start of the Games. He accepted the torch from the granddaughter of track icon Jesse Owens. Johnson was made a member of the National Track and Field Hall of Fame in 1974 and of the U.S. Olympic Hall of Fame in 1983.

Sources: Ashe, *A Hard Road to Glory*, vol. 2, pp. 184, 186; Henderson, *The Black Athlete*, p. 244; Page, *Black Olympian Medalists*, pp. 59–60; Smith, *Notable Black American Men*, pp. 638–39.

1960 • Wilma Glodean Rudolph (1940–1994) was born in St. Bethlehem, Tennessee. When she was four years old, she was diagnosed with polio, which left her paralyzed in the left leg and unable to walk well until age ten. She overcame these odds to become the first woman to win three track gold medals in a single Olympics. While a student at Tennessee State University, Nashville, Rudolph was a member of the famed Tigerbelles and became well known for her running technique and scissoring stride. She ran in the 100-meter, 200-meter, and relay, becoming also the first black woman winner of the 200-meter. After taking a bronze medal as a member of the women's 4 × 100-meter relay team at the Melbourne Olympics in 1956, Rudolph became the first black woman to win the

Sullivan Award (1961). She was the winner of numerous other awards as an outstanding athlete. Her autobiography, *Wilma,* was made into a television film in 1977. She became a well-known lecturer, talk show host, and goodwill ambassador, and served for a time as a vice president at Baptist Hospital in Nashville. Rudolph was one of five athletes and the only track star honored in June 1993 at the first annual National Sports Awards held in Washington, D.C. Rudolph grew up in Clarksville, Tennessee, and for years had to endure weekly visits to Nashville for therapy and daily massages at home. She wore a steel brace from the time she was five years old until she was eleven and did not enter school until she was seven years old, but was allowed to enter at the second-grade level. By the time she entered seventh grade, she was ready to begin her sports odyssey, and she began by playing basketball. She joined the track team the next year, but played basketball also until she was in the ninth grade. As a sophomore, Rudolph ran in five different events in twenty races; she won all of them. On the basketball floor, she set a new scoring record (803 points) for the girls' basketball team at her high school. Then she lost every event at a meet held at Tuskegee Institute (Alabama). Shortly after the meet, she went to Tennessee State's summer track camp, and when the team went to the National AAU meet in Philadelphia, Rudolph won all of the nine events she entered. From there it was on to the 1956 Olympics. She was the youngest member of the U.S. Olympic team. She moved about the country frequently after she stopped competitive running in 1960, almost always involved in some project that involved young people, community service, and/or track. Rudolph once served as a coach at DePauw University. She became a member of the Olympic Hall of Fame in 1983 and was also inducted into the National Track and Field Hall of Fame.

Wilma Rudolph

Sources: Ashe, *A Hard Road to Glory,* vol. 2, pp. 182, 185, 187, 189, 201; *Jet* 84 (12 July 1993): 56–58; 86 (5 September 1994): 22; Kane, *Famous First Facts,* p. 45; *Notable Black American Women,* pp. 958–61; Page, *Black Olympian Medalists,* pp. 102–3; *Contemporary Black Biography,* vol. 4, pp. 206–8.

1968 • Wyomia Tyus (1945–) the most successful U.S. woman track and field Olympic athlete, was the first athlete, male or female, to win an Olympic sprint title twice. She won a gold medal for the 100-meter run at the 1964 Olympics in Tokyo and a silver medal for the 4 × 100-meter relay at the same event. In 1968 she won the gold medal for the 100-meter run and the 4 × 100-meter relay in Mexico City. She set an Olympic and world record in the 100-meter run (the second time she had set a world record in the event) and helped set an Olympic and world record of 42.8 seconds in the latter event. The Los Angeles resident was born in Griffin, Georgia, and graduated from Tennessee State University, where she was a member of the Tigerbelles. Originally concentrating primarily on basketball while in high school, Tyus was a good sprinter but track was a sideline for her. She attended summer track camps at Tennessee State University for two summers before she enrolled there as a recreation major. She won several amateur championships while still in high school and continued to set records after she entered TSU. In 1963 she was clocked at running twenty-three miles an hour. In 1966, Tyus, a teammate and their coach, became goodwill ambassadors to Ethiopia, Kenya, Malawi, and Uganda. Tyus continued to win as an amateur until she retired from amateur sports after the 1968 Olympics. In 1974 she joined the first professional track and field association, where she was the tour's top money winner and had won all twenty-two races on the tour in her first season as a professional. Since her retirement from professional athletics, she has taught in junior and senior high school, coached at Beverly Hills (California) High School, and served as a consultant to the Olympic Experience Group. In 1974 she and other women athletes, including Billie Jean King, founded the Women's Sports Foundation, to enhance opportunities for girls in sports. She was also a commentator for the Montreal Olympic Games in 1976, has conducted many sports clinics, and has made numerous television appearances. Her many honors include election to the Georgia Athletic Hall of Fame in 1976 and to the U.S. Olympic Hall of Fame in 1985.

Sources: Ashe, *A Hard Road to Glory,* vol. 3, pp. 188, 197, 201, 205, 514, 515, 518; *Guinness Book of Olympic Records*; Henderson, *The Black Athlete,* pp. 263–65; *Jet* 98 (16 Octo-

The First Black Woman to Compete in Five Olympic Games

In 1972 Willye Brown White [Whyte] (1940–) became the first black woman to compete in five Olympic games. She won a silver medal for the long jump in 1956 and another silver for the 400-meter relay in 1964. White won the AAU long jump title ten times and the indoor, once. A native of Greenwood, Mississippi, she was the first black inducted into the Mississippi Hall of Fame in 1982.

Sources: Ashe, *A Hard Road to Glory,* vol. 3, p. 185; *Ebony* 18 (June 1963): 115–20; 32 (August 1977): 62; Lee, *Interesting People,* p. 186.

ber 2000): 19; Page, *Black Olympian Medalists,* p. 118; Smith, *Notable Black American Women,* Book II, pp. 661–63; *Who's Who among African Americans,* 26th ed., p. 1257.

1968 • On October 16 Tommie C. Smith (1944–) and John Wesley Carlos (1945–), were the first to refuse to recognize the American flag and national anthem at an Olympic event. During this event at the 1968 Olympics in Mexico City, they lowered their heads and raised a black glove-encased fist to make a black power salute reflecting the black power movement of the decade. Smith, who won a gold medal for the 200-meter run at the Olympics, and Carlos, who won a bronze medal for the 200-meter run, were expelled from the games. Vincent Matthews and Wayne Collett made a similar protest four years later in Munich when their attitude on the victory stand made clear their lack of respect for the American flag. They were banned from any future Olympic competition.

Sources: Ashe, *A Hard Road to Glory,* vol. 3, pp. 190–95, 199–200; Jones and Washington, *Black Champions Challenge American Sports,* pp. 134–36; Page, *Black Olympian Medalists,* pp. 20–21, 108.

1968 • Madeline Manning (1948–) was the first black woman to win a gold medal for the 800-meter race in the Olympics with an Olympic record time of 2 minutes 0.9 seconds. In the 1972 games in Munich she won a silver for the women's 4 × 400-meter relay. A Tennessee State track star, she won the 800-meters six times at the AAU level.

Sources: Alford, *Famous First Blacks,* p. 102; Ashe, *A Hard Road to Glory,* vol. 3, pp. 197, 200.

1969 • The first black American to sit on the U.S. Olympic committee's board of directors was Nell Cecilia Jackson. In 1977 Jackson was inducted into the Black Athletes Hall of Fame, in recognition of her achievements as track star and sports administrator.

Sources: Hine, *Black Women in America,* vol. II, p. 1328.

1980 • The first blacks to participate in the Winter Olympics were Jeff Gadley and Willie Davenport, a bobsled team.

Sources: Clark, *Sports Firsts,* p. 222; *People* (25 February 1980): 35.

1984 • Carl [Frederick Carlton] Lewis (1961–) was the first athlete to win four gold medals in a single Olympics since Jesse Owens. Lewis was influenced by Owens, whom he met at a school awards ceremony while in high school, and who told him, "Dedication will bring its rewards." At the Los Angeles meet in 1984 Lewis won gold medals for the 100-meter run, the 200-meter run, the long jump, and the 4 × 100-meter relay. He continued to win other honors and to set records. He won the long jump in the 1996 Summer Olympics. With this win, Lewis tied the Olympic record of nine gold medals. Lewis retired as a track and field competitor in 1997. Born in Birmingham, Alabama, but growing up in a Philadelphia suburb (Willingboro, New Jersey), he began running when he was eight years old and continued to run in high school and college. In high school, Lewis was the top-ranked high school track athlete in the United States. His parents taught at the Willingboro high school and founded the school's track club. Lewis entered the University of Houston in 1979, and while he was there he became the first athlete to win two events at an NCAA championship. At various points in his career he held the number-one rank in the world in the 100-meter race and the long jump, and held the number-two rank in the world in the 200-meter race. In 1999 Lewis was honored by receipt of a World Sports Award of the Century, being named the Greatest U.S. Olympian of the Century.

Carl Lewis

Sources: Ashe, *A Hard Road to Glory,* vol. 3, pp. 204–6; *Ebony* 39 (October 1984): 172; Page, *Black Olympian Medalists,* pp. 72–73, 154–56; *Sports Illustrated* (20 August 1984); *Who's Who among African Americans,* 26th ed., p. 767; *Contemporary Black Biography,* vol. 4, pp. 156–60; Salzman, *Encyclopedia of African-American Culture and History,* Supplement, pp. 106–07.

1984 • Valerie Ann Brisco-Hooks (1960–) won a gold medal and set world records at the 1984 Olympics in Los Angeles for both the 200-meter run and the 400-meter run and became the first athlete to win at both distances. Running on the winning relay team that year, she tied Wilma Rudolph as winner of three gold medals in United States women's track and field events. She also received a silver medal for the 4 × 400-meter relay in the 1988 Olympics in Seoul. Born in Greenwood, Mississippi, she attended California State University at Northridge.

Sources: Ashe, *A Hard Road to Glory,* vol. 3, pp. 189, 205; *Who's Who among African Americans,* 26th ed., pp. 143.

1984 • Cheryl De Ann Miller (1964–) was the first player, male or female, to be named to the *Parade* All-American basketball team for four consecutive years. She played in the 1984 Olympics in Los Angeles when the Americans won their first gold medal in women's basketball. Other black women on the United States team were Pam McGee, Lynette Woodard, Janice Lawrence, Cathy Boswell, and Teresa Edwards. Miller also led the United States team to gold medal victories in the World Championships and the Goodwill Games in Moscow, both in 1986. A native of Riverside, California, Miller was an outstanding college and amateur basketball player. She began with the Junior National Team in 1981, played with the U.S. National Team in 1982, and was on the World Championship Team in 1983. After graduation from the University of Southern California, where her major was communications (broadcast journalism), she worked as a sports commentator for ABC TV. She served as USC's head coach for the women's basketball team from 1993 to 1995, coached for the Phoenix Mercury in 1997, and later moved to Turner Sports as an NBA analyst for games broadcast on TBS-TV and TNT-TV. She was the Naismith Player of the Year three times in a row and has received more than 1,140 trophies and 125 plaques for her basketball exploits. As a broadcast journalist, she was the first female analyst to call a nationally televised NBA game. Miller honed her basketball skills early, by playing against her brothers. While she was in high school, she once set a California high school record by scoring 105 points in a game. She is also given credit for performing the first two dunks made by a woman in formal competition. She was elected to the Basketball Hall of Fame in 1995.

Sources: Ashe, *A Hard Road to Glory,* vol. 3, pp. 54, 57, 64, 254; Page, *Black Olympian Medalists,* pp. 83–84, 163; *Contemporary Black Biography,* vol. 10, pp. 177–79; *Who's Who among African Americans,* 26th ed., p. 873.

1984 • The first black referee and judge for the Olympic Games, one of four Americans, was Carmen Williamson.

Sources: *Jet* 66 (30 July 1984): 33.

1987 • Edwin Corley Moses (1955–), famous as a world-class hurdler, is the only athlete to perfect the technique of taking thirteen strides between each hurdle. This concentration on his event led to his being the first person to win 107 400-meter hurdles events in a row. His winning streak in the 400-meter intermediate hurdles began on September 2, 1977, in Dusseldorf, West Germany. The streak ended at the Madrid meet on June 4, 1987, when he was handed his first defeat in ten years. Moses won a gold medal at Montreal in 1976 for the 400-meter hurdles and set a world and Olympic record of 47.64 seconds, a time he lowered to 47.02 seconds when he set his fourth world record on August 31, 1983. He won a second gold medal in 1984 at Los Angeles for the 400-meter hurdle; and a bronze, also for the 400-meter hurdles, in Seoul in 1988. Moses dominated the 400-meter hurdles for almost ten years. He was the first U.S. athlete to be elected as a delegate to the International Amateur Athletic Federation. Moses won the prestigious Sullivan Award in 1983 and was elected to the Track and Field Hall of Fame in 1994. Born in Dayton, Ohio, he graduated from Morehouse College in Atlanta with a B.S. in physics in 1978, and earned the M.B.A. degree from Pepperdine University in 1994. He turned to track while in high school because his size did not lend itself to football or basketball. He became much taller and heavier while in college. Moses was appointed to the U.S. Olympic Committee on substance abuse in 1989, and also started training with a bobsled team, but he was not involved in the 1992 Olympics as a bobsledder and did not make a comeback as a hurdler. Moses, trained as an aeronautical engineer, became a partner in a corporate firm, and also a financial consultant after the 1992 Olympics.

Sources: Ashe, *A Hard Road to Glory,* vol. 3, pp. 201–2, 204; Page, *Black Olympian Medalists,* pp. 85–86, 153, 154; *Contemporary Black Biography,* vol. 8, pp. 178–81; *Who's Who among African Americans,* 26th ed., p. 912.

Jackie Joyner-Kersey

1988 • Jacqueline "Jackie" Joyner-Kersee (1962–) was the first U.S. woman to win the Olympic long jump and the first athlete in sixty-four years to win both a multi-event competition and an individual event in one Olympics. She won a silver medal for the heptathlon at the 1984 Olympics, and a gold medal in 1988 for the heptathlon, setting an Olympic and world record. This year she became the only woman to gain more than seven thousand points in the heptathlon. She became the first woman ever to repeat as Olympic heptathlon champion in 1992 when she won the two-day, seven-event marathon. She has been called the world's fastest woman and the greatest female athlete. Born in East Saint Louis, she married Bob Kersee, her sprint coach, in 1986. She was the first woman to receive *The Sporting News*'s Waterford Trophy, a prestigious annual award. Joyner-Kersee won her fourth world title in the heptathlon in Stuttgart, Germany, at the 1993 World Track and Field Championships, and in 1994 she set a new U.S. record (24 feet, 7 inches) in the long jump at the New York Games. She was less than two inches off of the world record. In 1996 she joined the Richmond Rage professional basketball team. She also held the presidency of Elite Sports Marketing at the time and is the founder of the Jackie Joyner-Kersee Foundation. Joyner-Kersee has received many honors, including the Sullivan Award as the Most Outstanding Amateur Athlete in 1986. She was *Track and Field News'* Woman Athlete of the Year in 1986 and 1987, and the University of Minnesota gave her an honorary doctorate degree in 1989. While a student at the University of California at Los Angeles, she was on both the basketball and track teams. She had been a high school champion in both sports. Joyner-Kersee's grandmother gave her the name Jacqueline, after then first lady Jacqueline Kennedy. When Joyner-Kersee officially retired from track at age thirty-eight, she certainly had become "first of something" many times over. At the time of her retirement, she had won six Olympic medals, the most at the time by any woman in the history of track and field.

Sources: Hine, *Black Women in America,* pp. 667–69; *Current Biography, 1987,* pp. 293–96; Smith, *Epic Lives,* pp. 305–11; Smith, *Notable Black American Women,* Book II, pp. 370–73; *Contemporary Black Biography,* vol. 4, pp. 152–55; *Who's Who among African Americans,* 26th ed., p. 710; *Jet* 86 (6 June 1994): 56; 93 (3 March 1998): 19; 99 (5 March 2001): 50.

1988 • Florence Delorez Griffith-Joyner (1959–1998) was the first American woman to win four medals in track and field at a single Olympics, in Seoul, South Korea. She won gold in the 100- and 200-meter dashes, and the 400-meter relays. She also won silver in the 1600-meter relay. Known affectionately by her fans as "Flo-Jo," she was born in Los Angeles, California, one of eleven children born to parents who were divorced when Griffith-Joyner was four years old. She was reared thereafter by her mother. Griffith-Joyner won her first track event when she was seven, in a competition sponsored by the Sugar Ray Robinson Youth Foundation. She excelled in track and field in high school, setting school records in the long jump and sprints. She entered California State-Northridge in 1978, but had to drop out for a year because of financial difficulties. With help from the black assistant track coach, Bob Kersee, she was able to return. When Kersee moved to coach at UCLA in 1980, Griffith-Joyner moved with him even though UCLA did not offer the business major she had been pursuing at CSU. She became a national champion while at UCLA, winning the NCAA championship in the 200-meter race in 1982. She made her first U.S. Olympic Team in 1984 and finished second in the 200-meter sprint. By this time she had begun growing the long fingernails that became one of her trademarks; the fingernails cost her a place on the 1984 sprint relay team. For a time after the Olympics her interest in track seemed to wane, but she kept track in the family by marrying Al Joyner, who had won a 1984 gold in the triple jump and just happened to be the brother of track star Jackie Joyner-Kersee, who just happened to be married to Bob Kersee, Griffith-Joyner's track coach. The stage was thus set for her triumphant performance in the 1988 Olympics. She was already a media attraction before she made Olympic history, having become known almost as much for her colorful garb as for her record-setting times in trial heats. She was the Associated Press Female Athlete of the Year in 1988, won both the Sullivan and Jesse Owens awards, and was also named Athlete of the Year by the Russian news agency Tass. She turned her hand to creative activities after the Olympics, designing fashions and writing children's books. She tried for a track comeback for the 1996 Olympics, but was unsuccessful. She kept busy, however, serving for a time as cochair of the President's Council on Physical Fitness in 1993. Her death at age thirty-eight of an apparent heart seizure came as a surprise to most, who may not have known that she had been diagnosed with a heart murmur when she was seven years old and had been hospitalized for one day in 1996 after a heart seizure. Amid the controversy surrounding her death, there were charges that she had been improperly medicated, and in August 2000 her family filed a wrongful death suit against the St. Louis (Missouri) hospital that had treated her in 1996. She had been elected to the Track and Field Hall of Fame in 1995.

Florence Griffith-Joyner

Sources: *Jet* 94 (12 October 1958): 52–61; Smith, *Notable Black American Women,* Book II, pp. 362–66; *Contemporary Black Biography,* vol. 28, pp. 78–80; Salzman, *Encyclopedia of African-American Culture and History,* Supplement, p. 119.

1988 • Anthony Nesty of Surinam was the first black swimming champion in Olympic games and the first swimming champion from South America. He won a gold medal at the Olympics in Seoul for the 100-meter butterfly in swimming to give Surinam its first Olympic medal. Nesty attended the University of Florida.

Sources: Page, *Black Olympian Medalists,* pp. 88, 167; *USA Today,* 3 October 1988.

1992 • Robert Erik Pipkins (1973–) became the first black member of the Olympic luge team and the first black in international competition. He won the junior world championship in Sapporo, Japan, in the same year. Born in Buffalo, New York, Pipkins received a B.S. degree from Drexel University in 1995 and went on to study architectural and civil engineering. He set the luge record at Lake Placid, New York, in his 1992 banner year and was U.S. National Champion from 1993 to 1995.

Sources: *Time* (10 February 1991); *Who's Who among African Americans,* 14th ed., p. 1037.

1992 • Sprinter Linford Christie (1960–) was the oldest man to date to win an Olympic gold medal in the 100-meter event, at Barcelona, confounding the track aficionados who had considered him too old to run effectively. Christie's family moved from his Jamaica birthplace to West London, England, when he was eight years old. He ran his first race that same year when he was in primary school, but it took him more than a decade to commit fully to the training he needed to advance in the sport. He won the European Championship in the 100-meter race in 1986, and in 1987 he finished third in the World Track and Field Championships in Rome. By the end of 1992, *Track & Field News* ranked him number-one in the world in the 100-meter event, and gave him the same rank in 1993. In 1993 Christie won twelve of the fifteen races he entered, including the World Track and Field Championship in his event.

Sources: *Contemporary Black Biography,* vol. 8, pp. 45–48.

1996 • Josia Thugwane (1971–) crossed the finish line in the marathon at the Summer Games in Atlanta and became the first black South African to win an Olympic gold medal. He grew up on his grandmother's farm after his parents were divorced when he was a baby. He was unable to attend school because of his remote location. A teenage soccer player, he changed to running because of his small size. He bought the shoes for his first race (which he won) on credit. He later found a job in a mine and moved to the township near the mine, where he built a house, continued to live under the restrictive conditions of apartheid, and underwent the prescribed rituals of manhood for men of the Ndebele tribe. He competed in several international marathons in 1994, and won a place on South Africa's 1996 Olympic team by first winning the South Africa marathon. His path to the Games could have been sidetracked by a carjacking in March 1996 during which he was shot in the face, but he refused to let this or the subsequent threats stop him. He was assaulted again in 1997, but won the Fukuoka Marathon in Japan that same year. He has since worked toward developing a network of sports programs for the youth of South Africa and toward overcoming his illiteracy.

Sources: *Contemporary Black Biography,* vol. 21, pp. 178–81.

1996 • The first man ever to win both the 200- and 400-meter sprints in the same Olympic Games was Michael Duane Johnson (1967–). The historic feat was nothing new for Johnson. He had been winning track events since his college days and setting records frequently both in college and after he became a more or less fulltime runner in 1990. Johnson, who was born in Dallas, Texas, graduated from Baylor University (Texas) in 1990 with a B.A. degree in business. He won his first Male Athlete of the Year award in that same year. While at Baylor, he won the NCAA indoor track championship and was the top-ranked runner in the 200- and 400-meter sprints. He was the first male athlete to hold the dual top rank. After his graduation, Johnson ran in Europe, and he won often. He was the world champion in the 200-meter event in 1991, the world champion in the 200 and 400 events in 1993 and 1995, and took the gold medal in the 400 event in the 1998 Goodwill Games. While making history in the 1996 Olympics for the 200 and 400 sprints, he also helped win the 400-meter relay, when he ran his leg in record-breaking time. Honors and awards have poured in for him. In 1997 he won the Amateur Athletic Union's (AAU) 67th Annual James E. Sullivan Award for his outstanding accomplishments in the 1996 Olympics held in Atlanta. He set a record of 43.49 seconds in the 400-meter race, and the Associated Press hailed Johnson as the top sports story of the year. In 1997 he won the Sullivan Award and the U.S. Olympic Committee's Man of the Year award. In 1998 he was inducted into the Texas Sports Hall of Fame, and in 1999 he was on the list of ten Outstanding Young Americans awards. Johnson once had a string of fifty-five straight wins in the 400-meter race, dating back to 1989. Running was always his favorite sport. Described as a loner who is both fiercely competitive and supremely self-confident, Johnson has secured a place in track and field history. He won the 400-meter event again in the 2000 Olympics, making him the first man to win this event in back-to-back Olympics.

Sources: *Contemporary Black Biography,* vol. 13, pp. 119–22; Salzman, *Encyclopedia of African-American Culture and History, Supplement,* p. 145; *Jet* 91 (20 January 1997): 57; 91 (7 April 1997): 48; 98 (23 October 2000): 52–57; *Who's Who among African Americans,* 26th ed., p. 676.

1996 • Teresa Edwards (1964–) became America's only four-time Olympian in basketball, in 1996, 1992, 1988, and 1984. She has won twelve international medals, including nine golds. USA Basketball named her the Female Athlete of the Year in 1996, for the third time. She was at the time the only three-time winner, male or female, of this award. The Georgia native became the player-coach of the American Basketball League's Atlanta Glory team in 1997. She joined the ABL's Philadelphia Rage team in 1998, playing as a guard. Edwards was named to the ABL board of directors in that same year.

Sources: *Jet* 93 (2 February 1998): 50; 94 (16 November 1998): 22; *Who's Who among African Americans,* 26th ed., p. 379.

2000 • Called the "fastest woman in the world," Marion Jones (1975–) won three gold medals and two bronze medals at the Sydney, Australia, Olympics and became the first woman to win five track medals in one Olympiad. The Associated Press named her Female Athlete of the Year, for 2000. Jones, who was born in Los Angeles, California, began participating in track when she was age seven and in basketball by the time she was in sixth grade. When she finished high school in 1993, Jones had set a high school track record in the 200-meter sprint, won state titles in both the 100 and 200 events, and been named the California Division I Player of the Year in basketball; she had also won two high school Athlete of the Year awards. In college, at the University of North Carolina in Chapel Hill, she continued to pursue both track and basketball. Jones did not decide to concentrate on track until after she graduated from college in 1997. Once she made the decision, she erupted into national view. At one point she had a streak of thirty-seven consecutive first-place finishes in the sprint and long jump. In 1998 she became the first woman since 1948 to win the 100-meter, 200-meter, and long jump, when she participated in the USA Outdoor Championships. *Track & Field* named her Woman of the Year in 1997 and Female Athlete of the Year in 1988. She won several other awards during this two-year period. With all of her achievements in track, Jones has managed to maintain a connection with basketball. She and then-husband C. J. Hunter, who was a coach at UNC when Jones was a student, have found time to coach a basketball team for young girls. After pleading guilty and lying about the use of steroids in 2000–01, and association with a check-fraud scheme, in 2008 Jones was sentenced to six months in prison and two years of probation and community service. She was released in September 2008. She had been stripped of all of her medals.

Marion Jones

Sources: Rapoport, *Marion Jones & the Making of a Champion; Jet* 98 (23 October 2000): 52–53; Salzman, *Encyclopedia of African-American Culture and History,* Supplement, p. 149; *Jet* 98 (23 October 2000): 52–57; *Ebony* 56 (March 2001): 150–54.

2000 • Maurice Greene (1974–), the fastest man on earth, won two gold medals (an individual gold in the 100-meter dash and a second as a member of the U.S. 4x100 relay team) and set a world record in the 100-meter dash at the Olympics held in Sydney, Australia. He had earlier set a record at the 1999 World Games in Athens, Greece. Called "The Kansas Cannonball," Greene was born in Kansas City, Kansas, and began running when he was a fourth grader. He played football and ran track in high school, and won his third straight high school state meet in the 100- and 200- meter sprint double in 1993. By 1997 he was ranked number-one in the U.S. and number-two in the world in the 100-meter event. In 1998 he set a world record in the 60-meter event in Madrid and had become number-one in the world, as well as in the U.S., in the 100-meter race. He set a new world record in the 100-meter dash at the Tsiklitiria Grand Prix meet in Athens, Greece, finishing in 9.79 seconds. He broke the record that Canadian sprinter Donovan Bailey set in the 1996 Olympics. He had more first-place victories, retained his number-one U.S. ranking in the 100-meter, and added a number-one U.S. ranking in the 200-meter in 1999.

Sources: Salzman, *Encyclopedia of African-American Culture and History,* Supplement, p. 116; *Who's Who among African Americans,* 26th ed., p, 496.

2000 • The first twins to run in the same relay in Olympic history and to win a gold medal were Alvin and Calvin Harrison. They were members of the 4x400 relay team.

Sources: *Jet* 98 (23 October 2000): 54.

2000 • The first Australian Aborigine to win Olympic gold in an individual event was Cathy Freeman (1973–), who won the 400-meter race. Born in Mackay, Queensland, Australia, Freeman is reported to have shown her running potential early, but it was not until 1988 that she came to national attention. In that year she had a good performance in Australia's National School Championships, and in 1990 she made the Commonwealth Games team as a sprinter and became a member of the 4x100 meter relay team that won the gold medal. She stopped competing in high school events after this, won the 200-meter title in the 1990 Australian National Championships, and participated in the World Games in Bulgaria. She was named Young Australian of the Year in 1990. She represented Australia

Olympic Swimming Firsts

n 2000 fifty-meter freestyler Anthony Ervin became the first black American swimmer to compete in the Olympic Games and to win a gold medal, at the Sydney Olympics.

Sources: *Jet* 98 (23 October 2000): 54.

in the 1992 Barcelona Olympics, running in the 400-meter event. Freeman won both the 200- and 400-meter events in the 1994 Commonwealth Games. After her win in the 400-meter race, she ran a victory lap with the Aboriginal flag draped around her neck instead of the Australian flag; this led to severe criticism. She did the same thing again after she won in the 200-meter race. By the time the 2000 games were held in Sydney, the Aboriginal flag was one of the flags given official recognition in the six designated Olympic areas of the city. Freeman at one time had won twenty-two consecutive 400-meter titles, including world championships in 1997 and 1999. Perhaps having been removed from the "young" list, she was named Australian of the Year in 1998. She was given the honor of lighting the Olympic cauldron when the Games came to Sydney. This time, when she ran her victory lap Freeman had both the Aboriginal flag and the Australian flag draped around her. She came to be regarded as a symbol of Australian unity and power.

Sources: *Jet* 98 (23 October 2000): 54; *Contemporary Black Biography,* vol. 29, pp. 64–67.

2002 • Bobsled brakeman Vonetta Flowers (1973–) became the first black American athlete to win a gold medal in a Winter Olympics, on February 19. She was also the first Alabamian to win a medal at the Winter Olympics. Held in Park City, Utah, this was a double-barrel historic event in that it was also the inaugural women's Olympic competition in the bobsled race. The medal was the first for the United States in the sport since 1948. The Bakken-Flowers team running in USA-II won out over the United State's best hope, the Gea Johnson/Jean Racine team. The twenty-eight-year-old former long jumper and seven-time All-American at the University of Alabama at Birmingham pushed the bobsled as Jill Bakken drove in the competition, as their two-time run was 1 minute and 37.76 seconds. Flowers had envisioned competing in the Summer Olympics but gave up hope after two knee operations and ankle surgery. She chose the bobsled in 1994 after her husband, Johnny, UABs track coach, saw Bonnie Warner's advertisement for a pusher at the U.S. Olympics track and field trials in Sacramento. In honor of her accomplishments, Birmingham mayor Bernard Kincaid declared March 23, 2002, "Vonetta Flowers Day."

Sources: *Crisis* 109 (March/April 2002): 8; *Jet* 101 (15 April 2002): 8; *Tennessean* (20 February 2002); *Who's Who among African Americans,* 26th ed., p. 417.

2002 • The U.S. men's bobsled team, running in the Winter Olympics, drove to the bronze medal in the four-man race at Utah Olympic Park on February 23, winning the first medal for a men's team in forty-six years. History was also made that day when Randy Jones and Garrett Hines became the first black men in the United States to win medals in the Winter Olympics. Their silver medals came five days after Vonetta Flowers became the first black to win gold in a Winter Olympics, participating in the inaugural race for women. Jones, brakeman Hines, and Bill Schuffenhauer were behind Todd Hayes when he drove the fire-engine red USA–1 sled to win in 3 minutes and 07.81 seconds

Sources: *Atlanta Journal/Constitution,* Sunday, Home ed. (24 February 2002); *Boston Globe,* third ed. (24 February 2002); *Tennessean* (24 February 2002).

2008 • Jamaican sprinter and five-time World and six-time Olympic gold medalist Usain Bolt (1986–) became the first black to hold simultaneously world and Olympic records in the 100-meter and 200-meter competition. In 2012, during the London Summer Olympics, he became the first man in modern Olympic history to win gold in the 100-meter, 200-meter, and 4 × 100-meter in consecutive Olmpics. "Lightning Bolt," as he is known, held the World Record and won gold at the 2008 Beijing Olympic games, when he ran the 4 × 100-meter, 200-meter, and 100-meter. In 2007 Bolt won silver in the World Championship, 200-meter held in Osaka. When he won gold in the 200-meter during the 2002 World Junior Championships, he was the first junior sprinter to run the 200-meter in under twenty seconds, and the youngest person ever to win gold. He turned professional in 2004, and continued to develop his sport. Born in Trelawny, Jamaca, his talent was recognized while in high school; his physical education teacher became his mentor and guided Bolt to success.

Sources: "Bolt Repeats Golden Double Spring," *Tennessean* (10 August 2012); "Olympics 2012: Usain Bolt Wins His Third London Gold Medal, Anchors Jamaica to World Record in the 4 × 100 Relay," *New York Daily News* (11 August 2012), http://www.nydailynews.com/sports/olympics-2012/olympics-2012-usain-bolt-wins-london-gold-medal-anchors-jamaica-world-record-4x100-relay-article-1.1134456, accessed October 2, 2012; *Who's Who among African Americans,* vol. 26, p. 117.

Usain Bolt

Poker

2002 • Professional poker player Phillip D. "Phil" Ivey (1976–) is regarded as one of the world's best all-round poker players. He honed his skills at an early age until he reached the legal age for gambling, then began a meteoric rise to the top of his sport. In this year he won three World Series of Poker bracelets, the youngest player ever to do so. By 2010 he had won eight bracelets. He had accumulated over $13.8 million in live tournament winnings by 2010. His total worth is said to be $100 billion. Born in Riverside, California, his family relocated to Roselle, New Jersey when he was an infant. His grandfather introduced him to gambling when his was eight years old. Ivey is seen regularly on televised poker games.

Sources: *Contemporary Black Biography,* vol. 72, pp. 62–64; Poker-King, "2012 Phil Ivey Poker Profile," http://www.poker-king.com/phil-ivey-profile.php, accessed October 2, 2012.

Rodeo

1876 • Nat Love (1844–?), former slave, frontiersman, and cowboy, was the only black claimant to the title Deadwood Dick and so claimed to be the first known black rodeo champion. His account of his life, as written in his autobiography, is sometimes unconvincing since none of the cowboys he worked with seemed to have ridden with other crews and records are lacking. Whatever its authenticity, the story does exist and makes interesting reading.

Sources: Durham and Jones, *The Negro Cowboys,* pp. 192–206; Katz, *Black People Who Made the Old West,* pp. 113–17; Katz, *The Black West,* 1993, pp. 150–52; *Contemporary Black Biography,* vol. 9, pp. 148–52.

1887 • Pinto Jim and Bronco Jim Davis are the first known blacks to participate in a rodeo, in October in Denver, Colorado. Pinto Jim could rope, bridle, saddle, and mount his horse in thirteen minutes. Bronco Jim Davis' contest was abandoned after thirty minutes of struggle in which the man and the horse appeared evenly matched.

Sources: Durham and Jones, *The Negro Cowboys,* p. 207.

1905 • Bill Pickett (1860–1932), rodeo cowboy and son of a former slave, is generally credited with being the first person to develop a way of bulldogging which made the act a spectacular performance. It is known that a black named Andy performed the maneuver bulldogging, which is now known as steer wrestling, in the 1870s, as Sam Johnson, a big and impressive man, did later. When Pickett joined the 101 Ranch in 1900, his new technique involved biting the upper lip of the steer after the throw and raising his hands to show that he was no longer holding. The 101 Ranch put on its first major rodeo in 1905 and continued until the outbreak of World War I in 1914. Pickett was presented to King

The First Black Rodeo Record

Early written accounts of rodeos are sparse, but the first black known to have set a record in steer roping in 1890 was an unnamed man in Mobeetie, Texas, with a time of one minute and forty-five seconds.

Sources: *Durham and Jones, The Negro Cowboys,* p. 206.

George V and Queen Mary after a special performance in that year. Pickett lived out his days on the 101 Ranch. On December 9, 1971, he became the first black elected to the National Cowboy Hall of Fame. He was later inducted into the ProRodeo Hall of Fame in 1989. Pickett was born in Travis County, Texas, near Austin, into a large family, which contained thirteen children. It has been suggested that he learned how to be a cowboy along with his brothers. He and several of his brothers opened their own stock business in the 1880s, in which their main job was breaking wild horses. The date of his first bull-dogging deed is not known, but he became a professional rodeo performer in 1888. He was successful both as a skilled cowboy and as an entertainer and acquired the nickname "The Dusky Demon." He was working as a ranch hand at the 101 Ranch when he died after being kicked in the head by a horse. In 1993 Pickett was one of the persons chosen to be on a twenty-nine-cent stamp in the "Legends of the West" series. Unfortunately, when the issue was released the picture on the Pickett stamp was that of his brother Sam. The mistake was corrected a few weeks later. He was honored again in 1984 when the first Bill Pickett Invitational Rodeo was held. The event continues as the only black rodeo; it is held annually. There is a bronze statue of Pickett at the North Fort Worth (Texas) Historical Society.

Sources: Alford, *Famous First Blacks,* p. 68; *Crisis* 77 (November 1970): 388; Durham and Jones, *Negro Cowboys,* pp. 209–19; *Ebony* 33 (May 1978): 58–62; *Jet* 93 (8 December 1997): 19; Katz, *The Black West,* 1983, pp. 160–62; Smith, *Encyclopedia of African American Popular Culture,* vol. 3, pp. 1087–89; Smith, *Notable Black American Men,* pp. 935–36; *Contemporary Black Biography,* vol. 4, pp. 198–201.

1982 • The first black World Rodeo champion was Charles Sampson (1957–) of Los Angeles. The bull rider won the National Finals Rodeo in 1981, and the next year won the Winston Rodeo Series and was awarded the world title. He won the Sierra Circuit title in 1984, and for five consecutive years, 1981–85, qualified for the National Finals Rodeo, appearing a total of ten times. His popularity as a rider made him a familiar media figure through his appearance in magazine advertisements and endorsement of a brand of jeans. Sampson attended Central Arizona College and joined the Professional Rodeo Cowboys Association in 1977. He was one of the performers in the 1983 Presidential Command Performance Rodeo. Sampson was named to the Professional Rodeo Hall of Fame in 1996. Sampson, who was short in stature and light in weight, was the first black to win a championship in the event of bull riding, and he set a record for money earned by bull riders in 1982. He was a top contender as a bull rider for more than a decade. Horses attracted his attention when he went on a pony ride when he was ten years old; he moved to bull riding after a trip to a riding stable that he took with the Boy Scouts the next year. He rode his first bucking bronco when he was twelve and earned his first money riding bulls when he was fifteen. A job at a stable when he was a teenager gave him the opportunity to hone his skills. He won a rodeo scholarship when he entered Central Arizona State. During the course of his career, Sampson's rodeo participation was derailed two separate times, when he broke the same leg twice. He also suffered injuries to his face, his ankle, his sternum, and a wrist at various points during his career. He retired as a professional rodeo cowboy in 1994. His activities since retirement have included producing professional bull riding competitions. He was named to the Professional Rodeo Cowboy Hall of Fame in 1996, and had earlier been the second black (after Bill Pickett) named to the National Cowboy Hall of Fame.

Sources: Ashe, *A Hard Road to Glory,* vol. 3, p. 234; *Jet* 65 (20 February 1984): 40; *Contemporary Black Biography,* vol. 4, pp. 175–78; *Who's Who among African Americans,* 26th ed., p. 1088.

1991 • Fred Whitfield (1967–) became the first black American to win the world title in calf roping. By the year 2000 Whitfield had won four World Calf Roping titles and had become the first black rodeo performer to earn more than $1 million. He reached this mark in eight years, faster than any other cowboy in the history of the PRCA at the time. In 2000 he became the first black to win the Professional Rodeo Cowboys Association's World Champion All-Around Cowboy title. Like other black rodeo performers, Whitfield took to the saddle early. The Texas native lived first in Cypress, Texas, moved to Houston with his mother when his parents divorced, but grew up primarily in Cypress, where he lived first with relatives and later with the son of the family for whom his mother had once worked as a housekeeper. He was five when he began watching calf roping, seven when he threw his first rope, and nine when he began competing in peewee rodeos and had his first victory. He joined the PRCA in 1989 and has been winning championships and setting records ever since.

Sources: *Jet* 94 (24 August 1998): 50; 97 (6 March 2000): 50; *Contemporary Black Biography,* vol. 23, pp. 214–17.

Rowing

1915 • Joseph E. Trigg manned the number seven oar at Syracuse University and became the first known black athlete on a varsity rowing team. Trigg was also an outstanding football player.

Sources: Ashe, *A Hard Road to Glory,* vol. 3, p. 215; Young, *Negro Firsts in Sports,* pp. 75, 176.

Sailing

1920 • The first excursion boat for blacks in Washington, D.C., began operating this year. The steamer was 160 feet long with a capacity of 400 gross tons and a seating capacity of eight. It also provided twenty state rooms. Called the *E. Madison Hall,* its owner, J. O. Holmes, purchased the boat in 1917 and allowed it to be used for government service for the first three years. After then, the boat was converted into an excursion steamer.

Sources: Jones, *Recreation and Amusement among Negroes in Washington, D.C.,* pp. 141–42.

1992 • Martin Stephan and Art Prince became the first black Americans to sail in the America's Cup.

Sources: *Emerge* 3 (October 1992): 38.

Skiing

2007 • Barbara Hillary, then seventy-five years old and a cancer survivor, completed a trek to the North Pole on skiis and is believed to be the first black woman to accomplish this feat. Hillary is one of the oldest people to reach the world's northernmost point. A resident of Averne, New York, she grew up in Harlem and enjoyed a career in nursing and community activism.

Sources: *Jet* 111 (28 May 2007): 36.

Soccer

1990 • Professional soccer player Roger Milla (1952–) of Cameroon, became the oldest player to score a goal in the history of the World Cup, on June 14. African soccer also reached a new level this year when the team from Cameroon advanced to the quarterfinals, becoming the first African team to reach that level. In the match between England and Cameroon, however, England won 3–2 in overtime. Milla grew up in Douala, and was a member of the 1975 team that won the African Cup, a tournament in which Africa's league champions competed. His performance in that tournament led to his being named African Football Player of the Year, which is the equivalent of the U.S. Most Valuable Player, in 1977. Milla then moved to France, where he played in the French First Division, a prestigious soccer league. Three of the teams on which he played reached the finals for the French championship while he was with them. He played for Cameroon in world matches during the same period. Briefly retired from play between 1988 and 1990, Milla was not expected to be on the team roster when Cameroon played in the 1990 World Cup, but at the last moment his name showed up. Of the four games that Cameroon played, Milla had a total of four goals, playing primarily as a substitute.

Sources: *Contemporary Black Biography,* vol. 2, pp. 162–63.

2000 • Briana Scurry (1971–), the only African American starter for the 1999 champion U.S. women's soccer team, became the first goalkeeper of any race or gender to play in one hundred international games. Scurry was born in St. Paul, Minnesota, but the Scurry family moved to Anoka, Minnesota, when Scurry was a youngster, and it was there that she was thrust into a soccer community. The Scurrys were the only black family within a radius of four miles, but this did not prevent the youngster from indulging in football, basketball, softball, and track before she tried out for soccer when she was in the fourth grade. At first she played on an all-boys team, while continuing to play basketball. She excelled in both sports, and when she graduated from high school she had made All-American as a goalie, was an All-State basketball player, and had been named the Minnesota high school Female Athlete of the Year. Colleges recruited her with a passion, most seeking her services as a soccer player. Scurry enrolled at the University of Massachusetts, where she was named Goalkeeper of the Year twice and was named National Goalkeeper of the Year by the Adidas Athletic Club in 1993. She joined the U.S. soccer team in 1994 and played in her first international match that year. The game was a shutout for the U.S.: no shot on goal got by her. When Scurry graduated from the University of Massachusetts in 1995, she put her law school plans on hold to rejoin the U.S. soccer team. Her future held more wins and more acclaim, including the Olympic gold medal in 1996 and the U.S. Women's World Cup gold medal in 1999. She was not the U.S. team's starting goalie when they went to the Olympics in 2000; Scurry had been out most of the year with injuries. The U.S. team won a silver medal in 2000. The Women's United Soccer Association team that was played in April 2001 was formed largely in response to the fan enthusiasm generated by the miraculous 1999 season of Scurry and her teammates. Scurry played for the Atlanta Beat of the WUSA.

Sources: *Contemporary Black Biography,* vol. 27, pp. 177–79; *Jet* 96 (2 August 1999): 49–50.

2007 • Victor B. McFarlane, then the new majority owner of the D.C. United soccer team, and co-owner Brian K. Davis became the first black owners in Major League Soccer. When the new owners were announced, McFarland acknowledged that soccer had become the number one sport but not so in the United States. "We want to be part of the change that is now on the horizon," he said, and added that he wanted to be part of the effort "to make soccer the sport that African Americans and other children of color first look to for recreation and entertainment."

Sources: *Jet* 110 (29 June 2007): 51.

Squash

1988 • The first black member of the men's All-American squash team of the National Intercollegiate Squash Racquets Association was Wendell Chestnut.

Sources: *Jet* 74 (23 May 1988): 20.

Swimming

1981 • Charles P. Chapman became the first black swimmer to cross the English Channel.

Sources: *Jet* 84 (5 July 1993): 18.

Taekwondo

2001 • Lauren Banks (1990–), a second-degree black belt, became the youngest and the only black belt in the American Taekwondo Association (ATA) (across all black belt girls divisions eight through sixteen) to win a world title in each of the last three consecutive tournament years, or 1999, 2000, and 2001. Since she was five years old, the eleven-year-old Blanks won over one hundred trophies. She has trained under ATA Master Carl Flotka, who is with Flotka's ATA Black Belt Academy located in Lansing, Michigan. Banks is a native of Lansing, Michigan, and a straight-A student.

Sources: *Jet* 101 (17 December 2001): 17.

Tennis

1899 • The first black to arrange an interstate tournament for black players was W. W. Walker of the Chautauqua Tennis Club. The Philadelphia event attracted competitors from several nearby states. Walker became the first of a long line of great black tennis coaches.

Sources: Ashe, *A Hard Road to Glory*, vol. 1, p. 59; *Encyclopedia of Black America*, p. 141; Jones and Washington, *Black Champions Challenge American Sports*, p. 21.

1917 • Tally Holmes of Washington, D.C. and Lucy Diggs Slowe (1885–1937) of Baltimore won the men's and women's singles, respectively, to become the first players to win the all-black American Tennis Association championships. The matches, the first ATA Nationals, were held in August this year at Druid Hill Park in Baltimore. Slowe also became the first black woman national champion in any sport.

Sources: Ashe, *A Hard Road to Glory*, pp. 60–61; Bennett, *Before the Mayflower*, p. 635; Young, *Negro Firsts in Sports*, pp. 183–84; Smith, *Notable Black American Women*, pp. 1031–33 (Slowe).

1935 • The first black woman to win seven consecutive titles in the American Tennis Association was Ora Washington (1898–1971). She began her career in 1924. During twelve undefeated years, she used her blazing pace to upset many of the American Tennis Association's top-seeded stars. She remained undefeated until 1936, when she became ill during play and lost the match, but she regained the championship in 1937. She was also on the ATA women's doubles team from 1930 through 1936. During her reign as ATA women's champion, the champion of the U.S. Lawn Tennis Association (Helen Wills Moody) refused to play Washington because of segregation and Moody's personal preference. Washington was also an outstanding basketball player, playing for the Germantown Hornets and starring as a center for the *Philadelphia Tribune* women's squad for eighteen years. She was also captain of the team. Washington won over 200 trophies in tennis and basketball. As late as 1961, she maintained her connection with tennis by giving free coaching and training for young people at community tennis courts in Germantown, Pennsylvania, where she first developed her own interest in tennis.

Ora Washington

Sources: Jones and Washington, *Black Champions Challenge American Sports*, pp. 54–56, 60, 80, 84; Young, *Black Firsts in Sports*, 183, 187, 194–96; Smith, *Notable Black American Women*, Book II, pp. 685–87.

1948 • Reginald Weir (1912–), a physician of New York City, was the first black to participate in the United States Indoor Lawn Tennis Association championship. He won his first match at the New York City event on March 11 and was eliminated on March 13.

Sources: Ashe, *A Hard Road to Glory,* vol. 2, pp. 61, 62, 64; Kane, *Famous First Facts,* p. 662; Young, *Negro Firsts in Sports,* pp. 184, 188.

1953 • Lorraine Williams (1939–) became the first black to win a nationally recognized tennis title when she won the junior girl's championship this year.

Sources: Bennett, *Before the Mayflower,* p. 635; *Ebony* 9 (January 1954): 24; 7 (June 1952): 41–45; Young, *Negro Firsts in Sports,* p. 280.

Althea Gibson

1956 • Althea Gibson (1927–2003) became the first black to win a major tennis title when she won the women's singles in the French Open on May 26. She won the Wimbledon championship the next year on July 6, 1957, when she also captured the women's singles, becoming the first black to win these honors. Gibson defended her Wimbledon championship successfully in 1958. She became the first black to win a major United States national championship on September 8, 1957, when she defeated Louise Brough at Forest Hills to win the women's singles. In 1991 she was the first black woman to receive the Theodore Roosevelt Award of the NCAA. Gibson was born in Silver, South Carolina, on a cotton farm where her father worked as a sharecropper, but the family moved to Harlem several years later. School was not her favorite activity, and she dropped out as soon as she could. Gibson became a ward of the state when she was fourteen, and subsequently was exposed to the programs of the Police Athletic League. The game of paddleball led her to tennis. She was so good at the game that the New York Cosmopolitan Club sponsored her for junior membership and private tennis lessons. In 1941 she won the New York State Open Championship. Following that, Gibson won New York State (1943) and National (1944 and 1945) Negro Girls Championships. She went back to school, graduated from high school in 1949, and entered Florida Agricultural and Mechanical College (now Florida A & M University) on a tennis scholarship. At first, Gibson had difficulty gaining access to major tennis matches. Her first real opportunity came when she was invited to play at Forest Hills in 1950. This first time, she lost to Louise Brough. Her game suffered a slump for several years, and she considered giving up tennis once she accepted a teaching job at Lincoln University (Missouri) after she graduated from college in 1953. But she stayed with the sport, going on a goodwill tour and playing tournaments abroad, where she won all but two of her eighteen matches. Her success in 1957 and the early part of 1958 provided a good backdrop for her 1958 championship match with Louise Brough. In addition to being the first black to win the Wimbledon title, she was the first black ever to enter the tournament (seeded first in both 1957 and 1958). For some reason, she turned to golf after her 1958 wins. Her career in golf was not a runaway success. Gibson married a New Jersey businessman and was active in civic affairs, retiring formally in 1992. In 1958 she was the first black voted Woman of the Year by the Associated Press. In 1968 Gibson was the first black inducted into the International Tennis Hall of Fame. When the Arthur Ashe Stadium was dedicated in New York in 1997, Gibson was honored. It happened on her 70th birthday.

Sources: Ashe, *A Hard Road to Glory,* pp. 58, 64, 100; Bennett, *Before the Mayflower,* pp. 635; *Encyclopedia of Black America,* p. 141; Smith, *Notable Black American Women,* pp. 397–402; *Contemporary Black Biography,* vol. 8, pp. 78–81; *Jet* 92 (26 May 1997): 19; 94 (6 July 1998): 19; 100 (9 July 2001): 19; *The Black New Yorkers,* p. 285.

1963 • Arthur Ashe (1943–1993) was the first black named to the American Davis Cup team. In 1961 the year he won the USLTA junior indoor title, another first, he had been named the first black on the United States Junior Davis Cup team. In 1968 he became the first black man to win a major tennis title, the national men's singles in the United States Lawn Tennis Association Open tournament at Forest Hills. This was the first time the contest was open to professionals as well as amateurs. He became the first black man to win a singles title at Wimbledon in 1975. In 1983 Ashe received a contract to produce the first complete book on blacks in sports, *A Hard Road to Glory.* He was the first black man inducted into the International Tennis Hall of Fame, in 1985. Ashe was stricken with a major heart attack in 1979 and retired from tennis in 1980. Subsequently he had a second heart attack and in 1988 had brain surgery. In 1993 Ashe died of AIDS acquired through a blood transfusion. In June 1993 President Bill Clinton honored him posthumously with the Presidential Medal of Freedom, awarded at the first annual National Sports Awards presentation in Washington, D.C. His Richmond hometown honored him by raising a statue of him on the city's main thoroughfare in 1996. The U.S. Tennis Association named the new U.S. Open stadium in honor of Ashe. Dedicated in 1997, the stadium is located at the USTA National Tennis Center at Flushing Meadows-Corona Park in Queens, New York. A native of Richmond, Virginia, Ashe grew up spending much of his time at a large city park for blacks, which his father managed. The Ashe family lived on the premises, and Ashe turned increasingly to books and sports after his mother died when he was six years old. Too light in weight for football and too slow for track, tennis became his choice. He began playing at age seven and was nationally ranked as an amateur by the time he was fourteen. His victories in the junior singles events brought him to the attention of a St. Louis tennis coach, and, while there, Ashe continued his tennis training while also being enrolled in high school. In 1962 he was ranked fifth as a U.S. junior player. Ashe's advances were not easy. He faced discrimination and racial prejudice with every step he took. Ashe has been reported to credit the education he received in his segregated Richmond school and the training he received from a Richmond tennis coach with helping him to endure racial affronts and maintain his composure, but he has also been reported to have felt isolated during much of his career. He graduated from UCLA in 1966. While there, he had served on the Davis Cup team twice, led UCLA to the NCAA championship, and advanced to rank number-two as an amateur. Military service, with tennis included, followed and brought him to the 1968 Open as the top-ranked player. He turned professional in 1969 and continued to be among the top five players between 1969 and 1975. Ashe's voice and his influence continued to be a force after his retirement. He became an author, lecturer, and a vocal humanitarian. And after he made his AIDS diagnosis public in 1992, he established the Arthur Ashe Foundation for the Defeat of AIDS.

Arthur Ashe

Sources: *Encyclopedia of Black America,* p. 142; *Jet* 84 (12 June 1993): 56, 58; 91 (10 March 1997): 49; Jones and Washington, *Black Champions Challenge American Sports,* p. 146; Smith, *Notable Black American Men,* pp. 36–40; *Contemporary Black Biography,* vol. 1, pp. 11–14, vol. 11, pp. 7–10; Salzman, *Encyclopedia of African-American Culture and History,* Supplement, p. 7.

1968 • The first black Davis Cup umpire was Huel Washington, who officiated in the United States vs. Mexico match at the Berkeley Tennis Club on May 24–26.

Sources: Documents from Huel Washington to the author, 26 July 2010; "Davis Cup Tie: United States vs. Mexico," Official Program, Berkeley Tennis Club, May 24–26, 1968.

1978 • Arthur Ashe (1943–1993) and Yannick Noah became the first black doubles team to play at Wimbledon. Ashe, who had helped the young boy from Cameroon to become a recognized tennis professional, had been a mentor for Noah. Noah was captain of the French Davis Cup team in 1995, the first black to have that honor.

Sources: *Jet* 87 (27 February 1995): 48–49.

1988 • Zina Lynna Garrison [Jackson] (1963–) won a gold medal in doubles and a bronze in the singles in the Olympics held in Seoul, Korea, becoming the first black Olympic winner in tennis. She was also the first black to rank in the top ten on the women's professional tour. Born in Houston, Texas, she was raised by her mother, after her father died before Garrison's first birthday. She began to develop her tennis skills when she was ten years old, and by age fourteen she ranked among the top players in her age group in the U.S. She was number-one among junior players at eighteen and had won both the Wimbledon and U.S. Open junior championships in 1981. Garrison played her first professional match in the 1982 French Open just after she graduated from high school. Her top-ten ranking came just a year later. She has been victorious in singles, doubles, and mixed doubles both in the U.S. and abroad. When Martina Navratilova defeated her in the 1990 Wimbledon tournament, Garrison was the first black woman to reach the finals in Wimbledon (or any other tennis Grand Slam competition) since Althea Gibson won the championship in 1957. The Zina Garrison Foundation, which supports a variety of causes (youth organizations, the homeless, and anti-drug organizations) was begun in 1988. Garrison is also well known for her personal community service activities. The Zina Garrison All-Court Tennis Academy was opened in 1992, designed to help youth with low self-esteem improve their self-confidence through achievements in tennis. Her plays on the court and her charitable activities have been recognized inside and outside the tennis world. In 1992 she received the *Family Circle* Player Who Makes a Difference Award, and she has held positions with the YWCA and on the board of directors of the World Tennis Association Player Council. In the period just before she became an Olympics champion, some bumps in the road led to a brief bout with bulimia. She was still mourning the death of her mother, suffering from an injury to her right foot, and experiencing problems in her relationship with her longtime doubles partner Lori McNeil. She managed to turn her life around. She became Garrison-Jackson in 1989 when she married Willard Jackson, who subsequently organized International Public Relations and Marketing for Athletes and became Garrison's manager.

Sources: Hine, *Black Women in America,* pp. 480–81; *Contemporary Black Biography,* vol. 2, pp. 89–92; *Jet* 78 (23 July 1990): 51; Smith, *Notable Black American Women,* Book II, pp. 243–46; *Who's Who among African Americans,* 26th ed., p. 451.

1994 • Lori Michelle McNeil (1963–) defeated five-time Wimbledon champion and number-one-ranked Steffi Graf in the first round of the Ladies' Singles held on the Centre Court. Until then, no reigning woman champion had lost in the first round to an unseeded opponent, making McNeil the first woman to accomplish this feat. It was McNeil's second straight victory over Graf. McNeil was born in San Diego, California, where her father was a San Diego Chargers football player. She began playing tennis there and continued play after the McNeil family moved to Houston, Texas. She entered Oklahoma State University when she graduated from high school, where she was the Big Eight Conference Tennis Singles Champion in 1983. McNeil turned professional in 1986 and was primarily known as a doubles player until she reached the Wimbledon quarterfinals in singles in 1986 and later defeated Chris Evert in the U.S. Open singles quarterfinals in 1987. The latter match gave her a number-one ranking in women's tennis. She later achieved rank number 9.

Sources: *Jet* 86 (11 July 1994):48–49; *Contemporary Black Biography,* vol. 1, pp. 156–57; *Who's Who among African Americans,* 26th ed., p. 860.

Venus and Serena Williams

1999 • Serena Williams (1981–) and her sister Venus Ebone Starr Williams (1980–) became the first black women's team to succeed at the U.S. Open on September 12 in New York City. They won the doubles title 4–6, 6–1, 6–4, defeating Chandra Rubin of America and Sandrine Testud of France. The Williams sisters had won the French Open championship in June and the Wimbledon women's doubles title in July, making this their third Grand Slam doubles title. These victories were just the beginning of the talented sisters' assault on major tennis championships. They took the gold medal in doubles at the 2000 Olympic games in Sydney, Australia, winning 6–1, 6–1 in straight sets. They were the first sisters to win Olympic gold in doubles, and extended their doubles winning streak to twenty-two matches. The sisters, Florida residents who were born in Compton, California, were coached at home by their father and were considered child tennis prodigies. With their lives and their careers nurtured carefully by their parents, they played junior tennis until Venus was eleven years old, when they dropped out and were mostly absent from the tennis scene until the mid–1990s. They began making news almost immediately, and by the time they came to the 1999 Open, they had made their presence felt on the women's tour. Inevitably, the time came when the sisters would have to play each other, not just in a routine match, but for a title. Several months prior to the Open, Venus defeated Serena in the WTA Lipton Championships match. It was the first time in 115 years that sisters had played each other for the title. In 2001, Venus defeated Serena again in the U.S. Open women's finals match. It was the first time two black players had faced each other in a Grand Slam singles match, but not the last. The Williams sisters repeated their finals match for the 2002 U.S. Open; this time, Serena won. The sisters are noted for the power they show on the court, but have not been the most popular players on the tour. Accused by other women on the tour

Women's Tennis Firsts

In 2002 Venus Ebone Starr Williams (1980–) achieved the top spot in the Women's Tennis Association's (WTA) world ranking, becoming the first black player with a number-one rating since 1975, when Arthur Ashe held that honor. In June 2002 Serena Williams was ranked number-two in the WTA Tour rankings, making the sisters the first siblings to reach a career high of 1–2. Playing in her third career Grand Slam, younger sister Serena defeated Venus Williams in the French Open women's singles finals on Saturday, June 8, 7–5, 6–3 to win the French Open.

Sources: *Jet* 101 (11 March 2002): 48; *Tennessean* (7 June 2002); (9 June 2002).

and by the press of being arrogant and part-time tennis players because they had not been playing the full tour, their image has become less harsh as their victories have increased. Although the drama increases when they play as partners or against each other, each sister is a star in her own right. They are the first sister duo in which each has won a Grand Slam championship. To date, no player has ever beaten both of the sisters in the same Grand Slam match.

Sources: *Jet* 98 (24 July 2000): 10–18, 51–100 (17 September 2001): 190; *Contemporary Black Biography,* vol. 20, pp. 227–29 (Serena); vol. 17, pp. 207–10 (Venus); *New York Times* (10 September 2000); (8 September 2001); (28 September 2000) Stein, "The Power Game," *Time* 158 (3 September 2001): 54–58, 61–63; *Who's Who among African Americans,* 26th ed., p. 1363.

1999 • The first black woman to win the U.S. Open since 1958, when tennis pioneer Althea Gibson won, was Serena Williams (1981–). She beat number-one-ranked Martina Hingis of Switzerland 6–3, 7–6, 7–4. Playing at first somewhat in the shadow of older sister Venus, she was the first sister to win a major championship. She was ranked number 4 in the world after her victory. She had won three titles earlier in the year. In 1998 she had won the mixed doubles title at Wimbledon. In 2012 she became a four-time winner of the U.S. Open, and won gold in women's singles at the London Olympics.

Sources: *Jet* 96 (30 August 1999): 52; 96 (12 September 1999): 51–55; *New York Times* (8 September 2001); *Who's Who among African Americans,* 26th ed., p. 1363.

2000 • Venus Ebone Starr Williams (1980–) won the Wimbledon 2000 Tennis Championship to become the first black woman winner since Althea Gibson in 1957 and 1958. She also won the U.S. Open Championship. Venus Williams won Olympic gold medals in singles and doubles in the summer Olympic Games held in Sydney, Australia this year, becoming the first black woman to achieve this honor. Her sister Serena was her doubles partner. She also signed a multiyear, $40 million contract with Reebok in what is believed to be the most lucrative deal for a woman athlete. In 2001 she won both the Wimbledon title and the U.S. Open title, giving her back-to-back titles in two of tennis' most prestigious events. No black person had won back-to-back titles at the Open since Althea Gibson in 1957 and 1958. Sister Serena was her opponent in the 2001 and 2002 U.S. Open finals matches.

Sources: *Jet* 99 (8 January 2001): 51; *New York Times* (8 September 2001); *Tennessean* (22 December 2000); *Who's Who among African Americans,* 26th ed., p. 1355.

2007 • Tennis coach Traci Green (1979–) became the first black woman to head any coaching staff for any Harvard University sport. Then twenty-eight years old, the former University of Florida tennis champion was mentored by Arthur Ashe. She also coached women's tennis at Temple University.

Sources: *Jet* 112 (9 July 2007): 53.

Track and Field

1912 • The first black to hold the record for the 100-yard dash was Howard Porter Drew (1890–1957), of Lexington, Virginia. He was called the world's fastest human and won the National Amateur Athletic Union championship on September 12. In this year also he won the 220-yard dash championship. He never competed in the Olympics.

Sources: Ashe, *A Hard Road to Glory*, vol. 1, pp. 64–65, 67; *Encyclopedia of Black America*, p. 139; Jones and Washington, *Black Champions Challenge American Sports*, pp. 39–40, 44, 45, 48.

1912 • Theodore "Ted" Cable of Harvard University, a hammer-throw specialist, was the first black to win an intercollegiate weight championship.

Sources: Ashe, *A Hard Road to Glory*, vol. 1, p. 64; Jones and Washington, *Black Champions Challenge American Sports*, p. 31; Young, *Negro Firsts in Sports*, pp. 84, 87.

1921 • Edward Orval Gourdin (1897–1966) was the first person of any race to long-jump more than twenty-five feet, surpassing that distance by three inches in a college international meet at Cambridge, Massachusetts, on July 23, 1921. This year he also was the first black to win the pentathlon in the National Amateur Athletic Union championships. In 1924 he won a silver medal in the Paris Olympics. Gourdin was born in Jacksonville, Florida, and graduated from Harvard University (B.A., 1921) and Harvard Law School (LL.N., 1924). He was admitted to the Massachusetts Bar and the Federal Bar. He became United States District Attorney in 1936 and in 1958 became the first black on the Massachusetts Supreme Court.

Sources: Ashe, *A Hard Road to Glory*, vol. 2, pp. 79–80; Logan and Winston, *Dictionary of American Negro Biography*, pp. 264–65; *Negro Year Book, 1921–1922*, pp. 30–31; Page, *Black Olympian Medalists*, pp. 44, 149; Young, *Negro Firsts in Sports*, p. 86.

1930 • Thomas Edward "Little Eddie" Tolan (1908–1967) ran in Evanston, Illinois, this year and was the first person officially credited with running 100 yards in 9.5 seconds. He set two Olympic records in the Los Angeles meet in 1932 and became the first black to win gold medals in both the 100- and 200-meter dash. He became the first black winner of two gold medals in the same meet. In his career he won three hundred races and lost seven. A graduate of the University of Michigan, he became an elementary school teacher in 1935.

Sources: Alford, *Famous First Blacks*, p. 99; *Encyclopedia of Black America*, p. 139; Young, *Negro Firsts in Sports*, pp. 84–85; Page, *Black Olympian Medalists*, pp. 116–17, 149.

Ralph H. Metcalfe

1934 • Ralph H. Metcalfe (1910–1978), while training for the Olympics, broke three world records on June 11—100 meters, 200 meters, and 220 yards. In 1934 he became the first man to win the NCAA doubles three times and the next year he became the only sprinter to win five times in a single event. In 1934–35 he was called the "world's fastest human." He and Jesse Owens were the first blacks to win a gold medal for the 400 × 100-meter relay, which they ran in Berlin in 1936. Metcalfe was born in Atlanta, Georgia, but moved with the family to Chicago, Illinois, when he was in elementary school. His interest in sports surfaced early, and he joined the track team when he was fifteen years old. A scant four years later, in 1929, Metcalfe won a national interscholastic sprint championship. He continued to star in track while a student at Marquette University, where he was captain of the track team, which set world and NCAA records in almost every sprint category. After the 1936 Olympics, Metcalfe taught political science and coached the track team at Xavier University in Louisiana until 1942. While at Xavier, he took a leave of absence to complete graduate studies at the University of Southern California. He earned his master's degree in physical education in 1939. From 1943 to March 1946 he served as a lieutenant in the U.S. Army. When discharged from the army, he held a number of government appointments, some of which were related to athletics. Metcalfe was appointed to the Illinois State Athletic Commission in 1949 and, in 1952, became actively involved in politics as a member of the Democratic Committee for Chicago's Third Ward; he held this position until 1971. Election as an alderman followed in 1955, and in 1970 he became a U.S. Congressman, elected from a Chicago district. He was still serving as a Congressman at the time of his death. Metcalfe was a multiple Olympic medal winner, and as such he received many honors, including election to the U.S. Track and Field Hall of Fame. As a congressman, he was noted for his concern for citizens' rights in all areas. There were ups and downs during his tenure in Congress, but his winning electoral margin when he was re-elected in 1974 was at the time the highest plurality achieved by a U.S. Congressman.

Sources: Jones and Washington, *Black Champions Challenge American Sports,* pp. 67–68, 69, 70; Page, *Black Olympian Medalists,* pp. 82, 149; Young, *Negro Firsts in Sports,* pp. 84–85; Smith, *Notable Black American Men,* pp. 803–06.

1936 • Cleveland Abbott (1894–1955) began a track program for women and organized a sports carnival for women in 1928. In 1936 his squads were the first black women's track teams to participate in the National Amateur Athletic Union Track and Field meeting in Providence, Rhode Island. From 1935 to 1950, Abbott's teams won AAU indoor and outdoor championships and also represented the United States in the London Olympics held in 1948. Abbott was born in South Dakota. In 1916 he joined the Tuskegee Institute (now Tuskegee University) faculty as athletic director and instructor, while also coaching four sports. He is credited with having built Tuskegee's athletic department and is regarded by some as Alabama's greatest black coach. In addition to his achievements as a track coach, Abbott also made his mark as a football coach. He had winning seasons, most by a wide margin, in every year from 1924 through 1931. He had a record of 199 wins, 94 losses, and 31 ties in his thirty-two years of coaching football, and his teams won the Southern Intercollegiate Championship twelve times. He was instrumental in establishing tournaments for Southern black colleges and established the National Intercollegiate Basketball Tournament at Tuskegee in 1935. Active in civic affairs, Abbott was buried next to two of Tuskegee's most well known figures, agricultural scientist George Washington Carver and founding president Booker T. Washington.

Sources: Bailey, *They Too Call Alabama Home,* pp. 3–4.

1937 • The women's track team of Tuskegee Institute (now University) was the first black team to win the National AAU women's track and field championship. Coached by Christine Evans Petty, Lulu Hymes sparked the team by winning the long jump, taking second place in the 50-meter dash, and helping the 400-meter relay team place second. The team continued winning the AAU title through 1942.

Sources: Ashe, *A Hard Road to Glory,* vol. 2, pp. 76–77; Young, *Negro Firsts in Sports,* p. 91.

1954 • Since 1930 the Amateur Athletic Union has presented annually the James E. Sullivan Memorial Trophy to the top amateur athletes in the United States. Track star Malvin Greston "Mal" Whitfield (1924–) of The Ohio State University was the first black man to win the award. From 1948 to 1954, Whitfield dominated the 800-meters; during this period he won sixty-nine races and lost three. He won five AAU titles and held five indoor and outdoor world records.

Sources: Ashe, *A Hard Road to Glory,* vol. 3, p. 182; Clark, *Sports Firsts,* p. 237; Kane, *Famous First Facts,* p. 45; Young, *Negro Firsts in Sports,* p. 86.

1956 • Charles Everett Dumas (1937–), who won a gold medal at the 1956 Olympics at Melbourne with an Olympic record leap of 6 feet 11¼ inches, was also the first man to break the 7-foot barrier, clearing 7 feet 5/8 inches at the Olympic finals trial at the Los Angeles Coliseum.

Sources: Ashe, *A Hard Road to Glory,* vol. 3, pp. 184, 516; Page, *Black Olympian Medalists,* p. 34; *Negro Almanac,* p. 1429.

1957 • Aubrey Lewis (1935?–2001) became the first black captain of an athletic team at the University of Notre Dame. He starred on the track squad from 1957 to 1958. When he went to the university he took a sterling athletic career with him, having been one of New Jersey's greatest high school athletes and an all-American halfback at Montclair High School in the early 1950s. He received some 200 scholarship offers from various schools.

At Notre Dame he was also a member of the football team, playing halfback from 1955 to 1957. In his senior year his team snapped Oklahoma's forty-seven-game winning streak. Although the Chicago Bears drafted him, his ankle injury at Notre Dame kept Lewis from becoming a professional football player. He had also concealed from his coaches in all of his sports that, since childhood, he had a heart murmur. Lewis was a native of Glen Ridge, New Jersey. After college he taught school and coached track and field. The Federal Bureau of Investigation recruited him in 1962, and he became one of the first two blacks to go through its training academy. He was also a commissioner of the New Jersey Sports and Exposition Authority and a commissioner of the Port Authority of New York and New Jersey. He died of a heart ailment on December 10, 2001.

Sources: *New York Times* Obituaries (13 December 2001).

1960 • The first black to clear 7 feet 3¾ inches in the high jump was John Thomas, at the 1960 United States Olympics trials. A foul-up by officials at the 1959 Millrose Games deprived him of the indoor world record when he first cleared seven feet as a seventeen-year-old. At the Olympics, Thomas had to settle for a bronze medal.

Sources: Ashe, *A Hard Road to Glory,* vol. 2, pp. 187, 192, 201; *Encyclopedia of Black America,* p. 141; Henderson, *The Black Athlete,* pp. 249–50.

1970 • Larry Ellis (1900?–1998) was the first black American coach in any Ivy League sport. Hired at Princeton from 1970 to 1992, he coached outdoor and indoor track and field for twenty years, and cross-country for twenty-two years. Ellis grew up in the Bronx (New York) and went on to put Princeton's track and field program on the map. During Ellis' time at Princeton, the institution was a member of the Heptagonal League and had never won a league title before he arrived. Before he left, Princeton had won nineteen Heptagonal titles, eleven in track and eight in cross-country. Ellis' track expertise was sufficiently recognized that his know-how was sought beyond Princeton. In 1984 he was head coach for the 1984 U.S. men's Olympic track and field team and president of USA Track and Field from 1992 to 1996. Just two months before his death, he had served as head coach of the U.S. men's team at the World Cup Competition in Johannesburg.

Sources: *Jet* 94 (23 November 1998): 55.

1987 • Karen C. Keith (1957–) was the first woman of any race to coach men's and women's teams at a major institution, Boston College. Keith, a native of Boston, did her undergraduate work at Florida Agricultural and Mechanical University, earning a bachelor's degree in education in 1978. She earned the M.Ed. degree in administration/supervision from Boston College in 1989. Keith joined the coaching staff there after having worked in several positions in education between 1978 and 1989. She was Division I Region Coach of the Year in 1987.

Sources: *Jet* 73 (23 November 1988): 46; *Who's Who Among African Americans,* 26th ed., p. 714.

1995 • Sprinter Michael Duane Johnson (1967–) won world championships in the 200- and 400-meter sprints in 1993, and again in Sweden in 1995. No other man had met this double-win record at the World Championship.

Sources: *Jet* 88 (28 August 1995): 51; Salzman, *Encyclopedia of African-American Culture and History,* Supplement, p. 145.

1997 • For the first time in the 101-year history of the Boston Marathon, African runners swept both the men's and the women's championships. Lameck Aguta of Kenya became the seventh straight men's champion from Kenya, while Ethiopia's Fatuma Roba became the first African women's champion. Roba had previously won gold in the 1996 Summer Olympics. When she won the Boston Marathon, it was the first time she had participated in the event.

Sources: *Jet* 91 (12 May 1997): 48.

2000 • Marcia Fletcher became the first black head coach of the women's track and field programs at Clemson University in South Carolina. She was Clemson's first black head coach in any sport. Fletcher came to the position less than a year after she took a job (in January 2000) as track and field coach at Stephen F. Austin State University in Texas. She had been an assistant coach at Yale University from 1995 to 1999. Fletcher graduated from Clemson in 1990. While there, she made All-American in the long jump.

Sources: *Jet* 98 (4 September 2000): 50.

2012 • Edward S. "Ed" Temple (1927–), Olympic track coach in 1960 and 1964, became the first track coach inducted into the U.S. Olympic Hall of Fame. The ceremony took place in Chicago's Harris Theater on July 12. In his position as head Tigerbelles track and field coach at Tennessee State University, he coached Wilma Rudolph, who claimed the goal medal in women's 100 meters at the 1960 Summer Games in Rome. Forty members of his team won twenty-three Olympic medals, including thirteen gold, six silver, and four bronze. Born in Harrisburg, Pennsylvania, Temple graduated from Tennessee State.

Volleyball

1994 • Beach volleyball pioneer Dain Blanton (1971–) was the first and only black American on the Association of Volleyball Professionals tour. In 1997 he became the first black to win a major tournament in that sport, at Hermosa Beach. His first victory on the professional tour—the Hermosa Beach AVP Grand Slam—paid $300,000, the richest payoff in professional beach volleyball history. Blanton and his teammate, Eric Fonoimoana, won gold medals at the Sydney Olympics in 2000. Blanton grew up in Laguna Beach, California, which acquired beach volleyball when he was twelve years old. He was already an athlete—playing baseball, basketball, and soccer—when he added volleyball to his activities. By the time he was a high school senior (1990) he made it to Orange County Player of the Year and was the Most Valuable Player of the Pacific Coast League. Blanton was offered basketball scholarships, but chose to enter Pepperdine University on a volleyball scholarship. The team won a national championship during his sophomore year. Qualified to teach when he graduated from Pepperdine, he chose professional volleyball instead. After his win at Hermosa Beach, Blanton set up volleyball clinics for young people in and around Los Angeles, with the aim of exposing them to the sport. After his Olympic victory, he was chosen to be the Grand Marshal for the Laguna Patriot's Day Parade in 2001. He and Fonoimoana also joined a new tour in 2001, Beach Volleyball America. Blanton is recognized as a pioneer in his sport. His success as a player opened doors for him in modeling and commercial endorsements. He has used these new doors in his continuing efforts to promote interest in volleyball.

Sources: *Contemporary Black Biography,* vol. 29, pp. 20–22; *Jet* 94 (31 August 1988): 51; 98 (23 October 2000): 56; *Who's Who among African Americans,* 26th ed., p. 111.

Wrestling

1992 • The first black heavyweight wrestling champion was Ron Simmons, three-time All-American nose tackle at Florida State. He captured the World Championship Wrestling title for a first in the sixty-year history of the sport. Operating first as a tag team member, he became an individual wrestler in 1988.

Sources: *Jet* 82 (21 September 1992): 50; *Who's Who among African Americans,* 26th ed., p. 1126.

1992 • Six-foot-eight, 700-pound sumo wrestler Manny Yarborough began his history-making events as the first black to win numerous sumo championships. Beginning with the Judo World Championship competition, he won second place this year, third place in 1993, second place in 1994, and first place in 1995. He won the Dutch Open in 1999. One of Yarborough's football teammates at Morgan State University in Maryland introduced him to sumo wrestling, and he became an All-American wrestler while in college. Since college, he has traveled abroad extensively to participate in sumo competitions and demonstrations. To Yarborough, who has worked as a club bouncer, sumo wrestling is said to be both a hobby and an occupation. Unlike many other professional sports, the claim is made that sumo wrestling welcomes multiculturalism, but it has not had great popularity with inner-city or minority youth. Yarborough, who attributes his size to the height of his paternal uncles (all tall) and the girth of his maternal uncles (all over 300 pounds), seems to have been made for the sport.

Sources: *Jet* 96 (9 August 1999): 46–50.

Sports Reporter

1972 • Lacy J. Banks (1994?–2012) became the first black full-time sports reporter for the Chicago *Sun-Times*. In the 1980s, he began covering the Chicago Bulls and reported on Michael Jordan during his entire NBA career. He also covered all six of the team's championships as well as hockey, women's pro basketball, college football and basketball, and professional boxing. A long-time Baptist preacher, Banks weaved his religious background into his writings as well as his interactions with players. The Lyon, Mississippi, native held a degree in French and was fluent in French and Spanish.

Sources: ESPN, "Lacy J. Banks dies at 68," http://espn.go.com/chicago/nba/story/_/id/77215 66/chicago-sun-times-sportswriter-lacy-j-banks-dies, accessed October 3. 2012.

WRITERS

Autobiography

1760 • Briton Hammon was the first black American writer of prose. The fourteen-page-work, *A Narrative of the Uncommon Sufferings and Surprising Deliverance of Briton Hammon, A Negro Man—Servant to General Winslow, of Marshfield in New England; Who Returned to Boston, after Having Been Absent almost Thirteen Years,* was published in Boston. This fourteen-page-account tells of his providential escape from captivity by Indians, and then from his Spanish rescuers. Although it is known that Hammon was an autobiographer, little else is known about him.

Sources: Logan and Winston, *Dictionary of American Negro Biography,* p. 281; Jackson, *A History of Afro-American Literature,* vol. 1, pp. 47–48.

1798 • *A Narrative of the Life and Adventure of Venture, a Native of Africa But Resident Above Sixty Years in the United States of America* was the first slave narrative written by a black American. The work is also important because it illustrates the life of slave and free blacks in Connnecticut during the eighteenth century. Venture [Broteer] [Smith] (1729–1805) recalls his royal descent in Africa, his slavery in Connecticut and Long Island, New York, and his prosperity after he was able to purchase his freedom by the age of forty-six. There are precursors to Venture's narrative, but they were written down by whites, like *Some Memoirs of the Life of Job* (1734), by Thomas Bluett; difficult to credit fully, like *A Narrative of the Lord's Dealings with John Marrant* (1789); or complete fictions. The author of the very important *The Interesting Narrative of the Life of Olaudah Equiano* (1789) spent only a few days in the American Colonies.

Sources: Logan and Winston, *Dictionary of American Negro Autobiography,* pp. 617–18; Jackson, *A History of Afro-American Literature,* vol. 1, pp. 61–62.

1831 • The first slave narrative published by a black woman in the Americas was *The History of Mary Prince, West Indian Slave.*

Sources: Hine, *Black Women in America,* vol. 2, p. 1311.

1836 • The first autobiography by an American black woman was *The Life and Religious Experiences of Jarena Lee, a Coloured Lady* by religious leader Jarena Lee (1783–?). Lee was a nineteenth-century evangelist and itinerant preacher who called herself "the first female preacher of the First African Methodist Episcopal Church." In her lifetime she published two autobiographies; the second, *Religious Experiences and Journal of Jarena Lee,* was published in 1849. Little is known about her life after that time.

Sources: Smith, *Notable Black American Women,* pp. 662–63; Hine, *Black Women in America,* vol. II, p. 1311; Andrews, *Sisters of the Spirit,* pp. 23–48.

1933 • *Along This Way: The Autobiography of James Weldon Johnson,* was the first autobiography by a black writer to be reviewed in the *New York Times.* In addition to the chronicle of his life, the autobiography tells the story of black Americans from post-Reconstruction to the end of the Harlem Renaissance. James Weldon Johnson (1871–1938) excelled as an educator, lawyer, diplomat, editor, lyricist, poet, essayist and political activist.

Sources: James Weldon Johnson Insitute, http://www.jamesweldonjohnson.emory.edu/subjames.htm. Accessed October 3, 2012.

Awards

Nella Larsen

1930 • Nella Marian Larsen (1893–1964) was the first black woman recipient of a Guggenheim Fellowship in creative writing. Her novels, *Quicksand* (1928) and *Passing* (1929), were highly acclaimed. Both deal with the tragic mulatto theme. She treated black women characters in urban settings, and was the foremother to African American novelists to follow her. Larsen was one of the first black women novelists to grapple with female sexuality and sexual politics. Born in Chicago to a Danish mother and West Indian father, Larsen grew up in a neighborhood of mixed cultures and then enrolled in the high school department at Fisk University where she had her first experiences in an all-black context. A year later she enrolled in classes at the University of Copenhagen, spent three years in New York City (during which time she became a nursing student at Lincoln Hospital), and spent one year at Tuskegee Institute. After 1916 she spent most of her life in or around New York City. Larsen worked as a nurse from 1916 to 1918 at Lincoln Hospital and as a nurse with the New York City Health Department from 1918 to 1921. She married physicist Elmer S. Imes around this time. Larsen completed training at the New York Public Library School and in 1923 received a certificate. In 1924 she became a children's librarian at the 135th Street Branch of the New York Public library, the location at which the Schomburg Center for Research in Black Culture had its founding. Both her marriage and her career gave her access to Harlem's social circles and enabled her to establish relationships with such influential people as Walter White and Carl Van Vechten. Soon Larsen abandoned her careers as nurse and librarian and launched her career as full-time novelist. Larsen won the Harmon Foundation's bronze medal for literature in 1928. Her ability as a writer placed her alongside prominent writers of her era. By 1941 she resumed nursing and worked Manhattan hospitals for about twenty years. By the time of her death in 1964, she had fallen into self-decreed literary oblivion.

Sources: Hine, *Black Women in America,* pp. 695–97; Smith, *Notable Black American Women,* pp. 652–57; Shockley, *Afro-American Women Writers 1746–1933,* p. 432.

1953 • Ralph Waldo Ellison (1914–1994) was the first black to win the National Book Award for his novel, *Invisible Man.* Written in 1952, the book deals with a black man's "place" in a white man's world. Born in Oklahoma City, Oklahoma, he studied at Tuskegee Institute (now University) before going to New York in 1936 intent on studying sculpture. He quickly met Langston Hughes who introduced him to Richard Wright. Ellison became interested in writing and joined the Federal Writer's Project in 1942 hoping to develop his skills. In 1944 he began to write what would become a celebrated novel, *Invisible Man,* which also won the Russwurm Award. Between 1943 and 1950 he worked on as many as four novels. His most distinguished short story, "Flying Home," was a long excerpt from one of his unfinished novels. He has published a collection of essays, *Shadow and Act* (1964). After *Invisible Man* was published, Ellison made a living primarily from teaching, lecturing, and royalties from his book. In 1999 Ellison's literary agents published *Juneteenth,* a novel completed before his death.

Sources: *Black Writers,* pp. 176–83; *Encyclopedia Americana,* vol. 10, p. 255; *Negro Almanac,* pp. 989–90; Smith, *Notable Black American Men,* pp. 369–73.

1986 • Wole Soyinka (1934–), Nigerian playwright, poet, and novelist, was the first African and the first black writer of any nation to win a Nobel Prize for literature. His works have been acclaimed for his portrayals of the human condition in emergent Africa. Soyinka was born in Abeokuta, a village on the banks of the River Ogun in western Nigeria. He was educated at Government College and University in Ibaden. He also received a degree in English from the University of Leeds in 1960 and worked as a teacher and scriptwriter in London at the Royal Court Theater. He returned to Nigeria in 1960 and soon established himself as a dramatist, actor, and director. In 1994 he went into exile in the United States and Europe. While in the United States, he was distinguished visiting professor at Emory University in Atlanta. In 1997 his home country Nigeria charged him with treason, asserting that he was involved with bombings against military installations, which he denied.

Sources: *Black Writers,* pp. 529–34; *Encyclopedia Americana,* vol. 25, p. 351; *Contemporary Black Biography,* vol. 4, pp. 333–38.

1992 • Derek Walcott (1930–), poet, educator, playwright, journalist, and painter, was the first African-Caribbean to be honored with the Nobel Prize in literature. The prize was given for his "melodious and sensitive" style and "historic vision." His writings reflect the cultural diversity of his native Caribbean homeland, St. Lucia. A teacher at Boston University, Walcott also won a $250,000 John D. and Catherine T. MacArthur Foundation grant eleven years earlier. He has been regarded as one of the finest living poets in England. Born of mixed racial and heritage background in Castries, St. Lucia, Walcott was educated as a British subject. He was founding director of Trinidad Theatre Workshop in 1959.

Sources: *Black Writers,* pp. 567–71; *Jet* 83 (26 October 1992): 14; *Time* 140 (19 October 1992), pp. 24, 65.

1993 • Toni Morrison (1931–), novelist, educator, and editor, was the first black American and the second American woman to win the Nobel Prize in literature, which was awarded on October 7. The Swedish Academy called her "a literary artist of first rank," one who "gives life to an essential aspect of American reality," and one who wrote prose "with the luster of poetry." Informed of the honor, Morrison said that her work was inspired by "huge silences in literature, things that had never been articulated, printed or imagined and they were the silences about black girls, black women." Her novel *Song of Solomon,* published in 1977, won the National Book Critics Award for fiction that year, and in 1988 she won the Pulitzer Prize for fiction for her work *Beloved.* Her other novels include *The Bluest Eye* (1970), *Sula* (1974), *Tar Baby* (1981), *Jazz* (1992), *Paradise* (1999), *Love* (2003), and *A Mercy* (2008). Morrison was born in Lorain, Ohio, and graduated from Howard University in Washington, D.C., in 1953. She received a master's degree in English from Cornell University in 1955. In 1965 Morrison became a textbook editor for a subsidiary of Random House Publishing in Syracuse, New York, and three years later she moved to New York City as a senior editor in the trade department at Random House. She mixed her editorial work with a teaching career and taught at a number of colleges. She left the publishing field in 1984, and in 1989 became the Robert F. Goheen Professor of the Council of the Humanities at Princeton University. She resigned from Princeton in 2006. In 1996 the National Endowment for the Humanities named her Jefferson Lecturer in the Humanities.

Toni Morrison

Sources: *Contemporary Biography,* vol. 2, pp. 167–72; Smith, *Notable Black American Women,* pp. 770–75; *Washington Post* (8 October 1993).

2001 • In 1993 historian and educator David Levering Lewis (1936–) won a Pulitzer Prize for his biography, *W.E.B. Du Bois: Biography of a Race: 1868–1919.* In 2001 he published the second volume of the Du Bois biography, *W.E.B. Du Bois: The Fight for Equality and the American Century, 1919–1963* and again won a Pulitzer Prize, becoming the first biographer to win twice for back-to-back books on the same subject. Lewis was born in Little Rock, Arkansas, and relocated with his parents to Wilberforce, Ohio. He entered

Fisk University in Nashville, Tennessee, in fall 1952, as a member of the university's Early Entrants Program for bright students who had not finished high school, graduating in 1956 with Phi Beta Kappa honors and a bachelor's degree in history. He received his master's degree in history from Columbia University in 1958 and enrolled in England's London School of Economics. There Lewis focused on Modern European and French history and received his doctorate in 1962. All the while he maintained an interest in U.S. history and continued to develop intellectually in that area. Lewis held a number of teaching posts at such institutions as the University of Ghana in Africa, Howard University, the University of Notre Dame, Morgan State University, the University of the District of Columbia, and finally Rutgers University, where he holds the Martin Luther King Jr. chair. His biography of Martin Luther King Jr. titled *King: A Biography,* published in 1978, was well received by the academic community. His book *When Harlem Was In Vogue,* published in 1981, was likewise well received and helped to extend the resources on that cultural period in history. Lewis's crowning achievement came with the publication of his monumental biographies of W. E. B. Du Bois that chronicle the life of one of the twentieth century's most brilliant and fertile minds.

Sources: *New York Times* (17 April 2001); Smith, *Notable Black American Men,* pp. 713–16; *Tennessean* (19 April 2001).

2007 • Poet, children's author, and prose writer for adults, Lucille Clifton (1936–2010) was the first black to win the Ruth Lilly Poetry Prize. The $100,000 award is one of the largest and most prestigious literary honors in the United States. Established in 1986, the annual prize honors the lifetime achievements of a U.S. poet. Two of Clifton's eleven books of poetry were nominated for a Pulitzer Prize. She has also written one book of prose and nineteen children's books. Born in Depew, New York, she later moved to Buffalo. She attended Howard University where she appeared in the first performance of James Baldwin's *The Amen Corner.* Later she transferred to Fredonia State Teacher's College (now State University of New York at Fredonia), joined a group of black intellectuals on campus, and began to come into her own as a writer. From 1974 to 1979, Clifton was poet-in-residence at Coppin State University and has held several distinguished positions at other colleges and universities.

Sources: *Contemporary Black Biography,* vol. 14, pp. 23–28, pp. 58–62, 64; *Jet* 111 (28 May 2007): 40; Smith, *Notable Black American Women,* Book II, pp. 108–12.

Comics

2011 • Miles Morales, a teen superhero, became the first biracial (half-black and half-Hispanic) Spider-Man in Marvel Comics' *Ultimate Comics Fallout #4.* For the first time, someone other than Peter Parker, who died in the series in June this year, became the superhero. The series editor noted that today's fans will have a Spider-Man "who's reflective of our culture and diversity."

Sources: Cavia, "Miles Morales & Me: Why the New Biracial Spider-Man Matters," http://www.washingtonpost.com/blogs/comic-riffs/post/miles-morales-and-me-why-the-new-biracial-spider-man-matters/2011/08/04/gIQABzlGuI_blog.html.

History

1836 • Robert Benjamin Lewis was the first black to publish a history, *Light and Truth.* Practically nothing is known about Lewis, except that he was a native of Boston and had both black and Indian ancestors. Characterized by a remarkable disregard for any standard of evidence, the book tries among other things to create a black presence in history and to establish Native Americans as the descendents of the lost tribes of Israel.

Sources: Jackson, *A History of Afro-American Literature,* vol. 1, pp. 200–01.

1841 • James William Charles Pennington (1807–1870) was the author of the first history of black people written by an African American for children, *A Text Book of the Origin and History … of the Colored People*. In 1850 he published *the Fugitive Blacksmith*, an account of his life. A slave blacksmith in Maryland, Pennington escaped and learned to read and write. He was an active and prominent abolitionist. Later on he officiated at the wedding of Frederick Douglass and his wife. Born Jim Pembroke on a farm in the Eastern Shore of Maryland, he and a part of his family were sold to another owner and moved to a farm in Washington County, near Hagerstown, Maryland. He escaped slavery on October 28, 1828, and went to Adams County, Pennsylvania, then to Chester County before moving to Brooklyn, New York. He worked as a coachman and earned an education by attending evening school and with private tutors. Pennington taught school in Newtown and then in Hartford, Connecticut, and also studied for the ministry. He was ordained a Presbyterian minister in 1837 and assigned to the newly founded Congregational church until July 1840, when he moved to the Talcott Street Colored Congregational Church in New Haven. He held other ministries and also worked for anti-slavery and civil rights causes. All the while, he was a fugitive slave, for it was not until May 27, 1851, that he won his freedom. In 1864 Pennington joined the African Methodist Episcopal Church and later did missionary work for the church in Mississippi. He also continued to work in the Congregational church.

James William Charles Pennington

Sources: Logan and Winston, *Dictionary of American Negro Biography,* pp. 488–90; Garrett, *Famous First Facts about Negroes,* p. 77; Jackson, *A History of Afro-American Literature,* vol. 1, p. 201; Smith, *Notable Black American Men,* pp. 923–25.

1855 • The first black history founded on written documentation is *The Colored Patriots of the American Revolution* by William Cooper Nell (1816–1874). Although deficient as history by modern standards, it nonetheless contains materials of lasting value. Nell's work began as a twenty-three-page pamphlet in 1851. A native of Boston, Nell came from a relatively privileged family. He joined the First African Baptist Church that Thomas Paul founded and was educated in the black school that operated in the church's basement. In 1826 he was a founding member of the Massachusetts General Colored Association and became an associate of David Walker who wrote *Walker's Appeal*. Nell was a major leader in the ultimately successful fight to desegregate the Massachusetts public schools, as well as an associate of William Lloyd Garrison and Frederick Douglass in the abolition movement.

Sources: Logan and Winston, *Dictionary of American Negro Biography,* pp. 472–73; Garrett, *Famous First Facts about Negroes,* p. 156; Jackson, *A History of Afro-American Literature,* vol. 1, pp. 201–2; Smith, *Notable Black American Men,* pp. 871–74.

1882 • George Washington Williams (1849–1891) was the author of the first major history of blacks in America. His *History of the Negro Race in America from 1619 to 1880,* in two volumes, was a major event and earned him respect for meeting the standards of professional historians. Williams was born in Bedford Springs, Pennsylvania, and spent time in a home for refugees. A wayward teenager, he changed his name and, in summer 1864, joined the Union Army. After his discharge in 1868, Williams received a license to preach in a church in Hannibal, Missouri, and attended Wayland Seminary in Washington, D.C. On June 10, 1874, he completed the theological program at Newton Theological Institution near Boston and he was ordained on June 11. While he was pastor of Twelfth Baptist Church in Boston, he wrote his first historical work, *History of the Twelfth Baptist Church.* In 1875 he was ordained as a Baptist minister but later turned to law and politics, serving a term in the Ohio legislature. Williams passed the Ohio Bar in 1881 and returned to Boston in 1883, where he became a member of the Massachusetts Bar. His active life did not preclude the collection of materials for his histories. His other writings include the valuable *History of the Negro Troops in the War of the Rebellion* in 1877. His last efforts were attacks on the inhumane government of the Congo Free State following a 1890 visit there.

Sources: Logan and Winston, *Dictionary of American Negro Biography,* pp. 657–59; Garrett, *Famous First Facts about Negroes,* p. 77; Jackson, *A History of Afro-American Literature,* vol.

1, pp. 211–18; Smith, *Notable Black American Men*, pp. 1233–36; Franklin, *George Washington Williams*.

1896 • W[illiam] E[dward] B[urghardt] Du Bois (1868–1963) wrote the first scientific historical monograph by a black American, *The Suppression of the African Slave Trade, 1638–1870*. The book was published as the first volume in the Harvard University Historical Studies. *The Souls of Black Folk* in 1903 established Du Bois as a peerless essayist. His 1935 study of Reconstructionism, *Black Reconstruction in America*, was the first account of the era from a black viewpoint. A founding member of the National Association for the Advancement of Colored People, Du Bois edited *Crisis*, the magazine of the NAACP, taught at Atlanta University for a number of years, and was an ardent supporter of African liberation movements. He was the leading black intellectual of the first half of the twentieth century.

Sources: Garrett, *Famous First Facts about Negroes*, pp. 77, 79–80; Logan and Winston, *Dictionary of American Negro Biography*, pp. 193–99; Smith, *Notable Black American Men*, pp. 336–41.

1916 • The *Journal of Negro History* was the first American black historical research journal. Carter Goodwin Woodson (1875–1950) was its founder and first editor. Born in New Canton, Virginia, Woodson found his early education limited due to his need to work for his family's support in the West Virginia coalfields. He completed his high school program in a year-and-a-half, and began a college career that led to a doctorate from Harvard in 1912. He was a co-founder and the first executive director of the Association for the Study of Negro Life and History, established on September 9, 1915. In 1926 Woodson launched the first Negro History Week (now Black History Month). In 1937 he began publishing *The Negro History Bulletin*. Throughout his life he was devoted both to the establishment of black history on a sound footing, and to the dissemination of historical knowledge about black people.

Sources: Garrett, *Famous First Facts about Negroes*, p. 77; Logan and Winston, *Dictionary of American Negro Biography*, pp. 665–67; Smith, *Notable Black American Men*, pp. 1256–59.

1978 • Sharon Harley (1948–) and Rosalyn M. Terborg-Penn (1941–) published *The Afro-American Woman: Struggle and Images*, the first anthology of black women's history. Both serve on the faculty at the University of Maryland, College Park. They also worked with Darlene Clark Hine on her work *Black Women in America*, published in 1993. Harley was on the Editorial Advisory Board; Terborg-Penn was an associate editor.

Sources: Hine, *Black Women in America*, vol. 2, p. 1330; Salem, *African American Women: A Biographical Dictionary*, p. 228 (Harley), 501–3 (Terborg-Penn).

Nonfiction

1742 • The first dissertation written by an African slave was *A Thesis on Slavery by the Former Slave, Jacobus Elisa Johannes Capitien, 1717–1747*. It is also the first scholarly work by an African slave. Capitien's master took him from Guinea to Holland in 1928 and freed him. After that, grants from the wealthy enabled him to receive an education at the University of Leiden. Capitien returned to Guinea as a missionary. His work refutes the authors of antiquity and shows that slavery violated the principles of natural freedom and equality. He also rebuts Aristotle's doctrine of natural slavery.

Sources: Prah, *Jacobus Eliza Johannes Capitien, 1717–1747*; Parker, *The Agony of Asar*.

1835 • Susan Paul (1809–1841) wrote *Memoir of James Jackson, the Attentive and Obedient Scholar, who Died in Boston, October 31, 1833, Aged Six Years and Eleven Months,* the first black American biography. She was also the first black American to write an evangelical juvenilia. The work was based on Paul's daily experiences as a teacher with a child named Jackson. The memoir was Paul's platform to promote the value of the black community and to argue that blacks were interested in education and enhancing their own lives. Susan Paul was a member of a prominent and influential family in Boston. Her father, Thomas Paul, was an abolitionist and Baptist minister, and her mother, Catherine Paul was a private-school teacher. While working as a teacher, Susan Paul organized the Garrison Juvenile Choir in 1832, using students from her school to form the group. The group was named in honor of abolitionist and journalist William Lloyd Garrison and performed at various anti-slavery gatherings. Proceeds from the choir's concert were used to support the abolitionist movement and Indian groups. Paul was one of the black women in Boston who joined the Boston Female Anti-Slavery Society, founded in 1832, and was one of the first black women to become well known in the anti-slavery movement.

Sources: Brown, *Memoir of James Jackson*; Salem, *African American Women,* pp. 392–93; Yee, *Black Women Abolitionists,* pp. 18–19, 66, 90.

1841 • Ann Plato (1820?–?) published *Essays; Including Biographies and Miscellaneous Pieces, in Prose and Poetry,* becoming the first black woman to publish a book of essays. The biographies included provide a capsule of what life for young, middle-class black women of New England was like at that time, and the twenty poems included are typical of early nineteenth-century works. James William Charles Pennington (1807–1870), pastor of Boston's Colored Congregational Church, introduced the book of essays and poems. Plato was born in Hartford, Connecticut, and became a teacher. A devout Congregationalist, she wrote about her experiences as a church member in the poem "Advice to young Ladies."

Sources: Smith, *Notable Black American Women,* p. 853–54; Potter and Clayton, *African American Firsts,* p. 148; Shockley, *Afro-American Women Writers, 1746–1933,* pp. 26–35.

1865 • Paul Jennings (1799–1874), who wrote *A Colored Man's Reminiscences of James Madison,* was the first White House memoirist. Jennings was born on Madison's Montpelier estate, the son of an English trader and a slave woman of African and Indian ancestry, and was Madison's constant body servant. Daniel Webster purchased Jennings following Madison's death. Webster manumitted Jennings on the condition that he work off the $120 fee at $8 a month. Having earned his freedom in 1846, Jennings became a leading plotter in Washington, D.C.'s great slave escape. His short memoir not only provides a portrait of Madison, it also describes the slaves' plot. He was also a supporter of sea captain and white abolitionist Daniel Drayton's failed plan to free enslaved blacks by shipping them out on the schooner *Pearl.* Although the slaves were recaptured, sold, or tried in the courts, Jennings was never implicated in the incident. Jennings was later employed by the Department of the Interior and was able to raise enough money to rescue a family from slavery.

Sources: Chase, "Plotting a Course for Freedom," *American Visions* (February–March 1995), pp. 52–55.

1878 • James Monroe Trotter (1842–1892) wrote the first important book on blacks in music, *Music and Some Highly Musical People.* The book contained valuable biographical material and an appendix reproducing the scores of thirteen black compositions. Trotter was born in Grand Gulf, Mississippi, the son of a white man and his slave, Letitia. While he was sent to Cincinnati to live and attended Gilmore school for freed slaves, Trotter was largely self-educated. John Mercer Langston recruited him for the black Fifty-fifth Massachusetts Regiment, where Trotter became a second lieutenant. He was mustered out in Boston in August 1865, settled there, and by 1878 he had addressed his lifelong interest in music. On March 3, 1887, he was confirmed by the U.S. Senate to become recorder of deeds, then the highest federal post available to blacks. Trotter died in Boston of tuberculosis.

Sources: Logan and Winston, *Dictionary of American Negro Biography,* pp. 602–3; Garrett, *Famous First Facts about Negroes,* p. 126; Smith, *Notable Black American Men,* pp. 1130–33.

1881 • William Sanders Scarborough (1852–1926) was the first black American scholar to publish a Greek language textbook. The widely used *First Lessons in Greek* won him recognition. In 1886, his *Birds of Aristophanes* was published. An African Methodist Episcopal minister, he was active in black intellectual circles and served as president of Wilberforce University from 1908 to 1920. Scarborough was born in Macon, Georgia, where he learned basic studies early on. By the start of the Civil War, he knew carpentry and was an apprentice to a master shoemaker. He attended various schools. In 1869 he enrolled in Atlanta University, where he learned Latin and Greek, and in 1875 he graduated from Oberlin College in Ohio. Scarborough returned to the South, where he taught at Lewis High School in Macon and later took charge of Payne Institute in Cokesbury, South Carolina. He studied theology at Oberlin, receiving a master's degree in 1878. He twice taught at Wilberforce University in Ohio, becoming vice president in 1897 and later president.

Sources: Logan and Winston, *Dictionary of American Negro Biography,* pp. 545–46; Garrett, *Famous First Facts about Negroes,* p. 102.

1890 • Amelia E. Johnson (1858–1922) published *Clarence and Corinne or God's Way,* the first book by a woman and the first by a black American published by the American Baptist Publication Society, one of the country's largest publishing houses. While the novel was only the second published by a black American in the United States, it was also the first Sunday school book published by a black American. Johnson, known also as Mrs. A. E. Johnson, was born in Toronto, Ontario, Canada, where she was educated. In 1874 she moved to Baltimore, the native home of her parents, and became a teacher. She began writing poems at an early age, publishing them in the *Baptist Messenger, Our Women and Children,* and the *American Baptist.* She was responsible for such publications as *Joy* (1887) that included other poems and stories, and *Ivy,* designed to promote African American history and to encourage young black Americans to read. In addition to her first novel, Johnson also published a second novel in 1894, *The Hazeley Family,* and in 1901 a third novel, *Martina Meridian; or, What Is My Motive?* As was the case with her first work, these novels were used as Sunday school literature to teach ethical behavior.

Sources: Smith, *Notable Black American Women,* Book II, pp. 237–39; Hine, *Black Women in America,* vol. II, p. 1316; Shockley, *Afro-American Women Writers, 1746–1933,* pp. 162–70.

1905 • The first book written by a black woman and published in Texas was *Moral and Mental Capsule for the Economic and Domestic Life of the Negro, as a Solution to the Race Problem,* by Josie Briggs Hall, of Waxahachie, a writer and teacher. In her book of essays and poems, Hall made a plea for the reversal of racial stereotypes and urged young women to raise the standard of womanhood.

Sources: *San Antonio Express-News* (5 February 1995); Winegarten, *Black Texas Women: 150 Years of Trial and Triumph,* pp. 143–44, 194.

Benjamin Brawley

1918 • Benjamin Griffith Brawley (1882–1939), college professor, dean, poet, and author, edited the first book devoted exclusively to black art and literature, *The Negro in Literature and Art.* The book was reprinted in 1937 as *The Negro Genius.* Born in Columbia, South Carolina, Brawley received his master's degree from Harvard University in 1908. A prolific writer of historical essays, social commentaries, and book reviews, Brawley's works were published in a number of journals, including *Lippincott's* Magazine, *Harvard Monthly,* and *The Sewanee Review.* He wrote twenty-three scholarly articles, seventeen of which were published in the *Dictionary of American Biography.* He also wrote books on English literature that were adopted as textbooks in several institutions. He had a distinguished teaching career at Atlanta Baptist Seminary (now Clark Atlanta University) and at Shaw and Howard universities.

Sources: Brown, Davis, and Lee, *The Negro Caravan,* p. 757; Hughes and Bontemps, *The Poetry of the Negro 1746–1949,* p. 390; Logan and Winston, *Dictionary of American Negro Biography,* pp. 60–61; Smith, *Notable Black American Men,* pp. 112–13.

1924 • Roger Arliner Young (1899–1964) published her first scientific paper, "On the Excretory Apparatus in the Paramecium," in the September 12, 1924, issue of *Science,* making her the first black woman to research and publish professionally in the field of science. A zoologist, she became a research assistant for eminent scholar Ernest Everett Just (1883–1941), head of Howard University's biology department. Her paper was the result of the research that she conducted with Just.

Sources: *Contemporary Black Biography,* vol. 29, pp. 195–97.

1935 • Folklorist Zora Neale Hurston (1891–1960) published *Mules and Men,* based on her field studies in Louisiana. Issued by Lippincott, this became the first such collection of folklore compiled and published by a black American woman. It is also the first by a woman indigenous to the culture from which the stories emerge. Born in Eatonville, Florida, sometimes called the first incorporated black town in America, Hurston left home at age fourteen to work with a traveling Gilbert and Sullivan theatrical troupe. She left the troupe when it arrived in Baltimore, Maryland, and entered high school, graduating in 1918. She entered Howard University in 1924, taking courses intermittently. In 1921 Hurston published her story, "John Redding Goes to Sea," in the school's literary magazine. Hurston moved to New York in 1925 and became absorbed in the Harlem Renaissance; she befriended and worked alongside such writers as Claude McKay, Eric Waldron, Jean Toomer, Langston Hughes, and Wallace Thurman. She also collaborated with Hughes and others in publishing the short-lived literary magazine *Fire!* In 1928 Hurston graduated from Barnard College and continued graduate study at Columbia University under renowned anthropologist Franz Boas. She returned to Eatonville and collected black folklore. Her book *Mules and Men,* published in 1935, includes the folklore that she collected in Florida and Alabama from 1929 to 1931 as well as her hoodoo essay written in 1931 for the *Journal of American Folklore.* Hurston's other works include *Jonah's Gourd Vine,* a novel (1934); *Their Eyes Were Watching God,* considered her best novel (1937); *Tell My Horse,* her second collection of folklore (1938); *Moses, Man of the Mountain,* her third novel (1939); *Dust Tracks on a Road,* her autobiography (1942); and *Seraphon the Sewanee,* her fourth and last novel (1948). Hurston's career began to slide in the 1950s, forcing her to take a series of menial jobs in Florida's small towns. After suffering a stroke in 1959, she was confined to Saint Lucie County Welfare Home in Fort Pierce, Florida, and she died in poverty on January 28, 1960. In August 1973 novelist and poet Alice Walker placed a stone marker at the approximate site of her grave in Fort Pierce. A Zora Neale Hurston festival held in Eatonville each year now honors the author's life and work. Hurston's play *Polk County* resurfaced in 1997 at the Library of Congress (where Hurston had deposited copies of ten of her unpublished and unproduced plays for copyright protection between 1925 and 1944) and was produced at the Arena Stage in Washington, D.C. In 1997 the Library of Congress rediscovered among its materials typescripts of ten plays by Hurston and subsequently placed them in its Manuscripts, Music, and Rare Books and Special Collections divisions.

Zora Neale Hurston

Sources: *The Black New Yorker,* p. 232; Smith, *Notable Black American Women,* pp. 543–48; *Washington Post* (7 April 2002).

1970 • Maya Angelou [Marguerite Johnson] (1928–) published *I Know Why the Caged Bird Sings* and became the first black woman to have a nonfiction work on the bestseller list.

Sources: *Contemporary Biography,* 1974, p. 12; Smith, *Notable Black American Women,* pp. 23–27.

1991 • Authors Dennis Kimbro (1950–) and Napoleon Hill published the first black self-help book *Think and Grow Rich: A Black Choice.* The work quickly found an audience, selling some 50,000 copies over the next two years. The book went through three printings. In 1992 and 1993 it was a best-seller among black nonfiction titles. Hill wrote a one-hundred-page manuscript that Kimbro used as a base but expanded to include many of America's most successful blacks. He interviewed such prominent people as Alice Walker, Leontyne Price, Earl Graves, and John H. Johnson and added his own comments for success-building.

Maya Angelou

Sources: *Contemporary Black Biography,* vol. 10, pp. 123–25; *Black Enterprise* 23 (November 1992), p. 105–11; 24 (January 1994), p. 79.

1993 • Darlene Clark Hine (1947–) edited and published a two-volume encyclopedia, *Black Women in America,* the first major work on that subject. Born in Morley, Missouri, Hine grew up in Chicago where her parents had relocated. She received her bachelor's degree from Roosevelt University in 1968 and her master's degree and doctorate from Kent State University in 1970 and 1975. In the course of her career she taught at South Carolina State College (now South Carolina State University) from 1972 to 1974 and Purdue University from 1979 to 1987. She was interim director of Purdue's Africana Studies and Research Center from 1978 to 1979, and from 1982 to 1986 she was vice provost. Hine left in 1987 to become John A. Hannah Professor of History at Michigan State University and later moved to Northwestern as Board of Trustees Professor of African American Studies and History. Her interest in black women's history began at Purdue, where she embarked on a project for the National Council of Negro Women. Her work resulted in the publication, *When the Truth Is Told: Black Women's Community and Culture in Indiana, 1875–1950*. She later received a grant from the National Endowment for the Humanities to establish the Black Women in the Middle West project, an archive of information on black women. Hine also co-edited a book about these sources in 1985 under the title *Black Women in the Middle West: A Comprehensive Research Guide, Indiana and Illinois*. Her two-volume work *Black Women in America*, for which Elsa Barkley Brown and Rosalyn Terborg-Penn served as associate editors, remained highly acclaimed. A second edition of the work, in three volumes, was published in 2005. Her other works include *Black Women in White: Racial Conflict and Cooperation in the Nursing Profession, 1890–1950* (1989); a sixteen-volume set, *Milestones in African-American History* (1993) which she co-edited; *Speak Truth to Power* (1996), and *Hine Sight* (1997).

Sources: *Contemporary Black Biography,* vol. 24, pp. 85–87.

1999 • Editor Hans J. Massaquoi (1926–) published a memoir *Destined to Witness: Growing Up Black in Nazi Germany,* marking the first time in literature that a black person has chronicled his life as he grew up in that country. The son of a well-to-do African and a white German nurse, Massaquoi wrote about his twelve years in Germany following Hitler's rise to power. Easily recognized because of his skin color, he lived in constant fear until the British liberated him in 1945. Massaquoi also severed as managing editor of *Ebony* magazine.

Sources: *Jet* 97 (6 December 1999): 13; *Who's Who among African Americans,* 14th ed., p. 851.

Novels

William Wells Brown

1853 • William Wells Brown (1814–1884) was the first black novelist. His novel, *Clotel; Or, The President's Daughter: A Narrative of Slave Life in the United States,* was published in England. The son of a slave mother and plantation owner, Brown was born near Lexington, Kentucky. In 1816 his master, John Young, moved his family and his slaves to a farm in the Missouri Territory and later to St. Louis. While in Missouri, Brown worked as Young's office boy and learned to prepare medicine and administer to slaves who were ill. After he being sold several times and several escape attempts, Brown successfully escaped on January 1, 1834. He became active in the abolitionist movement and in 1843 he became an agent of abolitionist societies. Brown spent five years in Europe championing emancipation and wrote the first book of travel, *Three Years in Europe,* in 1852, and the first dramatic work by an American black, *Experience; or How to Give a Northern Man a Backbone* in 1856. His second play, *Escape; or, A Leap for Freedom,* also written in 1856, was the first play published by an American black. Brown wrote more than a dozen books and pamphlets. He was also a physician and maintained a practice until his death; his interest also turned to writing the history of black achievement.

Sources: Logan and Winston, *Dictionary of American Negro Biography,* pp. 71–73; Jackson, *A History of Afro-American Literature,* vol. 1, pp. 322–42; Smith, *Notable Black American Men,* pp. 138–41.

1857 • Frank J. Webb (1828–1894) published (in England) the first novel to deal with the problems of Northern free blacks, *The Garies and Their Friends.* Its innovative themes include the first in-depth treatment of a mixed marriage, the first presentation of a lynch mob, and the first use of passing for white as a major theme. Webb was born in Philadelphia, spent some time in England and southern France, and in 1858 was appointed to a position in the post office in Jamaica. The next year he returned to the United States, spending some time in Washington, D.C. Around that time the *New Era* published two of his tales, three articles, and two poems. By 1878 he and his family had moved to Galveston, Texas. He edited a short-lived radical newspaper in 1871, became a postal clerk again, and was a school teacher and principal from 1881 until he died.

Sources: Jackson, *A History of Afro-American Literature,* vol. 1, pp. 343–50; Salzman, *Encyclopedia of African-American Culture and History,* vol. 5, p. 2796.

1857 • The earliest known manuscript of an unpublished novel by a black woman slave, *The Bondswoman's Narrative,* by Hannah Crafts, was written around this time. (Analysis of the document places its authorship between 1853 and 1860.) The manuscript, which was unnoticed for over 140 years, is probably the earliest known novel by a black woman anywhere, slave or free. It may be one of a few novels by black slaves in America as well. Years later a book dealer in New Jersey acquired the work. In 1948 Dorothy Porter Wesley (1905–1995), then head of the Moorland Spingarn Research Center at Howard University, acquired the manuscript on the belief that the author was a black American slave woman. She helped to authenticate her belief by noting that the author introduced and treated black characters as people without regard to race, while white writers introduced them with assured reference to their race. The manuscript surfaced again in 2001 at auction at the Swann Galleries in New York. Henry Louis Gates (1950–), chair of Harvard University's Black Studies Department, was the single bidder for the manuscript and acquired it for less than $10,000. He sold the rights to Warner Books for an undisclosed advance against royalties. The novelist, Hannah Crafts, was a slave on the John Hill plantation in North Carolina. In spring 1857 she escaped to New Jersey and wrote the novel, combining accounts of her life as a house slave, stories from works she had seen on Wheeler's shelves, and her experiences later on as a teacher in the North. Gates edited the work and it was published by Warner Books in April 2002.

Sources: Crafts, *The Bondwoman's Narrative*; *New York Times* (11 November 2001).

1859 • Harriet E. Adams Wilson (1827?–1870) was the first black woman to publish a novel. *Our Nig; or, Sketches from the Life of a Free Black, In A Two Story White House North, Showing That Slavery's Shadows Fall Even There* was published on August 18 in Boston, where she was living alone, after her husband had abandoned her and her son. She hoped to realize money from the book to reunite herself with her son, but he died before this was accomplished. The book was also the first novel published in the United States by a black man or woman; William Wells Brown's *Clotel,* and Frank J. Webb's *The Garies and Their Friends* were both published in England. *Our Nig* presents social, racial, and economic brutality suffered by a free mulatto woman in the antebellum North. Although several copies of the work are extant, in the early 1980s scholar Henry Louis Gates rediscovered the book and removed it from obscurity.

Sources: Jackson, *A History of Afro-American Literature,* vol. 1, p. 351–63; Smith, *Notable Black American Women,* p. 1266–68; Shockley, *Afro-American Women Writers 1746–1933,* p. 84.

1899 • Charles W. Chesnutt (1858–1932) became the first writer of fiction to explore black life from a variety of perspectives. Born in Cleveland, Ohio, to free black parents from Fayetteville, North Carolina, he spent his formative years in Fayetteville. He was a disciplined learner who studied Greek and German on his own, was well versed in English literature, and taught in several schools in North and South Carolina. In 1877 he became assistant principal of a newly-established school, State Colored Normal School, the forerunner of Fayetteville State University. After a brief stint in New York, he moved to Cleveland in 1884. The next year he began to study law with the legal counsel for Nickel Plate Railroad Company, where Chesnutt was employed. In 1887 he passed the Ohio bar and opened an office as a court reporter. His interest was in writing, however, and he closed the office between 1899 and 1901 to devote his time to writing. He continued to resort to his legal training to provide a livelihood whenever needed. Chesnutt traveled the United States and also lectured throughout the South, publishing articles on his impressions. Most of his literary work was published between 1899 and 1905. He published two

Charles Chesnutt

short-story collections, a biography, and three novels within a period of seven years. His short-story collection included *The Conjure Woman* published in 1899 and *The Wife of His Youth and Other Stories of the Color Line* published in 1900; his biography *Frederick Douglass* was published in 1899; and his first novel, *The House Behind the Cedars* appeared in 1901. Although he never tried to conceal his background, his racial identity was not always known. He was a precursor of the Harlem Renaissance and a positive influence on the young black writers of that time. In recognition of his pioneering work, the NAACP awarded him its Spingarn Medal in 1928.

Sources: *Contemporary Black Biography,* vol. 29, pp. 35–37; Smith, *Notable Black American Men,* pp. 193–97; Render, *Charles W. Chesnutt.*

1907 • Between 1907 and 1909 John Edward [Bruce Grit] Bruce (1856–1924) serialized *The Black Sleuth* in *McGirt's Magazine* between 1907 and 1909, and became the first known writer to depict a black detective in a novel. His work was a forerunner of detective novels by such authors as Rudolph Fisher and Chester Himes. Born a slave in Piscataway, Maryland, he studied at Howard University for a while and then became a journalist, editor, historian, and a popular public speaker. A militant writer for the black press, during his career he wrote for over twenty newspapers, some of which appeared in the white press. His famous column that appeared in the *Cleveland Gazette* and the *New York Age* was called "Bruce Grit," the name by which he was also known. In 1911 he was a co-founder with Arthur A. Schomburg and others of the Negro Society for Historical Research. John Cullen Gruesser of Kean University edited Bruce's work and published it in book form in June 2002.

Sources: *The Black Sleuth* (Northeastern Library of Black Literature); Logan and Winston, *Dictionary of American Negro Biography,* pp. 76–77; Penn, *The Afro-American Press and Its Editors,* pp. 344–47

1931 • Editor, journalist, and novelist George Schuyler (1895–1977) published *Black No More* this year. His work was the first full-length satire by a black author. Schuyler dropped out of high school in Syracuse, New York, and enlisted in the U.S. Army, becoming a member of the black 25th Infantry Division from 1912 to 1919. He moved to New York City in 1922 and later became a member of the editorial board for the *Messenger.* He was a columnist for the *Pittsburgh Courier* and wrote essays for *Nation* as well. He became a conservative in his final years, speaking out against Communism and the Civil Rights Movement.

Sources: Byrd, *Generations in Black and White,* p. 46.

1932 • Rudolph Fisher (1897–1934) was the first black writer to publish a detective novel in book form, *The Conjure Man Dies,* which revealed Fisher's medical and scientific knowledge within the storyline. The Federal Theater Project at the Lafayette Theater in Harlem produced his work as a play posthumously in 1936. In 2001 it was brought back to life and ran through February 11 at the Henry Street Settlement on the Lower East Side of New York City. Fisher was born in Washington, D.C., and earned both his bachelor's and master's degrees at Brown University. He received his medical degree from Howard University Medical School in 1924. The next year Fisher continued his medical education at Columbia University's College of Physicians and Surgeons. After that he trained for years in bacteriology, pathology, and roentgenology, becoming a radiologist. Fisher was said to have been conflicted over his involvement in two disparate professions—medicine and creative writing—but managed to do well in both. He wrote a number of very good short stories, and two novels (including *The Walls of Jericho,* 1928), in addition to his detective novel. He was considered one of the wittiest of the Harlem Renaissance group. Fisher died of cancer in 1934, while he worked on a dramatization of *The Conjure Man Dies.* He was only thirty-seven years old.

Sources: Brown, Davis, and Lee, *The Negro Caravan,* p. 54; Logan and Winston, *Dictionary of American Negro Biography,* pp. 222–23; *New York Times* (25 January 2001); Smith, *Notable Black American Men,* pp. 400–403.

1934 • Novelist and businessman George Lee (1894–1976) published his first novel, *Beale Street: Where the Blues Began,* that documented the life of middle-class blacks as well

The First Black Best-Selling Novel

The first best-selling novel by a black writer was *Home to Harlem* (1928), by Harlem Renaissance writer Claude McKay (1890?–1948). In 1929 the work won the Harmon Gold Award for literature; after only fourteen days, it soared to the best-seller list. Born Festus Claudius McKay, in Sunny Ville, Jamaica, he enjoyed reading English classics. By 1912 he had written two volumes of poetry—*Songs of Jamaica* and *Constab Ballads*—for which he received the Jamaican Medal of the Institute of Arts and Science. In that same year he immigrated to America, intending to study agriculture at Tuskegee Institute in Alabama. He was instead attracted to Harlem, where he found the intellectual ferment appropriate for an aspiring poet. He moved to Kansas State College and on to New York in 1914. McKay traveled back and forth to Europe, sometimes following the American literary expatriates to Europe. While in England in 1922 he published *Spring in New Hampshire*, a book of poetry that was enlarged and published in the United States in 1922 under the title *Harlem Shadows*. His sonnet "If We Must Die," which is concerned with racism and violence toward blacks in America and abroad, appeared in that work. This established him as a major Harlem Renaissance writer. Other works include the novel *Home to Harlem* (1928), the autobiography *A Long Way from Home* (1927), and the novels *Banjo* (1929), and *Banana Bottom* (1933). McKay returned to the United States in 1934 and published a few more works until he died in 1948.

Claude McKay

Sources: Smith, *Notable Black American Men*, pp. 791–94; *The Black New Yorkers*, p. 203; *Black Writers*, p. 398–401.

as the lives of dope peddlers, gamblers, easy riders, and others. It became the first book by a black writer to be advertised by the Book of the Month Club. He expanded a chapter of the book into a full-length novel, *River George* published in 1937. Lee served in the 92nd Division during World War II, and later settled in Memphis, Tennessee, where he became a successful businessman and politician.

Sources: Kellner, *The Harlem Renaissance: A Historical Dictionary for the Era*, p. 216; Gloster, *Negro Voices in American Fiction*, pp. 238–41; *Who's Who in Colored America*, 1938, p. 327.

1940 • *Native Son* by Richard Wright (1908–1960) was the first book by a black selected by the Book of the Month Club. The book was an outstanding critical and popular success, and became a significant milepost. It sold at the rate of 2,000 copies a day. However, his memoir *Black Boy,* published in 1945, was a bigger success, selling over a half-million copies while being named a Book of the Month Club pick. Born in poverty in Mississippi, Wright sought to escape ignorance and poverty with a move to Chicago. He became a member of the Federal Writers Project in 1935 and moved with the project to New York in 1937. In 1938 he won a Guggenheim Fellowship. His works include *Uncle Tom's Children* (1938), which established his reputation and won him a $500 prize. Wright established himself later in Paris, where he continued to write.

Sources: Logan and Winston, *Dictionary of American Negro Biography,* pp. 674–75; Hughes and Bontemps, *The Poetry of the Negro 1746–1949,* p. 408; *Negro Almanac*, pp. 1021–22; *New York Times* (26 August 2001); Smith, *Notable Black American Men*, pp. 1268–72.

Richard Wright

1946 • Ann Petry (1909–1997) became the first black woman to write a best-selling novel. Her book, *The Street,* published early this year, quickly became a sensation; over one million copies were sold. She was also one of the first black woman writers to address the problems that black women face. Petry was born in Old Saybrook, Connecticut, and decided early on that she wanted to become a writer. While in high school, she wrote one-act plays and poetry. Following family tradition, however, she entered the Connecticut College of Pharmacy, completed her program in 1931, and became a pharmacist. Petry worked for the *Amsterdam News* and the *People's Voice* but continued to hone her writing skills. After publishing several of her stories, in 1946 she published her novel, *The Street.* During her writing career she published a number of works, including two other novels— *Country Place* in 1947 and *The Narrows* in 1953.

Sources: *Contemporary Black Biography,* vol. 19, pp. 179–81; Smith, *Notable Black American Women,* pp. 844–47; *Current Biography,* 1946, pp. 476–77.

1949 • Frank Garvin Yerby (1916–1991) was the first black to write a series of bestselling novels. Beginning with *The Foxes of Harrow* in 1949, he concentrated on costume novels, producing an annual best seller. The general reading public was unaware of his racial identity, and there is little in the novels to suggest it. He became known also as one of the popular novelists who based his tales in the Old South. Yerby was born in Augusta, Georgia. He received his bachelor's degree from Paine College in 1937 and his master's degree from Fisk University in 1938. He also did graduate study at the University of Chicago. In 1952 he established himself in Europe, principally in Spain, where he died.

Sources: Hornsby, *Milestones in Twentieth-Century African-American History,* p. 484; *Negro Almanac,* p. 1022; Wilson and Ferris, *Encyclopedia of Southern Culture,* p. 1143.

Samuel R. Delany

1962 • The first black American to earn acclaim as a science fiction writer was Samuel R[ay] Delany (1942–). Delany was born in Harlem and had a privileged childhood. He was a versatile and talented person who began to write at an early age, was a talented musician and composer by age fourteen and who studied physics and mathematics in high school. It was then that he was diagnosed with dyslexia. Delany won a number of awards for his writing, including a fellowship to the Bread Loaf Writer's Conference in Vermont. There he met poet Robert Frost. Delany studied at City College of New York for a while, but failed to complete his degree. His first science fiction novel, *The Jewels of Aptor,* was published in 1962, when he was twenty-two years old. In 1973 he published a graphic novel, *The Tides of Lust.* That helped to set the course for his novels that followed. Around the mid–1970s he came to grips with his identity as a gay man. Delaney continued to write, producing in 1977 the first of his well-received works of criticism, *Jewel-Hinged Jaw,* followed by *The American Shore* in 1978. He has been highly recognized for his writings, receiving the Pilgrim Award in 1984 from the Science Fiction Research Association and the William Whitehead Memorial Award for Lifetime Contribution to Lesbian and Gay Writing in 1993.

Sources: Smith, *Notable Black American Men,* pp. 286–89; Hunter, *Contemporary Literary Criticism,* vol. 141, pp. 95–163.

1970 • Nuruddin Farah (1945–) published his debut novel in English, *From a Crooked Rib*; it was the first fictional work by a Somali writer printed in English. Farah has also been called "the first feminist writer to come out of Africa" who "describes and analyzes women as victims of male subjugation." As novelist and playwright, he became one of Africa's most influential writers. Born in Baidoa, Somalia, the son of a merchant and a poet, Farah graduated from Punjab University in India in 1970 and did postgraduate work in theater from 1974 to 1975 at the University of London, which is attached to the Royal Court Theater. He continued studies at the University of Essex. He has taught at the University of Ibadan and at the University of Bayreuth in West Germany. His numerous honors include the Tucholsky Prize in Stockholm in 1991 for his work as a literary exile, and being named the fifteenth Neustadt laureate in 1998.

Sources: *Contemporary Black Biography,* vol. 27, pp. 55–59.

1975 • Virginia Esther Hamilton [Adoff] (1936?–2002) became the first black to receive the Newbery Medal, the American Library Association's most prestigious award in American children's books. Her novel, *M. C. Higgins, the Great,* which won her the award, also garnered for her the National Book Award in 1975. The book won the *Boston Globe-Horn Book Magazine* Award, the Lewis Carroll Shelf Award, and the International Board on Books for Young People Award. In 1995 Hamilton became the first writer of children's books to receive a MacArthur Foundation "genius" grant. Hamilton was born in Yellow Springs, Ohio, and graduated from Antioch College in 1955, with a B.A. degree. She studied at The Ohio State University and the New School for Social Work. Her literary career began when she was around nine years old, when she began to write stories. She published her first book, *Zeely* in 1967, followed by such works as *The House of Dies Drear* in 1968, *The Time-Ago Tales of Jadhu* in 1969, *The Planet of Junior Brown* in 1971, and *M.C. Higgins, the Great* in 1974—the book that secured her literary reputation. After that her works included *Justice and her Brother* (1978), *The Gathering* (1981) *Sweet Whispers, Brother Rush* (1982), *The People Could Fly* (1985, *The Dark Way* (1990, *When Birds Could Talk and Bats Could Sing* (1996), *Second Cousins* (2000), and *The Girl Who Spun Gold* (2000). Altogether she wrote more than thirty-five children's books. Hamilton always considered herself a storyteller. In her tales she continued the African American tradition of recounting stories that tell the various experiences that they have faced. She became known as one of the most influential figures in twentieth-century American literature. Hamilton died of breast cancer on February 19, 2002, at age sixty-five, in Dayton, Ohio.

Sources: Hine, *Black Women in America,* vol. 1, pp. 521–24; *Contemporary Black Biography,* vol. 10, pp. 86–90; *Jet* 101 (18 March 2002): 18; *Black Issues Book Review 4* (May–June 2002), p. 12.

1976 • Octavia Butler (1947–2006) became the first black woman science-fiction writer to be published. Butler was born in Pasadena, California, and grew up in a racially integrated community. She suffered from unrecognized dyslexia, the consequence of which at first led to poor performance in school. However, her problem never interfered with the fantasy stories and romance that she wrote when she was ten and eleven years old. After graduating from high school, Butler worked during the day and enrolled in fiction writing courses at Pasadena City College at night. After completing the two-year program, she studied for a while at California State College. By now seriously interested in writing, she enrolled in writing courses at the University of California at Los Angeles, attended writing workshops that the Writers Guild of America West sponsored, and participated in the Clarion Writers Workshop in Clarion, Pennsylvania. Butler has published a number of short stories, several of which were award-winning. She also wrote a number of science-fiction novels, most falling within a series. Her most successful stand-alone novel is *Kindred* (1988), which she called "grim fantasy" and not science fiction, for there is no science in it.

Octavia Butler

Sources: Smith, *Notable Black American Women,* pp. 144–47; Potter and Claytor, *African American Firsts,* pp. 154–55; McHenry, "Octavia's Mind Trip Into the Near Future," *Black Issues Book Review,* pp. 14–18.

1983 • Alice Walker (1944–) was the first black woman writer to win a Pulitzer Prize for a work of fiction, on April 18. The novel, *The Color Purple,* was popular but controversial. It also won the American Book Award and established her as a major American writer. Her third novel, *The Color Purple* was made into an Oscar-nominated movie, which intensified discussion among black men and women over her presentation of black men. Walker is also a poet, essayist, and short fiction writer. The Georgia-born writer was labeled a rebel and forced to leave Spelman College; she graduated from the more liberal Sarah Lawrence College in 1965, and worked in the Civil Rights Movement in Mississippi after graduation. An ardent feminist, Walker uses the term "womanist" to describe her work. Her works include *The Third Life of Grange Copeland* (1970), *In Search of Our Mother's Garden: Womanist* Prose (1983), *Temple of My Familiar* (1989), *Meridian* (1999), and *The Way Forward Is with a Broken Heart* (2002).

Alice Walker

Sources: *Black Writers*, pp. 571–73; Lanker, *I Dream a World*, p. 24; Smith, *Notable Black American Women*, pp. 1178–82; Wilson and Ferris, *Encyclopedia of Southern Culture*, p. 898.

Pamphlets

1829 • David Walker (1796?–1830) published the first pamphlet by an American black calling for a slave revolt, *David Walker's Appeal*. Born in Wilmington, North Carolina, he was the son of a free mother and a slave father. Since his mother was free, by law he took her status and was also free. He wandered across the South before settling in Boston in 1825 where he was the proprietor of a shop buying and selling secondhand clothing. Walker worked quickly to make his mark on Boston's black community, becoming active in the Massachusetts General Colored Association. He assured his fame by publishing *Appeal, in Four Articles, Together with a Preamble, to the Colored Citizens of the World, But in Particular, and Very Expressly to Those of the United States of America*. Despite efforts to suppress it, the *Appeal* became one of the most widely circulated pamphlets of the time. The circulation of the work became a crime in the South, and a bounty was placed on Walker's life. In 1848 *The Appeal* was published with Henry Highland Garnet's *Address* (1843), another call to revolt, in a volume financially supported by John Brown.

Sources: Logan and Winston, *Dictionary of American Negro Biography*, pp. 622–23; Hornsby, *Chronology of African-American History*, p. 16; Jackson, *A History of Afro-American Literature*, vol. 1, pp. 100–102; Smith, *Notable Black American Men*, pp. 1165–66.

1852 • Martin Robinson Delany (1812–1885) wrote the first major appeal for emigration: *The Condition, Elevation, Emigration and Destiny of the Colored People of the United States, Politically Considered*. In 1859 Delany wrote *Blake*, the first black nationalist novel, which today exists only in an incomplete form, with the last six chapters missing.

Sources: Logan and Winston, *Dictionary of American Negro Biography*, pp. 169–72; Jackson, *A History of Afro-American Literature*, vol. 1, pp. 364–69; Robinson, *Historical Negro Biographies*, p. 72; Simmons, *Men of Mark*, pp. 1007–15; Smith, *Notable Black American Men*, pp. 282–86.

Poetry

1746 • Lucy Terry [Prince] (1730?–1821), a slave and orator, was the first black American poet. "Bars Fight," written this year (her only known poem), was inspired by an Indian ambush of haymakers in the Bars, a small plateau near Deerfield, Massachusetts. It was not published until 1855, in Josiah Gilbert Holland's *History of Western Massachusetts*. Terry was kidnapped as an infant in Africa and brought to Rhode Island. In 1756 Terry married Abijah Prince and obtained her freedom. She is also noted for her determined, if unsuccessful, attempt to persuade Williams College (Massachusetts) to accept her son as a student—she is reported to have argued before the board of trustees for three hours.

Sources: Jackson, *A History of Afro-American Literature*, vol. 1, pp. 29–33; Smith, *Notable Black American Women*, pp. 881–82; Shockley, *Afro-American Women Writers 1746–1933*, p. 13.

1760 • Jupiter Hammon (1711–1806?), poet and tract writer, was the first black to publish a poem, as a separate work, in America. This poem was the eighty-eight lines of "An Evening Thought. Salvation by Christ, with Penitential Cries: Composed by Jupiter Hammon, a Negro belonging to Mr. [Henry] Lloyd of Queen's Village on Long Island, the 25th of December, 1760." Born a slave on Long Island, Hammon revealed an intensely religious conviction of the Methodist variety in this and his other publications. He became noteworthy as well for providing the first and most comprehensive writing on black theology and was the first to write anti-slavery protest literature in America.

Sources: Logan and Winston, *Dictionary of American Negro Biography*, pp. 281–82; Jackson, *A History of Afro-American Literature*, vol. 1, pp. 33–37; Smith, *Notable Black American Men*, pp. 504–6.

1773 • Phillis Wheatley (1753?–1784), born on the west coast of Africa, published the first book of poetry by a black person in America (and the second published by a woman). *Poems on Various Subjects, Religious and Moral* was published in London, England. A Boston merchant, John Wheatley, had bought Phillis as a child of about seven or eight, and had allowed her to learn to read and write. Wheatley's first published poem, "On the Death of the Reverend George Whitefield," appeared in 1770 in a Boston broadside. In 1773 she traveled abroad with the Wheatleys' son, partially in the hope of restoring her health with exposure to sea air, and she attracted considerable attention in England as a poet. It was at about this time that she was freed. Deaths had ended the connection with the Wheatley family by 1788, when she married a freeman, John Peters. Her first two children died, and at the end of her life she worked as a maid in a boarding house to support herself. She died in December, followed the same day by her third child, an infant.

Sources: Logan and Winston, *Dictionary of American Negro Biography*, pp. 640–43; Jackson, *A History of Afro-American Literature*, vol. 1, pp. 38–46; Smith, *Notable Black American Women*, p. 1243–48.

Phillis Wheatley

1829 • George Moses Horton (1797–1883?) was the first Southern black to publish a collection of poetry. *The Hope of Liberty*, containing twenty-one poems, was published in Raleigh, North Carolina. He anticipated proceeds from this volume would pay his way to Liberia. As with all his attempts at gaining freedom before Emancipation, this was unsuccessful. Somehow Horton managed to educate himself and establish a connection with the University of North Carolina in Chapel Hill. He purchased his own time from his owners at twenty-five cents a day, later fifty cents. A tolerated character at the university, he seems to have earned part of his money by writing poems for undergraduates. In 1866 he had moved to Philadelphia and toward the end of his life wrote and published prose to earn a living. He also adapted Bible stories by changing names and events to fit the times. His works were found in different publications, since he sold then where he could. He may have returned South before he died around 1883.

Sources: Logan and Winston, *Dictionary of American Negro Autobiography*, pp. 327–28; Jackson, *A History of Afro-American Literature*, vol. 1, pp. 83–100; Smith, *Notable Black American Men*, pp. 571–73.

1845 • Armand Lanusse (1812–1867) compiled the first collection of American black poets, *Les Cenelles*, devoted to poetry in French. The work contained eighty-two poems written by seventeen Creoles of color, along with other selections. Eighteen of the poems are his. The title symbolizes the modesty and beauty of small pink and white blossoms on hawthorn shrubbery. Lanusse was a free man of color and the leader of a local group of young poets. He was born and died in New Orleans, and developed a love for classics. From 1852 to 1866 he was principal of the Bernard Couvent Institute for Indigent Catholic Orphans, where he exposed his students to the classics. Although he enjoyed some affluence, he identified himself with the underprivileged, preferring to live a simple life.

Sources: Logan and Winston, *Dictionary of American Negro Biography*, pp. 384–85; Hughes and Bontemps, *Poetry of the Negro 1746–l949*, p. 400; Jackson, *A History of Afro-American Literature*, vol. 1, pp. 225–34.

1877 • Albery Allson Whitman (1851–1902) was the first black American poet to publish a poem more than five thousand lines long, "Not a Man and Yet a Man." Born a slave near Munfordville, Kentucky, Whitman began life as a laborer, and had only a few months' formal education. He nevertheless became a very effective African Methodist Episcopal preacher. Alcoholism contributed to his short life. Whitman is considered the finest black poet of the Reconstruction era. (Whitman's poem was surpassed in length by some 3,500 lines with the publication of Robert E. Ford's "Brown Chapel, A Story in Verse," in 1903.)

Sources: Brown, Davis, and Lee, *The Negro Caravan*, p. 297; Logan and Winston, *Dictionary of American Negro Biography*, pp. 650–51; Jackson, *A History of Afro-American Literature*, vol. 1, pp. 272–92; Smith, *Notable Black American Men*, pp. 1213–14.

Albery Allson Whitman

Paul Laurence Dunbar

1893 • Paul Laurence Dunbar (1872–1906) was the first black poet to gain national fame. Born in Dayton, Ohio, Dunbar was accepted wholeheartedly as a writer and widely recognized in the late nineteenth century. His literary promise was recognized first when he graduated from high school in 1891. At that time he delivered the class poem that he had written. Financially unable to support himself while he studied law, Dunbar developed his literary talent and became a man of letters. He first worked as an elevator operator while he read widely and honed his writing skills, which led him to become founder and editor of the Dayton *Tattler* (1889–90). After that he worked briefly as a clerk at Chicago's World Columbian Exposition (1893), as court messenger (1896), and assistant clerk at the Library of Congress (1897–98). His writings began to appear in print and reflected his use of dialect and standard English in his work. Dunbar's poems were published in the *Dayton Herald* as early as 1888. His first book, *Oak and Ivy* appeared in 1893, and two years later his second book, *Majors and Minors*, attracted the attention of the celebrated critic William Dean Howells. His third book, *Lyrics of Lowly Life* (1896), gained him his national reputation. He published a number of other works, including collections of short stories, collections of poems, and works of fiction.

Sources: Brown, Davis, and Lee, *The Negro Caravan*, p. 303; Logan and Winston, *Dictionary of American Negro Biography*, pp. 200–203; Hughes and Bontemps, *The Poetry of the Negro 1746–1949*, p. 395; Smith, *Notable Black American Men*, pp. 344–48.

Gwendolyn Brooks

1950 • Gwendolyn Brooks (1917–2000), poet and novelist, was the first black to win a Pulitzer Prize for poetry with *Annie Allen*, on May 1. She became established as a major American poet, and in 1976, she was the first black woman inducted into the National Institute of Arts and Letters. A sensitive interpreter of Northern ghetto life, she began to write poetry at age seven; her first poems were published in the *Chicago Defender*. From 1969 on, she promoted the idea that blacks must develop their own culture. She changed her writing style in an effort to become accessible to the ordinary black reader. She was poet laureate of Illinois for sixteen years, and was named poetry consultant to the Library of Congress in 1985. Brooks was born in Topeka, Kansas, and began to write poetry when she was seven years old. While in high school, she met Langston Hughes who, on her request, read her poems and gave her enthusiastic inspiration. After graduation she attended Woodrow Wilson Junior College. In the 1940s and 1950s Brooks concentrated on learning poetry and on writing it as well. In 1945 she published *A Street in Bronzeville,* the book that launched her career. *Annie Allen,* her book of poetry published in 1949, won her a Pulitzer Prize. Her autobiographical novel, *Maude Martha,* was published in 1953, followed by the first of four books of poetry for children in 1956, then *The Bean Eaters* (1960), *In the Mecca* (1968), *The Riot* (1969), and other works.

Sources: *Hine, Black Women in America,* vol. 1, pp. 168–69; Hughes and Bontemps, *The Poetry of the Negro 1746–1949,* p. 390; Smith, *Notable Black American Women,* pp. 105–9.

1993 • Maya Angelou [Marguerite Johnson] (1928–) became the first black inaugural poet, at the swearing in of President Bill Clinton on January 20. Born Marguerite Johnson, in St. Louis, Missouri, she and her brother were sent to Stamps, Arkansas, to live with their paternal grandmother. Although the years of the Great Depression were severe for their grandmother, the family lived without government welfare. After graduating from the eighth grade, Angelou and her brother moved to San Francisco and lived with their mother. By the time she was twenty-four, she began a career as a dancer and performed in Chicago and New York; she also toured Europe and Africa in *Porgy and Bess.* It was around this time that she adopted her present name—Maya from her brother's nickname for her, and Angelou from a variation of her former husband's name. She returned to the United States and continued her career as a nightclub performer. But she also became a social activist and committed herself to the Southern Christian Leadership Conference. In 1961 she had a successful performance in Jean Genêt's play, *The Blacks.* By age thirty, Angelou was convinced that she wanted to become a writer. The Harlem Writer's Guild helped her along her newly chosen path. In 1979 Angelou published her first autobiography, *I Know Why the Caged Bird Sings,* which was made into a television movie. She earned an Emmy nomination for her appearance in Alex Haley's television production of *Roots,* and she contin-

The First Published Short Story

In 1859 Frances Ellen Watkins Harper (1825–1911) wrote "The Two Offers," the first short story published by a black woman in the United States. It appeared in the *Anglo-African* magazine in 1859. Harper was born in Baltimore, Maryland, of free parents. By age fourteen she had a fairly good education for the time and was already established as a writer and scholar. She became a noted speaker in the abolition movement, including that as permanent lecturer for the Maine Anti-Slavery Society. After the Civil War her lectures addressed such issues as the suffrage and temperance movements as well as women's rights. Often she interspersed poetry throughout her lectures. Although her poems addressed a variety of issues, Harper is often referred to as an abolitionist poet; she was also the most popular black poet of her time. Her first volume appeared in 1845, when she was twenty-one years old. She was an extremely successful poet—*Poems on Miscellaneous Subjects* launched her career and is reported to have sold fifty thousand copies by 1878—and her novel *Iola Leroy* (1892) had three editions printed.

Frances E. W. Harper

Sources: Brown, Davis, and Lee, *The Negro Caravan*, p. 293; Logan and Winston, *Dictionary of American Negro Biography*, pp. 289–90; Hughes and Bontemps, *The Poetry of the Negro 1746–1949*, p. 397; Jackson, *A History of Afro-American Literature*, vol. 1, pp. 265–72; 392–97; Smith, *Notable Black American Women*, pp. 457–62; Shockley, *Afro-American Women Writers 1746–1933*, p. 56.

ued her acting career while she developed a writing career as well. In 1981 Angelou accepted a lifetime appointment at Wake Forest University in Winston-Salem, as Reynolds Professor of American Studies. Angelou's numerous works include several volumes of poetry, yet critics consider her first autobiography and *The Heart of a Woman* her most outstanding works. With the publication of her sixth and final memoir, *A Song Flung up to Heaven* (2002), Angelou intends to "close the book on life," to the extent that it will be her concluding memoir. Juan Williams formerly with the National Public Radio, said that Angelou "occupies a singular space in American cultural history." Her inaugural poem was published as *On the Pulse of Morning* soon after the ceremony. Robert Frost was the first poet to read at the inauguration of a president, John F. Kennedy.

Sources: Smith, *Notable Black American Women*, pp. 23–27; *Jet* (8 February 1993): 4–10; *Tennessean* (20 January 1993); (17 April 2002); *USA Today* (21 January 1993).

Short Stories

1853 • Frederick Douglass (1817–1895) wrote the first short story published by a black, "The Heroic Slave." It appeared in four installments in his newspaper, *The North Star.* This long short story, almost a novella, is based on the real-life exploit of Madison Washington, a recaptured fugitive slave, who took the lead in seizing the ship on which he was being sent to be sold from Virginia to Louisiana, and regained his freedom by sailing the vessel to Nassau.

Sources: Jackson, *A History of Afro-American Literature*, vol. 1, pp. 118–20.

SOURCES

Aasang, Nathan. *African-American Athletes*. Rev. ed. New York: Facts on File, 2010.

Abdul, Raol. *Blacks in Classical Music: A Personal History*. New York: Dodd, Mead, 1977.

Abramson, Doris E. *Negro Playwrights in the American Theatre, 1925–1959*. New York: Columbia University Press, 1969.

Ackman, Martha. *Curveball: The Remarkable Story of Toni Stone, the First Woman to Play Professional Baseball in the Negro League*. Chicago: Lawrence Hill Books, 2010.

Adams, A. John, and Joan Martin Burke. *Civil Rights: A Current Guide to the People, Organizations, and Events*. New York: Bowker, 1970.

Adams, James Truslow, ed. *Dictionary of American History*. 7 vols. 2nd ed. New York: Charles Scribner's, 1968.

The African American Education Databook. Volume I: *Higher and Adult Education*. Fairfax, VA: Frederick D. Patterson Research Institute, 1997.

African American Legislators in Michigan 1893–2002: 109 Years of Service. Lansing: Michigan Legislative Black Caucus, 2002.

Afro-American Encyclopedia. North Miami, FL: Educational Book Publishers, 1974.

Alford, Sterling G. *Famous First Blacks*. New York: Vantage, 1974.

Anderson, Jervis. *This Was Harlem*. New York: Farrar Straus Giroux, 1982.

Andrews, William L. *Sisters of the Spirit: Three Black Women's Autobiographies of the Nineteenth Century*. Bloomington: Indiana University Press, 1986.

Angell, Stephen Ward. *Bishop Henry McNeal Turner and African-American Religion in the South*. Knoxville: University of Tennessee Press, 1992.

Archer, Jules. *They Had a Dream: The Civil Rights Struggle from Frederick Douglass to Marcus Garvey to Martin Luther King, Jr. and Malcolm X*. New York: Viking Children's Books, 1993.

Asante, Molefi, and Mark T. Mattson. *The Historical and Cultural Atlas of African Americans*. New York: Macmillan, 1991.

Ashe, Arthur R., Jr. *A Hard Road to Glory*. 3 vols. New York: Warner Books, 1988.

Bacote, Clarence. *The Story of Atlanta University.* New Haven, CT: Yale University Press, 1961.

Badger, Reid. *A Life in Ragtime: A Biography of James Reese Europe.* New York: Oxford University Press, 1995.

Baer, Hans A. *The Black Spiritual Movement.* Knoxville: University of Tennessee Press, 1984.

Baer, Hans A., and Merrill Singer. *African-American Religion in the Twentieth Century.* Knoxville: University of Tennessee Press, 1992.

Baer, Hans A., and Yvonne Jones, eds. *African Americans in the South.* Athens: University of Georgia Press, 1992.

Bailey, Richard. *They Too Call Alabama Home: African American Profiles, 1800–1999.* Montgomery, AL: Pyramid Publishing, 1999.

Barksdale, Richard, and Keneth Kinnamon. *Black Writers of America.* New York: Macmillan, 1972.

Baskin, Wade, and Richard Runes. *Dictionary of Black Culture.* New York: Philosophical Library, 1973.

Beasley, Delilah L. *The Negro Trailblazers in California.* Los Angeles: Times Mirror Printing and Binding House, 1919.

Bedini, Silvio A. *The Life of Benjamin Banneker.* New York: Scribner, 1971.

Bennett, Lerone, Jr. *Before the Mayflower.* 6th ed. Chicago: Johnson Publishing Co., 1987.

Bergman, Peter M. *The Chronological History of the Negro in America.* New York: Harper and Row, 1969.

Berry, Leonidas H. *I Wouldn't Take Nothin' for My Journey.* Chicago: Johnson Publishing Co., 1981.

Black Americans in Congress, 1870–2007. Prepared under the direction of the Committee on House Administration of the U.S. House of Representatives, by the Office of History and Preservation, Office of the Clerk, U.S. House of Representatives. Washington, DC: U.S. Government Printing Office, 2008.

Black Americans in Defense of Our Nation. Washington, DC: Department of Defense, 1982.

Black Writers. Detroit: Gale, 1989.

Blackett, R. J. M., ed. *Thomas Morris Chester, Black Civil War Correspondent.* New York: Da Capo Press, 1989.

Blassingame, John W. *Black New Orleans, 1860–1880.* Chicago: University of Chicago Press, 1973.

Blockson, Charles R., with Ron Fry. *Black Genealogy.* Englewood Cliffs, NJ: Prentice-Hall, 1977.

Bogle, Donald. *Dorothy Dandridge: A Biography.* New York: Amistad Press, 1997.

Bogle, Donald. *Primetime Blues: African Americans on Network Television.* New York: Farrar, Straus and Giroux, 2001.

Bogle, Donald. *Toms, Coons, Mulattoes, Mammies, and Bucks.* New York: Viking Press, 1973.

Bontemps, Arna. *The Harlem Renaissance Remembered.* New York: Dodd, Mead, 1972.

Bowles, Frank Hamilton, and Frank A. DeCosta. *Between Two Worlds.* New York: McGraw-Hill, 1971.

Bragg, George F. *Men of Maryland.* Baltimore: Church Advocate Press, 1925.

Bragg, George Freeman, Jr. *History of the Afro-American Group of the Episcopal Church.* Baltimore: Church Advocate Press, 1922.

Brawley, Benjamin. *The Negro Genius.* New York: Dodd, Mead, 1937.

Brooks, Christopher A., ed. *The African American Almanac.* 11th ed. Detroit: Gale, 2011.

Broughton, Viv. *Black Gospel: An Illustrated History of the Gospel Sound.* Poole, England: Blandford Press, 1985.

Brown, Elaine. *A Taste of Power: A Black Woman's Story.* New York: Pantheon Books, 1992.

Brown, Hallie Q., ed. *Homespun Heroines.* Xenia, OH: 1926.

Brown, Sterling, Arthur P. Davis, and Ulysses Lee, eds. *The Negro Caravan.* Reprint. New York: Arno Press, 1969.

Bruce, John Edward, and John Cullen Gruesser. *The Black Sleuth.* Boston: Northeastern University Press, 2002.

Burgess, Stanley M., and Gary B. McGee, eds. *Dictionary of Pentecostal and Charismatic Movements.* Grand Rapids, MI: Zondervan, 1988.

Burkett, Randall K., and Richard Newman, eds. *Black Apostles.* Boston: G. K. Hall, 1978.

Burrell, W. P., and D. E. Johnson, Sr. *Twenty-five Years History of the Grand Fountain of the United Order of True Reformers 1881–1905.* Richmond, VA: Grand Fountain, United Order of True Reformers, 1909.

Byrd, Rudolph. P., ed. *Generations in Black and White.* Athens: University of Georgia Press, 1993.

Cantor, George. *Historic Landmarks of Black America.* Detroit: Gale, 1991.

Cederholm, Teresa Dickason. *Afro-American Artists.* Boston: Boston Public Library, 1973.

Cha-Jua, Sundiata Keita. *America's First Black Town: Brooklyn, Illinois, 1830–1915.* Urbana: University of Illinois Press, 2000.

Chalk, Oceania. *Pioneers of Black Sport.* New York: Dodd, Mead, 1975.

Chilton, John. *Who's Who of Jazz.* Philadelphia: Chilton Book Company, 1972.

Chireau, Yvonne, and Nathaniel Deutsch, eds. *Black Zion.* New York: Oxford University Press, 2000.

Christmas, Walter. *Negroes in Public Affairs and Government.* Yonkers, NY: Educational Heritage, 1966.

Christopher, Maurine. *America's Black Congressmen.* New York: Thomas Y Crowell, 1971.

Clark, Patrick. *Sports Firsts.* New York: Facts on File, 1981.

Clayton, Edward T. *The Negro Politician.* Chicago, Johnson Publishing Co., 1964.

Clayton, Xernona. *I've Been Marching All the Time.* Atlanta: Longstreet Press, 1991.

Cobb, W. Montague. *The First Negro Medical Society: A History of the Medico-Chirurgical Society of the District of Columbia, 1884–1939.* Washington, DC: Associated Publishers, 1939.

Cohn, Lawrence, Mary Katherine Aldin, et al. *Nothing but the Blues.* New York: Abbeville Press, 1993.

Contemporary Black Biography. Vols. 1–98. Detroit: Gale, 1991–2012.

Cooley, Timothy Mather. *Sketches of the Life and Character of the Rev. Lemuel Hayes.* New York: Harper, 1837.

Crafts, Hannah. *The Bondwoman's Narrative.* Ed. Henry Louis Gates, Jr. New York: Warner Books, 2002.

Culhane, John. *The American Circus: An Illustrated History.* New York: Henry Holt, 1990.

Culp, Daniel W., ed. *Twentieth Century Negro Literature*. Naperville, IL: J. L. Nichols and Company, 1902.

Cunard, Nancy, ed. *Negro Anthology*. Reprint. New York: Negro Universities Press, 1969.

Current Biography. New York: H. W. Wilson.

Current, Richard Nelson. *Phi Beta Kappa in American Life*. New York: Oxford University Press, 1990.

Dabney, Lillian G. *The History of Schools for Negroes in the District of Columbia, 1807–1947*. Washington, DC: Catholic University of America Press, 1949.

Dannett, Sylvia G. L. *Profiles of Negro Womanhood*. Vol. 1. Yonkers, NY: Educational Heritage, 1964–1966.

Dates, Jannette L., and William Barlow, eds. *Split Image: African Americans in the Mass Media*. Washington: Howard University Press, 1990.

Davis, Cyprian. *The History of Black Catholics in the United States*. New York: Crossroad, 1990.

Delaney, John J. *Dictionary of Saints*. New York: Doubleday, 1980.

Dodson, Howard, Christopher Moore, and Roberta Yancy. *The Black New Yorkers: The Schomburg Illustrated Chronology*. New York: John Wiley, 2000.

Driskell, Claude Evans. *The History of Chicago Black Dental Professionals*. Chicago: privately printed, 1982.

Driskell, David C. *Two Centuries of Black American Art*. New York: Knopf, 1976.

Du Bois, W. E. Burghardt, ed. *Efforts for Social Betterment among Negro Americans*. Atlanta: Atlanta University Press, 1909.

Duberman, Martin B. *Paul Robeson*. New York: Knopf, 1988.

DuPree, Sherry Sherrod. *Biographical Dictionary of African-American Holiness-Pentecostals 1880–1990*. Washington, DC: Middle Atlantic Regional Press, 1989.

Durham, Philip, and Everett L. Jones, *The Negro Cowboys*. Reprint. Lincoln: University of Nebraska Press, 1983.

Dyson, Walter. *Howard University*. Washington, DC: Howard University, 1941.

The Ebony Success Library. Vols. 1 and 2. Nashville, TN: Southwestern, 1973.

Emery, Lynne Fauley. *Black Dance from 1619 to Today*. 2nd ed. Princeton, NJ: Princeton Book Company, 1988.

Encyclopedia Americana. Vol. 9. Danbury, CT: Grolier, 1988.

Encyclopedia of African American History, 1896 to the Present. Vol. 4. New York: Oxford University Press, 2009.

Encyclopedia of Ethnicity and Sports in the United States. Eds. George B. Kirsch, Othello Harris, and Claire E. Nolte. Westport, CT: Greenwood Press, 2000.

Ethel Thompson Overby. Richmond, VA: 1975.

Fax, Elton C. *Contemporary Black Leaders*. New York: Dodd, Mead, 1970.

Feather, Leonard G. *The Encyclopedia of Jazz*. New York: Horizon Press, 1965.

Field, Rob, and Alexander Bielakowski. *Buffalo Soldiers: African American Troops in the US Forces, 1866–1945*. New York: Osprey, 2008.

File, Nigel. *Black Settlers in Britain, 1555–1958*. London: Heinemann Educational Books, 1981.

Finkelman, Paul, ed. *Encyclopedia of African American History 1896 to the Present*. 2 vols. New York: Oxford University Press, 2009.

Fisk University. *Mission and Management: A Non-Traditional Self-Study of Fisk University*. Part 6. 1978.

Fisk University Bulletin, 1986–1989.

Flexner, Stuart Berg. *I Hear America Talking.* New York: Simon and Schuster, 1976.

Foner, Jack D. *Blacks and the Military in American History.* New York: Praeger, 1974.

Foner, Philip S. *Organized Labor and the Black Worker: 1619–1973.* New York: Praeger, 1974.

Foster, Frances Smith, ed. *A Brighter Coming Day: A Frances Ellen Watkins Harper Reader.* New York: The Feminist Press at The City University of New York, 1990.

Frank, Rusty E. *Tap! The Greatest Tap Dance Stars and Their Stories, 1900–1955.* New York: William Morrow, 1990.

Franklin, John Hope. *George Washington Williams, a Biography.* Chicago: University of Chicago Press, 1985.

Franklin, John Hope, and August Meier, eds. *Black Leaders of the Twentieth Century.* Urbana: University of Illinois Press, 1982.

Franklin, John Hope, and Evelyn Brooks Higginbotham. *From Slavery to Freedom.* 9th ed. New York: McGraw-Hill, 2011.

Frazier, E. Franklin. *The Negro Church in America.* Published with C. Eric Lincoln, *The Black Church since Frazier.* New York: Schocken Books, 1974.

Fuller, Edmund L. *Visions in Stone: The Sculpture of William Edmondson.* Pittsburgh: University of Pittsburgh Press, 1973.

Fuller, T. O. *History of the Negro Baptists of Tennessee.* Memphis: privately printed, 1936.

Furr, Arthur. *Democracy's Negroes.* Boston: The House of Edinboro, 1947.

Gale Directory of Publications and Broadcast Media. Detroit: Gale, 1993.

Garrett, Romeo B. *Famous First Facts about Negroes.* New York: Arno Press, 1972.

Garrity, John, and Mark C. Carnes, eds. *American National Biography.* New York: Oxford University Press, 1999.

Gates, Henry Louis, and Evelyn Brooks Higginbotham, eds. *African American National Biography,* 8 vols. New York: Oxford University Press, 2008.

Gatewood, Willard B. *Aristocrats of Color: The Black Elite, 1880–1890.* Bloomington: Indiana University Press, 1990.

Gaustad, Edwin Scott, and Philip Barlow. *New Historical Atlas of Religion in America.* New York: Oxford University Press, 2001.

Gavin, Christy, ed. *African American Women Playwrights: A Research Guide.* New York: Garland, 1999.

Gibb, H. A. R., and J. H. Kramers. *Shorter Encyclopaedia of Islam.* Ithaca, NY: Cornell University Press, 1953.

Gosnell, Harold F. *Negro Politicians.* Chicago: University of Chicago Press, 1935.

Great Athletes: The Twentieth Century. Vols. 14, 16. Englewood Cliffs, NJ: Salem Press, 1992.

Greenberg, Jonathan D. *Staking a Claim: Jake Simmons and the Making of an African-American Oil Dynasty.* New York: Atheneum, 1990.

Greene, Harry Washington. *Holders of Doctorates among American Negroes.* Boston: Meador Publishing, 1946.

Gubert, Betty Kaplan, Miriam Sawyer, and Caroline M. Fannin. *Distinguished African Americans in Aviation and Space Science.* Westport, CT: Oryx Press, 2002.

Haber, Louis. *Black Pioneers of Science and Invention.* New York: Harcourt, Brace and World, 1970.

Hamilton, Charles V. *Adam Clayton Powell, Jr.* New York: Atheneum, 1991.

Handy, D. Antoinette. *Black Women in American Bands and Orchestras.* Metuchen, NJ: Scarecrow Press, 1981.

Harlan, Louis R. *Booker T. Washington: The Making of a Black Leader, 1856–1901.* New York: Oxford University Press, 1972.

Harris, Michael W. *The Rise of Gospel Blues: The Music of Thomas Andrew Dorsey in the Urban Church.* New York: Oxford University Press, 1992.

Hartshorn, W. N., ed. *An Era of Progress and Promise, 1863–1910.* Boston: Priscilla Publishing Co., 1919.

Haskins, James. *Black Dance in America.* New York: Harper Trophy, 1990.

Haskins, James. *Outward Dreams: Black Inventors and their Dreams.* New York: Bantam, 1992.

Heilbut, Tony. *The Gospel Sound.* New York: Simon and Schuster, 1971.

Heiler, Allan. *Marian Anderson: A Songer's Journey.* New York: Scribner, 2000.

Henderson, Edwin B., and the editors of *Sport* magazine. *The Black Athlete.* New York: Publishers Company, 1980.

Higginbotham, Evelyn Brooks. *Righteous Discontent: The Women's Movement in the Black Baptist Church 1880–1920.* Cambridge: Harvard University Press, 1993.

Hill, Roy L. *Who's Who in the American Negro Press.* Dallas: Royal Publishing Company, 1960.

Hine, Darlene Clark., ed. *Black Women in America.* 2d ed. 3 vols. New York: Oxford University Press, 2005.

Hine, Darlene Clark., ed. *Black Women in America: An Historical Encyclopedia.* 2 vols. Brooklyn: Carlson Publishing, 1993.

Hine, Darlene Clark, and Earnestine Jenkins, eds. *A Question of Manhood.* Vol. 1. *"Manhood Rights": The Construction of Black Male History and Manhood, 1750–1870.* Bloomington: Indiana University Press, 1999.

History of Schools for the Colored Population. (Section C of the *Special Report of the Commissioner for Education on the Improvement of Public Schools in the District of Columbia, 1871.*) Reprint. New York: Arno Press and the *New York Times,* 1969.

Hoffschwelle, Mary S. *The Rosenwald Schools of the American South.* Gainesville: University Press of Florida, 2006.

Holmes, Dwight Oliver Wendell. *The Evolution of the Negro College.* New York: Teachers College, Columbia University, 1934.

Holway, John B. *The Great Black Jockeys: The Lives and Times of the Men Who Dominated America's First National Sport.* Rocklin, CA: Forum, 1999.

Hopkins, Lee Bennett. *Important Dates in Afro-American History.* New York: Franklin Watts, 1969.

Hornsby, Alton, Jr. *Chronology of African-American History.* Detroit: Gale, 1991.

Hornsby, Alton, Jr. *Milestones in Twentieth-Century African-American History.* Detroit: Visible Ink, 1993.

Horton, Carrell Peterson, and Jessie Carney Smith, eds. *Statistical Record of Black America.* Detroit: Gale, 1990.

Horton, James. *Free People of Color.* Washington, DC: Smithsonian Institution Press, 1993.

Houzeau, Jean-Charles. *My Passage at the New Orleans Tribune: A Memoir of the Civil War Era.* Ed. David C. Rankin. Baton Rouge: Louisiana State University Press, 1984.

Hubbard, G. W. *History of the Colored Schools of Nashville, Tennessee.* Wheeler, Marshall & Bruce, 1874.

Hudson, Karen E. *Paul R. Williams, Architect.* New York: Rizzoli, 1993.

Hughes, Langston, and Arna Bontemps. *Poetry of the Negro, 1746–1949*. Garden City, NY: Doubleday, 1949.

Hughes, Langston, and Milton Meltzer. *Black Magic*. Englewood Cliffs, NJ: Prentice-Hall, 1967.

Hughes, Langston, and Milton Meltzer. *A Pictorial History of the Negro in America*. 3rd. rev. ed. New York: Crown, 1968.

Hughes, Richard T. *Reviving the Ancient Faith: The Story of Churches of Christ in America*. Grand Rapids, MI: William B. Eerdsmans, 1996.

Hutchinson, Louise Daniel. *Anna J. Cooper*. Washington, DC: Smithsonian Institution Press, 1981.

I Have a Dream: A Collection of Black Americans on U.S. Postage Stamps. Washington, DC: U.S. Postal Service, 1991.

Ifill, Gwen. *The Breakthrough: Politics and Race in the Age of Obama*. New York: Doubleday, 2009.

Igus, Toyomi, ed. *Great Women in the Struggle*. Vol. 2 of *The Book of Black Heroes*. Orange, NJ: Just Us Books, 1991.

Inge, M. Thomas, ed. *Dark Laughter: The Satiric Art of Oliver W. Harrington*. Jackson: University Press of Mississippi, 1993.

Integration and the Negro Officer in the Armed Forces of the United States of America. Washington, DC: U.S. Government Printing Office, 1962.

Jackson, Blyden. *A History of Afro-American Literature*. Vol. 1. Baton Rouge: Louisiana State University Press, 1989.

Jackson, Giles B., and D. Webster Davis. *The Industrial History of the Negro Race of the United States*. Reprint. Freeport, NY: Books for Libraries Press, 1971.

Jackson-Coppin, Fanny. *Reminiscences of School Life, and Hints on Teaching*. Philadelphia: A.M.E. Book Concern, 1913.

James, Portia P. *The Real McCoy: African-American Invention and Innovation, 1619–1930*. Washington, DC: Smithsonian Institution Press, 1989.

Jaynes, Gerald Davis, and Robin M. Williams, eds. *A Common Destiny*. Washington, DC: National Academy Press, 1989.

Johnson, James Weldon. *Along This Way*. New York: Viking, 1933.

Johnson, James Weldon. *Black Manhattan*. New York: Knopf, 1940.

Johnson, John H., with Lerone Bennett. *Succeeding against the Odds*. New York: Warner Books, 1989.

Jones, James B., Jr. *Every Day in Tennessee History*. Winston-Salem, NC: John F. Blair, 1966.

Jones, Wally, and Jim Washington. *Black Champions Challenge American Sports*. New York: D. McKay, 1973.

Jones, William H. *Recreation and Amusement among Negroes in Washington, D.C.* Washington, DC: Howard University Press, 1927.

Jordan, Robert L. *Two Races in One Fellowship*. Oakland, CA: United Christian Church, 1944.

Jordan, Vernon E., Jr., with Annette Gordon-Reed. *Vernon Can Read: A Memoir*. New York: Public Affairs, 2001.

Josey, E. J., ed. *The Black Librarian in America*. Metuchen, NJ: Scarecrow Press, 1970.

Josey, E. J., and Ann Shockley, comps. and eds. *Handbook of Black Librarianship*. Littleton, CO: Libraries Unlimited, 1977.

Joyce, Donald Franklin. *Gatekeepers of Black Culture*. Westport, CO: Greenwood Press, 1983.

Kane, Joseph Nathan. *Famous First Facts*. New York: H. W. Wilson, 1981.

Karenga, Maulana. *The African American Holiday of Kwanzaa: A Celebration of Family, Community and Culture*. Los Angeles: University of Sankore Press, 1988.

Katz, William Loren. *Black Indians*. New York: Atheneum, 1986.

Katz, William Loren. *The Black West*. 3rd ed. Seattle, WA: Open Hand Publishing, 1987.

Katz, William Loren, ed. *Eyewitness: The Negro in American History*. 3rd ed. New York: Pitman, 1974.

Kellner, Bruce, ed. *The Harlem Renaissance*. Westport, CT: Greenwood Press, 1984.

Klever, Anita. *Women in Television*. Louisville, KY: Westminster Press, 1992.

Klotman, Phyllis Rauch. *Frame by Frame*. Bloomington: Indiana University Press, 1979.

Knight, Gladys L., ed. *Icons of African American Protest: Trailblazing Activists of the Civil Rights Movement*. Westport, CT: Greenwood Press, 2009.

Koger, A. Briscoe. *The Negro Lawyer in Maryland*. Baltimore: Clarke, 1948.

Krapp, Kristine, ed. *Notable Black American Scientists*. Detroit: Gale, 1999.

Lane, Roger. *William Dorsey's Philadelphia and Ours*. New York: Oxford University Press, 1991.

Lanker, Brian. *I Dream a World*. New York: Stewart, Tabori and Chang, 1989.

Leavell, Ullin Whitney. *Philanthropy in Negro Education*. Reprint. Westport, CT: Negro Universities Press, 1970.

Leckie, William H. *The Buffalo Soldiers: A Narrative of the Negro Cavalry in the West*. Norman: University of Oklahoma Press, 1967.

Lee, George L. *Interesting People: Black American History Makers*. New York: Ballantine Books, 1992.

Lee, Irvin H. *Negro Medal of Honor Men*. New York: Dodd, Mead, 1969.

Lerner, Gerda. *Black Women in White America*. New York: Pantheon, 1972.

Lewis, B., Ch. Pellat, and J. Schacht. *The Encyclopaedia of Islam*. New edition. London: Luzac and Company, 1959.

Lewis, David Levering. *When Harlem Was in Vogue*. New York: Knopf, 1981.

The Life and Teachings of Carrie Judd Montgomery, The Prayer of Faith. New York: Garland Publishing, 1985.

Lincoln, C. Eric. *The Black Church since Frazier*. Published with Frazier E. Franklin, *The Negro Church in America*. New York: Schocken Books, 1974.

Lincoln, C. Eric, and Lawrence H. Mamiya. *The Black Church in the African American Experience*. Durham, NC: Duke University Press, 1990.

Loewenberg, Bert J., and Ruth Bogin. *Black Women in Nineteenth-Century American Life*. University Park: Pennsylvania State University Press, 1976.

Logan, Rayford W. *Howard University*. New York: New York University Press, 1969.

Logan, Rayford W., and Michael R. Winston, eds. *Dictionary of American Negro Biography*. New York: Norton, 1982.

Lovett, Bobby L. *The African-American History of Nashville, Tennessee, 1780–1930*. Fayetteville: University of Arkansas Press, 1999.

Lovett, Bobby L. *The Civil Rights Movement in Tennessee: A Narrative History*. Knoxville: University of Tennessee Press, 2005.

Lovett, Bobby, and Linda T. Wynn, eds. *Profiles of African Americans in Tennessee*. Nashville: Annual Local Conference on Afro-American Culture and History, 1996.

Low, W. Augustus, and Virgil A. Clift, eds. *Encyclopedia of Black America.* New York: McGraw-Hill, 1981.

Lowery, Charles D., and John F. Marszalek, eds. *Greenwood Encyclopedia of African American Civil Rights.* 2 vols. Westport, CT: Greenwood Press, 2003.

Lykes, Richard Wayne. *Higher Education and the United States Office of Education (1967–1953).* Washington: Bureau of Postsecondary Education, United States Office of Education, 1975.

Macdonald, Anne L. *Feminine Ingenuity.* New York: Ballantine, 1992.

MacDonell, R. W. *Belle Harris Bennett: Her Life Work.* "Women in American Protest and Religion Series: 1800–1930," vol. 19. New York: Garland Press, 1987.

Mapp, Edward. *Blacks in American Films.* Metuchen, NJ: Scarecrow Press, 1972.

Marquis, Donald M. *In Search of Buddy Bolden: First Man of Jazz.* Baton Rouge: Louisiana State University Press, 1978.

Marshall, Herbert, and Mildred Stock. *Ira Aldridge.* Carbondale: Southern Illinois University Press, 1968.

Martin, Mart. *The Almanac of Women and Minorities in American Politics.* Boulder, CO: Westview Press, 1999.

Mason, Herman "Skip," Jr. *Going against the Wind.* Atlanta: Atlanta Journal and The APEX Museum, 1992.

May, Lynn E, Jr. *The First Baptist Church of Nashville 1820–1970.* Nashville: First Baptist Church, 1970.

Maynard, Robert, with Dori J. Maynard. *Letters to My Children.* Kansas City: Andrews and McMeel, 1995.

McClinton, Calvin A. *The Work of Vinnette Carroll, an African American Theatre Artist.* Lewiston, NY: Edwin Mellen Press, 2000.

McDonnell, Patrick, Karen O'Connell, and Georgia Riley de Havenon. *Krazy Kat.* New York: Abrams, 1986.

Melton, J. Gordon, ed. *The Encyclopedia of American Religions.* 3 vols. Tarrytown, NY: Triumph Books, 1991.

Montgomery, Carrie. *"Under His Wings": The Story of My Life.* Oakland, CA: Office of Triumphs of Faith, 1936.

Morais, Herbert M. *The History of the Negro in Medicine.* New York: Publishers Company, 1970.

Morton, David C., with Charles K. Wolfe. *DeFord Bailey.* Knoxville: University of Tennessee Press, 1991.

Moses, Wilson Jeremiah. *Alexander Crummell.* Amherst: University of Massachusetts Press, 1992.

Murphy, Larry G., ed. *Down by the Riverside: Readings in African American Religion.* New York: New York University Press, 2000.

The Negro Yearbook. Various editions. Tuskegee, AL: Tuskegee Institute, 1913-1952.

Noble, Peter. *The Negro in Films.* London: Skelton Robinson, 1969.

Notable American Women. 3 vols. Cambridge: Belknap Press of Harvard University Press, 1971–1980.

Ochs, Stephen J. *Desegregating the Altar.* Baton Rouge: Louisiana State University Press, 1990.

Odd, Gilbert. *The Encyclopedia of Boxing.* Secaucus, NJ: Chartwell Books, 1989.

Organ, Claude Y., and Margaret M. Kosiba, eds. *A Century of Black Surgeons: The U.S.A. Experience.* Vol. 1. Norman, OK: Transcript Press, 1987.

Othow, Helen Chavis. *John Chavis: African American Patriot, Preacher, Teacher, and Mentor (1763–1838)*. Jefferson, NC: McFarland, 2001.

Page, James A. *Black Olympian Medalists*. Englewood, CO: Libraries Unlimited, 1991.

Parker, Grant, trans. *The Agony of Asar: A Thesis on Slavery by the Former Slave, Jacobus Elisa Johannes Capitien, 1717–1747*. Princeton, NJ: Markus Wiener, 1999.

Paths Toward Freedom. Raleigh: Center for Urban Affairs, North Carolina State University at Raleigh, 1976.

Patterson, James T. *Brown v. Board of Education: A Civil Rights Milestone and Its Troubled Legacy*. New York: Oxford University Press, 2001.

Patton, Phil. *Made in USA*. New York: Grove Weidenfeld, 1992.

Payne, Daniel L. *History of the African Methodist Episcopal Church*. Vol. 1. Nashville, TN: A.M.E. Sunday-School Union, 1891. Announced as first volume, but completed by a supplemental volume: Charles Spencer Smith, *A History of the African Methodist Episcopal Church*. Philadelphia: Book Concern of the A.M.E. Church, 1922.

Payne, Wardell, ed. *Directory of African American Religious Bodies*. Washington, DC: Howard University Press, 1991.

Penn, Irvine Garland. *The Afro-American Press and Its Editors*. Reprint. New York: Arno Press, 1969.

Peterson, Bernard L., Jr. *Profiles of African American Stage Performers and Theatre People, 1816–1960*. Westport, CT: Greenwood Press, 2001.

Phi Beta Kappa. *Membership Directory, 2000*. Volume 1. New York: Bernard C. Harris Pub. Co., 2000.

Ploski, Harry A., and James Williams, eds. *The Negro Almanac*. 5th ed. Detroit: Gale Research, 1989.

Ploski, Harry A., and Warren Marr, II. *The Negro Almanac*. 3rd rev. ed. New York: Bellwether Company, 1976.

Powell, William J. *Black Wings*. Los Angeles: Ivan Deach, Jr., 1934.

Price, Valencia. "An Historical Perspective of the American Missionary Association and Its Establishment of LeMoyne College, 1871–1940." Ed.D. diss., Tennessee State University, 2001.

Pyles, Thomas. "The Real McCoy." *American Speech* 33 (December 1958): 297–298.

Raboteau, Albert J. *Slave Religion*. New York: Oxford University Press, 1978.

Rampersad, Arnold. *The Life of Langston Hughes*. 2 vols. New York: Oxford University Press, 1988.

Randall, Alice. *The Wind Done Gone*. Boston: Houghton Mifflin, 2001.

Randolph, Elizabeth S., ed. *An African-American Album*. Charlotte, NC: Public Library of Charlotte and Mecklenberg County, 1992.

Read, Florence M. *The Story of Spelman College*. Princeton: Princeton University Press, 1961.

Reasons, George. *They Had a Dream*. Vol. 2. New York: New American Library, 1971.

Render, Sylvia Lyons. *Charles W. Chesnutt*. Boston: Twayne Publishers, 1980.

Richards, Larry. *African American Films through 1959: A Comprehensive, Illustrated Filmography*. Jefferson, NC: McFarland, 1998.

Richardson, Joe M. *A History of Fisk University, 1865–1946*. Tuscaloosa: University of Alabama Press, 1980.

Robertson, Patrick. *The Book of Firsts*. New York: Clarkson N. Potter, 1974.

Robinson, Robert, with Jonathan Slevin. *Black on Red: My 44 Years inside the Soviet Union*. Washington, DC: Acropolis Books, 1988.

Robinson, Wilhelmina S. *Historical Negro Biographies*. New York: Publishers Company, 1970.

Roman, Charles Victor. *Meharry Medical College: A History*. Nashville, TN: Sunday School Publishing Board of the National Baptist Convention, 1934.

Rosen, Ruth. *The World Split Open: How the Modern Women's Movement Changed America*. New York: Viking, 2000.

Sadie, Stanley, ed. *The New Grove Dictionary of Music and Musicians*. 20 vols. London: Macmillan, 1980.

Sadie, Stanley, ed. *The New Grove Dictionary of Music and Musicians*. 2nd ed. New York: Grove, 2001.

Salem, Dorothy, ed. *African American Women: A Biographical Dictionary*. New York: Garland Publishing, 1993.

Salzman, Jack, ed. *Encyclopedia of African-American Culture and History, Supplement*. New York: Macmillan Reference USA, 2001.

Salzman, Jack, David Lionel Smith, and Cornel West, eds. *Encyclopedia of African-American Culture and History*. Vols. 1–5. New York: Macmillan Library Reference USA/Simon and Schuster Macmillan, 1996.

Scheuer, Steven H., ed. *Movies on TV and Videocassette, 1993–1994*. New York: Bantam Books, 1992.

Schultz, Rima Lunin, and Adele Hast, eds. *Women Building Chicago 1790–1990*. Bloomington: Indiana University Press, 2001.

Schweninger, Loren. *James T. Rapier and Reconstruction*. Chicago: University of Chicago Press, 1978.

Scobie, Edward. *Black Britannia*. Chicago: Johnson Publishing Co., 1972.

Scott, Emmett J. *The American Negro in the World War*. Chicago: Homewood Press, 1919.

Scott, Mingo, Jr. *The Negro in Tennessee Politics*. Nashville, TN: Rich Printing Company, 1964.

Senna, Carl. *The Black Press and the Struggle for Civil Rights*. New York: Franklin Watts, 1993.

Shannon, Sandra G. *The Dramatic Vision of August Wilson*. Washington, DC: Howard University Press, 1994.

Shockley, Ann Allen. *Afro-American Women Writers 1746–1933*. Boston: G. K. Hall, 1988.

Shockley, Ann Allen, and Sue P. Chandler. *Living Black Authors*. New York: Bowker, 1973.

Shockley, Grant S., ed. *Heritage and Hope: The African American Presence in United Methodism*. Nashville: Abington Press, 1991.

Simmons, William J. *Men of Mark*. Cleveland: Rewell, 1887.

Smith, Edward D. *Climbing Jacob's Ladder*. Washington, DC: Smithsonian Institution Press, 1988.

Smith, Eric Ledell. *Bert Williams: A Biography of the Pioneer Black Comedian*. Jefferson, NC: McFarland, 1992.

Smith, J. Clay, Jr. *Emancipation: The Making of the Black Lawyer, 1844–1944*. Philadelphia: University of Pennsylvania Press, 1993.

Smith. Jessie Carney. *Epic Lives*. Detroit: Visible Ink, 1993.

Smith, Jessie Carney. *Ethnic Genealogy*. Westport, CT: Greenwood Press, 1983.

Smith, Jessie Carney, ed. *Encyclopedia of African American Popular Culture*. 4 vols. Santa Barbara: Greenwood/ABC Clio, 2011.

Smith, Jessie Carney, ed. *Notable Black American Men.* Detroit: Gale, 1999.

Smith, Jessie Carney, ed. *Notable Black American Women.* Detroit: Gale, 1992.

Smith, Jessie Carney, ed. *Notable Black American Women, Book II.* Detroit: Gale, 1996.

Smith, Jessie Carney, and Linda T. Wynn. *Freedom Facts and Firsts: 400 Years of the African American Civil Rights Experience.* Detroit: Visible Ink Press, 2009.

Smith, Jessie Carney, and Joseph M. Palmisano, eds. *The African American Almanac.* 8th ed. Detroit: Gale, 2000.

Smith, Otis Milton, and Mary M. Stolberg. *Looking beyond Race: The Life of Otis Milton Smith.* Detroit: Wayne State University Press, 2000.

Sollors, Werner, Caldwell Titcomb, and Thomas A. Underwood, eds. *Blacks at Harvard: A Documentary History of African-American Experience at Harvard and Radcliffe.* New York: New York University Press, 1993.

Southern, Eileen. *Biographical Dictionary of Afro-American and African Musicians.* Westport, CT: Greenwood Press, 1982.

Southern, Eileen. *The Music of Black Americans.* 2nd ed. New York: Norton, 1983.

Spencer, Jon Michael. *Black Hymnody.* Knoxville: University of Tennessee Press, 1992.

Spradling, Mary Mace. *In Black and White.* 3rd ed. Vol. 1. Detroit: Gale, 1980.

The State of Black America 1992. New York: National Urban League, 1992.

The State of Black America 1993. New York: National Urban League, 1983.

Stein, M. L. *Blacks in Communications.* New York: Julian Messner, 1972.

Sterling, Dorothy, ed. *We Are Your Sisters.* New York: Norton, 1984.

Stewart, T. G. *Buffalo Soldiers: The Colored Regulars in the United States Army.* Amherst, NY: Humanity Books, 2003.

Stillwell, Paul, ed. *The Golden Thirteen: Recollections of the First Black Naval Officers.* Annapolis, MD: Naval Institute Press, 1993.

Story, Rosalyn. *And So I Sing.* New York: Warner Books, 1990.

Sumner, Charles. *Argument of Charles Sumner, Esq., Against the Constitutionality of Separate Colored Schools, in the Case of Sarah C. Roberts vs. the City of Boston before the Supreme Court of Mass. Dec. 4, 1849.* Boston: B. F. Roberts, 1849.

Synan, Vincent, ed. *The Century of the Holy Spirit.* Nashville, TN: Thomas Nelson, 2001.

Taylor, Alrutheus Ambush. *The Negro in Tennessee: 1865–1880.* Washington: Associated Publishers, 1941.

Taylor, Marshall W. *The Fastest Bicycle Rider in the World.* Reprint. Freeport, NY: Books for Libraries Press, 1971.

Thompson, George A., Jr. *A Documentary History of the African Theatre.* Evanston, IL: Northwestern University Press, 1998.

Thorn, John, and Pete Palmer, eds. *Total Baseball.* New York: Warner Books, 1989.

Thorpe, Edward. *Black Dance.* Woodstock, NY: Overlook Press, 1990.

Thurman, Howard. *With Head and Heart: The Autobiography of Howard Thurman.* New York: Harcourt Brace Jovanovich, 1979.

Toppin, Edgar. *A Biographical History of Blacks in America since 1528.* New York: McKay, 1971.

Treat, Robert L. *The Encyclopedia of Football.* Revised by Pete Palmer. South Brunswick, NJ: A. S. Barnes, 1975.

Trotter, James M. *Music and Some Highly Musical People.* Boston: Lee and Shepard, 1881.

Turner, Patricia. *Afro-American Singers: An Index and Preliminary Discography of Long-Playing Recordings of Opera, Choral Music, and Song.* Minneapolis: Challenge Productions, 1977.

Tuskegee Institute, Sixty-fifth Annual Catalog, 1946–47.

Tyson, Neil De Grasdse, Charles Liu, and Robert Irion. *The Universe.* Washington, DC: Joseph Henry Press, 2000.

U.S. Department of the Interior. Bureau of Education. Bulletin, 1928, No. 7. *Survey of Negro Colleges and Universities.* Reprint. New York: Negro Universities Press, 1969.

Vincent, Theodore G. *The Legacy of Vicente Guerrero, Mexico's First Black Indian President.* Gainesville, FL: University Press of Florida, 2001.

Waddell, William H. *The Black Man in Veterinary Medicine.* Rev. ed. Honolulu: W. H. Waddell, 1982.

Walker, Juliet E. K. *Free Frank: A Black Pioneer on the Antebellum Frontier.* Lexington: University Press of Kentucky, 1983.

Walker, Juliet E. K. *Encyclopedia of African American Business History.* Westport, CT: Greenwood Press, 1999.

Ward, Andrew. *Dark Midnight When I Rise: The Story of the Jubilee Singers Who Introduced the World to the Music of Black America.* New York: Farrar, Straus and Giroux, 2000.

Warren, Wini. *Black Women Scientists in the United States.* Bloomington: Indiana University Press, 1999.

Washington, Booker T., ed. *Tuskegee and Its People.* New York: D. Appleton, 1906.

Waters, Ethel. *His Eye Is on the Sparrow.* Garden City, NJ: Doubleday, 1951.

Watts, Jill. *God, Harlem U.S.A.: The Father Divine Story.* Berkeley: University of California Press, 1992.

Webster, Raymond B., ed. *African American Firsts in Science and Technology.* Detroit: Gale, 1999.

Westbrook, Peter, with Tej Hazarika. *Harnessing Anger: The Inner Discipline of Athletic Excellence.* New York: Seven Stories Press, 1997.

Whitaker, Matthew C., ed. *African American Icons of Sports: Triumph, Courage, and Excellence.* Westport, CT: Greenwood Press, 2008.

Who's Who among African Americans. Various editions. Detroit: Gale, 1998–2011.

Who's Who among Black Americans. Various editions. Detroit: Gale, 1988–1997.

Who's Who in America. Various editions. –2011.

Who's Who in American Politics, 1987–1988. 11th ed. New York: Bowker, 1987.

Who's Who in Colored America. Various editions, 1929–1950.

Williams, Gilbert A. *Legendary Pioneers of Black Radio.* Westport, CT: Praeger, 1998.

Williams, Joe Jr. *The 784th Tank Battalion in World War II: History of an African American Armored Unit in Europe.* Jefferson, NC: McFarland & Co., 2007.

Williams, Juan. *Thurgood Marshall: American Revolutionary.* New York: Times Books, 1998.

Wilmore, Gayraud S. *Black and Presbyterian.* Philadelphia: Geneva Press, 1983.

Wilson, Charles R., and William Ferris. *Encyclopedia of Southern Culture.* Chapel Hill: University of North Carolina Press, 1989.

Wilson, Emily Herring, and Susan Mullally. *Hope and Dignity: Older Black Women of the South.* Philadelphia: Temple University Press, 1983.

Wolseley, Roland E. *The Black Press.* 2nd ed. Ames: University of Iowa Press, 1990.

Woodson, C. G. *The Education of the Negro Prior to 1861.* New York: Putnam's, 1915.

INDEX

Note: (ill.) indicates photos and illustrations.